(9–2)

$$S_M^2 = \frac{\Sigma(M - GM)^2}{df_{\text{Between}}}$$

The estimated variance of the distribution of means is the sum of each sample mean's squared deviation from the grand mean, divided by the degrees of freedom for the between-groups population variance estimate.

(9–4)

$$S_{\text{Between}}^2 \text{ or } MS_{\text{Between}} = (S_M^2)(n)$$

The between-groups population variance estimate (or mean squares between) is the estimated variance of the distribution of means multiplied by the number of scores in each group.

(9–5)

$$F = \frac{S_{\text{Between}}^2}{S_{\text{Within}}^2} \text{ or } \frac{MS_{\text{Between}}}{MS_{\text{Within}}}$$

The F ratio is the between-groups population variance estimate (or mean squares between) divided by the within-groups population variance estimate (or mean squares within).

(9–10)

$$S_{\text{Between}}^2 = \frac{\Sigma(M - GM)^2}{df_{\text{Between}}} \text{ or }$$

$$MS_{\text{Between}} = \frac{SS_{\text{Between}}}{df_{\text{Between}}}$$

The between-groups population variance estimate is the sum of squared deviations of each score's group's mean from the grand mean divided by the degrees of freedom for the between-groups population variance estimate.

(9–11)

$$S_{\text{Within}}^2 = \frac{\Sigma(X - M)^2}{df_{\text{Within}}} \text{ or } MS_{\text{Within}} = \frac{SS_{\text{Within}}}{df_{\text{Within}}}$$

The within-groups population variance estimate is the sum of squared deviations of each score from its group's mean divided by the degrees of freedom for the within-groups population variance estimate.

(10–1)

$$SS_{\text{Rows}} = \Sigma(M_{\text{Row}} - GM)^2$$

The sum of squared deviations for rows is the sum of each score's row's mean's squared deviation from the grand mean.

(10–3)

$$SS_{\text{Interaction}} = \Sigma[(X - GM) - (X - M) \\ - (M_{\text{Row}} - GM) \\ - (M_{\text{Column}} - GM)]^2$$

The sum of squared deviations for the interaction is the sum of the squares of each score's deviation from the grand mean minus its deviation from its cell's mean, minus its row's mean's deviation from the grand mean, minus its column's mean's deviation from the grand mean.

(10–4)

$$SS_{\text{Within}} = \Sigma(X - M)^2$$

The sum of squared deviations within groups (within cells) is the sum of each score's squared deviation from its cell's mean.

(11–1)

$$r = \frac{\Sigma[(X - M_X)(Y - M_Y)]}{\sqrt{(SS_X)(SS_Y)}}$$

The correlation coefficient is the sum, over all the people in the study, of the product of each person's two deviation scores, divided by the square root of the result of multiplying the sum of everyone's squared deviation scores on the X variable by the sum of everyone's squared deviation scores on the Y variable.

(12–1)

$$\hat{Y} = a + (b)(X)$$

A person's predicted score on the criterion variable equals the regression constant plus the regression coefficient multiplied by that person's score on the predictor variable.

(13–1)

$$\chi^2 = \Sigma\frac{(O - E)^2}{E}$$

Chi-square is the sum, over all the categories or cells, of the squared difference between observed and expected frequencies divided by the expected frequency.

(13–2)

$$E = \left(\frac{R}{N}\right)(C)$$

A cell's expected frequency is the number in its row divided by the total number, multiplied by the number in its column.

Statistics for Psychology

Fifth Edition

Arthur Aron
State University of New York at Stony Brook

Elaine N. Aron
State University of New York at Stony Brook

Elliot J. Coups
Fox Chase Cancer Center

Upper Saddle River, New Jersey 07458

Library of Congress Cataloging-in-Publication Data

Aron, Arthur.
  Statistics for psychology / Arthur Aron, Elaine N. Aron, Elliot J.
Coups.—5th ed.
    p. cm.
  Includes bibliographical references and index.
  ISBN-13: 978-0-13-601057-9 (hardcover)
  ISBN-10: 0-13-601057-1 (hardcover)
  1. Psychology—Statistical methods. I. Aron, Elaine. II. Coups, Elliot J.
III. Title.
  BF39.A69 2009
  150.72'7—dc22

                                        2008000668

Publisher: Leah Jewell
Executive Editor: Jeff Marshall
Project Manager, Editorial: LeeAnn Doherty
Editorial Assistant: Aaron Talwar
Associate Managing Editor: Maureen Richardson
Production Liaison: Shelly Kupperman
Senior Operations Supervisor: Sherry Lewis
Director of Marketing: Brandy Dawson
Senior Marketing Manager: Jeanette Koskinas
Marketing Assistant: Laura Kennedy

AV Project Manager: Maria Piper
Associate Supplements Editor: Virginia Livsey
Manager, Cover Visual Research & Permissions: Karen Sanatar
Director, Cover Design: Jayne Conte
Cover Designer: Suzanne Behnke
Cover Image: Johnny Johnson/Photographer's Choice/Getty Images
Composition and Full-Service Project Management:
  ICC Macmillan Inc./Jill Traut
Printer/Binder: Edwards Brothers
Cover Printer: Coral Graphics

Credits and acknowledgments borrowed from other sources and reproduced, with permission, in this textbook appear on the appropriate page of appearance (or on page xv).

Pearson Education LTD., London
Pearson Education Singapore, Pte. Ltd
Pearson Education Canada, Inc.
Pearson Education—Japan
Pearson Education Australia PTY, Limited

Pearson Education North Asia Ltd., Hong Kong
Pearson Educación de Mexico, S.A. de C.V.
Pearson Education Malaysia, Pte. Ltd.
Pearson Education, Upper Saddle River, New Jersey

10 9 8 7 6 5 4

ISBN-13: 978-0-13-601057-9
ISBN-10:   0-13-601057-1

Brief Contents

Preface to the Instructor   xi

Introduction to the Student   xvi

Chapter 1 Displaying the Order in a Group of Numbers Using Tables and Graphs   1

Chapter 2 Central Tendency and Variability   33

Chapter 3 Some Key Ingredients for Inferential Statistics: *Z* Scores, the Normal Curve, Sample versus Population, and Probability   67

Chapter 4 Introduction to Hypothesis Testing   107

Chapter 5 Hypothesis Tests with Means of Samples   137

Chapter 6 Making Sense of Statistical Significance: Decision Errors, Effect Size, and Statistical Power   175

Chapter 7 Introduction to *t* Tests: Single Sample and Dependent Means   222

Chapter 8 The *t* Test for Independent Means   270

Chapter 9 Introduction to the Analysis of Variance   310

Chapter 10 Factorial Analysis of Variance   370

Chapter 11 Correlation   432

Chapter 12 Prediction   487

Chapter 13 Chi-Square Tests   536

Chapter 14 Strategies When Population Distributions Are Not Normal: Data Transformations and Rank-Order Tests   577

Chapter 15 The General Linear Model and Making Sense of Advanced Statistical Procedures in Research Articles   611

Appendix: Tables   664

Answers to Set I Practice Problems   673

Glossary   701

Glossary of Symbols   708

References   710

Index   719

Web Chapters (available at http://www.pearsonhighered.com**)**

Chapter W1 Overview of the Logic and Language of Psychology Research

Chapter W2 Applying Statistical Methods in Your Own Project

Chapter W3 Repeated-Measures Analysis of Variance

Chapter W4 Integration and the General Linear Model

Contents

Preface to the Instructor   xi

Introduction to the Student   xvi

Chapter 1   Displaying the Order in a Group of Numbers Using Tables and Graphs   1

The Two Branches of Statistical Methods   2

Some Basic Concepts   3

Box 1–1: Important Trivia for Poetic Statistics Students   6

Frequency Tables   7

Histograms   10

Box 1–2: Math Anxiety, Statistics Anxiety, and You: A Message for Those of You Who Are Truly Worried About This Course   12

Shapes of Frequency Distributions   15

Controversy: Misleading Graphs   19

Frequency Tables and Histograms in Research Articles   21

Summary   23

Key Terms   24

Example Worked-Out Problems   24

Practice Problems   25

Using SPSS   29

Chapter Note   32

Chapter 2   Central Tendency and Variability   33

Central Tendency   34

Variability   43

Box 2–1: The Sheer Joy (Yes, Joy) of Statistical Analysis   51

Controversy: The Tyranny of the Mean   52

Box 2–2: Gender, Ethnicity, and Math Performance   53

Central Tendency and Variability in Research Articles   55

Summary   57

Key Terms   57

Example Worked-Out Problems   57

Practice Problems   59

Using SPSS   62

Chapter Notes   65

Chapter 3   Some Key Ingredients for Inferential Statistics: Z Scores, the Normal Curve, Sample versus Population, and Probability   67

Z Scores   68

The Normal Curve   73

Box 3–1: de Moivre, the Eccentric Stranger Who Invented the Normal Curve   74

Sample and Population   83

Box 3–2: Surveys, Polls, and 1948's Costly "Free Sample"   86

Probability   88

Box 3–3: Pascal Begins Probability Theory at the Gambling Table, Then Learns to Bet on God   89

Controversies: Is the Normal Curve Really So Normal? and Using Nonrandom
Samples   93
Z Scores, Normal Curves, Samples and Populations, and Probabilities
in Research Articles   95
Advanced Topics: Probability Rules and Conditional Probabilities   96
Summary   97
Key Terms   98
Example Worked-Out Problems   99
Practice Problems   102
Using SPSS   105
Chapter Notes   106

Chapter 4   Introduction to Hypothesis Testing   107
A Hypothesis-Testing Example   108
The Core Logic of Hypothesis Testing   109
The Hypothesis-Testing Process   110
One-Tailed and Two-Tailed Hypothesis Tests   119
Controversy: Should Significance Tests Be Banned?   124
Box 4–1: Jacob Cohen, the Ultimate New Yorker: Funny, Pushy, Brilliant,
and Kind   126
Hypothesis Tests in Research Articles   127
Summary   128
Key Terms   129
Example Worked-Out Problems   129
Practice Problems   131
Chapter Notes   136

Chapter 5   Hypothesis Tests with Means of Samples   137
The Distribution of Means   138
Hypothesis Testing with a Distribution of Means: The *Z* Test   146
Box 5–1: More About Polls: Sampling Errors and Errors in Thinking
About Samples   147
Controversy: Marginal Significance   153
Hypothesis Tests About Means of Samples (*Z* Tests) and Standard Errors
in Research Articles   154
Advanced Topic: Estimation, Standard Errors, and Confidence Intervals   156
Advanced Topic Controversy: Confidence Intervals versus Significance Tests   162
Advanced Topic: Confidence Intervals in Research Articles   163
Summary   163
Key Terms   164
Example Worked-Out Problems   164
Practice Problems   167
Chapter Notes   173

**Chapter 6   Making Sense of Statistical Significance: Decision Errors,
Effect Size, and Statistical Power   175**
Decision Errors   175
Effect Size   179
Box 6–1: Effect Sizes for Relaxation and Meditation: A Restful Meta-Analysis   184
Statistical Power   187
What Determines the Power of a Study?   191
Box 6–2: The Power of Typical Psychology Experiments   199
The Role of Power When Planning a Study   203
The Role of Power When Interpreting the Results of a Study   205
Controversy: Statistical Significance versus Effect Size   208
Decision Errors, Effect Size, and Power in Research Articles   210
Advanced Topic: Figuring Statistical Power   212

Summary   214
Key Terms   215
Example Worked-Out Problems   215
Practice Problems   217
Chapter Note   221

**Chapter 7   Introduction to *t* Tests: Single Sample
and Dependent Means   222**
The *t* Test for a Single Sample   223
Box 7–1: William S. Gosset, Alias "Student": Not a Mathematician,
        But a Practical Man   224
The *t* Test for Dependent Means   236
Assumptions of the *t* Test for a Single Sample and the *t* Test for Dependent
        Means   247
Effect Size and Power for the *t* Test for Dependent Means   247
Controversy: Advantages and Disadvantages of Repeated-Measures
        Designs   250
Box 7–2: The Power of Studies Using Difference Scores: How the Lanarkshire Milk
        Experiment Could Have Been Milked for More   251
Single Sample *t* Tests and Dependent Means *t* Tests in Research Articles   252
Summary   253
Key Terms   254
Example Worked-Out Problems   254
Practice Problems   258
Using SPSS   265
Chapter Notes   268

Chapter 8   The *t* Test for Independent Means   270
The Distribution of Differences Between Means   271
Hypothesis Testing with a *t* Test for Independent Means   278
Assumptions of the *t* Test for Independent Means   286
Box 8–1: Monte Carlo Methods: When Mathematics Becomes Just an Experiment,
        and Statistics Depend on a Game of Chance   286
Effect Size and Power for the *t* Test for Independent Means   288
Review and Comparison of the Three Kinds of *t* Tests   290
Controversy: The Problem of Too Many *t* Tests   291
The *t* Test for Independent Means in Research Articles   292
Advanced Topic: Power for the *t* Test for Independent Means When Sample Sizes
        Are Not Equal   293
Summary   294
Key Terms   295
Example Worked-Out Problems   295
Practice Problems   298
Using SPSS   305
Chapter Notes   309

Chapter 9   Introduction to the Analysis of Variance   310
Basic Logic of the Analysis of Variance   311
Box 9–1: Sir Ronald Fisher, Caustic Genius of Statistics   317
Carrying Out an Analysis of Variance   319
Hypothesis Testing with the Analysis of Variance   327
Assumptions in the Analysis of Variance   331
Planned Contrasts   334
Post Hoc Comparisons   337
Effect Size and Power for the Analysis of Variance   339
Controversy: Omnibus Tests versus Planned Contrasts   343

Analyses of Variance in Research Articles   344
Advanced Topic: The Structural Model in the Analysis of Variance   345
Principles of the Structural Model   345
Summary   351
Key Terms   352
Example Worked-Out Problems   353
Practice Problems   357
Using SPSS   364
Chapter Notes   368

Chapter 10   Factorial Analysis of Variance   370
Basic Logic of Factorial Designs and Interaction Effects   371
Recognizing and Interpreting Interaction Effects   376
Basic Logic of the Two-Way Analysis of Variance   386
Box 10–1: Personality and Situational Influences on Behavior:
          An Interaction Effect   387
Assumptions in the Factorial Analysis of Variance   389
Extensions and Special Cases of the Analysis of Variance   389
Controversy: Dichotomizing Numeric Variables   391
Factorial Analysis of Variance in Research Articles   393
Advanced Topic: Figuring a Two-Way Analysis of Variance   395
Advanced Topic: Power and Effect Size in the Factorial Analysis
          of Variance   406
Summary   410
Key Terms   411
Example Worked-Out Problems   412
Practice Problems   415
Using SPSS   426
Chapter Notes   431

Chapter 11   Correlation   432
Graphing Correlations: The Scatter Diagram   434
Patterns of Correlation   437
The Correlation Coefficient   443
Box 11–1: Galton: Gentleman Genius   446
Significance of a Correlation Coefficient   452
Correlation and Causality   456
Issues in Interpreting the Correlation Coefficient   458
Box 11–2: Illusory Correlation: When You Know Perfectly Well That If It's Big,
          It's Fat—and You Are Perfectly Wrong   460
Effect Size and Power for the Correlation Coefficient   464
Controversy: What Is a Large Correlation?   466
Correlation in Research Articles   467
Summary   469
Key Terms   471
Example Worked-Out Problems   471
Practice Problems   474
Using SPSS   482
Chapter Notes   485

Chapter 12   Prediction   487
Predictor (X) and Criterion (Y) Variables   488
The Linear Prediction Rule   488
The Regression Line   492
Finding the Best Linear Prediction Rule   496
The Least Squared Error Principle   498

Issues in Prediction   503
Multiple Regression   506
Limitations of Prediction   508
Controversy: Unstandardized and Standardized Regression Coefficients;
    Comparing Predictors   509
Box 12–1: Clinical versus Statistical Prediction   510
Prediction in Research Articles   511
Advanced Topic: Error and Proportionate Reduction in Error   514
Summary   518
Key Terms   519
Example Worked-Out Problems   519
Practice Problems   524
Using SPSS   532
Chapter Notes   535

Chapter 13   Chi-Square Tests   536
Box 13–1: Karl Pearson, Inventor of Chi-Square and Center of Controversy   537
The Chi-Square Statistic and the Chi-Square Test for Goodness of Fit   538
The Chi-Square Test for Independence   546
Assumptions for Chi-Square Tests   554
Effect Size and Power for Chi-Square Tests for Independence   554
Controversy: The Minimum Expected Frequency   558
Chi-Square Tests in Research Articles   559
Summary   560
Key Terms   561
Example Worked-Out Problems   561
Practice Problems   565
Using SPSS   572
Chapter Notes   576

**Chapter 14   Strategies When Population Distributions
Are Not Normal: Data Transformations
and Rank-Order Tests   577**
Assumptions in the Standard Hypothesis-Testing Procedures   578
Data Transformations   580
Rank-Order Tests   585
Comparison of Methods   589
Controversy: Computer-Intensive Methods   591
Box 14–1: Where Do Random Numbers Come From?   594
Data Transformations and Rank-Order Tests in Research Articles   595
Summary   596
Key Terms   597
Example Worked-Out Problems   597
Practice Problems   597
Using SPSS   602
Chapter Notes   609

**Chapter 15   The General Linear Model and Making Sense of Advanced
Statistical Procedures in Research Articles   611**
The General Linear Model   612
Box 15–1: Two Women Make a Point About Gender and Statistics   616
Partial Correlation   617
Reliability   618
Multilevel Modeling   620
Factor Analysis   622
Causal Modeling   625

Box 15–2: The Golden Age of Statistics: Four Guys Around London   627
Procedures That Compare Groups   634
Analysis of Covariance (ANCOVA)   634
Multivariate Analysis of Variance (MANOVA) and Multivariate Analysis
    of Covariance (MANCOVA)   635
Overview of Statistical Techniques   636
Controversy: Should Statistics Be Controversial?   637
Box 15–3: The Forced Partnership of Fisher and Pearson   638
How to Read Results Using Unfamiliar Statistical Techniques   639
Summary   641
Key Terms   642
Practice Problems   642
Using SPSS   654
Chapter Notes   662

Appendix: Tables   664

Answers to Set I Practice Problems   673

Glossary   701

Glossary of Symbols   708

References   710

Index   719

Web Chapters (available at http://www.pearsonhighered.com)

**Chapter W1 Overview of the Logic and Language of Psychology
Research**

Chapter W2 Applying Statistical Methods in Your Own Project

Chapter W3 Repeated-Measures Analysis of Variance

Chapter W4 Integration and the General Linear Model

Preface to the Instructor

The heart of this book was written over a summer in a small apartment near the Place Saint Ferdinand, having been outlined in nearby cafés and on walks in the Bois de Boulogne. It is based on our collective many decades of experience teaching, researching, and writing. We believe that the result is a book as different from the conventional lot of statistics texts as Paris is from Pompeii, yet still comfortable and stimulating to the long-suffering community of statistics instructors.

Our approach was developed over decades of successful teaching—successful not only in the sense that students have consistently rated the course (a statistics course, remember) as a highlight of their major, but also in the sense that students come back to us long after graduating saying, "I was light years ahead of my fellow graduate students because of your course," or "Even though I don't do research, your course has really helped me read the journals in my field."

The response to the first four editions has been overwhelming. We have received hundreds of thank-you emails and letters from instructors (and from students themselves!) from all over the world. (The text has been translated into Traditional Chinese and Spanish.) Of course, we have also been delighted by the enthusiastic reviews it has received, starting with the first edition in *Contemporary Psychology* (Bourgeois, 1997) and continuing through recent years (Shevlin, 2005, in *Psychology Learning and Teaching*).

With each revision, we have tried to maintain those things about the book that have been especially appreciated, while reworking the text to take into account the feedback we have received, our own experiences, and advances and changes in the field. We have also added new pedagogical features to make the book even more accessible for students. (As we undertook this fifth edition we were particularly concerned that the book not become stale and that it remain as lively and as up-to-date as our very first edition.) However, before turning to what's new in this latest revision, we want to reiterate what we said with the first edition about how this book, from the beginning, has been so different from other statistics texts.

How This Book Was Dramatically Different from the Start

Different as this book is, it has from the start also done what the best of the better statistics texts of the last few years have been already doing pretty well: emphasizing the intuitive, de-emphasizing the mathematical, and explaining everything in direct, simple language. But what we have done continues to go beyond even the best of the current lot in 10 key respects.

1. *The definitional formulas are brought to center stage* because they provide a concise symbolic summary of the logic of each particular procedure. All our explanations, examples, practice problems, and test bank items are based on these definitional formulas. (The amount of data to be processed in practice problems and test bank items is reduced appropriately to keep computations manageable.)

Why this approach? Even in 2008, statistics texts have still not faced the technological realities. What is important today is *not* that the students learn to calculate a *t* test with a large data set—programs like SPSS can do this in an instant with a few mouse clicks. What is important today is that students work problems in a way that keeps them constantly aware of the underlying logic of what they are doing. Consider the population variance—the average of the squared deviations from the mean. This concept is directly displayed in the definitional formula (once the student is used to the symbols): Variance $= [\Sigma(X - M)^2]/N$. Repeatedly working problems using this formula ingrains the *meaning* in the student's mind. In contrast, the usual computational version of this formula only obscures this meaning: Variance $= [\Sigma X^2 - (\Sigma X)^2/N]/N$. Repeatedly working problems using this formula does nothing but teach the student the difference between ΣX^2 and $(\Sigma X)^2$!

Teaching these tired computational formulas today is an anachronism—at least 40 years out-of-date! Researchers do their statistics on computers now, and the use of statistical software makes the understanding of the basic principles, as they are symbolically expressed in the definitional formulas, more important than ever. Students still need to work lots of problems by hand to learn the material. But they need to work them using the definitional formulas that reinforce the concepts, not using the antiquated computational formulas that obscure them. Not since the era when Lyndon B. Johnson was U.S. president have those computational formulas made sense as time-savers when researchers had to work with large data sets by hand. Even then, however, they were poor teaching tools. (Because some instructors may feel naked without them, we still provide the computational formulas, usually in a brief note at the end of the chapter.)

2. *Each procedure is taught both verbally and numerically—and usually visually as well.* In fact, when we introduce *every* formula, it has attached to it a concise statement of the formula in words. (The major formulas *with their verbal descriptions* are also repeated on the inside front cover.) Typically, each example lays out the procedures in worked-out formulas, in words (often with a list of steps), and illustrated with easy-to-grasp figures. Practice problems and test bank items, in turn, require the student to calculate results, write a short explanation in layperson's language of what they have done, and make a sketch (for example, of the distributions involved in a *t* test). The chapter material completely prepares the student for these kinds of practice problems and test questions.

It is our repeated experience that these different ways of expressing an idea are crucial for establishing a concept in a student's mind. Many psychology students are more at ease with words than with numbers. In fact, some have a positive fear of all mathematics. Writing the formula in words and providing the lay-language explanation gives them an opportunity to do what they do best.

3. A main goal of any introductory statistics course in psychology is to ***prepare students to read research articles.*** The way a procedure such as a *t* test or an analysis of variance is described in a research article is often quite different from what the student expects from the standard textbook discussions. Therefore, as this book teaches a statistical method, it also gives examples of how that method is reported in current journal articles. And we don't just leave it there. The practice problems and test bank items also include excerpts from journal articles for the student to explain.

4. The book is ***unusually up-to-date.*** Most introductory statistics textbooks read as if they were written in the 1950s. The basics are still the basics, but statisticians and researchers think far more subtly about those basics now. Today, the basics are undergirded by a new appreciation of effect size, power, limitations of significance testing, the accumulation of results through meta-analysis, the critical role of models, the underlying unity of difference and association statistics, the growing prominence of regression and associated methods, and a host of new developments arising from the central role of the computer in statistical analyses. We are much engaged in the latest thinking in statistical theory and application, and this book reflects that engagement. For example, we devote an entire early chapter (Chapter 6) to effect size and power and then return to these topics as we teach each technique.

5. We ***capitalize on the students' motivations.*** We do this in two ways. First, our examples emphasize topics or populations that students seem to find most interesting. The very first is from a real study in which students in their first week of an introductory statistics class rated how much stress they felt they were under. Other examples emphasize clinical, organizational, social, and educational psychology while being sure to include sufficient interesting examples from cognitive, developmental, and behavioral psychology, as well as social and cognitive neuroscience, to inspire students with the value of those approaches. (Also, our examples continually emphasize the usefulness of statistical methods and ideas as tools in the research process, never allowing students to feel that what they are learning is theory for the sake of theory.)

Second, we have worked to make the book extremely straightforward and systematic in its explanation of basic concepts so that students can have frequent "aha" experiences. Such experiences bolster self-confidence and motivate further learning. It is quite inspiring to us to see even fairly modest students glow from having mastered some concept like negative correlation or the distinction between failing to reject the null hypothesis and supporting the null hypothesis. At the same time, we do not constantly remind them how greatly oversimplified we have made things, as some books do. Instead, we show students, in the controversy sections in particular, how much there is for them to consider deeply, even in an introductory course.

6. ***We emphasize statistical methods as a living, growing field of research.*** We take the time to describe the issues, such as the relative merits of both significance testing and confidence intervals. In addition, each chapter includes one or more "boxes" about famous statisticians or interesting sidelights. The goal is for students to see statistical methods as human efforts to make sense out of the jumble of numbers generated by a research study—to see that statistics are not "given" by nature, not infallible, not perfect descriptions of the events they try to describe, but rather a language that is constantly improving through the careful thought of those who use it. We hope that this orientation will help them maintain a questioning, alert attitude as students and later as professionals.

7. ***The final chapter looks at advanced procedures*** without actually teaching them in detail. It explains in simple terms how to make sense out of these statistics when they are encountered in research articles. Most psychology research articles today use methods such as analysis of covariance, multivariate analysis of variance, multilevel modeling, mediation, factor analysis, or structural equation modeling. Students completing the ordinary introductory statistics course are ill equipped to comprehend most of the articles they must read to prepare a paper or study a course topic in further depth. This chapter makes use of the basics that students have just learned (along with extensive excerpts from current research articles) to give a rudimentary understanding of these advanced procedures. This chapter also serves as a reference guide that students can keep and use in the future when reading such articles.

8. We have written an **Instructor's Manual** ***that really helps teach the course.*** The *Manual* begins with a chapter summarizing what we have gleaned from our own teaching experience and the research literature on effectiveness in college teaching. The next chapter discusses alternative organizations of the course, tables of possible schedules and a sample syllabus, advice on structuring exams and an example test, and more still! Then each chapter, corresponding to the text chapters, provides full lecture outlines and additional *worked-out examples not found in the text* (in a form suitable for copying for student handouts). These lecture outlines and worked-out examples are especially useful to new instructors or those using our book for the first time, since structuring lectures and creating good examples is one of the most demanding parts of teaching the course.

9. Our **Test Bank** *makes preparing exams easy.* We supply approximately 40 multiple-choice, 25 fill-in, and 10 to 12 problem/essay questions for each chapter. Considering that the emphasis of the course is so conceptual, the multiple-choice questions will be particularly useful for instructors who do not have the resources to grade essays.

10. The accompanying **Study Guide and Computer Workbook** focuses on mastering concepts and also includes instructions and examples for working problems with SPSS. Most study guides concentrate on plugging numbers into formulas and memorizing rules (which is consistent with the emphasis of the textbooks they accompany). For each chapter, our *Study Guide and Computer Workbook* provides learning objectives, the chapter's formulas (with all symbols defined), and summaries of steps of conducting each procedure covered in the chapter, plus a set of self tests, including multiple-choice, fill-in, and problem/essay questions.

Also, our *Study Guide and Computer Workbook* goes beyond the brief SPSS sections in each text chapter to provide the needed support for teaching students to become comfortable with this program and carrying out analyses on the computer. First, there is a special appendix on getting started with SPSS. Then, in each chapter corresponding to the text chapters, there is a section showing in detail how to carry out the chapter's procedures with SPSS. (These sections include step-by-step instructions, examples, and illustrations of how each menu and each output appears on the screen.) There are also special activities for using SPSS to strengthen understanding. As far as we know, no other statistics textbook package provides this much depth of explanation.

What's New in This Fifth Edition

With each new edition we have worked to improve the writing, update content, and make adjustments based on our experience teaching and the wonderful input we have received from instructors using the text.

A Web page, which is available to instructors who adopt the book and their students: http://www.pearsonhighered.com, supplements the text with four downloadable chapters: (1) the basics of research methods, (2) applying statistics in one's own research projects, (3) repeated-measures analysis of variance, and (4) integration of statistical tests and the general linear model (which also serves as an excellent review/overview of the entire book).

In the fourth edition, we reconceptualized the teaching of the material on correlation and regression. We had long resisted calls from instructors to move these topics to after the *t* test and analysis of variance, thinking that they worked best as descriptive statistics (in previous editions they came right after mean and standard deviation). On the other hand, many instructors will no doubt continue to prefer to follow our original order; so we have made sure in this edition that users can still go directly from Chapter 2 to correlation and regression (now Chapters 11 and 12), and then return to Chapter 3 to begin the discussion of inferential statistics.

In this fifth edition, we of course have continued to focus on simplifying exposition and have done our usual updating of content, examples, boxes, controversies, and other elements, in addition to making a host of minor adjustments to make the book more effective. And we have added further pedagogical aids, such as adding essay outlines before the *Practice Problems* section and including definitions of key terms in the margin. For several chapters, we expanded the *Using SPSS* section that shows students how to carry out the chapter's procedures. Also, we added a *Using SPSS* section to Chapter 15 that shows students how to use SPSS to figure a partial correlation, internal consistency reliability, and an analysis of covariance (ANCOVA). Yet another addition is a section on multilevel modeling analysis in Chapter 15.

Keep in Touch

Our goal is to do whatever we can to help you make your course a success. If you have any questions or suggestions, please send us an email (**Arthur.Aron@sunysb.edu** will do for all of us). Also, if you should find an error somewhere, for everyone's benefit, please let us know right away. When errors have come up in the past, we have usually been able to fix them in the very next printing.

Acknowledgments

First and foremost, we are grateful to our students through the years, who have shaped our approach to teaching by rewarding us with their appreciation for what we have done well as well as their various means of extinguishing what we have done not so well. We also deeply appreciate all those students and instructors who have sent us their ideas and encouragement.

We remain grateful to all of those who helped us with the first four editions of this book, as well as to those who helped with the four editions of the *Brief Course* version. For their very helpful input on the development of this fifth edition of *Statistics for Psychology,* we want to thank Mark Walter, Albion College; Helga Walz, University of Baltimore; Susan Nolan, Seton Hall University; Jwa K. Kim, Middle Tennessee State University; Steven Gangestad, University of New Mexico; Mark Vosvick, University of North Texas; Ann Lynn, Ithaca College; John Bechtold, Messiah College; Donald Sharpe, University of Regina; Terri-Lynn MacKay, University of Manitoba; and Jacqueline Bichsel, Penn State Harrisburg. We are extremely grateful to LeeAnn Doherty and Jeff Marshall of Prentice Hall for superbly leading us through the long revision process. Thanks are also due to Jill Traut, Lori Hazzard, and Fred Dahl for their excellent assistance with the production of this edition. We also particularly want to acknowledge Ted Whitley (East Carolina University) for identifying many crucial final changes to the text.

Arthur Aron

Elaine N. Aron

Elliot J. Coups

Credits

Data in Tables 7–11, 7–12, 8–4, 8–5, 9–9, 9–10, 10–15, 10–16, 11–7, 11–8, 13–9, and 13–10 are based on tables in Cohen, J. (1988). *Statistical power analysis for the behavioral sciences* (2nd ed.). Copyright © 1988 by Lawrence Erlbaum Associates, Inc. Reprinted by permission.

Introduction to the Student

The goal of this book is to help you *understand* statistics. We emphasize meaning and concepts, not just symbols and numbers.

This emphasis plays to your strength. Most psychology majors are not lovers of mathematics but are keenly attuned to ideas. And we want to underscore the following, based on our collective many decades of teaching experience: *We have never had a student who could do well in other college courses who could not also do well in this course.* (However, we admit that doing well in this course may require more work than doing well in others.)

In this introduction, we discuss why you are taking this course and how you can gain the most from it.

Why Learn Statistics, Other Than to Fulfill a Requirement?

1. *Understanding statistics is crucial to being able to read psychology research articles.* Nearly every course you will take as a psychology major will emphasize the results of research studies, and these almost always are expressed using statistics. If you do not understand the basic logic of statistics—if you cannot make sense of the jargon, the tables, and the graphs that are at the heart of any research report—your reading of research will be very superficial. (We also recommend that you take a course on how to design and evaluate good research. In this book, we focus on the statistical methods for making sense of the data collected through research. However, we have included a downloadable chapter on the Web site for the book—http://www.pearsonhighered.com—that provides an overview of the logic and language of psychology research.)

2. *Understanding statistics is crucial to doing research yourself.* Many psychology majors eventually decide to go on to graduate school. Graduate study in psychology—even in clinical and counseling psychology and other applied areas—almost always involves *doing* research. In fact, learning to do research on your own is often the main focus of graduate school, and doing research almost always involves statistics. This course gives you a solid foundation in the statistics you need for doing research. Further, by mastering the basic logic and ways of thinking about statistics, you will be unusually well prepared for the advanced courses, which focus on the nitty gritty of analyzing research results.

Many psychology programs also offer opportunities for undergraduates to do research. The main focus of this book is understanding statistics, not using statistics. Still, you will learn the basics you need to analyze the results of the kinds of research you are likely to do. (Also, the Web site that accompanies this book—http://www.pearsonhighered.com—has a special chapter to help you with practical issues in using what you learn in this book for analyzing results of your own research.)

3. *Understanding statistics develops your analytic and critical thinking.* Psychology majors are often most interested in people and in improving things in the practical world. This does not mean that you avoid abstractions. In fact, the students we know are exhilarated most by the almost philosophical levels of abstraction where the secrets of human experience so often seem to hide. Yet even this kind of abstraction often is grasped only superficially at first, as slogans instead of useful knowledge. Of all the courses you are likely to take in psychology, this one will probably do the most to help you learn to think precisely, to evaluate information, and to apply logical analysis at a very high level.

How to Gain the Most from This Course

There are five things we can advise:

1. *Keep your attention on the concepts.* Treat this course less like a math course and more like a course in logic. When you read a section of a chapter, your attention should be on grasping the principles. When working the exercises, think about why you are doing each step. If you simply try to memorize how to come up with the right numbers, you will have learned very little of use in your future studies—nor will you do very well on the tests in this course.

2. *Be sure you know each concept before you go on to the next.* Statistics is cumulative. Each new concept is built on the last one. There are short "How Are You Doing?" self-tests at the end of each main chapter section. Be sure you do them. You may also find it helpful to review the "How Are You Doing" sections before working on the practice problems and when studying for exams. If you are having trouble answering a question at any time—or even if you can answer it but aren't sure you really understand it—*stop*. Reread the section, rethink it, ask for help. Do whatever you need to do to grasp it. Don't go on to the next section until you are completely confident you have gotten this one. If you are not sure, and you've already done the "How are you doing?" questions, take a look at the *Example Worked-Out Problems* toward the end of the chapter, or try working a practice problem on this material from the end of the chapter. The answers to the Set I practice problems are given toward the end of the book so that you will be able to check your work.

Having to read the material in this book over and over does not mean that you are stupid. Most students have to read each chapter several times. And each reading in statistics is usually much slower than that in other textbooks. Statistics reading has to be pored over with clear, calm attention for it to sink in. Allow plenty of time for this kind of reading and rereading.

3. *Keep up.* Again, statistics is cumulative. If you fall behind in your reading or miss lectures, the lectures you do attend will be almost meaningless. It will get harder and harder to catch up.

4. *Study especially intensely in the first half of the course.* It is particularly important to master the material thoroughly at the start of the course. Everything else you learn in statistics is built on what you learn at the start. Yet the beginning of the semester is often when students study least.

If you have mastered the first half of the course—not just learned the general idea, but really know it—the second half will be easier. If you have not mastered the first half, the second half will be close to impossible.

5. *Help each other.* There is no better way to solidify and deepen your understanding of statistics than to try to explain it to someone who is having a harder time. (Of course, this explaining has to be done with patience and respect.) For those of you who are having a harder time, there is no better way to work through the difficult parts than by learning from another student who has just mastered the material.

Thus, we strongly urge you to form study groups with one to three other students. It is best if your group includes some who expect this material to come easily and some who don't. Those who learn statistics easily will get the most from helping others who have to struggle with it—the latter will tax the former's supposed understanding enormously. Those who fear trouble ahead need to work with those who do not (the blind leading the blind is no way to learn). Pick group members who live near you so that it is easy for you to get together. Also, meet often—between each class, if possible.

A Final Note

Believe it or not, we love teaching statistics. Time and again, we have had the wonderful experience of having beaming students come to us to say, "Professor, I got a 90% on this exam. I can't believe it! Me, a 90 on a statistics exam!" Or the student who tells us, "This is actually fun. Don't tell anyone, but I'm actually enjoying . . . statistics, of all things!" We hope you will have these kinds of experiences in this course.

Arthur Aron

Elaine N. Aron

Elliot J. Coups

CHAPTER 1

Displaying the Order in a Group of Numbers Using Tables and Graphs

Chapter Outline

- ✪ The Two Branches of Statistical Methods   2
- ✪ Some Basic Concepts   3
- ✪ Frequency Tables   7
- ✪ Histograms   10
- ✪ Shapes of Frequency Distributions   15
- ✪ Controversy: Misleading Graphs   19
- ✪ Frequency Tables and Histograms in Research Articles   21

- ✪ Summary   23
- ✪ Key Terms   24
- ✪ Example Worked-Out Problems   24
- ✪ Practice Problems   25
- ✪ Using SPSS   29
- ✪ Chapter Note   32

Welcome to *Statistics for Psychology*. We imagine you to be like other students we have known who have taken this course. You have chosen to major in psychology or a related field because you are fascinated by people—by the visible behaviors of the people around you, perhaps too by their inner lives as well as by your own. Some of you are highly scientific sorts; others are more intuitive. Some of you are fond of math; others are less so, or even afraid of it. Whatever your style, we welcome you. We want to assure you that if you give this book some special attention (perhaps a little more than most textbooks require), you *will* learn statistics. The approach used in this book has successfully taught all sorts of students before you, including those who had taken statistics previously and done poorly. With this book and your instructor's help, you will learn statistics and learn it well.

More importantly, we want to assure you that whatever your reason for studying psychology or a related field, this course is not a waste of time. Learning about statistics helps you to read the work of other psychologists, to do your own research if you so choose, and to hone both your reasoning and intuition. Formally, **statistics** is a branch of mathematics that focuses on the organization, analysis, and interpretation of a group of numbers. But really what is statistics? Think of statistics as a tool that has evolved from a basic thinking process employed by every human: you observe a thing; you wonder what it means or what caused it; you have an insight or make an intuitive guess; you observe again, but now in detail, or you try making little changes in the process to test your intuition. Then you face the eternal problem: was your hunch confirmed or not? What are the chances that what you observed this second time will happen again and again, so that you can announce your insight to the world as something probably true?

Statistics is a method of pursuing truth. As a minimum, statistics can tell you the likelihood that your hunch is true in this time and place and with these sorts of people. This pursuit of truth, or at least its future likelihood, is the essence of psychology, of science, and of human evolution. Think of the first research questions: what will the mammoths do next spring? What will happen if I eat this root? It is easy to see how the early accurate "researchers" survived. You are here today because your ancestors exercised brains as well as brawn. Do those who come after you the same favor: think carefully about outcomes. Statistics is one good way to do that.

Psychologists use statistical methods to help them make sense of the numbers they collect when conducting research. The issue of how to design good research is a topic in itself, summarized in a Web Chapter (*Overview of the Logic and Language of Psychology Research*) available on the Web site for this book *http://www.pearsonhighered.com/*. But in this text we confine ourselves to the statistical methods for making sense of the data collected through research.

Psychologists usually use a computer and statistical software to carry out statistical procedures, such as the ones you will learn in this book. However, the best way to develop a solid understanding of statistics is to learn how to do the procedures by hand (with the help of a calculator). To minimize the amount of figuring you have to do, we use relatively small groups of numbers in each chapter's examples and practice problems. We hope that this will also allow you to focus more on the *underlying principles and logic* of the statistical procedure, rather than on the mathematics of each practice problem (such as subtracting 3 from 7 and then dividing the result by 2 to give an answer of 2). (See the *Introduction to the Student* on pp. xvi–xviii for more information on the goals of this book.) Having said that, we also recognize the importance of learning how to do statistical procedures on a computer, as you most likely would when conducting your own research. So, at the end of relevant chapters, there is a section called *Using SPSS* (see also the *Study Guide and Computer Workbook* that accompanies this text and that includes a guide to getting started with SPSS). SPSS statistical software is commonly used by psychologists and other behavioral and social scientists to carry out statistical analyses. Check with your instructor to see if you have access to SPSS at your institution.

The Two Branches of Statistical Methods

There are two main branches of statistical methods.

1. **Descriptive statistics:** Psychologists use descriptive statistics to summarize and describe a group of numbers from a research study.
2. **Inferential statistics:** Psychologists use inferential statistics to draw conclusions and to make inferences that are based on the numbers from a research study but that go beyond the numbers. For example, inferential statistics allow researchers to make inferences about a large group of individuals based on a research study in which a much smaller number of individuals took part.

statistics   branch of mathematics that focuses on the organization, analysis, and interpretation of a group of numbers.

descriptive statistics   procedures for summarizing a group of scores or otherwise making them more comprehensible.

inferential statistics   procedures for drawing conclusions based on the scores collected in a research study but going beyond them.

In this chapter and the next, we focus on descriptive statistics. This topic is important in its own right, but it also prepares you to understand inferential statistics. Inferential statistics are the focus of the remainder of the book.

In this chapter we introduce you to some basic concepts, and then you will learn to use tables and graphs to describe a group of numbers. The purpose of descriptive statistics is to make a group of numbers easy to understand. As you will see, tables and graphs help a great deal.

purpose |.

Some Basic Concepts

Variables, Values, and Scores

As part of a larger study (Aron, Paris, & Aron, 1995), researchers gave a questionnaire to students in an introductory statistics class during the first week of the course. One question asked was, "How stressed have you been in the last 2½ weeks, on a scale of 0 to 10, with 0 being *not at all stressed* and 10 being *as stressed as possible?*" (How would *you* answer?) In this study, the researchers used a survey to examine students' level of stress. Other methods that researchers use to study stress include measuring stress-related hormones in human blood or conducting controlled laboratory studies with animals.

In this example, level of stress is a **variable,** which can have **values** from 0 to 10, and the value of any particular person's answer is the person's **score.** If you answered 6, your score is 6; your score has a value of 6 on the variable called "level of stress."

More formally, a variable is a condition or characteristic that can have different values. In short, it can *vary.* In our example, the variable was level of stress, which can have the values of 0 through 10. Height is a variable, social class is a variable, score on a creativity test is a variable, type of psychotherapy received by patients is a variable, speed on a reaction time test is a variable, number of people absent from work on a given day is a variable, and so forth.

A value is just a number, such as 4, –81, or 367.12. A value can also be a category, such as male or female, or a psychiatric diagnosis—major depression, post-traumatic stress disorder—and so forth.

Finally, on any variable, each person studied has a particular number or *score* that is his or her value on the variable. As we've said, your score on the stress variable might have a value of 6. Another student's score might have a value of 8.

Psychology research is about variables, values, and scores (see Table 1–1). The formal definitions are a bit abstract, but in practice, the meaning usually is clear.

Levels of Measurement (Kinds of Variables)

Most of the variables psychologists use are like those in the stress ratings example: the scores are numbers that tell you how much there is of what is being measured. In the stress ratings example, the higher the number is, the more stress there is. This is

variable   characteristic that can have different values.

values   possible number or category that a score can have.

score   particular person's value on a variable.

Table 1-1	Some Basic Terminology	
Term	**Definition**	**Examples**
Variable	Condition or characteristic that can have different values	Stress level, age, gender, religion
Value	Number or category	0, 1, 2, 3, 4, 25, 85, female, Catholic
Score	A particular person's value on a variable	0, 1, 2, 3, 4, 25, 85, female, Catholic

Quantitative variables (handwritten)

an example of a **numeric variable.** Numeric variables are also called *quantitative variables.*

There are several kinds of numeric variables. In psychology research the most important distinction is between two types: equal-interval variables and rank-order variables. An **equal-interval variable** is a variable in which the numbers stand for approximately equal amounts of what is being measured. For example, grade point average (GPA) is a roughly equal-interval variable, since the difference between a GPA of 2.5 and 2.8 means about as much as the difference between a GPA of 3.0 and 3.3 (each is a difference of 0.3 of a GPA). Most psychologists also consider scales like the 0-to-10 stress ratings as roughly equal interval. So, for example, a difference between stress ratings of 4 and 6 means about as much as the difference between 7 and 9.

Some equal-interval variables are measured on what is called a **ratio scale.** An equal-interval variable is measured on a ratio scale if it has an *absolute zero point.* An absolute zero point means that the value of zero on the variable indicates a complete absence of the variable. Most counts or accumulations of things use a ratio scale. For example, the number of siblings a person has is measured on a ratio scale, because a zero value means having no siblings. With variables that are measured on a ratio scale, you can make statements about the difference in magnitude between values. So, we can say that a person with four siblings has twice as many siblings as a person with two siblings. However, most of the variables in psychology are not on a ratio scale.

Equal-interval variables can also be distinguished as being either discrete variables or continuous variables. A **discrete variable** is one that has specific values and cannot have values between the specific values. The number of times you went to the dentist in the last 12 months is a discrete variable. You may have gone 0, 1, 2, 3, or more times, but you can't have gone 1.72 times or 2.34 times. With a **continuous variable,** there are in theory an infinite number of values between any two values. So, even though we usually answer the question "How old are you?" with a specific age, such as 19 or 20, you could also answer it by saying that you are 19.26 years old. Height, weight, and time are examples of other continuous variables.

The other main type of numeric variable, a **rank-order variable,** is a variable in which the numbers stand only for relative ranking. (Rank-order variables are also called *ordinal variables.*) A student's standing in his or her graduating class is an example. The amount of difference in underlying GPA between being second and third in class standing could be very unlike the amount of difference between being eighth and ninth.

A rank-order variable provides less information than an equal-interval variable. That is, the difference from one rank to the next doesn't tell you the exact difference in amount of what is being measured. However, psychologists often use rank-order variables because they are the only information available. Also, when people are being asked to rate something, it is sometimes easier and less arbitrary for them to make rank-order ratings. For example, when rating how much you like each of your friends, it may be easier to rank them by how much you like them than to rate your liking for them on a scale. Yet another reason researchers often use rank-order variables is that asking people to do rankings forces them to make distinctions. For example, if asked to rate how much you like each of your friends on a 1-to-10 scale, you might rate several of them at exactly the same level, but ranking would avoid such ties.

Another major type of variable used in psychology research, which is not a numeric variable at all, is a **nominal variable** in which the values are names or categories. The term *nominal* comes from the idea that its values are names. (Nominal

---

numeric variable variable whose values are numbers (as opposed to a nominal variable). Also called *quantitative variable.*

equal-interval variable variable in which the numbers stand for approximately equal amounts of what is being measured.

ratio scale an equal-interval variable is measured on a ratio scale if it has an *absolute zero point,* meaning that the value of zero on the variable indicates a complete absence of the variable.

discrete variable variable that has specific values and that cannot have values between these specific values.

continuous variable variable for which, in theory, there are an infinite number of values between any two values.

rank-order variable numeric variable in which the values are ranks, such as class standing or place finished in a race. Also called *ordinal variable.*

nominal variable variable with values that are categories (that is, they are names rather than numbers). Also called *categorical variable.*

Table 1-2   Levels of Measurement

Level	Definition	Example
Equal-interval	Numeric variable in which differences between values correspond to differences in the underlying thing being measured	Stress level, age
Rank-order	Numeric variable in which values correspond to the relative position of things measured	Class standing, position finished in a race
Nominal	Variable in which the values are categories	Gender, religion

variables are also called *categorical variables* because their values are categories.) For example, for the nominal variable gender, the values are female and male. A person's "score" on the variable gender is one of these two values. Another example is psychiatric diagnosis, which has values such as major depression, post-traumatic stress disorder, schizophrenia, and obsessive-compulsive disorder.

These different kinds of variables are based on different **levels of measurement** (see Table 1–2). Researchers sometimes have to decide how they will measure a particular variable. For example, they might use an equal-interval scale, a rank-order scale, or a nominal scale. The level of measurement selected affects the type of statistics that can be used with a variable. Suppose a researcher is studying the effects of a particular type of brain injury on being able to recognize objects. One approach the researcher might take would be to measure the number of different objects an injured person can observe at once. This is an example of an equal-interval level of measurement. Alternately, the researcher might rate people as able to observe no objects (rated 0), only one object at a time (rated 1), one object with a vague sense of other objects (rated 2), or ordinary vision (rated 3). This would be a rank-order approach. Finally, the researcher might divide people into those who are completely blind (rated B), those who can identify the location of an object but not what the object is (rated L), those who can identify what the object is but not locate it in space (rated I), those who can both locate and identify an object but have other abnormalities of object perception (rated O), and those with normal visual perception (rated N). This is a nominal level of measurement.

In this book, as in most psychology research, we focus mainly on numeric, equal-interval variables (or variables that roughly approximate equal-interval variables). We discuss statistical methods for working with nominal variables in Chapter 13 and methods for working with rank-order variables in Chapter 14.

levels of measurement   types of underlying numerical information provided by a measure, such as equal-interval, rank-order, and nominal (categorical).

How are you doing?

1. A father rates his daughter as a 2 on a 7-point scale (from 1 to 7) of crankiness. In this example, (a) what is the variable, (b) what is the score, and (c) what is the range of values?
2. What is the difference between a numeric and a nominal variable?
3. What is the difference between a discrete and a continuous variable?
4. Give the level of measurement of each of the following variables: (a) a person's nationality (Mexican, Spanish, Ethiopian, Australian, etc.), (b) a person's score on a standard IQ test, (c) a person's place on a waiting list (first in line, second in line, etc.).

BOX 1–1   Important Trivia for Poetic Statistics Students

The word *statistics* comes from the Italian word *statista,* a person dealing with affairs of state (from *stato,* "state"). It was originally called "state arithmetic," involving the tabulation of information about nations, especially for the purpose of taxation and planning the feasibility of wars.

Statistics were needed in ancient times to figure the odds of shipwrecks and piracy for marine insurance that would encourage voyages of commerce and exploration to far-flung places. The modern study of mortality rates and life insurance descended from the 17th-century plague pits—counting the bodies of persons cut down in the bloom of youth. The theory of errors (covered in Chapter 12) began in astronomy, that is, with stargazing; the theory of correlation (Chapter 11) has its roots in biology, from the observation of parent and child differences. Probability theory (Chapter 3) arose in the tense environs of the gambling table. The theory of analysis of experiments (Chapters 7 to 10) began in breweries and out among waving fields of wheat, where correct guesses determined not only the survival of a tasty beer but of thousands of marginal farmers. Theories of measurement and factor analysis (Chapter 15) derived from personality psychology, where the depths of human character were first explored with numbers. And chi-square (Chapter 13) came to us from sociology, where it was often a question of class.

In the early days of statistics, it was popular to use the new methods to prove the existence of God. For example, John Arbuthnot discovered that more male than female babies were born in London between 1629 and 1710. In what is considered the first use of a statistical test, he proved that the male birthrate was higher than could be expected by chance (assuming that 50:50 was chance) and concluded that there was a plan operating, since males face more danger to obtain food for their families, and only God, he said, could do such planning.

In 1767, John Michell also used probability theory to prove the existence of God when he argued that the odds were 500,000 to 1 against six stars being placed as close together as those in the constellation Pleiades; so their placement had to have been a deliberate act of the Creator.

Statistics in the "state arithmetic" sense are legally endorsed by most governments today. For example, the first article of the U.S. Constitution requires a census. And statistics helped the United States win the Revolutionary War. John Adams obtained critical aid from Holland by pointing out certain vital statistics, carefully gathered by the clergy in local parishes, demonstrating that the colonies had doubled their population every 18 years, adding 20,000 fighting men per annum. "Is this the case of our enemy, Great Britain?" Adams wrote. "Which then can maintain the war the longest?"

Similar statistics were observed by U.S. President Thomas Jefferson in 1786. He wrote that his people "become uneasy" when there are more of them than 10 per square mile and that given the population growth of the new country, within 40 years these restless souls would fill up all of their country's "vacant land." Some 17 years later, Jefferson doubled the size of the United States' "vacant" land through the Louisiana Purchase.

Frequency Tables

An Example

Let's return to the stress ratings example. Recall that in this study, students in an introductory statistics class during the first week of the course answered the question, "How stressed have you been in the last 2½ weeks, on a scale of 0 to 10, with 0 being *not at all stressed* and 10 being *as stressed as possible?*" The actual study included scores from 151 students. To ease the learning for this example, we are going to use a representative subset of scores from 30 of the 151 students (this also saves you time if you want to try it for yourself). The 30 students' scores (their ratings on the scale) are:

8, 7, 4, 10, 8, 6, 8, 9, 9, 7, 3, 7, 6, 5, 0, 9, 10, 7, 7, 3, 6, 7, 5, 2, 1, 6, 7, 10, 8, 8.

Looking through all these scores gives some sense of the overall tendencies, but this is hardly an accurate method. One solution is to make a table showing how many students used each of the 11 values that the ratings can have (0, 1, 2, and so on, through 10). We have done this in Table 1–3. We also figured the percentage each value's frequency is of the total number of scores. Tables like this sometimes give only the raw-number frequencies, not the percentages, or only the percentages and not the raw-number frequencies. In addition, some frequency tables include, for each value, the total number of scores with that value and all values preceding it. These are called *cumulative frequencies* because they tell how many scores are accumulated up to this point on the table. If percentages are used, cumulative percentages also may be included (for an example, see Figure 1–18 in the *Using SPSS* section on page 30). Cumulative percentages give, for each value, the percentage of scores up to and including that value. The cumulative percentage for any given value (or for a score having that value) is also called a *percentile*. Cumulative frequencies and cumulative percentages allow you to see where a particular score falls in the overall group of scores.

Table 1–3 is called a **frequency table** because it shows how frequently (how many times) each score was used. A frequency table makes the pattern of numbers easy to see. In this example, you can see that most of the students rated their stress level around 7 or 8, with few rating it very low.

Table 1-3 Frequency Table of Number of Students Rating Each Value of the Stress Scale

Stress Rating	Frequency	Percent
0	1	3.3
1	1	3.3
2	1	3.3
3	2	6.7
4	1	3.3
5	2	6.7
6	4	13.3
7	7	23.3
8	5	16.7
9	3	10.0
10	3	10.0

Source: Data based on Aron et al. (1995).

How to Make a Frequency Table

There are the four steps in making a frequency table.

❶ **Make a list down the page of each possible value, from lowest to highest.** In the stress ratings results, the list goes from 0, the lowest possible rating, up to 10, the highest possible rating.[1] Note that even if one of the ratings between 0 and 10 is not used, you still include that value in the listing, showing it as having a frequency of 0. For example, if no one gives a stress rating of 2, you still include 2 as one of the values on the frequency table.

❷ **Go one by one through the scores, making a mark for each next to its value on your list.** This is shown in Figure 1–1.

❸ **Make a table showing how many times each value on your list is used.** That is, add up the number of marks beside each value.

❹ **Figure the percentage of scores for each value.** To do this, take the frequency for that value, divide it by the total number of scores, and multiply by 100. You may need to round off the percentage. We recommend that you round percentages to one decimal place. Note that because of the rounding, your percentages do not usually add up to exactly 100% (but they should be close).

frequency table listing of number of individuals having each of the different values for a particular variable.

TIP FOR SUCCESS

When doing Step ❷, cross off each score as you mark it on the list. This should help you avoid mistakes, which are common in this step.

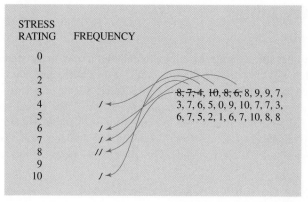

Figure 1–1   Making a frequency table for the stress ratings scores. (Data based on Aron et al., 1995.)

Table 1-4   Frequency Table for a Nominal Variable: Closest Person in Life for 208 Students

Closest Person	Frequency	Percent
Family member	33	15.9
Nonromantic friend	76	36.5
Romantic partner	92	44.2
Other	7	3.4

Source: Data from Aron et al. (1992).

0 -	17 - ////	34 -
1 - //	18 - 7HH	35 - //
2 - /	19 - ////	36 -
3 - 7HH	20 -	37 -
4 - ////	21 - ////	38 - /
5 - ///	22 - ///	39 -
6 - //	23 - /	40 - /
7 - //	24 - //	41 - /
8 - 7HH /	25 - ///	42 -
9 - ///	26 - //	43 -
10 - 7HH /	27 - /	44 - /
11 - ////	28 - /	45 -
12 - /	29 - ////	46 -
13 - //	30 - //	47 - //
14 - ///	31 -	48 - /
15 - /	32 - /	
16 - //	33 - /	

Figure 1-2   Making a frequency table of students' social interactions over a week. (Data from McLaughlin-Volpe et al., 2001.)

Frequency Tables for Nominal Variables

The preceding steps assume you are using numeric variables, the most common situation. However, you can also use a frequency table to show the number of scores in each value (or category) of a nominal variable. For example, researchers (Aron, Aron, & Smollan, 1992) asked 208 students to name the closest person in their life. As shown in Table 1–4, 33 students selected a family member, 76 a nonromantic friend, 92 a romantic partner, and 7 selected some other person. Also in Table 1–4, the values listed on the left hand side of the frequency table are the values (the categories) of the variable.

Another Example

Tracy McLaughlin-Volpe and her colleagues (2001) had 94 introductory psychology students keep a diary of their social interactions for a week during the regular semester. Each time a participant had a social interaction lasting 10 minutes or longer, he or she would fill out a card. The card had questions about various aspects of the conversation and the conversation partner. Excluding family and work situations, the number of social interactions 10 minutes or longer over a week for these students were as follows:

48, 15, 33, 3, 21, 19, 17, 16, 44, 25, 30, 3, 5, 9, 35, 32, 26, 13, 14, 14, 47, 47, 18, 11, 5, 19, 24, 17, 6, 25, 8, 18, 29, 1, 18, 22, 3, 22, 29, 2, 6, 10, 29, 10, 29, 21, 38, 41, 16, 17, 8, 40, 8, 10, 18, 7, 4, 4, 8, 11, 3, 23, 10, 19, 21, 13, 12, 10, 4, 17, 11, 21, 9, 8, 7, 5, 3, 22, 14, 25, 4, 11, 10, 18, 1, 28, 27, 19, 24, 35, 9, 30, 8, 26.

Now, let's follow our four steps for making a frequency table.

❶ **Make a list down the page of each possible value, from lowest to highest.** The lowest possible number of interactions is 0. In this study, the highest number of interactions could be any number. However, the highest actual number in this group is 48; so we can use 48 as the highest value. Thus, the first step is to list these values down a page. (It might be good to use several columns so that you can have all the scores on a single page.)

❷ **Go one by one through the scores, making a mark for each next to its value on your list.** Figure 1–2 shows the results of this step.

❸ **Make a table showing how many times each value on your list is used.** Table 1–5 is the result.

Table 1-5   Frequency Table for Number of Social Interactions During a Week for 94 College Students

Score	Frequency	Score	Frequency	Score	Frequency
0	0	17	4	34	0
1	2	18	5	35	2
2	1	19	4	36	0
3	5	20	0	37	0
4	4	21	4	38	1
5	3	22	3	39	0
6	2	23	1	40	1
7	2	24	2	41	1
8	6	25	3	42	0
9	3	26	2	43	0
10	6	27	1	44	1
11	4	28	1	45	0
12	1	29	4	46	0
13	2	30	2	47	2
14	3	31	0	48	1
15	1	32	1		
16	2	33	1		

Source: Data from McLaughlin-Volpe et al., (2001).

❹ **Figure the percentage of scores for each value.** We have *not* done so in this example because it would not help much for seeing the pattern of scores. However, if you want to check your understanding of this step, the first five percentages would be 0.0%, 2.1%, 1.1%, 5.3%, and 4.3%. (These are the percentages for frequencies of 0, 2, 1, 5, and 4, rounded to one decimal place.)

Grouped Frequency Tables

Sometimes there are so many possible values that an ordinary frequency table is too awkward to give a simple picture of the scores. The last example was a bit like that, wasn't it? The solution is to make groupings of values that include all values in a certain range. Consider the stress ratings example. Instead of having a separate frequency figure for the group of students who rated their stress as 8 and another for those who rated it as 9, you could have a combined category of 8 and 9. This combined category is a range of values that includes these two values. A combined category like this is called an **interval.** This particular interval of 8 and 9 has a frequency of 8 (the 5 scores with a value of 8 plus the 3 scores with a value of 9).

A frequency table that uses intervals is called a **grouped frequency table.** Table 1–6 is a grouped frequency table for the stress ratings example. (Note that in this example the full frequency table has only 11 different values. Thus, a grouped frequency table is not really necessary.) Table 1–7 is a grouped frequency table for the 94 students' number of social interactions over a week.

A grouped frequency table can make information even more directly understandable than an ordinary frequency table can. Of course, the greater understandability of a grouped frequency table is at a cost. You lose some information: the details of the breakdown of frequencies in each interval.

Table 1-6   Grouped Frequency Table for Stress Ratings

Stress Rating Interval	Frequency	Percent
0–1	2	6.7
2–3	3	10.0
4–5	3	10.0
6–7	11	36.7
8–9	8	26.7
10–11	3	10.0

Source: Data based on Aron et al. (1995).

TIP FOR SUCCESS

You can cross-check your work by adding the frequencies for all of the scores. This sum should equal the total number of scores you started with.

interval   range of values in a grouped frequency table that are grouped together. (For example, if the interval size is 10, one of the intervals might be from 10 to 19.)

grouped frequency table   frequency table in which the number of individuals (frequency) is given for each interval of values.

Table 1-7 Grouped Frequency Table for Numbers of Social Interactions During a Week for 94 College Students

Interval	Frequency	Percent
0–4	12	12.8
5–9	16	17.0
10–14	16	17.0
15–19	16	17.0
20–24	10	10.6
25–29	11	11.7
30–34	4	4.3
35–39	3	3.2
40–44	3	3.2
45–49	3	3.2

Source: Data from McLaughlin-Volpe et al., (2001).

When setting up a grouped frequency table, it makes a big difference how many intervals you use. There are guidelines to help researchers with this, but in practice it is done automatically by the researcher's computer (see the *Using SPSS* section for instructions on how to create frequency tables using statistical software). Thus, we will not focus on it in this book. However, should you have to make a grouped frequency table on your own, the key is to experiment with the interval size until you come up with one that is a round number (such as 2, 3, 5, or 10) and that creates about 5 to 15 intervals. Then, when actually setting up the table, be sure you set the start of each interval to a multiple of the interval size and the top end of each interval to the number just below the start of the next interval. For example, Table 1–6 uses six intervals with an interval size of 2. The intervals are 0–1, 2–3, 4–5, 6–7, 8–9, and 10–11. Note that each interval starts with a multiple of 2 (0, 2, 4, 6, 8, 10) and the top end of each interval (1, 3, 5, 7, 9) is the number just below the start of the next interval (2, 4, 6, 8, 10). Table 1–7 uses 10 intervals with an interval size of 5. The intervals are 0–4, 5–9, 10–14, 15–19, and so on, with a final interval of 45–49. Note that each interval starts with a multiple of 5 (0, 5, 10, 15, and so on) and that the top end of each interval (4, 9, 14, 19, and so on) is the number just below the start of the next interval (5, 10, 15, 20, and so on).

How are you doing?

1. What is a frequency table?
2. Why would a researcher want to make a frequency table?
3. Make a frequency table for the following scores: 5, 7, 4, 5, 6, 5, 4.
4. What does a grouped frequency table group?

Answers

1. A frequency table is a systematic listing of the number of scores (the frequency) of each value in the group studied.
2. A frequency table makes it easy to see the pattern in a large group of scores.

3.
Value	Frequency	Percent
4	2	28.6
5	3	42.9
6	1	14.3
7	1	14.3

4. A frequency table groups the frequencies of adjacent values into intervals.

Histograms

A graph is another good way to make a large group of scores easy to understand. A picture may be worth a thousand words, but it is sometimes worth a thousand numbers. A straightforward approach is to make a graph of the frequency table. One kind of graph of the information in a frequency table is a kind of bar chart called a **histogram.** In a histogram, the height of each bar is the frequency of each value in the frequency table. Ordinarily, in a histogram all the bars are put next to each other with no space in between. The result is that a histogram looks a bit like a city skyline. Figure 1–3 shows two histograms based on the stress ratings example (one based on the ordinary frequency table and one based on the grouped frequency table). Figure 1–4 shows a histogram based on the grouped frequency table for the example of the numbers of students' social interactions in a week.

histogram barlike graph of a frequency distribution in which the values are plotted along the horizontal axis and the height of each bar is the frequency of that value; the bars are usually placed next to each other without spaces, giving the appearance of a city skyline.

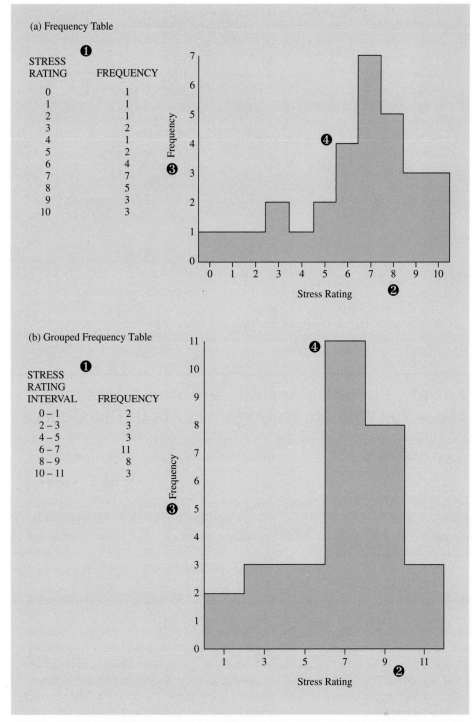

Figure 1–3 Histograms based on (a) frequency table and (b) a grouped frequency for the stress ratings example. (Data based on Aron et al., 1995.)

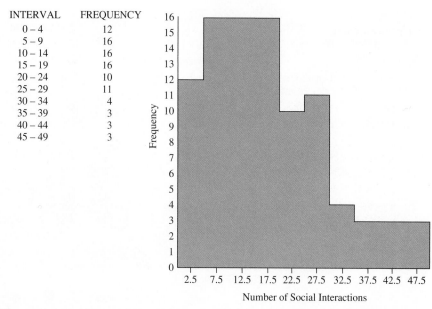

INTERVAL	FREQUENCY
0 – 4	12
5 – 9	16
10 – 14	16
15 – 19	16
20 – 24	10
25 – 29	11
30 – 34	4
35 – 39	3
40 – 44	3
45 – 49	3

Figure 1–4   Histogram for number of social interactions during a week for 94 college students based on grouped frequencies. (Data from McLaughlin-Volpe et al., 2001.)

BOX 1–2   Math Anxiety, Statistics Anxiety, and You: A Message for Those of You Who Are Truly Worried About This Course

Let's face it: Many of you dread this course, even to the point of having a full-blown case of "statistics anxiety" (Zeidner, 1991). If you become tense the minute you see numbers, we need to talk about that right now.

First, this course is a chance for a fresh start with digits. Your past performance in (or avoidance of) geometry, trigonometry, calculus, or similar horrors need not influence in any way how well you comprehend statistics. This is largely a different subject.

Second, if your worry persists, you need to determine where it is coming from. Math or statistics anxiety, test anxiety, general anxiety, and generally low self-confidence each seems to play its own role in students' difficulties with math courses (Cooper & Robinson, 1989; Dwinell & Higbee, 1991).

Is your problem mainly math or statistics anxiety? An Internet search will yield hundreds of wonderful books and Web sites to help you. We highly recommend Sheila Tobias's classics *Overcoming Math Anxiety* (1995) or *Succeed with Math: Every Student's Guide to Conquering Math Anxiety* (1987). Tobias, a former math avoider herself, suggests that your goal should be "math mental health," which she defines as "the willingness to learn the

math you need when you need it" (1995, p. 12). (Could it be that this course in statistics is one of those times?)

Tobias explains that math mental health is usually lost in elementary school, when you are called to the blackboard, your mind goes blank, and you are unable to produce the one right answer to an arithmetic problem. What confidence remained after such an experience probably faded during timed tests, which you did not realize were difficult for everyone except the most proficient few.

Tobias says that students who are good at math are not necessarily smarter than the rest of us, but they really know their strengths and weaknesses, and they have individual styles of thinking and feeling their way around a problem. They do not judge themselves harshly for mistakes. In particular, they do not expect to understand things instantly. Allowing yourself to be a "slow learner" does not mean that you are less intelligent. It shows that you are growing in math mental health.

Is your problem test anxiety? Test taking requires the use of the thinking part of our brain, the prefrontal cortex. When we are anxious, we naturally "downshift" to more basic, instinctual brain systems, and that effect ruins our thinking ability. Anxiety produces arousal, and one of the best understood relationships in psychology is between arousal and performance. Whereas moderate arousal helps performance, too much or too little dramatically reduces it. In the case of too much, things you have learned become harder to recall. Your mind starts to race, creating more anxiety, more arousal, and so on. Because during a test you may be fearing that you are "no good and never will be," it is important to rethink beforehand any poor grades you may have received in the past. They most likely reflected your problems with tests more than your abilities.

There are many ways to reduce anxiety and arousal in general, such as learning to breathe properly and to take a brief break to relax deeply. Your counseling center should be able to help you or direct you to some good books on the subject. Again, many Web sites deal with reducing anxiety.

Test anxiety specifically is first reduced by over-preparing for a few tests, so that you go in with the certainty that you cannot possibly fail, no matter how aroused you become. The best time to begin applying this tactic is the first test of this course. There will be no old material to review, success will not depend on having understood previous material, and initial success will help you do well throughout the course. (You also might enlist the sympathy of your instructor or teaching assistant. Bring in a list of what you have studied, state why you are being so exacting, and ask if you have missed anything.) Your preparation must be ridiculously thorough, but only for a few exams. After these successes, your test anxiety should decline.

Also, create a practice test situation as similar to a real test as possible, making a special effort to duplicate the aspects that bother you most. If feeling rushed is the troubling part, once you think you are well prepared, set yourself a time limit for solving some homework problems. Make yourself write out answers fully and legibly. This may be part of what makes you feel slow during a test. If the presence of others bothers you—the sound of their scurrying pencils while yours is frozen in midair—do your practice test with others in your course. Even make it an explicit contest to see who can finish first.

Is your problem a general lack of confidence? Is something else in your life causing you to worry or feel bad about yourself? Then we suggest that it is time you tried your friendly college counseling center.

Lastly, could you be highly sensitive? A final word about anxiety and arousal. About 15 to 20% of humans (and all higher animals) seem to be born with a temperament trait that has been seen traditionally as shyness, hesitancy, or introversion (Eysenck, 1981; Kagan, 1994). But this shyness or hesitancy seems actually due to a preference to observe and an ability to notice subtle stimulation and process information deeply (Aron, 1996; Aron & Aron, 1997). This often causes highly sensitive persons (HSPs) to be very intuitive or even gifted. But it also means they are more easily overaroused by high levels of stimulation, like tests.

You might want to find out if you are an HSP (at *http://www.hsperson.com*). If you are, appreciate the trait's assets and make some allowances for its one disadvantage, this tendency to become easily overaroused. It has to affect your performance on tests. What matters is what you actually know, which is probably quite a bit. This simple act of self-acceptance—that you are *not* less smart but *are* more sensitive—may in itself help ease your arousal when trying to express your statistical knowledge.

So good luck to all of you. We wish you the best while taking this course and in your lives.

How to Make a Histogram

There are four steps in making a histogram.

❶ **Make a frequency table (or grouped frequency table).**
❷ **Put the values along the bottom of the page, from left to right, from lowest to highest.** If you are making a histogram from a grouped frequency table, the values you put along the bottom of the page are the interval midpoints. The midpoint of an interval is halfway between the start of that interval and the start of the next highest interval. So, in Figure 1–4, the midpoint for the 0–4 interval is 2.5, because 2.5 is halfway between 0 (the start of the interval) and 5 (the start of the next highest interval). For the 5–9 interval, the midpoint is 7.5 because 7.5 is halfway between 5 (the start of the interval) and 10 (the start of the next highest interval). Do this for each interval. When you get to the last interval,

TIP FOR SUCCESS

Now try this yourself! Work out the interval midpoints for the grouped frequency table for the stress ratings example shown in Table 1–6. Your answers should be the same as the values shown along the bottom of Figure 1–3b.

find the midpoint between the start of the interval and the start of what would be the next highest interval. So, in Figure 1–4, the midpoint for the 45–49 interval is halfway between 45 (the start of the interval) and 50 (the start of what would be the next interval), which is 47.5.

❸ **Make a scale of frequencies along the left edge of the page that goes from 0 at the bottom to the highest frequency for any value.**

❹ **Make a bar above each value with a height for the frequency of that value.** For each bar, make sure that the middle of the bar is above its value.

When you have a nominal variable, the histogram is called a *bar graph.* Since the values of a nominal variable are not in any particular order, leave a space between the bars. Figure 1–5 shows a bar graph based on the frequency table in Table 1–4.

TIP FOR SUCCESS

You will probably find it easier to make a histogram if you use graph paper.

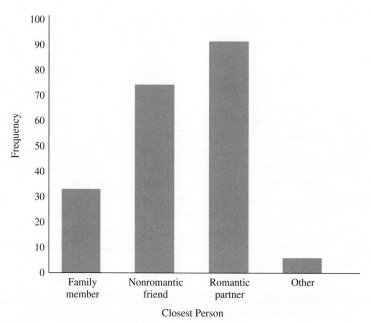

Figure 1–5 Bar graph for the closest person in life for 208 students (see Table 1–4). (Data from Aron et al., 1995.)

How are you doing?

1. Why do researchers make frequency graphs?
2. When making a histogram from a frequency table, (a) what goes along the bottom, (b) what goes along the left edge, and (c) what goes above each value?
3. Make a histogram based on the following frequency table:

Value	Frequency
1	3
2	4
3	8
4	5
5	2

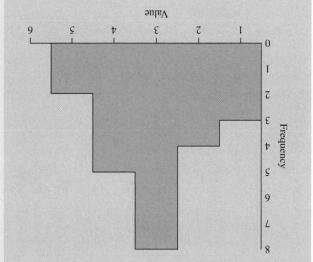

Figure 1–6
Histogram for "How Are
You Doing?" question 3.

3. See Figure 1–6.

value.

2. (a) The values, from lowest to highest go along the bottom; (b) the frequencies from 0 at the bottom to the highest frequency of any value at the top go along the left; (c) above each value is a bar with a height of the frequency for that

1. Researchers make frequency graphs to show the pattern visually in a frequency table.

Answers

frequency distribution   pattern of frequencies over the various values; what a frequency table, histogram, or frequency polygon describes.

unimodal distribution   frequency distribution with one value clearly having a larger frequency than any other.

bimodal distribution   frequency distribution with two approximately equal frequencies, each clearly larger than any of the others.

multimodal distribution   frequency distribution with two or more high frequencies separated by a lower frequency; a bimodal distribution is the special case of two high frequencies.

rectangular distribution   frequency distribution in which all values have approximately the same frequency.

Shapes of Frequency Distributions

A **frequency distribution** shows the pattern of frequencies over the various values. A frequency table or histogram describes a frequency distribution because each shows the pattern or shape of how the frequencies are spread out, or "distributed."

Psychologists also describe this shape in words. Describing the shape of a distribution is important both in the descriptive statistics of this chapter and the next and in the inferential statistics of later chapters.

Unimodal and Bimodal Frequency Distributions

One question is whether a distribution's shape has only one main high point: one high "tower" in the histogram. For example, in the stress ratings study, the most frequent value is 7, giving a graph only one very high area. This is a **unimodal distribution.** If a distribution has two fairly equal high points, it is a **bimodal distribution.** Any distribution with two or more high points is called a **multimodal distribution.** (Strictly speaking, a distribution is bimodal or multimodal only if the peaks are exactly equal. However, psychologists use these terms more informally to describe the general shape.) Finally, a distribution with values of all about the same frequency is a **rectangular distribution.** Figure 1–7 shows examples of these frequency distribution shapes. As you will see, the graphs in Figure 1–7 are not histograms, but special line graphs called *frequency polygons,* which are another way to graph a frequency table. In a frequency polygon, the line moves from point to point. The height of each point shows the number of scores with that value. This creates a mountain peak skyline.

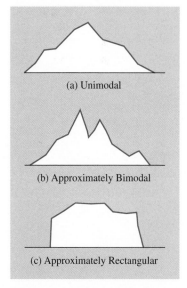

Figure 1–7 Examples of (a) unimodal, (b) approximately bimodal, and (c) approximately rectangular frequency polygons.

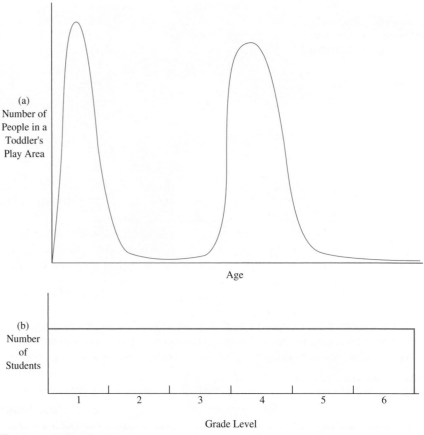

Figure 1–8 Fictional examples of distributions that are not unimodal: (a) A bimodal distribution showing the possible frequencies for people of different ages in a toddler's play area. (b) A regular distribution showing the possible frequencies of students at different grade levels in an elementary school.

The scores from most psychology studies are usually an approximately unimodal distribution. Bimodal and other multimodal distributions occasionally turn up. A bimodal example is the distribution of the ages of people in a toddler's play area in a park, who are mostly either toddlers with ages of around 2 to 4 or caretakers with ages of 20 to 40 or so (with few people aged 5 to 19 years or above 40). Thus, if you make a frequency distribution of these ages, the large frequencies are at the values for low ages (2 to 4) and for higher ages (20 to 40 or so). An example of a rectangular distribution is the number of children at each grade level at an elementary school; there is about the same number in first grade, second grade, and so on. Figure 1–8 shows these examples.

Symmetrical and Skewed Distributions

Look again at the histograms of the stress ratings example (Figure 1–3). The distribution is lopsided, with more scores near the high end. This is somewhat unusual. Most things we measure in psychology have about equal numbers on both sides of the middle. That is, most of the time in psychology, the scores follow an approximately

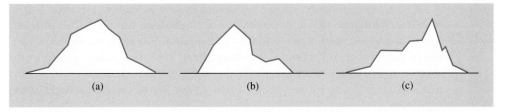

Figure 1–9 Examples of frequency polygons of distributions that are (a) approximately symmetrical, (b) skewed to the right (positively skewed), and (c) skewed to the left (negatively skewed).

symmetrical distribution (if you fold the graph of a symmetrical distribution in half, the two halves look the same).

A distribution that clearly is not symmetrical is called a **skewed distribution.** The stress ratings distribution is an example. A skewed distribution has one side that is long and spread out, somewhat like a tail. The side with the *fewer* scores (the side that looks like a tail) is considered the direction of the skew. Thus, the stress study example, which has too few scores at the low end, is skewed to the left. However, the social interactions example, which has too few scores at the high end, is skewed to the right (see Figure 1–4). Figure 1–9 shows examples of approximately symmetrical and skewed distributions.

A distribution that is skewed to the right is also called *positively skewed.* A distribution skewed to the left is also called *negatively skewed.*

Strongly skewed distributions come up in psychology research mainly when what is being measured has some upper or lower limit. For example, a family cannot have fewer than zero children. When many scores pile up at the low end because it is impossible to have a lower score, the result is called a **floor effect.** A skewed distribution caused by a lower limit is shown in Figure 1–10a.

symmetrical distribution distribution in which the pattern of frequencies on the left and right side are mirror images of each other.

skewed distribution distribution in which the scores pile up on one side of the middle and are spread out on the other side; distribution that is not symmetrical.

floor effect situation in which many scores pile up at the low end of a distribution (creating skewness) because it is not possible to have any lower score.

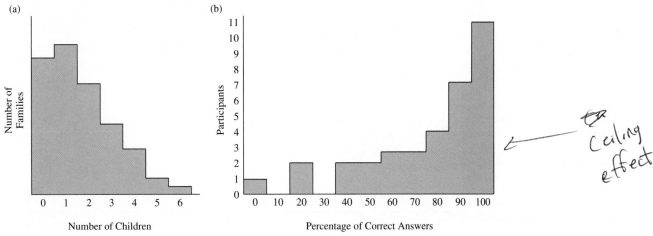

ceiling effect

Figure 1–10 (a) A distribution skewed to the right due to a floor effect: fictional distribution of the number of children in families. (b) A distribution skewed to the left due to a ceiling effect: fictional distribution of adults' scores on a multiplication table test.

A skewed distribution caused by an upper limit is shown in Figure 1–10b. This is a distribution of adults' scores on a multiplication table test. This distribution is strongly skewed to the left. Most of the scores pile up at the right, the high end (a perfect score). This shows a **ceiling effect.** The stress ratings example also shows a mild ceiling effect because many students had high levels of stress, the maximum rating was 10, and people often do not like to use ratings right at the maximum.

Normal and Kurtotic Distributions

Psychologists also describe a distribution in terms of whether the middle of the distribution is particularly peaked or flat. The standard of comparison is a bell-shaped curve. In psychology research and in nature generally, distributions often are similar to this bell-shaped standard, called the **normal curve.** We discuss this curve in some detail in later chapters. For now, however, the important thing is that the normal curve is a unimodal, symmetrical curve with an average peak—the sort of bell shape shown in Figure 1–11a. Both the stress ratings and the social interactions examples approximate a normal curve in a very general way—although, as we noted, both are somewhat skewed. In our experience, most distributions that result from psychology research are closer to the normal curve than are these two examples.

Kurtosis is how much the shape of a distribution differs from a normal curve in terms of whether its curve in the middle is more peaked or flat than the normal curve (DeCarlo, 1997). Kurtosis comes from the Greek word *kyrtos,* "curve." Figure 1–11b shows a kurtotic distribution with a more extreme peak than the normal curve. Figure 1–11c shows an extreme example of a kurtotic distribution, one with a very flat distribution. (A rectangular distribution would be even more extreme.)

Distributions that are more peaked or flat than a normal curve also tend to have a different shape in the tails. Those with a very peaked curve usually have more scores in the tails of the distribution than the normal curve (see Figure 1–11b). It is as if the normal curve got pinched in the middle and some of it went up into a sharp peak and the rest spread out into thick tails. Distributions with a flatter curve usually have fewer scores in the tails of the distribution than the normal curve (see Figure 1–11c). It is as if the tails and the top of the curve both got sucked in toward the middle on both sides. Although it is often easiest to identify kurtosis in terms of how peaked or flat the distribution is, the number of scores in the tails is what matters.

ceiling effect situation in which many scores pile up at the high end of a distribution (creating skewness) because it is not possible to have a higher score.

normal curve specific, mathematically defined, bell-shaped frequency distribution that is symmetrical and unimodal; distributions observed in nature and in research commonly approximate it.

kurtosis extent to which a frequency distribution deviates from a normal curve in terms of whether its curve in the middle is more peaked or flat than the normal curve.

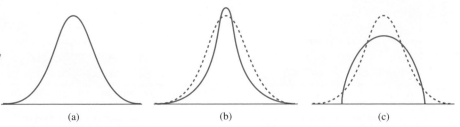

(a) (b) (c)

Figure 1–11 Examples of (a) normal, (b) peaked, and (c) flat distribution. The normal distribution is shown as a dashed line in (b) and (c).

Source: Adapted from DeCarlo, T. (1997). On the meaning and use of kurtosis. Psychological Methods, 3, 292–307, Figure 1. Published by the American Psychological Association. Adapted with permission.

Controversy: Misleading Graphs

The most serious controversy about frequency tables and histograms is not among psychologists, but among the general public. The misuse of these procedures by some public figures, advertisers, and the media seems to have created skepticism about the trustworthiness of statistics in general and of statistical tables and charts in particular. Everyone has heard that "statistics lie."

Of course, people can and do lie with statistics. It is just as easy to lie with words, but you may be less sure of your ability to recognize lies with numbers. In this section, we note two ways in which frequency tables and graphs can be misused and tell how to recognize such misuses. (Much of this material is based on the classic discussion of these issues in Tufte, 1983.)

Failure to Use Equal Interval Sizes

A key requirement of a grouped frequency table or graph is that the size of the intervals be equal. If they are not equal, the table or graph can be very misleading. Tufte (1983) gives an example, shown in Figure 1–12, from the respectable (and usually accurate) *New York Times*. This chart gives the impression that commissions paid to travel agents dropped dramatically in 1978. However, a close reading of the graph shows that the third bar for each airline is for only the first half of 1978. Thus, only half a year is being compared to each of the preceding full years. Assuming that the second half of 1978 was like the first half, the information in this graph actually tells us that 1978 shows an increase rather than a decrease. For example, Delta Airlines estimated a full-year 1978 figure of $72 million, much higher than 1977's $57 million.

Exaggeration of Proportions

The height of a histogram or bar graph (or frequency polygon) usually begins at 0 or the lowest value of the scale and continues to the highest value of the scale. Figure 1–13a shows a bar graph that does not follow this standard. The bar graph shows the mean

Figure 1-12 Misleading illustration of a frequency distribution due to unequal interval sizes.

Source: "Commission Payments to Travel Agents," From *The New York Times,* August 8, 1978. © 1978 The New York Times. Used by permission and protected by the Copyright Laws of the United States. The printing, copying, redistribution, or retransmission of the Material without express written permission is prohibited. *www.nytimes.com*

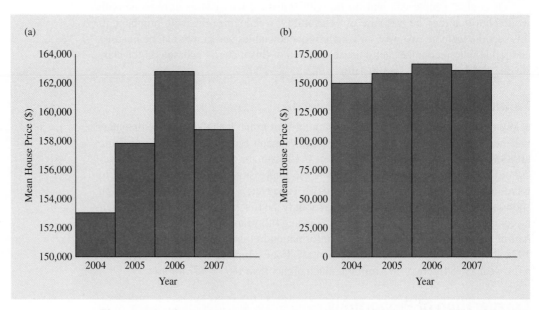

Figure 1-13 Misleading bar graph due to not starting at zero. The vertical axis starts at $150,000 for figure (a) compared to $0 for figure (b).

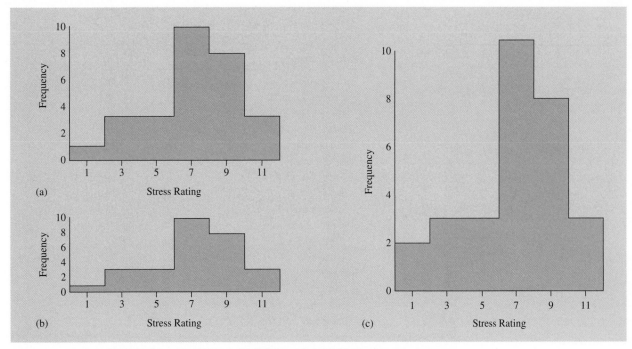

Figure 1–14   Histogram of students' stress ratings distorted from the standard of width 1 to 1.5 times height. (Data based on Aron et al., 1995.)

housing price in a particular region over a 4-year period (from 2004 to 2007). By starting the vertical axis at $150,000 (instead of 0, as is customary), the graph appears to exaggerate the changes in housing price over time. Figure 1–13b shows the same results with the vertical axis starting at $0. You can still see the changes in housing price from year to year in Figure 1–13b but the figure does a better job of showing the size of those changes.

The overall proportion of a histogram or bar graph should be about 1 to 1.5 times as wide as it is tall, as in Figure 1–14a for the stress ratings example. But look what happens if we make the graph much taller or shorter, as shown in Figures 1–14b and 1–14c. The effect is like that of a fun house mirror: the true picture is distorted. Any particular shape is in a sense accurate. But the 1-to-1.5 proportion has been adopted to give people a standard for comparison. Changing this proportion misleads the eye.

Frequency Tables and Histograms in Research Articles

Psychology researchers mainly use frequency tables and histograms as a first step in more elaborate statistical analyses. They are usually not included in research articles, and when they are, just because they are so rare, they are often not standard in some way. When they do appear, they are most likely to be in survey studies. For example, Raskauskas and Stoltz (2007) asked a group of 84 adolescents about their involvement in traditional and electronic bullying. The researchers defined electronic

Table 1-8 Incidence of Traditional and Electronic Bullying and Victimization ($N = 84$)

Form of bullying	N	%
Electronic victims	41	48.8
Text-message victim	27	32.1
Internet victim (Web sites, chatrooms)	13	15.5
Picture-phone victim	8	9.5
Traditional victims	60	71.4
Physical victim	38	45.2
Teasing victim	50	59.5
Rumors victim	32	38.6
Exclusion victim	30	50.0
Electronic bullies	18	21.4
Text-message bully	18	21.4
Internet bully	11	13.1
Traditional bullies	54	64.3
Physical bully	29	34.5
Teasing bully	38	45.2
Rumor bully	22	26.2
Exclusion bully	35	41.7

Source: Raskauskas, J., & Stoltz, A. D. (2007). Involvement in traditional and electronic bullying among adolescents. *Developmental Psychology, 43,* 564–575. Published by the American Psychological Association. Reprinted with permission.

bullying as ". . . a means of bullying in which peers use electronics [such as text messages, emails, and defaming Web sites] to taunt, threaten, harass, and/or intimidate a peer" (p. 565). Table 1–8 is a frequency table showing the adolescents' reported incidence of being victims or perpetrators of traditional and electronic bullying. The table shows, for example, that about half (48.8%) of the adolescents reported being the victim of electronic bullying, and the most common vehicle for electronic bullying (experienced by 32.1% of the adolescents) was text messaging.

Histograms are even more rare in research articles (except in articles *about* statistics), but they do appear occasionally. Maggi and colleagues (2007) conducted a study of age-related changes in cigarette smoking behaviors in Canadian adolescents. As shown in Figure 1–15, they created a histogram—from a grouped frequency table—to display their results. Their histogram shows the results from the two samples they studied (one shown in the light colored bars and the other in the dark colored bars). As you can see in the figure, less than 10% of the 10- and 11-year-olds reported that they had tried smoking, but more than half of the 16- and 17-year-olds said they had tried smoking. As already mentioned, such figures are often not standard in some way. In this example, the researchers drew the histogram with gaps between the bars, whereas it is standard not to use gaps (unless you are drawing a bar graph for a nominal variable). However, the histogram still does a good job of showing the distribution. Also, the researchers, to allow for a fair comparison of how the rate of smoking differed among adolescents of varying ages, plotted the percentage of adolescents on the vertical axis instead of the actual number of adolescents. (Plotting the actual number of adolescents who reported smoking would have been misleading, because there were not the same number of individuals in each of the age groups.)

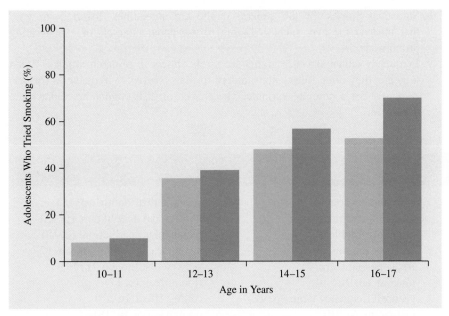

Figure 1–15 Change in the percentage of adolescents surveyed in the Canadian National Longitudinal Survey of Children and Youth longitudinal sample.

Source: Maggi, S., Hertzman, C., & Vaillancourt, T. (2007). Changes in smoking behaviors from late childhood to adolescence: Insights from the Canadian National Longitudinal Survey of Children and Youth. *Health Psychology, 26,* 232–240. Published by the American Psychological Association. Reprinted with permission.

Summary

1. Psychologists use descriptive statistics to describe and summarize a group of numbers from a research study.
2. A value is a number or category; a variable is a characteristic that can have different values; a score is a particular person's value on the variable.
3. Most variables in psychology research are numeric with approximately equal intervals. However, some numeric variables are rank-ordered (the values are ranks), and some variables are not numeric at all (the values are categories).
4. A frequency table organizes the scores into a table of each of the possible values with the frequency and percentage of scores with that value.
5. When there are many different values, a grouped frequency table is useful. It is like an ordinary frequency table except that the frequencies are given for intervals that include a range of values.
6. The pattern of frequencies in a distribution can be shown visually with a histogram (or bar graph), in which the height of each bar is the frequency for a particular value.
7. The general shape of a histogram can be unimodal (having a single peak), bimodal (having two peaks), multimodal (including bimodal), or rectangular (having no peak); it can be symmetrical or skewed (having a long tail) to the right or the left; and, compared to the bell-shaped normal curve, it can be kurtotic (having a peaked or flat distribution).

8. Statistical graphs for the general public are sometimes distorted in ways that mislead the eye, such as failing to use equal intervals or exaggerating proportions.
9. Frequency tables and histograms are rarely shown in research articles. When they are, they often follow nonstandard formats or involve frequencies (or percentages) for a nominal variable. The shapes of distributions are more often described.

Key Terms

statistics (p. 2)
descriptive statistics (p. 2)
inferential statistics (p. 2)
variable (p. 3)
values (p. 3)
score (p. 3)
numeric variable (p. 4)
equal-interval variable (p. 4)
ratio scale (p. 4)
discrete variable (p. 4)
continuous variable (p. 4)
rank-order variable (p. 4)
nominal variable (p. 4)
levels of measurement (p. 5)
frequency table (p. 7)
interval (p. 9)
grouped frequency table (p. 9)
histogram (p. 10)
frequency distribution (p. 15)
unimodal distribution (p. 15)
bimodal distribution (p. 15)
multimodal distribution (p. 15)
rectangular distribution (p. 15)
symmetrical distribution (p. 17)
skewed distribution (p. 17)
floor effect (p. 17)
ceiling effect (p. 18)
normal curve (p. 18)
kurtosis (p. 18)

Example Worked-Out Problems

Ten first-year students rated their interest in graduate school on a scale from 1 = *no interest at all* to 6 = *high interest.* Their scores were as follows: 2, 4, 5, 5, 1, 3, 6, 3, 6, 6.

Making a Frequency Table

See Figure 1–16.

❶ Interest in Graduate School	❸ Frequency	❹ Percent	❷
1	1	10	/
2	1	10	/
3	2	20	//
4	1	10	/
5	2	20	//
6	3	30	///

2, 4, 5, 5, 1, 3, 6, 3, 6, 6

Figure 1–16 Answer to Example Worked-Out Problem for making a frequency table. ❶ Make a list down the page of each possible value, from lowest to highest. ❷ Go one by one through the scores, making a mark for each next to its value on your list. ❸ Make a table showing how many times each value on your list is used. ❹ Figure the percentage of scores for each value.

Making a Histogram

See Figure 1–17.

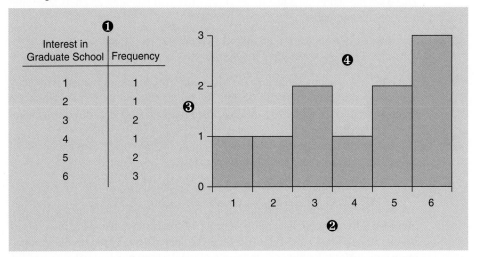

Figure 1–17   Answer to Worked-Out Problem for making a histogram. ❶ Make a frequency table (or grouped frequency table). ❷ Put the values along the bottom of the page, from left to right, from lowest to highest. ❸ Make a scale of frequencies along the left edge of the page that goes from 0 at the bottom to the highest frequency for any value. ❹ Make a bar above each value with a height for the frequency of that value.

Practice Problems

These problems involve tabulation and making graphs. Most real-life statistics problems are done on a computer with special statistical software. Even if you have such software, do these problems by hand to ingrain the method in your mind. To learn how to use a computer to solve statistics problems like those in this chapter, refer to the Using SPSS section at the end of this chapter and the *Study Guide and Computer Workbook* that accompanies this text.

All data are fictional unless an actual citation is given.

Set I (for Answers to Set I Problems, see pp. 673–674)

1. A client rates her satisfaction with her vocational counselor as a 3 on a 4-point scale from 1 = *not at all satisfied* to 4 = *very satisfied*. What is the (a) variable, (b) possible values, and (c) this client's score?
2. Give the level of measurement for each of the following variables: (a) ethnic group to which a person belongs, (b) number of times a mouse makes a wrong turn in a laboratory maze, and (c) position one finishes in a race.
3. A particular block in a suburban neighborhood has 20 households. The number of children in these households is as follows:

    2, 4, 2, 1, 0, 3, 6, 0, 1, 1, 2, 3, 2, 0, 1, 2, 1, 0, 2, 2

    Make (a) a frequency table and (b) a histogram. Then (c) describe the general shape of the distribution.

4. Fifty students were asked how many hours they studied this weekend. Here are their answers:

    11, 2, 0, 13, 5, 7, 1, 8, 12, 11, 7, 8, 9, 10, 7, 4, 6, 10, 4, 7, 8, 6, 7, 10, 7, 3,
       11, 18, 2, 9, 7, 3, 8, 7, 3, 13, 9, 8, 7, 7, 10, 4, 15, 3, 5, 6, 9, 7, 10, 6

Make (a) a frequency table and (b) a histogram. Then (c) describe the general shape of the distribution.

5. These are the scores on a test of sensitivity to smell taken by 25 chefs attending a national conference:

96, 83, 59, 64, 73, 74, 80, 68, 87, 67, 64, 92, 76, 71, 68, 50, 85, 75, 81, 70, 76, 91, 69, 83, 75

Make (a) a frequency table and (b) histogram. (c) Make a grouped frequency table using intervals of 50–59, 60–69, 70–79, 80–89, and 90–99. Based on the grouped frequency table, (d) make a histogram and (e) describe the general shape of the distribution.

6. The following data are the number of minutes it took each of a group of 34 10-year-olds to do a series of abstract puzzles:

24, 83, 36, 22, 81, 39, 60, 62, 38, 66, 38, 36, 45, 20, 20, 67, 41, 87, 41, 82, 35, 82, 28, 80, 80, 68, 40, 27, 43, 80, 31, 89, 83, 24

Make (a) a frequency table and (b) a grouped frequency table using intervals of 20–29, 30–39, 40–49, 50–59, 60–69, 70–79, and 80–89. Based on the grouped frequency table, (c) make a histogram and (d) describe the general shape of the distribution.

7. Describe the shapes of the three distributions illustrated.

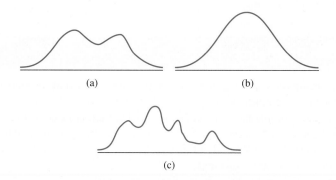

8. Draw an example of each of the following distributions: (a) symmetrical, (b) rectangular, and (c) skewed to the right.

9. Explain to a person who has never had a course in statistics what is meant by (a) a symmetrical unimodal distribution and (b) a negatively skewed unimodal distribution. (Be sure to include in your first answer an explanation of what "distribution" means.)

10. McKee and Ptacek (2001) asked 90 college students about a time they had delivered bad news to someone. Table 1–9 shows the results for the type of bad news given. (a) Using this table as an example, explain the idea of a frequency table to a person who has never had a course in statistics. (b) Explain the general meaning of the pattern of results.

Set II

11. A participant in a cognitive psychology study is given 50 words to remember and later asked to recall as many as he can of them. This participant recalls 17. What is the (a) variable, (b) possible values, and (c) score?

Category	Frequency	Percentage
1. Relationship with family	19	21.1
2. School	1	1.1
3. Job/work	6	6.7
4. Relationship with actual/potential girlfriend/boyfriend	17	18.9
5. Personal health	1	1.1
6. Finance	1	1.1
7. Relationship with friends	21	23.3
8. Health of family member/friend	23	25.6
9. Other	1	1.1

Table 1-9   Descriptive Statistics for the Type of News Given

Source: McKee, T. L. E., & Placek, J. T. (2001). I'm afraid I have something bad to tell you: Breaking bad news from the perspective of the given. *Journal of Applied Social Psychology, 31,* 246–273. Copyright © 2001 by Blackwell Publishing. Reprinted by permission of Blackwell Publishers Journals.

12. Explain and give an example for each of the following types of variables: (a) equal-interval, (b) rank-order, (c) nominal, (d) ratio scale, (e) continuous.

13. An organizational psychologist asks 20 employees in a company to rate their job satisfaction on a 5-point scale from 1 = *very unsatisfied* to 5 = *very satisfied.* The ratings are as follows:

    3, 2, 3, 4, 1, 3, 3, 4, 5, 2, 3, 5, 2, 3, 3, 4, 1, 3, 2, 4

    Make (a) a frequency table and (b) a histogram. Then (c) describe the general shape of the distribution.

14. A social psychologist asked 15 college students how many times they "fell in love" before they were 11 years old. The numbers of times were as follows:

    2, 0, 6, 0, 3, 1, 0, 4, 9, 0, 5, 6, 1, 0, 2

    Make (a) a frequency table and (b) a histogram. Then (c) describe the general shape of the distribution.

15. Following are the speeds of 40 cars clocked by radar on a particular road in a 35-mph zone on a particular afternoon:

    30, 36, 42, 36, 30, 52, 36, 34, 36, 33, 30, 32, 35, 32, 37, 34, 36, 31, 35, 20, 24, 46, 23, 31, 32, 45, 34, 37, 28, 40, 34, 38, 40, 52, 31, 33, 15, 27, 36, 40

    Make (a) a frequency table and (b) a histogram. Then (c) describe the general shape of the distribution.

16. Here are the number of holiday gifts purchased by 25 families randomly interviewed at a local mall at the end of the holiday season:

    22, 18, 22, 26, 19, 14, 23, 27, 2, 18, 28, 28, 11, 16, 34, 28, 13, 21, 32, 17, 6, 29, 23, 22, 19

    Make (a) a frequency table and (b) a grouped frequency table using intervals of 0–4, 5–9, 10–14, 15–19, 20–24, 25–29, and 30–34. Based on the grouped frequency table, (c) make a histogram and (d) describe the general shape of the distribution.

17. Pick a book and a page number of your choice. (Select a page with at least 30 lines; *do not pick a textbook or any book with tables or illustrations.*) Make a list of the number of words on each line; use that list as your data set. Make (a) a frequency table and (b) a histogram. Then (c) describe the general shape of the distribution. (Be sure to give the name, author, publisher, and year of the book you used, along with the page number, with your answer.)

18. Explain to a person who has never taken a course in statistics the meaning of a grouped frequency table.

19. Give an example of something having these distribution shapes: (a) bimodal, (b) approximately rectangular, and (c) positively skewed. Do not use an example given in this book or in class.

20. Find an example in a newspaper or magazine of a graph that misleads by failing to use equal interval sizes or by exaggerating proportions.

21. Nownes (2000) surveyed representatives of interest groups who were registered as lobbyists of three U.S. state legislatures. One of the issues he studied was whether interest groups are in competition with each other. Table 1–10 shows the results for one such question. (a) Using this table as an example, explain the idea of a frequency table to a person who has never had a course in statistics. (b) Explain the general meaning of the pattern of results.

22. Mouradian (2001) surveyed college students selected from a screening session to include two groups: (a) "Perpetrators"—students who reported at least one violent act (hitting, shoving, etc.) against their partner in their current or most recent relationship—and (b) "Comparisons"—students who did not report any such uses of violence in any of their last three relationships. At the actual testing session, the students first read a description of an aggressive behavior such as, "Throw something at his or her partner" or "Say something to upset his or her partner." They then were asked to write "as many examples of circumstances of situations as [they could] in which a person might engage in behaviors or acts of this sort with or towards their significant other." Table 1–11 shows the "Dominant Category of Explanation" (the category a participant used most) for females and males, broken down by comparisons and perpetrators. (a) Using this table as an example, explain the idea of a frequency table to a person who has never had a course in statistics. (b) Explain the general meaning of the pattern of results.

Table 1-10 Competition for Members and Other Resources

Answer	Question: How much competition does this group face from other groups with similar goals for members and other resources?	
	Percentage	Number
No competition	20	118
Some competition	58	342
A lot of competition	22	131
Total	100	591

Note: There were no statistically significant differences between states. For full results of significance tests, contact the author.
Source: Nownes, A. J. (2001). Policy conflict and the structure of interest communities. *American Politics Quarterly, 28,* 316.

Table 1-11 Dominant Category of Explanation for Intimate Aggression by Gender and Perpetrator Status

	Group							
	Female				Male			
	Comparisons ($n = 36$)		Perpetrators ($n = 33$)		Comparisons ($n = 32$)		Perpetrators ($n = 25$)	
Category	f	%	f	%	f	%	f	%
Self-defense	2	6	3	9	3	9	1	4
Control motives	8	22	9	27	9	28	3	12
Expressive aggression	4	11	3	9	3	9	8	32
Face/self-esteem preservation	1	3	2	6	2	6	3	12
Exculpatory explanations	5	14	3	9	3	9	3	12
Rejection of perpetrator or act	12	33	6	18	10	31	7	28
Prosocial/acceptable explanations	0	0	0	0	0	0	0	0
Tied categories	4	11	7	21	2	6	0	0

Note: f = frequency. % = percentage of respondents in a given group who provided a particular category of explanation.
Source: Mouradian, V. E. (2001). Applying schema theory to intimate aggression: Individual and gender differences in representation of contexts and goals. *Journal of Applied Social Psychology, 31,* 376–408. Copyright © 2001 by Blackwell Publishing. Reprinted by permission of Blackwell Publishers Journals.

Using SPSS

The ✐ in the following steps indicates a mouse click. (We used SPSS version 15.0 to carry out these analyses. The steps and output may be slightly different for other versions of SPSS.)

Creating a Frequency Table

❶ Enter the scores from your distribution in one column of the data window.
❷ ✐ *Analyze.*
❸ ✐ *Descriptive statistics.*
❹ ✐ *Frequencies.*
❺ ✐ the variable you want to make a frequency table of and then ✐ the arrow.
❻ ✐ *OK.*

Practice the preceding steps by creating a frequency table for the social interactions example in this chapter (the scores are listed on p. 8). After Step ❺, your screen should look like Figure 1–18. Your output window (which appears after you ✐ on *OK* in Step ❻) should look like Figure 1–19. As you will see, SPSS automatically produces a column with the cumulative percentage (or percentile) for each value. (Note that it is possible to create grouped frequency tables in SPSS, but since it is not a straightforward process, we do not cover it here.)

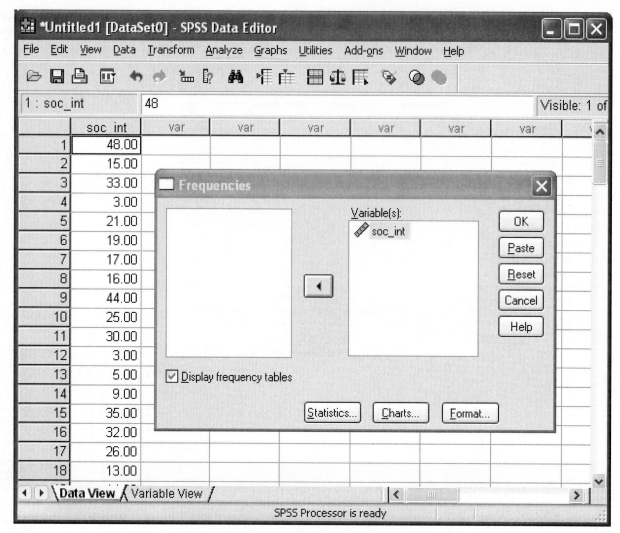

Figure 1–18 SPSS data window and frequencies window for the social interactions example. (Data from McLaughlin-Volpe et al., 2001.)

Creating a Histogram

❶ Enter the scores from your distribution in one column of the data window.
❷ ✎ *Analyze.*
❸ ✎ *Descriptive statistics.*
❹ ✎ *Frequencies.*
❺ ✎ the variable you want to make a histogram of and then ✎ on the arrow.
❻ ✎ *Charts,* ✎ *Histograms,* ✎ *Continue.*
❼ Optional: To instruct SPSS *not* to produce a frequency table, ✎ the box labeled *Display frequency tables* (this *un*checks the box).
❽ ✎ *OK.*

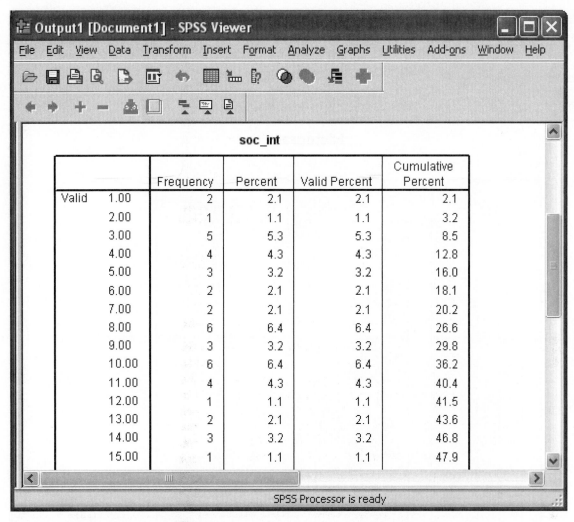

Figure 1–19 SPSS frequency table for the social interactions example. (Data from McLaughlin-Volpe et al., 2001.)

Practice these steps by creating a histogram for the social interactions example in this chapter (the scores are listed on p. 8). Your output window should look like Figure 1–20. Notice that SPSS automatically creates a histogram based on a grouped frequency table, with an interval in this case of 3 (1–3, 4–6, 7–9, and so on). (Should you wish, you can change the number of intervals or the interval size for the histogram by doing the following: Place your mouse cursor on the histogram and double ✍ to bring up a Chart Editor window; place your mouse cursor over one of the bars in the histogram and double ✍ to bring up a Properties window; ✍ the tab labeled *Binning;* ✍ *Custom;* then enter the number of intervals you want for the interval size, labeled *Interval Width;* ✍ *Apply.*) (If you want a nongrouped histogram, type in "1" for the interval size.)

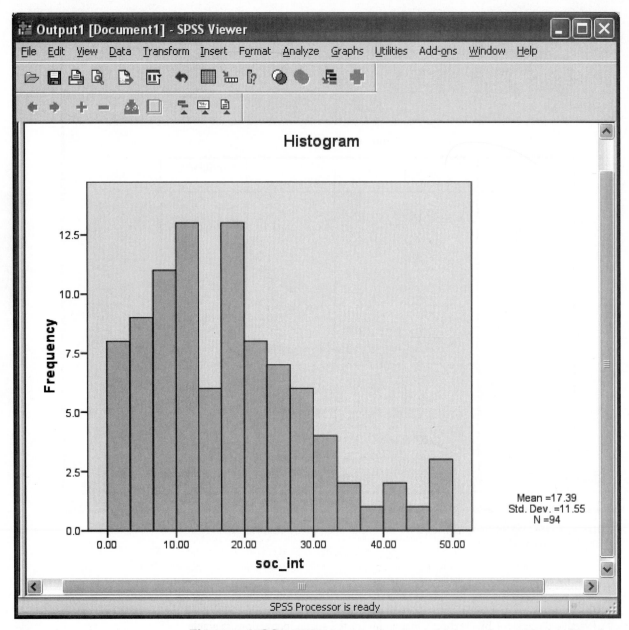

Figure 1–20 SPSS histogram for the social interactions example. (Data from McLaughlin-Volpe et al., 2001.)

Chapter Note

1. Most research articles follow the procedure we recommend here: going from lowest at the top to highest at the bottom. However, some statistics authorities recommend going from highest at the top to lowest at the bottom.

CHAPTER 2

Central Tendency and Variability

Chapter Outline

- Central Tendency   34
- Variability   43
- Controversy: The Tyranny of the Mean   52
- Central Tendency and Variability in Research Articles   55
- Summary   57
- Key Terms   57
- Example Worked-Out Problems   57
- Practice Problems   59
- Using SPSS   62
- Chapter Notes   65

As we noted in Chapter 1, the purpose of descriptive statistics is to make a group of scores understandable. We looked at some ways of getting that understanding through tables and graphs. In this chapter, we consider the main statistical techniques for describing a group of scores with numbers. First, you can describe a group of scores in terms of a *representative (or typical) value,* such as an average. A representative value gives the *central tendency* of a group of scores. A representative value is a simple way, with a single number, to describe a group of scores (and there may be hundreds or even thousands of scores). The main representative value we consider is *the mean.* Next, we focus on ways of describing how spread out the numbers are in a group of scores. In other words, we consider the amount of variation, or *variability,* among the scores. The two measures of variability you will learn about are called the *variance* and *standard deviation.*

In this chapter, for the first time in this book, you will use statistical formulas. Such formulas are not here to confuse you. Hopefully, you will come to see that they actually simplify things and provide a very straightforward, concise way of describing statistical procedures. To help you grasp what such formulas mean in words, whenever we present formulas in this book we always also give the "translation" in ordinary English.

> **TIP FOR SUCCESS**
>
> Before beginning this chapter, you should be sure you are comfortable with the key terms of *variable, score,* and *value* that we considered in Chapter 1.

Central Tendency

The **central tendency** of a group of scores (a distribution) refers to the middle of the group of scores. You will learn about three measures of central tendency: *mean, mode,* and *median.* Each measure of central tendency uses its own method to come up with a single number describing the middle of a group of scores. We start with the mean, the most commonly used measure of central tendency. Understanding the mean is also an important foundation for much of what you learn in later chapters.

The Mean

Usually the best measure of central tendency is the ordinary average, the sum of all the scores divided by the number of scores. In statistics, this is called the **mean.** The average, or mean, of a group of scores is a representative value.

Suppose 10 students, as part of a research study, record the total number of dreams they had during the last week. The numbers of dreams were as follows:

$$7, 8, 8, 7, 3, 1, 6, 9, 3, 8$$

The mean of these 10 scores is 6 (the sum of 60 dreams divided by 10 students). That is, on the average, each student had 6 dreams in the past week. The information for the 10 students is thus summarized by the single number 6.

You can think of the mean as a kind of balancing point for the distribution of scores. Try it by visualizing a board balanced over a log, like a rudimentary teeter-totter. Imagine piles of blocks set along the board according to their values, one for each score in the distribution (like a histogram made of blocks). The mean is the point on the board where the weight of the blocks on one side balances exactly with the weight on the other side. Figure 2–1 shows this for the number of dreams for the 10 students.

Mathematically, you can think of the mean as the point at which the total distance to all the scores above that point equals the total distance to all the scores below that point. Let's first figure the total distance from the mean to all the scores above the mean for the dreams example shown in Figure 2–1. There are two scores of 7, each of which is 1 unit above 6 (the mean). There are three scores of 8, each of which is 2 units above 6. And, there is one score of 9, which is 3 units above 6. This gives a total distance of 11 units (1 + 1 + 2 + 2 + 2 + 3) from the mean to all the scores above the mean. Now, let's look at the scores below the mean. There are two scores of 3, each of which is 3 units below 6 (the mean). And there is one score of 1, which is 5 units below 6. This gives a total distance of 11 units (3 + 3 + 5) from the mean to all of the scores below the mean. Thus, you can see that the total distance from the mean to the scores above the mean is the same as the total distance from the mean to the scores below the mean. The scores above the mean balance out the scores below the mean (and vice-versa).

central tendency   typical or most representative value of a group of scores.

mean   arithmetic average of a group of scores; sum of the scores divided by the number of scores.

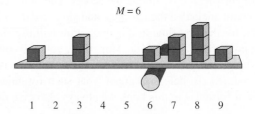

$M = 6$

1   2   3   4   5   6   7   8   9

Figure 2–1   Mean of the distribution of the number of dreams during a week for 10 students, illustrated using blocks on a board balanced on a log.

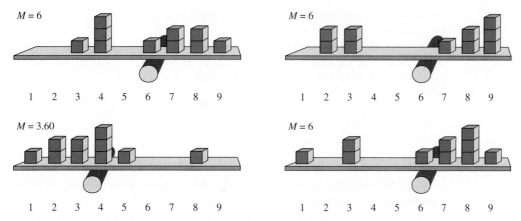

Figure 2-2   Means of various distributions illustrated with blocks on a board balanced on a log.

Some other examples are shown in Figure 2–2. Notice that there doesn't have to be a block right at the balance point. That is, the mean doesn't have to be a score actually in the distribution. The mean is the average of the scores, the balance point. The mean can be a decimal number, even if all the scores in the distribution have to be whole numbers (a mean of 2.30 children, for example). For each distribution in Figure 2–2, the total distance from the mean to the scores above the mean is the same as the total distance from the mean to the scores below the mean. (By the way, this analogy to blocks on a board, in reality, works out precisely only if the board has no weight of its own.)

Formula for the Mean and Statistical Symbols

The rule for figuring the mean is to add up all the scores and divide by the number of scores. Here is how this rule is written as a formula:

$$M = \frac{\Sigma X}{N} \qquad (2\text{–}1)$$

> The mean is the sum of the scores divided by the number of scores.

TIP FOR SUCCESS

Think of each formula as a statistical recipe, with statistical symbols as ingredients. Before you use each formula, be sure you know what each symbol stands for. Then carefully follow the formula to come up with the end result.

M is a symbol for the mean. An alternative symbol, $\overline{X}$ ("X-bar"), is sometimes used. However, M is almost always used in research articles in psychology, as recommended by the style guidelines of the American Psychological Association (2001). You will see $\overline{X}$ used mostly in advanced statistics books and in articles about statistics. In fact, there is not a general agreement for many of the symbols used in statistics. (In this book we generally use the symbols most widely found in psychology research articles.)

Σ, the capital Greek letter sigma, is the symbol for "sum of." It means "add up all the numbers for whatever follows." It is the most common special arithmetic symbol used in statistics.

X stands for the scores in the distribution of the variable X. We could have picked any letter. However, if there is only one variable, it is usually called X. In later chapters we use formulas with more than one variable. In those formulas, we use a second letter along with X (usually Y) or subscripts (such as X_1 and X_2).

ΣX is "the sum of X." This tells you to add up all the scores in the distribution of the variable X. Suppose X is the number of dreams of our 10 students: ΣX is $7 + 8 + 8 + 7 + 3 + 1 + 6 + 9 + 3 + 8$, which is 60.

M mean.

Σ sum of; add up all the scores following this symbol.

X scores in the distribution of the variable X.

N stands for number—the number of scores in a distribution. In our example, there are 10 scores. Thus, *N* equals 10.[1]

Overall, the formula says to divide the sum of all the scores in the distribution of the variable *X* by the total number of scores, *N*. In the dreams example, this means you divide 60 by 10. Put in terms of the formula,

$$M = \frac{\Sigma X}{N} = \frac{60}{10} = 6$$

Additional Examples of Figuring the Mean

Consider the examples from Chapter 1. The stress ratings of the 30 students in the first week of their statistics class (based on Aron et al., 1995) were:

8, 7, 4, 10, 8, 6, 8, 9, 9, 7, 3, 7, 6, 5, 0, 9, 10, 7, 7, 3, 6, 7, 5, 2, 1, 6, 7, 10, 8, 8

In Chapter 1 we summarized all these numbers into a frequency table (Table 1–3). You can now summarize all this information as a single number by figuring the mean. Figure the mean by adding up all the stress ratings and dividing by the number of stress ratings. That is, you add up the 30 stress ratings: 8 + 7 + 4 + 10 + 8 + 6 + 8 + 9 + 9 + 7 + 3 + 7 + 6 + 5 + 0 + 9 + 10 + 7 + 7 + 3 + 6 + 7 + 5 + 2 + 1 + 6 + 7 + 10 + 8 + 8, for a total of 193. Then you divide this total by the number of scores, 30. In terms of the formula,

$$M = \frac{\Sigma X}{N} = \frac{193}{30} = 6.43$$

This tells you that the average stress rating was 6.43 (after rounding off). This is clearly higher than the middle of the 0–10 scale. You can also see this on a graph. Think again of the histogram as a pile of blocks on a board and the mean of 6.43 as the point where the board balances on the fulcrum (see Figure 2–3). This single representative value simplifies the information in the 30 stress scores.

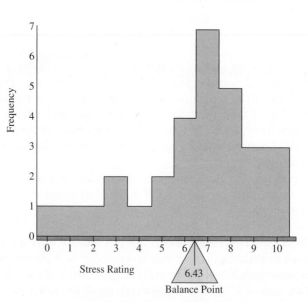

Figure 2–3 Analogy of blocks on a board balanced on a fulcrum showing the means for 30 statistics students' ratings of their stress level. (Data based on Aron et al., 1995.)

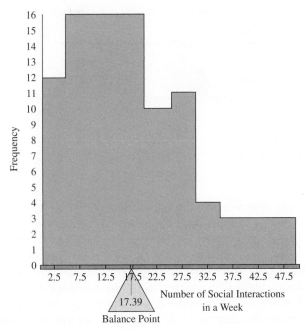

Figure 2–4 Analogy of blocks on a board balanced on a fulcrum illustrating the mean for number of social interactions during a week for 94 college students. (Data from McLaughlin-Volpe et al., 2001.)

Similarly, consider the Chapter 1 example of students' social interactions (McLaughlin-Volpe et al., 2001). The actual number of interactions over a week for the 94 students are listed on page 8. In Chapter 1, we organized the original scores into a frequency table (see Table 1–5). We can now take those same 94 scores, add them up, and divide by 94 to figure the mean:

$$M = \frac{\Sigma X}{N} = \frac{1,635}{94} = 17.39$$

This tells us that during this week these students had an average of 17.39 social interactions. Figure 2–4 shows the mean of 17.39 as the balance point for the 94 social interaction scores.

Steps for Figuring the Mean

Figure the mean in two steps.

❶ **Add up all the scores.** That is, figure ΣX.
❷ **Divide this sum by the number of scores.** That is, divide ΣX by N.

The Mode

The **mode** is another measure of central tendency. The mode is the most common single value in a distribution. In our dreams example, the mode is 8. This is because there are three students with 8 dreams and no other number of dreams with as many students. Another way to think of the mode is that it is the value with the largest frequency in a frequency table, the high point or peak of a distribution's histogram (as shown in Figure 2–5).

mode   value with the greatest frequency in a distribution.

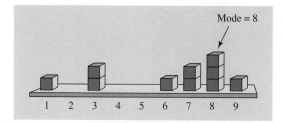

Figure 2-5 Mode as the high point in a distribution's histogram, using the example of the number of dreams during a week for 10 students.

In a perfectly symmetrical unimodal distribution, the mode is the same as the mean. However, what happens when the mean and the mode are not the same? In that situation, the mode is usually not a very good way of describing the central tendency of the scores in the distribution. In fact, sometimes researchers compare the mode to the mean to show that the distribution is *not* perfectly symmetrical. Also, the mode can be a particularly poor representative value because it does not reflect many aspects of the distribution. For example, you can change some of the scores in a distribution without affecting the mode—but this is not true of the mean, which is affected by any change in the distribution (see Figure 2–6).

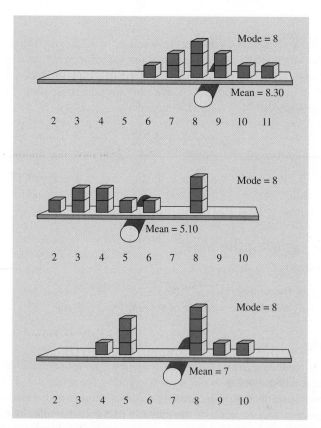

Figure 2-6 Effect on the mean and on the mode of changing some scores, using the example of the number of dreams during a week for 10 students.

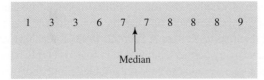

Figure 2–7   The median is the middle score when scores are lined up from lowest to highest, using the example of the number of dreams during a week for 10 students.

On the other hand, the mode *is* the usual way of describing the central tendency for a nominal variable. For example, if you know the religions of a particular group of people, the mode tells you which religion is the most frequent. However, when it comes to the numerical variables that are most common in psychology research, the mode is rarely used.

The Median

Another alternative to the mean is the **median.** If you line up all the scores from lowest to highest, the middle score is the median. Figure 2–7 shows the scores for the number of dreams lined up from lowest to highest. In this example, the fifth and sixth scores (the two middle ones) are both 7s. Either way, the median is 7.

When you have an even number of scores, the median is between two different scores. In that situation, the median is the average (the mean) of the two scores.

Steps for Finding the Median

Finding the median takes three steps.

❶ **Line up all the scores from lowest to highest.**
❷ **Figure how many scores there are to the middle score by adding 1 to the number of scores and dividing by 2.** For example, with 29 scores, adding 1 and dividing by 2 gives you 15. The 15th score is the middle score. If there are 50 scores, adding 1 and dividing by 2 gives you 25½. Because there are no half scores, the 25th and 26th scores (the scores on either side of 25½) are the middle scores.
❸ **Count up to the middle score or scores.** If you have one middle score, this is the median. If you have two middle scores, the median is the average (the mean) of these two scores.

Comparing the Mean, Mode, and Median

Sometimes, the median is better than the mean (and mode) as a representative value for a group of scores. This happens when a few extreme scores would strongly affect the mean but would not affect the median. Reaction time scores are a common example in psychology research. Suppose you are asked to press a key as quickly as possible when a green circle is shown on the computer screen. On five showings of the green circle, your times (in seconds) to respond are .74, .86, 2.32, .79, and .81. The mean of these five scores is 1.1040: that is, $(\Sigma X)/N = 5.52/5 = 1.1040$. However, this mean is very much influenced by the one very long time (2.32 seconds). (Perhaps you were distracted just when the green circle was shown.) The median is much less affected by the extreme score. The median of these five scores is .81—a value that is much more representative of most of the scores. Thus, using the median deemphasizes the one extreme time, which is probably appropriate. An extreme score like this is called an **outlier.** In this example, the outlier was much higher than the other scores, but in other cases an outlier may be much lower than the other scores in the distribution.

median   middle score when all the scores in a distribution are arranged from lowest to highest.

outlier   score with an extreme value (very high or very low) in relation to the other scores in the distribution.

The importance of whether you use the mean, mode, or median can be seen in a controversy among psychologists studying the evolutionary basis of human mate choice. One set of theorists (e.g., Buss & Schmitt, 1993) argue that over their lives, men should prefer to have many partners, but women should prefer to have just one reliable partner. This is because a woman can have only a small number of children in a lifetime and her genes are most likely to survive if those few children are well taken care of. Men, however, can have a great many children in a lifetime. Therefore, according to the theory, a shotgun approach is best for men, because their genes are most likely to survive if they have a great many partners. Consistent with this assumption, evolutionary psychologists have found that men report wanting far more partners than do women.

Other theorists (e.g., Miller & Fishkin, 1997), however, have questioned this view. They argue that women and men should prefer about the same number of partners. This is because individuals with a basic predisposition to seek a strong intimate bond are most likely to survive infancy. This desire for strong bonds, they argue, remains in adulthood. These theorists also asked women and men how many partners they wanted. They found the same result as the previous researchers when using the mean: men wanted an average of 64.3 partners, women an average of 2.8 partners. However, the picture looks drastically different if you look at the median or mode (see Table 2–1). Figure 2–8, taken directly from their article, shows why. Most women and most men want just one partner. A few want more, some many more. The big difference is that

Table 2-1 Responses of 106 Men and 160 Women to the Question, "How many partners would you ideally desire in the next 30 years?"

	Mean	Median	Mode
Women	2.8	1	1
Men	64.3	1	1

Source: Data from Miller & Fishkin (1997).

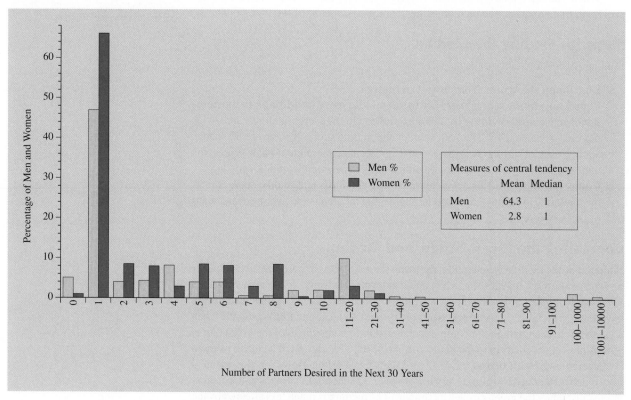

Figure 2-8 Distributions for men and women for the ideal number of partners desired over 30 years. *Note:* To include all the data, we collapsed across categories farther out on the tail of these distributions. If every category represented a single number, it would be more apparent that the tail is very flat and that distributions are even more skewed than is apparent here.

Source: Miller, L. C., & Fishkin, S. A. (1997). On the dynamics of human bonding and reproductive success: Seeking windows on the adapted-for-human-environmental interface. In J. Simpson & D. T. Kenrick (Eds.), *Evolutionary social psychology* (pp. 197–235). Mahwah, NJ: Erlbaum.

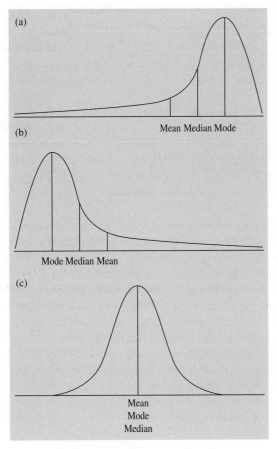

Figure 2–9 Locations of the mean, mode, and median on (a) a distribution skewed to the left, (b) a distribution skewed to the right, and (c) a normal curve.

there are a lot more men in the small group that want many more than one partner. These results were also replicated in a more recent study (Pedersen et al., 2002).

So which theory is right? You could argue either way from these results. The point is that focusing just on the mean can clearly misrepresent the reality of the distribution. As this example shows, the median is most likely to be used when a few extreme scores would make the mean unrepresentative of the main body of scores. Figure 2–9 illustrates this point, by showing the relative location of the mean, mode, and median for three types of distribution that you learned about in Chapter 1. The distribution in Figure 2–9a is skewed to the left (negatively skewed); the long tail of the distribution points to the left. The mode in this distribution is the highest point of the distribution, which is on the far right hand side of the distribution. The median is the point at which half of the scores are above that point and half are below. As you can see, for that to happen, the median must be a lower value than the mode. Finally, the mean is strongly influenced by the very low scores in the long tail of the distribution and is thus a lower value than the median. Figure 2–9b shows the location of the mean, mode, and median for a distribution that is skewed to the right (positively skewed). In this case, the mean is a higher value than either the mode or median because the mean is strongly influenced by the very *high* scores in the long tail of the distribution. Again, the mode is the highest point of the distribution, and the median is between the mode and the mean. In Figures 2–9a and 2–9b, the mean is not a good representative value of the scores, because it is unduly influenced by the extreme scores.

Table 2–2 Summary of Measures of Central Tendency

Measure	Definition	When Used
Mean	Sum of the scores divided by the number of scores	• With equal-interval variables • Very commonly used in psychology research
Mode	Value with the greatest frequency in a distribution	• With nominal variables • Rarely used in psychology research
Median	Middle score when all the scores in a distribution are arranged from lowest to highest	• With rank-ordered variables • When a distribution has one or more outliers • Rarely used in psychology research

Figure 2–9c shows a normal curve. As for any distribution, the mode is the highest point in the distribution. For a normal curve, the highest point falls exactly at the midpoint of the distribution. This midpoint is the median value, since half of the scores in the distribution are below that point and half are above it. The mean also falls at the same point because the normal curve is symmetrical about the midpoint, and every score in the left hand side of the curve has a matching score on the right hand side. So, for a normal curve, the mean, mode, and median are always the same value.

In some situations psychologists use the median as part of more complex statistical methods. Also, the median is the usual way of describing the central tendency for a rank-order variable. Otherwise, unless there are extreme scores, psychologists almost always use the mean as the representative value of a group of scores. In fact, as you will learn, the mean is a fundamental building block for most other statistical techniques.

A summary of the mean, mode, and median as measures of central tendency is shown in Table 2–2.

How are you doing?

1. Name and define three measures of central tendency.
2. Write the formula for the mean and define each of the symbols.
3. Figure the mean of the following scores: 2, 8, 3, 6, and 6.
4. For the following scores find (a) the mean, (b) the mode, and (c) the median: 5, 3, 2, 13, 2. (d) Why is the mean different from the median?

Answers

1. The mean is the ordinary average, the sum of the scores divided by the number of scores. The mode is the most frequent score in a distribution. The median is the middle score; that is, if you line the scores up from lowest to highest, it is the halfway score.
2. The formula for the mean is $M = (\Sigma X)/N$. M is the mean; Σ is the symbol for "sum of"—add up all the scores that follow; X is the variable whose scores you are adding up; N is the number of scores.
3. $M = (\Sigma X)/N = (2 + 8 + 3 + 6 + 6)/5 = 5$.
4. (a) The mean is 5; (b) the mode is 2; (c) the median is 3; (d) The mean is different from the median because the extreme score (13) makes the mean higher than the median.

Variability

Researchers also want to know how spread out the scores are in a distribution. This shows the amount of variability in the distribution. For example, suppose you were asked, "How old are the students in your statistics class?" At a city-based university with many returning and part-time students, the mean age might be 29. You could answer, "The average age of the students in my class is 29." However, this would not tell the whole story. You could have a mean of 29 because every student in the class was exactly 29 years old. If this is the case, the scores in the distribution are not spread out at all. In other words, there is no variation, or *variability*, among the scores. You could also have a mean of 29 because exactly half the class members were 19 and the other half 39. In this situation, the distribution is much more spread out; there is considerable variability among the scores in the distribution.

You can think of the variability of a distribution as the amount of spread of the scores around the mean. Distributions with the same mean can have very different amounts of spread around the mean; Figure 2–10a shows histograms for three different frequency distributions with the same mean but different amounts of spread around the mean. A real-life example of this is shown in Figure 2–11, which shows the distributions of the housing prices in two neighborhoods: one with diverse housing types and the other with a consistent type of housing. As with Figure 2–10a, the mean housing price is the same in each neighborhood. However, the distribution for

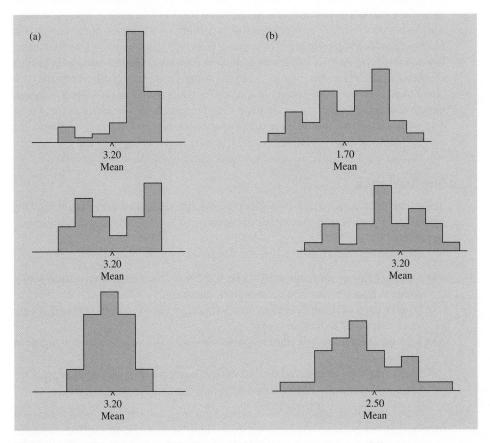

Figure 2–10 Examples of distributions with (a) the same mean but different amounts of spread, and (b) different means but the same amount of spread.

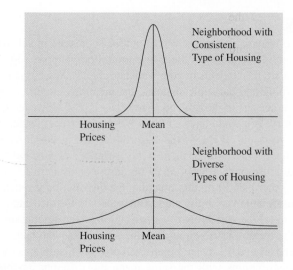

Figure 2–11 Example of two distributions with the same mean but different amounts of spread: housing prices for a neighborhood with diverse types of housing and for a neighborhood with a consistent type of housing.

the neighborhood with diverse housing types is much more spread out around the mean than the distribution for the neighborhood that has a consistent type of housing. This tells you that there is much greater variability in the prices of housing in the neighborhood with diverse types of housing than in the neighborhood with a consistent housing type. Also, distributions with different means can have the same amount of spread around the mean. Figure 2–10b shows three different distributions with different means but the same amount of spread. So, while the mean provides a representative value of a group of scores, it doesn't tell you about the variability of the scores. You will now learn about two measures of the variability of a group of scores: the *variance* and *standard deviation.*[2]

The Variance

The **variance** of a group of scores tells you how spread out the scores are around the mean. To be precise, the variance is the average of each score's squared difference from the mean.

Here are the four steps to figure the variance:

❶ **Subtract the mean from each score.** This gives each score's **deviation score,** which is how far away the score is from the mean.

❷ **Square each of these deviation scores** (multiply each by itself). This gives each score's **squared deviation score.**

❸ **Add up the squared deviation scores.** This total is called the **sum of squared deviations.**

❹ **Divide the sum of squared deviations by the number of scores.** This gives the average (the mean) of the squared deviations, called the variance.

Suppose one distribution is more spread out than another. The more spread-out distribution has a larger variance because being spread out makes the deviation scores bigger. If the deviation scores are bigger, the squared deviation scores and the average of the squared deviation scores (the variance) are also bigger.

variance   measure of how spread out a set of scores are; average of the squared deviations from the mean.

deviation score   score minus the mean.

squared deviation score   square of the difference between a score and the mean.

sum of squared deviations   total of all the scores of each score's squared difference from the mean.

In the example of the class in which everyone was exactly 29 years old, the variance would be exactly 0. That is, there would be no variance (which makes sense, because there is no variability among the ages). (In terms of the numbers, each person's deviation score would be $29 - 29 = 0$; 0 squared is 0. The average of a bunch of zeros is 0.) By contrast, the class of half 19-year-olds and half 39-year-olds would have a rather large variance of 100. (The 19-year-olds would each have deviation scores of $19 - 29 = -10$. The 39-year-olds would have deviation scores of $39 - 29 = 10$. All the squared deviation scores, which are either -10 squared or 10 squared, come out to 100. The average of all 100s is 100.)

The variance is extremely important in many statistical procedures you will learn about later. However, the variance is rarely used as a *descriptive statistic.* This is because the variance is based on *squared* deviation scores, which do not give a very easy-to-understand sense of how spread out the actual, nonsquared scores are. For example, a class with a variance of 400 clearly has a more spread-out distribution than one whose variance is 10. However, the number 400 does not give an obvious insight into the actual variation among the ages, none of which is anywhere near 400.[3]

The Standard Deviation

The most widely used way of *describing* the spread of a group of scores is the **standard deviation.** The standard deviation is directly related to the variance and is figured by taking the square root of the variance. There are two steps in figuring the standard deviation.

❶ **Figure the variance.**
❷ **Take the square root.** The standard deviation is the *positive* square root of the variance. (Any number has both a positive and a negative square root. For example, the square root of 9 is both $+3$ and -3.)

If the variance of a distribution is 400, the standard deviation is 20. If the variance is 9, the standard deviation is 3.

The variance is about squared deviations from the mean. Therefore, its square root, the standard deviation, is about direct, ordinary, not-squared deviations from the mean. *Roughly speaking, the standard deviation is the average amount that scores differ from the mean.* For example, consider a class where the ages have a standard deviation of 20 years. This tells you that the ages are spread out, on the average, about 20 years in each direction from the mean. Knowing the standard deviation gives you a general sense of the degree of spread.[4]

The standard deviation does not, however, perfectly describe the shape of the distribution. For example, suppose the distribution of the number of children in families in a particular country has a mean of 4 and standard deviation of 1. Figure 2–12 shows several possibilities of the distribution of number of children, all with a mean of 4 and a standard deviation of 1.

Formulas for the Variance and the Standard Deviation

We have seen that the variance is the average squared deviation from the mean. Here is the formula for the variance.

$$SD^2 = \frac{\sum(X - M)^2}{N}$$

(2–2)

standard deviation   square root of the average of the squared deviations from the mean; the most common descriptive statistic for variation; approximately the average amount that scores in a distribution vary from the mean.

> The variance is the sum of the squared deviations of the scores from the mean, divided by the number of scores.

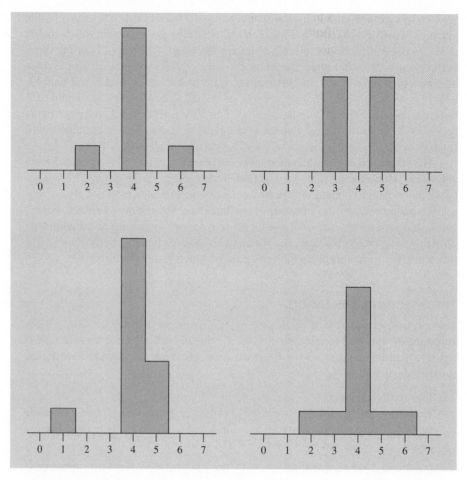

Figure 2–12 Some possible distributions for family size in a country where the mean is 4 and the standard deviation is 1.

SD² variance.

SD standard deviation.

sum of squares (SS) sum of squared deviations.

TIP FOR SUCCESS

The sum of squared deviations is an important part of many of the procedures you learn in later chapters; so be sure you fully understand it, as well as how it is figured.

The variance is the sum of squares divided by the number of scores.

SD^2 is the symbol for the *variance*. This may seem surprising. SD is short for *standard deviation*. The symbol SD^2 emphasizes that the variance is the standard deviation squared. (Later, you will learn other symbols for the variance, S^2 and σ^2—the lowercase Greek letter sigma squared. The different symbols are for different situations in which the variance is used. In some cases, it is figured slightly differently.)

The top part of the formula is the *sum of squared deviations*. X is for each score and M is the mean. Thus, $X - M$ is the score minus the mean, the deviation score. The superscript number (^{2}) tells you to square each deviation score. Finally, the sum sign (Σ) tells you to add up all these squared deviation scores.

The sum of squared deviations of the scores from the mean, which is called the **sum of squares** for short, has its own symbol, **SS.** Thus, the variance formula can be written using SS instead of $\Sigma(X - M)^2$:

$$SD^2 = \frac{SS}{N} \qquad (2\text{–}3)$$

Whether you use the simplified symbol SS or the full description of the sum of squared deviations, the bottom part of the formula is just N, the number of scores.

That is, the formula says to divide the sum of the squared deviation scores by the number of scores in the distribution.

The standard deviation is the square root of the variance. So, if you already know the variance, the formula is

$$SD = \sqrt{SD^2} \tag{2-4}$$

The formula for the standard deviation, starting from scratch, is the square root of what you figure for the variance:

$$SD = \sqrt{\frac{\Sigma(X - M)^2}{N}} \tag{2-5}$$

or

$$SD = \sqrt{\frac{SS}{N}} \tag{2-6}$$

> The standard deviation is the square root of the variance.

> The standard deviation is the square root of the result of taking the sum of the squared deviations of the scores from the mean divided by the number of scores.

> The standard deviation is the square root of the result of taking the sum of squares divided by the number of scores.

Examples of Figuring the Variance and Standard Deviation

Table 2–3 shows the figuring for the variance and standard deviation for the number of dreams example. (The table assumes you have already figured the mean to be 6 dreams.) Usually, it is easiest to do your figuring using a calculator, especially one with a square root key. The standard deviation of 2.57 tells you that roughly speaking, on the average, the number of dreams vary by about 2½ from the mean of 6.

Table 2–4 shows the figuring for the variance and standard deviation for the example of students' number of social interactions during a week (McLaughlin-Volpe et al., 2001). (To save space, the table shows only the first few and last few scores.) Roughly speaking, this result tells you that a student's number of social interactions in a week varies from the mean (of 17.39) by an average of 11.49. This can also be shown on a histogram (see Figure 2–13).

Measures of variability, such as the variance and standard deviation, are heavily influenced by the presence of one or more outliers (extreme values) in a distribution.

TIP FOR SUCCESS

Always check that your answers make *intuitive sense*. For example, looking at the scores for the dreams example, a standard deviation—which, roughly speaking, represents the average amount that the scores vary from the mean—of 2.57 makes sense. If your answer had been 21.23, however, it would mean that, on average, the number of dreams varied by more than 20 from the mean of 6. Looking at the group of scores, that just couldn't be true.

TIP FOR SUCCESS

Notice in Table 2–3 that the deviation scores (shown in the third column) add up to 0. The sum of the deviation scores is *always* 0 (or very close to 0, allowing for rounding error). So, to check your figuring, always sum the deviation scores. If they do not add up to 0, do your figuring again!

TIP FOR SUCCESS

When figuring the variance and standard deviation, lay your work out as in Tables 2–3 and 2–4. This helps you follow all the steps and end up with the correct answers.

Table 2-3 Figuring the Variance and Standard Deviation in the Number of Dreams Example

Score (Number of Dreams)	−	Mean Score (Mean Number of Dreams)	=	Deviation Score	Squared Deviation Score
7		6		1	1
8		6		2	4
8		6		2	4
7		6		1	1
3		6		−3	9
1		6		−5	25
6		6		0	0
9		6		3	9
3		6		−3	9
8		6		2	4
				Σ:0	66

Variance $= SD^2 = \dfrac{\Sigma(X-M)^2}{N} = \dfrac{SS}{N} = \dfrac{66}{10} = 6.60$

Standard deviation $= SD = \sqrt{SD^2} = \sqrt{6.60} = 2.57$

Table 2-4   Figuring the Variance and Standard Deviation for Number of Social Interactions During a Week for 94 College Students

Number of Interactions	−	Mean Number of Interactions	=	Deviation Score	Squared Deviation Score
48		17.39		30.61	936.97
15		17.39		−2.39	5.71
33		17.39		15.61	243.67
3		17.39		−14.39	207.07
21		17.39		3.61	13.03
·		·		·	·
·		·		·	·
·		·		·	·
35		17.39		17.61	310.11
9		17.39		−8.39	70.39
30		17.39		12.61	159.01
8		17.39		−9.39	88.17
26		17.39		8.61	74.13
				Σ: 0.00	12,406.44

$$\text{Variance} = SD^2 = \frac{\Sigma(X-M)^2}{N} = \frac{12{,}406.44}{94} = 131.98$$

$$\text{Standard deviation} = \sqrt{SD^2} = \sqrt{131.98} = 11.49$$

Source: Data from McLaughlin-Volpe et al. (2001).

INTERVAL	FREQUENCY
0 – 4	12
5 – 9	16
10 – 14	16
15 – 19	16
20 – 24	10
25 – 29	11
30 – 34	4
35 – 39	3
40 – 44	3
45 – 49	3

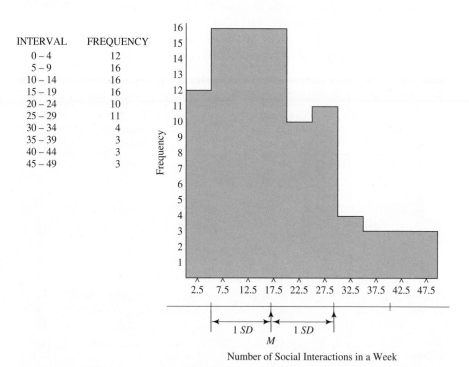

Figure 2-13   The standard deviation as the distance along the base of a histogram, using the example of number of social interactions in a week. (Data from McLaughlin-Volpe et al., 2001.)

The scores in the number of dreams example were 7, 8, 8, 7, 3, 1, 6, 9, 3, 8, and we figured the standard deviation of the scores to be 2.57. Now imagine that one additional person is added to the study and that the person reports having 21 dreams in the past week. The standard deviation of the scores would now be 4.96, which is almost double the size of the standard deviation without this additional single score.

Computational and Definitional Formulas

In actual research situations, psychologists must often figure the variance and the standard deviation for distributions with many scores, often involving decimals or large numbers. In the days before computers, this could make the whole process quite time-consuming, even with a calculator. To deal with this problem, in the old days researchers developed various shortcuts to simplify the figuring. A shortcut formula of this type is called a **computational formula.**

The traditional computational formula for the variance of the kind we are discussing in this chapter is as follows:

$$SD^2 = \frac{\sum X^2 - \left(\left(\sum X \right)^2 / N \right)}{N} \qquad (2\text{--}7)$$

$\sum X^2$ means that you square each score and then take the sum of the squared scores. However, $\left(\sum X \right)^2$ means that you first add up all the scores and then take the square of this sum. Although this sounds complicated, this formula was actually easier to use than the one you learned before if a researcher was figuring the variance for a lot of numbers by hand or even with an old-fashioned handheld calculator, because the researcher did not have to first find the deviation score for each score.

However, these days computational formulas are mainly of historical interest. They are used by researchers only on rare occasions when computers with statistics software are not readily available to do the figuring. In fact, today, even many handheld calculators are set up so that you need only enter the scores and press a button or two to get the variance and the standard deviation.

In this book we give a few computational formulas just so that you have them if you someday do a research project with a lot of numbers and you don't have access to statistical software. However, we very definitely recommend *not* using the computational formulas when you are learning statistics, even if they might save you a few minutes of figuring a practice problem. The computational formulas usually make it much harder to understand the *meaning* of what you are figuring. The only reason for figuring problems at all by hand when you are learning statistics is to reinforce the underlying principles. Thus, you would be undermining the whole point of the practice problems if you use a formula that had a complex relation to the basic logic. The formulas we give you for the practice problems and for all the examples in the book are designed to help strengthen your understanding of what the figuring *means*. Thus, the usual formula we give for each procedure is what statisticians call a **definitional formula.**

The Importance of Variability in Psychology Research

Variability is an important topic in psychology research because much of the research focuses on explaining variability. We will use a couple of examples to show what we mean by "explaining variability." As you might imagine, different students experience different levels of stress with regard to learning statistics: Some experience little stress; for other students, learning statistics can be a source of great stress. So, in this example, explaining variability means identifying the factors that explain why students differ in the amount of stress they experience. Perhaps how much experience students have had with math explains some of the variability. That is,

The variance is the sum of the squared scores minus the result of taking the sum of all the scores, squaring this sum and dividing by the number of scores, then taking this whole difference and dividing it by the number of scores.

computational formula equation mathematically equivalent to the definitional formula. Easier to use for figuring by hand, it does not directly show the meaning of the procedure.

definitional formula equation for a statistical procedure directly showing the meaning of the procedure.

according to this explanation, the differences (the variability) among students in amount of stress are partially due to the differences (the variability) among students in the amount of experience they have had with math. Thus, the variation in math experience partially explains, or accounts for, the variation in stress. What factors might explain the variation in students' number of weekly social interactions? Perhaps a factor is variation in the extraversion of students, with more extraverted students tending to have more interactions. Or perhaps it is variation in gender, with one gender having consistently more interactions than the other. Much of the rest of this book focuses on procedures for evaluating and testing whether variation in some specific factor (or factors) explains the variability in some variable of interest.

The Variance as the Sum of Squared Deviations Divided by $N - 1$

Researchers often use a slightly different kind of variance. We have defined the variance as the average of the squared deviation scores. Using that definition, you divide the sum of the squared deviation scores by the number of scores (that is, the variance is SS/N). But you will learn in Chapter 7 that for many purposes it is better to define the variance as the sum of squared deviation scores divided by *1 less than the number of scores*. In other words, for those purposes the variance is the sum of squared deviations divided by $N - 1$ (that is, variance is $SS/[N - 1]$). (As you will learn in Chapter 7, you use this dividing by $N - 1$ approach when you have scores from a particular group of people and you want to estimate what the variance would be for the larger group of people whom these individuals represent.)

The variances and standard deviations given in research articles are usually figured using $SS/(N - 1)$. Also, when calculators or computers give the variance or the standard deviation automatically, they are usually figured in this way (for example, see the *Using SPSS* section at the end of this chapter). But don't worry. The approach you are learning in this chapter of dividing by N (that is, figuring variance as SS/N) is entirely correct for our purpose here, which is to use descriptive statistics to describe the variation in a particular group of scores. It is also entirely correct for the material you learn in Chapters 3 through 6. We mention this other approach (variance as $SS/[N - 1]$) now only so that you will not be confused if you read about variance or standard deviation in other places or if your calculator or a computer program gives a surprising result. To keep things simple, we wait to discuss the dividing by $N - 1$ approach until it is needed, starting in Chapter 7.

How are you doing?

1. (a) Define the variance and (b) indicate what it tells you about a distribution and how this is different from what the mean tells you.
2. (a) Define the standard deviation; (b) describe its relation to the variance; and (c) explain what it tells you approximately about a group of scores.
3. Give the full formula for the variance and indicate what each of the symbols means.
4. Figure the (a) variance and (b) standard deviation for the following scores: 2, 4, 3, and 7 ($M = 4$).
5. Explain the difference between a definitional and a computational formula.
6. What is the difference between the formula for the variance you learned in this chapter and the formula that is typically used to figure the variance in research articles?

Answers

1. (a) The variance is the average of the squared deviation of each score from the mean. (b) The variance tells you about how spread out the scores are (that is, their variability), while the mean tells you the central tendency of the distribution.

2. (a) The standard deviation is the square root of the average of the squared deviations from the mean. (b) The standard deviation is the square root of the variance. (c) The standard deviation tells you approximately the average amount that scores differ from the mean.

3. $SD^2 = [\Sigma(X - M)^2]/N$. SD^2 is the variance. Σ means the sum of what follows. X is for the scores for the variable being studied. M is the mean of the scores. N is the number of scores.

4. (a) Variance: $SD^2 = [\Sigma(X - M)^2]/N = [(2 - 4)^2 + (4 - 4)^2 + (3 - 4)^2 + (7 - 4)^2]/4 = 14/4 = 3.50$.
(b) Standard deviation: $SD = \sqrt{SD^2} = \sqrt{3.50} = 1.87$.

5. A definitional formula is the straightforward form that shows the meaning of what the formula is figuring. A computational formula is a mathematically equivalent variation of the definitional formula, but the computational formula tends not to show the underlying meaning. Computational formulas were often used before computers were available and researchers had to do their figuring by hand with a lot of scores.

6. The formula for the variance in this chapter divides the sum of squares by the number of scores (that is, SS/N). The variance in research articles is usually figured by dividing the sum of squares by one less than the number of scores (that is, $SS/[N - 1]$).

BOX 2–1 The Sheer Joy (Yes, Joy) of Statistical Analysis

You are learning statistics for the fun of it, right? No? Or maybe so, after all. If you become a psychologist, at some time or other you will form a hypothesis, gather data, and analyze them. (Even if you plan a career as a psychotherapist or other mental health practitioner, you will probably eventually wish to test an idea about the nature of your patients and their difficulties.) That hypothesis—your own original idea—and the data you gather to test it are going to be very important to you. Your heart may well be pounding with excitement as you analyze the data.

Consider some of the comments of social psychologists we interviewed for our book *The Heart of Social Psychology* (Aron & Aron, 1989). Deborah Richardson, who studies interpersonal relationships, confided that her favorite part of being a social psychologist is looking at the statistical output of the computer analyses:

It's like putting together a puzzle. . . . It's a highly arousing, positive experience for me. I often go through periods of euphoria. Even when the data don't do what I want them to do . . . [there's a] physiological response. . . . It's exciting to see the numbers come off—Is it actually the way I thought it would be?—then thinking about the alternatives.

Harry Reis, former editor of the *Journal of Personality and Social Psychology,* sees his profession the same way:

By far the most rewarding part is when you get a new data set and start analyzing it and things pop out, partly a confirmation of what led you into the study in the first place, but then also other things. . . . "Why is that?" Trying to make sense of it. The kind of ideas that come from data. . . . I love analyzing data.

Bibb Latane, an eminent psychologist known for, among other things, his work on why people don't always intervene to help others who are in trouble, reports eagerly awaiting

... the first glimmerings of what came out ... [and] using them to shape what the next question should be ... You need to use everything you've got, ... every bit of your experience and intuition. It's where you have the biggest effect, it's the least routine. You're in the room with the tiger, face to face with the core of what you are doing, at the moment of truth.

Bill Graziano, whose work integrates developmental, personality, and social psychology, calls the analysis of his data "great fun, just great fun." And in the same vein, Margaret Clark, who studies emotion and cognition, declares that "the most fun of all is getting the data and looking at them."

So you see? Statistics in the service of your own creative ideas can be a pleasure indeed.

Controversy: The Tyranny of the Mean

Looking in the behavioral and social science research journals, you would think that statistical methods are their sole tool and language, but there have also been rebellions against the reign of statistics. We are most familiar with this issue in psychology, where the most unexpected opposition came from the leader of behaviorism, the school of psychology most dedicated to keeping the field strictly scientific.

Behaviorism opposed the study of inner states because inner events are impossible to observe objectively. (Today most research psychologists claim to measure inner events indirectly but objectively.) Behaviorism's most famous advocate, B. F. Skinner, was quite opposed to statistics. Skinner even said, "I would much rather see a graduate student in psychology taking a course in physical chemistry than in statistics. And I would include [before statistics] other sciences, even poetry, music, and art" (Evans, 1976, p. 93).

Skinner was constantly pointing to the information lost by averaging the results of a number of cases. For instance, Skinner (1956) cited the example of three overeating mice—one naturally obese, one poisoned with gold, and one whose hypothalamus had been altered. Each had a different curve for learning to press a bar for food. If these learning curves had been summed or merged statistically, the result would have represented no actual eating habits of any real mouse. As Skinner said, "These three individual curves contain more information than could probably ever be generated with measures requiring statistical treatment, yet they will be viewed with suspicion by many psychologists because they are single cases" (p. 232).

In clinical psychology and the study of personality, voices have always been raised in favor of the in-depth study of one person instead of or as well as the averaging of persons. The philosophical underpinnings of the in-depth study of individuals can be found in phenomenology, which began in Europe after World War I (Husserl, 1970). This viewpoint has been important throughout the social sciences, not just in psychology.

Today, the rebellion in psychology is led by qualitative research methodologists (e.g., McCracken, 1988), an approach that is much more prominent in other behavioral and social sciences. The qualitative research methods, developed mainly in anthropology, can involve long interviews or observations of a few individuals. The highly skilled researcher decides, as the event is taking place, what is important to remember, record, and pursue through more questions or observations. The mind of the researcher is the main tool because, according to this approach, only that mind can find the important relationships among the many categories of events arising in the respondent's speech.

Many who favor qualitative methods argue for a blend: First, discover the important categories through a qualitative approach. Then, determine their incidence in the larger population through quantitative methods. Too often, these advocates argue, quantitative researchers jump to conclusions about a phenomenon without first exploring the human experience of it through free-response interviews or observations.

Finally, Carl Jung, founder of Jungian psychology, sometimes spoke of the "statistical mood" and its effect on a person's feeling of uniqueness. Jung had no problem with statistics—he used them in his own research. He was concerned about the cultural impact of this "statistical mood"—much like the impact of being on a jammed subway and observing the hundreds of blank faces and feeling diminished, "one of a crowd." He held that the important contributions to culture tend to come from people who feel unique and not ordinary. As we increasingly describe ourselves statistically—"90% of men under thirty think . . ."—we tend to do just that, think like 90% of men under thirty. To counteract this mood, Jungian analyst Marie Louise von Franz (1979) wrote, "An act of loyalty is required towards one's own feelings" (pp. IV-18). Feeling "makes your life and your relationships and deeds feel unique and gives them a definite value" (pp. IV-18–IV-19). Your beloved is like no one else. Your own death is a face behind a door. And the meaning of 'civilian deaths this month due to the war were 20,964' is unfathomable horror—not a number.

In short, there have been many who have questioned an exclusively statistical view of our subject matter, and their voices should be considered too as you proceed with your study of what has become the predominant, but not exclusive, means of doing psychology research.

BOX 2–2   Gender, Ethnicity, and Math Performance

From time to time, someone tries to argue that because some groups of people score better on math tests and make careers out of mathematics, these groups have a genetic advantage in math (or statistics). Other groups are said or implied to be innately inferior at math. The issue comes up about gender, about racial and ethnic groups, and of course in arguments about overall intelligence as well as math. There's little evidence for such genetic differences (a must-see article is Block, 1995), but the stereotypes persist.

The impact of these stereotypes has been well established in research by Steele and his colleagues (1997), who have done numerous studies on what they call "stereotype threat." This phenomenon occurs when a negative stereotype about a group you belong to becomes relevant to you because of the situation you are in, like taking a math test, and provides an explanation for how you will behave. A typical experiment creating stereotype threat (Spencer et al., 1999) involved women taking a difficult math test. Half were told that men generally do better on the test, and the other half that women generally do equally well. Those who were told that women do worse did indeed score substantially lower than the other group. In the other condition, there was no difference. (In fact, in two separate studies, men performed a little worse when they were told there was no gender difference, as if they had lost some of their confidence.)

The same results occur when African Americans are given parts of the graduate record examination. They do fine on the test when they are told no racial differences in the scores have been found, and they do worse when they are told that such differences have been found (Steele, 1997).

Stereotype threat has also been found to occur in the United States for Latinos (Gonzales et al., 2002) and the poor (Croizet & Claire, 1998). Many lines of research indicate that prejudices, not genetics, are the probable cause of differences in test scores between groups. Although some researchers (Rushton & Jensen, 2005) continue to argue for genetic differences, the evidence is still substantial that stereotype threat plays the main role in lower test scores (Suzuki & Aronson, 2005). For example, the same difference of 15 IQ points between a dominant and minority group has been found all over the world, even when there is no genetic difference between the groups, and in cases where opportunities for a group have changed, such as when they emigrate, differences have rapidly disappeared (Block, 1995).

If groups such as women and African Americans are not inherently inferior but perform worse on tests, what might be the reasons? The usual explanation is that they have internalized the "superior" group's prejudices. Steele thinks the problem might not be so internal but may have to do with the situation. The stigmatized groups perform worse when they know that's what is expected—when they experience the threat of being stereotyped. They either become too anxious or give up and avoid the subject.

What Can You Do for Yourself?

So, do you feel you belong to a group that is expected to do poorly at math? (Perhaps the group of "math dumbbells" in the class?) What can you do to get out from under the shadow of stereotype threat as you take this course?

First, *care* about learning statistics. Don't discount it to save your self-esteem. Fight for your right to know this subject. Consider these words from the former president of the Mathematics Association of America:

> The paradox of our times is that as mathematics becomes increasingly powerful, only the powerful seem to benefit from it. The ability to think mathematically—broadly interpreted—is absolutely crucial to advancement in virtually every career. Confidence in dealing with data, skepticism in analyzing arguments, persistence in penetrating complex problems, and literacy in communicating about technical matters are the enabling arts offered by the new mathematical sciences. (Steen, 1987, p. xviii)

Second, once you care about succeeding at statistics, realize you are going to be affected by stereotype threat. Think of it as a stereotype-induced form of test anxiety and work on it that way (see Box 1–2).

Third, root out the effects of that stereotype in yourself as much as you can. It takes some effort. That's why we are spending time on it here. Research on stereotypes shows that they can be activated without our awareness (Fiske, 1998), even when we are otherwise low in prejudice or a member of the stereotyped group.

Some Points to Think About

For women, yes, the very top performers tend to be male, but the differences are slight, and the lowest performers are not more likely to be female. Indeed, gender differences on test performance have been declining (National Center for Education Statistics, 2001). Tobias (1982) cites numerous studies for why women might not make it to the very top in math. For example, in a study of students identified by a math talent search, it was found that few parents arranged for their daughters to be coached before the talent exams. Sons were almost invariably coached. In another study, parents of mathematically gifted girls were not even aware of their daughters' abilities, whereas parents of boys invariably were. In general, girls tend to avoid higher math classes, according to Tobias, because parents, peers, and even teachers often advise them against pursuing too much math. Indeed, mothers' views of their child's math abilities are strong predictors of their later performance (Bleeker & Jacobs, 2004). Girls frequently outperform boys in math, yet still greatly underestimate their abilities (Heller & Ziegler, 1996). So, even though women are earning more PhDs in math than ever before, it is not surprising that math is the field with the highest dropout rate for women.

We checked the grades in our own introductory statistics classes and found no reliable difference for gender. More generally, Schram (1996) analyzed results of 13 independent studies of performance in college statistics and found an overall average difference of almost exactly zero (the slight direction of difference favored females). Steele (1997) also found that the grades of African Americans, for example, rose substantially when they were enrolled in a transition-to-college program emphasizing that they were the cream of the crop and much was expected of them. Meanwhile, African American students at the same school who were enrolled in a remedial program for minorities received considerable attention, but their grades improved very little and many more of them dropped out of school than in the other group. Steele argues that the very idea of a remedial program exposed those students to a subtle stereotype threat.

Cognitive research on stereotype threat has demonstrated that it most affects math problems relying on long-term memory and spills over into subsequent tasks not normally affected by stereotype threat (Beilock et al., 2007).

Another point to ponder is a study cited by Tobias (1995) comparing students in Asia and the United States on an international mathematics test. The U.S. students were thoroughly outperformed, but more important was why: Interviews revealed that Asian students saw math as an ability fairly equally distributed among people and thought that differences in performance were due to hard work. Contrarily, U.S. students thought some people are just born better at math; so hard work matters little.

In short, our culture's belief that "math just comes naturally to some people" could be holding you back. But then, doing well in this course may even be more satisfying for you than for others.

Central Tendency and Variability in Research Articles

The mean and the standard deviation are very commonly reported in research articles. However, the mode, median, and variance are only occasionally reported. Sometimes the mean and standard deviation are included in the text of an article. For our dreams example, the researcher might write, "The mean number of dreams in the last week for the 10 students was 6.00 ($SD = 2.57$)." Means and standard deviations are also often listed in tables, especially if a study includes several groups or several different variables. For example, Selwyn (2007) conducted a study of gender-related perceptions of information and communication technologies (such as games machines, DVD players, and cell phones). The researcher asked 406 college students in Wales to rate 8 technologies in terms of their level of masculinity or femininity. The students rated each technology using a 7-point response scale, from -3 for very feminine to $+3$ for very masculine, with a midpoint of 0 for neither masculine or feminine. Table 2–5 (reproduced from Selwyn's article) shows the mean, standard deviation, and variance of the students' ratings of each technology. As the table shows, games machines were rated as being more masculine than feminine, and landline telephones were rated as being slightly more feminine than masculine. Notice that Table 2–5 is one of those rare examples where the variance is shown (usually just the standard deviation is given). Overall, the table provides a useful summary of the descriptive results of the study. In another part of the study, Selwyn compared women's and men's perceptions of the masculinity or femininity of different aspects of computers and computing. We will describe those results in Chapter 8; so be sure to look out for them!

Another interesting example is shown in Table 2–6 (reproduced from Norcross et al., 2005). The table shows the application and enrollment statistics for psychology doctoral programs in the United States, broken down by area of psychology and by year (1973, 1979, 1992, and 2003). The table does not give standard deviations, but it does give both means and medians. For example, in 2003 the mean number of applicants to doctoral counseling psychology programs was 71.0, but the median was only 59. This suggests that some programs had very high numbers of applicants that

Table 2-5   Mean Scores for Each Technology

	N	Mean	S.D.	Variance
Games machine (e.g., Playstation)	403	1.92	1.00	.98
DVD Player	406	.44	.85	.73
Personal Computer (PC)	400	.36	.82	.68
Digital radio (DAB)	399	.34	.99	.98
Television set	406	.26	.78	.62
Radio	404	−.01	.81	.65
Mobile phone	399	−.19	.88	.77
Landline telephone	404	−.77	1.03	1.07

Note: Mean scores range from -3 (*very feminine*) to $+3$ (*very masculine*). The midpoint score of .0 denotes "neither masculine nor feminine."
Source: Selwyn, N. (2007). Hi-tech = guy-tech? An exploration of undergraduate students' gendered perceptions of information and communication technologies. *Sex Roles, 56,* 525–536. Copyright © 2007. Reprinted by permission of Springer Science and Business Media.

Table 2–6   Application and Enrollment Statistics by Area and Year: Doctoral Programs

Program	N of programs				Applications								Enrollments			
					M				Mdn				M		Mdn	
	1973	1979	1992	2003	1973	1979	1992	2003	1973	1979	1992	2003	1992	2003	1992	2003
Clinical	105	130	225	216	314.4	252.6	191.1	142.0	290	234	168	126	12.0	15.4	8	8
Clinical neuro				20				72.3				37		10.7		6
Community	4	2	5	13	90.5		24.4	23.5	60		23	21	3.2	3.3	2	3
Counseling	29	43	62	66	133.4	90.9	120.2	71.0	120	84	110	59	7.3	6.8	6	7
Health			7	13			40.7	71.2			30	56	4.4	6.7	5	4
School	30	39	56	57	78.5	54.0	31.3	38.7	53	34	32	31	5.4	6.9	5	5
Other health service provider subfield				52				83.5				48		9.2		7
Cognitive			47	104			24.6	30.1			22	22	2.6	3.4	2	3
Developmental	56	72	97	111	54.1	38.9	27.6	25.5	41	30	24	22	2.8	3.4	2	3
Educational	23	28	30	35	67.8	39.7	20.0	19.7	34	26	12	13	6.0	4.9	4	4
Experimental	118	127	78	40	56.2	33.2	31.3	26.7	42	25	26	17	4.4	4.1	3	3
I/O	20	25	49	60	39.9	54.7	66.2	46.9	37	48	70	41	4.9	4.7	4	4
Neuroscience				53				22.0				16		2.8		2
Personality	23	15	10	18	42.5	24.7	12.3	47.8	33	17	6	31	1.0	2.8	1	2
Psychobiological/ physiological				18				21.1				17		2.4		2
Quantitative	40	43	76	17	33.2	29.3	20.0	11.2	29	24	20	11	3.9	1.9	2	1
Social	58	72	59	85	48.7	30.9	47.1	43.1	40	24	37	35	3.3	3.2	3	3
Other fields	60	47	288	101	61.6	74.1	26.6	26.0	27	25	15	17	3.3	3.8	2	3
Total	566	645	1,089	1,079	106.1	85.2	69.4	59.6			31	33	5.6	6.7	4	4

Note: The academic years correspond to the 1975–1976, 1981–1982, 1994 and 2005 editions of *Graduate Study in Psychology*, respectively. Clinical neuro = clinical neuropsychology; I/O = industrial-organizational.

Source: Norcross, J. C., Kohout, J. L., & Wicherski, M. (2005). Graduate study in psychology: 1971 to 2004. *American Psychologist, 60,* 959–975. Published by the American Psychological Association. Reprinted with permission.

skewed the distribution. In fact, you can see from the table that for almost every kind of program and for both applications and enrollments, the means are typically higher than the medians. You may also be struck by just how competitive it is to get into doctoral programs in many areas of psychology. It is our experience that one of the factors that makes a lot of difference is doing well in statistics courses!

Summary

1. The mean is the most commonly used measure of central tendency of a distribution of scores. The mean is the ordinary average—the sum of the scores divided by the number of scores. In symbols, $M = (\Sigma X)/N$.
2. Other, less commonly used ways of describing the central tendency of a distribution of scores are the mode (the most common single value) and the median (the value of the middle score when all the scores are lined up from lowest to highest).
3. The variability of a group of scores can be described by the variance and the standard deviation.
4. The variance is the average of the squared deviation of each score from the mean. In symbols, $SD^2 = [\Sigma(X - M)^2]/N$. The sum of squared deviations, $\Sigma(X - M)^2$, is also symbolized as SS. Thus $SD^2 = SS/N$.
5. The standard deviation is the square root of the variance. In symbols, $SD = \sqrt{SD^2}$. It is approximately the average amount that scores differ from the mean.
6. There have always been a few psychologists who have warned against statistical methodology because in the process of creating averages, knowledge about the individual case is lost.
7. Means and standard deviations are often given in research articles in the text or in tables.

Key Terms

central tendency (p. 34)
mean (M) (pp. 34, 35)
Σ (sum of) (p. 35)
X (p. 35)
N (number of scores) (p. 36)
mode (p. 37)
median (p. 39)

outlier (p. 39)
variance (SD^2) (p. 44)
deviation score (p. 44)
squared deviation score (p. 44)
sum of squared deviations (sum of
    squares) (SS) (pp. 44, 46)
standard deviation (SD) (p. 45)

SD^2 (p. 46)
SD (p. 46)
computational formula (p. 49)
definitional formula (p. 49)

Example Worked-Out Problems

Figuring the Mean

Find the mean for the following scores: 8, 6, 6, 9, 6, 5, 6, 2.

Answer

You can figure the mean using the formula or the steps.
    Using the formula: $M = (\Sigma X)/N = 48/8 = 6$
    Using the steps:

❶ **Add up all the scores.** $8 + 6 + 6 + 9 + 6 + 5 + 6 + 2 = 48$.
❷ **Divide this sum by the number of scores.** $48/8 = 6$.

Finding the Median

Find the median for the following scores: 1, 7, 4, 2, 3, 6, 2, 9, 7.

Answer

❶ **Line up all the scores from lowest to highest.** 1, 2, 2, 3, 4, 6, 7, 7, 9.
❷ **Figure how many scores there are to the middle score by adding 1 to the number of scores and dividing by 2.** There are 9 scores; so the middle score is the result of adding 1 to 9 and then dividing by 2, which is 5. The middle score is the fifth score.
❸ **Count up to the middle score or scores.** The fifth score from the bottom is 4; so the median is 4.

Figuring the Sum of Squares and the Variance

Find the sum of squares and the variance for the following scores: 8, 6, 6, 9, 6, 5, 6, 2. (These are the same scores used in the previous example for the mean: $M = 6$.)

Answer

You can figure the sum of squares and the variance using the formulas or the steps.
Using the formulas:

$$SS = \Sigma(X - M)^2 = (8 - 6)^2 + (6 - 6)^2 + (6 - 6)^2$$
$$+ (9 - 6)^2 + (6 - 6)^2 + (5 - 6)^2 + (6 - 6)^2 + (2 - 6)^2$$
$$= 2^2 + 0^2 + 0^2 + 3^2 + 0^2 + -1^2 + 0^2 + -4^2$$
$$= 4 + 0 + 0 + 9 + 0 + 1 + 0 + 16$$
$$= 30$$
$$SD^2 = SS/N = 30/8 = 3.75.$$

Table 2–7 shows the figuring, using the following steps:

❶ **Subtract the mean from each score.**
❷ **Square each of these deviation scores.**
❸ **Add up the squared deviation scores.** This gives the sum of squares (SS).
❹ **Divide the sum of squared deviations by the number of scores.** This gives the variance (SD^2).

Table 2-7 Figuring for Example Worked-Out Problem for the Sum of Squares and Variance Using Steps

Score	Mean	❶ Deviation	❷ Squared Deviation
8	6	2	4
6	6	0	0
6	6	0	0
9	6	3	9
6	6	0	0
5	6	−1	1
6	6	0	0
2	6	−4	16
			$\Sigma = SS = 30$ ❸

❹ Variance = 30/8 = 3.75

Figuring the Standard Deviation

Find the standard deviation for the following scores: 8, 6, 6, 9, 6, 5, 6, 2. (These are the same scores used above for the mean, sum of squares, and variance. $SD^2 = 3.75$.)

Answer

You can figure the standard deviation using the formula or the steps.
   Using the formula: $SD = \sqrt{SD^2} = \sqrt{3.75} = 1.94$.
   Using the steps:

 ❶ **Figure the variance.** The variance (from above) is 3.75.
 ❷ **Take the square root.** The square root of 3.75 is 1.94.

Outline for Writing Essays on Finding the Mean, Variance, and Standard Deviation

1. Explain that the mean is a measure of the central tendency of a group of scores. Mention that the mean is the ordinary average, that is, the sum of the scores divided by the number of scores.
2. Explain that the variance and standard deviation both measure the amount of variability (or spread) among a group of scores.
3. The variance is the average of each score's squared difference from the mean. Describe the steps for figuring the variance.
4. Roughly speaking, the standard deviation is the average amount that scores differ from the mean. Explain that the standard deviation is directly related to the variance and is figured by taking the square root of the variance.

Practice Problems

These problems involve figuring. Most real-life statistics problems are done on a computer with special statistical software. Even if you have such software, do these problems by hand to ingrain the method in your mind. To learn how to use a computer to solve statistics problems like those in this chapter, refer to the Using SPSS section at the end of this chapter and the *Study Guide and Computer Workbook* that accompanies this text.
   All data are fictional unless an actual citation is given.

Set I (for Answers to Set I Problems, see pp. 674–675)

1. For the following scores, find the (a) mean, (b) median, (c) sum of squared deviations, (d) variance, and (e) standard deviation:

$$32, 28, 24, 28, 28, 31, 35, 29, 26$$

2. For the following scores, find the (a) mean, (b) median, (c) sum of squared deviations, (d) variance, and (e) standard deviation:

$$6, 1, 4, 2, 3, 4, 6, 6$$

3. For the following scores, find the (a) mean, (b) median, (c) sum of squared deviations, (d) variance, and (e) standard deviation:

$$2.13, 6.01, 3.33, 5.78$$

4. Here are the noon temperatures (in degrees Celsius) in a particular Canadian city on Boxing Day (usually December 26) for the 10 years from 1998 through 2007: -5, -4, -1, -1, 0, -8, -5, -9, -13, and -24. Describe the typical temperature and the amount of variation to a person who has never had a course in statistics. Give three ways of describing the representative temperature and two ways of describing its variation, explaining the differences and how you figured each. (You will learn more if you try to write your own answer first, before reading our answer at the back of the book.)

5. A researcher is studying the amygdala (a part of the brain involved in emotion). Six participants in a particular fMRI (brain scan) study are measured for the increase in activation of their amygdala while they are viewing pictures of violent scenes. The activation increases are .43, .32, .64, .21, .29, and .51. Figure the (a) mean and (b) standard deviation for these six activation increases. (c) Explain what you have done and what the results mean to a person who has never had a course in statistics.

6. Describe and explain the location of the mean, mode, and median for a normal curve.

7. A researcher studied the number of anxiety attacks recounted over a two-week period by 30 people in psychotherapy for an anxiety disorder. In an article describing the results of the study, the researcher reports: "The mean number of anxiety attacks was 6.84 ($SD = 3.18$)." Explain these results to a person who has never had a course in statistics.

8. In a study by Gonzaga et al. (2001), romantic couples answered questions about how much they loved their partner and also were videotaped while revealing something about themselves to their partner. The videotapes were later rated by trained judges for various signs of affiliation. Table 2–8 (reproduced from their Table 2) shows some of the results. Explain to a person who has never had a course in statistics the results for self-reported love for the partner and for the number of seconds "leaning toward the partner."

Set II

9. (a) Describe and explain the difference between the mean, median, and mode. (b) Make up an example (not in the book or in your lectures) in which the median would be the preferred measure of central tendency.

Table 2-8 Mean Levels of Emotions and Cue Display in Study 1				
	Women ($n = 60$)		**Men ($n = 60$)**	
Indicator	**M**	**SD**	**M**	**SD**
Emotion reports				
Self-reported love	5.02	2.16	5.11	2.08
Partner-estimated love	4.85	2.13	4.58	2.20
Affiliation-cue display				
Affirmative head nods	1.28	2.89	1.21	1.91
Duchenne smiles	4.45	5.24	5.78	5.59
Leaning toward partner	32.27	20.36	31.36	21.08
Gesticulation	0.13	0.40	0.25	0.77

Note: Emotions are rated on a scale of 0 (*none*) to 8 (*extreme*). Cue displays are shown as mean seconds displayed per 60 s.
Source: Gonzaga, G. C., Keltner, D., Londahl, E. A., & Smith, M. D. (2001). Love and the commitment problem in romantic relationships and friendship. *Journal of Personality and Social Psychology, 81*, 247–262. Published by the American Psychological Association. Reprinted with permission.

10. (a) Describe the variance and standard deviation. (b) Explain why the standard deviation is more often used as a descriptive statistic than the variance.

11. For the following scores, find the (a) mean, (b) median, (c) sum of squared deviations, (d) variance, and (e) standard deviation:

$$2, 2, 0, 5, 1, 4, 1, 3, 0, 0, 1, 4, 4, 0, 1, 4, 3, 4, 2, 1, 0$$

12. For the following scores, find the (a) mean, (b) median, (c) sum of squared deviations, (d) variance, and (e) standard deviation:

$$1{,}112; 1{,}245; 1{,}361; 1{,}372; 1{,}472$$

13. For the following scores, find the (a) mean, (b) median, (c) sum of squared deviations, (d) variance, and (e) standard deviation:

$$3.0, 3.4, 2.6, 3.3, 3.5, 3.2$$

14. For the following scores, find the (a) mean, (b) median, (c) sum of squared deviations, (d) variance, and (e) standard deviation:

$$8, -5, 7, -10, 5$$

15. Make up three sets of scores: (a) one with the mean greater than the median, (b) one with the median and the mean the same, and (c) one with the mode greater than the median. (Each made-up set of scores should include at least five scores.)

16. A psychologist interested in political behavior measured the square footage of the desks in the official office of four U.S. governors and of four chief executive officers (CEOs) of major U.S. corporations. The figures for the governors were 44, 36, 52, and 40 square feet. The figures for the CEOs were 32, 60, 48, and 36 square feet. (a) Figure the means and standard deviations for the governors and for the CEOs. (b) Explain, to a person who has never had a course in statistics, what you have done. (c) Note the ways in which the means and standard deviations differ, and speculate on the possible meaning of these differences, presuming that they are representative of U.S. governors and large corporations' CEOs in general.

17. A developmental psychologist studies the number of words that seven infants have learned at a particular age. The numbers are 10, 12, 8, 0, 3, 40, and 18. Figure the (a) mean, (b) median, and (c) standard deviation for the number of words learned by these seven infants. (d) Explain what you have done and what the results mean to a person who has never had a course in statistics.

18. Describe and explain the location of the mean, mode, and median of a distribution of scores that is strongly skewed to the left.

19. You figure the variance of a distribution of scores to be -4.26. Explain why your answer cannot be correct.

20. A study involves measuring the number of days absent from work for 216 employees of a large company during the preceding year. As part of the results, the researcher reports, "The number of days absent during the preceding year ($M = 9.21$; $SD = 7.34$) was . . . ." Explain what is written in parentheses to a person who has never had a course in statistics.

21. Payne (2001) gave participants a computerized task in which they first see a face and then a picture of either a gun or a tool. The task was to press one button if it was a tool and a different one if it was a gun. Unknown to the participants while they were doing the study, the faces served as a "prime" (something that starts you thinking a particular way); half the time they were of a black person and half the time a white person. Table 2–9 shows the means and standard deviations for reaction times (the time to decide if the picture is of a gun or a tool) after either a black or white prime. (In Experiment 2, participants were told to

decide as fast as possible.) Explain the results to a person who has never had a course in statistics. (Be sure to explain some specific numbers as well as the general principle of the mean and standard deviation.)

Table 2-9	Mean Reaction Times (in Milliseconds) in Identifying Guns and Tools in Experiments 1 and 2				
	Prime				
	Black			White	
Target	*M*	*SD*		*M*	*SD*
Experiment 1					
Gun	423	64		441	73
Tool	454	57		446	60
Experiment 2					
Gun	299	28		295	31
Tool	307	29		304	29

Source: Payne, B. K. (2001). Prejudice and perception: The role of automatic and controlled processes in misperceiving a weapon. *Journal of Personality and Social Psychology, 81,* 181–192. Published by the American Psychological Association. Reprinted with permission.

Using SPSS

The ✐ in the following steps indicates a mouse click. (We used SPSS version 15.0 to carry out these analyses. The steps and output may be slightly different for other versions of SPSS.)

Finding the Mean, Mode, and Median

❶ Enter the scores from your distribution in one column of the data window.
❷ ✐ *Analyze.*
❸ ✐ *Descriptive statistics.*
❹ ✐ *Frequencies.*
❺ ✐ on the variable for which you want to find the mean, mode, and median, and then ✐ the arrow.
❻ *Statistics.*
❼ ✐ *Mean,* ✐ *Median,* ✐ *Mode,* ✐ *Continue.*
❽ Optional: To instruct SPSS *not* to produce a frequency table, ✐ the box labeled *Display frequency tables* (this *un*checks the box).
❾ ✐ *OK.*

Practice the steps above by finding the mean, mode, and median for the number of dreams example at the start of the chapter (the scores are 7, 8, 8, 7, 3, 1, 6, 9, 3, 8). Your output window should look like Figure 2–14. (If you instructed SPSS not to show the frequency table, your output will show only the mean, median, and mode.)

Finding the Variance and Standard Deviation

As mentioned earlier in the chapter, most calculators and computer software—including SPSS—calculate the variance and standard deviation using a formula that involves dividing by $N - 1$ instead of N. So, if you request the variance and standard

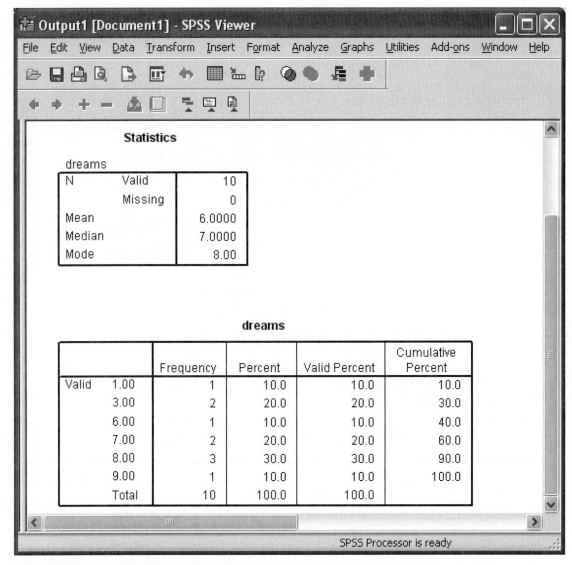

Figure 2–14   Using SPSS to find the mean, median, and mode for the number of dreams example.

deviation directly from SPSS (for example, by clicking *Variance* and *Std. deviation* in Step ❼), the answers provided by SPSS will be different from the answers in this chapter.[5] The following steps show you how to use SPSS to figure the variance and standard deviation using the dividing-by-*N* method you learned in this chapter. It is easier to learn these steps using actual numbers; so we will use the number of dreams example again.

❶ Enter the scores from your distribution in one column of the data window (the scores are 7, 8, 8, 7, 3, 1, 6, 9, 3, 8). We will call this variable "dreams."

❷ Find the mean of the scores by following the preceding steps for Finding the Mean, Mode, and Median. The mean of the dreams variable is 6.

❸ You are now going to create a new variable that shows each score's squared deviation from the mean. ✑ *Transform,* ✑ *Compute Variable.* You could call the new variable any name you want, but we will call it "sqdev" (for "squared

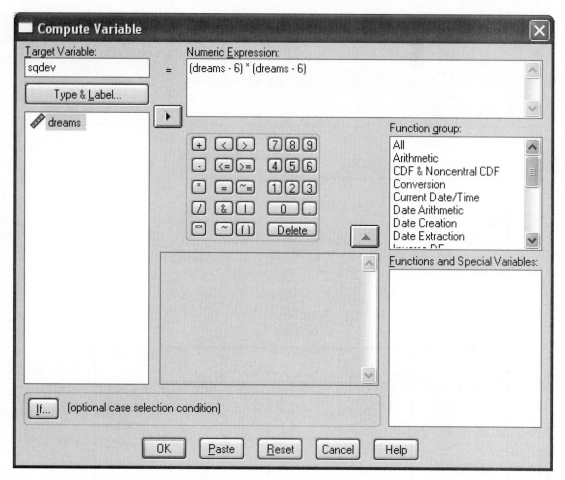

Figure 2–15 SPSS compute variable window for Step ❸ of finding the variance and standard deviation for the number of dreams example.

deviation"). So, write *sqdev* in the box labeled *Target Variable.* You are now going to tell SPSS how to figure *sqdev.* In the box labeled *Numeric Expression,* write (*dreams* − 6) * (*dreams* − 6). (The asterisk is how you show *multiplication* in SPSS.) As you can see, this formula takes each score's deviation score and multiplies it by itself to give the squared deviation score. Your Compute Variable window should look like Figure 2–15. ✍ *OK.* You will see that a new variable called *sqdev* has been added to the data window (see Figure 2–16). The scores are the squared deviations of each score from the mean.

❹ As you learned in this chapter, the variance is figured by dividing the sum of the squared deviations by the number of scores. This is the same as taking the mean of the squared deviation scores. So, to find the variance of the dreams scores, follow the steps shown earlier to find the mean of the *sqdev* variable. This comes out to 6.60; so the variance of the dreams scores is 6.60.

❺ To find the standard deviation, use a calculator to find the square root of 6.60, which is 2.57.

If you were conducting an actual research study, you would most likely request the variance and standard deviation directly from SPSS. However, for our purpose in this chapter (describing the variation in a group of scores), the steps we just outlined are entirely appropriate.

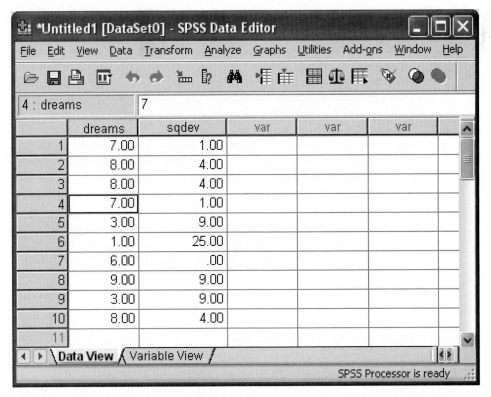

Figure 2–16 SPSS data window after Step ❸ for finding the variance and standard deviation for the number of dreams example.

Chapter Notes

1. In more formal, mathematical statistics writing, the symbols can be more complex. This complexity allows formulas to handle intricate situations without confusion. However, in books on statistics for psychologists, even fairly advanced texts, the symbols are kept simple. The simplified form rarely creates ambiguities in the kinds of statistical formulas psychologists use.

2. This section focuses on the variance and standard deviation as indicators of spread, or variability. Another way to describe the spread of a group of scores is in terms of the *range*—the highest score minus the lowest score. Suppose that in a particular class the oldest student is 39 years of age and the youngest is 19; the range is 20 (that is, $39 - 19 = 20$). Psychology researchers rarely use the range because it is such an imprecise way to describe the spread; it does not take into account how clumped together the scores are within the range.

3. Why don't statisticians use the deviation scores themselves, make all deviations positive, and just use their average? In fact, the average of the deviation scores (treating all deviations as positive) has a formal name—the *average deviation* or *mean deviation*. This procedure was actually used in the past, and some psychologists have noted subtle advantages of the average deviation (Catanzaro & Taylor, 1996). However, the average deviation does not work out very well as part of more complicated statistical procedures.

4. It is important to remember that the standard deviation is not *exactly* the average amount that scores differ from the mean. To be precise, the standard deviation is the square root of the average of scores' squared deviations from the mean. This squaring, averaging, and then taking the square root gives a slightly different result from simply averaging the scores' deviations from the mean. Still, the result of this approach has technical advantages that outweigh the slight disadvantage of giving only an approximate description of the average variation from the mean (see Chapter Note 3).

5. Note that if you request the variance from SPSS, you can convert it to the variance as we figure it in this chapter by multiplying the variance from SPSS by $N - 1$ (that is, the number of scores minus 1) and then dividing the result by N (the number of scores). (That is the variance as we are figuring it in this chapter = SPSS's variance multiplied by $[N - 1]/N$.) Taking the square root of the resulting value will give you the standard deviation (using the formula you learned in this chapter). We use a slightly longer approach to figuring the variance and standard deviation in order to show you how to create new variables in SPSS.

CHAPTER 3

Some Key Ingredients for Inferential Statistics

Z Scores, the Normal Curve, Sample versus Population, and Probability

Chapter Outline

- ✪ Z Scores   68
- ✪ The Normal Curve   73
- ✪ Sample and Population   83
- ✪ Probability   88
- ✪ Controversies: Is the Normal Curve Really So Normal? and Using Nonrandom Samples   93
- ✪ Z Scores, Normal Curves, Samples and Populations, and Probabilities in Research Articles   95

- ✪ Advanced Topic: Probability Rules and Conditional Probabilities   96
- ✪ Summary   97
- ✪ Key Terms   98
- ✪ Example Worked-Out Problems   99
- ✪ Practice Problems   102
- ✪ Using SPSS   105
- ✪ Chapter Notes   106

> **TIP FOR SUCCESS**
>
> Before beginning this chapter, be sure you have mastered the material in Chapter 1 on the shapes of distributions and the material in Chapter 2 on the mean and standard deviation.

Ordinarily, psychologists conduct research to test a theoretical principle or the effectiveness of a practical procedure. For example, a psychophysiologist might measure changes in heart rate from before to after solving a difficult problem. The measurements are then used to test a theory predicting that heart rate should change following successful problem solving. An applied social psychologist might examine the effectiveness of a program of neighborhood meetings intended to promote water conservation. Such studies are carried out with a particular group of research participants. But researchers use inferential statistics to make more general conclusions about the theoretical principle or procedure being studied. These conclusions go *beyond* the particular group of research participants studied.

This chapter and Chapters 4, 5, and 6 introduce inferential statistics. In this chapter, we consider four topics: *Z* scores, the normal curve, sample versus population, and probability. This chapter prepares the way for the next ones, which are more demanding conceptually.

Z Scores

In Chapter 2, you learned how to describe a group of scores in terms and the mean and variation around the mean. In this section you learn how to describe a particular score in terms of where it fits into the overall group of scores. That is, you learn how to use the mean and standard deviation to create a *Z* score; a *Z* score describes a score in terms of how much it is above or below the average.

Suppose you are told that a student, Jerome, is asked the question, "To what extent are you a morning person?" Jerome responds with a 5 on a 7-point scale, where 1 = *not at all* and 7 = *extremely*. Now suppose that we do not know anything about how other students answer this question. In this situation, it is hard to tell whether Jerome is more or less of a morning person in relation to other students. However, suppose that we know for students in general, the mean rating (*M*) is 3.40 and the standard deviation (*SD*) is 1.47. (These values are the actual mean and standard deviation that we found for this question in a large sample of statistics students from eight different universities across the United States and Canada.) With this knowledge, we can see that Jerome is more of a morning person than is typical among students. We can also see that Jerome is above the average (1.60 units more than average; that is, 5 − 3.40 = 1.60) by a bit more than students typically vary from the average (that is, students typically vary by about 1.47, the standard deviation). This is all shown in Figure 3–1.

What Is a *Z* Score?

A **Z score** makes use of the mean and standard deviation to describe a particular score. Specifically, a *Z* score is the number of standard deviations the actual score is above or below the mean. If the actual score is above the mean, the *Z* score is positive. If the actual score is below the mean, the *Z* score is negative. The standard deviation now becomes a kind of yardstick, a unit of measure in its own right.

In our example, Jerome has a score of 5, which is 1.60 units above the mean of 3.40. One standard deviation is 1.47 units; so Jerome's score is a little more than 1 standard

Z score   number of standard deviations that a score is above (or below, if it is negative) the mean of its distribution; it is thus an ordinary score transformed so that it better describes the score's location in a distribution.

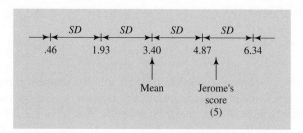

Figure 3–1   Score of one student, Jerome, in relation to the overall distribution on the measure of the extent to which students are morning people.

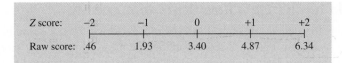

Figure 3-2 Scales of Z scores and raw scores for the example of the extent to which students are morning people.

deviation above the mean. To be precise, Jerome's Z score is +1.09 (that is, his score of 5 is 1.09 standard deviations above the mean). Another student, Michelle, has a score of 2. Her score is 1.40 units below the mean. Therefore, her score is a little less than 1 standard deviation below the mean (a Z score of −.95). So, Michelle's score is below the average by about as much as students typically vary from the average.

Z scores have many practical uses. As you will see later in this chapter, they are especially useful for showing exactly where a particular score falls on the normal curve.

Z Scores as a Scale

Figure 3–2 shows a scale of Z scores lined up against a scale of raw scores for our example of the degree to which students are morning people. A **raw score** is an ordinary score as opposed to a Z score. The two scales are something like a ruler with inches lined up on one side and centimeters on the other.

Changing a number to a Z score is a bit like converting words for measurement in various obscure languages into one language that everyone can understand—inches, cubits, and zingles (we made up that last one), for example, into centimeters. It is a very valuable tool.

Suppose that a developmental psychologist observed 3-year-old David in a laboratory situation playing with other children of the same age. During the observation, the psychologist counted the number of times David spoke to the other children. The result, over several observations, is that David spoke to other children about 8 times per hour of play. Without any standard of comparison, it would be hard to draw any conclusions from this. Let's assume, however, that it was known from previous research that under similar conditions, the mean number of times children speak is 12, with a standard deviation of 4. With that information, we can see that David spoke less often than other children in general, but not extremely less often. David would have a Z score of −1 ($M = 12$ and $SD = 4$, thus a score of 8 is 1 SD below M), as shown in Figure 3–3.

Suppose Ryan was observed speaking to other children 20 times in an hour. Ryan would clearly be unusually talkative, with a Z score of +2 (see Figure 3–3). Ryan speaks not merely more than the average but more by twice as much as children tend to vary from the average!

raw score ordinary score (or any number in a distribution before it has been made into a Z score or otherwise transformed).

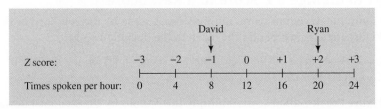

Figure 3-3 Number of times each hour that two children spoke, shown as raw scores and Z scores.

Formula to Change a Raw Score to a *Z* Score

A *Z* score is the number of standard deviations by which the raw score is above or below the mean. To figure a *Z* score, subtract the mean from the raw score, giving the deviation score. Then divide the deviation score by the standard deviation. The formula is

A *Z* score is the raw score minus the mean, divided by the standard deviation.	$$Z = \frac{X - M}{SD} \qquad (3\text{–}1)$$

For example, using the formula for David, the child who spoke to other children 8 times in an hour (where the mean number of times children speak is 12 and the standard deviation is 4),

$$Z = \frac{8 - 12}{4} = \frac{-4}{4} = -1$$

Steps to Change a Raw Score to a *Z* Score

❶ **Figure the deviation score: subtract the mean from the raw score.**
❷ **Figure the *Z* score: divide the deviation score by the standard deviation.**

Using these steps for David, the child who spoke with other children 8 times in an hour,

❶ **Figure the deviation score: subtract the mean from the raw score.**
   $8 - 12 = -4$.
❷ **Figure the *Z* score: divide the deviation score by the standard deviation.**
   $-4/4 = -1$.

Formula to Change a *Z* Score to a Raw Score

To change a *Z* score to a raw score, the process is reversed: multiply the *Z* score by the standard deviation and then add the mean. The formula is

The raw score is the *Z* score multiplied by the standard deviation, plus the mean.	$$X = (Z)(SD) + M \qquad (3\text{–}2)$$

Suppose a child has a *Z* score of 1.5 on the number of times spoken with another child during an hour. This child is 1.5 standard deviations above the mean. Because the standard deviation in this example is 4 raw score units (times spoken), the child is 6 raw score units above the mean, which is 12. Thus, 6 units above the mean is 18. Using the formula,

$$X = (Z)(SD) + M = (1.5)(4) + 12 = 6 + 12 = 18$$

Steps to Change a *Z* Score to a Raw Score

❶ **Figure the deviation score: multiply the *Z* score by the standard deviation.**
❷ **Figure the raw score: add the mean to the deviation score.**

Using these steps for the child with a *Z* score of 1.5 on the number of times spoken with another child during an hour:

❶ **Figure the deviation score: multiply the *Z* score by the standard deviation.**
   $1.5 \times 4 = 6$.
❷ **Figure the raw score: add the mean to the deviation score.** $6 + 12 = 18$.

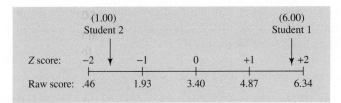

Figure 3–4 Scales of Z scores and raw scores for the example of the extent to which students are morning people, showing the scores of two sample students.

Additional Examples of Changing Z Scores to Raw Scores and Vice Versa

Consider again the example from the start of the chapter in which students were asked the extent to which they were a morning person. Using a scale from 1 (*not at all*) to 7 (*extremely*), the mean was 3.40 and the standard deviation was 1.47. Suppose a student's raw score is 6. That student is well above the mean. Specifically, using the formula,

$$Z = \frac{X - M}{SD} = \frac{6 - 3.40}{1.47} = \frac{2.60}{1.47} = 1.77$$

That is, the student's raw score is 1.77 standard deviations above the mean (see Figure 3–4, Student 1). Using the 7-point scale (from 1 = *not at all* to 7 = *extremely*), to what extent are *you* a morning person? Now figure the Z score for your raw score.

Another student has a Z score of −1.63, a score well below the mean. (This student is much less of a morning person than is typically the case for students.) You can find the exact raw score for this student using the formula

$$X = (Z)(SD) + M = (-1.63)(1.47) + 3.40 = -2.40 + 3.40 = 1.00$$

That is, the student's raw score is 1.00 (see Figure 3–4, Student 2).

Let's also consider some examples from the study of students' stress ratings. The mean stress rating of the 30 statistics students (using a 0–10 scale) was 6.43 (see Figure 2–3), and the standard deviation was 2.56. Figure 3–5 shows the raw score and Z score scales. Suppose a student's stress raw score is 10. That student is well above the mean. Specifically, using the formula

$$Z = \frac{X - M}{SD} = \frac{10 - 6.43}{2.56} = \frac{3.57}{2.56} = 1.39$$

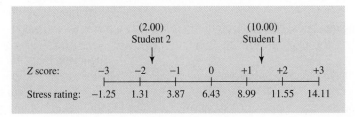

Figure 3–5 Scales of Z scores and raw scores for 30 statistics students' ratings of their stress level, showing the scores of two sample students. (Data based on Aron et al., 1995.)

The student's stress level is 1.39 standard deviations above the mean (see Figure 3–5, Student 1). On a scale of 0–10, how stressed have *you* been in the last 2½ weeks? Figure the Z score for your raw stress score.

Another student has a Z score of −1.73, a stress level well below the mean. You can find the exact raw stress score for this student using the formula

$$X = (Z)(SD) + M = (-1.73)(2.56) + 6.43 = -4.43 + 6.43 = 2.00$$

That is, the student's raw stress score is 2.00 (see Figure 3–5, Student 2).

The Mean and Standard Deviation of Z Scores

The mean of any distribution of Z scores is always 0. This is so because when you change each raw score to a Z score, you take the raw score minus the mean. So the mean is subtracted out of all the raw scores, making the overall mean come out to 0. In other words, in any distribution, the sum of the positive Z scores must always equal the sum of the negative Z scores. Thus, when you add them all up, you get 0.

The standard deviation of any distribution of Z scores is always 1. This is because when you change each raw score to a Z score, you divide by the standard deviation.

A Z score is sometimes called a *standard score*. There are two reasons: Z scores have standard values for the mean and the standard deviation, and, as we saw earlier, Z scores provide a kind of standard scale of measurement for any variable. (However, sometimes the term *standard score* is used only when the Z scores are for a distribution that follows a normal curve.)[1]

How are you doing?

1. How is a Z score related to a raw score?
2. Write the formula for changing a raw score to a Z score, and define each of the symbols.
3. For a particular group of scores, $M = 20$ and $SD = 5$. Give the Z score for (a) 30, (b) 15, (c) 20, and (d) 22.5.
4. Write the formula for changing a Z score to a raw score, and define each of the symbols.
5. For a particular group of scores, $M = 10$ and $SD = 2$. Give the raw score for a Z score of (a) +2, (b) +.5, (c) 0, and (d) −3.
6. Suppose a person has a Z score for overall health of +2 and a Z score for overall sense of humor of +1. What does it mean to say that this person is healthier than she is funny?

Answers

1. A Z score is the number of standard deviations a raw score is above or below the mean.
2. $Z = (X - M)/SD$. Z is the Z score; X is the raw score; M is the mean; SD is the standard deviation.
3. (a) $Z = (X - M)/SD = (30 - 20)/5 = 10/5 = 2$; (b) −1; (c) 0; (d) .5.
4. $X = (Z)(SD) + M$. X is the raw score; Z is the Z score; SD is the standard deviation; M is the mean.
5. (a) $X = (Z)(SD) + M = (2)(2) + 10 = 4 + 10 = 14$; (b) 11; (c) 10; (d) 4.
6. This person is more above the average in health (in terms of how much people typically vary from average in health) than she is above the average in humor (in terms of how much people typically vary from the average in humor).

The Normal Curve

As noted in Chapter 1, the graphs of the distributions of many of the variables that psychologists study follow a unimodal, roughly symmetrical, bell-shaped curve. These bell-shaped smooth histograms approximate a precise and important mathematical distribution called the **normal distribution,** or, more simply, the **normal curve.**[2] The normal curve is a mathematical (or theoretical) distribution. Researchers often compare the actual distributions of the variables they are studying (that is, the distributions they find in research studies) to the normal curve. They don't expect the distributions of their variables to match the normal curve *perfectly* (since the normal curve is a theoretical distribution), but researchers often check whether their variables *approximately* follow a normal curve. (The normal curve or normal distribution is also often called a *Gaussian distribution* after the astronomer Karl Friedrich Gauss. However, if its discovery can be attributed to anyone, it should really be to Abraham de Moivre—see Box 3–1.) An example of the normal curve is shown in Figure 3–6.

Why the Normal Curve Is So Common in Nature

Take, for example, the number of different letters a particular person can remember accurately on various testings (with different random letters each time). On some testings the number of letters remembered may be high, on others low, and on most somewhere in between. That is, the number of different letters a person can recall on various testings probably approximately follows a normal curve. Suppose that the person has a basic ability to recall, say, seven letters in this kind of memory task. Nevertheless, on any particular testing, the actual number recalled will be affected by various influences—noisiness of the room, the person's mood at the moment, a combination of random letters confused with a familiar name, and so on.

These various influences add up to make the person recall more than seven on some testings and less than seven on others. However, the particular combination of such influences that come up at any testing is essentially random; thus, on most testings, positive and negative influences should cancel out. The chances are not very good of all the negative influences happening to come together on a testing when none of the positive influences show up. Thus, in general, the person remembers a middle amount, an amount in which all the opposing influences cancel each other out. Very high or very low scores are much less common.

This creates a unimodal distribution with most of the scores near the middle and fewer at the extremes. It also creates a distribution that is symmetrical, because the number of letters recalled is as likely to be above as below the middle. Being a

normal distribution   frequency distribution that follows a normal curve.

normal curve   specific, mathematically defined, bell-shaped frequency distribution that is symmetrical and unimodal; distributions observed in nature and in research commonly approximate it.

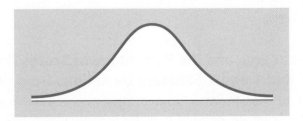

Figure 3–6   A normal curve.

BOX 3–1   de Moivre, the Eccentric Stranger Who Invented the Normal Curve

The normal curve is central to statistics and is the foundation of most statistical theories and procedures. If any one person can be said to have discovered this fundamental of the field, it was Abraham de Moivre. He was a French Protestant who came to England at the age of 21 because of religious persecution in France, which in 1685 denied Protestants all their civil liberties. In England, de Moivre became a friend of Isaac Newton, who was supposed to have often answered questions by saying, "Ask Mr. de Moivre—he knows all that better than I do." Yet because he was a foreigner, de Moivre was never able to rise to the same heights of fame as the British-born mathematicians who respected him so greatly.

Abraham de Moivre was mainly an expert on chance. In 1733, he wrote a "method of approximating the sum of the terms of the binomial expanded into a series." His paper essentially described the normal curve. The description was only in the form of a law, however; de Moivre never actually drew the curve itself. In fact, he was not very interested in it.

Credit for discovering the normal curve is often given to Pierre Laplace, a Frenchman who stayed home; or Karl Friedrich Gauss, a German; or Thomas Simpson, an Englishman. All worked on the problem of the distribution of errors around a mean, even going so far as describing the curve or drawing approximations of it. But even without drawing it, de Moivre was the first to compute the areas under the normal curve at 1, 2, and 3 standard deviations, and Karl Pearson (discussed in Chapter 13, Box 13–1), a distinguished later statistician, felt strongly that de Moivre was the true discoverer of this important concept.

In England, de Moivre was highly esteemed as a man of letters as well as of numbers, being familiar with all the classics and able to recite whole scenes from his beloved Moliére's *Misanthropist.* But for all his feelings for his native France, the French Academy elected him a *foreign* member of the Academy of Sciences just before his death. In England, he was ineligible for a university position because he was a foreigner there as well. He remained in poverty, unable even to marry. In his earlier years, he worked as a traveling teacher of mathematics. Later, he was famous for his daily sittings in Slaughter's Coffee House in Long Acre, making himself available to gamblers and insurance underwriters (two professions equally uncertain and hazardous before statistics were refined), who paid him a small sum for figuring odds for them.

De Moivre's unusual death generated several legends. He worked a great deal with infinite series, which always converge to a certain limit. One story has it that de Moivre began sleeping 15 more minutes each night until he was asleep all the time, then died. Another version claims that his work at the coffeehouse drove him to such despair that he simply went to sleep until he died. At any rate, in his 80s he could stay awake only four hours a day, although he was said to be as keenly intellectual in those hours as ever. Then his wakefulness was reduced to 1 hour, then none at all. At the age of 87, after eight days in bed, he failed to wake and was declared dead from "somnolence" (sleepiness).

Sources: Pearson (1978); Tankard (1984).

---

unimodal symmetrical curve does not guarantee that it will be a normal curve; it could be too flat or too pointed. However, it can be shown mathematically that in the long run, if the influences are truly random, and the number of different influences being combined is large, a precise normal curve will result. Mathematical statisticians call this principle the *central limit theorem.* We have more to say about this principle in Chapter 5.

The Normal Curve and the Percentage of Scores Between the Mean and 1 and 2 Standard Deviations from the Mean

The shape of the normal curve is standard. Thus, there is a known percentage of scores above or below any particular point. For example, exactly 50% of the scores in a normal curve are below the mean, because in any symmetrical distribution half

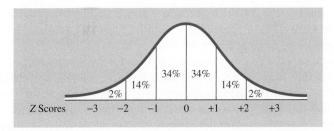

Figure 3–7   Normal curve with approximate percentages of scores between the mean and 1 and 2 standard deviations above and below the mean.

the scores are below the mean. More interestingly, as shown in Figure 3–7, approximately 34% of the scores are always between the mean and 1 standard deviation from the mean.

Consider IQ scores. On many widely used intelligence tests, the mean IQ is 100, the standard deviation is 16, and the distribution of IQs is roughly a normal curve (see Figure 3–8). Knowing about the normal curve and the percentage of scores between the mean and 1 standard deviation above the mean tells you that about 34% of people have IQs between 100, the mean IQ, and 116, the IQ score that is 1 standard deviation above the mean. Similarly, because the normal curve is symmetrical, about 34% of people have IQs between 100 and 84 (the score that is 1 standard deviation below the mean), and 68% (34% + 34%) have IQs between 84 and 116.

There are many fewer scores between 1 and 2 standard deviations from the mean than there are between the mean and 1 standard deviation from the mean. It turns out that about 14% of the scores are between 1 and 2 standard deviations above the mean (see Figure 3–7). (Similarly, about 14% of the scores are between 1 and 2 standard deviations below the mean.) Thus, about 14% of people have IQs between 116 (1 standard deviation above the mean) and 132 (2 standard deviations above the mean).

You will find it very useful to remember the 34% and 14% figures. These figures tell you the percentages of people above and below any particular score whenever you know that score's number of standard deviations above or below the mean. You can also reverse this approach and figure out a person's number of standard deviations from the mean from a percentage. Suppose you are told that a person scored in the top 2% on a test. Assuming that scores on the test are approximately normally distributed, the person must have a score that is at least 2 standard deviations above the mean. This is because a total of 50% of the scores are above the mean, but 34% are between the mean and 1 standard deviation above

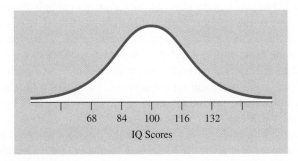

Figure 3–8   Distribution of IQ scores on many standard intelligence tests (with a mean of 100 and a standard deviation of 16).

the mean, and another 14% are between 1 and 2 standard deviations above the mean. That leaves 2% of scores (that is, 50% − 34% − 14% = 2%) that are 2 standard deviations or more above the mean.

Similarly, suppose you were selecting animals for a study and needed to consider their visual acuity. Suppose also that visual acuity was normally distributed and you wanted to use animals in the middle two-thirds (a figure close to 68%) for visual acuity. In this situation, you would select animals that scored between 1 standard deviation above and 1 standard deviation below the mean. (That is, about 34% are between the mean and 1 standard deviation above the mean and another 34% are between the mean and 1 standard deviation below the mean.) Also, remember that a Z score is the number of standard deviations that a score is above or below the mean—which is just what we are talking about here. Thus, if you knew the mean and the standard deviation of the visual acuity test, you could figure out the raw scores (the actual level of visual acuity) for being 1 standard deviation below and 1 standard deviation above the mean (that is, Z scores of −1 and +1). You would do this using the methods of changing raw scores to Z scores and vice versa that you learned earlier in this chapter, which are $Z = (X − M)/SD$ and $X = (Z)(SD) + M$.

The Normal Curve Table and Z Scores

The 50%, 34%, and 14% figures are important practical rules for working with a group of scores that follow a normal distribution. However, in many research and applied situations, psychologists need more accurate information. Because the normal curve is a precise mathematical curve, you can figure the exact percentage of scores between any two points on the normal curve (not just those that happen to be right at 1 or 2 standard deviations from the mean). For example, exactly 68.59% of scores have a Z score between +.62 and −1.68; exactly 2.81% of scores have a Z score between +.79 and +.89; and so forth.

You can figure these percentages using calculus, based on the formula for the normal curve. However, you can also do this much more simply (which you are probably glad to know!). Statisticians have worked out tables for the normal curve that give the percentage of scores between the mean (a Z score of 0) and any other Z score (as well as the percentage of scores in the tail for any Z score).

We have included a **normal curve table** in the Appendix (Table A–1, pp. 664–667). Table 3–1 shows the first part of the full table. The first column in the table lists the Z score. The second column, labeled "% Mean to Z," gives the percentage of scores between the mean and that Z score. The shaded area in the curve at the top of the column gives a visual reminder of the meaning of the percentages in the column. The third column, labeled "% in Tail," gives the percentage of scores in the tail for that Z score. The shaded tail area in the curve at the top of the column shows the meaning of the percentages in the column. Notice that the table lists only positive Z scores. This is because the normal curve is perfectly symmetrical. Thus, the percentage of scores between the mean and, say, a Z of +.98 (which is 33.65%) is exactly the same as the percentage of scores between the mean and a Z of −.98 (again 33.65%); and the percentage of scores in the tail for a Z score of +1.77 (3.84%) is the same as the percentage of scores in the tail for a Z score of −1.77 (again, 3.84%). Notice that for each Z score, the "% Mean to Z" value and the "% in Tail" value sum to 50.00. This is because exactly 50% of the scores are above the mean for a normal curve. For example, for the Z score of .57, the "% Mean to Z" value is 21.57% and the "% in Tail" value is 28.43%, and 21.57% + 28.43% = 50.00%.

Suppose you want to know the percentage of scores between the mean and a Z score of .64. You just look up .64 in the "Z" column of the table and the "% Mean

normal curve table table showing percentages of scores associated with the normal curve; the table usually includes percentages of scores between the mean and various numbers of standard deviations above the mean and percentages of scores more positive than various numbers of standard deviations above the mean.

Some Key Ingredients for Inferential Statistics

Table 3–1 Normal Curve Areas: Percentage of the Normal Curve Between the Mean and the Scores Shown and Percentage of Scores in the Tail for the *Z* Scores Shown (First part of table only: full table is Table A–1 in the Appendix. Highlighted values are examples from the text.)

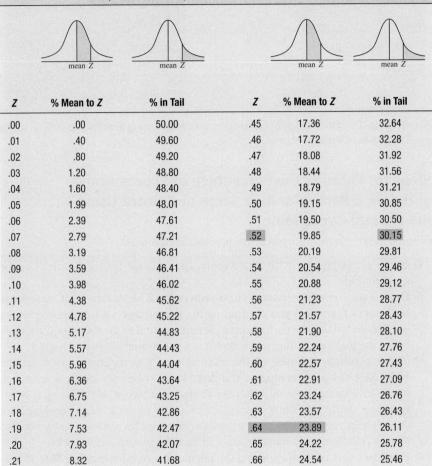

TIP FOR SUCCESS

Notice that the table repeats the basic three columns twice on the page. Be sure to look across to the columns you need.

Z	% Mean to Z	% in Tail	Z	% Mean to Z	% in Tail
.00	.00	50.00	.45	17.36	32.64
.01	.40	49.60	.46	17.72	32.28
.02	.80	49.20	.47	18.08	31.92
.03	1.20	48.80	.48	18.44	31.56
.04	1.60	48.40	.49	18.79	31.21
.05	1.99	48.01	.50	19.15	30.85
.06	2.39	47.61	.51	19.50	30.50
.07	2.79	47.21	.52	19.85	30.15
.08	3.19	46.81	.53	20.19	29.81
.09	3.59	46.41	.54	20.54	29.46
.10	3.98	46.02	.55	20.88	29.12
.11	4.38	45.62	.56	21.23	28.77
.12	4.78	45.22	.57	21.57	28.43
.13	5.17	44.83	.58	21.90	28.10
.14	5.57	44.43	.59	22.24	27.76
.15	5.96	44.04	.60	22.57	27.43
.16	6.36	43.64	.61	22.91	27.09
.17	6.75	43.25	.62	23.24	26.76
.18	7.14	42.86	.63	23.57	26.43
.19	7.53	42.47	.64	23.89	26.11
.20	7.93	42.07	.65	24.22	25.78
.21	8.32	41.68	.66	24.54	25.46

to *Z*" column tells you that 23.89% of the scores in a normal curve are between the mean and this *Z* score. These values are highlighted in Table 3–1.

You can also reverse the process and use the table to find the *Z* score for a particular percentage of scores. For example, imagine that 30% of ninth-grade students had a creativity score higher than Janice's. Assuming that creativity scores follow a normal curve, you can figure out her *Z* score as follows: if 30% of students scored higher than she did, then 30% of the scores are in the tail above her score. This is shown in Figure 3–9. So, you would look at the "% in Tail" column of the table until you found the percentage that was closest to 30%. In this example, the closest is 30.15%. Finally, look at the "*Z*" column to the left of this percentage, which lists a *Z* score of .52 (these values of 30.15% and .52 are highlighted in Table 3–1). Thus, Janice's *Z* score for her level of creativity is .52. If you know the mean and standard deviation for ninth-grade students' creativity scores, you can figure out Janice's actual raw score on the test by changing her *Z* score of .52 to a raw score using the usual formula, $X = (Z)(SD) + (M)$.

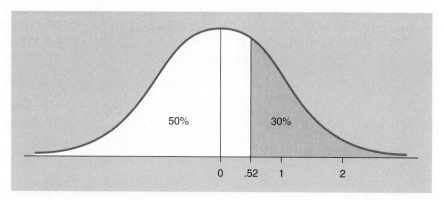

Figure 3–9 Distribution of creativity test scores showing area for top 30% of scores and *Z* score where this area begins.

Steps for Figuring the Percentage of Scores Above or Below a Particular Raw Score or *Z* Score Using the Normal Curve Table

Here are the five steps for figuring the percentage of scores.

❶ **If you are beginning with a raw score, first change it to a *Z* score.** Use the usual formula, $Z = (X - M)/SD$.

❷ **Draw a picture of the normal curve, where the *Z* score falls on it, and shade in the area for which you are finding the percentage.** (When marking where the *Z* score falls on the normal curve, be sure to put it in the right place above or below the mean according to whether it is a positive or negative *Z* score.)

❸ **Make a rough estimate of the shaded area's percentage based on the 50%–34%–14% percentages.** You don't need to be very exact; it is enough just to estimate a range in which the shaded area has to fall, figuring it is between two particular whole *Z* scores. This rough estimate step is designed not only to help you avoid errors (by providing a check for your figuring), but also to help you develop an intuitive sense of how the normal curve works.

❹ **Find the exact percentage using the normal curve table, adding 50% if necessary.** Look up the *Z* score in the "*Z*" column of Table A–1 and find the percentage in the "% Mean to *Z*" column or "% in Tail" column next to it. If you want the percentage of scores between the mean and this *Z* score, or if you want the percentage of scores in the tail for this *Z* score, the percentage in the table is your final answer. However, sometimes you need to add 50% to the percentage in the table. You need to do this if the *Z* score is positive and you want the total percentage below this *Z* score, or if the *Z* score is negative and you want the total percentage above this *Z* score. However, you don't need to memorize these rules; it is much easier to make a picture for the problem and reason out whether the percentage you have from the table is correct as is or if you need to add 50%.

❺ **Check that your exact percentage is within the range of your rough estimate from Step ❸.**

Examples

Here are two examples using IQ scores where $M = 100$ and $SD = 16$.

Example 1: If a person has an IQ of 125, what percentage of people have higher IQs?

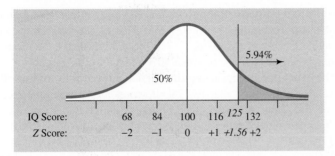

Figure 3–10 Distribution of IQ scores showing percentage of scores above an IQ score of 125 (shaded area).

❶ **If you are beginning with a raw score, first change it to a Z score.** Using the usual formula, $Z = (X - M)/SD$, $Z = (125 - 100)/16 = +1.56$.

❷ **Draw a picture of the normal curve, where the Z score falls on it, and shade in the area for which you are finding the percentage.** This is shown in Figure 3–10 (along with the exact percentages figured later).

❸ **Make a rough estimate of the shaded area's percentage based on the 50%–34%–14% percentages.** If the shaded area started at a Z score of 1, it would have 16% above it. If it started at a Z score of 2, it would have only 2% above it. So, with a Z score of 1.56, the number of scores above it has to be somewhere between 16% and 2%.

❹ **Find the exact percentage using the normal curve table, adding 50% if necessary.** In Table A–1, 1.56 in the "Z" column goes with 5.94 in the "% in Tail" column. Thus, 5.94% of people have IQ scores higher than 125. This is the answer to our problem. (There is no need to add 50% to the percentage.)

❺ **Check that your exact percentage is within the range of your rough estimate from Step ❸.** Our result, 5.94%, is within the 16-to-2% range we estimated.

Example 2: If a person has an IQ of 95, what percentage of people have higher IQs?

❶ **If you are beginning with a raw score, first change it to a Z score.** Using the usual formula, $Z = (95 - 100)/16 = -.31$.

❷ **Draw a picture of the normal curve, where the Z score falls on it, and shade in the area for which you are finding the percentage.** This is shown in Figure 3–11 (along with the percentages figured later).

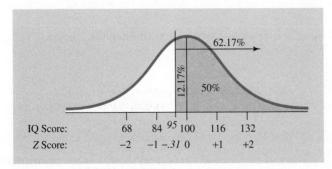

Figure 3–11 Distribution of IQ scores showing percentage of scores above an IQ score of 95 (shaded area).

❸ **Make a rough estimate of the shaded area's percentage based on the 50%–34%–14% percentages.** You know that 34% of the scores are between the mean and a Z score of −1. Also, 50% of the curve is above the mean. Thus, the Z score of −.31 has to have between 50% and 84% of scores above it.

❹ **Find the exact percentage using the normal curve table, adding 50% if necessary.** The table shows that 12.17% of scores are between the mean and a Z score of .31. Thus, the percentage of scores above a Z score of −.31 is the 12.17% between the Z score and the mean plus the 50% above the mean, which is 62.17%.

❺ **Check that your exact percentage is within the range of your rough estimate from Step ❸.** Our result of 62.17% is within the 50-to-84% range we estimated.

Figuring Z Scores and Raw Scores from Percentages Using the Normal Curve Table

Going from a percentage to a Z score or raw score is similar to going from a Z score or raw score to a percentage. However, you reverse the procedure when figuring the exact percentage. Also, any necessary changes from a Z score to a raw score are done at the end.

Here are the five steps.

❶ **Draw a picture of the normal curve, and shade in the approximate area for your percentage using the 50%–34%–14% percentages.**
❷ **Make a rough estimate of the Z score where the shaded area stops.**
❸ **Find the exact Z score using the normal curve table (subtracting 50% from your percentage if necessary before looking up the Z score).** Looking at your picture, figure out either the percentage in the shaded tail or the percentage between the mean and where the shading stops. For example, if your percentage is the bottom 35%, then the percentage in the shaded tail is 35%. Figuring the percentage between the mean and where the shading stops will sometimes involve subtracting 50% from the percentage in the problem. For example, if your percentage is the top 72%, then the percentage from the mean to where that shading stops is 22% (72% − 50% = 22%).

Once you have the percentage, look up the closest percentage in the appropriate column of the normal curve table ("% Mean to Z" or "% in Tail") and find the Z score for that percentage. That Z will be your answer—except it may be negative. The best way to tell if it is positive or negative is by looking at your picture.

❹ **Check that your exact Z score is within the range of your rough estimate from Step ❷.**
❺ **If you want to find a raw score, change it from the Z score.** Use the usual formula, $X = (Z)(SD) + M$.

Examples

Here are three examples. Once again, we use IQ for our examples, with $M = 100$ and $SD = 16$.

Example 1: What IQ score would a person need to be in the top 5%?

❶ **Draw a picture of the normal curve, and shade in the approximate area for your percentage using the 50%–34%–14% percentages.** We wanted the top 5%. Thus, the shading has to begin above (to the right of) 1 *SD* (there are 16%

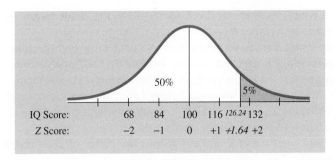

Figure 3–12 Finding the *Z* score and IQ raw score for where the top 5% of scores start.

of scores above 1 *SD*). However, it cannot start above 2 *SD* because only 2% of all the scores are above 2 *SD*. But 5% is a lot closer to 2% than to 16%. Thus, you would start shading a small way to the left of the 2 *SD* point. This is shown in Figure 3–12.

❷ **Make a rough estimate of the *Z* score where the shaded area stops.** The *Z* score is between +1 and +2.

❸ **Find the exact *Z* score using the normal curve table (subtracting 50% from your percentage if necessary before looking up the *Z* score).** We want the top 5%; so we can use the "% in Tail" column of the normal curve table. Looking in that column, the closest percentage to 5% is 5.05% (or you could use 4.95%). This goes with a *Z* score of 1.64 in the "*Z*" column.

❹ **Check that your exact *Z* score is within the range of your rough estimate from Step ❷.** As we estimated, +1.64 is between +1 and +2 (and closer to 2).

❺ **If you want to find a raw score, change it from the *Z* score.** Using the formula, $X = (Z)(SD) + M = (1.64)(16) + 100 = 126.24$. In sum, to be in the top 5%, a person would need an IQ of at least 126.24.

Example 2: What IQ score would a person need to be in the top 55%?

❶ **Draw a picture of the normal curve and shade in the approximate area for your percentage using the 50%–34%–14% percentages.** You want the top 55%. There are 50% of scores above the mean. So, the shading has to begin below (to the left of) the mean. There are 34% of scores between the mean and 1 *SD* below the mean; so the score is between the mean and 1 *SD* below the mean. You would shade the area to the right of that point. This is shown in Figure 3–13.

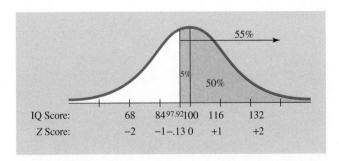

Figure 3–13 Finding the IQ score for where the top 55% of scores start.

❷ **Make a rough estimate of the Z score where the shaded area stops.** The Z score has to be between 0 and -1.

❸ **Find the exact Z score using the normal curve table (subtracting 50% from your percentage if necessary before looking up the Z score).** Being in the top 55% means that 5% of people have IQs between this IQ and the mean (that is, $55\% - 50\% = 5\%$). In the normal curve table, the closest percentage to 5% in the "% Mean to Z" column is 5.17%, which goes with a Z score of .13. Because you are below the mean, this becomes $-.13$.

❹ **Check that your exact Z score is within the range of your rough estimate from Step ❷.** As we estimated, $-.13$ is between 0 and -1.

❺ **If you want to find a raw score, change it from the Z score.** Using the usual formula, $X = (-.13)(16) + 100 = 97.92$. So, to be in the top 55% on IQ, a person needs an IQ score of 97.92 or higher.

Example 3: What range of IQ scores includes the 95% of people in the middle range of IQ scores?

This kind of problem—finding the middle percentage—may seem odd. However, it is actually a very common situation used in procedures you will learn in later chapters.

Think of this kind of problem in terms of finding the scores that go with the upper and lower ends of this percentage. Thus, in this example, you are trying to find the points where the bottom 2.5% ends and the top 2.5% begins (which, out of 100%, leaves the middle 95%).

❶ **Draw a picture of the normal curve, and shade in the approximate area for your percentage using the 50%–34%–14% percentages.** Let's start where the top 2.5% begins. This point has to be higher than 1 *SD* (16% of scores are higher than 1 *SD*). However, it cannot start above 2 *SD* because there are only 2% of scores above 2 *SD*. But 2.5% is very close to 2%. Thus, the top 2.5% starts just to the left of the 2 *SD* point. Similarly, the point where the bottom 2.5% comes in is just to the right of -2 *SD*. The result of all this is that we will shade in two tail areas on the curve: one starting just above -2 *SD* and the other starting just below $+2$ *SD*. This is shown in Figure 3–14.

❷ **Make a rough estimate of the Z score where the shaded area stops.** You can see from the picture that the Z score for where the shaded area stops above the mean is just below $+2$. Similarly, the Z score for where the shaded area stops below the mean is just above -2.

❸ **Find the exact Z score using the normal curve table (subtracting 50% from your percentage if necessary before looking up the Z score).** Being in the top 2.5% means that 2.5% of the IQ scores are in the upper tail. In the normal curve table, the closest percentage to 2.5% in the "% in Tail" column is exactly 2.50%,

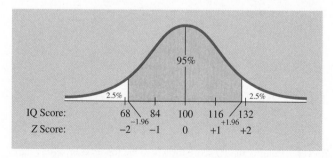

Figure 3–14 Finding the IQ scores for where the middle 95% of scores begins and ends.

which goes with a *Z* score of +1.96. The normal curve is symmetrical. Thus, the *Z* score for the lower tail is −1.96.

❹ **Check that your exact *Z* score is within the range of your rough estimate from Step ❷.** As we estimated, +1.96 is between +1 and +2 and is very close to +2, and −1.96 is between −1 and −2 and very close to −2.

❺ **If you want to find a raw score, change it from the *Z* score.** For the high end, using the usual formula, $X = (1.96)(16) + 100 = 131.36$. For the low end, $X = (-1.96)(16) + 100 = 68.64$. In sum, the middle 95% of IQ scores run from 68.64 to 131.36.

How are you doing?

1. Why is the normal curve (or at least a curve that is symmetrical and unimodal) so common in nature?
2. Without using a normal curve table, about what percentage of scores on a normal curve are (a) above the mean, (b) between the mean and 1 *SD* above the mean, (c) between 1 and 2 *SD*s above the mean, (d) below the mean, (e) between the mean and 1 *SD* below the mean, and (f) between 1 and 2 *SD*s below the mean?
3. Without using a normal curve table, about what percentage of scores on a normal curve are (a) between the mean and 2 *SD*s above the mean, (b) below 1 *SD* above the mean, (c) above 2 *SD*s below the mean?
4. Without using a normal curve table, about what *Z* score would a person have who is at the start of the top (a) 50%, (b) 16%, (c) 84%, (d) 2%?
5. Using the normal curve table, what percentage of scores are (a) between the mean and a *Z* score of 2.14, (b) above 2.14, (c) below 2.14?
6. Using the normal curve table, what *Z* score would you have if (a) 20% are above you and (b) 80% are below you?

Answers

1. It is common because any particular score is the result of the random combination of many effects, some of which make the score larger and some of which make the score smaller. Thus, on average these effects balance out near the middle, with relatively few at each extreme, because it is unlikely for most of the increasing and decreasing effects to come out in the same direction.
2. (a) Above the mean: 50%; (b) between the mean and 1 *SD* above the mean: 34%; (c) between 1 and 2 *SD*s above the mean: 14%; (d) below the mean: 50%; (e) between the mean and 1 *SD* below the mean: 34%; (f) between 1 and 2 *SD*s below the mean: 14%.
3. (a) Between the mean and 2 *SD*s above the mean: 48%; (b) below 1 *SD* above the mean: 84%; (c) above 2 *SD*s below the mean: 98%.
4. (a) 50%: 0; (b) 16%: 1; (c) 84%: −1; (d) 2%: 2.
5. (a) Between the mean and a *Z* score of 2.14: 48.38%; (b) above 2.14: 1.62%; (c) below 2.14: 98.38%.
6. (a) 20% above you: .84; (b) 80% below you: .84.

Sample and Population

We are going to introduce you to some important ideas by thinking of beans. Suppose you are cooking a pot of beans and taste a spoonful to see if they are done. In this example, the pot of beans is a **population,** the entire set of things of interest. The spoonful is a **sample,** the part of the population about which you actually have

population entire group of people to which a researcher intends the results of a study to apply; larger group to which inferences are made on the basis of the particular set of people (sample) studied.

sample scores of the particular group of people studied; usually considered to be representative of the scores in some larger population.

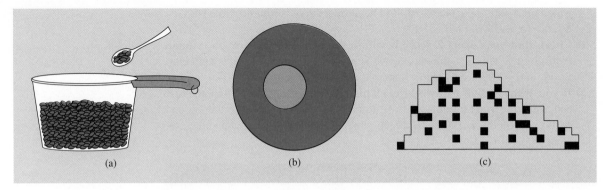

Figure 3–15   Populations and samples: (a) The entire pot of beans is the population, and the spoonful is the sample. (b) The entire larger circle is the population, and the circle within it is the sample. (c) The histogram is of the population, and the particular shaded scores make up the sample.

information. This is shown in Figure 3–15a. Figures 3–15b and 3–15c are other ways of showing the relation of a sample to a population.

In psychology research, we typically study samples not of beans but of individuals to make inferences about some larger group (a population). A sample might consist of the scores of 50 Canadian women who participate in a particular experiment, whereas the population might be intended to be the scores of all Canadian women. In an opinion survey, 1,000 people might be selected from the voting-age population of a particular district and asked for whom they plan to vote. The opinions of these 1,000 people are the sample. The opinions of the larger voting public in that country, to which the pollsters apply their results, is the population (see Figure 3–16).

Why Psychologists Study Samples Instead of Populations

If you want to know something about a population, your results would be most accurate if you could study the entire population rather than a subgroup from it. However, in most research situations this is not practical. More important, the whole point of research usually is to be able to make generalizations or predictions about events beyond your reach. We would not call it scientific research if we tested three particular cars to see which gets better gas mileage—unless you hoped to say something about the gas mileage of those models of cars in general. In other words, a researcher might do an experiment on how people store words in short-term memory using 20 students as the participants in the experiment. But the purpose of the experiment is not to find out how these *particular* 20 students respond to the experimental versus the control condition. Rather, the purpose is to learn something about human memory under these conditions *in general.*

The strategy in almost all psychology research is to study a sample of individuals who are believed to be representative of the general population (or of some particular population of interest). More realistically, researchers try to study people who do not differ from the general population in any systematic way that should matter for that topic of research.

The sample is what is studied, and the population is an unknown about which researchers draw conclusions based on the sample. Most of what you learn in the rest of this book is about the important work of drawing conclusions about populations based on information from samples.

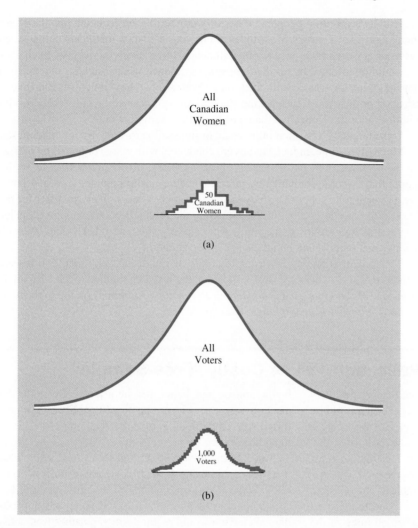

Figure 3–16 Additional examples of populations and samples: (a) The population is the scores of all Canadian women, and the sample is the scores of the 50 Canadian women studied. (b) The population is the voting preferences of the entire voting-age population, and the sample is the voting preferences of the 1,000 voting-age people who were surveyed.

Methods of Sampling

Usually, the ideal method of picking out a sample to study is called **random selection.** The researcher starts with a complete list of the population and randomly selects some of them to study. An example of random selection is to put each name on a table tennis ball, put all the balls into a big hopper, shake it up, and have a blindfolded person select as many as are needed. (In practice, most researchers use a computer-generated list of random numbers. Just how computers or persons can create a list of truly random numbers is an interesting question in its own right that we examine in Chapter 14, Box 14–1.)

It is important not to confuse truly random selection with what might be called *haphazard selection;* for example, just taking whoever is available or happens to be first on a list. When using haphazard selection, it is surprisingly easy to pick

random selection method for selecting a sample that uses truly random procedures (usually meaning that each person in the population has an equal chance of being selected); one procedure is for the researcher to begin with a complete list of all the people in the population and select a group of them to study using a table of random numbers.

accidentally a group of people that is really quite different from the population as a whole. Consider a survey of attitudes about your statistics instructor. Suppose you give your questionnaire only to other students sitting near you in class. Such a survey would be affected by all the things that influence where students choose to sit, some of which have to do with the topic of your study—how much students like the instructor or the class. Thus, asking students who sit near you would likely result in opinions more like your own than a truly random sample would.

Unfortunately, it is often impractical or impossible to study a truly random sample. Much of the time, in fact, studies are conducted with whoever is willing or available to be a research participant. At best, as noted, a researcher tries to study a sample that is not systematically unrepresentative of the population in any known way. For example, suppose a study is about a process that is likely to differ for people of different age groups. In this situation, the researcher may attempt to include people of all age groups in the study. Alternatively, the researcher would be careful to draw conclusions only about the age group studied.

Methods of sampling is a complex topic that is discussed in detail in research methods textbooks (also see Box 3–2) and in the research methods Web Chapter W1 (*Overview of the Logic and Language of Psychology Research*) on the Web site for this book *http://www.pearsonhighered.com/*.

BOX 3–2 **Surveys, Polls, and 1948's Costly "Free Sample"**

It is time to make you a more informed reader of polls in the media. Usually the results of properly done public polls are accompanied, somewhere in fine print, by a statement such as, "From a telephone poll of 1,000 American adults taken on June 4 and 5. Sampling error ±3%." What does a statement like this mean?

The Gallup poll is as good an example as any (Gallup, 1972; see also *http://www.gallup.com*), and there is no better place to begin than in 1948, when all three of the major polling organizations—Gallup, Crossley (for Hearst papers), and Roper (for *Fortune*)—wrongly predicted Thomas Dewey's victory over Harry Truman for the U.S. presidency. Yet Gallup's prediction was based on 50,000 interviews and Roper's on 15,000. By contrast, to predict George H. W. Bush's 1988 victory, Gallup used only 4,089. Since 1952, the pollsters have never used more than 8,144—but with very small error and no outright mistakes. What has changed?

The method used before 1948, and never repeated since, was called "quota sampling." Interviewers were assigned a fixed number of persons to interview, with strict quotas to fill in all the categories that seemed important, such as residence, sex, age, race, and economic status. Within these specifics, however, they were free to interview whomever they liked. Republicans generally tended to be easier to interview. They were more likely to have telephones and permanent addresses and to live in better houses and better neighborhoods. In 1948, the election was very close, and the Republican bias produced the embarrassing mistake that changed survey methods forever.

Since 1948, all survey organizations have used what is called a "probability method." Simple random sampling is the purest case of the probability method, but simple random sampling for a survey about a U.S. presidential election would require drawing names from a list of all the eligible voters in the nation—a lot of people. Each person selected would have to be found, in diversely scattered locales. So instead, "multistage cluster sampling" is used. The United States is divided into seven size-of-community groupings, from large cities to rural open country; these groupings are divided into seven geographic regions (New England, Middle Atlantic, and so on), after which smaller equal-sized groups are zoned, and then city blocks are drawn from the zones, with the probability of selection being proportional to the size of the population or number of dwelling units. Finally, an interviewer is given a randomly selected starting point on the map and is required to follow a given direction, taking households in sequence.

Actually, telephoning is often the favored method for polling today. Phone surveys cost about one-third of door-to-door polls. Since most people now own phones, this method is less biased than in Truman's time. Phoning also allows computers to randomly dial phone numbers and, unlike telephone directories, this method calls unlisted numbers. However, survey organizations in the United States typically do not call cell phone numbers. Thus, U.S. households that use a cell phone for all calls and do not have a home phone are not usually included in telephone opinion polls. Most survey organizations consider the current cell-phone-only rate to be low enough not to cause large biases in poll results (especially since the demographic characteristics of individuals without a home phone suggest that they are less likely to vote than individuals who live in households with a home phone). However, anticipated future increases in the cell-phone-only rate will likely make this an important issue for opinion polls. Survey organizations will need to consider

additional polling methods, perhaps using the Internet and email.

Whether by telephone or face to face, there will be about 35% nonrespondents after three attempts. This creates yet another bias, dealt with through questions about how much time a person spends at home, so that a slight extra weight can be given to the responses of those reached but usually at home less, to make up for those missed entirely.

Now you know quite a bit about opinion polls, but we have left two important questions unanswered: Why are only about 1,000 included in a poll meant to describe all U.S. adults, and what does the term *sampling error* mean? For these answers, you must wait for Chapter 5 (Box 5–1).

Statistical Terminology for Samples and Populations

The mean, variance, and standard deviation of a population are called **population parameters.** A population parameter usually is unknown and can be estimated only from what you know about a sample taken from that population. You do not taste all the beans, just the spoonful. "The beans are done" is an inference about the whole pot.

Population parameters are usually shown as Greek letters (e.g., μ). (This is a statistical convention with origins tracing back more than 2,000 years to the early Greek mathematicians.) The symbol for the mean of a population is μ, the Greek letter mu. The symbol for the variance of a population is σ^2, and the symbol for its standard deviation is σ, the lowercase Greek letter sigma. You won't see these symbols often, except while learning statistics. This is because, again, researchers seldom know the population parameters.

The mean, variance, and standard deviation you figure for the scores in a sample are called **sample statistics.** A sample statistic is figured from known information. Sample statistics are what we have been figuring all along and are expressed with the roman letters you learned in Chapter 2: M, SD^2, and SD. The population parameter and sample statistic symbols for the mean, variance, and standard deviation are summarized in Table 3–2.

The use of different types of symbols for population parameters (Greek letters) and sample statistics (roman letters) can take some getting used to; so don't worry if it seems tricky at first. It's important to know that the *statistical concepts* you are

population parameter   actual value of the mean, standard deviation, and so on, for the population; usually population parameters are not known, though often they are estimated based on information in samples.

μ population mean.

σ^2 population variance.

σ population standard deviation.

sample statistics   descriptive statistic, such as the mean or standard deviation, figured from the scores in a group of people studied.

Table 3-2 Population Parameters and Sample Statistics		
	Population Parameter (Usually Unknown)	**Sample Statistic (Figured from Known Data)**
Basis:	Scores of entire population	Scores of sample only
Symbols:		
Mean	μ	M
Standard deviation	σ	SD
Variance	σ^2	SD^2

learning—such as the mean, variance, and standard deviation—are the same for both a population and a sample. So, for example, you have learned that the standard deviation provides a measure of the variability of the scores in a distribution—whether we are talking about a sample or a population. (You will learn in later chapters that the variance and standard deviation are *figured* in a different way for a population than for a sample, but the *concepts* do not change). We use different symbols for population parameters and sample statistics to make it clear whether we are referring to a population or a sample. This is important, because some of the formulas you will encounter in later chapters use both sample statistics and population parameters.

How are you doing?

1. Explain the difference between the population and a sample for a research study.
2. Why do psychologists usually study samples and not populations?
3. Explain the difference between random sampling and haphazard sampling.
4. Explain the difference between a population parameter and a sample statistic.
5. Give the symbols for the population parameters for (a) the mean and (b) the standard deviation.
6. Why are different symbols (Greek versus roman letters) used for population parameters and sample statistics?

Answers

1. The population is the entire group to which results of a study are intended to apply. The sample is the particular, smaller group of individuals actually studied.
2. Psychologists usually study samples and not populations because it is not practical in most cases to study the entire population.
3. In random sampling, the sample is chosen from among the population using a completely random method, so that each individual has an equal chance of being included in the sample. In haphazard sampling, the researcher selects individuals who are easily available or who are convenient to study.
4. A population parameter is about the population (such as the mean of all the scores in the population); a sample statistic is about a particular sample (such as the mean of the scores of the people in the sample).
5. (a) Mean: μ; (b) standard deviation: σ.
6. Using different symbols for population parameters and sample statistics ensures that there is no confusion as to whether a symbol refers to a population or a sample.

Probability

The purpose of most psychological research is to examine the truth of a theory or the effectiveness of a procedure. But scientific research of any kind can only make that truth or effectiveness seem more or less likely; it cannot give us the luxury of knowing for certain. Probability is very important in science. In particular, probability is very important in inferential statistics, the methods psychologists use to go from results of research studies to conclusions about theories or applied procedures.

Probability has been studied for centuries by mathematicians and philosophers. Yet even today the topic is full of controversy. Fortunately, however, you need to know only a few key ideas to understand and carry out the inferential statistical procedures you learn in this book. These few key points are not very difficult; indeed, some students find them to be quite intuitive.

Interpretations of Probability

In statistics, we usually define **probability** as the expected relative frequency of a particular outcome. An **outcome** is the result of an experiment (or just about any situation in which the result is not known in advance, such as a coin coming up heads or it raining tomorrow). *Frequency* is how many times something happens. The *relative frequency* is the number of times something happens relative to the number of times it could have happened; that is, relative frequency is the proportion of times something happens. (A coin might come up heads 8 times out of 12 flips, for a relative frequency of 8/12, or 2/3.) **Expected relative frequency** is what you expect to get in the long run if you repeat the experiment many times. (In the case of a coin, in the long run you would expect to get 1/2 heads). This is called the **long-run relative-frequency interpretation of probability.**

We also use probability to express how certain we are that a particular thing will happen. This is called the **subjective interpretation of probability.** Suppose that you say there is a 95% chance that your favorite restaurant will be open tonight. You could be using a kind of relative frequency interpretation. This would imply that if you were to check whether this restaurant was open many times on days like today, you would find it open on 95% of those days. However, what you mean is probably more subjective: on a scale of 0% to 100%, you would rate your confidence that the restaurant is open at 95%. To put it another way, you would feel that a fair bet would have odds based on a 95% chance of the restaurant's being open.

The interpretation, however, does not affect how probability is figured. We mention these interpretations because we want to give you a deeper insight into the meaning of the term *probability,* which is such a prominent concept throughout statistics.

Figuring Probabilities

Probabilities are usually figured as the proportion of successful possible outcomes—the number of possible successful outcomes divided by the number of *all* possible outcomes. That is,

$$\text{Probability} = \frac{\text{Possible successful outcomes}}{\text{All possible outcomes}}$$

Consider the probability of getting heads when flipping a coin. There is one possible successful outcome (getting heads) out of two possible outcomes (getting heads or getting tails). This makes a probability of 1/2, or .5. In a throw of a single die, the probability of a 2 (or any other particular side of the six-sided die) is 1/6, or .17. This is because there can be only one successful outcome out of six possible outcomes. The probability of throwing a die and getting a number 3 or lower is 3/6, or .5. There are three possible successful outcomes (a 1, a 2, or a 3) out of six possible outcomes.

probability   expected relative frequency of an outcome; the proportion of successful outcomes to all outcomes.

outcome   term used in discussing probability for the result of an experiment (or almost any event, such as a coin coming up heads or it raining tomorrow).

expected relative frequency   number of successful outcomes divided by the number of total outcomes you would expect to get if you repeated an experiment a large number of times.

long-run relative-frequency interpretation of probability   understanding of probability as the proportion of a particular outcome that you would get if the experiment were repeated many times.

subjective interpretation of probability   way of understanding probability as the degree of one's certainty that a particular outcome will occur.

BOX 3–3   **Pascal Begins Probability Theory at the Gambling Table, Then Learns to Bet on God**

Whereas in England, statistics were used to keep track of death rates and to prove the existence of God (see Chapter 1, Box 1–1), the French and Italians developed statistics at the gaming table. In particular, there was the "problem of points"—the division of the stakes in a game after it has been interrupted. If a certain number of plays were planned, how much of the stakes should each player walk away with, given the percentage of plays completed?

The problem was discussed at least as early as 1494 by Luca Pacioli, a friend of Leonardo da Vinci. But it was unsolved until 1654, when it was presented to Blaise Pascal by the Chevalier de Méré. Pascal, a French child prodigy, attended meetings of the most famous adult French mathematicians and at 15 proved an important theorem in geometry. In correspondence with Pierre de Fermat, another famous French mathematician, Pascal solved the problem of points and in so doing began the field of probability theory and the work that would lead to the normal curve. (For more information on the problem of points, including its solution, see *http://mathforum. org/isaac/problems/prob1.html*).

Not long after solving this problem, Pascal became as religiously devout as the English statisticians. He was in a runaway horse-drawn coach on a bridge and was saved from drowning by the traces (the straps between the horses and the carriage) breaking at the last possible moment. He took this as a warning to abandon his mathematical work in favor of religious writings and later formulated "Pascal's wager": that the value of a game is the value of the prize times the probability of winning it; therefore, even if the probability is low that God exists, we should gamble on the affirmative because the value of the prize is infinite, whereas the value of not believing is only finite worldly pleasure.

Source: Tankard (1984).

Now consider a slightly more complicated example. Suppose a class has 200 people in it, and 30 are seniors. If you were to pick someone from the class at random, the probability of picking a senior would be 30/200, or .15. This is because there are 30 possible successful outcomes (getting a senior) out of 200 possible outcomes.

Steps for Finding Probabilities

There are three steps for finding probabilities.

❶ **Determine the number of possible successful outcomes.**
❷ **Determine the number of all possible outcomes.**
❸ **Divide the number of possible successful outcomes (Step ❶) by the number of all possible outcomes (Step ❷).**

Let's apply these steps to the probability of getting a number 3 or lower on a throw of a die.

❶ **Determine the number of possible successful outcomes.** There are three outcomes of 3 or lower: 1, 2, or 3.
❷ **Determine the number of all possible outcomes.** There are six possible outcomes in the throw of a die: 1, 2, 3, 4, 5, or 6.
❸ **Divide the number of possible successful outcomes (Step ❶) by the number of all possible outcomes (Step ❷).** $3/6 = .5$.

Range of Probabilities

A probability is a proportion, the number of possible successful outcomes to the total number of possible outcomes. A proportion cannot be less than 0 or greater than 1. In terms of percentages, proportions range from 0% to 100%. Something that has no chance of happening has a probability of 0, and something that is certain to happen has a probability of 1. Notice that when the probability of an event is 0, the event is completely *impossible;* it cannot happen. But when the probability of an event is low, say 5% or even 1%, the event is *improbable* or *unlikely,* but not impossible.

Probabilities Expressed as Symbols

Probability is usually symbolized by the letter *p.* The actual probability number is usually given as a decimal, though sometimes fractions or percentages are used. A 50-50 chance is usually written as $p = .5$, but it could also be written as $p = 1/2$ or

$p = 50\%$. It is also common to see probability written as being less than some number, using the "less than" sign. For example, $p < .05$ means "the probability is less than .05."

Probability Rules

As already noted, our discussion only scratches the surface of probability. One of the topics we have not considered is the rules for figuring probabilities for multiple outcomes: for example, what is the chance of flipping a coin twice and both times getting heads? These are called probability rules, and they are important in the mathematical foundation of many aspects of statistics. However, you don't need to know these probability rules to understand what we cover in this book. Also, the rules are rarely used directly in analyzing results of psychology research. Nevertheless, you occasionally see such procedures referred to in research articles. Thus, the most widely mentioned probability rules are described in the Advanced Topics section toward the end of this chapter.

Probability, *Z* Scores, and the Normal Distribution

So far, we mainly have discussed probabilities of specific events that might or might not happen. We also can talk about a range of events that might or might not happen. The throw of a die coming out 3 or lower is an example (it includes the range 1, 2, and 3). Another example is the probability of selecting someone on a city street who is between the ages of 30 and 40.

If you think of probability in terms of the proportion of scores, probability fits in well with frequency distributions (see Chapter 1). In the frequency distribution shown in Figure 3–17, 3 of the total of 50 people scored 9 or 10. If you were selecting people from this group of 50 at random, there would be 3 chances (possible successful outcomes) out of 50 (all possible outcomes) of selecting one that was 9 or 10. Thus, $p = 3/50 = .06$.

You can also think of the normal distribution as a probability distribution. With a normal curve, the percentage of scores between any two Z scores is known. The percentage of scores between any two Z scores is the same as the probability of selecting a score between those two Z scores. As you saw earlier in this chapter, approximately 34% of scores in a normal curve are between the mean and one standard deviation from the mean. You should therefore not be surprised to learn that the probability of a score being between the mean and a Z score of $+1$ is about .34 (that is, $p = .34$).

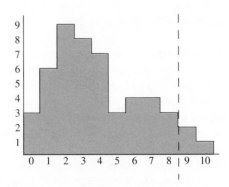

Figure 3–17 Frequency distribution (shown as a histogram) of 50 people, in which $p = .06$ (3/50) of randomly selecting a person with a score of 9 or 10.

In a previous IQ example in the normal curve section of this chapter, we figured that 95% of the scores in a normal curve are between a Z score of $+1.96$ and a Z score of -1.96 (see Figure 3–14). Thus, if you were to select a score at random from a distribution that follows a normal curve, the probability of selecting a score *between* Z scores of $+1.96$ and -1.96 is .95 (that is, a 95% chance). This is a very high probability. Also, the probability of selecting a score from such a distribution that is either *greater* than a Z score of $+1.96$ or *less than* a Z score of -1.96 is .05 (that is, a 5% chance). This is a very low probability. It helps to think about this visually. If you look back to Figure 3–14 on page 82, the .05 probability of selecting a score that is either *greater* than a Z score of $+1.96$ or *less than* a Z score of -1.96 is represented by the tail areas in the figure. The probability of a score being in the tail of a normal curve is a topic you will learn more about in the next chapter.

Probability, Samples, and Populations

Probability is also relevant to samples and populations. You will learn more about this topic in Chapters 4 and 5, but we will use an example to give you a sense of the role of probability in samples and populations. Imagine you are told that a sample of one person has a score of 4 on a certain measure. However, you do not know whether this person is from a population of women or of men. You are told that a population of women has scores on this measure that are normally distributed with a mean of 10 and a standard deviation of 3. How likely do you think it is that your sample of 1 person comes from this population of women? From your knowledge of the normal curve (see Figure 3–7), you know there are very few scores as low as 4 in a normal distribution that has a mean of 10 and a standard deviation of 3. So there is a very low likelihood that this person comes from the population of women. Now, what if the sample person had a score of 9? In this case, there is a much greater likelihood that this person comes from the population of women because there are many scores of 9 in that population. This kind of reasoning provides an introduction to the process of *hypothesis testing* that is the focus of the remainder of the book.

How are you doing?

1. The probability of an event is defined as the expected relative frequency of a particular outcome. Explain what is meant by (a) relative frequency and (b) outcome.
2. List and explain two interpretations of probability.
3. Suppose you have 400 coins in a jar and 40 of them are more than 9 years old. You then mix up the coins and pull one out. (a) What is the probability of getting one that is more than 9 years old? (b) What is the number of possible successful outcomes? (c) What is the number of all possible outcomes?
4. Suppose people's scores on a particular personality test are normally distributed with a mean of 50 and a standard deviation of 10. If you were to pick a person completely at random, what is the probability you would pick someone with a score on this test higher than 60?
5. What is meant by $p < .01$?

Controversies: Is the Normal Curve Really So Normal? and Using Nonrandom Samples

Basic though they are, there is considerable controversy about the topics we have introduced in this chapter. In this section we consider a major controversy about the normal curve and nonrandom samples.

Is the Normal Curve Really So Normal?

We've said that real distributions in the world often closely approximate the normal curve. Just how often real distributions closely follow a normal curve turns out to be very important, not just because normal curves make Z scores more useful. As you will learn in later chapters, the main statistical methods psychologists use assume that the samples studied come from populations that follow a normal curve. Researchers almost never know the true shape of the population distribution; so if they want to use the usual methods, they have to just *assume* it is normal, making this assumption because most populations are normal. Yet there is a long-standing debate in psychology about just how often populations really are normally distributed. The predominant view has been that, given how psychology measures are developed, a bell-shaped distribution "is almost guaranteed" (Walberg et al., 1984, p. 107). Or, as Hopkins and Glass (1978) put it, measurements in all disciplines are such good approximations to the curve that one might think "God loves the normal curve!"

On the other hand, there has been a persistent line of criticism about whether nature really packages itself so neatly. Micceri (1989) showed that many measures commonly used in psychology are *not* normally distributed "in nature." His study included achievement and ability tests (such as the SAT and the GRE) and personality tests (such as the Minnesota Multiphasic Personality Inventory, MMPI). Micceri examined the distributions of scores of 440 psychological and educational measures that had been used on very large samples. All of the measures he examined had been studied in samples of over 190 individuals, and the majority had samples of over 1,000 (14.3% even had samples of 5,000 to 10,293). Yet large samples were of no help. No measure he studied had a distribution that passed all checks for normality (mostly, Micceri looked for skewness, kurtosis, and "lumpiness"). Few measures had distributions that even came reasonably close to looking like the normal curve. Nor were these variations predictable: "The distributions studied here exhibited almost every conceivable type of contamination" (p. 162), although some were more common with certain types of tests. Micceri discusses many obvious reasons for this nonnormality, such as ceiling or floor effects (see Chapter 1).

How much has it mattered that the distributions for these measures were so far from normal? According to Micceri, the answer is just not known. And until more is known, the general opinion among psychologists will no doubt remain supportive of traditional statistical methods, with the underlying mathematics based on the assumption of normal population distributions.

What is the reason for this nonchalance in the face of findings such as Micceri's? It turns out that under most conditions in which the standard methods are used, they give results that are reasonably accurate even when the formal requirement of a normal population distribution is not met (e.g., Sawilowsky & Blair, 1992). In this book, we generally adopt this majority position favoring the use of the standard methods in all but the most extreme cases. But you should be aware that a vocal minority of psychologists disagrees. Some of the alternative statistical techniques they favor (ones that do not rely on assuming a normal distribution in the population) are presented in Chapter 14. These techniques include the use of *nonparametric statistics* that do not have assumptions about the shape of the population distribution.

Francis Galton (1889), one of the major pioneers of statistical methods (see Chapter 11, Box 11–1), said of the normal curve, "I know of scarcely anything so apt to impress the imagination. . . . [It] would have been personified by the Greeks and deified, if they had known of it. It reigns with serenity and in complete self-effacement amidst the wild confusion" (p. 66). Ironically, it may be true that in psychology, at least, it truly reigns in pure and austere isolation, with no even close-to-perfect real-life imitators.

Using Nonrandom Samples

Most of the procedures you learn in the rest of this book are based on mathematics that assume the sample studied is a random sample of the population. As we pointed out, however, in most psychology research the samples are nonrandom, including whatever individuals are available to participate in the experiment. Most studies are done with college students, volunteers, convenient laboratory animals, and the like.

Some psychologists are concerned about this problem and have suggested that researchers need to use different statistical approaches that make generalizations only to the kinds of people that are actually being used in the study.[3] For example, these psychologists would argue that, if your sample has a particular nonnormal distribution, you should assume that you can generalize only to a population with the same particular nonnormal distribution. We will have more to say about their suggested solutions in Chapter 14.

Sociologists, as compared to psychologists, are much more concerned about the representativeness of the groups they study. Studies reported in sociology journals (or in sociologically oriented social psychology journals) are much more likely to use formal methods of random selection and large samples, or at least to address the issue in their articles.

Why are psychologists more comfortable with using nonrandom samples? The main reason is that psychologists are mainly interested in the *relationships* among variables. If in one population the effect of experimentally changing X leads to a change in Y, this relationship should probably hold in other populations. This relationship should hold even if the actual levels of Y differ from population to population. Suppose that a researcher conducts an experiment testing the relation of number of exposures to a list of words to number of words remembered. Suppose further that this study is done with undergraduates taking introductory psychology and that the result is that the greater the number of exposures is, the greater is the number of words remembered. The actual number of words remembered from the list might well be different for people other than introductory psychology students. For example, chess masters (who probably have highly developed memories) may recall more words; people who have just been upset may recall fewer words. However, even in these groups, we would expect that the more times someone is exposed to the list, the more words will be remembered. That is, the *relation* of number of exposures to number of words recalled will probably be about the same in each population.

In sociology, the representativeness of samples is much more important. This is because sociologists are more concerned with the actual mean and variance of a variable in a particular society. Thus, a sociologist might be interested in the average attitude towards older people in the population of a particular country. For this purpose, how sampling is done is extremely important.

Z Scores, Normal Curves, Samples and Populations, and Probabilities in Research Articles

You need to understand the topics we covered in this chapter to learn what comes next. However, the topics of this chapter are rarely mentioned directly in research articles (except in articles *about* methods or statistics). Although Z scores are extremely important as steps in advanced statistical procedures, they are rarely reported directly in research articles. Sometimes you will see the normal curve mentioned, usually when a researcher is describing the pattern of scores on a particular variable. (We say more about this and give some examples from published articles in Chapter 14, where we consider situations in which the scores do not follow a normal curve.)

Research articles will sometimes briefly mention the method of selecting the sample from the population. For example, Viswanath and colleagues (2006) used data from the U.S. National Cancer Institute (NCI) Health Information National Trends Survey (HINTS) to examine differences in knowledge about cancer across individuals from varying socioeconomic and racial/ethnic groups. They described the method of their study as follows:

> The data from this study come from the NCI HINTS, based on a random-digit-dial (RDD) sample of all working telephones in the United States. One adult was selected at random within each household using the most recent birthday method in the case of more than three adults in a given household.... Vigorous efforts were made to increase response rates through advanced letters and $2 incentives to households. (p. 4)

Whenever possible, researchers report the proportion of individuals approached for the study who actually participated in the study. This is called the *response rate*. Viswanath and colleagues (2006) noted that "The final sample size was 6,369, yielding a response rate of 55%" (p. 4).

Researchers sometimes also check whether their sample is similar to the population as a whole, based on any information they may have about the overall population. For example, Schuster and colleagues (2001) conducted a national survey of stress reactions of U.S. adults after the September 11, 2001, terrorist attacks. In this study, the researchers compared their sample to 2001 census records and reported that the "sample slightly overrepresented women, non-Hispanic whites, and persons with higher levels of education and income" (p. 1507). Schuster and colleagues went on to note that overrepresentation of these groups "is typical of samples selected by means of random-digit dialing" (pp. 1507–1508).

However, even survey studies typically are not able to use such rigorous methods and have to rely on more haphazard methods of getting their samples. For example, in a study of relationship distress and partner abuse (Heyman et al., 2001), the researchers describe their method of gathering research participants to interview as follows: "Seventy-four couples of varying levels of relationship adjustment were recruited through community newspaper advertisements" (p. 336). In a study of this kind, one cannot very easily recruit a random sample of abusers since there is no list of all abusers to recruit from! This could be done with a very large national random sample of couples, who would then include a random sample of abusers. Indeed, the authors of this study are very aware of the issues. At the end of the article, when discussing "cautions necessary when interpreting our results," they note that before their conclusions can be taken as definitive "our study must be replicated with a representative sample" (p. 341).

Finally, probability is rarely discussed directly in research articles, except in relation to statistical significance, a topic we discuss in the next chapter. In almost any article you look at, the results section will be strewn with descriptions of various methods having to do with statistical significance, followed by something like "$p < .05$" or "$p < .01$." The p refers to probability, but the probability of what? This is the main topic of our discussion of statistical significance in the next chapter.

Advanced Topic: Probability Rules and Conditional Probabilities

This advanced topic section provides additional information on probability, focusing specifically on probability rules and conditional probabilities. Probability rules are procedures for figuring probabilities in more complex situations than we have considered so far. This section considers the two most widely used such rules and also explains the concept of conditional probabilities that is used in advanced discussions of probability.

Addition Rule

The *addition rule* (also called the *or rule*) is used when there are two or more *mutually exclusive outcomes*. "Mutually exclusive" means that, if one outcome happens, the others can't happen. For example, heads or tails on a single coin flip are mutually exclusive because the result has to be one or the other, but can't be both. With mutually exclusive outcomes, the total probability of getting either outcome is the sum of the individual probabilities. Thus, on a single coin flip, the total chance of getting either heads (which is .5) or tails (also .5) is 1.0 (.5 plus .5). Similarly, on a single throw of a die, the chance of getting either a 3 (1/6) or a 5 (1/6) is 1/3 (1/6 + 1/6). If you are picking a student at random from your university in which 30% are seniors and 25% are juniors, the chance of picking someone who is either a senior or a junior is 55%.

Even though we have not used the term *addition rule,* we have already used this rule in many of the examples we considered in this chapter. For example, we used this rule when we figured that the chance of getting a 3 or lower on the throw of a die is .5.

Multiplication Rule

The *multiplication rule* (also called the *and rule*), however, is completely new. You use the multiplication rule to figure the probability of getting *both* of two (or more) *independent outcomes.* Independent outcomes are those for which getting one has no effect on getting the other. For example, getting a head or tail on one flip of a coin is an independent outcome from getting a head or tail on a second flip of a coin. The probability of getting both of two independent outcomes is the product of (the result of multiplying) the individual probabilities. For example, on a single coin flip, the chance of getting a head is .5. On a second coin flip, the chance of getting a head (regardless of what you got on the first flip) is also .5. Thus, the probability of getting heads on *both* coin flips is .25 (.5 multiplied by .5). On two throws of a die, the chance of getting a 5 on *both* throws is 1/36—the probability of getting a 5 on the first throw (1/6) multiplied by the probability of getting a 5 on the second throw (1/6). Similarly, on a multiple choice exam with four possible answers to each item, the chance of getting both of two questions correct just by guessing is 1/16—that is, the chance of getting one question correct just by guessing (1/4) multiplied by the chance of getting the other correct just by guessing (1/4). To take one more example, suppose you have a 20% chance of getting accepted into one graduate school and a 30% chance of getting accepted into another graduate school. Your chance of getting accepted at *both* graduate schools is just 6% (that is, 20% × 30% = 6%).

Conditional Probabilities

There are several other probability rules, some of which are combinations of the addition and multiplication rules. Most of these other rules have to do with what are called *conditional probabilities.* A conditional probability is the probability of one outcome, assuming some other outcome will happen. That is, the probability of the one outcome depends on—is *conditional* on—the probability of the other outcome. Thus, suppose that college A has 50% women and college B has 60% women. If you select a person at random, what is the chance of getting a woman? If you know the person is from college A, the probability is 50%. That is, the probability of getting a woman, conditional upon her coming from college A, is 50%.

Summary

1. A Z score is the number of standard deviations that a raw score is above or below the mean.
2. The scores on many variables in psychology research approximately follow a bell-shaped, symmetrical, unimodal distribution called the normal curve. Because the shape of this curve follows an exact mathematical formula, there is a specific percentage of scores between any two points on a normal curve.
3. A useful working rule for normal curves is that 50% of the scores are above the mean, 34% are between the mean and 1 standard deviation above the mean, and 14% are between 1 and 2 standard deviations above the mean.

4. A normal curve table gives the percentage of scores between the mean and any particular Z score, as well as the percentage of scores in the tail for any Z score. Using this table, and knowing that the curve is symmetrical and that 50% of the scores are above the mean, you can figure the percentage of scores above or below any particular Z score. You can also use the table to figure the Z score for the point where a particular percentage of scores begins or ends.

5. A sample is an individual or group that is studied—usually as representative of some larger group or population that cannot be studied in its entirety. Ideally, the sample is selected from a population using a strictly random procedure. The mean (*M*), variance (*SD*²), standard deviation (*SD*), and so forth of a sample are called sample statistics. When of a population, the sample statistics are called population parameters and are symbolized by Greek letters—μ for mean, σ² for variance, and σ for standard deviation.

6. Most psychology researchers consider the probability of an event to be its expected relative frequency. However, some think of probability as the subjective degree of belief that the event will happen. Probability is figured as the proportion of successful outcomes to total possible outcomes. It is symbolized by *p* and has a range from 0 (event is impossible) to 1 (event is certain). The normal curve provides a way to know the probabilities of scores being within particular ranges of values.

7. There are controversies about many of the topics in this chapter. One is about whether normal distributions are truly typical of the populations of scores for the variables we study in psychology. In another controversy, some researchers have questioned the use of standard statistical methods in the typical psychology research situation that does not use strict random sampling.

8. Research articles rarely discuss Z scores, normal curves (except briefly when a variable being studied seems not to follow a normal curve), or probability (except in relation to statistical significance). Procedures of sampling, particularly when the study is a survey, are sometimes described, and the representativeness of a sample may also be discussed.

9. ADVANCED TOPIC: In situations where there are two or more mutually exclusive outcomes, probabilities are figured following an addition rule, in which the total probability is the sum of the individual probabilities. A multiplication rule (in which probabilities are multiplied together) is followed to figure the probability of getting both of two (or more) independent outcomes. A conditional probability is the probability of one outcome, assuming some other particular outcome will happen.

Key Terms

Z score (p. 68)
raw score (p. 69)
normal distribution (p. 73)
normal curve (p. 73)
normal curve table (p.76)
population (p. 83)
sample (p. 83)

random selection (p. 85)
population parameters (p. 87)
μ (population mean) (p. 87)
σ² (population variance) (p. 87)
σ (population standard
   deviation) (p. 87)
sample statistics (p. 87)

probability (*p*) (p. 89)
outcome (p. 89)
expected relative frequency (p. 89)
long-run relative-frequency interpretation of probability (p. 89)
subjective interpretation of probability (p. 89)

Example Worked-Out Problems

Changing a Raw Score to a *Z* Score

A distribution has a mean of 80 and a standard deviation of 20. Find the Z score for a raw score of 65.

Answer

You can change a raw score to a Z score using the formula or the steps.

Using the formula: $Z = (X - M)/SD = (65 - 80)/20 = -15/20 = -.75$.

Using the steps:

❶ **Figure the deviation score: subtract the mean from the raw score.** $65 - 80 = -15$.

❷ **Figure the *Z* score: divide the deviation score by the standard deviation.** $-15/20 = .75$.

Changing a *Z* Score to a Raw Score

A distribution has a mean of 200 and a standard deviation of 50. A person has a Z score of 1.26. What is the person's raw score?

Answer

You can change a Z score to a raw score using the formula or the steps.

Using the formula: $X = (Z)(SD) + M = (1.26)(50) + 200 = 63 + 200 = 263$.

Using the steps:

❶ **Figure the deviation score: multiply the *Z* score by the standard deviation.** $1.26 \times 50 = 63$.

❷ **Figure the raw score: add the mean to the deviation score.** $63 + 200 = 263$.

Outline for Writing Essays Involving *Z* Scores

1. If required by the question, explain the mean, variance, and standard deviation (using the points in the essay outlined in Chapter 2).
2. Describe the basic idea of a Z score as a way of describing where a particular score fits into an overall group of scores. Specifically, a Z score shows the number of standard deviations a score is above or below the mean.
3. Explain the steps for figuring a Z score from a raw (ordinary) score.
4. Mention that changing raw scores to Z scores puts scores that are for different variables onto the same scale, which makes it easier to make comparisons between scores on the variables.

Figuring the Percentage Above or Below a Particular Raw Score or *Z* Score

Suppose a test of sensitivity to violence is known to have a mean of 20, a standard deviation of 3, and a normal curve shape. What percentage of people have scores above 24?

Answer

❶ **If you are beginning with a raw score, first change it to a Z score.** Using the usual formula, $Z = (X - M)/SD$, $Z = (24 - 20)/3 = 1.33$.

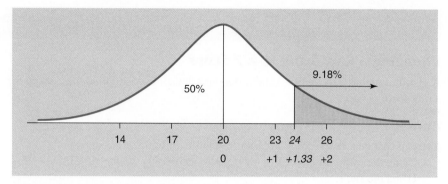

Figure 3–18   Distribution of sensitivity to violence scores showing the percentage of scores above a score of 24 (shaded area).

❷ **Draw a picture of the normal curve, decide where the Z score falls on it, and shade in the area for which you are finding the percentage.** This is shown in Figure 3–18.

❸ **Make a rough estimate of the shaded area's percentage based on the 50%–34%–14% percentages.** If the shaded area started at a Z score of 1, it would include 16%. If it started at a Z score of 2, it would include only 2%. So with a Z score of 1.33, it has to be somewhere between 16% and 2%.

❹ **Find the exact percentage using the normal curve table, adding 50% if necessary.** In Table A–1 (in the Appendix), 1.33 in the "Z" column goes with 9.18% in the "% in Tail" column. This is the answer to our problem: 9.18% of people have a higher score than 24 on the sensitivity to violence measure. (There is no need to add 50% to the percentage.)

❺ **Check that your exact percentage is within the range of your rough estimate from Step ❸.** Our result, 9.18%, is within the 16% to 2% range estimated.

Note: If the problem involves Z scores that are all 0, 1, or 2 (or −1 or −2), you can work the problem using the 50%–34%–14% figures and without using the normal curve table (although you should still draw a figure and shade in the appropriate area).

Figuring Z Scores and Raw Scores From Percentages

Consider the same situation: A test of sensitivity to violence is known to have a mean of 20, a standard deviation of 3, and a normal curve shape. What is the minimum score a person needs to be in the top 75%?

Answer

❶ **Draw a picture of the normal curve, and shade in the approximate area for your percentage using the 50%–34%–14% percentages.** The shading has to begin between the mean and 1 *SD* below the mean. (There are 50% above the mean and 84% above 1 *SD* below the mean). This is shown in Figure 3–19.

❷ **Make a rough estimate of the Z score where the shaded area stops.** The Z score has to be between 0 and −1.

❸ **Find the exact Z score using the normal curve table (subtracting 50% from your percentage if necessary before looking up the Z score).** Since 50% of people have IQs above the mean, for the top 75% you need to include the 25% below the mean (that is, 75% − 50% = 25%). Looking in the "% Mean to Z"

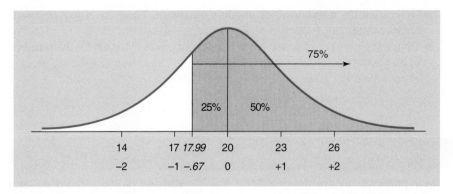

Figure 3–19   Finding the sensitivity to violence raw score for where the top 75% of scores start.

column of the normal curve table, the closest figure to 25% is 24.86, which goes with a Z of .67. Since we are interested in below the mean, we want −.67.
❹ **Check that your exact Z score is within the range of your rough estimate from Step ❷.** −.67 is between 0 and −1.
❺ **If you want to find a raw score, change it from the Z score.** Using the formula $X = (Z)(SD) + M$, $X = (−.67)(3) + 20 = −2.01 + 20 = 17.99$. That is, to be in the top 75%, a person needs to have a score on this test of at least 18.

Note: If the problem instructs you not to use a normal curve table, you should be able to work the problem using the 50%–34%–14% figures (although you should still draw a figure and shade in the appropriate area).

Outline for Writing Essays on the Logic and Computations for Figuring a Percentage from a Z Score and Vice Versa

1. Note that the normal curve is a mathematical (or theoretical) distribution, describe its shape (be sure to include a diagram of the normal curve), and mention that many variables in nature and in research approximately follow a normal curve.
2. If required by the question, explain the mean and standard deviation (using the points in the essay outline in Chapter 2).
3. Describe the link between the normal curve and the percentage of scores between the mean and any Z score. Be sure to include a description of the normal curve table and show how it is used.
4. Briefly describe the steps required to figure a percentage from a Z score or vice versa (as required by the question). Be sure to draw a diagram of the normal curve with appropriate numbers and shaded areas marked on it from the relevant question (e.g., the mean, one and two standard deviations above/below the mean, shaded area for which percentage or Z score is to be determined).

Finding a Probability

A candy dish has four kinds of fruit-flavored candy: 20 apple, 20 strawberry, 5 cherry, and 5 grape. If you close your eyes and pick one piece of candy at random, what is the probability it will be either cherry or grape?

Answer

❶ **Determine the number of possible successful outcomes.** There are 10 possible successful outcomes—5 cherry and 5 grape.

❷ **Determine the number of all possible outcomes.** There are 50 possible outcomes overall: $20 + 20 + 5 + 5 = 50$.

❸ **Divide the number of possible successful outcomes (Step ❶) by the number of all possible outcomes (Step ❷).** $10/50 = .2$. Thus, the probability of picking either a cherry or grape candy is .2.

Practice Problems

These problems involve figuring. Most real-life statistics problems are done on a computer with special statistical software. Even if you have such software, do these problems by hand to ingrain the method in your mind. To learn how to use a computer to solve statistics problems like those in this chapter, refer to the Using SPSS section at the end of this chapter and the *Study Guide and Computer Workbook* that accompanies this text.

All data are fictional unless an actual citation is given.

Set I (for Answers to Set I Practice Problems, see p. 675)

1. On a measure of anxiety, the mean is 79 and the standard deviation is 12. What are the Z scores for each of the following raw scores? (a) 91, (b) 68, and (c) 103.

2. On an intelligence test, the mean number of raw items correct is 231 and the standard deviation is 41. What are the raw (actual) scores on the test for people with IQs of (a) 107, (b) 83, and (c) 100? To do this problem, first figure the Z score for the particular IQ score; then use that Z score to find the raw score. Note that IQ scores have a mean of 100 and a standard deviation of 16.

3. Six months after a divorce, the former wife and husband each take a test that measures divorce adjustment. The wife's score is 63, and the husband's score is 59. Overall, the mean score for divorced women on this test is 60 ($SD = 6$); the mean score for divorced men is 55 ($SD = 4$). Which of the two has adjusted better to the divorce in relation to other divorced people of the same gender? Explain your answer to a person who has never had a course in statistics.

4. Suppose the people living in a city have a mean score of 40 and a standard deviation of 5 on a measure of concern about the environment. Assume that these concern scores are normally distributed. Using the 50%–34%–14% figures, approximately what percentage of people have a score (a) above 40, (b) above 45, (c) above 30, (d) above 35, (e) below 40, (f) below 45, (g) below 30, and (h) below 35?

5. Using the information in problem 4 and the 50%–34%–14% figures, what is the minimum score a person has to have to be in the top (a) 2%, (b) 16%, (c) 50%, (d) 84%, and (e) 98%?

6. A psychologist has been studying eye fatigue using a particular measure, which she administers to students after they have worked for 1 hour writing on a computer. On this measure, she has found that the distribution follows a normal curve. Using a normal curve table, what percentage of students have Z scores (a) below 1.5, (b) above 1.5, (c) below −1.5, (d) above −1.5, (e) above 2.10, (f) below 2.10, (g) above .45, (h) below −1.78, and (i) above 1.68?

7. In the previous problem, the test of eye fatigue has a mean of 15 and a standard deviation of 5. Using a normal curve table, what percentage of students have scores (a) above 16, (b) above 17, (c) above 18, (d) below 18, and (e) below 14?

8. In the eye fatigue example of problems 6 and 7, using a normal curve table, what is the lowest score on the eye fatigue measure a person has to have to be in (a) the top 40%, (b) the top 30%, (c) the top 20%?

9. Using a normal curve table, give the percentage of scores between the mean and a Z score of (a) .58, (b) .59, (c) 1.46, (d) 1.56, (e) −.58.

10. Consider a test of coordination that has a normal distribution, a mean of 50, and a standard deviation of 10. (a) How high a score would a person need to be in the top 5%? (b) Explain your answer to someone who has never had a course in statistics.

11. Altman et al. (1997) conducted a telephone survey of the attitudes of the U.S. adult public toward tobacco farmers. In the method section of their article, they explained that their respondents were "randomly selected from a nationwide list of telephone numbers" (p. 117). Explain to a person who has never had a course in statistics or research methods what this means and why it is important.

12. The following numbers of individuals in a company received special assistance from the personnel department last year:

Drug/alcohol	10
Family crisis counseling	20
Other	20
Total	50

If you were to select someone at random from the records for last year, what is the probability that the person would be in each of the following categories: (a) drug/alcohol, (b) family, (c) drug/alcohol or family, (d) any category except "Other," or (e) any of the three categories? (f) Explain your answers to someone who has never had a course in statistics.

Set II

13. On a measure of artistic ability, the mean for college students in New Zealand is 150 and the standard deviation is 25. Give the Z scores for New Zealand college students who score (a) 100, (b) 120, (c) 140, and (d) 160. Give the raw scores for persons whose Z scores on this test are (e) −1, (f) −.8, (g) −.2, and (h) +1.38.

14. On a standard measure of hearing ability, the mean is 300 and the standard deviation is 20. Give the Z scores for persons who score (a) 340, (b) 310, and (c) 260. Give the raw scores for persons whose Z scores on this test are (d) 2.4, (e) 1.5, (f) 0, and (g) −4.5.

15. A person scores 81 on a test of verbal ability and 6.4 on a test of quantitative ability. For the verbal ability test, the mean for people in general is 50 and the standard deviation is 20. For the quantitative ability test, the mean for people in general is 0 and the standard deviation is 5. Which is this person's stronger ability: verbal or quantitative? Explain your answer to a person who has never had a course in statistics.

16. The amount of time it takes to recover physiologically from a certain kind of sudden noise is found to be normally distributed with a mean of 80 seconds and a standard deviation of 10 seconds. Using the 50%–34%–14% figures, approximately what percentage of scores (on time to recover) will be (a) above 100, (b) below 100, (c) above 90, (d) below 90, (e) above 80, (f) below 80, (g) above 70, (h) below 70, (i) above 60, and (j) below 60?

17. Using the information in problem 16 and the 50%–34%–14% figures, what is the longest time to recover that a person can take and still be in the bottom (a) 2%, (b) 16%, (c) 50%, (d) 84%, and (e) 98%?

18. Suppose that the scores of architects on a particular creativity test are normally distributed. Using a normal curve table, what percentage of architects have Z scores (a) above .10, (b) below .10, (c) above .20, (d) below .20, (e) above 1.10, (f) below 1.10, (g) above −.10, and (h) below −.10?

19. In the example in problem 18, using a normal curve table, what is the minimum Z score an architect can have on the creativity test to be in the (a) top 50%, (b) top 40%, (c) top 60%, (d) top 30%, and (e) top 20%?

20. In the example in problem 18, assume that the mean is 300 and the standard deviation is 25. Using a normal curve table, what scores would be the top and bottom scores to find (a) the middle 50% of architects, (b) the middle 90% of architects, and (c) the middle 99% of architects?

21. Suppose that you are designing an instrument panel for a large industrial machine. The machine requires the person using it to reach 2 feet from a particular position. The reach from this position for adult women is known to have a mean of 2.8 feet with a standard deviation of .5. The reach for adult men is known to have a mean of 3.1 feet with a standard deviation of .6. Both women's and men's reach from this position is normally distributed. If this design is implemented, (a) what percentage of women will not be able to work on this instrument panel? (b) What percentage of men will not be able to work on this instrument panel? (c) Explain your answers to a person who has never had a course in statistics.

22. Suppose you want to conduct a survey of the attitude of psychology graduate students studying clinical psychology toward psychoanalytic methods of psychotherapy. One approach would be to contact every psychology graduate student you know and ask them to fill out a questionnaire about it. (a) What kind of sampling method is this? (b) What is a major limitation of this kind of approach?

23. A large study of how people make future plans and the relation of this to their life satisfaction (Prenda & Lachman, 2001) recruited participants "through random-digit dialing procedures." These are procedures in which phone numbers to call potential participants are randomly generated by a computer. Explain to a person who has never had a course in statistics (a) why this method of sampling might be used and (b) why it may be a problem if not everyone called agreed to be interviewed.

24. Suppose that you were going to conduct a survey of visitors to your campus. You want the survey to be as representative as possible. (a) How would you select the people to survey? (b) Why would that be your best method?

25. You are conducting a survey at a college with 800 students, 50 faculty members, and 150 administrators. Each of these 1,000 individuals has a single listing in the campus phone directory. Suppose you were to cut up the directory and pull out one listing at random to contact. What is the probability it would be (a) a student, (b) a faculty member, (c) an administrator, (d) a faculty member or administrator, and (e) anyone except an administrator? (f) Explain your answers to someone who has never had a course in statistics.

26. You apply to 20 graduate programs, 10 of which are in clinical psychology, 5 of which are in counseling psychology, and 5 of which are in social work. You get a message from home that you have a letter from one of the programs you applied to, but nothing is said about which one. Give the probabilities it is from (a) a clinical psychology program, (b) a counseling psychology program, (c) from any program other than social work. (d) Explain your answers to someone who has never had a course in statistics.

Using SPSS

The ✐ in the following steps indicates a mouse click. (We used SPSS version 15.0 to carry out these analyses. The steps and output may be slightly different for other versions of SPSS.)

Changing Raw Scores to *Z* Scores

It is easier to learn these steps using actual numbers, so we will use the number of dreams example from Chapter 2.

❶ Enter the scores from your distribution in one column of the data window (the scores are 7, 8, 8, 7, 3, 1, 6, 9, 3, 8). We will call this variable "dreams."

❷ Find the mean and standard deviation of the scores. You learned how to do this in the Chapter 2 Using SPSS section (see p. 62). The mean is 6 and the standard deviation is 2.57.

❸ You are now going to create a new variable that shows the *Z* score for each raw score. ✐ *Transform,* ✐ *Compute Variable.* You can call the new variable any name that you want, but we will call it "zdreams." So, write *zdreams* in the box labeled *Target Variable.* In the box labeled *Numeric Expression,* write (*dreams* − 6)/2.57. As you can see, this formula creates a deviation score (by subtracting the mean from the raw score) and divides the deviation score by the standard deviation. ✐ *OK.* You will see that a new variable called *zdreams* has been added to the data window. The scores for this *zdreams* variable are the *Z* scores for the dreams variable.[4] Your data window should now look like Figure 3–20.

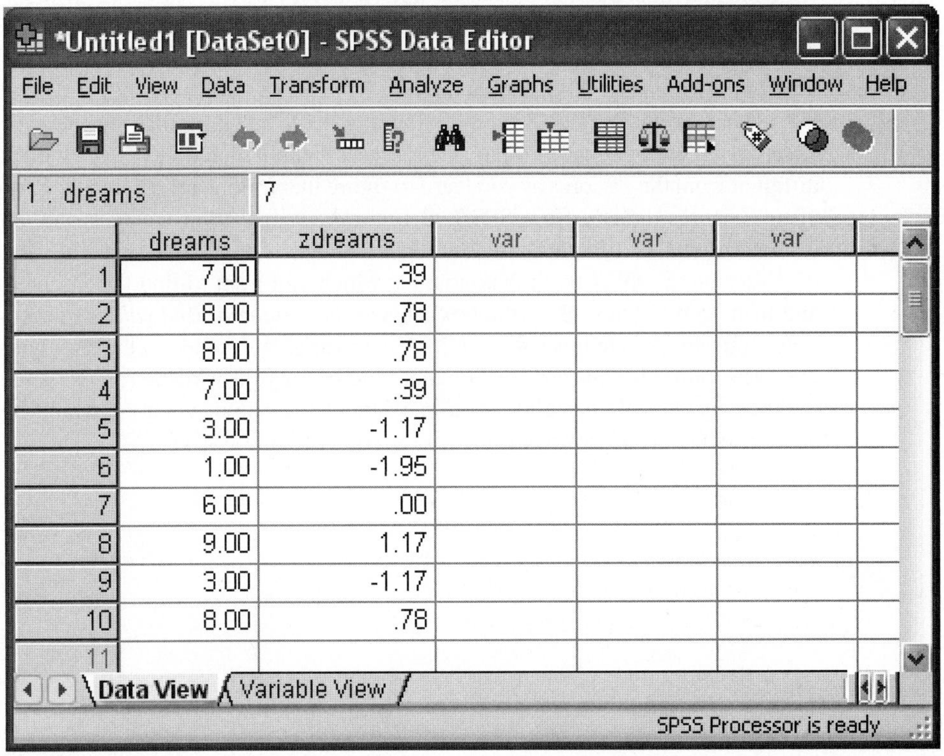

	dreams	zdreams	var	var	var
1	7.00	.39			
2	8.00	.78			
3	8.00	.78			
4	7.00	.39			
5	3.00	-1.17			
6	1.00	-1.95			
7	6.00	.00			
8	9.00	1.17			
9	3.00	-1.17			
10	8.00	.78			
11					

Figure 3-20 Using SPSS to change raw scores to *Z* scores for the number of dreams example.

Chapter Notes

1. Also, sometimes used are scores similar to Z scores, called T scores, in which the mean is 50 and the standard deviation is 10. For example, some tests used by clinical psychologists use a T score scale. Thus, a 65 on a scale of T scores equals a Z score of 1.5.

2. The formula for the normal curve (when the mean is 0 and the standard deviation is 1) is

$$f(x) = \frac{1}{\sqrt{2\pi}} e^{-x^2/2}$$

where $f(x)$ is the height of the curve at point x and π and e are the usual mathematical constants (approximately 3.14 and 2.72, respectively). However, psychology researchers almost never use this formula because it is built into the statistics software that do calculations involving normal curves. When work must be done by hand, any needed information about the normal curve is provided in tables in statistics books (for example, Table A–1 in the Appendix).

3. Frick (1998) argued that in most cases psychology researchers should not think in terms of samples and populations at all. Rather, he argues, researchers should think of themselves as studying processes. An experiment examines some process in a group of individuals. Then the researcher evaluates the probability that the pattern of results could have been caused by chance factors. For example, the researcher examines whether a difference in means between an experimental and a control group could have been caused by factors other than by the experimental manipulation. Frick claims that this way of thinking is much closer to the way researchers actually work, and argues that it has various advantages in terms of the subtle logic of inferential statistical procedures.

4. You can also request the Z scores directly from SPSS. However, SPSS figures the standard deviation based on the "dividing by $N - 1$ formula" for the variance (see Chapters 2 and 6). Thus, the Z scores figured directly by SPSS will be different from the Z scores as you learn to figure them. Here are the steps for figuring Z scores directly from SPSS: ❶ Enter the scores from your distribution in one column of the data window. ❷ ✑ *Analyze,* ✑ *Descriptive statistics,* ✑ *Descriptives.* ❸ ✑ on the variable for which you want to find the Z scores, and then ✑ the arrow. ❹ ✑ the box labeled *Save standardized values as variables* (this checks the box). ❺ ✑ *OK.* A new variable is added to the data window. The values for this variable are the Z scores for your variable (based on the dividing by $N - 1$ formula). (You can ignore the output window, which by default will show descriptive statistics for your variable.)

CHAPTER 4

Introduction to Hypothesis Testing

Chapter Outline

- ✪ A Hypothesis-Testing Example   108
- ✪ The Core Logic of Hypothesis Testing   109
- ✪ The Hypothesis-Testing Process   110
- ✪ One-Tailed and Two-Tailed Hypothesis Tests   119
- ✪ Controversy: Should Significance Tests Be Banned?   124

- ✪ Hypothesis Tests in Research Articles   127
- ✪ Summary   128
- ✪ Key Terms   129
- ✪ Example Worked-Out Problems   129
- ✪ Practice Problems   131
- ✪ Chapter Notes   136

I n this chapter, we introduce the crucial topic of **hypothesis testing. A hypothesis** is a prediction intended to be tested in a research study. The prediction may be based on informal observation (as in clinical or applied settings regarding a possible practical innovation), on related results of previous studies, or on a broader *theory* about what is being studied. You can think of a **theory** as a set of principles that attempt to explain an important psychological process. A theory usually leads to various specific hypotheses that can be tested in research studies.

This chapter focuses on the basic logic for analyzing results of a research study to test a hypothesis. The central theme of hypothesis testing has to do with the important distinction between sample and population discussed in the last chapter: hypothesis testing is a systematic procedure for deciding whether the results of a research study, which examines a sample, support a hypothesis which applies to a population. Hypothesis testing is the central theme in all the remaining chapters of this book, as it is in most research in psychology and related fields.

Many students find the most difficult part of the course to be mastering the basic logic of this chapter and the next two. This chapter in particular requires some mental gymnastics. Even if you follow everything the first time through, you will be wise to

hypothesis testing   procedure for deciding whether the outcome of a study (results for a sample) support a particular theory or practical innovation (which is thought to apply to a population).

hypothesis   prediction, often based on informal observation, previous research, or theory, that is tested in a research study.

theory   set of principles that attempt to explain one or more facts, relationships, or events; psychologists often derive specific predictions from theories that are then tested in research studies.

review the chapter thoroughly. Hypothesis testing involves grasping ideas that make little sense covered separately; so in this chapter you learn several new ideas all at once. However, once you understand the material in this chapter and the two that follow, your mind will be used to this sort of thing, and the rest of the course should seem easier.

At the same time, we have kept this introduction to hypothesis testing as simple as possible, putting off what we could for later chapters. For example, real-life psychology research involves samples of many individuals. However, to minimize how much you have to learn at one time, this chapter's examples are about studies in which the sample is a single individual. To do this, we use some odd examples. Just remember that you are building a foundation that will, by Chapter 7, prepare you to understand hypothesis testing as it is actually done in real research.

A Hypothesis-Testing Example

Here is our first necessarily odd example that we made up to keep this introduction to hypothesis testing as straightforward as possible. A large research project has been going on for several years. In this project, new babies are given a particular vitamin and then the research team follows their development during the first 2 years of life. So far, the vitamin has not speeded up the development of the babies. The ages at which these and all other babies start to walk is shown in Figure 4–1. The mean is 14 months ($\mu = 14$), the standard deviation is 3 months ($\sigma = 3$), and the ages follow a normal curve. Based on the normal curve percentages, you can figure that fewer than 2% of babies start walking before 8 months of age; these are the babies who are more than 2 standard deviations below the mean. [This fictional distribution is close to the true distribution psychologists have found for European babies, although that true distribution is slightly skewed to the right (Hindley et al., 1966).]

One of the researchers working on the project has an idea. If the vitamin the babies are taking could be more highly refined, perhaps its effect would be dramatically increased: babies taking the highly purified version should start walking much earlier than other babies. (We will assume that the purification process could not possibly make the vitamin harmful.) However, refining the vitamin in this way is extremely expensive for each dose; so the research team decides to try the procedure with just enough purified doses for one baby. A newborn in the project is then randomly selected to take the highly purified version of the vitamin, and the researchers then

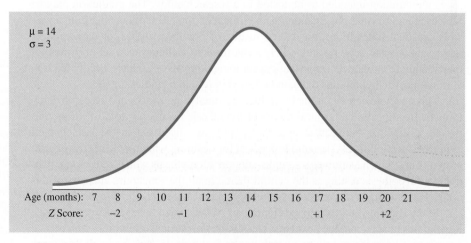

Figure 4–1 Distribution of when babies begin to walk (fictional data).

follow this baby's progress for 2 years. What kind of result should lead the researchers to conclude that the highly purified vitamin allows babies to walk earlier?

This is a hypothesis-testing problem. The researchers want to draw a general conclusion about whether the purified vitamin allows babies *in general* to walk earlier. The conclusion will be about babies in general (a population of babies). However, the conclusion will be based on results of studying a sample. In this example, the sample consists of a single baby.

The Core Logic of Hypothesis Testing

There is a standard way researchers approach any hypothesis-testing problem. For this example, it works as follows. Consider first the population of babies in general (those who are not given the specially purified vitamin). In this population, the chance of a baby's starting to walk at age 8 months or earlier would be less than 2%. (As shown in Figure 4–1, the mean walking age is 14 months with a standard deviation of 3 months.) Thus, walking at 8 months or earlier is highly unlikely among such babies. But what if the randomly selected sample of one baby in our study does start walking by 8 months? If the specially purified vitamin had no effect on this particular baby's walking age (which means that the baby's walking age should be similar to that of babies who were not given the vitamin), it is highly unlikely (less than a 2% chance) that the particular baby we selected at random would start walking by 8 months. So, if the baby in our study does in fact start walking by 8 months, that allows us to *reject* the idea that the specially purified vitamin has *no* effect. And if we reject the idea that the specially purified vitamin has no effect, then we must also *accept* the idea that the specially purified vitamin *does* have an effect.

Using the same reasoning, if the baby starts walking by 8 months, we can reject the idea that this baby comes from a population of babies like that of the general population with a mean walking age of 14 months. We therefore conclude that babies given the specially purified vitamin will on the average start to walk before 14 months. Our explanation for the baby's early walking age in the study is that the specially purified vitamin speeded up the baby's development.

In this example, the researchers first spelled out what would have to happen for them to conclude that the special purification procedure makes a difference. Having laid this out in advance, the researchers then conducted their study. Conducting the study in this case meant giving the specially purified vitamin to a randomly selected baby and watching to see how early that baby walked. We supposed that the result of the study is that the baby started walking before 8 months. The researchers then concluded that it is unlikely the specially purified vitamin makes *no* difference and thus also that it *does* make a difference.

This kind of testing, with its opposite-of-what-you-predict, roundabout reasoning, is at the heart of inferential statistics in psychology. It is something like a double negative. One reason for this approach is that we have the information to figure the probability of getting a particular experimental result if the situation of there being *no difference* is true. In the purified vitamin example, the researchers know what the probabilities are of babies walking at different ages if the specially purified vitamin does not have any effect. The probabilities of babies walking at various ages are already known from studies of babies in general—that is, babies who have not received the specially purified vitamin. If the specially purified vitamin has no effect, then the ages at which babies start walking are the same with or without the specially purified vitamin. Thus, the distribution is that shown in Figure 4–1, based on ages at which babies start walking in general.

TIP FOR SUCCESS

This section, The Core Logic of Hypothesis Testing, is central to everything else we do in the book. Thus, you may want to read it a few times. You should also be certain that you understand the logic of hypothesis testing before reading later chapters.

Without such a tortuous way of going at the problem, in most cases you could not test hypotheses scientifically at all. In almost all psychology research, we base our conclusions on the question, "What is the probability of getting our research results if the opposite of what we are predicting were true?" That is, we usually predict an effect of some kind. However, we decide on whether there *is* such an effect by seeing if it is unlikely that there is *not* such an effect. If it is highly unlikely that we would get our research results if the opposite of what we are predicting were true, that finding allows us to reject the opposite prediction. If we reject the opposite prediction, we are able to accept our prediction. However, if it is likely that we would get our research results if the opposite of what we are predicting were true, we are not able to reject the opposite prediction. If we are not able to reject the opposite prediction, we are not able to accept our prediction.

The Hypothesis-Testing Process

Let's look at our example again, this time going over each step in some detail. Along the way, we cover the special terminology of hypothesis testing. Most important, we introduce the five steps of hypothesis testing that you use for the rest of this book.

Step ❶: Restate the Question as a Research Hypothesis and a Null Hypothesis About the Populations

Our researchers are interested in the effects on babies in general (not just on this particular baby). That is, the purpose of studying samples is to know about populations. Thus, it is useful to restate the research question in terms of populations. In our example, we can think of two populations of babies:

Population 1: Babies who take the specially purified vitamin.
Population 2: Babies in general (that is, babies who do not take the specially purified vitamin).

Population 1 consists of babies who receive the experimental treatment (the specially purified vitamin). In our example, we use a sample of one baby to draw a conclusion about the age at which babies in Population 1 start to walk. Population 2 is a kind of comparison baseline of what is already known about babies in general.

The prediction of our research team is that Population 1 babies (those who take the specially purified vitamin) will on the average walk earlier than Population 2 babies (babies in general who do not take the specially purified vitamin). This prediction is based on the researchers' theory of how these vitamins work. A prediction like this about the difference between populations is called a **research hypothesis.** Put more formally, the prediction is that the mean of Population 1 is lower (babies receiving the special vitamin walk earlier) than the mean of Population 2. In symbols, the research hypothesis for this example is $\mu_1 < \mu_2$.

The opposite of the research hypothesis is that the populations are not different in the way predicted. Under this scenario, Population 1 babies (those who take the specially purified vitamin) will on the average *not* walk earlier than Population 2 babies (babies in general—those who do not take the specially purified vitamin). That is, the prediction is that there is no difference in the ages at which Population 1 and Population 2 babies start walking. On the average, they start at the same time. A statement like this, about a lack of difference between populations, is the crucial *opposite* of the research hypothesis. It is called a **null hypothesis.** It has this name

research hypothesis statement in hypothesis testing about the predicted relation between populations (often a prediction of a difference between population means).

null hypothesis statement about a relation between populations that is the opposite of the research hypothesis; statement that in the population there is no difference (or a difference opposite to that predicted) between populations; contrived statement set up to examine whether it can be rejected as part of hypothesis testing.

because it states the situation in which there is no difference (the difference is "null") between the populations. In symbols, the null hypothesis is $\mu_1 = \mu_2$.[1]

The research hypothesis and the null hypothesis are complete opposites: if one is true, the other cannot be. In fact, the research hypothesis is sometimes called the *alternative hypothesis*—that is, it is the alternative to the null hypothesis. This term is a bit ironic. As researchers, we care most about the research hypothesis. But when doing the steps of hypothesis testing, we use this roundabout method of seeing whether or not we can reject the null hypothesis so that we can decide about its alternative (the research hypothesis).

Step ❷: Determine the Characteristics of the Comparison Distribution

Recall that the overall logic of hypothesis testing involves figuring out the probability of getting a particular result if the null hypothesis is true. Thus, you need to know what the situation would be if the null hypothesis were true. In our example, we start out knowing the key information about Population 2, babies in the general population (see Figure 4–1): we know it follows a normal curve, $\mu = 14$, and $\sigma = 3$. If the null hypothesis is true, Population 1 and Population 2 are the same; in our example, this would mean Populations 1 and 2 both follow a normal curve, $\mu = 14$, and $\sigma = 3$.

In the hypothesis-testing process, you want to find out the probability that you could have gotten a sample score as extreme as what you got (say, a baby walking very early) if your sample were from a population with a distribution of the sort you would have if the null hypothesis were true. Thus, in this book we call this distribution a **comparison distribution.** (The comparison distribution is sometimes called a *sampling distribution*—an idea we discuss in Chapter 5.) That is, in the hypothesis-testing process, you compare the actual sample's score to this comparison distribution.

In our vitamin example, the null hypothesis is that there is no difference in walking age between babies who take the specially purified vitamin (Population 1) and babies in general who do not take the specially purified vitamin (Population 2). The comparison distribution is the distribution for Population 2, since this population represents the walking age of babies if the null hypothesis is true. In later chapters, you will learn about different types of comparison distributions, but the same principle applies in all cases: The comparison distribution is the distribution that represents the population situation if the null hypothesis is true.

Step ❸: Determine the Cutoff Sample Score on the Comparison Distribution at Which the Null Hypothesis Should Be Rejected

Ideally, before conducting a study, researchers set a target against which they will compare their result: how extreme a sample score they would need to decide against the null hypothesis, that is, how extreme the sample score would have to be for it to be too unlikely that they could get such an extreme score if the null hypothesis were true. This is called the **cutoff sample score.** (The cutoff sample score is also known as the *critical value*.)

Consider our purified vitamin example, in which the null hypothesis is that walking age is not influenced by whether babies take the specially purified vitamin. The researchers might decide that, if the null hypothesis were true, a randomly

comparison distribution distribution used in hypothesis testing. It represents the population situation if the null hypothesis is true. It is the distribution to which you compare the score based on your sample's results.

cutoff sample score point in hypothesis testing, on the comparison distribution at which, if reached or exceeded by the sample score, you reject the null hypothesis. Also called *critical value*.

selected baby walking before 8 months would be very unlikely. With a normal distribution, being 2 or more standard deviations below the mean (walking by 8 months) could occur less than 2% of the time. Thus, based on the comparison distribution, the researchers set their cutoff sample score even before doing the study. They decide in advance that *if* the result of their study is a baby who walks by 8 months, they will reject the null hypothesis.

But what if the baby does not start walking until after 8 months? If that happens, the researchers will not be able to reject the null hypothesis.

When setting in advance how extreme a sample's score needs to be to reject the null hypothesis, researchers use Z scores and percentages. In our purified vitamin example, the researchers might decide that if a result were less likely than 2%, they would reject the null hypothesis. Being in the bottom 2% of a normal curve means having a Z score of about -2 or lower. Thus, the researchers would set -2 as their Z-score cutoff point on the comparison distribution for deciding that a result is extreme enough to reject the null hypothesis. So, if the actual sample Z score is -2 or lower, the researchers will reject the null hypothesis. However, if the actual sample Z score is greater than -2, the researchers will not reject the null hypothesis.

Suppose that the researchers are even more cautious about too easily rejecting the null hypothesis. They might decide that they will reject the null hypothesis only if they get a result that could occur by chance 1% of the time or less. They could then figure out the Z-score cutoff for 1%. Using the normal curve table, to have a score in the lower 1% of a normal curve, you need a Z score of -2.33 or less. (In our example, a Z score of -2.33 means 7 months.) In Figure 4–2, we have shaded the 1% of the comparison distribution in which a sample would be considered so extreme that the possibility that it came from a distribution like this would be rejected. Now the researchers will reject the null hypothesis only if the actual sample Z score is -2.33 or lower—that is, if it falls in the shaded area in Figure 4–2. If the sample Z score falls outside the shaded area in Figure 4–2, the researchers will *not* reject the null hypothesis.

In general, psychology researchers use a cutoff on the comparison distribution with a probability of 5% that a score will be at least that extreme if the null hypothesis were true. That is, researchers reject the null hypothesis if the probability of getting a sample score this extreme (if the null hypothesis were true) is less than 5%. This probability is usually written as $p < .05$. However, in some areas of research, or when researchers want to be especially cautious, they use a cutoff of 1% $(p < .01)$.[2]

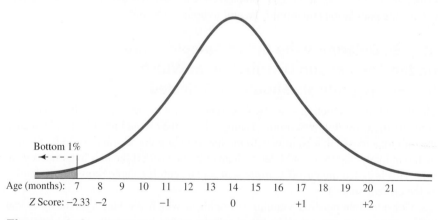

Figure 4–2 Distribution of when babies begin to walk, with bottom 1% shaded (fictional data).

These are called **conventional levels of significance.** They are described as the *.05 significance level* and the *.01 significance level.* We also refer to them as the 5% significance level and the 1% significance level. (We discuss in more detail in Chapter 6 the issues in deciding on the significance level to use.) When a sample score is so extreme that researchers reject the null hypothesis, the result is said to be **statistically significant** (or *significant,* as it is often abbreviated).

Step ❹: Determine Your Sample's Score on the Comparison Distribution

The next step is to carry out the study and get the actual results for your sample. Once you have the results for your sample, you figure the Z score for the sample's raw score based on the population mean and standard deviation of the comparison distribution.

Assume that the researchers did the study and the baby who was given the specially purified vitamin started walking at 6 months. The mean of the comparison distribution to which we are comparing these results is 14 months and the standard deviation is 3 months. That is, $\mu = 14$ and $\sigma = 3$. Thus, a baby who walks at 6 months is 8 months below the population mean. This puts the baby 2⅔ standard deviations below the population mean. The Z score for this sample baby on the comparison distribution is thus -2.67 [that is, $Z = (6 - 14)/3 = -2.67$]. Figure 4–3 shows the score of our sample baby on the comparison distribution.

Step ❺: Decide Whether to Reject the Null Hypothesis

To decide whether to reject the null hypothesis, compare your actual sample's Z score (from Step ❹) to the cutoff Z score (from Step ❸). In our example, the actual result was -2.67. Let's suppose the researchers had decided in advance that they would reject the null hypothesis if the sample's Z score was below -2. Since -2.67 is below -2, the researchers would reject the null hypothesis.

Alternatively, suppose the researchers had used the more conservative 1% significance level. The needed Z score to reject the null hypothesis would then have

> **TIP FOR SUCCESS**
>
> If you are unsure about these symbols for population parameters (μ, σ), be sure to review Table 3–2 on p. 87.

conventional levels of significance $(p < .05, p < .01)$ levels of significance widely used in psychology.

statistically significant   conclusion that the results of a study would be unlikely if in fact the sample studied represents a population that is no different from the population in general; an outcome of hypothesis testing in which the null hypothesis is rejected.

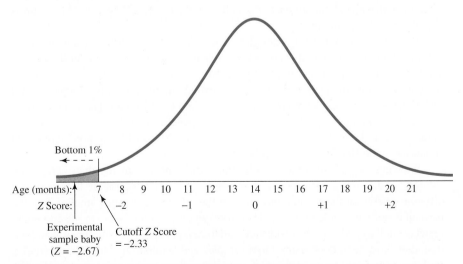

Figure 4–3   Distribution of when babies begin to walk, showing both the bottom 1% and the single baby who is the sample studied (fictional data).

been −2.33 or lower. But, again, the actual *Z* for the randomly selected baby was −2.67 (a more extreme score than −2.33). Thus, even with this more conservative cutoff, they would still reject the null hypothesis. This situation is shown in Figure 4–3. As you can see in the figure, the bottom 1% of the distribution is shaded. We recommend that you always draw such a picture of the distribution. Be sure to shade in the part of the distribution that is *more extreme* (that is, farther out in the tail) than the cutoff sample score. If your actual sample *Z* score falls within the shaded region, you can reject the null hypothesis. Since the sample *Z* score (−2.67) in this example falls within the shaded tail region, the researchers can reject the null hypothesis.

If the researchers reject the null hypothesis, what remains is the research hypothesis. In this example, the research team can conclude that the results of their study support the research hypothesis that babies who take the specially purified vitamin walk earlier than babies in general.

Implications of Rejecting or Failing to Reject the Null Hypothesis

It is important to emphasize two points about the conclusions you can make from the hypothesis-testing process. First, when you reject the null hypothesis, all you are saying is that your results support the research hypothesis (as in our example). You would not go on to say that the results *prove* the research hypothesis or that the results show that the research hypothesis is *true*. Terms such as *prove* and *true* are too strong because the results of research studies are based on probabilities. Specifically, they are based on the probability being low of getting your result if the null hypothesis were true. *Proven* and *true* are okay terms in logic and mathematics, but to use these words in conclusions from scientific research is unprofessional. (It is okay to use *true* when speaking hypothetically—for example, "*if* this hypothesis *were* true, then . . ."—but not when speaking of conclusions about an actual result.) What you do say when you reject the null hypothesis is that the results are *statistically significant*. You can also say that the results "support" or "provide evidence for" the research hypothesis.

Second, when a result is not extreme enough to reject the null hypothesis, you do not say that the result *supports* the null hypothesis. You simply say the result is *not statistically significant*.

A result that is not strong enough to reject the null hypothesis means the study was inconclusive. The results may not be extreme enough to reject the null hypothesis, but the null hypothesis might still be false (and the research hypothesis true). Suppose in our example that the specially purified vitamin had only a slight but still real effect. In that case, we would not expect to find a baby who is given the purified vitamin to be walking a lot earlier than babies in general. Thus, we would not be able to reject the null hypothesis, even though it is false. (You will learn more about such situations in the Decision Errors section in Chapter 6.)

Showing the null hypothesis to be true would mean showing that there is absolutely no difference between the populations. It is always possible that there is a difference between the populations but that the difference is much smaller than the particular study was able to detect. Therefore, when a result is not extreme enough to reject the null hypothesis, the results are said to be *inconclusive*. Sometimes, however, if studies have been done using large samples and accurate measuring procedures, evidence may build up in support of something close to the null hypothesis—that there is at most very little difference between the populations. (We have more to say

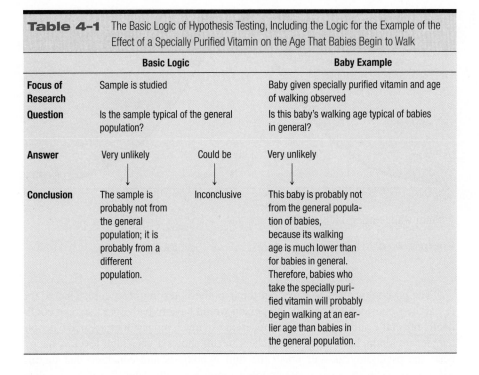

Table 4-1   The Basic Logic of Hypothesis Testing, Including the Logic for the Example of the Effect of a Specially Purified Vitamin on the Age That Babies Begin to Walk

	Basic Logic		Baby Example
Focus of Research	Sample is studied		Baby given specially purified vitamin and age of walking observed
Question	Is the sample typical of the general population?		Is this baby's walking age typical of babies in general?
Answer	Very unlikely	Could be	Very unlikely
	↓	↓	↓
Conclusion	The sample is probably not from the general population; it is probably from a different population.	Inconclusive	This baby is probably not from the general population of babies, because its walking age is much lower than for babies in general. Therefore, babies who take the specially purified vitamin will probably begin walking at an earlier age than babies in the general population.

on this important issue later in this chapter and in Chapter 6.) The basic logic of hypothesis testing is summarized in Table 4–1, which also includes the logic for our example of a baby who is given a specially purified vitamin.

Summary of Steps of Hypothesis Testing

Here is a summary of the five steps of hypothesis testing.

❶ **Restate the question as a research hypothesis and a null hypothesis about the populations.**
❷ **Determine the characteristics of the comparison distribution.**
❸ **Determine the cutoff sample score on the comparison distribution at which the null hypothesis should be rejected.**
❹ **Determine your sample's score on the comparison distribution.**
❺ **Decide whether to reject the null hypothesis.**

A Second Example

Here is another fictional example. Two happy-go-lucky personality psychologists are examining the theory that happiness comes from positive experiences. In particular, these researchers argue that if people have something very fortunate happen to them, they become very happy and will still be happy 6 months later. So the researchers plan the following experiment: a person will be randomly selected from the North American adult public and given $10 million. Six months later, the person's happiness will be measured. It is already known (in this fictional example) what the distribution of happiness is like in the general population of North American adults, and this is shown in Figure 4–4. On the test being used, the mean happiness score is 70, the standard deviation is 10, and the distribution is approximately normal.

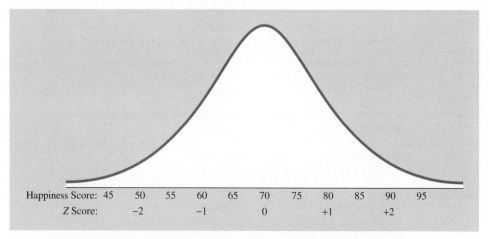

Happiness Score:	45	50	55	60	65	70	75	80	85	90	95
Z Score:		−2		−1		0		+1		+2	

Figure 4–4 Distribution of happiness sources (fictional data).

The psychologists now carry out the hypothesis-testing procedure. That is, the researchers consider how happy the person would have to be before they can confidently reject the null hypothesis that receiving so much money does *not* make people happier 6 months later. If the researchers' result shows a very high level of happiness, the psychologists will *reject* the null hypothesis and conclude that getting $10 million probably *does* make people happier 6 months later. But if the result is not very extreme, the researchers will conclude that there is not sufficient evidence to reject the null hypothesis, and the results of the experiment are inconclusive.

Now let us consider the hypothesis-testing procedure in more detail in this example, following the five steps.

❶ **Restate the question as a research hypothesis and a null hypothesis about the populations.** There are two populations of interest:

Population 1: People who 6 months ago received $10 million.
Population 2: The general population (consisting of people who 6 months ago did not receive $10 million).

The prediction of the personality psychologists, based on their theory of happiness, is that Population 1 people will on the average be happier than Population 2 people: in symbols, $\mu_1 > \mu_2$. The null hypothesis is that Population 1 people (those who get $10 million) will not be happier than Population 2 people (people in general who do not get $10 million).

❷ **Determine the characteristics of the comparison distribution.** The comparison distribution is the distribution that represents the population situation if the null hypothesis is true. If the null hypothesis is true, the distributions of Populations 1 and 2 are the same. We know Population 2's distribution (it is normally distributed with $\mu = 70$ and $\sigma = 10$); so we can use it as the comparison distribution.

❸ **Determine the cutoff sample score on the comparison distribution at which the null hypothesis should be rejected.** What kind of result would be extreme enough to convince us to reject the null hypothesis? In this example, assume that the researchers decided the following in advance: they will reject the null hypothesis as too unlikely if the results would occur less than 5% of the time if this null hypothesis were true. We know that the comparison distribution is a normal curve. Thus, we can figure that the top 5% of scores from the normal curve table begin at a Z score of about 1.64. Thus the researchers set as the cutoff point for rejecting the null hypothesis a result in which the sample's Z score on the comparison distribution is at or above 1.64. (The mean of the comparison distribution is 70 and the standard deviation is 10. Therefore, the null hypothesis will be rejected if the sample result is at or above 86.4.)

❹ **Determine your sample's score on the comparison distribution.** Now for the results: six months after giving the randomly selected person $10 million, the now very wealthy research participant takes the happiness test. The person's score is 80. As you can see from Figure 4–4, a score of 80 has a Z score of +1 on the comparison distribution.

❺ **Decide whether to reject the null hypothesis.** The Z score of the sample individual is +1. The researchers set the minimum Z score to reject the null hypothesis at +1.64. Thus, the sample score is not extreme enough to reject the null hypothesis. The experiment is inconclusive; researchers would say the results are "not statistically significant." Figure 4–5 shows the comparison distribution with the top 5% shaded and the location of the sample participant who received $10 million.

You may be interested to know that Brickman et al. (1978) carried out a more elaborate study based on the same question. They studied lottery winners as examples of people suddenly having a very positive event happen to them. Their results were similar to those in our fictional example: those who won the lottery were not much happier 6 months later than people who did not win the lottery. Also, another group they studied, people who had become paraplegics through a random accident, were not much less happy than other people 6 months later. These researchers concluded that if a major event does have a lasting effect on happiness, it is probably not a very big one. This conclusion is consistent with the findings of more recent studies (e.g., Suh et al., 1996). Indeed, in recent years, a great deal of research has examined what factors contribute to people's level of happiness. If you are interested in knowing more about this topic, we highly recommend an article by Diener and colleagues (2006) and social psychologist Daniel Gilbert's (2006) engaging best seller, *Stumbling on Happiness.*

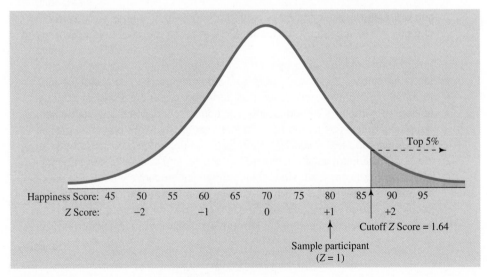

Figure 4–5 Distribution of happiness scores with upper 5% shaded and showing the location of the sample participant (fictional data).

How are you doing?

1. A sample of rats in a laboratory is given an experimental treatment intended to make them learn a maze faster than other rats. State (a) the null hypothesis and (b) the research hypothesis.
2. (a) What is a comparison distribution? (b) What role does it play in hypothesis testing?
3. What is the cutoff sample score?
4. Why do we say that hypothesis testing involves a double negative logic?
5. What can you conclude when (a) a result is so extreme that you reject the null hypothesis and (b) a result is not very extreme so that you cannot reject the null hypothesis?
6. A training program to increase friendliness is tried on one individual randomly selected from the general public. Among the general public (who do not get this training program), the mean on the friendliness measure is 30 with a standard deviation of 4. The researchers want to test their hypothesis at the 5% significance level. After going through the training program, this individual takes the friendliness measure and gets a score of 40. What should the researchers conclude?

Answers

1. (a) The population of rats like those that get the experimental treatment score the same on the time to learn the maze as the population of rats in general that do not get the experimental treatment. (b) The population of rats like those that get the experimental treatment learn the maze faster than the population of rats in general that do not get the experimental treatment.
2. (a) A comparison distribution is a distribution to which you compare the results of your study. (b) In hypothesis testing, the comparison distribution is the distribution for the situation when the null hypothesis is true. To decide whether to reject the null hypothesis, you check how extreme the score of your sample is on this comparison distribution—how likely it would be to get a score this extreme if your sample came from this comparison distribution.
3. The cutoff sample score is the Z score at which, if the sample's Z score is more extreme than it is on the comparison distribution, you reject the null hypothesis.
4. We say that hypothesis testing involves a double negative logic because we are interested in the research hypothesis, but we test whether it is true by seeing if we can reject its opposite, the null hypothesis.
5. (a) The research hypothesis is supported when a result is so extreme that you reject the null hypothesis; the result is statistically significant. (b) The result is not statistically significant when a result is not very extreme; the result is inconclusive.
6. The training program increases friendliness. (The cutoff sample Z score on the comparison distribution is 1.64. The actual sample's Z score of 2.50 is more extreme—that is, farther in the tail—than the cutoff Z score. Therefore, reject the null hypothesis; the research hypothesis is supported; the result is statistically significant.)

One-Tailed and Two-Tailed Hypothesis Tests

In our examples so far, the researchers were interested in only one direction of result. In our first example, researchers tested whether babies given the specially purified vitamin would walk *earlier* than babies in general. In the happiness example, the personality psychologists predicted the person who received $10 million would be *happier* than other people. The researchers in these studies were not interested in the possibility that giving the specially purified vitamin would cause babies to start walking *later* or that people getting $10 million might become *less* happy.

Directional Hypotheses and One-Tailed Tests

The purified vitamin and happiness studies are examples of testing a **directional hypothesis.** Both studies focused on a specific direction of effect. When a researcher makes a directional hypothesis, the null hypothesis is also, in a sense, directional. Suppose the research hypothesis is that getting $10 million will make a person happier than the general population. The null hypothesis, then, is that the money will either have no effect or make the person less happy. [In symbols, if the research hypothesis is $\mu_1 > \mu_2$, then the null hypothesis is $\mu_1 \leq \mu_2$ ("$\leq$" is the symbol for less than or equal to).] Thus, in Figure 4–5, to reject the null hypothesis, the sample has to have a score in one tail of the comparison distribution: the upper extreme or tail (in this example, the top 5%) of the comparison distribution. (When it comes to rejecting the null hypothesis with a directional hypothesis, a score at the other tail is the same as a score in the middle; that is, such a score does not allow you to reject the null hypothesis.) For this reason, the test of a directional hypothesis is called a **one-tailed test.** A one-tailed test can be one-tailed in either direction. In the happiness study example, the tail for the predicted effect was at the high end. In the baby study example, the tail for the predicted effect was at the low end (that is, the prediction tested was that babies given the specially purified vitamin would start walking unusually *early*).

Nondirectional Hypotheses and Two-Tailed Tests

Sometimes, a research hypothesis states that an experimental procedure will have an effect, without saying whether it will produce a very high score or a very low score. Suppose an organizational psychologist is interested in how a new social skills program will affect productivity. The program could either improve productivity by making the working environment more pleasant or hurt productivity by encouraging people to socialize instead of work. The research hypothesis is that the social skills program *changes* the level of productivity; the null hypothesis is that the program does not change productivity one way or the other. In symbols, the research hypothesis is $\mu_1 \neq \mu_2$ ("$\neq$" is the symbol for not equal); the null hypothesis is $\mu_1 = \mu_2$.

When a research hypothesis predicts an effect but does not predict a direction for the effect, it is called a **nondirectional hypothesis.** To test the significance of a nondirectional hypothesis, you have to consider the possibility that the sample could be extreme at either tail of the comparison distribution. Thus, this is called a **two-tailed test.**

directional hypothesis   research hypothesis predicting a particular direction of difference between populations—for example, a prediction that the population like the sample studied has a higher mean than the population in general.

one-tailed test   hypothesis-testing procedure for a directional hypothesis; situation in which the region of the comparison distribution in which the null hypothesis would be rejected is all on one side (tail) of the distribution.

nondirectional hypothesis   research hypothesis that does not predict a particular direction of difference between the population like the sample studied and the population in general.

two-tailed test   hypothesis-testing procedure for a nondirectional hypothesis; the situation in which the region of the comparison distribution in which the null hypothesis would be rejected is divided between the two sides (tails) of the distribution.

Determining Cutoff Scores with Two-Tailed Tests

There is a special complication in a two-tailed test. You have to divide the significance percentage between the two tails. For example, with a 5% significance level, you reject a null hypothesis only if the sample is so extreme that it is in either the top 2.5% or the bottom 2.5% of the comparison distribution. This keeps the overall level of significance at a total of 5%.

Note that a two-tailed test makes the cutoff Z scores for the 5% level +1.96 and −1.96. For a one-tailed test at the 5% level, the cutoff is not so extreme: only +1.64 or −1.64. But with a one-tailed test, only one side of the distribution is considered. These situations are shown in Figure 4–6a.

Using the 1% significance level, a two-tailed test (.5% at each tail) has cutoffs of +2.58 and −2.58, while a one-tailed test's cutoff is either +2.33 or −2.33. These situations are shown in Figure 4–6b. The Z score cutoffs for one-tailed and two-tailed tests for the .05 and .01 significance levels are also summarized in Table 4–2.

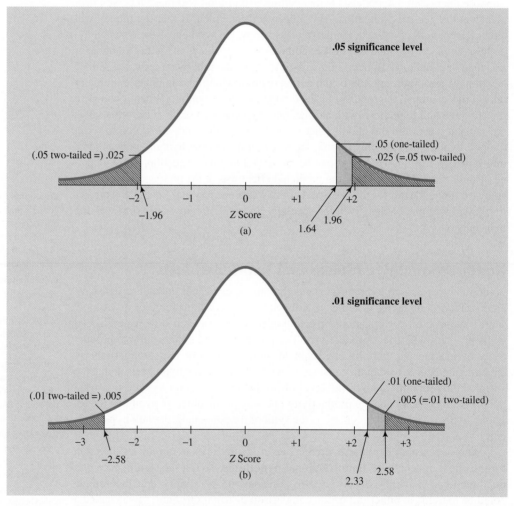

Figure 4–6 Significance level cutoffs for one-tailed and two-tailed tests: (a) .05 significance level; (b) .01 significance level. (The one-tailed tests in these examples assume the prediction was for a high score. You could instead have a one-tailed test where the prediction is for the lower, left tail.)

Table 4–2 One-Tailed and Two-Tailed Cutoff Z Scores for the .05 and .01 Significance Levels

		Type of Test	
		One-Tailed	Two-Tailed
Significance	*.05*	-1.64 *or* 1.64	-1.96 *and* 1.96
Level	*.01*	-2.33 *or* 2.33	-2.58 *and* 2.58

When to Use One-Tailed or Two-Tailed Tests

If the researcher decides in advance to use a one-tailed test, then the sample's score does not need to be so extreme to be significant compared to what would be needed with a two-tailed test. Yet there is a price. If the result is extreme in the direction opposite to what was predicted—no matter how extreme—the result cannot be considered statistically significant.

In principle, you plan to use a one-tailed test when you have a clearly directional hypothesis and a two-tailed test when you have a clearly nondirectional hypothesis. In practice, the decision is not so simple. Even when a theory clearly predicts a particular result, the actual result may come out opposite to what you expected. Sometimes, the opposite may be more interesting than what you had predicted. (For example, what if, as in all the fairy tales about wish-granting genies and fish, receiving $10 million and being able to fulfill almost any desire had made that individual miserable?) By using one-tailed tests, we risk having to ignore possibly important results.

For these reasons, researchers disagree about whether one-tailed tests should be used, even when there is a clearly directional hypothesis. To be safe, many researchers use two-tailed tests for both nondirectional and directional hypotheses. If the two-tailed test is significant, then the researcher looks at the result to see the direction and considers the study significant in that direction. In practice, always using two-tailed tests is a conservative procedure because the cutoff scores are more extreme for a two-tailed test and so it is less likely that a two-tailed test will give a significant result. Thus, if you do get a significant result with a two-tailed test, you are more confident about the conclusion. In fact, in most psychology research articles, unless the researcher specifically states that a one-tailed test was used, it is assumed that the test was two-tailed.

In practice, however, our experience is that most research results are either so extreme that they will be significant whether you use a one-tailed or two-tailed test or so far from extreme that they would not be significant in either kind of test. But what happens when a result is less certain? The researcher's decision about one- or two-tailed tests now can make a big difference. In this situation the researcher tries to use the type of test that will give the most accurate and noncontroversial conclusion. The idea is to let nature—not a researcher's decisions—determine the conclusion as much as possible. Further, whenever a result is less than completely clear one way or the other, most researchers are not comfortable drawing strong conclusions until more research is done.

Example of Hypothesis Testing with a Two-Tailed Test

Here is one more fictional example, this time using a two-tailed test. Clinical psychologists at a residential treatment center have developed a new type of therapy to reduce depression that they believe is more effective than the current therapy.

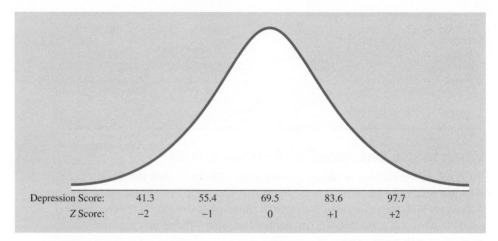

| Depression Score: | 41.3 | 55.4 | 69.5 | 83.6 | 97.7 |
| Z Score: | −2 | −1 | 0 | +1 | +2 |

Figure 4–7 Distribution of depression scores at 4 weeks after admission for diagnosed depressed psychiatric patients receiving the standard therapy (fictional data).

However, as with any treatment, it could make patients' depression worse. Thus, the clinical psychologists make a nondirectional hypothesis.

The psychologists randomly select an incoming patient to receive the new form of therapy instead of the usual therapy. (In a real study, of course, more than one patient would be selected, but let's assume that only one person has been trained to do the new therapy and she has time to treat only one patient.) After 4 weeks, the patient fills out a standard depression scale that is given automatically to all patients after 4 weeks. The standard scale has been given at this treatment center for a long time. Thus, the psychologists know in advance the distribution of depression scores at 4 weeks for those who receive the usual therapy: it follows a normal curve with a mean of 69.5 and a standard deviation of 14.1. [These figures correspond roughly to the depression scores found in a national survey of 75,000 psychiatric patients given a widely used standard test (Dahlstrom et al., 1986).] This distribution is shown in Figure 4–7.

The clinical psychologists then carry out the five steps of hypothesis-testing.

❶ **Restate the question as a research hypothesis and a null hypothesis about the populations.** There are two populations of interest:

Population 1: Patients diagnosed as depressed who receive the new therapy.
Population 2: Patients diagnosed as depressed in general (who receive the usual therapy).

The research hypothesis is that when measured on depression 4 weeks after admission, patients who receive the new therapy (Population 1) will on the average score differently from patients who receive the current therapy (Population 2).
In symbols, the research hypothesis is $\mu_1 \neq \mu_2$. The opposite of the research hypothesis, the null hypothesis, is that patients who receive the new therapy will have the same average depression level as the patients who receive the usual therapy. (That is, the depression level measured after 4 weeks will have the same mean for Populations 1 and 2.) In symbols, the null hypothesis is $\mu_1 = \mu_2$.

❷ **Determine the characteristics of the comparison distribution.** If the null hypothesis is true, the distributions of Populations 1 and 2 are the same. We know the distribution of Population 2 (it is the one shown in Figure 4–7). Thus, we can use Population 2 as our comparison distribution. As noted, it follows a normal curve, with $\mu = 69.5$ and $\sigma = 14.1$.

❸ **Determine the cutoff sample score on the comparison distribution at which the null hypothesis should be rejected.** The clinical psychologists select the 5% significance level. They have made a nondirectional hypothesis and will therefore use a two-tailed test. Thus, they will reject the null hypothesis only if the patient's depression score is in either the top or bottom 2.5% of the comparison distribution. In terms of Z scores, these cutoffs are $+1.96$ and -1.96 (see Figure 4–6 and Table 4–2).

❹ **Determine your sample's score on the comparison distribution.** The patient who received the new therapy was measured 4 weeks after admission. The patient's score on the depression scale was 41, which is a Z score on the comparison distribution of -2.02. That is, $Z = (X - M)/SD = (41 - 69.5)/14.1 = -2.02$. Figure 4–8 shows the distribution of Population 2 for this study, with the upper and lower 2.5% areas shaded; the depression score of the sample patient is also shown.

❺ **Decide whether to reject the null hypothesis.** A Z score of -2.02 is slightly more extreme than a Z score of -1.96, which is where the lower 2.5% of the comparison distribution begins. Notice in Figure 4–8 that the Z score of -2.02 falls within the shaded area in the left tail of the comparison distribution. This Z score of -2.02 is a result so extreme that it is unlikely to have occurred if this patient were from a population no different from Population 2. Therefore, the clinical psychologists reject the null hypothesis. The result is statistically significant, and it supports the research hypothesis that depressed patients receiving the new therapy have different depression levels than depressed patients in general who receive the usual therapy.

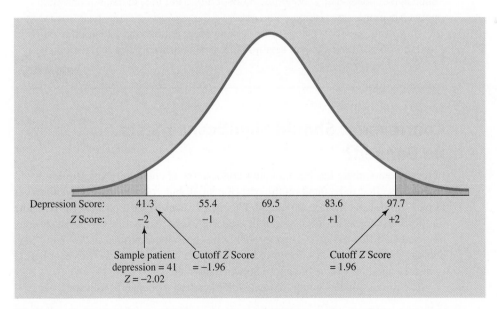

Figure 4–8 Distribution of depression scores with upper and lower 2.5% shaded and showing the sample patient who received the new therapy (fictional data).

How are you doing?

1. What is a nondirectional hypothesis test?
2. What is a two-tailed test?
3. Why do you use a two-tailed test when testing a nondirectional hypothesis?
4. What is the advantage of using a one-tailed test when your theory predicts a particular direction of result?
5. Why might you use a two-tailed test even when your theory predicts a particular direction of result?
6. A researcher predicts that making people hungry will affect how they do on a coordination test. A randomly selected person is asked not to eat for 24 hours before taking a standard coordination test and gets a score of 400. For people in general of this age group and gender, tested under normal conditions, coordination scores are normally distributed with a mean of 500 and a standard deviation of 40. Using the .01 significance level, what should the researcher conclude?

Answers

1. A nondirectional hypothesis test is a hypothesis test in which you do not predict a particular direction of difference.
2. A two-tailed test is one in which the overall percentage for the cutoff is divided between the two tails of the comparison distribution. A two-tailed test is used to test the significance of a nondirectional hypothesis.
3. You use a two-tailed test when testing a nondirectional hypothesis because an extreme result in either direction supports the research hypothesis.
4. The cutoff for a one-tailed test is not so extreme; thus, if your result comes out in the predicted direction, it is more likely to be significant. The cutoff is not so extreme because the entire percentage (say 5%) is put in one tail instead of being divided between two tails.
5. It lets you count as significant an extreme result in either direction; if you used a one-tailed test and the result came out opposite to the prediction, it could not be called statistically significant.
6. The cutoffs are +2.58 and −2.58. The sample person's Z score is $(400 − 500)/40 = −2.5$. The result is not significant; the study is inconclusive.

Controversy: Should Significance Tests Be Banned?

In recent years, there has been a major controversy about significance testing itself, with a concerted movement on the part of a small but vocal group of psychologists to ban significance tests completely! This is a radical suggestion with far-reaching implications: for at least half a century, nearly every research study in psychology has used significance tests. There probably has been more written in the major psychology journals in the last dozen years or so about this controversy than ever before in history about any issue having to do with statistics.

The discussion has gotten so heated that one article began as follows:

It is not true that a group of radical activists held 10 statisticians and six editors hostage at the . . . convention of the American Psychological Society and chanted, "Support the total test ban!" and "Nix the null!" (Abelson, 1997, p. 12)

Since this is by far the most important controversy in years regarding statistics as used in psychology, we discuss the issues in at least three different places. In this chapter we focus on some basic challenges to hypothesis testing. In Chapters 5 and 6, we cover other topics that relate to aspects of hypothesis testing that you will learn about in those chapters.

Before discussing this controversy, you should be reassured that you are not learning about hypothesis testing for nothing. Whatever happens in the future, you absolutely have to understand hypothesis testing to make sense of virtually every research article published in the past. Further, in spite of the controversy that has raged for more than a decade, it is extremely rare to see new articles that do not use significance testing. Thus, it is doubtful that any major shifts will occur in the near future. Finally, even if hypothesis testing is completely abandoned, the alternatives (which involve procedures you will learn about in Chapters 5 and 6) require understanding virtually all of the logic and procedures we are covering here.

So what is the big controversy? Some of the debate concerns subtle points of logic. For example, one issue relates to whether it makes sense to worry about rejecting the null hypothesis when a hypothesis of no effect whatsoever is extremely unlikely to be true. Another issue is about the foundation of hypothesis testing in terms of populations and samples, since in most experiments the samples we use are not randomly selected from any definable population. We discussed some points relating to this issue in Chapter 3. Finally, some have questioned the appropriateness of concluding that if the data are inconsistent with the null hypothesis, this should be counted as evidence for the research hypothesis. This controversy becomes rather technical, but our own view is that, given recent considerations of the issues, the way researchers in psychology use hypothesis testing is reasonable (Balluerka et al., 2005; Iacobucci, 2005; Nickerson, 2000).

However, the biggest complaint against significance tests, and the one that has received almost universal agreement, is that they are misused (Balluerka et al., 2005). In fact, opponents of significance tests argue that even if there were no other problems with the tests, they should be banned simply because they are so often and so badly misused. They are misused in two main ways: one we can consider now; the other must wait until we have covered a topic you learn in Chapter 6.

A major misuse of significance tests is the tendency for researchers to decide that if a result is not significant, the null hypothesis is shown to be true (see Box 4–1). We have emphasized that when you can't reject the null hypothesis, the results are simply inconclusive. The error of concluding the null hypothesis is true from failing to reject it is extremely serious, because important theories and methods may be considered false just because a particular study did not get strong enough results. [You learn in Chapter 6 that it is quite easy for a true research hypothesis not to come out significant just because there were too few people in the study or the measures were not very accurate. In fact, Hunter (1997) argues that in about 60% of psychology studies, we are likely to get nonsignificant results even when the research hypothesis is actually true.]

What should be done? The general consensus seems to be that we should keep significance tests, but better train our students not to misuse them (hence the emphasis on these points in this book). We should not, as it were, throw the baby out with the bathwater. To address this controversy, the American Psychological Association (APA) established a committee of eminent psychologists renowned for their statistical expertise. The committee met over a two-year period, circulated a preliminary report, and considered reactions to it from a large number of researchers. In the end, they strongly condemned various misuses of significance testing of the kind we have been discussing, but they left its use up to the decision of each researcher. In their report they concluded:

> Some had hoped that this task force would vote to recommend an outright ban on the use of significance tests in psychology journals. Although this might eliminate some abuses, the committee thought there were enough counterexamples (e.g., Abelson, 1997) to justify forbearance. (Wilkinson & Task Force on Statistical Inference, 1999, pp. 602–603)

Balluerka and colleagues (2005) reviewed the arguments for and against significance testing. Their conclusion, with which we agree (as do probably most psychology researchers), is that "...rigorous research activity requires the use of ... [significance testing] in the appropriate context, the complementary use of other methods which provide information about aspects not addressed by ... [significance testing], and adherence to a series of recommendations which promote its rational use in psychological research" (p. 55).

BOX 4–1   Jacob Cohen, the Ultimate New Yorker: Funny, Pushy, Brilliant, and Kind

New Yorkers can be proud of Jacob Cohen, who single-handedly introduced to behavioral and social scientists some of our most important statistical tools. Never worried about being popular—although he was—he almost single-handedly forced the current debate over significance testing, which he liked to joke was entrenched like a "secular religion." About the asterisk that accompanies a significant result, he said the religion must be "of Judeo-Christian derivation, as it employs as its most powerful icon a six-pointed cross" (1990, p. 1307).

Jacob entered graduate school at New York University (NYU) in clinical psychology in 1947 and three years later had a masters and a doctorate. He then worked in rather lowly roles for the Veterans Administration, doing research on various practical topics, until he returned to NYU in 1959. There he became a very famous faculty member because of his creative, offbeat ideas about statistics. Amazingly, he made his contributions having no mathematics training beyond high school algebra.

But a lack of formal training may have been Jacob Cohen's advantage because he emphasized looking at data and thinking about them, not just applying a standard analysis. In particular, he demonstrated that the standard methods were not working very well, especially for the "soft" fields of psychology such as clinical, personality, and social psychology. Many of his ideas were hailed as great breakthroughs. Starting in the 1990s he really began to force the issue of the mindless use of significance testing. But he still used humor to tease behavioral and social scientists for their failure to see the problems inherent in the arbitrary yes-no decision feature of null hypothesis testing. For example, he liked to remind everyone that significance testing came out of Sir Ronald Fisher's work in agriculture (see Box 9–1), in which the decisions were yes-no matters such as whether a crop needed manure. He pointed out that behavioral and social scientists "do not deal in manure, at least not knowingly" (Cohen, 1990, p. 1307)! He really disliked the fact that Fisher-style decision making is used to determine the fate of not only doctoral dissertations, research funds, publications, and promotions, "but whether to have a baby just now" (1990, p. 1307). And getting more serious, he charged that significance testing's "arbitrary unreasonable tyranny has led to data fudging of varying degrees of subtlety, from grossly altering data to dropping cases where there 'must have been' errors" (p. 1307).

Cohen was active in many social causes, especially desegregation in the schools and fighting discrimination in police departments. He cared passionately about everything he did. He was deeply loved. And he suffered from major depression, becoming incapacitated by it four times in his life.

Got troubles? Got no more math than high school algebra? It doesn't have to stop you from contributing to science.

Hypothesis Tests in Research Articles

In general, hypothesis testing is reported in research articles using one of the specific methods of hypothesis testing you learn in later chapters. For each result of interest, the researcher usually first indicates whether the result was statistically significant. (Note that, as with the first of the following examples, the researcher will not necessarily use the word *significant;* so look out for other indicators, such as reporting that scores on a variable decreased, increased, or were associated with scores on another variable.) Next, the researcher usually gives the symbol associated with the specific method used in figuring the probability that the result would have occurred if the null hypothesis was true, such as t, F, r, or χ^2 (see Chapters 7 to 13). Finally, there will be an indication of the significance level, such as $p < .05$ or $p < .01$. (The researcher will usually also provide other information, such as the mean and standard deviation of sample scores.) For example, in a study of competitive Scrabble players, Halpern and Wai (2007) reported: "Contrary to expectations, the number of correctly defined words correlated significantly with participants' official Scrabble rating, $r(21) = .45$, $p < .05$, showing a moderate relationship (Cohen & Cohen, 1983), with higher-rated players defining more words correctly." There is a lot here that you will learn about in later chapters, but the key thing to understand now about this result is the "$p < .05$." This means that the probability of the results if the null hypothesis were true is less than .05 (5%).

When a result is close but does not reach the significance level chosen, it may be reported anyway as a "near significant trend" or as having "approached significance." When a result is not even close to being extreme enough to reject the null hypothesis, it may be reported as "not significant," or the abbreviation *ns* will be used. Finally, whether or not a result is significant, it is increasingly common for researchers to report the exact p level, such as $p = .03$ or $p = .27$ (these are given in computer outputs of hypothesis testing results). The p reported here is based on the proportion of the comparison distribution that is more extreme than the sample score information that you could figure from the Z score for your sample and a normal curve table.

A researcher will usually note if he or she used a one-tailed test. When reading research articles, assume the researcher used a two-tailed test if nothing is said otherwise. Even though a researcher has chosen a significance level in advance, such as .05, the researcher may note that results meet more rigorous standards. Thus, in the same article, you may see some results noted as "$p < .05$," others as "$p < .01$," and still others as "$p < .001$."

Finally, often researchers show hypothesis testing results only as asterisks (stars) in a table of results. In such tables, a result with an asterisk means it is significant, while a result without an asterisk is not. For example, Table 4–3 shows the results of part of a study by Bohnert and colleagues (2007) comparing various aspects of social adjustment to college of male and female college students during the summer before their first year of college (Time 1) and 10 months later (Time 2). The table gives figures for means, standard deviations, and t statistics—the "$t(83)$" is about details of the specific hypothesis testing procedure used in this study called a t test, which you will learn in Chapters 7 and 8. The important things to look at now are the asterisks (and the notes at the bottom of the table that go with them). The asterisks tell you the significance levels for the various comparisons. For example, females had a higher level of friendship quality at Time 1 ($M = 2.82$) than males ($M = 2.49$); thus there are three asterisks at the end of the row for this result, which the note at the bottom tells you means that the probability of getting this big a difference

Table 4-3 Means and Standard Deviation for Main Study Variables by Gender

	Total (n = 85)		Males (n = 31)		Females (n = 54)		
	M	**SD**	**M**	**SD**	**M**	**SD**	**t(83)**
Adolescence (Time 1)							
Friendship quality	2.70	0.40	2.49	0.46	2.82	0.32	13.98***
Loneliness	36.39	8.71	39.30	9.98	34.78	7.56	5.47*
Emerging adulthood (Time 2)							
Friendship quality	3.10	0.48	2.84	0.57	3.21	0.38	11.31***
Loneliness	35.84	9.98	37.88	11.38	34.71	9.21	1.76
Activities: Intensity	8.09	8.27	10.00	10.19	7.18	7.18	0.98
Activities: Breadth	1.71	1.06	1.84	1.18	1.65	1.01	0.51

$*p < .05. **p < .01. ***p < .001.$

Source: Bohnert, A. M., Aikins, J. W., & Edidin, J. (2007). The role of organized activities in facilitating social adaptation across the transition to college. *Journal of Adolescent Research, 22,* 189–208. Sage Publications, Ltd. Reprinted by permission of Sage Publications, Thousands Oaks, London, and New Delhi.

if the null hypothesis was true is less than one in a thousand (.001). At Time 1, males reported being more lonely ($M = 39.30$) than females ($M = 34.78$), but you can see that there was no significant gender difference in loneliness at Time 2 (the means were 37.88 and 34.71, and the lack of an asterisk in this row indicates that these were not different enough to be significant in this study). At Time 2, females again reported a significantly higher level of friendship quality ($M = 3.21$) than males ($M = 2.84$); the asterisks show that the difference was significant at the .001 (one in a thousand) level.

In reporting results of significance testing, researchers rarely talk explicitly about the research hypothesis or the null hypothesis, nor do they describe any of the other steps of the process in detail. It is assumed that readers of psychology research understand all of this very well.

Summary

1. Hypothesis testing considers the probability that the result of a study could have come about even if the experimental procedure had no effect. If this probability is low, the scenario of no effect is rejected and the hypothesis behind the experimental procedure is supported.
2. The expectation of an effect is the research hypothesis, and the hypothetical situation of no effect is the null hypothesis.
3. When a result (that is, a sample score) is so extreme that the result would be very unlikely if the null hypothesis were true, the researcher rejects the null hypothesis and describes the research hypothesis as supported. If the result is not that extreme, the researcher does not reject the null hypothesis, and the study is inconclusive.
4. Psychologists usually consider a result too extreme if it is less likely than 5% (that is, a significance level of $p < .05$) to have come about if the null hypothesis were true. Psychologists sometimes use a more stringent 1% ($p < .01$ significance level), or even .1% ($p < .001$ significance level), cutoff.

5. The cutoff percentage is the probability of the result being extreme in a predicted direction in a directional or one-tailed test. The cutoff percentages are the probability of the result being extreme in either direction in a nondirectional or two-tailed test.

6. The five steps of hypothesis testing are:

   ❶ **Restate the question as a research hypothesis and a null hypothesis about the populations.**

   ❷ **Determine the characteristics of the comparison distribution.**

   ❸ **Determine the cutoff sample score on the comparison distribution at which the null hypothesis should be rejected.**

   ❹ **Determine your sample's score on the comparison distribution.**

   ❺ **Decide whether to reject the null hypothesis.**

7. There has been much controversy about significance tests, including critiques of the basic logic and, especially, that they are often misused. One major way researchers misuse significance tests is by interpreting not rejecting the null hypothesis as demonstrating that the null hypothesis is true.

8. Research articles typically report the results of hypothesis testing by saying a result was or was not significant and giving the probability level cutoff (usually 5% or 1%) that the decision was based on.

Key Terms

hypothesis testing (p. 107)
hypothesis (p. 107)
theory (p. 107)
research hypothesis (p. 110)
null hypothesis (p. 110)

comparison distribution (p. 111)
cutoff sample score (p. 111)
conventional levels of significance
  ($p < .05, p < .01$) (p. 113)
statistically significant (p. 113)

directional hypothesis (p. 119)
one-tailed test (p. 119)
nondirectional hypothesis
  (p. 119)
two-tailed test (p. 119)

Example Worked-Out Problems

A randomly selected individual, after going through an experimental treatment, has a score of 27 on a particular measure. The scores of people in general on this measure are normally distributed with a mean of 19 and a standard deviation of 4. The researcher predicts an effect, but does not predict a particular direction of effect. Using the 5% significance level, what should you conclude? Solve this problem explicitly using all five steps of hypothesis testing and illustrate your answer with a sketch showing the comparison distribution, the cutoff (or cutoffs), and the score of the sample on this distribution.

Answer

❶ **Restate the question as a research hypothesis and a null hypothesis about the populations.** There are two populations of interest:

Population 1: People who go through the experimental procedure.
Population 2: People in general (that is, people who do not go through the experimental procedure).

The research hypothesis is that Population 1 will score differently than Population 2 on the particular measure. The null hypothesis is that the two populations are not different on the measure.

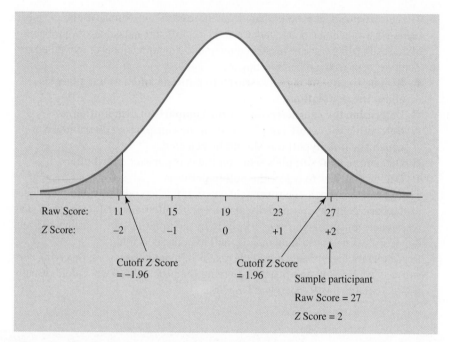

Figure 4–9   Diagram for Example Worked-Out Problem showing comparison distribution, cutoffs (2.5% shaded area in each tail), and sample score.

❷ **Determine the characteristics of the comparison distribution:** $\mu = 19$, $\sigma = 4$, normally distributed.

❸ **Determine the cutoff sample score on the comparison distribution at which the null hypothesis should be rejected.** For a two-tailed test at the 5% level (2.5% at each tail), the cutoff scores are $+1.96$ and -1.96 (see Figure 4–6 or Table 4–2).

❹ **Determine your sample's score on the comparison distribution.** $Z = (27 - 19)/4 = 2$.

❺ **Decide whether to reject the null hypothesis.** A Z score of 2 is more extreme than the cutoff Z of ± 1.96. Reject the null hypothesis; the result is significant. The experimental procedure affects scores on this measure. The diagram is shown in Figure 4–9.

Outline for Writing Essays for Hypothesis-Testing Problems Involving a Single Sample of One Participant and a Known Population

1. Describe the core logic of hypothesis testing. Be sure to explain terminology such as research hypothesis and null hypothesis, and explain the concept of providing support for the research hypothesis when the study results are strong enough to reject the null hypothesis.

2. Explain the concept of the comparison distribution. Be sure to mention that it is the distribution that represents the population situation if the null hypothesis is true. Note that the key characteristics of the comparison distribution are its mean, standard deviation, and shape.

3. Describe the logic and process for determining (using the normal curve) the cut-off sample scores on the comparison distribution at which you should reject the null hypothesis.
4. Describe how to figure the sample's score on the comparison distribution.
5. Explain how and why the scores from Steps ❸ and ❹ of the hypothesis-testing process are compared. Explain the meaning of the result of this comparison with regard to the specific research and null hypotheses being tested.

Practice Problems

These problems involve figuring. Most real-life statistics problems are done on a computer with special statistical software. Even if you have such software, do these problems by hand to ingrain the method in your mind.

All data are fictional unless an actual citation is given.

Set I (for Answers to Set I Problems, see pp. 675–677)

1. Define the following terms in your own words: (a) hypothesis-testing procedure, (b) .05 significance level, and (c) two-tailed test.
2. When a result is not extreme enough to reject the null hypothesis, explain why it is wrong to conclude that your result supports the null hypothesis.
3. For each of the following, (a) say which two populations are being compared, (b) state the research hypothesis, (c) state the null hypothesis, and (d) say whether you should use a one-tailed or two-tailed test and why.
   i. Do Canadian children whose parents are librarians score higher than Canadian children in general on reading ability?
   ii. Is the level of income for residents of a particular city different from the level of income for people in the region?
   iii. Do people who have experienced an earthquake have more or less self-confidence than the general population?
4. Based on the information given for each of the following studies, decide whether to reject the null hypothesis. For each, give (a) the Z-score cutoff (or cutoffs) on the comparison distribution at which the null hypothesis should be rejected, (b) the Z score on the comparison distribution for the sample score, and (c) your conclusion. Assume that all populations are normally distributed.

Study	Population μ	σ	Sample Score	p	Tails of Test
A	10	2	14	.05	1 (high predicted)
B	10	2	14	.05	2
C	10	2	14	.01	1 (high predicted)
D	10	2	14	.01	2
E	10	4	14	.05	1 (high predicted)

5. Based on the information given for each of the following studies, decide whether to reject the null hypothesis. For each, give (a) the Z-score cutoff (or cutoffs) on the comparison distribution at which the null hypothesis should be rejected, (b) the Z score on the comparison distribution for the sample score, and (c) your conclusion. Assume that all populations are normally distributed.

Study	Population μ	σ	Sample Score	p	Tails of Test
A	70	4	74	.05	1 (high predicted)
B	70	1	74	.01	2
C	70	2	76	.01	2
D	72	2	77	.01	2
E	72	2	68	.05	1 (low predicted)

6. A psychologist studying the senses of taste and smell has carried out many studies in which students are given each of 20 different foods (apricot, chocolate, cherry, coffee, garlic, and so on). She administers each food by dropping a liquid on the tongue. Based on her past research, she knows that for students overall at the university, the mean number of the 20 foods that students can identify correctly is 14, with a standard deviation of 4, and the distribution of scores follows a normal curve. The psychologist wants to know whether people's accuracy on this task has more to do with smell than with taste. In other words, she wants to test whether people do *worse* on the task when they are only able to taste the liquid compared to when they can both taste and smell it (note that this is a directional hypothesis). Thus, she sets up special procedures that keep a person from being able to use the sense of smell during the task. The psychologist then tries the procedure on one randomly selected student. This student is able to identify only 5 correctly. (a) Using the .05 significance level, what should the psychologist conclude? Solve this problem explicitly using all five steps of hypothesis testing and illustrate your answer with a sketch showing the comparison distribution, the cutoff (or cutoffs), and the score of the sample on this distribution. (b) Then explain your answer to someone who has never had a course in statistics (but who is familiar with mean, standard deviation, and Z scores).

7. A psychologist is working with people who have had a particular type of major surgery. This psychologist proposes that people will recover from the operation more quickly if friends and family are in the room with them for the first 48 hours after the operation. It is known that time to recover from this kind of surgery is normally distributed with a mean of 12 days and a standard deviation of 5 days. The procedure of having friends and family in the room for the period after the surgery is tried with a randomly selected patient. This patient recovers in 18 days. (a) Using the .01 significance level, what should the researcher conclude? Solve this problem explicitly using all five steps of hypothesis testing, and illustrate your answer with a sketch showing the comparison distribution, the cutoff (or cutoffs), and the score of the sample on this distribution. (b) Then explain your answer to someone who has never had a course in statistics (but who is familiar with mean, standard deviation, and Z scores).

8. What is the effect of going through a natural disaster on the attitude of police chiefs about the goodness of the people in their city? A researcher studying this expects a more positive attitude (because of the many acts of heroism and helping of neighbors), but a more negative attitude is also possible (because of looting and scams). It is known that, using a 1-to-10 scale (from 1 = extremely negative attitude to 10 = extremely positive attitude), in general police chiefs' attitudes about the goodness of the people in their cities is normally distributed,

with a mean of 6.5 and a standard deviation of 2.1. A major earthquake has just occurred in an isolated city, and shortly afterward the researcher is able to give the attitude questionnaire to the police chief of that city. The chief's score is 8.2. (a) Using the .05 significance level, what should the researcher conclude? Solve this problem explicitly using all five steps of hypothesis testing and illustrate your answer with a sketch showing the comparison distribution, the cutoff (or cutoffs), and the score of the sample on this distribution. (b) Then explain your answer to someone who has never had a course in statistics (but who is familiar with mean, standard deviation, and Z scores).

9. Robins and John (1997) carried out a study on narcissism (self-love), comparing people who scored high versus low on a narcissism questionnaire. (An example item was, "If I ruled the world it would be a better place.") They also had other questionnaires, including one that had an item about how many times the participant looked in the mirror on a typical day. In their results section, the researchers noted "... as predicted, high-narcissism individuals reported looking at themselves in the mirror more frequently than did low narcissism individuals (Ms = 5.7 vs. 4.8), ... $p < .05$" (p. 39). Explain this result to a person who has never had a course in statistics. (Focus on the meaning of this result in terms of the general logic of hypothesis testing and statistical significance.)

10. Reber and Kotovsky (1997), in a study of problem solving, described one of their results comparing a specific group of participants within their overall control condition as follows: "This group took an average of 179 moves to solve the puzzle, whereas the rest of the control participants took an average of 74 moves, $t(19) = 3.31, p < .01$" (p. 183). Explain this result to a person who has never had a course in statistics. (Focus on the meaning of this result in terms of the general logic of hypothesis testing and statistical significance.)

Set II

11. List the five steps of hypothesis testing, and explain the procedure and logic of each.

12. When a result is significant, explain why it is wrong to say the result "proves" the research hypothesis.

13. For each of the following, (a) state which two populations are being compared, (b) state the research hypothesis, (c) state the null hypothesis, and (d) say whether you should use a one-tailed or two-tailed test and why.

   i. In an experiment, people are told to solve a problem by focusing on the details. Is the speed of solving the problem different for people who get such instructions compared to the speed for people who are given no special instructions?

   ii. Based on anthropological reports in which the status of women is scored on a 10-point scale, the mean and standard deviation across many cultures are known. A new culture is found in which there is an unusual family arrangement. The status of women is also rated in this culture. Do cultures with the unusual family arrangement provide higher status to women than cultures in general?

   iii. Do people who live in big cities develop more stress-related conditions than people in general?

14. Based on the information given for each of the following studies, decide whether to reject the null hypothesis. For each, give (a) the Z-score cutoff (or cutoffs) on the comparison distribution at which the null hypothesis should be rejected, (b) the Z score on the comparison distribution for the sample score, and (c) your conclusion. Assume that all populations are normally distributed.

Study	Population μ	σ	Sample Score	p	Tails of Test
A	5	1	7	.05	1 (high predicted)
B	5	1	7	.05	2
C	5	1	7	.01	1 (high predicted)
D	5	1	7	.01	2

15. Based on the information given for each of the following studies, decide whether to reject the null hypothesis. For each, give (a) the Z-score cutoff (or cutoffs) on the comparison distribution at which the null hypothesis should be rejected, (b) the Z score on the comparison distribution for the sample score, and (c) your conclusion. Assume that all populations are normally distributed.

Study	Population μ	σ	Sample Score	p	Tails of Test
A	100.0	10.0	80	.05	1 (low predicted)
B	100.0	20.0	80	.01	2
C	74.3	11.8	80	.01	2
D	16.9	1.2	80	.05	1 (low predicted)
E	88.1	12.7	80	.05	2

16. A researcher wants to test whether a certain sound will make rats do worse on learning tasks. It is known that an ordinary rat can learn to run a particular maze correctly in 18 trials, with a standard deviation of 6. (The number of trials to learn this maze is normally distributed.) The researcher now tries an ordinary rat in the maze, but with the sound. The rat takes 38 trials to learn the maze. (a) Using the .05 level, what should the researcher conclude? Solve this problem explicitly using all five steps of hypothesis testing, and illustrate your answer with a sketch showing the comparison distribution, the cutoff (or cutoffs), and the score of the sample on this distribution. (b) Then explain your answer to someone who has never had a course in statistics (but who is familiar with mean, standard deviation, and Z scores).

17. A family psychologist developed an elaborate training program to reduce the stress of childless men who marry women with adolescent children. It is known from previous research that such men, one month after moving in with their new wife and her children, have a stress level of 85 with a standard deviation of 15, and the stress levels are normally distributed. The training program is tried on one man randomly selected from all those in a particular city who during the preceding month have married a woman with an adolescent child. After the training program, this man's stress level is 60. (a) Using the .05 level, what should the researcher conclude? Solve this problem explicitly using all five steps of hypothesis testing and illustrate your answer with a sketch showing the comparison distribution, the cutoff (or cutoffs), and the score of the sample on this distribution. (b) Then explain your answer to someone who has never had a course in statistics (but who is familiar with mean, standard deviation, and Z scores).

18. A researcher predicts that listening to music while solving math problems will make a particular brain area more active. To test this, a research participant has her brain scanned while listening to music and solving math problems, and the brain area of interest has a percentage signal change of 58. From many previous studies with this same math problems procedure (but not listening to music), it is known that the signal change in this brain area is normally distributed with a mean of 35 and a standard deviation of 10. (a) Using the .01 level, what should the researcher conclude? Solve this problem explicitly using all five steps of hypothesis testing, and illustrate your answer with a sketch showing the comparison distribution, the cutoff (or cutoffs), and the score of the sample on this distribution. (b) Then explain your answer to someone who has never had a course in statistics (but who is familiar with mean, standard deviation, and Z scores).

19. Pecukonis (1990), as part of a larger study, measured ego development (a measure of overall maturity) and ability to empathize with others among a group of 24 aggressive adolescent girls in a residential treatment center. The girls were divided into high- and low-ego development groups, and the empathy ("cognitive empathy") scores of these two groups were compared. In his results section, Pecukonis reported, "The average score on cognitive empathy for subjects scoring high on ego development was 22.1 as compared with 16.3 for low scorers, ... $p < .005$" (p. 68). Explain this result to a person who has never had a course in statistics. (Focus on the meaning of this result in terms of the general logic of hypothesis testing and statistical significance.)

20. In an article about antitobacco campaigns, Siegel and Biener (1997) discuss the results of a survey of tobacco usage and attitudes, conducted in Massachusetts in 1993 and 1995; Table 4–4 shows the results of this survey. Focusing on just

Table 4-4   Selected Indicators of Change in Tobacco Use, ETS Exposure, and Public Attitudes toward Tobacco Control Policies—Massachusetts, 1993–1995

	1993	1995
Adult Smoking Behavior		
Percentage smoking >25 cigarettes daily	24	10*
Percentage smoking <15 cigarettes daily	31	49*
Percentage smoking within 30 minutes of waking	54	41
Environmental Tobacco Smoke Exposure		
Percentage of workers reporting a smoke free worksite	53	65*
Mean hours of ETS exposure at work during prior week	4.2	2.3*
Percentage of homes in which smoking is banned	41	51*
Attitudes Toward Tobacco Control Policies		
Percentage supporting further increase in tax on tobacco with funds earmarked for tobacco control	78	81
Percentage believing ETS is harmful	90	84
Percentage supporting ban on vending machines	54	64*
Percentage supporting ban on support of sports and cultural events by tobacco companies	59	53*

* $p < .05$
Source: Siegel, M., & Biener, L. (1997). Evaluating the impact of statewide anti-tobacco campaigns: The Massachusetts and California tobacco control programs. *Journal of Social Issues, 53,* 147–168. Copyright © 1997 by Blackwell Publishing. Reprinted by permission of Blackwell Publishers Journals.

the first line (the percentage smoking >25 cigarettes daily), explain what this result means to a person who has never had a course in statistics. (Focus on the meaning of this result in terms of the general logic of hypothesis testing and statistical significance.)

Chapter Notes

1. We are oversimplifying a bit to make the initial learning easier. The research hypothesis is that one population will walk earlier than the other, $\mu_1 < \mu_2$. Thus, to be precise, its opposite is that the other group will either walk at the same time or later. That is, the opposite of the research hypothesis in this example includes both no difference and a difference in the direction opposite to what we predicted. In terms of symbols, if our research hypothesis is $\mu_1 < \mu_2$, then its opposite is $\mu_1 \geq \mu_2$ (the symbol "$\geq$" means "greater than or equal to"). We discuss this issue in some detail later in the chapter.

2. In practice, since hypothesis testing is usually done on a computer, you have to decide in advance only on the cutoff probability. The computer prints out the exact probability of getting your result if the null hypothesis were true. You then just compare the printed-out probability to see if it is less than the cutoff probability level you set in advance. However, to *understand* what these probability levels mean, you need to learn the entire process, including how to figure the Z score for a particular cutoff probability.

CHAPTER 5

Hypothesis Tests with Means of Samples

Chapter Outline

- The Distribution of Means   138
- Hypothesis Testing with a Distribution of Means: The *Z* Test   146
- Controversy: Marginal Significance   153
- Hypothesis Tests About Means of Samples (*Z* Tests) and Standard Errors in Research Articles   154
- Advanced Topic: Estimation, Standard Errors, and Confidence Intervals   156
- Advanced Topic Controversy: Confidence Intervals versus Significance Tests   162
- Advanced Topic: Confidence Intervals in Research Articles   163
- Summary   163
- Key Terms   164
- Example Worked-Out Problems   164
- Practice Problems   167
- Chapter Notes   173

In Chapter 4, we introduced the basic logic of hypothesis testing. The studies we used as examples had a sample of a single individual. As we noted, however, in actual practice, psychology research almost always involves a sample of many individuals. In this chapter, we build on what you have learned so far and consider hypothesis testing with a sample of more than one individual. For example, a social psychologist is interested in the potential effect of perceptions of people's personality on perceptions of their physical attractiveness. The researcher's theory predicts that, if a you are told that a person has positive personality qualities (such as kindness, warmth, a sense of humor, and intelligence), you will rate that person as more attractive than if no mention had been made of the person's personality qualities. From extensive previous research (in which no mention was made of personality qualities), the researcher has established the population mean and standard deviation of the attractiveness rating of a photo of a particular person. The researcher then recruits a sample of 64 individuals to rate the attractiveness of the person in the photograph. However, prior to rating the person, each individual is told that the person whose photograph they are going to rate has many positive personality qualities. In this chapter, you will learn how to test hypotheses in situations such as those presented in this example, situations in which the population has a *known mean and standard deviation* and in which a sample has *more than one individual.* Mainly, this requires examining in some detail a new kind of distribution, called a "distribution of means." (We will return to this example later in the chapter.)

The Distribution of Means

Hypothesis testing in the usual research situation, where you are studying a sample of many individuals, is exactly the same as you learned in Chapter 4—with an important exception. When you have more than one person in your sample, there is a special problem with Step ❷, determining the characteristics of the comparison distribution. In each of our examples so far, the comparison distribution has been a distribution of *individual scores* (such as the population of ages when individual babies start walking). A distribution of individual scores has been the correct comparison distribution because we have used examples with a sample of *one individual.* That is, there has been consistency between the type of sample score we have been dealing with (a score from *one individual*) and the comparison distribution (a distribution of *individual scores*).

Now, consider the situation when you have a sample of, say, 64 individuals (as in the attractiveness rating example). You now have a *group of 64 scores* (an attractiveness rating from each of the 64 people in the study). As you will recall from Chapter 2, the mean is a very useful representative value of a group of scores. Thus, the score you care about when there is more than one individual in your sample is the *mean of the group of scores.* In this example, you would focus on the mean of the 64 individuals' scores. If you were to compare the mean of this sample of 64 individuals' scores to a distribution of a population of individual scores, this would be a mismatch—like comparing apples to oranges. *Instead, when you are interested in the mean of a sample of 64 scores, you need a comparison distribution that is a distribution of means of samples of 64 scores.* We call such a comparison distribution a **distribution of means.** So, the scores in a distribution of means are *means,* not scores of individuals.

A distribution of means is a distribution of the means of each of lots and lots of samples of the same size, with each sample randomly taken from the same population of individuals. (Statisticians also call this distribution of means a *sampling distribution of the mean.* In this book, however, we use the term *distribution of means* to keep it clear that we are talking about populations of *means,* not samples or some kind of distribution of samples.)

The distribution of means is the correct comparison distribution when there is more than one person in a sample. Thus, in most research situations, determining the characteristics of a distribution of means is necessary for Step ❷ of the hypothesis-testing procedure, determining the characteristics of the comparison distribution.

Building a Distribution of Means

To help you understand the idea of a distribution of means, we consider how you could build up such a distribution from an ordinary population distribution of individual scores. Suppose our population of individual scores was of the grade levels of the

distribution of means distribution of means of samples of a given size from a population (also called a *sampling distribution of the mean*); comparison distribution when testing hypotheses involving a single sample of more than one individual.

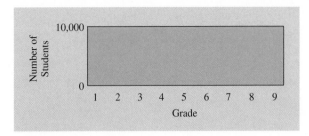

Figure 5–1 Distribution of grade levels among 90,000 schoolchildren (fictional data).

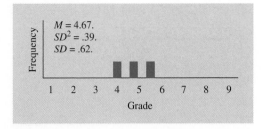

Figure 5–2 Distribution of the means of three randomly taken samples of two schoolchildren's grade levels each from a population of grade levels of 90,000 schoolchildren (fictional data).

90,000 elementary and junior-high schoolchildren in a particular region. Suppose further (to keep the example simple) that there are exactly 10,000 children at each grade level, from first through ninth grade. This population distribution would be rectangular, with a mean of 5, a variance of 6.67, and a standard deviation of 2.58 (see Figure 5–1).

Next, suppose that you wrote each child's grade level on a table tennis ball and put all 90,000 balls into a giant tub. The tub would have 10,000 balls with a 1 on them, 10,000 with a 2 on them, and so forth. You stir up the balls in the tub and then take two of them out. You have taken a random sample of two balls. Suppose one ball has a 2 on it and the other has a 9 on it. The mean grade level of this sample of two children's grade levels is 5.5, the average of 2 and 9. Now you put the balls back, mix up all the balls, and select two balls again. Maybe this time you get two 4s, making the mean of your second sample 4. Then you try again; this time you get a 2 and a 7, making your mean 4.5. So far you have three means: 5.5, 4, and 4.5.

Each of these three numbers is a mean of a sample of grade levels of two school children. And these three means can be thought of as a small distribution in its own right. The mean of this little distribution of means is 4.67 (the sum of 5.5, 4, and 4.5, divided by 3). The variance of this distribution of means is .39 (the variance of 5.5, 4, and 4.5). The standard deviation of this distribution of means is .62 (the square root of .39). A histogram of this distribution of three means is shown in Figure 5–2.

Suppose you continued selecting samples of two balls and taking the mean of the numbers on each pair of balls. The histogram of means would continue to grow. Figure 5–3 shows examples of distributions of means varying from a sample with just 50 means, up to a sample with 1,000 means (with each mean being of a sample of two randomly drawn balls). (We actually made the histograms shown in Figure 5–3 using a computer to make the random selections instead of using 90,000 table tennis balls and a giant tub.)

As you can imagine, the method we just described is not a practical way of determining the characteristics of a distribution of means. Fortunately, however, you can figure out the characteristics of a distribution of means directly, using some simple rules, without taking even one sample. The only information you need is (a) the characteristics of the distribution of the population of individuals and (b) the number of scores in each sample. (Don't worry for now about how you could know the characteristics of the population of individuals.) The laborious method of building up a distribution of means in the way we have just considered and the concise method you will learn shortly give the same result. We have had you think of the process in terms of the painstaking method only because it helps you understand the idea of a distribution of means.

TIP FOR SUCCESS

Before moving on to later chapters, be sure you fully understand the idea of a distribution of means (and why it is the correct comparison distribution when a sample contains more than one individual). You may need to go through this chapter a couple of times to achieve full understanding of this crucial concept.

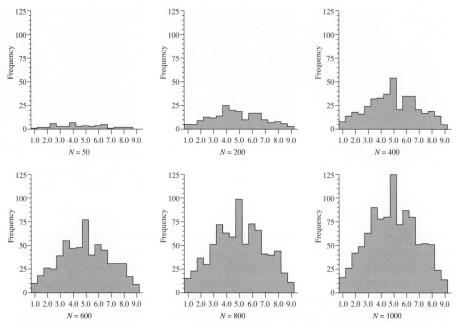

Figure 5–3 Histograms of means of two grade levels randomly selected from a large group of students with equal numbers of grades 1 through 9. Histograms are shown for 50 such means, 200 such means, 400 such means, 600 such means, 800 such means, and 1,000 such means. Notice that the histograms become increasingly like a normal curve as the number of means increases.

Determining the Characteristics of a Distribution of Means

Recall that Step ❷ of hypothesis testing involves determining the characteristics of the comparison distribution. The three key characteristics of the comparison distribution that you need to determine are:

1. Its mean.
2. Its spread (which you can measure using the variance and standard deviation).
3. Its shape.

Notice three things about the distribution of means we built in our example, as shown in Figure 5–3:

1. The mean of the distribution of means is about the same as the mean of the original population of individuals (both are 5).
2. The spread of the distribution of means is less than the spread of the distribution of the population of individuals.
3. The shape of the distribution of means is approximately normal.

The first two observations, regarding the mean and the spread, are true for all distributions of means. The third, regarding the shape, is true for most distributions of means. These three observations, in fact, illustrate three basic rules you can use to find the mean, the spread (that is, variance and standard deviation), and the shape of any distribution of means without having to write on plastic balls and take endless samples.

Now let's look at the three rules more closely. The first is for the **mean of a distribution of means.**

mean of a distribution of means the mean of a distribution of means of samples of a given size from a population; the same as the mean of the population of individuals.

Rule 1: The mean of a distribution of means is the same as the mean of the population of individuals. Stated as a formula,

$$\mu_M = \mu \qquad \qquad \textbf{(5–1)}$$

> The mean of a distribution of means is equal to the mean of the population of individuals.

μ_M is the mean of the distribution of means (it uses a Greek letter because the distribution of means is also a kind of population). μ is the mean of the population of individuals.

Each sample is based on randomly selected individuals from the population of individuals. Thus, the mean of a sample will sometimes be higher and sometimes lower than the mean of the whole population of individuals. However, because the selection process is random and we are taking a very large number of samples, eventually the high means and the low means perfectly balance each other out.

In Figure 5–3, as the number of sample means in the distributions of means increases, the mean of the distribution of means becomes more similar to the mean of the population of individuals, which in this example was 5. It can be proven mathematically that, if you took an infinite number of samples, the mean of the distribution of means of these samples would come out to be exactly the same as the mean of the distribution of individuals.

The second rule is about spread. Rule 2a is for the **variance of a distribution of means.**

Rule 2a: The variance of a distribution of means is the variance of the population of individuals divided by the number of individuals in each sample. A distribution of means will be less spread out than the distribution of individuals from which the samples are taken. If you are taking a sample of two scores, it is less likely that *both* scores will be extreme. Further, for a particular random sample to have an extreme mean, the two extreme scores would both have to be extreme in the same direction (both very high or both very low). Thus, having more than a single score in each sample has a moderating effect on the mean of such samples. In any one sample, the extremes tend to be balanced out by a middle score or by an extreme in the opposite direction. This makes each sample mean tend toward the middle and away from extreme values. With fewer extreme means, the variance of the means is less than the variance of the population of individuals.

Consider again our example. There were plenty of 1s and 9s in the population, making a fair amount of spread. That is, about a ninth of the time, if you were taking samples of single scores, you would get a 1 and about a ninth of the time you would get a 9. If you are taking samples of two at a time, you would get a sample with a mean of 1 (that is, in which *both* balls were 1s) or a mean of 9 (both balls 9s) much less often. Getting two balls that average out to a middle value such as 5 is much more likely. (This is because several combinations could give this result—1 and 9, 2 and 8, 3 and 7, 4 and 6, or two 5s).

The more individuals in each sample, the less spread out will be the means of the samples. This is because, the more scores in each sample, the rarer it will be for extremes in any particular sample not to be balanced out by middle scores or extremes in the other direction. In terms of the table tennis balls in our example, we rarely got a mean of 1 when taking samples of two balls at a time. If we were taking three balls at a time, getting a sample with a mean of 1 (all three balls would have to be 1s) is even less likely. Getting middle values for the means becomes even more likely.

Using samples of two balls at a time, the variance of the distribution of means came out to about 3.34. This is half of the variance of the population of individuals, which was 6.67. If we had built up a distribution of means using samples of three

μ_M mean of a distribution of means.

variance of a distribution of means variance of the population divided by the number of scores in each sample.

balls each, the variance of the distribution of means would have been 2.22. This is one-third of the variance of our population of individuals. Had we randomly selected five balls for each sample, the variance of the distribution of means would have been one-fifth of the variance of the population of individuals.

These examples follow a general rule—our Rule 2a for the distribution of means: the variance of a distribution of means is the variance of the population of individuals divided by the number of individuals in each of the samples. This rule holds in all situations and can be proven mathematically.

Here is Rule 2a stated as a formula:

$$\sigma_M^2 = \frac{\sigma^2}{N} \tag{5-2}$$

> The variance of a distribution of means is the variance of the population of individuals divided by the number of individuals in each sample.

σ_M^2 is the variance of the distribution of means (it uses a Greek letter because the distribution of means is also a kind of population). σ^2 is the variance of the population of individuals, and N is the number of individuals in each sample.

In our example, the variance of the population of individual children's grade levels was 6.67, and there were two children's grade levels in each sample. Thus,

$$\sigma_M^2 = \frac{\sigma^2}{N} = \frac{6.67}{2} = 3.34$$

To use a different example, suppose a population had a variance of 400 and you wanted to know the variance of a distribution of means of 25 individuals each:

$$\sigma_M^2 = \frac{\sigma^2}{N} = \frac{400}{25} = 16$$

The second rule also tells us about the **standard deviation of a distribution of means.**

Rule 2b: The standard deviation of a distribution of means is the square root of the variance of the distribution of means.   Stated as a formula,

$$\sigma_M = \sqrt{\sigma_M^2} = \sqrt{\frac{\sigma^2}{N}} \tag{5-3}$$

> The standard deviation of a distribution of means is the square root of the variance of the distribution of means and also the square root of the result of dividing the variance of the population of individuals by the number of individuals in each sample.

σ_M is the standard deviation of the distribution of means.[1]

The standard deviation of the distribution of means also has a special name of its own, the **standard error of the mean (SEM)**, or the **standard error (SE)**, for short. (Thus, σ_M also stands for the standard error.) It has this name because it tells you how much the means of samples are typically "in error" as estimates of the mean of the population of individuals. That is, it tells you how much the various means in the distribution of means deviate from the mean of the population. We have more to say about the standard error later in the chapter.

Finally, the third rule for finding the characteristics of a distribution of means focuses on its shape.

σ_M^2 variance of a distribution of means.

standard deviation of a distribution of means   square root of the variance of a distribution of means; also called *standard error of the mean (SEM)* and *standard error (SE).*

σ_M standard deviation of a distribution of means.

standard error of the mean (SEM)   same as *standard deviation of a distribution of means;* also called *standard error (SE).*

standard error (SE)   same as *standard deviation of a distribution of means;* also called *standard error of the mean (SEM).*

Rule 3: The shape of a distribution of means is approximately normal if either (a) each sample is of 30 or more individuals or (b) the distribution of the population of individuals is normal.   Whatever the shape of the distribution of the population of individuals, the distribution of means tends to be unimodal and symmetrical. In the grade-level example, the population distribution was rectangular.

(It had an equal number at each value.) However, the shape of the distribution of 1,000 sample means (see Figure 5–3) was roughly that of a bell—unimodal and symmetrical. Had we taken many more than 1,000 samples, the shape would have been even more clearly unimodal and symmetrical.

A distribution of means tends to be unimodal because of the same basic process of extremes balancing each other out that we noted in the discussion of the variance: middle scores for means are more likely, and extreme means are less likely. A distribution of means tends to be symmetrical because a lack of symmetry (skew) is caused by extremes. With fewer extremes, there is less asymmetry. In our grade-level example, the distribution of means we built up also came out so clearly symmetrical because the population distribution of individual grade levels was symmetrical. Had the population distribution of individuals been skewed to one side, the distribution of means would have still been skewed, but not as much.

The more individuals in each sample, the closer the distribution of means will be to a normal curve. Although the distribution of means will rarely be an exactly normal curve, with samples of 30 or more individuals (even with a nonnormal population of individuals), the approximation of the distribution of means to a normal curve is very close and the percentages in the normal curve table will be extremely accurate.[2,3] (That is, samples that are larger than 30 make for even slightly better approximations, but for most practical research purposes, the approximation with 30 is quite good enough.) Finally, whenever the population distribution of individuals is normal, the distribution of means will be normal, regardless of the number of individuals in each sample.

Summary of Rules and Formulas for Determining the Characteristics of a Distribution of Means

Rule 1: The mean of a distribution of means is the same as the mean of the population of individuals:

$$\mu_M = \mu$$

Rule 2a: The variance of a distribution of means is the variance of the population of individuals divided by the number of individuals in each sample:

$$\sigma_M^2 = \frac{\sigma^2}{N}$$

Rule 2b: The standard deviation of a distribution of means is the square root of the variance of the distribution of means:

$$\sigma_M = \sqrt{\sigma_M^2} = \sqrt{\frac{\sigma^2}{N}}$$

Rule 3: The shape of a distribution of means is approximately normal if either (a) each sample is of 30 or more individuals or (b) the distribution of the population of individuals is normal. Figure 5–4 shows these three rules graphically.

These three rules are based on the *central limit theorem,* a fundamental principle in mathematical statistics we mentioned in Chapter 3. A notable strength of the central limit theorem is that it provides the key characteristics (central tendency, variability, and shape) of a distribution of means for a population with a distribution *of any shape.*

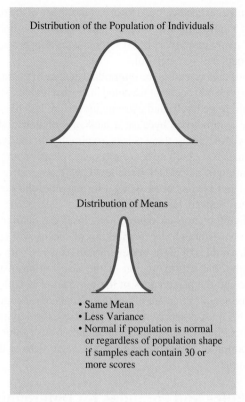

Figure 5–4 Comparing the distribution of the population of individuals (upper curve) and the distribution of means (lower curve).

Example of Determining the Characteristics of a Distribution of Means

Think back to the example from the start of the chapter in which students rated the attractiveness of a person in a photograph. Consider the population of students' ratings of the person in the photograph (when students are told nothing about the personality characteristics of the person in the photograph). Suppose the distribution is approximately normal with a mean of 200 and a standard deviation of 48. What will be the characteristics of the distribution of means for samples of 64 students?

Rule 1: The mean of a distribution of means is the same as the mean of the population of individuals. The mean of the population is 200. Thus, the mean of the distribution of means will also be 200. That is, $\mu_M = \mu = 200$.

Rule 2a: The variance of a distribution of means is the variance of the population of individuals divided by the number of individuals in each sample. The standard deviation of the population of individuals is 48; thus, the variance of the population of individuals is 48^2, which is 2,304. The variance of the distribution of means is therefore 2,304 divided by 64 (the size of the sample). This comes out to 36. That is, $\sigma_M^2 = \sigma^2/N = 2{,}304/64 = 36$.

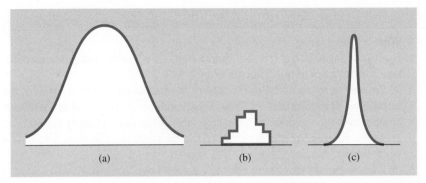

Figure 5–5   Three kinds of distributions: (a) the distribution of a population of individuals, (b) the distribution of a particular sample taken from that population, and (c) the distribution of means.

Rule 2b: The standard deviation of a distribution of means is the square root of the variance of the distribution of means.   The standard deviation of the distribution of means is the square root of 36, which is 6. That is, $\sigma_M = \sqrt{\sigma_M^2} = \sqrt{36} = 6$.

Rule 3: The shape of a distribution of means is approximately normal if either (a) each sample is of 30 or more individuals or (b) the distribution of the population of individuals is normal.   Our situation meets both of these conditions—the sample of 64 students is more than 30, and the population of individuals follows a normal distribution. Thus, the distribution of means will follow a normal curve. (It would have been enough even if only one of the two conditions had been met.)

Review of the Three Kinds of Distributions

We have considered three kinds of distributions: (1) the distribution of a population of individuals, (2) the distribution of a particular sample of individuals from that population, and (3) the distribution of means. Figure 5–5 shows these three kinds of distributions graphically and Table 5–1 describes them.

Table 5–1   Comparison of Three Types of Distributions

	Population's Distribution	Particular Sample's Distribution	Distribution of Means
Content	Scores of all individuals in the population	Scores of the individuals in a single sample	Means of samples randomly taken from the population
Shape	Could be any shape; often normal	Could be any shape	Approximately normal if samples have ≥ 30 individuals in each or if population is normal
Mean	μ	$M = (\Sigma X)/N$	$\mu_M = \mu$
Variance	σ^2	$SD^2 = [\Sigma(X - M)^2]/N$	$\sigma_M^2 = \sigma^2/N$
Standard deviation	σ	$SD = \sqrt{SD^2}$	$\sigma_M = \sqrt{\sigma_M^2}$

TIP FOR SUCCESS

Be sure you fully understand the different types of distribution shown in Table 5–1 before you move on to later chapters. To check your understanding, cover up portions of the table and then try to recall the hidden information.

How are you doing?

1. What is a distribution of means?
2. Explain how you could create a distribution of means by taking a large number of samples of four individuals each.
3. (a) Why is the mean of the distribution of means the same as the mean of the population of individuals? (b) Why is the variance of a distribution of means smaller than the variance of the distribution of the population of individuals?
4. Write the formula for the variance of the distribution of means, and define each of the symbols.
5. (a) What is the standard error? (b) Why does it have this name?
6. A population of individuals that follows a normal curve has a mean of 60 and a standard deviation of 10. What are the characteristics of a distribution of means from this population for samples of four each?

Answers

1. A distribution of means is a distribution of the means of a very large number of samples of the same size taken randomly from a population of individuals.
2. Take a random sample of four from the population and figure its mean. Do this a very large number of times. Make a distribution of these means.
3. (a) With randomly taken samples, some will have higher means and some lower means than those of the population of individuals; these should balance out. (b) You are less likely to get a sample of several scores with an extreme mean than you are to get a single extreme score. This is because in any random sample it is highly unlikely to get several extremes in the same direction; extreme scores tend to be balanced out by middle scores or extremes in the opposite direction. Thus, with fewer extreme scores and more middle scores, there is less variance.
4. The formula for the variance of the distribution of means is $\sigma_M^2 = \sigma^2/N$. σ_M^2 is the variance of the distribution of means; σ^2 is the variance of the population of individuals; N is the number of individuals in your sample.
5. (a) The standard error is the standard deviation of the distribution of means. (b) It has this name because it tells you about how much the means of samples typically (standardly) differ from the population mean, and thus the typical amount that the means of samples are in error as estimates of the population mean.
6. The characteristics of a distribution of means for samples of four are as follows: $\mu_M = \mu = 60$; $\sigma_M^2 = \sigma^2/N = 10^2/4 = 25$; $\sigma_M = 5$; shape = normal.

Hypothesis Testing with a Distribution of Means: The Z Test

Now we are ready to turn to hypothesis testing when there is more than one individual in the study's sample. The hypothesis testing procedure you will learn is called a Z test.

The Distribution of Means as the Comparison Distribution in Hypothesis Testing

In the usual research situation, a psychologist studies a sample of more than one person. In this situation, the distribution of means is the comparison distribution. It is the distribution whose characteristics need to be determined in Step ❷ of the

BOX 5–1   **More About Polls: Sampling Errors and Errors in Thinking About Samples**

If you think back to Box 3–3 on surveys and the Gallup poll, you will recall that we left two important questions unanswered about fine print included with the results of a poll, saying something like, "From a telephone poll of 1,000 American adults taken on June 4 and 5. Sampling error ±3%." First, you might wonder how such small numbers, like 1,000 (but rarely much less), can be used to predict the opinion of the entire U.S. population. Second, after working through the material in this chapter on the standard deviation of the distribution of means, you may wonder what the term *sampling error* means when a sample is not randomly sampled but rather selected by the complicated probability method used for polls.

Regarding sample size, you know from this chapter that large sample sizes, like 1,000, greatly reduce the standard deviation of the distribution of means. That is, the curve becomes very high and narrow, gathered all around the population mean. The mean of any sample of that size is very close to being the population mean.

When a sample is only a small part of a very large population, the sample's *absolute size* is the only determiner of accuracy. This absolute size determines the impact of the random errors of measurement and selection. What remains important is reducing bias or systematic error, which can be done only by careful planning.

As for the term *sampling error,* it is worked out according to past experience with the sampling procedures used. It is given in tables for different sample sizes (usually below 1,000, because that is where error increases dramatically).

So the number of people polled is not very important (provided that it is at least 1,000 or so), but what matters very much are the methods of sampling and estimating error, which will not be reported in the detail necessary to judge whether the results are reliable. The reputation of the organization doing the survey is probably the best criterion. If the sampling and error-estimating approach is not revealed at all, be cautious. For more information about how polls are conducted, go to   *http://media.gallup.com/PDF/FAQ/HowArePolls.pdf* (note that sampling error is referred to as "margin of error" on the Web site).

hypothesis-testing process. The distribution of means is the distribution to which you compare your sample's mean to see how likely it is that you could have selected a sample with a mean that is extreme *if the null hypothesis were true.*

Figuring the *Z* Score of a Sample's Mean on the Distribution of Means

There can be some confusion in figuring the location of your sample on the comparison distribution in hypothesis testing with a sample of more than one. In this situation, you are finding a *Z* score of your sample's mean on a distribution of means. (Before, you were finding the *Z* score of a single individual on a distribution of a population of single individuals.) The method of changing the sample's mean to a *Z* score is the same as the usual way of changing a raw score to a *Z* score. However, you have to be careful not to get mixed up because more than one mean is involved. It is important to remember that you are treating the sample mean like a single score. Recall that the ordinary formula (from Chapter 3) for changing a raw score to a *Z* score is $Z = (X - M)/SD$. In the present situation, you are actually using the following formula:

$$Z = \frac{M - \mu_M}{\sigma_M} \qquad (5\text{–}4)$$

> The Z score for the sample's mean on the distribution of means is the sample's mean minus the mean of the distribution of means, divided by the standard deviation of the distribution of means.

For example, suppose your sample's mean is 18 and the distribution of means has a mean of 10 and a standard deviation of 4. The *Z* score of this sample mean is +2. Using the formula,

$$Z = \frac{M - \mu_M}{\sigma_M} = \frac{18 - 10}{4} = \frac{8}{4} = 2$$

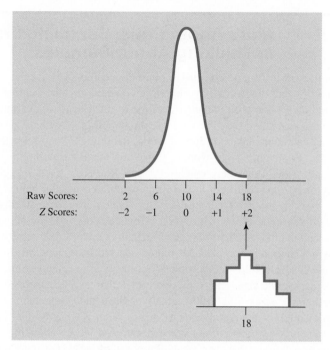

Raw Scores: 2   6   10   14   18
Z Scores: −2 −1   0   +1   +2

18

Figure 5-6 *Z* score for the mean of a particular sample on the distribution of means.

This is shown in Figure 5–6.

The hypothesis test you are learning in this chapter is called a **Z test,** because you figure the Z score for your sample's mean.

Example

Let's return again to our example in which a social psychologist is interested in whether being told a person has positive personality qualities increases ratings of the physical attractiveness of that person. The psychologist asks 64 randomly selected students to rate the attractiveness of a particular person in a photograph. Prior to rating the attractiveness of the person, each student is told that the person has positive personality qualities (kindness, warmth, a sense of humor, and intelligence). On a scale of 0 (the lowest possible attractiveness) to 400 (the highest possible attractiveness), the mean attractiveness rating given by the 64 students is 220. From previous research, the psychologist knows that the attractiveness ratings of the person in the photograph (when no mention is made of the person's positive personality qualities) have a mean of 200 and a standard deviation of 48, and they follow an approximately normal distribution. This distribution is shown in Figure 5–7a.[4]

Now let's carry out the Z test by following the five steps of hypothesis testing you learned in Chapter 4:

❶ **Restate the question as a research hypothesis and a null hypothesis about the populations.** The two populations are these:

Population 1: Students who are told that the person has positive personality qualities.
Population 2: Students in general (who are told nothing about the person's personality qualities).

***Z* test** hypothesis-testing procedure in which there is a single sample and the population variance is known.

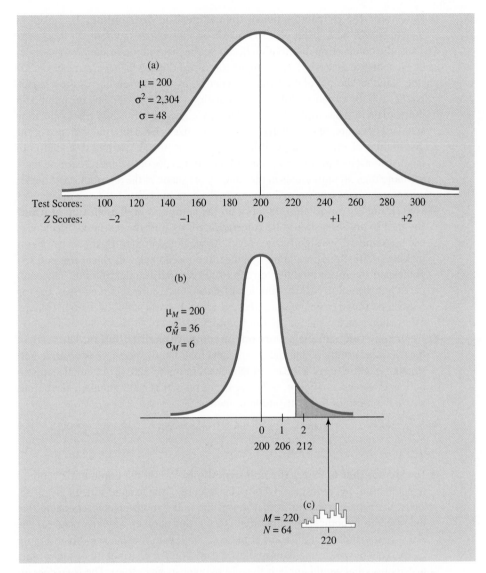

Figure 5-7 For the fictional study of positive personality qualities and ratings of physical attractiveness, (a) the distribution of the population of individuals, (b) the distribution of means (the comparison distribution), and (c) the sample's distribution. The shaded area in the distribution of means is the rejection region—the area in which the null hypothesis will be rejected if the study's sample mean turns out to be in that area.

The research hypothesis is that the population of students who are told that the person has positive personality qualities will on the average give higher attractiveness scores for that person than the population of students who are told nothing about the person's personality qualities: $\mu_1 > \mu_2$. The null hypothesis is that Population 1's scores will not on the average be higher than Population 2's: $\mu_1 \leq \mu_2$. Note that these are directional hypotheses. The researcher wants to know if being told that the person has positive personality qualities will increase attractiveness scores; a result in the opposite direction would not be relevant to the theory the researcher is testing.

❷ **Determine the characteristics of the comparison distribution.** The result of the study will be a mean of a sample of 64 individuals (students in this case). Thus, the comparison distribution has to be the distribution of means of samples of 64 individuals each. This comparison distribution will have a mean of 200 (the same as the population mean). That is, as we saw earlier in the chapter, $\mu_M = 200$. Its variance will be the population variance divided by the number of individuals in the sample. The population variance, σ^2, is 2,304 (the population standard deviation of 48 squared); the sample size is 64. Thus, the variance of the distribution of means, σ_M^2, will be 2,304/64, or 36. The standard deviation of the distribution of means, σ_M, is the square root of 36, or 6. Finally, because there are more than 30 individuals in the sample, the shape of the distribution of means will be approximately normal. Figure 5–7b shows this distribution of means.

❸ **Determine the cutoff sample score on the comparison distribution at which the null hypothesis should be rejected.** Let's assume the researcher decides to use the standard 5% significance level. As we noted in Step ❶, the researcher is making a directional prediction. Hence, the researcher will reject the null hypothesis if the result is in the top 5% of the comparison distribution. The comparison distribution (the distribution of means) is a normal curve. Thus, the top 5% can be found from the normal curve table. It starts at a Z of +1.64. This top 5% is shown as the shaded area in Figure 5–7b.

❹ **Determine your sample's score on the comparison distribution.** The result of the (fictional) study is that the 64 students told that the person has positive personality qualities gave a mean attractiveness rating of 220. (This sample's distribution is shown in Figure 5–7c.) A mean of 220 is 3.33 standard deviations above the mean of the distribution of means:

$$Z = \frac{M - \mu_M}{\sigma_M} = \frac{220 - 200}{6} = \frac{20}{6} = 3.33$$

❺ **Decide whether to reject the null hypothesis.** We set the minimum Z score to reject the null hypothesis to +1.64. The Z score of the sample's mean is +3.33. Thus, the social psychologist can reject the null hypothesis and conclude that the research hypothesis is supported. To put this another way, the result of the Z test is statistically significant at the $p < .05$ level. You can see this in Figure 5–7b. Note how extreme the sample's mean is on the distribution of means (the distribution that would apply if the null hypothesis were true). The final conclusion is that, among students, being told that a person has positive personality qualities does increase the attractiveness ratings of that person. (Results of actual studies show this effect, as well as showing that if you have heard negative information about a person, you then rate them as less physically attractive; e.g., Lewandowski, Aron, & Gee, 2007.)

A Second Example

Suppose a researcher wants to test the effect of a communication skills seminar on students' use of verbal fillers during a presentation. Verbal fillers are words such as "um," "uh," and "you know," that people commonly use in conversations and when giving presentations. The researcher conducts a study in which 25 students attend a communication skills seminar and then give a half-hour presentation on a topic of their choice. The presentations are tape-recorded and a research assistant later counts the number of verbal fillers used by each student during his or her presentation. In this fictional example, we assume that the researcher knows from previous studies that students typically use a mean of 53 verbal fillers during a half-hour presentation

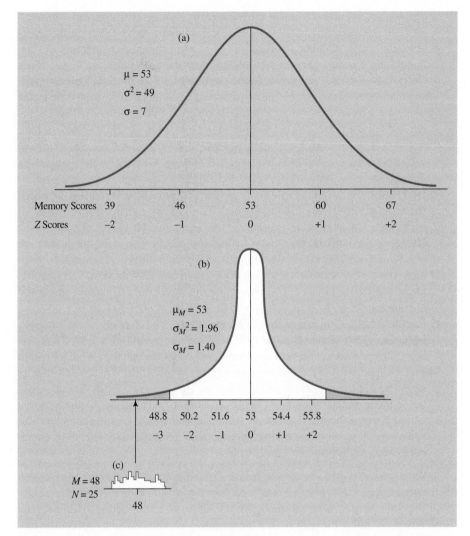

Figure 5–8   For the fictional study of the use of verbal filters in a presentation, (a) the distribution of the population of individuals, (b) the distribution of means (the comparison distribution), and (c) the sample's distribution. The shaded areas in the distribution of means are the rejection regions—the areas in which the null hypothesis will be rejected if the study's sample mean turns out to be in that area.

of this kind, with a standard deviation of 7, and the distribution of verbal fillers follows a normal curve (see Figure 5–8a). The 25 students who take the communication skills seminar use a mean of 48 verbal fillers. The researcher wants to carry out the Z test using the 1% significance level, and an effect in either direction would be important (that is, the researcher is interested in whether the communications seminar could increase or decrease the use of verbal fillers).

❶ **Restate the question as a research hypothesis and a null hypothesis about the populations.** The two populations are:

Population 1: Students who attend a communication skills seminar.
Population 2: Students in general (who do not attend a communication skills seminar).

The research hypothesis is that the population of students who attend a communication skills seminar will use a different number of verbal fillers during a presentation than students in general: $\mu_1 \neq \mu_2$. The null hypothesis is that Population 1's scores are on the average the same as Population 2's: $\mu_1 = \mu_2$.

❷ **Determine the characteristics of the comparison distribution.** This comparison distribution is a distribution of means. It has a mean of 53 (the same as the population mean). Its variance is the population variance divided by 25, the number of individuals in the sample: $\sigma_M^2 = \sigma^2/N = 7^2/25 = 49/25 = 1.96$; $\sigma_M = \sqrt{1.96} = 1.40$. Its shape is normal, since the population of individual verbal filler scores is normally distributed. (Figure 5–8b shows the comparison distribution.)

❸ **Determine the cutoff sample score on the comparison distribution at which the null hypothesis should be rejected.** This is a two-tailed test (the researcher is interested in an effect in either direction) at the overall 1% significance level. Based on the normal curve table for the top and bottom .5%, the cutoffs are +2.57 and −2.57 (see tiny shaded areas in Figure 5–8b).

❹ **Determine your sample's score on the comparison distribution.** The sample's mean was 48 (see Figure 5–8c). This comes out to a Z of −3.57 on the comparison distribution: $Z = (M - \mu_M)/\sigma_M = (48 - 53)/1.40 = -5/1.40 = -3.57$.

❺ **Decide whether to reject the null hypothesis.** The Z score of the sample's mean is −3.57, which is more extreme than the cutoffs of ±2.57. Thus, the researchers can reject the null hypothesis and conclude that the research hypothesis is supported. To put this another way, the result of the Z test is statistically significant at the $p < .01$ level. You can see this in Figure 5–8b. Note how extreme the sample's mean is on the distribution of means (the distribution that would apply if the null hypothesis were true). The final conclusion is that students' use of verbal fillers during a presentation decreases after attending a communication skills seminar.

When you next give a presentation, ask a friend to count the number of times you use verbal fillers (such as "um," "uh," and "you know"), or tape-record the presentation and count your own verbal fillers. Verbal fillers can be distracting to listeners and may adversely affect the quality of a presentation. Communications specialists recommend replacing verbal fillers with brief pauses (that allow you to gather your thoughts).

How are you doing?

1. How is hypothesis testing with a sample of more than one person different from hypothesis testing with a sample of a single person?
2. How do you find the Z score for the sample's mean on the distribution of means?
3. A researcher predicts that showing a certain film will change people's attitudes toward alcohol. The researchers then randomly select 36 people, show them the film, and give them an attitude questionnaire. The mean score on the attitude test for these 36 people is 70. The score for people in general on this test is 75, with a standard deviation of 12. Using the five steps of hypothesis testing and the 5% significance level, carry out a Z test to see if viewing the film changes people's attitudes toward alcohol.

Answers

1. In hypothesis testing with a sample of more than one person, the comparison distribution is a distribution of means.

2. You use the usual formula for changing a raw score to a Z score, but using the mean and standard deviation of the distribution of means. The formula is $Z = (M - \mu_M)/\sigma_M$.

3. ❶ Restate the question as a research hypothesis and a null hypothesis about the populations. The two populations are:

Population 1: People shown the film.
Population 2: People in general (who are not shown the film).

The research hypothesis is that the mean attitude of the population shown the film is different from the mean attitude of the population of people in general: $\mu_1 \neq \mu_2$. The null hypothesis is that the populations have the same mean attitude score: $\mu_1 = \mu_2$.

❷ Determine the characteristics of the comparison distribution. $\mu_M = \mu = 75$; $\sigma_M^2 = \sigma^2/N = 12^2/36 = 144/36 = 4$; $\sigma_M = 2$; shape is normal.

❸ Determine the cutoff sample score on the comparison distribution at which the null hypothesis should be rejected. Two-tailed cutoffs, 5% significance levels are $+1.96$ and -1.96.

❹ Determine your sample's score on the comparison distribution. $Z = (M - \mu_M)/\sigma_M = (70 - 75)/2 = -2.50$.

❺ Decide whether to reject the null hypothesis. The Z score of the sample's mean is -2.50, which is more extreme than -1.96; reject the null hypothesis. Seeing the film does change attitudes.

Controversy: Marginal Significance

A long-standing controversy regarding significance testing is what to do when a result does not make the cutoff value at the usual 5% level but comes very close (say, $p < .10$). This is often called "marginal significance," "approaching significance," or a "near significant trend." A couple of years ago, the controversy was spotlighted on an email listserv for social and personality psychologists. The discussion began when the following note was posted by Todd Nelson (California State University at Stanislaw):

> Throughout my ph.d. training...it was common parlance to refer to...P-values of between .05 and .10 as "marginally significant." It was a very common term in all the major social psychological journals...and among my professors.
>
> The other day, in a thesis defense I was chairing, I was dumfounded when the other thesis committee members strongly objected to the term "marginally significant" in the student's results section...both saying they had NEVER heard of the term (!).
>
> Wanting to make sure I was still on planet Earth, I consulted several statistics and research textbooks in my office, and found a few that referred to "marginal significance" and several articles by noted statisticians who make the case for discussing results in the .05–.10 range...
>
> [H]ave you heard of this term...? Do you use it and teach it? If so, why? If not, what is your objection?

Almost immediately there were more than 100 responses! First, it quickly became clear that calling results that are close "marginally significant" is indeed a common practice in many areas of psychology. As Frank LoSchiavo (Ohio University) put it, "It sounds like it is the other committee members who are not on Earth."

But it also became clear that while it may be fairly common, many think it is a bad idea. Charles Stangor (University of Maryland) called it a "completely bogus concept . . . used to make us poor scientists feel better when our results are close but no cigar." Tricia Yurak (Rowan University) called it "a fudge term that I won't use" adding that "even if I get a p value of .07, I will report it as not significant." Richard St. Jean (University of Prince Edward Island) recalls "one of my stats professors said calling a finding marginally significant is like calling a woman marginally pregnant! The principle is that it is an all or none decision . . ." David Washburn (Georgia State University) explains the logic: "One decides in advance or by convention to call $p < .05$ effects 'significant' . . . . [T]erms like 'marginally significant' are counterfactuals—like saying you 'almost did' something that you didn't do." As several of the email posts noted, the argument was spelled out in some detail in an article by Chet Insko (2003; University of North Carolina):

> . . . null-hypothesis testing depends on traditional two-valued logic. Thus, one either rejects or fails to reject the null hypothesis, and rejection of the null hypothesis allows for acceptance of the logical contradictory of the null hypothesis, the research hypothesis. The crucial point here is that deductive logic is two valued; for example, Socrates is or is not mortal. . . . A logician would not, for example, conclude that Socrates is marginally mortal. Since null-hypothesis testing depends on logic, only two-valued distinctions can be made, and this, of course, requires a single cut point to differentiate significant test statistics from nonsignificant test statistics. (p. 1331)

However, the majority opinion among those responding was expressed by Warren Thorngate (Carleton University): " . . . people who adhere to the '0.05 or nothing!' philosophy either need to be reeducated or enter therapy." Phoebe Ellsworth (University of Michigan) added that "to act as though there is a gulf between .05 and .06 is not maintaining high standards; it is idiocy." The point here is that .05 is an arbitrary convention. Indeed, many quoted a comment in an influential article by Rosnow and Rosenthal (1989) " . . . surely God loves the .06 nearly as much as the .05" (p. 1277). In addition, many noted that it is more important to emphasize the size of the effect and the power of the study, issues we consider in the next chapter. Also, several mentioned that such "near significant results" may be appropriate particularly when there are related results that are clearly significant (for example, if a study of the effects on stress is significant when using a questionnaire measure and is also near significant when using a physiological measure). Finally, quite a few people emphasized that the acceptability of reporting such results varies considerably among different specialty areas of psychology.

Hypothesis Tests About Means of Samples (*Z* Tests) and Standard Errors in Research Articles

As we have noted several times, research in which there is a known population mean and standard deviation is quite rare in psychology. Thus, you will not often see a Z test in a research article. We have asked you to learn about this situation mainly as a building block for understanding hypothesis testing in more common research situations. Still, Z tests do show up now and then.

Here is an example. As part of a larger study, Wiseman (1997) gave a loneliness test to a group of college students in Israel. As a first step in examining the results, Wiseman checked that the average score on the loneliness test was not significantly different from a known population distribution based on a large U.S.

study of university students that had been conducted earlier by Russell and colleagues (1980). Wiseman reported:

> . . . [T]he mean loneliness scores of the current Israeli sample were similar to those of Russell et al.'s (1980) university sample for both males (Israeli: $M = 38.74$, $SD = 9.30$; Russell: $M = 37.06$, $SD = 10.91$; $z = 1.09$, NS) and females (Israeli: $M = 36.39$, $SD = 8.87$; Russell: $M = 36.06$, $SD = 10.11$; $z = .25$, NS). (p. 291)

In this example, the researcher gives the standard deviation for both the sample studied (the Israeli group) and the population (the data from Russell). However, in the steps of figuring each Z (the sample's score on the distribution of means), the researcher would have used the standard deviation only of the population. Notice also that the researcher took the nonsignificance of the difference as support for the sample means being "similar" to the population means. However, the researcher was very careful not to claim that these results showed there was "no difference."

Of the topics we have covered in this chapter, the one you are most likely to see in a research article is the standard deviation of the distribution of means, used to describe the amount of variation that might be expected among means of samples of a given size from this population. In this context, it is usually called the *standard error* (*SE*) or *standard error of the mean* (*SEM*). Standard errors are typically shown in research articles as the lines that go above (and sometimes also below) the tops of the bars in a bar graph; these lines are called *error bars*. For example, Stankiewicz and colleagues (2006) examined how limitations in human perception and memory (and other factors) affect people's ability to find their way in indoor spaces. In one of their experiments, eight students used a computer keyboard to move through a virtual indoor space of corridors and hallways shown on a computer monitor. The researchers calculated how efficiently students moved through the space, with efficiency ranging from 0 (extremely inefficient) to 1 (extremely efficient). The researchers compared the efficiency of moving through the space when students had a limited view of the space versus when they had a clear (or unlimited) view of the space. Their results, shown in Figure 5–9, include error bars.

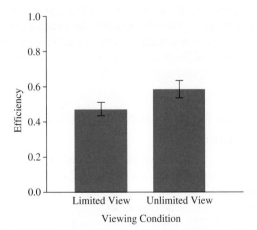

Figure 5–9   The mean navigation efficiency when navigating in the unlimited and limited viewing condition in Experiment 2. In the limited-view condition, visual information was available as far as the next intersection (further details were obscured by "fog"). In the unlimited-view condition, visual information was available to the end of the corridor. Error bars represent 1 standard error of the mean.

Source: Stankiewicz, B. J., Legge, G. E., Mansfield, J. S., & Schlicht, E. J. (2006). Lost in virtual space: Studies in human and ideal spatial navigation. *Journal of Experimental Psychology: Human Perception and Performance, 32,* 688–704. Copyright © 2006 by the American Psychological Association.

Error bars on graphs are common in psychology research articles, particularly in the more experimental areas such as perception and cognitive neuroscience.

Advanced Topic: Estimation, Standard Errors, and Confidence Intervals

Hypothesis testing is our main focus in this book. However, there is another kind of statistical question related to the distribution of means that is also important in psychology: estimating the population mean based on the scores in a sample. Traditionally, this has been very important in survey research. In recent years it is also becoming important in experimental research (e.g., Wilkinson and Task Force on Statistical Inference, 1999) and can even serve as an alternative approach to hypothesis testing.

Estimating the Population Mean When It Is Unknown

When the population mean is unknown, *the best estimate of the population mean is the sample mean.* In the study of students who were told about a person's positive personality qualities, the mean attractiveness rating given to that person by the sample of 64 students was 220. Thus, 220 is the best estimate of the mean attractiveness rating that would be given by the unknown population of students who would ever be told about a person's positive personality qualities.

How accurate is the sample mean as an estimate of the population mean? A way to get at this question is to ask, "How much do means of samples from a population vary?" Fortunately we have already thought about this question when considering the distribution of means. The variation in means of samples from a population is the variation in the distribution of means. The standard deviation of this distribution of means, the standard error of the mean, is thus a measure of how much the means of samples vary from the overall population mean. (As we noted earlier, just because researchers are often interested in using a mean of a sample to estimate the population mean, this variation in the distribution of means is thought of as "error" and we give the name "standard error of the mean" to the standard deviation of a distribution of means.)

In our example, the accuracy of our estimate of 220 for the mean of the population of students who are told about the person's positive personality qualities is the standard error, which we figured earlier to be 6.

Range of Possible Means Likely to Include the Population Mean

You can also estimate the *range* of possible means that are likely to include the population mean. Consider our estimate of 220 with a standard error of 6. Now follow this closely: suppose you took a mean from our distribution of means; it is 34% likely you would get a mean between 220 (the mean of the distribution of means) and 226 (one standard error above 220). This is because the distribution of means is a normal curve. Thus, the standard error is 1 standard deviation on that curve, and 34% of a normal curve is between the mean and 1 standard deviation above the mean. From this reasoning, we could also figure that another 34% should be between 220 and 214 (1 standard error below 220). Putting this together, we have a region from 214 to 226 that we are 68% confident should include the population mean if our sample was randomly taken from this population. (See Figure 5–10a.)

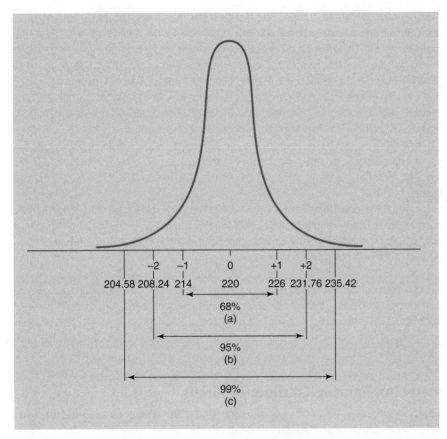

Figure 5-10   A distribution of means and the (a) 68%, (b) 95%, and (c) 99% confidence intervals for students rating the physical attractiveness of a person after being told that the person has positive personality qualities (fictional data).

This is an example of a **confidence interval** (usually abbreviated CI). We would call it the "68% confidence interval." The upper and lower ends of a confidence interval are called **confidence limits.** In this example, the confidence limits for the 68% confidence interval are 214 and 226 (see Figure 5–10a).

Let's review the logic: based on our knowledge of a sample's mean, we are trying to estimate the mean of the population that sample came from. Our best estimate of the population mean has to be our sample mean. What we don't know is how good an estimate it is. If sample means from that population could vary a lot, then we cannot be very confident that our estimate is close to the true population mean. But if the sample means are likely all to be very close to the true population mean, we can assume our estimate is pretty close. To get a sense of how accurate our estimate is, we can use our knowledge of the normal curve to estimate the *range* of possible means that are likely to include the population mean. This estimate of the range of means is called a confidence interval.

The 95% and 99% Confidence Intervals

Normally, you would want to be more than 68% confident about your estimates. Thus, when figuring confidence intervals, psychologists use 95% or even 99% confidence intervals. These are figured based on the distribution of means for the area

confidence interval (CI)   roughly speaking, the range of scores (that is, the scores between an upper and lower value) that is likely to include the true population mean; more precisely, the range of possible population means from which it is not highly unlikely that you could have obtained your sample mean.

confidence limit   upper or lower value of a confidence interval.

that includes the middle 95% or middle 99%. For the **95% confidence interval,** you want the area in a normal curve on each side between the mean and the Z score that includes 47.5% (47.5% plus 47.5% adds up to 95%). The normal curve table shows this to be 1.96. Thus, in terms of Z scores, the 95% confidence interval is from -1.96 to $+1.96$ on the distribution of means. Changing these Z scores to raw scores for the attractiveness ratings example gives an interval of 208.24 to 231.76 (see Figure 5–10b). That is, for the lower confidence limit, $(-1.96)(6) + 220 = -11.76 + 220 = 208.24$; for the upper confidence limit, $(1.96)(6) + 220 = 11.76 + 220 = 231.76$. In sum, based on the sample of 64 students who were told about the person's positive personality qualities, you can be 95% confident that the true population mean for such students is between 208.24 and 231.76 (see Figure 5–10b).

For a **99% confidence interval,** you use the Z scores for the middle 99% of the normal curve (the part that includes 49.5% above and below the mean). This comes out to ± 2.57. Changing this to raw scores, the 99% confidence interval is from 204.58 to 235.42 (see Figure 5–10c).

Notice in Figure 5–10 that the greater the confidence is, the broader is the confidence interval. In our example, you could be 68% confident that the true population mean is between 214 and 226; but you could be 95% confident that it is between 208.24 and 231.76 and 99% confident it is between 204.58 and 235.42. This is a general principle. It makes sense that you need a wider range of possibility to be more sure you are right.

Steps for Figuring Confidence Limits

There are two steps for figuring confidence limits. These steps assume that the distribution of means is approximately a normal distribution.

❶ **Figure the standard error.** That is, find the standard deviation of the distribution of means in the usual way:

$$\sigma_M = \sqrt{\sigma_M^2} = \sqrt{\frac{\sigma^2}{N}}$$

❷ **For the 95% confidence interval, figure the raw scores for 1.96 standard errors above and below the sample mean; for the 99% confidence interval, figure the raw scores for 2.57 standard errors above and below the sample mean.** To figure these raw scores, first multiply 1.96 or 2.57 by the standard error, then add this to the mean for the upper limit and subtract this from the mean for the lower limit.

In terms of the overall figuring, once you know the standard error, the upper limit of the 95% confidence interval is equal to the sample mean *plus* 1.96 multiplied by the standard error of the mean: upper limit $= M + (1.96)(\sigma_M)$; the lower limit is the sample mean *minus* 1.96 multiplied by the standard error: lower limit $= M - (1.96)(\sigma_M)$. For the 99% CI, the computation for the upper limit is: $M + (2.57)(\sigma_M)$; the lower 99% CI limit is $M - (2.57)(\sigma_M)$.

95% confidence interval confidence interval in which, roughly speaking, there is a 95% chance that the population mean falls within this interval.

99% confidence interval confidence interval in which, roughly speaking, there is a 99% chance that the population mean falls within this interval.

Example Let's find the 99% confidence interval for the verbal fillers example from earlier in the chapter. Recall that, in that example, the number of verbal fillers used by students in the general population (that is, students who had not attended a communication skills seminar) was normally distributed with a mean of 53 and a standard deviation of 7. The 25 students who attended a presentation skills seminar used a mean of 48 fillers.

❶ **Figure the standard error.** $\sigma_M = \sqrt{\dfrac{\sigma^2}{N}} = \sqrt{\dfrac{7^2}{25}} = \sqrt{1.96} = 1.40$.

❷ **For the 95% confidence interval, figure the raw scores for 1.96 standard errors above and below the sample mean; for the 99% confidence interval, figure the raw scores for 2.57 standard errors above and below the sample mean.** You want the 99% confidence interval. Thus, first multiply 2.57 by 1.40 to get 3.60, which is how far the confidence limit is from the mean. For the upper confidence limit, add this distance to the sample mean: $48 + 3.60 = 51.60$. In terms of the overall calculations, upper limit $= M + (2.57)$ $(\sigma_M = 48 + (2.57)(1.40) = 51.60$. For the lower confidence limit, subtract 3.60 (the results of multiplying 2.57 by 1.40) from 48, the mean of the sample, which gives 44.40. In terms of the overall calculations, lower limit $= M - (2.57)(1.40) = 44.40$.

Thus, based on this sample of 25 students, you can be 99% confident that an interval from 44.40 to 51.60 includes the true population mean.

The Subtle Logic of Confidence Intervals

If you understand the preceding explanation, it will be sufficient for practical purposes in working with confidence intervals. Basically, confidence intervals tell you the range of means that you can be pretty sure include the true population mean. However, if you want to think deeply about the situation, there is a subtle issue about precisely what these numbers mean. (What follows is kind of an "advanced, advanced" topic section!)

Strictly speaking, consider what we are figuring to be, say, a 95% confidence interval. We are figuring it as the range of means that are 95% likely to come from a population *with a true mean that happens to be the mean of our sample.* However, what we really want to know is the range that is 95% likely to include the true population mean. This we cannot know. That is, we are figuring one thing and really want to know another. Read this paragraph again and think about it. It is easy to miss this subtle but logically significant twist.

The way this awkward situation has been dealt with traditionally by most researchers is just to ignore this subtlety. Researchers who are more sophisticated statistically are comfortable with the situation by emphasizing that what we actually say is that we are 95% *confident* that the true mean is in this range. That is, by using this language, we are acknowledging that what we are doing is really a bit backward, but it is the best we can do! "Confidence" is closer to the subjective interpretation of probability we discussed in Chapter 3. In fact, "confidence" is meant to be a slightly vaguer term than probability. Nevertheless, it is not completely vague. What we are doing does have a solid basis.

Here is how to understand this: suppose in our attractiveness ratings example, the true mean was indeed 220. As we have seen, this would give a 95% confidence interval of 208.24 to 231.76, as shown in Figure 5–11a. We don't know what the true population mean is. But suppose the true population mean was 208.24. The range that includes 95% of sample means from this population's distribution of means would be from 196.48 to 220.00, as shown in Figure 5–11b. (You can work this out yourself following the two steps for figuring confidence limits.) Similarly, for the population with a mean of 231.76, the range that includes 95% of sample means from this population's distribution of means is from 220.00 to 243.52, as shown in Figure 5–11c.

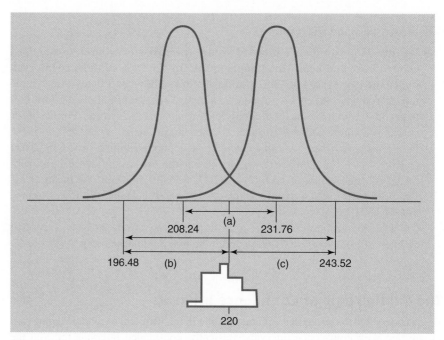

Figure 5–11   (a) 95% confidence interval based on sample mean of 220 for students rating the physical attractiveness of a person after being told that the person has positive personality qualities (fictional data); (b) range including 95% of sample means, based on distribution of means shown above it with μ_{Mb} = lower limit of the 95% confidence interval for $M = 220$; (c) range including 95% of sample means, based on distribution of means above it with μ_{Mc} = upper limit of the 95% confidence interval for $M = 220$.

What this shows is a general principle: for a 95% confidence interval, the lower confidence limit is the lowest possible population mean that would have a 95% probability of including our sample mean; the upper confidence limit is the highest possible population mean that would have a 95% probability of including our sample mean.

This convoluted logic is a bit like the double-negative logic behind hypothesis testing. This is no accident, since both are making inferences from samples to populations using the same information.

Confidence Intervals and Hypothesis Testing

A practical implication of the link of confidence intervals and hypothesis testing is that you can use confidence intervals to do hypothesis testing! If the confidence interval does not include the mean of the null hypothesis distribution, then the result is significant. For example, in the attractiveness ratings study, the 95% confidence interval for those who were told that the person has positive personality qualities was from 208.24 to 231.76. However, the population that was told nothing about the person's personality qualities had a mean of 200. This population mean is outside the range of the confidence interval. Thus, if you are 95% confident that the true range is 208.24 to 231.76 and the population mean for those who were told nothing about the person's personality qualities is not in this range, you are 95% confident that that population is not the same as the one your sample came from.

Another way to understand this is in terms of the idea that the confidence limits are the points at which a more extreme true population would not include your sample mean 95% of the time. The population mean for those who were told nothing about the person's personality qualities was 200. If this were the true mean also for the group that was told about the person's positive personality qualities, 95% of the time it would not produce a sample mean as high as the one we got.

How are you doing?

1. (a) What is the best estimate of a population mean? (b) Why?
2. (a) What number is used to indicate the accuracy of an estimate of the population mean? (b) Why?
3. What is a 95% confidence interval?
4. A researcher predicts that showing a certain film will change people's attitudes toward alcohol. The researchers then randomly select 36 people, show them the film, and give them an attitude questionnaire. The mean score on the attitude test for these 36 people is 70. The score on this test for people in the general population (who do not see the film) is 75, with a standard deviation of 12. (a) Find the best estimate of the mean of people who see the film and (b) its 95% confidence interval. (c) Compare this result to the conclusion you drew for this same situation when you used this example in the How are you doing? section for hypothesis testing with a distribution of means.
5. (a) Why is it wrong to say that the 95% confidence interval is the region in which there is a 95% probability of finding the true population mean? (b) What is the basis for our 95% confidence?

Answers

1. (a) The best estimate of a population mean is the sample mean. (b) It is more likely to have come from a population with the same mean than from any other population.
2. (a) The standard error (or standard deviation of the distribution of means) is used to indicate the accuracy of an estimate of the population mean. (b) The standard error (or standard deviation of the distribution of means) is roughly the average amount that means vary from the mean of the distribution of means.
3. The range of values that you are 95% confident includes the population mean, estimated based on the scores in a sample.
4. (a) The best estimate is the sample mean: 70.
   (b) Standard error (σ_M) is $\sqrt{\sigma^2/N} = \sqrt{144/36} = 2$. The lower confidence limit $= M - (1.96)(\sigma_M) = 70 - (1.96)(2) = 70 - 3.92 = 66.08$; upper confidence limit $= M + (1.96)(\sigma_M) = 70 + (1.96)(2) = 70 + 3.92 = 73.92$. The 95% confidence interval is from 66.08 to 73.92.
   (c) The 95% confidence interval does not include the mean of the general population (which was 75). Thus, you can reject the null hypothesis that the two populations are the same. This is the same conclusion as when using this example for hypothesis testing.
5. (a) It is wrong to say that the 95% confidence interval is the region in which there is a 95% probability of finding the true population mean because you do not know the true population mean; so you have no way of knowing for sure what to start with when figuring 95% probability.
   (b) The lower confidence limit is the point at which a true population any lower would not have a 95% probability of including a sample with our mean; similarly, the upper confidence limit is the point at which a true population any higher would not have a 95% probability of including a sample with our mean.

Advanced Topic Controversy: Confidence Intervals versus Significance Tests

You may recall from Chapter 4 that for a number of years there has been a lively debate among psychologists about significance testing. Among the major issues in that debate is a proposal that psychologists should use confidence intervals instead of significance tests.

Those who favor replacing significance tests with confidence intervals (e.g., Cohen, 1994; Hunter, 1997; Schmidt, 1996) cite several major advantages. First, as we noted above, confidence intervals contain all the key information in a significance test,[5] but also give additional information—the estimation of the range of values that you can be quite confident include the true population mean. A second advantage is that they focus attention on the estimation of effects instead of on hypothesis testing. Some researchers argue that the goal of science is to provide numeric estimates of effects (and the accuracy of those estimates), not just decisions as to whether an effect is different from zero.

Confidence intervals are particularly valuable when the results are not significant (Frick, 1995). This is, because knowing the confidence interval gives you an idea of just how far from no effect you can be confident that the true mean is to be found. If the results are not significant and the entire confidence interval is near to no effect, you can feel confident that, even if there is some true effect, it is probably small. However, if the results are not significant and the confidence interval, while including no effect, also spreads out to include means far from no effect, it would tell us that the study is really very inconclusive: it is possible that there is little or no effect, but it is also possible that there is a substantial effect.

A third advantage claimed by proponents of confidence intervals over significance testing is that researchers are less likely to misuse them. As we noted in Chapter 4, a common error in the use of significance tests is to conclude that a nonsignificant result means there is no effect. With confidence intervals, it is harder to fall into this kind of error.

In light of these various advantages, the most recent *Publication Manual of the American Psychological Association* (2001) takes the position that "The use of confidence intervals is . . . strongly recommended" (p. 22).

However, it is still relatively uncommon to find confidence intervals in many types of psychology research articles. In part, this is probably due to tradition and to most psychologists having been trained with significance tests and having become used to them.

Other researchers (e.g., Abelson, 1997; Harris, 1997; Nickerson, 2000) emphasize two reasons for not abandoning significance testing in favor of confidence intervals. First, for some advanced statistical procedures, it is possible to do significance testing but not to figure confidence intervals. Second, just as it is possible to make mistakes with significance tests, it is also possible to make other kinds of mistakes with confidence intervals—especially since most research psychologists are less experienced in using them.

Whatever the outcome of this controversy about confidence intervals, it is valuable to understand them, since you will run into them occasionally when reading research literature, and you are likely to see them more often in the future. On the other hand, they now appear only occasionally, and there is no sign that they are likely to replace significance testing any time soon. For this reason (and to keep the amount of material to be learned manageable), we have made confidence intervals an advanced topic and decided not to emphasize them in subsequent chapters of this book, which are mainly on significance testing in various types of research situations.

Advanced Topic: Confidence Intervals in Research Articles

As we noted, confidence intervals (usually abbreviated as CI), while far from standard, are sometimes reported in research articles. For example, consider a study by Christakis and Fowler (2007). They studied more than 12,000 people over a 32-year period to examine whether people's chances of becoming obese are related to whether they have friends and family who become obese. They reported that "A person's chance of becoming obese increased by 57% (95% confidence interval [CI], 6 to 123) if he or she had a friend who became obese in a given interval" (p. 370). This means that we can be 95% confident that the true increase in obesity risk was between 6% and 123%. As another example, an organizational psychologist might explain that the average number of overtime hours per week worked in a particular industry is 3.7 with a 95% confidence interval of 2.5 to 4.9. This would tell you that the true average number of overtime hours is probably somewhere between 2.5 and 4.9.

A shortcut that many researchers find helpful in reading research articles that give standard errors but not confidence intervals is that the 95% confidence interval is approximately 2 standard errors in both directions (it is exactly 1.96 *SE*s) and the 99% confidence interval is approximately 2.5 standard errors in both directions (it is exactly 2.57 *SE*s).

Summary

1. When studying a sample of more than one individual, the comparison distribution in the hypothesis-testing process is a distribution of means. It can be thought of as what would result from (a) taking a very large number of samples, each of the same number of scores taken randomly from the population of individuals, and then (b) making a distribution of the means of these samples.

2. The distribution of means has the same mean as the corresponding population of individuals. However, it has a smaller variance because the means of samples are less likely to be extreme than individual scores. (In any one sample, extreme scores are likely to be balanced by middle scores or extreme scores in the other direction.) Specifically, the variance of the distribution of means is the variance of the population of individuals divided by the number of individuals in each sample. Its standard deviation is the square root of its variance. The shape of the distribution of means approximates a normal curve if either (a) the samples are each of 30 or more scores or (b) the population of individuals follows a normal curve.

3. Hypothesis tests with a single sample of more than one individual and a known population are called *Z* tests and are done the same way as the hypothesis tests of Chapter 4 (where the studies were of a single individual compared to a population of individuals). The main exception is that the comparison distribution in a hypothesis test with a single sample of more than one individual and a known population is a distribution of means.

4. There is some controversy about the use of terms such as *marginal significance, approaching significance,* and *near significant trend* to describe results that come close to the significance cutoff value. Critics of these terms note that hypothesis testing is an all or nothing decision. However, other researchers advocate for greater flexibility and point out that the .05 and .01 significance levels are arbitrary conventions.

5. The kind of hypothesis testing described in this chapter (the *Z* test) is rarely used in research practice; you have learned it as a stepping-stone. The standard deviation of the distribution of means (the standard error) is commonly used to describe the expected variability of means, particularly in bar graphs in which the standard error may be shown as the length of a line above (and sometimes below) the top of each bar.

6. ADVANCED TOPIC: The sample mean is the best estimate for the population mean when the population mean is unknown. The accuracy of the estimate is the standard deviation of the distribution of means (also known as the standard error), which tells you roughly the amount by which means vary. Based on the distribution of means, you can figure the range of possible means that are likely to include the population mean. If we assume the distribution of means follows a normal curve, the 95% confidence interval includes the range from 1.96 standard deviations below the sample mean (the lower confidence limit) to 1.96 standard deviations above the sample mean (the upper confidence limit). Strictly speaking, the 95% confidence interval around a sample mean is the range in which the lower limit is the mean of the lowest population that would have a 95% probability of including a sample with this sample mean, and the upper limit is the corresponding mean of the highest population. The 99% confidence interval includes the range from 2.57 standard deviations below the sample mean (the lower confidence limit) to 2.57 standard deviations above the sample mean (the upper confidence limit).

7. ADVANCED TOPIC: An aspect of the ongoing controversy about significance tests is whether researchers should replace them with confidence intervals. Proponents of confidence intervals argue that they provide additional information, put the focus on estimation, and reduce misuses common with significance tests. Confidence intervals have become more common in recent years in psychology research articles, but they are still relatively unusual, in part due to tradition and unfamiliarity with them. In addition, opponents of relying exclusively on confidence intervals argue that they cannot be used in some advanced procedures, estimation is not always the goal, and they can have misuses of their own. When confidence intervals are reported in research articles, it is usually with the abbreviation *CI*.

Key Terms

distribution of means (p. 138)
mean of a distribution of means
  (p. 140)
μ_M (p. 141)
variance of a distribution of means
  (p. 141)

σ^2_M (p. 142)
standard deviation of a distribution
  of means (p. 142)
σ_M (p. 142)
standard error of the mean
  (*SEM*) (p. 142)

standard error (*SE*) (p. 142)
Z test (p. 148)
confidence interval (CI) (p. 157)
confidence limit (p. 157)
95% confidence interval (p. 158)
99% confidence interval (p. 158)

Example Worked-Out Problems

Figuring the Standard Deviation of the Distribution of Means

Find the standard deviation of the distribution of means for a population with $\sigma = 13$ and a sample size of 20.

Answer

Using Rules 2a and 2b for the characteristics of a distribution of means: **The variance of a distribution of means is the variance of the population of individuals divided by the number of individuals in each sample. The standard deviation of a distribution of means is the square root of the variance of the distribution of means.** The variance of the population is 169 (that is, 13 squared is 169); dividing this by 20 gives a variance of the distribution of means of 8.45. The square root of this, 2.91, is the standard deviation of the distribution of means.

Using the formula,

$$\sigma_M = \sqrt{\frac{\sigma^2}{N}} = \sqrt{\frac{13^2}{20}} = \sqrt{\frac{169}{20}} = \sqrt{8.45} = 2.91$$

Hypothesis Testing with a Sample of More Than One: The Z Test

A sample of 75 was given an experimental treatment and had a mean of 16 on a particular measure. The general population of individuals has a mean of 15 on this measure and a standard deviation of 5. Carry out a Z test using the five steps of hypothesis testing with a two-tailed test at the .05 significance level, and make a drawing of the distributions involved.

Answer

❶ **Restate the question as a research hypothesis and a null hypothesis about the populations.** The two populations are:

Population 1: Those given the experimental treatment.
Population 2: People in the general population (who are not given the experimental treatment).

The research hypothesis is that the population given the experimental treatment will have a different mean on the particular measure from the mean of people in the general population (who are not given the experimental treatment): $\mu_1 \neq \mu_2$. The null hypothesis is that the populations have the same mean score on this measure: $\mu_1 = \mu_2$.

❷ **Determine the characteristics of the comparison distribution.** $\mu_M = \mu = 15$; $\sigma_M = \sqrt{\frac{\sigma^2}{N}} = \sqrt{\frac{5^2}{75}} = \sqrt{.33} = .57$; shape is normal (sample size is greater than 30).

❸ **Determine the cutoff sample score on the comparison distribution at which the null hypothesis should be rejected.** Two-tailed cutoffs, 5% significance level, are $+1.96$ and -1.96.

❹ **Determine your sample's score on the comparison distribution.** Using the formula, $Z = (M - \mu_M)/\sigma_M$, $Z = (16 - 15)/.57 = 1/.57 = 1.75$.

❺ **Decide whether to reject the null hypothesis.** The sample's Z score of 1.75 is *not* more extreme than the cutoffs of ± 1.96; do not reject the null hypothesis. Results are inconclusive. The distributions involved are shown in Figure 5–12.

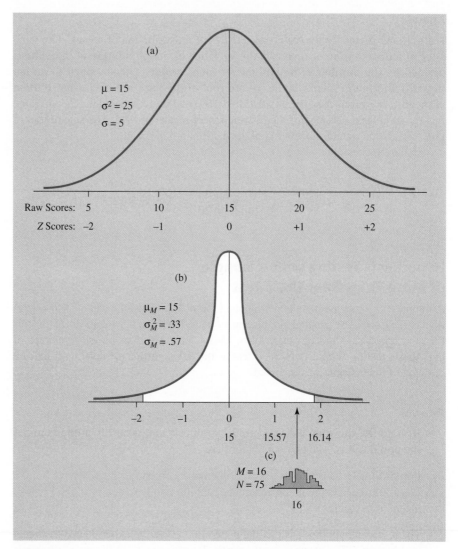

Figure 5-12 Answer to the hypothesis-testing problem in Example Worked-Out Problems: (a) the distribution of the population of individuals, (b) the distribution of means (the comparison distribution), and (c) the sample's distribution.

Outline for Writing Essays for Hypothesis-Testing Problems Involving a Single Sample of More Than One and a Known Population (*Z* Test)

1. Describe the core logic of hypothesis testing in this situation. Be sure to explain the meaning of the research hypothesis and the null hypothesis in this situation where we focus on the mean of a sample and compare it to a known population mean. Explain the concept of support being provided for the research hypothesis when the study results allow the null hypothesis to be rejected.

2. Explain the concept of the comparison distribution. Be sure to mention that, with a sample of more than one, the comparison distribution is a distribution of means because the information from the study is a mean of a sample. Mention that the distribution of means has the same mean as the population mean

because there is no reason for random samples in the long run to have a different mean; the distribution of means has a smaller variance (the variance of the population divided by the number in each sample) because it is harder to get extreme means than extreme individual cases by chance, and the larger the samples are, the rarer it is to get extreme means.

3. Describe the logic and process for determining (using the normal curve) the cut-off sample score(s) on the comparison distribution at which the null hypothesis should be rejected.
4. Describe why and how you figure the Z score of the sample mean on the comparison distribution.
5. Explain how and why the scores from Steps ❸ and ❹ of the hypothesis-testing process are compared. Explain the meaning of the result of this comparison with regard to the specific research and null hypotheses being tested.

Advanced Topic: Finding Confidence Intervals

Find the 99% confidence interval for the sample mean in the study just described.

Answer

❶ **Figure the standard error.** The standard error is the standard deviation of the distribution of means. In the preceding problem, it was .57.

❷ **For the 95% confidence interval, figure the raw scores for 1.96 standard errors above and below the sample mean; for the 99% confidence interval, figure the raw scores for 2.57 standard errors above and below the sample mean.** For the 99% confidence interval, upper limit = $M + (2.57)(\sigma_M) = 16 + (2.57)(.57) = 16 + 1.46 = 17.46$; lower limit = $M - (2.57)(\sigma_M) = 16 - (2.57)(.57) = 16 - 1.46 = 14.54$. Thus, the 99% confidence interval is from 14.54 to 17.46.

Advanced Topic: Outline for Writing Essays for Finding Confidence Intervals

1. Explain that a confidence interval is an estimate (based on your sample's mean and the standard deviation of the distribution of means) of the range of values that is likely to include the true population mean for the group studied (Population 1). Be sure to mention that the 95% (or 99%) confidence interval is the range of values you are 95% (or 99%) confident include the true population mean.
2. Explain that the first step in figuring a confidence interval is to estimate the population mean (for which the best estimate is the sample mean), and figure the standard deviation of the distribution of means.
3. Mention that you next find the Z scores that go with the confidence interval that you want.
4. Describe how to change the Z scores to raw scores to find the confidence interval.

Practice Problems

These problems involve figuring. Most real-life statistics problems are done on a computer with special statistical software. Even if you have such software, do these problems by hand to ingrain the method in your mind.

All data are fictional unless an actual citation is given.

Set I (for Answers to Set I Problems, see pp. 677–678)

1. Why is the standard deviation of the distribution of means generally smaller than the standard deviation of the distribution of the population of individuals?

2. For a population that has a standard deviation of 10, figure the standard deviation of the distribution of means for samples of size (a) 2, (b) 3, (c) 4, and (d) 9.

3. For a population that has a standard deviation of 20, figure the standard deviation of the distribution of means for samples of size (a) 2, (b) 3, (c) 4, and (d) 9.

4. ADVANCED TOPIC: Figure the 95% confidence interval (that is, the lower and upper confidence limits) for each part of problem 2. Assume that in each case the researcher's sample has a mean of 100 and that the population of individuals is known to follow a normal curve.

5. ADVANCED TOPIC: Figure the 99% confidence interval (that is, the lower and upper confidence limits) for each part of problem 3. Assume that in each case the researcher's sample has a mean of 10 and that the population of individuals is known to follow a normal curve.

6. For each of the following samples that were given an experimental treatment, test whether they are different from the general population: (a) a sample of 10 with a mean of 44, (b) a sample of 1 with a mean of 48. The general population of individuals has a mean of 40, a standard deviation of 6, and follows a normal curve. For each sample, carry out a Z test using the five steps of hypothesis testing with a two-tailed test at the .05 significance level, and make a drawing of the distributions involved. (c) ADVANCED TOPIC: Figure the 95% confidence interval for parts (a) and (b).

7. For each of the following samples that were given an experimental treatment, test whether they scored significantly higher than the general population: (a) a sample of 100 with a mean of 82, (b) a sample of 10 with a mean of 84. The general population of individuals has a mean of 81, a standard deviation of 8, and follows a normal curve. For each sample, carry out a Z test using the five steps of hypothesis testing with a one-tailed test at the .01 significance level, and make a drawing of the distributions involved. (c) ADVANCED TOPIC: Figure the 99% confidence interval for parts (a) and (b).

8. Twenty-five women between the ages of 70 and 80 were randomly selected from the general population of women their age to take part in a special program to decrease reaction time (speed). After the course, the women had an average reaction time of 1.5 seconds. Assume that the mean reaction time for the general population of women of this age group is 1.8, with a standard deviation of .5 seconds. (Also assume that the population is approximately normal.) What should you conclude about the effectiveness of the course? (a) Carry out a Z test using the five steps of hypothesis testing (use the .01 level). (b) Make a drawing of the distributions involved. (c) Explain your answer to someone who is familiar with the general logic of hypothesis testing, the normal curve, Z scores, and probability, but not with the idea of a distribution of means. (d) ADVANCED TOPIC: Figure the 99% confidence interval and explain your answer to someone who is familiar with the general logic of hypothesis testing, the normal curve, Z scores, probability, and the idea of a distribution of means, but has not heard of confidence intervals.

9. A large number of people were shown a particular film of an automobile collision between a moving car and a stopped car. Each person then filled out a questionnaire about how likely it was that the driver of the moving car was at fault, on a scale from 0 = *not at fault* to 10 = *completely at fault*. The distribution of

ratings under ordinary conditions follows a normal curve with $\mu = 5.5$ and $\sigma = .8$. Sixteen randomly selected individuals are tested in a condition in which the wording of the question is changed so that the question asks, "How likely is it that the driver of the car who crashed into the other was at fault?" (The difference is that in this changed condition, instead of describing the event in a neutral way, the question uses the phrase "crashed into.") Using the changed instruction, these 16 research participants gave a mean at-fault rating of 5.9. Did the changed instructions significantly increase the rating of being at fault? (a) Carry out a Z test using the five steps of hypothesis testing (use the .05 level). (b) Make a drawing of the distributions involved. (c) Explain your answer to someone who has never taken statistics. (d) ADVANCED TOPIC: Figure the 95% confidence interval.

10. Lee and colleagues (2000) tested a theory of the role of distinctiveness in face perception. In their study, participants indicated whether they recognized each of 48 faces of male celebrities when they were shown rapidly on a computer screen. A third of the faces were shown in caricature form, in which facial features were electronically modified so that distinctive features were exaggerated; a third were shown in veridical form, in which the faces were not modified at all; and a third were shown in anticaricature form, in which facial features were modified to be slightly more like the average of the celebrities' faces. The average percentage correct across their participants is shown in Figure 5–13. Explain the meaning of the error bars in this figure to a person who understands mean, standard deviation, and variance, but nothing else about statistics.

11. ADVANCED TOPIC: Anderson and colleagues (2000) studied the rate of HIV testing among adults in the United States and reported one of their findings as follows: "Responses from the NHIS [National Health Interview Survey] indicate that by 1995, 39.7% of adults (95% CI = 38.8%, 40.5%) had been tested at least once. . . ." (p. 1090). Explain what "(95% CI = 38.8%, 40.5%)" means to a person who understands hypothesis testing with the mean of a sample of more than one but who has never heard of confidence intervals.

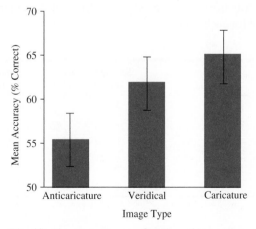

Figure 5–13 Identification accuracy as a function of image type. Standard error bars are shown.

Source: Lee, K., Byatt, G., & Rhodes, G. (2000). Caricature effects, distinctiveness, and identification: Testing the face-space framework. *Psychological Science, 11,* 381. Copyright © 2000 by Blackwell Publishing. Reprinted by permission of Blackwell Publishers Journals.

Set II

12. Under what conditions is it reasonable to assume that a distribution of means will follow a normal curve?

13. Indicate the mean and the standard deviation of the distribution of means for each of the following situations.

	Population		Sample Size
	Mean	*Variance*	*N*
(a)	100	40	10
(b)	100	30	10
(c)	100	20	10
(d)	100	10	10
(e)	50	10	10
(f)	100	40	20
(g)	100	10	20

14. Figure the standard deviation of the distribution of means for a population with a standard deviation of 20 and sample sizes of (a) 10, (b) 11, (c) 100, and (d) 101.

15. ADVANCED TOPIC: Figure the 95% confidence interval (that is, the lower and upper confidence limits) for each part of problem 13. Assume that in each case the researcher's sample has a mean of 80 and the population of individuals is known to follow a normal curve.

16. ADVANCED TOPIC: Figure the 99% confidence interval (that is, the lower and upper confidence limits) for each part of problem 14. Assume that in each case the researcher's sample has a mean of 50 and that the population of individuals is known to follow a normal curve.

17. For each of the following studies, the samples were given an experimental treatment and the researchers compared their results to the general population. (Assume all populations are normally distributed.) For each, carry out a Z test using the five steps of hypothesis testing for a two-tailed test, and make a drawing of the distributions involved. ADVANCED TOPIC: Figure the 95% confidence interval for each study.

	Population		Sample Size	Sample Mean	Significance Level
	μ	σ	*N*		
(a)	36	8	16	38	.05
(b)	36	6	16	38	.05
(c)	36	4	16	38	.05
(d)	36	4	16	38	.01
(e)	34	4	16	38	.01

18. For each of the following studies, the samples were given an experimental treatment and the researchers compared their results to the general population. For each, carry out a Z test using the five steps of hypothesis testing for a two-tailed test at the .01 level, and make a drawing of the distributions involved. ADVANCED TOPIC: Figure the 99% confidence interval for each study.

	Population		Sample Size	Sample Mean
	μ	σ	N	
(a)	10	2	50	12
(b)	10	2	100	12
(c)	12	4	50	12
(d)	14	4	100	12

19. A researcher is interested in whether people are able to identify emotions correctly when they are extremely tired. It is known that, using a particular method of measurement, the accuracy ratings of people in the general population (who are not extremely tired) are normally distributed with a mean of 82 and a variance of 20. In the present study, however, the researcher arranges to test 50 people who had no sleep the previous night. The mean accuracy for these 50 individuals was 78. Using the .05 level, what should the researcher conclude? (a) Carry out a Z test using the five steps of hypothesis testing. (b) Make a drawing of the distributions involved. (c) Explain your answer to someone who knows about hypothesis testing with a sample of a single individual but who knows nothing about hypothesis testing with a sample of more than one individual. (d) ADVANCED TOPIC: Figure the 95% confidence interval and explain your answer to someone who is familiar with the general logic of hypothesis testing, the normal curve, Z scores, probability, and the idea of a distribution of means, but who has not heard of confidence intervals.

20. A psychologist is interested in the conditions that affect the number of dreams per month that people report in which they are alone. We will assume that based on extensive previous research, it is known that in the general population the number of such dreams per month follows a normal curve, with $\mu = 5$ and $\sigma = 4$. The researcher wants to test the prediction that the number of such dreams will be greater among people who have recently experienced a traumatic event. Thus, the psychologist studies 36 individuals who have recently experienced a traumatic event, having them keep a record of their dreams for a month. Their mean number of alone dreams is 8. Should you conclude that people who have recently had a traumatic experience have a significantly different number of dreams in which they are alone? (a) Carry out a Z test using the five steps of hypothesis testing (use the .05 level). (b) Make a drawing of the distributions involved. (c) Explain your answer to a person who has never had a course in statistics. (d) ADVANCED TOPIC: Figure the 95% confidence interval.

21. A government-sponsored telephone counseling service for adolescents tested whether the length of calls would be affected by a special telephone system that had a better sound quality. Over the past several years, the lengths of telephone calls (in minutes) were normally distributed with $\mu = 18$ and $\sigma = 8$. They arranged to have the special phone system loaned to them for one day. On that day, the mean length of the 46 calls they received was 21 minutes. Test whether the length of calls has changed using the 5% significance level. (a) Carry out a Z test using the five steps of hypothesis testing. (b) Make a drawing of the distributions involved. (c) Explain your answer to someone who knows about hypothesis testing with a sample of a single individual but who knows nothing about hypothesis testing with samples of more than one individual. (d) ADVANCED TOPIC: Figure the 95% confidence interval.

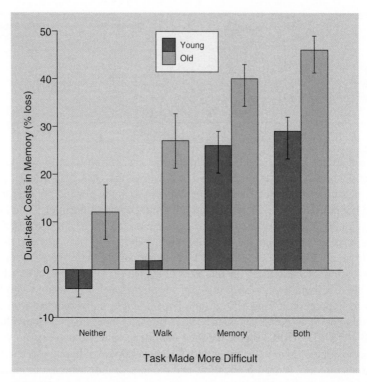

Figure 5–14 Dual-task costs in memory as a function of age group and difficulty condition. Error bars represent ±1 SEM.

Source: Li, K. Z. H., Lindenberger, U., Freund, A. M., & Baltes, P. B. (2001). Walking while memorizing: Age-related differences in compensatory behavior. *Psychological Science, 12,* 230–237. Copyright © 2001 by Blackwell Publishing. Reprinted by permission of Blackwell Publishers Journals.

22. Li and colleagues (2001) compared older (aged 60 to 75) and younger (aged 20 to 30) adults on the impact on memory of making some aspect of what they were doing more difficult. Figure 5–14 shows some of their results. In the figure caption they note that "Error bars represent ±1 *SEM*" (standard error of the mean). Explain the meaning of this statement, using one of the error bars as an example, to a person who understands mean and standard deviation, but knows nothing else about statistics.

23. ADVANCED TOPIC: Perna and colleagues (2003) tested whether a stress management intervention could reduce injury and illness among college athletes. In their study, 34 college athletes were randomly assigned to be in one of two groups: (1) a stress management intervention group: this group received a cognitive behavioral stress management (CBSM) intervention during preseason training; (2) a control group: this group did not receive the intervention. At the end of the season, for each athlete, the researchers recorded the number of health center visits (including visits to the athletic training center) and the number of days of illness or injury during the season. The results are shown in Figure 5–15. In the figure caption, the researchers note that the figure show shows the "Mean (+*SE*)". This tells you that the line above the top of each bar represents the standard error. Explain what this means, using one of the error bars as an example, to a person who understands mean and standard deviation, but knows nothing else about statistics.

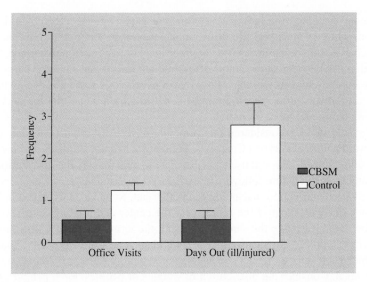

Figure 5–15   Mean ($+SE$) number of accumulated days injured or ill and athletic training room and health center office visits for cognitive behavioral stress management (*CBSM*) ($n = 18$) and control groups ($n = 16$) from study entry to season's end.

Source: Perna, F. M., Antoni, M. H., Baum, A., Gordon, P., & Schneiderman, N. (2003). Cognitive behavior stress management effects on injury and illness among competitive athletes: A randomized clinical trial. *Annals of Behavioral Medicine, 25,* 66–73. Copyright © Lawrence Erlbaum Associates, Inc. Reprinted with permission.

24. Cut up 90 small slips of paper, and write each number from 1 to 9 on 10 slips each. Put the slips in a large bowl and mix them up. (a) Take out a slip, write down the number on it, and put it back. Do this 20 times. Make a histogram, and figure the mean and the variance of the result. You should get an approximately rectangular distribution. (b) Take two slips out, figure out their mean, write it down, and put the slips back.[6] Repeat this process 20 times. Make a histogram; then figure the mean and the variance of this distribution of means. The variance should be about half of the variance of the distribution of individual scores. (c) Repeat the process again, this time taking three slips at a time. Again, make a histogram and figure the mean and the variance of the distribution of means. The distribution of means of three slips each should have a variance of about a third of the distribution of individual scores. Also note that as the sample size increases, your distributions get closer to normal. (Had you begun with a normally distributed distribution of slips, your distributions of means would have been fairly close to normal regardless of the number of slips in each sample.)

Chapter Notes

1. The formula for figuring the standard deviation of a distribution of means can also be written as $\sigma_M = \dfrac{\sigma}{\sqrt{N}}$. We prefer to use Formula 5–3, because it provides a reminder of the basic logic that the variance of a distribution of means is figured by dividing the variance of the population of individuals by the number of individuals in each sample.

2. We have ignored the fact that a normal curve is a smooth theoretical distribution, while in most real-life distributions, scores are only at specific numbers, such as a child being in a particular grade and not in a fraction of a grade. So one difference between our example distribution of means and a normal curve is that the normal curve is smooth. However, in psychology research, even when our measurements are at specific numbers, we usually assume that the underlying thing being measured is continuous.

3. We have already considered this principle of a distribution of means tending toward a normal curve in Chapter 3. Though we had not yet discussed the distribution of means, we still used this principle to explain why the distribution of so many things in nature follows a normal curve. In that chapter, we explained it as the various influences balancing each other out, to make an averaged influence come out with most of the scores near the center and a few at either extreme. Now we have made the same point using the terminology of a distribution of means. Think of any distribution of individual scores in nature as a situation in which each score is actually an average of a random set of influences on that individual. Consider the distribution of weights of pebbles. Each pebble's weight is a kind of average of all the different forces that went into making the pebble have a particular weight.

4. This fictional study would be much better if the researchers also had another group of students who were randomly assigned to rate the attractiveness of the person after being told nothing about the person's personality qualities. Relying on the attractiveness ratings for a known population of students is a bit hazardous because the circumstances in the experiment might be somewhat different from that of the usual situation in which students rated the attractiveness of the person. However, we have taken liberties with this example to help introduce the hypothesis-testing process to you one step at a time. In this example and the others in this chapter, we use situations in which a single sample is contrasted with a "known" population. Starting in Chapter 7, we extend the hypothesis-testing procedure to more realistic research situations, those involving more than one group of participants and those involving populations whose characteristics are not known.

5. Some proponents of confidence intervals over significance testing argue that we should ignore the link with hypothesis testing altogether. This is the most radical antisignificance-test position. That is, these psychologists argue that our entire focus should be on estimation, and significance testing of any kind should be irrelevant. In Chapter 6, we will discuss the rationale for their position, along with the counterarguments.

6. Technically, when taking the samples of two slips, this should be done by taking one, writing it down, putting it back, then taking the next, writing it down, and putting it back. You would consider these two scores as one sample for which you figure a mean. The same applies for samples of three slips. This is called sampling *with replacement*. However, with 90 slips in the bowl, taking two or three slips at a time and putting them back will be a close enough approximation for this exercise and will save you some time.

CHAPTER 6

Making Sense of Statistical Significance

Decision Errors, Effect Size, and Statistical Power

Chapter Outline

- Decision Errors   175
- Effect Size   179
- Statistical Power   187
- What Determines the Power of a Study?   191
- The Role of Power When Planning a Study   203
- The Role of Power When Interpreting the Results of a Study   205
- Controversy: Statistical Significance versus Effect Size   208
- Decision Errors, Effect Size, and Power in Research Articles   210
- Advanced Topic: Figuring Statistical Power   212
- Summary   214
- Key Terms   215
- Example Worked-Out Problems   215
- Practice Problems   217
- Chapter Note   221

S tatistical significance is extremely important in psychology research, but sophisticated researchers and readers of research understand that there is more to the story of a study's result than $p < .05$ or *ns* (not significant). This chapter helps you become sophisticated about making sense of significance. Gaining this sophistication means learning about three interrelated issues: decision errors, effect size, and statistical power.

Decision Errors

A crucial topic for making sense of statistical significance is the kinds of errors that are possible in the hypothesis-testing process. The kind of errors we consider here are about how, in spite of doing all your figuring correctly, your conclusions from hypothesis testing can still be incorrect. It is *not* about making mistakes in calculations or even about using the wrong procedures. That is, **decision errors** are situations in which the *right procedures* lead to the *wrong decisions.*

Decision errors are possible in hypothesis testing because you are making decisions about populations based on information in samples. The whole hypothesis-testing process is based on probabilities; it is set up to make the probability of decision errors as small as possible. For example, we decide to reject the null hypothesis only if a sample's mean is so extreme that there is a very small probability (say, less than 5%) that we could have gotten such an extreme sample if the null hypothesis is true. But a very small probability is not the same as a zero probability! Thus, in spite of your best intentions, decision errors are always possible.

There are two kinds of decision errors in hypothesis testing: Type I error and Type II error.

Type I Error

You make a **Type I error** if you reject the null hypothesis when in fact the null hypothesis is true. Or, to put it in terms of the research hypothesis, you make a Type I error when you conclude that the study supports the research hypothesis when in reality the research hypothesis is false.

Suppose you carried out a study in which you had set the significance level cutoff at a very lenient probability level, such as 20%. This would mean that it would not take a very extreme result to reject the null hypothesis. If you did many studies like this, you would often (about 20% of the time) be deciding to consider the research hypothesis supported when you should not. That is, you would have a 20% chance of making a Type I error.

Even when you set the probability at the conventional .05 or .01 levels, you will still make a Type I error sometimes (5% or 1% of the time). Consider again the example of giving the new therapy to a depressed patient. Suppose the new therapy is not more effective than the usual therapy. However, in randomly picking a sample of one depressed patient to study, the clinical psychologists might just happen to pick a patient whose depression would respond equally well to the new therapy and the usual therapy. Randomly selecting a sample patient like this is *unlikely*. But such extreme samples are possible. Should this happen, the clinical psychologists would reject the null hypothesis and conclude that the new therapy is different than the usual therapy. Their decision to reject the null hypothesis would be wrong—a Type I error. Of course, the researchers could not know they had made a decision error of this kind. What reassures researchers is that they know from the logic of hypothesis testing that the probability of making such a decision error is kept low (less than 5% if you use the .05 significance level).

Still, the fact that Type I errors can happen at all is of serious concern to psychologists, who might construct entire theories and research programs, not to mention practical applications, based on a conclusion from hypothesis testing that is in fact mistaken. It is because these errors are of such serious concern that they are called Type I.

As we have noted, researchers cannot tell when they have made a Type I error. However, they can try to carry out studies so that the chance of making a Type I error is as small as possible.

What is the chance of making a Type I error? It is the same as the significance level you set. If you set the significance level at $p < .05$, you are saying you will reject the null hypothesis if there is less than a 5% (.05) chance that you could have

decision error   incorrect conclusion in hypothesis testing in relation to the real (but unknown) situation, such as deciding the null hypothesis is false when it is really true.

Type I error   rejecting the null hypothesis when in fact it is true; getting a statistically significant result when in fact the research hypothesis is not true.

gotten your result if the null hypothesis were true. When rejecting the null hypothesis in this way, you are allowing up to a 5% chance that you got your results even though the null hypothesis was actually true. That is, you are allowing a 5% chance of a Type I error.

The significance level, which is the chance of making a Type I error, is called **alpha** (the Greek letter α). The lower the alpha, the smaller the chance of a Type I error. Researchers who do not want to take a lot of risk set alpha lower than .05, such as $p < .001$. In this way the result of a study has to be very extreme for the hypothesis-testing process to reject the null hypothesis.

Using a .001 significance level is like buying insurance against making a Type I error. However, as when buying insurance, the better the protection, the higher the cost. There is a cost in setting the significance level at too extreme a level. We turn to that cost next.

Type II Error

If you set a very extreme significance level, such as $p < .001$, you run a different kind of risk: you may carry out a study in which, in reality, the research hypothesis is true but the result does not come out extreme enough to reject the null hypothesis. Thus, the decision error you would make is in *not* rejecting the null hypothesis when in reality the null hypothesis is false. To put this in terms of the research hypothesis, you make this kind of decision error when the hypothesis-testing procedure leads you to decide that the results of the study are inconclusive when in reality the research hypothesis is true. This is called a **Type II error.** The probability of making a Type II error is called **beta** (the Greek letter β). (Do not confuse this beta with the standardized regression coefficient that you will learn about in Chapter 12, which is also called beta.)

Consider again our depression therapy example. Suppose that, in truth, the new therapy is better at treating depression than the usual therapy. However, in conducting your study, the results for the sample patient are not strong enough to allow you to reject the null hypothesis. Perhaps the random sample patient that you selected to try out the new therapy happened to be a person who would not respond to either the new therapy or the usual therapy. The results would not be significant. Having decided not to reject the null hypothesis, and thus refusing to draw a conclusion, would be a Type II error.

Type II errors especially concern psychologists interested in practical applications. This is because a Type II error could mean that a valuable practical procedure is not used.

As with a Type I error, you cannot know when you have made a Type II error. But researchers can try to carry out studies so as to reduce the chance of making one. One way of buying insurance against a Type II error is to set a very lenient significance level, such as $p < .10$ or even $p < .20$. In this way, even if a study produces only a very small effect, this effect has a good chance of being significant. There is a cost to this insurance policy too.

Relationship Between Type I and Type II Errors

When it comes to setting significance levels, protecting against one kind of decision error increases the chance of making the other. The insurance policy against Type I error (setting a significance level of, say, .001) has the cost of increasing the chance of making a Type II error. (This is because with an extreme significance level like .001, even if the research hypothesis is true, the results have to be quite strong for you to reject the null hypothesis.) The insurance policy against Type II error (setting a significance level of, say, .20) has the cost of increasing the chance of making a Type I

alpha (α)   probability of making a Type I error; same as *significance level.*

Type II error   failing to reject the null hypothesis when in fact it is false; failing to get a statistically significant result when in fact the research hypothesis is true.

beta (β)   probability of making a Type I error.

error. (This is because, with a level of significance like .20, even if the null hypothesis is true, it is fairly easy to get a significant result just by accidentally getting a sample that is higher or lower than the general population before doing the study.)

The trade-off between these two conflicting concerns usually is worked out by compromise—thus the standard 5% ($p < .05$) and 1% ($p < .01$) significance levels.

Summary of Possible Outcomes of Hypothesis Testing

The entire issue of possibly correct or mistaken conclusions in hypothesis testing is shown in Table 6–1. Along the top of this table are the two possibilities about whether the null hypothesis or the research hypothesis is really true. (Remember, you never actually know this.)

Along the side is whether, after hypothesis testing, you decide that the research hypothesis is supported (reject the null hypothesis) or decide that the results are inconclusive (do not reject the null hypothesis). Table 6–1 shows that there are two ways to be correct and two ways to be in error in any hypothesis-testing situation.

How are you doing?

1. What is a decision error?
2. (a) What is a Type I error? (b) Why is it possible? (c) What is its probability? (d) What is this probability called?
3. (a) What is a Type II error? (b) Why is it possible? (c) What is its probability called?
4. If you set a lenient alpha level (say .25), what is the effect on the probability of (a) Type I error and (b) Type II error?
5. If you set an extreme alpha level (say .001), what is the effect on the probability of (a) Type I error and (b) Type II error?

Answers

1. A decision error is a conclusion from hypothesis testing that does not match reality.
2. (a) Rejecting the null hypothesis (and thus supporting the research hypothesis) when the null hypothesis is actually true (and the research hypothesis is actually false) is a Type I error. (b) You reject the null hypothesis when a sample's result is so extreme that it is unlikely you would have gotten that result if the null hypothesis is true. However, even though it is unlikely, it is still possible that the null hypothesis is true. (c) A Type I error's probability is the significance level (such as .05). (d) The probability is called alpha.
3. (a) Failing to reject the null hypothesis (and thus failing to support the research hypothesis) when the null hypothesis is actually false (and the research hypothesis is actually true) is a Type II error. (b) You reject the null hypothesis when a sample's result is so extreme it is unlikely you would have gotten that result if the null hypothesis is true. However, the null hypothesis could be false, but the sample may not be extreme enough to reject the null hypothesis. (c) A Type II error's probability is called beta.
4. (a) The probability is high; (b) the probability is low.
5. (a) The probability is low; (b) the probability is high.

Table 6-1   Possible Correct and Incorrect Decisions in Hypothesis Testing

		Real Situation (in practice, unknown)	
		Null Hypothesis True	Research Hypothesis True
Conclusion Using Hypothesis-testing Procedure	Research hypothesis supported (reject null hypothesis)	Error (Type I) α	Correct decision
	Study is inconclusive (do not reject null hypothesis)	Correct decision	Error (Type II) β

Effect Size

Consider again our example from Chapter 5, in which people rated the physical attractiveness of a person after being told that the person has positive personality qualities. In the hypothesis-testing procedure for this example (the Z test), we compared two populations:

Population 1: Students who are told that the person has positive personality qualities.
Population 2: Students in general (who are told nothing about the person's personality qualities).

The research hypothesis was that Population 1 would on the average give higher attractiveness ratings to the person in the photograph than Population 2. Population 2 is known to have a mean of 200. In the example, we said the researcher found that the sample of 64 students who were told that the person has positive personality qualities gave a mean attractiveness rating of 220. Following the hypothesis-testing procedure, we rejected the null hypothesis that the two populations are the same. This was because it was extremely unlikely that we would get a sample with a score as high as 220 from a population like Population 2 (see Figure 6–1, which is the same as Figure 5–7 from the last chapter). Thus, we could conclude the result is "statistically significant." In this example, the best estimate of the mean of Population 1 is the sample's mean, which is 220. Thus, we can estimate that telling students about the person's positive personality qualities has an average effect of increasing the students' ratings of the physical attractiveness of the person by 20 points.

Now look again at Figure 6–1. Suppose the sample's score had been only 210. This would have given a Z score of 1.67 (that is, $[210 - 200]/6 = 1.67$). This is more extreme than the cutoff in this example, which was 1.64, so the result would still have been significant. However, in this situation we would estimate that the average effect of telling students about the person's positive personality qualities was only 10 points.

Notice that both results are significant, but in one example the effect is twice as big as in the other example. The point is that knowing statistical significance does not give you much information about the *size* of the effect. Significance tells us that the results of the experiment should convince us that there is an effect (that it is not "due to chance"). But significance does not tell us how *big* this nonchance effect is.

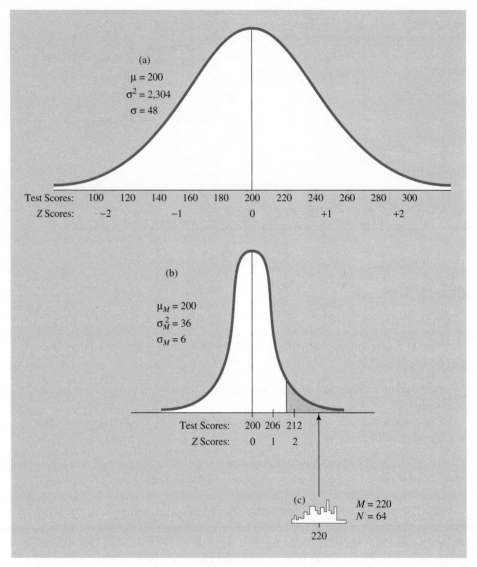

Figure 6–1   For the fictional study of positive personality qualities and ratings of physical attractiveness, (a) the distribution of the population of individuals, (b) the distribution of means for Population 2 (the comparison distribution), and (c) the sample's distribution. The shaded area in the distribution of means is the rejection region—the area in which the null hypothesis will be rejected if the study's sample mean turns out to be in that area.

Put another way, **effect size** is a measure of the difference between population means. You can think of effect size as how much something changes after a specific intervention. Effect size indicates the extent to which two populations do *not* overlap—that is, how much they are separated due to the experimental procedure. In the attractiveness ratings example, Population 2 (the known population) had a mean of 200; based on our original sample's mean of 220, we estimated that Population 1 (those told that the person has positive personality qualities) would have a mean of 220. The left curve in Figure 6–2 is the distribution (*of individual scores*) for Population 2; the right curve is the distribution for Population 1. Now look at Figure 6–3. Again, the left curve is for Population 2 and is the same as in Figure 6–2. However,

effect size   standardized measure of difference (lack of overlap) between populations. Effect size increases with greater differences between means.

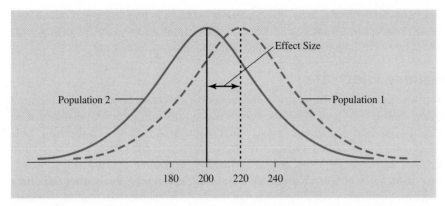

Figure 6–2   The distributions for the fictional study of positive personality qualities and ratings of physical attractiveness. Right curve: Population 1, those students told that the person has positive personality qualities. Left curve: Population 2, students told nothing about the person's personality. Population 1's mean is estimated based on the sample mean of 220, as originally described in Chapter 5; its standard deviation of 48 is assumed to be the same as Population 2's, which is known.

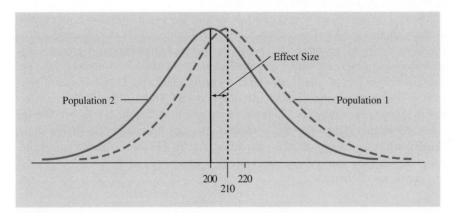

Figure 6–3   The distributions for the fictional study of positive personality qualities and ratings of physical attractiveness. Right curve: Population 1, those students told that the person has positive personality qualities. Left curve: Population 2, students told nothing about the person's personality. Population 1's mean is estimated based on a sample mean of 210; its standard deviation of 48 is assumed to be the same as Population 2's, which is known.

this time the right curve for Population 1 is estimated based on a sample (the sample told that the person has positive personality qualities) with a mean of 210. Here you can see that the effect size is smaller and that the two populations overlap even more.

We often want to know not only whether a result is significant, but how big the effect is. As we will discuss later, an effect could well be statistically significant but not of much practical significance. (That is, suppose an increase of only 10 points on the attractiveness measure is not considered important.) Further, we may want to compare the results of this procedure to that of other procedures studied in the past. For these reasons, the latest edition of the *Publication Manual of the American Psychological Association* (APA, 2001), the accepted standard for how to present psychology research results, states, "For the reader to fully understand the importance of your findings, it is almost always necessary to include some index of effect size . . ." (p. 25). Thus, whenever you use a hypothesis-testing procedure, you should also figure effect size. You can think of it as a sixth step in our standard hypothesis-testing procedure: *figure the effect size.* As you will see later in the chapter, effect size plays an important role in two other important statistical topics: meta-analysis and power.

Figuring Effect Size

You just learned that effect size is a measure of the difference between two population means. In Figure 6–2, the effect size is shown as the difference between the Population 1 mean and the Population 2 mean, which is 20 (that is, $220 - 200 = 20$). This effect size of 20 is called a *raw score effect size,* because the effect size is given in terms of the raw score on the measure (which in this case is a measure of attractiveness, from a low of 0 to a high of 400). But what if you want to compare this effect size with the result of a similar study that used a different measure of attractiveness? This similar study used a measure with a 1-to-10 scale, and the researchers reported an estimated Population 2 mean of 5, a Population 1 mean of 6, and a population standard deviation of 2. The raw score effect size in this study is 1 (that is, $6 - 5 = 1$). How do we compare this raw score effect size of 1 with the raw score effect size of 20 in our original study? The solution to this problem is to use a *standardized effect size*—that is, to divide the raw score effect size for each study by its respective population standard deviation.

In the original attractiveness ratings example, the population standard deviation (of individuals) was 48. Thus, a raw score of effect size of 20 gives a standardized effect size of 20/48, which is .42. That is, the effect of knowing positive personality qualities was to increase attractiveness ratings by .42 of a standard deviation. The raw score effect size of 1 in the similar study (which had a population standard deviation of 2) is a standardized effect size of $1/2 = .50$. Thus, in this study, the effect was to increase the ratings by .50 (half) of a standard deviation. So, in this case the effect size in our original example is smaller than the effect size in the similar study. Usually, when psychologists refer to an effect size in a situation like we are considering, they mean a standardized effect size.

Stated as a formula,

The standardized effect size is the difference between the population means divided by the population's standard deviation.

$$d = \frac{\mu_1 - \mu_2}{\sigma} \qquad (6-1)$$

In this formula, d (also known as *Cohen's d*) is a symbol for effect size. (In later chapters, you learn other measures of effect size that are appropriate to different hypothesis–testing situations.) μ_1 is the mean of Population 1 (the mean for the population that receives the experimental manipulation); μ_2 is the mean of Population 2 (the known population, the basis for the comparison distribution); and σ is the population standard deviation.

Notice that when figuring effect size, you don't use σ_M, the standard deviation of the distribution of means. Instead, you use σ, the standard deviation of the population of individuals. Also notice that you are only concerned with one population's standard deviation. This is because in hypothesis testing you usually assume that both populations have the same standard deviation. (We say more about this in later chapters.)

Consider again the attractiveness ratings example shown in Figure 6–1. The mean of Population 1 was 220, the mean of Population 2 was 200, and the population standard deviation was 48. (In hypothesis-testing situations you don't know the mean of Population 1; so you actually use an *estimated mean;* thus, you are actually figuring an *estimated effect size.*) Using these numbers,

d effect size

$$d = (\mu_1 - \mu_2)/\sigma = (220 - 200)/48 = 20/48 = .42.$$

For the example in which the sample mean was 210, we estimated Population 1's mean to be 210. Thus,

$$d = (\mu_1 - \mu_2)/\sigma = (210 - 200)/48 = 10/48 = .21$$

However, suppose the procedure actually reduced the score, so that those who were given the special instructions had a mean of 170:

$$d = (\mu_1 - \mu_2)/\sigma = (170 - 200)/48 = -30/48 = -.63.$$

The minus sign means that the effect is a decrease.

Table 6-2 Summary of Cohen's Effect Size Conventions for Mean Differences	
Verbal Description	**Effect Size (*d*)**
Small	.20
Medium	.50
Large	.80

Effect Size Conventions

What should you consider to be a "big" effect, and what is a "small" effect? Jacob Cohen (1988, 1992), a renowned psychologist who you learned about in Box 4–1 in Chapter 4, helped solve this problem. Cohen came up with some **effect size conventions** based on the effects found in psychology research in general. Specifically, Cohen recommended that, for the kind of situation we are considering in this chapter, we should think of a small effect size as about .20. With a *d* of .20, the populations of individuals have an overlap of about 85%. This small effect size of .20 is, for example, the average difference in height between 15- and 16-year-old girls (see Figure 6–4a), which is about a half-inch difference with a standard deviation of about 2.1 inches. Cohen considered a medium effect size to be .50, which means an overlap of about 67%. This is about the average difference in heights between 14- and 18-year-old girls (see Figure 6–4b). Finally, Cohen defined a large effect size as .80. This is only about a 53% overlap. It is about the average difference in height between 13- and 18-year-old girls (see Figure 6–4c). These three effect size conventions are summarized in Table 6–2. (Note that these effect size conventions apply in

effect size conventions   standard rules about what to consider a small, medium, and large effect size, based on what is typical in psychology research; also known as Cohen's conventions.

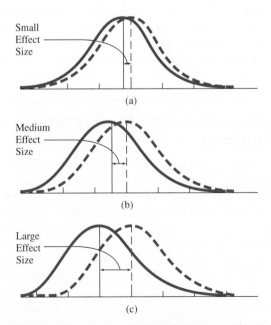

Figure 6-4 Comparisons of pairs of population distributions of individuals showing Cohen's conventions for effect size: (a) small effect size (*d* = .20), (b) medium effect size (*d* = .50), (c) large effect size (*d* = .80).

the same way to both positive and negative effect sizes. So, $-.20$ is a small effect size, $-.50$ is a medium effect size, and $-.80$ is a large effect size.)

Consider another example. As noted earlier in the book, many IQ tests have a standard deviation of 16 points. An experimental procedure with a small effect size would create an increase in IQ of 3.2 IQ points. (A difference of 3.2 IQ points between the mean of the population who goes through the experimental procedure and the mean of the population that does not, divided by the population standard deviation of 16, gives an effect size of .20. That is, $d = 3.2/16 = .20$.) An experimental procedure with a medium effect size would increase IQ by 8 points. An experimental procedure with a large effect size would increase IQ by 12.8 points.

Cohen's effect sizes provide a standard for deciding on the importance of the effect of a study in relation to what is typical in psychology.

Meta-Analysis

Meta-analysis is an important development in statistics that has had a profound effect on psychology, especially clinical and social psychology, and on many other scientific fields, such as medicine, education, and organizational behavior. This procedure combines results from different studies, even results using different methods of measurement. When combining results, the crucial thing is the *effect sizes*. As an example, a social psychologist might be interested in the effects of cross-race friendships on prejudice, a topic on which there has been a large number of studies. Using meta-analysis, the social psychologist could combine the results of these studies. This would provide an overall effect size. It would also tell how effect sizes differ for studies done in different countries or about prejudice toward different ethnic groups. (For an example of such a meta-analysis, see Pettigrew & Tropp, 2006. For another example of meta-analysis, see Box 6–1.) An educational psychologist might be interested in the effects of different educational methods on students' educational achievement. Walberg and Lai (1999) carried out a large meta-analysis on this very topic and provided effect size estimates for 275 educational methods and conditions. The effect sizes for selected general educational methods are shown in Table 6–3. As you can see in the table, many of the methods are associated with medium effect sizes and several have large (or very large) effect sizes.

meta-analysis statistical method for combining effect sizes from different studies.

BOX 6–1   **Effect Sizes for Relaxation and Meditation: A Restful Meta-Analysis**

In the 1970s and 1980s, the results of research on meditation and relaxation were the subject of considerable controversy. Eppley, Abrams, and Shear (1989) decided to look at the issue systematically by conducting a meta-analysis of the effects of various relaxation techniques on trait anxiety (that is, ongoing anxiety as opposed to a temporary state). Eppley and colleagues chose trait anxiety for their meta-analysis because it is a definite problem related to many other mental health issues, yet in itself is fairly consistent from test to test.

Following the usual procedure, the researchers searched the scientific literature for studies—not only research journals, but books and unpublished doctoral dissertations. Finding all the relevant research studies is one of the most difficult parts of meta-analysis.

To find the "bottom line," these researchers compared effect sizes for each of the four widely studied methods of meditation and relaxation. The result was that the average effect size for the 35 transcendental meditation (TM) studies was .70 (meaning an average difference of .70 standard deviations in anxiety scores between those who practiced this meditation procedure and those in the control groups). This effect size was significantly larger than the average effect size of .28 for the 44 studies on all other types of meditation, the average effect size of .38 for the 30 studies on "progressive relaxation" (a widely used method by clinical psychologists), and the average effect size of .40 for the 37 studies on other forms of relaxation.

Looking at different populations of research participants, they discovered that people who were screened to be highly anxious contributed more to the effect size, and prison populations and younger participants seemed to gain more from TM. There was little or no impact on effect size of the skill of the instructors, expectations of the participants, whether participants had volunteered or been randomly assigned to conditions, experimenter bias (the TM results were actually stronger when any apparently pro-TM researchers' studies were eliminated), the various measures of anxiety, and the research designs.

The researchers thought that one clue to TM's high performance might be that techniques involving concentration produced a significantly smaller effect, whereas TM makes a point of teaching an "effortless, spontaneous" method. Also, TM uses Sanskrit mantras (special sounds) said to come from a very old tradition and selected for each student by the instructor. Results were lower for methods employing randomly selected Sanskrit sounds or personally selected English words.

Whatever the reasons, the authors concluded that there are "grounds for optimism that at least some current treatment procedures can effectively reduce trait anxiety" (p. 973). So if you are prone to worry about matters like statistics exams, consider these results.

Reviews of the collection of studies on a particular topic that use meta-analysis are an alternative to the traditional "narrative" literature review article. Such traditional reviews describe and evaluate each study and then attempt to draw some overall conclusion. The first formal meta-analysis in psychology, which focused on the effects of psychotherapy, was published more than 30 years ago (Smith & Glass, 1977).

Table 6-3   Effect Sizes of Selected General Educational Methods

Elements of Instruction	
Cues	1.25
Reinforcement	1.17
Corrective feedback	.94
Engagement	.88
Mastery Learning	.73
Computer-Assisted Instruction	
For early elementary students	1.05
For handicapped students	.66
Teaching	
Direct instruction	.71
Comprehension instruction	.55
Teaching Techniques	
Homework with teacher comments	.83
Graded homework	.78
Frequent testing	.49
Pretests	.48
Adjunct questions	.40
Goal setting	.40
Assigned homework	.28
Explanatory Graphics	.75

Source: Adapted from Walberg, H. J., & Lai, J. S. (1999). Meta-analytic effects for policy. In G. J. Cizek (Ed.). *Handbook of Educational Policy* (pp. 419–453). San Diego, CA. Academic Press. Copyright © 1999 by Elsevier. Reprinted by permission of Elsevier.

Table 6–4	Number of Publications on Meta-Analysis in the Psychological Research Literature During Each 3-Year Period from 1977 Through 2006
Publication Dates	**Number of Publications**
1977–1979	17
1980–1982	86
1983–1985	277
1986–1988	398
1989–1991	550
1992–1994	652
1995–1997	806
1998–2000	850
2001–2003	1176
2004–2006	1588

Source: PsycINFO.

Since then, meta-analysis has become an increasingly popular statistical procedure. To get a sense of the popularity of meta-analysis, we used a research database commonly used by psychologists (called PsycINFO) to search for publications on meta-analysis in the psychological research literature during each three-year period from 1977 through 2006. As you can see in Table 6–4, the number of research publications (research articles, books, book chapters, and dissertations) on meta-analysis has increased during every successive three-year period.

How are you doing?

1. What does effect size add to just knowing whether a result is significant?
2. Why do researchers usually use a *standardized* effect size?
3. Write the formula for effect size in the situation we have been considering, and define each of the symbols.
4. On a standard test, the population is known to have a mean of 500 and a standard deviation of 100. Those receiving an experimental treatment have a mean of 540. What is the effect size?
5. (a) Why are effect size conventions useful? (b) What are the effect size conventions for *d*?
6. (a) What is meta-analysis? (b) What is the role of effect size in a meta-analysis?

3. The formula for effect size is $d = (\mu_1 - \mu_2)/\sigma$. d is effect size; μ_1 is the mean of Population 1 (the mean for the population that receives the experimental manipulation); μ_2 is the mean of Population 2 (the known population, the basis for the comparison distribution); and σ is the population standard deviation.
4. The effect size is $d = (\mu_1 - \mu_2)/\sigma = (540 - 500)/100 = .40$.
5. (a) Effect size conventions allow you to compare the effect size of a study to what is typically found in psychology research. (b) The effect size conventions for *d* are small = .20, medium = .50, large = .80.
6. (a) Meta-analysis is a systematic procedure for combining results of different studies. (b) Meta-analyses usually come up with average effect sizes across studies and compare effect sizes for different subgroups of studies.

Statistical Power

Power is the ability to achieve your goals. A goal of a researcher conducting a study is to get a significant result—but only *if* the research hypothesis really is true. The **statistical power** of a research study is the probability that the study will produce a statistically significant result if the research hypothesis is true. Power is *not* the probability that a study will produce a statistically significant result; it is the probability that a study will produce a statistically significant result, *if the research hypothesis is true*. If the research hypothesis is false, you do not want to get significant results. (That would be a Type I error, as you learned earlier in the chapter.) Remember, however, even if the research hypothesis is true, a study will not automatically give a significant result; the sample that happens to be selected from the population may not turn out to be extreme enough to reject the null hypothesis.

Statistical power is important for several reasons. As you will learn later in the chapter, figuring power when planning a study helps you determine how many participants you need. As you will also learn later in the chapter, understanding power is extremely important when you read a research article, particularly for making sense of results that are not significant or results that are statistically but not practically significant.

Consider once again our example in which students rated the physical attractiveness of a person after being told that the person has positive personality qualities. Recall that we compared two populations:

Population 1: Students who are told that the person has positive personality qualities.

Population 2: Students in general (who are told nothing about the person's personality qualities).

Also recall that the research hypothesis was that Population 1 would give higher attractiveness ratings than Population 2.

The curve in Figure 6–5 shows the distribution of means for Population 2. (Be careful: when discussing effect size, we showed figures, such as Figures 6–2 and 6–3, for populations of individuals; now we are back to focusing on distributions of means.) This curve is the comparison distribution, the distribution of means that you would expect for both populations if the null hypothesis were true. The mean of this distribution of means is 200 and its standard deviation is 6. In Chapter 5, we found that using the 5% significance level, one-tailed, you need a Z score for the mean of your sample of at least 1.64 to reject the null hypothesis. Using the formula for converting Z scores to raw scores, this comes out to a raw score of 209.84; that is, $(1.64)(6) + 200 = 209.84$. Therefore, we have shaded the tail of the distribution above a raw score of 209.84 (a Z score of 1.64 on this distribution). This is the area where you would reject the null hypothesis if, as a result of your study, the mean of your sample was in this area. This shaded area is labeled "alpha" because alpha is a name for the significance level (which in this example is 5%, or $p < .05$).

statistical power probability that the study will give a significant result if the research hypothesis is true.

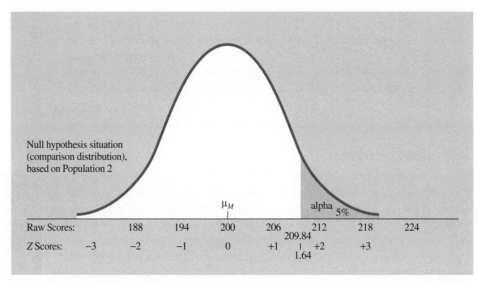

Figure 6–5   For the fictional study of positive personality qualities and ratings of physical attractiveness, distribution of means for Population 2 (the comparison distribution), students told nothing about the person's personality. Significance cutoff score (209.84) shown for *p* < .05, one-tailed.

Imagine that the researcher predicts that telling students about the positive personality qualities of the person will increase the attractiveness rating of the person to 208. (This is an increase of 8 points from the mean of 200 when no mention is made about the person's personality). If this prediction is correct, the research hypothesis is true and the mean of Population 1 (the population of students who are told about the person's positive personality qualities) is indeed greater than the mean of Population 2. The distribution of means for Population 1 for this *hypothetical predicted situation* is shown in the top part of Figure 6–6. Notice that the distribution has a mean of 208.

Now take a look at the curve shown in the bottom part of Figure 6–6. This curve is exactly the same as the one shown in Figure 6–5: the comparison distribution, the distribution of means for Population 2. Notice that the distribution of means for Population 1 (the top curve) is set off to the right of the distribution of means for Population 2 (the bottom curve). This is because the researcher predicts the mean of Population 1 to be higher (a mean of 208) than the mean of Population 1 (which we know is 200). (If Population 1's mean is predicted to be *lower* than Population 2's mean, then Population 1 would be set off to the *left*.) If the null hypothesis is true, the true distribution for Population 1 is the same as the distribution based on Population 2. Thus, the Population 1 distribution would be lined up directly above the Population 2 distribution and would not be set off to the right (or the left).

Recall that the cutoff score for rejecting the null hypothesis in this example is 209.84. Thus, the shaded rejection area for Population 2's distribution of means (shown in the bottom curve in Figure 6–6) starts at 209.84. We can also create a rejection area for the distribution of means for Population 1. This rejection area will also start at 209.84 (see the shaded area in the top curve in Figure 6–6). Remember that, in this example, Population 1's distribution of means represents the possible sample means that we would get if we randomly selected 64 students from a population of students with a mean of 208 (and a standard deviation of 48).

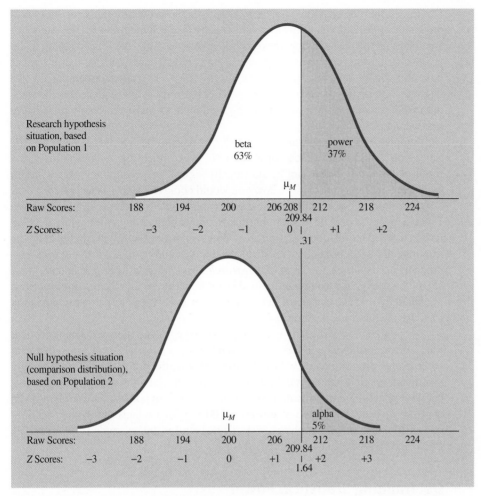

Figure 6-6   Distributions of means for the fictional study of positive personality qualities and ratings of physical attractiveness. Upper curve: Population 1 based on predicted population mean of 208. Lower curve: Population 2 (the comparison distribution) based on known population mean of 200. Significance cutoff score (209.84) shown for $p < .05$, one-tailed. Power = 37%.

Now, suppose the researcher carries out the study. The researcher randomly selects a sample of 64 students, tells them that a particular person has positive personality qualities, and then asks them to rate the attractiveness of that person. The researcher finds the mean of the attractiveness ratings given by the sample of 64 students in the study. And suppose this sample's mean turns out to be in the shaded area of the distributions (that is, a mean of 209.84 or higher). If that happens, the researcher will reject the null hypothesis. What Figure 6–6 shows us is that most of the means from Population 1's distribution of means (assuming that its mean is 208) will not be large enough to reject the null hypothesis. Less than half of the upper distribution is shaded. Put another way, if the research hypothesis is true, as the researcher predicts, the sample studied is a random sample from this Population 1 distribution of means. However, there is less than a 50-50 chance that the mean of a random sample from this distribution will be in the shaded rejection area.

Recall that the statistical power of a study is the probability that the study will produce a statistically significant result if the research hypothesis is true. Since we are assuming the research hypothesis is true in this example, the shaded region in the upper distribution represents the power of the study. It turns out that the power for this situation (shown in Figure 6–6) is only 37%. Therefore, assuming the researcher's prediction is correct, the researcher has only a 37% chance that the sample of 64 students will have a mean high enough to make the result statistically significant.

Suppose that the particular sample of 64 students studied had a mean of 203. Since you would need a mean of at least 209.84 to reject the null hypothesis, the result of this study would not be statistically significant, even though the research hypothesis really is true. This is how you would come to make a Type II error.

It is entirely possible that the researcher might select a sample from Population 1 with a mean far enough to the right (that is, with a high enough mean attractiveness rating) to be in the shaded rejection area. However, given the way we have set up the example, there is a better than even chance that the study will *not* turn out to be significant, *even though we know the research hypothesis is true.* (Of course, once again, the researcher would not know this.) When a study like the one in this example has only a small chance of being significant even if the research hypothesis is true, we say the study has *low power.*

As you learned earlier in the chapter, you make a Type II error if you do *not* get a significant result when in fact the research hypothesis is true. You learned that *beta* is the probability of making a Type II error—that is, the probability of *not* getting a significant result when the research hypothesis is true. Notice that power, the probability of getting a significant result if the research hypothesis is true, is just the *opposite* of beta. Thus, beta + power = 100%, which means that beta is 100% − power. In this example, power is 37%. Thus, beta for this example is 63% (that is, 100% − 37% = 63%) (see Figure 6–6).

Determining Statistical Power

The statistical power of a study can be figured. In a situation like the attractiveness ratings example (when you have a known population and a single sample), figuring power involves figuring out the area of the shaded portion of the upper distribution in Figure 6–6 (for more details, see the Advanced Topic section later in this chapter). The research situations faced by researchers (including those we consider in the next several chapters) are usually more complex than our current example, and figuring power is much more complicated. Thus, researchers do not usually figure power themselves and instead rely on alternate approaches.

Researchers can use a power software package to determine power. There are also power calculators available on the Internet. When using a power software package or Internet power calculator, the researcher puts in the values for the various aspects of the research study (such as the known population mean, the predicted population mean, the population standard deviation, the sample size, the significance level, and whether the test is one- or two-tailed), and the figuring is done automatically.

Finally, researchers can find the power of a study using special charts, called **power tables.** [Such tables have been prepared by Cohen (1988) and by Kraemer & Thiemann (1987), among others.] In the following chapters, with each method you learn, we provide basic power tables and discuss how to use them. Table A–5 in the Appendix is an index to these tables.

TIP FOR SUCCESS

Remember that power is expressed as a probability or percentage, and effect size (in the hypothesis testing situation you are learning about in this chapter) is a measure of the distance between two population means.

---

power table table for a hypothesis-testing procedure showing the statistical power of a study for various effect sizes and sample sizes.

1. (a) What is statistical power? (b) How is it different from just the probability of getting a significant result? (c) What is the probability of getting a significant result if the research hypothesis is false?
2. Give two reasons why statistical power is important.
3. (a) What is the relationship of power to beta? (b) How is beta figured?
4. (a) Name three approaches that researchers typically use to determine power. (b) Why do researchers use these approaches, as opposed to figuring power themselves by hand?

Answers

1. (a) Statistical power is the probability of getting a significant result if the research hypothesis is true. (b) It is the probability of getting a significant result if *the research hypothesis is true*. (c) The probability of getting a significant result if the research hypothesis is false is alpha, the significance level (that is, the probability of making a Type I error).
2. Statistical power is important because (i) it can help you determine how many participants are needed for a study you are planning, and (ii) understanding power can help you make sense of results that are not significant or results that are statistically but not practically significant.
3. (a) Beta, the probability of *not* getting a significant result if the research hypothesis is true, is the opposite of power, the probability of getting a significant result if the research hypothesis is true. (b) Beta is 100% minus power.
4. (a) Three approaches that researchers typically use to determine power are (i) power software packages, (ii) Internet power calculators, and (iii) power tables. (b) In common hypothesis-testing situations, figuring power by hand is very complicated.

What Determines the Power of a Study?

It is very important that you understand what power is about. It is especially important to understand the factors that affect the power of a study and how to use power when planning a study and when making sense of a study you read.

The statistical power of a study depends on two main factors: (1) how big an effect (the effect size) the research hypothesis predicts and (2) how many participants are in the study (the sample size). Power is also affected by the significance level chosen, whether a one-tailed or two-tailed test is used, and the kind of hypothesis-testing procedure used.

Effect Size

Figure 6–6 shows the situation in our attractiveness ratings example in which the researcher had reason to predict that students told that the person has positive personality qualities (Population 1, the upper curve) would have a mean score *8 points higher* than students who were not told anything about the person's personality (Population 2, the lower curve). Figure 6–7 shows the same study for a situation in which the researcher had reason to expect that Population 1 would have a mean score *16 points higher* than Population 2. Comparing Figure 6–7 to Figure 6–6, you are more likely to get a significant result in the situation shown in Figure 6–7. In fact, we noted earlier that the Figure 6–6 situation, in which the researcher had reason to

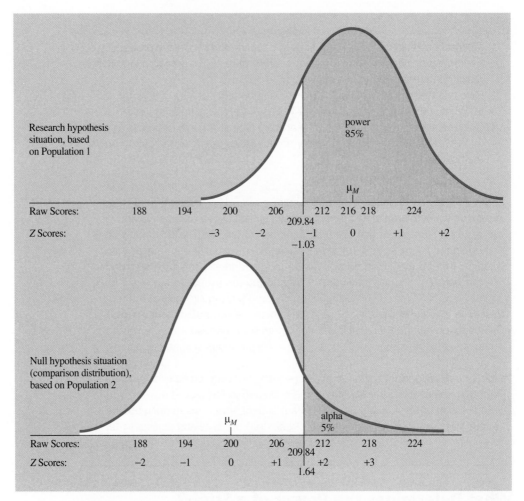

Raw Scores: 188   194   200   206   212   216   218   224

209.84

Z Scores: −3   −2   −1   0   +1   +2

−1.03

Figure 6–7 Distributions of means for the fictional study of positive personality qualities and ratings of physical attractiveness. Upper curve: Population 1, based on predicted population mean of 216. Bottom curve: Population 2 (the comparison distribution), based on the known population mean of 200. Significance cutoff score (209.84) shown for $p < .05$, one-tailed. Power = 85%. Compare with Figure 6–6, in which the predicted population mean was 208 and power was 37%.

predict a mean of only 208, has a power of 37%. However, the Figure 6–7 situation, in which there was a basis for the researcher to predict a mean of 216, comes out to a power of 85%. In any study, the bigger the difference that your theory or previous research says you should expect between the two populations, the more power there is in the study. That is, if in fact there is a big mean difference in the population, you have more chance of getting a significant result in the study. So if you predict a bigger mean difference, the power you figure based on that prediction will be greater. (Thus if you figure power based on a prediction that is unrealistically big, you are just fooling yourself about the power of the study.)

    The difference in the means between populations we saw earlier is part of what goes into effect size. Thus, the bigger the effect size is, the greater the power is. The effect size for the situation in Figure 6–6, in which the researcher predicted Population 1 to have a mean of 208, is .17. That is, $d = (\mu_1 - \mu_2)/\sigma = (208 - 200)/48 = 8/48 = .17$. The effect size for the situation in Figure 6–7, in which the

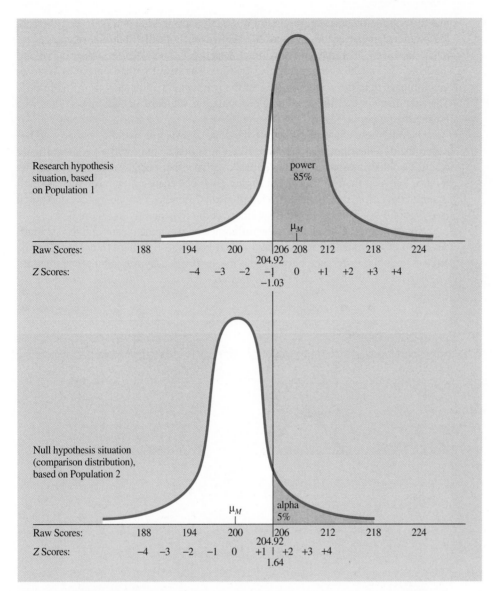

Figure 6–8 Distributions of means for the fictional study of positive personality qualities and ratings of physical attractiveness. Upper curve: Population 1, based on predicted population mean of 208. Bottom curve: Population 2 (the comparison distribution), based on the known population mean of 200. In this example, the population standard deviation is half as large as that shown for this example in previous figures. Significance cutoff score (204.92) shown for $p < .05$, one-tailed. Power = 85%. Compare with Figure 6–6, which had the original population standard deviation and power was 37%.

researcher predicted Population 1 to have a mean of 216, is .33. That is, $d = (\mu_1 - \mu_2)/\sigma = (216 - 200)/48 = .33$.

Effect size, however, is also affected by the population standard deviation. The smaller the standard deviation is, the bigger the effect size is. In terms of the effect size formula, this is because, if you divide by a smaller number, the result is bigger. In terms of the actual distributions, this is because, if two distributions that are separated are narrower, they *overlap less*. Figure 6–8 shows two distributions of means based on the same example. However, this time we have changed the example so that the population standard deviation is exactly half of what it was. In this version, the predicted mean is the original 208. However, both distributions of means are much narrower. Therefore, there is much less overlap between the upper curve and the lower curve (the comparison distribution). The result is that the power is 85%, much higher than the power of 37% in the original situation shown in Figure 6–6. The idea here is that the smaller the population standard deviation becomes, the greater the power is.

Overall, these examples illustrate the general principle that the less overlap between the two distributions, the more likely it is that a study will give a significant result. Two distributions might have little overlap either because there is a large difference between their means (as in Figure 6–7) or because they have such a small standard deviation, that even with a small mean difference they do not overlap much (see Figure 6–8). This principle is summarized more generally in Figure 6–9.

Notice that these two factors, the difference between the means and the standard deviation of the population, are exactly what goes into figuring effect size. That is, effect size is the difference between the means divided by the population standard

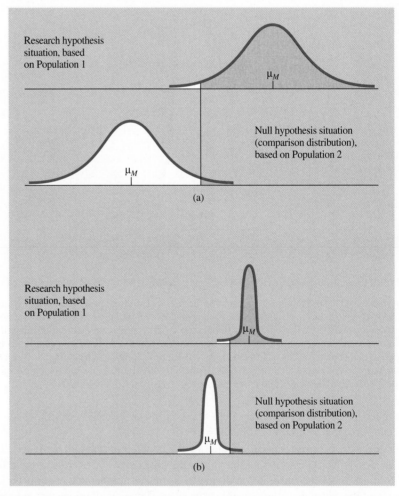

Figure 6-9   The predicted and comparison distributions of means might have little overlap (and thus the study would have high power) because either (a) the two means are very different or (b) the population standard deviation is very small.

deviation: $d = (\mu_1 - \mu_2)/\sigma$. Thus, the larger the expected difference is between the two population means (that is, the larger $\mu_1 - \mu_2$ is), the greater the effect size becomes; and the smaller the standard deviation is within the two populations (that is, the smaller σ^2 is and thus the smaller σ is), the greater the effect size becomes. And the greater the effect size is, the greater the power is.

When figuring power in advance of doing a study, the difference between the means of the two populations is the difference between the known population mean (Population 2) and the researcher's prediction for the population to be given the experimental manipulation (Population 1). This prediction is based on a precise theory, on previous experience with research of this kind, or on what would be the smallest difference that would be useful. In the situations we have considered so far, the population standard deviation, the other number you need to figure the effect size, is known in advance.

Determining Power from Predicted Effect Sizes

Sometimes, instead of predicting a particular mean, researchers predict an effect size. Especially when studying something for the first time, researchers make this prediction using Cohen's conventions. That is, they may have only a fairly vague idea of how big an effect to expect, so if they expect a small effect, for example, they use a predicted effect size of .20.

Once the researchers have predicted an effect size, in whatever way, they can use their predicted effect size to figure the predicted mean (the mean for Population 1), and then find the power in the usual way (using a power software package, an Internet power calculator, or a power table, or using the figuring shown in the Advanced Topic section later in this chapter). Consider our example in which the known population (Population 2) has a mean of 200 and a standard deviation of 48. Suppose the researcher predicts an effect size of .20 (a small effect size, using Cohen's conventions). In this situation, the predicted mean has to be enough higher than 200 so that the overall effect size, after dividing by 48, comes out to .20. That is, the mean difference has to increase by .20 standard deviations. In the example, .20 of 48 is 9.60. Thus, the predicted mean has to be 9.60 higher than the known mean. In this example, the known mean is 200; so the predicted mean for an effect size of .20 would be 209.60.

Stating this principle in terms of a formula,

$$\text{Predicted } \mu_1 = \mu_2 + (d)(\sigma) \tag{6-2}$$

Using the formula for a predicted effect size of .20 (a small effect size),

$$\text{Predicted } \mu_1 = \mu_2 + (d)(\sigma) = 200 + (.20)(48) = 200 + 9.60 = 209.60.$$

Using the formula for a predicted effect size of .50 (a medium effect size),

$$\text{Predicted } \mu_1 = \mu_2 + (d)(\sigma) = 200 + (.50)(48) = 200 + 24.00 = 224.00.$$

Figure 6–10 shows, for our attractiveness ratings example, the distributions of means for small (middle curve) and medium (upper curve) predicted effect sizes, along with the power for each situation.

> The predicted mean of the population to which the experimental procedure will be applied is the known population mean plus the result of multiplying the predicted effect size by the known population standard deviation.

Sample Size

The other major influence on power, besides effect size, is the number of people in the sample studied, the sample size. Basically, the more people there are in the study, the more power there is.

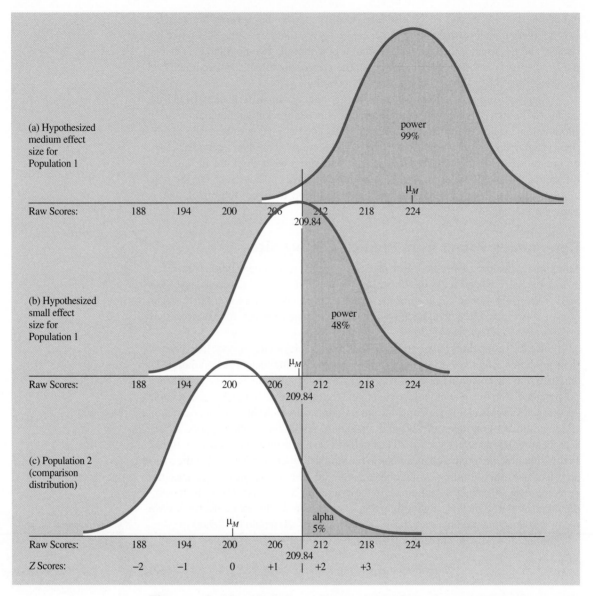

Figure 6-10 Distributions of means for the fictional study of positive personality qualities and ratings of physical attractiveness: (a) and (b) are based on predicted distributions of populations of individuals; (c) is based on a known distribution of population of individuals. Significance cutoff score (209.84) shown for $p < .05$, one-tailed. In this example, (a) is the predicted distribution with a medium effect size ($d = .50$, power = 99%); and (b) is the predicted distribution with a small effect size ($d = .20$, power = 48%).

Sample size affects power because, the larger the sample size is, the smaller the standard deviation of the distribution of means becomes. If these distributions have a smaller standard deviation, they are narrower. And if they are narrower, there is less overlap between them. Figure 6–11 shows the situation for our attractiveness ratings example if the study included 100 students, instead of the 64 in the original example, with a predicted mean of 208 and a population standard deviation of 48. The power now is 51%. (It was 37% with 64 students.) With 500 participants in the study, power is 99% (see Figure 6–12).

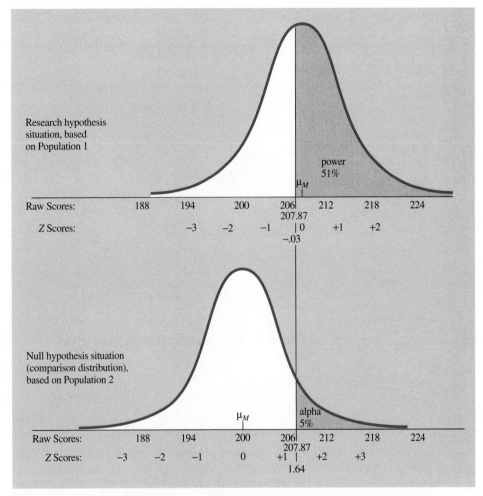

Figure 6–11   Distributions of means for the fictional study of positive personality qualities and ratings of physical attractiveness. Upper curve: Population 1, based on predicted population mean of 208. Bottom curve: Population 2 (the comparison distribution), based on the known population mean of 200. In this example, the sample size is 100, compared to 64 in the original example. Significance cutoff score (207.87) shown for $p < .05$, one-tailed. Power = 51%. Compare with Figure 6–6, which had the original sample size and power was 37%.

Don't get mixed up. The distributions of means can be narrow (and thus have less overlap and more power) for two very different reasons. One reason is that the population of individuals may have a small standard deviation; this has to do with effect size. The other reason is that the sample size is large. This reason is completely separate. Sample size has nothing to do with effect size. Both effect size and sample size affect power. However, as we will see shortly, these two different influences on power lead to completely different kinds of practical steps for increasing power when planning a study.

Figuring Needed Sample Size for a Given Level of Power

When planning a study, the main reason researchers consider power is to help decide how many participants to include in the study. Sample size has an important influence on power. Thus, a researcher wants to be sure to have enough people in the

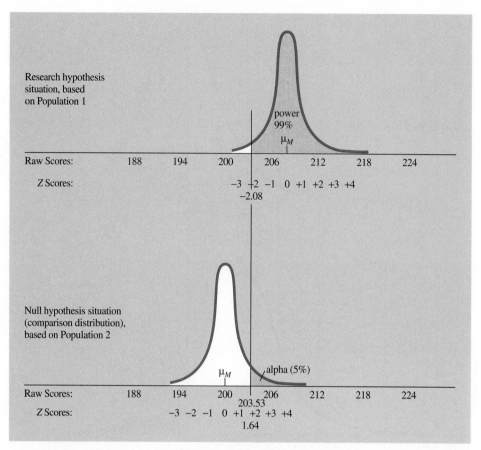

Figure 6–12 Distributions of means for the fictional distribution of positive personality qualities and ratings of physical attractiveness. Upper curve: Population 1, based on predicted population mean of 208. Bottom curve: Population 2 (the comparison distribution), based on the known population mean of 200. In this example, the sample size is 500, compared to 64 in the original example. Significance cutoff score (203.53) shown for $p < .05$, one-tailed. Power = 99%. Compare with Figure 6–6, which had the original sample size and power was 37%, and with Figure 6–7, which had a sample of 100 and a power of 51%.

study for the study to have fairly high power. (Too often, researchers carry out studies in which the power is so low that it is unlikely they will get a significant result even if the research hypothesis is true. See Box 6–2.)

A researcher can figure out the needed number of participants by turning the steps of figuring power on their head. You begin with the level of power you want—say, 80%—and then figure how many participants you need to get that level of power. Suppose the researcher in our attractiveness ratings example was planning the study and wanted to figure out how many students to include in the sample. Let us presume that based on previous research for a situation like this, the researcher predicts a mean difference of 8 and there is a known population standard deviation of 48. In this case, it turns out that the researcher would need 222 students to have 80% power. We won't go into the computational details here. (However, if you read the Advanced Procedures section later in the chapter, you might want to try figuring this out on your own. See if you can get the same answer as we did, starting with 80% power and following the steps backward to get the number of participants needed.)

In practice, researchers use power software packages, Internet power calculators, or special power tables that tell you how many participants you need in a study

BOX 6-2 **The Power of Typical Psychology Experiments**

More than four decades ago, Jacob Cohen (1962), a psychologist specializing in statistical methods (see Box 4–1), published in the *Journal of Abnormal and Social Psychology* a now well-known analysis of the statistical power of studies. He had observed that great attention was given to significance, or the issue of whether a Type I error had been made (that the null hypothesis was mistakenly rejected and some effect was being assumed from the results that in fact did not exist). But essentially no attention was given to the possibility of a Type II error (that the null hypothesis had been mistakenly not rejected and a real effect was ignored—indeed, often treated as nonexistent—because of inconclusive results). Power was not even mentioned in the studies he was discussing.

Cohen computed the power for the results in these articles. Not being familiar with the many content areas involved, he looked at power under three assumptions of effect size: small, medium, and large. If small, he found, the studies published had only one chance in six of detecting a significant effect because of their small sample sizes. Not had a better than 50-50 chance. If he assumed a medium effect in the population, the studies had a slightly better than 50-50 chance of detecting this effect. One quarter still had less than one chance in three. Only if one assumes large effect sizes did the studies as they were designed have a good chance of rejecting the null hypothesis. As Cohen (1962) put it, "A generation of researchers could be suitably employed in repeating interesting studies which originally used inadequate sample sizes" (p. 153).

These experiments that "failed," when in fact their hypotheses were never adequately tested, represented tremendous knowledge that may have been lost, perhaps never to be explored again. And this loss was simply because of a failure to be concerned about power—most often a failure to calculate, through a consideration of effect size, significance level, and power, the sample size that would best test the hypothesis.

In 1969, Cohen published a handbook for analyzing power in the social sciences, and a revised version appeared in 1988. Still, in an article published in 1989, Sedlmeier and Gigerenzer observed that Cohen's admonitions apparently had had no effect during the intervening years. In fact, the power of studies in the same journal that Cohen had studied (now the *Journal of Abnormal Psychology*) had actually decreased over those years. And low power still went unnoticed. Only 2 of 64 experiments even discussed power, and these two had

not estimated it. Meanwhile, in 11% of the studies published in that issue, nonsignificance was considered a confirmation of the null hypothesis, perhaps in an attempt to adhere to the traditional admonitions we questioned in Chapter 4, Box 4–1. Yet Sedlmeier and Gigerenzer found that the median power in these particular studies was only 25%. Certainly, if we are to consider it valuable information in itself when results favor the null hypothesis (again, see Box 4–1), it can be taken that way only when power is high enough so that, if the research hypothesis was true, the study would at least have an even chance of showing it.

A number of analyses of the power of studies in specific journals and research fields suggest that many studies are conducted with low power (e.g., Bezeau and Graves's 2001 analysis of three clinical neuropsychology journals, Clark-Carters's 1997 study of the *British Journal of Psychology*, and Woods et al.'s 2006 study of the cognitive effect of subthalamic nucleus deep brain stimulation in Parkinson's disease). However, this trend may not hold for all areas of psychological research. For example, Maddock and Rossi (2001) reported that studies published in three health psychology-related journals had, on average, enough power to identify both large and medium-sized effects. Maxwell (2004) suggested that this may in part be due to the fact that many health psychology studies are funded by government research grants, for which researchers submit a grant proposal containing an analysis of the power of the proposed study.

Still, the stubborn failure by many researchers to consider power is a bit shocking. More often than not, it means that researchers are going through all their work for nothing. The odds are against their finding what they seek, even if it is true. But in an article in *American Psychologist* titled "Things I Have Learned (So Far)," Jacob Cohen (1990) looked back over the decades philosophically:

I do not despair. I remember that W. S. Gosset, the fellow who worked in a brewery and appeared in print modestly as "Student," published the *t* test a decade before we entered World War I, and the test didn't get into the psychological statistics textbooks until after World War II.

These things take time. So, if you publish something that you think is really good, and a year or a decade or two go by and hardly anyone seems to have taken notice, remember the *t* test, and take heart. (p. 1311)

to have a high level of power, given a certain predicted effect size. We provide simplified versions of power tables for each of the main hypothesis-testing procedures you learn in upcoming chapters.

Other Influences on Power

Three other factors, besides effect size and sample size, affect power.

1. **Significance level (alpha).** Less extreme significance levels (such as $p < .10$ or $p < .20$) mean more power. More extreme significance levels ($p < .01$ or $p < .001$) mean less power. Less extreme significance levels result in more power because the shaded rejection area on the lower curve is bigger. Thus, more of the area in the upper curve is shaded. More extreme significance levels result in less power because the shaded rejection region on the lower curve is smaller. Suppose in our attractiveness ratings example we had used the .01 significance level instead. The power would have dropped from 37% to only 16% (see Figure 6–13).

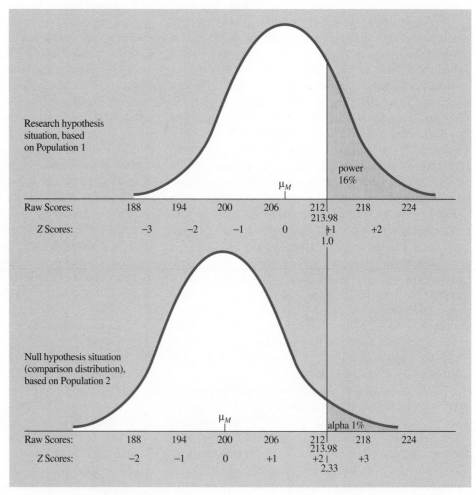

Figure 6–13 Distributions of means for the fictional study of positive personality qualities and ratings of physical attractiveness. Upper curve: Population 1, based on predicted population mean of 208. Bottom curve: Population 2 (the comparison distribution), based on the known population mean of 200. Significance cutoff score (213.98) now shown for $p < .01$, one-tailed. Power = 16%. Compare with Figure 6–6, which used a significance level of $p < .05$, one-tailed, and power was 37%.

It is important to bear in mind that using a less extreme significance level (such as $p < .10$ or $p < .20$) increases the chance of making a Type I error. Also, using an extreme significance level (such as $p < .01$ or $p < .001$) increases the chance of making a Type II error.

2. **One- versus two-tailed tests.** Using a two-tailed test makes it harder to get significance on any one tail. Thus, keeping everything else the same, power is less with a two-tailed test than with a one-tailed test. Suppose in our attractiveness ratings example we had used a two-tailed test instead of a one-tailed test (but still using 5% overall). As shown in Figure 6–14, power would be only 26% (compared to 37% in the original one-tailed version).

3. **Type of hypothesis-testing procedure.** Sometimes the researcher has a choice of more than one hypothesis-testing procedure to use for a particular study. We have not considered any such situations so far in this book, but we will do so in Chapter 14.

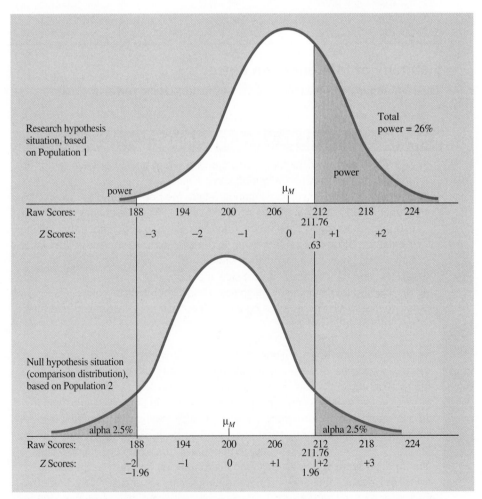

Figure 6–14   Distributions of means for the fictional study of positive personality qualities and ratings of physical attractiveness. Upper curve: Population 1, based on predicted population mean of 208. Bottom curve: Population 2 (the comparison distribution), based on the known population mean of 200. Significance cutoff score (211.76) now shown for $p < .05$, two-tailed. Power = 26%. Compare with Figure 6–6, which used a significance level of $p < .05$, one-tailed, and power was 37%.

Table 6-5 Influences on Power

Feature of the Study	Increases Power	Decreases Power
Effect size (d) $(d = [\mu_1 - \mu_2]/\sigma)$	Large d	Small d
Effect size combines the following two features:		
Predicted difference between population means $(\mu_1 - \mu_2)$	Large differences	Small differences
Population standard deviation (σ)	Small (σ)	Large (σ)
Sample size (N)	Large N	Small N
Significance level (α)	Lenient, high α (such as .05 or .10)	Extreme, low α (such as .01 or .001)
One-tailed versus two-tailed test	One-tailed	Two-tailed
Type of hypothesis-testing procedure used	Varies	Varies

Summary of Influences on Power

Table 6–5 summarizes the effects of various factors on the power of a study.

How are you doing?

1. (a) What are the two factors that determine effect size? For each factor [(b) and (c)], explain how and why it affects power.
2. In a planned study involving a standard test, the population is known to have a mean of 500 and a standard deviation of 100. The researchers predict that their planned experimental procedure will produce a large effect (that is, they predict an effect size of .80). What is the predicted mean of the population that will be given the experimental procedure?
3. (a) How and (b) why does sample size affect power?
4. (a) How and (b) why does the significance level used affect power?
5. (a) How and (b) why does using a one-tailed versus a two-tailed test affect power?

of dividing the population variance by the sample size) and thus have less
overlap; so the area in the predicted distribution that is more extreme than the
cutoff in the known distribution is greater.
4. (a) The more lenient the significance level is (for example, .10 versus .05), the
more power there is. (b) This is because it makes the cutoff in the known distribution less extreme; so the corresponding area that is more extreme than
this cutoff in the predicted distribution of means is larger.
5. (a) A study with a one-tailed test has more power (for a result in the predicted
direction) than a two-tailed test. (b) This is because with a one-tailed test, the
cutoff in the predicted direction in the known distribution is less extreme; so the
corresponding area that is more extreme than this cutoff in the predicted distribution of means is larger. There is an added cutoff in the opposite side with a two-
tailed test, but this is so far out on the distribution that it has little effect on power.

Answers

1. (a) The two factors that determine effect size are (i) the difference between the known and predicted population means and (ii) the population standard deviation.
(b) The more difference there is between the means, the larger the effect size is, and the more power. This is because it drives the distributions of means farther apart and thus they have less overlap; so the area in the predicted distribution that is more extreme than the cutoff in the known distribution is greater.
(c) The smaller the population standard deviation is, the larger the effect size becomes, and the greater the power. This is because it makes the distributions of means narrower and thus have less overlap. Therefore, the area in the predicted distribution that is more extreme than the cutoff in the known distribution is greater.

2. The predicted mean of the population that will be given the experimental procedure is $\mu_1 = \mu_2 + (d)(\sigma) = 500 + (.80)(100) = 580$.

3. (a) The larger the sample size is, the more power there is. (b) This is because a larger sample size makes the distributions of means narrower (because the standard deviation of the distribution of means is the square root of the result

The Role of Power When Planning a Study

Determining power is very important when planning a study. If you do a study in which the power is low, even if the research hypothesis is true, the study will probably not give statistically significant results. Thus, the time and expense of carrying out the study, as it is currently planned, would probably not be worthwhile. So when the power of a planned study is found to be low, researchers look for practical ways to increase the power to an acceptable level.

What is an acceptable level of power? A widely used rule is that a study should have 80% power to be worth doing (see Cohen, 1988). Power of 80% means that there is an 80% (8 out of 10) chance that the study will produce a statistically significant result if the research hypothesis is true. Obviously, the more power the better. However, the costs of greater power, such as studying more people, often make even 80% power beyond your reach.

How can you increase the power of a planned study? In principle, you can do so by changing any of the factors summarized in Table 6–5. Let's consider each.

1. **Increase effect size by increasing the predicted difference between population means.** You can't just arbitrarily predict a bigger effect. There has to be a basis for your prediction. Thus, to increase the predicted difference, your method in carrying out the study must make it reasonable to expect a bigger effect. Consider again our example of the experiment about the impact of telling students about the positive personality characteristics of a person on the attractiveness ratings of that person. One way to increase the expected mean difference might be to use a more intense experimental procedure (such as telling students that the person has a great many positive personality qualities and does not have a single negative personality quality). A disadvantage of this approach of increasing the impact of the experimental procedure is that you may have to use an experimental procedure that is not like the one to which you want the results of your study to apply. It can also sometimes be difficult or costly. In some studies, another way to increase the expected

mean difference might be to make the instructions more elaborate, spending more time explaining them, perhaps allowing time for practice, and so forth.

2. **Increase effect size by decreasing the population standard deviation.** You can decrease the population standard deviation in a planned study in at least two ways. One way is to study a population that has less variance within it than the one originally planned. For example, in a study of fifth-graders' performance on a test, you might only use fifth-graders in a particular suburban school system. The disadvantage is that your results will then apply only to the more limited population.

   Another way to decrease the population standard deviation is to use conditions of testing that are more standardized and measures that are more precise. For example, testing in a controlled laboratory setting usually makes for less variation among scores in results (meaning a smaller standard deviation). Similarly, using measures and tests with very clear wording also reduces variation. When practical, this is an excellent way to increase power, but often the study is already as rigorous as it can be.

3. **Increase the sample size.** The most straightforward way to increase power is to study more people. Of course, if you are studying billionaires who have made their fortune by founding an Internet company, there is a limit to how many are available. Also, using a larger sample size often adds to the time and cost of conducting the research study. In most research situations, though, increasing sample size is the main way to change a planned study to raise its power.

4. **Use a less extreme level of significance (such as $p < .10$ or $p < .20$).** Ordinarily, the level of significance you use should be the least extreme that reasonably protects against Type I error. Normally, in psychology research, this will be $p < .05$. In general, we don't recommend using a less extreme significance level to increase power because this increases the chances of making a Type I error.

5. **Use a one-tailed test.** Whether you use a one- or two-tailed test depends on the logic of the hypothesis being studied. As with significance level, it is rare that you have much of a choice about this factor.

6. **Use a more sensitive hypothesis-testing procedure.** This is fine if alternatives are available. We consider some options of this kind in Chapter 14. Usually, however, the researcher begins with the most sensitive method available; so little more can be done.

Table 6–6 summarizes some practical ways to increase the power of a planned experiment.

Table 6-6   Summary of Practical Ways of Increasing the Power of a Planned Study

Feature of the Study	Practical Way of Raising Power	Disadvantages
Predicted difference between population means ($\mu_1 - \mu_2$)	Increase the intensity of experimental procedure.	May not be practical or may distort study's meaning.
Standard deviation (σ)	Use a less diverse population.	May not be available; decreases generalizability.
	Use standardized, controlled circumstances of testing or more precise measurement.	Not always practical.
Sample size (N)	Use a larger sample size.	Not always practical; can be costly.
Significance level (α)	Use a more lenient level of significance (such as .10).	Raises alpha, the probability of Type I error.
One-tailed versus two-tailed test	Use a one-tailed test.	May not be appropriate for the logic of the study.
Type of hypothesis-testing procedure	Use a more sensitive procedure.	None may be available or appropriate.

The Role of Power When Interpreting the Results of a Study

Understanding statistical power and what affects it is very important in drawing conclusions from the results of research.

When a Result Is Statistically Significant: Statistical Significance versus Practical Significance

You have learned that a study with a larger effect size is more likely to come out statistically significant. It also is possible for a study with a very small effect size to come out significant. This is likely to happen when a study has high power due to other factors, especially a large sample size. Consider a sample of 10,000 adults who complete a new Internet-based counseling program designed to increase their level of happiness. At the end of the program, their mean happiness score is 100.6, compared to the mean happiness score of 100 ($\sigma = 10$) for adults in general. This result would be significant at the .001 level. So the researchers could be confident that the new program increases people's level of happiness. But the effect size is a tiny .06. This means that the new program increases happiness by only a very small amount. Such a small increase is unlikely to make a noticeable difference in people's lives and thus the researchers might conclude that the effect of the program is statistically significant but has little practical significance.

Clinical psychologists often distinguish between a result being statistically significant and clinically significant. The latter phrase means that the result is big enough to make a difference that matters in treating people. Chambless and Hollon (1998) stated the issue quite simply: "If a treatment is to be useful to practitioners it is not enough for treatment effects to be statistically significant: they also need to be large enough to be clinically meaningful" (p. 11).

The message here is that when judging a study's results, there are two questions. First, is the result statistically significant? If it is, you can consider there to be a *real effect*. The next question is whether the effect size is large enough for the result to be *useful or interesting*. This second question is especially important if the study has practical implications. (Sometimes, in a study testing purely theoretical issues, it may be enough just to be confident that there is an effect at all in a particular direction. We have more to say about this later when discussing controversies.)

If the sample was small, you can assume that a statistically significant result is probably also practically important. On the other hand, if the sample size is very large, you must consider the effect size directly, because it is quite possible that the effect size is too small to be useful. As Bakeman (2006) succinctly noted: "...statistical significance should not overly impress us. After all, even the most miniscule effect can achieve statistical significance if the sample size is large enough" (pp. 136–137).

What we just said may seem a bit of a paradox. Most people assume that the more people there are in the study, the more important its results will be. In a sense, just the reverse is true. All other things being equal, if a study with only a few participants manages to be significant, that significance must be due to a large effect size. A study with a large number of people that is statistically significant may or may not have a large effect size. This is why the American Psychological Association (2001) urges researchers to include effect sizes when they describe the results of studies in research articles.

Also notice that it is usually not a good idea to compare the significance level of two studies to see which has the more important result. For example, a study with a small number of participants that is significant at the .05 level might well have a large effect size. At the same time, a study with a large number of participants that is significant at the .001 level might well have a small effect size.

The level of significance does tell you something. It tells you how confident you can be that you can reject the null hypothesis. The more extreme (lower) the p level is, the stronger the evidence is for a nonzero effect size (Frick, 1996). However, it is definitely *not* the case that the more extreme (smaller) the p level is, the larger the effect will be. If two studies were identical in every other way, a more extreme (smaller) p level would mean a bigger effect. But if the studies differ, especially if they differ in sample size, p level is ambiguous in its relation to effect size. A small p level could be due to a large effect size, but it could just as well be due to a large sample size. Thus, the p level tells you the strength of the evidence that there is a nonzero effect, but it does not tell you how big that nonzero effect is.

The most important lesson from all this is that the word *significant* in statistically significant has a very special meaning. It means that you can be pretty confident that there is some real effect. But it does *not* mean that the effect is significant in a practical sense, that it is important or noteworthy.

Role of Power When a Result Is Not Statistically Significant

We saw in Chapter 4 that a result that is not statistically significant is inconclusive. Often, however, we really would like to conclude that there is little or no difference between the populations. Can we ever do that?

Consider the relationship of power to a nonsignificant result. Suppose you carried out a study that had low power and did not get a significant result. In this situation, the result is entirely inconclusive. Not getting a significant result may have come about because the research hypothesis was false or because the study had too little power (for example, because it had too few participants).

On the other hand, suppose you carried out a study that had high power and you did not get a significant result. In this situation, it seems unlikely that the research hypothesis is true. In this situation (where there is high power), a nonsignificant result is a fairly strong argument against the research hypothesis. This does not mean that all versions of the research hypothesis are false. For example, it is possible that the research hypothesis is true and the populations are only very slightly different (and you figured power based on predicting a large difference).

In sum, a nonsignificant result from a study with low power is truly inconclusive. However, a nonsignificant result from a study with high power does suggest either that the research hypothesis is false or that there is less of an effect than was predicted when figuring power.

Summary of the Role of Power When Evaluating Results of a Study

Table 6–7 summarizes the role of significance and sample size in interpreting research results.

Table 6-7 Role of Significance and Sample Size in Interpreting Research Results		
Result Statistically Significant	**Sample Size**	**Conclusion**
Yes	Small	Important result
Yes	Large	Might or might not have practical importance
No	Small	Inconclusive
No	Large	Research hypothesis probably false

How are you doing?

1. (a) What are the two basic ways of increasing the effect size of a planned study? For each [(b) and (c)], how can it be done, and what are the disadvantages?
2. What is usually the easiest way to increase the power of a planned study?
3. What are the disadvantages of increasing the power of a planned study by using (a) a more lenient significance level or (b) a one-tailed test rather than a two-tailed test?
4. Why is statistical significance not the same as practical importance?
5. You are comparing two studies in which one is significant at $p < .01$ and the other is significant at $p < .05$. (a) What can you conclude about the two studies? (b) What can you *not* conclude about the two studies?
6. When a result is significant, what can you conclude about effect size if the study had (a) a very large sample size or (b) a very small sample size?
7. When a result is not significant, what can you conclude about the truth of the research hypothesis if the study had (a) a very large sample size or (b) a very small sample size?

7. (a) The research hypothesis is probably not true (or has a much smaller effect size than predicted). (b) You can conclude very little about the truth of the research hypothesis.
6. (a) Given a very large sample size, the effect size could be small or large. (b) Given a very small sample size, the effect size is probably large.
5. (a) We can be more confident that the first study's result is not due to chance. (b) We *cannot* conclude which one has the bigger effect size.
4. A statistically significant result means that you can be confident the effect did not occur by chance; it does not, however, mean that it is a large or substantial effect.
3. (a) Increasing the power of a planned study by using a more lenient significance level increases the probability of a Type I error. (b) A one-tailed test rather than a two-tailed test may not be appropriate to the logic of the study; and if the result comes out opposite to predictions, in principle, it would have to be considered nonsignificant.
2. Usually, the easiest way to increase the power of a planned study is to increase the sample size.
1. (c) You can decrease the population standard deviation by using a less diverse population (which has the disadvantage of not permitting you to apply your results to a more general population) and by using more standardized procedures or more accurate measurement (which may not be practical).

Controversy: Statistical Significance versus Effect Size

In Chapter 4 we discussed an ongoing, heated controversy about the value of significance tests, including the argument that they are often misused. We said that significance tests are misused in two main ways that seriously concern psychologists. One
of them is that nonsignificant results are unthinkingly interpreted as showing there is
in fact no effect. In light of this chapter, you should be able to see even more clearly
why this mistake is a problem: nonsignificant results could be due either to little or
no true effect or simply to the low power of the experiment.

In Chapter 4, we said we would postpone discussing the other way significance
tests are often misused until we had covered material in a later chapter. That material
was effect size, and we are now in a position to examine this issue. This misuse
occurs when a significant result is unthinkingly interpreted as being an "important"
result; that is, significance is confused with a large effect size.

Loosely speaking, statistical significance is about the probability that we could
have gotten our pattern of results by chance. As Frick (1996) put it, significance is
about the strength of the evidence that we have a nonzero effect. If our result is
significant at the .05 level, that is pretty good evidence; if it is significant at the .01
level, that is even better evidence (see also the marginal significance controversy
section in Chapter 5).

However, as we have seen in this chapter, a significant result may not be important in the sense of meaning a large effect size or having practical importance.
For example, if the sample size was large, a result with a tiny effect size could be
statistically significant at $p < .001$. In this situation we would be very confident
that the true effect was other than zero. But the size of this true nonzero effect
would still be very small. We would be concluding that we have a real, but slight,
effect. Similarly, if the sample size was small enough, a result with a huge effect
size might not be statistically significant at all. In this situation, our best estimate of
the size of the effect is that it is large. But we would have no confidence that this effect is really there at all; it could be that the true effect is very small or even in the
opposite direction.

Several researchers have observed that the word *significant* is the cause of
some confusion. Fidler and colleagues (2005) noted: "Confusion of clinical and statistical significance often manifests itself in ambiguous language: Researchers describe their results as *significant* or *nonsignificant* without distinguishing whether
they are speaking statistically or substantively" (p. 137). One solution might be
to change the term *statistically significant,* but it is unlikely that this will happen
anytime soon. Thus, it is important that when reading or conducting psychology
research, you keep in mind the distinction between the special way the word

significance is used in psychology versus the way it is used in ordinary language. As we noted in Chapter 4, most psychologists do not see the misuses as a reason to abandon significance testing. Instead, they argue, we should make more of an effort to prevent such misuse.

However, this is not the end of the matter. Many of those who oppose significance testing argue that, even if properly used, significance testing misses the point. What psychology is fundamentally about, they argue, is effect size. It is not about whether a result is nonzero. We already saw a version of this argument in an Advanced Topic section in Chapter 5, with the suggestion that researchers use confidence intervals instead of significance testing. The full version of that proposal is that researchers should really be reporting effect sizes (ideally, with confidence intervals around the effect sizes).

Proponents of emphasizing effect size argue that effect sizes provide information that can be compared to other studies and used in accumulating information over independent studies as research in a field progresses. Effect sizes are crucial ingredients in meta-analysis, and many of the proponents of effect size see meta-analysis as *the* wave of the future of psychology.

There are, however, counterarguments in favor of significance testing (and against using effect sizes alone). One such counterargument is that, when sample size is small, it is still possible for a study to come out with a large effect size just by chance. Thus, if we are interested in the result of a particular study that used a small sample, significance tests protect against taking the results of such a study too seriously. Similarly, at times a very small effect size is nevertheless important. In such a situation, it is crucial to know whether the result should be trusted as not due to chance. Still, many of those making these counterarguments agree that significance has been overemphasized. Most hold that significance should always be reported but that effect size should also be given more emphasis in the discussion of results.

There is yet another view: in some circumstances effect sizes are actually misleading, and we should rely only on significance testing. Chow (1988, 1996), for example, makes a distinction between applied and theoretically oriented research. In applied research, psychologists want to know the actual amount of effect a particular program has or how big is the actual difference between two particular groups. In these circumstances, Chow agrees, effect size is a good idea. However, when doing theoretical research, Chow argues, the situation is quite different. In this situation, he says, effect sizes are irrelevant and even misleading.

Consider an experiment on the effect of familiarity on recognizing information. The point of such a study is to examine the basic way that familiarity affects information processing. A particular study might show people familiar and unfamiliar words to see how many milliseconds it takes to recognize them. The effect size of such a study would tell us very little to help interpret the results of the study. It depends on all sorts of details of how the study was done, such as just how familiar and unfamiliar the words were, the specific way the words were presented, and so forth. What matters in a study like this, Chow says, is that (a) the prediction of a difference in recognizing familiar versus unfamiliar words was based on theory, (b) the results were consistent with what was predicted (as shown by the statistical significance), and (c) the theory was thus supported.

It is not only in cognitive psychology that research is primarily theoretical in this way. Some other examples of research that are primarily theoretical include experimental studies of motivations for interpersonal attraction, of how neural processes are influenced by chemical changes, of how infants develop language, or of how memory differs for emotional and nonemotional events.

In fact, the current balance of the use of significance tests and effect sizes is probably just what one might expect from the points that Chow makes. In applied areas of psychology, there is an increasing emphasis on effect size. But in more theoretical areas of psychology, explicit mentions of effect size are less common. The prevailing view among statistics experts in psychology seems to be that, even in theoretically oriented research, the potential loss (due to misplaced emphasis) by including effect size is probably offset by, among other benefits, the usefulness to future researchers of having such information to help them in figuring power when planning their own studies and, most important, for future meta-analysts who will combine the results of this study with other related studies.

Decision Errors, Effect Size, and Power in Research Articles

Decision errors are rarely mentioned in research articles. They might be mentioned if the study did not find statistically significant results and also had low power. In this situation, the researchers might mention that the lack of significant results may represent a Type II error. Since most academic journals generally avoid publishing such studies, you will seldom see such discussions. However, it is increasingly common for articles to mention effect size. For example, Morehouse and Tobler (2000) studied the effectiveness of an intervention program for "high-risk, multiproblem, inner-city, primarily African-American and Latino youth." The authors reported, "Youth who received 5–30 hours of intervention ([the high dosage group], $n = 101$) were compared with those who received 1–4 hours (the low-dosage group, $n = 31$). ... The difference between the groups in terms of reduction in [alcohol and drug] use was highly significant. A between-groups effect size of .68 was achieved for the high-dosage group when compared with the low-dosage group." (Their wording about the study is a bit confusing; they are using *dosage* here to mean the amount of intervention, not the amount of drugs anyone was taking!) The meaning of the .68 effect size is that the group getting 5 to 30 hours of intervention was .68 standard deviations higher in terms of reduction on their drug and alcohol use than the group getting only 1 to 4 hours of the intervention. This is a medium to large effect size.

Effect size is most commonly reported in meta-analyses, in which results from different articles are being combined and compared. We have given several examples of such meta-analytic studies, including one in Box 6–1. As an example of how these studies actually describe results in terms of effect size, consider a meta-analysis conducted by Roberts, Walton, and Viechtbauer (2006). They reviewed 92 research studies (some of which provided results for several different samples) that examined whether people's personality characteristics change over their lifetime. One of the personality characteristics examined in the meta-analysis was openness to experience. People with a high openness to experience tend to be curious and imaginative; they enjoy novel experiences and ideas. Table 6–8 shows the results of the meta-analysis for openness to experience. Specifically, the table shows the extent to which openness to experience changes during different ages (from age 10 to 18 years, from age 18 to 22 years, and so on). For each age grouping, Table 6–8 shows the number of samples studied, the number of study participants, and the standardized effect size. (The final two columns of the table present information that is beyond our discussion of meta-analysis.) From the table you can see that the largest change in

Table 6-8	Population Estimates of Mean-Level Change in Openness to Experience Across the Life Course				
Age	**K**	**N**	**d**	**CI**	**Q_h**
10–18	13	2,911	.23	.00, .48	37.2*
18–22	37	3,998	.37*	.18, .56	76.6*
22–30	12	702	−.01	−.14, .12	27.8*
30–40	11	541	.07	−.06, .21	6.8
40–50	12	2,660	−.01	−.07, .04	10.6
50–60	6	317	.11	−.16, .39	21.1*
60–70	8	507	−.19*	−.37, −.02	11.3
70+	8	458	−.08	−.16, .01	5.1

Note: K = number of samples; d = standardized mean difference; CI = 95% fixed effects confidence intervals; Q_h = heterogeneity statistic.
*$p < .05$.
Source: Roberts, B. W., Walton, K. E., & Viechtbauer, W. (2006). Patterns of mean-level change in personality traits across the life course: A meta-analysis of longitudinal studies. *Psychological Bulletin, 132,* 1–25. Published by the American Psychological Association. Reprinted with permission.

openness to experience occurs from age 18 to 22 years. Roberts and colleagues note in the text of their paper that this change represents an increase in openness to experience. Based on Cohen's conventions, the effect size of $d = .37$ for this change represents a small to medium effect size.

You mainly think about power when planning research. (Power, for example, is often a major topic in grant proposals requesting funding for research and in thesis proposals.) As for research articles, power is sometimes mentioned in the final section of an article where the author discusses the meaning of the results or in discussions of results of other studies. In either situation, the emphasis tends to be on the meaning of nonsignificant results. Also, when power is discussed, it may be explained in some detail because only recently have most psychologists begun to be knowledgeable about power.

For example, Denenberg (1999), in discussing the basis for his own study, makes the following comments about a relevant previous study by Mody, Kennedy, and Brady (1997) that had not found significant results.

> [T]hey were confronted with the serious problem of having to accept the null hypothesis. ...we can view this issue in terms of statistical power. ...A minimal statistical power of .80 [80%] is required before one can consider the argument that the lack of significance may be interpreted as evidence that Ho [the null hypothesis] is true. To conduct a power analysis, it is necessary to specify an expected mean difference, the alpha level, and whether a one-tailed or two-tailed test will be used. Given a power requirement of .80 [80%], one can then determine the N necessary. Once these conditions are satisfied, if the experiment fails to find a significant difference, then one can make the following kind of a statement: "We have designed an experiment with a .8 probability of finding a significant difference, if such exists in the population. Because we failed to find a significant effect, we think it quite unlikely that one exists. Even if it does exist, its contribution would appear to be minimal...."
>
> Mody et al. never discussed power, even though they interpreted negative findings as proof of the validity of the null hypothesis in all of their experiments....

Because the participants were split in this experiment, the *ns* [sample sizes] were reduced to 10 per group. Under such conditions one would not expect to find a significant difference, unless the experimental variable was very powerful. In other words, it is more difficult to reject the null hypothesis when working with small *ns* [sample sizes]. The only meaningful conclusion that can be drawn from this study is that no meaningful interpretation can be made of the lack of findings. (pp. 380–381)

Advanced Topic: Figuring Statistical Power

In this section, you will learn how to figure statistical power by hand for research situations in which the mean and standard deviation of the comparison distribution are known and a mean is predicted for the population of individuals receiving the experimental procedure. Learning to figure power by hand will greatly deepen your understanding of this important topic.

Consider again the attractiveness ratings example shown in Figure 6–6. The population of individuals who were not told anything about the person's positive personality qualities (Population 1) had a mean of 200 and a standard deviation of 48 (a variance of 2,304). The researcher studied a sample of 64 students. Thus, we figured the standard deviation of the distribution of means to be 6; that is, $\sigma_M = \sqrt{\dfrac{\sigma^2}{N}} = \sqrt{\dfrac{2,304}{64}} = 6$. We have presumed that the researcher predicted that telling students that the person had positive personality qualities would raise the mean attractiveness rating to 208.

You learned earlier that the power of the study is represented by the shaded region in the upper curve in Figure 6–6, the distribution of means for Population 1. Thus, figuring the percentage of the curve in that shaded area will tell us the power of the study. Recall that the cutoff Z score on Populations 2's distribution of means (the lower distribution in Figure 6–6) was 1.64. This corresponded to a raw score cutoff of 209.84. Now, look at the top curve in Figure 6–6, the distribution of means for Population 1. This raw score cutoff of 209.84 corresponds to a Z score on that distribution of .31; that is, $Z = (M - \mu_M)/\sigma_M = (209.84 - 208)/6 = .31$.

The normal curve table (Table A–1 in the Appendix) shows that 38% of a normal curve is in the tail region above a Z of .31. In other words, 38% of the means in predicted Population 1's distribution of means are above a Z score of .31 (and therefore 38% of the means are above a raw score of 209.84). Thus, the power of the study is 38%. (The exact percentage shown in the table is 37.83%, but we can round power to the nearest whole percentage.) Recall that we told you earlier the power for the study was 37%. This difference between 37% and 37.83% occurs due to rounding error.

Notice that the way we figured power had nothing to do with the actual results of the study. It was based on predictions. In fact, researchers usually figure power *before* doing the study.

Steps for Figuring Power

In our situation (the mean of a single sample compared to a known population), there are four steps to figure power:

❶ **Gather the needed information: the mean and standard deviation of Population 2's distribution of means (the comparison distribution) and the predicted mean of Population 1's distribution of means (the population given the experimental procedure).** The mean of Population 2's distribution of means is 200 and its standard deviation is 6. The predicted mean of Population 1's distribution of means is 208.

❷ **Figure the raw-score cutoff point on the comparison distribution to reject the null hypothesis.** For the 5% significance level, one-tailed, the Z score cutoff is +1.64. A Z of +1.64 is a raw score of 209.84. Thus, in the lower curve (the comparison distribution) in Figure 6–6, we have shaded the area to the right of 209.84. This is the alpha region.

❸ **Figure the Z score for this same point, but on the distribution of means for the population that receives the experimental procedure (Population 1).** On this distribution (based on the predicted scores for Population 1), a raw score of 209.84 is the same as a Z score of .31; that is, $Z = (M - \mu_M)/\sigma_M = (209.84 - 208)/6 = .31$. Thus, in the upper curve in Figure 6–6, we have shaded the area to the right of .31. This shaded area shows the power of the study, the area in which a mean of an actual sample would produce statistically significant results for the study.

❹ **Using the normal curve table, figure the probability of getting a score more extreme than that Z score.[1]** The normal curve table shows 38% in the tail region above a Z of .31. The power of this study is 38%. (Beta is thus 100% − 38% = 62%.)

How are you doing?

1. In a planned study, the population is known to have a mean of 500 and a standard deviation of 100. The researchers will give the experimental treatment to 60 people and predict that the mean for those 60 will be 540. They will use the .05 significance level. (a) Figure the power of this study and (b) sketch the distributions involved. (c) What is beta in this study?

Figure 6–15 Distributions of means for "How Are You Doing?" question 1. Upper curve: Predicted. Lower curve: Known.

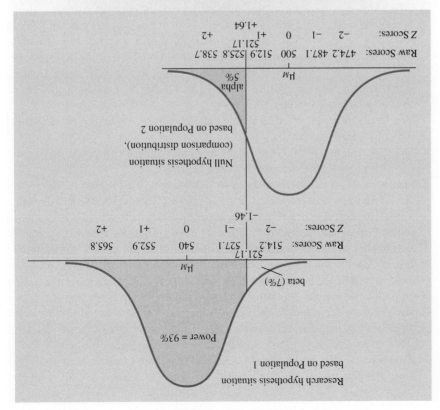

214 Chapter 6

Answer

1. (a) ❶ **Gather the needed information.** The mean of the comparison distribution is 500. The predicted mean of the population that receives the experimental procedure is 540. The standard deviation of the distribution of means, σ_M, is $\sqrt{\sigma^2/N} = \sqrt{100^2/60} = 12.91$.

❷ **Figure the raw-score cutoff point on the comparison distribution to reject the null hypothesis.** A Z of $+1.64$ (for the 5% significance level) gives a raw score of 521.17.

❸ **Figure the Z score for this same point, but on the distribution of means for the population that receives the experimental procedure (Population 1).** A raw score of 521.17 on this distribution is a Z score of -1.46.

❹ **Using the normal curve table, figure the probability of getting a score more extreme than that Z score. Power = 93%** (that is, 43% between the mean and a Z of -1.46, plus 50% above the mean).

(b) The distributions involved are shown in Figure 6–15.

(c) Beta is 7%: that is, $100\% - 93\% = 7\%$.

Summary

1. There are two kinds of possible decision errors in hypothesis testing. A Type I error is when a researcher rejects the null hypothesis, but the null hypothesis is actually true. A Type II error is when a researcher does not reject the null hypothesis, but the null hypothesis is actually false.

2. Effect size is a measure of the difference between population means. In the hypothesis-testing situations you learned about in this chapter, you can think of effect size as how much something changes after a specific intervention. A widely used standardized measure of effect size, Cohen's d, is the difference between population means divided by the population standard deviation. Cohen's effect size conventions consider a small effect to be .20, a medium effect to be .50, and a large effect to be .80.

3. Meta-analysis is a procedure for systematically combining and comparing effect sizes of separate studies.

4. The statistical power of a study is the probability that it will give a statistically significant result *if the research hypothesis is true.*

5. The larger the effect size is, the greater the power is. This is because the greater the difference is between means or the smaller the population standard deviation is (the two ingredients in effect size), the less overlap there is between the known and predicted populations' distributions of means. Thus, the area in the predicted distribution that is more extreme than the cutoff in the known distribution is greater. Also, if you know or predict the effect size, you can figure the predicted mean; it will be the known mean plus the result of multiplying the effect size by the population standard deviation. You can then use this to figure power.

6. The larger the sample size is, the greater the power is. This is because the larger the sample is, the smaller is the variance of the distribution of means. So, for a given effect size, there is less overlap between distributions of means.

7. Power is also affected by significance level (the more extreme, such as .01, the lower the power), by whether a one-tailed or two-tailed test is used (with less

power for a two-tailed test), and by the type of hypothesis-testing procedure used (in the occasional situation where there is a choice of procedure).

8. Statistically significant results from a study with high power (such as one with a large sample size) may not have practical importance. Results that are not statistically significant from a study with low power (such as one with a small sample size) leave open the possibility that significant results might show up if power were increased.

9. Psychologists disagree about whether statistical significance or effect size is more important in interpreting experimental results; theoretically oriented psychologists seem to emphasize statistical significance, and applied researchers emphasize effect size.

10. Research articles increasingly report effect size, and effect sizes are almost always reported in meta-analyses. Research articles sometimes include discussions of power, especially when evaluating nonsignificant results.

11. ADVANCED TOPIC: To figure power (in the situation of a known population and a single sample), you first find the cutoff point for significance, in raw-score terms, on the comparison distribution. Based on a specific predicted mean, you can find the Z score for this cutoff on the distribution of means for the population given the experimental procedure. Power is the probability of exceeding this Z score, the area greater than this Z score, which you can find from the normal curve table.

Key Terms

decision errors (p. 176)
Type I error (p. 176)
alpha (α) (p. 177)
Type II error (p. 177)

beta (β) (p. 177)
effect size (d) (p. 180)
d (p. 182)
effect size conventions (p. 183)

meta-analysis (p. 184)
statistical power (p. 187)
power tables (p. 190)

Example Worked-Out Problems

Each problem below is based on a known population with a normal distribution, $\mu = 40$, and $\sigma = 10$.

Figuring the Effect Size

A sample given an experimental treatment has a mean of 37. What is the effect size? Is this approximately small, medium, or large?

Answer

$d = (\mu_1 - \mu_2)/\sigma = (37 - 40)/10 = -3/10 = -.30$; approximately small.

Find the Predicted Mean from an Effect Size

The researcher predicts a small negative effect size. What is the predicted mean?

Answer

A small negative effect size is $-.20$. Predicted $\mu_1 = \mu_2 + (d)(\sigma) = 40 + (-.20)(10) = 40 + (-2) = 38$.

Outline for Writing Essays on Power and Effect Size for Studies Involving a Sample of More Than One Individual and a Known Population

1. Explain the idea of power as the probability of getting significant results if the research hypothesis is true. Be sure to mention that the minimum acceptable level of power for a research study is 80%. Explain the role played by power when you are interpreting the results of a study (both when a study is and is not significant), taking into account significance levels and sample size in relation to the likely effect size.
2. Explain the idea of effect size as the degree of overlap between distributions, noting how this overlap is a function of mean difference and population standard deviation (and describing precisely how it is figured and why it is figured that way). If required by the question, discuss the effect size conventions.
3. Explain the relationship between effect size and power.

Advanced Topic: Figuring Power

The researcher plans to conduct a new study with a sample of 25 and predicts that, when given a new experimental treatment, this group will have a mean of 49. The researcher plans to use the 1% significance level (one-tailed). What is the power of the planned study? What is beta in this study? Make a diagram of the distributions on which you show the areas for alpha, beta, and power.

Answer

❶ **Gather the needed information: the mean and standard deviation of Population 2's distribution of means (the comparison distribution) and the predicted mean of Population 1's distribution of means (the population given the experimental procedure).** The mean of the comparison distribution is 40. The predicted mean of the distribution of means for the population that receives the experimental procedure is 49. The standard deviation of the distribution of means, σ_M, is $\sqrt{10^2/25} = \sqrt{100/25} = \sqrt{4} = 2$.

❷ **Figure the raw-score cutoff point on the comparison distribution to reject the null hypothesis.** A Z of $+2.33$ (for the 1% significance level) gives a raw score of $40 + (2.33)(2) = 44.66$.

❸ **Figure the Z score for this same point, but on the distribution of means for the population that receives the experimental procedure (Population 1).** A raw score of 44.66 on the distribution that will be given the experimental treatment is a Z score of $(44.66 - 49)/2 = -4.34/2 = -2.17$.

❹ **Using the normal curve table, figure the probability of getting a score more extreme than that Z score.** From the normal curve table, the area between the mean and a Z of 2.17 is 48.5%. Since -2.17 is below the mean, and there is another 50% above the mean, power $= 98.5\%$, which we can round to 99%.

The distributions involved are shown in Figure 6–16.
Beta is $100\% -$ power. Thus, beta $= 100\% - 99\% = 1\%$.

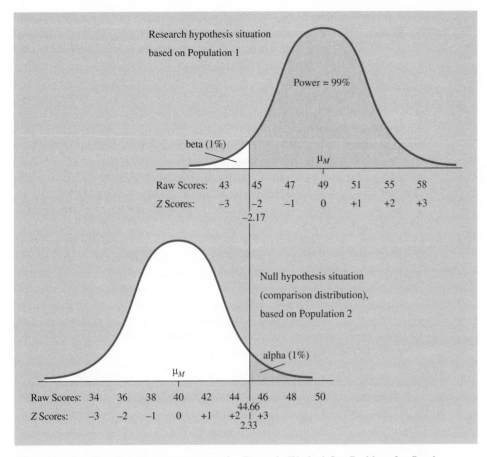

Figure 6-16 Distributions of means for Example Worked-Out Problem for figuring power. Upper curve: Predicted. Bottom curve: Known.

Practice Problems

These problems involve figuring. Most real-life statistics problems are done on a computer with special statistical software. Even if you have such software, do these problems by hand to ingrain the method in your mind.

All data are fictional unless an actual citation is given.

Set I (for Answers to Set I Problems, see pp. 678–681)

1. Define alpha and beta.
2. For each of the following studies, make a chart of the four possible correct and incorrect decisions, and explain what each would mean. Each chart should be laid out like Table 6–1, but put into the boxes the possible results, using the names of the variables involved in the study.
    (a) A study of whether increasing the amount of recess time improves school-children's in-class behavior.

    (b) A study of whether color-blind individuals can distinguish gray shades better than the population at large.

    (c) A study comparing individuals who have ever been in psychotherapy to the general public to see if they are more tolerant of other people's upsets than is the general population.

3. In a completed study, there is a known population with a normal distribution, $\mu = 25$, and $\sigma = 12$. What is the estimated effect size if a sample given an experimental procedure has a mean of (a) 19, (b) 22, (c) 25, (d) 30, and (e) 35? For each part, also indicate whether the effect is approximately small, medium, or large.

4. In a planned study, there is a known population with a normal distribution, $\mu = 50$, and $\sigma = 5$. What is the predicted effect size (d) if the researchers predict that those given an experimental treatment have a mean of (a) 50, (b) 52, (c) 54, (d) 56, and (e) 47? For each part, also indicate whether the effect is approximately small, medium, or large.

5. In a planned study, there is a known population with a normal distribution, $\mu = 15$, and $\sigma = 2$. What is the predicted mean if the researcher predicts (a) a small positive effect size, (b) a medium negative effect size, (c) a large positive effect size, (d) an effect size of $d = .35$, and (e) and effect size of $d = -1.50$?

6. Here is information about several possible versions of a planned experiment. Figure effect size for each; sketch the distributions involved, showing the area for alpha, beta, and power. (Assume all populations have a normal distribution.) ADVANCED TOPIC: Figure the power for each version.

	Population		Predicted Mean	*N*	Significance Level	One- or Two-Tailed
	μ	σ				
(a)	90	4	91	100	.05	1
(b)	90	4	92	100	.05	1
(c)	90	2	91	100	.05	1
(d)	90	4	91	16	.05	1
(e)	90	4	91	100	.01	1
(f)	90	4	91	100	.05	2

7. You read a study in which the result is significant ($p < .05$). You then look at the size of the sample. If the sample is very large (rather than very small), how should this affect your interpretation of (a) the probability that the null hypothesis is actually true and (b) the practical importance of the result? (c) Explain your answers to a person who understands hypothesis testing but has never learned about effect size or power.

8. Aron and colleagues (1997) placed strangers in pairs and asked them to talk together following a series of instructions designed to help them become close. At the end of 45 minutes, individuals privately answered some questions about how close they now felt to their partners. (The researchers combined the answers into a "closeness composite.") One key question was whether closeness would be affected by either (a) matching strangers based on their attitude agreement or (b) leading participants to believe that they had been put together with someone who would like them. The result for both agreement and expecting to be liked was that "there was no significant differences on the closeness composite" (p. 367). The researchers went on to argue that the results suggested that there was little true effect of these variables on closeness:

There was about 90% power in this study of achieving significant effects… for the two manipulated variables if in fact there were a large effect of this kind ($d = .8$). Indeed, the power is about 90% for finding at least a near-significant ($p < .10$) medium-sized effect ($d = .5$). Thus, it seems unlikely that we would have obtained the present results if in fact there is more than a small effect.…(p. 367)

Explain this result to a person who understands hypothesis testing but has never learned about power or effect size.

9. How does each of the following affect the power of a planned study?
   (a) A larger predicted difference between the means of the populations.
   (b) A larger population standard deviation.
   (c) A larger sample size.
   (d) Using a more extreme significance level (e.g., .01 instead of .05).
   (e) Using a two-tailed test instead of a one-tailed test.

10. List two situations in which it is useful to consider power, indicating what the use is for each.

11. ADVANCED TOPIC: Based on a particular theory of creativity, a psychologist predicts that artists will be greater risk takers than the general population. The general population is normally distributed with a mean of 50 and a standard deviation of 12 on the risk-taking questionnaire this psychologist plans to use. The psychologist expects that artists will score, on the average, 55 on this questionnaire. The psychologist plans to study 36 artists and test the hypothesis at the .05 level. (a) What is the power of this study? (b) Sketch the distributions involved, showing the areas for alpha, beta, and power. (c) Explain your answer to someone who understands hypothesis testing with means of samples but has never learned about power.

12. ADVANCED TOPIC: On a memory task in which words are learned in a random order, it is known that people can recall a mean of 11 words with a standard deviation of 4 and that the distribution follows a normal curve. A cognitive psychologist, to test a theory, modifies that task so that the words are presented in a way in which words that have a related meaning are presented together. The cognitive psychologist predicts that, under these conditions, people will recall so many more words that there will be a large effect size. She plans to test this with a sample of 20 people, using the .01 significance level, two-tailed. (a) What is the power of this study? (b) Sketch the distributions involved, showing the areas for alpha, beta, and power. (c) Explain your answer to someone who understands hypothesis testing involving means of samples but has never learned about effect size or power.

Set II

13. For each of the following studies, make a chart of the four possible correct and incorrect decisions, and explain what each would mean. (Each chart should be laid out like Table 6–1, but put into the boxes the possible results, using the names of the variables involved in the study.)
    (a) A study of whether infants born prematurely begin to recognize faces later than do infants in general.
    (b) A study of whether high school students who receive an AIDS prevention program in their school are more likely to practice safe sex than are other high school students.
    (c) A study of whether memory for abstract ideas is reduced if the information is presented in distracting colors.

14. In a completed study, there is a known population with a normal distribution, $\mu = 122$, and $\sigma = 8$. What is the estimated effect size if a sample given an experimental procedure has a mean of (a) 100, (b) 110, (c) 120, (d) 130, and (e) 140? For each part, also indicate whether the effect is approximately small, medium, or large.

15. In a planned study, there is a known population with a normal distribution, $\mu = 0$, and $\sigma = 10$. What is the predicted effect size (d) if the researchers predict that those given an experimental treatment have a mean of (a) -8, (b) -5, (c) -2, (d) 0, and (e) 10? For each part, also indicate whether the effect is approximately small, medium, or large.

16. In a planned study, there is a known population with a normal distribution, $\mu = 17.5$, and $\sigma = 3.2$. What is the predicted mean if the researcher predicts (a) a small positive effect size, (b) a medium negative effect size, (c) an effect size of $d = .40$, (d) an effect size of $d = -.40$, (e) an effect size of $d = 3$?

17. Here is information about several possible versions of a planned experiment, each with a single sample. Figure effect size for each; then sketch the distributions involved, showing the areas for alpha, beta, and power. (Assume all populations have a normal distribution.) ADVANCED TOPIC: Figure the power for each version.

	Population		Predicted Mean	N	Significance Level	One- or Two-Tailed
	μ	σ				
(a)	0	.5	.1	50	.05	1
(b)	0	.5	.5	50	.05	1
(c)	0	.5	1.0	50	.05	1
(d)	0	.5	.5	100	.05	1
(e)	0	.5	.5	200	.05	1
(f)	0	.5	.5	400	.05	1

18. You read a study that just barely fails to be significant at the .05 level. That is, the result is not significant. You then look at the size of the sample. If the sample is very large (rather than very small), how should this affect your interpretation of (a) the probability that the null hypothesis is actually true and (b) the probability that the null hypothesis is actually false? (c) Explain your answers to a person who understands hypothesis testing but has never learned about power.

19. Caspi and colleagues (1997) analyzed results from a large-scale longitudinal study of a sample of children born around 1972 in Dunedin, New Zealand. As one part of their study, the researchers compared the 94 in their sample who were, at age 21, alcohol dependent (clearly alcoholic) versus the 863 who were not alcohol dependent. The researchers compared these two groups in terms of personality test scores from when they were 18 years old. After noting that all results were significant, they reported the following results:

> Young adults who were alcohol dependent at age 21 scored lower at age 18 on Traditionalism ($d = .49$), Harm Avoidance ($d = .44$), Control ($d = .64$), and Social Closeness ($d = .40$), and higher on Aggression ($d = .86$), Alienation ($d = .66$), and Stress Reaction ($d = .50$).

Explain these results, including why it was especially important for the researchers in this study to give effect sizes, to a person who understands hypothesis testing but has never learned about effect size or power.

20. You are planning a study that you compute as having quite low power. Name six things that you might do to increase power.

21. ADVANCED TOPIC: A psychologist is planning a study on the effect of motivation on performance on an attention task. In this task, participants try to identify target letters in a stream of letters passing by at a rapid rate. The researcher knows from long experience that, under ordinary experimental conditions, the population of students who participate in this task identify a mean of 71 of the key letters, that the standard deviation is 10, and that the distribution is approximately normal. The psychologist predicts that, if the participant is paid a dollar for each letter identified correctly, the number correctly identified will increase to 74. The psychologist plans to test 20 participants under these conditions, using the .05 level. (a) What is the power of this study? (b) Sketch the distributions involved, showing the areas for alpha, beta, and power. (c) Explain your answer to someone who understands hypothesis testing involving means of samples but has never learned about power.

22. ADVANCED TOPIC: An organizational psychologist predicts that assembly workers will have a somewhat higher level of job satisfaction if they are given a new kind of incentive program (that is, he predicts a medium effect size). On a standard job satisfaction scale, for assembly workers in this company overall, the distribution is normal, with $\mu = 82$ and $\sigma = 7$. The psychologist plans to provide the new incentive program to 25 randomly selected assembly workers. (a) What is the power of this study (using $p < .01$)? (b) Sketch the distributions involved, showing the areas for alpha, beta, and power. (c) Explain your answer to someone who understands hypothesis testing involving means of samples but has never learned about effect size or power.

Chapter Note

1. This method of figuring power (which is the only method for figuring power covered in this book) assumes that the distributions of means are normally distributed.

CHAPTER 7

Introduction to *t* Tests

Single Sample and Dependent Means

Chapter Outline

- The *t* Test for a Single Sample   223
- The *t* Test for Dependent Means   236
- Assumptions of the *t* Test for a Single Sample and the *t* Test for Dependent Means   247
- Effect Size and Power for the *t* Test for Dependent Means   247
- Controversy: Advantages and Disadvantages of Repeated-Measures Designs   250
- Single Sample *t* Tests and Dependent Means *t* Tests in Research Articles   252
- Summary   253
- Key Terms   254
- Example Worked-Out Problems   254
- Practice Problems   258
- Using SPSS   265
- Chapter Notes   268

At this point, you may think you know all about hypothesis testing. Here's a surprise: what you know will not help you much as a researcher. Why? The procedures for testing hypotheses described up to this point were, of course, absolutely necessary for what you will now learn. However, these procedures involved comparing a group of scores to a *known population*. In real research practice, you often compare two or more groups of scores to each other, without any direct information about populations. For example, you may have two scores for each person in a group of people, such as scores on an anxiety test before and after psychotherapy or number of familiar versus unfamiliar words recalled in a memory experiment. Or you might have one score per person for two groups of people, such as an experimental group and a control group in a study of the effect of sleep loss on problem solving, or comparing the self-esteem test scores of a group of 10-year-old girls to a group of 10-year-old boys.

These kinds of research situations are among the most common in psychology, where usually the only information available is from samples. Nothing is known about the populations that the samples are supposed to come from. In particular, the researcher does not know the variance of the populations involved, which is a crucial ingredient in Step ❷ of the hypothesis-testing process (determining the characteristics of the comparison distribution).

In this chapter, we first look at the solution to the problem of not knowing the population variance by focusing on a special situation: comparing the mean of a single sample to a population with a known mean but an unknown variance. Then, after describing how to handle this problem of not knowing the population variance, we go on to consider the situation in which there is no known population at all—the situation in which all we have are two scores for each of a number of people.

The hypothesis-testing procedures you learn in this chapter, those in which the population variance is unknown, are examples of ***t* tests.** The *t* test is sometimes called "Student's *t*" because its main principles were originally developed by William S. Gosset, who published his research articles anonymously using the name "Student" (see Box 7–1).

The *t* Test for a Single Sample

Let's begin with an example. Suppose your college newspaper reports an informal survey showing that students at your college study an average of 17 hours per week. However, you think that the students in your dormitory study much more than that. You randomly pick 16 students from your dormitory and ask them how much they study each day. (We will assume that they are all honest and accurate.) Your result is that these 16 students study an average of 21 hours per week. Should you conclude that students in your dormitory study more than the college average? Or should you conclude that your results are close enough to the college average that the small difference of 4 hours might well be due to your having picked, purely by chance, 16 of the more studious residents in your dormitory?

In this example you have scores for a sample of individuals and you want to compare the mean of this sample to a population for which you know the mean but not the variance. Hypothesis testing in this situation is called a ***t* test for a single sample.** (It is also called a *one-sample t test.*) The *t* test for a single sample works basically the same way as the Z test you learned in Chapter 5. In the studies we considered in that chapter, you had scores for a sample of individuals (such as a group of 64 students rating the attractiveness of a person in a photograph after being told that the person has positive personality qualities) and you wanted to compare the mean of this sample to a population (in this case, a population of students not told about the person's personality qualities). However, in the studies we considered in Chapter 5, you knew both the mean and variance of the general population to which you were going to compare your sample. In the situations we are now going to consider, everything is the same, but you don't know the population variance. This presents two important new wrinkles affecting the details of how you carry out two of the steps of the hypothesis-testing process.

The first important new wrinkle is in Step ❷. Because the population variance is not known, you have to estimate it. So the first new wrinkle we consider is how to estimate an unknown population variance. The other important new wrinkle affects Steps ❷ and ❸. When the population variance has to be estimated, the shape of the comparison

***t* test** hypothesis-testing procedure in which the population variance is unknown; it compares *t* scores from a sample to a comparison distribution called a *t* distribution.

***t* test for a single sample** hypothesis-testing procedure in which a sample mean is being compared to a known population mean and the population variance is unknown.

BOX 7–1   **William S. Gosset, Alias "Student":
Not a Mathematician, But a Practical Man**

The Granger Collection

William S. Gosset graduated from Oxford University in 1899 with degrees in mathematics and chemistry. It happened that in the same year the Guinness brewers in Dublin, Ireland, were seeking a few young scientists to take a first-ever scientific look at beer making. Gosset took one of these jobs and soon had immersed himself in barley, hops, and vats of brew.

The problem was how to make beer of a consistently high quality. Scientists such as Gosset wanted to make the quality of beer less variable, and they were especially interested in finding the cause of bad batches. A proper scientist would say, "Conduct experiments!" But a business such as a brewery could not afford to waste money on experiments involving large numbers of vats, some of which any brewer worth his hops knew would fail. So Gosset was forced to contemplate the probability of, say, a certain strain of barley producing terrible beer when the experiment could consist of only a few batches of each strain. Adding to the problem was that he had no idea of the variability of a given strain of barley—perhaps some fields planted with the same strain grew better barley. (Does this sound familiar? Poor Gosset, like today's psychologists, had no idea of his population's variance.)

Gosset was up to the task, although at the time only he knew that. To his colleagues at the brewery, he was a professor of mathematics and not a proper brewer at all. To his statistical colleagues, mainly at the Biometric Laboratory at University College in London, he was a mere brewer and not a proper mathematician.

So Gosset discovered the *t* distribution and invented the *t* test—simplicity itself (compared to most of statistics)—for situations when samples are small and the variability of the larger population is unknown. However, the Guinness brewery did not allow its scientists to publish papers, because one Guinness scientist had revealed brewery secrets. To this day, most statisticians call the *t* distribution "Student's *t*" because Gosset wrote under the anonymous name "Student." A few of his fellow statisticians knew who "Student" was, but apparently meetings with others involved the secrecy worthy of a spy novel. The brewery learned of his scientific fame only at his death, when colleagues wanted to honor him.

In spite of his great achievements, Gosset often wrote in letters that his own work provided "only a rough idea of the thing" or so-and-so "really worked out the complete mathematics." He was remembered as a thoughtful, kind, humble man, sensitive to others' feelings. Gosset's friendliness and generosity with his time and ideas also resulted in many students and younger colleagues making major breakthroughs based on his help.

To learn more about William Gosset, go to *http://www-history.mcs.st-andrews.ac.uk/Biographies/Gosset.html*.

Sources: Peters (1987); Salsburg (2001); Stigler (1986); Tankard (1984).

distribution is not quite a normal curve; so the second new wrinkle we consider is the shape of the comparison distribution (for Step ❷) and how to use a special table to find the cutoff (Step ❸) on what is a slightly differently shaped distribution.

Let's return to the amount of studying example. Step ❶ of the hypothesis-testing procedure is to restate the problem as hypotheses about populations. There are two populations:

Population 1: The kind of students who live in your dormitory.
Population 2: The kind of students in general at your college.

The research hypothesis is that Population 1 students study more than Population 2 students; the null hypothesis is that Population 1 students do not study more than Population 2 students. So far, the problem is no different from those in Chapter 5.

Step ❷ is to determine the characteristics of the comparison distribution. In this example, its mean will be 17, what the survey found for students at your college generally (Population 2).

The next part of Step ❷ is finding the variance of the distribution of means. Now you face a problem. Up to now in this book, you have always known the variance of the population of individuals. Using that variance, you then figured the variance of the distribution of means. However, in the present example, the variance of the number of hours studied for students at your college (the Population 2 students) was not reported in the newspaper article. So you email the paper. Unfortunately, the reporter did not figure the variance, and the original survey results are no longer available. What to do?

Basic Principle of the *t* Test: Estimating the Population Variance from the Sample Scores

If you do not know the variance of the population of individuals, you can *estimate* it from what you do know—the scores of the people in your sample.

In the logic of hypothesis testing, the group of people you study is considered to be a random sample from a particular population. The variance of this sample ought to reflect the variance of that population. If the scores in the population have *a lot* of variation, then the scores in a sample randomly selected from that population should also have *a lot* of variation. If the population has *very little* variation, the scores in a sample from that population should also have *very little* variation. Thus, it should be possible to use the variation among the scores in the sample to make an informed guess about the spread of the scores in the population. That is, you could figure the variance of the sample's scores, and that should be *similar* to the variance of the scores in the population. (See Figure 7–1.)

There is, however, one small hitch. The variance of a sample will generally be slightly smaller than the variance of the population from which it is taken. For this reason, the variance of the sample is a **biased estimate** of the population variance.[1] It is a *biased estimate* because it consistently *underestimates* the actual variance of the population. (For example, if a population has a variance of 180, a typical sample

biased estimate estimate of a population parameter that is likely systematically to overestimate or underestimate the true value of the population parameter. For example, SD^2 would be a biased estimate of the population variance (it would systematically underestimate it).

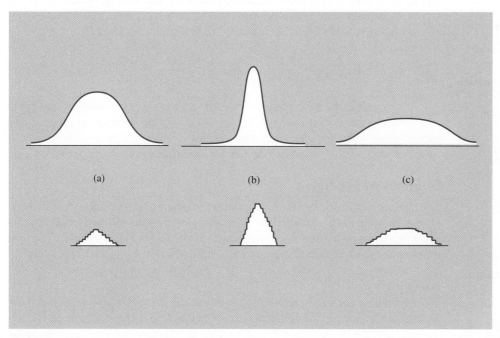

Figure 7–1 The variation in samples (as in each of the lower distributions) is similar to the variations in the populations they are taken from (each of the upper distributions).

unbiased estimate of the population variance (S^2) estimate of the population variance, based on sample scores, which has been corrected so that it is equally likely to overestimate or underestimate the true population variance; the correction used is dividing the sum of squared deviations by the sample size minus 1, instead of the usual procedure of dividing by the sample size directly.

degrees of freedom (*df*) number of scores free to vary when estimating a population parameter; usually part of a formula for making that estimate—for example, in the formula for estimating the population variance from a single sample, the degrees of freedom is the number of scores minus 1.

> The estimated population variance is the sum of the squared deviation scores divided by the number of scores minus 1.

> The estimated population standard deviation is the square root of the estimated population variance.

of 20 scores might have a variance of only 171.) If we used a biased estimate of the population variance in our research studies, our results would not be accurate. Therefore, we need to identify an *unbiased estimate* of the population variance.

Fortunately, you can figure an **unbiased estimate of the population variance** by slightly changing the ordinary variance formula. The ordinary variance formula is the sum of the squared deviation scores divided by the number of scores. The changed formula still starts with the sum of the squared deviation scores, but divides this by the number of scores *minus 1*. Dividing by a slightly smaller number makes the result slightly larger. Dividing by the number of scores minus 1 makes the variance you get just enough larger to make it an *unbiased estimate* of the population variance. (This unbiased estimate is our best estimate of the population variance. However, it is still an *estimate*, so it is unlikely to be exactly the same as the true population variance. But we can be certain that our unbiased estimate of the population variance is equally likely to be too high as it is to be too low. This is what makes the estimate *unbiased.*)

The symbol we will use for the unbiased estimate of the population variance is S^2. The formula is the usual variance formula, but now dividing by $N - 1$:

$$S^2 = \frac{\sum(X - M)^2}{N - 1} = \frac{SS}{N - 1} \quad \text{(7–1)}$$

$$S = \sqrt{S^2} \quad \text{(7–2)}$$

Let's return again to the example of hours spent studying and figure the estimated population variance from the sample's 16 scores. First, you figure the sum of squared deviation scores. (Subtract the mean from each of the scores, square those deviation scores, and add them.) Presume in our example that this comes out to 694 ($SS = 694$). To get the estimated population variance, you divide this sum of squared deviation scores by the number of scores minus 1; that is, in this example, you divide 694 by $16 - 1$; 694 divided by 15 comes out to 46.27. In terms of the formula,

$$S^2 = \frac{\sum(X - M)^2}{N - 1} = \frac{SS}{N - 1} = \frac{694}{16 - 1} = \frac{694}{15} = 46.27$$

At this point, you have now seen several different types of standard deviation and variance (that is, for a sample, for a population, and unbiased estimates); and each of these types has used a different symbol. To help you keep them straight, a summary of the types of standard deviation and variance is shown in Table 7–1.

Degrees of Freedom

The number you divide by (the number of scores minus 1) to get the estimated population variance has a special name. It is called the **degrees of freedom.** It has this name because it is the number of scores in a sample that are "free to vary." The idea is that, when figuring the variance, you first have to know the mean. If you know the mean and all but one of the scores in the sample, you can figure out the one you don't know with a little arithmetic. Thus, once you know the mean, one of the scores in the sample is not free to have any possible value. So in this kind of situation the degrees of freedom are the number of scores minus 1. In terms of a formula,

$$df = N - 1 \quad \text{(7–3)}$$

df is the degrees of freedom.

Table 7-1 Summary of Different Types of Standard Deviation and Variance

Statistical Term	Symbol
Sample standard deviation	SD
Population standard deviation	σ
Estimated population standard deviation	S
Sample variance	SD^2
Population variance	σ^2
Estimated population variance	S^2

> The degrees of freedom are the number of scores in the sample minus 1.

In our example, $df = 16 - 1 = 15$. (In some situations you learn about in later chapters, the degrees of freedom are figured a bit differently. This is because in those situations, the number of scores free to vary is different. For all the situations you learn about in this chapter, $df = N - 1$.)

The formula for the estimated population variance is often written using df instead of $N - 1$:

$$S^2 = \frac{\sum(X - M)^2}{df} = \frac{SS}{df} \tag{7-4}$$

> The estimated population variance is the sum of squared deviations divided by the degrees of freedom.

The Standard Deviation of the Distribution of Means

Once you have figured the estimated population variance, you can figure the standard deviation of the comparison distribution using the same procedures you learned in Chapter 5. Just as before, when you have a sample of more than one, the comparison distribution is a *distribution of means,* and the variance of a distribution of means is the variance of the population of individuals divided by the sample size. You have just estimated the variance of the population. Thus, you can estimate the variance of the distribution of means by dividing the estimated population variance by the sample size. The standard deviation of the distribution of means is the square root of its variance. Stated as formulas,

$$S_M^2 = \frac{S^2}{N} \tag{7-5}$$

> The variance of the distribution of means based on an estimated population variance is the estimated population variance divided by the number of scores in the sample.

$$S_M = \sqrt{S_M^2} \tag{7-6}$$

> The standard deviation of the distribution of means based on an estimated population variance is the square root of the variance of the distribution of means based on an estimated population variance.

Note that, with an estimated population variance, the symbols for the variance and standard deviation of the distribution of means use S instead of σ.

In our example, the sample size was 16 and we worked out the estimated population variance to be 46.27. The variance of the distribution of means, based on that estimate, will be 2.89. That is, 46.27 divided by 16 equals 2.89. The standard deviation is 1.70, the square root of 2.89. In terms of the formulas,

$$S_M^2 = \frac{S^2}{N} = \frac{46.27}{16} = 2.89$$

$$S_M = \sqrt{S_M^2} = \sqrt{2.89} = 1.70$$

The Shape of the Comparison Distribution When Using an Estimated Population Variance: The *t* Distribution

In Chapter 5 you learned that when the population distribution follows a normal curve, the shape of the distribution of means will also be a normal curve. However, this changes when you do hypothesis testing with an estimated population variance. When you are using an estimated population variance, you have less true information and more room for error. The mathematical effect is that there are likely to be slightly more extreme means than in an exact normal curve. Further, the smaller your

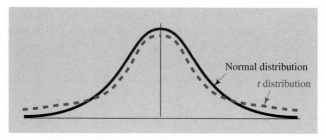

Figure 7–2 A *t* distribution (dashed blue line) compared to the normal curve (solid black line).

sample size, the bigger this tendency. This is because, with a smaller sample size, your estimate of the population variance is based on less information.

The result of all this is that, when doing hypothesis testing using an estimated variance, your comparison distribution will not be a normal curve. Instead, the comparison distribution will be a slightly different curve called a *t* **distribution.**

Actually, there is a whole family of *t* distributions. They vary in shape according to the degrees of freedom you used to estimate the population variance. However, for any particular degrees of freedom, there is only one *t* distribution.

Generally, *t* distributions look to the eye like a normal curve—bell-shaped, symmetrical, and unimodal. A *t* distribution differs subtly in having heavier tails (that is, slightly more scores at the extremes). Figure 7–2 shows the shape of a *t* distribution compared to a normal curve.

This slight difference in shape affects how extreme a score you need to reject the null hypothesis. As always, to reject the null hypothesis, your sample mean has to be in an extreme section of the comparison distribution of means, such as the top 5%. However, if the comparison distribution has more of its means in the tails than a normal curve would have, then the point where the top 5% begins has to be farther out on this comparison distribution. The result is that it takes a slightly more extreme sample mean to get a significant result when using a *t* distribution than when using a normal curve.

Just how much the *t* distribution differs from the normal curve depends on the degrees of freedom, the amount of information used in estimating the population variance. The *t* distribution differs most from the normal curve when the degrees of freedom are low (because your estimate of the population variance is based on a very small sample). For example, using the normal curve, you may recall that 1.64 is the cutoff for a one-tailed test at the .05 level. On a *t* distribution with 7 degrees of freedom (that is, with a sample size of 8), the cutoff is 1.895 for a one-tailed test at the .05 level. If your estimate is based on a larger sample, say a sample of 25 (so that $df = 24$), the cutoff is 1.711, a cutoff much closer to that for the normal curve. If your sample size is infinite, the *t* distribution is the same as the normal curve. (Of course, if your sample size were infinite, it would include the entire population!) But even with sample sizes of 30 or more, the *t* distribution is nearly identical to the normal curve.

Shortly, you will learn how to find the cutoff using a *t* distribution, but let's first return briefly to the example of how much students in your dorm study each week. You finally have everything you need for Step ❷ about the characteristics of the comparison distribution. We have already seen that the distribution of means in this example has a mean of 17 hours and a standard deviation of 1.70. You can now add that the shape of the comparison distribution will be a *t* distribution with 15 degrees of freedom.[2]

t **distribution**   mathematically defined curve that is the comparison distribution used in a *t* test.

The Cutoff Sample Score for Rejecting the Null Hypothesis: Using the *t* Table

Step ❸ of hypothesis testing is determining the cutoff for rejecting the null hypothesis. There is a different *t* distribution for any particular degrees of freedom. However, to avoid taking up pages and pages with tables for each possible *t* distribution, you use a simplified table that gives only the crucial cutoff points. We have included such a **t table** in the Appendix (Table A–2). Just as with the normal curve table, the *t* table shows only positive *t* scores. If you have a one-tailed test, you need to decide whether your cutoff score is a positive *t* score or a negative *t* score. If your one-tailed test is testing whether the mean of Population 1 is greater than the mean of Population 2, the cutoff *t* score is positive. However, if your one-tailed test is testing whether the mean of Population 1 is less than the mean of Population 2, the cutoff *t* score is negative.

In the hours-studied example, you have a one-tailed test. (You want to know whether students in your dorm study *more* than students in general at your college study.) You will probably want to use the 5% significance level, because the cost of a Type I error (mistakenly rejecting the null hypothesis) is not great. You have 16 participants, making 15 degrees of freedom for your estimate of the population variance.

Table 7–2 shows a portion of the *t* table from Table A–2 in the Appendix. Find the column for the .05 significance level for one-tailed tests and move down to the row for 15 degrees of freedom. The crucial cutoff is 1.753. In this example, you are testing whether students in your dormitory (Population 1) study *more* than students in general at your college (Population 2). In other words, you are testing whether

t table table of cutoff scores on the *t* distribution for various degrees of freedom, significance levels, and one- and two-tailed tests.

Table 7-2 Cutoff Scores for *t* Distributions with 1 Through 17 Degrees of Freedom (Highlighting Cutoff for Hours-Studied Example)

df	One-Tailed Tests .10	.05	.01	Two-Tailed Tests .10	.05	.01
1	3.078	6.314	31.821	6.314	12.706	63.657
2	1.886	2.920	6.965	2.920	4.303	9.925
3	1.638	2.353	4.541	2.353	3.182	5.841
4	1.533	2.132	3.747	2.132	2.776	4.604
5	1.476	2.015	3.365	2.015	2.571	4.032
6	1.440	1.943	3.143	1.943	2.447	3.708
7	1.415	1.895	2.998	1.895	2.365	3.500
8	1.397	1.860	2.897	1.860	2.306	3.356
9	1.383	1.833	2.822	1.833	2.262	3.250
10	1.372	1.813	2.764	1.813	2.228	3.170
11	1.364	1.796	2.718	1.796	2.201	3.106
12	1.356	1.783	2.681	1.783	2.179	3.055
13	1.350	1.771	2.651	1.771	2.161	3.013
14	1.345	1.762	2.625	1.762	2.145	2.977
15	1.341	1.753	2.603	1.753	2.132	2.947
16	1.337	1.746	2.584	1.746	2.120	2.921
17	1.334	1.740	2.567	1.740	2.110	2.898

students in your dormitory have a higher *t* score than students in general. This means that the cutoff *t* score is positive. Thus, you will reject the null hypothesis if your sample's mean is 1.753 or more standard deviations above the mean on the comparison distribution. (If you were using a known variance, you would have found your cutoff from a normal curve table. The *Z* score to reject the null hypothesis based on the normal curve would have been 1.645.)

One other point about using the *t* table: In the full *t* table in the Appendix, there are rows for each degree of freedom from 1 through 30, then for 35, 40, 45, and so on up to 100. Suppose your study has degrees of freedom between two of these higher values. To be safe, you should use the nearest degrees of freedom to yours given on the table that is less than yours. For example, in a study with 43 degrees of freedom, you would use the cutoff for $df = 40$.

The Sample Mean's Score on the Comparison Distribution: The *t* Score

Step ❹ of hypothesis testing is figuring your sample mean's score on the comparison distribution. In Chapter 5, this meant finding the *Z* score on the comparison distribution—the number of standard deviations your sample's mean is from the mean on the distribution. You do exactly the same thing when your comparison distribution is a *t* distribution. The only difference is that, instead of calling this a *Z* score, because it is from a *t* distribution, you call it a *t* **score.** In terms of a formula,

> The *t* score is your sample's mean minus the population mean, divided by the standard deviation of the distribution of means.

$$t = \frac{M - \mu}{S_M} \tag{7-7}$$

In the example, your sample's mean of 21 is 4 hours from the mean of the distribution of means, which amounts to 2.35 standard deviations from the mean (4 hours divided by the standard deviation of 1.70 hours).[3] That is, the *t* score in the example is 2.35. In terms of the formula,

$$t = \frac{M - \mu}{S_M} = \frac{21 - 17}{1.70} = \frac{4}{1.70} = 2.35$$

Deciding Whether to Reject the Null Hypothesis

Step ❺ of hypothesis testing is deciding whether to reject the null hypothesis. This step is exactly the same with a *t* test, as it was in the hypothesis-testing situations discussed in previous chapters. In the example, the cutoff *t* score was 1.753 and the actual *t* score for your sample was 2.35. Conclusion: reject the null hypothesis. The research hypothesis is supported that students in your dorm study more than students in the college overall.

Figure 7–3 shows the various distributions for this example.

Summary of Hypothesis Testing When the Population Variance Is Not Known

Table 7–3 compares the hypothesis-testing procedure we just considered (for a *t* test for a single sample) with the hypothesis-testing procedure for a *Z* test from Chapter 5. That is, we are comparing the current situation in which you know the population's mean but not its variance to the Chapter 5 situation, where you knew the population's mean *and* variance.

t **score**   on a *t* distribution, number of standard deviations from the mean (like a *Z* score, but on a *t* distribution).

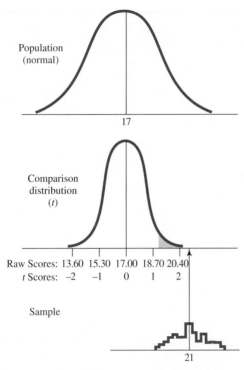

Figure 7–3 Distribution for the hours-studied example.

Another Example of a *t* Test for a Single Sample

Consider another fictional example. Suppose a researcher was studying the psychological effects of a devastating flood in a small rural community. Specifically, the researcher was interested in how hopeful (versus unhopeful) people felt after the flood. The

Table 7-3	Hypothesis Testing with a Single Sample Mean When Population Variance Is Unknown (*t* Test for a Single Sample) Compared to When Population Variance Is Known (*Z* Test)

Steps in Hypothesis Testing	Difference From When Population Variance Is Known
❶ Restate the question as a research hypothesis and a null hypothesis about the populations.	No difference in method.
❷ Determine the characteristics of the comparison distribution:	
Population mean	No difference in method.
Population variance	*Estimate* from the sample.
Standard deviation of the distribution of sample means	No difference in method (but based on *estimated* population variance).
Shape of the comparison distribution	Use the *t* distribution with *df* = *N* − 1.
❸ Determine the significance cutoff.	Use the *t* table.
❹ Determine your sample's score on the comparison distribution.	No difference in method (but called a *t* score).
❺ Decide whether to reject the null hypothesis.	No difference in method.

Table 7-4	Results and Figuring for a Single-Sample *t* Test for a Study of 10 People's Ratings of Hopefulness Following a Devastating Flood (Fictional Data)

Rating (X)	Difference From the Mean (X − M)	Squared Difference From the Mean (X − M)²
5	.30	.09
3	−1.70	2.89
6	1.30	1.69
2	−2.70	7.29
7	2.30	5.29
6	1.30	1.69
7	−2.30	5.29
4	−.70	.49
2	−2.70	7.29
5	.30	.09
Σ: 47		32.10

$M = (\Sigma X)/N = 47/10 = 4.70.$

$df = N - 1 = 10 - 1 = 9.$

$\mu = 4.00.$

$S^2 = SS/df = 32.10/(10 - 1) = 32.10/9 = 3.57.$

$S_M^2 = S^2/N = 3.57/10 = .36$

$S_M = \sqrt{S_M^2} = \sqrt{.36} = .60.$

t with $df = 9$ needed for 1% significance level, two-tailed $= \pm 3.250.$

Actual sample $t = (M - \mu)/S_M = (4.70 - 4.00)/.60 = .70/.60 = 1.17.$

Decision: Do not reject the null hypothesis.

researcher randomly selected 10 people from this community to complete a short questionnaire. The key item on the questionnaire asked how hopeful they felt, using a 7-point scale from *extremely unhopeful* (1) to *neutral* (4) to *extremely hopeful* (7). The researcher wanted to know whether the ratings of hopefulness for people who had been through the flood would be consistently above or below the neutral point on the scale (4).

Table 7–4 shows the results and figuring for the *t* test for a single sample; Figure 7–4 shows the distributions involved. Here are the steps of hypothesis testing.

❶ **Restate the question as a research hypothesis and a null hypothesis about the populations.** There are two populations:

Population 1: People who experienced the flood.
Population 2: People who are neither hopeful nor unhopeful.

The research hypothesis is that the two populations will score differently. The null hypothesis is that they will score the same.

❷ **Determine the characteristics of the comparison distribution.** If the null hypothesis is true, the mean of both populations is 4. The variance of these populations is not known, so you have to estimate it from the sample. As shown in Table 7–4, the sum of the squared deviations of the sample's scores from the sample's mean is 32.10. Thus, the estimated population variance is 32.10 divided by 9 degrees of freedom (10 – 1), which comes out to 3.57.

The distribution of means has a mean of 4 (the same as the population mean). Its variance is the estimated population variance divided by the sample size (3.57

TIP FOR SUCCESS

Be careful. To find the variance of a distribution of means, you always divide the population variance by the sample size. This is true whether the population's variance is known or only estimated. It is only when making the estimate of the population variance that you divide by the sample size minus 1. That is, the degrees of freedom are used only when estimating the variance of the population of individuals.

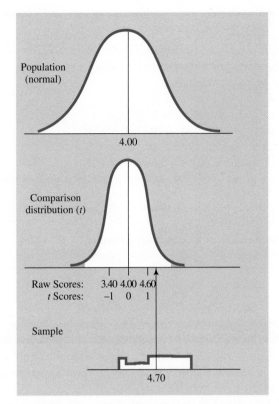

Figure 7–4   Distributions for the example of how hopeful individuals felt following a devastating flood.

divided by 10 equals .36). The square root of this, the standard deviation of the distribution of means, is .60. Its shape will be a *t* distribution for *df* = 9.

❸ **Determine the cutoff sample score on the comparison distribution at which the null hypothesis should be rejected.** The researcher wanted to be very cautious about mistakenly concluding that the flood made a difference. Thus, she decided to use the .01 significance level. The hypothesis was nondirectional (that is, no specific direction of difference from the mean of 4 was specified; either result would have been of interest); so the researcher used a two-tailed test. The researcher looked up the cutoff in Table 7–2 (or Table A–2 in the Appendix) for a two-tailed test and 9 degrees of freedom. The cutoff given in the table is 3.250. Thus, to reject the null hypothesis, the sample's score on the comparison distribution must be 3.250 or higher, or −3.250 or lower.

❹ **Determine your sample's score on the comparison distribution.** The sample's mean of 4.70 is .70 scale points from the null hypothesis mean of 4.00. That makes it 1.17 standard deviations on the comparison distribution from that distribution's mean (.70/.60 = 1.17); *t* = 1.17.

❺ **Decide whether to reject the null hypothesis.** The *t* of 1.17 is not as extreme as the needed *t* of ±3.250. Therefore, the researcher cannot reject the null hypothesis. The study is inconclusive. (If the researcher had used a larger sample, giving more power, the result might have been quite different.)

Summary of Steps for a *t* Test for a Single Sample

Table 7–5 summarizes the steps of hypothesis testing when you have scores from a single sample and a population with a known mean but an unknown variance.[4]

Table 7-5   Steps for a *t* Test for a Single Sample

❶ **Restate the question as a research hypothesis and a null hypothesis about the populations.**

❷ **Determine the characteristics of the comparison distribution.**
  a. The mean is the same as the known population mean.
  b. The standard deviation is figured as follows:
    Ⓐ Figure the estimated population variance: $S^2 = SS/df$.
    Ⓑ Figure the variance of the distribution of means: $S_M^2 = S^2/N$.
    Ⓒ Figure the standard deviation of the distribution of means: $S_M = \sqrt{S_M^2}$.
  c. The shape will be a *t* distribution with $N - 1$ degrees of freedom.

❸ **Determine the cutoff sample score on the comparison distribution at which the null hypothesis should be rejected.**
  a. Decide the significance level and whether to use a one-tailed or a two-tailed test.
  b. Look up the appropriate cutoff in a *t* table.

❹ **Determine your sample's score on the comparison distribution:** $t = (M - \mu)/S_M$.

❺ **Decide whether to reject the null hypothesis:** Compare the scores from Steps ❸ and ❹.

How are you doing?

1. In what sense is a sample's variance a biased estimate of the variance of the population the sample is taken from? That is, in what way does the sample's variance typically differ from the population's?

2. What is the difference between the usual formula for figuring the variance and the formula for estimating a population's variance from the scores in a sample (that is, the formula for an unbiased estimate of the population variance)?

3. (a) What are degrees of freedom? (b) How do you figure the degrees of freedom in a *t* test for a single sample? (c) What do they have to do with estimating the population variance? (d) What do they have to do with the *t* distribution?

4. (a) How does a *t* distribution differ from a normal curve? (b) How do degrees of freedom affect this? (c) What is the effect of the difference on hypothesis testing?

5. List three differences in how you do hypothesis testing for a *t* test for a single sample versus for the *Z* test (you learned in Chapter 5).

6. A population has a mean of 23. A sample of 4 is given an experimental procedure and has scores of 20, 22, 22, and 20. Test the hypothesis that the procedure produces a lower score. Use the .05 significance level. (a) Use the steps of hypothesis testing and (b) make a sketch of the distributions involved.

❸ **Determine the cutoff sample score on the comparison distribution at which the null hypothesis should be rejected.** From Table A-2, the cutoff for a one-tailed *t* test at the .05 level for $df = 3$ is -2.353. The cutoff *t* score is negative, since the research hypothesis is that the procedure produces a *lower score*.

❹ **Determine your sample's score on the comparison distribution.**
$t = (M - \mu)/S_M = (21 - 23)/.57 = -2/.57 = -3.51$.

❺ **Decide whether to reject the null hypothesis.** The *t* of -3.51 is more extreme than the needed *t* of -2.353. Therefore, reject the null hypothesis; the research hypothesis is supported.

(b) Sketches of distributions are shown in Figure 7-5.

6. (a) Steps of hypothesis testing:

❶ **Restate the question as a research hypothesis and a null hypothesis about the populations.** There are two populations:

Population 1: People who are given the experimental procedure.

Population 2: The general population.

The research hypothesis is that Population 1 will score lower than Population 2. The null hypothesis is that Population 1 will not score lower than Population 2.

❷ **Determine the characteristics of the comparison distribution.**

   a. The mean of the distribution of means is 23.

   b. The standard deviation is figured as follows:

   ❶ Figure the estimated population variance. You first need to figure the sample mean, which is $(20 + 22 + 22 + 20)/4 = 84/4 = 21$. The estimated population variance is $S^2 = SS/(N - 1) = [(20 - 21)^2 + (22 - 21)^2 + (22 - 21)^2 + (20 - 21)^2]/(4 - 1) = (-1^2 + 1^2 + 1^2 + -1^2)/3 = (1 + 1 + 1 + 1)/3 = 4/3 = 1.33$.

   ❷ Figure the variance of the distribution of means:
   $$S_M^2 = S^2/N = 1.33/4 = .33$$

   ❸ Figure the standard deviation of the distribution of means:
   $$S_M = \sqrt{S_M^2} = \sqrt{.33} = .57$$

   c. The shape of the comparison distribution will be a *t* distribution with *df* = 3.

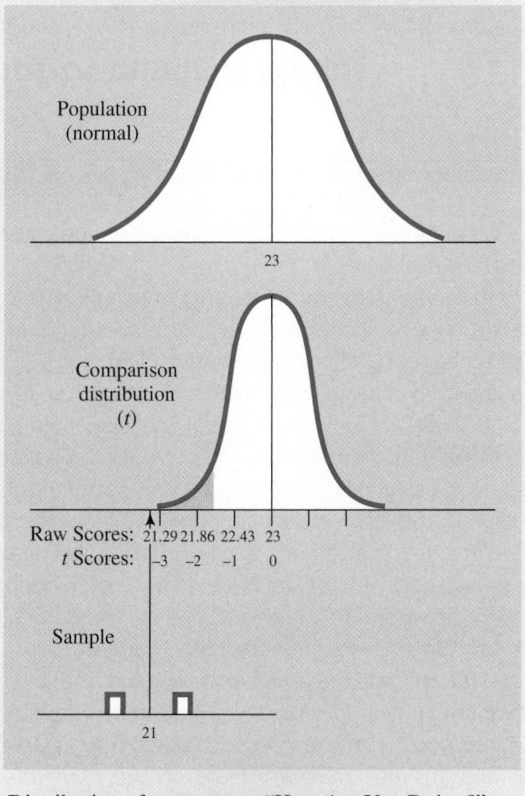

Figure 7-5 Distributions for answer to "How Are You Doing?" question 6b.

Answers

1. The sample's variance will in general be smaller than the variance of the population the sample is taken from.

2. In the usual formula you divide by the number of participants (*N*); in the formula for estimating a population's variance from the scores in a sample, you divide by the number of participants in the sample minus 1 (that is, *N* − 1).

3. (a) Degrees of freedom consist of the number of scores free to vary. (b) The degrees of freedom in a *t* test for a single sample consist of the number of scores in the sample minus 1. (c) In estimating the population variance, the formula is the sum of squared deviations divided by the degrees of freedom. (d) *t* distributions differ slightly from each other according to the degrees of freedom.

4. (a) A *t* distribution differs from a normal curve in that it has heavier tails; that is, more scores at the extremes. (b) The more degrees of freedom, the closer the shape (including the tails) is to a normal curve. (c) The cutoffs for significance are more extreme for a *t* distribution than for a normal curve.

5. In the *t* test you (a) estimate the population variance from the sample (it is not known in advance); (b) you look up the cutoff on a *t* table in which you also have to take into account the degrees of freedom (you don't use a normal curve table); and (c) your sample's score on the comparison distribution, which is a *t* distribution (not a normal curve), is a *t* score (not a *Z* score).

The *t* Test for Dependent Means

The situation you just learned about (the *t* test for a single sample) is for when you know the population mean but not its variance and you have a single sample of scores. It turns out that in most research you do not even know the population's *mean;* plus, in most research situations you usually have not one set, but *two* sets, of scores. These two things, not knowing the population mean and having two sets of scores, is very, very common.

The rest of this chapter focuses specifically on this important research situation in which you have two scores from each person in your sample. This kind of research situation is called a **repeated-measures design** (also known as a *within subjects design*). A common example is when you measure the same people before and after some psychological or social intervention. For example, a psychologist might measure the quality of men's communication before and after receiving premarital counseling.

The hypothesis-testing procedure for the situation in which each person is measured twice (that is, for the situation in which we have a repeated-measures design) is a **t test for dependent means.** It has the name "dependent means" because the mean for each group of scores (for example, a group of before-scores and a group of after-scores) are dependent on each other in that they are both from the same people. (In Chapter 8, we consider the situation in which you compare scores from two different groups of people, a research situation you analyze using a *t* test for *independent* means.)

You do a *t* test for dependent means exactly the same way as a *t* test for a single sample, except that (a) you use something called *difference scores,* and (b) you assume that the population mean (of the difference scores) is 0. We will now consider each of these two new aspects.

Difference Scores

With a repeated-measures design, your sample includes two scores for each person instead of just one. The way you handle this is to make the two scores per person into one

repeated-measures design research strategy in which each person is tested more than once; same as *within subjects design*.

t test for dependent means hypothesis-testing procedure in which there are two scores for each person and the population variance is not known; it determines the significance of a hypothesis that is being tested using difference or change scores from a single group of people.

score per person! You do this magic by creating **difference scores:** For each person, you subtract one score from the other. If the difference is before versus after, difference scores are also called *change scores.*

Consider the example of the quality of men's communication before and after receiving premarital counseling. The psychologist subtracts the communication quality score before the counseling from the communication quality score after the counseling. This gives an after-minus-before difference score for each man. When the two scores are a before-score and an after-score, we usually take the after-score minus the before-score to indicate the *change.*

Once you have the difference score for each person in the study, you do the rest of the hypothesis testing with difference scores. That is, you treat the study as if there were a single sample of scores (scores that in this situation happen to be difference scores).

Population of Difference Scores with a Mean of 0

So far in the research situations we have considered in this book, you have always known the mean of the population to which you compared your sample's mean. For example, in the college dormitory survey of hours studied, you knew the population mean was 17 hours. However, now we are using difference scores, and we usually don't know the mean of the population of difference scores.

Here is the solution. Ordinarily, the null hypothesis in a repeated-measures design is that on the average there is *no difference* between the two groups of scores. For example, the null hypothesis in a study of the quality of men's communication before and after receiving premarital counseling is that on the average there is no difference between communication quality before and after the counseling. What does no *difference* mean? Saying there is on the average no difference is the same as saying that the mean of the population of the difference scores is 0. Therefore, when working with difference scores, you are comparing the population of difference scores that your sample of difference scores comes from to a population of difference scores with a mean of 0. In other words, with a *t* test for dependent means, what we call Population 2 will ordinarily have a mean of 0 (that is, it is a population of difference scores that has a mean of 0).

Example of a *t* Test for Dependent Means

Olthoff (1989) tested the communication quality of couples three months before and again three months after marriage. One group studied was 19 couples who had received ordinary (very minimal) premarital counseling from the ministers who were going to marry them. (To keep the example simple, we will focus on just this one group and only on the husbands in the group. Scores for wives were similar, though somewhat more varied, making it a more complicated example for learning the *t* test procedure.)

The scores for the 19 husbands are listed in the "Before" and "After" columns in Table 7–6, followed by all the *t* test figuring. (The distributions involved are shown in Figure 7–6.) The crucial column for starting the analysis is the difference scores. For example, the first husband, whose communication quality was 126 before marriage and 115 after had a difference of −11. (We figured after minus before, so that an increase is positive and a decrease, as for this husband, is negative.) The mean of the difference scores is −12.05. That is, on the average, these 19 husbands' communication quality decreased by about 12 points.

Is this decrease significant? In other words, how likely is it that this sample of difference scores is a random sample from a population of difference scores whose mean is 0?

difference scores   difference between a person's score on one testing and the same person's score on another testing; often an after-score minus a before-score, in which case it is also called a *change* score.

Table 7-6 *t* Test for Communication Quality Scores Before and After Marriage for 19 Husbands Who Received Ordinary Premarital Counseling

Husband	Communication Quality		Difference (After − Before)	Deviation (Difference − M)	Squared Deviation
	Before	*After*			
A	126	115	−11	1.05	1.10
B	133	125	−8	4.05	16.40
C	126	96	−30	−17.95	322.20
D	115	115	0	12.05	145.20
E	108	119	11	23.05	531.30
F	109	82	−27	−14.95	223.50
G	124	93	−31	−18.95	359.10
H	98	109	11	23.05	531.30
I	95	72	−23	−10.95	119.90
J	120	104	−16	−3.95	15.60
K	118	107	−11	1.05	1.10
L	126	118	−8	4.05	16.40
M	121	102	−19	−6.95	48.30
N	116	115	−1	11.05	122.10
O	94	83	−11	1.05	1.10
P	105	87	−18	−5.95	35.40
Q	123	121	−2	10.05	101.00
R	125	100	−25	−12.95	167.70
S	128	118	−10	2.05	4.20
Σ:	2,210	1,981	−229		2,762.90

For difference scores:

$M = -229/19 = -12.05$.

$\mu = 0$ (assumed as a no-change baseline of comparison).

$S^2 = SS/df = 2,762.90/(19 - 1) = 153.49$.

$S_M^2 = S^2/N = 153.49/19 = 8.08$.

$S_M = \sqrt{S_M^2} = \sqrt{8.08} = 2.84$.

t with $df = 18$ needed for 5% level, two-tailed $= \pm 2.101$.

$t = (M - \mu)/S_M = (-12.05 - 0)/2.84 = -4.24$.

Decision: Reject the null hypothesis.

Source: Data from Olthoff (1989).

❶ **Restate the question as a research hypothesis and a null hypothesis about the populations.** There are two populations:

Population 1: Husbands who receive ordinary premarital counseling.
Population 2: Husbands whose communication quality does not change from before to after marriage. (In other words, it is a population of husbands whose mean difference in communication quality from before to after marriage is 0.)

The research hypothesis is that Population 1's mean difference score (communication quality after marriage minus communication quality before marriage) is different from Population 2's mean difference score (of zero). That is, the

TIP FOR SUCCESS

As in previous chapters, Population 2 is the population for when the null hypothesis is true.

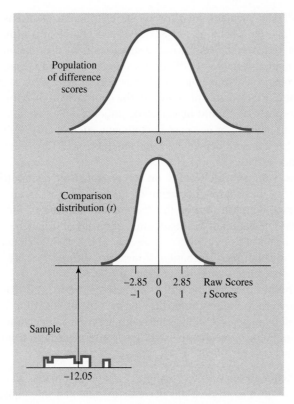

Figure 7–6 Distributions for the Olthoff (1989) example of a *t* test for dependent means.

research hypothesis is that husbands who receive ordinary premarital counseling, like the husbands Olthoff studied, *do* change in communication quality from before to after marriage. The null hypothesis is that the populations are the same— that the husbands who receive ordinary premarital counseling *do not* change in their communication quality from before to after marriage.

Notice that you have no actual information about Population 2 husbands. The husbands in the study are a sample of Population 1 husbands. For the purposes of hypothesis testing, you set up Population 2 as a kind of straw man comparison group. That is, for the purpose of the analysis, you set up a comparison group of husbands who, if measured before and after marriage, would on the average show no difference.

❷ **Determine the characteristics of the comparison distribution.** If the null hypothesis is true, the mean of the population of difference scores is 0. The variance of the population of difference scores can be estimated from the sample of difference scores. As shown in Table 7–6, the sum of squared deviations of the difference scores from the mean of the difference scores is 2,762.90. With 19 husbands in the study, there are 18 degrees of freedom. Dividing the sum of squared deviation scores by the degrees of freedom gives an estimated population variance of difference scores of 153.49.

The distribution of means (from this population of difference scores) has a mean of 0, the same as the mean of the population of difference scores. The variance of the distribution of means of difference scores is the estimated population variance of difference scores (153.49) divided by the sample size (19), which gives 8.08. The standard deviation of the distribution of means of difference scores is 2.84, the square root of 8.08. Because Olthoff was using an estimated population variance, the comparison distribution is a *t* distribution. The estimate of the population variance of difference scores is based on 18 degrees of freedom; so this comparison distribution is a *t* distribution for 18 degrees of freedom.

❸ **Determine the cutoff sample score on the comparison distribution at which the null hypothesis should be rejected.** Olthoff used a two-tailed test to allow for either an increase or decrease in communication quality. Using the .05 significance level and 18 degrees of freedom, Table A–2 shows cutoff *t* scores of +2.101 and −2.101.

❹ **Determine your sample's score on the comparison distribution.** Olthoff's sample had a mean difference score of −12.05. That is, the mean was 12.05 points below the mean of 0 on the distribution of means of difference scores. The standard deviation of the distribution of means of difference scores is 2.84. Thus, the mean of the difference scores of −12.05 is 4.24 standard deviations below the mean of the distribution of means of difference scores. So Olthoff's sample of difference scores has a *t* score of −4.24.

❺ **Decide whether to reject the null hypothesis.** The *t* of −4.24 for the sample of difference scores is more extreme than the needed *t* of ±2.101. Thus, you can reject the null hypothesis: Olthoff's husbands are from a population in which husbands' communication quality is different after marriage from what it was before (it is lower).

Olthoff's actual study was more complex. You may be interested to know that he found that the wives also showed this decrease in communication quality after marriage. But a group of similar engaged couples who were given special communication skills training by their ministers (much more than the usual short session) had no significant decline in marital communication quality after marriage. In fact, there is a great deal of research showing that on the average marital happiness declines steeply over time (VanLaningham et al., 2001). And many studies have now shown the value of a full course of premarital communications training. For example, a recent representative survey of 3,344 adults in the United States showed that those who had attended a premarital communication program had significantly greater marital satisfaction, had less marital conflict, and were 31% less likely to divorce (Stanley et al., 2006). Further, benefits were greatest for those with a college education!

Summary of Steps for a *t* Test for Dependent Means

Table 7–7 summarizes the steps for a *t* test for dependent means.[5]

A Second Example of a *t* Test for Dependent Means

Here is another example. A team of researchers examined the brain systems involved in human romantic love (Aron et al., 2005). One issue was whether romantic love engages a part of the brain called the caudate (a brain structure that is engaged when people win money, are given cocaine, and other such "rewards"). Thus, the researchers recruited people who had very recently fallen "madly in love." (For example, to be in the study participants had to think about their partner at least 80% of their waking hours.) Participants brought a picture of their beloved with them, plus a picture of a familiar, neutral person of the same age and sex as their beloved. Participants then went in to the functional magnetic resonance imaging (fMRI) machine and their brain was scanned while they looked at the two pictures—30 seconds at the neutral person's picture, 30 seconds at their beloved, 30 seconds at the neutral person, and so forth.

Table 7-7   Steps for a *t* Test for Dependent Means

❶ **Restate the question as a research hypothesis and a null hypothesis about the populations.**
❷ **Determine the characteristics of the comparison distribution.**
  a. Make each person's two scores into a difference score. Do all the remaining steps using these difference scores.
  b. Figure the mean of the difference scores.
  c. Assume a mean of the distribution of means of difference scores of 0: $\mu = 0$.
  d. The standard deviation of the distribution of means of difference scores is figured as follows:
    Ⓐ Figure the estimated population variance of difference scores: $S^2 = SS/df$.
    Ⓑ Figure the variance of the distribution of means of difference scores: $S_M^2 = S^2/N$.
    Ⓒ Figure the standard deviation of the distribution of means of difference scores: $S_M = \sqrt{S_M^2}$.
  e. The shape is a *t* distribution with $df = N - 1$.
❸ **Determine the cutoff sample score on the comparison distribution at which the null hypothesis should be rejected.**
  a. Decide the significance level and whether to use a one-tailed or a two-tailed test.
  b. Look up the appropriate cutoff in a *t* table.
❹ **Determine your sample's score on the comparison distribution:** $t = (M - \mu)/S_M$.
❺ **Decide whether to reject the null hypothesis:** Compare the scores from Steps ❸ and ❹.

Table 7–8 shows average brain activations (mean fMRI scanner values) in the caudate area of interest during the two kinds of pictures. (We have simplified the example for teaching purposes, including using only 10 participants when the actual study had 17.) It also shows the figuring of the difference scores and all the other

Table 7-8   *t* Test for a Study of Romantic Love and Brain Activation in Part of the Caudate

Student	Brain Activation		Difference (Beloved − Control)	Deviation (Difference − M)	Squared Deviation
	Beloved's photo	Control photo			
1	1487.8	1487.2	.6	−.800	.640
2	1329.4	1328.1	1.3	−.100	.010
3	1407.9	1405.9	2.0	.600	.360
4	1236.1	1234.0	2.1	.700	.490
5	1299.8	1298.2	1.6	.200	.040
6	1447.2	1444.7	2.5	1.100	1.210
7	1354.1	1354.3	−.2	−1.600	2.560
8	1204.6	1203.7	.9	−.500	.250
9	1322.3	1320.8	1.5	.100	.010
10	1388.5	1386.8	1.7	.300	.090
Σ:	13477.7	13463.7	14.0		5.660

For difference scores:
  $M = 14.0/10 = 1.400$.
  $\mu = 0$ (assumed as a no-change baseline of comparison).
  $S^2 = SS/df = 5.660/(10 - 1) = 5.660/9 = .629$.
  $S_M^2 = S^2/N = .629/10 = .063$.
  $S_M = \sqrt{S_M^2} = \sqrt{.063} = .251$.
  t with $df = 9$ needed for 5% level, one-tailed $= 1.833$.
  $t = (M - \mu)/S_M = (1.400 - 0)/.251 = 5.58$.

  Decision: Reject the null hypothesis.

Source: Data based on Aron et al. (2005).

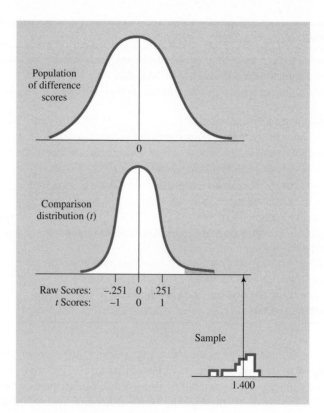

Figure 7–7   Distributions for the example of romantic love and brain activation in part of the caudate.

figuring for the *t* test for dependent means. Figure 7–7 shows the distributions involved. Here are the steps of hypothesis testing:

❶ **Restate the question as a research hypothesis and a null hypothesis about the populations.** There are two populations:

Population 1: Individuals like those tested in this study.
Population 2: Individuals whose brain activation in the caudate area of interest is the same when looking at a picture of their beloved and a picture of a familiar, neutral person.

The research hypothesis is that Population 1's mean difference score (brain activation when viewing the beloved's picture minus brain activation when viewing the neutral person's picture) is greater than Population 2's mean difference score (of no difference). That is, the research hypothesis is that brain activation in the caudate area of interest is greater when viewing the beloved person's picture than when viewing the neutral person's picture. The null hypothesis is that Population 1's mean difference score is not greater than Population 2's. That is, the null hypothesis is that brain activation in the caudate area of interest is not greater when viewing the beloved person's picture than when viewing the neutral person's picture.

❷ **Determine the characteristics of the comparison distribution.**
  a. **Make each person's two scores into a difference score. This is shown in the column labeled "Difference" in Table 7–8. You do all the remaining steps using these difference scores.**

b. Figure the mean of the difference scores. The sum of the difference scores (14.0) divided by the number of difference scores (10) gives a mean of the difference scores of 1.400. So, $M = 1.400$.

c. Assume a mean of the distribution of means of difference scores of 0: $\mu = 0$.

d. The standard deviation of the distribution of means of difference scores is figured as follows:

Ⓐ Figure the estimated population variance of difference scores: $S^2 = SS/df = 5.660/(10 - 1) = .629$.

Ⓑ Figure the variance of the distribution of means of difference scores: $S_M^2 = S^2/N = .629/10 = .063$.

Ⓒ Figure the standard deviation of the distribution of means of difference scores: $S_M = \sqrt{S_M^2} = \sqrt{.063} = .251$.

e. The shape is a *t* distribution with $df = N - 1$. Therefore, the comparison distribution is a *t* distribution for 9 degrees of freedom. It is a *t* distribution because we figured its variance based on an estimated population variance. It has 9 degrees of freedom because there were 9 degrees of freedom in the estimate of the population variance.

❖ **Determine the cutoff sample score on the comparison distribution at which the null hypothesis should be rejected.**

a. We will use the standard .05 significance level. This is a one-tailed test because the researchers were interested only in a specific direction of difference.

b. Using the .05 significance level with 9 degrees of freedom, Table A–2 shows a cutoff *t* of 1.833. In Table 7–8, the difference score is figured as brain activation when viewing the beloved's picture minus brain activation when viewing the neutral person's picture. Thus, the research hypothesis predicts a positive difference score, which means that our cutoff is +1.833.

❖ **Determine your sample's score on the comparison distribution.** $t = (M - \mu)/S_M = (1.400 - 0)/.251 = 5.58$. The sample's mean difference of 1.400 is 5.58 standard deviations (of .251 each) above the mean of 0 on the distribution of means of difference scores.

❖ **Decide whether to reject the null hypothesis.** The sample's *t* score of 5.58 is more extreme than the cutoff *t* of 1.833. You can reject the null hypothesis. Brain activation in the caudate area of interest is greater when viewing a beloved's picture than when viewing a neutral person's picture. The results of this study are not limited to North Americans. Recently, the study was replicated, with virtually identical results, in Beijing with Chinese students who were intensely in love (Xu et al., 2007).

t Test for Dependent Means with Scores from Pairs of Research Participants

The *t* test for dependent means is also called a *paired-samples t test, t test for correlated means, t test for matched samples,* and *t test for matched pairs.* Each of these names comes from the same idea that in this kind of *t* test you are comparing two sets of scores that are related to each other in a direct way. In the *t* test for dependent means examples in this chapter, the two sets of scores have been related because each individual had a score in both sets of scores (for example, a score before a procedure and a score after a procedure). However, you can also use a *t* test for dependent means with scores from *pairs of research participants,* considering each pair as if it were one person, and figuring the difference score for each pair. For example, suppose you have 30 married couples and want to test whether wives consistently do more housework than husbands.

Table 7-9 Review of the Z Test, the t Test for a Single Sample, and the t Test for Dependent Means

| | Type of Test | | |
Features	Z Test	t Test for a Single Sample	t Test for Dependent Means
Population variance is known	Yes	No	No
Population mean is known	Yes	Yes	No
Number of scores for each participant	1	1	2
Shape of comparison distribution	Z distribution	t distribution	t distribution
Formula for degrees of freedom	Not applicable	$df = N - 1$	$df = N - 1$
Formula	$Z = (M - \mu_M)/\sigma_M$	$t = (M - \mu)/S_M$	$t = (M - \mu)/S_M$

You could figure for each couple a difference score of the wife's hours of housework per week minus her husband's number of hours of housework per week. There are also situations in which experimenters *create* pairs. For example, a researcher might put participants into pairs to do a puzzle task together and, for each pair, assign one to be a leader and one a follower. At the end of the study, participants privately fill out a questionnaire about how much they enjoyed the interaction. The procedure for analyzing this study would be to create a difference score for each pair by taking the enjoyment rating of the leader minus the enjoyment rating of the follower.

Review and Comparison of Z Test, t Test for a Single Sample, and t test for Dependent Means

In Chapter 5 you learned about the Z test; in this chapter you have learned about the t test for a single sample and the t test for dependent means. Table 7–9 provides a review and comparison of the Z test, the t test for a single sample, and the t test for dependent means.

How are you doing?

1. Describe the situation in which you would use a t test for dependent means.
2. When doing a t test for dependent means, what do you do with the two scores you have for each participant?
3. In a t test for dependent means, (a) what is usually considered to be the mean of the "known" population (Population 2). (b) Why?
4. Five individuals are tested before and after an experimental procedure; their scores are given in the following table. Test the hypothesis that there is no change, using the .05 significance level. (a) Use the steps of hypothesis testing and (b) sketch the distributions involved.

Person	Before	After
1	20	30
2	30	50
3	20	10
4	40	30
5	30	40

5. What about the research situation makes the difference in whether you should carry out a *Z* test or a *t* test for a single sample?

6. What about the research situation makes the difference in whether you should carry out a *t* test for a single sample or a *t* test for dependent means?

4. (b) The distributions are shown in Figure 7–8.

5. As shown in Table 7–9, whether the population variance is known determines whether you should carry out a *Z* test or a *t* test for a single sample. You use a *Z* test when the population variance is known and you use the *t* test for a single sample when it is not known.

6. As shown in Table 7–9, whether the population mean is known and whether there are one or two scores for each participant determines whether you should carry out a *t* test for a single sample or a *t* test for dependent means. You use a *t* test for a single sample when you know the population mean and you have one score for each participant; you use the *t* test for dependent means when you do not know the population mean and there are two scores for each participant.

⑥ **Decide whether to reject the null hypothesis.** The sample's *t* score of .67 is not more extreme than the cutoff *t* of ±2.776. Therefore, do *not* reject the null hypothesis.

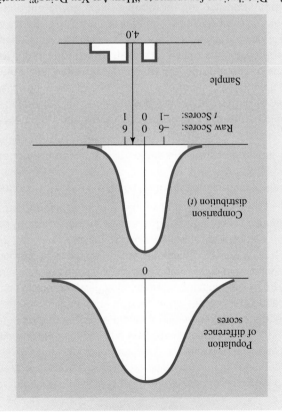

Figure 7–8 Distributions for answer to "How Are You Doing?" question 4.

Answers

1. A t test for dependent means is used when you are doing hypothesis testing and you have two scores for each participant (such as a before-score and an after-score) and the population variance is unknown. It is also used when a study compares participants who are organized into pairs.

2. Subtract one from the other to create a difference (or change) score for each person. The t test is then done with these difference (or change) scores.

3. (a) The mean of the "known" population (Population 2) is 0. (b) You are comparing your sample to a situation in which there is no difference—a population of difference scores in which the average difference is 0.

4. (a) Steps of hypothesis testing (all figuring is shown in Table 7–10):

❶ **Restate the question as a research hypothesis and a null hypothesis about the populations.** There are two populations:

Population 1: People like those tested before and after the experimental procedure.

Population 2: People whose scores are the same before and after the experimental procedure.

The research hypothesis is that Population 1's mean change score (after minus before) is different from Population 2's. The null hypothesis is that Population 1's mean change score is the same as Population 2's.

❷ **Determine the characteristics of the comparison distribution.** The mean of the distribution of means of difference scores (the comparison distribution) is 0; the standard deviation of the distribution of means of difference scores is 6; it is a t distribution with 4 degrees of freedom.

❸ **Determine the cutoff sample score on the comparison distribution at which the null hypothesis should be rejected.** For a two-tailed test at the .05 level, the cutoff sample scores are +2.776 and −2.776.

❹ **Determine your sample's score on the comparison distribution.**

$$t = (4 - 0)/6 = .67.$$

Table 7-10 Figuring for Answer to "How Are You Doing?" Question 4

Person	Score Before	Score After	Difference (After − Before)	Deviation (Difference − M)	Deviation Squared
1	20	30	10	6	36
2	30	50	20	16	256
3	20	10	−10	−14	196
4	40	30	−10	−14	196
5	30	40	10	6	36
Σ:	140	160	20		720

For difference scores:

$M = 20/5 = 4.00.$

$\mu = 0.$

$S^2 = SS/df = 720/(5 - 1) = 720/4 = 180.$

$S^2_M = S^2/N = 180/5 = 36.$

$S_M = \sqrt{S^2_M} = \sqrt{36} = 6.$

t for $df = 4$ needed for 5% significance level, two-tailed $= \pm 2.776.$

$t = (M - \mu)/S_M = (4 - 0)/6 = .67$

Decision: Do not reject the null hypothesis.

Assumptions of the *t* Test for a Single Sample and the *t* Test for Dependent Means

As we have seen, when you are using an estimated population variance, the comparison distribution is a *t* distribution. However, the comparison distribution will be exactly a *t* distribution only if the distribution of individuals follows a normal curve. Otherwise, the comparison distribution will follow some other (usually unknown) shape.

Thus, strictly speaking, a normal population is a requirement within the logic and mathematics of the *t* test. A requirement like this for a hypothesis-testing procedure is called an **assumption.** That is, a normal population distribution is one assumption of the *t* test. The effect of this assumption is that if the population distribution is not normal, the comparison distribution will be some indeterminate shape other than a *t* distribution—and thus the cutoffs on the *t* table will be incorrect.

Unfortunately, when you do a *t* test, you don't know whether the population is normal. This is because, when doing a *t* test, usually all you have to go on are the scores in your sample. Fortunately, however, as we saw in Chapter 3, distributions in psychology research quite often approximate a normal curve. (This also applies to distributions of difference scores.) Also, statisticians have found that, in practice, you get reasonably accurate results with *t* tests even when the population is rather far from normal. In other words, the *t* test is said to be *robust* over moderate violations of the assumption of a normal population distribution. How statisticians figure out the **robustness** of a test is an interesting topic, which is described in Box 8–1 in Chapter 8.

The only very common situation in which using a *t* test for dependent means is likely to give a seriously distorted result is when you are using a one-tailed test and the population is highly skewed (is very asymmetrical, with a much longer tail on one side than the other). Thus, you need to be cautious about your conclusions when doing a one-tailed test if the sample of difference scores is highly skewed, suggesting the population it comes from is also highly skewed.

Effect Size and Power for the *t* Test for Dependent Means

Effect Size

You can figure the effect size for a study using a *t* test for dependent means the same way as in Chapter 6.[6] *t* is the difference between the population means divided by the population standard deviation: $d = (\mu_1 - \mu_2)/\sigma$. When using this formula for a *t* test for dependent means, μ_1 is for the predicted mean of the population of difference scores, μ_2 (the "known" population mean) is almost always 0, and σ usually stands for the standard deviation of the population of difference scores. The conventions for effect size for a *t* test for dependent means are also the same as you learned for the situation we considered in Chapter 6: A small effect size is .20, a medium effect size is .50, and a large effect size is .80.

Consider an example. A sports psychologist plans a study on attitudes toward teammates before versus after a game. She will administer an attitude questionnaire twice, once before and once after a game. Suppose that the smallest before-after difference that would be of any importance is 4 points on the questionnaire. Also suppose that, based on related research, the researcher figures that the standard deviation of difference scores on this attitude questionnaire is about 8 points. Thus, $\mu_1 = 4$ and $\sigma = 8$. Applying the effect size formula, $d = (\mu_1 - \mu_2)/\sigma = (4 - 0)/8 = .50$. In terms of the effect size conventions, her planned study has a medium effect size.

assumption   condition, such as a population's having a normal distribution, required for carrying out a particular hypothesis-testing procedure; a part of the mathematical foundation for the accuracy of the tables used in determining cutoff values.

robustness   extent to which a particular hypothesis-testing procedure is reasonably accurate even when its assumptions are violated.

To estimate the effect size after a study, use the actual mean of your sample's difference scores as your estimate of μ_1, and use S (for the population of difference scores) as your estimate of σ.

Consider our first example of a t test for dependent means, the study of husbands' change in communication quality. In that study, the mean of the difference scores was -12.05. The estimated population standard deviation of the difference scores would be 12.41. That is, we figured the estimated variance of the difference scores (S^2) to be 153.49; $\sqrt{S^2} = 12.39$. Therefore, the estimated effect size is $d = (\mu_1 - \mu_2)/\sigma = (M - 0)/S = (-12.05 - 0)/12.39 = -.97$. This is a very large effect size. (The negative sign for the effect size means that the large effect was a decrease.)

Power

Power for a t test for dependent means can be determined using a power table, a power software package, or an Internet power calculator. Table 7–11 gives the approximate power at the .05 significance level for small, medium, and large effect sizes and one-tailed and two-tailed tests. In the sports psychology example, the researcher expected a medium effect size ($d = .50$). If she planned to conduct the study using the .05 level, two-tailed, with 20 participants, the study would have a power of .59. This means that, if the research hypothesis is true and has a medium effect size, there is a 59% chance that this study will come out significant.

The power table (Table 7–11) is also useful when you are reading about a non-significant result in a published study. Suppose that a study using a t test for dependent means has a nonsignificant result. The study tested significance at the .05 level, was two-tailed, and had 10 participants. Should you conclude that there is in fact no difference at all in the populations? Probably not. Even assuming a medium effect size, Table 7–11 shows that there is only a 32% chance of getting a significant result in this study.

TIP FOR SUCCESS

Recall from Chapter 6 that power can be expressed as a probability (such as .71) or as a percentage (such as 71%). Power is expressed as a probability in Table 7–11 (as well as in power tables in later chapters).

Table 7–11 Approximate Power for Studies Using the t Test for Dependent Means for Testing Hypotheses at the .05 Significance Level

Difference Scores in Sample (N)	Effect Size		
	Small ($d = .20$)	**Medium** ($d = .50$)	**Large** ($d = .80$)
One-tailed test			
10	.15	.46	.78
20	.22	.71	.96
30	.29	.86	*
40	.35	.93	*
50	.40	.97	*
100	.63	*	*
Two-tailed test			
10	.09	.32	.66
20	.14	.59	.93
30	.19	.77	.99
40	.24	.88	*
50	.29	.94	*
100	.55	*	*

*Power is nearly 1.

Table 7-12	Approximate Number of Research Participants Needed for 80% Power for the *t* Test for Dependent Means in Testing Hypotheses at the .05 Significance Level		
	Effect Size		
	Small **(*d* = .20)**	**Medium** **(*d* = .50)**	**Large** **(*d* = .80)**
One-tailed	156	26	12
Two-tailed	196	33	14

Consider another study that was not significant. This study also used the .05 significance level, two-tailed. This study had 100 research participants. Table 7–11 tells you that there would be a 55% chance of the study's coming out significant if there were even a true small effect size in the population. If there were a medium effect size in the population, the table indicates that there is almost a 100% chance that this study would have come out significant. Thus, in this study with 100 participants, we could conclude from the results that in the population there is probably at most a small difference.

To keep Table 7–11 simple, we have given power figures for only a few different numbers of participants (10, 20, 30, 40, 50, and 100). This should be adequate for the kinds of rough evaluations you need to make when evaluating results of research articles.[7]

Planning Sample Size

Table 7–12 gives the approximate number of participants needed for 80% power for a planned study. (Eighty percent is a common figure used by researchers for the minimum power to make a study worth doing.) Suppose you plan a study in which you expect a large effect size and you use the .05 significance level, two-tailed. The table shows you would only need 14 participants to have 80% power. On the other hand, a study using the same significance level, also two-tailed, but in which you expect only a small effect size would need 196 participants for 80% power.[8]

How are you doing?

1. (a) What is an assumption in hypothesis testing? (b) Describe a specific assumption for a *t* test for dependent means. (c) What is the effect of violating this assumption? (d) What does it mean to say that the *t* test for dependent means is robust? (e) Describe a situation in which it is not robust.
2. How can you tell if you have violated the normal curve assumption?
3. (a) Write the formula for effect size; (b) describe each of its terms as they apply to a planned *t* test for dependent means; (c) describe what you use for each of its terms in figuring effect size for a completed study that used a *t* test for dependent means.
4. You are planning a study in which you predict the mean of the population of difference scores to be 40, and the population standard deviation is 80. You plan to test significance using a *t* test for dependent means, one-tailed, with an alpha of .05. (a) What is the predicted effect size? (b) What is the power of this study if you carry it out with 20 participants? (c) How many participants would you need to have 80% power?

Answers

1. (a) An assumption is a requirement that you must meet for the results of the hypothesis testing procedure to be accurate. (b) The population of individuals' difference scores is assumed to be a normal distribution. (c) The significance level cutoff from the *t* table is not accurate. (d) Unless you very strongly violate the assumption (that is, unless the population distribution is very far from normal), the cutoff is fairly accurate. (e) The *t* test for dependent means is not robust when you are doing a one-tailed test and the population distribution is highly skewed.

2. You look at the distribution of the sample of difference scores to see if it is dramatically different from a normal curve.

3. (a) $d = (\mu_1 - \mu_2)/\sigma$. (b) d is the effect size; μ_1 is for the predicted mean of the population of difference scores; μ_2 is the mean of the known population, which for a population of difference scores is almost always 0; σ is for the standard deviation of the population of difference scores. (c) To estimate μ_1, you use M, the actual mean of your sample's difference scores; μ_2 remains as 0; and for σ, you use S, the estimated standard deviation of the population of difference scores.

4. (a) Predicted effect size: $d = (\mu_1 - \mu_2)/\sigma = (40 - 0)/80 = .50$. (b) Power of this study: .71. (c) Number of participants for 80% power: 26.

Controversy: Advantages and Disadvantages of Repeated-Measures Designs

The main controversies about *t* tests have to do with their relative advantages and disadvantages compared to various alternatives (alternatives we will discuss in Chapter 14). There is, however, one consideration that we want to comment on now. It is about all research designs in which the same participants are tested before and after some experimental intervention (the kind of situation the *t* test for dependent means is often used for).

Studies using difference scores (that is, studies using a repeated-measures design) often have much larger effect sizes for the same amount of expected difference between means than other kinds of research designs. That is, testing each of a group of participants twice (once under one condition and once under a different condition) usually produces a study with high power. In particular, this kind of study gives more power than dividing the participants up into two groups and testing each group once (one group tested under one condition and the other tested under another condition). In fact, studies using difference scores usually have even more power than those in which you have twice as many participants, but each is tested only once.

Why do repeated-measures designs have so much power? The reason is that the standard deviation of difference scores is usually quite low. (The standard deviation of difference scores is what you divide by to get the effect size when using difference scores.) This produces a large effect size, which increases the power. In a repeated-measures design, the only variation is in the difference scores. Variation among participants on each testing's scores is not part of the variation involved in the analysis. As an example, look back at Table 7–8 from our romantic love and brain imaging study. Notice that there were very great differences between the scores (fMRI scanner activation values) for each participant. The first participant's scores were around 1,487, the second's was around 1,328, and so forth. Each person has a quite different overall level of activation. But the *differences* between the two conditions were relatively small. What we see in this example is that, because difference scores are all comparing participants to themselves, the variation in them is much less (and does not include the variation between participants). William S. Gosset, who essentially invented the *t* test (see Box 7–1), made much of the higher power of repeated-measures studies in a historically interesting controversy over an experiment about milk, which is described in Box 7–2.

On the other hand, testing a group of people before and after an experimental procedure, without any kind of control group that does not go through the procedure, is a weak research design (Cook & Campbell, 1979). Even if such a study produces a significant difference, it leaves many alternative explanations for that difference. For example, the research participants might have matured or improved during that period anyway, or perhaps other events happened between tests, or the participants not getting benefits may have dropped out. It is even possible that the initial test itself caused changes.

Note, however, that the difficulties of research that tests people before and after some intervention are shared only slightly with the kind of study in which participants are tested under two conditions, such as viewing a beloved person's picture and a neutral person's picture, with half tested first viewing the beloved's picture and half tested first viewing the neutral person's picture. Another example would be a study examining the hand-eye coordination of a group of surgeons under both quiet and noisy conditions (not while doing surgery, of course). Each surgeon would perform the test of hand-eye

---

BOX 7–2 **The Power of Studies Using Difference Scores: How the Lanarkshire Milk Experiment Could Have Been Milked for More**

In 1930, a major health experiment was conducted in Scotland involving 20,000 schoolchildren. Its main purpose was to compare the growth of a group of children who were assigned to drink milk regularly to those who were in a control group. The results were that those who drank milk showed more growth.

However, William Gosset, a contemporary statistician and inventor of the *t* test (see Box 7–1), was appalled at the way the experiment was conducted. It had cost about £7,500, which in 1930 was a huge amount of money, and was done wrong! Large studies such as this were very popular among statisticians in those days because they seemed to imitate the large numbers found in nature. Gosset, by contrast, being a brewer, was forced to use very small numbers in his studies—experimental batches of beer were too costly. And he was often chided by the "real statisticians" for his small sample sizes. But Gosset argued that no number of participants was large enough when strict random assignment was not followed. And in this study, teachers were permitted to switch children from group to group if they took pity on a child whom they felt would benefit from receiving milk!

However, even more interesting in light of the present chapter, Gosset demonstrated that the researchers could have obtained the same result with 50 pairs of identical twins, flipping a coin to determine which of each pair was in the milk group (and sticking to it). Of course, the statistic you would use is the *t* test as taught in this chapter—the *t* test for dependent means.

More recently, the development of power analysis, which we introduced in Chapter 6, has thoroughly vindicated Gosset. It is now clear just how surprisingly few participants are needed when a researcher can find a way to set up a repeated-measures design in which difference scores are the basic unit of analysis. (In this case, each *pair* of twins would be one "participant.") As Gosset could have told them, studies that use the *t* test for dependent means can be extremely sensitive.

Sources: Peters (1987); Tankard (1984).

coordination during quiet conditions and noisy conditions. Ideally, any effects of practice or fatigue from taking the test twice would be equalized by testing half of the surgeons under noisy conditions first, and half under quiet conditions first.

Single Sample *t* Tests and Dependent Means *t* Tests in Research Articles

Research articles usually describe *t* tests in a fairly standard format that includes the degrees of freedom, the *t* score, and the significance level. For example, " $t(24) = 2.80, p < .05$" tells you that the researcher used a *t* test with 24 degrees of freedom, found a *t* score of 2.80, and the result was significant at the .05 level. Whether a one-tailed or two-tailed test was used may also be noted. (If not, assume that it was two-tailed.) Usually the means, and sometimes the standard deviations, are given for each testing. Rarely does an article report the standard deviation of the difference scores.

Had our student in the dormitory example reported the results in a research article, she would have written something like this: "The sample from my dormitory studied a mean of 21 hours ($SD = 6.80$). Based on a *t* test for a single sample, this was significantly different from the known mean of 17 for the college as a whole, $t(15) = 2.35, p < .05$, one-tailed." The researchers in our fictional flood victims example might have written up their results as follows: "The reported hopefulness of our sample of flood victims ($M = 4.70, SD = 1.89$) was not significantly different from the midpoint of the scale, $t(9) = 1.17$."

As we noted earlier, psychologists only occasionally use the *t* test for a single sample. We introduced it mainly as a stepping-stone to the more widely used *t* test for dependent means. Nevertheless, one sometimes sees the *t* test for a single sample in research articles. For example, Soproni and colleagues (2001), as part of a larger study, had pet dogs respond to a series of eight trials in which the owner would look at one of two bowls of dog food and the researchers measured whether the dog went to the correct bowl. (The researchers called these "at trials" because the owner looked directly *at* the target.) For each dog, this produced an average percentage correct that was compared to chance, which would be 50% correct. Here is part of their results: "During the eight test trials for gesture, dogs performed significantly above chance on at target trials: one sample *t* test, $t(13) = 5.3, p < .01 . . .$" (p. 124).

As we have said, the *t* test for dependent means is much more commonly used. Olthoff (1989) might have reported the result of his study of husbands' communication quality as follows: "There was a significant decline in communication quality, dropping from a mean of 116.32 before marriage to a mean of 104.26 after marriage, $t(18) = -4.24, p < .05$."

As another example, Rashotte and Webster (2005) carried out a study about people's general expectations about the abilities of men and women. In the study, the researchers showed 174 college students photos of women and men (referred to as the female and male targets, respectively). The students rated the person in each photo in terms of that person's general abilities (e.g., in terms of the person's intelligence, abstract abilities, capability at most tasks, and so on). For each participant, these ratings were combined to create a measure of the perceived status of the female targets and of the male targets. The researchers then compared the status ratings given for the female targets and male targets. Since each participant in the study rated *both* the female and the male targets, the researchers compared the status ratings assigned to the female and male targets using a *t* test for dependent means. Table 7–13 shows the results. The row entitled "Whole sample ($N = 174$)" gives the

Table 7-13   Status Scale: Mean (and *SE*) General Expectations for Female and Male Targets

Respondents	Mean Score (*SE*)		M − F Target Difference	*t*(1-tailed *p*)
	Female Target	Male Target		
Whole sample (*N* = 174)	5.60 (.06)	5.85 (.07)	.25	3.46 (<.001)
Female respondents (*N* = 111)	5.62 (.07)	5.84 (.081)	.22	2.62 (<.05)
Male respondents (*N* = 63)	5.57 (.10)	5.86 (.11)	.29	2.26 (<.05)

Source: Rashotte, L. S., & Webster, M., Jr. (2005). Gender status beliefs. *Social Science Research, 34*, 618–633. Copyright © 2005 by Elsevier. Reprinted by permission of Elsevier.

result of the *t* test for all 174 participants and shows that the status rating assigned to the male targets was significantly higher than the rating assigned to the female targets ($t = 3.46, p < .001$). As shown in the table, the researchers also conducted two additional *t* tests to see if this effect was the same among the female participants and the male participants. The results showed that both the female and the male participants assigned higher ratings to the male targets.

Summary

1. You use the standard steps of hypothesis testing even when you don't know the population variance. However, in this situation you have to estimate the population variance from the scores in the sample, using a formula that divides the sum of squared deviation scores by the degrees of freedom ($df = N - 1$).

2. When the population variance is estimated, the comparison distribution of means is a *t* distribution (with cutoffs given in a *t* table). A *t* distribution has slightly heavier tails than a normal curve (just how much heavier depends on how few the degrees of freedom are). Also, in this situation, a sample's number of standard deviations from the mean of the comparison distribution is called a *t* score.

3. You use a *t* test for a single sample when a sample mean is being compared to a known population mean and the population variance is unknown.

4. You use a *t* test for dependent means in studies where each participant has two scores, such as a before-score and an after-score or a score in each of two experimental conditions. A *t* test for dependent means is also used when you have scores from pairs of research participants. In this *t* test, you first figure a difference or change score for each participant, then go through the usual five steps of hypothesis testing with the modifications described in summary points 1 and 2 and making Population 2 a population of difference scores with a mean of 0 (no difference).

5. An assumption of the *t* test is that the population distribution is a normal curve. However, even when it is not, the *t* test is usually fairly accurate.

6. The effect size of a study using a *t* test for dependent means is the mean of the difference scores divided by the standard deviation of the difference scores. You can look up power and needed sample size for any particular level of power using power software packages, an Internet power calculator, or special tables.

7. The power of studies using difference scores is usually much higher than that of studies using other designs with the same number of participants. However, research using a single group tested before and after some intervening event, without a control group, allows for many alternative explanations of any observed changes.

8. *t* tests are reported in research articles using a standard format. For example, "$t(24) = 2.80, p < .05$."

Key Terms

t tests (p. 223)
t test for a single sample (p. 223)
biased estimate (p. 225)
unbiased estimate of the population
variance (S^2) (p. 226)

degrees of freedom (*df*) (p. 226)
t distribution (p. 228)
t table (p. 229)
t score (p. 230)
repeated-measures design (p. 236)

t test for dependent means (p. 236)
difference scores (p. 237)
assumption (p. 247)
robustness (p. 247)

Example Worked-Out Problems

t Test for a Single Sample

Eight participants are tested after being given an experimental procedure. Their scores are 14, 8, 6, 5, 13, 10, 10, and 6. The population of people not given this procedure is normally distributed with a mean of 6. Using the .05 level, two-tailed, does the experimental procedure make a difference? (a) Use the five steps of hypothesis testing and (b) sketch the distributions involved.

Answer

(a) Steps of hypothesis testing:

❶ **Restate the question as a research hypothesis and a null hypothesis about the populations.** There are two populations:

Population 1: People who are given the experimental procedure.
Population 2: The general population.

The research hypothesis is that the Population 1 will score differently than Population 2. The null hypothesis is that Population 1 will score the same as Population 2.

❷ **Determine the characteristics of the comparison distribution.** The mean of the distribution of means is 6 (the known population mean). To figure the estimated population variance, you first need to figure the sample mean, which is $(14 + 8 + 6 + 5 + 13 + 10 + 10 + 6)/8 = 72/8 = 9$. The estimated population variance is $S^2 = SS/df = 78/7 = 11.14$; the variance of the distribution of means is $S_M^2 = S^2/N = 11.14/8 = 1.39$. The standard deviation of the distribution of means is $S_M = \sqrt{S_M^2} = \sqrt{1.39} = 1.18$. Its shape will be a *t* distribution for $df = 7$.

❸ **Determine the cutoff sample score on the comparison distribution at which the null hypothesis should be rejected.** From Table A–2, the cutoffs for a two-tailed *t* test at the .05 level for $df = 7$ are +2.365 and −2.365.

❹ **Determine your sample's score on the comparison distribution.** $t = (M - \mu)/S_M = (9 - 6)/1.18 = 3/1.18 = 2.54$.

❺ **Decide whether to reject the null hypothesis.** The *t* of 2.54 is more extreme than the needed *t* of ±2.365. Therefore, reject the null hypothesis; the research hypothesis is supported. The experimental procedure does make a difference.

(b) Sketches of distributions are shown in Figure 7–9.

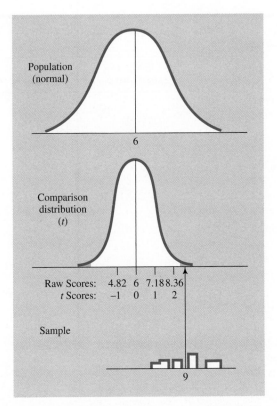

Figure 7–9   Distributions for answer to Example Worked-Out Example Problem for *t* test for a single sample.

t Test for Dependent Means

A researcher tests 10 individuals before and after an experimental procedure. The results are as follows:

Participant	Before	After
1	10.4	10.8
2	12.6	12.1
3	11.2	12.1
4	10.9	11.4
5	14.3	13.9
6	13.2	13.5
7	9.7	10.9
8	11.5	11.5
9	10.8	10.4
10	13.1	12.5

Test the hypothesis that there is an increase in scores, using the .05 significance level. (a) Use the five steps of hypothesis testing and (b) sketch the distributions involved.

Table 7–14 Figuring for Answer to Example Worked-Out Problem for *t* Test for Dependent Means

Participant	Score		Difference (After − Before)	Deviation (Difference − *M*)	Squared Deviation
	Before	*After*			
1	10.4	10.8	.4	.260	.068
2	12.6	12.1	−.5	−.640	.410
3	11.2	12.1	.9	.760	.578
4	10.9	11.4	.5	.360	.130
5	14.3	13.9	−.4	−.540	.292
6	13.2	13.5	.3	.160	.026
7	9.7	10.9	1.2	1.060	1.124
8	11.5	11.5	0.0	−.140	.020
9	10.8	10.4	−.4	−.540	.292
10	13.1	12.5	−.6	−.740	.548
Σ:	117.7	119.1	1.4		3.488

For difference scores:

$M = 1.4/10 = .140$.

$\mu = 0$.

$S^2 = SS/df = 3.488/(10 - 1) = 3.488/9 = .388$.

$S_M^2 = S^2/N = .388/10 = .039$.

$S_M = \sqrt{S_M^2} = \sqrt{.039} = .197$.

t for *df* = 9 needed for 5% significance level, one-tailed = 1.833.

$t = (M - \mu)/S_M = (.140 - 0)/.197 = .71$.

Decision: Do not reject the null hypothesis.

Answer

(a) Table 7–14 shows the results, including the figuring of difference scores and all the other figuring for the *t* test for dependent means. Here are the steps of hypothesis testing:

❶ **Restate the question as a research hypothesis and a null hypothesis about the populations.** There are two populations:

Population 1: People like those who are given the experimental procedure.
Population 2: People who show no change from before to after.

The research hypothesis is that Population 1's mean difference score (figured using "after" scores minus "before" scores) is greater than Population 2's mean difference score. The null hypothesis is that Population 1's mean difference score is not greater than Population 2's.

❷ **Determine the characteristics of the comparison distribution.** Its population mean is 0 difference. The estimated population variance of difference scores, S^2, is shown in Table 7–14 to be .388. As shown in Table 7–14, the standard deviation of the distribution of means of difference scores, S_M, is .197. Therefore, the comparison distribution has a mean of 0 and a standard deviation of .197. It will be a *t* distribution for *df* = 9.

❸ **Determine the cutoff sample score on the comparison distribution at which the null hypothesis should be rejected.** For a one-tailed test at the .05 level with *df* = 9, the cutoff is 1.833. (The cutoff is positive as the research hypothesis is that Population 1's mean difference score will be *greater* than Population 2's.)

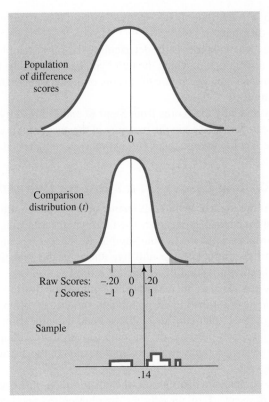

Figure 7–10 Distributions for answer to Example Worked-Out Problem for *t* test for dependent means.

❹ **Determine your sample's score on the comparison distribution.** The sample's mean change of .140 is .71 standard deviations (of .197 each) on the distribution of means above that distribution's mean of 0. That is, $t = (M - \mu)/S_M = (.140 - 0)/.197 = .71$.

❺ **Decide whether to reject the null hypothesis.** The sample's *t* of .71 is less extreme than the needed *t* of 1.833. Thus, you cannot reject the null hypothesis. The study is inconclusive.

(b) Sketches of distributions are shown in Figure 7–10.

Outline for Writing Essays for a *t* Test for a Single Sample

1. Describe the core logic of hypothesis testing in this situation. Be sure to mention that the *t* test for a single sample is used for hypothesis testing when you have scores for a sample of individuals and you want to compare the mean of this sample to a population for which the mean is known but the variance is unknown. Be sure to explain the meaning of the research hypothesis and the null hypothesis in this situation.

2. Outline the logic of estimating the population variance from the sample scores. Explain the idea of biased and unbiased estimates of the population variance, and describe the formula for estimating the population variance and why it is different from the ordinary variance formula.

3. Describe the comparison distribution (the *t* distribution) that is used with a *t* test for a single sample, noting how it is different from a normal curve and why.

Explain why a *t* distribution (as opposed to the normal curve) is used as the comparison distribution.

4. Describe the logic and process for determining the cutoff sample score(s) on the comparison distribution at which the null hypothesis should be rejected.

5. Describe why and how you figure the *t* score of the sample mean on the comparison distribution.

6. Explain how and why the scores from Steps ❸ and ❹ of the hypothesis-testing process are compared. Explain the meaning of the result of this comparison with regard to the specific research and null hypotheses being tested.

Outline for Writing Essays for a *t* Test for Dependent Means

1. Describe the core logic of hypothesis testing in this situation. Be sure to mention that the *t* test for dependent means is used for hypothesis testing when you have two scores from each person in your sample. Be sure to explain the meaning of the research hypothesis and the null hypothesis in this situation. Explain the logic and procedure for creating difference scores.

2. Explain why you use 0 as the mean for the comparison distribution.

3. Outline the logic of estimating the population variance of difference scores from the sample scores. Explain the idea of biased and unbiased estimates of the population variance, and describe the formula for estimating the population variance. Describe how to figure the standard deviation of the distribution of means of difference scores.

4. Describe the comparison distribution (the *t* distribution) that is used with a *t* test for dependent means. Explain why a *t* distribution (as opposed to the normal curve) is used as the comparison distribution.

5. Describe the logic and process for determining the cutoff sample score(s) on the comparison distribution at which the null hypothesis should be rejected.

6. Describe why and how you figure the *t* score of the sample mean on the comparison distribution.

7. Explain how and why the scores from Steps ❸ and ❹ of the hypothesis-testing process are compared. Explain the meaning of the result of this comparison with regard to the specific research and null hypotheses being tested.

Practice Problems

These problems involve figuring. Most real-life statistics problems are done on a computer with special statistical software. Even if you have such software, do these problems by hand to ingrain the method in your mind. To learn how to use a computer to solve statistics problems like those in this chapter, refer to the Using SPSS section at the end of this chapter and the *Study Guide and Computer Workbook* that accompanies this text.

All data are fictional unless an actual citation is given.

Set I (for Answers to Set I Problems, see pp. 681–683)

1. In each of the following studies, a single sample's mean is being compared to a population with a known mean but an unknown variance. For each study, decide whether the result is significant. (Be sure to show all of your calculations.)

	Sample Size (*N*)	Population Mean (μ)	Estimated Population Variance (*S*²)	Sample Mean (*M*)	Tails	Significance Level (α)
(a)	64	12.40	9.00	11.00	1 (low predicted)	.05
(b)	49	1,006.35	317.91	1,009.72	2	.01
(c)	400	52.00	7.02	52.41	1 (high predicted)	.01

2. Suppose a candidate running for sheriff in a rural community claims that she will reduce the average speed of emergency response to less than 30 minutes, which is thought to be the average response time with the current sheriff. There are no past records; so the actual standard deviation of such response times cannot be determined. Thanks to this campaign, she is elected sheriff, and careful records are now kept. The response times for the first month are 26, 30, 28, 29, 25, 28, 32, 35, 24, and 23 minutes.

   Using the .05 level of significance, did she keep her promise? (a) Use the steps of hypothesis testing. (b) Sketch the distributions involved. (c) Explain your answer to someone who has never taken a course in statistics.

3. A researcher tests five individuals who have seen paid political ads about a particular issue. These individuals take a multiple-choice test about the issue in which people in general (who know nothing about the issue) usually get 40 questions correct. The number correct for these five individuals was 48, 41, 40, 51, and 50.

   Using the .05 level of significance, two-tailed, do people who see the ads do better on this test? (a) Use the steps of hypothesis testing. (b) Sketch the distributions involved. (c) Explain your answer to someone who is familiar with the *Z* test (from Chapter 5) but is unfamiliar with *t* tests.

4. For each of the following studies using difference scores, test the significance using a *t* test for dependent means.

	Number of Difference Scores in Sample	Mean of Difference Scores in Sample	Estimated Population Variance of Difference Scores	Tails	Significance Level
(a)	20	1.7	8.29	1 (high predicted)	.05
(b)	164	2.3	414.53	2	.05
(c)	15	−2.2	4.00	1 (low predicted)	.01

5. A program to decrease littering was carried out in four cities in California's Central Valley starting in August 2007. The amount of litter in the streets (average pounds of litter collected per block per day) was measured during July before the program started and then the next July, after the program had been in effect for a year. The results were as follows:

City	July 2007	July 2008
Fresno	9	2
Merced	10	4
Bakersfield	8	9
Stockton	9	1

Using the .01 level of significance, was there a significant decrease in the amount of litter? (a) Use the five steps of hypothesis testing. (b) Sketch the distributions involved. (c) Explain your answer to someone who understands mean, standard deviation, and variance, but knows nothing else about statistics.

6. A researcher assesses the level of a particular hormone in the blood in five patients before and after they begin taking a hormone treatment program. Results for the five are as follows:

Patient	Before	After
A	.20	.18
B	.16	.16
C	.24	.23
D	.22	.19
E	.17	.16

Using the .05 significance level, was there a significant change in the level of this hormone? (a) Use the steps of hypothesis testing. (b) Sketch the distributions involved. (c) Explain your answer to someone who understands the *t* test for a single sample but is unfamiliar with the *t* test for dependent means.

7. Figure the estimated effect size and indicate whether it is approximately small, medium, or large, for each of the following studies:

	Mean Change	S
(a)	20	32
(b)	5	10
(c)	.1	.4
(d)	100	500

8. What is the power of each of the following studies, using a *t* test for dependent means (based on the .05 significance level)?

	Effect Size	N	Tails
(a)	Small	20	One
(b)	Medium	20	One
(c)	Medium	30	One
(d)	Medium	30	Two
(e)	Large	30	Two

9. About how many participants are needed for 80% power in each of the following planned studies that will use a *t* test for dependent means with $p < .05$?

	Predicted Effect Size	Tails
(a)	Medium	Two
(b)	Large	One
(c)	Small	One

10. Weller and Weller (1997) conducted a study of the tendency for the menstrual cycles of women who live together (such as sisters) to become synchronized. For their statistical analysis, they compared scores on a measure of synchronization of pairs of sisters living together versus the degree of synchronization that would be expected by chance (lower scores mean more synchronization). Their key results (reported in a table not reproduced here) were synchrony scores of 6.32 for the 30 roommate sister pairs in their sample compared to an expected synchrony score of 7.76; they then reported a *t* score of 2.27 and a *p* level of .011 for this difference. Explain this result to a person who is familiar with hypothesis testing with a known population variance, but not with the *t* test for a single sample.

11. A psychologist conducts a study of perceptual illusions under two different lighting conditions. Twenty participants were each tested under both of the two different conditions. The experimenter reported: "The mean number of effective illusions was 6.72 under the bright conditions and 6.85 under the dimly lit conditions, a difference that was not significant, $t(19) = 1.62$." Explain this result to a person who has never had a course in statistics. Be sure to use sketches of the distributions in your answer.

12. A study was done of personality characteristics of 100 students who were tested at the beginning and end of their first year of college. The researchers reported the results in the following table:

Personality Scale	Fall M	Fall SD	Spring M	Spring SD	Difference M	Difference SD
Anxiety	16.82	4.21	15.32	3.84	1.50**	1.85
Depression	89.32	8.39	86.24	8.91	3.08**	4.23
Introversion	59.89	6.87	60.12	7.11	−.23	2.22
Neuroticism	38.11	5.39	37.22	6.02	.89*	4.21

*$p < .05$.
**$p < .01$.

(a) Focusing on the difference scores, figure the *t* values for each personality scale. (Assume that *SD* in the table is for what we have called *S*, the unbiased estimate of the population standard deviation.)
(b) Explain to a person who has never had a course in statistics what this table means.

Set II

13. In each of the following studies, a single sample's mean is being compared to a population with a known mean but an unknown variance. For each study, decide whether the result is significant.

	Sample Size (*N*)	Population Mean (μ)	Estimated Population Standard Deviation (*S*)	Sample Mean (*M*)	Tails	Significance Level (α)
(a)	16	100.31	2.00	100.98	1 (high predicted)	.05
(b)	16	.47	4.00	.00	2	.05
(c)	16	68.90	9.00	34.00	1 (low predicted)	.01

14. Evolutionary theories often emphasize that humans have adapted to their physical environment. One such theory hypothesizes that people should spontaneously follow a 24-hour cycle of sleeping and waking—even if they are not exposed to the usual pattern of sunlight. To test this notion, eight paid volunteers were placed (individually) in a room in which there was no light from the outside and no clocks or other indications of time. They could turn the lights on and off as they wished. After a month in the room, each individual tended to develop a steady cycle. Their cycles at the end of the study were as follows: 25, 27, 25, 23, 24, 25, 26, and 25.

Using the .05 level of significance, what should we conclude about the theory that 24 hours is the natural cycle? (That is, does the average cycle length under these conditions differ significantly from 24 hours?) (a) Use the steps of hypothesis testing. (b) Sketch the distributions involved. (c) Explain your answer to someone who has never taken a course in statistics.

15. In a particular country, it is known that college seniors report falling in love an average of 2.20 times during their college years. A sample of five seniors, originally from that country but who have spent their entire college career in the United States, were asked how many times they had fallen in love during their college years. Their numbers were 2, 3, 5, 5, and 2. Using the .05 significance level, do students like these who go to college in the United States fall in love more often than those from their country who go to college in their own country? (a) Use the steps of hypothesis testing. (b) Sketch the distributions involved. (c) Explain your answer to someone who is familiar with the Z test (from Chapter 5) but is unfamiliar with the *t* test for a single sample.

16. For each of the following studies using difference scores, test the significance using a *t* test for dependent means.

	Number of Difference Scores in Sample	Mean of Difference Scores	S^2 for Difference Scores	Tails	Significance Level
(a)	10	3.8	50	One (high)	.05
(b)	100	3.8	50	One (high)	.05
(c)	100	1.9	50	One (high)	.05
(d)	100	1.9	50	Two	.05
(e)	100	1.9	25	Two	.05

17. Four individuals with high levels of cholesterol went on a special crash diet, avoiding high-cholesterol foods and taking special supplements. Their total cholesterol levels before and after the diet were as follows:

Participant	Before	After
J. K.	287	255
L. M. M	305	269
A. K.	243	245
R. O. S.	309	247

Using the .05 level of significance, was there a significant change in cholesterol level? (a) Use the steps of hypothesis testing. (b) Sketch the distributions involved. (c) Explain your answer to someone who has never taken a course in statistics.

18. Five people who were convicted of speeding were ordered by the court to attend a workshop. A special device put into their cars kept records of their speeds for two weeks before and after the workshop. The maximum speeds for each person during the two weeks before and the two weeks after the workshop follow.

Participant	Before	After
L. B.	65	58
J. K.	62	65
R .C.	60	56
R. T.	70	66
J. M.	68	60

Using the .05 significance level, should we conclude that people are likely to drive more slowly after such a workshop? (a) Use the steps of hypothesis testing. (b) Sketch the distributions involved. (c) Explain your answer to someone who is familiar with hypothesis testing involving known populations, but has never learned anything about *t* tests.

19. The amount of oxygen consumption was measured in six individuals over two 10-minute periods while sitting with their eyes closed. During one period, they listened to an exciting adventure story; during the other, they heard restful music.

Participant	Story	Music
1	6.12	5.39
2	7.25	6.72
3	5.70	5.42
4	6.40	6.16
5	5.82	5.96
6	6.24	6.08

Based on the results shown, is oxygen consumption less when listening to the music? Use the .01 significance level. (a) Use the steps of hypothesis testing. (b) Sketch the distributions involved. (c) Explain your answer to someone who understands mean, standard deviation, and variance but knows nothing else about statistics.

20. Five sophomores were given an English achievement test before and after receiving instruction in basic grammar. Their scores are shown below.

Student	Before	After
A	20	18
B	18	22
C	17	15
D	16	17
E	12	9

Is it reasonable to conclude that future students would show higher scores after instruction? Use the .05 significance level. (a) Use the steps of hypothesis testing. (b) Sketch the distributions involved (c) Explain your answer to someone who understands mean, standard deviation, and variance but knows nothing else about statistics.

21. Figure the predicted effect size and indicate whether it is approximately small, medium, or large, for each of the following planned studies:

	Predicted Mean Change	σ
(a)	8	30
(b)	8	10
(c)	16	30
(d)	16	10

22. What is the power of each of the following studies, using a *t* test for dependent means (based on the .05 significance level)?

	Effect Size	N	Tails
(a)	Small	50	Two
(b)	Medium	50	Two
(c)	Large	50	Two
(d)	Small	10	Two
(e)	Small	40	Two
(f)	Small	100	Two
(g)	Small	100	One

23. About how many participants are needed for 80% power in each of the following planned studies that will use a *t* test for dependent means with $p < .05$?

	Predicted Effect Size	Tails
(a)	Small	Two
(b)	Medium	One
(c)	Large	Two

24. A study compared union activity of employees in 10 plants during two different decades. The researchers reported "a significant increase in union activity, $t(9) = 3.28, p < .01$." Explain this result to a person who has never had a course in statistics. Be sure to use sketches of the distributions in your answer.

25. Holden and colleagues (1997) compared mothers' reported attitudes toward corporal punishment of their children from before to 3 years after having their first child. "The average change in the women's prior-to-current attitudes was significant, $t(107) = 10.32, p < .001 \ldots$" (p. 485). (The change was that they felt more negatively about corporal punishment after having their child.) Explain this result to someone who is familiar with the *t* test for a single sample, but not with the *t* test for dependent means.

26. Table 7–15 (reproduced from Table 4 of Larson et al., 2001) shows ratings of various aspects of work and home life of 100 middle-class men in India who were fathers. Pick three rows of interest to you and explain the results to someone who is familiar with the mean, variance, and *Z* scores but knows nothing else about statistics.

Table 7-15 Comparison of Fathers' Mean Psychological States in the Job and Home Spheres (*N* = 100)

		Sphere		
Scale	Range	Work	Home	Work vs. Home
Important	0–9	5.98	5.06	6.86***
Attention	0–9	6.15	5.13	7.96***
Challenge	0–9	4.11	2.41	11.49***
Choice	0–9	4.28	4.74	−3.38***
Wish doing else	0–9	1.50	1.44	0.61
Hurried	0–3	1.80	1.39	3.21**
Social anxiety	0–3	0.81	0.64	3.17**
Affect	1–7	4.84	4.98	−2.64**
Social climate	1–7	5.64	5.95	4.17***

Note: Values for column 3 are *t* scores; *df* = 90 for all *t* tests.
**p < .01.
***p < .001.
Source: Larson, R., Dworkin, J., & Verma, S. (2001). Men's work and family lives in India: The daily organization of time and emotions. *Journal of Family Psychology, 15,* 206–224. Copyright © 2001 by the American Psychological Association.

Using SPSS

The ✑ in the following steps indicates a mouse click. (We used SPSS version 15.0 for Windows to carry out these analyses. The steps and output may be slightly different for other versions of SPSS.)

t Test for a Single Sample

❶ Enter the scores from your distribution in one column of the data window.
❷ ✑ *Analyze.*
❸ ✑ *Compare means.*
❹ ✑ *One-sample T test* (this is the name SPSS uses for a *t* test for a single sample).
❺ ✑ on the variable for which you want to carry out the *t* test and then ✑ the arrow.
❻ Enter the population mean in the "Test Value" box.
❼ ✑ *OK.*

Practice these steps by carrying out a single sample *t* test for the example shown earlier in this chapter of 10 people's ratings of hopefulness after a flood. The sample scores, population mean, and figuring for that study are shown in Table 7–4 on page 232. Your SPSS output window should look like Figure 7–11. The first table provides information about the variable: the number of scores ("N"); the mean of the scores ("Mean"); the estimated population standard deviation, *S* ("Std. Deviation"); and the standard deviation of the distribution of means, S_M ("Std. Error Mean"). Check that the values in that table are consistent (allowing for rounding error) with the values in Table 7–4.

The second table in the SPSS output window gives the outcome of the *t* test. Compare the values of *t* and *df* in that table and the values shown in Table 7–4. The exact two-tailed significance level of the *t* test is given in the "Sig. (2-tailed)" column. In this study, the researcher was using the .01 significance level. The significance level given by SPSS (.271) is not more extreme than .01, which means that the researcher cannot reject the null hypothesis and the study is inconclusive.

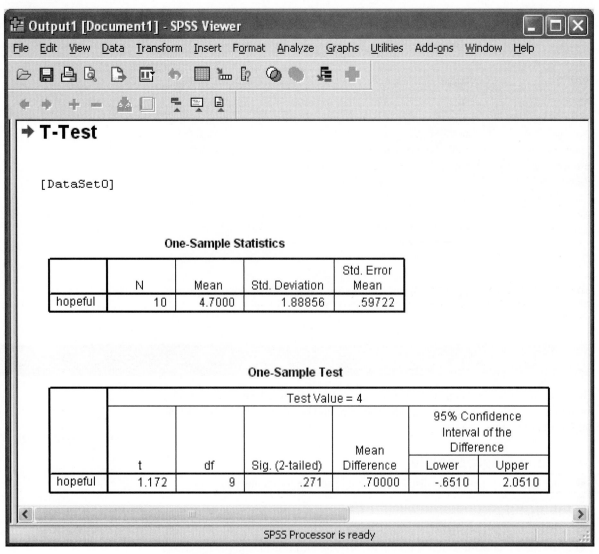

Figure 7-11 Using SPSS to carry out a *t* test for a single sample for the example of 10 people's ratings of hopefulness after a flood.

t Test for Dependent Means

❶ Enter one set of scores (for example, the "before" scores) in the first column of the data window. Then enter the second set of scores (for example, the "after" scores) in the second column of the data window. (Be sure to enter the scores in the order they are listed.) Since each row in the SPSS data window represents a separate person, it is important that you enter each person's scores in two separate columns (for example, a "before" column and an "after" column).

❷ ✑ *Analyze.*

❸ ✑ *Compare means.*

❹ ✑ *Paired-Samples T Test* (this is the name SPSS uses for a *t* test for dependent means).

❺ ✎ on the first variable (this will highlight the variable). ✎ on the second variable (this will highlight the variable). ✎ the arrow. The two variables will now appear in the "Paired Variables" box.

❻ ✎ *OK*.

Practice these steps by carrying out a *t* test for dependent means for Olthoff's (1989) study of communication quality of 19 men who received ordinary premarital counseling. The scores and figuring for that study are shown in Table 7–6 on page 238. Your SPSS output window should look like Figure 7–12. The key information is contained in the third table (labeled "Paired Samples Test"). The final three columns of this table give the *t* score (4.240), the degrees of freedom (18), and the two-tailed significance level (.000 in this case) of the *t* test. The significance level is so small that, even after rounding to three decimal places, it is less than .001. Since the significance level is more extreme than the .05 significance level we set for this study, you can reject the null hypothesis. By looking at the means for the "before" variable and the "after" variable in the first table (labeled "Paired Samples Statistics"), you can see that

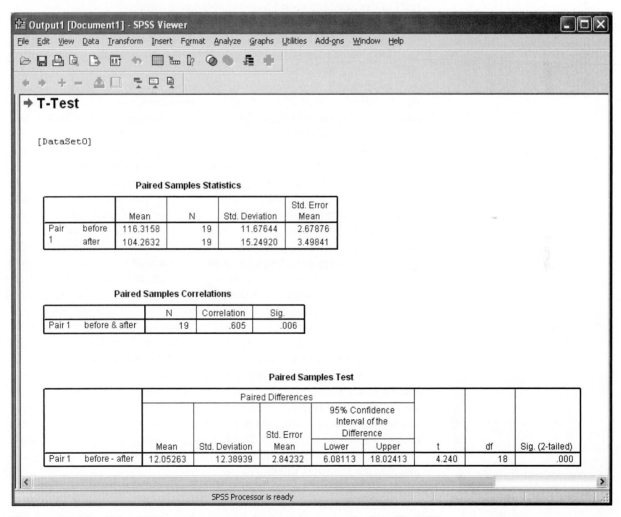

Figure 7–12 Using SPSS to carry out a *t* test for dependent means for Olthoff's (1989) study of communication quality of 19 men who received ordinary premarital counseling.

the husbands' communication quality was lower after marriage (a mean of 104.2632) than before marriage (a mean 116.3158). Don't worry that the t value figured in Table 7–6 was negative, whereas the t value in the SPSS output is positive. This happens because the difference score in Table 7–6 was figured as after minus before, but SPSS figured the difference scores as before minus after. Both ways of figuring the difference score are mathematically correct and the overall result is the same in each case.

Chapter Notes

1. A sample's variance is slightly smaller than the population's because it is based on deviations from the sample's mean. A sample's mean is the optimal balance point for its scores. Thus, deviations of a sample's scores from its mean will be smaller than deviations from any other number. The mean of a sample generally is not exactly the same as the mean of the population it comes from. Thus, deviations of a sample's scores from its mean will generally be smaller than deviations of that sample's scores from the population mean.

2. Statisticians make a subtle distinction in this situation between the comparison distribution and the distribution of means. (We avoid this distinction to simplify your learning of what is already fairly difficult.) The general procedure of hypothesis testing, as we introduced it in Chapter 5, can be described as comparing a Z score to your sample's mean, where $Z = (M - \mu)/\sigma_M$ and then comparing this Z score to a cutoff Z score from the normal curve table. We described this process as using the distribution of means as your comparison distribution. Statisticians would say that actually you are comparing the Z score you figured for your sample mean to a distribution of Z scores (which is simply a standard normal curve). Similarly, for a t test, statisticians think of the procedure as figuring a t score (like a Z score, but figured using an estimated standard deviation) where $t = (M - \mu)/S_M$ and then comparing your computed t score to a cutoff t score from a t distribution table. Thus, according to the formal statistical logic, the comparison distribution is a distribution of t scores, not of means.

3. In line with the terminology we used in Chapter 5, the symbol μ in the formula should read μ_M, since it refers to the population mean of a *distribution of means*. In Chapter 5, we used the μ_M terminology to emphasize the conceptual difference between the mean of a population of individuals and the mean of a population of means. But μ and μ_M are always equal. Thus, to keep the terminology as straightforward as possible in this and subsequent chapters, we refer to the mean of a distribution of means as μ. (If we were even more formal, we might use μ_2 or even μ_{M_2} since we are referring to the mean of Population 2.)

4. The steps of carrying out a t test for a single sample can be combined into a computational formula for t based on difference scores. For learning purposes in your class, you should use the steps as we have discussed them in this chapter. In a real research situation, the figuring is usually all done by computer (see this chapter's *Using SPSS* section). Should you ever have to do a t test for a single sample for an actual research study by hand (or just with a hand calculator), you may find the following formula useful:

$$t = \frac{M - \mu}{\sqrt{\dfrac{\sum X^2 - ((\sum X)^2/N)}{(N - 1)(N)}}}$$

The t score for a t test for a single sample is the result of subtracting the population mean from the sample mean and dividing that difference by the square root of the following: the sum of the squared scores minus the result of taking the sum of all the scores, squaring this sum and dividing by the number of scores, then taking this whole difference and dividing it by the result of multiplying the number of scores minus 1 by the number of scores.

5. The steps of carrying out a *t* test for dependent means can be combined into a computational formula for *t* based on difference scores. For learning purposes in your class, you should use the steps as we have discussed them in this chapter. In a real research situation, the figuring is usually all done by computer (see the *Using SPSS* section at the end of this chapter). However, if you ever have to do a *t* test for dependent means for an actual research study by hand (or with just a hand calculator), you may find the formula useful:

$$t = \frac{(\Sigma D)/N}{\sqrt{\dfrac{\Sigma D^2 - ((\Sigma D)^2/N)}{(N-1)(N)}}}$$

6. Single sample *t* tests are quite rare in practice; so we didn't include a discussion of effect size or power for them in the main text. However, the effect size for a single sample *t* test can be figured using the same approach as in Chapter 6 (which is the same as the approach for figuring effect size for the *t* test for dependent means). It is the difference between the population means divided by the population standard deviation: $d = (\mu_1 - \mu_2)/\sigma$. When using this formula for a *t* test for a single sample, μ_1 is the predicted mean of Population 1 (the population from which you are studying a sample), μ_2 is the mean of the "known" population, and σ is the population standard deviation. The conventions for effect size for a *t* test for a single sample are the same as you learned for the situation we considered in Chapter 6: A small effect size is .20, a medium effect size is .50, and a large effect size is .80.

7. Cohen (1988, pp. 28–39) provides more detailed tables in terms of numbers of participants, levels of effect size, and significance levels. If you use his tables, note that the *d* referred to is actually based on a *t* test for independent means (the situation we consider in Chapter 8). To use these tables for a *t* test for dependent means, first multiply your effect size by 1.4. For example, if your effect size is .30, for purposes of using Cohen's tables, you would consider it to be .42 (that is, .30 × 1.4 = .42). The only other difference from our table is that Cohen describes the significance level by the letter *a* (for "alpha level"), with a subscript of either 1 or 2, referring to a one-tailed or two-tailed test. For example, a table that refers to "$a_1 = .05$" at the top means that this is the table for $p < .05$, one-tailed.

8. More detailed tables, giving the needed numbers of participants for levels of power other than 80% (and also for effect sizes other than .20, .50, and .80 and for other significance levels) are provided in Cohen (1988, pp. 54–55). However, see Chapter Note 7 about using Cohen's tables for a *t* test for dependent means.

The *t* score for a *t* test for dependent means is the result of dividing the sum of the difference scores by the number of difference scores and then dividing that result by the square root of the following: the sum of the squared difference scores minus the result of taking the sum of all the difference scores, squaring this sum and dividing by the number of difference scores, then taking this whole difference and dividing it by the result of multiplying the number of difference scores minus 1 by the number of difference scores.

CHAPTER 8

The *t* Test for Independent Means

Chapter Outline

- ✪ The Distribution of Differences Between Means   271
- ✪ Hypothesis Testing with a *t* Test for Independent Means   278
- ✪ Assumptions of the *t* Test for Independent Means   286
- ✪ Effect Size and Power for the *t* Test for Independent Means   288
- ✪ Review and Comparison of the Three Kinds of *t* Tests   290
- ✪ Controversy: The Problem of Too Many *t* Tests   291
- ✪ The *t* Test for Independent Means in Research Articles   292
- ✪ Advanced Topic: Power for the *t* Test for Independent Means When Sample Sizes Are Not Equal   293
- ✪ Summary   294
- ✪ Key Terms   295
- ✪ Example Worked-Out Problems   295
- ✪ Practice Problems   298
- ✪ Using SPSS   305
- ✪ Chapter Notes   309

I n the previous chapter, you learned how to use the *t* test for dependent means to compare two sets of scores from a *single group of people* (such as the same men measured on communication quality before and after premarital counseling).

In this chapter, you learn how to compare two sets of scores, one from each of *two entirely separate groups of people*. This is a very common situation in psychology research. For example, a study may compare the scores from individuals in an experimental group and individuals in a control group (or from a group of men and a group of women). This is a *t* test situation because you don't know the population variances (so they must be estimated). The scores of the two groups are independent of each other; so the test you learn in this chapter is called a **t test for independent means**.

t test for independent means   hypothesis-testing procedure in which there are two separate groups of people tested and in which the population variance is not known.

Let's consider an example. A team of researchers is interested in the effect on physical health of writing about thoughts and feelings associated with traumatic life events. This kind of writing is called expressive writing. Suppose the researchers recruit undergraduate students to take part in a study and randomly assign them to be in an expressive writing group or a control group. Students in the expressive writing group are instructed to write four 20-minute essays over four consecutive days about their most traumatic life experiences. Students in the control group write four 20-minute essays over four consecutive days describing their plans for that day. One month later, the researchers ask the students to rate their overall level of physical health (on a scale from $0 = $ *very poor health* to $100 = $ *perfect health*). Since the expressive writing and the control group contain different students, a *t* test for independent means is the appropriate test of the effect of expressive writing on physical health. We will return to this example later in the chapter. But first, you will learn about the logic of the *t* test for independent means, which involves learning about a new kind of distribution (called the *distribution of differences between means*).

The Distribution of Differences Between Means

In the previous chapter, you learned the logic and figuring for the *t* test for dependent means. In that chapter, the same group of people each had two scores; that is, you had a pair of scores for each person. This allowed you to figure a difference score for each person. You then carried out the hypothesis-testing procedure using these difference scores. The comparison distribution you used for this hypothesis testing was a *distribution of means of difference scores.*

In the situation you face in this chapter, the scores in one group are for different people than the scores in the other group. So you don't have any pairs of scores, as you did when the same group of people each had two scores. Thus, it wouldn't make sense to create difference scores, and you can't use difference scores for the hypothesis-testing procedure in this chapter. Instead, when the scores in one group are for different people than the scores in the other group, what you can compare is the *mean* of one group to the *mean* of the other group.

So the *t* test for independent means focuses on the *difference between the means* of the two groups. The hypothesis-testing procedure, however, for the most part works just like the hypothesis-testing procedures you have already learned. Since the focus is now on the difference between means, the comparison distribution is a **distribution of differences between means.**

A distribution of differences between means is, in a sense, two steps removed from the populations of individuals: First, there is a distribution of means from each population of individuals; second, there is a distribution of differences between pairs of means, one of each pair from each of these distributions of means.

Think of this distribution of differences between means as being built up as follows: (a) randomly select one mean from the distribution of means for the first group's population, (b) randomly select one mean from the distribution of means for the second group's population, and (c) subtract. (That is, take the mean from the first distribution of means and subtract the mean from the second distribution of means.) This gives a difference score between the two selected means. Then repeat the process. This creates a second difference score, a difference between the two newly selected means. Repeating this process a large number of times creates a distribution of differences between means. You would never actually create a distribution of differences between means using this lengthy method. But it shows clearly what makes up the distribution.

TIP FOR SUCCESS

The comparison distributions for the *t* test for dependent means and the *t* test for independent means have similar names: a distribution of means of difference scores, and a distribution of differences between means, respectively. Thus, it can be easy to confuse these comparison distributions. To remember which is which, think of the logic of each *t* test. The *t* test for dependent means involves *difference scores*. So, its comparison distribution is a distribution of means of *difference scores*. The *t* test for independent means involves *differences between means*. Thus, its comparison distribution is a distribution of *differences between means*.

distribution of differences between means   distribution of differences between means of pairs of samples such that, for each pair of means, one is from one population and the other is from a second population; the comparison distribution in a *t* test for independent means.

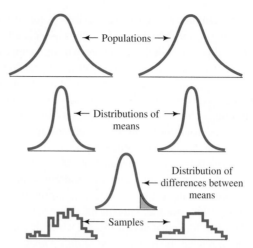

Figure 8–1 Diagram of the logic of a distribution of differences between means.

The Logic

Figure 8–1 shows the entire logical construction for a distribution of differences between means. At the top are the two population distributions. We do not know the characteristics of these population distributions, but we do know that if the null hypothesis is true, the two population means are the same. That is, the null hypothesis is that $\mu_1 = \mu_2$. We also can estimate the variance of these populations based on the sample information (these estimated variances will be S_1^2 and S_2^2).

Below each population distribution is the distribution of means for that population. Using the estimated population variance and knowing the size of each sample, you can figure the variance of each distribution of means in the usual way. (It is the estimated variance of its parent population divided by the size of the sample from that population that is being studied.)

Below these two distributions of means, and built from them, is the crucial *distribution of differences between means*. This distribution's variance is ultimately based on estimated population variances. Thus, we can think of it as a *t* distribution. The goal of a *t* test for independent means is to decide whether the difference between the means of your two actual samples is a more extreme difference than the cutoff difference on this distribution of differences between means. The two actual samples are shown (as histograms) at the bottom.

Remember, this whole procedure is really a kind of complicated castle in the air. It exists only in our minds to help us make decisions based on the results of an actual experiment. The only concrete reality in all of this is the actual scores in the two samples. You estimate the population variances from these sample scores. The variances of the two distributions of means are based entirely on these estimated population variances (and the sample sizes). And, as you will see shortly, the characteristics of the distribution of differences between means are based on these two distributions of means.

Still, the procedure is a powerful one. It has the power of mathematics and logic behind it. It helps you develop general knowledge based on the specifics of a particular study.

With this overview of the basic logic, we now turn to six key details: (1) the mean of the distribution of differences between means, (2) the estimated population variance, (3) the variance of the two distributions of means, (4) the variance and standard deviation of the distribution of differences between means, (5) the shape of the distribution of differences between means, and (6) the *t* score for the difference between the two means being compared.

Mean of the Distribution of Differences Between Means

In a *t* test for independent means, you are considering two populations: for example, one population from which an experimental group is taken and one population from which a control group is taken. In practice, you don't know the mean of either population. You do know that if the null hypothesis is true, these two populations have equal means. Also, if these two populations have equal means, the two distributions of means have equal means. (This is because each distribution of means has the same mean as its parent population of individuals.) Finally, if you take random samples from two distributions with equal means, the differences between the means of these random samples, in the long run, balance out to 0. The result of all this is the following: whatever the specifics of the study, you know that, if the null hypothesis is true, the distribution of differences between means has a mean of 0.

Estimating the Population Variance

In Chapter 7, you learned to estimate the population variance from the scores in your sample. It is the sum of squared deviation scores divided by the degrees of freedom (the number in the sample minus 1). To do a *t* test for independent means, it has to be reasonable to assume that the populations the two samples come from have the same variance (which, in statistical terms, is called *homogeneity of variance*). (If the null hypothesis is true, they also have the same mean. However, whether or not the null hypothesis is true, you must be able to assume that the two populations have the same variance.) Therefore, when you estimate the variance from the scores in either sample, you are getting two separate estimates of what should be the same number. In practice, the two estimates will almost never be exactly identical. Since they are both supposed to be estimating the same thing, the best solution is to average the two estimates to get the best single overall estimate. This is called the **pooled estimate of the population variance (S^2_{Pooled}).**

In making this average, however, you also have to take into account that the two samples may not be the same size. If one sample is larger than the other, the estimate it provides is likely to be more accurate (because it is based on more information). If both samples are exactly the same size, you could just take an ordinary average of the two estimates. On the other hand, when they are not the same size, you need to make some adjustment in the averaging to give more weight to the larger sample. That is, you need a **weighted average,** an average weighted by the amount of information each sample provides.

Also, to be precise, the amount of information each sample provides is not its number of scores, but its degrees of freedom (its number of scores minus 1). Thus, your weighted average needs to be based on the degrees of freedom each sample provides. To find the weighted average, you figure out what proportion of the total degrees of freedom each sample contributes and multiply that proportion by the population variance estimate from that sample. Finally, you add up the two results, and that is your weighted, pooled estimate. In terms of a formula,

$$S^2_{Pooled} = \frac{df_1}{df_{Total}}(S^2_1) + \frac{df_2}{df_{Total}}(S^2_2) \tag{8-1}$$

In this formula, S^2_{Pooled} is the pooled estimate of the population variance. df_1 is the degrees of freedom in the sample from Population 1, and df_2 is the degrees of freedom in the sample from Population 2. (Remember, each sample's *df* is its number of scores minus 1.) df_{Total} is the total degrees of freedom ($df_{Total} = df_1 + df_2$). S^2_1 is the

pooled estimate of the population variance (S^2_{Pooled}) in a *t* test for independent means, weighted average of the estimates of the population variance from two samples (each estimate weighted by the proportion consisting of its sample's degrees of freedom divided by the total degrees of freedom for both samples).

weighted average average in which the scores being averaged do not have equal influence on the total, as in figuring the pooled variance estimate in a *t* test for independent means.

The pooled estimate of the population variance is the degrees of freedom in the first sample divided by the total degrees of freedom (from both samples), multiplied by the population estimate based on the first sample, plus the degrees of freedom in the second sample divided by the total degrees of freedom multiplied by the population variance estimate based on the second sample.

estimate of the population variance based on the scores in Population 1's sample; is the estimate based on the scores in Population 2's sample.

Consider a study in which the population variance estimate based on an experimental group of 11 participants is 60, and the population variance estimate based on a control group of 31 participants is 80. The estimate from the experimental group is based on 10 degrees of freedom (11 participants minus 1), and the estimate from the control group is based on 30 degrees of freedom (31 minus 1). The total information on which the estimate is based is the total degrees of freedom—in this example, 40 (that is, $10 + 30$). Thus, the experimental group provides one-quarter of the information ($10/40 = 1/4$), and the control group provides three-quarters of the information ($30/40 = 3/4$).

You then multiply the estimate from the experimental group by 1/4, making 15 (that is, $60 \times 1/4 = 15$), and you multiply the estimate from the control group by 3/4, making 60 (that is, $80 \times 3/4 = 60$). Adding the two gives an overall estimate of 15 plus 60, which is 75. Using the formula,

$$S^2_{Pooled} = \frac{df_1}{df_{Total}}(S^2_1) + \frac{df_2}{df_{Total}}(S^2_2) = \frac{10}{40}(60) + \frac{30}{40}(80)$$

$$= \frac{1}{4}(60) + \frac{3}{4}(80) = 15 + 60 = 75.$$

TIP FOR SUCCESS

You know you have made a mistake in figuring S^2_{Pooled} if it does not come out between the two estimates of the population variance. (You also know you have made a mistake if it does not come out closer to the estimate from the larger sample.)

Notice that this procedure does not give the same result as ordinary averaging (without weighting).

Ordinary averaging would give an estimate of 70 (that is, $[60 + 80]/2 = 70$). Your weighted, pooled estimate of the population variance of 75 is closer to the estimate based on the control group alone than to the estimate based on the experimental group alone. This is as it should be, because the control group estimate in this example was based on more information.

Figuring the Variance of Each of the Two Distributions of Means

The pooled estimate of the population variance is the best estimate for both populations. (Remember, to do a *t* test for independent means, you have to be able to assume that the two populations have the same variance.) However, even though the two populations have the same variance, if the samples are not the same size, the distributions of means taken from them do not have the same variance. That is because the variance of a distribution of means is the population variance divided by the sample size. In terms of formulas,

The variance of the distribution of means for the first population (based on an estimated population variance) is the pooled estimate of the population variance divided by the number of participants in the sample from the first population.

$$S^2_{M_1} = \frac{S^2_{Pooled}}{N_1} \tag{8–2}$$

$$S^2_{M_2} = \frac{S^2_{Pooled}}{N_2} \tag{8-3}$$

The variance of the distribution of means for the second population (based on an estimated population variance) is the pooled estimate of the population variance divided by the number of participants in the sample from the second population.

Consider again the study with 11 in the experimental group and 31 in the control group. We figured the pooled estimate of the population variance to be 75. For the experimental group, the variance of the distribution of means would be 75/11, which is 6.82. For the control group, the variance would be 75/31, which is 2.42. Using the formulas,

$$S^2_{M_1} = \frac{S^2_{Pooled}}{N_1} = \frac{75}{11} = 6.82$$

$$S^2_{M_2} = \frac{S^2_{Pooled}}{N_2} = \frac{75}{31} = 2.42.$$

TIP FOR SUCCESS

Remember that when figuring estimated variances, you divide by the degrees of freedom. But when figuring the variance of **a** distribution of means, which does not involve any additional estimation, you divide by the actual number in the sample.

The Variance and Standard Deviation of the Distribution of Differences Between Means

The **variance of the distribution of differences between means ($S^2_{Difference}$)** is the variance of Population 1's distribution of means plus the variance of Population 2's distribution of means. (This is because, in a difference between two numbers, the variation in each contributes to the overall variation in their difference. It is like subtracting a moving number from a moving target.) Stated as a formula,

$$S^2_{Difference} = S^2_{M_1} + S^2_{M_2} \tag{8-4}$$

The **standard deviation of the distribution of differences between means ($S_{Difference}$)** is the square root of the variance:

The variance of the distribution of differences between means is the variance of the distribution of means for the first population (based on an estimated population variance) plus the variance of the distribution of means for the second population (based on an estimated population variance).

$$S_{Difference} = \sqrt{S^2_{Difference}} \tag{8-5}$$

In the example we have been considering, the variance of the distribution of means for the experimental group was 6.82, and the variance of the distribution of means for the control group was 2.42; the variance of the distribution of the difference between means is thus 6.82 plus 2.42, which is 9.24. This makes the standard deviation of this distribution the square root of 9.24, which is 3.04. In terms of the formulas,

$$S^2_{Difference} = S^2_{M_1} + S^2_{M_2} = 6.82 + 2.42 = 9.24$$

$$S_{Difference} = \sqrt{S^2_{Difference}} = \sqrt{9.24} = 3.04.$$

The standard deviation of the distribution of differences between means is the square root of the variance of the distribution of differences between means.

Steps to Find the Standard Deviation of the Distribution of Differences Between Means

Ⓐ Figure the estimated population variances based on each sample. That is, figure one estimate for each population using the formula $S^2 = SS/(N-1)$.

variance of a distribution of differences between means ($S^2_{Difference}$) one of the numbers figured as part of a *t* test for independent means; it equals the sum of the variances of the distributions of means associated with each of the two samples.

standard deviation of the distribution of differences between means ($S_{Difference}$) in a *t* test for independent means, square root of the variance of the distribution of differences between means.

❸ **Figure the pooled estimate of the population variance:**

$$S^2_{\text{Pooled}} = \frac{df_1}{df_{\text{Total}}}(S^2_1) + \frac{df_2}{df_{\text{Total}}}(S^2_2)$$

$$(df_1 = N_1 - 1 \text{ and } df_2 = N_2 - 1; df_{\text{Total}} = df_1 + df_2)$$

❹ **Figure the variance of each distribution of means:** $S^2_{M_1} = S^2_{\text{Pooled}}/N_1$ and $S^2_{M_2} = S^2_{\text{Pooled}}/N_2$.

❺ **Figure the variance of the distribution of differences between means:** $S^2_{\text{Difference}} = S^2_{M_1} + S^2_{M_2}$.

❻ **Figure the standard deviation of the distribution of differences between means:** $S_{\text{Difference}} = \sqrt{S^2_{\text{Difference}}}$.

The Shape of the Distribution of Differences Between Means

The distribution of differences between means is based on estimated population variances. Thus, the distribution of differences between means (the comparison distribution) is a t distribution. The variance of this distribution is figured based on population variance estimates from two samples. Therefore, the degrees of freedom for this t distribution are the sum of the degrees of freedom of the two samples. In terms of a formula,

> The total degrees of freedom for a *t* test for independent means is the degrees of freedom in the first sample plus the degrees of freedom in the second sample.

$$df_{\text{Total}} = df_1 + df_2 \tag{8–6}$$

In the example we have been considering with an experimental group of 11 and a control group of 31, we saw earlier that the total degrees of freedom is 40 (that is, $11 - 1 = 10$; $31 - 1 = 30$; and $10 + 30 = 40$). To find the t score needed for significance, you look up the cutoff point in the t table in the row with 40 degrees of freedom. Suppose you are conducting a one-tailed test using the .05 significance level. The t table in the Appendix (Table A–2) shows a cutoff of 1.684 for 40 degrees of freedom. That is, for a result to be significant, the difference between the means has to be at least 1.684 standard deviations above the mean difference of 0 on the distribution of differences between means.

The t Score for the Difference Between the Two Actual Means

Here is how you figure the t score for Step ❹ of the hypothesis testing: First, figure the difference between your two samples' means. (That is, subtract one from the other). Then, figure out where this difference is on the distribution of differences between means. You do this by dividing your difference by the standard deviation of this distribution. In terms of a formula,

> The *t* score is the difference between the two sample means divided by the standard deviation of the distribution of differences between means.

$$t = \frac{M_1 - M_2}{S_{\text{Difference}}} \tag{8–7}$$

For our example, suppose the mean of the first sample is 198 and the mean of the second sample is 190. The difference between these two means is 8 (that is, $198 - 190 = 8$). Earlier we figured the standard deviation of the distribution of differences between means in this example to be 3.04. That would make a t score of 2.63 (that is, $8/3.04 = 2.63$). In other words, in this example the difference between the two means is 2.63 standard deviations above the mean of the distribution of differences between means. In terms of the formula,

$$t = \frac{M_1 - M_2}{S_{\text{Difference}}} = \frac{198 - 190}{3.04} = \frac{8}{3.04} = 2.63$$

How are you doing?

1. (a) When would you carry out a *t* test for independent means? (b) How is this different from the situation in which you would carry out a *t* test for dependent means?

2. (a) What is the comparison distribution in a *t* test for independent means? (b) Explain the logic of going from scores in two samples to an estimate of the variance of this comparison distribution. (c) Illustrate your answer with sketches of the distributions involved. (d) Why is the mean of this distribution 0?

3. Write the formula for each of the following: (a) pooled estimate of the population variance, (b) variance of the distribution of means for the first population, (c) variance of the distribution of differences between means, and (d) *t* score in a *t* test for independent means. (e) Define all the symbols used in these formulas.

4. Explain (a) why a *t* test for independent means uses a single pooled estimate of the population variance, and (b) why and (c) how this estimate is "weighted."

5. For a particular study comparing means of two samples, the first sample has 21 participants and an estimated population variance of 100; the second sample has 31 participants and an estimated population variance of 200. (a) What is the standard deviation of the distribution of differences between means? (b) What is its mean? (c) What will be its shape? (d) Illustrate your answer with sketches of the distributions involved.

1. (a) You carry out a *t* test for independent means when you have done a study in which you have scores from two samples of different individuals and you don't know the population variance. (b) In a *t* test for dependent means, the scores are from one group of individuals—such as the same people measured before and after some procedure.

2. (a) The comparison distribution in a *t* test for independent means is a distribution of differences between means. (b) You start with the two groups' scores. Based on each group's scores, you estimate the variance of its population of individuals. You figure a pooled estimate of the population variance based on these two estimates. Using this pooled estimate, you figure the variance of each group's distribution of means. Adding these two variances of distributions of means gives the variance of the distribution of differences between means. (c) [sketches] (d) On the average, the two populations have the same mean; thus the difference between them averages to 0.

3. (a) $S^2_{Pooled} = \dfrac{df_1}{df_{Total}}(S^2_1) + \dfrac{df_2}{df_{Total}}(S^2_2)$; (b) $S^2_{M_1} = \dfrac{S^2_{Pooled}}{N_1}$; (c) $S^2_{Difference} = S^2_{M_1} + S^2_{M_2}$; (d) $t = \dfrac{M_1 - M_2}{S_{Difference}}$. (e) S^2_{Pooled} is the pooled estimate of the population variance; df_1 and df_2 are the degrees of freedom in the samples from the first and second populations, respectively; df_{Total} is the total degrees of freedom (the sum of df_1 and df_2); S^2_1 and S^2_2 are the population variance estimates based on the samples from the first and second populations, respectively; $S^2_{M_1}$ is the variance of the distribution of means for the first population based on an estimated variance of the population of individuals; N_1 is the number of participants in the sample from the first population; $S^2_{Difference}$ is the variance of the distribution of differences between means based on estimated variances of the populations of individuals; *t* is the *t* score for a *t* test for independent means (the number of standard deviations from the mean on the distribution of differences between means); M_1 and M_2 are the means of the samples from the first and second populations, respectively; and $S_{Difference}$ is the standard deviation of the distribution of differences between means based on estimated variances of the populations of individuals.

4. (a) You assume that both populations have the same variance; thus the estimates from the two samples should be estimates of the same number. (b) We weight (give more influence to) an estimate from a larger sample because, being based on more information, it is likely to be more accurate. (c) The actual weighting is done by multiplying each sample's estimate by the degrees of freedom for that sample divided by the total degrees of freedom; you then sum these two products.

5. (a) Standard deviation of the distribution of differences between means:
$S^2_{Pooled} = (20/50)(100) + (30/50)(200) = 40 + 120 = 160$.
$S^2_{M_1} = 160/21 = 7.62$; $S^2_{M_2} = 160/31 = 5.16$;
$S^2_{Difference} = 7.62 + 5.16 = 12.78$;
$S_{Difference} = \sqrt{12.78} = 3.57$.
(b) Mean: 0; (c) Shape: *t* distribution with $df = 50$; (d) Should look like Figure 8–1 with numbers written in (see Figure 8–2 for an example).

Answers

1. (a) You carry out a t test for independent means when you have done a study in which you have scores from two samples of different individuals and you do not know the population variance.

(b) In a t test for dependent means you have two scores from each of several individuals.

2. (a) The comparison distribution in a t test for independent means is a distribution of differences between means.

(b) You estimate the population variance from each sample's scores. Since you assume the populations have the same variance, you then pool the two estimates (giving proportionately more weight in this averaging to the sample that has more degrees of freedom in its estimate). Using this pooled estimate, you figure the variance of the distribution of means for each sample's population by dividing this pooled estimate by the sample's number of participants. Finally, since your interest is in a difference between means, you create a comparison distribution of differences between means. This comparison distribution will have a variance equal to the sum of the variances of the two distributions of means. (Because the distribution of differences between means is made up of pairs of means, one taken from each distribution of means, the variance of both of these distributions of means contributes to the variance of the comparison distribution.)

(c) Your sketch should look like Figure 8–1.

(d) The mean of this distribution will be zero because, if the null hypothesis is true, the two populations have the same mean. So differences between means would on the average come out to zero.

3. (a) Pooled estimate of the population variance:
$$S^2_{Pooled} = \frac{df_1}{df_{Total}}(S^2_1) + \frac{df_2}{df_{Total}}(S^2_2).$$

(b) Variance of the distribution of means for the first population:
$$S^2_{M_1} = \frac{S^2_{Pooled}}{N_1}.$$

(c) Variance of the distribution of differences between means:
$$S^2_{Difference} = S^2_{M_1} + S^2_{M_2}.$$

(d) t score in a t test for independent means: $t = \dfrac{M_1 - M_2}{S_{Difference}}$.

Hypothesis Testing with a *t* Test for Independent Means

Considering the five steps of hypothesis testing, there are three new wrinkles for a *t* test for independent means: (1) the comparison distribution is now a distribution of differences between means (this affects Step ❷); (2) the degrees of freedom for finding the cutoff on the *t* table is based on two samples (this affects Step ❸); and (3) your sample's score on the comparison distribution is based on the difference between your two means (this affects Step ❹).

Example of a *t* Test for Independent Means

Let's return to the expressive writing study that we introduced at the start of the chapter. Twenty students were recruited to take part in the study. The 10 students

Table 8-1 *t* Test for Independent Means for a Fictional Study of the Effect of Expressive Writing on Physical Health

Expressive Writing Group			Control Writing Group		
Score	Deviation from Mean (Score – M)	Squared Deviation from Mean	Score	Deviation from Mean (Score – M)	Squared Deviation from Mean
77	−2	4	87	19	361
88	9	81	77	9	81
77	−2	4	71	3	9
90	11	121	70	2	4
68	−11	121	63	−5	25
74	−5	25	50	−18	324
62	−17	289	58	−10	100
93	14	196	63	−5	25
82	3	9	76	8	64
79	0	0	65	−3	9
Σ: 790		850	680		1002

$M_1 = 79.00; S_1^2 = 850/9 = 94.44; M_2 = 68.00\ S_1^2 = 1002/9 = 111.33$

$N_1 = 10; df_1 = N_1 - 1 = 9; N_2 = 10; df_2 = N_2 - 1 = 9$

$df_{Total} = df_1 + df_2 = 9 + 9 = 18$

$S_{Pooled}^2 = \dfrac{df_1}{df_{Total}}(S_1^2) + \dfrac{df_2}{df_{Total}}(S_2^2) = \dfrac{9}{18}(94.44) + \dfrac{9}{18}(111.33) = 47.22 + 55.67 = 102.89$

$S_{M_1}^2 = S_{Pooled}^2/N_1 = 102.89/10 = 10.29$

$S_{M_2}^2 = S_{Pooled}^2/N_2 = 102.89/10 = 10.29$

$S_{Difference}^2 = S_{M_1}^2 + S_{M_2}^2 = 10.29 + 10.29 = 20.58$

$S_{Difference} = \sqrt{S_{Difference}^2} = \sqrt{20.58} = 4.54$

Needed *t* with $df = 18$, 5% level, two-tailed $= \pm 2.101$

$t = (M_1 - M_2)/S_{Difference} = (79.00 - 68.00)/4.54 = 2.42$

Decision: Reject the null hypothesis.

randomly assigned to the expressive writing group wrote about their thoughts and feelings associated with their most traumatic life events. The 10 students randomly assigned to the control group wrote about their plans for the day. One month later, all of the students rated their overall level of physical health on a scale from $0 = very\ poor\ health$ to $100 = perfect\ health$.

The scores and figuring for the *t* test are shown in Table 8–1. Figure 8–2 shows the distributions involved. Let's go through the five steps of hypothesis testing.

❶ **Restate the question as a research hypothesis and a null hypothesis about the populations.** There are two populations:

Population 1: Students who engage in expressive writing.
Population 2: Students who write about a neutral topic (their plans for the day).

The researchers were interested in identifying a positive or a negative health effect of expressive writing. Thus, the research hypothesis was that Population 1 students would rate their health differently from Population 2 students: $\mu_1 \neq \mu_2$. The null hypothesis was that Population 1 students would rate their health the same as Population 2 students: $\mu_1 = \mu_2$.

❷ **Determine the characteristics of the comparison distribution.** The comparison distribution is a distribution of differences between means. (a) Its mean is

TIP FOR SUCCESS

Note that in previous chapters, Population 2 represented the population situation if the null hypothesis is true.

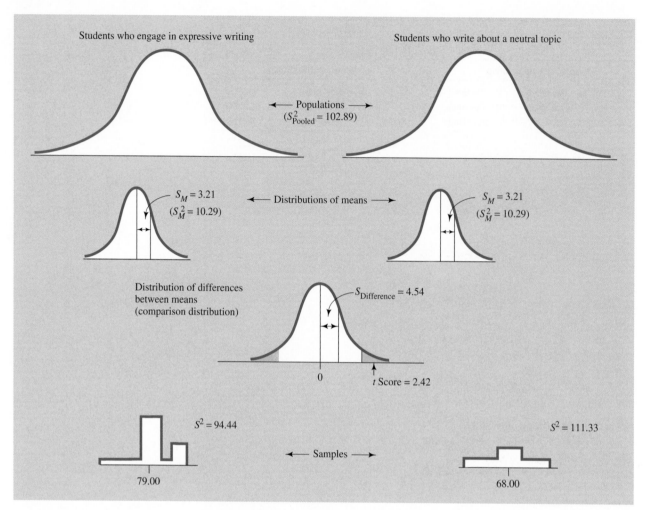

Figure 8-2   Distributions for a *t* test for independent means for the expressive writing example.

0 (as it almost always is in a *t* test for independent means, because we are interested in whether there is more than 0 difference between the two populations). (b) Regarding its standard deviation,

❶ **Figure the estimated population variances based on each sample.** As shown in Table 8–1, S^2_1 comes out to 94.44 and $S^2_2 = 111.33$.

❷ **Figure the pooled estimate of the population variance:** As shown in Table 8–1, the figuring for S^2_{Pooled} gives a result of 102.89.

❸ **Figure the variance of each distribution of means:** Dividing S^2_{Pooled} by the *N* in each sample, as shown in Table 8–1, gives $S^2_{M_1} = 10.29$ and $S^2_{M_2} = 10.29$.

❹ **Figure the variance of the distribution of differences between means:** Adding up the variances of the two distributions of means, as shown in Table 8–1, comes out to $S^2_{\text{Difference}} = 20.58$.

❺ **Figure the standard deviation of the distribution of differences between means:** $S_{\text{Difference}} = \sqrt{S^2_{\text{Difference}}} = \sqrt{20.58} = 4.54$.

(c) The shape of this comparison distribution will be a *t* distribution with a total of 18 degrees of freedom.

❸ **Determine the cutoff sample score on the comparison distribution at which the null hypothesis should be rejected.** This requires a two-tailed test because the researchers were interested in an effect in either direction. As shown in Table A–2 (in the Appendix), the cutoff *t* scores at the .05 level are 2.101 and −2.101.

❹ **Determine your sample's score on the comparison distribution.** The *t* score is the difference between the two sample means (79.00 − 68.00, which is 11.00), divided by the standard deviation of the distribution of differences between means (which is 4.54). This comes out to 2.42.

❺ **Decide whether to reject the null hypothesis.** The *t* score of 2.42 for the difference between the two actual means is larger than the cutoff *t* score of 2.101. You can reject the null hypothesis. The research hypothesis is supported: students who engage in expressive writing report a higher level of health than students who write about a neutral topic.

Although the actual numbers in this study were fictional, the results are consistent with those from many actual studies that have shown beneficial effects of expressive writing on self-reported health outcomes, as well as additional outcomes such as psychological well-being (e.g., Pennebaker & Beall, 1986; Warner et al., 2006; see also Frattaroli, 2006).

Summary of Steps for a t Test for Independent Means

Table 8–2 summarizes the steps for a *t* test for independent means.[1]

Table 8-2   Steps for a *t* Test for Independent Means

❶ **Restate the question as a research hypothesis and a null hypothesis about the populations.**

❷ **Determine the characteristics of the comparison distribution.**

a. Its mean will be 0.

b. Figure its standard deviation.

Ⓐ **Figure the estimated population variances based on each sample.** For each population,

$S^2 = SS/(N - 1)$.

Ⓑ **Figure the pooled estimate of the population variance:**

$$S^2_{Pooled} = \frac{df_1}{df_{Total}}(S^2_1) + \frac{df_2}{df_{Total}}(S^2_2)$$

$(df_1 = N_1 - 1 \text{ and } df_2 = N_2 - 1; df_{Total} = df_1 + df_2)$

Ⓒ **Figure the variance of each distribution of means:**

$S^2_{M_1} = S^2_{Pooled}/N_1 \text{ and } S^2_{M_2} = S^2_{Pooled}/N_2$

Ⓓ **Figure the variance of the distribution of differences between means:**

$S^2_{Difference} = S^2_{M_1} + S^2_{M_2}$

Ⓔ **Figure the standard deviation of the distribution of differences between means:**

$S_{Difference} = \sqrt{S^2_{Difference}}$

c. Determine its shape: It will be a t distribution with df_{Total} degrees of freedom.

❸ **Determine the cutoff sample score on the comparison distribution at which the null hypothesis should be rejected.**

a. Determine the degrees of freedom (df_{Total}), desired significance level, and tails in the test (one or two).

b. Look up the appropriate cutoff in a *t* table. If the exact *df* is not given, use the *df* below it.

❹ **Determine your sample's score on the comparison distribution:**

$t = (M_1 - M_2)/S_{Difference}$

❺ **Decide whether to reject the null hypothesis:** Compare the scores from Steps ❸ and ❹.

A Second Example of a *t* Test for Independent Means

Valenzuela (1997) compared the mothering received by poor children who either were or were not undernourished. One of her measures was systematic ratings of how well the mother assisted her child in a standard puzzle-solving task (observed during home visits). The mothers of the 43 adequately nourished children had a mean quality of assistance of 33.10 and an estimated population variance of 201.64. The mothers of the 42 chronically undernourished children had a mean of 27.00 on this measure, with an estimated population variance of 134.56.

The figuring for the *t* test comparing the quality of assistance scores for the two conditions is shown in Table 8–3. The distributions involved are shown in Figure 8–3. Next, we go through the five steps of hypothesis testing.

❶ **Restate the question as a research hypothesis and a null hypothesis about the populations.** There are two populations:

Population 1: Mothers of adequately nourished poor children.
Population 2: Mothers of chronically undernourished poor children.

The research hypothesis was that Population 1 mothers would score differently from Population 2 mothers on the quality of assistance to their children. Valenzuela predicted that Population 1 would score higher than Population 2. However, following conventional practice in studies like this, she used a nondirectional (two-tailed) significance test. (This had the advantage of allowing the possibility of finding significant results in the direction opposite to her prediction.) Thus, the research hypothesis actually tested was that Population 1 mothers would score differently from Population 2 mothers: $\mu_1 \neq \mu_2$. The null hypothesis was that the Population 1 mothers would score the same as Population 2 mothers: $\mu_1 = \mu_2$.

❷ **Determine the characteristics of the comparison distribution.** (a) Its mean will be 0. (b) Figure its standard deviation (see Table 8–3 for the figuring for each step below),

❹ **Figure the estimated population variances based on each sample.** These are already figured for us: $S_1^2 = 201.64$ and $S_2^2 = 134.56$.

Table 8-3   *t* Test for Independent Means in Study of Quality of Assistance of Mothers of Adequately Nourished Versus Chronically Undernourished Poor Chilean Children

Adequately Nourished Children:
$$N_1 = 43; df_1 = N_1 - 1 = 42; M_1 = 33.10; S_1^2 = 201.64$$
Chronically Undernourished Children:
$$N_2 = 42; df_2 = N_2 - 1 = 41; M_2 = 27.00; S_2^2 = 134.56$$

$df_{Total} = df_1 + df_2 = 42 + 41 = 83$

$S_{Pooled}^2 = \dfrac{df_1}{df_{Total}}(S_1^2) + \dfrac{df_2}{df_{Total}}(S_2^2) = \dfrac{42}{83}(201.64) + \dfrac{41}{83}(134.56)$
$\qquad = .51(201.64) + .49(134.56) = 102.84 + 65.93 = 168.77$

$S_{M_1}^2 = S_{Pooled}^2/N_1 = 168.77/43 = 3.92$

$S_{M_2}^2 = S_{Pooled}^2/N_2 = 168.77/42 = 4.02$

$S_{Difference}^2 = S_{M_1}^2 + S_{M_2}^2 = 3.92 + 4.02 = 7.94$

$S_{Difference} = \sqrt{S_{Difference}^2} = \sqrt{7.94} = 2.82$

Needed *t* with $df = 83$ (using $df = 80$ in the table), 5% level, two-tailed $= \pm 1.990$

$t = (M_1 - M_2)/S_{Difference} = (33.10 - 27.00)/2.82 = 6.10/2.82 = 2.16$

Decision: Reject the null hypothesis; the research hypothesis is supported.

Source: Data from Valenzuela (1997).

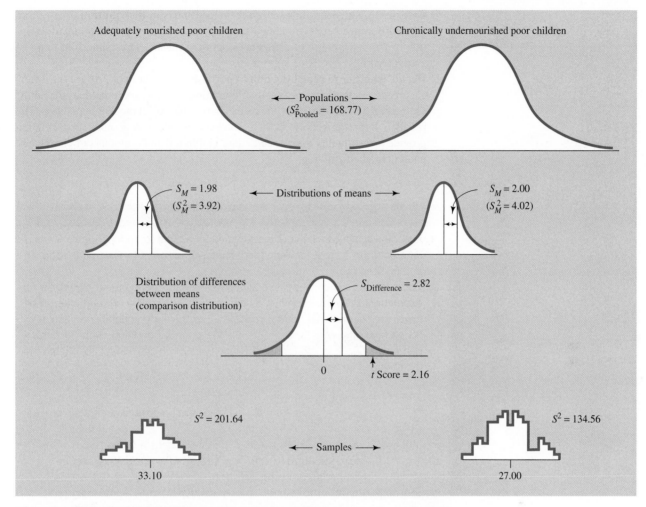

Figure 8–3 Distributions for a *t* test for independent means for the mothers of adequately nourished versus chronically undernourished poor children.

Source: Data from Valenzuela, 1997.

- ❶ **Figure the pooled estimate of the population variance:** The figuring for S^2_{Pooled} gives a result of 168.77.
- ❷ **Figure the variance of each distribution of means:** Dividing S^2_{Pooled} by the *N* in each sample gives $S^2_{M_1} = 3.92$ and $S^2_{M_2} = 4.02$.
- ❸ **Figure the variance of the distribution of differences between means:** Adding up the variances of the two distributions of means comes out to $S^2_{\text{Difference}} = 7.94$.
- ❹ **Figure the standard deviation of the distribution of differences between means:** $S_{\text{Difference}} = \sqrt{S^2_{\text{Difference}}} = \sqrt{7.94} = 2.82$.

(c) The shape of this comparison distribution will be a *t* distribution with df_{Total} of 83.

❷ **Determine the cutoff sample score on the comparison distribution at which the null hypothesis should be rejected.** The cutoff you need is for a two-tailed test (because the research hypothesis is nondirectional) at the usual .05 level, with 83 degrees of freedom. The *t* table in the Appendix (Table A–2) does not have a listing for 83 degrees of freedom. Thus, you use the next lowest *df* available, which is 80. This gives cutoff *t* scores of +1.990 and −1.990.

❹ **Determine your sample's score on the comparison distribution.** The *t* score is the difference between the two sample means divided by the standard deviation of the distribution of differences between means. This comes out to a *t* of 2.16. (That is, $t = 6.10/2.82 = 2.16$.)

❺ **Decide whether to reject the null hypothesis.** The *t* score of 2.16 for the difference between the means of the two conditions is more extreme than the cutoff *t* score of ±1.990. Therefore, the researchers could reject the null hypothesis. The research hypothesis is supported: mothers of adequately nourished children provide better-quality assistance to their children than do mothers of chronically undernourished children.

How are you doing?

1. List the ways in which hypothesis testing for a *t* test for independent means is different from a *t* test for dependent means in terms of (a) Step ❷, (b) Step ❸, and (c) Step ❹.
2. Using the .05 significance level, figure a *t* test for independent means for an experiment in which scores in an experimental condition are predicted to be lower than scores in a control condition. For the experimental condition, with 26 participants, $M = 5$, $S^2 = 10$; for the control condition, with 36 participants, $M = 8$, $S^2 = 12$. (a) Use the steps of hypothesis testing. (b) Sketch the distributions involved.

2. ❷ **Determine the characteristics of the comparison distribution.**
   (a) Its mean will be 0.
   (b) Figure its standard deviation,
   ❶ **Figure the estimated population variances based on each sample:** $S_1^2 = 10$; $S_2^2 = 12$.
   ❷ **Figure the pooled estimate of the population variance:** $S_{Pooled}^2 = (25/60)(10) + (35/60)(12) = 4.17 + 7.00 = 11.17$.
   ❸ **Figure the variance of each distribution of means:** $S_{M_1}^2 = 11.17/26 = .43$ and $S_{M_2}^2 = 11.17/36 = .31$.
   ❹ **Figure the variance of the distribution of differences between means:** $S_{Difference}^2 = .43 + .31 = .74$.
   ❺ **Figure the standard deviation of the distribution of differences between means:** $S_{Difference} = \sqrt{S_{Difference}^2} = \sqrt{.74} = .86$.
   (c) The shape is a *t* distribution with $df_{Total} = 60$.
   ❸ **Determine the cutoff sample score on the comparison distribution at which the null hypothesis should be rejected.** The *t* cutoff for .05 level, one-tailed, $df_{Total} = 60$ is -1.671. (The cutoff is a negative *t* score, because the research hypothesis is that the mean of Population 1 will be *lower* than the mean of Population 2.)
   ❹ **Determine your sample's score on the comparison distribution.** $t = (M_1 - M_2)/S_{Difference} = (5 - 8)/.86 = -3.49$.
   ❺ **Decide whether to reject the null hypothesis.** The *t* of -3.49 is more extreme than the cutoff *t* of -1.671. Therefore, reject the null hypothesis.
   (b) The distributions involved are shown in Figure 8–4.

Answers

1. (a) The comparison distribution for a *t* test for independent means is a distribution of differences between means.

(b) The degrees of freedom for a *t* test for independent means is the sum of the degrees of freedom for the two samples.

(c) The *t* score for a *t* test for independent means is based on differences between means (divided by the standard deviation of the distribution of differences between means).

2. (a) Steps of hypothesis testing:

❶ **Restate the question as a research hypothesis and a null hypothesis about the populations.** There are two populations.

Population 1: People given the experimental procedure.
Population 2: People given the control procedure.

The research hypothesis is that the mean of Population 1 is less than the mean of Population 2: $\mu_1 < \mu_2$. The null hypothesis is that the mean of Population 1 is not less than the mean of Population 2: $\mu_1 \geq \mu_2$.

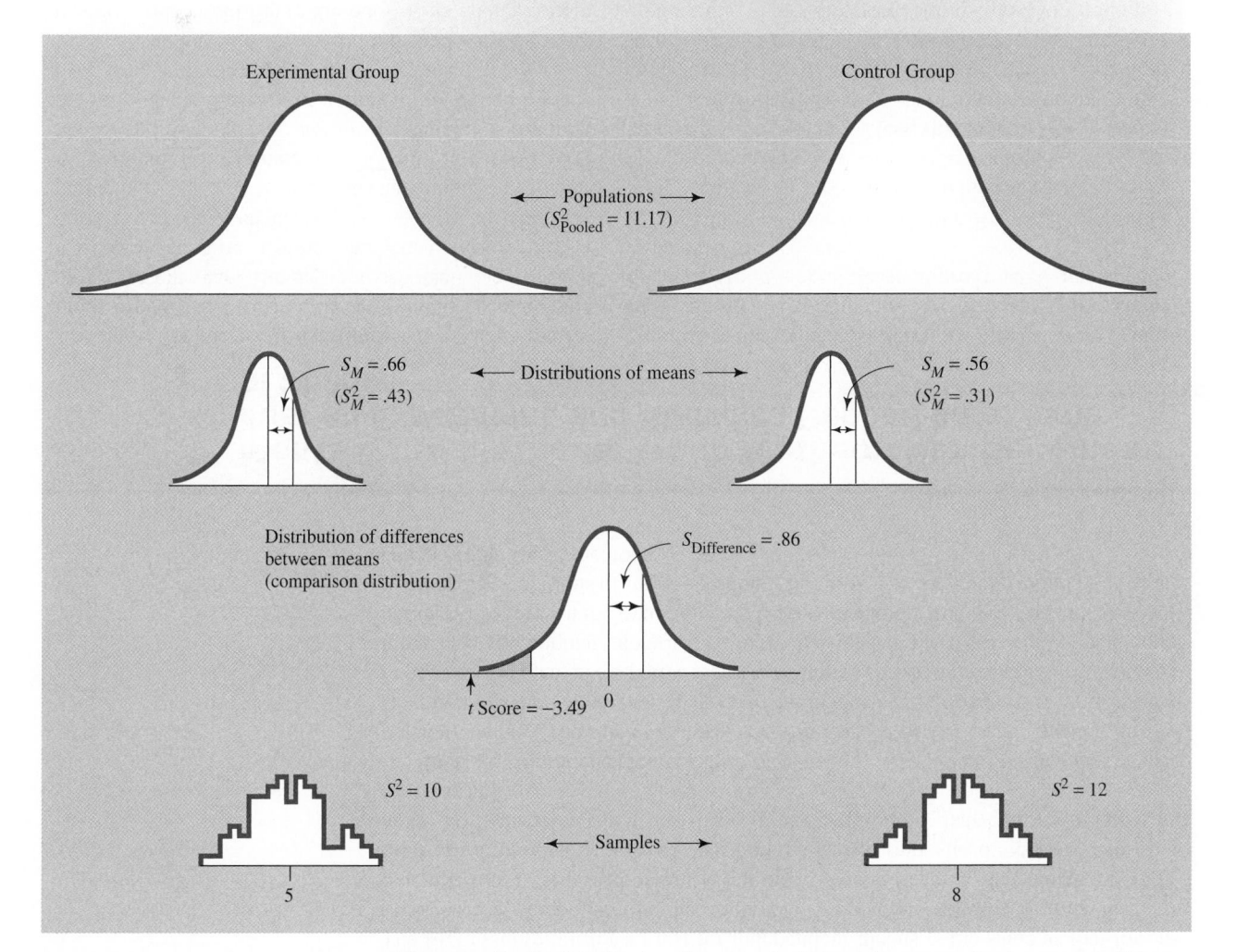

Figure 8–4   Distributions for a *t* test for independent means for the answer to "How Are You Doing" question 2.

Assumptions of the *t* Test for Independent Means

The first assumption for a *t* test for independent means is the same as that for any *t* test: each of the population distributions is assumed to follow a normal curve. In practice, this is only a problem if you have reason to think that the two populations are dramatically skewed distributions and in opposite directions. The *t* test holds up well even when the shape of the population distributions is fairly far from normal.

In a *t* test for independent means, you also have to be able to assume that the two populations have the same variance. (As you learned earlier in the chapter, this assumption is called *homogeneity of variance*.) Once again, however, it turns out that in practice the *t* test gives pretty accurate results even when there are fairly large differences in the population variances, particularly when there are equal or near equal numbers of scores in the two samples. (How do we know that the *t* test holds up well to moderate violations of its assumptions? See Box 8–1 for a description of what are called Monte Carlo methods.)

BOX 8–1   **Monte Carlo Methods: When Mathematics Becomes Just an Experiment, and Statistics Depend on a Game of Chance**

The name for the methods, *Monte Carlo* (after the famous Monegasque casino resort city), has been adopted only in recent years. But the approach itself dates back at least a few centuries to when mathematicians would set down their pens or chalk and go out and try an actual experiment to test a particular understanding of a probability problem. For example, in 1777 Buffon described, in his *Essai d'Arithmétique morale,* a method of computing the ratio of the diameter of a circle to its circumference by tossing a needle onto a flat surface containing parallel lines. Assuming that the needle fell randomly into any position, one could figure the odds of its taking certain positions, such as touching the lines or not and lying at certain angles. The term *Monte Carlo* no doubt reflects the early understanding of mathematicians and statisticians that many of their problems were like those involving games of chance. (Recall Pascal and the problem of points from Chapter 3, Box 3–3.)

Wide use of Monte Carlo methods by statisticians became possible with the advent of computers. This is because the essence of Monte Carlo studies is the interaction of randomness and probabilities, which means testing out a great many possibilities. Indeed, the first application of Monte Carlo methods was in neutron physics because the behavior of particles when scattered by a neutron beam is so complicated and so close to random that solving the problem mathematically from equations was practically impossible. But by artificially simulating the statistical conditions of what were essentially physical experiments, the physical world could be understood—or at least approximated in an adequate way.

Do you remember being shown Brownian motion in your chemistry or physics class in high school? Its study is a good example of a Monte Carlo problem. Here are atomic particles, more or less, this time in fluids, free to do an almost limitless number of almost random things. In fact, Brownian motion has been likened to a "random walk" of a drunkard. At any moment, the drunkard could move in any direction. But the problem is simplified by limiting the drunkard (or particle) to an imaginary grid.

Picture the grid of a city's streets. Further imagine that there is a wall around the city that the drunkard cannot escape (just as all particles must come to a limit; they cannot go on forever). At the limit, the wall, the drunkard must pay a fine, which also varies randomly. The point of this example is how much is random—all the movements and also all the ultimate consequences. So the number of possible paths is enormous.

The random walk example brings us to the main feature of Monte Carlo methods: they require the use of random numbers. And for an explanation of them, you can look forward to Chapter 14, Box 14–1.

Now, let's return to what interests us here: the use of Monte Carlo studies to check out what will be the result of the violations of assumptions of statistical tests. For example, the computer may set up two populations with identical means, but the other parameters are supplied by the statistical researcher so that these violate some important assumption. Perhaps the populations are skewed a certain way or the two populations have different variances.

Then, samples are randomly selected from each of these two offbeat populations (remember, they were invented by the computer). The means of these samples are compared using the usual *t*-test procedure with the usual *t* tables with all their assumptions. A large number, often around 10,000, of such pairs of samples are selected, and a *t* test is figured for each. The question is, "How many of these 10,000 *t* tests will come out significant at the 5% significance level?" Ideally, the result would be about 5%, or 50 of the 10,000. But what if 10% (1,000) of these supposedly 5%-level tests come out significant? What if only 1% do? If these kinds of results arise, then this particular violation of the assumptions of the *t* test cannot be tolerated. But, in fact, most violations (except for very extreme ones) checked with these methods do not create very large changes in the *p* values.

Monte Carlo methods are a boon to statistics, but like everything else, they have their drawbacks as well and consequently their critics. One problem is that the ways in which populations can violate assumptions are almost limitless in their variations. But even computers have their limits; Monte Carlo studies are tried on only a representative set of those variations. A more specific problem is that there is good reason to think that some of the variations that are not studied are far more like the real world than those that have been studied (see the discussion in Chapter 3 of the controversy about how common the normal curve really is). Finally, when we are deciding whether to use a particular statistic in any specific situation, we have no idea about the population our sample came from; is it like any on which there has been a Monte Carlo study performed, or not? Simply knowing that Monte Carlo studies have shown some statistic to be robust in the face of many kinds of assumption violations does not prove that it is robust in a given situation. We can only hope that it increases the chances that using the statistic is safe and justifiable.

At any rate, Monte Carlo studies are a perfect example of how the computer has changed science. Shreider (1966) expressed it this way:

> Computers have led to a novel revolution in mathematics. Whereas previously an investigation of a random process was regarded as complete as soon as it was reduced to an analytic description, nowadays it is convenient in many cases to solve an analytic problem by reducing it to a corresponding random process and then simulating that process. (p. vii)

In other words, instead of math helping us analyze experiments, experiments are helping us analyze math.

However, the *t* test can give quite misleading results if (a) the scores in the samples suggest that the populations are very far from normal, (b) the variances are very different, or (c) there are both problems. In these situations, there are alternatives to the ordinary *t* test procedure, some of which we will consider in Chapter 14.

Many computer programs for figuring the *t* test for independent means actually provide two sets of results. One set of results figures the *t* test assuming the population variances are equal. This method is the standard one, the one you have learned in this chapter. A second set of results uses a special alternative procedure that takes into account that the population variances may be unequal. (But it still assumes that the populations follow a normal distribution.) An example of these two sets of results is shown in the Using SPSS section at the end of this chapter (see Figure 8–8). However, in most situations we can assume that the population variances are equal. Thus, researchers usually use the standard method. Using the special alternative procedure has the advantage that you don't have to worry about whether you met the equal population variance assumption. But it has the disadvantage that if you have met that assumption, with this special method you have less power. That is, when you do meet the assumption, you are slightly less likely to get a significant result using the special method.

Effect Size and Power for the *t* Test for Independent Means

Effect Size

Effect size for the *t* test for independent means is figured in basically the same way as we have been using all along:

> The effect size is the difference between the population means divided by the population's standard deviation.

$$d = \frac{\mu_1 - \mu_2}{\sigma} \qquad (8\text{–}8)$$

Cohen's (1988) conventions for the *t* test for independent means are the same as in all the situations we have considered so far: .20 for a small effect size, .50 for a medium effect size, and .80 for a large effect size.

Suppose that an environmental psychologist is working in a city with high levels of air pollution. This psychologist plans a study of the number of problems completed on a creativity test over a one-hour period. The study compares performance under two conditions. In the experimental condition, each participant takes the test in a room with a special air purifier. In the control condition, each participant takes the test in a room without the air purifier. The researcher expects that the control group will probably score like others who have taken this test in the past, which is a mean of 21. But the researcher expects that the experimental group will perform better, scoring about 29. This test is known from previous research to have a standard deviation of about 10. Thus, $\mu_1 = 29$, $\mu_2 = 21$, and $\sigma = 10$. Given these figures, $d = (\mu_1 - \mu_2)/\sigma = (29 - 21)/10 = .80$, a large effect size.

When you have results of a completed study, you estimate the effect size as the difference between the sample means divided by the pooled estimate of the population standard deviation (the square root of the pooled estimate of the population variance). You use the sample means because they are the best estimate of the population means, and you use S_{Pooled} because it is the best estimate of σ. Stated as a formula,

> The estimated effect size is the difference between the sample means divided by the pooled estimate of the population's standard deviation.

$$\text{Estimated } d = \frac{M_1 - M_2}{S_{\text{Pooled}}} \qquad (8\text{–}9)$$

Consider Valenzuela's (1997) study of the quality of instructional assistance provided by mothers of poor children. The mean for the sample of mothers of the adequately nourished children was 33.10; the mean for the sample of mothers of chronically undernourished children was 27.00. We figured the pooled estimate of the population variance to be 168.77; the standard deviation is thus 12.99. The difference in means of 6.10, divided by 12.99, gives an effect size of .47—a medium effect size. In terms of the formula,

$$\text{Estimated } d = \frac{M_1 - M_2}{S_{\text{Pooled}}} = \frac{33.10 - 27.00}{12.99} = \frac{6.10}{12.99} = .47$$

Power

Power for a *t* test for independent means can be determined using a power table, a power software package, or an Internet power calculator. The power table shown in

Table 8-4 Approximate Power for Studies Using the *t* Test for Independent Means Testing Hypotheses at the .05 Significance Level

Number of Participants in Each Group	Effect Size		
	Small (.20)	Medium (.50)	Large (.80)
One-tailed test			
10	.11	.29	.53
20	.15	.46	.80
30	.19	.61	.92
40	.22	.72	.97
50	.26	.80	.99
100	.41	.97	*
Two-tailed test			
10	.07	.18	.39
20	.09	.33	.69
30	.12	.47	.86
40	.14	.60	.94
50	.17	.70	.98
100	.29	.94	*

*Nearly 1.

Table 8–4 gives the approximate power for the .05 significance level for small, medium, and large effect sizes, and one-tailed or two-tailed tests.[2] Consider again the environmental psychology example of a planned study, where the researchers expected a large effect size ($d = .80$). Suppose this researcher plans to use the .05 level, one-tailed, with 10 participants. Based on Table 8–4, the study would have a power of .53. This means that, even if the research hypothesis is in fact true and has a large effect size, there is only a 53% chance that the study will come out significant.

Now consider an example of a completed study. Suppose you have read a study using a *t* test for independent means that had a nonsignificant result using the .05 significance level, two-tailed. There were 40 participants in each group. Should you conclude that there is in fact no difference at all in the populations? This conclusion seems quite unjustified. Table 8–4 shows a power of only .14 for a small effect size. This suggests that even if such a small effect does indeed exist in the populations, this study would probably not come out significant. Still, we can also conclude that, if there is a true difference in the populations, it is probably not large. Table 8–4 shows a power of .94 for a large effect size. This suggests that, if a large effect exists, it almost surely would have produced a significant result.

Planning Sample Size

Table 8–5 gives the approximate number of participants needed for 80% power for estimated small, medium, and large effect sizes, using one-tailed and two-tailed tests, all using the .05 significance level.[3] Suppose you plan a study in which you expect a medium effect size and will use the .05 significance level, one-tailed. Based on Table 8–5, you need 50 people in each group (100 total) to have 80% power. However, if you did a study using the same significance level but expected a large effect size, you would need only 20 people in each group (40 total).

Table 8-5 Approximate Number of Participants Needed in Each Group (Assuming Equal Sample Sizes) for 80% Power for the *t* Test for Independent Means, Testing Hypotheses at the .05 Significance Level

	Effect Size		
	Small (.20)	Medium (.50)	Large (.80)
One-tailed	310	50	20
Two-tailed	393	64	26

How are you doing?

1. List two assumptions for the *t* test for independent means. For each, give the situations in which violations of these assumptions would be seriously problematic.
2. Why do you need to assume the populations have the same variance?
3. What is the effect size for a planned study in which Population 1 is predicted to have a mean of 17, Population 2 is predicted to have a mean of 25, and the population standard deviation is assumed to be about 20?
4. What is the power of a study using a *t* test for independent means, with a two-tailed test at the .05 significance level, in which the researchers predict a large effect size and there are 20 participants in each group?
5. How many participants do you need in each group for 80% power in a planned study in which you predict a small effect size and will be using a *t* test for independent means, one-tailed, at the .05 significance level?

Answers

1. One assumption is that the two populations are normally distributed; this is mainly a problem if you have reason to think the two populations are strongly skewed in opposite directions. A second assumption is that the two populations have the same variance; this is mainly a problem if you believe the two distributions have quite different variances *and* the sample sizes are different.
2. You need to assume the populations have the same variance because you make a pooled estimate of the population variance. The pooling would not make sense if the estimates from the two samples were for populations with different variances.
3. The effect size is $d = (17 - 25)/20 = -8/20 = -.40$.
4. The power is .69.
5. You need 310 participants.

Review and Comparison of the Three Kinds of *t* Tests

You have now learned about three kinds of *t* tests: In Chapter 7, you learned about the *t* test for a single sample and the *t* test for dependent means, and in this chapter you learned about the *t* test for independent means. Table 8–6 provides a review and comparison of these three kinds of *t* tests.

As you can see in Table 8–6, the population variance is not known for each test, and the shape of the comparison distribution for each test is a *t* distribution. The

Table 8-6   Review of the Three Kinds of *t* Tests

Feature of the *t* Tests	Type of *t* Test		
	Single Sample	**Dependent Means**	**Independent Means**
Population variance is known	No	No	No
Population mean is known	Yes	No	No
Number of scores for each participant	1	2	1
t test carried out on difference scores	No	Yes	No
Shape of comparison distribution	*t* distribution	*t* distribution	*t* distribution
Formula for degrees of freedom	$df = N - 1$	$df = N - 1$	$df_{Total} = df_1 + df_2$ $(df_1 = N_1 - 1; df_2 = N_2 - 1)$
Formula for *t*	$t = (M - \mu)/S_M$	$t = (M - \mu)/S_M$	$t = (M_1 - M_2)/S_{Difference}$

TIP FOR SUCCESS

We recommend that you spend some time carefully going through Table 8–6. Test your understanding of the three kinds of *t* tests by covering up portions of the table and trying to recall the hidden information. If you are at all unsure about any information in the table, be sure to review the relevant material in this chapter and in Chapter 7.

single sample *t* test is used for hypothesis testing when you are comparing the mean of a single sample to a known population mean. However, in most research in psychology, you do not know the population mean. With an unknown population mean, the *t* test for dependent means is the appropriate *t* test when each participant has two scores (such as a before-score and an after-score) and you want to see if, on average, there is a difference between the participants' pairs of scores. The *t* test for independent means is used for hypothesis testing when you are comparing the mean of scores from of one group of individuals (such as an experimental group) with the mean of scores from a different group of individuals (such as a control group).

Controversy: The Problem of Too Many *t* Tests

A long-standing controversy is what is usually called the problem of "too many *t* tests." The basic issues come up in all types of hypothesis testing, not just in the *t* test. However, we introduce this problem now because it has traditionally been brought up in this context.

Suppose you do a large number of *t* tests for the same study. For example, you might compare two groups on each of 17 different measures, such as different indicators of memory on a recall task, various intelligence test subscales, or different aspects of observed interactions between infants. When you do several *t* tests in the same study, the chance of any one of them coming out significant at, say, the 5% level is really greater than 5%. If you make 100 independent comparisons, on the average five of them will come out significant at the 5% level just by chance. That is, about five will come out significant even if there is no true difference at all between the populations the *t* tests are comparing.

The fundamental issue is not controversial. Everyone agrees that there is a problem in a study involving a large number of comparisons. And everyone agrees that in a study like this, if only a few results come out significant, these differences should be viewed very cautiously. The controversy is about how cautious to be and about how few is "only a few." One reason there is room for controversy is that, in most cases, the many comparisons being made are not independent; the chance of one coming out significant is related to the chance of another coming out significant.

Here is an example. A study compares a sample of lawyers to a sample of doctors on 100 personality traits. Now suppose the researcher simply conducts 100 t tests. If these 100 t tests were truly independent, we would expect that on the average five would come out significant just by chance. In fact, tables exist that tell you quite precisely the chance of any particular number of t tests coming out significant. The problem, however, is that in practice these 100 t tests are *not* independent. Many of the various personality traits are probably related: if doctors and lawyers differ on assertiveness, they probably also differ on self-confidence. Thus, certain sets of comparisons may be more or less likely to come out significant by chance so that 5 in 100 may not be what you should expect by chance.

There is yet another complication: in most cases, differences on some of the variables are more important than on others. Some comparisons may directly test a theory or the effectiveness of some practical procedure; other comparisons may be more "exploratory."

Here is another kind of example. In studies using brain imaging procedures [such as functional magnetic resonance imagery (fMRI)], the way the analysis works for a typical study is like this: a person's brain is scanned every few seconds over a 10- or 15-minute period. During this time, the person is sometimes looking at one kind of image, say a picture of a person smiling, and at other times is looking at a different kind of image, say a picture of the same person frowning. For each little area of the brain, the fMRI produces a number for how active that area was during each 2- to 3-second scan. Thus, for each little area of the brain, you might have 60 numbers for activation when looking at the smile and 60 numbers for when looking at the frown. Thus, for each little area, you can figure a t test for dependent means. In fact, this is exactly what is done in this kind of research. (We considered an example like this in Chapter 7.) The problem, however, is that you have a great many little areas of the brain. (Typically, in fMRI research, each little area may be about a 1/4-inch cube or smaller.) Thus, you have several thousand t tests, and you would expect some of them to be significant just by chance. This whole situation is further complicated by the issue that some brain areas might be expected to be more likely to show different levels of activity for this kind of image. In addition, the situation is still further complicated by the fact that you might want to pay more attention when two or more little areas that are right next to each other show significant differences.

In these various examples, there are a variety of contending solutions. We introduce one kind of solution in Chapter 9 (the Bonferroni procedure), when we consider a related situation, one that comes up in studies comparing more than two groups. However, the issue remains at the forefront of work on the development of statistical methods. [Aron et al. (2005) used one of the more conservative methods in the study that was the basis of the Chapter 7 example; so they were very confident of their results—but, using that method, they might have missed finding even more differences.] In the neuroimaging research literature, this issue has been a particularly lively topic of late (e.g., Nancy & Cordes, 2007; Nichols & Hayasaka, 2003).

The t Test for Independent Means in Research Articles

A t test for independent means is usually described in a research article by giving the means (and sometimes the standard deviations) of the two samples, plus the usual way of reporting any kind of t test—for example, $t(38) = 4.72$, $p < .01$ (recall that the number in parentheses is the degrees of freedom). The result of the study of the health effects of expressive writing might be written up as follows: "The mean level

Table 8-7 Mean and Standard Deviation of Scores for Women and Men on Measures of Machismo, Attitudes Toward Women, and Adoption Beliefs

	Women (*n* = 64)	Men (*n* = 88)	*t*	*p*
Machismo	1.17 ± .15	1.32 ± .20	4.77	<.001
AWSA	3.26 ± .31	2.98 ± .35	5.00	<.001
Adoption	3.10 ± .39	2.85 ± .41	3.07	<.01

Source: Gibbons, J. L., Wilson, S. L., & Rufener, C. A. (2006). Gender attitudes mediate gender differences in attitudes towards adoption in Guatemala. *Sex Roles, 54,* 139–145. Copyright © 2006. Reprinted by permission of Springer Science and Business Media.

of self-reported health in the expressive writing group was 79.00 ($SD = 9.72$), and the mean for the control writing group was 68.00 ($SD = 10.55$); $t(18) = 2.42$, $p < .05$, two-tailed."

Here is another example. Dodge and Kaufman (2007) conducted a study of college students' use of and attitudes toward dietary supplements. Here is an excerpt from their results section: "Men were more likely than women to report they had used a dietary supplement to improve physical performance, $t(61) = 4.03$, $p < .01$, whereas women were more likely than men to report having used a dietary supplement to help with weight loss, $t(61) = -2.74$, $p < .01$" (p. 515).

Table 8–7 is an example in which the results of several *t* tests are given in a table. This table is taken from a study conducted by Gibbons and colleagues (2006). In that study, 152 college students in Guatemala were surveyed on their beliefs about machismo (a strong sense of masculinity), their attitudes toward women, and their beliefs about adoption. As shown in Table 8–7, the researchers used three *t* tests for independent means to examine whether female and male students differed on these beliefs and attitudes. The scales were scored so that higher scores were for more positive attitudes about machismo, more egalitarian (equal) gender beliefs (which were measured using the Attitudes Towards Women Scale for Adolescents, abbreviated as AWSA in Table 8–7), and more favorable beliefs about adoption. The first line of the table shows that men (with a mean score of 1.32) had more positive attitudes about machismo than women (mean score of 1.17). The *t* score for this comparison was 4.77 and it was statistically significant at $p < .001$. The results in Table 8–7 also show that women had more positive attitudes toward women than men did and that women had more favorable beliefs regarding adoption than men. (The number after each ± sign is the standard deviation for that particular group.)

Advanced Topic: Power for the *t* Test for Independent Means When Sample Sizes are Not Equal

For a study with any given total number of participants, power is greatest when the participants are divided into two equal groups. Recall the example from earlier in this chapter where the 42 participants were divided into 11 in the experimental group and 31 in the control group. This study has much less power than it would have if the researchers had been able to divide their 42 participants into 21 in each group.

There is a practical problem in figuring power from tables when sample sizes are not equal. (Power software packages and Internet power calculators require you to specify the sample sizes, which are then taken into account when they figure power.) Like most power tables, Table 8–4 assumes equal numbers in each of the two groups. What do you do when your two samples have different numbers of people in them? It turns out that in terms of power, the **harmonic mean** of the numbers of participants in two unequal sample sizes gives the equivalent sample size for what you would have with two equal samples. There are several accounts as to the origin of the harmonic mean, but it seems most likely that it originated from ancient Greek times (around 350 BCE) in the context of music and harmonious tones. The harmonic mean sample size is given by this formula:

> The harmonic mean is two times the first sample size times the second sample size, all divided by the sum of the two sample sizes.

$$\text{Harmonic mean} = \frac{(2)(N_1)(N_2)}{N_1 + N_2} \tag{8-10}$$

In our example with 11 in one group and 31 in the other, the harmonic mean is 16.24:

$$\text{Harmonic mean} = \frac{(2)(N_1)(N_2)}{N_1 + N_2} = \frac{(2)(11)(31)}{11 + 31} = \frac{682}{42} = 16.24$$

Thus, even though you have a total of 42 participants, the study has the power of a study with equal sample sizes of only about 16 in each group. (This means that a study with a total of 32 participants divided equally would have had about the same power.)

How are you doing?

1. What is the approximate power of a study using a *t* test for independent means, with a two-tailed test at the .05 significance level, in which the researchers predict a large effect size, and there are 6 participants in one group and 34 participants in the other group?

harmonic mean   special average influenced disproportionately by smaller numbers; in a *t* test for independent means when the number of scores in the two groups differ, the harmonic mean is used as the equivalent of each group's sample size when determining power.

Answer

1. Harmonic mean $= (2)(6)(34)/(6 + 34) = 408/40 = 10.20$. Power for a study like this with 10 in each group $= .39$ (see Table 8–4).

Summary

1. A *t* test for independent means is used for hypothesis testing with scores from two entirely separate groups of people. The comparison distribution for a *t* test for independent means is a distribution of differences between means of samples. This distribution can be thought of as being built up in two steps: each population of individuals produces a distribution of means, and then a new distribution is created of differences between pairs of means selected from these two distributions of means.

2. The distribution of differences between means has a mean of 0 and is a *t* distribution with the total of the degrees of freedom from the two samples. Its standard deviation is figured in several steps:
   - ❶ **Figure the estimated population variances based on each sample.**
   - ❷ **Figure the pooled estimate of the population variance.**
   - ❸ **Figure the variance of each distribution of means.**
   - ❹ **Figure the variance of the distribution of differences between means.**
   - ❺ **Figure the standard deviation of the distribution of differences between means.**

3. The assumptions of the *t* test for independent means are that the two populations are normally distributed and have the same variance. However, the *t* test gives fairly accurate results when the true situation is moderately different from the assumptions.

4. Effect size for a *t* test for independent means is the difference between the means divided by the population standard deviation. Power for a *t* test for independent means can be determined using a table (see Table 8–4), a power software package, or an Internet power calculator.

5. When you carry out many significance tests in the same study, such as a series of *t* tests comparing two groups on various measures, the possibility that any one of the comparisons may turn out significant at the .05 level by chance is greater than .05. There is controversy about how to adjust for this problem, though most agree that results should be interpreted cautiously in a situation of this kind.

6. *t* tests for independent means are usually reported in research articles with the means of the two groups plus the degrees of freedom, *t* score, and significance level. Results may also be reported in a table in which each significant difference may be shown by asterisks.

7. ADVANCED TOPIC: Power is greatest when the sample sizes of the two groups are equal. When they are not equal, you use the harmonic mean of the two sample sizes when looking up power in a table.

Key Terms

t test for independent means (p. 270)
distribution of differences between means (p. 271)
pooled estimate of the population variance (S^2_{Pooled}) (p. 273)

weighted average (p. 273)
variance of the distribution of differences between means ($S^2_{Difference}$) (p. 275)

standard deviation of the distribution of differences between means ($S_{Difference}$) (p. 275)
harmonic mean (p. 294)

Example Worked-Out Problems

Figuring the Standard Deviation of the Distribution of Differences Between Means

Figure $S_{Difference}$ for the following study: $N_1 = 40$, $S^2_1 = 15$; $N_2 = 60$; $S^2_2 = 12$.

Answer

❶ **Figure the estimated population variances based on each sample:** $S^2_1 = 15$; $S^2_2 = 12$.

❷ **Figure the pooled estimate of the population variance:**

$$df_1 = N_1 - 1 = 40 - 1 = 39; df_2 = N_2 - 1 = 60 - 1 = 59;$$

$$df_{Total} = df_1 + df_2 = 39 + 59 = 98$$

$$S^2_{Pooled} = \frac{df_1}{df_{Total}}(S^2_1) + \frac{df_2}{df_{Total}}(S^2_2) = (39/98)(15) + (59/98)(12) = 13.19$$

❸ **Figure the variance of each distribution of means:**

$$S^2_{M_1} = S^2_{Pooled}/N_1 = 13.19/40 = .33$$
$$S^2_{M_2} = S^2_{Pooled}/N_2 = 13.19/60 = .22.$$

⓪ Figure the variance of the distribution of differences between means:

$$S^2_{\text{Difference}} = S^2_{M_1} + S^2_{M_2} = .33 + .22 = .55$$

⓫ Figure the standard deviation of the distribution of differences between means:

$$S_{\text{Difference}} = \sqrt{S^2_{\text{Difference}}} = \sqrt{.55} = .74$$

Hypothesis Testing Using the *t* Test for Independent Means

A researcher randomly assigns seven individuals to receive a new experimental procedure and seven to a control condition. At the end of the study, all 14 are measured. Scores for those in the experimental group were 6, 4, 9, 7, 7, 3, and 6. Scores for those in the control group were 6, 1, 5, 3, 1, 1, and 4. Carry out a *t* test for independent means using the .05 level of significance, two-tailed. Use the five steps of hypothesis testing and sketch the distributions involved.

Answer

The figuring is shown in Table 8–8; the distributions are shown in Figure 8–5. Here are the steps of hypothesis testing.

Table 8-8 Example Worked-Out Problem for Hypothesis Testing Using the *t* Test Independent Means

	Experimental Group			Control Group		
Score	Deviation From Mean	Squared Deviation From Mean		Score	Deviation From Mean	Squared Deviation From Mean
6	0	0		6	3	9
4	−2	4		1	−2	4
9	3	9		5	2	4
7	1	1		3	0	0
7	1	1		1	−2	4
3	−3	9		1	−2	4
6	0	0		4	1	1
Σ: 42	0	24		21	0	26

$M_1 = 6; S^2_1 = 24/6 = 4.00; M_2 = 3; S^2_2 = 26/6 = 4.33$
$N_1 = 7; df_1 = N_1 - 1 = 6; N_2 = 7; df_2 = N_2 - 1 = 6$
$df_{\text{Total}} = df_1 + df_2 = 6 + 6 = 12$
$S^2_{\text{Pooled}} = \dfrac{df_1}{df_{\text{Total}}}(S^2_1) + \dfrac{df_2}{df_{\text{Total}}}(S^2_2) = \dfrac{6}{12}(4) + \dfrac{6}{12}(4.33) = .5(4) + .5(4.33) = 2.00 + 2.17 = 4.17$
$S^2_{M_1} = S^2_{\text{Pooled}}/N_1 = 4.17/7 = .60$
$S^2_{M_2} = S^2_{\text{Pooled}}/N_2 = 4.17/7 = .60$
$S^2_{\text{Difference}} = S^2_{M_1} + S^2_{M_2} = .60 + .60 = 1.20$
$S_{\text{Difference}} = \sqrt{S^2_{\text{Difference}}} = \sqrt{1.20} = 1.10$
Needed *t* with $df = 12$, 5% level, two-tailed $= \pm 2.179$
$t = (M_1 - M_2)/S_{\text{Difference}} = (6.00 - 3.00)/1.10 = 3.00/1.10 = 2.73$
Decision: Reject the null hypothesis; the research hypothesis is supported.

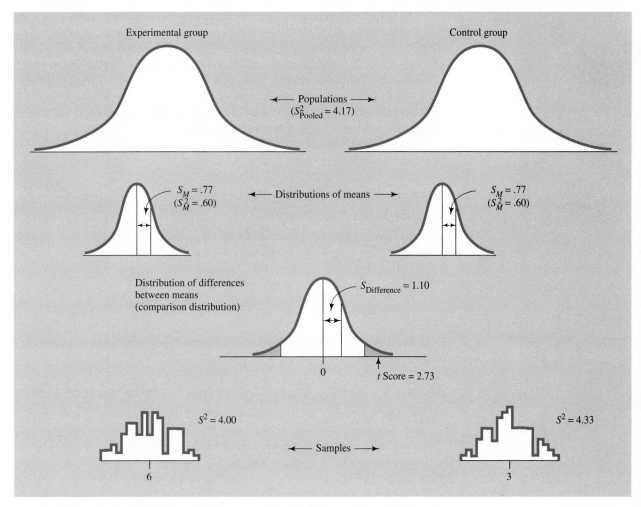

Figure 8–5   Distributions for the Example Worked-Out Problem for hypothesis testing using the *t* test for independent means.

❶ **Restate the question as a research hypothesis and a null hypothesis about the populations.** There are two populations:

Population 1: People like those who receive the experimental procedure.
Population 2: People like those who receive the control procedure.

The research hypothesis is that the means of the two populations are different: $\mu_1 \neq \mu_2$. The null hypothesis is that the means of the two populations are the same: $\mu_1 = \mu_2$.

❷ **Determine the characteristics of the comparison distribution.**
   (a) The distribution of differences between means has a mean of 0. (b) Regarding its standard deviation,
      ❹ **Figure the estimated population variances based on each sample:** $S_1^2 = 4.00$; $S_2^2 = 4.33$.
      ❷ **Figure the pooled estimate of the population variance:** $S_{Pooled}^2 = 4.17$.
      ❸ **Figure the variance of each distribution of means:** $S_{M_1}^2 = .60$; $S_{M_2}^2 = .60$.
      ❹ **Figure the variance of the distribution of differences between means:** $S_{Difference}^2 = 1.20$.

❶ **Figure the standard deviation of the distribution of differences between means:** $S_{\text{Difference}} = 1.10$.

(c) The shape of the comparison distribution is a t distribution with $df_{\text{Total}} = 12$.

❸ **Determine the cutoff sample score on the comparison distribution at which the null hypothesis should be rejected.** With $df_{\text{Total}} = 12$, .05 significance level, two-tailed test, the cutoffs are $+2.179$ and -2.179.

❹ **Determine the sample's score on the comparison distribution.** $t = 2.73$.

❺ **Decide whether to reject the null hypothesis.** The t of 2.73 is more extreme than the cutoffs of ± 2.179. Thus, you can reject the null hypothesis. The research hypothesis is supported.

Advanced Topic: Finding Power When Sample Sizes Are Unequal

A planned study with a predicted small effect size has 22 in one group and 51 in the other. What is the approximate power for a one-tailed test at the .05 significance level?

Answer

$$\text{Harmonic mean} = \frac{(2)(N_1)(N_2)}{N_1 + N_2} = \frac{(2)(22)(51)}{22 + 51} = \frac{2244}{73} = 30.7$$

From Table 8–4, for a one-tailed test with 30 participants in each group, power for a small effect size is .19.

Outline for Writing Essays for a *t* Test for Independent Means

1. Describe the core logic of hypothesis testing in this situation. Be sure to mention that the t test for independent is used for hypothesis testing when you have scores from two entirely separate groups of people. Be sure to explain the meaning of the research hypothesis and the null hypothesis in this situation.

2. Explain the logic of the comparison distribution that is used with a t test for independent means (the distribution of differences between means). Be sure to explain why you use 0 as its mean.

3. Outline the logic of estimating the population variance and the variance of the two distributions of means. Describe how to figure the standard deviation of the distribution of differences between means.

4. Explain why the shape of the comparison distribution that is used with a t test for independent means is a t distribution (as opposed to the normal curve).

5. Describe the logic and process for determining the cutoff sample score(s) on the comparison distribution at which the null hypothesis should be rejected.

6. Describe why and how you figure the t score of the sample mean on the comparison distribution.

7. Explain how and why the scores from Steps ❸ and ❹ of the hypothesis-testing process are compared. Explain the meaning of the result of this comparison with regard to the specific research and null hypotheses being tested.

Practice Problems

These problems involve figuring. Most real-life statistics problems are done on a computer with special statistical software. Even if you have such software, do these problems by hand to ingrain the method in your mind. To learn how to use a computer to solve statistics problems like those in this chapter, refer to the Using SPSS section at the end of this chapter and the *Study Guide and Computer Workbook* that accompanies this text.

All data are fictional unless an actual citation is given.

Set I (for Answers to Set I Problems, see pp. 683–685)

1. For each of the following studies, say whether you would use a *t* test for dependent means or a *t* test for independent means.
   (a) A researcher randomly assigns a group of 25 unemployed workers to receive a new job skills program and 24 other workers to receive the standard job skills program, and then measures how well they all do on a job skills test.
   (b) A researcher measures self-esteem in 21 students before and after taking a difficult exam.
   (c) A researcher tests reaction time of each member of a group of 14 individuals twice, once while in a very hot room and once while in a normal-temperature room.

2. Figure $S_{\text{Difference}}$ for each of the following studies:

	N_1	S_1^2	N_2	S_2^2
(a)	20	1	20	2
(b)	20	1	40	2
(c)	40	1	20	2
(d)	40	1	40	2
(e)	40	1	40	4

3. For each of the following experiments, decide whether the difference between conditions is statistically significant at the .05 level (two-tailed).

	Experimental Group			Control Group		
	N	M	S^2	N	M	S^2
(a)	30	12.0	2.4	30	11.1	2.8
(b)	20	12.0	2.4	40	11.1	2.8
(c)	30	12.0	2.2	30	11.1	3.0

4. A social psychologist studying mass communication randomly assigned 82 volunteers to one of two experimental groups. Sixty-one were instructed to get their news for a month only from television, and 21 were instructed to get their news for a month only from the Internet. (Why the researcher didn't assign equal numbers to the two conditions is a mystery!) After the month was up, all participants were tested on their knowledge of several political issues. The researcher did not have a prediction as to which news source would make people more knowledgeable. That is, the researcher simply predicted that there is some kind of difference. These were the results of the study. TV group: $M = 24$, $S^2 = 4$; Internet group: $M = 26$, $S^2 = 6$. Using the .01 level, what should the social psychologist conclude? (a) Use the steps of hypothesis testing, (b) sketch the distributions involved, and (c) explain your answers to someone who is familiar with the *t* test for a single sample, but not with the *t* test for independent means.

5. An educational psychologist was interested in whether using a student's own name in a story affected children's attention span while reading. Six children were randomly assigned to read a story under ordinary conditions (using names

like Dick and Jane). Five other children read versions of the same story, but with each child's own name substituted for one of the children in the story. The researcher kept a careful measure of how long it took each child to read the story. The results are shown in the following table. Using the .05 level, does including the child's name make any difference? (a) Use the steps of hypothesis testing, (b) sketch the distributions involved, and (c) explain your answers to someone who has never had a course in statistics.

Ordinary Story		Own-Name Story	
Student	Reading Time	Student	Reading Time
A	2	G	4
B	5	H	16
C	7	I	11
D	9	J	9
E	6	K	8
F	7		

6. A developmental psychologist compares 4-year-olds and 8-year-olds on their ability to understand the analogies used in stories. The scores for the five 4-year-olds tested were 7, 6, 2, 3, and 8. The scores for the three 8-year-olds tested were 9, 2, and 5. Using the .05 level, do older children do better? (a) Use the steps of hypothesis testing, (b) sketch the distributions involved, and (c) explain your answers to someone who understands the *t* test for a single sample but does not know anything about the *t* test for independent means.

7. Figure the estimated effect size for problems (a) 4, (b) 5, and (c) 6. (d) Explain what you have done in part (a) to someone who understands the *t* test for independent means but knows nothing about effect size.

8. Figure the approximate power of a *t* test for independent means for each of the following planned studies:

	Number of People in Each Group	One- or Two-Tailed	Effect Size
(a)	30	1	Small (.20)
(b)	100	2	Large (.80)
(c)	40	1	Medium (.50)
(d)	40	1	Large (.80)

9. ADVANCED TOPIC: Figure the approximate power of each of the following planned studies, all using a *t* test for independent means at the .05 significance level, one-tailed, with a predicted small effect size:

	N_1	N_2
(a)	3	57
(b)	10	50
(c)	20	40
(d)	30	30

10. What are the approximate numbers of participants needed for each of the following planned studies to have 80% power, assuming equal numbers in the two groups and all using the .05 significance level? (Be sure to give the total number of participants needed, not just the number needed for each group.)

	Expected			
	μ_1	μ_2	σ	**Tails**
(a)	107.0	149.0	84.0	1
(b)	22.5	16.2	31.5	2
(c)	14.0	12.0	2.5	1
(d)	480.0	520.0	50.0	2

11. Van Aken and Asendorpf (1997) studied 139 German 12-year-olds. All of the children completed a general self-worth questionnaire and were interviewed about the supportiveness they experienced from their mothers, fathers, and class-mates. The researchers then compared the self-worth of those with high and low levels of support of each type. The researchers reported that "lower general self-worth was found for children with a low-supportive mother ($t(137) = 4.52$, $p < .001$, $d = 0.78$) and with a low-supportive father ($t(137) = 4.03$, $p < .001$, $d = 0.69$).... A lower general self-worth was also found for children with only low supportive classmates ($t(137) = 2.04$, $p < .05$, $d = 0.35$)." (a) Explain what these results mean to a person who has never had a course in statistics. (b) Include a discussion of effect size and power. (When figuring power, you can assume that the two groups in each comparison had about equal sample sizes.)

12. Gallagher-Thompson and her colleagues (2001) compared 27 wives who were caring for their husbands who had Alzheimer's disease to 27 wives in which nei-ther partner had Alzheimer's. The two groups of wives were otherwise similar in terms of age, number of years married, and social economic status. Table 8–9 (reproduced from their Table 1) shows some of their results. Focusing on the

Table 8-9   Comparison of Caregiving and Noncaregiving Wives on Select Psychosocial Variables

	Caregiving Wives ($n = 27$)			**Noncaregiving Wives ($n = 27$)**				
	M	*SD*	Range	*M*	*SD*	Range	*t*	*p*
Geriatric Depression Scale[a]	9.42	6.59	1–25	2.37	2.54	0–8	5.14	.0001
Perceived Stress Scale[b]	22.29	8.34	6–36	15.33	6.36	7–30	3.44	.001
Hope questionnaire[c]								
Agency	11.88	1.63	9–16	13.23	1.39	10–16	3.20	.002
Resilience	11.89	0.91	10–14	13.08	1.60	10–16	3.31	.002
Total	23.77	2.03	21–29	26.31	2.56	22–31	3.97	.0001
Mutuality Scale[d]								
Closeness	3.51	.81	.33–4	3.70	.41	2.67–4	−1.02	.315
Reciprocity	2.25	1.19	.17–4	3.25	.55	1.67–4	−3.68	.001
Shared pleasures	2.65	1.00	0–4	3.52	.61	1.75–4	−3.66	.001
Shared values	3.15	.89	0–4	3.46	.45	2.4–4	−1.51	.138

Note: For all measures, higher scores indicate more of the construct being measured.
[a]Maximum score is 30.
[b]Maximum score is 56.
[c]Four questions in each subscale, with a maximum total score of 32.
[d]Maximum mean for each subscale is 4.
Source: Gallagher-Thompson, D., Dal Canto, P. G., Jacob, T., & Thompson, L. W. (2001). A comparison of marital interaction patterns between couples in which the husband does or does not have Alzheimer's disease. *The Journals of Gerontology Series B: Psychology Sciences and Social Sciences, 56,* 5140–5150. Copy-right © 2001 by the Gerontological Society of America. Reprinted by permission of the publishers.

Geriatric Depression Scale (the first row of the table) and the Mutuality Scale for Shared Values (the last row in the table), explain these results to a person who knows about the *t* test for a single sample but is unfamiliar with the *t* test for independent means.

Set II

13. Make up two examples of studies (not in the book or from your lectures) that would be tested with a *t* test for independent means.

14. For each of the following studies, say whether you would use a *t* test for dependent means or a *t* test for independent means.
    (a) A researcher measures the heights of 40 university students who are the firstborn in their families and compares the 15 who come from large families to the 25 who come from smaller families.
    (b) A researcher tests performance on a math skills test of each of 250 individuals before and after they complete a one-day seminar on managing test anxiety.
    (c) A researcher compares the resting heart rate of 15 individuals who have been taking a particular drug to the resting heart rate of 48 other individuals who have not been taking the drug.

15. Figure $S_{\text{Difference}}$ for each of the following studies:

	N_1	S_1^2	N_2	S_2^2
(a)	30	5	20	4
(b)	30	5	30	4
(c)	30	5	50	4
(d)	20	5	30	4
(e)	30	5	20	2

16. For each of the following experiments, decide whether the difference between conditions is statistically significant at the .05 level (two-tailed).

	Experimental Group			Control Group		
	N	M	S^2	N	M	S^2
(a)	10	604	60	10	607	50
(b)	40	604	60	40	607	50
(c)	10	604	20	40	607	16

17. A psychologist theorized that people can hear better when they have just eaten a large meal. Six individuals were randomly assigned to eat either a large meal or a small meal. After eating the meal, their hearing was tested. The hearing ability scores (high numbers indicate greater ability) are given in the following table. Using the .05 level, do the results support the psychologist's theory? (a) Use the steps of hypothesis testing, (b) sketch the distributions involved, and (c) explain your answers to someone who has never had a course in statistics.

Big Meal Group		Small Meal Group	
Subject	**Hearing**	**Subject**	**Hearing**
A	22	D	19
B	25	E	23
C	25	F	21

18. Twenty students randomly assigned to an experimental group receive an instructional program; 30 in a control group do not. After 6 months, both groups are tested on their knowledge. The experimental group has a mean of 38 on the test (with an estimated population standard deviation of 3); the control group has a mean of 35 (with an estimated population standard deviation of 5). Using the .05 level, what should the experimenter conclude? (a) Use the steps of hypothesis testing, (b) sketch the distributions involved, and (c) explain your answer to someone who is familiar with the *t* test for a single sample but not with the *t* test for independent means.

19. A study of the effects of color on easing anxiety compared anxiety test scores of participants who completed the test printed on either soft yellow paper or on harsh green paper. The scores for five participants who completed the test printed on the yellow paper were 17, 19, 28, 21, and 18. The scores for four participants who completed the test on the green paper were 20, 26, 17, and 24. Using the .05 level, one-tailed (predicting lower anxiety scores for the yellow paper), what should the researcher conclude? (a) Use the steps of hypothesis testing, (b) sketch the distributions involved, and (c) explain your answers to someone who is familiar with the *t* test for a single sample but not with the *t* test for independent means.

20. Figure the estimated effect size for problems (a) 16, (b) 17, and (c) 18. (d) Explain your answer to part (a) to a person who understands the *t* test for independent means but is unfamiliar with effect size.

21. Figure the approximate power of a *t* test for independent means for each of the following planned studies:

	Number of People in Each Group	One- or Two-Tailed	Effect Size
(a)	60	1	Small (.20)
(b)	60	2	Large (.80)
(c)	10	2	Medium (.50)
(d)	100	2	Medium (.50)

22. ADVANCED TOPIC: What is the approximate power of each of the following planned studies, all using a *t* test for independent means at the .05 significance level, two-tailed, with a predicted medium effect size?

	N_1	N_2
(a)	90	10
(b)	50	50
(c)	6	34
(d)	20	20

23. What are the approximate numbers of participants needed for each of the following planned studies to have 80% power, assuming equal numbers in the two groups and all using the .05 significance level? (Be sure to give the total number of participants needed, not just the number needed for each group.)

	Expected			
	μ_1	μ_2	σ	Tails
(a)	10	15	25	1
(b)	10	30	25	1
(c)	10	30	40	1
(d)	10	15	25	2

24. Escudero and colleagues (1997) videotaped 30 couples discussing a marital problem in their laboratory. The videotapes were later systematically rated for various aspects of the couple's communication, such as domineeringness and the positive or negative quality of affect (emotion) expressed between them. A major interest of their study was to compare couples who were having relationship problems with those who were not. The 18 couples in the group having problems were recruited from those who had gone to a marital clinic for help; they were called the Clinic group. The 12 couples in the group not having problems were recruited through advertisements and were called the Nonclinic group. (The two groups in fact had dramatically different scores on a standard test of marital satisfaction.) Table 8–10 presents some of their results. (You can ignore the arrows and plus and minus signs, which have to do with how they rated the interactions. Also, ignore the note at the bottom about "arcsine transformation"; we will explain this in Chapter 14.) (a) Focusing on Domineeringness and Submissiveness, explain these results to a person who has never had a course in statistics. (b) ADVANCED TOPIC: Include a discussion of effect size and power.

Table 8-10 Base-Rate Differences between Clinic and Nonclinic Couples on Relational Control and Nonverbal Affect Codes Expressed in Proportions (*SDs* in Parentheses)

	Couple Status		Between-Group Differences
	Clinic Mean	Nonclinic Mean	t
Domineeringness ($\uparrow$)	.452 (107)	.307 (.152)	3.06[*]
Levelingness ($\rightarrow$)	.305 (.061)	.438 (.065)	5.77[**]
Submissiveness ($\downarrow$)	.183 (.097)	.226 (.111)	1.12
Double-codes	.050 (.028)	.024 (.017)	2.92[*]
Positive affect (+)	.127 (.090)	.280 (.173)	3.22[*]
Negative affect (−)	.509 (.192)	.127 (.133)	5.38[**]
Neutral affect (0)	.344 (.110)	.582 (.089)	6.44[**]
Double-codes (+/−)	.019 (.028)	.008 (.017)	2.96[*]

Note: Proportions of each control and affect code were converted using arcsine transformation for use in between-group comparisons. *$p < .01$, **$p < .001$, (d.f. = 28).
Source: Escudero, V., Rogers, L. E., & Gutierrez, E. (1997). Patterns of relational control and nonverbal affect in clinic and nonclinic couples. *Journal of Social and Personal Relationships, 14,* 5–29. Copyright © 1997 by Sage Publications, Ltd. Reprinted by permission of Sage Publications, Thousand Oaks, London, and New Delhi.

Table 8–11 Gender Differences in Internet Use and Potential Mediators

	Males[a]	Females[b]	*t*-value	*df*	*p*-value
E-mail use	4.16 (0.66)	4.30 (0.57)	2.81	626	.005
Web use	3.57 (0.67)	3.30 (0.67)	−4.84	627	.000
Overall Internet use	3.86 (0.58)	3.80 (0.53)	−1.44	627	.130
Computer anxiety	1.67 (0.56)	1.80 (0.57)	4.03	612	.000
Computer self-efficacy	3.89 (0.52)	3.71 (0.62)	−3.49	608	.001
Loneliness	2.06 (0.64)	1.96 (0.64)	−1.88	607	.061
Depression	1.22 (0.32)	1.28 (0.34)	2.36	609	.019
E-mail privacy	4.04 (0.78)	4.10 (0.69)	−0.97	609	.516
E-mail trust	3.50 (0.77)	3.46 (0.75)	−0.65	610	.516
Web privacy	4.06 (0.74)	4.09 (0.71)	0.62	623	.534
Web trust	3.14 (0.73)	3.12 (0.73)	−0.28	624	.780
Web search success	4.05 (0.85)	4.13 (0.81)	1.12	568	.262
Importance of computer skills	2.54 (1.03)	2.31 (0.90)	−2.57	477	.011
Computers cause health problems	2.67 (1.00)	3.00 (1.08)	3.36	476	.001
Gender stereotypes about computer skills	3.45 (1.15)	4.33 (0.96)	−8.95	476	.000
Racial/ethnic stereotypes about computer skills	3.63 (1.17)	3.99 (1.07)	3.40	477	.001
Computers are taking over	3.08 (1.19)	2.87 (1.08)	−1.89	476	.059

Note: For the attitude items, 1 = strongly agree, 2 = strongly disagree. For gender, 1 = male, 2 = female. Numbers in parentheses are standard deviations.
[a]*n* = 227.
[b]*n* = 403.
Source: Jackson, L. A., Ervin, K. S., Gardner, P. D., & Schmitt, N. (2004). Gender and the Internet Women communicating and men searching. *Sex Roles, 44,* 363–379. Copyright © 2004. Reprinted by permission of Springer Science and Business Media.

25. Jackson and colleagues (2001) gave a questionnaire about Internet usage to university students. Table 8–11 (their Table 1) shows their results comparing men and women. (a) Select one significant and one nonsignificant result and explain these two results to a person who understands the *t* test for a single sample but does not know anything about the *t* test for independent means. (b) ADVANCED TOPIC: Include a discussion of effect size and power (note that the sample sizes for the male and female groups are shown in the table footnote).

Using SPSS

The ✑ in the following steps indicates a mouse click. (We used SPSS version 15.0 for Windows to carry out these analyses. The steps and output may be slightly different for other versions of SPSS.)

t Test for Independent Means

It is easier to learn these steps using actual numbers, so we will use the expressive writing example from earlier in the chapter. The scores for that example are shown in Table 8–1 on page 279.

❶ Enter the scores into SPSS. SPSS assumes that all scores in a row are from the same person. In this example, each person is in only one of the two groups (*either* the expressive writing group *or* the control writing group). Thus, to tell SPSS which person is in each group, you should enter the numbers as shown in Figure 8–6. In the first column (labeled "group"), we used the number "1" to indicate that a person is in the expressive writing group and the number "2" to indicate that a person is in the control writing group. Each person's score on the health measure is listed in the second column (labeled "health"). (For the *t* test for dependent means in the previous chapter, you set up the SPSS data with a before-scores column and an after-scores column so that both scores for a particular person were on the same line. In this example, you have only one score

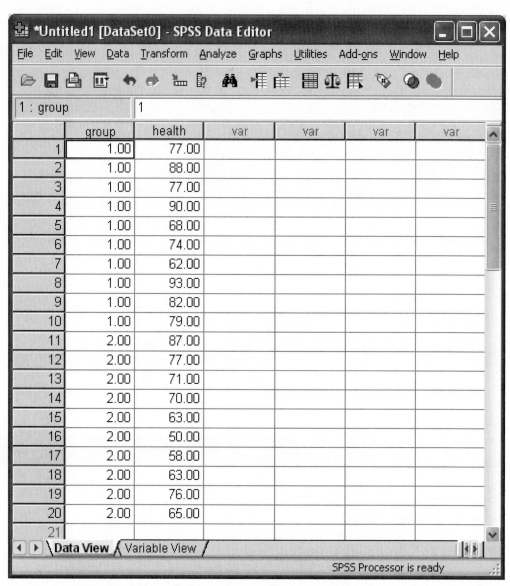

Figure 8–6   SPSS data editor window for the expressive writing example (in which 20 students were randomly assigned to be in an expressive writing group or a control writing group).

per person; so you have one column of scores and another column to show which experimental group each person is in; that is, you have a score column and a group column.)

❷ ✍ *Analyze.*

❸ ✍ *Compare means.*

❹ ✍ *Independent-Samples T Test* (this is the name SPSS uses for a *t* test for independent means).

❺ ✍ on the variable called "health" and then ✍ the arrow next to the box labeled "Test Variable(s)." This tells SPSS that the *t* test should be carried out on the scores for the "health" variable.

❻ ✍ the variable called "group" and then ✍ the arrow next to the the box labeled "Grouping Variable." This tells SPSS that the variable called "group" shows which person is in which group. ✍ *Define Groups.* You now tell SPSS the values you used to label each group. Put 1 in the Group 1 box and put 2 in the Group 2 box. Your screen should now look like Figure 8–7. ✍ *Continue.*

❼ ✍ *OK.* Your SPSS output window should look like Figure 8–8.

The first table in the SPSS output provides information about the two variables. The first column gives the levels of the grouping variable (1 and 2, which indicate the expressive writing group and the control writing group, respectively). The second, third, and fourth columns give, respectively, the number of individuals (N), mean (M), and estimated population standard deviation (S) for each group. The fifth column, labeled "Std. error mean," is the standard deviation of the distribution of means, S_M, for each group. Note that these values for the standard error of the mean are based on each population variance estimate and not on the pooled estimate; so they are not quite the same for each group as the square root of each S_M^2 figured in the text. (See Table 8–1 for the figuring for this example.)

The second table in the SPSS output shows the actual results of the *t* test for independent means. Before the *t* test results, SPSS shows the results of "Levene's

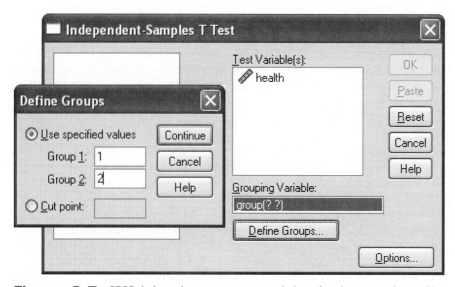

Figure 8–7 SPSS independent means *t* test window for the expressive writing example.

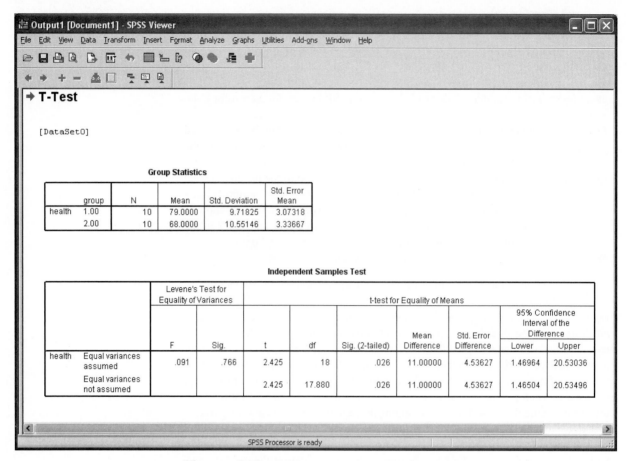

Figure 8–8 SPSS output window for a *t* test for independent means for the expressive writing example.

Test for Equality of Variances," which is a test of whether the *variances* of the two populations are the same. This test is important mainly as a check on whether you have met the assumption of equal population variances (called "homogeneity of variance"). If this test is significant (that is, the value in the "Sig." column is less than .05), this assumption is brought into question. However, in this example, the result is clearly not significant (.766 is well above .05), so we have no reason to doubt the assumption of equal population variances. Thus, we can feel more confident that whatever conclusion we draw from the *t* test will be accurate.

The *t* test results begin with the column labeled "*t*." Note that there are two rows of *t* test results. The first row (a *t* of 2.425, *df* of 18, and so on), labeled "Equal variances assumed" (on the left hand side of the table), shows the *t* test results assuming the population variances are equal. The second row (a *t* of 2.425, *df* of 17.880, and so on), labeled "Equal variances not assumed," shows the *t* test results if we do not assume that the population variances are equal. In the present example (as in most real-life cases), the Levene test was not significant; so we use the *t* test results assuming equal population variances. Notice that the values for "*t*" (the sample's *t* score), "*df*" (degrees of freedom), and "Std. Error Difference" (the standard deviation of the distribution of differences between means, $S_{\text{Difference}}$) in Figure 8–8 are the same (within rounding error) as their respective values we figured by hand in Table 8–1. The column labeled "Sig. (2-tailed)" shows the exact significance level of the sample's *t* score. The significance level of .026 is less than our .05 cutoff for this example, which means that you can reject the null hypothesis and the research hypothesis is supported. (You can ignore the final two columns of the table, listed under the heading "95% Confidence Interval of the Difference." These columns refer to the raw scores corresponding to the *t* scores at the bottom 2.5% and the top 2.5% of the *t* distribution; see Chapter 5 for a discussion of confidence intervals). Note that SPSS does not know if you are doing a one-tailed or a two-tailed test. So it always gives results for a two-tailed test. If you are doing a one-tailed test, the true significance level is exactly half of what is given by SPSS.

Chapter Notes

1. In a real research situation, the figuring for a *t* test for independent means is usually all done by computer (see this chapter's *Using SPSS* section). However, if you ever have to do a *t* test for independent means for an actual research study by hand (or with just a hand calculator), you may find the following formula useful:

$$t = \frac{M_1 - M_2}{\sqrt{\frac{(N_1 - 1)(S_1^2) + (N_2 - 1)(S_2^2)}{N_1 + N_2 - 2}\left(\frac{1}{N_1} + \frac{1}{N_2}\right)}}$$

2. Cohen (1988, pp. 28–39) provides more detailed tables in terms of number of participants, levels of effect size, and significance levels. Note that Cohen describes the significance level by the letter *a* (for "alpha level"), with a subscript of either 1 or 2, referring to a one-tailed or two-tailed test. For example, a table that refers to "$a_1 = .05$" at the top means that this is the table for $p < .05$, one-tailed.

3. Cohen (1988, pp. 54–55) provides fuller tables, indicating needed numbers of participants for levels of power other than 80%; for effect sizes other than .20, .50, and .80; and for other significance levels. If you just need a rough approximation, Dunlap and Myers (1997) have developed a shortcut for finding the approximate number of participants needed for studies using the *t* test for independent means. For 50% power, the number of participants needed per group is approximately $8/d^2 + 1$. For 80%–90% power, $16/d^2 + 2$.

The *t* score for a *t* test for independent means is the result of subtracting Sample 2's mean from Sample 1's mean and dividing that difference by the square root of the following: multiplying one less than the number of scores in Sample 1 by Population 1's estimated population variance and adding this product to the result of multiplying one less than the number of scores in Sample 2 by Population 2's estimated population variance, and then dividing this summed result by two less than the sum of the number of scores in Sample 1 and the number of scores in Sample 2, and then taking the result of this division and multiplying it by the result of adding one divided by the number of scores in Sample 1 to one divided by the number of scores in Sample 2.

CHAPTER 9

Introduction to the Analysis of Variance

Chapter Outline

- ✪ Basic Logic of the Analysis of Variance   311
- ✪ Carrying Out an Analysis of Variance   319
- ✪ Hypothesis Testing with the Analysis of Variance   327
- ✪ Assumptions in the Analysis of Variance   331
- ✪ Planned Contrasts   334
- ✪ Post Hoc Comparisons   337
- ✪ Effect Size and Power for the Analysis of Variance   339
- ✪ Controversy: Omnibus Tests versus Planned Contrasts   343

- ✪ Analyses of Variance in Research Articles   344
- ✪ Advanced Topic: The Structural Model in the Analysis of Variance   345
- ✪ Summary   351
- ✪ Key Terms   352
- ✪ Example Worked-Out Problems   353
- ✪ Practice Problems   357
- ✪ Using SPSS   364
- ✪ Chapter Notes   368

TIP FOR SUCCESS

This chapter assumes you understand the logic of hypothesis testing and the *t* test (particularly estimated population variance and the distribution of means). So be sure you understand the relevant material in Chapters 4, 5, 7, and 8 before starting this chapter.

In Chapter 8, you learned about the *t* test for independent means, a procedure for comparing *two groups of scores* from *entirely separate groups of people* (such as an experimental group and a control group). In this chapter, you will learn about a procedure for comparing *more than two groups of scores,* each of which is from an *entirely separate group of people.*

We will begin with an example. Cindy Hazan and Philip Shaver (1987) arranged to have the *Rocky Mountain News,* a large Denver area newspaper, print a mail-in survey. The survey included the question shown in Table 9–1 to measure what is called attachment style. (How would *you* answer this item?) Those who selected the first choice are "secure"; those who selected the second, "avoidant"; and those who selected

Table 9-1 Question Used in Hazan and Shaver (1987) Newspaper Survey
Which of the following best describes your feelings? [Check one]
[ ] I find it relatively easy to get close to others and am comfortable depending on them and having them depend on me. I don't often worry about being abandoned or about someone getting too close to me.
[ ] I am somewhat uncomfortable being close to others; I find it difficult to trust them completely, difficult to allow myself to depend on them. I am nervous when anyone gets too close, and often, love partners want me to be more intimate than I feel comfortable being.
[ ] I find that others are reluctant to get as close as I would like. I often worry that my partner doesn't really love me or won't want to stay with me. I want to merge completely with another person, and this desire sometimes scares people away.

Source: Hazan and Shaver (1987, p. 515).

the third, "anxious-ambivalent." These attachment styles are thought to be different ways of behaving and thinking in close relationships that develop from a person's experience with early caretakers (Mikulincer & Shaver, 2007). (Of course, this single item is only a very rough measure that works for a large survey but is certainly not definitive in any particular person.) Readers also answered questions about various aspects of love, including amount of jealousy. Hazan and Shaver then compared the amount of jealousy reported by people with the three different attachment styles.

With a *t* test for independent means, Hazan and Shaver could have compared the mean jealousy scores of any two of the attachment styles. Instead, they were interested in differences among all three attachment styles. The statistical procedure for testing variation among the means of *more than two groups* is called the **analysis of variance,** abbreviated as **ANOVA.** (You could use the analysis of variance for a study with only two groups, but the simpler *t* test gives the same result.)

In this chapter, we introduce the analysis of variance, focusing on the situation in which the different groups being compared each have the same number of scores. In an Advanced Topic section later in the chapter, we describe a more flexible way of thinking about analysis of variance that allows groups to have different numbers of scores. In Chapter 10, we consider situations in which the different groups are arrayed across more than one dimension. For example, in the same analysis we might consider both gender and attachment style, making six groups in all (female secure, male secure, female avoidant, etc.), arrayed across the two dimensions of gender and attachment style. This situation is known as a *factorial analysis of variance.* To emphasize the difference from factorial analysis of variance, what you learn in this chapter is often called a *one-way analysis of variance.* (If this is confusing, don't worry. We will go through it slowly and systematically in Chapter 10. We only mention this now so that, if you hear these terms, you will not be surprised.)

Basic Logic of the Analysis of Variance

The null hypothesis in an analysis of variance is that the several populations being compared all have the same mean. For example, in the attachment style example, the null hypothesis is that the populations of secure, avoidant, and anxious-ambivalent people all have the same degree of jealousy. The research hypothesis would be that the degree of jealousy differs among these three populations.

Hypothesis testing in analysis of variance is about whether the means of the samples differ more than you would expect if the null hypothesis were true. This question about *means* is answered, surprisingly, by analyzing *variances* (hence the name

analysis of variance (ANOVA)
hypothesis-testing procedure for studies with three or more groups.

analysis of variance). Among other reasons, you focus on variances because, when you want to know how several means differ, you are asking about the variation among those means.

Thus, to understand the logic of analysis of variance, we consider variances. In particular, we begin by discussing *two different ways* of estimating population variances. As you will see, the analysis of variance is about a comparison of the results of these two different ways of estimating population variances.

Estimating Population Variance from Variation Within Each Sample

With the analysis of variance, as with the *t* test, you do not know the true population variances. However, as with the *t* test, you can estimate the variance of each of the populations from the scores in the samples. Also, as with the *t* test, you assume in the analysis of variance that all populations have the *same* variance. This allows you to average the estimates from each sample into a single pooled estimate, called the **within-groups estimate of the population variance.** It is an average of estimates figured entirely from the scores *within* each of the samples.

One of the most important things to remember about this within-groups estimate is that it is not affected by whether the null hypothesis is true. This estimate comes out the same whether the means of the populations are all the same (the null hypothesis is true) or the means of the populations are not all the same (the null hypothesis is false). This estimate comes out the same because it focuses only on the variation *inside* each population. Thus, it doesn't matter how far apart the means of the different populations are.

If the variation in scores within each sample is not affected by whether the null hypothesis is true, what determines the level of within-group variation? The answer is that chance factors (that is, factors that are unknown to the researcher) account for why different people in a sample have different scores. These chance factors include the fact that different people respond differently to the same situation or treatment and that there may be some experimental error associated with the measurement of the variable of interest. Thus, we can think of the within-groups population variance estimate as an estimate based on chance (or unknown) factors that cause different people in a study to have different scores.

Estimating the Population Variance from Variation Between the Means of the Samples

There is also a second way to estimate the population variance. Each sample's mean is a number in its own right. If there are several samples, there are several such numbers, and these numbers will have some variation among them. The variation among these means gives another way to estimate the variance in the populations that the samples come from. Just how this works is a bit tricky; so follow the next two sections closely.

When the Null Hypothesis Is True   First, consider the situation in which the null hypothesis is true. In this situation, all samples come from populations that have the same mean. Remember, we are always assuming that all populations have the same variance (and also that they are all normal curves). Thus, if the null hypothesis is true, all populations are identical and thus they have the same mean, variance, and shape.

within-groups estimate of the population variance   estimate of the variance of the population of individuals based on the variation among the scores in each of the actual groups studied.

However, even when the populations are identical (that is, even when the null hypothesis is true), samples from the different populations will each be a little different. How different can the sample means be? That depends on how much variation there is in each population. If a population has very little variation in the scores in it, then the means of samples from that population (or any identical population) will tend to be very similar to each other. When the null hypothesis is true, the variability among the sample means is influenced by the same chance factors that influence the variability among the scores within each sample.

What if several identical populations (with the same population mean) have a lot of variation in the scores within each? In that situation, if you take one sample from each population, the means of those samples could easily be very different from each other. Being very different, the variance of these means will be large. The point is that the more variance within each of several identical populations, the more variance there will be among the means of samples when you take a random sample from each population.

Suppose you were studying samples of six children from each of three large playgrounds (the populations in this example). If each playground had children who were all either 7 or 8 years old, the means of your three samples would all be between 7 and 8. Thus, there would not be much variance among those means. However, if each playground had children ranging from 3 to 12 years old, the means of the three samples would probably vary quite a bit. What this shows is that the variation among the means of samples is related directly to the amount of variation in each of the populations from which the samples are taken. The more variation in each population, the more variation there is among the means of samples taken from those populations.

This principle is shown in Figure 9–1. The three identical populations on the left have small variances, and the three identical populations on the right have large variances. In each set of three identical populations, even though the *means of the populations* (shown by triangles) are exactly the same, the *means of the samples* from those populations (shown by Xs) are not exactly the same. Most important, the sample means from the populations that each have a small amount of variance are closer together (have less variance among them). The sample means from the populations that each have more variance are more spread out (have more variance among them).

We have now seen that the variation among the means of samples taken from identical populations is related directly to the variation of the scores in each of those populations. This has a very important and perhaps surprising implication: it should be possible to estimate the variance in each population from the variation among the means of our samples.

Such an estimate is called a **between-groups estimate of the population variance.** (It has this name because it is based on the variation between the means of the samples, the "groups." Grammatically, it ought to be *among* groups, but *between* groups is traditional.) You will learn how to figure this estimate later in the chapter.

So far, all of this logic we have considered has assumed that the null hypothesis is true, so that there is no variation among the means of the *populations.* In this situation, the between-groups estimate of the population variance (which reflects variability in the means of the samples) is influenced by the chance factors that cause different people in the same sample to have different scores. Let's now consider what happens when the null hypothesis is not true, when instead the research hypothesis is true.

When the Null Hypothesis Is Not True   If the null hypothesis is not true (and thus the research hypothesis is true), the populations themselves have different means. In this situation, variation among the means of samples taken from these

between-groups estimate of the population variance   estimate of the variance of the population of individuals based on the variation among the means of the groups studied.

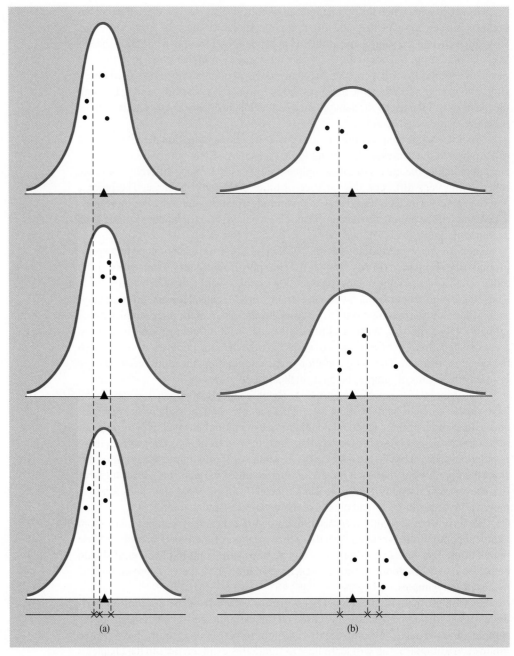

Figure 9–1 Means of samples from identical populations will not be identical. (a) Sample means from populations with less variation will vary less. (b) Sample means from populations with more variation will vary more. (Population means are indicated by a triangle, sample means by an X.)

populations is still caused by the chance factors that cause variation within the populations. So the larger the variation within the populations, the larger the variation will be among the means of samples taken from the populations. However, in this situation, in which the research hypothesis is true, variation among the means of the samples *also* is caused by variation among the population means. You can think of

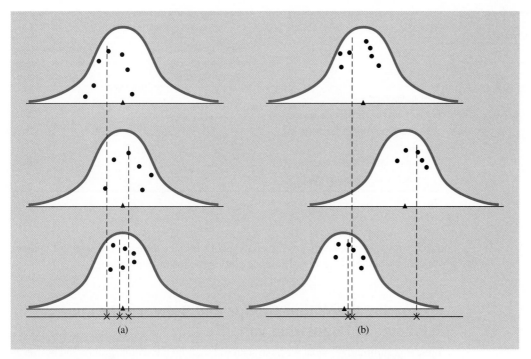

Figure 9–2   Means of samples from populations whose means differ (b) will vary more than sample means taken from populations whose means are the same (a). (Population means are indicated by a triangle, sample means by an X.)

this variation among population means as resulting from a treatment effect—that is, the different treatment received by the groups (as in an experiment) causes the groups to have different means. So, when the research hypothesis is true, the means of the samples are spread out for two different reasons: (1) because of variation in each of the populations (due to chance factors) and (2) because of variation among the population means (that is, a treatment effect). The left side of Figure 9–2 shows populations with the same means (shown by triangles) and the means of samples taken from them (shown by Xs). (This is the same situation as in both sides of Figure 9–1.) The right side of Figure 9–2 shows three populations with different means (shown by triangles) and the means of samples taken from them (shown by Xs). (This is the situation we have just been discussing.) Notice that the means of the samples are more spread out in the situation on the right side of Figure 9–2. This is true even though the variations in the populations are the same for the situation on both sides of Figure 9–2. This additional spread (variance) for the means on the right side of Figure 9–2 is due to the populations having different means.

In summary, the between-groups estimate of the population variance is figured based on the variation among the means of the samples. If the null hypothesis is true, this estimate gives an accurate indication of the variation within the populations (that is, the variation due to chance factors). But if the null hypothesis is false, this method of estimating the population variance is influenced both by the variation within the populations (the variation due to chance factors) and the variation among the population means (the variation due to a treatment effect). It will not give an accurate estimate of the variation within the populations because it also will be affected by the variation among the populations. This difference between the two situations has important

TIP FOR SUCCESS

You may want to read this paragraph again to ensure that you fully understand the logic we are presenting.

TIP FOR SUCCESS

Table 9–2 summarizes the logic of the analysis of variance. Test your understanding of this logic by trying to explain Table 9–2, without referring to the book. You might try writing your answer down and swapping it with someone else in your class.

Table 9–2   Sources of Variation in Within-Groups and Between-Groups Variance Estimates

	Variation Within Populations (Due to Chance Factors)	Variation Between Populations (Due to a Treatment Effect)
Null hypothesis is true		
Within-groups estimate reflects	✓	
Between-groups estimate reflects	✓	
Research hypothesis is true		
Within-groups estimate reflects	✓	
Between-groups estimate reflects	✓	✓

implications. It is what makes the analysis of variance a method of testing hypotheses about whether there is a difference among means of populations.

Comparing the Within-Groups and Between-Groups Estimates of Population Variance

Table 9–2 summarizes what we have seen so far about the within-groups and between-groups estimates of population variance, both when the null hypothesis is true and when the research hypothesis is true. When the null hypothesis is true, the within-groups and between-groups estimates are based on the same thing (that is, the chance variation within populations). Literally, they are estimates of the same population variance. Therefore, when the null hypothesis is true, both estimates should be about the same. (Only *about* the same; these are estimates). Here is another way of describing this similarity of the between-groups estimate and the within-groups estimate when the null hypothesis is true: In this situation, the ratio of the between-groups estimate to the within-groups estimate should be approximately one to one. For example, if the within-groups estimate is 107.5, the between-groups estimate should be around 107.5, so that the ratio would be about 1. (A ratio is found by dividing one number by the other; thus $107.5/107.5 = 1$.)

The situation is quite different when the null hypothesis is not true. As shown in Table 9–2, when the research hypothesis is true, the between-groups estimate is influenced by two sources of variation: (a) the variation of the scores in each population (due to chance factors) and (b) the variation of the means of the populations from each other (due to a treatment effect). Yet even when the research hypothesis is true, the within-groups estimate still is influenced *only* by the variation in the populations. Therefore, when the research hypothesis is true, the between-groups estimate should be *larger* than the within-groups estimate. In this situation, the ratio of the between-groups estimate to the within-groups estimate should be greater than 1. For example, the between-groups estimate might be 638.9 and the within-groups estimate 107.5, making a ratio of 638.9 to 107.5, or 5.94. In this example the between-groups estimate is nearly six times bigger (5.94 times to be exact) than the within-groups estimate.

This is the central principle of the analysis of variance: *When the null hypothesis is true, the ratio of the between-groups population variance estimate to the within-groups population variance estimate should be about 1. When the research hypothesis is true, this ratio should be greater than 1.* If you figure this ratio and it comes out much

BOX 9–1   Sir Ronald Fisher, Caustic Genius of Statistics

Courtesy of the Library of Congress

Ronald A. Fisher, a contemporary of William Gosset (see Chapter 7, Box 7–1) and Karl Pearson (see Chapter 13, Box 13–1), was probably the brightest and certainly the most productive of this close-knit group of British statisticians. In the process of writing 300 papers and seven books, he developed many of the modern field's key concepts: variance, analysis of variance, significance levels, the null hypothesis, and almost all of our basic ideas of research design, including the fundamental importance of randomization.

A family legend is that little Ronald, born in 1890, was so fascinated by math that one day, at age 3, when put into his highchair for breakfast, he asked his nurse, "What is a half of a half?" Told it was a quarter, he asked, "What's half of a quarter?" To that answer he wanted to know what was half of an eighth. At the next answer he purportedly thought a moment and said, "Then I suppose that a half of a sixteenth must be a thirty-toof." Ah, baby stories.

As a grown man, however, Fisher seems to have been anything but darling. Some observers ascribe this to a cold and unemotional mother, but, whatever the reason, throughout his life he was embroiled in bitter feuds, even with scholars who had previously been his closest allies and who certainly ought to have been comrades in research.

Fisher's thin ration of compassion extended to his readers as well; not only was his writing hopelessly obscure, but it often simply failed to supply important assumptions and proofs. Gosset said that when Fisher began a sentence with "Evidently," it meant two hours of hard work before one could hope to see why the point was evident.

Indeed, his lack of empathy extended to all of humankind. Like Galton, Fisher was fond of eugenics, favoring anything that might increase the birthrate of the upper and professional classes and skilled artisans. Not only did he see contraception as a poor idea—fearing that the least desirable persons would use it least—but he defended infanticide as serving an evolutionary function. It may be just as well that his opportunities to experiment with breeding never extended beyond the raising of his own children and some crops of potatoes and wheat.

Although Fisher eventually became the Galton Professor of Eugenics at University College, his most influential appointment probably came when he was invited to Iowa State College in Ames for the summers of 1931 and 1936 (where he was said to be so put out with the terrible heat that he stored his sheets in the refrigerator all day). At Ames, Fisher greatly impressed George Snedecor, an American professor of mathematics also working on agricultural problems. Consequently, Snedecor wrote a textbook of statistics for agriculture that borrowed heavily from Fisher's work. The book so popularized Fisher's ideas about statistics and research design that its second edition sold 100,000 copies.

You can learn more about Fisher at the following Web site: *http://www-groups.dcs.st-and.ac.uk/~history/ Biographies/Fisher.html.*

Sources: Peters (1987); Salsburg (2001); Stigler (1986); Tankard (1984).

---

greater than 1, you can reject the null hypothesis. That is, it is unlikely that the null hypothesis could be true and the between-groups estimate be a lot bigger than the within-groups estimate.

The *F* Ratio

This crucial ratio of the between-groups to the within-groups population variance estimate is called an ***F* ratio.** (The *F* is for Sir Ronald Fisher, an eminent statistician who developed the analysis of variance; see Box 9–1.)

The *F* Distribution and the *F* Table

We have said that if the crucial ratio of between-groups estimate to within-groups estimate (the *F* ratio) is a lot larger than 1, you can reject the null hypothesis. The next question is, "Just how much bigger than 1 should it be?"

***F* ratio**   ratio of the between-groups population variance estimate to the within-groups population variance estimate.

Statisticians have developed the mathematics of an *F* **distribution** and have prepared tables of *F* ratios. For any given situation, you merely look up in an *F* **table** how extreme an *F* ratio is needed to reject the null hypothesis at, say, the .05 level. (You learn to use the *F* table later in the chapter.)

For an example of an *F* ratio, let's return to the attachment style study. The results of that study, for jealousy, were as follows: The between-groups population variance estimate was 23.27, and the within-groups population variance estimate was .53. (You learn shortly how to figure these estimates on your own.) The ratio of the between-groups to the within-groups variance estimates (23.27/.53) came out to 43.91; that is, $F = 43.91$. This *F* ratio is considerably larger than 1. The *F* ratio needed to reject the null hypothesis at the .05 level in this study is only 3.01. Thus, the researchers confidently rejected the null hypothesis and concluded that the amount of jealousy is not the same for the three attachment styles. (Mean jealous ratings were 2.17 for secures, 2.57 for avoidants, and 2.88 for anxious-ambivalents.)

An Analogy

Some students find an analogy helpful in understanding the analysis of variance. The analogy is to what engineers call the signal-to-noise ratio. For example, your ability to make out the words in a staticky cell phone conversation depends on the strength of the signal versus the amount of random noise. With the *F* ratio in the analysis of variance, the difference among the means of the samples is like the signal; it is the information of interest. The variation within the samples is like the noise. When the variation among the samples is sufficiently great in comparison to the variation within the samples, you conclude that there is a significant effect.

How are you doing?

1. When do you use an analysis of variance?
2. (a) What is the within-groups population variance estimate based on? (b) How is it affected by the null hypothesis being true or not? (c) Why?
3. (a) What is the between-groups population variance estimate based on? (b) How is it affected by the null hypothesis being true or not? (c) Why?
4. What are two sources of variation that can contribute to the between-groups population variance estimate?
5. (a) What is the *F* ratio; (b) why is it usually about 1 when the null hypothesis is true; and (c) why is it usually larger than 1 when the null hypothesis is false?

F **distribution** mathematically defined curve that is the comparison distribution used in an analysis of variance.

F **table** table of cutoff scores on the *F* distribution.

4. Two sources of variation that can contribute to the between-groups population variance estimate are (i) variation among the scores in each of the populations (that is, variation due to chance factors) and (ii) variation among the means of the populations (that is, variation due to a treatment effect).
5. (a) The *F* ratio is the ratio of the between-groups population variance estimate to the within-groups population variance estimate. (b) Both estimates are based entirely on the same source of variation—the variation among the scores in each of the populations (that is, due to chance factors). (c) The between-groups estimate is also influenced by the variation among the means of the populations (that is, a treatment effect) whereas the within-groups estimate is not. Thus, when the null hypothesis is false (and thus the means of the populations are not the same), the between-groups estimate will be bigger than the within-groups estimate.

Carrying Out an Analysis of Variance

Now that we have considered the basic logic of the analysis of variance, we will go through an example to illustrate the details. (We use a fictional study to keep the numbers simple.)

Suppose a social psychologist is studying the influence of knowledge of previous criminal record on juries' perceptions of the guilt or innocence of defendants. The researcher recruits 15 volunteers who have been selected for jury duty (but have not yet served at a trial). The researcher shows them a video of a four-hour trial in which a woman is accused of passing bad checks. Before viewing the tape, however, all of the research participants are given a "background sheet" with age, marital status, education, and other such information about the accused woman. The sheet is the same for all 15 participants, with one difference. For five of the participants, the last section of the sheet says that the woman has been convicted several times before of passing bad checks; we will call those participants the Criminal Record group. For five other participants, the last section of the sheet says the woman has a completely clean criminal record—the Clean Record group. For the remaining five participants, the sheet does not mention anything about criminal record one way or the other—the No Information group.

The participants are randomly assigned to the groups. After viewing the tape of the trial, all 15 participants make a rating on a 10-point scale, which runs from completely sure she is innocent (1) to completely sure she is guilty (10). The results of this fictional study are shown in Table 9–3. As you can see, the means of the three groups are different (8, 4, and 5). Yet there is also quite a bit of variation within each of the three groups. Population variance estimates from the scores in each of these three groups are 4.5, 5.0, and 6.5.

You need to figure the following numbers to test the hypothesis that the three populations are different: (a) a population variance estimate based on the variation of the scores in each of the samples, (b) a population variance estimate based on the

Table 9-3 Results of the Criminal Record Study (Fictional Data)

Criminal Record Group			Clean Record Group			No Information Group		
Rating	Deviation from Mean	Squared Deviation from Mean	Rating	Deviation from Mean	Squared Deviation from Mean	Rating	Deviation from Mean	Squared Deviation from Mean
10	2	4	5	1	1	4	−1	1
7	−1	1	1	−3	9	6	1	1
5	−3	9	3	−1	1	9	4	16
10	2	4	7	3	9	3	−2	4
8	0	0	4	0	0	3	−2	4
Σ: 40	0	18	20	0	20	25	0	26

$M = 40/5 = 8.$
$S^2 = 18/4 = 4.5.$

$M = 20/5 = 4.$
$S^2 = 20/4 = 5.0.$

$M = 25/5 = 5.$
$S^2 = 26/4 = 6.5.$

differences among the group means, and (c) the ratio of the two, the F ratio. (In addition, you need the significance cutoff F from an F table.)

Figuring the Within-Groups Estimate of the Population Variance

You can estimate the population variance from any one group (that is, from any one sample) using the usual method of estimating a population variance from a sample. First, you figure the sum of the squared deviation scores. That is, you take the deviation of each score from its group's mean, square that deviation score, and sum all the squared deviation scores. Second, you divide that sum of squared deviation scores by that group's degrees of freedom. (The degrees of freedom for a group are the number of scores in the group minus 1.) For the example, as shown in Table 9–3, this gives an estimated population variance of 4.5 based on the Criminal Record group's scores, an estimate of 5.0 based on the Clean Record group's scores, and an estimate of 6.5 based on the No Information group's scores.

Once again, in the analysis of variance, as with the t test, we assume that the populations have the same variance and that the estimates based on each sample's scores are all estimating the same true population variance. The sample sizes are equal in this example; so the estimate for each group is based on an equal amount of information. Thus (unlike with the t test), you can pool these variance estimates by straight averaging. This gives an overall estimate of the population variance based on the variation within groups of 5.33 (that is, the sum of 4.5, 5.0, and 6.5, which is 16, divided by 3, the number of groups).

To summarize, the two steps are:

Ⓐ **Figure population variance estimates based on each group's scores.**
Ⓑ **Average these variance estimates.** The estimated population variance based on the variation of the scores within each of the groups is the within-groups variance estimate. This is symbolized as S^2_{Within} or MS_{Within}. MS_{Within} is short for *mean squares within.* The term *mean squares* is another name for the variance, because the variance is the mean of the squared deviations. (S^2_{Within} or MS_{Within} is also sometimes called the error variance and symbolized as S^2_{Error} or MS_{Error}.)

S^2_{Within} **or** MS_{Within} within-groups estimate of the population variance.

In terms of a formula,

$$S^2_{\text{Within}} \text{ or } MS_{\text{Within}} = \frac{S^2_1 + S^2_2 + \cdots + S^2_{\text{Last}}}{N_{\text{Groups}}} \qquad \textbf{(9–1)}$$

> The within-groups population variance estimate is the sum of the population variance estimates based on each sample, divided by the number of groups.

In this formula, S^2_1 is the estimated population variance based on the scores in the first group (the group from Population 1), S^2_2 is the estimated population variance based on the scores in the second group, and S^2_{Last} is the estimated population variance based on the scores in the last group. (The dots, or ellipsis, in the formula show that you are to fill in a population variance estimate for as many other groups as there are in the analysis.) N_{Groups} is the number of groups.

Using this formula for our figuring, we get

$$S^2_{\text{Within}} = \frac{S^2_1 + S^2_2 + \cdots + S^2_{\text{Last}}}{N_{\text{Groups}}} = \frac{4.5 + 5.0 + 6.5}{3} = \frac{16}{3} = 5.33$$

Figuring the Between-Groups Estimate of the Population Variance

Figuring the between-groups estimate of the population variance also involves two steps (though quite different ones from the within-groups estimate). First estimate, from the means of your samples, the variance of a distribution of means. Second, based on the variance of this distribution of means, figure the variance of the population of individuals. Here are the two steps in more detail:

❶ **Estimate the variance of the distribution of means:** Add up the sample means' squared deviations from the overall mean (the mean of all the scores) and divide this by the number of means minus 1.

You can think of the means of your samples as taken from a distribution of means. Follow the standard procedure of using the scores in a sample to estimate the variance of the population from which these scores are taken. In this situation, you think of the means of your samples as the scores and the distribution of means as the population from which these scores come. What this all boils down to are the following procedures. You begin by figuring the sum of squared deviations. (You find the mean of your sample means, figure the deviation of each sample mean from this mean of means, square each of these deviations, and then sum these squared deviations.) Then, divide this sum of squared deviations by the degrees of freedom, which is the number of means minus 1. In terms of a formula (when sample sizes are all equal),

> **grand mean (*GM*)**   overall mean of all the scores, regardless of what group they are in; when group sizes are equal, mean of the group means.

$$S^2_M = \frac{\sum (M - GM)^2}{df_{\text{Between}}} \qquad \textbf{(9–2)}$$

> The estimated variance of the distribution of means is the sum of each sample mean's squared deviation from the grand mean, divided by the degrees of freedom for the between-groups population variance estimate.

In this formula, S^2_M is the estimated variance of the distribution of means (estimated based on the means of the samples in your study). M is the mean of each of your samples. GM is the **grand mean,** the overall mean of all your scores, which is also the mean of your means. df_{Between} is the degrees of freedom in the between-groups estimate, the number of groups minus 1. Stated as a formula,

$$df_{\text{Between}} = N_{\text{Groups}} - 1 \qquad \textbf{(9–3)}$$

> The degrees of freedom for the between-groups population variance estimate is the number of groups minus 1.

In the criminal record example, the three means are 8, 4, and 5. The figuring of S^2_M is shown in Table 9–4.

Table 9–4   Estimated Variance of the Distribution of Means Based on Means of the Three Experimental Groups in the Criminal Record Study (Fictional Data)

Sample Means	Deviation from Grand Mean	Squared Deviation from Grand Mean
(M)	$(M - GM)$	$(M - GM)^2$
4	−1.67	2.79
8	2.33	5.43
5	−.67	.45
Σ 17	−0.01	8.67

$GM = (\Sigma M)/N_{\text{Groups}} = 17/3 = 5.67$; $S_M^2 = \Sigma(M - GM)^2/df_{\text{Between}} = 8.67/2 = 4.34$.

Source: Hazan, C., & Shaver, P. (1987). Romantic love conceptualized as an attachment process. *Journal of Personality and Social Psychology, 52,* 515. Published by the American Psychological Association. Reprinted with permission.

❷ **Figure the estimated variance of the population of individual scores:** Multiply the variance of the distribution of means by the number of scores in each group.

What we just figured in Step ❶, from a sample of a few means, is the estimated variance of a distribution of means. From this we want to estimate the variance of the population (the distribution of individuals) on which the distribution of means is based. We saw in Chapter 5 that the variance of a distribution of means is smaller than the variance of the population (the distribution of individuals) that it is based on. This is because means are less likely to be extreme than are individual scores (because any one sample is unlikely to include several scores that are extreme in the same direction). Specifically, you learned in Chapter 5 that the variance of a distribution of means is the variance of the distribution of individual scores divided by the number of scores in each sample.

Now, however, we are going to reverse what we did in Chapter 5. In Chapter 5 you figured the variance of the distribution of means by *dividing* the variance of the distribution of individuals by the sample size. Now you are going to figure the variance of the distribution of individuals by *multiplying* the variance of the distribution of means by the sample size (see Table 9–5). That is, to come up with the variance of the population of individuals, you multiply your estimate of the variance of the distribution of means by the sample size in each of the groups. The result of all this is the between-groups variance estimate. Stated as a formula (for when sample sizes are equal),

$$S_{\text{Between}}^2 \text{ or } MS_{\text{Between}} = S_M^2(n) \tag{9–4}$$

> The between-groups population variance estimate (or mean squares between) is the estimated variance of the distribution of means multiplied by the number of scores in each group.
>
> S_{Between}^2 or MS_{Between} between-groups estimate of the population variance.

In this formula, S_{Between}^2 or MS_{Between} is the estimate of the population variance based on the variation between the means (the between-groups population variance estimate). n is the number of participants in each sample.

Let's return to our example in which there were five participants in each sample and an estimated variance of the distribution of means of 4.34. In this example,

Table 9–5   Comparison of Figuring the Variance of a Distribution of Means from the Variance of a Distribution of Individuals, and the Reverse

- From distribution of individuals to distribution of means: $S_M^2 = S^2/n$
- From distribution of means to distribution of individuals: $S^2 = (S_M^2)(n)$

multiplying 4.34 by 5 gives a between-groups population variance estimate of 21.70. In terms of the formula,

$$S^2_{\text{Between}} \text{ or } MS_{\text{Between}} = (S^2_M)(n) = (4.34)(5) = 21.70$$

Figuring the *F* Ratio

The *F* ratio is the ratio of the between-groups to the within-groups estimate of the population variance. Stated as a formula,

$$F = \frac{S^2_{\text{Between}}}{S^2_{\text{Within}}} \text{ or } \frac{MS_{\text{Between}}}{MS_{\text{Within}}} \qquad (9\text{–}5)$$

> The *F* ratio is the between-groups population variance estimate (or mean squares between) divided by the within-groups population variance estimate (or mean squares within).

In the example, the ratio of between to within is 21.70 to 5.33. Carrying out the division gives an *F* ratio of 4.07. In terms of the formula,

$$F = \frac{S^2_{\text{Between}}}{S^2_{\text{Within}}} \text{ or } \frac{MS_{\text{Between}}}{MS_{\text{Within}}} = \frac{21.70}{5.33} = 4.07$$

The *F* Distribution

You are not quite done. You still need to find the cutoff for the *F* ratio that is large enough to reject the null hypothesis. This requires a distribution of *F* ratios that you can use to figure out what is an extreme *F* ratio.

In practice, you simply look up the needed cutoff on a table (or read the exact significance from the computer output). To understand where that number on the table comes from, you need to understand the *F* distribution. The easiest way to understand this distribution is to think about how you would go about making one.

Start with three identical populations. Next, randomly select five scores from each. Then, on the basis of these three samples (of five scores each), figure the *F* ratio. (That is, use these scores to make a within-groups estimate and a between-groups estimate, then divide the between estimate by the within estimate.) Let's say that you do this and the *F* ratio you come up with is 1.36. Now you select three new random samples of five scores each and figure the *F* ratio using these three samples. Perhaps you get an *F* of .93. If you do this whole process many, many times, you will eventually get a lot of *F* ratios. The distribution of all possible *F* ratios figured in this way (from random samples from identical populations) is called the *F* distribution. Figure 9–3 shows an example of an *F* distribution. (There are many different *F* distributions, and each has a slightly different shape. The exact shape depends on how many samples you take each time and how many scores are in each sample. The general shape is like that shown in the figure.)

No one actually goes about making *F* distributions in this way. It is a mathematical distribution whose exact characteristics can be found from a formula. Statisticians can also prove that, if you had the patience to follow this procedure of taking random samples and figuring the *F* ratio of each for a very long time, you would get the same result.

As you can see in Figure 9–3, the *F* distribution is not symmetrical but has a long tail on the right. The reason for the positive skew is that an *F* distribution is a distribution of ratios of variances. Variances are always positive numbers. (A variance is an average of squared deviations, and anything squared is a positive number.) A ratio of a positive number to a positive number can never be less than 0. Yet there is nothing to stop a ratio from being a very high number. Thus, the *F* ratio's

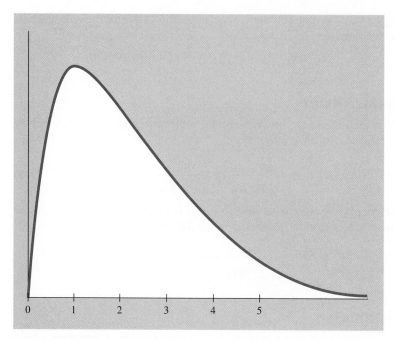

Figure 9-3 An *F* distribution.

between-groups (or numerator) degrees of freedom (df_{Between}) degrees of freedom used in the between-groups estimate of the population variance in an analysis of variance (the numerator of the *F* ratio); number of scores free to vary (number of means minus 1) in figuring the between-groups estimate of the population variance.

within-groups (or denominator) degrees of freedom (df_{Within}) degrees of freedom used in the within-groups estimate of the population variance in an analysis of variance, denominator of the *F* ratio; number of scores free to vary (number of scores in each group minus 1, summed over all the groups) in figuring the within-groups population variance estimate.

> The degrees of freedom for the within-groups population variance estimate is the sum of the degrees of freedom used in making estimates of the population variance from each sample.

distribution cannot be lower than 0 and can rise quite high.[1] (Most *F* ratios pile up near 1, but they spread out more on the positive side, where they have more room to spread out.)

The *F* Table

The *F* table is a little more complicated than the *t* table. This is because there is a different *F* distribution according to both the degrees of freedom used in the between-groups variance estimate and the degrees of freedom used in the within-groups variance estimate. That is, you have to take into account two different degrees of freedom to look up the needed cutoff. One is the **between-groups degrees of freedom.** It is also called the *numerator degrees of freedom.* This is the degrees of freedom you use in the between-groups variance estimate, the numerator of the *F* ratio. As shown earlier in Formula 9–3, the degrees of freedom for the between-groups population variance estimate is equal to the number of groups minus 1 ($df_{\text{Between}} = N_{\text{Groups}} - 1$).

The other type of degrees of freedom is the **within-groups degrees of freedom,** also called the *denominator degrees of freedom.* This is the sum of the degrees of freedom from each sample you use when figuring out the within-groups variance estimate, the denominator of the *F* ratio.

Stated as a formula,

$$df_{\text{Within}} = df_1 + df_2 + \cdots + df_{\text{Last}} \tag{9-6}$$

In the criminal record study example, the between-groups degrees of freedom is 2. (There are 3 means, minus 1.) In terms of the formula,

$$df_{\text{Between}} = N_{\text{Groups}} - 1 = 3 - 1 = 2$$

Table 9-6 Selected Cutoffs for the *F* Distribution (with Values Highlighted for the Criminal Record Study)

Denominator Degrees of Freedom	Significance Level	Numerator Degrees of Freedom					
		1	2	3	4	5	6
10	.01	10.05	7.56	6.55	6.00	5.64	5.39
	.05	4.97	4.10	3.71	3.48	3.33	3.22
	.10	3.29	2.93	2.73	2.61	2.52	2.46
11	.01	9.65	7.21	6.22	5.67	5.32	5.07
	.05	4.85	3.98	3.59	3.36	3.20	3.10
	.10	3.23	2.86	2.66	2.54	2.45	2.39
12	.01	9.33	6.93	5.95	5.41	5.07	4.82
	.05	4.75	3.89	3.49	3.26	3.11	3.00
	.10	3.18	2.81	2.61	2.48	2.40	2.33
13	.01	9.07	6.70	5.74	5.21	4.86	4.62
	.05	4.67	3.81	3.41	3.18	3.03	2.92
	.10	3.14	2.76	2.56	2.43	2.35	2.28

Note: Full table is Table A–3 in the Appendix.

The within-groups degrees of freedom is 12. This is because each of the groups has 4 degrees of freedom on which the estimate is based (5 scores minus 1) and there are 3 groups overall, making a total of 12 degrees of freedom. In terms of the formula,

$$df_{\text{Within}} = df_1 + df_2 + \cdots + df_{\text{Last}} = (5 - 1) + (5 - 1) + (5 - 1)$$
$$= 4 + 4 + 4 = 12$$

You would look up the cutoff for an *F* distribution "with 2 and 12" degrees of freedom. As shown in Table 9–6, for the .05 level, you need an *F* ratio of 3.89 to reject the null hypothesis. (The full *F* table is Table A–3 in the Appendix.)

How are you doing?

For part (c) of each question, use the following scores involving three samples: The scores in Sample A are 5 and 7 ($M = 6$), the scores in Sample B are 6 and 10 ($M = 8$), and the scores in Sample C are 8 and 9 ($M = 8.5$).

1. (a) Write the formula for the within-groups population variance estimate and (b) define each of the symbols. (c) Figure the within-groups population variance estimate for these scores.
2. (a) Write the formula for the variance of the distribution of means when using it as part of an analysis of variance and (b) define each of the symbols. (c) Figure the variance of the distribution of means for these scores.
3. (a) Write the formula for the between-groups population variance estimate based on the variance of the distribution of means and (b) define each of the symbols and explain the logic behind this formula. (c) Figure the between-groups population variance estimate for these scores.
4. (a) Write the formula for the *F* ratio and (b) define each of the symbols. (c) Figure the *F* ratio for these scores.

5. (a) Write the formulas for the between-groups and within-groups degrees of freedom and (b) define each of the symbols. (c) Figure the between-groups and within-groups degrees of freedom for these scores.

6. (a) What is the F distribution? (b) Why is it skewed to the right? (c) What is the cutoff F for these scores for the .05 significance level?

samples. GM is the grand mean, the overall mean of all your scores, which is also the mean of your means. $df_{Between}$ is the degrees of freedom in the between-groups estimate, the number of groups minus 1.

(c) Grand mean (GM) is $(6 + 8 + 8.5)/3 = 7.5$.

$$S_M^2 = \Sigma(M - GM)^2/df_{Between}$$
$$= ([6 - 7.5]^2 + [8 - 7.5]^2 + [8.5 - 7.5]^2)/(3 - 1)$$
$$= (2.25 + .25 + 1)/2 = 3.5/2 = 1.75.$$

3. (a) $S_{Between}^2 = (S_M^2)(n)$.

(b) $S_{Between}^2$ is the between-groups population variance estimate; S_M^2 is the es-timated variance of the distribution of means (estimated based on the means of the samples in your study); n is the number of participants in each sample. The goal is to have a variance of a distribution of individuals based on the vari-ation among the means of the groups. S_M^2 is the estimate of the variance of a distribution of means from the overall population based on the means of the samples. To go from the variance of a distribution of means to the variance of a distribution of individuals, you multiply by the size of each sample. This is be-cause the variance of the distribution of means is always smaller than the dis-tribution of individuals (because samples of means are less likely to be extreme than are individual scores); the exact relation is that the variance of distribution of means is the variance of the distribution of individuals divided by the sam-ple size; thus you reverse that process here.

(c) $S_{Between}^2 = (S_M^2)(n) = (1.75)(2) = 3.5$

4. (a) $F = S_{Between}^2/S_{Within}^2$.

(b) F is the F ratio; $S_{Between}^2$ is the between-groups population variance estimate; S_{Within}^2 is the within-groups population variance estimate.

(c) $F = S_{Between}^2/S_{Within}^2 = 3.5/3.5 = 1.0$.

5. (a) $df_{Between} = N_{Groups} - 1$ and $df_{Within} = df_1 + df_2 + \cdots + df_{Last}$.

(b) $df_{Between}$ is the between-groups degrees of freedom; N_{Groups} is the number of groups; df_{Within} is the within-groups degrees of freedom; df_1 is the degrees of freedom for the population variance estimate based on the scores in the first sample; df_2 is the degrees of freedom for the population variance esti-mate based on the scores in the second sample; df_{Last} is the degrees of free-dom for the population variance estimate based on the scores in the last sample; the dots show that you are to fill in the population degrees of freedom for as many other samples as there are in the analysis.

(c) $df_{Between} = N_{Groups} - 1 = 3 - 1 = 2$; $df_{Within} = df_1 + df_2 + \cdots + df_{Last} = 1 + 1 + 1 = 3$.

6. (a) The distribution of F ratios you would expect by chance. (b) F ratios, because they are a ratio of variances (which as averages of squared numbers have to be positive), are ratios of two positive numbers, which always have to be pos-itive. Thus, they can't be less than 0. But there is no limit to how high an F ratio can be. Thus, the scores bunch up at the left (near 0) and spread out to the right.

(c) Cutoff F for the .05 significance level: 9.55.

Answers

1. (a) Formula for the within-groups population variance estimate:

$$S^2_{Within} = (S^2_1 + S^2_2 + \cdots + S^2_{Last})/N_{Groups}.$$

(b) S^2_{Within} is the within-groups population variance estimate; S^2_1 is the estimated population variance based on the scores in the first group (the group from Population A); S^2_2 is the estimated population variance based on the scores in the second group; S^2_{Last} is the estimated population variance based on the scores in the last group; the dots show that you are to fill in a population variance estimate for as many other groups as there are in the analysis; N_{Groups} is the number of groups.

(c) Figuring for the within-groups population variance estimate:

$S^2_1 = ([5 - 6]^2 + [7 - 6]^2)/(2 - 1) = (1 + 1)/1 = 2.$

$S^2_2 = ([6 - 8]^2 + [10 - 8]^2)/(2 - 1) = (4 + 4)/1 = 8.$

$S^2_3 = ([8 - 8.5]^2 + [9 - 8.5]^2)/(2 - 1) = (.25 + .25)/1 = .5.$

$S^2_{Within} = (S^2_1 + S^2_2 + \cdots + S^2_{Last})/N_{Groups} = (2 + 8 + .5)/3 = 10.5/3 = 3.5.$

2. (a) $S^2_M = \Sigma(M - GM)^2/df_{Between}.$

(b) S^2_M is the estimated variance of the distribution of means (estimated based on the means of the samples in your study). M is the mean of each of your

Hypothesis Testing with the Analysis of Variance

Here are the five steps of hypothesis testing for the criminal record study. The distributions involved are shown in Figure 9–4.

❶ **Restate the question as a research hypothesis and a null hypothesis about the populations.** There are three populations:

Population 1: Jurors told that the defendant has a criminal record.
Population 2: Jurors told that the defendant has a clean record.
Population 3: Jurors given no information about the defendant's record.

The null hypothesis is that these three populations have the same mean ($\mu_1 = \mu_2 = \mu_3$). The research hypothesis is that the populations' means are not the same.

❷ **Determine the characteristics of the comparison distribution.** The comparison distribution is an F distribution with 2 and 12 degrees of freedom.

❸ **Determine the cutoff sample score on the comparison distribution at which the null hypothesis should be rejected.** Using the F table for the .05 significance level, the cutoff F ratio is 3.89.

❹ **Determine your sample's score on the comparison distribution.** In the analysis of variance, the comparison distribution is an F distribution, and the sample's score on that distribution is thus its F ratio. In the example, the F ratio was 4.07.

❺ **Decide whether to reject the null hypothesis.** In the example, the F ratio of 4.07 is more extreme than the .05 significance level cutoff of 3.89. Thus, the researcher would reject the null hypothesis that the three groups come from populations with the same mean. This suggests that they come from populations with different means: that people exposed to different kinds of information (or no information) about the criminal record of a defendant in a situation of this kind will differ in their ratings of the defendant's guilt.

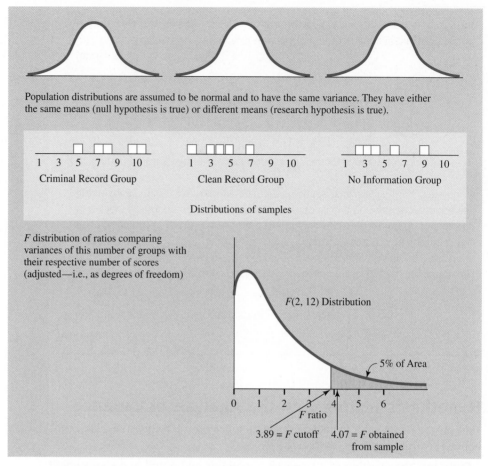

Figure 9–4 Distributions involved in the criminal record study example (fictitious data).

You may be interested to know that several real studies have looked at whether knowing a defendant's prior criminal record affects the likelihood of conviction. The overall conclusion seems to be reasonably consistent with that of the fictional study described here. For a review of such studies, see Dane and Wrightsman (1982). (For an example of a study showing this pattern see Greene & Dodge, 1995.)

Another Example

Mikulincer (1998) conducted a series of studies in Israel using the same attachment style classification measure we discussed earlier in the chapter (see Table 9–1). One of his studies included 30 university students (10 of each attachment style), all of whom were in serious romantic relationships. As part of the study, each evening the students wrote down whether during that day their partner had done something to violate their trust. Participants noted such events as the partner being very late for a promised meeting or "forgetting" to tell the participant about some important plan. The results, along with the analysis of variance figuring, are shown in Table 9–7. The distributions involved are shown in Figure 9–5. The steps of the hypothesis testing follow.

Table 9-7   Number of Trust Violation Events by Romantic Partners Over 3 Weeks Reported by Individuals of Three Attachment Styles

	Attachment Style		
	Secure	Avoidant	Anxious-Ambivalent
n	10	10	10
M	2.10	3.70	4.20
S	1.66	1.89	1.93
S^2	2.76	3.57	3.72

F distribution:

$df_{Between} = N_{Groups} - 1 = 3 - 1 = 2$

$df_{Within} = df_1 + df_2 + \cdots + df_{Last} = (10 - 1) + (10 - 1) + (10 - 1) = 9 + 9 + 9 = 27$

F needed for significance at .05 level from F table, $df = 2, 27$: 3.36

Between-groups population variance estimate:

Table for finding S^2 for the three means

	M	Deviation	Squared Deviation
Secure	2.10	−1.23	1.51
Avoidant	3.70	.37	.14
Anxious-Ambivalent	4.20	.87	.76
	Σ: 10.00		$\Sigma(M - GM)^2$: 2.41
	GM: 3.33		

$S_M^2 = \Sigma(M - GM)^2 / df_{Between} = 2.41/2 = 1.205$

$S_{Between}^2$ or $MS_{Between} = (S_M^2)(n) = (1.205)(10) = 12.05$

Within-groups population variance estimate:

S_{Within}^2 or $MS_{Within} = \dfrac{S_1^2 + S_2^2 + \cdots + S_{Last}^2}{N_{groups}} = \dfrac{2.76 + 3.57 + 3.72}{3} = \dfrac{10.05}{3} = 3.35$

F ratio: $F = S_{Between}^2 / S_{Within}^2$ or $MS_{Between} / MS_{Within} = 12.05/3.35 = 3.60$

Decision: Reject the null hypothesis.

Source: Data from Mikulincer (1998)

❶ **Restate the question as a research hypothesis and a null hypothesis about the populations.** There are three populations.

Population 1: Students with a secure attachment style.
Population 2: Students with an avoidant attachment style.
Population 3: Students with an anxious-ambivalent attachment style.

The null hypothesis is that these three populations have the same mean ($\mu_1 = \mu_2 = \mu_3$). The research hypothesis is that their means are not the same.

❷ **Determine the characteristics of the comparison distribution.** The comparison distribution will be an F distribution. Its degrees of freedom are figured as follows: the between-groups variance estimate is based on three groups, making 2 degrees of freedom. The within-groups estimate is based on 9 degrees of freedom (10 participants) in each of the three groups, making a total of 27 degrees of freedom.

❸ **Determine the cutoff sample score on the comparison distribution at which the null hypothesis should be rejected.** Using Table A–3 in the Appendix, look down the column for 2 degrees of freedom in the numerator and stop at the row

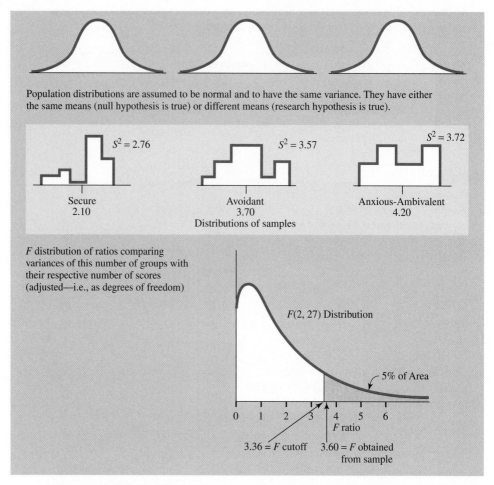

Population distributions are assumed to be normal and to have the same variance. They have either the same means (null hypothesis is true) or different means (research hypothesis is true).

$S^2 = 2.76$ $S^2 = 3.57$ $S^2 = 3.72$

Secure
2.10

Avoidant
3.70

Anxious-Ambivalent
4.20

Distributions of samples

F distribution of ratios comparing variances of this number of groups with their respective number of scores (adjusted—i.e., as degrees of freedom)

$F(2, 27)$ Distribution

5% of Area

0   1   2   3   4   5   6
F ratio

3.36 = *F* cutoff   3.60 = *F* obtained from sample

Figure 9–5   Distributions involved in the attachment style example. (*Source:* Data from Mikulincer, 1998.)

for our denominator degrees of freedom of 27. We will use the .05 significance level. This gives a cutoff *F* of 3.36.

❹ **Determine your sample's score on the comparison distribution.** This step requires determining the sample's *F* ratio. You find the between-groups variance estimate (the numerator of the *F* ratio) in two steps.

Ⓐ **Estimate the variance of the distribution of means:** Add up the sample means' squared deviations from the grand mean, and divide by the number of means minus 1. From Table 9–7, this comes out to 1.205.

Ⓑ **Figure the estimated variance of the population of individual scores:** Multiply the variance of the distribution of means by the number of scores in each group. From Table 9–7, this comes out to 12.05.

You find the within-groups variance estimate (the denominator of the *F* ratio) in two steps.

Ⓐ **Figure population variance estimates based on each group's scores:** As shown in Table 9–7, the population variance estimates are 2.76, 3.57, and 3.72.

Ⓑ **Average these variance estimates:** The average of 2.76, 3.57, and 3.72 comes out to 3.35.

Table 9–8   Steps for the Analysis of Variance (When Sample Sizes Are Equal)

❶ **Restate the question as a research hypothesis and a null hypothesis about the populations.**

❷ **Determine the characteristics of the comparison distribution.**

  a. The comparison distribution is an *F* distribution.

  b. The between-groups (numerator) degrees of freedom is the number of groups minus 1:
   $df_{Between} = N_{Groups} - 1$.

  c. The within-groups (denominator) degrees of freedom is the sum of the degrees of freedom in each group (the number in the group minus 1):
   $df_{Within} = df_1 + df_2 + \cdots + df_{Last}$.

❸ **Determine the cutoff sample score on the comparison distribution at which the null hypothesis should be rejected.**

  a. Decide the significance level.

  b. Look up the appropriate cutoff in an *F* table, using the degrees of freedom from Step ❷.

❹ **Determine your sample's score on the comparison distribution.** This will be an *F* ratio.

  a. Figure the between-groups population variance estimate ($S^2_{Between}$ or $MS_{Between}$). Figure the means of each group.

  ❶ **Estimate the variance of the distribution of means:** $S^2_M = \Sigma(M - GM)^2/df_{Between}$.

  ❷ **Figure the estimated variance of the population of individual scores:**
   $S^2_{Between}$ or $MS_{Between} = (S^2_M)(n)$

  b. Figure the within-groups population variance estimate (S^2_{Within} or MS_{Within}).

  ❶ **Figure population variance estimates based on each group's scores:** For each group,
   $S^2 = \Sigma(X - M)^2/(n - 1) = SS/df$.

  ❷ **Average these variance estimates:**
   S^2_{Within} or $MS_{Within} = (S^2_1 + S^2_2 + \cdots + S^2_{Last})/N_{Groups}$.

  c. Figure the *F* ratio: $F = S^2_{Between}/S^2_{Within}$ or $F = MS_{Between}/MS_{Within}$.

❺ **Decide whether to reject the null hypothesis:** Compare the scores from Steps ❸ and ❹.

The *F* ratio is the between-groups variance estimate divided by the within-groups variance estimate, which comes out to 3.60 (that is, $12.05/3.35 = 3.60$).

❺ **Decide whether to reject the null hypothesis.** The *F* ratio of 3.60 is more extreme than the .05 significance level cutoff *F* of 3.36. Therefore, Mikulincer (1998) rejected the null hypothesis. He was able to conclude that students having the three attachment styles differ in the number of trust violations by their romantic partners they reported over a 3-week period. This conclusion was consistent with Mikulincer's hypotheses based on attachment theory.

Summary of Steps for Hypothesis Testing with the Analysis of Variance

Table 9–8 summarizes the steps of an analysis of variance of the kind we have been considering in this chapter.

Assumptions in the Analysis of Variance

The assumptions for the analysis of variance are basically the same as for the *t* test for independent means. That is, the cutoff *F* ratio from the table (or the exact *p* level from the computer output) is strictly accurate only when the populations follow a normal curve and have equal variances. As with the *t* test, in practice the cutoffs are reasonably accurate even when your populations are moderately far from normal and have moderately different variances. As a general rule, if the variance estimate of the group with the largest estimate is no more than four or five times that of the smallest and the sample sizes are equal, the conclusions using the *F* distribution should be adequately accurate. In Chapter 14 we consider what to do when your populations are a long way from meeting these assumptions.

How are you doing?

1. A study compares the effects of three experimental treatments, A, B, and C, by giving each treatment to 16 participants and then assessing their performance on a standard measure. The results on the standard measure are as follows. Treatment A group: $M = 20$, $S^2 = 8$; Treatment B group: $M = 22$, $S^2 = 9$; Treatment C group: $M = 18$, $S^2 = 7$. Using the .01 significance level, do the three experimental treatments create any difference among the populations these groups represent? (a) Use the steps of hypothesis testing and (b) sketch the distributions involved.
2. Give the two main assumptions for the analysis of variance.
3. Why do we need the equal variance assumption?
4. What is the general rule about when violations of the equal variance assumption are likely to lead to serious inaccuracies in results?

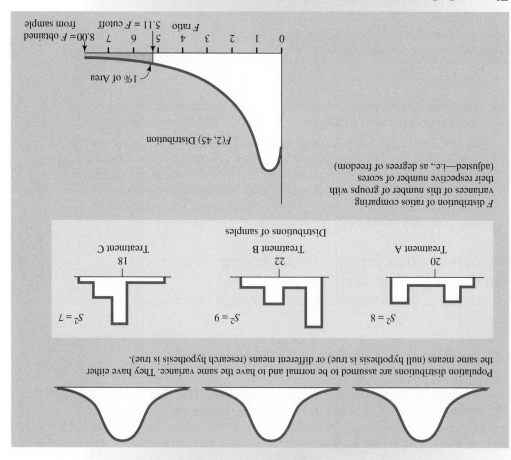

Figure 9–6 Distributions for "How Are You Doing?" question 1.

Answers

1. (a) Steps of hypothesis testing:

❶ Restate the question as a research hypothesis and a null hypothesis about the populations. There are three populations.

Population 1: People given experimental treatment A.

Population 2: People given experimental treatment B.

Population 3: People given experimental treatment C.

The null hypothesis is that these three populations have the same mean ($\mu_1 = \mu_2 = \mu_3$). The research hypothesis is that their means are not the same.

❷ Determine the characteristics of the comparison distribution. The comparison distribution will be an F distribution. Its degrees of freedom are figured as follows: The between-groups variance estimate is based on three groups, making 2 degrees of freedom. The within-groups estimate is based on 15 degrees of freedom (16 participants) in each of the three groups, making 45 degrees of freedom.

❸ Determine the cutoff sample score on the comparison distribution at which the null hypothesis should be rejected. Using Table A-3 in the Appendix, the cutoff F for $df = 2$, 45 at the .01 level is 5.11.

❹ Determine your sample's score on the comparison distribution.

(a) Figure the between-groups population variance estimate ($S^2_{Between}$): First, figure the mean of each group. The group means are 20, 22, and 18.

   ❶ Estimate the variance of the distribution of means: Add up the sample means' squared deviations from the grand mean and divide by the number of means minus 1:

$$S^2_M = [(20 - 20)^2 + (22 - 20)^2 + (18 - 20)^2]/(3 - 1)$$
$$= (0 + 4 + 4)/2 = 4$$

   ❷ **Figure the estimated variance of the population of individual scores:** Multiply the variance of the distribution of means by the number of scores in each group.

$$S^2_{Between} = (4)(16) = 64$$

(b) Figure the within-groups population variance estimate (S^2_{Within}):

   ❸ **Figure population variance estimates based on each group's scores:** Treatment A group, $S^2 = 8$; Treatment B group, $S^2 = 9$; Treatment C group, $S^2 = 7$.

   ❹ **Average these estimates:** $S^2_{Within} = (8 + 9 + 7)/3 = 8$.

   The F ratio is the between-groups estimate divided by the within-groups estimate: $F = 64/8 = 8.00$.

❺ Decide whether to reject the null hypothesis. The F of 8.00 is more extreme than the .01 cutoff F of 5.11. Therefore, reject the null hypothesis. The research hypothesis is supported; the different experimental treatments do produce different effects on the standard performance measure.

(b) The distributions involved are shown in Figure 9–6.

2. The populations are assumed to be normally distributed with equal variances.

3. We need the equal variance assumption to be able to justify averaging the estimates from each sample into an overall within-groups population variance estimate.

4. The analysis can lead to inaccurate results when the variance estimate from the group with the largest estimate is more than four or five times the smallest variance estimate.

Planned Contrasts

When you reject the null hypothesis in an analysis of variance, this implies that the population means are not all the same. What is not clear, however, is which population means differ from which. For example, in the criminal record study, the Criminal Record group jurors had the highest ratings for the defendant's guilt ($M = 8$); the No Information group jurors, the second highest ($M = 5$); and the Clean Record group jurors, the lowest ($M = 4$). From the analysis of variance results, we concluded that the true means of the three populations these groups represent are not all the same. (That is, the overall analysis of variance was significant.) However, we do not know which populations' means are significantly different from each other.

In practice, in most research situations involving more than two groups, our real interest is not in an overall, or *omnibus,* difference among the several groups, but rather in more specific comparisons. For example, in the criminal record study, the researchers' prediction in advance would probably have been that the Criminal Record group would rate the defendant's guilt higher than both the No Information group and the Clean Record group. If, in fact, the researchers had made these predictions, these predictions would be examples of what are called **planned contrasts** (They are called "contrasts" because they contrast the results from specific groups.)

Researchers use planned contrasts to look at some particular, focused differences between groups that directly follow from a theory or that are related directly to some practical application. Planned contrasts are also sometimes called *a priori comparisons* because they have been planned in advance of the study. They may also be called *planned comparisons* because they compare the results for specific groups. Finally, a general name you may see for most contrasts you would figure is *linear contrasts.*

Figuring Planned Contrasts

The procedure to compare the means of a particular pair of groups is a direct extension of what you already know: figure a between-groups population variance estimate, a within-groups population variance estimate, and an F.

The within-groups population variance estimate will be the same as for the overall analysis of variance. This is because, regardless of the particular groups you are comparing, you are still assuming that all groups are from populations with the same variance. Thus, your best estimate of that variance is the one that makes use of the information from all the groups, the average of the population variance estimates from each of the samples.

The between-groups population variance estimate, however, in a planned contrast is different from the between-groups variance estimate in the overall analysis. It is different because in a planned contrast you are interested in the variation only between a particular pair of means. Specifically, in a planned contrast between two group means, you figure the between-groups population variance estimate with the usual two-step procedure, but using just the two means of interest.[2]

Once you have the two variance estimates for the planned contrast, you figure the F in the usual way, and compare it to a cutoff from the F table based on the df that go into the two estimates, which are the same as the overall analysis for df_{Within} and are usually exactly 1 for $df_{Between}$ (because the between estimate is based on two means, and $2 - 1 = 1$).

An Example

Consider the planned contrast of the Criminal Record group ($M = 8$) to the No Information group ($M = 5$).

planned contrast comparison in which the particular means to be compared were decided in advance. Also called *planned comparison.*

The within-groups population variance estimate for a planned contrast is always the same as the within-groups estimate from the overall analysis: In the criminal record example S^2_{Within} was 5.33.

For the between-groups population variance estimate, you follow the usual two-step procedure, but using only the two means you plan to compare.

❶ Estimate the variance of the distribution of means: Add up the sample means' squared deviations from the grand mean and divide by the number of means minus 1. The grand mean for these two means would be 6.5 [that is, $(8 + 5)/2 = 6.5$] and $df_{Between}$ when there are two means being compared is $2 - 1 = 1$. Thus,

$$S^2_M = \Sigma(M - GM)^2/df_{Between} = [(8 - 6.5)^2 + (5 - 6.5)^2]/1$$
$$= [1.5^2 + (-1.5^2)]/1 = 2.25 + 2.25 = 4.5.$$

❷ Figure the estimated variance of the population of individual scores: Multiply the variance of the distribution of means by the number of scores in each group. There are five scores in each group in this study. Thus,

$$S^2_{Between} = (S^2_M)(n) = (4.5)(5) = 22.5$$

Thus, for this planned contrast, $F = S^2_{Between}/S^2_{Within} = 22.5/5.33 = 4.22$. The .05 cutoff F for $df = 1, 12$ is 4.75. Thus, the planned contrast is not significant. You can conclude that the three means differ overall (from the original analysis of variance, which was significant), but you cannot conclude specifically that the Criminal Record condition makes a person rate guilt differently from being in the No Information condition.

A Second Example

What about the other planned contrast of the Criminal Record Group ($M = 8$) to the Clean Record group ($M = 4$)?

For the between-groups population variance estimate,

❶ Estimate the variance of the distribution of means: Add the sample means' squared deviations from the grand mean and divide by the number of means minus 1. The grand mean for these two means is $(8 + 4)/2 = 6.0$ and $df_{Between} = 2 - 1 = 1$. Thus,

$$S^2_M = [(8 - 6.0)^2 + (4 - 6.0)^2]/1 = [2.0^2 + (-2.0^2)]/1 = 4.0 + 4.0 = 8.0$$

❷ Figure the estimated variance of the population of individual scores: Multiply the variance of the distribution of means by the number of scores in each group:

$$S^2_{Between} = (S^2_M)(n) = (8)(5) = 40.0$$

The within-groups estimate, again, is the same as we figured for the overall analysis—5.33.

Thus, $F = S^2_{Between}/S^2_{Within} = 40.0/5.33 = 7.50$. This F of 7.50 is larger than 4.75 (the .05 cutoff F for $df = 1, 12$), which means that the planned contrast is significant. Thus, you can conclude that the Criminal Record condition makes a person rate guilt differently from the Clean Record condition.

The Bonferroni Procedure

There is a problem when you carry out several planned contrasts. Normally, when you set the .05 significance level, this means you have selected a cutoff so extreme that you have only a .05 chance of getting a significant result if the null hypothesis is true. However, with multiple contrasts, if you use the .05 cutoff, you can actually have much *more* than a .05 chance of getting a significant result if the null hypothesis is true!

The reason is this: if you are making several contrasts (comparisons), each at the .05 level, the chance of any one of them coming out significant is more than .05. (It is like flipping coins. If you flip any one coin, it has only a 50% chance of coming up heads. But if you flip five coins, there is a lot better than 50% chance at least one of them will come up heads.) In fact, if you make two contrasts, each at the .05 significance level, there is about a .10 chance that at least one will come out significant just by chance (that is, if the null hypothesis is true). If you make three planned contrasts at the .05 level, there is about a .15 chance.

A widely used approach for dealing with this problem with planned contrasts is the **Bonferroni procedure.** The idea of the Bonferroni procedure is that you use a more stringent significance level for each contrast. The result is that the overall chance of any one of the contrasts being mistakenly significant is still reasonably low. For example, if each of two planned contrasts used the .025 significance level, the overall chance of any one of them being mistakenly significant would still be less than .05. (That is, $.05/2 = .025$.) With three planned contrasts, you could use the .017 level ($.05/3 = .017$).

The general principle is that the Bonferroni corrected cutoff you use is the true significance level you want divided by the number of planned contrasts. Thus, if you want to test your hypothesis at the .01 level and you will make three planned contrasts, you would test each planned contrast using the .0033 significance level. That is, $.01/3 = .0033$.

If you are doing your analyses on a computer, it gives exact significance probabilities as part of the output—that is, it might give a *p* of .037 or .0054, not just whether you are beyond the .05 or .01 level. However, if you are using tables, normally only the .01 or .05 cutoffs would be available. Thus, even though almost all researchers use computers for their analyses, this situation has led to some traditions that are still followed today. Specifically, for simplicity, when the Bonferroni corrected cutoff might be .017 or even .025, researchers often use the .01 significance level. Also, if there are only two planned contrasts (or even three), it is common for researchers not to correct at all.

How are you doing?

1. (a) What is a planned contrast? (b) Why do researchers make them?
2. How is the procedure for figuring a planned contrast between two particular groups different from the overall analysis of variance?
3. A study has three groups of 25 participants each in the overall analysis of variance, and S^2_{Within} is 100. The researcher makes a single planned contrast between a group that has a mean of 10 and another group that has a mean of 16. Is it significant? (Use the .05 significance level.)
4. (a) Why do researchers making planned contrasts need to make the Bonferroni correction? (b) What is the principle of the Bonferroni correction?
5. If a researcher is making four planned contrasts using the .05 significance level, what would be the Bonferroni corrected significance level?

Bonferroni procedure multiple-comparison procedure in which the total alpha percentage is divided among the set of comparisons so that each is tested at a more stringent significance level.

Answers

1. (a) A planned contrast is a focused comparison of two groups in an overall analysis of variance that the researcher planned in advance of the study based on a theory or practical issue.
(b) Researchers make them because they are more likely to be of theoretical or practical interest than the overall difference among means.

2. The procedure for figuring a planned contrast between two particular groups is the same except that you make the between-groups estimate using only the means of the two groups being compared.

3. It is significant. For the between-groups population variance estimate for the planned contrast.

❶ **Estimate the variance of the distribution of means:**

$GM = (10 + 16)/2 = 13;$ $df_{Between} = 2 - 1 = 1.$

$$S_M^2 = [(10 - 13)^2 + (16 - 13)^2]/1 = 18$$

❷ **Figure the estimated variance of the population of individual scores:**

$$S_{Between}^2 = (18)(25) = 450$$

The within-groups estimate is the same as the overall within-groups estimate, 100.

$$F = 450/100 = 4.5.$$

The cutoff for $df = 1, 72$ (actually 1, 70, since 1, 72 is not in the table) is 3.98. You can reject the null hypothesis. The planned contrast is significant.

4. (a) With more than one contrast, the chance of any one coming out significant is greater than the direct significance level used.
(b) You divide your overall desired true significance level by the number of contrasts. This way, the chance of any one of them coming out significant is taken into account.

5. The Bonferroni corrected significance level is $.05/4 = .0125.$

Post Hoc Comparisons

As we have noted, rejecting the null hypothesis in an analysis of variance implies that the population means are not all the same, but it does not tell you which population means differ from which. As you learned in the preceding section on planned contrasts, researchers often plan specific comparisons based on theory or practical considerations. Sometimes, however, researchers take a more exploratory approach, for example, comparing all the different pairings of means to discover which ones do and do not differ significantly. (We call this making *pairwise comparisons,* because you are comparing all possible pairings of means.) That is, after the study is done, the researcher is fishing through the results to see which groups differ from each other. These are called **post hoc comparisons** (or *a posteriori comparisons*) because they are after the fact and not planned in advance.

In post hoc comparisons, all possible comparisons have to be taken into account when figuring the overall chance of any one of them turning out significant. Using the Bonferroni procedure for post hoc comparisons is safe, in the sense that you are confident you won't get too many results significant by chance. But in post hoc comparisons there are often so many comparisons to consider that the overall significance level is divided into such a small number by the Bonferroni procedure that getting any one

post hoc comparisons multiple comparisons, not specified in advance; procedure conducted as part of an exploratory analysis after an analysis of variance.

comparison to come out significant would be a long shot. For example, with four groups, there are six possible pairs to compare; so using a Bonferroni correction and an overall significance level of .05, you would have to test each comparison at .05/6 or .0083. If there are five groups, there are 10 possible comparisons; .05 overall becomes .005 for each comparison. And so forth. Thus, the power for any one comparison becomes very low.

Of course, you might think, "I'll just test the pairs of means that have the biggest difference so that the number of comparisons won't be so great." Unfortunately, this strategy won't work. Since you did not decide in advance which pairs of means would be compared, when exploring after the fact, you have to take into account that any of the pairs might have been the biggest ones. So unless you made specific predictions in advance—and had a sound theoretical or practical basis for those predictions—all the possible pairings have to be counted.

For this reason, statisticians have developed a variety of procedures to use in these fishing expeditions. These procedures attempt to keep the overall risk of a Type I error at some level like .05, while at the same time not too drastically reducing statistical power. You may see some of these referred to in articles you read, described by the names of their developers; the **Scheffé test** and *Tukey test* are the most widely used, with the *Neuman-Keuls* and *Duncan* procedures almost as common. Which procedure is best under various conditions remains a topic of dispute. You can learn the details about the possibilities and controversies in intermediate statistics.

The Scheffé Test

As a post hoc test, the Scheffé method has the advantage of being the most widely applicable method. We say that because it is the only one that can be used when you are making relatively simple comparisons (such as the ones we have considered in which two groups are being compared), as well as when you are making more complex comparisons (for example, comparing the average of two groups to a third group). Its disadvantage, however, is that, compared to the Tukey and other procedures, it is the most conservative. That is, for any given post hoc comparison, its chance of being significant using the Scheffé is usually still better than the Bonferroni, but worse than the Tukey or any of the other post hoc contrasts.

To use the Scheffé test, you first figure the F for your comparison in the usual way. But then you divide that F by the overall study's df_{Between} (the number of groups minus 1). You then compare this much smaller F to the overall study's F cutoff.

Here is an example. Recall that for the comparison of the Criminal Record group versus the No Information group, we figured an F of 4.22. Since the overall df_{Between} in that study was 2 (there were three groups), for a Scheffé test, you would actually consider the F for this contrast to be an F of only $4.22/2 = 2.11$. You would then compare this Scheffé corrected F of 2.11 to the cutoff F for the overall between effect (in this example, the F for $df = 2, 12$), which was 3.89. Thus, the comparison is not significant using the Scheffé test.

How are you doing?

1. (a) What are post hoc comparisons? (b) Why do researchers make them?
2. (a) Why do researchers typically not use the Bonferroni procedure for post hoc comparisons?
   (b) What is the advantage over the Bonferroni procedure of procedures such as the Tukey and Scheffé tests?
3. What are the (a) advantages and (b) disadvantages of the Scheffé procedure versus other post hoc tests (such as the Tukey)?
4. How do you carry out the Scheffé procedure?

Scheffé test method of figuring the significance of post hoc comparisons that takes into account all possible comparisons that could be made.

5. Suppose in a study with four groups of 50 participants each, for a particular contrast, you figure an F of 12.60. Using a Scheffé test, is this significant at the .05 significance level?

Answers

1. (a) Post hoc comparisons are comparisons figured after an analysis of variance, such as between two groups, that were not planned in advance.
(b) Researchers make them as an exploratory procedure to see what patterns of relations among populations are suggested by the data over and above any comparisons that were planned in advance.
2. (a) In any follow-up analysis, there are usually so many possible post hoc comparisons that, if you used the Bonferroni procedure, your corrected significance level would be so extreme that it would be very hard for any result to be significant.
(b) The effect of the Tukey and Scheffé tests, and others like them, when doing multiple post hoc comparisons and correctly adjusting for the many comparisons being made, is that a result does not have to be quite so extreme to be significant.
3. (a) You can use the Scheffé procedure for any number of comparisons, including complex comparisons.
(b) The Scheffé procedure is more conservative: the chance of any comparison being significant is less.
4. Figure the comparison in the usual way, but divide the F by the overall study's $df_{Between}$ and use the overall study's F cutoff.
5. Overall study's $df_{Between} = 4 - 1 = 3$; $df_{Within} = 49 + 49 + 49 + 49 = 196$. Scheffé corrected $F = 12.60/3 = 4.20$. Overall study's .05 cutoff F ($df = 3$, 196; closest on table = 3, 100) is 2.70. Thus, even with the Scheffé correction, this comparison is significant.

Effect Size and Power for the Analysis of Variance
Effect Size

Effect size for the analysis of variance is a little more complex than for a t test. With the t test, you took the difference between the two means and divided by the standard deviation. In the analysis of variance, you have more than two means; so it is not obvious just what is the equivalent to the difference between the means—the numerator in figuring effect size.[3] Thus, in this section we consider a quite different approach to effect size, the **proportion of variance accounted for (R^2).**

To be precise, R^2 is the proportion of the total variation of scores from the grand mean that is accounted for by the variation between the means of the groups. (In other words, you consider how much of the variance in the measured variable—such as ratings of guilt—is accounted for by the variable that divides up the groups—such as what experimental condition one is in.) In terms of a formula,

$$R^2 = \frac{(S^2_{Between})(df_{Between})}{(S^2_{Between})(df_{Between}) + (S^2_{Within})(df_{Within})} \qquad (9\text{--}7)$$

The between- and within-groups degrees of freedom are included in the formula to take into account the number of participants and the number of groups used in the study.

Consider once again the criminal record study. In that example, $S^2_{Between} = 21.70$, $df_{Between} = 2$, $S^2_{Within} = 5.33$, and $df_{Within} = 12$. Thus, the

proportion of variance accounted for (R^2) proportion of the total variation of scores from the grand mean that is accounted for by the variation between the means of the groups.

The proportion of variance accounted for is the between-groups population variance estimate multiplied by the between-groups degrees of freedom, divided by the sum of the between-groups population variance estimate multiplied by the between-groups degrees of freedom, plus the within-groups population variance estimate multiplied by the within-groups degrees of freedom.

proportion of the total variation accounted for by the variation between groups is $(21.70)(2)/[(21.70)(2) + (5.33)(12)]$, which is .40 (or 40%). In terms of the formula,

$$R^2 = \frac{(S^2_{Between})(df_{Between})}{(S^2_{Between})(df_{Between}) + (S^2_{Within})(df_{Within})}$$

$$= \frac{(21.70)(2)}{(21.70)(2) + (5.33)(12)} = \frac{43.40}{107.36} = .40$$

The proportion of variance accounted for is the *F* ratio multiplied by the between-groups degrees of freedom (the degrees of freedom for the between-groups population variance estimate), divided by the sum of the *F* ratio multiplied by the between-groups degrees of freedom, plus the degrees of freedom for the within-groups population variance estimate.

What if the between-groups and within-groups variance estimates are not available, as is often true in published studies? It is also possible to figure R^2 directly from F and the degrees of freedom. The formula is

$$R^2 = \frac{(F)(df_{Between})}{(F)(df_{Between}) + df_{Within}} \tag{9-8}$$

For example, in the criminal record study,

$$R^2 = \frac{(F)(df_{Between})}{(F)(df_{Between}) + df_{Within}} = \frac{(4.07)(2)}{(4.07)(2) + 12} = \frac{8.14}{20.14} = .40$$

You should also know that another common name for this measure of effect size (besides R^2) is $\mathbf{\eta^2}$, the Greek letter *eta* **squared**; η^2 is also known as the *correlation ratio*.

The proportion of variance accounted for is a useful measure of effect size because it has the direct meaning suggested by its name. [Further, researchers are familiar with R^2 from its use in regression (see Chapter 12) and its square root, R, is a kind of correlation coefficient that is very familiar to most researchers (see Chapter 11).]

R^2 has a minimum of 0 and a maximum of 1. However, in practice it is rare in most psychology research for an analysis of variance to have an R^2 even as high as .20. Cohen's (1988) conventions for R^2 are .01, a small effect size; .06, a medium effect size; and .14, a large effect size.

Power

Table 9–9 shows the approximate power for the .05 significance level for small, medium, and large effect sizes; sample sizes of 10, 20, 30, 40, 50, and 100 per group; and three, four, and five groups.[4]

Consider a planned study with five groups of 10 participants each and an expected large effect size (.14). Using the .05 significance level, the study would have a power of .56. Thus, even if the research hypothesis is in fact true and has a large effect size, there is only a little greater than even chance (56%) that the study will come out significant.

As we have noted in previous chapters, determining power is especially useful when interpreting the practical implication of a nonsignificant result. For example, suppose that you have read a study using an analysis of variance with four groups of 30 participants each, and there is a nonsignificant result at the .05 level. Table 9–9 shows a power of only .13 for a small effect size. This suggests that even if such a small effect exists in the population, this study would be very unlikely to have come out

eta squared (η^2) common name for the R^2 measure of effect size for the analysis of variance. Also called *correlation ratio*.

Table 9-9 Approximate Power for Studies Using the Analysis of Variance Testing Hypotheses at the .05 Significance Level

Participants per Group (n)	Small ($R^2 = .01$)	Medium ($R^2 = .06$)	Large ($R^2 = .14$)
Three groups ($df_{Between} = 2$)			
10	.07	.20	.45
20	.09	.38	.78
30	.12	.55	.93
40	.15	.68	.98
50	.18	.79	.99
100	.32	.98	*
Four groups ($df_{Between} = 3$)			
10	.07	.21	.51
20	.10	.43	.85
30	.13	.61	.96
40	.16	.76	.99
50	.19	.85	*
100	.36	.99	*
Five groups ($df_{Between} = 4$)			
10	.07	.23	.56
20	.10	.47	.90
30	.13	.67	.98
40	.17	.81	*
50	.21	.90	*
100	.40	*	*

*Nearly 1.

significant. But the table shows a power of .96 for a large effect size. This suggests that if a large effect existed in the population, it almost surely would have shown up in that study.

Planning Sample Size

Table 9–10 gives the approximate number of participants you need in each group for 80% power at the .05 significance level for estimated small, medium, and large effect sizes for studies with three, four, and five groups.[5]

Table 9-10 Approximate Number of Participants Needed in Each Group (Assuming Equal Sample Sizes) for 80% Power for the One-Way Analysis of Variance Testing Hypotheses at the .05 Significance Level

	Small ($R^2 = .01$)	Medium ($R^2 = .06$)	Large ($R^2 = .14$)
Three groups ($df_{Between} = 2$)	322	52	21
Four groups ($df_{Between} = 3$)	274	45	18
Five groups ($df_{Between} = 4$)	240	39	16

For example, suppose you are planning a study involving four groups and you expect a small effect size (and will use the .05 significance level). For 80% power, you would need 274 participants in each group, a total of 1,096 in all. However, suppose you could adjust the research plan so that it was now reasonable to predict a large effect size (perhaps by using more accurate measures and a stronger experimental manipulation). Now you would need only 18 in each of the four groups, for a total of 72.

How are you doing?

1. (a) Why is the method of figuring effect size for analysis of variance quite different from that used for the t tests? (b) Explain the logic of why proportion of variance accounted for can serve as an effect size in analysis of variance.
2. (a) Write the formula for effect size in analysis of variance using $S^2_{Between}$ and S^2_{Within}; (b) define each of the symbols; (c) give an alternative symbol for R^2; and (d) figure the effect size for a study in which $S^2_{Between} = 12.22$, $S^2_{Within} = 7.20$, $df_{Between} = 2$, and $df_{Within} = 8$.
3. (a) Write the formula for effect size in analysis of variance from a study in which only the F ratio and degrees of freedom are available; (b) define each of the symbols; and (c) figure the effect size for a study with 18 participants in each of the three groups and an F of 4.50.
4. What is the power of a study with four groups of approximately 40 participants each to be tested at the .05 significance level, in which the researchers predict a large effect size?
5. About how many participants do you need in each group for 80% power in a planned study with five groups in which you predict a medium effect size and will be using the .05 significance level?

Answers

1. (a) With t tests, your focus is on the difference between two means; there is no direct equivalent in the analysis of variance. (b) You are figuring the percentage of the total variation among the scores that is accounted for by which group the participant is in.
2. (a) The formula for effect size in analysis of variance: $R^2 = (S^2_{Between})(df_{Between})/[(S^2_{Between})(df_{Between}) + (S^2_{Within})(df_{Within})]$. (b) R^2 is the proportion of variance accounted for; $S^2_{Between}$ is the between-groups population variance estimate; $df_{Between}$ is the between-groups degrees of freedom (number of groups minus 1); S^2_{Within} is the within-groups population variance estimate; df_{Within} is the within-groups degrees of freedom (the sum of the degrees of freedom for each group's population variance estimate). (c) η^2. (d) Effect size: .30.
3. (a) $R^2 = (F)(df_{Between})/[(F)(df_{Between}) + df_{Within}]$. (b) R^2 is the proportion of variance accounted for; F is the F ratio from the study; $df_{Between}$ is the between-groups degrees of freedom; and df_{Within} is the within-groups degrees of freedom. (c) Effect size: $df_{Between} = 3 - 1 = 2$; $df_{Within} = 17 + 17 + 17 = 51$. $R^2 = (F)(df_{Between})/[(F)(df_{Between}) + df_{Within}] = (4.5)(2)/[(4.5)(2) + 51] = 9/[9 + 51] = 9/60 = .15$.
4. The power of the study is .99.
5. The number of participants needed in each group is 39.

Controversy: Omnibus Tests versus Planned Contrasts

The analysis of variance is commonly used in situations comparing three or more groups. (If you are comparing two groups, you can use a *t* test.) However, following the logic we introduced earlier, Rosnow and Rosenthal (1989) argue that such diffuse or omnibus tests are not very useful. They say that, in almost all cases when we test the overall difference among three or more groups, "we have tested a question in which we almost surely are not interested" (p. 1281). In which questions *are* we interested? We are interested in specific comparisons, such as between two particular groups.

Rosnow and Rosenthal (1989; see also Furr & Rosenthal, 2003) advocate that, when figuring an analysis of variance, you should analyze *only* planned contrasts. These should replace entirely the overall *F* test (that is, the diffuse or omnibus *F* test) for whether you can reject the hypothesis of no difference among population means. Traditionally, planned contrasts, when used at all, are a supplement to the overall *F* test. So this has been a rather revolutionary idea.

Consider an example. Orbach and colleagues (1997) compared a group of suicidal mental hospital patients (individuals who had made serious suicide attempts), nonsuicidal mental hospital patients with similar diagnoses, and a control group of volunteers from the community. The purpose of the study was to test the theory that suicidal individuals have a higher tolerance for physical pain. The idea is that their higher pain threshold makes it easier for them to do the painful acts usually involved in suicide. The researchers carried out standard pain threshold and other sensory tests and administered a variety of questionnaires to all three groups. Here is how they describe their analysis:

> To examine the study hypothesis, we performed a set of two linear contrasts for each pain measure.... The first linear contrast, *suicidality contrast,* compared the suicidal group with the two nonsuicidal groups (psychiatric inpatients and control participants). The second contrast compared the two nonsuicidal groups.... We did not make a previous omnibus *F* because we conducted preplanned group comparisons testing the study hypothesis. Because of multiple comparisons needed, the critical alpha was set at .01, to avoid Type I error....
>
> The suicidality contrast was significant for thermal sensation threshold, $F(1, 95) = 21.64$, $p < .01$; pain threshold, $F(1, 95) = 23.65$, $p < .01$; pain tolerance $F(1, 95) = 6.55$, $p < .01$; and maximum tolerance $F(1, 95) = 16.05$. No significant difference was found between the suicidal and nonsuicidal groups in the magnitude estimate measure. An examination of the means... supports our main hypothesis: Suicidal participants, as expected, had high sensation and pain thresholds, high pain tolerance, and were more likely to tolerate the maximum temperature administered than inpatients and control participants. Interestingly, the second set of contrasts revealed no significant differences between the psychiatric inpatients and control participants in any of the five pain measures. (p. 648)

The study by Orbach and colleagues study exemplifies Rosnow and Rosenthal's advice to use planned contrasts instead of an overall analysis of variance. But, although the idea was originally proposed nearly two decades ago, this approach has not yet been widely adopted and is still controversial. The main concern is much like the issue we considered in Chapter 4 regarding one-tailed and two-tailed tests. If we adopt the highly targeted, planned contrasts recommended by Rosnow and

Rosenthal, critics argue, we lose out on finding unexpected differences not initially planned, and we put too much control of what is found in the hands of the researcher (versus nature).

Analyses of Variance in Research Articles

Analyses of variance (of the kind we have considered in this chapter) are usually described in a research article by giving the F, the degrees of freedom, and the significance level. For example, "$F(3, 68) = 5.21, p < .01$." The means for the groups usually are given in a table, although if there are only a few groups and only one or a few measures, the means may be given in the regular text of the article. Usually, there is also some report of follow-up analyses, such as planned contrasts.

Returning again to the criminal record study example, we could describe the analysis of variance results this way: "The means for the Criminal Record, Clean Record, and No Information groups were 8.0, 4.0, and 5.0, respectively. These were significantly different, $F(2, 12) = 4.07, p < .05$. We also carried out two planned contrasts: The Criminal Record versus the No Information condition, $F(1, 12) = 4.22$, $p < .10$; and the Criminal Record versus the Clean Record condition, $F(1, 12) = 7.50, p < .05$. The first contrast approached significance, but after a Bonferroni correction (for two planned contrasts), it would not even reach the .10 level."

Note that it is also common for researchers to report planned contrasts using t tests. These are not ordinary t tests for independent means, but rather special t tests for the comparisons that are mathematically equivalent to the method we described—that is, the results in terms of significance are identical (see Chapter Note 2).

Researchers often report results of post hoc comparisons among all pairs of means. The most common method of doing this is by putting small letters by the means in the tables. Usually, means with the same letter are *not* significantly different from each other; those with different letters are. For example, Table 9–11 presents the actual results on the love experience measures in the Hazan and Shaver (1987) study (our

Table 9-11 Love Subscale Means for the Three Attachment Types (Newspaper Sample)

Scale Name	Avoidant	Anxious/ Ambivalent	Secure	$F(2, 571)$
Happiness	3.19$_a$	3.31$_a$	3.51$_b$	14.21***
Friendship	3.18$_a$	3.19$_a$	3.50$_b$	22.96***
Trust	3.11$_a$	3.13$_a$	3.43$_b$	16.21***
Fear of closeness	2.30$_a$	2.15$_a$	1.88$_b$	22.65***
Acceptance	2.86$_a$	3.03$_b$	3.01$_b$	4.66**
Emotional extremes	2.75$_a$	3.05$_b$	2.36$_c$	27.54***
Jealousy	2.57$_a$	2.88$_b$	2.17$_c$	43.91***
Obsessive preoccupation	3.01$_a$	3.29$_b$	3.01$_a$	9.47***
Sexual attraction	3.27$_a$	3.43$_b$	3.27$_a$	4.08*
Desire for union	2.81$_a$	3.25$_b$	2.69$_a$	22.67***
Desire for reciprocation	3.24$_a$	3.55$_b$	3.22$_a$	14.90***
Love at first sight	2.91$_a$	3.17$_b$	2.97$_a$	6.00**

Note: Within each row, means with different subscripts differ at the .05 level of significance according to a Scheffé test.
*$p < .05$; ** $p < .01$; ***$p < .001$.
Source: Hazan, C., & Shaver, P. (1987). Romantic love conceptualized as an attachment process. *Journal of Personality and Social Psychology, 52,* 511–524. Published by the American Psychological Association. Reprinted with permission.

example at the start of the chapter). Consider the first row (the happiness results). The avoidant and anxious-ambivalent groups are not significantly different from each other, since they have the same letter (*a*). But both are significantly different on happiness compared to the secure group, which has a different letter (*b*). In the jealousy row, however, all three groups differ from one another.

When reading results of post hoc comparisons, you will see many different procedures named. For example, Table 9–11 (from the Hazan and Shaver study) explicitly mentions that the results are "according to a Scheffé test."

Advanced Topic: The Structural Model in the Analysis of Variance

This chapter introduced the basic logic of the analysis of variance. Building on this understanding, we now briefly describe an alternative but mathematically equivalent way of understanding the analysis of variance. This alternative is called the **structural model.** The core logic you learned earlier in the chapter still applies. However, the structural model provides a different and more flexible way of figuring the two population variance estimates. Understanding the structural model provides deeper insights into the underlying logic of the analysis of variance, including helping you understand the way analysis of variance results are laid out in computer printouts. Also, the structural method more easily handles the situation in which the number of individuals in each group is not equal. Finally, the structural model method is related to a fundamental mathematical approach to which we want to expose those of you who might be going on to more advanced statistics courses.

Principles of the Structural Model

Dividing Up the Deviations

The structural model is all about deviations. To start with, there is the deviation of a score from the grand mean. In the criminal record example earlier in the chapter (see Tables 9–3 and 9–4), the grand mean of the 15 scores was $85/15 = 5.67$.

The deviation from the grand mean is just the beginning. You then think of this deviation from the grand mean as having two parts: (a) the deviation of the score from the mean of its group and (b) the deviation of the mean of its group from the grand mean. Consider a participant in the criminal record study who rated the defendant's guilt as a 10. The grand mean of all participants' guilt ratings was 5.67. This person's score has a total deviation of 4.33 (that is, $10 - 5.67 = 4.33$). The mean of the Criminal Record group by itself was 8. Thus, the deviation of this person's score from his or her group's mean is 2 (that is, $10 - 8 = 2$), and the deviation of that group's mean from the grand mean is 2.33 (that is, $8 - 5.67 = 2.33$). Note that these two deviations (2 and 2.33) add up to the total deviation of 4.33. This is shown in Figure 9–7. We encourage you to study this figure until you grasp it well.

Summing the Squared Deviations

The next step in the structural model is to square each of these deviation scores and add up the squared deviations of each type for all the participants. This gives a *sum of squared deviations* for each type of deviation score. It turns out that the sum of squared deviations of each score from the grand mean is equal to (a) the sum of the squared deviations of each score from its group's mean plus (b) the sum of the squared

structural model way of understanding the analysis of variance as a division of the deviation of each score from the overall mean into two parts: the variation in groups (its deviation from its group's mean) and the variation between groups (its group's mean's deviation from the overall mean); an alternative (but mathematically equivalent) way of understanding the analysis of variance.

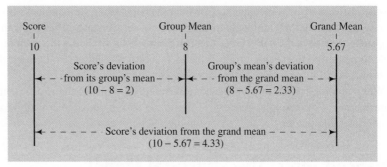

Figure 9–7 Example from the fictional criminal record study of the deviation of one individual's score from the grand mean being that individual's score's deviation from his or her group's mean plus that individual's group's mean's deviation from the grand mean.

> The sum of squared deviations of each score from the grand mean is the sum of squared deviations of each score from its group's mean plus the sum of squared deviations of each score's group's mean from the grand mean.

deviations of each score's group's mean from the grand mean. This principle can be stated as a formula:

$$\Sigma(X - GM) = \Sigma(X - M)^2 + \Sigma(M - GM)^2 \text{ or}$$

$$SS_{\text{Total}} = SS_{\text{Within}} + SS_{\text{Between}} \qquad (9\text{–}9)$$

In this formula, $\Sigma(X - GM)^2$ or $\mathbf{SS_{Total}}$ is the sum of squared deviations of each score from the grand mean, completely ignoring the group a score is in. $\Sigma(X - M)^2$ or $\mathbf{SS_{Within}}$ is the sum of squared deviations of each score from its group's mean, added up for all participants. $\Sigma(M - GM)^2$ or $\mathbf{SS_{Between}}$ is the sum of squared deviations of each score's group's mean from the grand mean—again, added up for all participants.

This rule applies only to the *sums* of the squared deviations. For each individual score, the deviations themselves, but not the squared deviations, always add up.

> SS_{Total} sum of squared deviations of each score from the overall mean of all scores, completely ignoring the group a score is in.
>
> SS_{Within} sum of squared deviations of each score from its group's mean.
>
> SS_{Between} sum of squared deviations of each score's group's mean from the grand mean.

From the Sums of Squared Deviations to the Population Variance Estimates

Now we are ready to use these sums of squared deviations to figure the needed population variance estimates for an analysis of variance. To do this, you divide each sum of squared deviations by an appropriate degrees of freedom. The between-groups population variance estimate (S^2_{Between} or MS_{Between}) is the sum of squared deviations of each score's group's mean from the grand mean (SS_{Between}) divided by the degrees of freedom on which it is based (df_{Between}, the number of groups minus 1). Stated as a formula,

> The between-groups population variance estimate is the sum of squared deviations of each score's group's mean from the grand mean divided by the degrees of freedom for the between-groups population variance estimate.

$$S^2_{\text{Between}} = \frac{\Sigma(M - GM)^2}{df_{\text{Between}}} \quad \text{or} \quad MS_{\text{Between}} = \frac{SS_{\text{Between}}}{df_{\text{Between}}} \qquad (9\text{–}10)$$

The within-groups population variance estimate (S^2_{Within} or MS_{Within}) is the sum of squared deviations of each score from its group's mean (SS_{Within}) divided by the total degrees of freedom on which this is based (df_{Within}; the sum of the degrees of freedom over all the groups—the number of scores in the first group minus 1, plus the number in the second group minus 1, etc.). Stated as a formula,

> The within-groups population variance estimate is the sum of squared deviations of each score from its group's mean divided by the degrees of freedom for the within-groups population variance estimate.

$$S^2_{\text{Within}} = \frac{\Sigma(X - M)^2}{df_{\text{Within}}} \quad \text{or} \quad MS_{\text{Within}} = \frac{SS_{\text{Within}}}{df_{\text{Within}}} \qquad (9\text{–}11)$$

Notice that we have ignored the sum of squared deviations of each score from the grand mean (SS_{Total}). This sum of squares is useful mainly for checking our arithmetic. Recall that $SS_{\text{Total}} = SS_{\text{Within}} + SS_{\text{Between}}$.

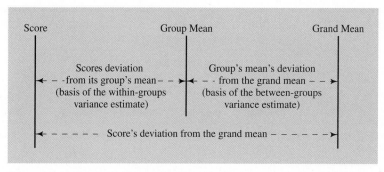

Figure 9–8   The score's deviations from its group's mean is the basis for the within-groups population variance estimate; the group's mean's deviation from the grand mean is the basis for the between-groups population variance estimate.

Figure 9–8 again shows the division of the deviation score into two parts, but this time emphasizes which deviations are associated with which population variance estimates.

Relation of the Structural Model Method to the Method You Learned Earlier in the Chapter

The methods we have just described for figuring the within-groups and between-groups population variance estimates using the structural model approach give exactly the same result as the methods you learned earlier in the chapter. (If you enjoy algebra, you might see whether you can derive the earlier formulas from the ones you have just learned.) However, the procedures you follow to figure those estimates are quite different. In the structural model method, when figuring the within-groups variance estimate method, you never actually figure the variance estimate for each group and average them. Similarly, for the between-groups estimate, with the structural model method, you never multiply anything by the number of scores in each sample. The point is that, with either method, you get the same within-groups and between-groups variance estimates, and thus the same F and the same overall result.

The deeper logic of the analysis of variance with the structural model is also essentially the same as what you learned earlier in the chapter, with a twist. The twist is one of emphasis. The method you learned earlier in the chapter emphasizes entire groups, comparing a variance based on differences among group means to a variance based on averaging variances of the groups. The structural model method emphasizes individual scores. It compares a variance based on deviations of individual scores' groups' means from the grand mean to a variance based on deviations of individual scores from their group's mean. The method earlier in the chapter focuses directly on what contributes to the overall population variance estimates; the structural model method focuses directly on what contributes to the divisions of the deviations of scores from the grand mean.

An Example

Table 9–12 shows all the figuring using the structural model for an analysis of variance for the criminal record study. This table shows all three types of deviations and squared deviations for each score. For example, for the first person, the deviation from the grand mean is 4.33 (the score of 10 minus the grand mean of 5.67). This

Table 9-12 Analysis of Variance for the Criminal Record Study (Fictional Data) Using the Structural Model Method (Compare to Tables 9–3 and 9–4)

Criminal Record Group

X	X − GM Deviation	X − GM Squared Deviation	X − M Deviation	X − M Squared Deviation	M − GM Deviation	M − GM Squared Deviation
10	4.33	18.75	2	4	2.33	5.43
7	1.33	1.77	−1	1	2.33	5.43
5	−.67	.45	−3	9	2.33	5.43
10	4.33	18.75	2	4	2.33	5.43
8	2.33	5.43	0	0	2.33	5.43
40		45.15		18		27.15

$M = 40/5 = 8$

Clean Record Group

X	X − GM Deviation	X − GM Squared Deviation	X − M Deviation	X − M Squared Deviation	M − GM Deviation	M − GM Squared Deviation
5	−.67	.45	1	1	−1.67	2.79
1	−4.67	21.81	−3	9	−1.67	2.79
3	−2.67	7.13	−1	1	−1.67	2.79
7	1.33	1.77	3	9	−1.67	2.79
4	−1.67	2.79	0	0	−1.67	2.79
20		33.95		20		13.95

$M = 20/5 = 4$

No Information Group

X	X − GM Deviation	X − GM Squared Deviation	X − M Deviation	X − M Squared Deviation	M − GM Deviation	M − GM Squared Deviation
4	−1.67	2.79	−1	1	−.67	.45
6	.33	.11	1	1	−.67	.45
9	3.33	11.09	4	16	−.67	.45
3	−2.67	7.13	−2	4	−.67	.45
3	−2.67	7.13	−2	4	−.67	.45
25		28.25		26		2.25

$M = 25/5 = 5$

Sums of squared deviations:

$\Sigma(X - GM)^2$ or $SS_{Total} = 45.15 + 33.95 + 28.25 = 107.35$

$\Sigma(X - M)^2$ or $SS_{Within} = 18 + 20 + 26 = 64$

$\Sigma(M - GM)^2$ or $SS_{Between} = 27.15 + 13.95 + 2.25 = 43.35$

Check ($SS_{Total} = SS_{Within} + SS_{Between}$):

$SS_{Total} = 107.35$; $SS_{Within} + SS_{Between} = 64 + 43.35 = 107.35$

Degrees of freedom:

$df_{Total} = N - 1 = 15 - 1 = 14$

$df_{Within} = df_1 + df_2 + \cdots + df_{Last} = (5 - 1) + (5 - 1) + (5 - 1) = 4 + 4 + 4 = 12$

$df_{Between} = N_{Groups} - 1 = 3 - 1 = 2$

Check ($df_{Total} = df_{Within} + df_{Between}$): $14 = 12 + 2$

Population variance estimates:

S^2_{Within} or $MS_{Within} = SS_{Within}/df_{Within} = 64/12 = 5.33$

$S^2_{Between}$ or $MS_{Between} = SS_{Between}/df_{Between} = 43.35/2 = 21.68$

F ratio: $F = S^2_{Between}/S^2_{Within}$ or $MS_{Between}/MS_{Within} = 21.68/5.33 = 4.07$

deviation squared is 18.75. The deviation of the score from its group's mean is 2; this deviation squared is 4. Finally, the deviation of the score's group's mean from the grand mean is 2.33; this deviation squared is 5.43. Notice that the deviations of each score's group's mean from the grand mean (in this case, 2.33) is the same number for all the scores in a group. At the bottom of each column, we have also summed the squared deviations of each type.

The bottom part of Table 9–12 shows the analysis of variance figuring. First, you figure the three sums of squared deviations (SS_{Total}, SS_{Within}, and $SS_{Between}$). The next step is to check for accuracy. You do this following the principle that the sum of squared deviations of each score from the grand mean comes out to the total of the other two kinds of sums of squared deviations.

The degrees of freedom, the next step shown in the table, is figured the same way as you learned earlier in the chapter. Then, the table shows the figuring of the two crucial population variance estimates. You figure them by dividing each sum of squared deviations by the appropriate degrees of freedom. Finally, the table shows the figuring of the F ratio in the usual way—dividing the between-groups variance estimate by the within-groups variance estimate. All these results, degrees of freedom, variance estimates, and F come out exactly the same (within rounding error) as we figured earlier in the chapter.

Analysis of Variance Tables

An **analysis of variance table** lays out the results of an analysis of variance based on the structural model method. These kinds of charts are automatically produced by most analysis of variance computer programs (see, for example, Figure 9–11 later in the chapter). A standard analysis of variance table has five columns. Table 9–13 shows an analysis of variance table for the criminal record study.

The first column in a standard analysis of variance table is labeled "Source"; it lists the type of variance estimate or deviation score involved ["between" (groups), "within" (groups), and "total"]. The next column is usually labeled "SS" (sum of squares); it lists the different types of sums of squared deviations. The third column is "df" (the degrees of freedom of each type). The fourth column is "MS" (mean square); this refers to mean squares, that is, MS is SS divided by df, the variance estimate. MS is, as usual, the same thing as S^2. However, in an analysis of variance table the variance is almost always referred to as MS. The last column is "F," the F ratio. (In a computer printout there may be additional columns, listing the exact p value and possibly effect size or confidence intervals.) Each row of the table refers to one of the variance estimates. The first row is for the between-groups variance estimate. It is usually listed under Source as "Between" or "Group," although you will sometimes see it called "Model" or "Treatment." The second row is for the within-groups variance estimate, though it is sometimes labeled as "Error." The final row is for the sum of squares based on the total deviation of each score from the grand mean. Note, however, that computer printouts will sometimes use a different order for the columns and will sometimes omit either SS or MS, but not both.

analysis of variance table chart showing the major elements in figuring an analysis of variance using the structural model approach.

Table 9-13 Analysis of Variance Table for the Criminal Record Study (Fictional Data)

Source	SS	df	MS	F
Between	43.35	2	21.68	4.07
Within	64	12	5.33	
Total	107.35	14		

Table 9-14 Hypothesis Testing Steps for an Analysis of Variance Using the Structural Model Approach (Equal- or Unequal-Sized Groups)

❶ **Restate the question as a research hypothesis and a null hypothesis about the populations.**

❷ **Determine the characteristics of the comparison distribution.**

   a. The comparison distribution will be an F distribution.

   b. The between-groups (numerator) degrees of freedom is the number of groups minus 1:
   $$df_{Between} = N_{Groups} - 1.$$

   c. The within-groups (denominator) degrees of freedom is the sum of the degrees of freedom in each group (the number of scores in the group minus 1):
   $$df_{Within} = df_1 + df_2 + \cdots + df_{Last}.$$

   d. Check the accuracy of your figuring by making sure that df_{Within} and $df_{Between}$ sum to df_{Total} (which is the total number of participants minus 1).

❸ **Determine the cutoff sample score on the comparison distribution at which the null hypothesis should be rejected.**

   a. Decide the significance level.

   b. Look up the appropriate cutoff in an F table, using the degrees of freedom from Step ❷.

❹ **Determine your sample's score on the comparison distribution.** This will be an F ratio.

   a. Figure the mean of each group and the grand mean of all scores.

   b. Figure the following deviations for each score:

      i. Its deviation from the grand mean $(X - GM)$.

      ii. Its deviation from its group's mean $(X - M)$.

      iii. Its group's mean's deviation from the grand mean $(M - GM)$.

   c. Square each of these deviation scores.

   d. Figure the sums of each of these three types of deviation scores (SS_{Total}, SS_{Within}, and $SS_{Between}$).

   e. Check the accuracy of your figuring by making sure that $SS_{Within} + SS_{Between} = SS_{Total}$.

   f. Figure the between-groups variance estimate: $SS_{Between}/df_{Between}$.

   g. Figure the within-groups variance estimate: SS_{Within}/df_{Within}.

   h. Figure the F ratio: $F = S^2_{Between}/S^2_{Within}$ or $F = MS_{Between}/MS_{Within}$.

❺ **Decide whether to reject the null hypothesis:** Compare scores from Steps ❸ and ❹.

TIP FOR SUCCESS

Check your understanding of the structural model method for analysis of variance by covering up portions of Table 9–15 and trying to recall the hidden material.

Table 9-15 Analysis of Variance Table Showing Symbols and Formulas for Figuring the Analysis of Variance

Symbols Corresponding to Each Part of an Analysis of Variance Table				
Source	**SS**	**df**	**MS**	**F**
Between	$SS_{Between}$	$df_{Between}$	$MS_{Between}$ (or $S^2_{Between}$)	F
Within	SS_{Within}	df_{Within}	MS_{Within} (or S^2_{Within})	
Total	SS_{Total}	df_{Total}		

Formulas for Each Part of an Analysis of Variance Table				
Source	**SS**	**df**	**MS**	**F**
Between	$\Sigma(M - GM)^2$	$N_{Groups} - 1$	$SS_{Between}/df_{Between}$	$MS_{Between}/MS_{Within}$
Within	$\Sigma(X - M)^2$	$df_1 + df_2 + \cdots + df_{Last}$	SS_{Within}/df_{Within}	
Total	$\Sigma(X - GM)^2$	$N - 1$		

Summary of Procedures for an Analysis of Variance Using the Structural Model

Table 9–14 summarizes the steps in an analysis of variance using the structural model method. Note that the only difference from what you learned earlier in this chapter is in Step ❹, substeps b through g (compare to Table 9–8). Table 9–15 shows an analysis of variance table with the symbols for all the parts put in each section where the numbers would usually go. It is followed by the same style of analysis of variance table with the various formulas filled in where the numbers would usually go.[6]

Summary

1. The analysis of variance (ANOVA) is used to test hypotheses based on differences among means of more than two samples. The procedure compares two estimates of population variance. One, the within-groups estimate, is the average of the variance estimates from each of the samples. The other, the between-groups estimate, is based on the variation among the means of the samples.
2. The F ratio is the between-groups estimate divided by the within-groups estimate. The null hypothesis is that all the samples come from populations with the same mean. If the null hypothesis is true, the F ratio should be about 1. This is because the two population variance estimates are based on the same thing, the variation within each of the populations (due to chance factors). If the research hypothesis is true, so that the samples come from populations with different means, the F ratio should be larger than 1. This is because the between-groups estimate is now influenced by the variation both within the populations (due to chance factors) and among them (due to a treatment effect). But the within-groups estimate is still affected only by the variation within each of the populations.
3. When the samples are of equal size, the within-groups population variance estimate is the ordinary average of the estimates of the population variance figured from each sample. The between-groups population variance estimate is done in two steps. First, you estimate the variance of the distribution of means based on the means of your samples. (This is figured with the usual formula for estimating population variance from sample scores.) Second, you multiply this estimate by the number of participants in each group. This step takes you from the variance of the distribution of means to the variance of the distribution of individual scores.
4. The distribution of F ratios when the null hypothesis is true is a mathematically defined distribution that is skewed to the right. Significance cutoffs are given on an F table according to the degrees of freedom for each population variance estimate: the between-groups (numerator) degrees of freedom is the number of groups minus 1, and the within-groups (denominator) degrees of freedom is the sum of the degrees of freedom within all samples.
5. The assumptions for the analysis of variance are the same as for the t test. The populations must be normally distributed, with equal variances. Like the t test, the analysis of variance is robust to moderate violations of these assumptions.
6. The overall results of an analysis of variance are often followed up by planned contrasts, based on theory or a specific practical need, that examine differences such as those between specific pairs of means. These contrasts (or comparisons) are figured using the usual analysis of variance method, but with the between-groups estimate based on the variation between the two means being compared.

7. When making more than one planned contrast, researchers often protect against the possibility of getting some contrasts significant just by chance by making a Bonferroni correction of the significance level (dividing the overall desired significance level by the number of contrasts).

8. An analysis of variance may be followed up by exploratory, post hoc comparisons. Such comparisons have to protect against the possibility of getting some significant results just by chance because of the great many comparisons that could be made. There are a number of methods for dealing with this problem that are not as severe as the Bonferroni correction. In one such method, the Scheffé test, you figure each comparison of interest in the usual way and then divide its F by the between-groups degrees of freedom from the overall analysis of variance.

9. The proportion of variance accounted for (R^2), also called "eta squared" (η^2), is a measure of analysis of variance effect size. The formula for R^2 is: $R^2 = (S^2_{Between})(df_{Between})/[(S^2_{Between})(df_{Between}) + (S^2_{Within})(df_{Within})]$. Power depends on effect size, number of people in the study, significance level, and number of groups.

10. Some experts recommend that, instead of using an analysis of variance to make diffuse, overall comparisons among several means, researchers should plan in advance to conduct only specific planned contrasts, targeted directly to their theoretical or practical questions.

11. Analysis of variance results are reported in a standard fashion, such as $F(3, 68) = 5.21$, $p < .01$. Results of planned contrasts are also commonly reported (sometimes using special t tests instead of analysis of variance). Results of post hoc comparisons are usually shown by putting small letters by the means in tables.

12. ADVANCED TOPIC: An alternative approach to the analysis of variance uses the structural model. In the structural model method, the deviation of each score from the grand mean is divided into two parts: (a) the score's difference from its group's mean and (b) its group's mean's difference from the grand mean. These deviations, when squared, summed, and divided by the appropriate degrees of freedom, give the same within-groups and between-groups estimates as using the standard analysis of variance method you learned. However, the structural model is more flexible and can be applied to studies with unequal sample sizes. Computations using the structural model are usually summarized in an analysis of variance table, with a column for source of variation (between, within, and total), sums of squared deviations (SS), degrees of freedom (df), population variance estimates (MS, which equals SS/df), and F (which equals $MS_{Between}/MS_{Within}$).

Key Terms

analysis of variance (ANOVA) (p. 311)
within-groups estimate of the population variance (S^2_{Within} or MS_{Within}) (p. 312)
between-groups estimate of the population variance ($S^2_{Between}$ or $MS_{Between}$) (p. 313)
F ratio (p. 317)
F distribution (p. 318)
F table (p. 318)

S^2_{Within} or MS_{Within} (p. 320)
grand mean (GM) (p. 321)
$S^2_{Between}$ or $MS_{Between}$ (p. 322)
between-groups (or numerator) degrees of freedom ($df_{Between}$) (p. 324)
within-groups (or denominator) degrees of freedom (df_{Within}) (p. 324)
planned contrasts (p. 334)
Bonferroni procedure (p. 336)

post hoc comparisons (p. 337)
Scheffé test (p. 338)
proportion of variance accounted for (R^2) (p. 339)
eta squared (η^2) (p. 340)
structural model (p. 345)
SS_{Total}, SS_{Within}, $SS_{Between}$ (p. 346)
analysis of variance table (p. 349)

Example Worked-Out Problems

Overall Analysis of Variance

An experiment compares the effects of four treatments, giving each treatment to 20 participants and then assessing their performance on a standard measure. The results on the standard measure are as follows. Treatment 1: $M = 15$, $S^2 = 20$; Treatment 2: $M = 12$, $S^2 = 25$; Treatment 3: $M = 18$, $S^2 = 14$; Treatment 4: $M = 15$, $S^2 = 27$. Using the .05 significance level, does treatment matter? Use the five steps of hypothesis testing and sketch the distributions involved.

Answer

The distributions involved are shown in Figure 9–9.

❶ **Restate the question as a research hypothesis and a null hypothesis about the populations.** There are four populations.

Population 1: People given experimental treatment 1.
Population 2: People given experimental treatment 2.
Population 3: People given experimental treatment 3.
Population 4: People given experimental treatment 4.

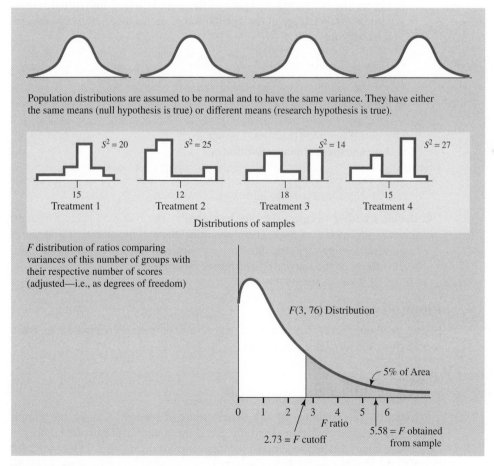

Figure 9–9   Distributions involved in Example Worked-Out Problem for overall analysis of variance.

The null hypothesis is that these four populations have the same mean ($\mu_1 = \mu_2 = \mu_3 = \mu_4$). The research hypothesis is that the four population means are not the same.

❷ **Determine the characteristics of the comparison distribution.** The comparison distribution will be an F distribution. $df_{\text{Between}} = N_{\text{Groups}} - 1 = 4 - 1 = 3$; $df_{\text{Within}} = df_1 + df_2 + \cdots + df_{\text{Last}} = 19 + 19 + 19 + 19 = 76$.

❸ **Determine the cutoff sample score on the comparison distribution at which the null hypothesis should be rejected.** Using Table A–3 in the Appendix for $df = 3, 75$ (the closest below 3, 76) at the .05 level, the cutoff F is 2.73.

❹ **Determine your sample's score on the comparison distribution.**

a. Figure the between-groups population variance estimate (S^2_{Between}):

Figure the mean of each group. The group means are 15, 12, 18, and 15.

Ⓐ **Estimate the variance of the distribution of means:** Add up the sample means' squared deviations from the grand mean and divide by the number of means minus 1:

$$GM = (15 + 12 + 18 + 15)/4 = 15$$
$$S^2_M = \Sigma(M - GM)^2/df_{\text{Between}}$$
$$= ([15 - 15]^2 + [12 - 15]^2 + [18 - 15]^2 + [15 - 15]^2)/(4-1)$$
$$= (0 + 9 + 9 + 0)/3 = 18/3 = 6.$$

Ⓑ **Figure the estimated variance of the population of individual scores:** Multiply the variance of the distribution of means by the number of scores in each group.

$$S^2_{\text{Between}} = (S^2_M)(n) = (6)(20) = 120.$$

b. Figure the within-groups population variance estimate (S^2_{Within}):

Ⓐ **Figure population variance estimates based on each group's scores:** Treatment 1 group, $S^2 = 20$; Treatment 2 group, $S^2 = 25$; Treatment 3 group, $S^2 = 14$; Treatment 4 group, $S^2 = 27$.

Ⓑ **Average these variance estimates:**

$$S^2_{\text{Within}} = (20 + 25 + 14 + 27)/4 = 86/4 = 21.5.$$
$$F = S^2_{\text{Between}}/S^2_{\text{Within}} = 120/21.5 = 5.58.$$

❺ **Decide whether to reject the null hypothesis.** The F of 5.58 is more extreme than the .05 cutoff F of 2.73. Therefore, reject the null hypothesis. The research hypothesis is supported; the different experimental treatments do produce different effects on the standard performance measure.

Planned Contrasts

For the preceding study, figure a planned contrast comparing Treatment 2 to Treatment 3 using the .01 significance level.

Answer

For the between-groups population variance estimate,

Ⓐ **Estimate the variance of the distribution of means:** Add up the sample means' squared deviations from the grand mean and divide by the number of means minus 1. The grand mean for these two means is $(12 + 18)/2 = 15$ and $df_{\text{Between}} = N_{\text{Groups}} - 1 = 2 - 1 = 1$.

$$S_M^2 = \Sigma(M - GM)^2/df_{\text{Between}}$$
$$= [(12 - 15)^2 + (18 - 15)^2]/1$$
$$= [(-3)^2 + 3^2]/1 = (9 + 9)/1 = 18.$$

❶ **Figure the estimated variance of the population of individual scores:** Multiply the variance of the distribution of means by the number of scores in each group.

$$S_{\text{Between}}^2 = (S_M^2)(n) = (18)(20) = 360$$
$$S_{\text{Within}}^2 \text{ (from the overall analysis)} = 21.5$$
$$F = S_{\text{Between}}^2/S_{\text{Within}}^2 = 360/21.5 = 16.74.$$

The cutoff F for .05, $df = 1, 75$ (the closest on the table below the true df of 1, 76) $= 3.97$.

Reject the null hypothesis; the contrast is significant.

Bonferroni Procedure

What is the Bonferroni corrected significance level for each of six planned contrasts at the overall .05 significance level?

Answer

Bonferroni corrected significance $= .05/6 = .0083$.

Post Hoc Comparisons Using the Scheffé Method

A study has five groups with 10 participants in each. Using a Scheffé test, is a comparison with a computed F of 11.21 significant at the .01 significance level?

Answer

The overall study's $df_{\text{Between}} = 5 - 1 = 4$; $df_{\text{Within}} = 9 + 9 + 9 + 9 + 9 = 45$.

The Scheffé corrected F for this contrast is $11.21/4 = 2.80$. The overall study's .01 cutoff F ($df = 4, 45$) is 3.77. The contrast is not significant.

Figuring Effect Size for an Analysis of Variance

Figure the effect size for the overall analysis of variance Example Worked-Out Problem.

Answer

$$R^2 = (S_{\text{Between}}^2)(df_{\text{Between}})/[(S_{\text{Between}}^2)(df_{\text{Between}}) + (S_{\text{Within}}^2)(df_{\text{Within}})]$$
$$= (120)(3)/[(120)(3) + (21.5)(76)] = (360)/[(360) + (1634)] = .18.$$

Advanced Topic: Figuring an Analysis of Variance Using the Structural Model Method

A researcher at an alcohol treatment center conducts a study of client satisfaction with treatment methods A, B, and C. The researcher randomly assigns each of the available 10 clients to receive one of these treatments; four clients end up with Treatment A, three with Treatment B, and three with Treatment C. Two weeks later, the researcher measures client satisfaction with the three treatments on a scale from 1 (low satisfaction) to 20 (high satisfaction). Scores for Treatment A were 8, 13, 10, and 9. Scores for Treatment B were 7, 3, and 8. Scores for Treatment C were 6, 4, and 2. Use the steps of hypothesis testing and figure an analysis of variance (at the .05 level) using the structural model method. (Although the example we used for the structural model method earlier in the chapter had the same number of participants in each group, you can use the same method in this example with unequal sized groups. Just remember to figure the grand mean, *GM*, as the average of all of the scores.)

Answer

Table 9–16 shows the figuring and the analysis of variance table.

❶ **Restate the question as a research hypothesis and a null hypothesis about the populations.** There are three populations:

Population 1: Alcoholics receiving Treatment A.
Population 2: Alcoholics receiving Treatment B.
Population 3: Alcoholics receiving Treatment C.

The null hypothesis is that these three populations have the same mean ($\mu_1 = \mu_2 = \mu_3$). The research hypothesis is that they do not all have the same mean.

❷ **Determine the characteristics of the comparison distribution.** An *F* distribution; from Table 9–16, $df = 2, 7$.

Table 9-16 Analysis of Variance Figuring and Analysis of Variance Table Problem for an Alcohol Treatment Study (Fictional Data)

Treatment A						Treatment B						Treatment C					
X	*X − GM*		*X − M*		*M − GM*		*X*	*X − GM*		*X − M*		*M − GM*		*X*	*X − GM*		*X − M*		*M − GM*
	Dev	Dev²	Dev	Dev²	Dev	Dev²		Dev	Dev²	Dev	Dev²	Dev	Dev²		Dev	Dev²	Dev	Dev²	Dev	Dev²
8	1	1	−2	4	3	9	7	0	0	1	1	−1	1	6	−1	1	2	4	−3	9
13	6	36	3	9	3	9	3	−4	16	−3	9	−1	1	4	−3	9	0	0	−3	9
10	3	9	0	0	3	9	8	1	1	2	4	−1	1	2	−5	25	−2	4	−3	9
9	2	4	−1	1	3	9														
40		50		14		36	18		17		14		3	12		35		8		27

$M = 40/4 = 10$ $M = 18/3 = 6$ $M = 12/3 = 4$

Note: Dev = Deviation; Dev² = Squared deviation.

$GM = (40 + 18 + 12)/10 = 70/10 = 7$
$df_{Total} = N - 1 = 10 - 1 = 9$
$df_{Within} = df_1 + df_2 + \cdots + df_{Last} = (4 - 1) + (3 - 1) + (3 - 1) = 3 + 2 + 2 = 7$
$df_{Between} = N_{Groups} - 1 = 3 - 1 = 2$
F needed for $df = 2, 7$ at the .05 level $= 4.74$
$SS_{Total} = 50 + 17 + 35 = 102$
$SS_{Within} = 14 + 14 + 8 = 36$
$SS_{Between} = 36 + 3 + 27 = 66$

ANALYSIS OF VARIANCE TABLE:

Source	SS	df	MS	F
Between	66	2	33	6.42
Within	36	7	5.14	
Total	102	9		

Decision: Reject the null hypothesis.

❸ **Determine the cutoff sample score on the comparison distribution at which the null hypothesis should be rejected.** Using Table A–3, for $df = 2, 7$ and a .05 significance level, the cutoff F is 4.74.

❹ **Determine your sample's score on the comparison distribution.**   From the figuring shown in Table 9–16, $F = 6.42$.

❺ **Decide whether to reject the null hypothesis.** The F ratio of 6.42 is more extreme than the .05 significance level cutoff F of 4.74. Thus, the researcher can reject the null hypothesis. If these were real data, the researcher could conclude that the three kinds of treatment have different effects on how satisfied clients like theirs are with their treatment.

Outline for Writing Essays for a One-Way Analysis of Variance

1. Explain that the one-way analysis of variance is used for hypothesis testing when you have scores from three or more entirely separate groups of people. Be sure to explain the meaning of the research hypothesis and the null hypothesis in this situation.

2. Describe the core logic of hypothesis testing in this situation. Be sure to mention that the analysis of variance involves comparing the results of two ways of estimating the population variance. One population variance estimate (the within-groups estimate) is based on the variation within each sample and the other estimate (the between-groups estimate) is based on the variation among the means of the samples. Be sure to describe these estimates in detail (including how they are figured, why they are figured that way, and how each is affected by whether the null hypothesis is true); explain how and why they are used to figure an F ratio.

3. Explain the logic of the comparison distribution that is used with a one-way analysis of varianance (the F distribution).

4. Describe the logic and process for determining the cutoff sample F score on the comparison distribution at which the null hypothesis should be rejected.

5. Explain how and why the scores from Steps ❸ and ❹ of the hypothesis-testing process are compared. Explain the meaning of the result of this comparison with regard to the specific research and null hypotheses being tested.

Practice Problems

These problems involve figuring. Most real-life statistics problems are done on a computer with special statistical software. Even if you have such software, do these problems by hand to ingrain the method in your mind. To learn how to use a computer to solve statistics problems like those in this chapter, refer to the Using SPSS section at the end of this chapter and the *Study Guide and Computer Workbook* that accompanies this text.

All data are fictional unless an actual citation is given.

Set I (for Answers to Set I Problems, see pp. 685–688)

1. For each of the following studies, decide whether you can reject the null hypothesis that the groups come from identical populations. Use the .05 level. Note that study (b) provides S, not S^2.

(a)	Group 1	Group 2	Group 3	
n	10	10	10	
M	7.4	6.8	6.8	
S^2	.82	.90	.80	

(b)	Group 1	Group 2	Group 3	Group 4
n	25	25	25	25
M	94	101	124	105
S	24	28	31	25

2. For each of the following studies, (a) and (b), decide whether you can reject the null hypothesis that the groups come from identical populations. Use the .01 level. (c) Figure the effect size for each study. (d) ADVANCED TOPIC: For study (a), carry out an analysis of variance using the structural model method.

(a)	Group 1	Group 2	Group 3
	8	6	4
	8	6	4
	7	5	3
	9	7	5

(b)	Group 1	Group 2	Group 3
	12	10	8
	4	2	0
	12	10	8
	4	2	0

3. A psychologist at a private mental hospital was asked to determine whether there was any clear difference in the length of stay of patients with different categories of diagnosis. Looking at the last four patients in each of the three major categories, the results (in terms of weeks of stay) were as follows:

Diagnosis Category		
Affective Disorders	Cognitive Disorders	Drug-Related Conditions
7	12	8
6	8	10
5	9	12
6	11	10

(a) Using the .05 level and the five steps of hypothesis testing, is there a significant difference in length of stay among diagnosis categories? (b) Sketch the distributions involved. (c) Figure the effect size for the study. (d) Explain your answer to part (a) to someone who understands everything involved in conducting a *t* test for independent means but is unfamiliar with the analysis of variance. (e) Test the significance of planned contrasts (using the .05 level without a Bonferroni correction) for affective disorders versus drug-related conditions and (f) cognitive disorders versus drug-related conditions. (g) Explain your answers to parts (e) and (f) to a person who understands analysis of variance but is unfamiliar with planned contrasts.

4. A study compared the felt intensity of unrequited love (loving someone who doesn't love you) among three groups: 50 individuals who were currently experiencing unrequited love who had a mean experienced intensity $= 3.5$, $S^2 = 5.2$; 50 who had previously experienced unrequited love and described their experiences retrospectively, $M = 3.2$, $S^2 = 5.8$; and 50 who had never experienced unrequited love but described how they thought they would feel if they were to experience it, $M = 3.8$, $S^2 = 4.8$. Determine the significance of the difference among groups, using the 5% level. (a) Use the steps of hypothesis testing; (b) sketch the distributions involved; (c) figure the effect size for the study; and (d) explain your answer to part (a) to someone who has never had a course in statistics.

5. A researcher studying genetic influences on learning compares the maze performance of four genetically different strains of mice, using eight mice per strain. Performance for the four strains were as follows:

Strain	Mean	S
J	41	3.5
M	38	4.6
Q	14	3.8
W	37	4.9

Using the .01 significance level, is there an overall difference in maze performance among the four strains? (a) Use the steps of hypothesis testing; (b) sketch the distributions involved; (c) figure the effect size for the study; and (d) explain your answer to part (a) to someone who is familiar with hypothesis testing with known populations but unfamiliar with the t test or the analysis of variance. (e) Test the significance of planned contrasts using the overall .05 level (with a Bonferroni correction for testing each of the five contrasts) for strain J versus strain M, (f) for strain J versus strain Q, (g) for strain J versus strain W, (h) for strain Q versus strain M, and (i) for strain Q versus strain W. (j) Explain your answers to parts (e) through (i) to a person who understands analysis of variance but is unfamiliar with planned contrasts and the Bonferroni correction.

6. What is the Bonferroni corrected significance level for each of the following situations?

Situation	(a)	(b)	(c)	(d)
Overall significance level	.05	.05	.01	.01
Number of planned contrasts	2	4	3	5

7. For each of the following studies, test whether a comparison in which the researcher figures an F of 17.21 would be significant using the Scheffé method.

	Number of Groups	Participants in Each Group	Significance Level
(a)	5	10	.05
(b)	6	10	.05
(c)	5	20	.05
(d)	5	10	.01

8. What is the power of each of the following planned studies, using the analysis of variance with $p < .05$?

	Predicted Effect Size	Number of Groups	Participants in Each Group
(a)	Small	3	20
(b)	Small	3	30
(c)	Small	4	20
(d)	Medium	3	20

9. About how many participants do you need in each group for 80% power in each of the following planned studies, using the analysis of variance with $p < .05$?

	Predicted Effect Size	Number of Groups
(a)	Small	3
(b)	Large	3
(c)	Small	4
(d)	Medium	3

10. Grilo and colleagues (1997) are clinical psychologists interested in the relationship of depression and substance use to personality disorders. Personality disorders are persistent, problematic traits and behaviors that exceed the usual range of individual differences. The researchers conducted interviews assessing personality disorders with adolescents who were psychiatric inpatients and had one of three diagnoses: (1) those with major depression, (2) those with substance abuse, and (3) those with both major depression and substance abuse. The mean number of disorders was as follows: major depression $M = 1.0$, substance abuse $M = .7$, those with both conditions $M = 1.9$. The researchers reported, "The three study groups differed in the average number of diagnosed personality disorders, $F(2, 112) = 10.18, p < .0001$." Explain this result to someone who is familiar with hypothesis testing with known populations but is unfamiliar with the t test or the analysis of variance.

11. A researcher wants to know whether the need for mental health care among prisoners varies according to the different types of prison facilities. The researcher randomly selects 40 prisoners from each of the three main types of prisons in a particular Canadian province and conducts exams to determine their need for mental health care. In the article describing the results, the researcher reported the means for each group and then added: "The need for mental health care among prisoners in the three types of prison systems appeared to be clearly different, $F(2, 117) = 5.62, p < .01$. A planned comparison [contrast] of System 1 to System 2 was significant, $F(1, 117) = 4.03, p < .05$." Explain this result to a person who has never had a course in statistics.

12. Based on Table 9–11 from the Hazan and Shaver (1987) study, indicate for which variables, if any, (a) the Avoidants are significantly different from the other two groups, (b) the Anxious-Ambivalents are different from the other two groups, (c) the Secures are different from the other two groups, and (d) all three groups are different. (e) Explain, to a person who understands analysis of variance but does not know anything about post hoc comparisons, what is meant in the table note that the results are "according to a Scheffé test."

13. Which type of English words are longer: nouns, verbs, or adjectives? Go to a book of at least 400 pages (not this book) and turn to random pages using the random numbers listed at the end of this paragraph. Go down the page until you come to a noun. Note its length (in number of letters). Do this for 10 different nouns. Do the same for 10 verbs and then for 10 adjectives. Using the .05 significance level, (a) carry out an analysis of variance comparing the three types of words, and (b) figure a planned contrast of nouns versus verbs. (Be sure also to give the full bibliographic information on the book you used: authors, title, year published, publisher, city.)

    73, 320, 179, 323, 219, 176, 167, 102, 228, 352, 4, 335, 118, 12, 333, 123, 38, 49, 399, 17, 188, 264, 342, 89, 13, 77, 378, 223, 92, 77, 152, 34, 214, 75, 83, 198, 210

Set II

14. For each of the following studies, decide whether you can reject the null hypothesis that the groups come from identical populations. Use the .05 level.

(a)	Group 1	Group 2	Group 3
n	5	5	5
M	10	12	14
S^2	4	6	5

(b)	Group 1	Group 2	Group 3
n	10	10	10
M	10	12	14
S^2	4	6	5

15. For each of the following studies, (a) and (b), decide whether you can reject the null hypothesis that the groups come from identical populations. Use the .01 level. (c) Figure the effect size for each study. (d) ADVANCED TOPIC: Carry out an analysis of variance for study (a) using the structural model method.

(a)	Group 1	Group 2	Group 3
	1	1	8
	2	2	7
	1	1	8
	2	2	7

(b)	Group 1	Group 2	Group 3
	1	4	8
	2	5	7
	1	4	8
	2	5	7

16. An organizational psychologist was interested in whether individuals working in different sectors of a company differed in their attitudes toward the company. The results for the three people surveyed in development were 10, 12, and 11; for the three in the marketing department, 6, 6, and 8; for the three in accounting, 7, 4, and 4; and for the three in production, 14, 16, and 13 (higher numbers mean more

positive attitudes). Was there a significant difference in attitude toward the company among employees working in different sectors of the company at the .05 level? (a) Use the steps of hypothesis testing; (b) sketch the distributions involved; (c) figure the effect size for the study; (d) explain your answer to part (a) to someone who understands everything involved in conducting a t test for independent means but is unfamiliar with the analysis of variance; (e) test the significance of planned contrasts using the overall .05 level (with a Bonferroni correction for testing each of the five contrasts) for engineering versus production, (f) marketing versus production, (g) accounting versus production, (h) development versus marketing, and (i) development versus accounting. (j) Explain your answers to parts (e) through (i) to a person who understands analysis of variance but is unfamiliar with planned contrasts or Bonferroni corrections. (k) ADVANCED TOPIC: Carry out an analysis of variance for the study using the structural model method.

17. Do students at various universities differ in how sociable they are? Twenty-five students were randomly selected from each of three universities in a region and were asked to report on the amount of time they spent socializing each day with other students. The result for University X was a mean of 5 hours and an estimated population variance of 2 hours; for University Y, $M = 4$, $S^2 = 1.5$; and for University Z, $M = 6$, $S^2 = 2.5$. What should you conclude? Use the .05 level. (a) Use the steps of hypothesis testing, (b) figure the effect size for the study; and (c) explain your answers to parts (a) and (b) to someone who has never had a course in statistics.

18. A psychologist studying artistic preference randomly assigns a group of 45 participants to one of three conditions in which they view a series of unfamiliar abstract paintings. The 15 participants in the Famous condition are led to believe that these are each famous paintings; their mean rating for liking the paintings is 6.5 ($S = 3.5$). The 15 in the Critically Acclaimed condition are led to believe that these are paintings that are not famous but are very highly thought of by a group of professional art critics; their mean rating is 8.5 ($S = 4.2$). The 15 in the Control condition are given no special information about the paintings; their mean rating is 3.1 ($S = 2.9$). Does what people are told about paintings make a difference in how well they are liked? Use the .05 level. (a) Use the steps of hypothesis testing; (b) sketch the distributions involved; (c) figure the effect size for the study; (d) explain your answer to part (a) to someone who is familiar with the t test for independent means but is unfamiliar with analysis of variance; (e) test the significance of planned contrasts (using the .05 significance level without a Bonferroni correction) for Famous versus Control and (f) Critically Acclaimed versus Control. (g) Explain your answers to parts (e) and (f) to a person who understands analysis of variance but is unfamiliar with planned contrasts.

19. What is the Bonferroni corrected significance level for each of the following situations?

Situation	(a)	(b)	(c)	(d)
Overall significance level	.01	.01	.05	.05
Number of planned contrasts	4	2	4	3

20. For each of the following studies, test whether a comparison in which the researcher figures an F of 8.12 would be significant using the Scheffé method.

	Number of Groups	Participants in Each Group	Significance Level
(a)	4	30	.05
(b)	5	80	.05
(c)	4	5	.05
(d)	8	30	.01

21. What is the power of each of the following planned studies, using the analysis of variance with $p < .05$?

	Predicted Effect Size	Number of Groups	Participants in Each Group
(a)	Small	4	50
(b)	Medium	4	50
(c)	Large	4	50
(d)	Medium	5	50

22. About how many participants do you need in each group for 80% power in each of the following planned studies, using the analysis of variance with $p < .05$?

	Predicted Effect Size	Number of Groups
(a)	Small	5
(b)	Medium	5
(c)	Large	5
(d)	Medium	3

23. An experiment is conducted in which 60 participants each fill out a personality test, but not according to the way the participants see themselves. Instead, 15 are randomly assigned to fill it out according to the way they think their mothers see them (that is, the way they think their mothers would fill it out to describe the participants); 15 as their fathers would fill it out for them; 15 as their best friends would fill it out for them; and 15 as the professors they know best would fill it out for them. The main results appear in Table 9–17. Explain these results to a person who has never had a course in statistics.

24. Rosalie Friend (2001), an educational psychologist, compared three methods of teaching writing. Students were randomly assigned to three different experimental conditions involving different methods of writing a summary. At the

Table 9-17 Means for Main Personality Scales for Each Experimental Condition (Fictional Data)

Scale	Mother	Father	Friend	Professor	$F(3, 56)$
Conformity	24	21	12	16	4.21**
Extroversion	14	13	15	13	2.05
Maturity	15	15	22	19	3.11*
Self-confidence	38	42	27	32	3.58*

*$p < .05$, **$p < .01$.

Table 9-18 Effects of Relationship Status

Dependent measure	Relationship Status		
	Dating No One	**Casual Dating**	**Exclusive Dating**
Skin conductance	19.5_b	19.1_b	15.8_a
Desire to meet target	14.6_b	15.3_b	11.2_a
Perceived physical attractiveness of target	15.6_b	17.1_b	13.8_a

Note: Higher numbers reflect greater arousal, desire to meet target, and perceived attractiveness; for the latter two items the possible range was 1–19. Within each row, means with different subscripts differ significantly ($p < .05$) by Duncan's multiple range test.
Source: Miller, R.S. (1997). Inattentive and contented: Relationship commitment and attention to alternatives. *Journal of Personality and Social Psychology, 73,* 758–766. Published by the American Psychological Association. Reprinted with permission.

end of the two days of instructions, participants wrote a summary. One of the ways it was scored was the percentage of specific details of information it included from the original material. Here is a selection from her article describing one of the findings:

> The effect of summarization method on inclusion of important information was significant: $F(2, 144) = 4.1032, p < .019$. The mean scores (with standard deviations in parentheses) were as follows: Argument Repetition, 59.6% (17.9); Generalization, 59.8% (15.2); and Self-Reflection, 50.2% (18.0). (p. 14)
>
> (a) Explain these results to a person who has never had a course in statistics. (b) Using the information in the preceding description, figure the effect size for the study.

25. Miller (1997) asked 147 female students to view slides of magazine ads that included, among other things, pictures of attractive men. The participants were measured for physiological arousal (skin conductance) while viewing the ads and also after viewing them; they were asked to rate the attractiveness and how much they would like to meet each person in the ads. As part of the analysis, Miller compared results for women dating no one, women in casual dating relationships, and women in exclusive dating relationships. Table 9–18 shows Miller's results. (a), (b), and (c) Describe the pattern of results on each variable. (d) Explain, to a person who understands analysis of variance but is unfamiliar with post hoc comparisons, what is meant in a general way by the table note that the results are based on "Duncan's multiple range test." (That is, you don't need to explain this specific test, but you do need to explain why a test like this was used and what it attempts to accomplish.)

Using SPSS

The ✐ in the following steps indicates a mouse click. (We used SPSS version 15.0 for Windows to carry out these analyses. The steps and output may be slightly different for other versions of SPSS.)

It is easier to learn these steps using actual numbers; so we will use the criminal record example from earlier in the chapter. The scores for that example are shown in Table 9–3 on page 320.

Figuring a One-Way Analysis of Variance

❶ Enter the scores into SPSS. SPSS assumes that all scores in a row are from the same person. In this example, each person is in only one of the three groups (the Criminal Record group, the Clean Record group, or the No Information group). Thus, to tell SPSS which person is in each group, enter the numbers as shown in Figure 9–10. In the first column (labeled "group"), we used the number "1" to indicate that a person is in the Criminal Record group, the number "2" to indicate a person in the Clean Record group, and the number "3" to indicate a person in the No Information group.

❷ ✑ *Analyze.*

❸ ✑ *Compare means.*

❹ ✑ *One-Way ANOVA.*

❺ ✑ on the variable called "guilt" and then ✑ the arrow next to the box labeled "Dependent List." This tells SPSS that the analysis of variance should be carried out on the scores for the "guilt" variable.

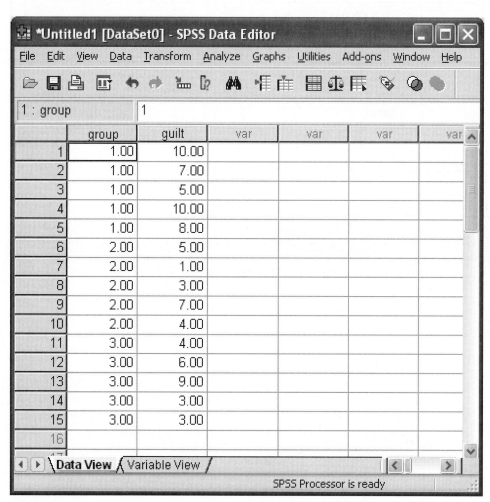

Figure 9–10 SPSS data editor window for the criminal record example (in which 15 individuals rated the guilt of a defendant after being randomly assigned to one of the three groups that were given different information about the defendant's previous criminal record).

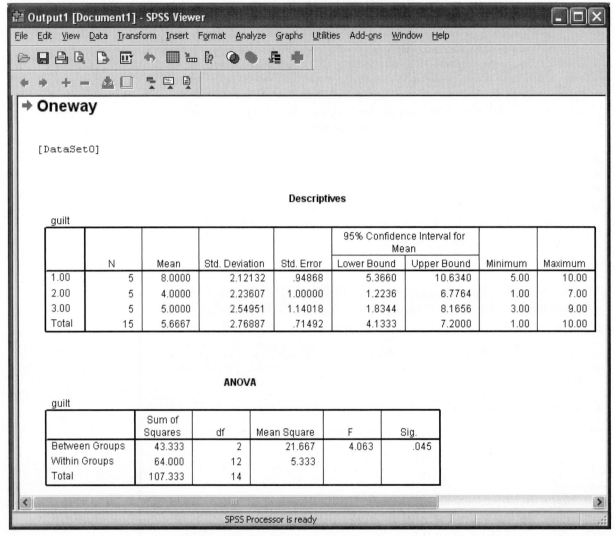

Figure 9–11 SPSS output window for a one-way analysis of variance for the criminal record example.

⑥ ✑ the variable called "group" and then ✑ the arrow next to the box labeled "Factor." This tells SPSS that the variable called "group" shows which person is in which group.

⑦ ✑ *Options.* ✑ the box labeled *Descriptive* (this checks the box). This tells SPSS to provide descriptive statistics (such as the mean and standard deviation) for each group. ✑ *Continue.* (Step ⑦ is optional, but we recommend always requesting descriptive statistics for any hypothesis testing situation.)

⑧ ✑ *OK.* Your SPSS output window should look like Figure 9–11.

The first table in the SPSS output provides descriptive statistics (number of individuals, mean, estimated population standard deviation, and other statistics) for the "guilt" scores for each of the three groups.

The second table in the SPSS output shows the actual results of the one-way analysis of variance. The first column lists the types of population variance estimates (between groups and within groups). The second column lists the between groups and within groups sums of squares: these are described in the Advanced Topic section earlier in this chapter, but ignore this column if you did not read that section. The third column, "df," gives the degrees of freedom. In the between groups row, this corresponds to df_{Between}; in the within groups row, this corresponds to df_{Within}. The fourth column, "Mean Square," gives the population variance estimates (S^2_{Between} and S^2_{Within}), with the between-groups estimate first and then the within-groups estimate. The next column gives the F ratio for the analysis of variance. Allowing for rounding error, the values for "df," "Mean Square," and "F" (and "Sum of Squares") are the same as those reported earlier in the chapter (allowing for rounding error). The final column, "Sig.," shows the exact significance level of the F ratio. The significance level of .045 is less than our .05 cutoff for this example. Thus, you can reject the null hypothesis and the research hypothesis is supported (that is, the result is statistically significant).

Post Hoc Tests for a One-Way Analysis of Variance

We will again use the criminal record example that we used for the one-way analysis of variance. Note that, before going through the following steps, we went to the "Variable View" window in SPSS and entered value labels (in the "Values" column) for the "guilt" variable (1 = "criminal record"; 2 = "clean record"; 3 = "no information"). Doing this makes it easier to read the SPSS output for the post hoc tests.

First, follow Steps ❶ through ❼ shown above for a one-way analysis of variance.

❽ ✐ *Post Hoc.* As you will see in the window that appears, there are many different types of post hoc tests available. In this chapter, we focused on the Scheffé test, so ✐ the box labeled *Scheffe* (this checks the box). ✐ *Continue.*

❾ ✐ *OK.*

The first two tables shown in your SPSS output window will be the same as the tables shown in Figure 9–11. There will also be two new tables in your SPSS output window; the first of these tables, labeled "Post Hoc Tests," is the most important and is shown in Figure 9–12. The table shows the results of all possible comparisons of the study groups (Criminal Record, No Record, and No Information). Let's start by looking at the first row of numbers, which shows the comparison of the Criminal Record group to the Clean Record group. The value of 4 in the "Mean Difference" column tells you that the difference between the means of these groups was 4. The "Sig." column tells you the exact significance level associated with a difference of that size. The value of .054 is not less than our standard .05 cutoff value, which tells you that the means of the criminal record and Clean Record groups are not significantly different. (For the current purposes, you do not need to worry about the columns labeled "Std. Error" or "95% Confidence Interval.") The second row of numbers shows the result of comparing the Criminal Record group to the No Information group. As you can see in the "Mean Difference" column, the difference between the means of these groups was 3; this difference is not statistically significant since the significance level of .164 is greater than our standard .05 cutoff. You can ignore the third row of numbers because it shows the result of comparing the Clean Record group to the Criminal Record group, and you have already seen the result of that comparison in the first row of the table. The only remaining comparison to consider is the difference between the Clean Record group and the No Information group. That comparison is shown in the fourth row of numbers. The difference between the means of those groups was −1 and the significance level of .795 tells you that this difference is not statistically significant. So, overall, none of the three Scheffé post hoc comparisons was statistically significant.

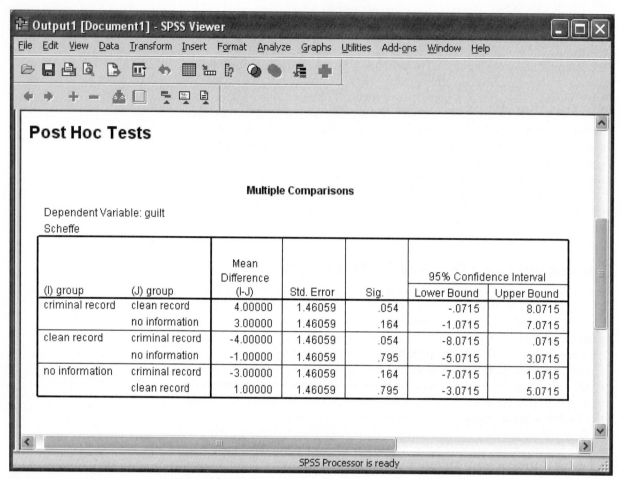

Figure 9–12 SPSS output window for post hoc tests for a one-way analysis of variance for the criminal record example.

Chapter Notes

1. It is possible, by chance, for F to be larger or smaller than 1 in any particular situation. Both the between-groups and the within-groups estimates are only *estimates* and can each vary a fair amount even when the null hypothesis is perfectly true. If F is considerably larger than 1, you reject the null hypothesis that the populations all have the same mean. But what if F is substantially smaller than 1? This rarely happens. When it does, it could mean that there is *less* variation among the groups than would be expected by chance—something is restricting the variation between groups.

2. Why not just use a t test to compare the two groups? If you used an ordinary t test, your pooled estimate of the population variance would be based on only these two groups. Thus, you would be ignoring the information about the population variance provided by the scores in the other groups. One way to deal with this would be to do the ordinary t test in the usual way at every step, except wherever you would ordinarily use the pooled estimate, you would instead use the within-groups

population variance estimate from the overall analysis of variance. Also, you would determine your significance cutoff using the *df* for the overall within-groups estimate. Actually, this modified *t* test procedure for a planned contrast and the one we describe using the *F* test are mathematically equivalent and give exactly the same final result in terms of whether or not your result is significant. (See Chapter 15 for a more general discussion of the relation of the *t* test to the analysis of variance.) We emphasize the *F* test approach here because it is more straightforward in terms of the rest of the material in this chapter.

3. There actually *is* a kind of analysis of variance equivalent to the difference between means—the variation among the means. In fact, Cohen (1988) recommends using the standard deviation of the distribution of means. Thus, he defines what he calls *f* as an effect size for the analysis of variance, which is figured as the standard deviation of the distribution of means (estimated as S_M) divided by the standard deviation of the individuals (estimated as S_{Within}). However, this measure of effect size is rarely used in research articles and is less intuitively meaningful than the more common one we discuss here.

4. More detailed tables are provided in Cohen (1988, pp. 289–354). When using these tables, note that the value of *u* at the top of each of his tables refers to df_{Between}, which for a one-way analysis of variance is the number of groups minus 1, not the number of groups as used in our Table 9–9.

5. More detailed tables are provided in Cohen (1988, pp. 381–389). If you use these, see Chapter Note 4.

6. There are also computational formulas for figuring an analysis of variance with the structural model method. For learning purposes in your class, you should use the steps as we have discussed them in this *Advanced Topic* section. In a real research situation, the figuring is usually all done by computer (see this chapter's *Using SPSS* section). However, if you are ever in the unlikely situation of having to do a one-way analysis of variance for an actual research study by hand (or just using a hand calculator), you may find the following formulas useful:

$$SS_{\text{Total}} = \Sigma X^2 - \frac{(\Sigma X)^2}{N}$$

$$SS_{\text{Between}} = \frac{(\Sigma X_1)^2}{n_1} + \frac{(\Sigma X_2)^2}{n_2} + \cdots + \frac{(\Sigma X_{\text{Last}})^2}{n_{\text{Last}}} - \frac{(\Sigma X)^2}{N}$$

$$SS_{\text{Within}} = SS_{\text{Total}} - SS_{\text{Between}}$$

Chapter Outline

✪ Basic Logic of Factorial Designs
and Interaction Effects   371

✪ Recognizing and Interpreting
Interaction Effects   376

✪ Basic Logic of the Two-Way Analysis
of Variance   386

✪ Assumptions in the Factorial Analysis
of Variance   389

✪ Extensions and Special Cases
of the Analysis of Variance   389

✪ Controversy: Dichotomizing Numeric
Variables   391

✪ Factorial Analysis of Variance
in Research Articles   393

✪ Advanced Topic: Figuring
a Two-Way Analysis of
Variance   395

✪ Advanced Topic: Power and Effect
Size in the Factorial Analysis
of Variance   406

✪ Summary   410

✪ Key Terms   411

✪ Example Worked-Out
Problems   412

✪ Practice Problems   415

✪ Using SPSS   426

✪ Chapter Notes   431

factorial analysis of variance analysis of variance for a factorial research design.

factorial research design way of organizing a study in which the effects of two or more variables are studied at once by making groupings of every combination of the variables.

Factorial analysis of variance is an extension of the procedures you learned in Chapter 9. This method provides a flexible and efficient approach to analyzing results of studies that use what is called a **factorial research design.** As you will learn in this chapter, in a factorial research design, the effects of *two or more variables* are examined at the same time by making groupings of every combination of the variables. Factorial research designs are widely used in psychology.

We first consider in depth the nature of the research approach used in these kinds of studies. We then go on to a discussion of the reasoning for, and basic logic of, a factorial analysis of variance. We also discuss some extensions to the analysis of variance. (We cover a particular type of advanced analysis of variance called *repeated-measures analysis of variance* in a Web Chapter available on the Web site for the book, *http://www.pearsonhighered.com/*). We present the computational procedures for a factorial analysis of variance in an Advanced Topic section. Power and effect size for a factorial analysis of variance are also covered in an Advanced Topic section.

Basic Logic of Factorial Designs and Interaction Effects

An Example

E. Aron and A. Aron (1997) proposed that people differ on a basic, inherited tendency they call "sensory-processing sensitivity" that is found in about a fourth of humans and in many animal species. People with this trait process information especially thoroughly. Table 10–1 gives six items from their Highly Sensitive Person Scale. If you score high on most of the items, you are probably among the 25% of people who are "highly sensitive."

One implication of being a highly sensitive person, according to this model, is that such people are more affected than others by success and failure. This is because they process all experiences more completely. So one would expect highly sensitive people to feel especially good when they succeed and especially bad when they fail. To test this prediction, E. Aron, A. Aron, and Davies (2005, Study 4) conducted an experiment. In the experiment, students first completed the sensitivity questions in Table 10–1. (This permitted the researchers when analyzing the results to divide them into highly sensitive and not highly sensitive.) Later, as part of a series of tests on attitudes and other topics, everyone was given a timed test of their "applied reasoning ability," something important to most students. But without their knowing it, half took an extremely easy version and half took a version so difficult that some problems had no right answer. The questionnaires were handed out to people in alternate seats (it was randomly determined where this process began in each row); so if you had the hard version of the test, the people on either side had an easy version and you were probably aware that they finished quickly while you were still struggling. On the other hand, if you had the easy version, you were probably aware that you had finished easily while the others around you were still working on what you presumed to be the same test.

Right after the test, everyone was asked some items about their mood, how depressed, anxious, and sad they felt at the moment. (The mood items were buried in

Table 10–1   Selected Items from the Highly Sensitive Person Scale

1. Do you find it unpleasant to have a lot going on at once?
2. Do you find yourself wanting to withdraw during busy days, into bed or into a darkened room or any place where you can have some privacy and relief from stimulation?
3. Are you easily overwhelmed by things like bright lights, strong smells, coarse fabrics, or sirens close by?
4. Do you get rattled when you have a lot to do in a short amount of time?
5. Do changes in your life shake you up?
6. Are you bothered by intense stimuli, like loud noises and chaotic scenes?

Note: Each item is answered on a scale from 1 "Not at all" to 7 "Extremely."
Source: Aron, E., & Aron, A. (1997). Sensory-processing sensitivity and its relation to introversion and emotionality. *Journal of Personality and Social Psychology, 73,* 345–368. Published by the American Psychological Association. Reprinted with permission.

Table 10-2 Factorial Research Design Employed by E. Aron and colleagues (2005)

		Test Difficulty	
		Easy	Hard
Sensitivity	Not High	a	c
	High	b	d

other questions.) Responses to the mood items were averaged to create a measure of overall negative mood.

In sum, the study looked at the effect of *two different factors* on negative mood: (1) whether a person was highly sensitive or not highly sensitive and (2) whether a person had taken the easy test (which caused them to feel they had succeeded) or the hard test (which caused them to feel they had failed).

Aron and colleagues could have done two studies, one comparing highly sensitive versus not highly sensitive individuals and one comparing people who took the easy test versus people who took the hard test. Instead, they studied the effects of both sensitivity and test difficulty in a single study. With this setup there were four groups of participants (see Table 10–2): (1) those who are not highly sensitive and took the easy test, (2) those who are highly sensitive and took the easy test, (3) those who are not highly sensitive and took the hard test, and (4) those who are highly sensitive and took the hard test.

Factorial Research Design Defined

The E. Aron and colleagues (2005) study is an example of a factorial research design. As you learned at the beginning of the chapter, in a factorial research design the effects of *two or more variables* are examined at once by making groupings of every combination of the variables. In this example, there are two levels of sensitivity (not high and high) and two levels of test difficulty (easy and hard). This creates four possible group combinations, and the researchers used all of them in their study.

A factorial research design has a major advantage over conducting separate studies of each variable: efficiency. With a factorial design, you can study both variables at once, without needing twice as many participants. In the example, Aron and colleagues were able to use a single group of participants to study the effects of sensitivity and test difficulty on negative mood. (The two "studies" don't get in each other's way because for each part of each comparison, there are equal numbers in each part of the other conditions.)

Interaction Effects

There is, however, an even more important advantage of a factorial research design. A factorial design lets you study the effects of *combining two or more variables.* In this example, sensitivity and test difficulty might affect negative mood in a simple additive way. By additive, we mean that their combined influence is the sum of their separate influences; if you are more of one and also more of the other, then the overall effect is the total of the two individual effects. For example, suppose being highly sensitive makes you more likely to experience a negative mood; similarly, suppose the test being hard makes you more likely to experience a negative mood. If these two effects are additive, then participants in the high sensitivity, hard test group will be most likely to experience a negative mood; participants who are not highly sensitive and take the easy test will be the least likely to experience a negative mood; and those in the other two conditions would have an intermediate likelihood of experiencing a negative mood.

It could also be that one variable but not the other has an effect. Or perhaps neither variable has any effect. In the additive situation, or when only one variable or neither has an effect, looking at the two variables in combination does not give any interesting additional information.

However, it is also possible that the *combination of the two variables* changes the result. In fact, as noted earlier, Aron and colleagues predicted that the effect of being highly sensitive would be especially strong in the hard test condition. A situation where the *combination* of variables has a special effect is called an **interaction effect.** An interaction effect is an effect in which the effect of one variable (that divides the groups) on the measured variable is different across the levels of the other variable that divides the groups.

In the Aron and colleagues study, there was an interaction effect. Look at Table 10–3. The result was that the students in the High Sensitivity/Hard Test group had the most negative mood (remember, a high number means a more negative mood), and the students in the High Sensitivity/Easy Test group had the least negative mood. The level of negative mood in the other two groups (the Not High Sensitivity groups) was similar and between that of the two High Sensitivity groups. These results show that the effect of test difficulty (on negative mood) is different according to the level of sensitivity: for students who are not highly sensitive, their level of negative mood is slightly higher with a hard test (2.56) compared to an easy test (2.43); but for students who are highly sensitive, their level of negative mood is much higher with a hard test (3.01) compared to an easy test (2.19).

Suppose the researchers had studied sensitivity and test difficulty in two separate studies. In the study of sensitivity (assuming equal numbers of students in each group), they would have concluded that sensitivity had little (if any) effect on negative mood: the average level of negative mood for students who are not highly sensitive is 2.50 (that is, the average of 2.43 and 2.56) and for highly sensitive students 2.60 (the average of 2.19 and 3.01). In the study of test difficulty (again assuming equal numbers of students in each group), they would have concluded that students experienced a lower level of negative mood when taking an easy test than a hard test: The average level of negative mood for students taking the easy test was 2.31 (the average of 2.43 and 2.19), and the average for those taking the hard test was 2.79 (the average of 2.56 and 3.01). Thus, following the approach of two separate studies, the researchers would have completely missed the most important result. The most important result had to do with the *combination of the two factors.*

Some Terminology

The Aron and colleagues study used a **two-way factorial research design.** It would be analyzed with what is called a **two-way analysis of variance** because it considers the effects of two variables that divide the groups. These variables are called **grouping variables.** By contrast, the situations in Chapter 9 (such as the attachment style study or the criminal record study) used a **one-way analysis of variance.** Such analyses are called *one-way* because they consider the effect of only one grouping variable (such as a person's attachment style or kind of information about a defendant's criminal record).

In a two-way analysis of variance, each grouping variable or "way" (each dimension in the diagram) is a possible **main effect.** If the result for a grouping variable, averaging across the other grouping variable(s), is significant, it is a *main effect.* This is entirely different from an *interaction effect,* which is based on the *combination of grouping variables.* In the two-way Aron and colleagues study, there was a possibility of two main effects and one interaction effect. The two possible main effects are one for sensitivity and one for test difficulty. The possible interaction effect is for the combination of sensitivity and test difficulty. In a two-way analysis of variance you are always testing two possible main effects and one possible interaction effect.

Table 10–3 Mean Levels of Negative Mood in the E. Aron and colleagues (2005) Study

		Test Difficulty	
		Easy	Hard
Sensitivity	Not High	2.43	2.56
	High	2.19	3.01

interaction effect   situation in the factorial analysis of variance in which a combination of variables has an effect that could not be predicted from the effects of the two variables individually; situation in which the effect of one variable (that divides the groups) on the measured variable is different across the levels of the other variable that divides the groups.

two-way factorial research design   factorial research design in analysis of variance with two variables that each divide the groups.

two-way analysis of variance   analysis of variance for a two-way factorial research design.

grouping variable   a variable that separates groups in analysis of variance.

one-way analysis of variance   analysis of variance in which there is only one grouping variable.

main effect   difference between groups on one grouping variable in a factorial design in analysis of variance; result for a grouping variable, averaging across the levels of the other grouping variable(s).

Each grouping combination in a factorial design is called a **cell.** The mean of the scores in each cell is a **cell mean.** In the Aron and colleagues study, there are four cells and thus four cell means, one for each combination of the levels of sensitivity and test difficulty. That is, one cell is Not High Sensitivity and an Easy Test (as shown in Table 10–3, its cell mean is 2.43); one cell is High Sensitivity and an Easy Test (2.19); one cell is Not High Sensitivity and a Hard Test (2.56); and one cell is High Sensitivity and a Hard Test (3.01).

The means of one grouping variable alone are called **marginal means.** For example, in the Aron and colleagues study there are two marginal means for each grouping variable. For sensitivity, there is one marginal mean for all the students who are not highly sensitive (as we saw earlier, 2.50) and one for all the students who are highly sensitive (2.60). For the test difficulty grouping variable, there is one marginal mean for all the students who took the easy test (2.31) and one marginal mean for all the students who took the hard test (2.79). (Because we were mainly interested in the interaction, we did not show these marginal means in our tables.)

To look at a main effect, you focus on the marginal means for each grouping variable. To look at the interaction effect, you focus on the pattern of individual cell means.

Some studies investigate the effect of three or more grouping variables at a time. For example, Aron and colleagues could have looked at whether their results were different for women and men. To do this, they would have divided each of their four groups into two subgroups, women and men. This would have created eight grouping combinations: Not High Sensitivity/Easy Test/Women; Not High Sensitivity/Easy Test/Men; Not High Sensitivity/Hard Test/Women; and so forth. The complete set of groupings is shown in Figure 10–1. This analysis would examine the influence of three grouping variables at one time: sensitivity, test difficulty, and gender. It takes three dimensions to diagram such a study. Thus, this is an example of a *three-way factorial design.* You can do studies with four-way and even higher factorial designs, though you can't diagram such studies in any simple way. However, most psychology research is limited to two-way and occasionally three-way factorial designs.

Factorial research designs are often described in terms of the number of grouping variables in the study and the number of levels that each grouping variable has. So, for example, consider a study of the effects of two grouping variables in which the first grouping variable has two levels (such as low and high) and the second

cell in a factorial design, particular combination of levels of the variables that divide the group.

cell mean mean of a particular combination of levels of the variables that divide the groups in a factorial design in analysis of variance.

marginal means in a factorial design in analysis of variance, mean score for all the participants at a particular level of one of the grouping variables.

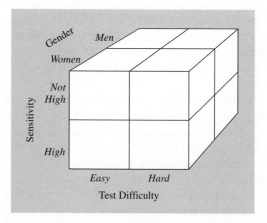

Figure 10–1 Possible three-way factorial research design for the E. Aron and colleagues (2005) study.

grouping variable has three levels (such as small, medium, and large). This would be called a 2×3 *factorial design*—the 2 is for the number of levels of the first grouping variable and the 3 is for the number of levels of the second grouping variable. As another example, consider a study with three grouping variables, with the first grouping variable having two levels and the other two grouping variables each having three levels. This would be a $2 \times 3 \times 3$ design.

How are you doing?

1. (a) What is a factorial research design? (b) and (c) Give two advantages of a factorial research design over doing two separate studies.
2. In a factorial design, (a) what is a main effect, and (b) what is an interaction effect?
3. In the following table are the means from a study in which participants rated the originality of paintings under various conditions. For each mean, indicate its grouping and whether it is a cell or marginal mean.

	Contemporary	Renaissance	Overall
Landscape	6.5	5.5	6
Portrait	3.5	2.5	3
Overall	5	4	

4. In each of the following studies, participants' performance on a coordination task was measured under various conditions or compared for different groups. For each study, make a diagram of the research design and indicate whether it is a one-way, two-way, or three-way design: (a) a study in which people are assigned to either a high-stress condition or a low-stress condition, and, in each of these conditions, half are assigned to work alone and half to work in a room with other people; (b) a study comparing students majoring in physics, chemistry, or engineering; (c) a study comparing people doing a task in a hot room versus a cold room, with half in each room doing the task with their right hand and half with their left hand, and within each of these various temperature/hand combinations, half are blindfolded and half are not.
5. Explain what it means to say that a study is using a 2×4 research design.

5. A study is using a 2×4 research design when it has two grouping variables, one that has two levels and one that has four levels.

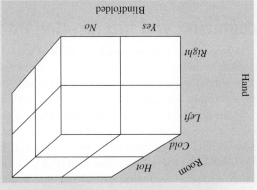

(c) Three-way.

Answers

1. (a) A factorial research design is a research design in which the effect of two or more grouping variables is examined at once by making groupings of every combination of the variables.

(b) A factorial research design is more efficient. For example, you can study the effects of two grouping variables at once with only a single group of participants.

(c) A factorial research design makes it possible to see if there are interaction effects.

2. (a) A main effect in a factorial research design is the effect of one of the grouping variables, ignoring the pattern of results on the other grouping variable(s) (or a difference in the marginal means for the different levels of a particular grouping variable).

(b) An interaction effect is the different effect of one grouping variable according to the level of the other grouping variable(s).

3. 6.5 = cell mean for Contemporary/Landscape group; 5.5 = cell mean for Renaissance/Landscape group; 6 = marginal mean for Landscape groups; 3.5 = cell mean for Contemporary/Portrait group; 2.5 = cell mean for Renaissance/Portrait group; 3 = marginal mean for Portrait groups; 5 = marginal mean for Contemporary groups; and 4 = marginal mean for Renaissance groups.

4. (a) Two-way.

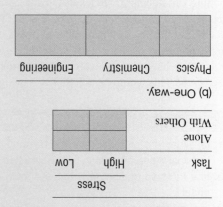

	Stress	
Task	High	Low
Alone		
With Others		

(b) One-way.

Physics	Chemistry	Engineering

Recognizing and Interpreting Interaction Effects

It is very important to understand interaction effects. In many studies the interaction effect is the main point of the research. As we have seen, an interaction effect is an effect in which the impact of one grouping variable depends on the level of another grouping variable. You can think out and describe an interaction effect in three ways: in words, in numbers, or in a graph. Note that, in discussing the examples in this section on interaction effects, we will treat all differences that have the pattern of an interaction effect or of a main effect as if they were statistically significant. (In reality, you would carry out hypothesis testing steps to test whether the particular patterns were strong enough to be statistically *significant*.) We are taking this approach here to keep the focus on the *idea* of interaction effects while you are learning this fairly abstract notion.

Identifying Interaction Effects in Words and Numbers

You can think out an interaction effect in words by saying that you have an interaction effect when the effect of one grouping variable varies according to the level of another grouping variable. In the Aron and colleagues example, the effect of test difficulty (easy versus hard) varies according to the level of sensitivity (not high versus high). Another way of saying this is that the effect of test difficulty depends on the level of sensitivity (the effect of test difficulty is different for highly sensitive individuals than for individuals who are not highly sensitive).

(You can also talk about this interaction effect by focusing on the other grouping variable first. So you could say that the effect of sensitivity varies according to the level of test difficulty, or that the effect of sensitivity depends on the level of test difficulty. Interaction effects are completely symmetrical in that you can describe them from the point of view of either grouping variable.)

You can see an interaction effect numerically by looking at the pattern of cell means. If there is an interaction effect, the *pattern of differences in cell means* across one row will not be the same as the patterns of differences in cell means across another row. (Again, all of this is symmetrical: you can also look at the differences in cell means for one column compared to another column, but we will focus here on rows.) Consider the Aron and colleagues example. In the Not High Sensitivity row, the cell mean for negative mood of the Easy Test students (2.43) was just slightly lower than the cell mean for negative mood of the Hard Test students (2.56). This is a difference of $-.13$ (that is, $2.43 - 2.56 = -.13$). However, now look at the High Sensitivity row. In this row, the cell mean for Easy Test students' negative mood (2.19) was a lot lower than the cell mean for negative mood for the Hard Test students (3.01). This difference of $-.82$ is not at all the same as the difference of $-.13$ in the Not High Sensitivity row; this *dissimilar pattern of differences in cell means* indicates an interaction effect.

Some Examples

Table 10–4 gives cell means and marginal means for six possible results of a fictional two-way factorial study on the relation of age and education (the grouping variables) to income (the measured variable). The grouping variable age has two levels (younger, such as 25 to 34, versus older, such as 35 to 44), and the grouping variable education has two levels (high school versus college). Thus, the study is using a 2×2 research design. These fictional results are exaggerated to make clear when there are interactions and main effects. Before you look at the six possible results, take a minute to think about what kind of results you might expect (and hope!) to see. For example, do you expect that people with a college education will earn less than or more than people with only a high school education? Would you expect younger people to earn more than or less than older people? Most importantly (since we are focusing on interaction effects), what about the possibility of an interaction effect? Do you think that the effect of education (college versus high school) will be different according to age (younger versus older)? Let's take a look at the six possible results and then we'll tell you what the results of actual research show.

Result A   Interaction. Note that in the Younger row, education makes no difference, but in the Older row, the college cell mean is much higher than the high-school cell mean. One way to say this is that for the younger group, education is unrelated to income; but for the older group, people with a college education earn much more than

Table 10-4 Possible Means for Results of a Study of the Relation of Age and Education to Income (in Thousands of Dollars)

	Result A			Result B			Result C		
Age	High School	College	Overall	High School	College	Overall	High School	College	Overall
Younger	40	40	40	60	40	50	20	60	40
Older	40	60	50	40	60	50	40	80	60
Overall	40	50		50	50		30	70	

	Result D			Result E			Result F		
Age	High School	College	Overall	High School	College	Overall	High School	College	Overall
Younger	20	20	20	40	60	50	30	45	37.5
Older	120	120	120	40	80	60	35	60	47.5
Overall	70	70		40	70		32.5	52.5	

those with less education. There are also two main effects: overall, older people earn more than younger people, and overall, people with a college education earn more than those with only a high school education.

Result B Interaction. This is because, in the Younger row, the high school mean income is higher than the college mean income, but in the Older row the high-school mean income is lower. Put in words, among younger people, those with only a high school education make more money (perhaps because they entered the workplace earlier or the kinds of jobs they have start out at a higher level); but among older people, those with a college education make more money. (There are no main effects in Result B, since the marginal means for the two rows are the same and the marginal means for the two columns are the same.)

Result C No interaction. In the Younger row, the high-school mean is 40 lower than the college mean, and the same is true in the Older row. Whether young or old, people with college educations earn $40,000 more. (There are also main effects for both age and education.)

Result D No interaction. There is no difference in the pattern of income between the two rows. Regardless of education, older people earn $100,000 more. (There is also a main effect for age, but no main effect for education.)

Result E Interaction. In the Younger row, the college mean is 20 higher than the high-school mean, but in the Older row, the college mean is 40 higher than the high-school mean. So among young people, college-educated people earn a little more; but, among older people, those with a college education earn much more. (There are also main effects for both age and education.)

Result F Interaction. There is a smaller difference between the high school and college mean in the Younger row than in the Older row. As with Result E, for people with a college education, income increases more with age than it does for those with only a high school education. (There are also main effects for both age and education.)

Based on 1997–1999 statistics from the U.S. Census Bureau, the actual situation in the United States is closest to Result F (Day & Newberger, 2002). People with a college education earn more than those with only a high school education in both age groups, but the difference is somewhat greater for the older group. [You may be interested to know that, over a typical working life, people in the United States with a college degree earn an average of 1.8 times more than those with only a high school education (Day & Newberger, 2002). However, it is important to keep in mind that whether people receive a college education is also related to the social class of their parents and other factors that may affect income as much as education does.]

More Examples

Table 10–5 shows possible results of another fictional study. In this factorial experiment, the two experimentally manipulated variables are difficulty of the task (which has two levels: easy versus hard) and level of physiological arousal (which has three levels: low, moderate, or high). (This study is using a 2×3 research design.) Arousal in this study is how anxious the participant is made to feel about the importance of doing well. The variable being measured is how well the participant performs a set of arithmetic tasks. Let's consider each possible pattern of results.

Result A   No interaction. The pattern of cell means in the Easy row is the same as the pattern of cell means in the Hard row. In each row, the cell means are the same for each level of arousal. (There is one main effect: task difficulty affects performance; arousal does not.)

Result B   No interaction. The cell means in the Easy row increase by 10 from low to moderate and from moderate to high. The cell means in the Hard row do the same. (Again, there is only one main effect: arousal affects performance; task difficulty does not.)

Result C   No interaction. The cell means in the Easy row increase by 10 from low to moderate and from moderate to high; the cell means in the Hard row do the same. (In this example, there are two main effects: arousal affects performance and task difficulty affects performance.)

Result D   Interaction. The pattern of cell means in the Easy row is an increase of 10 from low to moderate and another increase of 10 from moderate to high. This pattern

Table 10-5   Some Possible Results of an Experiment on the Effect of Task Difficulty and Arousal Level on Performance (Fictional Data)

		Result A					Result B					Result C		
		Arousal					**Arousal**					**Arousal**		
Task	**Low**	**Moderate**	**High**	**Overall**	**Low**	**Moderate**	**High**	**Overall**	**Low**	**Moderate**	**High**	**Overall**
Easy	10	10	10	10	10	20	30	20	10	20	30	20
Hard	20	20	20	20	10	20	30	20	20	30	40	30
Overall	15	15	15		10	20	30		15	25	35	

Task		**Result D**				**Result E**				**Result F**		
Easy	10	20	30	20	10	20	10	13.3	10	20	30	20
Hard	10	20	60	30	20	10	20	16.7	30	20	10	20
Overall	10	20	45		15	15	15		20	20	20	

is not the same as the pattern of cell means in the Hard row, where there is again an increase of 10 from low to moderate, but there is an increase of 40 from moderate to high. Thus, in all cases, performance on easy and hard tasks tends to improve with greater arousal. However, the impact of high versus moderate arousal is much greater for hard than for easy tasks. (There are two main effects: arousal affects performance and task difficulty affects performance.)

Result E   Interaction. The pattern of cell means in the Easy row is an increase of 10 and then a decrease of 10. This is quite different from the Hard row, where the pattern is a decrease of 10 and then an increase of 10. For easy tasks, performance is best under moderate arousal, but, for hard tasks, performance is worst under moderate arousal. (There is only one main effect: task difficulty affects performance; arousal does not.)

Result F   Interaction. In the Easy row, the cell means increase as you go across; in the Hard row, they decrease as you go across. For easy tasks, the more arousal, the better; for hard tasks, arousal interferes with performance. (There are no main effects.) (Result F is closest to a well established finding in psychology known as the Yerkes-Dodson law.)

Identifying Interaction Effects Graphically

Another common way of making sense of interaction effects is by graphing the pattern of cell means. This is usually done with a bar graph, although a line graph is sometimes used. The bar graph in Figure 10–2 shows the results from Aron and colleagues' (2005) study. Figure 10–3 is a line graph that shows the same results as the bar graph in Figure 10–2. (We will use bar graphs for future examples, although we will revisit the issue of using a bar graph versus a line graph in the section on factorial analyses of variance in research articles.) Figures 10–4 and 10–5 show the bar graphs for the fictional results we just considered from Tables 10–3 and 10–4, respectively.

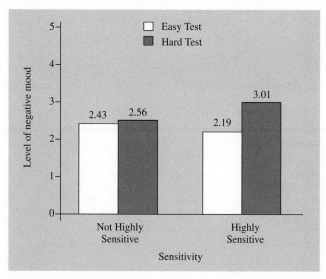

Figure 10–2   Bar graph for level of negative mood as a function of sensitivity (not high versus high) and test difficulty (easy versus hard).

Source: Based on Aron, E., Aron, A., & Davies, K. M. (2005). Adult shyness: The interaction of temporal sensitivity and an adverse childhood environment. *Personality and Social Psychology Bulletin, 31,* 1–17. Copyright © 2005 by Sage Publications, Ltd. Reprinted by permission of Sage Publications, Thousands Oaks, London, and New Delhi.

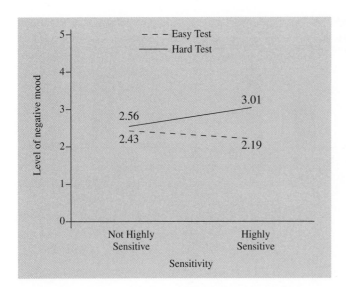

Figure 10-3 Line graph for level of negative mood as a function of sensitivity (not high versus high) and test difficulty (easy versus hard).

Source: Based on Aron, E., Aron, A., & Davies, K. M. (2005). Adult shyness: The interaction of temporal sensitivity and an adverse childhood environment. *Personality and Social Psychology Bulletin, 31,* 1–17. Copyright © 2000 by Society for Personality and Social Psychology, Inc. Reprinted by permission of Sage Publications, Inc.

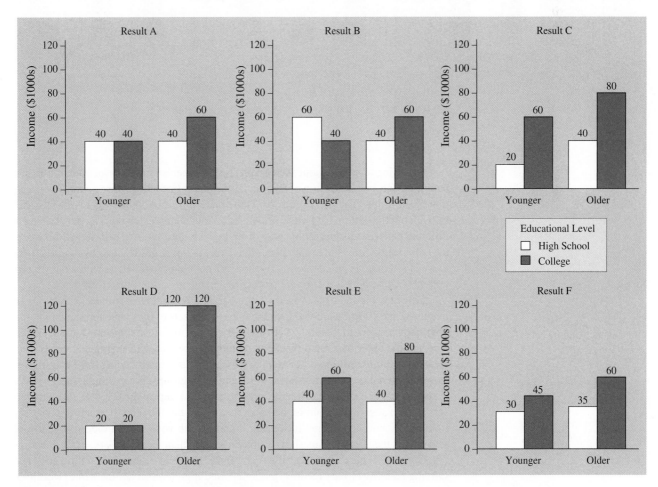

Figure 10-4 Bar graphs of fictional results in Table 10–4.

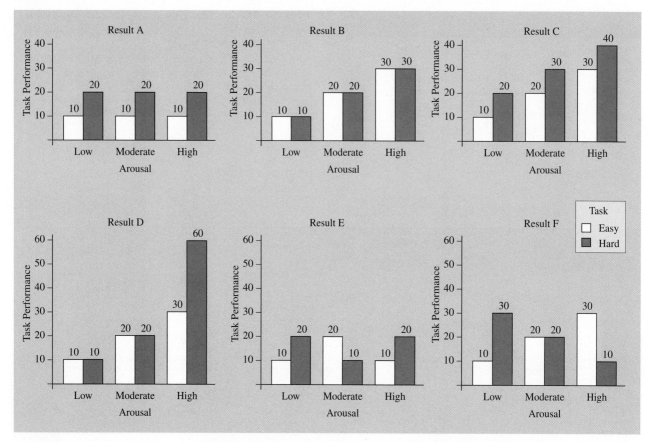

Figure 10–5 Bar graphs of fictional results in Table 10–5.

One thing to notice about such graphs is this: whenever there is an interaction, the pattern of bars on one section of the graph is different from the pattern on the other section of the graph. Thus, in Figure 10–2, the pattern for not highly sensitive is a small step up, but the pattern for highly sensitive is a much larger step up. The bars having a different pattern is just a graphic way of saying that the pattern of differences between the cell means from row to row is not the same. In a line graph, such as Figure 10–3, you can tell there is an interaction by the *lines* not being parallel; as with a bar graph, this shows that there is a different pattern of cell means from row to row.

Consider Figure 10–4, based on the age and education examples. First look at Results C and D. In Result C the younger and older sets of bars have the same pattern: both step up by 40. In Result D, both are flat. Within both Results C and D, the younger bars and the older bars have the same pattern. These were the examples that *did not have interactions*. All the other results, which did have interactions, have patterns of bars that are not the same for the younger and older groups. For example, in Result A, the two younger bars are flat, but the older bars show a step up. In Result B, the younger bars show a step down from high school to college, but the older bars show a step up from high school to college. In Results E and F, both younger and older bars show a step up, but the younger bars show a smaller step up than the older bars.

Consider Figure 10–5. Results A, B, and C show no interaction; within each result, the patterns of bars for low, moderate, and high arousal are the same. Result D

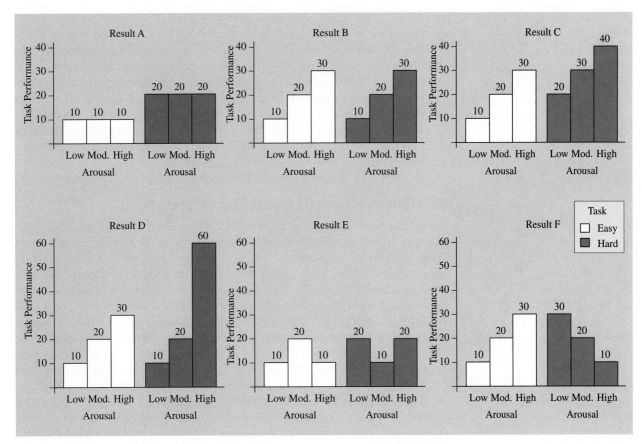

Figure 10–6 Alternative bar graphs (compared to Figure 10–5) of fictional results in Table 10–5.

is an interaction. You can see this in the figure as follows: the bars within low are flat and the bars within moderate are flat; but for the high arousal bars, there is a step up from easy to hard tasks. Result E's interaction shows steps up for low and high arousal, but a step down for moderate arousal. Result F's interaction is seen in there being a step up for low, flat for moderate, and a step down for hard.

Figure 10–6 shows an alternate way of graphing the results from Table 10–5 than shown in Figure 10–5. Here we have grouped the bars according to hard versus easy. The easy task bars for low, moderate, and high arousal are next to each other and the hard task bars for low, moderate, and high arousal are next to each other. This alternate way of grouping is completely equivalent in meaning and leads to exactly the same conclusions. For example, in Result A the three hard-task bars are flat and the three easy-task bars are flat. In Results B and C, where there is also no interaction, the three easy-task bars rise up in the same step pattern as the three hard task bars. However, consider Result D, where there is an interaction. The pattern of the easy task bars is different from the pattern of the hard task bars. There is a bigger step up from moderate to high arousal in the hard task bars than there is in the easy task bars.

You can also see *main effects* from these graphs. In Figure 10–4, a main effect for age would be shown by the bars for younger being overall higher or lower than the bars for older. For example, in Result C, the bars for older are clearly higher than the bars for younger. What about the main effect for the bars that are not grouped together—college versus high school in this example? With these bars, you have to see whether the overall step pattern goes up or down. For example, in Result C, there is also a main effect for education, because the general pattern of the bars for high school to college goes up, and it does this for both the younger and older bars. Result D shows a main effect for age (the older bars are higher than the younger bars). But Result D does not show a main effect for education; the pattern is flat for both the older and younger bars. Result A in Figure 10–5 shows a main effect for task difficulty but no main effect for arousal. This is because the average heights of the bars are the same for low, moderate, and high arousal, while within each arousal level, the bars step up from easy to hard.

Relation of Interaction and Main Effects

A study can have any combination of main and interaction effects. For example, you can have both main effects and the interaction, as in the pattern in Result F of Table 10–4. In this result, as you saw, older students earn more (a main effect for age), college students earn more (a main effect for level of education), and how much more college students earn depends on age (the interaction effect). Similarly, in Result D of Table 10–5, on the average people perform better at hard tasks (a main effect for task difficulty) and at higher levels of arousal (a main effect for arousal level), but the effect of task difficulty shows up only at high levels of arousal (the interaction). (Notice, however, that the main effect for task difficulty—the higher average for hard tasks—is entirely due to the high arousal condition. We have more to say about this kind of situation shortly.)

There can also be an interaction effect with no main effects. Result B of Table 10–4 is an example. The average level of income is the same for younger and older (no main effect for age), and it is the same for college and high school (no main effect for level of education). Similarly, in Result F of Table 10–5, the average performance is the same for low, moderate, and high arousal (no main effect for arousal level) and is the same for easy and hard tasks (no main effect for task difficulty). However, in both examples there are clear interactions.

It is also possible for there to be one main effect along with an interaction, one main effect by itself, or no main or interaction effects.

When there is no interaction, a main effect has a straightforward meaning. However, when there is an interaction along with a main effect, things are more complicated. Consider Result D in the arousal and task difficulty example (Table 10–5). There are two main effects and an interaction. But as we noted earlier, the main effect for task difficulty is entirely due to the high arousal hard task cell. It would be misleading to say anything about hard versus easy tasks overall without also saying that the effect really depends on the level of arousal. You should be especially cautious about the meaning of a main effect when the direction of the effect is reversed for some levels of the other grouping variable.

On the other hand, even when there is an interaction, sometimes the main effect clearly holds up over and above the interaction. That is, the main effect may be there at every level of the other grouping variable, but even more strongly at some points than at others. Consider again Result D in the arousal and task difficulty example (Table 10–5). In this result, the main effect for arousal holds up over and above the interaction. The effect for arousal is there for both easy and hard tasks; in both cases, low arousal produces the least performance, moderate the next most, and high arousal the most. (There is still an interaction because how much high arousal produces better performance than moderate arousal is more for hard than for easy tasks.)

How are you doing?

Questions 1 to 3 are based on the following results for a fictional study of the effects of vividness and length of examples (the grouping variables) on number of examples recalled (the measured variables).

	Vividness		
Example Length	**Low**	**High**	**Overall**
Short	5	7	6
Long	3	1	2
Overall	4	4	

1. Describe the pattern of results in words.
2. Explain the pattern in terms of numbers.
3. (a) and (b) Make two bar graphs of these results.
4. For a two-way factorial research design, what are the possible combinations of main and interaction effects?
5. When there is both a main and an interaction effect, (a) under what conditions must you be careful in interpreting the main effect, and (b) under what conditions can you still be confident in the overall main effect?

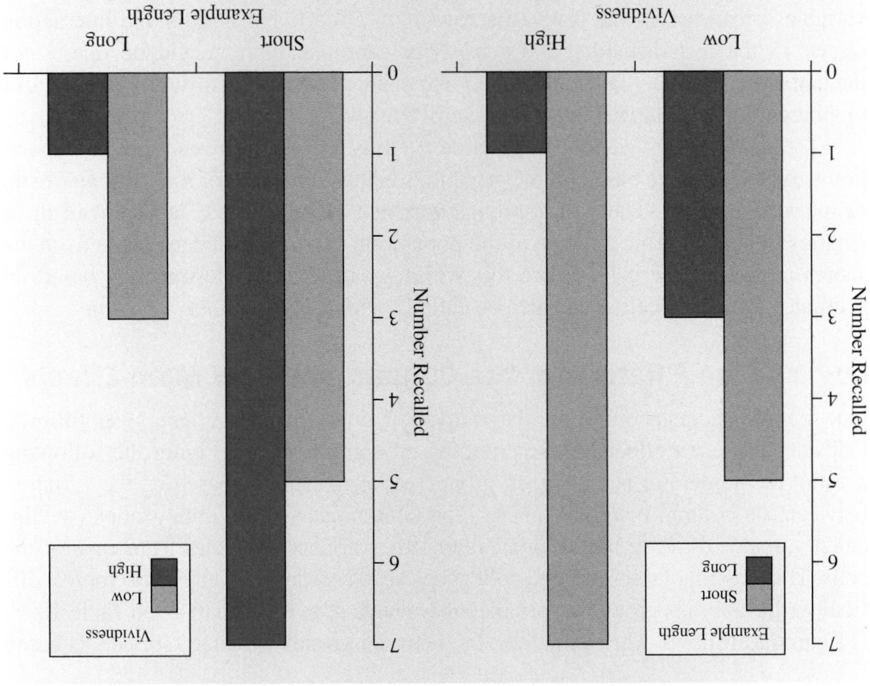

Figure 10-7 Answer to "How Are You Doing" question 3.

interaction effect with either main effect; or an interaction effect with both main effects.

5. (a) You should be careful in interpreting the main effect when it is found for only one level of the other grouping variable or when its direction is reversed at different levels of the other grouping variable.
(b) You can still be confident in the overall main effect when it holds and is in the same direction at each level of the other grouping variable.

Answers

1. There is a main effect in which short examples are recalled better; there is no main effect for vividness, and there is an interaction effect in which there is a bigger advantage of short over long examples when they are highly vivid.

2. The main effect is that on the average people recall six short examples but only two long examples. There is no main effect for vividness because people on the average recall four examples, regardless of how vivid the examples are. The interaction effect is that for short examples, people recall two more highly vivid than low vivid; but for long examples, they recall two fewer highly vivid than low vivid.

3. See Figure 10–7.

4. All possible combinations: no main or interaction effects; either main effect only; the interaction only; both main effects but no interaction effect; an

Basic Logic of the Two-Way Analysis of Variance

The statistical procedure for analyzing the results of a two-way factorial study is called a *two-way analysis of variance.* The basic logic is the same as you learned in Chapter 9. In any analysis of variance, you figure an F ratio, and this F ratio compares a population variance estimate based on the variation *between* the means of the groupings of interest to a population variance estimate based on variation *within* groups.

The Three F Ratios in a Two-Way Analysis of Variance

In a two-way analysis of variance, there are three F ratios: one for the grouping variable spread across the columns (the column main effect), one for the grouping variable spread across the rows (the row main effect), and one for the interaction effect. In the test difficulty and sensitivity example, there would be one F for the main effect for Test Difficulty, one F for main effect for Sensitivity, and one F for the interaction of Test Difficulty with Sensitivity.

The numerator of each of these three F ratios will be a between-groups population variance estimate based on the groupings being compared for the particular main or interaction effect. The within-groups variance estimate is the same for all three F ratios; it is always the average of the population variance estimates made from the scores in each of the cells. Since this within-groups variance estimate is based on estimates from each cell, it can also be called a *within-cells variance estimate.*

Logic of the F Ratios for the Column and Row Main Effects

One way of understanding how the analysis is done for main effects is as follows. Consider the main effect for the columns grouping variable. Figure the following F ratio: the numerator is a between-groups variance estimate based on the variation between the column marginal means. The denominator is a within-groups (within-cells) variance estimate based on averaging the variance estimates from each of the cells. Think again of the Aron and colleagues (2005) example. The F ratio for test difficulty (the columns grouping variable, as we have drawn the chart—see Table 10–6) is figured as follows. The numerator, the between-groups variance estimate, is based

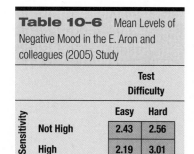

Table 10–6 Mean Levels of Negative Mood in the E. Aron and colleagues (2005) Study

		Test Difficulty	
		Easy	Hard
Sensitivity	Not High	2.43	2.56
	High	2.19	3.01

BOX 10–1   **Personality and Situational Influences on Behavior: An Interaction Effect**

In a certain sense, the study of statistics is training in a style of seeing the world.

Regardless of whether psychological researchers draw an explicit comparison between analysis of variance and the way they think, they probably often use the crisp model of analysis of variance as a guide to their own logic. They do this not only when analyzing data or even when designing research, but they probably also use the analysis of variance as a metaphor when theorizing as well.

An important example of how statistics has influenced the way psychologists think about their subject matter, not just their data, is in the history of the study of personality. In the 1960s, the field of personality was forever changed by the work of Walter Mischel (1968; for an insider's description, see Mischel, 2007). Mischel appeared to have demonstrated that, as a rule, *situation* (a street signal turning red, for example, or a well-dressed person asking for help) is a far better predictor of how a person will act than any *personality trait* (for example, that a person is by nature cautious or altruistic). The embattled personality theorists, typically trained in psychodynamics, struggled to defend themselves within the rules of the game as Mischel had defined them: how much of the variation in behavior could really be predicted by their personality measures? That is, personality theorists were forced to think statistically.

One result of this challenge was something called "interactionism" (e.g., Endler & Magnusson, 1976). That is the idea that behavior is best predicted by the interaction of person and situation. You can instantly guess what statistical method has had its influence. (You are studying it in this chapter!)

For example, according to interactionism, neither the personality trait of anxiety nor the situation of taking the SAT is nearly as good a predictor of anxiety as knowing that a person with a given tendency toward anxiety perceives the taking of the SAT as an anxiety-producing situation. The emphasis is that behavior is being altered constantly by the individual's internal disposition interacting with his or her perception of the changing situation. [In fact, even Walter Mischel (2004) later proposed a theory of this kind.]

Let's follow an anxious man through some situations. He may feel even more—or perhaps less—anxiety while proceeding from the testing situation to a dark, empty parking lot, depending again on the interaction of his trait anxiety and his perception of this new situation. The same is true as he proceeds to drive home on the highway, to open the garage door, to enter an empty house.

According to interactionism, the person is not a passive component but an "intentional active agent in this interaction process" (Endler & Magnusson, 1976, p. 968).

The important part of the person aspect of the interaction is how a person thinks about a situation. The important part of the situation aspect of the interaction is, again, its meaning for the person. [Note that the Aron et al. (2005) study we have been using as an example in this chapter is a current version of just such an interaction of personality (sensitivity) with a situation (being faced with an easy or a hard test).] Some form of interactionism now appears to be true in general for explaining what people do and the idea continues to be highly important in personality psychology. For example, whether one is a "morning person" or a "night person" (the personality trait) interacts with one's work schedule in predicting one's alertness (Cavallera & Giudici, 2008). [It is now turning out that interactionism may even explain the way ordinary people typically *understand* other people's behavior (Kammrath et al., 2005). That is, people may be intuitive statisticians!]

This influence of statistics on theory has been happening throughout the history of nearly every area of psychology. Indeed, the influence of recent statistical developments on thinking has become particularly important in recent years as new ideas are developed in statistical methods (such as multilevel modeling; see Chapter 15) and as new opportunities emerge as psychologists more thoroughly take into account the role of culture, genetics, and neural processes in predicting behavior. In a sense, we could say that pioneers in statistics are now determining not only the complexity of psychological research that is possible, but the depth of theorizing itself. They are carving out the channels through which psychologists' actual thinking patterns flow and therefore are shaping and directing much of our understanding of psychology.

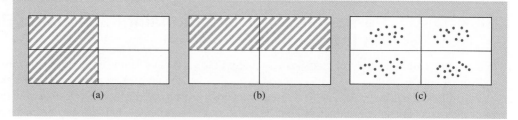

Figure 10–8 A diagram to help you understand a two-way factorial analysis of variance: (a) the column between-groups variance estimate as based on the difference between the mean of the participants in the first (shaded) and second (unshaded) columns; (b) the row between-groups variance estimate as based on the difference between the mean of the participants in the top (shaded) and bottom (unshaded) rows; and (c) the within-groups (within-cells) variance estimate as based on the variation among scores in each cell.

on the difference between the easy test difficulty marginal mean and the hard test difficulty marginal mean. The denominator, the within-groups (within-cells) variance estimate, is based on averaging the population variance estimates from within each of the four cells.

The procedure for the row main effect is the same idea. You figure it using a between-groups variance estimate based on the difference between the two row marginal means. (The Aron and colleagues study was designed so that the row marginal means are the mean for all the nonhighly sensitive participants and the mean for all the highly sensitive participants.)

Figure 10–8a shows the column between-groups variance estimate as based on the difference between the mean of the scores in the first column (the shaded area) and the mean of the scores in the second column (the unshaded area). Figure 10–8b shows the row between-groups estimate as based on the difference between the mean of the scores in its top row (the shaded area) and the mean of the scores in the bottom row (the unshaded area). And Figure 10–8c shows the within-groups variance estimate (used for all the *F* ratios) as based on the variation among the scores in each of the cells.

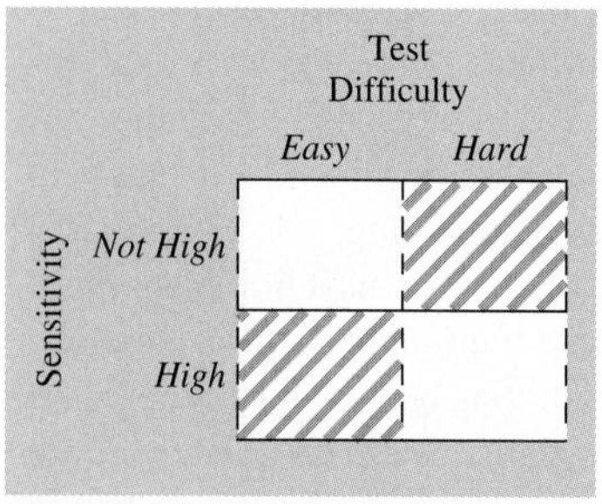

Logic of the *F* Ratio for the Interaction Effect

The logic of the *F* ratio for the interaction effect is a bit more complex. One approach is to think of the interaction effect as the combinations left over after considering the row and column main effects. Consider a study with two grouping variables, each of which has two levels. (As you learned earlier, this is called a 2 × 2 research design.) In this study, the main effects have grouped the four cells into rows and columns. But it is also possible to divide the cells into other kinds of groupings. Figure 10–9, based on the Aron and colleagues (2005) study, shows a remaining possible organization of the four cells into two larger groupings: (a) one grouping of two cells consisting of the upper left cell (Not High Sensitivity/Easy Test Difficulty) along with the lower right cell (High Sensitivity/Hard Test Difficulty), and (b) another grouping of two cells consisting of the lower left cell (High Sensitivity/ Easy Test Difficulty) and the upper right cell (Not High Sensitivity/Hard Test Difficulty). The between-groups variance estimate for the interaction effect can then be figured from the variation between the means of these two groupings. (In this example, these two groupings of cells are the diagonals.)

Figure 10–9 Interaction as a comparison of scores in the shaded cells (easy test difficulty and high sensitivity; hard test difficulty and not high sensitivity) to the mean of the scores in the unshaded cells (easy test difficulty and not high sensitivity; hard test difficulty and high sensitivity) in the study by E. Aron and colleagues (2005).

With a 2×2 design, there is only one organization of pairs of cells that is not already accounted for by the row and column organizations: the grouping pattern (of diagonals) shown in the example in Figure 10–9. But the situation is not so simple with a larger two-way design, such as a 2×3 study (a study in which the first variable has two levels and the second variable has three levels, such as the study of task difficulty and arousal we considered earlier). In such a study, there is more than one way to make the groupings, and all must be taken into account. Thus, it can be quite complicated to figure the between-groups variance estimate for the interaction effect when dealing with situations other than a 2×2 design. Fortunately, it turns out that figuring the between-groups variance estimate for the interaction is much more straightforward when using the structural model approach that was presented in an Advanced Topic section in Chapter 9. Thus, we describe the actual figuring for the factorial analysis of variance using the structural model approach in a later Advanced Topic section in this chapter. (But the procedures we have just described actually work quite well and simply when you have the very common 2×2 situation.)

Assumptions in the Factorial Analysis of Variance

The assumptions for a factorial analysis of variance are the same as for the one-way analysis of variance. However, in a factorial analysis of variance, the requirements of population normality and equal variances apply to the populations that go with each cell.

Extensions and Special Cases of the Analysis of Variance

The analysis of variance is an extremely versatile technique. We cannot, in this introductory book, go into the details of the statistical procedures for handling all the possibilities. (These are covered in most intermediate statistics texts in psychology as well as in what are often called "experimental design" textbooks.) However, it is possible to describe some of the main variations and to provide some insight into the basic modifications to what you have already learned.

Three-Way and Higher Analysis of Variance Designs

The most straightforward extension of the two-way analysis of variance is to studies involving three-way designs (in which there are three grouping variables) or even four-way and higher designs. The basic logic of such studies is the same as we have described in this chapter, except that there are additional main and interaction effects.

Sometimes a study involves secondary grouping variables, such as the order of the presentation of different parts of an experimental task or which of two experimenters conducted the study for each participant. Such secondary grouping variables are usually of interest only if they interact with the major grouping variables. In these situations, the researcher may start with a multiway factorial analysis of variance. If these grouping variables of secondary interest do not have significant interaction effects with the grouping variables of primary interest, you run the analysis again, ignoring these secondary variables. The design then becomes a more manageable two-way or three-way analysis of variance. The resulting analysis is said to be *collapsed* over the variables that are being ignored.

Repeated-Measures Analysis of Variance

In all the situations in this chapter and Chapter 9, the different cells or groupings are based on scores from *different individuals*. Sometimes, however, a researcher measures the same individual in several different situations. (In a study with only one grouping variable of this kind that has two levels, such as the levels of before and after some treatment, you can use a *t* test for dependent means, as described in Chapter 7. But if there are more than two levels or if there is another grouping variable involved as well, you have to use analysis of variance.) Consider a study in which, for each participant, you measure speed of recognizing a syllable when embedded in three word types: familiar words, unfamiliar words, and nonword sounds. The result is that for each participant you have an average number of errors for each word type. Or suppose you do a study of psychotherapy effects testing patients on their depression before, immediately following, and again three months after therapy. In each of these examples, you have three groups of scores, but in each example, all three scores are from the same people. These studies are examples of repeated-measures designs.

Repeated-measures designs are analyzed with a **repeated-measures analysis of variance.** It has this name because the same participants are being measured repeatedly. This kind of design and analysis is also called a *within-subjects design* or *within-subjects analysis of variance* because the comparison is within, not between, the different participants or subjects. (The American Psychological Association recommends the use of the term *participants* rather than "subjects.")

Sometimes a repeated-measures variable is crossed in the same study with an ordinary between-participants variable. For example, in the therapy study, there might be a control group not getting the therapy but tested at the same three points in time. This would be a *mixed* 2 (therapy versus control group) $\times$ 3 (before, after, 3 months after) design in which the first variable is the usual between-subjects type and the second is a repeated-measures type. It is even possible to have two repeated-measures factors or even more complicated combinations.

We cover *repeated-measures analysis of variance* in more detail in a Web Chapter available on the Web site for the book (*http://www.pearsonhighered.com/*).

repeated-measures analysis of variance analysis of variance for a repeated-measures design in which each person is tested more than once so that the levels of the grouping variable(s) are different times or types of testing for the same persons.

How are you doing?

1. In a two-way analysis of variance, what is the numerator of the *F* ratio for the row main effect?
2. In a 2 $\times$ 2 analysis of variance, what is the numerator of the *F* ratio for the interaction effect?
3. In any two-way analysis of variance, what is the denominator of the *F* ratio for (a) each main effect and (b) the interaction?
4. What are the assumptions for a factorial analysis of variance?
5. (a) What does it mean when a research study reports that "results were collapsed over order of testing"? (b) How is a repeated-measures analysis of variance different from an ordinary between-subjects analysis of variance? (c) What is a mixed design?

Controversy: Dichotomizing Numeric Variables

Suppose a developmental psychologist measured anxiety and social skills in a group of children. The psychologist then observed their behavior in a playgroup with other children, focusing on their aggressive responses. To examine the results of this study, the researcher divided the children in half on their anxiety scores (making a high anxiety and a low anxiety group), then divided them in half on social skills (making a high and low social skills group). The combinations resulted in four groups: High Anxiety/High Social Skills; High Anxiety/Low Social Skills; and so forth. Having divided up the children in this way, the researcher then carried out a two-way (2 × 2) factorial analysis of variance, with grouping variables of anxiety (high versus low) and social skills (high versus low). With this analysis, the researcher could see whether there was a main effect of anxiety on aggression, a main effect of social skills on aggression, and/or an interaction effect of anxiety and social skills on aggression.

The thing to notice here is that the researcher divided up the children into two groups on anxiety and two groups on social skills. Consider anxiety first. In this study anxiety was a numeric, quantitative variable measured along a continuum. Nevertheless, the researcher ignored all the fine gradations and simply divided the group in half, making a high anxiety and a low anxiety grouping. This resulted in everyone in the high anxiety grouping being treated as having the same (high) level of anxiety and everyone in the low anxiety grouping being treated as having the same (low) level of anxiety.

This kind of division is called **dichotomizing**—making into a dichotomy, or two groupings. Since the dichotomizing is usually done by taking those above and below the median, it is also called making a *median split* of the scores. In this example, the researcher also dichotomized (made a median split) on social skills.

The advantage of dichotomizing numeric variables is that you can then do a factorial analysis of variance, with all of its advantages of efficiency and testing interaction

dichotomizing   dividing the scores for a variable into two groups. Also called *median split*.

effects. Also, most psychologists are familiar with factorial analysis of variance. Many psychologists are less familiar with alternative procedures that accomplish much the same thing but do not require dichotomizing. (The alternative procedures one would use in these cases are mainly those based on multiple regression, see Chapters 12 and 15.)

A major disadvantage of dichotomizing is that you lose information when you reduce a whole range of scores to just two, high and low; it is just less accurate. Owen and Froman (2005) outlined the problem clearly: "With a median split, a person's score barely above the median is now put into the same category (*high*) as a person three standard deviations above the mean. That does not make good sense or good use of the data" (p. 499). One result is that the effect size and power of a study that dichotomizes is lower than when using the original scores (MacCallum et al., 2002; Taylor et al., 2006). Cohen (1983) calculated this reduction in power and effect size to be between 20% and 66%! It is equivalent, he suggested, to "discarding one-third to two-thirds of the sample" (p. 253).

On the other hand, many researchers dichotomize their variables, claiming that the effect is "conservative"—that, while it may increase the chance of a Type II error (failing to reject the null hypothesis when in fact it is false), it does not increase the chance of a Type I error (rejecting the null hypothesis when it is true). Put another way, dichotomizing reduces accuracy so that it is harder, not easier, to get significant results.

However, even assuming that, on the average, the effect of dichotomizing a single variable is conservative, there are still problems. One concern is that the analysis is now *overly* conservative in the sense that true results will go undiscovered (you will make Type II errors) and true effect sizes will be underestimated. There is also a general inaccuracy. Dichotomizing is conservative *on the average*. But in any particular case the inaccuracy in dichotomizing could happen to work in favor of the researcher's hypothesis, making a true nondifference come out significant in the study and a true large effect size come out smaller.

Indeed, Maxwell and Delaney (1993) have shown that, when both variables in a two-way factorial design are dichotomized (as in our example of anxiety and social skills), the effect is *not* automatically conservative. Under a number of common conditions in psychology research, dichotomizing two variables can produce the opposite of conservative effects even on the average. According to Maxwell and Delaney, you should be especially skeptical of the results of studies using a two-way analysis of variance in which both variables have been dichotomized.

There are, however, a few limited instances when dichotomization is appropriate. For example, MacCallum and colleagues (2002) note that it is appropriate when there is clear and convincing evidence that the two groups created by dichotomization represent very different types of people. Recall in the Aron and colleagues (2005) example that the researchers dichotomized scores on the measure of sensitivity to create a group of individuals who were not highly sensitive and a group who were highly sensitive. In their article, Aron and colleagues cited evidence from a variety of sources, including research on sensitivity in both infants and animals, indicating that sensitivity is best considered as a dichotomous variable rather than as a continuous variable. That is, the evidence is that people are essentially either highly sensitive or not, and variations along the scale are just due to the test's not being perfectly accurate.

In spite of the common problems of dichotomization, dichotomizing (even of both variables in two-way analysis of variance) is still surprisingly common in psychology research. It is our impression, though, that it is dying out.

Factorial Analysis of Variance in Research Articles

In a factorial analysis of variance, researchers usually give a description plus a table. The description gives the F ratio and the information that goes with it for each main and interaction effect. The table gives the cell means and sometimes the marginal means. If there is a significant interaction effect, there may also be a graph.

Van Prooijen and colleagues (2004) carried out a series of studies focusing on the effect of belongingness (whether a person feels included in, or excluded from, a group) and being able to voice one's opinion about a decision. The researchers examined the effect of these two variables on a person's satisfaction with the decision-making process (also known as *procedural satisfaction*). The participants were Dutch university students who were asked to imagine themselves as members of a team working on a project. They were then told that one member of the team would have to be excluded from a hypothetical project. Some students were told that they were not chosen to be excluded (the *inclusion* condition), other students were told that they were the person selected to be excluded from the project (the *exclusion* condition), and a final group of students were told that it was unclear whether they would be excluded (the *not yet known* condition). (Thus, the belongingness grouping variable had three levels: inclusion, exclusion, and not yet known.) Then, each student was either told that he or she would or would not be able to voice an opinion about a financial bonus to be received by the group (the *voice* condition and *no voice* condition, respectively). (Thus, the procedure grouping variable—as the researchers called it—had two levels: voice and no voice.) The researchers measured procedural satisfaction by asking the students to rate how satisfied they were with the way they were treated by the other people on their team. Here is how they reported the results:

> A 3×2 analysis of variance (ANOVA) on the procedural satisfaction scale showed main effects of both procedure, $F(1, 136) = 94.28$, $p < .01$, $\eta^2 = .41$, and group belongingness, $F(2, 136) = 3.70$, $p < .03$, $\eta^2 = .05$. More important…was that this analysis also yielded the predicted interaction effect, $F(2, 136) = 3.46$, $p < .04$, $\eta^2 = .05$. The cell means and standard deviations are shown in Table [10–7]….Findings…showed that inclusion in a group leads to stronger effects of voice as opposed to no-voice procedures on participants' ratings of procedural satisfaction than exclusion from a group. (p. 70)

Note that van Prooijen and colleagues (2004) provided the effect size for each main effect and the interaction effect. The effect sizes were shown as values of eta squared, η^2, which is another name for R^2 (which you learned about in Chapter 9). In an Advanced Topic section later in this chapter, we describe how to figure R^2 for a factorial analysis of variance. Notice in Table 10–7 that the researchers used subscript letters ($_a, _b, _c$) to show the results of post hoc comparisons of the means.

As we mentioned earlier in the chapter, researchers sometimes show interaction effects using a kind of line graph. Consider an example. Gump and Kulik (1997) tested a theory about the conditions that promote interpersonal affiliation. Specifically, they predicted that one is more likely to affiliate with another person when one is under threat and when the other person is facing the same threat. In their study, participants were randomly assigned to either expect or not expect a painful experimental procedure. This was the threat manipulation grouping variable (high versus low). In all conditions there was another participant in the room. Half the participants were told this other participant was in the same experiment and thus facing a similar situation of threat or nonthreat; for the other half, the other participant was supposedly taking part in a completely different experiment and thus not expecting the same

Table 10-7 Means and Standard Deviations of Participants' Procedural Satisfaction Ratings as a Function of Group Belongingness and Procedure, Experiment 1

	Group Belongingness					
	Inclusion		Exclusion		Not yet known	
Procedure	*M*	*SD*	*M*	*SD*	*M*	*SD*
Voice	4.86$_a$	1.82	3.31$_b$	1.83	4.46$_a$	1.95
No voice	1.89$_c$	1.14	1.81$_c$	0.84	1.69$_c$	0.83

Note: Means are on 7-point scales, with higher values indicating more positive ratings of procedural satisfaction. Means with no subscript in common differ as indicated by a least significant difference test for multiple comparisons between means ($p < .05$).
Source: van Prooijen, J. W., van den Bos, K., & Wilke, H. A. M. (2004). Group belongingness and procedural justice: Social inclusion and exclusion by peers affects the psychology of voice. *Journal of Personality and Social Psychology, 87,* 66–79. Published by the American Psychological Association. Reprinted with permission.

threatening or nonthreatening situation. This was the manipulation of similarity of situation grouping variable (similar versus dissimilar). As the participant was being told about the threat over an earphone, the experimenters observed how much time each participant spent looking at his or her partner. The results were as predicted:

> In this analysis, a significant interaction between participant threat and situational similarity emerged, $F(1, 77) = 5.57$, $p = .02$. No other effects were significant. As can be seen in Figure [10–10], it is clear that high threat produced more looking at an affiliate who was believed to be facing the same, compared with a different, situation, whereas no such differentiation occurred for low-threat participants. (p. 309)

The type of graph Gump and Kulik presented (Figure 10–10) has the advantage of making the pattern of interaction very vivid, even compared to the usual bar graph. However, line graphs like this have become less common in recent years, because they are slightly misleading in that the line implies that there is a *continuum of effect*.

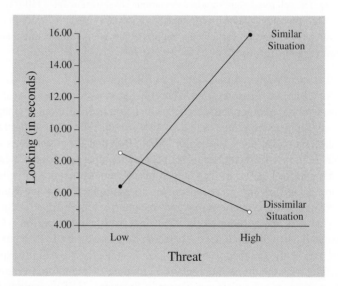

Figure 10-10 Study 1: The effect of threat and situational similarity on time spent looking at an affiliate.

Source: Gump, B. B., & Kulik, J. A. (1997). Stress, affiliation, and emotional contagion. *Journal of Personality and Social Psychology, 72,* 305–319. Published by the American Psychological Association. Reprinted with permission.

However, we only have information about the *two extreme points*. For example, in the Gump and Kulik study, there was a high threat and a low threat condition. The lines give the impression that the pattern for each similarity condition is continuous from low to high threat. Suppose the researchers had included an intermediate threat condition. It is possible that the result for this condition would be not at all where the line in the present graph says it should be. The bar graph approach, in contrast, does not imply anything about in-between levels; it simply shows the results at each level of the variable tested.

Advanced Topic: Figuring a Two-Way Analysis of Variance

As we noted earlier, to figure the interaction effect in a factorial analysis of variance beyond a 2 × 2 design, it is much easier to use the structural model approach you learned in the Advanced Topic sections of Chapter 9. Rather than mix approaches, researchers carry out the entire factorial analysis of variance using the structural model approach. Thus, in this section we first consider the structural model approach as it applies to factorial analysis of variance and then go into the details of how to do the figuring for a full factorial analysis of variance. As you will soon see, this Advanced Topic section builds directly on the Advanced Topic section in Chapter 9 on the structural model in the analysis of variance.

> **TIP FOR SUCCESS**
> Be sure you have mastered the material in the Advanced Topic section in Chapter 9 before reading on in this Advanced Topic section.

The Structural Model for the Two-Way Analysis of Variance

From the structural model perspective, each score's overall deviation from the grand mean of all scores can be divided into several parts. In a two-way analysis, there are four such parts of this overall deviation (see Figure 10–11):

> **TIP FOR SUCCESS**
> Be sure to study Figure 10–11 very carefully. It is the best way to understand and remember the structural model for the two-way analysis of variance.

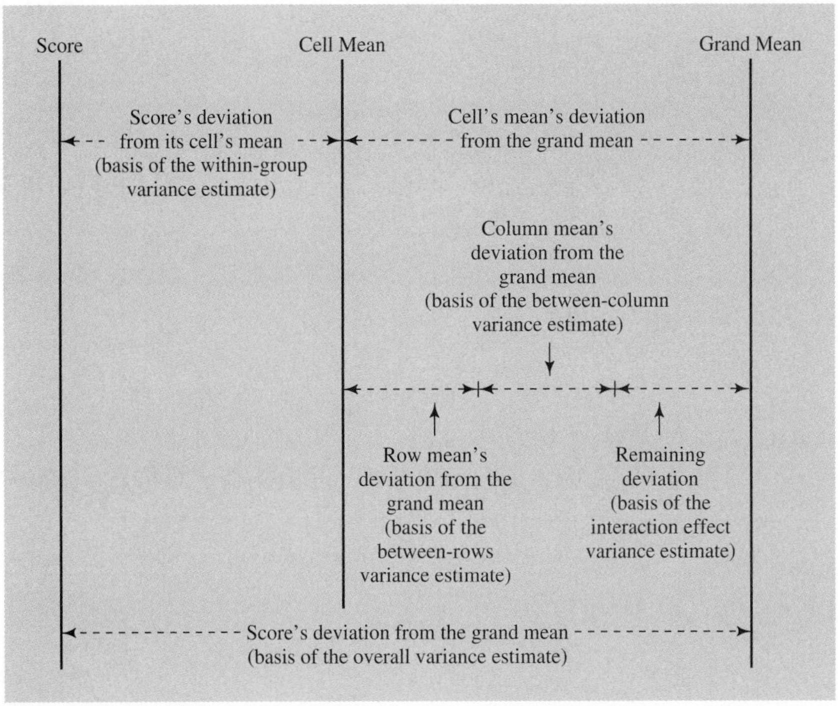

Figure 10-11   Dividing each score's deviation from the grand mean.

1. The score's deviation from the mean of its cell (used for the within-groups population variance estimate).
2. The deviation of the score's row's mean from the grand mean (used for the between-groups population variance estimate for the main effect for the grouping variable that divides the rows).
3. The deviation of the score's column's mean from the grand mean (used for the between-groups population variance estimate for the main effect for the grouping variable that divides the columns).
4. What remains after subtracting the other three deviations from the overall deviation from the grand mean (used for the between-groups estimate for the interaction effect).

Steps for the Two-Way Analysis of Variance

When figuring an analysis of variance using the structural model, you figure the *F* ratios as follows:

Ⓐ Figure the mean of each cell, row, and column, plus the grand mean of all scores.
Ⓑ Figure all the deviation scores of each type.
Ⓒ Square each deviation score. This gives the squared deviations.
Ⓓ Add up the squared deviation scores of each type. This gives the sums of squared deviations.
Ⓔ Divide each sum of squared deviations by its appropriate degrees of freedom. This gives the variance estimates.
Ⓕ Divide the various between-groups variance estimates by the within-groups variance estimate. This gives the *F* ratios.

In terms of formulas, the sums of squares are as follows:

The sum of squared deviations for rows is the sum of each score's row's mean's squared deviation from the grand mean.

$$SS_{\text{Rows}} = \Sigma(M_{\text{Row}} - GM)^2 \qquad (10\text{–}1)$$

The sum of squared deviations for columns is the sum of each score's column's mean's squared deviation from the grand mean.

$$SS_{\text{Columns}} = \Sigma(M_{\text{Column}} - GM)^2 \qquad (10\text{–}2)$$

The sum of squared deviations for the interaction is the sum of the squares of each score's deviation from the grand mean minus its deviation from its cell's mean, minus its row's mean's deviation from the grand mean, minus its column's mean's deviation from the grand mean.

$$SS_{\text{Interaction}} = \Sigma[(X - GM) \\ - (X - M) - (M_{\text{Row}} - GM) - (M_{\text{Column}} - GM)]^2 \qquad (10\text{–}3)$$

$$SS_{\text{Within}} = \Sigma(X - M)^2 \qquad \textbf{(10-4)}$$

$$SS_{\text{Total}} = \Sigma(X - GM)^2 \qquad \textbf{(10-5)}$$

In these formulas, SS_{Rows}, SS_{Columns}, $SS_{\text{Interaction}}$, and SS_{Within} are the sums of squared deviations for rows, columns, interaction, and within groups (within cells). The sum sign (Σ) tells you to add up over all scores (not just over all rows or columns or cells). GM is the grand mean; X is the score. M_{Row} and M_{Column} are the mean of a score's row or column, and M is the mean of a score's cell.

As was the case for the one-way analysis of variance, here too the different individual sums of squares add up to the total sums of squares. (You can use this as a check on your arithmetic.) Stated as a formula,

$$SS_{\text{Total}} = SS_{\text{Rows}} + SS_{\text{Columns}} + SS_{\text{Interaction}} + SS_{\text{Within}} \qquad \textbf{(10-6)}$$

The formulas for the population variance estimates are, as was the case for the one-way analysis of variance using the structural model approach, the sums of squares divided by the degrees of freedom:

$$S_{\text{Rows}}^2 \text{ or } MS_{\text{Rows}} = \frac{SS_{\text{Rows}}}{df_{\text{Rows}}} \qquad \textbf{(10-7)}$$

$$S_{\text{Columns}}^2 \text{ or } MS_{\text{Columns}} = \frac{SS_{\text{Columns}}}{df_{\text{Columns}}} \qquad \textbf{(10-8)}$$

$$S_{\text{Interaction}}^2 \text{ or } MS_{\text{Interaction}} = \frac{SS_{\text{Interaction}}}{df_{\text{Interaction}}} \qquad \textbf{(10-9)}$$

$$S_{\text{Within}}^2 \text{ or } MS_{\text{Within}} = \frac{SS_{\text{Within}}}{df_{\text{Within}}} \qquad \textbf{(10-10)}$$

The *F* ratio for the row main effect is the population variance estimate based on the variation between rows divided rows divided by the population variance estimate based on the variation within groups (within cells).

The *F* ratio for the column main effect is the population variance estimate based on the variation between columns divided by the population variance estimate based on the variation within groups (within cells).

The *F* ratio for the interaction effect is the population variance estimate based on the variation associated with the interaction divided by the population variance estimate based on the variation within groups (within cells).

The *F* ratios are the population variance estimates for the different effects, each divided by the within-groups population variance estimate:

$$F_{\text{Rows}} = \frac{S_{\text{Rows}}^2}{S_{\text{Within}}^2} \text{ or } \frac{MS_{\text{Rows}}}{MS_{\text{Within}}} \quad (10\text{–}11)$$

$$F_{\text{Columns}} = \frac{S_{\text{Columns}}^2}{S_{\text{Within}}^2} \text{ or } \frac{MS_{\text{Columns}}}{MS_{\text{Within}}} \quad (10\text{–}12)$$

$$F_{\text{Interaction}} = \frac{S_{\text{Interaction}}^2}{S_{\text{Within}}^2} \text{ or } \frac{MS_{\text{Interaction}}}{MS_{\text{Within}}} \quad (10\text{–}13)$$

Degrees of Freedom in a Two-Way Analysis of Variance

Degrees of Freedom for Between-Groups Variance Estimates for the Main Effects   The degrees of freedom for each main effect (each between-groups variance estimate) is the number of levels of the grouping variable minus 1. For example, if there are two levels to a grouping variable, as in each main effect in the Aron and colleagues (2005) study, there is one degree of freedom for each of these main effects. In the arousal levels and task difficulty examples we considered earlier, the columns grouping variable (arousal level) main effect had three levels. Thus, there were two degrees of freedom for this grouping variable's main effect.

Stated as formulas,

The degrees of freedom for the rows main effect is the number of rows minus 1.

$$df_{\text{Rows}} = N_{\text{Rows}} - 1 \quad (10\text{–}14)$$

The degrees of freedom for the columns main effect is the number of columns minus 1.

$$df_{\text{Columns}} = N_{\text{Columns}} - 1 \quad (10\text{–}15)$$

Degrees of Freedom for the Interaction Effect Variance Estimate   The degrees of freedom for the variance estimate for the interaction effect is the total number of cells minus the number of degrees of freedom for both main effects, minus 1. In the Aron and colleagues (2005) study, there were four cells and one degree of freedom for each main effect. This leaves two degrees of freedom, minus 1 more, leaving one degree of freedom for the interaction. In the arousal level and task difficulty examples, there were six cells. There were two degrees of freedom for the column effect and one for the row effect (easy versus hard task). This leaves three degrees of freedom. When one more is subtracted, there are two degrees of freedom left for the interaction.

Stated as a formula,

$$df_{\text{Interaction}} = N_{\text{Cells}} - df_{\text{Rows}} - df_{\text{Columns}} - 1 \qquad \textbf{(10–16)}$$

Applying the formula to the Aron and colleagues study,

$$df_{\text{Interaction}} = N_{\text{Cells}} - df_{\text{Rows}} - df_{\text{Columns}} - 1 = 4 - 1 - 1 - 1 = 1.$$

Applying the formula to the arousal and task difficulty example,

$$df_{\text{Interaction}} = N_{\text{Cells}} - df_{\text{Rows}} - df_{\text{Columns}} - 1 = 6 - 1 - 2 - 1 = 2.$$

Degrees of Freedom for the Within-Groups Population Variance Estimate
As usual, the within-groups degrees of freedom is the sum of the degrees of freedom for all the groups (in this case, all the cells). For each cell, you take its number of scores minus 1, then add up what you get for all the cells. In terms of a formula,

$$df_{\text{Within}} = df_1 + df_2 + \cdots + df_{\text{Last}} \qquad \textbf{(10–17)}$$

In this formula, $df_1, df_2, \ldots, df_{\text{Last}}$ are the degrees of freedom for each cell (the number of scores in the cell minus 1), in succession, from the first cell to the last.

Total Degrees of Freedom   The total degrees of freedom, as usual, is the number of scores minus 1. In terms of a formula,

$$df_{\text{Total}} = N - 1 \qquad \textbf{(10–18)}$$

You can also figure the total degrees of freedom by adding up all the individual degrees of freedom (for columns, rows, interaction, and within). This provides a check of your arithmetic in figuring degrees of freedom. In terms of a formula,

$$df_{\text{Total}} = df_{\text{Rows}} + df_{\text{Columns}} + df_{\text{Interaction}} + df_{\text{Within}} \qquad \textbf{(10–19)}$$

Table for a Two-Way Analysis of Variance

The analysis of variance table in a two-way analysis is similar to the ones in Chapter 9 (where you were doing one-way analyses of variance). However, with a two-way analysis of variance there is a line in the table for each between-groups effect (that is, for the columns main effect, the rows main effect, and the interaction). Table 10–8 shows the layout.

Example   Let's return to the Aron and colleagues (2005) example, in which students, who were either highly sensitive or not highly sensitive, took an easy test or a hard test. The study was a 2×2 factorial design, with grouping variables of sensitivity and test difficulty. The variable measured was students' level of negative mood. There were 160 students in the original study, but, to keep the figuring simple, we have made up scores that give the same cell and marginal means, but with only five students per cell. The cell means and marginal means are shown in Table 10–9. The scores and the figuring for all the deviations are shown in Table 10–10.

The degrees of freedom for the interaction effect is the number of cells minus the degrees of freedom for the row main effect minus the degrees of freedom for the column main effect minus 1.

The degrees of freedom for the within-groups (within-cells) population variance estimate is the sum of the degrees of freedom for all the cells.

The total degrees of freedom is the number of scores minus 1.

The total degrees of freedom are the degrees of freedom for the row main effect plus the degrees of freedom for the column main effect plus the degrees of freedom for the interaction effect plus the degrees of freedom for the within-groups (within-cells) population variance estimate.

Table 10-8 Layout of an Analysis of Variance Table for a Two-Way Analysis of Variance

Source	SS	df	MS	F
Between:				
Columns	$SS_{Columns}$	$df_{Columns}$	$MS_{Columns}$	$F_{Columns}$
Rows	SS_{Rows}	df_{Rows}	MS_{Rows}	F_{Rows}
Interaction	$SS_{Interaction}$	$df_{Interaction}$	$MS_{Interaction}$	$F_{Interaction}$
Within	SS_{Within}	df_{Within}	MS_{Within}	
Total	SS_{Total}	df_{Total}		

Table 10-9 Cell and Marginal Means for Level of Negative Mood

		Test Difficulty		
		Easy	Hard	
Sensitivity	Not High	2.43	2.56	2.50
	High	2.19	3.01	2.60
		2.31	2.79	

Source: Data from E. Aron et al. (2005).

Table 10–11 shows the cutoff F values and the analysis of variance table. Figure 10–2 (earlier in the chapter) graphs the results. We can explore the example following the usual step-by-step hypothesis-testing procedure.

❶ **Restate the question as a research hypothesis and a null hypothesis about the populations for each main effect and the interaction effect.** There are four populations:

Population 1, 1: People who are not highly sensitive and take an easy test.
Population 1, 2: People who are not highly sensitive and take a hard test.
Population 2, 1: People who are highly sensitive and take an easy test.
Population 2, 2: People who are highly sensitive and take a hard test.

The first null hypothesis is that the combined populations for individuals who are not highly sensitive (Populations 1, 1 and 1, 2) have the same level of negative mood as the combined populations for individuals who are highly sensitive (Populations 2, 1 and 2, 2). This is the null hypothesis for testing the main effect for sensitivity (not highly sensitive versus highly sensitive). The research hypothesis is that the populations of not highly sensitive and highly sensitive individuals have different means.

The second null hypothesis is that the combined populations for those who take an easy test (Populations 1, 1 and 2, 1) have the same level of negative mood as the combined populations for those who take a hard test (Populations 1, 2 and 2, 2). This is the null hypothesis for testing the main effect for test difficulty (easy versus hard). The research hypothesis is that populations taking easy and hard tests have different means.

The third null hypothesis is that the difference between the level of negative mood of the two populations for individuals who are not highly sensitive (Population 1, 1 minus Population 1, 2) will be the same as the difference between the means of the two populations for individuals who are highly sensitive (Population 2, 1 minus Population 2, 2). This is the null hypothesis for testing the interaction effect. (We could also say the same thing, with no change in meaning, as the difference between the two populations for the easy test equaling the difference between the two populations for the hard test.) The research hypothesis is that these differences will not be the same.

❷ **Determine the characteristics of the comparison distributions.** The three comparison distributions will be F distributions. The denominator degrees of freedom are the sum of the degrees of freedom in each of the cells (the number of scores in the cell minus 1). In this example, there are five participants in each

Table 10–10 Scores, Squared Deviations, and Sums of Squared Deviations for Fictional Data Based on the E. Aron and Colleagues (2005) Study

Easy Test Difficulty					Hard Test Difficulty				
X	$(X - GM)^2$	$(X - M)^2$	$(M_{Row} - GM)^2$	$(M_{Column} - GM)^2$ INT^2	X	$(X - GM)^2$	$(X - M)^2$	$(M_{Row} - GM)^2$	$(M_{Column} - GM)^2$ INT^2
Not Highly Sensitive									
2.63	.01	.04	.00	.06 .03	2.69	.02	.02	.00	.06 .03
2.53	.00	.01	.00	.06 .03	2.31	.06	.06	.00	.06 .03
2.25	.09	.03	.00	.06 .03	2.45	.01	.01	.00	.06 .03
2.22	.11	.04	.00	.06 .03	2.80	.06	.06	.00	.06 .03
2.52	.00	.01	.00	.06 .03	2.55	.00	.00	.00	.06 .03
12.15	.21	.13	.00	.30 .15	12.80	.15	.15	.00	.30 .15
Highly Sensitive									
2.06	.24	.02	.00	.06 .03	3.21	.44	.04	.00	.06 .03
2.32	.05	.02	.00	.06 .03	3.21	.44	.04	.00	.06 .03
2.04	.26	.02	.00	.06 .03	2.77	.05	.06	.00	.06 .03
2.31	.06	.01	.00	.06 .03	2.83	.08	.03	.00	.06 .03
2.22	.11	.00	.00	.06 .03	3.03	.23	.00	.00	.06 .03
10.95	.72	.07	.00	.30 .15	15.05	1.24	.17	.00	.30 .15

GM = grand mean (mean of all the scores)

M = mean of the score's cell

M_{Row} = mean of the score's row

M_{Column} = mean of the score's column

INT = score's remaining deviation for the interaction

Examples of figuring of deviations, using the first score in the Not Highly Sensitive/Easy Test cell:

$$(X - GM)^2 = (2.63 - 2.55)^2 = .08^2 = .01$$
$$(X - M)^2 = (2.63 - 2.43)^2 = .20^2 = .04$$
$$(M_{Row} - GM)^2 = (2.50 - 2.55)^2 = -.05^2 = .00$$
$$(M_{Column} - GM)^2 = (2.31 - 2.55)^2 = -.24^2 = .06$$
$$INT^2 = [(X - GM) - (X - M) - (M_{Row} - GM) - (M_{Column} - GM)]^2$$
$$= [(.08) - (.20) - (-.05) - (-.24)]^2 = (.08 - .20 + .05 + .24)^2 = .17^2 = .03$$
$$SS_{Total} = .21 + .15 + .72 + 1.24 = 2.32$$
$$SS_{Within} = .13 + .15 + .07 + .17 = .52$$
$$SS_{Row} = .00 + .00 + .00 + .00 = .00$$
$$SS_{Column} = .30 + .30 + .30 + .30 = 1.20$$
$$SS_{Interaction} = .15 + .15 + .15 + .15 = .60$$

Accuracy check: $SS_{Total} = 2.32$, $SS_{Within} + SS_{Rows} + SS_{Columns} + SS_{Interaction} = .52 + .00 + 1.20 + .60 = 2.32$

Table 10–11 Factorial Analysis of Variance Based on the E. Aron and Colleagues (2005) Study (Fictional Data)

F needed for Sensitivity main effect ($df = 1, 16$; $p < .05$) = 4.49.
F needed for Test Difficulty main effect ($df = 1, 16$; $p < .05$) = 4.49.
F needed for Interaction effect ($df = 1, 16$; $p < .05$) = 4.49.

Source	SS	df	MS	F	Decision
Sensitivity	.00	1	.00	0.00	Do not reject the null hypothesis
Test Difficulty	1.20	1	1.20	40.00	Reject the null hypothesis
Sensitivity × Test Difficulty	.60	1	.60	20.00	Reject the null hypothesis
Within groups	.52	16	.03		

TIP FOR SUCCESS

As a check of the accuracy of the degrees of freedom calculations, the three numerators plus the denominator degrees of freedom come out to 19 (that is, $1 + 1 + 1 + 16 = 19$). This is the same as the total degrees of freedom figured as number of participants minus 1, which is also 19 (that is, $20 - 1 = 19$).

of the four cells. This makes four degrees of freedom per cell, for a total of 16 within-groups degrees of freedom. The numerator for the comparison distribution for the sensitivity main effect has one degree of freedom (two rows minus 1); the numerator for the test difficulty main effect also has one degree of freedom; and the numerator degrees of freedom for the interaction effect is, again, 1 (it is the number of cells, four, minus the degrees of freedom for columns, minus the degrees of freedom for rows, minus 1).

❸ **Determine the cutoff sample scores on the comparison distributions at which each null hypothesis should be rejected.** Using the .05 significance level, Table A–3 (in the Appendix) gives a cutoff for 1 and 16 degrees of freedom of 4.49. The degrees of freedom and the significance level are the same in this example for both main effects and the interaction, so the cutoff is the same for all three (see Table 10–11).

❹ **Determine your samples' scores on each comparison distribution.** This requires figuring three F ratios.

  ❹ **Figure the mean of each cell, row, and column, plus the grand mean of all scores.** The cell means, row means, and column means are shown in Table 10–9. The grand mean of all the scores (the sum of all the scores, divided by the total number of scores) is 2.55.

  ❸ **Figure all the deviation scores of each type.** To save space, Table 10–10 shows only the squared deviations. However, following the table of squared deviations, we show how we figured all the deviations for the first score. For example, the deviation of the first score from the grand mean is 2.63 minus 2.55.

  ❸ **Square each deviation score.** All of these squared deviations are shown in Table 10–10. For example, the first score's deviation of .12 from the grand mean, when squared, is .01.

  ❶ **Add up the squared deviation scores of each type.** For example, for the sum of squared deviations from the grand mean, the total in the first cell (Not Highly Sensitive/Easy Test) is .21; for the second cell, .15; for the third, .72; and for the fourth, 1.24. This adds up to a total of 2.32. That is, $SS_{Total} = 2.32$. Remember that the *sums* of the various squared deviations (SS_{Within}, SS_{Rows}, $SS_{Columns}$, $SS_{Interaction}$) add up.

TIP FOR SUCCESS

When figuring the deviation for the interaction effect, keep close track of the signs of the deviations you are subtracting and remember that this interaction deviation, prior to squaring, is figured from the original unsquared deviations, not the squared deviations.

  But within a single participant, the various squared deviations do not add up to the overall squared deviation of the score from the grand mean. Table 10–10 also shows the check for accuracy: The sum of the squared deviations from the grand mean equals the total of the sums of the other four kinds of squared deviations (within rounding error).

  ❶ **Divide each sum of squared deviations by its appropriate degrees of freedom.** This is shown in Table 10–11. For example, the population variance estimate for Test Difficulty (the columns) comes out to 1.20, the sum of squares of 1.20 divided by the degrees of freedom of 1.

  ❶ **Divide the various between-groups variance estimates by the within-groups variance estimate.** This gives the F ratios and is shown in Table 10–11. For example, the F for Test Difficulty comes out to 40.00, the between-rows population variance estimate of 1.20 divided by the within-groups population variance estimate of .03.

❺ **Decide whether to reject the null hypotheses.** The F ratio for the test difficulty main effect of 40.00 is much larger than the cutoff of 4.49. Thus, you can reject the null hypothesis that the populations of individuals who take an easy test and a difficult test have the same mean level of negative mood. That is, the test difficulty effect is significant. The F of 0.00 for the sensitivity main effect did not reach the necessary 4.49 cutoff. Finally, the interaction effect F of 20.00 exceeds 4.49; so the interaction effect is significant.

As can be seen from the cell means in Table 10–9 (and from Figure 10–2), the test difficulty main effect is due to individuals taking the hard test having a higher level of negative mood than individuals who take the easy test. The interaction effect is due to a different effect of test difficulty on negative mood according to the level of sensitivity. The level of negative mood of students who are not highly sensitive is slightly higher with a hard test compared to an easy test; but the level of negative mood of students who are highly sensitive is much higher with a hard test compared to an easy test. You can see how using an analysis of variance to look at interaction effects uncovered an interesting relationship among the variables.

Summary of Procedures for a Two-Way Analysis of Variance   Table 10–12 summarizes the steps of hypothesis testing and Table 10–13 shows the analysis of variance table and the formulas for a two-way analysis of variance.[1]

Table 10-12   Steps of Hypothesis Testing for a Two-Way Analysis of Variance

❶ **Restate the question as a research hypothesis and a null hypothesis about the populations for each main effect and the interaction effect.**

❷ **Determine the characteristics of the comparison distributions.**
  a. The numerator degrees of freedom for the F distribution for the columns main effect is the number of columns minus 1: $df_{Columns} = N_{Columns} - 1$.
  b. The numerator degrees of freedom for the F distribution for the rows main effect is the number of rows minus 1: $df_{Rows} = N_{Rows} - 1$.
  c. The numerator degrees of freedom for the F distribution for the interaction effect is the number of cells minus the degrees of freedom for columns minus the degrees of freedom for rows minus 1: $df_{Interaction} = N_{Cells} - df_{Columns} - df_{Rows} - 1$.
  d. The comparison distributions will be F distributions with denominator degrees of freedom equal to the sum of the degrees of freedom in each of the cells (the number of scores in the cell minus 1): $df_{Within} = df_1 + df_2 + \cdots + df_{Last}$.
  e. Check the accuracy of your figuring by making sure that all of the degrees of freedom add up to the total degrees of freedom: $df_{Total} = N - 1 = df_{Within} + df_{Columns} + df_{Rows} + df_{Interaction}$.

❸ **Determine the cutoff sample scores on the comparison distributions at which each null hypothesis should be rejected.**
  a. Determine the desired significance levels.
  b. Look up the appropriate cutoffs in an F table (Table A–3 in the Appendix).

❹ **Determine your samples' scores on each comparison distribution.**
  Ⓐ **Figure the mean of each cell, row, and column, plus the grand mean of all scores.**
  Ⓑ **Figure all the deviation scores of each type. For each score figure:**
    i. Its deviation from the grand mean: $X - GM$.
    ii. Its deviation from its cell's mean: $X - M$.
    iii. Its row's mean's deviation from the grand mean: $M_{Row} - GM$.
    iv. Its column's mean's deviation from the grand mean: $M_{Column} - GM$.
    v. Its deviation from the grand mean minus all the other deviations: Interaction deviation $= (X - GM) - (X - M) - (M_{Row} - GM) - (M_{Column} - GM)$.
  Ⓒ **Square each deviation score.** This gives the squared deviations.
  Ⓓ **Add up the squared deviation scores of each type.** This gives the sums of squared deviations: SS_{Total}, SS_{Within}, $SS_{Columns}$, SS_{Rows}, and $SS_{Interaction}$.
  Ⓔ **Divide each sum of squared deviations by its appropriate degrees of freedom.** This gives the variance estimates. That is, $MS_{Columns}$ or $S^2_{Columns} = SS_{Columns}/df_{Columns}$; MS_{Rows} or $S^2_{Rows} = SS_{Rows}/df_{Rows}$; $MS_{Interaction}$ or $S^2_{Interaction} = SS_{Interaction}/df_{Interaction}$.
  Ⓕ **Divide the various between-groups variance estimates by the within-groups variance estimate.** This gives the F ratios: $F_{Columns} = S^2_{Columns}/S^2_{Within}$ or $MS_{Columns}/MS_{Within}$; $F_{Rows} = S^2_{Rows}/S^2_{Within}$ or MS_{Rows}/MS_{Within}; $F_{Interaction} = S^2_{Interaction}/S^2_{Within}$ or $MS_{Interaction}/MS_{Within}$.

❺ **Decide whether to reject the null hypotheses.** Compare scores in Steps ❸ and ❹.

Table 10-13 Analysis of Variance Table and Formulas for a Two-Way Analysis of Variance

Analysis of variance table:

Source	SS	df	MS	F
Between:				
Columns	$SS_{Columns}$	$df_{Columns}$	$MS_{Columns}$ (or $S^2_{Columns}$)	$F_{Columns}$
Rows	SS_{Rows}	df_{Rows}	MS_{Rows} (or S^2_{Rows})	F_{Rows}
Interaction	$SS_{Interaction}$	$df_{Interaction}$	$MS_{Interaction}$ (or $S^2_{Interaction}$)	$F_{Interaction}$
Within	SS_{Within}	df_{Within}	MS_{Within} (or S^2_{Within})	
Total	SS_{Total}	df_{Total}		

Formulas for each section of the analysis of variance table:

Source	SS	df	MS	F
Between:				
Columns	$\Sigma(M_{Column} - GM)^2$	$N_{Columns} - 1$	$SS_{Columns}/df_{Columns}$	$MS_{Columns}/MS_{Within}$
Rows	$\Sigma(M_{Row} - GM)^2$	$N_{Rows} - 1$	SS_{Rows}/df_{Rows}	MS_{Rows}/MS_{Within}
Interaction	$\Sigma[(X - GM)$ $- (X - M)$ $- (M_{Row} - GM)$ $- (M_{Column} - GM)]^2$	$N_{Cells} - df_{Columns} - df_{Rows} - 1$	$SS_{Interaction}/df_{Interaction}$	$MS_{Interaction}/MS_{Within}$
Within	$\Sigma(X - M)^2$	$df_1 + df_2 + \cdots + df_{Last}$	SS_{Within}/df_{Within}	
Total	$\Sigma(X - GM)^2$	$N - 1$		

Definitions of basic symbols:

Σ = sum of the appropriate numbers for all *scores* (not all cells)

M = mean of a score's cell

M_{Row} = mean of a score's row

M_{Column} = mean of a score's column

GM = grand mean of all scores

N_{Cells} = number of cells

N_{Rows} = number of rows

$N_{Columns}$ = number of columns

X = each score

N = total number of scores in the study

How are you doing?

1. List the steps for figuring the *F* ratios in a two-way factorial analysis of variance.
2. Write the formula for the sum of squares for rows and define each of the symbols.
3. Write the formula for the sum of squares for the interaction and define each of the symbols.
4. Write the formula for the degrees of freedom for the interaction and define each of the symbols.

5. Here are the scores for participants A through H (a total of eight; two participants per cell) for the fictional study of the effects of vividness and length of examples on the number of examples recalled used in an earlier "How Are You Doing?" question. Find the three *F* ratios (and test their significance at $p < .05$).

Participant	Vividness Condition	Length Condition	Number Recalled
A	Low	Short	6
B	Low	Short	4
C	High	Short	9
D	High	Short	5
E	Low	Long	2
F	Low	Long	4
G	High	Long	1
H	High	Long	1

Table 10-14 Figuring for "How Are You Doing?" question 5

F needed for main effect for Vividness ($df = 1, 4; p < .05$) = 7.71.
F needed for main effect for Length ($df = 1, 4; p < .05$) = 7.71.
F needed for interaction effect ($df = 1, 4; p < .05$) = 7.71.

	Low Vividness					High Vividness						
	X	$(X - GM)^2$	INT^2	$(M_{Column} - GM)^2$	$(M_{Row} - GM)^2$	$(X - M)^2$	X	INT^2	$(M_{Column} - GM)^2$	$(M_{Row} - GM)^2$	$(X - M)^2$	$(X - GM)^2$
Short												
6	4	4	1	0	1	1	9	4	1	25	4	1
4	0	1	1	0	1	1	5	4	1	26	4	1
	2	4	2	0	8	8	2	8	2		8	2
Long												
4	4	4	1	0	1	1	9	4	1	9	4	1
4	0	1	1	0	1	1	6	4	1	18	0	1
	4	8	2	0	8	8	2	8	2		0	2

$SS_{Total} = 4 + 26 + 4 + 18 = 52$
$SS_{Within} = 2 + 8 + 2 + 0 = 12$
$SS_{Rows} = 8 + 8 + 8 + 8 = 32$
$SS_{Columns} = 0 + 0 + 0 + 0 = 0$
$SS_{Interaction} = 2 + 2 + 2 + 2 = 8$
Accuracy check: $SS_{Total} = SS_{Within} + SS_{Rows} + SS_{Columns} + SS_{Interaction} = 12 + 32 + 0 + 8 = 52$

Source	SS	df	MS	F	Decision
Length (rows)	32	1	32	10.67	Reject the null hypothesis.
Vividness (columns)	0	1	0	0	Do not reject the null hypothesis.
Interaction (Length × Vividness)	8	1	8	2.67	Do not reject the null hypothesis.
Within groups	12	4	3		

5. The major figuring is shown in Table 10-14. For the Length effect, $F = 10.67$; significant. For the Vividness effect, $F = 0$; not significant. For the interaction effect, $F = 2.67$; not significant.

Answers

1. ⓐ **Figure the mean of each cell, row, and column, plus the grand mean of all scores.**
   ⓑ **Figure all the deviation scores of each type.**
   ⓒ **Square each deviation score.**
   ⓓ **Add up the squared deviation scores of each type.**
   ⓔ **Divide each sum of squared deviations by its appropriate degrees of freedom.**
   ⓕ **Divide the various between-groups variance estimates by the within-groups variance estimate.**

2. Formula for the sum of squares for rows: $SS_{\text{Rows}} = \Sigma(M_{\text{Row}} - GM)^2$. SS_{Rows} is the sum of squared deviations for rows; Σ tells you to add up what follows over all scores; M_{Row} is the mean of a score's row; and GM is the grand mean (the mean of all the scores).

3. Formula for the sum of squares for the interaction: $SS_{\text{Interaction}} = \Sigma[(X - GM) - (X - M) - (M_{\text{Row}} - GM) - (M_{\text{Column}} - GM)]^2$. $SS_{\text{Interaction}}$ is the sum of squared deviations for the interaction; Σ tells you to add up what follows over all scores; X is each score; GM is the grand mean (the mean of all the scores); M is the mean of a score's cell; and M_{Row} and M_{Column} are the means, respectively, of a score's row and column.

4. Formula for the degrees of freedom for the interaction: $df_{\text{Interaction}} = N_{\text{Cells}} - df_{\text{Columns}} - df_{\text{Rows}} - 1$. $df_{\text{Interaction}}$ is the degrees of freedom for the interaction effect; N_{Cells} is the number of cells; df_{Columns} is the degrees of freedom for columns (the number of columns − 1); and df_{Rows} is the number of rows (the number of rows − 1).

Advanced Topic: Power and Effect Size in the Factorial Analysis of Variance

You figure power and effect size in a factorial analysis of variance using the same approach as for a one-way analysis of variance (see Chapter 9), except that you figure power and effect size separately for each main effect and the interaction.

Effect Size

You can figure the effect size for each main and interaction effect as an R^2, the proportion of variance accounted for (also called eta squared, symbolized as η^2) by the effect. In Chapter 9 we described the proportion of variance accounted for in a one-way analysis of variance as the proportion of the total variation of scores from the grand mean that is accounted for by the variation between the means of the groups. In a one-way analysis of variance, $R^2 = [(S^2_{\text{Between}})(df_{\text{Between}})]/[(S^2_{\text{Between}})(df_{\text{Between}}) + (S^2_{\text{Within}})(df_{\text{Within}})]$. Now, consider the situation of the column effect in a two-way analysis of variance. We can certainly substitute S^2_{Columns} for S^2_{Between} and df_{Columns} for df_{Between} in the numerator of the equation. S^2_{Columns} (the sum of squared deviations of the columns' means from the grand mean) is the variance created by the effect of the grouping variable that divides the groups across the columns and is otherwise not accounted for.

However, what about the denominator—the baseline, which is the variance that is to be accounted for in the proportion of variance accounted for? In a two-way analysis, the squared deviations of each score from the grand mean are now partly accounted for by the column effect, the row effect, and the interaction effect. But the column effect should not be held responsible for variance already accounted for by the row and interaction effects; the squared deviations to be accounted for by columns should include only those squared deviations not already accounted for by rows or the interaction. Thus, we can substitute S^2_{Columns} for S^2_{Between} and df_{Columns} for df_{Between} in the denominator of the equation. To put this in terms of a formula,

$$R^2_{\text{Columns}} = \frac{(S^2_{\text{Columns}})\,(df_{\text{Columns}})}{(S^2_{\text{Columns}})\,(df_{\text{Columns}}) + (S^2_{\text{Within}})\,(df_{\text{Within}})} \qquad \textbf{(10–20)}$$

> The proportion of variance accounted for by variation between columns is the product of the F ratio for columns multiplied by its degrees of freedom divided by the sum of the F ratio for columns multiplied by its degrees of freedom plus the degrees of freedom within groups (within cells).

The same principle holds for the row and interaction effects. Stated as formulas,

$$R^2_{\text{Rows}} = \frac{(S^2_{\text{Rows}})\,(df_{\text{Rows}})}{(S^2_{\text{Rows}})\,(df_{\text{Rows}}) + (S^2_{\text{Within}})(df_{\text{Within}})} \qquad \textbf{(10–21)}$$

> The proportion of variance accounted for by variation between rows is the population variance estimate based on the variation between rows multiplied by the degrees of freedom for the rows, divided by the sum of the population variance estimate based on the variation between rows multiplied by the degrees of freedom for the rows, plus the within-groups (within-cells) population variance estimate multiplied by the within-groups (within-cells) degrees of freedom.

$$R^2_{\text{Interaction}} = \frac{(S^2_{\text{Interaction}})\,(df_{\text{Interaction}})}{(S^2_{\text{Interaction}})\,(df_{\text{Interaction}}) + (S^2_{\text{Within}})\,(df_{\text{Within}})} \qquad \textbf{(10–22)}$$

> The proportion of variance accounted for by the interaction is the population variance estimate based on the variation associated with the interaction multiplied by the degrees of freedom for the interaction, divided by the sum of the population variance estimate based on the variation associated with the interaction multiplied by the degrees of freedom for the interaction, plus the within-groups (within-cells) population variance estimate multiplied by the within-groups (within-cells) degrees of freedom.

Technically, each of these is a "partial" R^2 because it describes the proportion of variance accounted for by an effect after "partialing out" the other effects. (We say more about partial correlations in Chapters 15.)

In our example based on the Aron and colleagues (2005) study, R^2 would be figured as follows:

$$R^2_{\text{Columns}} \text{ (Test Difficulty)} = \frac{(S^2_{\text{Columns}})\,(df_{\text{Columns}})}{(S^2_{\text{Columns}})\,(df_{\text{Columns}}) + (S^2_{\text{Within}})\,(df_{\text{Within}})}$$

$$= \frac{(1.20)\,(1)}{(1.20)\,(1) + (.03)\,(16)} = .71.$$

$$R^2_{\text{Rows}} \text{ (Sensitivity)} = \frac{(S^2_{\text{Rows}})\,(df_{\text{Rows}})}{(S^2_{\text{Rows}})\,(df_{\text{Rows}}) + (S^2_{\text{Within}})\,(df_{\text{Within}})}$$

$$= \frac{(.00)\,(1)}{(.00)\,(1) + (.03)\,(16)} = .00.$$

$$R^2_{\text{Interaction}} \text{ (Interaction)} = \frac{(S^2_{\text{Interaction}})\,(df_{\text{Interaction}})}{(S^2_{\text{Interaction}})\,(df_{\text{Interaction}}) + (S^2_{\text{Within}})\,(df_{\text{Within}})}$$

$$= \frac{(.60)\,(1)}{(.60)\,(1) + (.03)\,(16)} = .56$$

Based on Cohen's conventions for R^2 in the analysis of variance (.01, small effect size; .06, medium effect size; .14, large effect size), there is an enormous effect size—a high R^2—for test difficulty and also an extremely large effect size for the interaction. The nonsignificant effect for affiliation had a zero effect size. (In the actual study, the effect sizes were much smaller. The effect sizes for test difficulty and the interaction are so large in the example because we made up scores with much less variance than in the actual study. We did this to help you see the patterns very clearly.)

Power

In a factorial analysis of variance, the power of each effect is influenced by the overall design. For example, a three-level column effect will have different power if it is crossed with a two-level row effect than if it is crossed with a three-level row effect. To keep things simple, we present power figures for only the three most common two-way analysis of situations: all effects in a 2 × 2 design, a two-level (two-row or two-column) main effect in a 2 × 3 design, and a three-level (three-row or three-column) main effect in a 2 × 3 design. (The power of the interaction in a 2 × 3 design is the same as for the three-level main effect.)

Table 10–15 presents approximate power at the .05 significance level for each of these situations for small, medium, and large effect sizes and for cell sizes of 10, 20, 30, 40, 50, and 100.[2]

Consider a planned 2 × 2 study with 30 participants in each cell and an expected medium effect size ($R^2 = .06$) for the row main effect (and using the .05 significance level). The row main effect for this planned study would have a power of .78, meaning that, if the research hypothesis for this row main effect is in fact true and has a medium effect size, the chance that the study will come out significant is about 78%.

Or consider an example of a published study in which a nonsignificant result is found for an interaction effect in a 2 × 3 analysis of variance with 20 participants per cell. Based on the table, power is only .14 for a small effect size. This means that,

Table 10-15   Approximate Power for Studies Using 2 × 2 or 2 × 3 Analysis of Variance for Hypotheses Tested at the .05 Significance Level

	Effect Size		
N Per Cell	**Small** $(R^2 = .01)$	**Medium** $(R^2 = .06)$	**Large** $(R^2 = .14)$
All effects in a 2 × 2 analysis:			
10	.09	.33	.68
20	.13	.60	.94
30	.19	.78	.99
40	.24	.89	*
50	.29	.94	*
100	.52	*	*
Two-level main effect in a 2 × 3 analysis:			
10	.11	.46	.84
20	.18	.77	.99
30	.26	.92	*
40	.34	.97	*
50	.41	.99	*
100	.70	*	*
Three-level main effect and interaction effect in a 2 × 3 analysis:			
10	.09	.36	.76
20	.14	.67	.98
30	.21	.86	*
40	.27	.94	*
50	.32	.98	*
100	.59	*	*

*Nearly 1.

even if such a small effect exists in the population, this study would be very unlikely to have come out significant. By contrast, the table shows a power of .98 for a large effect size. This means that. if a large interaction effect existed in the population, it would almost certainly have been significant in this study.

Planning Sample Size

Table 10–16 gives the approximate number of participants *per cell* needed for 80% power at the .05 significance level for estimated small, medium, and large effect sizes for the same situations as were included in the power table.[3]

Suppose that you are planning a 2 × 3 analysis of variance in which you are predicting a large effect size for the main effect on the three-level variable and a medium effect size for the other main effect and interaction. For 80% power (at the .05 significance level), you need 11 participants per cell for the three-level main effect, 22 per cell for the two-level main effect, and 27 per cell for the interaction effect. Of course, you have to do the whole study at once. Thus, you need at least 27 per cell (unless you choose to risk lower power for the interaction effect). This would mean recruiting 162 participants (27 for each of the six cells of the 2 × 3 design).

| Table 10–16 | Approximate Number of Participants Needed in Each Cell (Assuming Equal Sample Sizes) for 80% Power for Studies Using a 2 × 2 or 2 × 3 Analysis of Variance, Testing Hypotheses at the .05 Significance Level |

	Effect Size		
	Small $(R^2 = .01)$	**Medium** $(R^2 = .06)$	**Large** $(R^2 = .14)$
2 × 2: All effects	197	33	14
2 × 3: Two-level main effect	132	22	9
Three-level main effect and interaction	162	27	11

How are you doing?

1. (a) Write the formula for the effect size for rows in a two-way analysis of variance, (b) define each of the symbols, and (c) figure the effect size for a study in which S^2_{Rows} is 9.45, S^2_{Within} is 3.67, df_{Rows} is 1, and df_{Within} is 36.
2. (a) What is the power of the two-level main effect in a 2 × 3 analysis of variance with approximately 40 participants in each group to be tested at the .05 significance level, in which the researchers predict a medium effect size? (b) About how many participants do you need in each cell for 80% power in a planned 2 × 2 study in which you predict a medium effect size and will be using the .05 significance level?

Answers

1. (a) E Effect size for rows in a two-way analysis of variance:

$$R^2_{Rows} = \frac{(S^2_{Rows})(df_{Rows})}{(S^2_{Rows})(df_{Rows}) + (S^2_{Within})(df_{Within})}.$$

(b) R^2_{Rows} is the proportion of variance accounted for by variation between rows; S^2_{Rows} is the population variance estimate for rows; df_{Rows} is the degrees of freedom for rows (number of rows minus 1); S^2_{Within} is the within-groups population variance estimate; and df_{Within} is the degrees of freedom within groups (the number of scores in each cell minus 1, added up over all cells).

(c) $R^2_{Rows} = (9.45)(1)/[(9.45)(1) + (3.67)(36)] = 9.45/141.57 = .07.$

2. (a) Power: 97. (b) Number of participants: 33.

Summary

1. In a factorial research design, participants are put into groupings according to the combinations of the grouping variables whose effects are being studied. In such designs, you can study the effects of two grouping variables without needing twice as many participants. Also, such designs allow you to study the effects of combinations of the two grouping variables.
2. An interaction effect is when the impact of one grouping variable varies according to the level of the other grouping variable. A main effect is the impact of one grouping variable, ignoring the effect of the other grouping variable. Interaction

effects and main effects can be described verbally, numerically, and graphically (usually on a graph with bars for each combination of the grouping variables, with the height of the bar being the score on the measured variable). When there is an interaction along with a main effect, you have to be cautious in drawing conclusions about the main effect.

3. In a two-way analysis of variance, there are three types of between-groups variance estimates: one for differences on the grouping variable dividing the rows, one for differences on the grouping variable dividing the columns, and one for the interaction of the row and column variables. Since the within-groups variance estimate is based on estimates from each cell, it can also be called a *within-cells* variance estimate.

4. The assumptions for a factorial analysis of variance are the same as for the one-way analysis of variance except that the requirements of population normality and equal variances apply to the populations that go with each cell.

5. The factorial analysis of variance can be extended beyond two-way designs and can also be used for repeated-measures studies. (For more information on repeated-measures analysis of variance, see the Web chapter at *http://www.pearsonhighered.com/*).

6. There is a long-standing controversy about whether to dichotomize continuous variables to do an analysis of variance. This is a decreasingly common procedure; alternative procedures that use the full range of values of each variable are generally considered the better approach.

7. Results of factorial analyses of variance often include graphical descriptions of results, particularly when the interaction effect is significant. These are usually bar graphs but sometimes include line graphs.

8. ADVANCED TOPIC: The figuring for a two-way analysis of variance uses an expanded version of the structural model approach. The within-groups estimate is based on deviations of each score from its cell's mean. The row effect is based on deviations between row means and the grand mean; the column main effect, on deviations between column means and the grand mean. The interaction effect is based on the deviation of scores from the grand mean remaining after subtracting all the other deviations from the grand mean (deviations from the cell mean, the row means, and the column means). To get the actual population variance estimates, the various deviations (within, rows, columns, and interaction) are squared, summed, and divided by their degrees of freedom. The F ratios for row, column, and interaction effects are the population variance estimates for each of these divided by the within-groups (within-cells) population variance estimate.

9. ADVANCED TOPIC: In a factorial analysis of variance, you figure effect size and power separately for each main and interaction effect. R^2 is the variance estimate for that particular effect multiplied by the degrees of freedom for that effect, divided by the sum of the variance estimate for that particular effect multiplied by the degrees of freedom for that effect, plus the within-groups variance estimate multiplied by the within-groups degrees of freedom.

Key Terms

factorial analysis of variance (p. 370)
factorial research design (p. 370)

interaction effect (p. 373)
two-way factorial research design (p. 373)

two-way analysis of variance (p. 373)
grouping variable (p. 373)

one-way analysis of variance (p. 373)
main effect (p. 373)

cell (p. 374)
cell mean (p. 374)
marginal means (p. 374)

repeated-measures analysis of variance (p. 390)
dichotomizing (p. 391)

Example Worked-Out Problems

Recognizing and Interpreting Main Effects and Interaction Effects

Each of the following tables of means shows the result of a fictional study using a two-way factorial research design. Assuming that any differences are statistically significant, for each table, (a) indicate which effects (main and interaction), if any, are found, and (b) describe the meaning of the pattern of means (that is, any main or interaction effects or the lack thereof).

1. Measured variable: Level of happiness

		Stress		
		Low	*High*	*Overall*
Age	*Young*	8	4	6
	Old	8	4	6
	Overall	8	4	6

2. Measured variable: Symptoms of depression

		Therapy		
		No	*Yes*	*Overall*
Medication	*No*	9	6	7.5
	Yes	6	2	4
	Overall	7.5	4	5.75

Answers

1. (a) Main effect for stress, no main effect for age, no interaction effect; (b) happiness is lower for people with high stress, but there is no difference in happiness between younger and older people, and each combination of stress and age has the level of happiness you would expect knowing the level of each variable.
2. (a) Main effects for therapy and medication, interaction effect; (b) fewer symptoms of depression are found for people who have therapy and people who take medication, and people who have therapy and take medication have an especially low number of symptoms.

Bar Graphs and Figuring a Two-Way Analysis of Variance

In a 3×2 experiment, Variable A has three levels (1, 2, and 3), and Variable B has two levels (1 and 2). Four participants are randomly assigned to each combination of Variables A and B and are then observed on the measured variable. Scores of the 24 participants follow:

	Variable B	
	Level 1	*Level 2*
Variable A Level 1	25	19
	20	24
	23	21
	24	20
Variable A Level 2	22	24
	19	18
	22	22
	21	20
Variable A Level 3	16	18
	19	21
	13	16
	16	17

(a) Make a table of cell and marginal means. (b) Make a bar graph of the cell means. (c) ADVANCED TOPIC: Are there any significant main or interaction effects (use the .05 significance level)?

Answers

(a)

		Variable B		
		Level 1	*Level 2*	*Overall*
Variable A	*Level 1*	23	21	22
	Level 2	21	21	21
	Level 3	16	18	17
	Overall	20	20	20

(b) See Figure 10–12.

(c) Table 10–17 shows the figuring and conclusions.

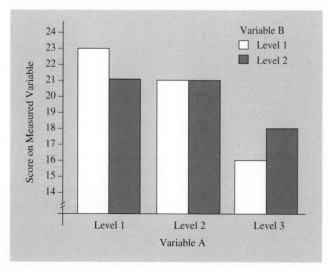

Figure 10–12   Bar graph for Example Worked-Out Problem.

Table 10-17 Figuring for Two-Way Factorial Analysis of Variance Example Worked-Out Problem

F needed for main effect for Variable B (*df* = 1, 18; *p* < .05) = 4.41.
F needed for main effect for Variable A (*df* = 2, 18; *p* < .05) = 3.56.
F needed for interaction effect (*df* = 2, 18; *p* < .05) = 3.56.

		Variable B Level 1						Variable B Level 2			
X	$(X - GM)^2$	$(X - M)^2$	$(M_{Row} - GM)^2$	$(M_{Column} - GM)^2$	INT^2	X	$(X - GM)^2$	$(X - M)^2$	$(M_{Row} - GM)^2$	$(M_{Column} - GM)^2$	INT^2
Variable A Level 1											
25	25	4	4	0	1	19	1	4	4	0	1
20	0	9	4	0	1	24	16	9	4	0	1
23	9	0	4	0	1	21	1	0	4	0	1
24	16	1	4	0	1	20	0	1	4	0	1
	50	14	16	0	4		18	14	16	0	4
Variable A Level 2											
22	4	1	1	0	0	24	16	9	1	0	0
19	1	4	1	0	0	18	4	9	1	0	0
22	4	1	1	0	0	22	4	1	1	0	0
21	1	0	1	0	0	20	0	1	1	0	0
	10	6	4	0	0		24	20	4	0	0
Variable A Level 3											
16	16	0	9	0	1	18	4	0	9	0	1
19	1	9	9	0	1	21	1	9	9	0	1
13	49	9	9	0	1	16	16	4	9	0	1
16	16	0	9	0	1	17	9	1	9	0	1
	82	18	36	0	4		30	14	36	0	4

M = mean of the score's cell
M_{Row} = mean of the score's row
M_{Column} = mean of the score's column
INT = score's remaining deviation for the interaction

Sample figuring of deviations, using the first score in the Variable A Level 1/Variable B Level 1 cell:

$(X - GM)^2$ = $(25 - 20)^2 = 5^2 = 25$.
$(X - M)^2$ = $(25 - 23)^2 = 2^2 = 4$.
$(M_{Row} - GM)^2$ = $(22 - 20)^2 = 2^2 = 4$.
$(M_{Column} - GM)^2$ = $(20 - 20)^2 = 0^2 = 0$.
INT^2 = $[(X - GM) - (X - M) - (M_{Row} - GM) - (M_{Column} - GM)]^2 = (5 - 2 - 2 - 0)^2 = 1^2 = 1$
SS_{Total} = $50 + 18 + 10 + 24 + 82 + 30 = 214$
SS_{Within} = $14 + 14 + 6 + 20 + 18 + 14 = 86$
SS_{Column} = $0 + 0 + 0 + 0 + 0 + 0 = 0$
SS_{Row} = $16 + 16 + 4 + 4 + 36 + 36 = 112$
$SS_{Interaction}$ = $4 + 4 + 0 + 0 + 4 + 4 = 16$

Accuracy check: $SS_{Total} = 214$; $SS_{Within} + SS_{Rows} + SS_{Columns} + SS_{Interaction} = 86 + 0 + 112 + 16 = 214$

Source	SS	df	MS	F	Decision
Variable B (columns)	0	1	0	0.0	Do not reject the null hypothesis.
Variable A (rows)	112	2	56	11.7	Reject the null hypothesis.
Interaction (columns × rows)	16	2	8	1.7	Do not reject the null hypothesis.
Within groups	86	18	4.8		

Source: Brockner, J., Ackerman, G., Greenberg, J., Gelfand, M. J., Francesco, A. M., Chen, Z. X., Leung, K., Bierbraner, G., Gomez, C., Kirkman, B. L., & Shapiro, D. (2001). Culture and procedural justice: The influence of power distance on reactions to voice. *Journal of Experimental Social Psychology, 37*, 300–315. Copyright © 2001 with permission from Elsevier.

Outline for Writing Essays for a Two-Way Analysis of Variance

1. Explain that the two-way analysis of variance is used for hypothesis testing when a study uses a two-way factorial research design; with such a design, participants are put into groupings according to the combinations of the variables whose effects are being studied.
2. Describe the core logic of hypothesis testing in this situation. Be sure to explain what is meant by the terms *main effect* and *interaction effect*. Also, describe the three F ratios that are tested in a two-way analysis of variance, including how each F ratio is figured.
3. Describe the assumptions of a two-way analysis of variance.
4. ADVANCED TOPIC: Describe the structural model for the analysis of variance, including how each score's overall deviation from the grand mean can be divided into several components. Explain the logic of the comparison distributions that are used with the two-way analysis of variance. Describe the logic and process for determining the cutoff sample F scores at which each null hypothesis should be rejected. Explain how and why the scores from Steps ❸ and ❹ of the hypothesis-testing process are compared. Explain the meaning of the results of these comparisons with regard to the specific research and null hypotheses being tested.

Practice Problems

These problems involve figuring. Most real-life statistics problems are done on a computer with special statistical software. Even if you have such software, do these problems by hand to ingrain the method in your mind. To learn how to use a computer to solve statistics problems like those in this chapter, refer to the Using SPSS section at the end of this chapter and the *Study Guide and Computer Workbook* that accompanies this text.

All data are fictional unless an actual citation is given.

Set I (for Answers to Set I Problems, see pp. 688–690)

1. Each of the following is a table of means showing the results of a study using a factorial design. Assuming that any differences are statistically significant, for each table, (a) and (b) make two bar graphs showing the results (in one graph grouping the bars according to one variable and in the other graph grouping the bars according to the other variable); (c) indicate which effects (main and interaction), if any, are found; and (d) describe the meaning of the pattern of means (that is, any main or interaction effects or the lack thereof) in words.

    (i) Measured variable: Income (thousands of dollars)

	Age	
Class	*Young*	*Old*
Lower	20	35
Upper	25	100

    (ii) Measured variable: Grade point average

	Major	
College	*Science*	*Arts*
Community	2.1	2.8
Liberal Arts	2.8	2.1

(iii) Measured variable: Days sick per month

Gender

	Females	Males
Exercisers	2.0	2.5
Controls	3.1	3.6

(Group)

2. Each of the following is a table of means showing the results of a study using a factorial design. Assuming that any differences are statistically significant, for each table, (a) and (b) make two bar graphs showing the results (in one graph grouping the bars according to one variable and in the other graph grouping the bars according to the other variable); (c) indicate which effects (main and interaction), if any, are found; and (d) describe the meaning of the pattern of means (that is, any main or interaction effects or the lack thereof) in words.

(i) Measured variable: Conversation length

Topic

	Nonpersonal	Personal
Friend	16	20
Parent	10	6

(Relationship)

(ii) Measured variable: Rated restaurant quality

City

	New York	Chicago	Vancouver
Expensive	9	5	7
Moderate	6	4	6
Inexpensive	4	3	5

(Cost)

(iii) Measured variable: Ratings of flavor

Coffee Brand

	X	Y	Z
Regular	7	4	6
Decaf	5	2	6

(Type)

3. A sports psychologist studied the effect of a motivational program on injuries among players of three different sports. The following chart shows the design. For each of the following possible patterns of results, make up a set of cell means, figure the marginal means, and make a bar graph of the results (assume that any differences are statistically significant): (a) a main effect for type of sport and no other main effect or interaction; (b) a main effect for program and no other main effect or interaction; (c) both main effects but no interaction; (d) a main effect for program and an interaction, but no main effect for type of sport; (e) both main effects and an interaction.

Measured Variable: Number of injuries per person over 10 weeks

Sport

	Baseball	Football	Basketball
With motivational program			
Without motivational program			

(Sport)

4. Kunda and Oleson (1997) studied the effect on stereotypes of counterinformation, learning about someone who is opposite to what you would expect from the stereotype. They predicted that extreme counterinformation may have a boomerang effect—making the stereotype even stronger. Participants were preselected to be in the study based on a questionnaire in which they rated public relations (PR) agents for their typical degree of extroversion: an "extreme-stereotype" group of participants who had rated PR agents as extremely extroverted and a "moderate-stereotype" group of participants who had rated PR agents as only moderately extroverted. During the actual study, some participants were given a description of a particular PR agent who was highly introverted, the extreme deviant condition; the other participants were given no special description, the control condition. Finally, all participants were asked about their beliefs about PR agents. Kunda and Oleson (1997) reported the results as follows:

> A 2 (prior stereotype) $\times$ 2 (condition) ANOVA yielded a significant interaction, $F(1, 42) = 5.69$, $p < .05$, indicating that the impact of the target on participants' stereotypes depended on their prior stereotypes. As can be seen in Figure [10–13], extreme-stereotype participants exposed to the highly introverted target came to view PR agents as even more extroverted than did extreme controls ... [a] boomerang effect. ... A different pattern was observed for the moderate-stereotype participants: Their stereotypes were unaffected by exposure to the same target .... The ANOVA also revealed a large effect for prior stereotypes, $F(1, 42) = 38.94$, $p < .0001$ indicating, not surprisingly, that extreme-stereotype participants continued to view PR agents as more extroverted than did moderate-stereotype participants. There was also a marginal effect for condition, $F(1, 42) = 2.89$, $p < .10$, which was clearly due entirely to the extreme-stereotype participants. (p. 974)

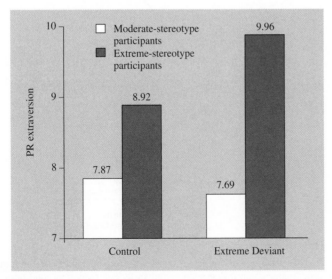

Figure 10–13 Mean ratings of the extraversion of public relations (PR) agents made by participants with moderate or extreme prior stereotypes who were exposed to an extremely introverted PR agent or to no target (controls). Higher numbers indicate a greater PR extraversion.

Source: Kunda, Z., & Oleson, K. C. (1997). When exceptions prove the rule: However extremity of deviance determines the impact of defiant examples on stereotypes. *Journal of Personality and Social Psychology, 72,* 965–979. Published by the American Psychological Association. Reprinted with permission.

Briefly describe the meaning of these results to a person who has never had a course in statistics. (Do not go into the computational details, just the basic logic of the pattern of means, the significant results, and issues of interpreting nonsignificant results.)

5. Yamagishi and Melara (2001) studied people's ability to separate visual images from the background. Participants were shown images differing from the background in either just chromaticity (color) or just luminescence (brightness). Also, they made the figures more difficult to identify by degrading (distorting) either the contour (shape of the edges) or the surface of the figure. The key measure was "difference in sensitivity from baseline," which the researchers abbreviated as Δd_a. Here is an excerpt from their results (note that MS_e refers to mean squared error, which is the same as MS_{Within}, the population variance estimate based on the variation within groups (within cells).

> The only factor to yield a significant main effect was task $[F(1, 3) = 373.35, MS_e = 0.01, p < .001]$. Greater overall loss was observed in the chromacity tasks $(\Delta d_a = -0.86)$ than in the luminance tasks $(\Delta d_a = -0.37)$ ....[T]he critical effect is found in the interaction between degradation and task. This interaction, depicted in Figure [10–14], was highly significant $[F(1, 3) = 178.77, MS_e = 0.02, p < .001]$. As one can see, figural

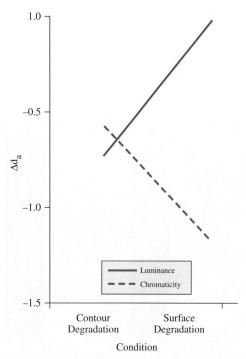

Figure 10–14 Average difference in sensitivity from baseline (Δd_a) in luminance and chromaticity tasks under contour-degradation and surface-degradation conditions across Experiments IA and IB. Note the crossover interaction between degradation and task: performance in the luminance tasks was most disrupted by contour degradation, whereas performance in the chromaticity tasks was most disrupted by surface degradation.

Source: Yamagishi, N., & Melara, R. D. (2001). Informational primacy of visual dimensions: Specialized roles for luminance and chromaticity in figure-ground perception. *Perception and Psychophysics, 63,* 824–846. Reprinted with permission.

identification in the luminance tasks was disrupted by contour degradation, but not by surface degradation. On the other hand, figural identification in the chromacity task was disrupted by both forms of degradation; however, surface degradation was twice as harmful to performance in these tasks as contour degradation. (p. 831)

Describe the meaning of these results to a person who understands one-way analysis of variance but is completely unfamiliar with factorial designs or the two-way analysis of variance.

6. ADVANCED TOPIC: For each of the following data sets, carry out an analysis of variance, including making a table of cell and marginal means and making a bar graph of the cell means. Use the .05 significance level.

(a)	Experimental Condition	
	A	B
Group 1	0	3
	1	2
	1	3
Group 2	3	0
	2	1
	3	1

(b)	Experimental Condition	
	A	B
Group 1	0	0
	1	1
	1	1
Group 2	3	3
	2	2
	3	3

(c)	Experimental Condition	
	A	B
Group 1	0	3
	1	2
	1	3
Group 2	0	3
	1	2
	1	3

7. ADVANCED TOPIC: Patients with two kinds of diagnoses were randomly assigned to one of three types of therapy and the effectiveness of the therapy was measured on a 1-to-15 scale (with a higher number indicating greater effectiveness). There were two patients per cell. Based on the following results, (a) carry out the analysis of variance (use the .05 significance level), (b) make a table of cell and marginal means, (c) make a bar graph of the results, and (d) describe the results in words (indicate which effects are significant and, on the basis of the significant effects, how to understand the pattern of cell means).

	Therapy A	Therapy B	Therapy C
Diagnosis I	6	3	2
	2	1	4
Diagnosis II	11	7	8
	9	9	10

8. ADVANCED TOPIC: A psychologist who studies the legal system conducted a study of the effect of defendants' likability and nervousness on willingness to convict the defendant. Each participant read the same transcript, taken from an actual trial, in which the guilt or innocence of a male defendant was quite ambiguous. All participants also saw a brief videotape that supposedly showed the defendant on the witness stand. However, the way the actor played the part on the videotape differed for different participants, including the four possibilities of likable versus not and nervous versus not. After viewing the tape, participants rated the likelihood that the defendant is innocent (on a scale of 1, *very unlikely,* to 10, *very likely*). The results for the first 12 participants in the study were as follows:

	Likeable	Not Likeable
Nervous	7	3
	8	4
	6	2
Not nervous	3	7
	3	5
	3	9

(a) Carry out the analysis of variance (use the .05 significance level). (b) Make a table of cell and marginal means. (c) Make a bar graph of the results. (d) Explain the results and the way you arrived at them to someone who is familiar with the one-way analysis of variance (including the structural model approach) but not with the factorial analysis of variance.

9. ADVANCED TOPIC: Figure the effect size for each main and interaction effect for problems (a) 6a, (b) 6b, (c) 6c, (d) 7, and (e) 8.

10. ADVANCED TOPIC: What is the power of the effect in the following planned studies using the analysis of variance with $p < .05$?

	Predicted Effect Size	Overall Design	Number of Levels of the Effect	Participants Per Cell
(a)	Small	2 × 2	2	30
(b)	Small	2 × 2	2	50
(c)	Small	2 × 3	2	30
(d)	Small	2 × 3	3	30
(e)	Medium	2 × 2	2	30

11. ADVANCED TOPIC: About how many participants do you need in each cell for 80% power in each of the following planned studies, using the analysis of variance with $p < .05$?

	Predicted Effect Size	Design	Effect
(a)	Small	2 × 2	Main effect
(b)	Small	2 × 2	Interaction effect
(c)	Medium	2 × 2	Main effect
(d)	Small	2 × 3	Two-level main effect
(e)	Small	2 × 3	Three-level main effect
(f)	Small	2 × 3	Interaction effect

Set II

12. Each of the following tables of means shows the results of a study using a factorial design. Assuming that any differences are statistically significant, for each table (a) and (b), make two bar graphs showing the results (in one graph grouping the bars according to one variable and in the other graph grouping the bars according to the other variable); (c) indicate which effects (main and interaction), if any, are found; and (d) describe the meaning of the pattern of means (that is, any main or interaction effects or the lack thereof) in words.

(i) Measured variable: Degree of envy of another person's success

Degree of Success

Status of Other	Great	Small
Friend	8	5
Stranger	1	4

(ii) Measured variable: Observed engagement in the activity

Play Activity

Situation	Blocks	Dress Up
Alone	4.5	2.5
With playmate	2.5	4.5

(iii) Measured variable: Intensity of attention

Program

Type of Balletgoer	The Nutcracker	Modern
Regular	20	15
Sometime	15	15
Novice	10	5

13. Each of the following tables of means shows the results of a study using a factorial design. Assuming that any differences are statistically significant, for each table (a) and (b), make two bar graphs showing the results (in one graph grouping the bars according to one variable and in the other graph grouping the bars according to the other variable); (c) indicate which effects (main and interaction), if

any, are found; and (d) describe the meaning of the pattern of means (that is, any main or interaction effects or the lack thereof) in words.

(i) Measured variable: Right frontal neural activity in brain during memory task

Items Remembered

Times Presented	Words	Pictures
Once	45	68
Twice	30	30

(ii) Measured variable: Approval rating of the U.S. president

Region

Class	West	East	Midwest	South
Middle	70	45	55	50
Lower	50	25	35	30

(iii) Measured variable: Satisfaction with education

Gender

Time After Obtaining BA	Females	Males
1 month	3	3
1 year	4	4
5 years	9	9

14. In this study, English-speaking participants were instructed to try to read a paragraph for a half hour in one of three languages they did not understand. They read the paragraph after either being told the main idea of the paragraph, told the main idea of the first sentence only, or not told anything about the meaning. They were given translations of some words. The researchers then measured how many of the other words they could correctly translate. The following chart shows the design. For each of the following possible patterns of results, make up a set of cell means, figure the marginal means, and make a bar graph of the results: (a) a main effect for language and no other main effect or interaction; (b) a main effect for knowledge of meaning and no other main effect or interaction; (c) both main effects but no interaction; (d) a main effect for language and an interaction, but no main effect for knowledge of meaning; (e) both main effects and an interaction.

Measured variable: Number of words not given that participant could correctly translate

Language

Knowledge of Meaning	Dutch	Rumanian	Swedish
Paragraph			
Sentence			
None			

15. Brockner and colleagues (2001) studied the effect of cultural values about the appropriateness of power differentials on how employees feel about having input to managers about important decisions. Their participants were business students in China (a culture in which power differentials are considered appropriate and normal), a "high power distance" culture, and in the United States, a "low power distance" culture. The students were asked to imagine that they were working in a company and had just been put under the direction of a new manager; they were then assigned to one of three conditions: (1) the new manager discouraged input from them (the low voice condition), (2) the new manager encouraged input from them (high voice), or (3) no information was given about the manager's style (the control condition). They then had the students answer questions about how committed they would feel to the organization. Here is how the researchers reported the results:

> A two-factor ANOVA yielded a significant main effect of voice, $F(2, 245) = 26.30$, $p < .001$. As expected, participants responded less favorably in the low voice condition ($M = 2.93$) than in the high voice condition ($M = 3.58$). The mean rating in the control condition ($M = 3.34$) fell between these two extremes. Of greater importance, the interaction between culture and voice was also significant, $F(2, 245) = 4.11$, $p < .02$.... As can be seen in Table [10–18] the voice effect was more pronounced in the low power distance culture (the United States) than in the high power distance culture (the People's Republic of China). (p. 304)

Briefly describe the meaning of these results to a person who has never had a course in statistics. (Do not go into the computational details, just the basic logic of the pattern of means, the significant results, and issues of interpreting non-significant results.)

16. Sinclair and Kunda (2000) tested the idea that, if you want to think well of someone (for example, because he or she has said positive things about you), you are less influenced by the normal stereotypes when evaluating them. Participants filled out a questionnaire on their social skills, then either a male or female "manager in training" gave them feedback, rigged so that half the participants were given positive feedback and half, negative feedback. Finally, the participants rated the managers for their skill at evaluating them. The question was whether

Table 10-18 Mean Level of Organizational Commitment as a Function of Culture and Level of Voice (Study 1)

Culture	Level of Voice		Control
	Low	High	
United States (low power distance)	2.63 (0.72)	3.57 (0.56)	3.17 (0.66)
People's Republic of China (high power distance)	3.27 (0.68)	3.60 (0.43)	3.52 (0.55)

Note: Scores could range from 1 to 5, with higher scores reflecting greater organizational commitment. Standard deviations are in parentheses.
Source: Brockner, J., Ackerman, G., Greenberg, J., Gelfand, M. J., Francesco, A. M., Chen, Z. X., Leung, K., Bierbrauer, G., Gomez, C., Kirkman, B.L., & Shapiro, D. (2001). Culture and procedural justice: The influence of power distance on reactions to voice. *Journal of Experimental Social Psychology, 37,* 300–315. Copyright © 2001 with permission from Elsevier.

the usual tendency to stereotype women as less skillful managers would be undermined when people got positive ratings. Here are the results:

> Participants' ratings of the manager's skill at evaluating them were analyzed with a 2 (feedback) $\times$ 2 (manager gender) ANOVA. Managers who had provided positive feedback ($M = 9.08$) were rated more highly than were managers who had provided negative feedback ($M = 7.46$), $F(1, 46) = 19.44$, $p < .0001$. However, as may be seen in Figure [10–15], the effect was qualified by a significant interaction, $F(1, 46) = 4.71$, $p < .05$. . . . (pp. 1335–1336)

Describe the meaning of these results to a person who understands one-way analysis of variance but is completely unfamiliar with factorial designs or the two-way analysis of variance.

17. ADVANCED TOPIC: For each of the following data sets, carry out an analysis of variance, including making a table of cell and marginal means and making a bar graph of the cell means. Use the .05 significance level.

(a)	Group	
	I	**II**
Experimental Condition A	8	8
	6	6
Experimental Condition B	3	3
	1	1

(b)	Group	
	I	**II**
Experimental Condition A	9	9
	5	5
Experimental Condition B	4	4
	0	0

18. ADVANCED TOPIC: A developmental psychologist studied the effects of loudness of a sudden noise on infants of different inherited temperaments. The infants were exposed either to a sudden loud noise or a sudden soft noise, then the infants' startle reactions were observed. The startle reaction scores were as follows:

	Sudden Noise	
	Loud	**Soft**
Temperament K	14	7
	10	5
	9	9
Temperament R	3	8
	8	8
	7	2

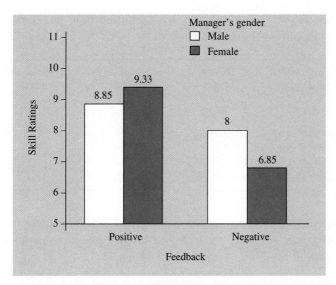

Figure 10–15   Participants' ratings of the manager's skill at evaluating them as a function of feedback favorability and the manager's gender (Study 2).

Source: Sinclair, L., & Kunda, Z. (2000). Motivated stereotyping of women: She's fine if she praised me but incompetent if she criticized me. *Personality and Social Psychology Bulletin, 26,* 1329–1342. Copyright © 2000 by Society for Personality and Social Psychology, Inc. Reprinted by permission of Sage Publications, Inc.

(a) Make a table of cell and marginal means; (b) draw a bar graph of them; (c) carry out the five steps of hypothesis testing (use the .05 significance level); and (d) describe the results in words (indicate which effects are significant and, on the basis of the significant effects, how to understand the pattern of cell means).

19. ADVANCED TOPIC: In a particular high school, three types of videotaped teaching programs were each tried for English, history, and math. The researchers then measured amount learned. There were two students per cell. Based on the following results, (a) make a table of cell and marginal means, (b) draw a bar graph of them, (c) carry out the five steps of hypothesis testing (use the .05 significance level), and (d) explain the results and the way you arrived at them to someone who is familiar with the one-way analysis of variance (including the structural model approach), but not with the factorial analysis of variance.

	English	History	Math
Program Type A	3	15	2
	3	14	3
Program Type B	6	18	6
	8	10	5
Program Type C	1	13	2
	3	4	0

20. ADVANCED TOPIC: Figure the effect size for each main and interaction effect for problems (a) 17a, (b) 17b, (c) 18, and (d) 19.

21. ADVANCED TOPIC: What is the power of the effect in the following planned studies using the analysis of variance with $p < .05$?

	Predicted Effect Size	Overall Design	Number of Levels of the Effect	Participants Per Cell
(a)	Small	2 × 2	2	10
(b)	Medium	2 × 2	2	10
(c)	Large	2 × 2	2	10
(d)	Medium	2 × 3	3	10
(e)	Medium	2 × 3	3	20
(f)	Medium	2 × 2	Interaction	20

22. ADVANCED TOPIC: About how many participants do you need in each cell for 80% power in each of the following planned studies, using the analysis of variance with $p < .05$?

	Predicted Effect Size	Design	Effect
(a)	Medium	2 × 2	Main effect
(b)	Large	2 × 2	Main effect
(c)	Medium	2 × 2	Interaction effect
(d)	Medium	2 × 3	Three-level main effect
(e)	Large	2 × 3	Three-level main effect
(f)	Medium	2 × 3	Interaction effect

Using SPSS

The ✑ in the following steps indicates a mouse click. (We used SPSS version 15.0 for Windows to carry out these analyses. The steps and output may be slightly different for other versions of SPSS.)

Figuring a Two-Way Analysis of Variance

It is easier to learn these steps using actual numbers; so we will use the study of the effects of vividness (low versus high) and length of examples (short versus long) on the number of examples recalled. The scores for that example are shown in How Are You Doing question 5 on p. 405, and the figuring is shown in Table 10–14 on p. 405.

❶ Enter the scores into SPSS. SPSS assumes that all scores in a row are from the same person. In this example, each person is in only one of the four cells. Further, we want to be able to tell SPSS what each score means in terms of the grouping variables. Thus, you should enter the numbers as shown in Figure 10–16. In the first column (labeled "vivid"), we used the number "1" to indicate that a person is in the low vividness condition and the number "2" to indicate a person is in the high vividness condition. That is, the first column is for the first grouping variable (vividness in this case), and we arbitrarily used a 1 or a 2 to show which level a person is in on this grouping variable (we could have used any two numbers, but 1 and 2 are simple). In the second column (labeled "length"), we used the number "1" for a person being in the short length condition and "2" for a person

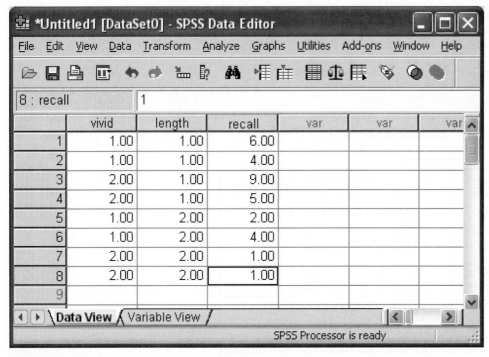

Figure 10–16 SPSS data editor window for the fictional study of the effects of vividness and length of examples on the number of examples recalled.

being in the long length condition. In the third column (labeled "recall"), we put in each person's score on the measured variable (that is, the number of examples each person recalled).

❷ ✍ *Analyze.*

❸ ✍ *General Linear Model.*

❹ ✍ *Univariate.*

❺ ✍ the variable called "recall" and then ✍ the arrow next to the box labeled "Dependent Variable." This tells SPSS that the analysis of variance should be carried out on the scores for the "recall" variable. ("Dependent variable" is another name for the measured variable.)

❻ ✍ the variable called "length" and then ✍ the arrow next to the box labeled "Fixed Factor(s)." This tells SPSS that the grouping variable called "length" shows whether people saw examples that were short or long. ("Fixed factors" is another name for the kind of grouping variables usually used in a factorial analysis of variance.)

❼ ✍ the variable called "vivid" and then ✍ the arrow next to the box labeled "Fixed Factor(s)." This tells SPSS that the grouping variable called "vivid" shows whether people saw examples that had low or high vividness.

❽ ✍ *Options.* Click the box labeled *Descriptive statistics* (this checks the box). This tells SPSS to provide descriptive statistics (means, standard deviations, etc.) for each cell. ✍ *Continue.* (Step ❽ is optional, but we strongly recommend requesting descriptive statistics for any hypothesis-testing situation.)

❾ ✍ *OK.* Your SPSS output window should look like Figure 10–17.

The first table in the SPSS output (which is not shown in Figure 10–17) gives the number of individuals in each level of the two grouping variables ("length" and

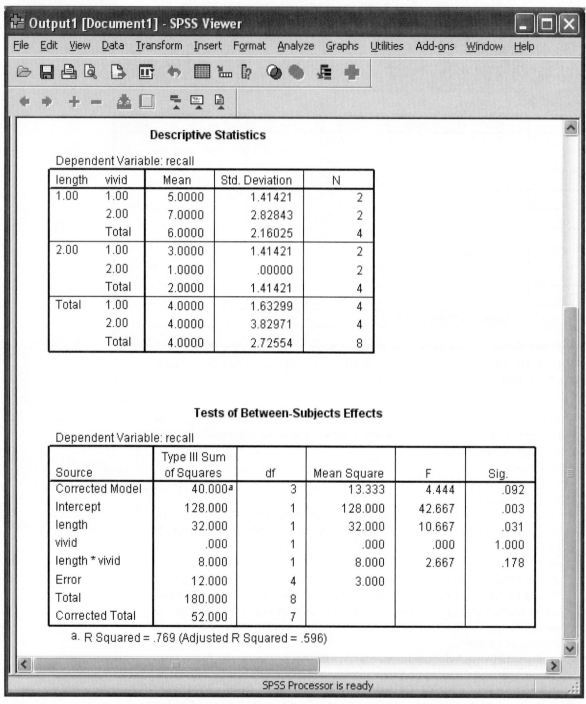

Figure 10–17 SPSS output window for a two-way analysis of variance for the fictional study of the effects of vividness and length of examples on the number of examples recalled.

"vivid"). Be sure to look at this closely to check that the analysis actually used the participants and variables you intended! The second table (labeled "Descriptive Statistics") provides descriptive statistics (mean, estimated population standard deviation, and number of individuals) for the "recall" scores for each cell. Knowing the mean value of each cell is important when it comes to interpreting significant results from an analysis of variance. This table also provides marginal means for each row and column and the overall mean. These are shown in the "Total" rows and "Total" section.

The third table in the SPSS output (labeled "Tests of Between-Subjects Effects") shows the actual results of the two-way analysis of variance. You can ignore the results shown in the rows labeled "Corrected Model," "Intercept," and "Corrected Total." The first column ("Source") lists the types of population variance estimates, including the effects for "length," "vivid," the interaction ("length * vivid"), and the within-groups estimate ("Error"). The second column lists the sums of squares: these are described in the Advanced Topic section earlier in this chapter, but ignore this column if you did not read that section. The third column, "df," gives each type of degrees of freedom. The fourth column, "Mean Square," gives the population variance estimates for each main effect (length, vivid), for the interaction, and for the within-groups (or "Error"). The next column gives the F ratio for each main effect and for the interaction. The values for "df," "Mean Square," and "F" (and "Sum of Squares") are consistent with those shown in Table 10–14, where we worked this out by hand using the procedures in the Advanced Topic section. The final column, "Sig.," shows the exact significance level of each F ratio. The significance level of .031 for the "length" effect is less than our .05 cutoff for this example, which means that you can reject the null hypothesis and the research hypothesis is supported (that is, the result is statistically significant). For the "vivid" effect, the significance level of 1.000 is greater than our .05 cutoff, which means that you cannot reject the null hypothesis. The significance level of .178 for the interaction effect is also greater than our .05 cutoff, which means that you cannot reject the null hypothesis.

Making a Bar Graph of the Results of a Two-Way Analysis of Variance

As you learned earlier in the chapter, it is often helpful to make a bar graph to visualize the results of a two-way analysis of variance. We will use the same example from the preceding two-way analysis of variance to show how to create such a bar graph. Note that, before we undertook the following steps to produce the bar graph, we went to the "Variable View" window in SPSS and entered value labels (in the "Values" column) for the "vivid" (1 = "Low"; 2 = "High") and "length" (1 = "Short"; 2 = "Long") variables. This makes it easier to understand the bar graph, as these value labels are then shown on the graph.

❶ Enter the scores into SPSS as shown in Figure 10–16.

❷ ✐ *Graphs.*

❸ ✐ *Legacy Dialogs.*

❹ ✐ *Bar.*

❺ ✐ the graph next to "Clustered." ✐ *Define.*

❻ ✐ the circle labeled *Other statistic (e.g., mean).* ✐ the variable called "recall" and ✐ the arrow next to the box labeled "Variable:". This tells SPSS to plot mean scores of the "recall" grouping variable on the vertical axis.

❼ ✐ the variable called "vivid" and ✐ the arrow next to the box labeled "Category Axis:". This tells SPSS to plot separate sets of bars according to the levels of the "vivid" grouping variable on the horizontal axis.

❽ ✐ the variable called "length" and ✐ the arrow next to the box labeled "Defined Clusters by:". This tells SPSS to plot separate bars for each level of the grouping variable "length."

❾ ✐ *OK.* Your SPSS output window should look like Figure 10–18. As you can see, the bar graph shown in Figure 10–18 is the same as the bar graph shown in

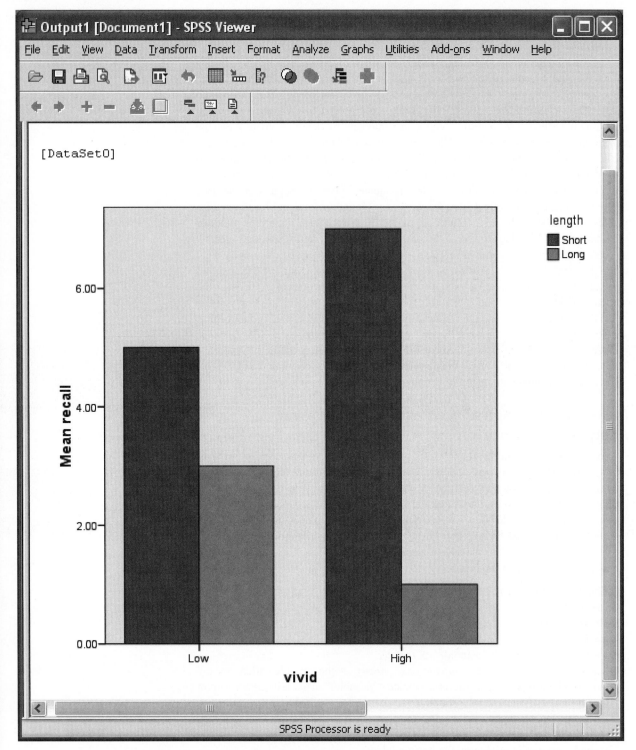

Figure 10–18 SPSS output window for a bar graph of the fictional study of the effects of vividness and length of examples on the number of examples recalled.

the left hand side of Figure 10–7 on p. 385. (Note that in Step ❼ we could have told SPSS to use "length" as the "category axis" variable. Had we done that, we would have also told it to use "vivid" for the "define clusters" variable in Step ❽. The resulting bar graph would then have looked like the right hand side of Figure 10–7.)

Chapter Notes

1. There are also calculational formulas for the sums of squares that researchers used in the days before the computer. These formulas made it easier to carry out the figuring by hand (or with a hand calculator) when working with the results of a real study with a large number of scores in each cell. We strongly urge you to use the definitional formulas and procedures shown in Tables 10–11 and 10–12 when working the practice problems in this book. These definitional formulas reinforce the underlying principles that are the main things you are trying to learn. However, should you have need of them, here are the computational formulas:

$$SS_{\text{Total}} = \Sigma X^2 - \frac{(\Sigma X)^2}{N}$$

$$SS_{\text{Between}} = \frac{(\Sigma X_1)^2}{n} + \frac{(\Sigma X_2)^2}{n} + \cdots + \frac{(\Sigma X_{\text{Last}})^2}{n} - \frac{(\Sigma X)^2}{N}$$

$$SS_{\text{Within}} = SS_{\text{Total}} - SS_{\text{Between}}$$

$$SS_{\text{Rows}} = \frac{(\Sigma X_{\text{Row}_1})^2}{n_{\text{Row}}} + \frac{(\Sigma X_{\text{Row}_2})^2}{n_{\text{Row}}} + \cdots + \frac{(\Sigma X_{\text{Last}})^2}{n_{\text{Row}}} - \frac{(\Sigma X)^2}{N}$$

$$SS_{\text{Columns}} = \frac{(\Sigma X_{\text{Column}_1})^2}{n_{\text{Column}}} + \frac{(\Sigma X_{\text{Column}_2})^2}{n_{\text{Column}}} + \cdots + \frac{(\Sigma X_{\text{Column}_{\text{Last}}})^2}{n_{\text{Column}}} - \frac{(\Sigma X)^2}{N}$$

$$SS_{\text{Interaction}} = SS_{\text{Between}} - SS_{\text{Rows}} - SS_{\text{Columns}}$$

In these formulas, ΣX^2 is the sum of each squared score, $(\Sigma X)^2$ is the square of the sum of all the scores; N is the total number of scores; $(\Sigma X_1)^2, (\Sigma X_2)^2, \ldots, (\Sigma X_{\text{Last}})^2$ are the squares of the sums of all scores in each cell; n is the number of participants in each cell; $(\Sigma X_{\text{Row}_1})^2, (\Sigma X_{\text{Row}_2})^2, \ldots, (\Sigma X_{\text{Last}})^2$ are the squares of the sums of all scores in each row; n_{Row} is the number of participants in each row; $(\Sigma X_{\text{Column}_1})^2, (\Sigma X_{\text{Column}_2})^2, \ldots, (\Sigma X_{\text{Column}_{\text{Last}}})^2$ are the squares of the sums of all scores in each column; and n_{Column} is the number of participants in each column.

2. More detailed tables are provided in Cohen (1988, pp. 389–354). However, using these tables with a factorial design requires some preliminary figuring, as Cohen explains on pages 364–379.

3. More detailed tables are provided in Cohen (1988, pp. 381–389). If you use these, be sure to read Cohen's pages 396–403.

CHAPTER 11

Correlation

Chapter Outline

- Graphing Correlations: The Scatter Diagram   434
- Patterns of Correlation   437
- The Correlation Coefficient   443
- Significance of a Correlation Coefficient   452
- Correlation and Causality   456
- Issues in Interpreting the Correlation Coefficient   458
- Effect Size and Power for the Correlation Coefficient   464
- Controversy: What Is a Large Correlation?   466
- Correlation in Research Articles   467
- Summary   469
- Key Terms   471
- Example Worked-Out Problems   471
- Practice Problems   474
- Using SPSS   482
- Chapter Notes   485

This chapter is about a statistical procedure that allows you to look at the relationship between two groups of scores. To give you an idea of what we mean, let's consider some common real-world examples. Among students, there is a relationship between high school grades and college grades. It isn't a perfect relationship, but generally speaking students with better high school grades tend to get better grades in college. Similarly, there is a relationship between parents' heights and the adult height of their children. Taller parents tend to give birth to children who grow up to be taller than the children of shorter parents. Again, the relationship isn't perfect, but the general pattern is clear. Now we'll look at an example in detail.

One hundred thirteen married people in the small college town of Santa Cruz, California, responded to a questionnaire in the local newspaper about their marriage. [This was part of a larger study reported by Aron and colleagues (2000).] As part of the questionnaire, they answered the question, "How exciting are the things you do together with your partner?" using a scale from 1, *not exciting at all* to 5, *extremely exciting*. The questionnaire also included a standard measure of marital satisfaction (that included items such as, "In general, how often do you think that things between you and your partner are going well?").

The researchers were interested in finding out the relationship between doing exciting things with a marital partner and the level of marital satisfaction people reported. In other words, they wanted to look at the relationship between two groups of scores: the group of scores for doing exciting things and the group of scores for marital satisfaction. As shown in Figure 11–1, the relationship between these two groups of scores can be shown very clearly using a graph. The horizontal axis is for people's answers to the question, "How exciting are the things you do together with your partner?" The vertical axis is for the marital satisfaction scores. Each person's score on the two variables is shown as a dot.

The overall pattern is that the dots go from the lower left to the upper right. That is, lower scores on the variable "doing exciting activities with your partner" more often go with lower scores on the variable "marital satisfaction," and higher with higher. So, in general, this graph shows that the more that people did exciting activities with their partner, the more satisfied they were in their marriage. Even though the pattern is far from one to one, you can see a general trend. This general pattern is of high scores on one variable going with high scores on the other variable, low scores going with low scores, and mediums with mediums. This is an example of a **correlation.**

A correlation describes the relationship between two variables. More precisely, the usual measure of a correlation describes the relationship between *two equal-interval numeric variables*. As you learned in Chapter 1, the differences between values for

correlation association between scores on two variables.

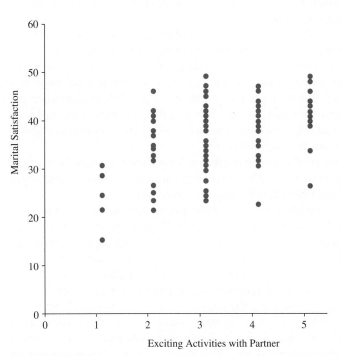

Figure 11–1 Scatter diagram showing the correlation for 113 married individuals between doing exciting activities with their partner and their marital satisfaction. (Data from Aron et al., 2000.)

equal-interval numeric variables correspond to differences in the underlying thing being measured. (Most psychologists consider scales like a 1-to-10 rating scale as approximately equal-interval scales.) There are countless examples of correlations: in children, there is a correlation between age and coordination skills; among students, there is a correlation between amount of time studying and amount learned; in the marketplace, we often assume that a correlation exists between price and quality—that high prices go with high quality and low with low.

This chapter explores correlation, including how to describe it graphically, different types of correlations, how to figure the correlation coefficient (which gives a number for the degree of correlation), the statistical significance of a correlation coefficient, issues about how to interpret a correlation coefficient, and effect size and power for a correlation coefficient.

Graphing Correlations: The Scatter Diagram

Figure 11–1 shows the correlation between exciting activities and marital satisfaction and is an example of a **scatter diagram** (also called a *scatterplot*). A scatter diagram shows you at a glance the pattern of the relationship between the two variables.

How to Make a Scatter Diagram

There are three steps to making a scatter diagram:

❶ **Draw the axes and decide which variable goes on which axis.** Often, it doesn't matter which variable goes on which axis. However, sometimes the researchers are thinking of one of the variables as predicting or causing the other. In that case, the variable that is doing the predicting or causing goes on the horizontal axis and the variable that is being predicted about or caused goes on the vertical axis. In Figure 11–1, we put exciting activities on the horizontal axis and marital satisfaction on the vertical axis. This was because the study was based on a theory that the more the activities that a couple does together are exciting, the more the couple is satisfied with their marriage. (We will have more to say about this later in the chapter when we discuss causality and also in Chapter 12 when we discuss prediction.)

❷ **Determine the range of values to use for each variable and mark them on the axes.** Your numbers should go from low to high on each axis, starting from where the axes meet. Your low value on each axis should be 0.

Each axis should continue to the highest value your measure can possibly have. When there is no obvious highest possible value, make the axis go to a value that is as high as people ordinarily score in the group of people of interest for your study. Note that scatter diagrams are usually made roughly square, with the horizontal and vertical axes being about the same length (a 1:1 ratio).

❸ **Mark a dot for each pair of scores.** Find the place on the horizontal axis for the first pair of scores on the horizontal-axis variable. Next, move up to the height for the score for the first pair of scores on the vertical-axis variable. Then mark a clear dot. Continue this process for the remaining pairs of scores. Sometimes the same pair of scores occurs twice (or more times). This means that the dots for these pairs would go in the same place. When this happens, you can put a second dot as near as possible to the first—touching, if possible—but making it clear that there are in fact two dots in the one place. Alternatively, you can put the number 2 in that place.

scatter diagram   graph showing the relationship between two variables: the values of one variable are along the horizontal axis and the values of the other variable are along the vertical axis; each score is shown as a dot in this two-dimensional space.

An Example

Suppose a researcher is studying the relationship of sleep to mood. As an initial test, the researcher asks six students in her morning seminar two questions:

1. How many hours did you sleep last night?
2. How happy do you feel right now on a scale from 0, *not at all happy*, to 8, *extremely happy?*

The (fictional) results are shown in Table 11–1. (In practice, a much larger group would be used in this kind of research. We are using an example with just six to keep things simple for learning. In fact, we have done a real version of this study. Results of the real study are similar to what we show here, except not as strong as the ones we made up to make the pattern clear for learning.)

Table 11-1	Hours Slept Last Night and Happy Mood Example (Fictional Data)
Hours Slept	**Happy Mood**
7	4
5	2
8	7
6	2
6	3
10	6

❶ **Draw the axes and decide which variable goes on which axis.** Because sleep comes before mood in this study, it makes most sense to think of sleep as the predictor. Thus, as shown in Figure 11–2a, we put hours slept on the horizontal axis and happy mood on the vertical axis.

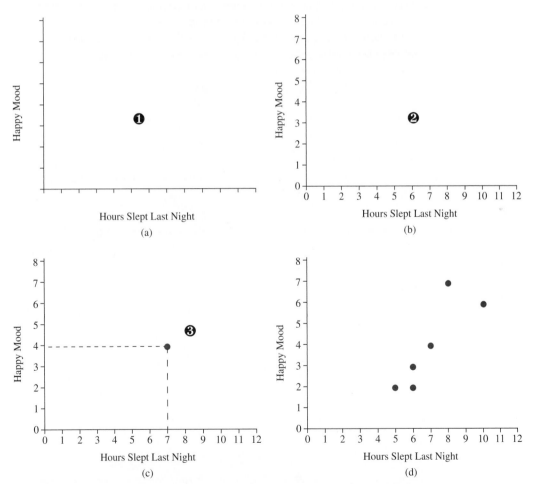

Figure 11–2   Steps for making a scatter diagram. (a) ❶ Draw the axes and decide which variable goes on which axis—the predictor variable (Hours Slept Last Night) on the horizontal axis, the other (Happy Mood) on the vertical axis. (b) ❷ Determine the range of values to use for each variable and mark them on the axes. (c) ❸ Mark a dot for the pair of scores for the first student. (d) ❸ continued: Mark dots for the remaining pairs of scores.

❷ **Determine the range of values to use for each variable and mark them on the axes.** For the horizontal axis, we start at 0 as usual. We do not know the maximum possible, but let us assume that students rarely sleep more than 12 hours. The vertical axis goes from 0 to 8, the lowest and highest scores possible on the happiness question. See Figure 11–2b.

❸ **Mark a dot for each pair of scores.** For the first student, the number of hours slept last night was 7. Move across to 7 on the horizontal axis. The happy mood rating for the first student was 4, so move up to the point across from the 4 on the vertical axis. Place a dot at this point, as shown in Figure 11–2c. Do the same for each of the other five students. The result should look like Figure 11–2d.

How are you doing?

1. What does a scatter diagram show, and what does it consist of?
2. (a) When it is the kind of study in which one variable can be thought of as predicting another variable, which variable goes on the horizontal axis? (b) Which goes on the vertical axis?
3. Make a scatter diagram for the following scores for four people who were each tested on two variables, X and Y. X is the variable we are predicting from; it can have scores ranging from 0 to 6. Y is the variable being predicted; it can have scores from 0 to 7.

Person	X	Y
A	3	4
B	6	7
C	1	2
D	4	6

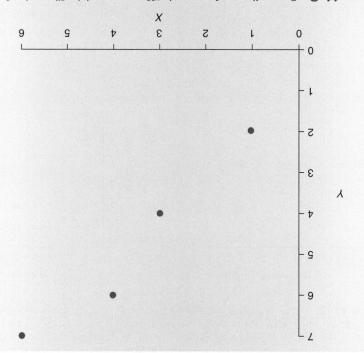

Figure 11–3 Scatter diagram for scores in "How are you doing?" question 3.

Patterns of Correlation

Linear and Curvilinear Correlations

In each example so far, the pattern in the scatter diagram very roughly approximates a straight line. Thus, each is an example of a **linear correlation.** In the scatter diagram for the study of happy mood and sleep (Figure 11–2d), you could draw a line showing the general trend of the dots, as we have done in Figure 11–4. Notice that the scores do not all fall right on the line. Notice, however, that the line does describe the general tendency of the scores. (In Chapter 12 you learn the precise rules for drawing such a line.)

Sometimes, however, the general relationship between two variables does not follow a straight line at all, but instead follows the more complex pattern of a **curvilinear correlation.** Consider, for example, the relationship between a person's level of kindness and the degree to which that person is desired by others as a potential romantic partner. There is evidence suggesting that, up to a point, a greater level of kindness increases a person's desirability as a romantic partner. However, beyond that point, additional kindness does little to increase desirability (Li et al., 2002). This particular curvilinear pattern is shown in Figure 11–5. Notice that you could not draw a straight line to describe this pattern. Some other examples of curvilinear relationships are shown in Figure 11–6.

linear correlation relation between two variables that shows up on a scatter diagram as the dots roughly following a straight line.

curvilinear correlation relation between two variables that shows up on a scatter diagram as dots following a systematic pattern that is not a straight line.

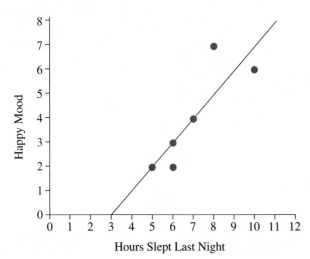

Figure 11–4 Scatter diagram from Figure 11–2d with a line drawn to show the general trend.

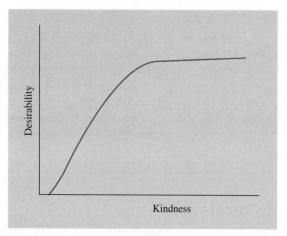

Figure 11–5   Example of a curvilinear relationship: desirability and kindness.

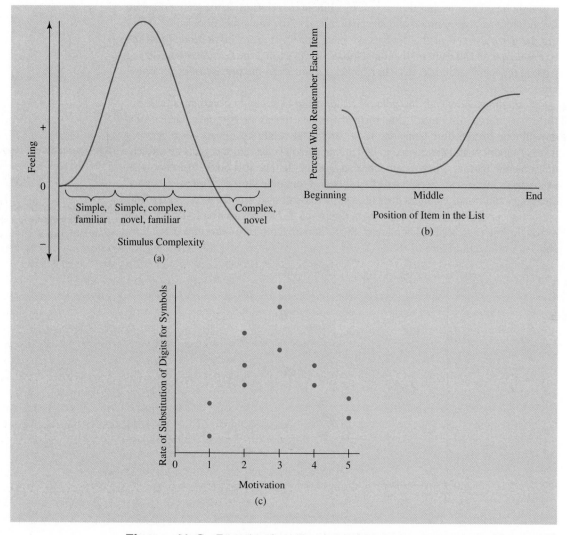

Figure 11–6   Examples of curvilinear relationships: (a) the way we feel and the complexity of a stimulus; (b) the number of people who remember an item and its position on a list; and (c) children's rate of and motivation for substituting digits for symbols.

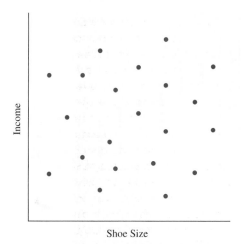

Figure 11–7   Two variables with no association with each other: income and shoe size (fictional data).

The usual way of figuring the correlation (the one you learn shortly in this chapter) gives the degree of *linear* correlation. If the true pattern of association is curvilinear, figuring the correlation in the usual way could show little or no correlation. Thus, it is important to look at scatter diagrams to identify these richer relationships rather than automatically figuring correlations in the usual way, assuming that the only relationship is a straight line.

No Correlation

It is also possible for two variables to be essentially unrelated to each other. For example, if you were to do a study of income and shoe size, your results might appear as shown in Figure 11–7. The dots are spread everywhere, and there is no line, straight or otherwise, that is any reasonable representation of a trend. There is simply **no correlation.**

Positive and Negative Linear Correlations

In the examples so far of linear correlations, such as exciting activities and martial satisfaction, high scores go with high scores, lows with lows, and mediums with mediums. This is called a **positive correlation.** (One reason for the term "positive" is that in geometry, the slope of a line is positive when it goes up and to the right on a graph like this. Notice that in Figure 11–4 the positive correlation between happy mood and sleep is shown by a line that goes up and to the right.)

Sometimes, however, high scores on one variable go with low scores on the other variable and lows with highs. This is called a **negative correlation.** For example, in the newspaper survey about marriage, the researchers also asked about boredom with the relationship and the partner. Not surprisingly, the more bored a person was, the *lower* was the person's marital satisfaction. That is, low scores on one variable went with high scores on the other. Similarly, the less bored a person was, the higher the marital satisfaction. This is shown in Figure 11–8, where we also put in a line to emphasize the general trend. You can see that as it goes from left to right, the line slopes slightly downward.

Another example of a negative correlation is from organizational psychology. A well established finding in that field is that absenteeism from work has a negative

no correlation   no systematic relationship between two variables.

positive correlation   relation between two variables in which high scores on one go with high scores on the other, mediums with mediums, and lows with lows; on a scatter diagram, the dots roughly follow a straight line sloping up and to the right.

negative correlation   relation between two variables in which high scores on one go with low scores on the other, mediums with mediums, and lows with highs; on a scatter diagram, the dots roughly follow a straight line sloping down and to the right.

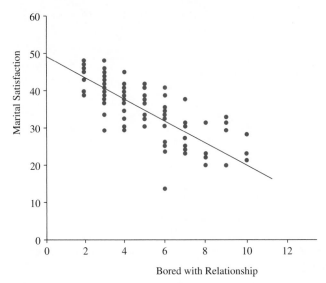

Figure 11–8   Scatter diagram with the line drawn in to show the general trend for a negative correlation between two variables: greater boredom with the relationship goes with lower marital satisfaction. (Data from Aron et al., 2000.)

linear correlation with satisfaction with the job (e.g., Mirvis & Lawler, 1977): that is, the higher the level of job satisfaction, the lower the level of absenteeism. Put another way, the lower the level of job satisfaction is, the higher the absenteeism becomes. Research on this topic has continued to show this pattern all over the world (e.g., Punnett et al., 2007), and the same pattern is found for university classes: the more satisfied students are, the less they miss class (Yorges et al., 2007).

Strength of the Correlation

What we mean by the *strength of the correlation* is how much there is a clear pattern of some particular relationship between two variables. For example, we saw that a positive linear correlation is when high scores go with highs, mediums with mediums, lows with lows. The strength (or degree) of such a correlation, then, is how much highs go with highs, and so on. Similarly, the strength of a negative linear correlation is how much the highs on one variable go with the lows on the other, and so forth. In terms of a scatter diagram, there is a "large" (or "strong") linear correlation if the dots fall close to a straight line (the line sloping up or down depending on whether the linear correlation is positive or negative). A perfect linear correlation means all the dots fall exactly on the straight line. There is a "small" (or "weak") correlation when you can barely tell there is a correlation at all; the dots fall far from a straight line. The correlation is "moderate" (also called a "medium" correlation) if the pattern of dots is somewhere between a small and a large correlation.

Importance of Identifying the Pattern of Correlation

The procedure you learn in the next main section is for figuring the direction and strength of linear correlation. As we suggested earlier, the best approach to such a problem is *first* to make a scatter diagram and to identify the pattern of correlation. If the pattern is curvilinear, then you would not go on to figure the linear correlation. This is important because figuring the linear correlation when the true correlation is curvilinear would be misleading. (For example, you might conclude that there is little or no correlation when in fact there is a quite strong relationship; it is just not linear.) You should assume that the correlation is linear, unless the scatter diagram shows a curvilinear correlation. We say this, because when the linear correlation is small, the dots will fall far from a straight line. In such situations, it can sometimes be hard to imagine a straight line that roughly shows the pattern of dots.

If the correlation appears to be linear, it is also important to "eyeball" the scatter diagram a bit more. The idea is to note the direction (positive or negative) of the linear correlation and also to make a rough guess as to the strength of the correlation. Scatter diagrams with varying directions and strengths of correlation are shown in Figure 11–9. For example, scatter diagram (a) in Figure 11–9 shows a large positive correlation, because the dots fall relatively close to a straight line, with low scores

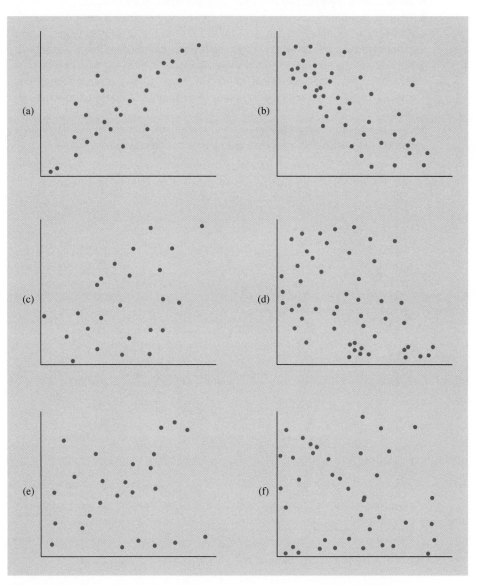

Figure 11–9 Examples of scatter diagrams with different degrees of correlation.

going with low scores and highs with highs. Scatter diagram (d), however, shows a negative correlation (there is a general tendency for lows to be with highs and highs with lows) that is of a moderate size (the dots fall too far from a straight line to be a large correlation, but are not so far apart that it is a small correlation). Using a scatter diagram to examine the direction and approximate strength of correlation is important because it lets you check to see whether you have made a major mistake when you then do the figuring you learn in the next section.

How are you doing?

1. What is the difference between a linear and curvilinear correlation in terms of how they appear in a scatter diagram?
2. What does it mean to say that two variables have no correlation?
3. What is the difference between a positive and negative linear correlation? Answer this question in terms of (a) the patterns in a scatter diagram and (b) what those patterns tell you about the relationship between the two variables.
4. For each of the scatter diagrams shown in Figure 11–10, say whether the pattern is roughly linear, curvilinear, or no correlation. If the pattern is roughly linear, also say if it is positive or negative, and whether it is large, moderate, or small.
5. Give two reasons why it is important to identify the pattern of correlation in a scatter diagram before proceeding to figure the precise correlation.

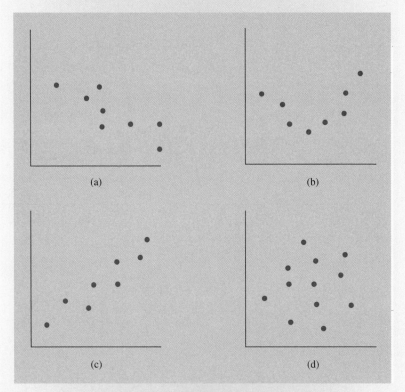

Figure 11–10 Scatter diagrams for "How are you doing?" question 4.

The Correlation Coefficient

Looking at a scatter diagram gives you a rough idea of the relationship between two variables, but it is not a very precise approach. What you need is a number that gives the exact correlation (in terms of its direction and strength).

Logic of Figuring the Linear Correlation

A linear correlation (when it is positive) means that highs go with highs and lows with lows. Thus, the first thing you need in figuring the correlation is some consistent way to measure what is a high score and what is a low score. An efficient way to solve this problem is to use *deviation scores*—that is, the raw score minus the mean (deviation scores = $X - M_X$ for one variable and $Y - M_Y$ for the other variable). A raw score above the mean (that is, a *high* score) will always give a positive deviation score and a raw score below the mean (that is, a *low* score) will always give a negative deviation score.

There is an additional and very important reason why deviation scores are so useful when figuring the correlation. It has to do with what happens if you multiply a score on one variable by a score on the other variable and get the product. When using deviation scores, this is called a **product of deviation scores** (or *product of deviations*). If you multiply a positive deviation score on one variable by a positive deviation score on another variable (each positive deviation score represents a raw score above the mean), you will always get a *positive product*. Further—and here is where it gets interesting—if you multiply a negative deviation score by a negative deviation score (each negative deviation score represents a raw score below the mean), you also get a *positive product*.

product of deviation scores the result of multiplying the deviation score on one variable by the deviation score on another variable.

So, if highs on one variable go with highs on the other, and lows on one go with lows on the other, the products of deviation scores always will be positive. Considering a whole distribution of scores, suppose you take each person's deviation score on one variable and multiply it by that person's deviation score on the other variable. The result of doing this when highs go with highs and lows with lows is that the products all come out positive. If you sum up these products of deviation scores for all the people in the study, which are all positive, you will end up with a *big positive number.*

On the other hand, with a negative correlation, highs go with lows and lows with highs. In terms of deviation scores, this would mean positives with negatives and negatives with positives. Multiplied out, that gives all negative products of deviations scores. If you add all these negative products together, you get a *big negative number.*

Finally, suppose there is no linear correlation. In this situation, for some people highs on one variable would go with highs on the other variable (and some lows would go with lows), making positive products of deviations. For other people, highs on one variable would go with lows on the other variable (and some lows would go with highs), making negative products. Adding up these products for all the people in the study would result in the positive products and the negative products canceling each other out, giving a result around 0.

In each situation, we changed all the scores to deviation scores, multiplied the two deviation scores for each person by each other, and added up these products of deviations. The result was a large positive number if there was a positive linear correlation, a large negative number if there was a negative linear correlation, and 0 if there was no linear correlation.

Table 11–2 summarizes the logic up to this point. The table shows the effect on the correlation of different patterns of raw scores and resulting deviation scores. For example, the first row shows a high score on X going with a high score on Y. In this situation, the deviation score for variable X is a positive number (since X is a high number, above the mean of X), and similarly the deviation score for variable Y is a positive number (since Y is a high number, above the mean of Y). Thus, the product of these two positive deviation scores must be a positive number (since a positive number multiplied by a positive number always gives a positive number). The overall

TIP FOR SUCCESS

Test your understanding of correlation by covering up portions of Table 11–2 and trying to recall the hidden information.

Table 11-2 The Effect on the Correlation of Different Patterns of Raw Scores and Deviation Scores

Pair of Scores		Deviation Scores		Product of Deviation Scores	Effect on Correlation
X	Y	$X - M_X$	$Y - M_Y$	$(X - M_X)(Y - M_Y)$	
High	High	+	+	+	Contributes to positive correlation
Low	Low	−	−	+	Contributes to positive correlation
High	Low	+	−	−	Contributes to negative correlation
Low	High	−	+	−	Contributes to negative correlation
Middle	Any	Zero	+, −, or Zero	Zero	Makes correlation near zero
Any	Middle	+, −, or Zero	Zero	Zero	Makes correlation near zero

Note: + indicates a positive number; − indicates a negative number

effect is that when a high score on X goes with a high score on Y, the pair of scores contribute toward making a positive correlation. The table shows that positive products of deviation scores contribute toward making a positive correlation, negative products of deviation scores contribute toward making a negative correlation, and products of deviation scores that are zero (or close to zero) contribute toward making a correlation of zero.

However, you are still left with the problem of figuring the precise strength of a positive or negative correlation. The larger the number is (that is, the farther from zero), the stronger the correlation will be. But how large is large, and how large is not very large? You can't judge from the sum of the products of deviations alone, which gets bigger just by adding the products of more persons together. For example, a study with 100 people would have a larger sum of products of deviations than the same study with only 25 people. The sum of the products also gets larger if the scores are on a more spread-out scale. For example, a study in which the scores on the two variables have a lot of variation, so they range from, say, 0 to 50, will have much larger products of deviation scores (and thus a larger sum of the products) than a study in which the scores on the two variables have less variation and range from, say, 0 to 10. This is because you are multiplying larger deviation scores by each other.

The upshot of all this is the sign ($+$ or $-$) of the sum of the products of deviation scores tells you the direction of the correlation. And the bigger it is (ignoring the sign), the more positive or negative it is. But it is hard to know from the sum of the products of deviation scores just how strong the correlation is because the number of people in the study and the amount of variation of the scores for each variable both affect the size of the sum of the products of deviation scores.

The solution to finding the precise degree of correlation is to divide this sum of the products of deviations by a number that corrects for both the number of people in the study and the variation of the scores for each variable. It turns out that this number is based on the sum of the squared deviations of each variable. This is because the more people there are in the study, the more squared deviations are being summed and because the more variation there is in the scores for each variable, the larger will be the squared deviations being summed. That is, to adjust our sum of products, we use a *correction number* that has two properties:

1. It gets larger with more people.
2. It gets larger as the scores for each variable have more variation.

These two properties of the correction number mean that it serves two very important purposes: it adjusts for the number of people in the study, and it adjusts for the different variation in scores for each variable.

The actual specific correction number that is used is the square root of what you get when you take the sum of squared deviations for each variable (the SS or sum of squares you figure when figuring the variance), multiply the two sums of squares by each other, and take the square root: $\sqrt{(SS_X)\,(SS_Y)}$. However, we will turn to the formulas shortly.

So how do you actually use this number to make the correction? You divide the sum of products of deviations by this correction number. It turns out that the result of dividing the sum of the product of deviation scores by the correction number can never be more than $+1$, which would be a perfect positive linear correlation. It can never be less than -1, which would be a perfect negative linear correlation. In the situation of no linear correlation, the result is 0.

TIP FOR SUCCESS

If you figure a correlation coefficient to be larger than +1 or less than −1, you have made a mistake in your figuring.

For a positive linear correlation that is not perfect (it is extremely rare to find a perfect correlation), the result of taking the sum of the products of deviation scores and dividing by the correction number is a number between 0 and +1. To put this another way, if the general trend of the dots is upward and to the right, but they do not fall exactly on a single straight line, the result of this process is between 0 and +1. The same rule holds for negative correlations: they fall between 0 and −1. So, overall, a correlation varies from −1 to +1.

Interpreting the Correlation Coefficient

correlation coefficient (r)   measure of degree of linear correlation between two variables ranging from −1 (a perfect negative linear correlation) through 0 (no correlation) to +1 (a perfect positive correlation).

The result of dividing the sum of the products of deviation scores by the correction number is called the **correlation coefficient.** It is also called the Pearson correlation coefficient (or the Pearson product-moment correlation coefficient, to be very traditional). It is named after Karl Pearson (whom you meet in Box 13–1). Pearson, along with Francis Galton (see Box 11–1 in this chapter), played a major role in developing the correlation coefficient. The correlation coefficient is abbreviated by

---

BOX 11–1   Galton: Gentleman Genius

Corbiss/Bettman

Francis Galton is credited with inventing the correlation statistic. (Karl Pearson, the hero of our Chapter 13, worked out the formulas, but Pearson was a student of Galton and gave Galton all the credit.) Statistics at this time (around the end of the 19th century) was a tight little British club. In fact, most of science was an only slightly larger club. Galton also was influenced greatly by his own cousin, Charles Darwin.

Galton was a typical eccentric, independently wealthy gentleman scientist. Aside from his work in statistics, he possessed a medical degree, had explored "darkest Africa," invented glasses for reading underwater, experimented with stereoscopic maps, dabbled in meteorology and anthropology, and wrote a paper about receiving intelligible signals from the stars.

Above all, Galton was a compulsive counter. Some of his counts are rather infamous. Once while attending a lecture he counted the fidgets of an audience per minute, looking for variations with the boringness of the subject matter. While twice having his picture painted, he counted the artist's brush strokes per hour, concluding that each portrait required an average of 20,000 strokes. While walking the streets of various towns in the British Isles, he classified the beauty of the female inhabitants by fingering a recording device in his pocket to register good, medium, or bad.

Galton's consuming interest, however, was the counting of geniuses, criminals, and other types in families. He wanted to understand how each type was produced so that science could improve the human race by encouraging governments to enforce eugenics—selective breeding for intelligence, proper moral behavior, and other qualities—to be determined, of course, by the eugenicists. (Eugenics has since been generally discredited.) The concept of correlation came directly from his first simple efforts in this area, the study of the relation of the height of children to their parents.

At first, Galton's method of exactly measuring the tendency for "one thing to go with another" seemed almost the same as proving the cause of something. For example, if it could be shown mathematically that most of the brightest people came from a few highborn British families and most of the least intelligent people came from poor families, that seemed at first to "prove" that intelligence was caused by the inheritance of certain genes (provided that you were prejudiced enough to overlook the differences in educational opportunities). Now the study only proves that if you were a member of one of those highborn British families, history would make you a prime example of how easy it is to misinterpret the meaning of a correlation.

You can learn more about Galton on the following Web page: *http://www-history.mcs.st-andrews.ac.uk/Biographies/Galton.html.*

Sources: Peters (1987); Salsburg (2001); Tankard (1984).

the letter *r*, which is short for regression, an idea closely related to correlation (see Chapter 12).

The sign (+ or −) of a correlation coefficient tells you the *direction* of the linear correlation between two variables (a positive correlation or a negative correlation). The actual value of the correlation coefficient—from a low of 0 to a high of 1, ignoring the sign of the correlation coefficient—tells you the *strength* of the linear correlation. So, a correlation coefficient of +.85 represents a larger linear correlation than a correlation of +.42. Similarly, a correlation of −.90 represents a larger linear correlation than +.85 (since .90 is bigger than .85). Another way of thinking of this is that, in a scatter diagram, the closer the dots are to falling on a single straight line, the larger the linear correlation. Figure 11–11 shows the scatter diagrams from Figure 11–9, with the correlation coefficient shown for each

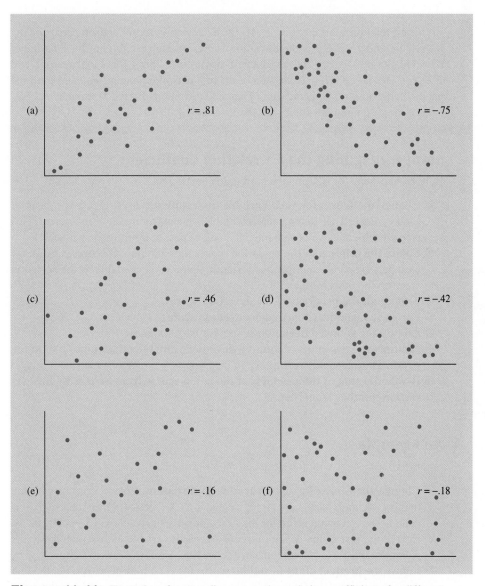

Figure 11–11   Examples of scatter diagrams and correlation coefficients for different degrees of linear correlation.

scatter diagram. Be sure that the correlation coefficient for each scatter diagram agrees roughly with the correlation coefficient you would expect based on the pattern of dots.

Formula for the Correlation Coefficient

The correlation coefficient, as we have seen, is the sum of the products of deviation scores divided by a correction number that takes into account the number of people and the variation on each variable being correlated. Put as a formula,

> The correlation coefficient is the sum, over all the people in the study, of the product of each person's two deviation scores, divided by the result of taking the square root of what you get when you multiply the sum of everyone's squared deviation scores on the X variable by the sum of everyone's squared deviation scores on the Y variable.

$$r = \frac{\sum[(X - M_X)(Y - M_Y)]}{\sqrt{(SS_X)(SS_Y)}} \qquad (11\text{--}1)$$

r is the correlation coefficient. $X - M_X$ is the deviation score for each person on the X variable and $Y - M_Y$ is the deviation score for each person on the Y variable; $(X - M_X)(Y - M_Y)$ is the product of deviation scores for each person; and $\sum[(X - M_X)(Y - M_Y)]$ is the sum of the products of deviation scores over all the people in the study. SS_X is the sum of squared deviations for the X variable and SS_Y is the sum of squared deviations for the Y variable.[1]

Steps for Figuring the Correlation Coefficient

Here are the steps for figuring the correlation coefficient.

❶ **Change the scores for each variable to deviation scores.** Figure the mean of each variable. Then subtract each variable's mean from each of its scores. (This is just what you have been doing all along as part of figuring the variance.)

❷ **Figure the product of the deviation scores for each pair of scores.** That is, for each pair of scores, multiply the deviation score on one variable by the deviation score on the other variable.

❸ **Add up all the products of the deviation scores.**

❹ **For each variable, square each deviation score.**

❺ **Add up the squared deviation scores for each variable.**

❻ **Multiply the two sums of squared deviations and take the square root of the result.** This creates a correction number.

❼ **Divide the sum of the products of deviation scores from Step ❸ by the correction number from Step ❻.**

An Example

Let us try these steps with the sleep and mood example.

❶ **Change the scores for each variable to deviation scores.** Starting with the number of hours slept last night, the mean is 7 (sum of 42 divided by 6 students). The deviation score for the first student's sleep score is $7 - 7 = 0$. We figured the rest of the deviation scores for each variable and show them in the $X - M_X$ and $Y - M_Y$ columns in Table 11–3.

❷ **Figure the product of the deviation scores for each pair of scores.** For the first student, multiply 0 by 0 to give 0. The products of deviation scores for all the students are shown in the last column of Table 11–3.

Table 11-3   Figuring the Correlation Coefficient for the Sleep and Mood Study (Fictional Data)

Number of Hours Slept (X)			Happy Mood (Y)			Products of ❷ Deviation Scores
	Deviation ❶	Deviation Squared ❹		Deviation ❶	Deviation Squared ❹	
X	$X - M_X$	$(X - M_X)^2$	Y	$Y - M_Y$	$(Y - M_Y)^2$	$(X - M_X)(Y - M_Y)$
7	0	0	4	0	0	0
5	−2	4	2	−2	4	4
8	1	1	7	3	9	3
6	−1	1	2	−2	4	2
6	−1	1	3	−1	1	1
10	3	9	6	2	4	6
$\Sigma = 42$		$\Sigma = SS_X = 16$ ❺	$\Sigma = 24$		$\Sigma = SS_Y = 22$ ❺	$\Sigma = 16$ ❸
$M = 7$			$M = 4$			

$$r = \frac{\Sigma[(X - M_X)(Y - M_Y)]}{\sqrt{(SS_X)(SS_Y)}} = \frac{16}{\sqrt{(16)(22)}} = \frac{16}{\sqrt{352}} = \frac{16}{18.76} = .85 \, ❼$$
❻

❸ **Add up all the products of the deviation scores.** Adding up all the products of the deviation scores, as shown in Table 11–3, gives a sum of 16.

❹ **For each variable, square each deviation score.** For the first student, the squared deviation for the sleep variable is 0 multiplied by 0, which is 0. The squared deviation scores for all the students for the sleep variable are shown in the $(X - M_X)^2$ column of Table 11–3. The squared deviation scores for all the students for the happy mood variable are shown in the $(Y - M_Y)^2$ column.

❺ **Add up the squared deviation scores for each variable.** As shown in Table 11–3, the sum of squared deviations for the sleep variable is 16 and the sum of squared deviations for the happy mood variable is 22.

❻ **Multiply the two sums of squared deviations and take the square root of the result.** Multiplying 16 by 22 is 352, and the square root of 352 is 18.76.

❼ **Divide the sum of the products of deviation scores from Step ❸ by the correction number from Step ❻.** Dividing 16 by 18.76 gives a result of .85. This is the correlation coefficient. (Note that correlation coefficients are usually rounded to two decimal places.)

In terms of the correlation coefficient formula,

$$r = \frac{\Sigma[(X - M_X)(Y - M_Y)]}{\sqrt{(SS_X)(SS_Y)}} = \frac{16}{18.76} = .85$$

Because this correlation coefficient is positive and near 1, the highest possible value, this is a very large positive linear correlation.

A Second Example

Suppose that a memory researcher does an experiment to test a theory predicting that the number of exposures to a word increases the chance that the word will be remembered. One research participant is randomly assigned to be exposed to the list of 10 words once, one participant to be exposed to the list twice, and so forth, up to a total of eight exposures to each word. This makes eight participants in all, one for

Table 11-4 Effect of Number of Exposures to Words on the Number of Words Recalled (Fictional Data)

Number of Exposures	Number of Words Recalled
1	3
2	2
3	6
4	4
5	5
6	5
7	6
8	9

each of the eight levels of exposure. The researchers record how many of the 10 words each participant is able to remember. Results are shown in Table 11–4. (An actual study of this kind would probably show a pattern in which the relative improvement in recall is less at higher numbers of exposures.) The steps for figuring the correlation coefficient are shown in Table 11–5.

❶ **Change the scores for each variable to deviation scores.** The mean of the number of exposures is 4.5. Thus, the first exposure score of 1 gives a deviation score of $1 - 4.5 = -3.5$. Using the same procedure for all the other scores gives the deviation scores shown in the $X - M_X$ and $Y - M_Y$ columns in Table 11–5.

❷ **Figure the product of the deviation scores for each pair of scores.** For the first person, multiply -3.5 by -2 to give 7. The products of deviation scores for all the scores are shown in the last column of Table 11–5.

❸ **Add up all the products of the deviation scores.** Adding up all the products of the deviation scores, as shown in Table 11–5, gives a sum of 30.

❹ **For each variable, square each deviation score.** For the first person, the squared deviation for the number of exposures variable is -3.5 multiplied by -3.5, which is 12.25. The squared deviation scores for all the scores are shown in the $(X - M_X)^2$ and $(Y - M_Y)^2$ columns of Table 11–5.

❺ **Add up the squared deviation scores for each variable.** As shown in Table 11–5, the sum of squared deviations for the number of exposures variable is 42, and the sum of squared deviations for the number of words recalled variable is 32.

❻ **Multiply the two sums of squared deviations and take the square root of the result.** Multiplying 42 by 32 is 1344, and the square root of 1344 is 36.66.

❼ **Divide the sum of the products of deviation scores from Step ❸ by the correction number from Step ❻.** Dividing 30 by 36.66 gives a result of .82. This is the correlation coefficient.

Table 11-5 Figuring the Correlation Coefficient for the Effect of Number of Exposures to Each Word on the Number of Words Recalled (Fictional Data)

Number of Exposures (X)			Number of Words Recalled (Y)			Products of ❷ Deviation Scores
	Deviation ❶	Deviation Squared ❹		Deviation ❶	Deviation Squared ❹	
X	X − M_X	(X − M_X)²	Y	Y − M_Y	(Y − M_Y)²	(X − M_X)(Y − M_Y)
1	−3.5	12.25	3	−2	4	7.0
2	−2.5	6.25	2	−3	9	7.5
3	−1.5	2.25	6	1	1	−1.5
4	−.5	.25	4	−1	1	.5
5	.5	.25	5	0	0	0
6	1.5	2.25	5	0	0	0
7	2.5	6.25	6	1	1	2.5
8	3.5	12.25	9	4	16	14
Σ = 36		Σ = SS_X = 42 ❺	Σ = 40		Σ = SS_Y = 32 ❺	Σ = 30 ❸
M = 4.5			M = 5			

$$r = \frac{\Sigma[(X - M_X)(Y - M_Y)]}{\sqrt{(SS_X)(SS_Y)}} = \frac{30}{\sqrt{(42)(32)}} = \frac{30}{\sqrt{1344}}_{❻} = \frac{30}{36.66} = .82^{❼}$$

In terms of the correlation coefficient formula,

$$r = \frac{\sum[(X - M_X)(Y - M_Y)]}{\sqrt{(SS_X)(SS_Y)}} = \frac{30}{36.66} = .82$$

Because this correlation coefficient is positive and near 1, the highest possible value, this is a very large positive linear correlation.

How are you doing?

1. Why do we change the scores for each variable into deviation scores in the first step of figuring the correlation coefficient?
2. Explain the logic of using the sum of the products of deviation scores as the numerator of the formula for the correlation coefficient.
3. When figuring the correlation coefficient, why do you divide the sum of the products of deviation scores by a correction number?
4. Write the formula for the correlation coefficient and define each of the symbols.
5. Figure the correlation coefficient for the following scores for three people who were each tested on two variables, X and Y.

Person	X	Y
K	5	10
L	4	10
M	3	13

5. As shown in Table 11–6, $r = -.87$.

4. Formula for the correlation coefficient: $r = \frac{\sum[(X - M_X)(Y - M_Y)]}{\sqrt{(SS_X)(SS_Y)}}$. r is the correlation coefficient; $\sum$ is the symbol for sum of—add up all the scores that follow (in this formula, you add up all the products of deviation scores that follow); $X - M_X$ is the deviation score for each person on the X variable; $Y - M_Y$ is the deviation score for each person on the Y variable; SS_X is the sum of squared deviations for the X variable; SS_Y is the sum of squared deviations for the Y variable.

Table 11-6 Figuring the Correlation Coefficient for "How are you doing?" Question 5

X	Deviation ❶ (X − M_X)	Squared Deviation ❹ (X − M_X)²	Y	Deviation ❶ (Y − M_Y)	Squared Deviation ❹ (Y − M_Y)²	Products of ❷ Deviation Scores (X − M_X)(Y − M_Y)
5	1	1	10	−1	1	−1
4	0	0	10	−1	1	0
3	−1	1	13	2	4	−2
Σ = 12		Σ = SS_X = 2 ❸	Σ = 33		Σ = SS_Y = 6 ❸	Σ = −3 ❺
M = 4			M = 11			

$$r = \frac{\sum[(X - M_X)(Y - M_Y)]}{\sqrt{(SS_X)(SS_Y)}} = \frac{-3}{\sqrt{(2)(6)}} = \frac{-3}{\sqrt{12}} = \frac{-3}{3.46} = -.87 \;❼$$ ❻

TIP FOR SUCCESS
You will not be able to make much
sense of this section if you have
not yet studied Chapters 3
through 7.

Significance of a Correlation Coefficient

The correlation coefficient is a descriptive statistic, like the mean or standard deviation. The correlation coefficient describes the linear relationship between two variables. However, in addition to *describing* this relationship, we may also want to test whether it is statistically significant. In the case of a correlation, the question is usually whether it is significantly different from zero. That is, the null hypothesis in hypothesis testing for a correlation is usually that in the population the true relation between the two variable is no correlation ($r = 0$).[2]

The overall logic is much like that we have considered for the various *t* test and analysis of variance situations discussed in previous chapters. Suppose for a particular population we had the distribution of two variables, *X* and *Y*. And suppose further that in this population there was no correlation between these two variables. The scatter diagram might look like that shown in Figure 11–12. Thus, if you were to consider the dot for one random person from this scatter diagram, the scores might be $X = 4$ and $Y = 2$. For another random person, it might be $X = 2$ and $Y = 1$. For a third person, $X = 3$ and $Y = 5$. The correlation for these three persons would be $r = .24$. If you then took out another three persons and figured the correlation it might come out to $r = -.12$. Presuming there was no actual correlation in the population, if you did this lots and lots of times, you would end up with a distribution of correlations with a mean of zero. This is a distribution of correlations of three persons' each. As shown in Figure 11–13, it would have a mean of zero and be spread out in both directions up to a maximum of 1 and a minimum of -1.

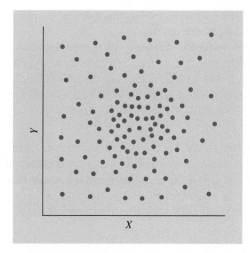

Figure 11–12   Scatter diagram for variables X and Y for a population in which there is no relationship between X and Y.

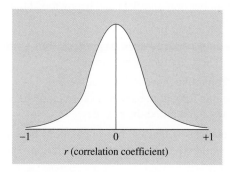

r (correlation coefficient)

Figure 11–13   Distribution of correlation coefficients for a large number of samples ($N = 3$) drawn from a population with no correlation between variables X and Y.

It would actually be possible to figure out the cutoffs for significance on such a distribution of correlation coefficients, just as we did for example for the F distribution. Then you could just compare your actual r to that cutoff to see if it was significant. However, we do not need to introduce a whole new distribution with its own tables and such. It turns out that we can figure out a number based on the correlation coefficient that will follow a t distribution. This number is figured using the following formula:

$$t = \frac{r}{\sqrt{(1 - r^2)/(N - 2)}} \tag{11–2}$$

Notice that in this formula if $r = 0$, $t = 0$. This is because the numerator would be 0 and the result of dividing 0 by any number is 0. Also notice that the bigger the r, the bigger the t.

If you were to take three persons' scores at random from the distribution with no true correlation, you could figure this t value. For example, for the first three-person example we just considered, the correlation was .24. So, $t = .24/\sqrt{(1 - .24^2)/(3 - 2)} = .24/\sqrt{(.9424)/(1)} = .25$. If you took a large number of such samples of three persons each, computed the correlation and then the t for each, you would eventually have a distribution of t scores. And here is the main point: you

The t score for a correlation coefficient is the result of dividing the correlation coefficient by the square root of what you get when you divide one minus the correlation coefficient squared by two less than the number of people in the study.

could then compare the *t* score figured in this way for the actual correlation in the study, using the standard *t* table cutoffs.

As usual with the *t* statistic, there are different *t* distributions for different degrees of freedom. In the case of the *t* test for a correlation, *df* is the number of people in the sample minus 2. (We subtract 2 because the whole figuring involved two different means, the mean of *X* and the mean of *Y*.) In terms of a formula,

$$df = N - 2 \qquad (11\text{–}3)$$

> The degrees of freedom for the *t* test for a correlation are the number of people in the sample minus 2.

Finally, note that the *t* value will be positive or negative, according to whether your correlation is positive or negative. Thus, as with any *t* test, the *t* test for a correlation can be either one-tailed or two-tailed. A one-tailed test means that the researcher has predicted the sign (+ or −) of the correlation. However, in practice, even when a researcher expects a certain direction of correlation, correlations are usually tested with two-tailed tests.

An Example

In the sleep and mood study example, let's suppose that the researchers predicted a correlation between number of hours slept and happy mood the next day, to be tested at the .05 level, two-tailed.

❶ Restate the question as a research hypothesis and a null hypothesis about the populations. There are two populations:

Population 1: People like those in this study.
Population 2: People for whom there is no correlation between number of hours slept the night before and mood the next day.

The null hypothesis is that the two populations have the same correlation. The research hypothesis is that the two populations do not have the same correlation.

❷ Determine the characteristics of the comparison distribution. The comparison distribution is a *t* distribution with $df = 4$. (That is, $df = N - 2 = 6 - 2 = 4$.)

❸ Determine the cutoff sample score on the comparison distribution at which the null hypothesis should be rejected. The *t* table (Table A–2 in the Appendix) shows that for a two-tailed test at the .05 level, with 4 degrees of freedom, the cutoff *t* scores are 2.776 and −2.776.

❹ Determine your sample's score on the comparison distribution. We figured a correlation of $r = .85$. Applying the formula to find the equivalent *t*, we get

$$t = \frac{r}{\sqrt{(1 - r^2)/(N - 2)}} = \frac{.85}{\sqrt{(1 - .85^2)/(6 - 2)}} = \frac{.85}{\sqrt{.0694}} = 3.23$$

❺ Decide whether to reject the null hypothesis. The *t* score of 3.23 for our sample correlation is more extreme than a cutoff *t* score of 2.776. Thus, we can reject the null hypothesis and the research hypothesis is supported.

Assumptions for the Significance Test of a Correlation Coefficient

The assumptions for testing the significance of a correlation coefficient are similar to those for the *t* test for independent means and analysis of variance. In those situations you have to assume the population for each group follows a normal distribution and has the same variance as the population for the other groups. With the correlation you have to assume that:

1. **The population of each variable (X and Y) follows a normal distribution.** Actually you also assume that the relationship *between* the two variables also follows a normal curve. This creates what is called a *bivariate normal distribution*. In practice, however, we usually check whether we have met the requirement by checking whether the distribution in the sample for each of our variables is roughly normal.

2. **There is an equal distribution of each variable at each point of the other variable.** For example, in a scatter diagram, if there is much more variation at the low end than at the high end (or vice versa), this suggests a problem. In practice, you should look at the scatter diagram for your study to see if it looks like the dots are much more spread out at the low or high end (or both). A lot of dots in the middle are to be expected. So long as the greater number of dots in the middle are not a lot more spread out than those at either end, this does not suggest a problem with the assumptions.

Like the t tests you have already learned and like the analysis of variance, the t test for the significance of a correlation coefficient is pretty robust to all but extreme violations of its assumptions.

How are you doing?

1. What is the usual null hypothesis in hypothesis testing with a correlation coefficient?
2. Write the formula for testing the significance of a correlation coefficient, and define each of the symbols.
3. Use the five steps of hypothesis testing to determine whether a correlation coefficient of $r = -.31$ from a study with a sample of 60 people is significant at the .05 level, two-tailed.
4. What are the assumptions for the significance test of a correlation coefficient?

Appendix) shows that for a two-tailed test at the .05 level, with 58 degrees of freedom, the cutoff t scores are 2.004 and −2.004 (we used the cutoffs for $df = 55$, the closest df in the table below 58).

❹ **Determine your sample's score on the comparison distribution.** The correlation in the study was −.31. Applying the formula to find the equivalent t, we get

$$t = \frac{r}{\sqrt{(1 - r^2)/(N - 2)}} = \frac{-.31}{\sqrt{(1 - (-.31^2))/(58)}} = \frac{-.31}{.125} = -2.48.$$

❺ **Decide whether to reject the null hypothesis.** The t score of −2.48 for our sample correlation is more extreme than a cutoff t score of −2.004. Thus, we can reject the null hypothesis and the research hypothesis is supported.

4. The population of each variable (and the relationship between them) follows a normal distribution, and there is an equal distribution of each variable at each point of the other variable.

Answers

1. In hypothesis testing with a correlation coefficient, the usual null hypothesis is that in the population the true relation between the two variables is no correlation ($r = 0$).

2. Formula for testing the significance of a correlation coefficient: $t = \dfrac{r}{\sqrt{(1 - r^2)/(N - 2)}}$. t is the t statistic for testing the significance of the correlation coefficient; r is the correlation coefficient; N is the number of people in the study.

3. ❶ **Restate the question as a research hypothesis and a null hypothesis about the populations.** There are two populations:

Population 1: People like those in this study.
Population 2: People for whom there is no correlation between the two variables.

The null hypothesis is that the two populations have the same correlation. The research hypothesis is that the two populations do not have the same correlation.

❷ **Determine the characteristics of the comparison distribution.** The comparison distribution is a t distribution with $df = N - 2 = 58$. (That is, $df = N - 2 = 60 - 2 = 58$.)

❸ **Determine the cutoff sample score on the comparison distribution at which the null hypothesis should be rejected.** The t table (Table A–2) in the

Correlation and Causality

If two variables have a significant linear correlation, we normally assume that there is something causing them to go together. However, you can't know the **direction of causality** (what is causing what) just from the fact that the two variables are correlated.

Three Possible Directions of Causality

Consider the example with which we started the chapter, the correlation between doing exciting activities with your partner and satisfaction with the relationship. There are three possible directions of causality for these two variables:

1. It could be that doing exciting activities together causes the partners to be more satisfied with their relationship.
2. It could also be that people who are more satisfied with their relationship choose to do more exciting activities together.
3. Another possibility is that something like having less pressure (versus more pressure) at work makes people happier in their marriage and also gives them more time and energy to do exciting activities with their partner.

These three possible directions of causality are shown in Figure 11–14a.

The principle is that for any correlation between variables X and Y, there are at least three possible directions of causality:

1. X could be causing Y.
2. Y could be causing X.
3. Some third factor could be causing both X and Y.

These three possible directions of causality are shown in Figure 11–14b.

direction of causality path of causal effect; if X is thought to cause Y then the direction of causality is from X to Y.

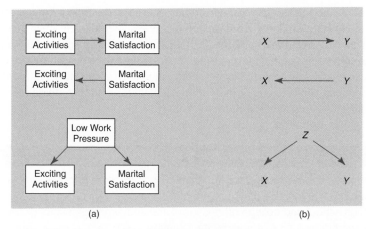

Figure 11–14   Three possible directions of causality (shown with arrows) for a correlation for (a) the exciting activities and marital satisfaction example and (b) the general principle for any two variables X and Y.

It is also possible (and often likely) that there is more than one direction of causality making two variables correlated.

Ruling Out Some Possible Directions of Causality

Sometimes you can rule out one or more of these three possible directions based on additional knowledge of the situation. For example, the correlation between sleep the night before and a happy mood the next day cannot be due to happy mood the next day causing you to sleep more the night before (causality doesn't go backward in time). But we still do not know whether the sleep the night before caused the happy mood or some third factor, such as a general tendency to be happy, caused people both to sleep well and to be happy on any particular day.

Another way we can rule out alternative directions of causality is by conducting a true experiment. In a true experiment, participants are randomly assigned to a particular level of a variable and then measured on another variable. An example of this is the study in which participants were randomly assigned (say, by flipping a coin) to different numbers of exposures to a list of words, and then the number of words they could remember was measured. There was an .82 correlation between number of exposures and number of words recalled. In this situation, any causality has to be from the variable that was manipulated (number of exposures) to the variable that is measured (words recalled). The number of words recalled can't cause more exposures, because the exposures came first. And a third variable can't be causing both number of exposures and words recalled because number of exposures was determined randomly; nothing can be causing it other than the random method we used (such as flipping a coin).

Correlational Statistical Procedures versus Correlation Research Methods

Discussions of correlation and causality in psychology research are often confused by there being two uses of the word *correlation*. Sometimes the word is used as the name of a statistical procedure, the correlation coefficient (as we have done in this chapter). At other times, the term *correlation* is used to describe a kind of research design. A **correlational research design** is any research design other than a true experiment. A correlational research design is not necessarily statistically analyzed using the correlation coefficient, and some studies using experimental research designs are most appropriately analyzed using a correlation coefficient. Hence the confusion. We recommend you take one or more research methods courses to learn more about research designs used in research in psychology.

How are you doing?

1. If anxiety and depression are correlated, what are three possible directions of causality that might explain this correlation?
2. If high school and college grades are correlated, what directions of causality can and cannot be ruled out by the situation?
3. A researcher randomly assigns participants to eat either zero or four cookies and then asks them how full they feel. The number of cookies eaten and feeling full are highly correlated. What directions of causality can and cannot be ruled out?
4. What is the difference between correlation as a statistical procedure and a correlational research design?

Answers

1. Being depressed can cause a person to be anxious; being anxious can cause a person to be depressed; some third variable (such as some aspect of heredity or childhood traumas) could be causing both anxiety and depression.
2. College grades cannot be causing high school grades (causality doesn't go backward), but high school grades could be causing college grades (maybe knowing you did well in high school gives you more confidence), and some third variable (such as general academic ability) could be causing students to do well in both high school and college.
3. Eating more cookies can cause participants to feel full. Feeling full cannot have caused participants to have eaten more cookies, because how many cookies were eaten was determined randomly. Third variables can't cause both, because how many cookies were eaten was determined randomly.
4. The statistical procedure of correlation is about using the formula for the correlation coefficient, regardless of how the study was done. A correlational research design is any research design other than a true experiment.

Issues in Interpreting the Correlation Coefficient

There are a number of subtle cautions in interpreting a correlation coefficient.

The Correlation Coefficient and the Proportionate Reduction in Error or Proportion of Variance Accounted For

A correlation coefficient tells you the direction and strength of a linear correlation. Bigger *r*s (values farther from 0) mean a higher degree of correlation. That is, an *r* of .60 is a larger correlation than an *r* of .30. However, most researchers would hold

correlational research design any research design other than a true experiment.

that an r of .60 is *more than* twice as large as an r of .30. To compare correlations with each other, most researchers square the correlations (that is, they use r^2 instead of r). This is called, for reasons you will learn in an Advanced Topic section of Chapter 12, the **proportionate reduction in error** (and also the *proportion of variance accounted for*).

For example, a correlation of .30 is an r^2 of .09 and a correlation of .60 is an r^2 of .36. Thus, a correlation of .60 is actually four times as large as one of .30 (that is, .36 is four times as big as .09).

Restriction in Range

Suppose an educational psychologist studies the relation of grade level to knowledge of geography. If this researcher studied students from the entire range of school grade levels, the results might appear as shown in the scatter diagram in Figure 11–15a. That is, the researcher might find a large positive correlation. But suppose the researcher had studied students only from the first three grades. The scatter diagram (see Figure 11–15b) would show a much smaller correlation (the general increasing tendency is in relation to much more noise). However, the researcher would be making a mistake by concluding that grade level is only slightly related to knowledge of geography over all grades.

The problem in this situation is that the correlation is based on people who include only a limited range of the possible values on one of the variables. (In this example, there is a limited range of grade levels.) It is misleading to think of the correlation as if it applied to the entire range of values the variable might have. This situation is called **restriction in range.**

It is easy to make such mistakes in interpreting correlations. (You will occasionally see them even in published research articles.) Consider another example. Businesses sometimes try to decide whether their hiring tests are correlated with how successful the persons hired turn out on the job. Often, they find very little relationship. What they fail to take into account is that they hired only people who did well on the tests. Their study of job success included only the subgroup of high scorers. This example is shown in Figure 11–16.

proportionate reduction in error (r^2) measure of association between variables that is used when comparing associations. Also called *proportion of variance accounted for.*

restriction in range situation in which you figure a correlation but only a limited range of the possible values on one of the variables is included in the group studied.

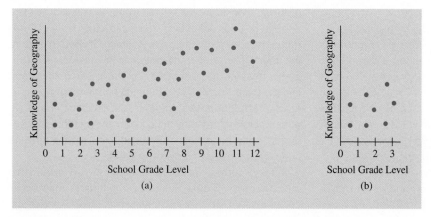

Figure 11–15   Example of restriction in range comparing two scatter diagrams (a) when the entire range is shown (of school grade level and knowledge of geography) and (b) when the range is restricted (to the first three grades) (fictional data).

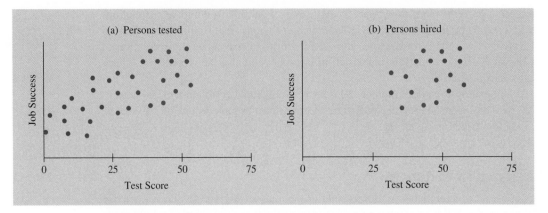

Figure 11–16 Additional example of restriction in range comparing two scatter diagrams (a) when the entire range is shown (of all persons tested) and (b) when the range is restricted (to just those persons who were hired) (fictional data).

Yet another example is any study that tries to correlate intelligence with other variables that uses only college students. The problem here is that college students do not include many lower or below-average intelligence students. Thus, a researcher could find a low correlation in such a study. But if the researcher did the same study with people who included the full range of intelligence levels, there could well be a high correlation.

BOX 11–2　Illusory Correlation: When You Know Perfectly Well That If It's Big, It's Fat—and You Are Perfectly Wrong

The concept of correlation was not really invented by statisticians. It is one of the most basic of human mental processes. The first humans must have thought in terms of correlation all the time—at least those who survived. "Every time it snows, the animals we hunt go away. Snow belongs with no animals. When the snow comes again, if we follow the animals, we may not starve."

In fact, correlation is such a typically human and highly successful thought process that we seem to be psychologically organized to see more correlation than is there—like the Aztecs, who thought that good crops correlated with human sacrifices (let's hope they were wrong), and like the following examples from social psychology of what is called *illusory correlation* (Hamilton, 1981; Hamilton & Gifford, 1976; Johnson & Mullen, 1994).

Illusory correlation is the term for the overestimation of the strength of the relationship between two variables (the term has also had other special meanings in the past). Right away, you may think of some harmful illusory correlations related to ethnicity, race, gender, and age. One source of illusory correlation is the tendency to link two infrequent and therefore highly memorable events. Suppose Group B is smaller than Group A, and in *both* groups one-third of the people are known to commit certain infrequent but undesirable acts. In this kind of situation, research shows that Group B, whose members are less frequently encountered, will in fact be blamed for far more of these undesirable acts than Group A. This is true even though the odds are greater that a particular act was committed by a member of Group A, since Group A has more members. The problem is that infrequent events stick together in memory. Membership in the less frequent group and the occurrence of less frequent behaviors form an illusory correlation. One obvious consequence is that we remember anything unusual done by the member of a minority group better than we remember anything unusual done by a member of a majority group.

Illusory correlation due to "paired distinctiveness" (two unusual events being linked in our minds) may occur because when we first encounter distinctive experiences, we think more about them, processing them more deeply so that they are more accessible in memory later (Johnson &

Mullen, 1994). If we encounter, for example, members of a minority we don't see often, or negative acts that we rarely see or hear about, we really think about them. If they are paired, we study them both and they are quicker to return to memory. It also seems that we can continue to process information about groups, people, and their behaviors without any awareness of doing so. Sometime along the way, or when we go to make a judgment, we overassociate the unusual groups or people with the unusual (negative) behaviors (McConnell et al., 1994). This effect is stronger when information about the groups or people is sparse, as if we try even harder in ambiguous situations to make sense of what we have seen (Berndsen et al., 2001).

Indeed, observing a single instance of a rare group showing some unusual behavior, a "one-shot illusory correlation," is sufficient to create the effect (Risen et al., 2007).

Most illusory correlations, however, occur simply because of prejudices. Prejudices are implicit, erroneous theories that we carry around with us. For example, we estimate that we have seen more support for an association between two social traits than we have actually seen:

driving skills and a particular age group; level of academic achievement and a specific ethnic group; certain speech, dress, or social behaviors and residence in some region of the country. One especially interesting example is that most people in business believe that job satisfaction and job performance are closely linked, when in fact the correlation is quite low. People who do not like their jobs can still put in a good day's work; people who rave about their job can still be lazy about doing it.

By the way, some people form their implicit theories impulsively and hold them rigidly; others seem to base them according to what they remember about people and change their theories as they have new experiences (McConnell, 2001). Which are you?

The point is, the next time you ask yourself why you are struggling to learn statistics, it might help to think of it as a quest to make ordinary thought processes more moral and fair. So, again, we assert that statistics can be downright romantic: it can be about conquering dark, evil mistakes with the pure light of numbers, subduing the lie of prejudices with the honesty of data.

Unreliability of Measurement

Suppose the number of hours slept and mood the next day have a very high degree of correlation. However, suppose also that in a particular study the researcher had asked people about their sleep on a particular night three weeks ago and about their mood on the day after that particular night. There are many problems with this kind of study, but one is that the measurement of hours slept and mood would not be very accurate. For example, what a person recalls about how many hours were slept on a particular night three weeks ago is probably not very close to how many hours the person actually slept. Thus, the true correlation between sleep and mood could be high, but the correlation in the particular study might be quite low, just because there is lots of "random noise" (random inaccuracy) in the scores.

Here is another way to understand this issue: think of a correlation in terms of how close the dots in the scatter diagram fall to a straight line. One of the reasons why dots may not fall close to the line is inaccurate measurement.

Consider another example. Height and social power have been found in many studies to have a moderate degree of correlation. However, if someone were to do this study and measure each person's height using an elastic measuring tape, the correlation would be much lower. Some other examples of not fully accurate measurement are personality questionnaires that include items that are difficult to understand (or are understood differently by different people), ratings of behavior (such as children's play activity) that require some subjective judgment, or physiological measures that are influenced by things like ambient magnetic fields.

Often in psychology research our measures are not perfectly accurate or *reliable* (this idea is discussed in more detail in Chapter 15). The result is that a correlation between any two variables is lower than it would be if you had perfect measures of the two variables.

The reduction in a correlation due to unreliability of measures is called *attenuation.* More advanced statistics texts and psychological measurement texts describe formulas for *correction for attenuation* that can be used under some conditions. However, studies using such procedures are relatively rare in most areas of psychology research.

The main thing to remember from all of this is that, to the extent the measures used in a study are less than perfectly accurate, the correlations reported in that study usually underestimate the true correlation between the variables (the correlation that would be found if there was perfect measurement).

Influence of Outliers

The direction and strength of a correlation can be drastically distorted by one or more individual's scores on the two variables if each pair of scores is a very unusual combination. For example, suppose in the sleep and mood example that an additional person was added to the study who had not slept at all (0 hours sleep) and yet was extremely happy the next day (8 on the happiness scale). (Maybe the person was going through some sort of manic phase!) We have shown this situation in the scatter diagram in Figure 11–17. It turns out that the correlation, which without this added person was a *large positive correlation* ($r = .85$), now becomes a *small to moderate negative correlation* ($r = -.18$)!

As we mentioned in Chapter 2, extreme scores are called **outliers** (they lie outside of the usual range of scores, a little like "outlaws"). Outliers are actually a problem in most kinds of statistical analyses and we will have more to say about them in Chapter 14. However, the main point for now is this: if the scatter diagram shows one or more unusual combinations, you need to be aware that these individuals have an especially large influence on the correlation.

outliers scores with an extreme (very high or very low) value in relation to the other scores in the distribution.

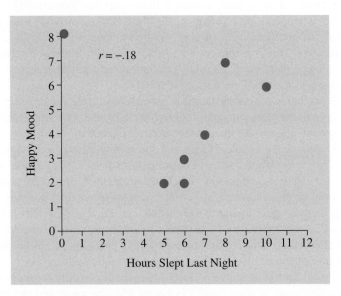

Figure 11–17 A scatter diagram for the hours slept last night and happy mood example (see Table 11–1 and Figure 11–2d) with an outlier combination of scores (0 hours slept and happy mood of 8) for an extra person (correlation is now $r = -.18$ compared to $r = .85$ without the extra person).

What If There Is Some Curvilinearity? The Spearman Rho

The correlation coefficient, as we have seen, describes the direction and strength of the *linear* relationship between two variables. It shows us how well the dots in a scatter diagram follow a straight line in which highs go with highs and lows go with lows (a positive correlation) or highs go with lows and lows with highs (a negative correlation). Sometimes however, as you saw earlier in the chapter, the pattern of dots follow a precise pattern, but that pattern is curved. For example, consider Figure 11–6b. In this example, highs go with highs, middle scores go with lows, and low scores go with highs. It is a kind of U shape. There are methods of figuring the degree to which the dots follow such a curved line; these procedures are considered in advanced textbooks (e.g., Cohen et al., 2003).

Sometimes however, as shown in Figure 11–5, highs go with highs and lows with lows, but the pattern is still not quite linear. In these particular kinds of situations we can in a sense straighten out the line and then use the ordinary correlation. One way this can be done is by changing all the scores to their rank order. So, separately for each variable, you would rank the scores from lowest to highest (starting with 1 for the lowest score and continuing until all the scores have been ranked). This makes the pattern more linear. In fact, we could now proceed to figure the correlation coefficient in the usual way, but using the rank-order scores instead of the original scores. A correlation figured in this way is called **Spearman's rho.** (It was developed in the 1920s by Charles Spearman, an important British psychologist who invented many statistical procedures to help him solve the problems he was working on, mainly involving the nature and measurement of human intelligence.)

We discuss changing scores to ranks more generally in Chapter 14, and consider Spearman's rho again in that context. We bring it up now, however, because in some areas of psychology it is common practice to use Spearman's rho instead of the ordinary correlation coefficient, even if the dots do not show curvilinearity. Some researchers prefer Spearman's rho because it works correctly even if the original scores are not based on true equal-interval measurement (as we discussed in Chapter 1). Finally, many researchers like to use Spearman's rho because it is much less affected by outliers.

Spearman's rho   the equivalent of a correlation coefficient for rank-ordered scores.

How are you doing?

1. (a) What numbers do psychologists use when they compare the size of two correlation coefficients? (b) What are these numbers called? (c) How much larger is a correlation of .80 than a correlation of .20?
2. (a) What is restriction in range? (b) What is its effect on the correlation coefficient?
3. (a) What is unreliability of measurement? (b) What is its effect on the correlation coefficient?
4. (a) What is the outlier combination of scores in the set of scores below? (b) Why are outliers a potential problem with regard to correlation?

X	Y
10	41
8	35
12	46
9	37
2	70

5. Give three reasons why a researcher might choose to use Spearman's rho instead of the regular correlation coefficient.

Answers

1. (a) When psychologists compare the size of two correlation coefficients, they use the correlation coefficients squared. (b) The correlation coefficient squared is called the proportionate reduction in error (or proportion of variance accounted for). (c) A correlation of .80 is 16 times larger than a correlation of .20 (for $r = .80$, $r^2 = .64$; for $r = .20$, $r^2 = .04$; and .64 is 16 times larger than .04).

2. (a) Restriction in range is a situation in correlation in which the scores of the group of people studied on one of the variables do not include the full range of scores that are found among people more generally. (b) The effect is often to drastically reduce the correlation compared to what it would be if people more generally were included in the study (presuming there would be a correlation among people more generally).

3. (a) Unreliability of measurement is when the procedures used to measure a particular variable are not perfectly accurate. (b) The effect is to make the correlation smaller than it would be if perfectly accurate measures were used (presuming there would be a correlation if perfectly accurate measures were used).

4. (a) The outlier combination of scores is the final pair of scores ($X = 2$ and $Y = 70$). The other four pairs of scores all suggest a positive correlation between variables X and Y, but the final pair of scores is a very low score for variable X and a very high score for variable Y. (b) Outliers have a larger effect on the correlation than other combinations of scores.

5. First, Spearman's rho can be used in certain situations when the scatter diagram suggests a curvilinear relationship between two variables. Second, Spearman's rho can be used in certain situations to figure a correlation when the original scores are not based on true equal-interval measurement. Finally, Spearman's rho is less affected by outliers than the regular correlation coefficient.

Effect Size and Power for the Correlation Coefficient

The correlation coefficient itself is a measure of effect size. (Thus, in the study of sleep and mood, effect size was $r = .85$.) Cohen's (1988) conventions for the correlation coefficient are .10 for a small effect size, .30 for a medium (or moderate) effect size, and .50 for a large effect size.

Power for a correlation can be determined using a power table, a power software package, or an Internet power calculator. Table 11–7 gives the approximate power for the .05 significance level for small, medium, and large correlations, and one-tailed or two-tailed tests.[3] For example, the power for a study with an expected medium effect size ($r = .30$), two-tailed, with 50 participants, is .57 (which is below the standard desired level of at least .80 power). This means that even if the research hypothesis is in fact true and has a medium effect size (that is, the two variables are correlated at $r = .30$ in the population), there is only a 57% chance that the study will produce a significant correlation.

Planning Sample Size

Table 11–8 gives the approximate number of participants needed for 80% power for estimated small, medium, and large correlations, using one-tailed and two-tailed tests, all using the .05 significance level.[4]

Table 11-7 Approximate Power of Studies Using the Correlation Coefficient (r) for Testing Hypotheses at the .05 Level of Significance

		Effect Size		
		Small ($r = .10$)	**Medium** ($r = .30$)	**Large** ($r = .50$)
Two-tailed				
Total N:	10	.06	.13	.33
	20	.07	.25	.64
	30	.08	.37	.83
	40	.09	.48	.92
	50	.11	.57	.97
	100	.17	.86	*
One-tailed				
Total N:	10	.08	.22	.46
	20	.11	.37	.75
	30	.13	.50	.90
	40	.15	.60	.96
	50	.17	.69	.98
	100	.26	.92	*

*Power is nearly 1.

Table 11-8 Approximate Number of Participants Needed for 80% Power for a Study Using the Correlation Coefficient (r) for Testing a Hypothesis at the .05 Significance Level

	Effect Size		
	Small ($r = .10$)	**Medium** ($r = .30$)	**Large** ($r = .50$)
Two-tailed	783	85	28
One-tailed	617	68	22

How are you doing?

1. What are the conventions for effect size for correlation coefficients?
2. What is the power of a study using a correlation, with a two-tailed test at the .05 significance level, in which the researchers predict a large effect size and there are 50 participants?
3. How many participants do you need for 80% power in a planned study in which you predict a small effect size and will be using a correlation, two-tailed, at the .05 significance level?

Answers

1. The conventions for effect size and correlation coefficients: $r = .10$, small effect size; $r = .30$, medium effect size; $r = .50$, large effect size.
2. Power is .97.
3. The number of participants needed is 783.

Controversy: What Is a Large Correlation?

An ongoing controversy about the correlation coefficient is, "What is a large *r*?" Traditionally in psychology, a large correlation is considered to be about .50 or above, a moderate correlation to be about .30, and a small correlation to be about .10 (Cohen, 1988). In fact, in many areas of psychology it is rare to find correlations that are greater than .40. Even when we are confident that *X* causes *Y*, *X* will not be the *only* cause of *Y*. For example, doing exciting activities together may cause people to be happier in their marriage. (In fact, we have done a number of true experiments supporting this direction of causality; Aron et al., 2000.) However, exciting activities is still only one of a great many factors that affect marital satisfaction. All those other factors are not part of our correlation. No one correlation could possibly tell the whole story. Small correlations are also due to the unavoidably low reliability of many measures in psychology.

It is traditional to caution that a low correlation is not very important even if it is statistically significant. (A small correlation can be statistically significant if the study includes a very large number of participants.)

Further, even experienced research psychologists tend to treat any particular size of correlation as meaning more of an association between two variables than it actually does. Michael Oakes (1982) at the University of Sussex gave 30 research psychologists the two columns of numbers shown in Table 11–9. He then asked them to estimate *r* (without doing any calculations). What is your guess? The intuitions of the British researchers (who are as a group at least as well trained in statistics as psychologists anywhere in the world) ranged from −.20 to +.60, with a mean of .24. You can figure the true correlation for yourself. It comes out to .50! That is, what psychologists think a correlation of .50 means in the abstract is a much stronger degree of correlation than what they think when they see the actual numbers (which even at *r* = .50 only *look* like .24).

Oakes (1982) gave a different group of 30 researchers just the *X* column and asked them to fill in numbers in the *Y* column that would come out to a correlation of .50 (again, just using their intuition and without any figuring). When Oakes figured the actual correlations from their answers, these correlations averaged .68. In other words, once again, even experienced researchers think of a correlation coefficient as meaning more linkage between the two variables than it actually does.

In contrast, other psychologists hold that small correlations can be very important theoretically. They also can have major practical implications in that small effects may accumulate over time (Prentice & Miller, 1992).

To demonstrate the practical importance of small correlations, Rosnow and Rosenthal (1989) give an example of a now famous study (Steering Committee of the Physicians' Health Study Research Group, 1988) in which doctors either did or did not take aspirin each day. Whether or not they took aspirin each day was then correlated with heart attacks. The results were that taking aspirin was correlated −.034 with heart attacks.[5] This means that taking aspirin explains only .1% ($r^2 = -034 \times -034 = .001$, which is .1%) of the variation in whether people get heart attacks. So taking aspirin is only a small part of what affects people getting heart attacks; 99.9% of the variation in whether people get heart attacks is due to other factors (diet, exercise, genetic factors, etc.). However, Rosnow and Rosenthal point out that this correlation of "only −.034" meant that among the more than 20,000 doctors who were in the study, there were 72 more heart attacks in the group that did not take aspirin. (In fact, there were also 13 more heart attack deaths in the group that did not take aspirin.) Certainly, this difference in getting heart attacks is a difference we care about.

Table 11–9 Table Presented to 30 Psychologists to Estimate *r*

X	Y
1	1
2	10
3	2
4	9
5	5
6	4
7	6
8	3
9	11
10	8
11	7
12	12

Source: Based on Oakes (1982).

Another argument for the importance of small correlations emphasizes research methods. Prentice and Miller (1992) explain:

> Showing that an effect holds even under the most unlikely circumstances possible can be as impressive as (or in some cases, perhaps even more impressive) than showing that it accounts for a great deal of variance. (p. 163)

Some examples they give are studies showing correlations between attractiveness and judgments of guilt or innocence in court cases (e.g., Sigall & Ostrove, 1975). The point is that "legal judgments are supposed to be unaffected by such extraneous factors as attractiveness." Thus, if studies show that attractiveness is associated with legal judgments even slightly, we are persuaded of just how important attractiveness could be in influencing social judgments in general.

Finally, you should be aware that there is even controversy about the widespread use of Cohen's (1988) conventions for the correlation coefficient (that is, .10 for a small effect size, .30 for a medium effect size, and .50 for a large effect size). When proposing conventions for effect size estimates, such as the correlation coefficient (r), Cohen himself noted: ". . . these proposed conventions were set forth throughout with much diffidence, qualifications, and invitations not to employ them if possible. The values chosen had no more a reliable basis than my own intuition. They were offered as conventions because they were needed in a research climate characterized by a neglect of issues of [effect size] magnitude" (p. 532). Thus, some researchers strongly suggest that the magnitude of effects found in research studies should not be compared with Cohen's conventions, but rather with the effects reported in previous similar research studies (Thompson, 2007).

Correlation in Research Articles

Scatter diagrams are occasionally included in research articles. For example, Gump and colleagues (2007) conducted a study of the level of lead in children's blood and the socioeconomic status of their family. The participants were 122 children who were taking part in an ongoing study of the developmental effects of environmental toxicants. Between the age of 2 and 3 years, a blood sample was taken from each child (with parental permission), and the amount of lead in each sample was determined with a laboratory test. The researchers measured the socioeconomic status of each child's family based on the parents' self-reported occupation and education level. As shown in Figure 11–18 Gump et al. (2007) used a scatter diagram to describe the relationship between childhood blood levels and family socioeconomic status. There was a clear linear negative trend, with the researchers noting ". . . increasing family SES [socioeconomic status] was significantly associated with declining blood levels" (p. 300). The scatter diagram shows that children from families with a higher socioeconomic status had lower levels of lead in their blood. Of course, this is a correlational result; so it does not necessarily mean that family socioeconomic status directly influences the amount of lead in children's blood. It is possible that some other factor may explain this association, such as a person's level of education.

Correlation coefficients are very commonly reported in research articles, both in the text of articles and in tables. The result with which we started the chapter would be described as follows: there was a positive correlation ($r = .51$) between excitement of activities done with partner and marital satisfaction. Usually, the statistical significance of the correlation will also be reported; in this example, it would be $r = .51$, $p < .05$.

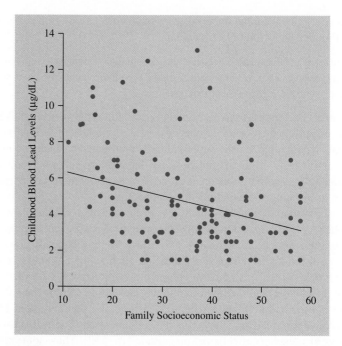

Figure 11–18 Children's family socioeconomic status (Hollingshead Index) as a function of childhood lead levels.

Source: Gump, B. B., Reihman, J., Stewart, P., Lonky, E., Darvill, T., & Matthews, K. A. (2007). Blood lead (Pb) levels: A potential environmental mechanism explaining the relation between socioeconomic status and cardiovascular reactivity in children. *Health Psychology, 26,* 296–304. Published by the American Psychological Association. Reprinted with permission.

correlation matrix common way of reporting the correlation coefficients among several variables in a research article; table in which the variables are named on the top and along the side and the correlations among them are all shown.

Tables of correlations are common when several variables are involved. Usually, the table is set up so that each variable is listed down the left and also across the top. The correlation of each pair of variables is shown inside the table. This is called a **correlation matrix.**

Table 11–10 is a correlation matrix from a study of 114 expert Scrabble players (Halpern & Wai, 2007). (You may remember that we first mentioned this study in

Table 11–10 Correlations with Official Scrabble Ratings (Experts Only)

Variable	1	2	3	4	5	6	7	8	9
1. Official Scrabble rating	—	−.178	.116	−.173	−.202*	.021	−.128	.227*	.224*
2. Gender		—	.318*	.094	.265*	.104	−.181	.220*	.242*
3. Current age			—	.167	.727**	.088	−.094	.769**	.515**
4. Age started playing Scrabble				—	.355*	.233*	.094	−.501**	.058
5. Age started competing					—	.096	.112	.386*	.121
6. Days of year playing Scrabble						—	.050	−.093	−.196
7. Hours per day playing Scrabble							—	−.134	.377*
8. Years of practice								—	.492**
9. Total hours playing (Years × Hours)									—

*$p < .05$. **$p < .01$.

Source: Halpern, D. F., & Wai, J. (2007). The world of competitive Scrabble: Novice and expert differences in visiospatial and verbal abilities. *Journal of Experimental Psychology: Applied, 13,* 79–94. Published by the American Psychological Association. Reprinted with permission.

Chapter 4.) The researchers asked the expert Scrabble players a series of questions about their Scrabble playing, including the age at which they started playing and the age at which they started competing, the number of days a year and the number of hours per day they play Scrabble, and the number of years they had been practicing. The expert Scrabble players also provided their official Scrabble rating to the researchers. Table 11–10 shows the correlations among all the study measures.

This example shows several features that are typical of the way correlation matrixes are laid out. First, notice that the correlation of a variable with itself is not given. In this example, a short line is put in instead; sometimes they are just left blank. Also notice that only the upper triangle is filled in. This is because the lower left triangle would contain exactly the same information. For example, the correlation of official Scrabble rating with current age (which is .116) has to be the same as the correlation of current age with official Scrabble rating. Another shortcut saves space across the page: the names of the variables are listed only on the side of the table, with the numbers for them put across the top.

Looking at this example, among other results, you can see that there is a small to moderate negative correlation between official Scrabble rating and the age at which a person started competing in Scrabble. Also, there is a small to moderate correlation between official Scrabble rating and the years of practice. The asterisks—* and **— after some of the correlation coefficients tell you that those correlations are statistically significant. The note at the bottom of the table tells you the significance levels associated with the asterisks.

Summary

1. When two variables are associated in a clear pattern (for example, when high scores on one consistently go with high scores on the other, and lows on one go with lows on the other) the two variables are correlated.
2. A scatter diagram shows the relation between two variables. The lowest to highest possible values of one variable (the one you are predicting from if one variable can be thought of as predicting the other variable) are marked on the horizontal axis. The lowest to highest possible values of the other variable are marked on the vertical axis. Each individual's pair of scores is shown as a dot.
3. When the dots in the scatter diagram generally follow a straight line, this is called a linear correlation. In a curvilinear correlation, the dots follow a line pattern other than a simple straight line. There is no correlation when the dots do not follow any kind of line. In a positive linear correlation, the line goes upward to the right (so that low scores go with lows, mediums with mediums, and highs with highs). In a negative linear correlation, the line goes downward to the right (so that low scores go with highs, mediums with mediums, and highs with lows). The strength of the correlation refers to the degree to which there is a clear pattern of relationship between the two variables.
4. The correlation coefficient (r) gives the precise linear correlation between two equal-interval numeric variables. The correlation coefficient is the product of the deviation scores ($X - M_X$ and $Y - M_Y$) divided by a correction number that takes into account the number of people in the study and the variation of each variable's scores. The correction number is figured as the square root of the result of multiplying the sum of squared deviations for one variable (SS_X) by the sum of squared deviations for the other variable (SS_Y). The correlation coefficient is highly positive when there is a large positive linear correlation. This is

because positive deviation scores are multiplied by positive, and negative by negative (giving all positive products of deviation scores). The correlation coefficient is highly negative when there is a large negative linear correlation. This is because negative deviation scores are multiplied by positive deviation scores and positive by negative (giving all negative products of deviation scores). The correlation coefficient is 0 when there is no linear correlation. This is because positives are sometimes multiplied by positives and sometimes by negatives (and vice versa), so that positive and negative products of deviation scores cancel each other out.

5. The sign (+ or −) of a correlation coefficient tells you the *direction* of the linear correlation between two variables. The actual value of the correlation coefficient (ignoring the sign) tells you the *strength* of the linear correlation. The maximum positive value of r is $+1$. $r = +1$ when there is a perfect positive linear correlation. The maximum negative value of r is -1. $r = -1$ when there is a perfect negative linear correlation.

6. The statistical significance of a correlation coefficient can be tested by changing the correlation coefficient into a t score and using cutoffs on a t distribution with degrees of freedom equal to the number of people in the study minus two. The t score for a correlation coefficient is the result of dividing the correlation coefficient by the square root of what you get when you divide one minus the correlation coefficient squared by two less than the number of people in the study. The null hypothesis for hypothesis testing with a correlation coefficient is that the true relation between the two variables in the population is no correlation ($r = 0$).

7. The assumptions for the significance test of a correlation coefficient are that the population of each variable (and the relationship between them) follows a normal distribution, and that there is an equal distribution of each variable at each point of the other variable.

8. Correlation does not tell you the direction of causation. If two variables, X and Y, are correlated, the correlation could be because X is causing Y, Y is causing X, or a third factor is causing both X and Y.

9. Comparisons of the degree of linear correlation are considered most accurate in terms of the correlation coefficient squared (r^2), called the proportionate reduction in error or proportion of variance accounted for.

10. A correlation coefficient will be lower (closer to 0) than the true correlation if it is based on scores from a group selected for study that is restricted in its range of scores (compared to people in general) or if the scores are based on unreliable measures.

11. The direction and strength of a correlation can be drastically distorted by extreme combinations of scores called outliers.

12. Spearman's rho is a special type of correlation based on rank-order scores. It can be used in certain situations when the scatter diagram suggests a curvilinear relationship between two variables. Spearman's rho is less affected than the regular correlation by outliers, and it works correctly even if the original scores are not based on true equal-interval measurement.

13. The correlation itself is a measure of effect size. Power and needed sample size for 80% power for a correlation coefficient can be determined using special power tables, a power software package, or an Internet power calculator.

14. Studies suggest that psychologists tend to think of any particular correlation coefficient as meaning more association than actually exists. However, small

correlations may have practical importance and may also be impressive in demonstrating the importance of a relationship when a study shows that the correlation holds even under what would seem to be unlikely conditions.

15. Correlational results are usually presented in research articles either in the text with the value of r (and usually the significance level) or in a special table (a correlation matrix) showing the correlations among several variables.

Key Terms

correlation (p. 433)
scatter diagram (p. 434)
linear correlation (p. 437)
curvilinear correlation (p. 437)
no correlation (p. 439)
positive correlation (p. 439)

negative correlation (p. 439)
product of deviation scores (p. 443)
correlation coefficient (p. 446)
direction of causality (p. 456)
correlational research
    design (p. 458)

proportionate reduction in
    error (p. 459)
restriction in range (p. 459)
outliers (p. 462)
Spearman's rho (p. 463)
correlation matrix (p. 468)

Example Worked-Out Problems

Making a Scatter Diagram and Describing the General Pattern of Association

Based on the class size and average achievement test scores for five elementary schools in the following table, make a scatter diagram and describe in words the general pattern of association.

Elementary School	Class Size	Achievement Test Score
Main Street	25	80
Casat	14	98
Harland	33	50
Shady Grove	28	82
Jefferson	20	90

Answer

The steps in solving the problem follow; Figure 11–19 shows the scatter diagram with markers for each step.

❶ **Draw the axes and decide which variable goes on which axis.** It seems more reasonable to think of class size as predicting achievement test scores rather than the other way around. Thus, you can draw the axis with class size along the bottom. (However, the prediction was not explicitly stated in the problem; so the other direction of prediction is certainly possible. Thus, putting either variable on either axis would be acceptable.)

❷ **Determine the range of values to use for each variable and mark them on the axes.** We will assume that the achievement test scores go from 0 to 100. We don't know the maximum class size; so we guessed 50. (The range of the variables

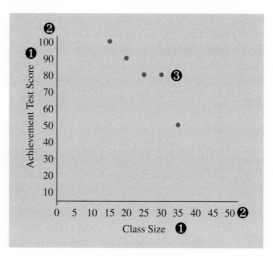

Figure 11–19 Scatter diagram for scores in Example Worked-Out Problem. ❶ Draw the axes and decide which variable goes on which axis. ❷ Determine the range of values to use for each variable and mark them on the axes. ❸ Mark a dot for each pair of scores.

was not given in the problem; thus any reasonable range would be acceptable as long as it includes the values of the scores in the actual study.)

❸ **Mark a dot for each pair of scores.** For example, to mark the dot for Main Street School, you go across to 25 and up to 80.

The general pattern is roughly linear. Its direction is negative (it goes down and to the right, with larger class sizes going with smaller achievement scores and vice versa). It is a quite large correlation, since the dots all fall fairly close to a straight line; it should be fairly close to –1. In words, it is a large, linear, negative correlation.

Figuring the Correlation Coefficient

Figure the correlation coefficient for the class size and achievement test in the preceding example.

Answer

You can figure the correlation using either the formula or the steps. The basic figuring is shown in Table 11–11 with markers for each of the steps.

Using the formula,

$$r = \frac{\sum[(X-M_X)(Y-M_Y)]}{\sqrt{(SS_X)(SS_Y)}} = \frac{-482}{533.10} = -.90$$

Using the steps,

❶ **Change the scores for each variable to deviation scores.** The mean of the class size is 24. Thus, the first class size score of 25 gives a deviation score of $25 - 24 = 1$. Using the same procedure for all the other scores gives the deviation scores shown in the $X - M_X$ and $Y - M_Y$ columns in Table 11–11.

❷ **Figure the product of the deviation scores for each pair of scores.** For the first school, multiply 1 by 0 to give 0. The products of deviation scores for all the scores are shown in the last column of Table 11–11.

Table 11–11 Figuring the Correlation Coefficient Between Class Size and Achievement Test Score for the Example Worked-Out Problem

Class Size (X)			Achievement Test Score (Y)			Products of ❷ Deviation Scores
Deviation ❶	Deviation Squared ❹		Deviation ❶		Deviation Squared ❹	
X	$X - M_X$	$(X - M_X)^2$	Y	$Y - M_Y$	$(Y - M_Y)^2$	$(X - M_X)(Y - M_Y)$
25	1	1	80	0	0	0
14	−10	100	98	18	324	−180
33	9	81	50	−30	900	−270
28	4	16	82	2	4	8
20	−4	16	90	10	100	−40
$\Sigma = 120$		$\Sigma = SS_X = 214$ ❺	$\Sigma = 400$		$\Sigma = SS_Y = 1328$ ❺	$\Sigma = -482$ ❸
$M = 24$			$M = 80$			

$$r = \frac{\Sigma[(X - M_X)(Y - M_Y)]}{\sqrt{(SS_X)(SS_Y)}} = \frac{-482}{\sqrt{(214)(1328)}} = \frac{-482}{533.10} = -.90 \; ❼$$
❻

❸ **Add up all the products of the deviation scores.** Adding up all the products of the deviation scores, as shown in Table 11–11, gives a sum of −482.

❹ **For each variable, square each deviation score.** For the first school, the squared deviation for the class size variable is 1 multiplied by 1, which is 1. The squared deviation scores for all the scores are shown in the $(X - M_X)^2$ and $(Y - M_Y)^2$ columns of Table 11–11.

❺ **Add up the squared deviation scores for each variable.** As shown in Table 11–11, the sum of squared deviations for the class size variable is 214 and the sum of squared deviations for the achievement test score variable is 1,328.

❻ **Multiply the two sums of squared deviations and take the square root of the result.** Multiplying 214 by 1,328 is 284,192 and the square root of 284,192 is 533.10.

❼ **Divide the sum of the products of deviation scores from Step ❸ by the correction number from Step ❻.** Dividing −482 by 533.10 gives a result of −.90. This is the correlation coefficient.

Figuring the Significance of a Correlation Coefficient

Figure whether the correlation between class size and achievement test score in the preceding example is statistically significant (use the .05 level, two-tailed).

Answer

❶ **Restate the question as a research hypothesis and a null hypothesis about the populations.** There are two populations:

Population 1: Schools like those in this study.
Population 2: Schools for whom there is no correlation between the two variables.

The null hypothesis is that the two populations have the same correlation. The research hypothesis is that the two populations do not have the same correlation.

❷ **Determine the characteristics of the comparison distribution.** The comparison distribution is a *t* distribution with $df = 3$. (That is, $df = N - 2 = 5 - 2 = 3$.)

❸ **Determine the cutoff sample score on the comparison distribution at which the null hypothesis should be rejected.** The *t* table (Table A–2 in the Appendix) shows that for a two-tailed test at the .05 level, with 3 degrees of freedom, the cutoff *t* scores are 3.182 and −3.182.

❹ **Determine your sample's score on the comparison distribution.** The correlation in the study was –.90. Applying the formula to find the equivalent *t*, we get

$$t = \frac{r}{\sqrt{(1 - r^2)/(N-2)}} = \frac{-.90}{\sqrt{(1 - (-.90^2))/(3)}} = \frac{-.90}{\sqrt{.0633}} = -3.58.$$

❺ **Decide whether to reject the null hypothesis.** The *t* score of −3.58 for our sample correlation is more extreme than a cutoff *t* score of −3.182. Thus, we can reject the null hypothesis and the research hypothesis is supported.

Outline for Writing Essays on the Logic and Figuring of a Correlation Coefficient

1. If the question involves creating a scatter diagram, explain how and why you created the diagram to show the pattern of relationship between the two variables. Explain the meaning of the term *correlation*. Mention the type of correlation (e.g., linear; positive or negative; small, moderate, or large) shown by the scatter diagram.

2. Explain the idea that a correlation coefficient tells you the direction and strength of linear correlation between two variables.

3. Outline and explain the steps for figuring the correlation coefficient. Be sure to mention that the first step involves changing the scores for each variable to deviation scores. Describe how to figure the product of the deviation scores. Explain why the product of deviation scores will tend to be positive if the correlation is positive and will tend to be negative if the correlation is negative. Explain the two reasons why it is necessary to use a correction number to adjust the sum of the products of deviation scores. Describe how that correction number is figured and how it acts to adjust the sum of the products of deviation scores. Explain what the value of the correlation coefficient means in terms of the direction and strength of linear correlation.

4. Be sure to discuss the direction and strength of correlation of your particular result. As needed for the specific question you are answering, discuss whether the correlation is statistically significant.

Practice Problems

These problems involve figuring. Most real-life statistics problems are done on a computer with special statistical software. Even if you have such software, do these problems by hand to ingrain the method in your mind. To learn how to use a computer to solve statistics problems like those in this chapter, refer to the Using SPSS section at the end of this chapter and the *Study Guide and Computer Workbook* that accompanies this text.

All data are fictional unless an actual citation is given.

Set I (for Answers to Set I Problems, see pp. 690–692)

1. For each of the following scatter diagrams, indicate whether the pattern is linear, curvilinear, or no correlation; if it is linear, indicate whether it is positive or negative and the approximate strength (large, moderate, small) of the correlation.

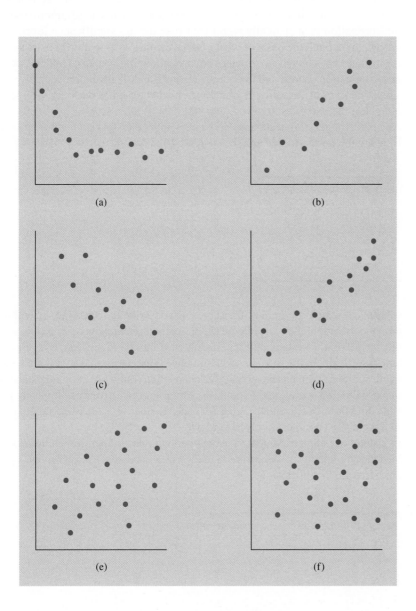

2. A researcher studied the relation between psychotherapists' degree of empathy and their patients' satisfaction with therapy. As a pilot study, four patient–therapist pairs were studied. Here are the results:

Pair Number	Therapist Empathy	Patient Satisfaction
1	70	4
2	94	5
3	36	2
4	48	1

(a) Make a scatter diagram of the scores; (b) describe in words the general pattern of correlation, if any; (c) figure the correlation coefficient; (d) figure whether the correlation is statistically significant (use the .05 significance level, two-tailed); (e) explain the logic of what you have done, writing as if you are speaking to someone who has never heard of correlation (but who does understand the mean, deviation scores, and hypothesis testing); and (f) give three logically possible directions of causality, saying for each whether it is a reasonable direction in light of the variables involved (and why).

3. An instructor asked five students how many hours they had studied for an exam. Here are the hours studied and the students' grades:

Hours Studied	Test Grade
0	52
10	95
6	83
8	71
6	64

(a) Make a scatter diagram of the scores; (b) describe in words the general pattern of correlation, if any; (c) figure the correlation coefficient; (d) figure whether the correlation is statistically significant (use the .05 significance level, two-tailed); (e) explain the logic of what you have done, writing as if you are speaking to someone who has never heard of correlation (but who does understand the mean, deviation scores, and hypothesis testing); and (f) give three logically possible directions of causality, saying for each whether it is a reasonable direction in light of the variables involved (and why).

4. In a study of people first getting acquainted with each other, researchers examined the amount of self-disclosure of one's partner and one's liking for one's partner. Here are the results:

Partner's Self-Disclosure	Liking for Partner
8	7
7	9
10	6
3	7
1	4

(a) Make a scatter diagram of the scores; (b) describe in words the general pattern of correlation, if any; (c) figure the correlation coefficient; and (d) figure whether the correlation is statistically significant (use the .05 significance level, two-tailed).

5. The following have been prepared so that data sets B through D are slightly modified versions of data set A. For each data set, (a) make a scatter diagram, (b) figure the correlation coefficient, and (c) figure whether the correlation is statistically significant (use the .05 significance level, two-tailed).

Data Set A	Data Set B	Data Set C	Data Set D
X Y	X Y	X Y	X Y
1 1	1 1	1 5	1 1
2 2	2 2	2 2	2 4
3 3	3 3	3 3	3 3
4 4	4 5	4 4	4 2
5 5	5 4	5 1	5 5

6. For each of the following situations, indicate why the correlation coefficient might be a distorted estimate of the true correlation (and what kind of distortion you would expect):
   (a) Scores on two questionnaire measures of personality are correlated.
   (b) Comfort of living situation and happiness are correlated among a group of millionaires.

7. What is the power of each of the following studies using a correlation coefficient and the .05 significance level?

	Effect Size (r)	N	Tails
(a)	.10	50	2
(b)	.30	100	1
(c)	.50	30	2
(d)	.30	40	1
(e)	.10	100	2

8. About how many participants are needed for 80% power in each of the following planned studies that will use a correlation coefficient and the .05 significance level?

	Effect Size (r)	Tails
(a)	.50	2
(b)	.30	1
(c)	.10	2

9. Chapman et al. (1997) interviewed 68 inner city pregnant women and their husbands (or boyfriends) twice during their pregnancy, once between three and six months into the pregnancy and again between six and nine months into the pregnancy. Table 11–12 shows the correlations among several of their measures. ("Zero-Order Correlations" means the same thing as ordinary correlations.) Most important in this table are the correlations among women's reports of their own stress, men's reports of their partners' stress, women's perception of their partners' support at the first and at the second interviews, and women's depression at the first and at the second interviews.

Table 11-12 Zero-Order Correlations for Study Variables

Variable	1	2	3	4	5	6	7	8	9	10
1. Women's report of stress	—									
2. Men's report of women's stress	.17	—								
3. Partner Support 1	−.28*	−.18	—							
4. Partner Support 2	−.27*	−.18	.44***	—						
5. Depressed Mood 1	.23*	.10	−.34**	−.17	—					
6. Depressed Mood 2	.50***	.14	−.42***	−.41***	.55***	—				
7. Women's age	.06	.16	.04	−.24*	−.35*	−.09	—			
8. Women's ethnicity	−.19	−.09	−.16	−.14	.11	.13	−.02	—		
9. Women's marital status	−.18	.01	.12	.24*	−.04	−.20	.05	−.34**	—	
10. Parity	.19	.13	−.11	−.17	.10	.16	.26*	.31*	−.12	—

$*p < .05, **p < .01, ***p < .001.$

Source: Chapman, H. A., Hobfoll, S. E., & Ritter, C. (1997). Partners' stress underestimations lead to women's distress: A study of pregnant inner-city women. *Journal of Personality and Social Psychology, 73,* 418–425. Published by the American Psychological Association. Reprinted with permission.

Explain the results on these measures as if you were writing to a person who has never had a course in statistics. Specifically, (a) explain what is meant by a correlation coefficient using one of the correlations as an example; (b) study the table and then comment on the patterns of results in terms of which variables are relatively strongly correlated and which are not very strongly correlated; and (c) comment on the limitations of making conclusions about the direction of causality based on these data, using a specific correlation as an example (noting at least one plausible alternative causal direction and why that alternative is plausible).

Set II

10. For each of the following scatter diagrams, indicate whether the pattern is linear, curvilinear, or no correlation; if it is linear, indicate whether it is positive or negative and the approximate strength (large, moderate, small) of the correlation.

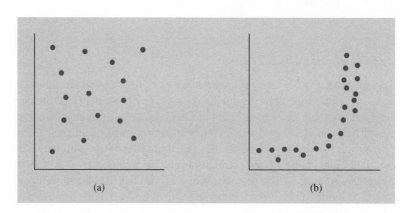

(a) (b)

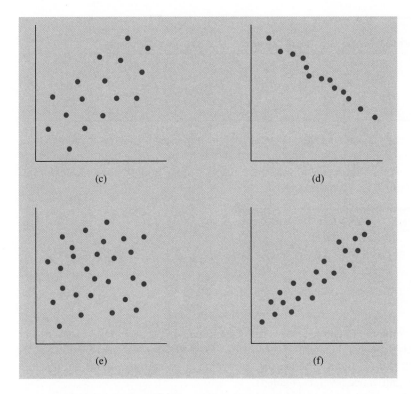

11. Make up a scatter diagram with 10 dots for each of the following situations: (a) perfect positive linear correlation, (b) large but not perfect positive linear correlation, (c) small positive linear correlation, (d) large but not perfect negative linear correlation, (e) no correlation, (f) clear curvilinear correlation.

  For problems 12 to 14, do the following: (a) Make a scatter diagram of the scores; (b) describe in words the general pattern of correlation, if any; (c) figure the correlation coefficient; (d) figure whether the correlation is statistically significant (use the .05 significance level, two-tailed); (e) explain the logic of what you have done, writing as if you are speaking to someone who has never heard of correlation (but who does understand the mean, deviation scores, and hypothesis testing); and (f) give three logically possible directions of causality, indicating for each direction whether it is a reasonable explanation for the correlation in light of the variables involved (and why).

12. Four research participants take a test of manual dexterity (high scores mean better dexterity) and an anxiety test (high scores mean more anxiety). The scores are as follows.

Person	Dexterity	Anxiety
1	1	10
2	1	8
3	2	4
4	4	−2

13. Four young children were monitored closely over a period of several weeks to measure how much they watched violent television programs and their amount of violent behavior toward their playmates. The results were as follows:

Child's Code Number	Weekly Viewing of Violent TV (hours)	Number of Violent or Aggressive Acts Toward Playmates
G3368	14	9
R8904	8	6
C9890	6	1
L8722	12	8

14. Five college students were asked about how important a goal it is to them to have a family and about how important a goal it is for them to be highly successful in their work. Each variable was measured on a scale from 0, *not at all important goal* to 10, *very important goal.*

Student	Family Goal	Work Goal
A	7	5
B	6	4
C	8	2
D	3	9
E	4	1

For problems 15 and 16, (a) make a scatter diagram of the scores; (b) describe in words the general pattern of correlation, if any; (c) figure the correlation coefficient; and (d) figure whether the correlation is statistically significant (use the .05 significance level, two-tailed).

15. The Louvre Museum is interested in the relation of the age of a painting to public interest in it. The number of people stopping to look at each of 10 randomly selected paintings is observed over a week. The results are as shown:

Painting Title	Approximate Age (Years) *X*	Number of People Stopping to Look *Y*
The Entombment	465	68
Mys Mar Sainte Catherine	515	71
The Bathers	240	123
The Toilette	107	112
Portrait of Castiglione	376	48
Charles I of England	355	84
Crispin and Scapin	140	66
Nude in the Sun	115	148
The Balcony	122	71
The Circus	99	91

16. A developmental psychologist studying people in their eighties was interested in the relation between number of very close friends and overall health. The scores for six research participants follow.

Research Participant	Number of Friends *X*	Overall Health *Y*
A	2	41
B	4	72
C	0	37
D	3	84
E	2	52
F	1	49

17. What is the power of each of the following studies using a correlation coefficient and the .05 significance level?

	Effect Size (*r*)	N	Tails
(a)	.10	30	1
(b)	.30	40	2
(c)	.50	50	2
(d)	.30	100	2
(e)	.10	20	1

18. About how many participants are needed for 80% power in each of the following planned studies that will use a correlation coefficient and the .05 significance level?

	Effect Size (*r*)	Tails
(a)	.10	1
(b)	.30	2
(c)	.50	1

19. As part of a larger study, Speed and Gangstead (1997) collected ratings and nominations on a number of characteristics for 66 fraternity men from their fellow fraternity members. The following paragraph is taken from their Results section:

> . . . men's romantic popularity significantly correlated with several characteristics: best dressed (*r* = .48), most physically attractive (*r* = .47), most outgoing (*r* = .47), most self-confident (*r* = .44), best trendsetters (*r* = .38), funniest (*r* = .37), most satisfied (*r* = .32), and most independent (*r* = .28). Unexpectedly, however, men's potential for financial success did not significantly correlate with romantic popularity (*r* = .10). (p. 931)

Explain these results as if you were writing to a person who has never had a course in statistics. Specifically, (a) explain what is meant by a correlation coefficient using one of the correlations as an example; (b) explain in a general way what is meant by "significantly" and "not significantly," referring to at least one specific example; and (c) speculate on the meaning of the pattern of results, taking into account the issue of direction of causality.

20. Gable and Lutz (2000) studied 65 children, 3 to 10 years old, and their parents. One of their results was "Parental control of child eating showed a negative association with children's participation in extracurricular activities (*r* = .34; *p* < .01)" (p. 296). Another result was "Parents who held less appropriate beliefs about children's nutrition reported that their children watched more hours of television per day (*r* = .36; *p* < .01)" (p. 296). Explain these results as if you were writing to a person who has never had a course in statistics. Be sure to comment on possible directions of causality for each result.

21. Table 11–13 is from a study by Baldwin and colleagues (2006) that examined the associations among feelings of shame, guilt, and self-efficacy in a sample of 194 college students. Self-efficacy refers to people's beliefs about their ability to be successful at various things they may try to do. (For example, the students indicated how much they agreed with statements such as, "When I make

Table 11-13 Correlations Among Shame, Guilt, and Self-Efficacy Subscales

	1	2	3	4	5
1. Shame					
2. Guilt	.34**				
3. General Self-efficacy	−.29**	.12			
4. Social Self-efficacy	−.18*	−.06	.47**		
5. Total Self-efficacy	−.29**	.07	.94**	.74**	

$*p < .01$, $**p < .001$. For all correlations, n is between 184 and 190.

Source: Baldwin, K. M., Baldwin, J. R., & Ewald, T. (2006). The relationship among shame, guilt, and self-efficacy. *American Journal of Psychotherapy, 60,* 1–21. Copyright © 2006 by The Association for the Advancement of Psychotherapy. Reprinted by permission of the publisher.

plans, I am certain I can make them work.") Table 11-13 shows the correlations among the questionnaire measures of shame, guilt, general self-efficacy, social self-efficacy, and total self-efficacy (general self-efficacy plus social self-efficacy).

Explain the results as if you were writing to a person who has never had a course in statistics. Specifically, (a) explain what is meant by a correlation coefficient using one of the correlations as an example; (b) study the table and then comment on the patterns of results in terms of which variables are relatively strongly correlated and which are not very strongly correlated; and (c) comment on the limitations of making conclusions about the direction of causality based on these data, using a specific correlation as an example (noting at least one plausible alternative causal direction and why that alternative is plausible).

22. Arbitrarily select eight people from your class. Do each of the following: (a) Make a scatter diagram for the relation between the number of letters in each person's first and last name; (b) figure the correlation coefficient for the relation between the number of letters in each person's first and last name; (c) figure whether the correlation is statistically significant (use the .05 significance level, two-tailed); (d) describe the result in words; and (e) suggest a possible interpretation for your results.

Using SPSS

The ✎ in the following steps indicates a mouse click. (We used SPSS version 15.0 for Windows to carry out these analyses. The steps and output may be slightly different for other versions of SPSS.)

In the following steps for the scatter diagram and correlation coefficient, we will use the example of the sleep and happy mood study. The scores for that study are shown in Table 11–1 on p. 435, the scatter diagram is shown in Figure 11–2 on p. 435, and the figuring for the correlation coefficient and its significance is shown in Table 11–3 on p. 449.

Creating a Scatter Diagram

❶ Enter the scores into SPSS. Enter the scores as shown in Figure 11–20.

❷ ✎ *Graphs.*

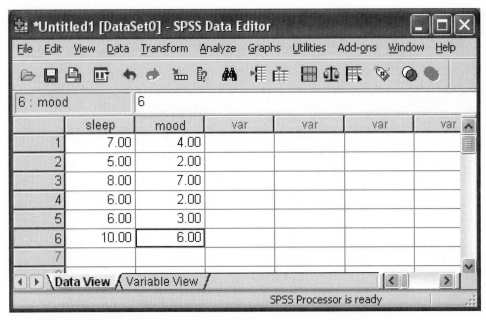

Figure 11–20 SPSS data editor window for the fictional study of the relationship between hours slept last night and mood.

❸ ✐ *Legacy/Dialogs,* ✐ *Scatter/Dot.* A box will appear that allows you to select different types of scatter diagrams. You want the "Simple Scatter" diagram. This is selected as the default type of diagram; so you just need to ✐ *Define.*

❹ ✐ the variable called "mood" and then ✐ the arrow next to the box labeled "Y axis." This tells SPSS that the scores for the "mood" variable should go on the vertical (or Y) axis of the scatter diagram. ✐ the variable called "sleep" and then ✐ the arrow next to the box labeled "X axis." This tells SPSS that the scores for the "sleep" variable should go on the horizontal (or X) axis of the scatter diagram.

❺ ✐ *OK.* Your SPSS output window should look like Figure 11–21.

Finding the Correlation Coefficient

❶ Enter the scores into SPSS. Enter the scores as shown in Figure 11–20.

❷ ✐ *Analyze.*

❸ ✐ *Correlate.*

❹ ✐ *Bivariate.*

❺ ✐ on the variable called "mood" and then ✐ the arrow next to the box labeled "Variables." ✐ on the variable called "sleep" and then ✐ the arrow next to the box labeled "Variables." This tells SPSS to figure the correlation between the "mood" and "sleep" variables. (If you wanted to find the correlation between each of several variables, you would put all of them into the "Variables" box.) Notice that by default SPSS carries out a Pearson correlation (the type of correlation you have learned in this chapter), gives the significance level using a two-tailed test, and flags statistically significant correlations using the .05 significance level. (Clicking the box next to "Spearman" requests Spearman's rho, which is a special type of correlation we briefly discussed earlier in the chapter.)

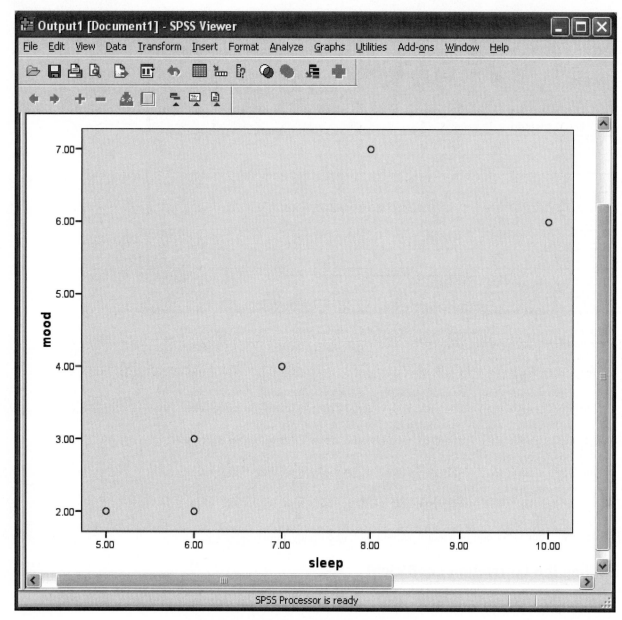

Figure 11–21 An SPSS scatter diagram showing the relationship between hours slept last night and mood (fictional data).

❻ ✎ *OK.* Your SPSS output window should look like Figure 11–22.

The table shown in Figure 11-22 is a small correlation matrix (there are only two variables). (If you were interested in the correlations among more than two variables—which is often the case in psychology research—SPSS would produce a larger correlation matrix.) The correlation matrix shows the correlation coefficient ("Pearson Correlation"), the exact significance level of the correlation coefficient ["Sig. (2-tailed)"], and the number of people in the correlation analysis ("N"). Note that two of the cells of the correlation matrix show a correlation coefficient of exactly 1. You can ignore these cells; they simply show that each variable is perfectly correlated with

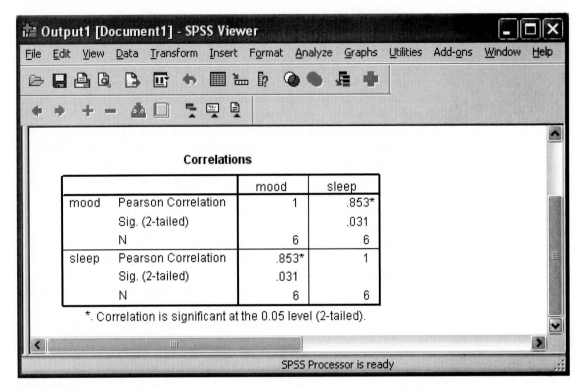

Figure 11–22   SPSS output window for the correlation between hours slept and mood (fictional data).

itself. (In larger correlation matrixes all of the cells on the diagonal from the top left to the bottom right of the table will have a correlation coefficient of 1.) You will also notice that the remaining two cells provide identical information. This is because the table shows the correlations between sleep and mood and also between mood and sleep (which are, of course, identical correlations). So you can look at either one. (In a larger correlation matrix, you need only look either at all of the correlations above the diagonal that goes from top left to bottom right or at all of the correlations below that diagonal.) The correlation coefficient is .853 (which is usually rounded to two decimal places in research articles). The significance level of .031 is less than our .05 cutoff, which means that it is a statistically significant correlation. The asterisk (*) by the correlation of .853 also shows that it is statistically significant (at the .05 significance level, as shown by the note under the table).

Chapter Notes

1. There is also a "computational" version of this formula that is mathematically equivalent and thus gives the same result:

$$r = \frac{N\sum(XY) - (\sum X)(\sum Y)}{\sqrt{[N\sum X^2 - (\sum X)^2]}\sqrt{[N\sum Y^2 - (\sum Y)^2]}}$$

This formula is easier to use when computing by hand (or with a hand calculator) when you have a large number of people in the study, because you don't have to first figure out all the deviation scores. However, researchers rarely use computational formulas like this any more because the actual figuring is done by a computer. As a student learning statistics, it is much better to use the definitional formula (11–1). This is because when solving problems using the definitional formula, you are strengthening your understanding of what the correlation coefficient means. In all examples in this chapter, we use the definitional formula and we urge you to use it in doing the chapter's practice problems.

2. As we noted in Chapter 3, statisticians usually use Greek letters to denote a population parameter. The population parameter for a correlation is ρ (rho). However, for ease of learning (and to avoid potential confusion with a term we introduce later in the chapter) we use the ordinary letter r for both the correlation you figure from a sample and the correlation in a population.

3. More complete tables are provided in Cohen (1988, pp. 84–95).

4. More complete tables are provided in Cohen (1988, pp. 101–102).

5. To figure the correlation between getting a heart attack and taking aspirin, you would have to make the two variables into numbers. For example, you could make getting a heart attack equal 1 and not getting a heart attack equal 0; similarly, you could make being in the aspirin group equal 1 and being in the control group equal 0. It would not matter which two numbers you used for the two values for each variable. Whichever two numbers you use, the result will come out the same after converting to deviation scores and using the correction number. The only difference that the two numbers you use makes is that the value that gets the higher number determines whether the correlation will be positive or negative.

CHAPTER 12

Prediction

Chapter Outline

- Predictor (*X*) and Criterion (*Y*) Variables   488
- The Linear Prediction Rule   488
- The Regression Line   492
- Finding the Best Linear Prediction Rule   496
- The Least Squared Error Principle   498
- Issues in Prediction   503
- Multiple Regression   506
- Limitations of Prediction   508
- Controversy: Unstandardized and Standardized Regression
- Coefficients; Comparing Predictors   509
- Prediction in Research Articles   511
- Advanced Topic: Error and Proportionate Reduction in Error   514
- Summary   518
- Key Terms   519
- Example Worked-Out Problems   519
- Practice Problems   524
- Using SPSS   532
- Chapter Notes   535

I n this chapter, building on what you learned in Chapter 11, we consider a major practical application of statistical methods: making predictions. Psychologists of various kinds are called on to make informed (and precise) guesses about such things as how well a particular job applicant is likely to perform if hired, how much a reading program is likely to help a particular third grader, how likely a particular patient is to commit suicide, or how likely a potential parolee is to commit a violent crime if released. Statistical prediction also plays a major part in helping research psychologists understand how various factors affect outcomes of interest. For example, what factors in people who marry predict whether they will be happy and together 10 years later; what are the factors in childhood that predict depression and anxiety in adulthood; what are the circumstances of learning something that predict

TIP FOR SUCCESS

Be sure you have fully mastered the material on correlation in Chapter 11 before reading this chapter.

good or poor memory for it years later; or what are the various kinds of support from friends and family that predict how quickly or poorly someone recovers from the death of a loved one? Finally, learning the intricacies of statistical prediction deepens your insight into other statistical topics and prepares you for central themes in more advanced statistics courses.

The main part of this chapter considers in some detail the logic and procedures for making predictions about one variable, such as predicting college grade point average (GPA), based on information about another variable, such as SAT scores. We then briefly introduce procedures for situations in which predictions about one variable, such as college GPA, are made based on information about two or more other variables, such as using both SAT scores and high school GPA. Finally, as an Advanced Topic, we discuss how to estimate the expected accuracy of the predictions we make using these procedures.

As you learn these new topics, you will find that they are closely linked with the topic of correlation we considered in the last chapter. That is because if two variables are correlated it means that you can predict one from the other. So if sleep the night before is correlated with happiness the next day, this means that you should be able, to some extent, to predict how happy a person will be the next day from knowing how much sleep the person got the night before. But if two variables are not correlated, then knowing about one does not help you predict the other. So if shoe size and income have a zero correlation, knowing a person's shoe size does not allow you to predict anything about the person's income. As we proceed, we will be referring again to the connections of correlation with prediction. But for now let us turn to prediction before we come back to correlation.

Predictor (*X*) and Criterion (*Y*) Variables

One of the ways correlation and prediction look different is this: with correlation it did not matter much which variable was which. But with prediction we have to decide which variable is *being predicted from* and which variable is *being predicted.* The variable being predicted from is called the **predictor variable.** The variable being predicted is called the **criterion variable.** In formulas the predictor variable is usually labeled *X*, and the criterion variable is usually labeled *Y*. That is, *X* predicts *Y*. In the example we just considered, SAT scores would be the predictor variable or *X*, and college grades would be the criterion variable or *Y*. (See Table 12–1.)

The Linear Prediction Rule

predictor variable (usually *X*) in prediction, variable that is used to predict scores of individuals on another variable.

criterion variable (usually *Y*) in prediction, a variable that is predicted.

Suppose we want to predict students' GPA at a particular college from their SAT scores. We could go about predicting college GPA by ignoring the SAT scores and just predicting that everyone will have an average level of college GPA. But we would not be taking advantage of knowing the SAT scores. Another possibility

Table 12-1 Predictor and Criterion Variables		
	Variable Predicted from	**Variable Predicted to**
	Predictor Variable	**Criterion Variable**
Symbol	*X*	*Y*
Example	SAT scores	College GPA

would be to use the information we have about SAT and GPA from recent students at this college to set up a complicated set of rules about what GPA we predict for each possible SAT score. For example, suppose in the past few years that students who came to this college with an SAT of 580 had an average GPA at graduation of 2.72; for students with an SAT of 590 the average GPA was 2.76; for students with an SAT of 600 the average GPA was 2.74; and so forth. We could then use these numbers to set up a rule that, for future students who come in with an SAT of 580, we would predict they would graduate with a GPA of 2.72; for those who come in with an SAT of 590, we would predict they would graduate with a GPA of 2.76; and so forth. This would be a pretty good rule and probably would make reasonably accurate predictions. However, the problem with this kind of rule is that it is quite complicated. Also because some SAT scores may have only a few students, it might not be that accurate for students with those SAT scores.

Ideally we would like a prediction rule that is not only simpler than this kind of complicated rule but also does not depend on only a few cases for each prediction. The solution that is favored by research psychologists is a rule of the form "to predict a person's score on Y, start with some baseline number, which we will call a, then add to it the result of multiplying a special predictor value, which we will call b, by the person's score on X." For our SAT and GPA example, the rule might be "to predict a person's graduating GPA, start with .3 and add the result of multiplying .004 by the person's SAT score." That is, the baseline number (a) would be .3 and the predictor value (b) is .004. Thus, if a person had an SAT of 600, we would predict the person would graduate with a GPA of 2.7. That is, the baseline number of .3 plus the result of multiplying the predictor value of .004 by 600 gives .3 plus 2.4, which equals 2.7. For a student with an SAT of 700, we would predict a graduating GPA of 3.1 [that is, $.3 + (.004 \times 700) = 3.1$].

This is an example of a **linear prediction rule** (or *linear prediction model*). We will see in the next main section why it is called "linear." For now it is enough just to note that "linear" here means the same thing as it did when we considered correlation in the last chapter: Lows go with lows and highs with highs (or lows with highs and highs with lows). In our SAT score and college GPA example, a low score on the predictor variable (SAT score) predicts a low score on the criterion variable (college GPA), and a high score on the predictor variable predicts a high score on the criterion variable.

In a linear prediction rule the formal name for the baseline number or a is the **regression constant** or just *constant*. It has the name "constant" because it is a fixed value that you always use when making a prediction. *Regression* is another name statisticians use for prediction; that is why it is called the regression constant. The number you multiply by the person's score on the predictor variable, b, is called the **regression coefficient** because a coefficient is a number you multiply by something. Later in the chapter, you will learn how to figure the values of a and b, and you will use them to draw a figure that shows the linear prediction rule, but for now we are focusing on the logic for making predictions about one variable (the criterion variable) based on information about another variable (the predictor variable).

All linear prediction rules have this formula:

$$\hat{Y} = a + (b)(X) \tag{12-1}$$

In this formula, $\hat{Y}$ is the person's predicted score on the criterion variable; a is the regression constant, b is the regression coefficient, and X is the person's score on the predictor variable. The symbol over the Y means "predicted value of" and is called a *hat* (so, $\hat{Y}$ is said "Y hat").

linear prediction rule   formula for making predictions; that is, formula for predicting a person's score on a criterion variable based on the person's score on one or more predictor variables.

regression constant (a)   in a linear prediction rule, particular fixed number added into the prediction.

regression coefficient (b)   number multiplied by a person's score on a predictor variable as part of a linear prediction rule.

A person's predicted score on the criterion variable equals the regression constant plus the regression coefficient multiplied by that person's score on the predictor variable.

An Example

In the example of using SAT scores to predict college GPA, the regression constant (*a*) was .3 and the regression coefficient (*b*) was .004. So, to predict a person's GPA, you start with a score of .3 and add .004 multiplied by the SAT score. In terms of the linear prediction rule formula,

$$\hat{Y} = a + (b)(X) = .3 + (.004)(X).$$

Or in terms of the variable names,

$$\text{Predicted GPA} = .3 + (.004)(\text{SAT score}).$$

Applying this formula to predicting GPA from a SAT score of 700,

$$\text{Predicted GPA} = .3 + (.004)(700) = .3 + 2.80 = 3.10.$$

You may be interested to know that research studies have consistently shown that SAT scores (and high school GPA) predict students' GPA in college (e.g., Schmitt et al., 2007). As you can imagine (and may know from personal experience), SAT scores are not the only factor that predict students' college GPA.

Another Example

Recall the example from Chapter 11 in which we considered the relationship between the number of hours of sleep and happy mood the next day for six students. In this example, hours of sleep is the predictor variable (*X*) and happy mood is the criterion variable (*Y*). The regression constant (*a*) in this example is −3 and the regression coefficient (*b*) is 1. (You will learn in a later section how to figure these values of *a* and *b*.) So, to predict a person's mood level, you start with a score of −3 and add 1 multiplied by the number of hours of sleep. In terms of the linear prediction rule formula,

$$\hat{Y} = a + (b)(X) = -3 + (1)(X).$$

Or in terms of the variable names,

$$\text{Predicted mood} = -3 + (1)(\text{hours of sleep}).$$

Applying this formula to predicting mood after having 9 hours of sleep,

$$\text{Predicted mood} = -3 + (1)(9) = -3 + 9 = 6.$$

Table 12–2 shows the worked-out linear prediction rule formula for the predicted mood scores for scores on sleep ranging from 0 to 16 hours. An important thing to notice from Table 12–2 is that in actual prediction situations it is not a good idea to predict from scores on the predictor variable that are much higher or lower than those in the study you used to figure the original correlation. You can see in this example that when a person sleeps a very small number of hours, you predict negative scores on the mood scale, which is impossible (the scale goes from 0 to 8); and when the person sleeps a great many hours, you predict scores on the mood scale that are higher than the limits of the scale. (In fact, it does not even make sense; sleeping 16 hours would probably not make you incredibly happy.) This is why a prediction rule should be used only for making predictions within the same range of scores for the predictor variable that were used to come up with the original correlation on which the prediction rule is based.

Table 12-2 Using the Linear Prediction Rule Formula for the Fictional Sleep and Mood Example for 0 to 16 Hours of Sleep

Linear prediction rule: $\hat{Y} = a + (b)(X)$
Predicted mood $= -3 + (1)$(hours of sleep)

0 hours sleep	$-3 = -3 + (1)(0)$
1 hours sleep	$-2 = -3 + (1)(1)$
2 hours sleep	$-1 = -3 + (1)(2)$
3 hours sleep	$0 = -3 + (1)(3)$
4 hours sleep	$1 = -3 + (1)(4)$
5 hours sleep	$2 = -3 + (1)(5)$
6 hours sleep	$3 = -3 + (1)(6)$
7 hours sleep	$4 = -3 + (1)(7)$
8 hours sleep	$5 = -3 + (1)(8)$
9 hours sleep	$6 = -3 + (1)(9)$
10 hours sleep	$7 = -3 + (1)(10)$
11 hours sleep	$8 = -3 + (1)(11)$
12 hours sleep	$9 = -3 + (1)(12)$
13 hours sleep	$10 = -3 + (1)(13)$
14 hours sleep	$11 = -3 + (1)(14)$
15 hours sleep	$12 = -3 + (1)(15)$
16 hours sleep	$13 = -3 + (1)(16)$

How are you doing?

1. *Fill in the blanks:* The variable being predicted from is called the ____ variable and the variable being predicted is called the ____ variable.
2. What is the linear prediction rule in words?
3. Write the formula for the linear prediction rule and define each of the symbols.
4. In a particular prediction rule, $a = -1.23$ and $b = 6.11$. What is the predicted score on the criterion variable if the score on the predictor variable is (a) 2.00; (b) 4.87; (c) −1.92?
5. Why should the linear prediction rule be used for making predictions only within the same range of scores in the group of people studied that was the basis for forming the particular prediction rule?

Answers

1. The variable being predicted from is called the *predictor* variable and the variable being predicted is called the *criterion* variable.
2. To predict a person's score on a criterion variable (Y), start with a particular regression constant and add to it the result of multiplying the particular regression coefficient by the person's score on the predictor variable (X).
3. Formula for the linear prediction rule: $\hat{Y} = a + (b)(X)$. $\hat{Y}$ is the predicted score on the criterion variable (Y); a is the regression constant; b is the regression coefficient; and X is the score on the predictor variable (X).
4. Predicted scores: (a) $\hat{Y} = a + (b)(X) = -1.23 + (6.11)(2.00) = 10.99$; (b) $-1.23 + (6.11)(4.87) = 28.53$; (c) $-1.23 + (6.11)(-1.92) = -12.96$.
5. Using scores outside the range for the predictor variable may give unrealistic (or even impossible) predicted scores for the criterion variable.

The Regression Line

You can visualize a linear prediction rule as a line on a graph in which the horizontal axis is for values of the predictor variable (X) and the vertical axis is for predicted scores for the criterion variable ($\hat{Y}$). (The graph is set up like the scatter diagrams you learned to make in Chapter 11.) The line is called a **regression line** and shows the relation between values of the predictor variable and the *predicted values* of the criterion variable.

Figure 12–1 shows the regression line for the SAT scores (predictor variable) and college GPA (criterion variable) example. By following the regression line, you can find the GPA score that is predicted from any particular SAT score. The dotted lines show the prediction for having an SAT score of 700. From the figure, the predicted GPA score for an SAT score of 700 is a little more than 3.0, which is consistent with the precise predicted value of 3.1 we found earlier when using the linear prediction rule formula. So, as you can see, the regression line acts as a visual equivalent of the linear prediction rule formula.

The regression line for the hours slept last night (predictor variable) and happy mood (criterion variable) example is shown in Figure 12–2. The dotted lines show that having 9 hours of sleep gives a predicted happy mood score of 6, which is the same value we found when using the linear prediction rule formula.

regression line line on a graph such as a scatter diagram showing the predicted value of the criterion variable for each value of the predictor variable; visual equivalent of the linear prediction rule.

slope steepness of the angle of a regression line in a graph of the relation of scores on a predictor variable and predicted scores on a criterion variable; number of units the line goes up for every unit it goes across.

Slope of the Regression Line

The steepness of the angle of the regression line, called its **slope,** is the amount the line moves up for every unit it moves across. In the example in Figure 12–1, the line moves up .004 on the GPA scale for every additional point on the SAT. In fact, the slope of the line is exactly b, the regression coefficient. (We don't usually think of SAT scores increasing by as little as 1 point—say, from 600 to 601. So instead of thinking about a 1-point increase in SAT giving a .004-point increase in GPA, it may be easier to think in terms of a 100-point increase in SAT giving a .4-point increase in GPA.)

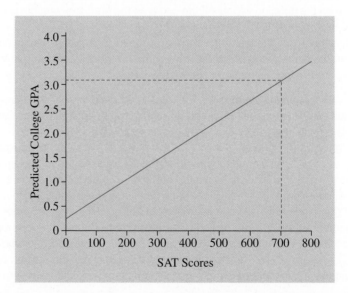

Figure 12–1 Regression line for the SAT scores and college GPA example, showing predicted college GPA for a person with an SAT score of 700 (fictional data).

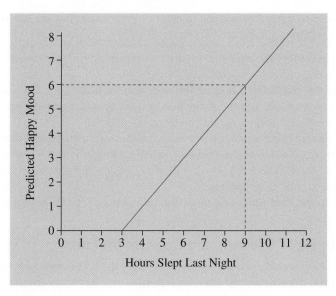

Figure 12-2 Regression line for the hours of sleep and happy mood example, showing predicted happy mood for a person who slept 9 hours (fictional data).

For the hours of sleep and happy mood example shown in Figure 12–2, the value of the regression coefficient, b, is 1. So, the line moves up 1 on the happy mood scale for every additional hour of sleep.

The Intercept of the Regression Line

The point at which the regression line crosses (or "intercepts") the vertical axis is called the **intercept** (or sometimes the *Y intercept*). (This assumes you have drawn the vertical axis so it is at the 0 point on the horizontal axis.) The intercept is the predicted score on the criterion variable ($\hat{Y}$) when the score on the predictor variable (X) is 0. It turns out that the intercept is the same as the regression constant. This works because the regression constant is the number you always add in—a kind of baseline number, the number you start with. And it is reasonable that the best baseline number would be the number you predict from a score of 0 on the predictor variable. In Figure 12–1, the line crosses the vertical axis at .3. That is, when a person has an SAT score of 0, they are predicted to have a college GPA of .3. In fact, the intercept of the line is exactly a, the regression constant. Another way of thinking of this is in terms of the linear prediction rule formula, $\hat{Y} = a + (b)(X)$. If X is 0, then whatever the value of b, when you multiply it by X you get 0. Thus, if b multiplied by X comes out to 0, all that is left of the prediction formula is $\hat{Y} = a + 0$. That is, if X is 0, then $\hat{Y} = a$.

For the hours of sleep and happy mood example, the regression constant, a, was -3. If you were to extend the regression line in Figure 12–2, it would cross the vertical axis at -3.

How to Draw the Regression Line

The first steps are setting up the axes and labels of your graph—the same steps that you learned in Chapter 11 for setting up a scatter diagram. The regression line is a straight line and thus shows a *linear* prediction. Thus, to draw the regression line,

intercept the point where the regression line crosses the vertical axis; the regression constant (a).

you only have to figure the location of any two points and draw the line that passes through them. Overall, there are four steps:

❶ **Draw and label the axes for a scatter diagram.** Remember to put the predictor variable on the horizontal axis.

❷ **Figure the predicted value on the criterion variable for a low value of the predictor variable and mark the point on the graph.** You make the prediction using the linear prediction rule you learned earlier: $\hat{Y} = a + (b)(X)$.

❸ **Do the same thing again, but for a high value on the predictor variable.** It is best to pick a value of the predictor variable (X) that is much higher than you used in Step ❷. This is because it will make the dots fairly far apart, so that your drawing will be more accurate.

❹ **Draw a line that passes through the two marks.** This is the regression line.

An Example of Drawing the Regression Line

Here is how you would draw the regression line for the SAT scores and college GPA example. (The steps are shown in Figure 12–3.)

❶ **Draw and label the axes for a scatter diagram.** Note that we labeled the Y axis "Predicted" college GPA, as the regression line shows the relationship between actual scores of the predictor variable (X) and *predicted scores* of the criterion variable ($\hat{Y}$).

❷ **Figure the predicted value on the criterion variable for a low value of the predictor variable and mark the point on the graph.** Recall from earlier that the linear prediction rule formula for predicting college GPA from an SAT score is $\hat{Y} = .3 + (.004)(X)$. So, for an SAT score of 200 (a low SAT score), the predicted college GPA is $.3 + (.004)(200)$, which is 1.1. Thus, you mark this point ($X = 200$, $\hat{Y} = 1.1$) on the graph, as shown in Figure 12–3.

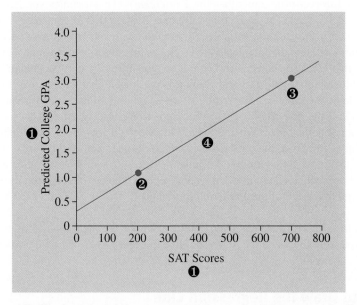

Figure 12–3 Steps in drawing a regression line for the SAT scores and college GPA example. ❶ Draw and label the axes, ❷ mark a point for a low value of the predictor variable and its predicted value on the criterion variable, ❸ mark a point for a high value of the predictor variable and its predicted value on the criterion variable, and ❹ draw the regression line.

❸ **Do the same thing again, but for a high value on the predictor variable.** We saw earlier that if a person has an SAT score of 700 (a high SAT score), we predict a college GPA of 3.1 [that is, .3 + (.004)(700) = 3.1]. Thus, you mark this point ($X = 700$, $\hat{Y} = 3.1$) on the graph, as shown in Figure 12–3.

❹ **Draw a line that passes through the two marks.** The line is shown in Figure 12–3.

Another Example of Drawing the Regression Line

Here is how you would draw the regression line for the hours of sleep and happy mood example. (The steps are shown in Figure 12–4.)

❶ **Draw and label the axes for a scatter diagram.**

❷ **Figure the predicted value on the criterion variable for a low value of the predictor variable and mark the point on the graph.** Recall that the linear prediction rule for predicting happy mood from the number of hours of sleep is $\hat{Y} = -3 + (1)(X)$. So, for 3 hours of sleep (a low amount of sleep), the predicted happy mood is $-3 + (1)(3)$, which is 0. Thus, you mark this point ($X = 3$, $\hat{Y} = 0$) on the graph, as shown in Figure 12–4.

❸ **Do the same thing again, but for a high value on the predictor variable.** If a person has 10 hours of sleep (a large amount of sleep), we predict a happy mood of 7 [that is, $-3 + (1)(10) = 7$]. Thus you mark this point ($X = 10$, $\hat{Y} = 7$) on the graph, as shown in Figure 12–4.

❹ **Draw a line that passes through the two marks.** The line is shown in Figure 12–4.

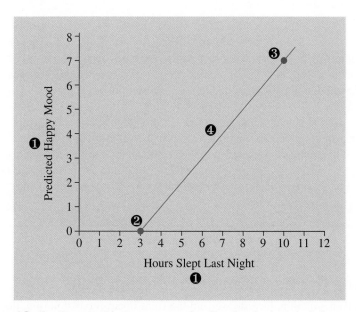

Figure 12–4 Steps in drawing a regression line for the hours of sleep and happy mood example. ❶ Draw and label the axes, ❷ mark a point for a low value of the predictor variable and its predicted value on the criterion variable, ❸ mark a point for a high value of the predictor variable and its predicted value on the criterion variable, and ❹ draw the regression line.

How are you doing?

1. What does the regression line show?
2. What is the relationship between the regression line and the linear prediction rule?
3. (a) What is the slope of the regression line? (b) What is it equivalent to in the linear prediction rule?
4. (a) What is the intercept of the regression line? (b) What is it equivalent to in the linear prediction rule?
5. Draw the regression line for X and $\hat{Y}$ where $a = 4$ and $b = 1.33$ (put values from 0 to 12 on the X axis and values of 0 to 20 on the Y axis.)

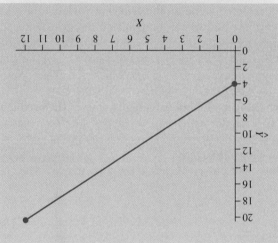

Figure 12–5 Regression line for "How are you doing?" question 5.

Answers

1. The regression line shows the relationship between the predictor variable (X) and predicted values of the criterion variable (Y).
2. The regression line is a visual equivalent of the linear prediction rule.
3. (a) The slope of the regression line is the amount the line goes up for every one unit it moves across. (b) In the linear prediction rule, it is equivalent to b, the regression coefficient.
4. (a) The intercept of the regression line is the point at which the regression line crosses the vertical axis (assuming the vertical axis is at 0 on the horizontal axis). (b) In the linear prediction rule, it is equivalent to a, the regression constant.
5. See Figure 12–5.

Finding the Best Linear Prediction Rule

In any given situation, how do we find the right linear prediction rule, the correct numbers for the regression constant, a, and the regression coefficient, b? Whether we think of it as a rule in words, a formula, or a regression line on a graph, we still have to know these two numbers. Figure 12–6 shows the scatter diagram for the six students in the hours of sleep and happy mood example. Four different regression

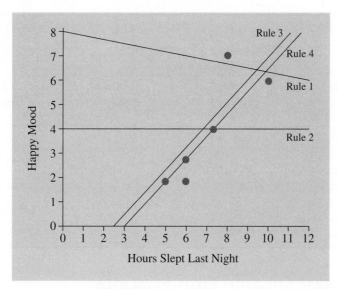

Figure 12–6   Actual scores from six students (shown as dots) and four prediction rules (shown as regression lines) for predicting happy mood from hours of sleep (fictional data).

lines (each showing a different linear prediction rule) are shown in the figure. In the figure, the dots show the actual scores of the six students, and the lines show different prediction rules for predicting happy mood from hours of sleep. So the closer a line comes to matching the actual results (the dots), the better the job it does as a prediction rule. In reality, there is only *one* best linear prediction rule, but for learning purposes, imagine you have four rules to pick from. Which rule in Figure 12–6 will do the best job of predicting happy mood scores from the number of hours slept?

Suppose we used Rule 1 as our linear prediction rule. This would be a rule $\hat{Y} = 8 - (.18)(X)$. For example, if we used this rule to make a prediction for a person who had 6 hours of sleep, we would predict a happy mood of 6.92 [that is, $8 - (.18)(6) = 6.92$], which would be way off from the actual scores of the two people in the study who slept for 6 hours (one of whom had a mood score of 2, the other a 3). In fact, you can see from the line that most of the predictions based on Rule 1 would be way off from the actual happy mood scores. Rule 2 is a prediction rule of $\hat{Y} = 4 + (0)(X)$, which more simply is $\hat{Y} = 4$. (Since the mean of the Y values in this example is 4, this rule involves always predicting the mean of Y.) If we used this rule we would make a reasonable prediction for a person with 6 hours of sleep: we would predict a happy mood of 4, which would be pretty close to the true scores. But using this prediction rule would not do so well if we were predicting for a person with 5 hours of sleep or 8 hours of sleep. Overall, Rule 3 does a good job of predicting actual happy mood scores (it is quite close to most of the dots), but Rule 4 does an even better job.

Table 12–3 summarizes how well each of the four rules predicts the actual happy mood scores of the six students in this example. The table shows the hours slept (X), the actual happy mood score (Y), and the predicted happy mood score ($\hat{Y}$) for each student using each of the four prediction rules. The table shows that Rules 3 and 4 have predicted values of the happy mood criterion variable ($\hat{Y}$) that are much closer to the actual values of the criterion variable (Y) than is the case for Rules 1 and 2.

Table 12-3 Comparing Actual and Predicted Happy Mood Scores for Six Students Using Four Linear Prediction Rules (shown as Rules 1, 2, 3, and 4 in Figure 12–6)

		Happy Mood			
Hours Slept	Actual Mood	Rule 1 Predicted Mood $\hat{Y} = 8 - (.18)(X)$	Rule 2 Predicted Mood $\hat{Y} = 4 + (0)(X)$	Rule 3 Predicted Mood $\hat{Y} = -2.5 + (1)(X)$	Rule 4 Predicted Mood $\hat{Y} = -3 + (1)(X)$
X	Y	$\hat{Y}$	$\hat{Y}$	$\hat{Y}$	$\hat{Y}$
5	2	7.10	4.00	2.50	2.00
6	2	6.92	4.00	3.50	3.00
6	3	6.92	4.00	3.50	3.00
7	4	6.74	4.00	4.50	4.00
8	7	6.56	4.00	5.50	5.00
10	6	6.20	4.00	7.50	7.00

The Least Squared Error Principle

One way to come up with a prediction rule is by eyeballing and trial and error. Using such a method we might come up with Rule 3 or 4 in Figure 12–6 or a similar rule (each of which would be a lot better than Rule 1 or Rule 2). However, what we really need is some method of coming up with the precise, very best linear prediction rule (that is, the best regression line); and this method should not be subjective or based on eyeballing (where different researchers may decide on different lines). Remember, we are trying to find the *one best rule;* we considered four rules for the mood and sleep example in Figure 12–6 to show the logic of linear prediction rules.

Coming up with the best prediction rule means we first have to decide on what we mean by "best." In terms of a regression line, we basically mean the line that comes closest to the true scores on the criterion variable, that makes predictions that are as little off from the true scores as possible. The difference between a prediction rule's predicted score on the criterion variable and a person's actual score on the criterion variable is called **error.**

We, of course, want as little error as possible over the whole range of scores we would predict, so what we want is the *smallest* sum of errors. But there is one more problem here. Sometimes the errors will be positive (the rule will predict too low), and sometimes they will be negative (the rule will predict too high). The positive and negative errors will cancel each other out. So, to avoid this problem, we use *squared errors.* That is, we take each amount of error and square it (multiply it by itself), then we add up the squared errors. (This is the same solution we used in a similar situation in Chapter 2 when figuring the variance and standard deviation.) Using squared errors also has various other statistical advantages over alternative approaches. For example, this approach penalizes large errors more than small errors; this approach also makes it easier to do more advanced computations.

Thus, to evaluate how good a prediction rule is, we figure the **sum of the squared errors** that we would make using that rule. Table 12–4 gives the sum of squared errors for each of the four prediction rules shown in Figure 12–6 and Table 12–3. To avoid making Table 12–4 too complex, we show only the actual figuring of the sum of squared errors for Rule 1 and Rule 4. The scores in each "Error" column show the result of subtracting the predicted score on the criterion variable ($\hat{Y}$) using the rule from the actual score on the criterion variable (Y) for each of the six students in the example (error $= Y - \hat{Y}$). We then squared each error score for

error in prediction, the difference between a person's predicted score on the criterion variable and the person's actual score on the criterion variable.

sum of the squared errors sum of the squared differences between each predicted score and actual score on the criterion variable.

Table 12-4 The Sum of Squared Errors for Rules 1, 2, 3, and 4 (from Figure 12–6 and Table 12–3), Showing the Figuring for Rule 1 and Rule 4

		Rule 1			Rule 4		
Hours Slept	Actual Mood	Rule 1 Predicted Mood $\hat{Y} = 8 - (.18)(X)$	Rule 1 Error	Rule 1 Squared Error	Rule 4 Predicted Mood $\hat{Y} = -3 + (1)(X)$	Rule 4 Error	Rule 4 Squared Error
X	Y	$\hat{Y}$	$(Y - \hat{Y})$	$(Y - \hat{Y})^2$	$\hat{Y}$	$(Y - \hat{Y})$	$(Y - \hat{Y})^2$
5	2	7.10	−5.10	26.01	2.00	.00	.00
6	2	6.92	−4.92	24.21	3.00	−1.00	1.00
6	3	6.92	−3.92	15.37	3.00	.00	.00
7	4	6.74	−2.74	7.51	4.00	.00	.00
8	7	6.56	.44	.19	5.00	2.00	4.00
10	6	6.20	−.20	.04	7.00	−1.00	1.00
				$\Sigma = 73.33$			$\Sigma = 6.00$

Rule 1 sum of squared errors = 73.33
Rule 2 sum of squared errors = 22.00
Rule 3 sum of squared errors = 7.50
Rule 4 sum of squared errors = 6.00

each rule. The sum of these squared error scores was 73.33 for Rule 1 and 6.00 for Rule 4. We repeated this process for Rules 2 and 3. Overall, the results for the sum of squared errors for Rules 1, 2, 3, and 4 were 73.33, 22.00, 7.50, and 6.00, respectively. Because the goal is to come up with a linear prediction rule—values for a and b in the formula $\hat{Y} = a + (b)(X)$—that creates the *smallest sum of squared errors,* we would in this case pick Rule 4.

In picking this linear prediction rule, we have used what statisticians call the *least squares criterion.* That is, we found the regression line that gave the lowest sum of squared errors between the *actual scores* on the criterion variable (Y) and the *predicted scores* on the criterion variable ($\hat{Y}$). In the next section, you learn how to find the values of a and b for the linear prediction rule that gives the very smallest sum of squared errors possible.

TIP FOR SUCCESS
Remember, the regression line is a visual equivalent of the linear prediction rule.

Finding a and b for the Least Squares Linear Prediction Rule

There are straightforward formulas for figuring the values of a (the regression constant) and b (the regression coefficient) that will give the linear prediction rule with the smallest possible sum of squared errors. These formulas give you the linear prediction rule guaranteed to produce less squared error than any other possible prediction rule.

Here are the formulas:

$$b = \frac{\Sigma[(X - M_X)(Y - M_Y)]}{SS_X} \quad (12\text{–}2)$$

In this formula, b is the regression coefficient. $X - M_X$ is the deviation score for each person on the X variable and $Y - M_Y$ is the deviation score for each person on the Y variable; $(X - M_X)(Y - M_Y)$ is the product of deviation scores for each person; and $\Sigma[(X - M_X)(Y - M_Y)]$ is the sum of the products of deviation

The regression coefficient is the sum, over all the people in the study, of the product of each person's two deviation scores, divided by the sum of everyone's squared deviation scores on the predictor variable.

The regression constant is the mean of the criterion variable minus the result of multiplying the regression coefficient by the mean of the predictor variable.

TIP FOR SUCCESS

You may have noticed that the formula for b is similar to the formula for the correlation coefficient, r, from Chapter 11. Be sure to use the appropriate formula for each statistic. The numerators of the two formulas are indeed the same (both are the sum of the products of the deviation scores), but the denominators are different.

scores over all the people in the study. SS_X is the sum of squared deviations for the X variable.

$$a = M_Y - (b)(M_X) \qquad \text{(12–3)}$$

Notice that you need to know the value of b in order to figure the value of a. So you first use formula (12–2) to find the value of b and then use formula (12–3) to figure the value of a.

Here are the steps for figuring the regression coefficient, b:

❶ **Change the scores for each variable to deviation scores.** Figure the mean of each variable. Then subtract each variable's mean from each of its scores.
❷ **Figure the product of the deviation scores for each pair of scores.** That is, for each pair of scores, multiply the deviation score on one variable by the deviation score on the other variable.
❸ **Add up all the products of the deviation scores.**
❹ **Square each deviation score for the predictor variable (X).**
❺ **Add up the squared deviation scores for the predictor variable (X).**
❻ **Divide the sum of the products of deviation scores from Step ❸ by the sum of squared deviations for the predictor variable (X) from Step ❺.** This gives the regression coefficient, b.

Here are the steps for figuring the regression constant, a:

❶ **Multiply the regression coefficient, b, by the mean of the X variable.**
❷ **Subtract the result of Step ❶ from the mean of the Y variable.** This gives the regression constant, a.

Earlier in the chapter, we told you that the regression coefficient, b, for the hours of sleep and mood example was 1, and the regression constant, a, was –3. Now let's see how we figured those values. The figuring for the regression coefficient, b, is shown in Table 12–5. Using the steps,

❶ **Change the scores for each variable to deviation scores.** Figure the mean of each variable. Then subtract each variable's mean from each of its scores. The deviation scores are shown in the $X - M_X$ and $Y - M_Y$ columns in Table 12–5.
❷ **Figure the product of the deviation scores for each pair of scores.** That is, for each pair of scores, multiply the deviation score on one variable by the deviation score on the other variable.
❸ **Add up all the products of the deviation scores.** Adding up all the products of the deviation scores, as shown in the final column of Table 12–5, gives a sum of 16.
❹ **Square each deviation score for the predictor variable (X).**
❺ **Add up the squared deviation scores for the predictor variable (X).** As shown in the $(X - M_X)^2$ column of Table 12–5, the sum of squared deviations for the sleep variable is 16.
❻ **Divide the sum of the products of deviation scores from Step ❸ by the sum of squared deviations for the predictor variable (X) from Step ❺.** Dividing 16 by 16 gives a result of 1. This is the regression coefficient. In terms of the formula,

$$b = \frac{\Sigma[(X - M_X)(Y - M_Y)]}{SS_X} = \frac{16}{16} = 1$$

Table 12-5 Figuring the Regression Coefficient (b), Regression Constant (a), and the Linear Prediction Rule for Predicting Happy Mood from Hours of Sleep (Fictional Data)

Number of Hours Slept (X)			Happy Mood (Y)		Products of ❷ Deviation Scores
	Deviation ❶	Deviation Squared ❹		Deviation ❶	
X	$X - M_X$	$(X - M_X)^2$	Y	$Y - M_Y$	$(X - M_X)(Y - M_Y)$
7	0	0	4	0	0
5	−2	4	2	−2	4
8	1	1	7	3	3
6	−1	1	2	−2	2
6	−1	1	3	−1	1
10	3	9	6	2	6
$\Sigma = 42$		$\Sigma = SS_X = 16$ ❺	$\Sigma = 24$		$\Sigma = 16$ ❸
$M = 7$			$M = 4$		

$$b = \frac{\Sigma[(X - M_X)(Y - M_Y)]}{SS_X} \overset{❻}{=} \frac{16}{16} = 1$$

$$a = M_Y - (b)(M_X) = 4 - (1)(7) = 4 - 7 = -3$$

Linear prediction rule: Using formula $\hat{Y} = a + (b)(X)$, $\hat{Y} = -3 + (1)(X)$

Note: The circled numbers refer to the steps for figuring the regression coefficient, b.

The figuring for the regression constant, a, is also shown in Table 12–5. Using the steps,

❶ **Multiply the regression coefficient, b, by the mean of the X variable.** We just figured the value of b to be 1, and 1 multiplied by 7 (the mean of X) gives 7.

❷ **Subtract the result of Step ❶ from the mean of the Y variable.** Subtracting 7 (the result of Step ❶) from 4 (the mean of Y) gives −3. This is the regression constant, a. In terms of the formula,

$$a = M_Y - (b)(M_X) = 4 - (1)(7) = -3.$$

So, for the sleep and happy mood example, the (least squares) linear prediction rule for predicting mood from hours of sleep—using our formula $\hat{Y} = a + (b)(X)$—is $\hat{Y} = -3 + (1)(X)$. As we showed earlier in the chapter (see Table 12–2), you can enter values for X (hours of sleep) into this formula to give predicted values of happy mood.

How are you doing?

1. What is the least squared error principle?
2. Give three advantages of using squared errors, as opposed to unsquared errors, when figuring the best linear prediction rule.
3. (a) Write the formula for the regression coefficient, b, and define each of the symbols. (b) Write the formula for the regression constant, a, and define each of the symbols.
4. (a) Find the linear prediction rule for predicting Y scores from X scores based on the following numbers. (b) Figure the sum of the squared errors when using the

linear prediction rule from part (a) to predict the scores for the four people in this study. (c) Repeat part (b), this time using the prediction rule $\hat{Y} = 9 - (.7)(X)$. (d) Why *must* your answer to (b) be lower than your answer to (c)?

X	Y
4	6
6	8
7	3
3	7

4. (a) The figuring is shown in Table 12–6. The linear prediction rule is $\hat{Y} = 9 - (.6)(X)$. (b) As shown in Table 12–7, the sum of squared errors is 10.40. (c) As shown in Table 12–7, the sum of squared errors is 11.50. (d) The linear prediction rule figured in part (a) is the rule that gives the *smallest* sum of squared errors; so the sum of squared errors for any other rule will be larger than this sum.

Table 12–7 Figuring the Sums of Squared Errors for "How Are You Doing?" Questions 4b and 4c

		Prediction Rule from Part (a)			Prediction Rule from Part (c)		
		$\hat{Y} = 9 - (.6)(X)$	Error	Squared Error	$\hat{Y} = 9 - (.7)(X)$	Error	Squared Error
X	Y	$\hat{Y}$	$(Y - \hat{Y})$	$(Y - \hat{Y})^2$	$\hat{Y}$	$(Y - \hat{Y})$	$(Y - \hat{Y})^2$
4	6	6.6	−.6	.36	6.2	−.2	.04
6	8	5.4	2.6	6.76	4.8	3.2	10.24
7	3	4.8	−1.8	3.24	4.1	−1.1	1.21
3	7	7.2	−.2	.04	6.9	.1	.01
				Σ = 10.40			Σ = 11.50

Source: Oettingen, G., Schnetter, K., & Pak, H. (2001). Self-regulations of goal setting: Turning free fantasies about the future into binding goals. *Journal of Personality and Social Psychology, 80,* 736–753. Published by the American Psychological Association. Reprinted with permission.

Table 12–6 Figuring the Linear Prediction Rule for "How Are You Doing?" Question 4

X			Y		
	Deviation ①	Squared Deviation ④		Deviation ①	Products of ② Deviation Scores
X	$X - M_X$	$(X - M_X)^2$	Y	$Y - M_Y$	$(X - M_X)(Y - M_Y)$
4	−1	1	6	0	0
6	1	1	8	2	2
7	2	4	3	−3	−6
3	−2	4	7	1	−2
Σ = 20		Σ = SS_X = 10 ⑤	Σ = 24		Σ = −6 ⑤
M = 5 ③			M = 6		

$$b = \frac{\Sigma[(X - M_X)(Y - M_Y)]}{SS_X} = \frac{-6}{10} = -.6 \quad ⑥$$

$$a = M_Y - (b)(M_X) = 6 - (-.6)(5) = 6 + 3 = 9$$

Linear prediction rule: Using formula $\hat{Y} = a + (b)(X)$, $\hat{Y} = 9 - (.6)(X)$.

Note: The circled numbers refer to the steps for figuring the regression coefficient, b.

Answers

1. The least squared error principle is the principle that the best prediction rule is the rule that gives the lowest sum of squared errors between the actual scores on the criterion variable and the predicted scores on the criterion variable.

2. Unlike unsquared errors, squared errors do not cancel each other out. Using squared errors penalizes large errors more than small errors; they also make it easier to do more advanced computations.

3. (a) The formula for the regression coefficient: $b = \dfrac{\sum[(X - M_X)(Y - M_Y)]}{SS_X}$. b is the regression coefficient; $\sum$ is the symbol for sum of—add up all the scores that follow (in this formula, you add up all the products of deviation scores that follow): $X - M_X$ is the deviation score for each person on the predictor variable; $Y - M_Y$ is the deviation score for each person on the predictor variable; SS_X is the sum of squared deviations for the predictor variable.
(b) $a = M_Y - (b)(M_X)$. a is the regression constant; M_Y is the mean of the criterion variable; b is the regression coefficient; M_X is the mean of the predictor variable.

Issues in Prediction

In this section, you will learn about two issues in prediction: the standardized regression coefficient; and hypothesis testing and prediction.[1]

The Standardized Regression Coefficient

The linear prediction rule you have learned provides a useful and practical way of making predictions on a criterion variable from scores on a predictor variable. Recall from the hours of sleep and happy mood example that the prediction rule for predicting mood from sleep was: $\hat{Y} = -3 + (1)(X)$. Now, imagine that another group of researchers carry out the same study and find the prediction rule to be $\hat{Y} = -3 + (2)(X)$. In this new study, the regression coefficient (of 2) is much larger than the regression coefficient (of 1) in the original study. Recall that the regression coefficient tells you the slope of the regression line. That is, the regression coefficient is the predicted amount of increase in units for the criterion variable when the predictor variable increases by one unit. So the original study shows a 1-unit increase in sleep is associated with a 1-unit increase in mood. The new study, however, shows a 1-unit increase in sleep is associated with a 2-unit increase in mood. With this in mind, you might conclude that the larger regression coefficient in the new study shows that sleep has a much stronger effect on mood.

At this point, however, we should note one important difference between the two studies of sleep and happy mood. In the original study, happy mood was measured on a scale going from 0 to 8. However, the researchers in the new study used a scale of 0 to 20. Thus, with the first study, a 1-hour increase in sleep predicts a 1-point increase in mood on a scale from 0 to 8, but in the second study a 1-hour increase in sleep predicts a 2-point increase in mood but on a scale of 0 to 20. Thus, the second study might actually have found a slightly smaller effect of sleep!

Researchers in psychology quite often use slightly different measures or the same measure with a different scale (1 to 5 versus 10 to 100, for example) for

The standardized regression coefficient is equal to the regular, unstandardized regression coefficient multiplied by the result of dividing the square root of the sum of squared deviations for the predictor variable by the square root of the sum of squared deviations for the criterion variable.

the same variable. This can make it hard to compare the linear prediction rule for the same type of effect (such as the effect of sleep on happy mood) across studies. This is because the scale used for the predictor and criterion variables will affect the value of b (the regression coefficient) in the linear prediction rule. (The value of a, the regression constant, will also be affected by the scales used. But researchers in psychology are usually more interested in the actual value of b than a.)

Does this type of problem seem familiar to you? Recall from Chapter 3 that you learned how to change a raw score into a Z score, which is a score on a scale of standard deviation units. For example, a Z score of 1.23 is a score that is 1.23 standard deviation units above the mean of the scores, and a Z score of $-.62$ is $-.62$ standard deviation units below the mean. This allowed you to compare the score on one variable relative to the score on another variable, even when the two variables used different scales. In the case of the regression coefficient in this chapter, we need a type of regression coefficient that can be compared across studies (that may have used different scales for the same variable).

It turns out that, just as there was a formula for changing a raw score to a Z score, there is a formula for changing a regression coefficient into what is known as a **standardized regression coefficient.** A standardized regression coefficient, which is referred to using the Greek symbol β (beta), shows the predicted amount of change in standard deviation units of the criterion variable if the value of the predicted variable increases by one standard deviation. For example, a standardized regression coefficient of .63 would mean for every increase of 1 standard deviation on X, we predict an increase of .63 standard deviations on Y. The formula for the standardized regression coefficient (β) is

$$\beta = (b)\frac{\sqrt{SS_X}}{\sqrt{SS_Y}} \qquad \text{(12–4)}$$

This formula has the effect of changing the regular (unstandardized) regression coefficient (b), the size of which is related to the specific scales for the predictor and criterion variables, to a standardized regression coefficient (β) that shows the relationship between the predictor and criterion variables in terms of standard deviation units.

An Example

For the sleep and mood example shown in Table 12–5, $SS_X = 16$. Table 12–5 doesn't show the value of SS_Y, but we can figure it by squaring each score in the $Y - M_Y$ column and summing the resulting values. Thus, $SS_Y = 0^2 + (-2^2) + 3^2 + (-2^2) + (-1^2) + 2^2 = 0 + 4 + 9 + 4 + 1 + 4 = 22$. The value of b was 1; so the standardized regression coefficient for the sleep and mood example is

$$\beta = (b)\frac{\sqrt{SS_X}}{\sqrt{SS_Y}} = (1)\frac{\sqrt{16}}{\sqrt{22}} = (1)\frac{4}{4.69} = .85.$$

This means that for every standard deviation increase in sleep, the predicted level of mood increases by .85 standard deviations. You could then compare this value of β = .85 to the standardized regression coefficient (β) from other studies, such as the study we described earlier that used a 0 to 20 mood scale instead of the 0 to 8 mood in the original study.

Later in the chapter, we will discuss when researchers describe their results in terms of the regular (unstandardized) regression coefficient (b) and when they report the standardized regression coefficient (β).

standardized regression coefficient (β) regression coefficient in standard deviation units. It shows the predicted amount of change in standard deviation units of the criterion variable if the value of the predictor variable increases by one standard deviation.

The Standardized Regression Coefficient (β) and the Correlation Coefficient (r)

In the examples we have used so far in this chapter, in which scores on a criterion variable are predicted based on scores from *one predictor variable,* the standardized regression coefficient (β) has the same value as the correlation coefficient (r) between the two variables. So, the β of .85 for the sleep and mood example is the same as the r of .85 between sleep and mood we figured in Chapter 11 (see Table 11–2). However, in formula (12–4), we gave a more general method for figuring a standardized regression coefficient, because the standardized regression coefficient is *not* the same as the correlation coefficient when scores on a criterion variable are predicted based on scores from *more than one predictor variable* (a situation we examine in the next main section).

Hypothesis Testing and Prediction

In Chapter 11, you learned that hypothesis testing with a correlation coefficient meant examining whether the coefficient was significantly different than 0 (no correlation). You learned how to use a *t* test to determine whether a correlation coefficient was statistically significant. Since the standardized regression coefficient is the same as the correlation coefficient (when predicting a criterion variable from one predictor variable), the *t* test for the correlation between the two variables also acts as the *t* test for the prediction of the criterion variable from the predictor variable. The standardized regression coefficient is just another way of presenting the regular regression coefficient; so the *t* test for the correlation applies to both types of regression coefficients. In terms of prediction, the hypothesis test for a regression coefficient (for both *b* and β) tests whether the regression coefficient is significantly different from 0. A regression coefficient of 0 means that knowing a person's score on the predictor variable does not give you any useful information for predicting that person's score on the criterion variable. However, if the hypothesis testing result shows that the regression coefficient is significantly different from 0, then knowing a person's score on the predictor variable gives you useful information for predicting a person's score on the criterion variable.

How are you doing?

1. What does a standardized regression coefficient show?
2. (a) Write the formula for the standardized regression coefficient, β, and define each of the symbols. (b) Figure the value of β when $b = -1.21$, $SS_X = 2.57$, and $SS_Y = 7.21$.
3. When predicting scores on a criterion variable from scores on one predictor variable, the standardized regression coefficient has the same value as what other statistic?
4. How is hypothesis testing carried out with a regression coefficient?

4. When predicting a criterion variable based on scores on one predictor variable, the hypothesis test for a regression coefficient is the same as the hypothesis test for the correlation between the two variables. The test uses a *t* statistic and tests whether the regression coefficient is significantly different from 0. A statistically significant regression coefficient means that knowing a person's score on the predictor variable provides useful information for predicting a person's score on the criterion variable.

Multiple Regression

So far, we have predicted a person's score on a criterion variable using the person's score on a single predictor variable. That is, each example so far was for **bivariate prediction** (or *bivariate regression*)—bivariate means two variable—and the prediction rules we used were *bivariate prediction rules.*

Suppose you could use more than one predictor variable. For example, in predicting happy mood, all you had to work with was the number of hours slept the night before. Suppose you also knew how well the person had slept and how many dreams the person had had. With this added information, you might be able to make a much more accurate prediction of mood.

The association between a criterion variable and two or more predictor variables is called **multiple correlation.**[2] Making predictions in this situation is called **multiple regression.**

We explore these topics only briefly because the details are beyond the level of an introductory book. However, multiple regression and multiple correlation are very frequently used in research articles in psychology, especially in fields like clinical, developmental, personality, and social psychology. So it is valuable for you to have a general understanding of them. (We build on your general understanding of multiple regression in Chapter 15.)

Multiple Regression Prediction Rules

A multiple regression linear prediction rule with three predictor variables goes like this:

$$\hat{Y} = a + (b_1)(X_1) + (b_2)(X_2) + (b_3)(X_3) \qquad \textbf{(12–5)}$$

In this formula, $\hat{Y}$ is the predicted score on the criterion variable; a is the regression constant; b_1, b_2, and b_3 are the regression coefficients for the first, second, and third predictor variables, respectively; and X_1, X_2, and X_3 are the person's scores on the first, second, and third predictor variables, respectively. Notice that there is one regression constant and each predictor variable has its own regression coefficient.

bivariate prediction prediction of scores on one variable based on scores of one other variable. Also called *bivariate regression.*

multiple correlation correlation of a criterion variable with two or more predictor variables.

multiple regression procedure for predicting scores on a criterion variable from scores on two or more predictor variables.

A person's predicted score on the criterion variable is the regression constant, plus the regression coefficient for the first predictor variable multiplied by the person's score on the first predictor variable, plus the regression coefficient for the second predictor variable multiplied by the person's score on the second predictor variable, plus the regression coefficient for the third predictor variable multiplied by the person's score on the third predictor variable.

For example, in the sleep and mood study, a multiple regression linear prediction rule for predicting mood with three predictor variables might be as follows:

$$\text{Predicted mood} = -3.78 + (.87)(\text{hours of sleep}) + (.33)(\text{how well slept}) + (.20)(\text{number of dreams})$$

Suppose a particular person had slept 7 hours the night before, rated how well slept as a 3, and had 1 dream. Their predicted mood would be

$$\text{Predicted mood} = -3.78 + (.87)(7) + (.33)(3) + (.20)(1)$$
$$= -3.78 + 6.09 + .99 + .20 = 3.50$$

An Important Difference Between Multiple Regression and Bivariate Prediction

There is one particularly important difference between multiple regression and bivariate prediction. In ordinary bivariate prediction the standardized regression coefficient is the same as the correlation coefficient. But, as we noted earlier, the standardized regression coefficient (β) for each predictor variable in multiple regression is *not* the same as the ordinary correlation coefficient (r) of that predictor with the criterion variable.

Usually, a β will be closer to 0 than r. The reason is that part of what makes any one predictor successful in predicting the criterion will usually overlap with what makes the other predictors successful in predicting the criterion variable. In multiple regression, both the standardized and the regular regression coefficients are about the unique, distinctive contribution of the variable, excluding any overlap with other predictor variables.

Consider the sleep and mood example. When we were predicting mood using just the number of hours slept, β was the same as the correlation coefficient of .85. Now, with multiple regression, the β for number of hours slept turns out to be .74. It is less because part of what makes number of hours slept predict mood overlaps with what makes sleeping well and number of dreams predict mood. (In this fictional example, people who sleep more hours usually sleep well and have more dreams.)

In multiple regression, the correlation between the criterion variable and all the predictor variables taken together is called the **multiple correlation coefficient** and is symbolized as **R.** However, because of the usual overlap among predictor variables, the multiple correlation is usually smaller than the sum of the individual rs of each predictor with the criterion variable. The squared multiple correlation, R^2, gives the proportionate reduction in error or proportion of variance accounted for in the criterion variable by all the predictor variables taken together. For example, an R of .40 gives an R^2 of .16, which means that the predictor variables together account for 16% (.40 $\times$ .40 = .16, which is the same as 16%) of the variation in the scores in the criterion variable.

In multiple regression, there are a number of possible hypothesis tests. First, you can test the significance of the multiple correlation (and the squared multiple correlation) using a procedure in which the null hypothesis is that in the population the multiple correlation is 0. This tests whether the variables as a whole are associated with the criterion variable. You can also test the significance of each individual predictor variable using a t test in a similar manner for hypothesis testing with bivariate prediction. Each test shows whether the regression coefficient for that variable is

multiple correlation coefficient
(R) in multiple regression, the correlation between the criterion variable and all the predictor variables taken together.

significantly different from 0. As with bivariate prediction, a significant regression coefficient for a predictor variable means that knowing a person's score on that predictor variable gives you useful information for predicting a person's score on the criterion variable. However, here the focus is on whether this predictor variable adds more than 0 to the prediction over and above what the other predictor variables already predict. Finally, there is also a hypothesis test for whether the regression constant is significantly different from 0. However, researchers in psychology typically do not pay much attention to this test, because the actual value of the regression constant (and whether it is different from 0) is usually not of great importance in many areas of research.

Limitations of Prediction

All of the limitations for correlation we discussed in Chapter 11 apply to prediction. The procedures we have considered in this chapter are inaccurate if the correlation is curvilinear, the group studied is restricted in range, the measures are unreliable, or there are outliers. That is, in each of these situations the regression coefficients (whether bivariate or multiple) are smaller than they should be to reflect the true association of the predictor variables with the criterion variable. Nor do these prediction procedures by themselves tell you anything about the direction of causality. Even in published articles, researchers sometimes overlook these limitations when considering complex regression results. We will not go in to detail, but prior to doing prediction (and correlation) analyses, researchers often check to see if any of the preceding limitations are relevant in their research situation. For example, a scatter diagram can help to identify outliers. The researcher can then conduct the analysis two ways. In one analysis, the outliers are included in the figuring; and in a separate analysis, the outliers are excluded from the figuring. By doing this, the researcher can see how the outliers influence the overall results.

How are you doing?

1. What is multiple regression?
2. Write the multiple regression linear prediction rule with two predictors and define each of the symbols.
3. In a multiple regression linear prediction rule, the regression constant is 2.19, the regression coefficient for the first variable is -3.16, and the regression coefficient for the second variable is .99. What is the predicted score on the criterion variable for (a) a person with a score of .40 on the first predictor variable and a score of 10.50 on the second predictor variable, and (b) a person with a score of .15 on the first predictor variable and a score of 5.50 on the second predictor variable?
4. In multiple regression, why are the standardized regression coefficients for each predictor variable often smaller than the ordinary correlation coefficient of that predictor variable with the criterion variable?
5. What are the different hypothesis tests for multiple regression?
6. List four conditions in which regression coefficients you figure will be closer to zero than they would be if they represented the true linear prediction rule.

Answers

1. Multiple regression is the procedure for predicting a criterion variable from a prediction rule that includes more than one predictor variable.

2. The multiple regression linear prediction rule is $\hat{Y} = a + (b_1)(X_1) + (b_2)(X_2)$. $\hat{Y}$ is the predicted score on the criterion variable; a is the regression constant; b_1 is the regression coefficient for the first predictor variable; X_1 is the person's score on the first predictor variable; b_2 is the regression coefficient for the second predictor variable; and X_2 is the person's score on the second predictor variable.

3. Predicted scores on the criterion variable:
(a) $\hat{Y} = 2.19 - (3.16)(.40) + (.99)(10.50) = 2.19 - 1.26 + 10.40 = 11.33$.
(b) $\hat{Y} = 2.19 - (3.16)(.15) + (.99)(5.50) = 2.19 - .47 + 5.45 = 7.17$.

4. In multiple regression, a predictor variable's association with the criterion variable usually overlaps with the other predictor variables' association with the criterion variable. Thus, the unique association of a predictor variable with the criterion variable (as shown by the standardized regression coefficient) is usually smaller than the ordinary correlation of the predictor variable with the criterion variable.

5. There is a hypothesis test to test the significance of the multiple correlation. Also, a hypothesis test can be carried out for each predictor variable to test whether its regression coefficient is significantly different from 0. Finally, there is a hypothesis test to test whether the regression constant is significantly different from 0.

6. Four conditions in which regression coefficients you figure will be closer to zero than they would be if they represented the true linear prediction rule: (i) restriction in range, (ii) curvilinear associations, (iii) unreliable measurement, and (iv) outliers.

Controversy: Unstandardized and Standardized Regression Coefficients; Comparing Predictors

There is some debate in the psychological research literature about whether research studies should present their results in terms of unstandardized regression coefficients (βs), standardized regression coefficients (bs), or both types of coefficient. The publication guidelines of the American Psychological Association (2001) recommend listing only regular unstandardized regression coefficients when the study is purely applied, only standardized regression coefficients when the study is purely theoretical, and both the regular and standardized regression coefficients in all other cases. While this appears to be a straightforward solution to the issue, researchers do not always agree as to when a study is *purely* applied or *purely* theoretical. This issue is further complicated by the fact that standardized regression coefficients can be less than consistent across different samples because they are influenced by the range (and variance) of the scores in the samples, while unstandardized regression coefficients are not so influenced. Overall, we generally recommend that, unless there is a good reason not to do so, you present the results of your own research studies in terms of both unstandardized and standardized regression coefficients.

Related to these issues, recall from earlier in the chapter that we introduced the standardized regression coefficient as a useful way to compare a regression coefficient from one study with a regression coefficient from another study. Similarly, when comparing the size of the regression coefficients for each of several predictor variables in a multiple regression, you should compare the standardized regression coefficients (the βs), as opposed to the regular unstandardized regression coefficients (the bs). This is because a larger value of b for one predictor variable compared to another predictor variable may simply reflect the different scales for each variable (0 to 10 versus 0 to 100, for example).

However, even assuming we want to focus on standardized values for some purposes, there is an ongoing controversy in multiple regression about how to judge the relative importance of each predictor variable in predicting the criterion variable. The question is whether (i) you should use the standardized regression coefficients (the βs) of the predictor variables from the overall regression equation, or (ii) you should instead use the bivariate correlation coefficients (the rs) of each predictor variable with the criterion variable. Both are standardized in that they adjust for the variation in the variables used, and in bivariate regression they are the same thing. But in multiple regression, as we noted, they are not the same thing. Specifically, a regression coefficient tells you the unique contribution of the predictor variable to the prediction, over and above all the other predictors. When predicting by itself, without considering the other predictors (that is, using its ordinary correlation, r, with the criterion variable), a predictor variable may seem to have a quite different importance relative to the other predictor variables.

For example, if there are three predictors, the standardized regression coefficients (the βs) could be .4, .6, and .8. But in that particular study, the rs for these three predictors might be .4, .2, and .3. Thus, if you looked at the βs, you would think the third predictor was most important; but if you looked at the rs, you would think the first predictor was the most important.

Many approaches to this problem have been considered over the years, but all are controversial. What most experts recommend is to use all the information you have; consider *both* the rs *and* the βs, keeping in mind the difference in what they tell you. The r tells you the overall association of the predictor variable with the criterion variable. The β tells you the unique association of this predictor variable, over and above the other predictor variables, with the criterion variable.

In addition to these and other controversies relating to the statistical aspects, there has been an ongoing controversy for many years about the superiority of statistical prediction over more intuitive, humanistic, or clinical approaches. This issue is addressed in Box 12–1.

BOX 12–1 **Clinical versus Statistical Prediction**

More than fifty years ago, Paul Meehl (1954) wrote an unsettling little book called *Clinical vs. Statistical Prediction*. He argued that when experts such as clinical psychologists (or business managers, economic forecasters, engineers, or doctors, among others) use the kinds of unspecified internal cognitive processes that are usually called "trained intuitions," they are not very accurate. On the average their decisions are no better than those anybody could make by using very simple, straightforward prediction *formulas*. For example, in psychiatric diagnosing, a supposedly well-trained clinician's interview and diagnosis are less useful than a mere rule such as "if the person has been admitted to the hospital twice before, is over 50, and appears suicidal, then . . ."—the kind of rule generated by using a multiple regression model.

In the first decade after Meehl questioned the accuracy of experts, considerable efforts were made to disprove him. But on the whole, Meehl's discovery has held up. He noted this himself 30 years later in an article entitled "Causes and Effects of My Disturbing Little Book" (Meehl, 1986). Looking specifically at predictions in clinical psychology, a recent meta-analysis of nearly a hundred research studies (Ægisdóttir et al., 2006) continues to support his basic conclusion, with some caveats. It is important that clinicians be allowed to follow a client model-building process, in which clinicians act like scientists, forming a hypothesis about a patient based on statistical information and then applying it to see if it holds up (Strohmer & Arm, 2006). Perhaps with this client the hypothesis needs revising because new facts have come to light, making other research more relevant. Then the clinician hears some other new aspect that requires the hypothesis to be revised again, on the basis of research on this aspect, and so on. What is important is that this scientific model-building process replace jumping to the wrong conclusion, which could happen either with intuition or a formula.

Further, this issue tends to become polarized between "therapy-as-an-art" and "formulas-beat-clinicians." In fact "Although the statistical method is almost always the equal of the clinical method and is often better, the improvement is not overwhelming" (Ægisdóttir et al., 2006, p. 367). It amounts in study after study to be about a 13% increase in accuracy. Formulas, therefore, seem most important when making a mistake is especially dangerous. That is in fact how formulas have been most often used so far—to predict suicide, violence, and recidivism.

Remember, this is an issue of prediction, and statistical methods often cannot do all that well at predicting violence or suicide either. Their main advantage is consistency, like a gambler with a system.

Naturally, the focus has turned to how cognition operates, why it is flawed, and what, if anything, can be done to improve it. The flaws are mainly that people make illusory correlations (see Chapter 11, Box 11–2). Or they are overconfident; they do not keep a record of their successes and failures to see whether they are in fact accurate, but instead put too much weight on their remembered successes and forget their failures. Also, overconfidence comes in part from lack of feedback; clinicians may make hundreds of diagnoses without learning whether they were correct. Finally, human memory and cognition may not have the capacity to handle the information and operations required to make certain complex decisions. And that capacity varies. Some people have a high "need for cognition," the desire to think about things. Those with a low need are less consistent and accurate (Ruscio, 2000).

A great deal of research has addressed how to "de-bias" human decisions. People can be shown when they must rely on their intuition—for example, when there is not enough time to apply a formula or when simple averaging will suffice. At other times they need to understand that a formula is more accurate—for example, when rules are complicated.

There is also considerable work on decision aids, such as computer programs with built-in decision rules supplied by experts. Sometimes, more intuitive or subjective information can be added at the last minute by experts knowledgeable about the particular situation (Holzworth, 1996; Whitecotton, 1996). What cannot be allowed with any decision aid is that it be abandoned when someone has a hunch they can do better without the aid.

The use of decision support systems is on the rise. For example, expert chess players have developed aids that can sometimes outwit their own creators, merely by being thoroughly consistent. Thus, some chess players have become comfortable using decision support systems to keep themselves on track during a game. And as health care is forced to become more cost conscious, it may have to use impartial decision aids about who receives what treatment. And the public may benefit. For example, a decision aid for helping doctors who are not dermatologists decide if something might be skin cancer and require referral to a specialist was found to decrease errors by 64% (Gerbert et al., 1999). Another decision aid reduced serious medication errors by 55% (Bates et al., 1998).

Prediction in Research Articles

It is rare for bivariate linear prediction rules to be reported in psychology research articles; usually, simple correlations are reported. Sometimes, however, you will see regression lines from bivariate predictions. This is usually done when there is more than one group and the researcher wants to illustrate the difference in the linear prediction rule between the two groups.

For example, consider an experiment Oettingen and her colleagues (2001) conducted with German university students. This experiment focused on the students' thoughts about the possibility of studying abroad. First, the students were asked about how much they expected to succeed (that is, how likely it was that they would study abroad). In the next part of the study, participants were divided into one of three groups. Participants in the positive fantasy group were instructed to spend some time thinking about specific positive aspects of studying abroad; those in the negative reality group, were instructed to spend some time thinking about specific obstacles that stand in the way of studying abroad; and those in the contrast group were instructed to spend some time thinking about both positive possibilities and negative realities. Afterward, participants answered questions about how disappointed they would be if they were never able to study abroad.

Figure 12–7 (from Oettingen et al., 2001) shows a regression line for each of the three experimental groups. Each regression line shows how much expectation of success predicts anticipated disappointment. The major result is shown in the solid blue line: For students in the contrast group (those who thought about both the positive possibilities and realistic obstacles), the greater their initial expectations of success, the more disappointed they would be if they were not able to study abroad.

The researchers see the pattern for the contrast group as what would be expected: that people are most disappointed when they expect to succeed and least disappointed when they don't. But either having positive fantasies or dwelling on negative obstacles interferes with this normal process; so level of disappointment is much less related to expectations of success.

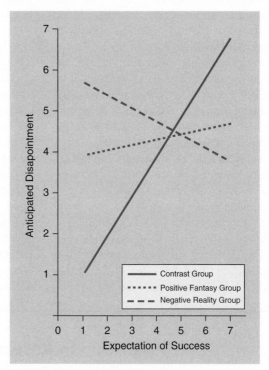

Figure 12–7 Regression lines depicting the link of expectation of success to anticipated disappointment as a function of self-regulatory thought.

Source: Oettingen, G., Schnetter, K., and Pak, H. (2001). Self-regulation of goal setting: Turning free fantasies about the future into binding goals. *Journal of Personality and Social Psychology, 80,* 736–753. Published by the American Psychological Association. Reprinted with permission.

Multiple regression results are common in research articles and are often reported in tables. Usually, the table lays out the regression coefficient for each predictor variable, which can be either the regular unstandardized (b), standardized (β), or both, along with the overall R or R^2 in a note at the bottom of the table. [As we noted earlier in this chapter, the publication guidelines of the American Psychological Association (2001) recommend listing only regular unstandardized regression coefficients when the study is purely applied, only standardized regression coefficients when the study is purely theoretical, and both the regular and standardized regression coefficients in all other cases.] The table may also give the correlation coefficient (r) for each predictor variable with the criterion variable. This lets you compare the unique association of each predictor to the criterion variable (what the regression coefficient tells you) with the overall association (what the correlation coefficient tells you). As we saw in Chapter 11 with correlation tables, regression tables also usually give the statistical significance for the various statistics reported. Finally, many tables will provide a variety of other statistics that go beyond what we have covered. But if you understand the basics, you should be able to make good sense of the key information in such tables.

Consider an example from a study (Hahlweg et al., 2001) of a treatment method for agoraphobia, a condition that affects about 4% of the population and involves unpredictable panic attacks in public places such as crowded restaurants, buses, or movie theaters. Table 12–8 (from Hahlweg et al., 2001) shows the correlation coefficients (rs) and standardized regression coefficients (βs) for four variables predicting the effectiveness of the treatment. (The actual criterion variable is labeled "Average Intragroup Effect Size at Postassessment." The article explains that this is each patient's change from before to after treatment, averaged across several measures of mental health.)

Looking at the β column, you can see that the standardized regression coefficients were very small for number of sessions attended and the duration of the disorder. At the same time, age and BDI (a measure of depression at the start of treatment) were much more important unique predictors of the outcome of treatment. Notice from the asterisks and the note at the bottom of the table that the regression coefficients for the number of sessions and duration of disorder were not statistically significant, whereas the coefficients for BDI and age were significant. Also notice (from the bottom of the table) that the overall correlation of the four predictors with treatment outcome had an R of .36 and an R^2 of .13. This is a moderate overall relationship, but

Table 12-8 Multiple Regression Analysis Predicting Average Intragroup Effect Size at Postassessment

Independent Variable	r	β
BDI	.30***	.30***
Age	−.21***	−.20**
No. of sessions	.12*	.08
Duration of disorder	−.13*	−.02

Note: $R = .36$; $R^2 = .13$. BDI = Beck Depression Inventory.

*$p < .05$. **$p < .01$. ***$p < .000$.

Source: Hahlweg, K., Fiegenbaum, W., Frank, M., Schroeder, B., & von Witzleben, I. (2001). Short- and long-term effectiveness of an empirically supported treatment of agoraphobia. *Journal of Consulting and Clinical Psychology, 69,* 375–382. Published by the American Psychological Association. Reprinted with permission.

not substantial; that is, only 13% of the overall variation in treatment outcome was predicted by these four variables. Notice also the r column. For BDI and age, the βs and rs are about the same. Note, however, that number of sessions and durations have larger rs than βs. This suggests that these two variables have considerable overlap with each other or other variables in the prediction rule, so that their unique contribution to predicting treatment outcome is rather small.

Advanced Topic: Error and Proportionate Reduction in Error

How accurate are the predictions you make using regression? Normally, you predict the future; so there is no way to know how accurate you are in advance. However, you can estimate your likely accuracy. What you do is figure how accurate your prediction rule would have been if you had used it to make "predictions" for the scores you used to figure the linear regression rule (and correlation coefficient) in the first place. We did this earlier in the chapter when we figured the sum of squared errors for the linear prediction rule for the sleep and mood example. The linear prediction rule for this example was $\hat{Y} = -3 + (1)(X)$. This rule was shown as regression line "Rule 4" in Figure 12–6. The figuring of the squared error for the rule is shown in Table 12–4.

Proportionate Reduction in Error

Now, how is knowing the squared errors useful? The most common way to think about the accuracy of a prediction rule is to compare the amount of squared error using your prediction rule to the amount of squared error you would have without the prediction rule.

First, you figure the amount of squared error using the prediction rule. Next, you figure the squared error you would make predicting without the prediction rule. Finally, you compare the two amounts of squared error.

The squared error using the prediction rule is the *sum of the squared errors*. That is, you just add up the squared errors of the individuals in the study. In the sleep and mood example, this is the sum of the last column in Table 12–4, which is 6.00. The sum of squared errors is abbreviated as SS_{Error}. In our example, $SS_{\text{Error}} = 6.00$.

How do you figure the amount of squared error predicting without the prediction rule? If you cannot use the prediction rule, the most accurate prediction for anyone will be the criterion variable's mean. In our example, suppose you knew nothing about how much a person slept the night before. Your best strategy for any student would be to predict that the student will have the mean score on happy mood. That is, your best strategy would be to predict a mood score of 4. (Earlier in the chapter we called this particular rule of predicting 4 for each person "Rule 2" and showed the regression line for it in Figure 12–6.) Consider another example. Suppose you wanted to predict a person's college GPA, but you had no information about any predictor variables. Your best bet here is to predict that the person will have the mean college GPA for students at that college.

Thus, predictions without a prediction rule involve predicting the mean. This means that *the amount of squared error when predicting without a rule is the amount of squared error when predicting each score to be the mean.* Error in general is the actual score on the criterion variable minus the predicted score on the criterion variable. When the predicted score is the mean, error is the actual score minus the mean.

SS_{Error} (sum of the squared errors) sum of the squared differences between each score on the criterion variable and its predicted score.

Squared error is the square of this number. The sum of these squared errors is the **total squared error when predicting from the mean; we call this number SS_{Total}.** (What we are now calling SS_{Total} is the same as what we called SS in Chapter 2 when figuring the variance, and is also the same as what we call SS_Y in this chapter and Chapter 11. In Chapter 2, we defined SS as the sum of squared deviations from the mean. A deviation from the mean is the score minus the mean. This is exactly the same as the error that results when our prediction is the mean.)

The value of a prediction rule is how much *less* error you make using the prediction rule (SS_{Error}) compared to using the mean (SS_{Total}). With a good prediction rule, SS_{Error} should be much smaller than SS_{Total}.

The key comparison is the *proportionate reduction in error:* The reduction in error ($SS_{Total} - SS_{Error}$), divided by the total amount that could be reduced (SS_{Total}). In terms of a formula,

$$\text{Proportionate reduction in error} = \frac{SS_{Total} - SS_{Error}}{SS_{Total}} \qquad (12\text{--}6)$$

> The proportionate reduction in error is the sum of squared error when predicting from the mean minus the sum of squared error when predicting from the bivariate prediction rule, all divided by the sum of squared error when predicting from the mean.

To put this another way, using the mean to predict is not a very precise method because it leaves a lot of error. So now you are seeing how much better you can do—how much the proportion of the squared error you would make using the mean is reduced by using the prediction rule.

Suppose a prediction rule is no improvement over predicting from the mean. In this situation, SS_{Error} equals SS_{Total} (SS_{Error} can never be worse than SS_{Total}). The prediction rule has reduced zero error ($SS_{Total} - SS_{Error} = 0$), and it has reduced 0% of the total error ($0/SS_{Total} = 0$).

Now suppose a prediction rule gives perfect predictions with no error whatsoever. The prediction rule has reduced the error by 100%. (In terms of the equation, if $SS_{Error} = 0$, then the numerator will be $SS_{Total} - 0$, or SS_{Total}; dividing SS_{Total} by SS_{Total} gives 1, or 100%.)

In most actual situations, the proportionate reduction in error will be somewhere between 0% and 100%.

Steps for Figuring the Proportionate Reduction in Error

❶ **Figure the sum of squared errors using the mean to predict.** Take each score minus the mean, square it, and add these up. This gives SS_{Total}.

❷ **Figure the sum of squared errors using the prediction rule.** Take each score minus the predicted score for this person, square it, and add these up. This gives SS_{Error}.

❸ **Figure the reduction in squared error.** This is the sum of squared errors using the mean to predict (from Step ❶) minus the sum of squared errors using the prediction rule (from Step ❷).

❹ **Figure the proportionate reduction in squared error.** This is the reduction in squared error (from Step ❸) divided by the total squared error when using the mean to predict (from Step ❶).

An Example

Table 12–9 shows the actual scores, predicted scores, errors, squared errors, sums of squared errors, and proportionate reduction in error for the sleep and mood example. Using the steps,

total squared error when predicting from the mean (SS_{Total}) sum of squared differences of each score on the criterion variable from the predicted score when predicting from the mean.

Table 12-9 Figuring Proportionate Reduction in Error for the Fictional Sleep and Mood Example

Hours Slept	Actual Mood	Predicted Mood Using Mean ❶			Predicted Mood Using Prediction Rule ❷		
		Mean Mood	Error	Error^2	Predicted Mood	Error	Error^2
X	Y	M	$(Y - M)$	$(Y - M)^2$	$\hat{Y}$	$(Y - \hat{Y})$	$(Y - \hat{Y})^2$
5	2	4	−2	4	2.00	.00	.00
6	2	4	−2	4	3.00	−1.00	1.00
6	3	4	−1	1	3.00	.00	.00
7	4	4	0	0	4.00	.00	.00
8	7	4	3	9	5.00	2.00	4.00
10	6	4	2	4	7.00	−1.00	1.00
				$\Sigma = SS_{\text{Total}} = 22$			$\Sigma = SS_{\text{Error}} = 6.00$

Proportionate reduction in error $= \dfrac{❸SS_{\text{Total}} - SS_{\text{Error}}}{SS_{\text{Total}}} = \dfrac{22 - 6}{22} = \dfrac{16}{22} = .73$ ❹

❶ **Figure the sum of squared errors using the mean to predict.** Take each score minus the mean, square it, and add these up. From Table 12–9, $SS_{\text{Total}} = 22$. (Note that this is the same as SS_Y we figured for happy mood in the last chapter and again in this one as part of the figuring for the standardized regression coefficient.)

❷ **Figure the sum of squared errors using the prediction rule.** Take each score on the criterion variable (Y) minus the predicted score on the criterion variable ($\hat{Y}$) for this person, square it, and add these up. From Table 12–9, $SS_{\text{Error}} = 6.00$.

❸ **Figure the reduction in squared error.** This is the sum of squared errors using the mean to predict (from Step ❶) minus the sum of squared errors using the prediction rule (from Step ❷). Reduction in squared error $= 22 - 6 = 16$.

❹ **Figure the proportionate reduction in squared error.** This is the reduction in squared error (from Step ❸) divided by the total squared error when using the mean to predict (from Step ❶). Proportionate reduction in squared error $= 16/22 = .73$.

Thus, when predicting happy mood from sleep the night before, the prediction rule, based on the scores from our group of 6 students, provides a 73% reduction in error over using the mean to predict.

Proportionate Reduction in Error as r^2

The proportionate reduction in error turns out to equal the correlation coefficient squared. That is,

$$\text{Proportionate reduction in error} = r^2 \qquad \text{(12–7)}$$

> The proportionate reduction in error is equal to the correlation coefficient squared.

Because of this equivalence, r^2 is typically used as the symbol for the proportionate reduction in error with bivariate prediction. (As we noted earlier in the chapter, R^2 is the symbol for the proportionate reduction in error for multiple regression.)

For example, in the sleep and mood study, the correlation coefficient was .85, and .85 squared is .72. That is, $r^2 = .72$. Notice that, within rounding error, this number (.72) is the same as we just figured (.73) by finding predicted scores, errors, squared errors, sums of squared errors, and proportionate reduction in squared error.

We figured the proportionate reduction in error so laboriously in this example only to help you understand this important concept. However, in an actual research situation, you would use the simpler procedure of squaring the correlation coefficient. (Also note that this works in reverse also. If you know the proportionate reduction in error, you can find the correlation coefficient by taking the square root of the proportionate reduction in error. Since a square root can be positive or negative, look at the pattern of numbers to determine if the correlation is positive or negative.)

How are you doing?

1. Explain in words how you figure (a) the sum of squared error predicting from the mean, and (b) the sum of squared error using the prediction rule.
2. Write the formula for figuring the proportionate reduction in error and define each of its symbols in words.
3. Explain why the procedure for figuring the proportionate reduction in error tells you about the accuracy of the prediction rule.
4. The following scores and predicted scores are for four people on a particular criterion variable using a prediction rule based on the scores from these four people. Figure the proportionate reduction in error and correlation coefficient.

Score	Predicted Score
Y	$\hat{Y}$
6	5.7
4	4.3
2	2.9
8	7.1

Answers

3. The procedure for figuring the proportionate reduction in error tells you about the accuracy of the prediction rule because it tells you the proportion of total error (the error you would make if just predicting from the mean) you are reducing by using the prediction rule (where your error is based on predicting from the prediction rule). That is, the larger proportion of total error you reduce, the more accurate your prediction rule will be. Perfect prediction would be 100% reduction.

4.

Score	Mean	Error	Error²	Predicted Score	Error	Error²
Y	M	$(Y-M)$	$(Y-M)^2$	$\hat{Y}$	$(Y-\hat{Y})$	$(Y-\hat{Y})^2$
6	5	1	1	5.7	.3	.09
4	5	−1	1	4.3	−.3	.09
2	5	−3	9	2.9	−.9	.81
8	5	3	9	7.1	.9	.81
		$\Sigma = SS_\text{Total} = 20$				$\Sigma = SS_\text{Error} = 1.80$

Proportionate reduction in error $= (SS_\text{Total} - SS_\text{Error})/SS_\text{Total} = (20 - 1.80)/20 = 18.20/20 = .91$. $r = \sqrt{r^2} = \sqrt{.91} = .95$. (It is a positive correlation, as low scores go with lows and highs with highs.)

Summary

1. Prediction (or regression) involves making predictions about scores on a criterion variable based on scores on a predictor variable.
2. The linear prediction rule for predicting scores on a criterion variable from scores on a predictor variable is $\hat{Y} = a + (b)(X)$, where $\hat{Y}$ is the predicted score on the criterion variable, a is the regression constant, b is the regression coefficient, and X is the score on the predictor variable.
3. A regression line, which is drawn in the same kind of graph as a scatter diagram, shows the predicted criterion variable value ($\hat{Y}$) for each value of the predictor variable (X). The slope of this line equals b; a is where this line crosses the vertical axis (the intercept). A regression line is a visual equivalent of a linear prediction rule.
4. The best linear prediction rule is the rule that gives the lowest sum of squared errors between the actual scores on the criterion variable and the predicted scores on the criterion variable. There are formulas for figuring the regression constant (a) and the regression coefficient (b) that will give the linear prediction rule with the smallest sum of squared errors.
5. A standardized regression coefficient (β) shows how much of a standard deviation the predicted value of the criterion variable changes when the predictor variable changes by one standard deviation. The standardized regression coefficient can be figured from the regular regression coefficient and the sum of squared deviations for the predictor and criterion variables. When predicting scores on the criterion variable from scores on one other variable (bivariate prediction), the standardized regression coefficient (β) is the same as the correlation coefficient (r) between the two variables.
6. In bivariate prediction, the hypothesis test for a regression coefficient is the same as the hypothesis test for the correlation between the two variables.
7. In multiple regression, a criterion variable is predicted from two or more predictor variables. In a multiple regression linear prediction rule, there is a regression constant, the score for each predictor variable is multiplied by its own regression coefficient, and the results are added up to make the prediction. Each regression coefficient tells you the unique relation of the predictor to the criterion variable in the context of the other predictor variables. The multiple correlation

coefficient (R) is the overall degree of association between the criterion variable and the predictor variables taken together. R^2 is the overall proportionate reduction in error for multiple regression.

8. Bivariate prediction and multiple regression have the same limitations as ordinary correlation. In addition, in multiple regression there is ambiguity in interpreting the relative importance of the predictor variables.

9. Bivariate prediction results are rarely described directly in research articles, but regression lines are sometimes shown when prediction rules for more than one group are being compared. Multiple regressions are commonly reported in articles, often in a table that includes the regression coefficients and overall proportionate reduction in error (R^2).

10. ADVANCED TOPIC: The proportionate reduction in error, an indicator of the accuracy of a prediction rule, is figured by applying the prediction rule to the scores on which the prediction rule was based. The sum of squared error when using the prediction rule (SS_{Error}) is the sum of the squared differences between each actual score and the predicted score for that individual; the sum of squared error total (SS_{Total}) is the sum of the squared differences between each actual score and the mean; the proportionate reduction in error is the reduction in squared error gained by using the prediction rule ($SS_{Total} - SS_{Error}$) divided by the squared error when predicting from the mean (SS_{Total}). The proportionate reduction in error (or proportion of variance accounted for) in bivariate prediction equals the correlation coefficient squared (r^2).

Key Terms

predictor variable (X) (p. 488)
criterion variable (Y) (p. 488)
linear prediction rule (p. 489)
regression constant (a) (p. 489)
regression coefficient (b) (p. 489)
regression line (p. 492)
slope (p. 492)

intercept (p. 493)
error (p. 498)
sum of the squared errors (p. 498)
standardized regression coefficient (β) (p. 504)
bivariate prediction (p. 506)
multiple correlation (p. 506)

multiple regression (p. 506)
multiple correlation coefficient (R) (p. 507)
SS_{Error} (sum of the squared errors) (p. 514)
total squared error when predicting from the mean (SS_{Total}) (p. 515)

Example Worked-Out Problems

The following bivariate problems are based on the following data set. (This is the same data for the example worked-out problems in Chapter 11.) In this study, the researchers want to predict achievement test score from class size.

Elementary School	Class Size	Achievement Test Score
Main Street	25	80
Casat	14	98
Harland	33	50
Shady Grove	28	82
Jefferson	20	90
M	24	80
$r = -.90$		

Using the Linear Prediction Rule

If the regression constant for predicting achievement test scores from class size is 134 and the regression coefficient is −2.25 (you will figure these values for yourself in a later example worked-out problem), what is the predicted achievement test score for a school with a class size of (a) 23, and (b) 14?

Answer

Using the linear prediction rule $\hat{Y} = a + (b)(X)$, $\hat{Y} = 134 − (2.25)(X)$.

  (a) If class size is 23, then the predicted achievement test score $= 134 − (2.25)(23) = 82.25$.
  (b) Predicted achievement test score $= 134 − (2.25)(14) = 102.50$.

Drawing a Regression Line

Draw the regression line for predicting achievement test scores from class size.

Answer

The result of each step is shown in Figure 12–8.

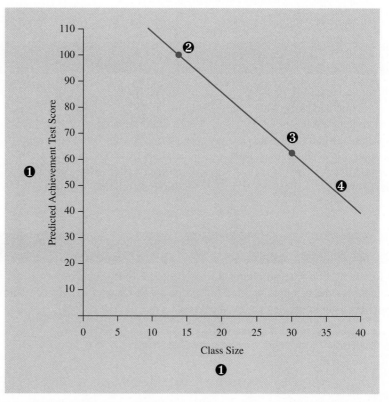

Figure 12–8   Steps in drawing a regression line for the class size and achievement test score Example Worked-Out Problem. ❶ Draw and label the axes, ❷ mark a point for a low value of the predictor variable and its predicted value on the criterion variable, ❸ mark a point for a high value of the predictor variable and its predicted value on the criterion variable, and ❹ draw the regression line.

❶ **Draw and label the axes for a scatter diagram.**

❷ **Figure the predicted value on the criterion variable for a low value on the predictor variable, and mark the point on the graph.** From the answer to the previous problem, the predicted achievement test score for a school with a class size of 14 is 102.50. Thus, you mark the point $(X = 14, \hat{Y} = 102.50)$.

❸ **Do the same thing again, but for a high value on the predictor variable.** For a class size of 30, the predicted achievement test score is $134 - (2.25)(30)$, which is 66.50. Thus, you mark the point $(X = 30, \hat{Y} = 66.50)$.

❹ **Draw a line that passes through the two marks.**

Finding the Values of a and b

Earlier we told you that the regression constant (a) for predicting achievement test scores from class size was 134 and the regression coefficient (b) was -2.25. Carry out the figuring for a and b to make sure these are the correct values.

Answer

The figuring for a and b is shown in Table 12–10.

Here are the steps for figuring the regression coefficient, b:

❶ **Change the scores for each variable to deviation scores.** Figure the mean of each variable. Then subtract each variable's mean from each of its scores.

❷ **Figure the product of the deviation scores for each pair of scores.** That is, for each pair of scores, multiply the deviation score on one variable by the deviation score on the other variable.

❸ **Add up all the products of the deviation scores.** This gives a total of -482.

❹ **Square each deviation score for the predictor variable (X).**

❺ **Add up the squared deviation scores for the predictor variable (X).** This gives a total of 214.

Table 12-10   Figuring the Values of a and b for the Example Worked-Out Problem

Class Size (X)			Achievement Test Score (Y)		
	Deviation ❶	Deviation Squared ❹		Deviation ❶	Products of ❷ Deviation Scores
X	$X - M_X$	$(X - M_X)^2$	Y	$Y - M_Y$	$(X - M_X)(Y - M_Y)$
25	1	1	80	0	0
14	-10	100	98	18	-180
33	9	81	50	-30	-270
28	4	16	82	2	8
20	-4	16	90	10	-40
$\Sigma = 120$		$\Sigma = SS_X = 214$	$\Sigma = 400$		$\Sigma = -482$
$M = 24$		❺	$M = 80$		❸

$$b = \frac{\Sigma[(X - M_X)(Y - M_Y)]}{SS_X} = \frac{\overset{❻}{-482}}{214} = -2.25$$

$$a = M_Y - (b)(M_X) = 80 - (-2.25)(24) = 134$$

Note: The circled numbers refer to the steps for figuring the regression coefficient, b.

❻ **Divide the sum of the products of deviation scores from Step ❸ by the sum of squared deviations for the predictor variable (*X*) from Step ❺.** This gives the regression coefficient, *b*. Dividing −482 by 214 gives a *b* of −2.25.

Here are the steps for figuring the regression constant, *a:*

❶ **Multiply the regression coefficient, *b*, by the mean of the *X* variable.** Multiplying −2.25 by 24 gives −54.

❷ **Subtract the result of Step ❶ from the mean of the *Y* variable.** This gives the regression constant, *a*. Subtracting −54 from 80 gives 80 − (−54), which is 134.

So the value of *b* is −2.25 and the value of *a* is 134.

Figuring the Standardized Regression Coefficient

Figure the standardized regression for predicting achievement test scores from class size.

Answer

The formula for a standardized regression coefficient is

$$\beta = (b)\frac{\sqrt{SS_X}}{\sqrt{SS_Y}}.$$

From Table 12–10, SS_X is 214. Table 12–10 doesn't show the value of SS_Y, but we can figure it by squaring each score in the $Y - M_Y$ column and summing the resulting values. Thus, $SS_Y = 0^2 + 18^2 + (-30^2) + 2^2 + 10^2 = 1328$. The value of *b* was −2.25; so the standardized regression coefficient for predicting achievement test scores from class size is

$$\beta = (b)\frac{\sqrt{SS_X}}{\sqrt{SS_Y}} = (-2.25)\frac{\sqrt{214}}{\sqrt{1328}} = (-2.25)\frac{14.63}{36.44} = -.90.$$

Multiple Regression Predictions

A (fictional) psychologist studied the talkativeness of children in families with a mother, father, and one grandparent. The psychologist found that the child's talkativeness score depended on the quality of the child's relationship with each of these people. The multiple regression linear prediction rule was as follows:

Child's predicted talkativeness = 2.13 + (1.32)(mother) + (1.21)(father)
+ (1.41)(grandparent).

Predict a child's talkativeness score who had scores for relationship quality of 4 with mother, 5 with father, and 3 with grandparent.

Answer

Child's predicted talkativeness = 2.13 + (1.32)(mother) + (1.21)(father)
+ (1.41)(grandparent).
= 2.13 + (1.32)(4) + (1.21)(5)
+ (1.41)(3) = 17.69.

Advanced Topic: Figuring the Proportionate Reduction in Error

Using the method of finding SS_{Total} and SS_{Error}, find the proportionate reduction in error for predicting achievement test scores from class size.

Answer

We first need to find the predicted achievement score for each school using the linear prediction rule. The rule in this example is $\hat{Y} = 134 - (2.25)(X)$. So, for the first school, Main Street, $\hat{Y} = 134 - (2.25)(25) = 77.74$. Repeating this process for the other schools gives predicted achievement test scores of: Casat, 102.50; Harland, 59.75; Shady Grove, 71.00; Jefferson, 89.00.

The figuring for the proportionate reduction of error is shown in Table 12–11, and the steps follow.

❶ **Figure the sum of squared error using the mean to predict.** Take each score minus the mean, square it, and add these up. From Table 12–11, $SS_{Total} = 1328$.

❷ **Figure the sum of squared errors using the prediction rule.** Take each score minus the predicted score for this person, square it, and add these up. From Table 12–11, $SS_{Error} = 242.37$.

❸ **Figure the reduction in squared error.** This is the sum of squared errors using the mean to predict (from Step ❶) minus the sum of squared errors using the prediction rule (from Step ❷). Reduction in squared error $= 1328 - 242.37 = 1085.63$.

❹ **Figure the proportionate reduction in squared error.** This is the reduction in squared error (from Step ❸) divided by the total squared error when using the mean to predict (from Step ❶). Proportionate reduction in squared error $= 1085.63/1328 = .82$. You can interpret this in terms of 82% of the variation in test scores being accounted for by class size.

> **TIP FOR SUCCESS**
>
> The square root of the proportionate reduction in error should equal the correlation. In this problem, $\sqrt{.82} = -.91$ (it is a negative correlation in this example, because low scores go with high scores and highs with lows), which is consistent (allowing for rounding error) with the correlation we began with of $-.90$.

Table 12-11 Figuring Proportionate Reduction in Error for the Example Worked-Out Problem

Class Size	Actual Test Score	Mean Test Score	Predicted Test Score ❶ Using Mean		Predicted Test Score ❷ Using Prediction Rule		
			Error	Error²	Predicted Test Score	Error	Error²
X	Y	M	$(Y - M)$	$(Y - M)^2$	$\hat{Y}$	$(Y - \hat{Y})$	$(Y - \hat{Y})^2$
25	80	80	0	0	77.75	2.25	5.06
14	98	80	18	324	102.50	−4.50	20.25
33	50	80	−30	900	59.75	−9.75	95.06
28	82	80	2	4	71.00	11.00	121.00
20	90	80	10	100	89.00	1.00	1.00
				$\Sigma = SS_{Total} = 1328$			$\Sigma = SS_{Error} = 242.37$

$$\text{Proportionate reduction in error} = \frac{\overset{❸}{SS_{Total} - SS_{Error}}}{SS_{Total}} = \frac{1328 - 242.37}{1328} = \frac{1085.63}{1328} \overset{❹}{=} .82.$$

Outline for Writing Essays on the Logic and Figuring of Bivariate Prediction

1. Explain the meaning of the term *prediction* as it is used in the context of statistics. Be sure to mention and explain key terms such as *predictor variable* and *criterion variable.*

2. Explain the concept of the linear prediction rule, including its formula. As part of this explanation, be sure to emphasize the meaning of the regression coefficient and regression constant.

3. Explain how the linear prediction rule can be shown as a line on a graph, called a *regression line.* Be sure to describe how to draw the regression line and what it shows.

4. Explain how the regression coefficient and regression constant are each related to the regression line.

5. Explain the idea of the best linear prediction rule in terms of the notion of least squared error.

6. Explain the meaning of the standardized regression coefficient, why it is useful, and how it is figured.

7. In the context of these explanations, describe the meaning of the numeric results of the particular question you are answering.

Practice Problems

These problems involve figuring. Most real-life statistics problems are done on a computer with special statistical software. Even if you have such software, do these problems by hand to ingrain the method in your mind. To learn how to use a computer to solve statistics problems like those in this chapter, refer to the Using SPSS section at the end of this chapter and the *Study Guide and Computer Workbook* that accompanies this text.

All data are fictional unless an actual citation is given.

Set I (for Answers to Set I Problems, see pp. 692–695)

1. A sports psychologist working with hockey players has found that players' knowledge of physiology predicts the number of injuries received over the subsequent year. The regression constant in the linear prediction rule for predicting injuries from knowledge of physiology is 10.30 and the regression coefficient is $-.70$. (a) Indicate the predictor variable, and (b) the criterion variable. (c) Write the linear prediction rule for this example. Indicate the predicted number of injuries for athletes whose scores on the physiology test are (d) 0, (e) 1, (f) 2, (g) 5, and (h) 6.

2. A professor has found that scores on the midterm exam in her classes predict scores on the final exam. The regression constant in the linear prediction rule for predicting final exam scores from midterm exam scores is 40 and the regression coefficient is .5. (a) Indicate the predictor variable, and (b) the criterion variable. (c) Write the linear prediction rule for this example. Figure the predicted final exam scores for each of eight students whose scores on the midterm were (d) 30, (e) 40, (f) 50, (g) 60, (h) 70, (i) 80, (j) 90, and (k) 100.

3. For each of the following, (a) through (d), determine the linear prediction rule for predicting criterion variable Y from predictor variable X. Then (e) make a

single graph (with values from 0 to 10 on both axes) showing all the regression lines, labeling each by its letter. (Be sure to make your graph large enough so that the lines are clearly separate.)

	Regression Constant *a*	Regression Coefficient *b*
(a)	1.5	.8
(b)	10.0	−.4
(c)	2.0	.2
(d)	9.5	−.8

4. Problem 3 in Chapter 11 was about an instructor who asked five students how many hours they had studied for an exam. The number of hours studied and their grades, along with the means, are shown here. (a) Determine the linear prediction rule for predicting test grade from hours studied, and (b) draw the regression line. Use the linear prediction rule to figure the predicted test grade of students who studied for each of the following number of hours: (c) 3, (d) 5, and (e) 7. (f) Determine the standardized regression coefficient, and (g) explain what you have done in all the previous parts of this question to someone who understands the mean and deviation scores but does not know any more about statistics. (h) Add the dots for the pairs of scores for the five students to your figure from part (b) and also add a regression line for the linear prediction rule $\hat{Y} = 60 + (5.00)(X)$. (i) Which regression line does a better job of coming close to the dots in your figure for part (h), and why? (j) Figure the sum of squared errors for your linear prediction rule from part (a) and for the prediction rule $\hat{Y} = 60 + (5.00)(X)$. (k) ADVANCED TOPIC: Find the proportionate reduction in error (using SS_{Error} and SS_{Total}).

	Hours Studied	Test Grade
	0	52
	10	95
	6	83
	8	71
	6	64
M	6	73

5. Repeat problem 4, doing parts (a) through (f), but this time predicting hours studied from test grade, and using values of 70, 75, and 80 for parts (c), (d), and (e), respectively.

6. Problem 2 in Chapter 11 described a pilot study of the relation between psychotherapists' degree of empathy and their patients' satisfaction with therapy. Four patient–therapist pairs were studied. The results are presented here, including the means.

Pair Number	Therapist Empathy	Patient Satisfaction
1	70	4
2	94	5
3	36	2
4	48	1
M	62	3

(a) Determine the linear prediction rule for predicting satisfaction from empathy, and (b) draw the regression line. Use the linear prediction rule to figure the predicted satisfaction of patients whose therapist had the following amount of empathy: (c) 50, (d) 64, and (e) 80. (f) Determine the standardized regression coefficient, and (g) explain what you have done in all the previous parts of this question to someone who understands the mean and deviation scores but does not know any more about statistics. (h) ADVANCED TOPIC: Find the proportionate reduction in error (using SS_{Error} and SS_{Total}).

7. Repeat problem 6, doing parts (a) through (f), but this time predicting empathy from satisfaction, and using values of 3, 2, and 1 for parts (c), (d), and (e), respectively.

8. Repeat problem 6, doing parts (a) through (f), but this time adding an additional pair of scores, with a therapist empathy value of 95 and a patient satisfaction value of 1 (this pair of scores can be thought of as an outlier). (g) Discuss how the results from problem 6 compare with the results of this problem.

9. For each of the following, (a) through (d), determine the multiple linear prediction rule for predicting criterion variable Y from predictor variables X_1, X_2, and X_3. Then (e) figure the predicted score on the criterion variable for part (a) for a person with scores on the predictor variables of $X_1 = 2$, $X_2 = 5$, and $X_3 = 9$.

	Regression Constant	Regression Coefficient	Regression Coefficient	Regression Coefficient
	a	b_1	b_2	b_3
(a)	1.5	.8	−.3	9.99
(b)	10.0	−.4	11.0	−8.62
(c)	2.0	.2	6.13	2.12
(d)	9.5	−.8	21.23	1.02

10. In the Oettingen and colleagues (2001) study described earlier (in the "Prediction in Research Articles" section), in addition to studying anticipated disappointment, the researchers conducted an experiment focusing on number of plans and on taking responsibility. Their results are shown in Figure 12–9. Explain the meaning of each graph to a person who has never had a course in statistics.

11. Mize and Petit (1997) were interested in the impact of a mother's style of helping her child understand social interactions on the child's social life. These researchers arranged for 43 volunteer mothers and their 3- to 5-year-old children to be videotaped in three separate sessions. In the key session, the mothers and children were shown videotapes of other children behaving in hostile or rejecting ways with each other; then the mothers discussed the tapes with their children. Later, the psychologists rated each mother for "social coaching"—such as how well the mothers helped the children understand what they had seen and suggested more positive ways to handle the situation. Tapes of the mothers and children playing together were rated for the mothers' "responsive style"—warmth and attunement to the children. Finally, in the last session, tapes of the children solving a puzzle were rated for the mothers' "nonsocial teaching"—how well they helped the children develop problem-solving skills. In another part of the study, the researchers had all the children

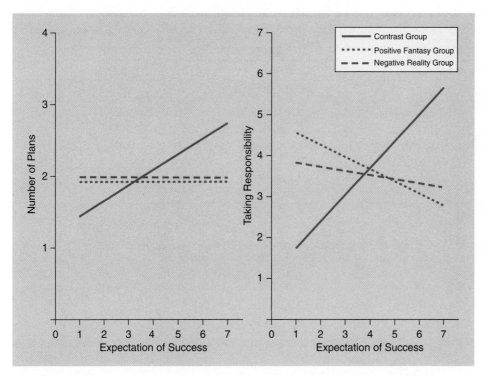

Figure 12–9   Regression lines depicting the link of expectation of success to formulating plans (left) and to taking responsibility (right) as a function of self-regulatory thought.

Source: Oettingen, G., Schnetter, K., & Pak, H. (2001). Self-regulations of goal setting: Turning free fantasies about the future into binding goals. *Journal of Personality and Social Psychology, 80,* 736–753. Published by the American Psychological Association. Reprinted with permission.

answer questions about how much they liked the other children. Using this information, they were able to come up with an overall measure of how much each child was liked, which they called "peer acceptance."

The researchers hypothesized that the extent to which a mother was good at social coaching would predict her child's peer acceptance. They also hypothesized that the relation of a mother's social coaching to peer acceptance would hold up even in a multiple regression equation (prediction rule) that included nonsocial coaching and would also hold up in a regression equation that included responsive style. (That is, including the other predictors in the model would still leave a substantial unique association of social coaching with peer acceptance.)

The Peer Acceptance section of Table 12–12 shows their results. Equation 1 shows the results of the multiple regression analysis in which nonsocial teaching and social coaching are included as predictors of peer acceptance. Equation 2 shows the results of a separate multiple regression analysis in which responsive style and social coaching are included as predictors of peer acceptance. (In each case, standardized regression coefficients are shown, not regular regression coefficients.) Explain the meaning of the peer acceptance results as if you were writing to a person who understands bivariate prediction, but does not understand multiple regression. (You can ignore the column for sr_1, the *semipartial correlation.* All the information you need to interpret this table is included in the r, R^2, and beta columns.)

Table 12-12 Simultaneous Regression Analyses Predicting Teacher-Rated Social Skills, Aggression, and Peer Acceptance in Study 1

Predictor Variables	Peer Acceptance				Social Skills				Aggression			
	r	R^2	sr_1	Beta	*r*	R^2	sr_1	Beta	*r*	R^2	sr_1	Beta
Equation 1:												
Nonsocial teaching	.21*		.10	.10	.15		.05	.06	−.35*		−.23	−.24
Social coaching	.36*	.14*	.30	.32	.31*	.10	.28	.29	−.41***	.22**	−.32	−.33*
Equation 2:												
Responsive style	.34*		.26	.27	.25		.18	.18	−.26		−.16	−.17
Social coaching	.36*	.19*	.28	.29	.31*	.13	.25	.26	−.41***	.20*	−.36	−.37*

Note: sr_1 = semipartial correlation; n = 38.

*$p < .10$; **$p < .05$; ***$p < .01$.

Source: Mize, J., & Pettit, G. S. (1997). Mothers' social coaching, mother-child relationship style, and children's peer competence: Is the medium the message? *Child Development, 68,* 312–332. Copyright © 1997 by the Society for Research in Child Development, Inc. Reprinted with permission.

Set II

12. A personnel psychologist studying adjustment to the job of new employees found that employees' amount of education (in number of years) predicts ratings by job supervisors two months later. The regression constant in the linear prediction rule for predicting job ratings from education is 0.5 and the regression coefficient is .40. (a) Indicate the predictor variable, and (b) the criterion variable. (c) Write the linear prediction rule for this example. Indicate the predicted job rating for employees with each of the following amount of education (in years): (d) 8, (e) 10, (f) 17, (g) 19, and (h) 21.

13. A clinical psychologist has found that scores on a new depression scale predict satisfaction with psychotherapy. The regression constant in the linear prediction rule for predicting satisfaction from the depression score is 12 and the regression coefficient is −.4. (a) Indicate the predictor variable and (b) the criterion variable. (c) Write the linear prediction rule for this example. Indicate the predicted satisfaction for people with each of the following depression scores: (d) 8, (e) 6, (f) 5, (g) 3, and (h) 0.

14. For each of the following, (a) through (d), determine the linear prediction rule for predicting criterion variable *Y* from predictor variable *X*. Then (e) make a single graph (with values from 0 to 100 on both axes) showing all the regression lines, labeling each by its letter. (Be sure to make your graph large enough so that the lines are clearly separate.)

	Regression Constant *a*	Regression Coefficient *b*
(a)	89.0	−.8
(b)	5.0	.7
(c)	50.0	.1
(d)	20.0	.4

15. In problem 12 of Chapter 11, four individuals were given a test of manual dexterity (high scores mean better dexterity) and an anxiety test (high scores mean more anxiety). The results are presented here, including the means.

Person	Dexterity	Anxiety
1	1	10
2	1	8
3	2	4
4	4	−2
M	2	5

(a) Determine the linear prediction rule for predicting anxiety from dexterity, and (b) draw the regression line. Use the linear prediction rule to figure the predicted anxiety of people with dexterity scores as follows: (c) 1, (d) 2, and (e) 3. (f) Determine the standardized regression coefficient, and (g) explain what you have done in all the previous parts of this question to someone who understands the mean and deviation scores but does not know any more about statistics. (h) ADVANCED TOPIC: Find the proportionate reduction in error (using SS_{Error} and SS_{Total}).

16. Repeat problem 15, doing parts (a) through (f), but this time predicting dexterity from anxiety, and using values of 0, 4, and 7 for parts (c), (d), and (e), respectively.

17. Repeat problem 15, doing parts (a) through (f), but this time adding an additional pair of scores, with a dexterity value of 4 and an value of 10 (this pair of scores can be thought of as an outlier). (g) Discuss how the results from problem 15 compare with the results of this problem.

18. Problem 13 from Chapter 11 was about the amount of violent television watched and the amount of violent behavior toward their playmates for four young children. The results are presented here, including the means.

Child's Code Number	Weekly Viewing of Violent TV (hours)	Number of Violent or Aggressive Acts Toward Playmates
G3368	14	9
R8904	8	6
C9890	6	1
L8722	12	8
M	10	6

(a) Determine the linear prediction rule for predicting violent acts from watching violent television, and (b) draw the regression line. Use the linear prediction rule to figure the predicted number of violent acts for children watching the following number of hours of violent television: (c) 7, (d) 9, and (e) 11. (f) Determine the standardized regression coefficient, and (g) explain what you have done in all the previous parts of this question to someone who understands the mean and deviation scores but does not know any more about statistics. (h) Add the dots for the pairs of scores for the four children to your figure from part (b) and also add a regression line for the linear prediction rule $\hat{Y} = -2 + (.20)(X)$. (i) Figure the sum of squared errors for your linear prediction rule from part (a) and for the prediction rule $\hat{Y} = -2 + (.20)(X)$. (j) Explain why the sum of squared errors for your linear prediction rule from (a) must be lower than the sum of squared errors for any other linear prediction rule. (k) ADVANCED TOPIC: Find the proportionate reduction in error (using SS_{Error} and SS_{Total}).

19. Repeat problem 18, doing parts (a) through (f), but this time predicting the number of hours of watching violent television from violent acts, and using values of 2, 5, and 7 for parts (c), (d), and (e), respectively.

20. For each of the following, (a) through (d), determine the multiple linear prediction rule for predicting criterion variable Y from predictor variables X_1, X_2, and X_3. Then (e) figure the predicted score on the criterion variable for part (a) for a person with scores on the predictor variables of $X_1 = 12$, $X_2 = 8$, and $X_3 = 1$.

	Regression Constant	Regression Coefficient	Regression Coefficient	Regression Coefficient
	a	b_1	b_2	b_3
(a)	3.8	4.1	.9	7.1
(b)	11.2	.9	2.5	3.9
(c)	.8	.1	1.0	1.5
(d)	−3.1	.8	12.4	4.3

21. Nezlek and colleagues (1997) had participants first write self-descriptions and then exchange them with four other students also taking part in the study. Then the students privately ranked the other students on how much they would like to work with them on the next task. One group of participants were then told that they had been selected to work on the next task with the rest of the group; this was the inclusion condition. The remaining participants were told that they had not been chosen to work with the others and would work alone—the exclusion condition. At this point, participants were asked about how accepted they felt. Earlier, at the start of the study, they had completed a self-esteem scale. Figure 12–10 shows regression lines for the two experimental groups. Explain what these two lines mean to a person who understands correlation but knows nothing about prediction.

22. Social psychologists studying criminal justice issues have long been interested in what influences people's attitudes about punishment of criminal offenders. Graham and her colleagues (1997) took advantage of the very public trial of U.S. football star O. J. Simpson to test some basic issues in this area. In the first few days after Simpson was accused of having murdered his ex-wife, the researchers asked people a series of questions about the case. The researchers were mainly interested in the responses of the 177 individuals who believed Simpson was probably guilty, particularly their belief about retribution—how much they agreed or disagreed with the statement, "The punishment should make O. J. suffer as he made others suffer." The researchers were interested in a number of possible influences on this belief. These included "control" (how much control they believed Simpson had over his actions at the time of the crime), "responsibility" (how much they believed he was responsible for the crime), "anger" they felt toward him, "sympathy" they felt for him, "stability" (how much they believed his actions represented a stable versus temporary way

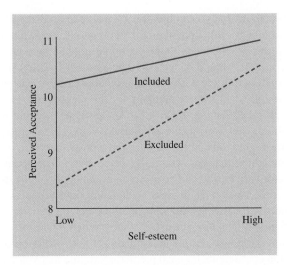

Figure 12–10 Effects of inclusion/exclusion and traits self-esteem on perceived acceptance.

Source: Nezlek, J. B., Kowalski, R. M., Leary, M. R., Blevins, T., & Holgate, S. (1997). Personality moderators of reactions to interpersonal rejection: Depression and trait self-esteem. *Personality and Social Psychology Bulletin, 23,* 1235–1244. Copyright © 1997 by Sage Publications, Ltd. Reprinted by permission of Sage Publications, Thousands Oaks, London, and New Delhi.

of behaving), and "expectancy" (if they thought he would commit such a crime again). Graham and her colleagues reported

. . . Table [12–13] reveals partial support for our hypotheses. As expected, the strongest predictors of the retributive goal of making Simpson suffer were inferences about responsibility and the moral emotions of anger and sympathy. [S]tability and expectancy . . . were relatively weak [predictors]. (p. 337)

Explain these results as if you were writing to a person who understands bivariate prediction but does not understand multiple regression. (Refer only to the retribution part of the table. You may ignore the *t* column, which is about the statistical significance of the results.)

Table 12-13 Multiple Regressions Predicting Punishment Goals from the Attributional Variables, Study 1

	Punishment Goal							
	Retribution		**Rehabilition**		**Protection**		**Deterrence**	
Predictors	β	*t*	β	*t*	β	*t*	β	*t*
Control	−.05	<1	−.05	<1	−.03	<1	.15	1.90
Responsibility	.17	2.07*	−.00	<1	−.04	<1	.19	2.15*
Anger	.30	4.04***	.11	1.54	−.03	<1	−.04	<1
Sympathy	−.30	−3.68***	.39	5.18***	−.07	<1	−.13	−1.54
Stability	−.01	<1	−.34	−4.85***	−.19	2.33*	.04	<1
Expectancy	−.10	−1.33	−.06	<1	−.27	3.36***	.08	1.04
R^2		.27		.37		.17		.18

Note: β = standardized regression coefficient.

*p < .05; ***p < .001.

Source: Graham, S., Weiner, B., & Zucker, G. S. (1997). An attributional analysis of punishment goals and public reactions to O. J. Simpson. *Personality and Social Psychology Bulletin, 23,* 331–346. Copyright © 1997 by the Society for Personality and Social Psychology, Inc. Reprinted by permission of Sage Publications, Inc.

23. Think of something that you would like to be able to predict and what predictor variable would be useful in predicting it. (This should be different from any example given in class, included in the textbook, or used for a previous problem. Also, both variables should be measured on a numeric scale.) (a) Write a linear prediction rule, noting the name of the predictor variable and the name of the criterion variable. (b) Estimate numbers for the regression constant and the regression coefficient that you think make some sense based on what you know about the things you are making predictions about. Finally, explain why you picked (c) the regression constant and (d) the regression coefficient size you did.

24. Think of something that you would like to be able to predict and what *two or more* predictor variables would be useful in predicting it. (This should be different from any example given in class, included in the textbook, or used in a previous problem. All variables should be measured on numeric scales.) (a) Write a linear prediction rule, noting the name of the predictor variables and the name of the criterion variable. (b) Estimate numbers for the regression constant and for the regression coefficients for each predictor variable that you think make some sense based on what you know about the things you are making predictions about. Finally, explain why you picked (c) the regression constant, and (d) the regression coefficient sizes you did.

25. Ask five other students of the same gender as yourself (each from different families) to give you their own height and also their mother's height. Determine the linear prediction rule for predicting a person's height from his or her mother's height, and make a graph showing the regression line. Finally, based on your prediction rule, predict the height of a person of your gender whose mother's height is (a) 5 feet, (b) 5 feet 6 inches, and (c) 6 feet. (*Note:* Either convert inches to decimals of feet or do the whole problem using inches.)

Using SPSS

The ✐ in the following steps indicates a mouse click. (We used SPSS version 15.0 for Windows to carry out these analyses. The steps and output may be slightly different for other versions of SPSS.)

In the following steps for figuring the bivariate linear prediction rule, we use the example of the sleep and happy mood study. The scores and figuring of the regression constant (a) and the regression coefficient (b) for that study are shown in Table 12–5 on p. 501.

Figuring the Bivariate Linear Prediction Rule

❶ Enter the scores into SPSS. Enter the scores as shown in Figure 12–11 (which is the same as Figure 11–20 in Chapter 11).

❷ ✐ *Analyze.*

❸ ✐ *Regression.* ✐ *Linear.* This tells SPSS that you are figuring a *linear* prediction rule, as opposed to any one of a number of other types of prediction rules.

❹ ✐ the variable called "mood" and then ✐ the arrow next to the box labeled "Dependent." This tells SPSS that the "mood" variable is the criterion variable (which is also called the *dependent variable* in prediction, because it "depends" on the predictor variable's score). ✐ the variable called "sleep" and then ✐ the arrow next to the box labeled "Independent(s)." This tells SPSS that the "sleep" variable is the predictor variable (which is also called the *independent variable*

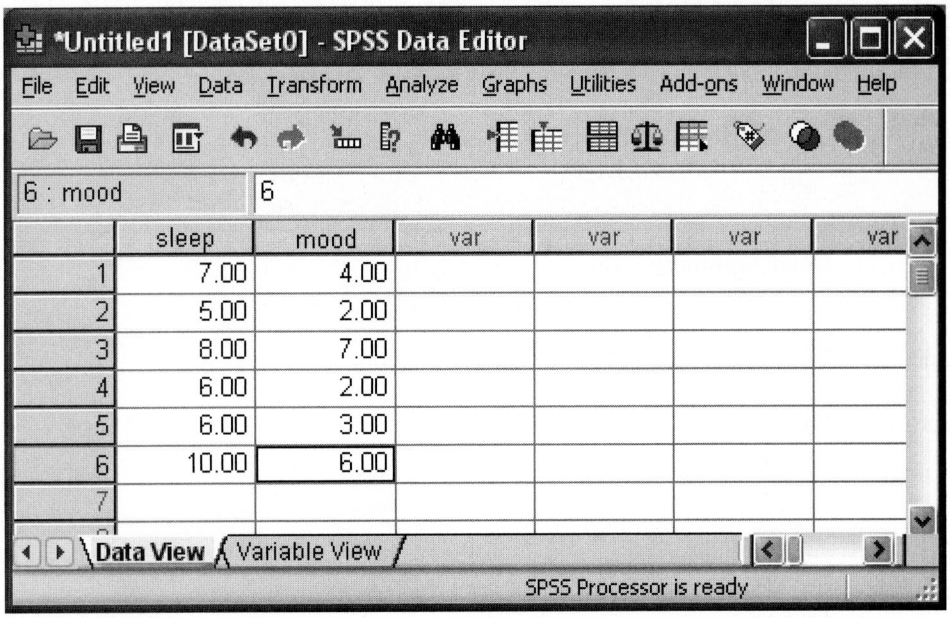

Figure 12–11 SPSS data editor window for the fictional study of the relationship between hours slept last night and mood.

in prediction). (If you were figuring a multiple regression, you would put all of the predictor variables in the "Independent(s)" box.)

❺ ⬧ *Statistics,* ⬧ *Descriptives,* ⬧ *Continue.* This requests useful descriptive information on the variables (such as the mean and estimated population standard deviation) and also gives the correlation between the variables. (Step ❺ is optional, but we strongly recommend requesting descriptive statistics for any hypothesis-testing situation.)

❻ ⬧ *OK.* Your SPSS output window should look like Figure 12–12.

SPSS provides six tables in the output. (It provides four tables if you do not select "Descriptives," as shown in Step ❺ above.) The first two tables show descriptive statistics and a correlation matrix. The third table shows which variable was the predictor variable ("variable entered") and which was the criterion variable ("dependent variable"). Always check to see that you used the correct variables. These first three tables are not shown in Figure 12–12. The fourth table (labeled "Model Summary") gives the correlation coefficient ("R") between the two variables and the proportionate reduction in error ("R square" or R^2), which we discussed in the Advanced Topic section of this chapter. (With bivariate prediction, SPSS uses R and R^2 for what we refer to as r and r^2 in the chapter. Following the usual way of doing this in psychology, we used lower case r and r^2 with bivariate regression, and capital R and R^2 with multiple correlation and the proportionate reduction in error for multiple regression. But SPSS just uses capitals for both.) You can ignore the final two columns of the "Model Summary" table. You can also ignore the table in the output labeled "ANOVA." (However, if you read the Advanced Topic section in this chapter on error and proportionate reduction in error, note that SS_{Error} is shown as the "Sums of Squares" for "Regression" in the second column and the SS_{Total} is the "Sums of Squares Total" shown in the same column. The "Residual" in the "Sums of Squares" column shows the difference between SS_{Total} and SS_{Error}.)

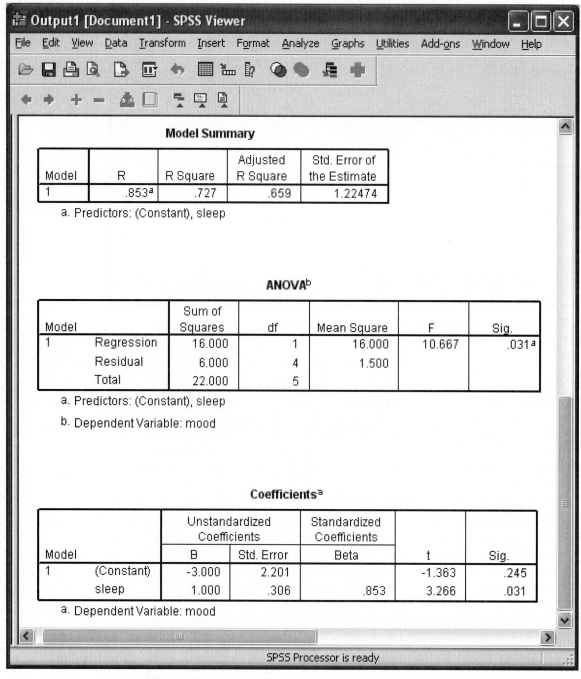

Figure 12–12 SPSS output window for the bivariate prediction rule predicting mood from hours slept last night (fictional data).

The final table (labeled "Coefficients") gives the information for the linear prediction rule. This is what you want to focus on. The first row of the table gives the regression constant, which in this case is −3.000. (It also gives some other statistics related to the constant, such as a *t* test of whether the constant is significantly different from 0.) So, using the terminology from this chapter, $a = -3.00$. The regression coefficients are shown in the second row of the table. (In a multiple regression, there would a row of regression coefficients for each predictor variable.) The value of 1.000 in the "B" column ("B" is the same as b you learned in this chapter) is the regular, unstandardized regression coefficient. So, using the terminology from this chapter, $b = 1.000$. We now have the necessary information—a and b—for the linear prediction rule. Thus, the linear prediction rule is Predicted mood $= -3 + (1)$ (hours of sleep). The table also shows the standardized regression coefficient, which is .853. The final two columns for the "sleep" row give the statistical test of whether each regression coefficient is significantly different from 0. The significance level of .031 is less than our usual .05 cutoff, which means that the number of hours slept is a statistically significant predictor of mood the next day. Notice that the t value of 3.226 for the sleep predictor variable is consistent (within rounding error) with the t (of 3.21) we figured for this example in the previous chapter.

Chapter Notes

1. Psychologists often call the kind of prediction in this chapter *regression*. Regression means, literally, going back or returning. The term *regression* is used here because, for any individual, the predicted score on the criterion variable is closer (in terms of standard deviation units) to the mean of the criterion variable compared to the distance from the person's predictor variable score to the mean of the predictor variable. This would be true in all cases except for a perfect correlation between the two variables. So you can think of this in terms of the predicted value of the criterion variable regressing, or going back, toward the mean of the criterion variable.

2. There are also procedures that allow you to use more than one criterion variable. For example, you might want to know how good a predictor hours slept is for both mood and peace of mind. Procedures involving more than one criterion variable are called "multivariate statistics" and are quite advanced. We introduce you to some examples in Chapter 15.

CHAPTER 13

Chi-Square Tests

Chapter Outline

✪ The Chi-Square Statistic and the Chi-Square Test for Goodness of Fit 538

✪ The Chi-Square Test for Independence 546

✪ Assumptions for Chi-Square Tests 554

✪ Effect Size and Power for Chi-Square Tests for Independence 554

✪ Controversy: The Minimum Expected Frequency 558

✪ Chi-Square Tests in Research Articles 559

✪ Summary 560

✪ Key Terms 561

✪ Example Worked-Out Problems 561

✪ Practice Problems 565

✪ Using SPSS 572

✪ Chapter Notes 576

chi-square tests hypothesis-testing procedures used when the variables of interest are nominal variables.

The hypothesis testing procedures you learned in Chapters 7 through 12 (*t* tests, analysis of variance, correlation, and prediction) are very versatile, but there are certain research situations in which these methods cannot be used. One such situation is hypothesis testing for variables whose values are categories, such as a person's region of the country, religious preference, or hair color. The *t* test, analysis of variance, correlation, and prediction all required that the measured variable or variables have scores that are quantitative, such as a rating on a 7-point scale or number of years served as mayor. This chapter focuses on **chi-square tests,** which are used when the scores are on a *nominal variable* (that is, a variable with values that are categories). (Chi is the Greek letter χ; it is pronounced *ki,* rhyming with high and pie.) Therefore, the scores that you will encounter in this chapter represent *frequencies:* that is, how many people or observations fall into different categories. The chi-square test was originally developed by Karl Pearson (see Box 13–1) and is sometimes called the Pearson chi-square.

BOX 13–1   ## Karl Pearson, Inventor of Chi-Square and Center of Controversy

Topham/The Image Works

Karl Pearson, sometimes hailed as the founder of the science of statistics, was born in 1857. Both his virtues and vices are revealed in what he reported to his colleague Julia Bell as his earliest memory: he was sitting in his highchair, sucking his thumb, when he was told to stop or his thumb would wither away. Pearson silently thought, "I can't see that the thumb I suck is any smaller than the other. I wonder if she could be lying to me." Here we see Pearson's faith in himself and in observational evidence, as well as his rejection of authority. We also see his tendency to doubt the character of people with whom he disagreed.

Pearson studied mathematics at Cambridge. Soon after he arrived, he requested to be excused from compulsory chapel. As soon as his request was granted, however, he appeared in chapel. The dean summoned him for an explanation, and Pearson declared that he had asked to be excused not from chapel "but from *compulsory* chapel."

After graduation, Pearson studied in Germany, becoming a socialist and a self-described "free-thinker." Returning to England, he changed his name from Carl to Karl (in honor of Karl Marx) and wrote an attack on Christianity under a pen name. In 1885 he founded a Men and Women's Club to promote equality between the sexes.

Most of Pearson's research from 1893 to 1901 focused on the laws of heredity, but he needed better statistical methods, leading to his most famous contribution, the chi-square test. Pearson also invented the method of computing correlation used today and coined the terms *histogram, skew,* and *spurious correlation.* When he felt that biology journals failed to appreciate his work, he founded the famous journal *Biometrika.*

Unfortunately, Pearson was a great fan of eugenics, and his work was later used by the Nazis as justification for their treatment of the Jews. Toward the end of his life he fought back, writing a paper using clear logic and data on Jews and Gentiles from all over the world to demonstrate that the Nazis' ideas were sheer nonsense.

Indeed, throughout his life, Pearson's strong opinions created a long list of enemies, especially as other, younger statisticians passed him by, while he refused to publish their work in *Biometrika.* William S. Gosset (Box 7–1) was one of his friends. Sir Ronald Fisher (Box 9–1) was one of Pearson's worst enemies. The kindly Gosset was always trying to smooth matters between them. In 1933, Pearson finally retired, and Fisher, of all persons, took over his chair, the Galton Professorship of Eugenics at University College in London. In 1936, the two entered into their bitterest argument yet; Pearson died the same year.

For more information about Pearson, see *http://en.wikipedia.org/wiki/Karl_Pearson* and *http://www.human-nature.com/nibbs/03/kpearson.html.*

Sources: Peters (1987); Salsburg (2001); Stigler (1986); Tankard (1984).

An Example

Harter and colleagues (1997) were interested in three styles of relating to romantic partners: a self-focused autonomy style, an other-focused connection style, and a mutuality style. The researchers conducted a newspaper survey that included items about the respondents' relationship styles and their perceptions of their partners' styles. One of the researchers' predictions was that men who described themselves as having the self-focused autonomy style would be most likely to describe their partners as having the other-focused style. And sure enough, of the 101 self-focused men in their study, 49.5% "reported the predicted pairing, compared to 25.5% who reported self-focused autonomous partners and 24.5% who reported partners displaying mutuality..." (p. 156). In terms of raw numbers, of the 101 self-focused men, 50 had other-focused partners, 26 had self-focused partners, and 25 had mutuality-style partners.

Table 13-1 Observed and Expected Frequencies for Relationship Styles of Partners of Self-Focused Autonomous Men

Partner Style	Observed Frequency[a] (O)	Expected Frequency (E)	Difference (O − E)	Difference Squared (O − E)²	Difference Squared Weighted by Expected Frequency (O − E)²/E
Other-Focused Connection	50	33.67	16.33	266.67	7.92
Self-Focused Autonomous	26	33.67	−7.67	58.83	1.75
Mutuality	25	33.67	−8.67	75.17	2.23

[a]Data from Harter et al. (1997).

Suppose the partners of these 101 self-focused men had been equally likely to be of each of the three relationship styles. If that were the situation, then about 33.67 (one-third of the 101) of the partners of these men should have been of each style. This information is laid out in the "Observed Frequency" and "Expected Frequency" columns of Table 13–1. The "Observed Frequency" column shows the breakdown of relationship styles of partners actually *observed*. The "Expected Frequency" column shows the breakdown you would *expect* if the different partner styles had been exactly equally likely. (Note that it won't always be the case that you expect an *equal breakdown* across the categories. In other situations, the expected frequency for each category may be based on theory or on a distribution in another study or circumstance.)

Clearly, there is a discrepancy between what was actually observed and the breakdown you would expect if each of the three partner styles were equally likely. The question is, "Should you assume that this discrepancy is no more than would easily occur just by chance for a sample of this size?" Suppose that self-focused men in general (the population) are equally likely to have partners of all three styles. Still, in any particular sample from that population, you would not get a perfectly equal breakdown of partners' styles. But if the breakdown in the sample is a long way from equal, you would doubt that the partner styles in the population really are equal. In other words, you are in a hypothesis-testing situation, much like the ones we have been considering all along. But with a big difference too.

In the situations in previous chapters, the scores have all been *numerical values* on some dimension, such as a score on a standard achievement test, length of time in a relationship, an employer's rating of an employee's job effectiveness on a 9-point scale, and so forth; often we figured means of these numbers. By contrast, relationship style of a man's partner is an example of what in Chapter 1 we called a *nominal variable* (or a *categorical variable*). A nominal variable is one in which the information is the number of people—or the frequency—in each category. Therefore, the numbers associated with nominal variables are frequencies (and not means at all); the frequency tells you how many people fall into each category of the variable. We use the term *nominal variable* because the different categories or levels of the variable have names instead of numbers. Hypothesis testing with nominal variables uses *chi-square tests*.

The Chi-Square Statistic and the Chi-Square Test for Goodness of Fit

The basic idea of any chi-square test is that you compare how well an *observed breakdown* of people over various categories fits some *expected breakdown*. In this chapter you will learn about two types of chi-square tests: First, you will learn about the

chi-square test for goodness of fit, which is a chi-square test involving levels of a *single nominal variable.* Later in the chapter, you will learn about the **chi-square test for independence,** which is used when there are *two nominal variables,* each with several categories.

In the relationship style example—in which there is a single nominal variable with three categories—you are comparing the observed breakdown of 50, 26, and 25 to the expected breakdown of about 34 (33.67) for each style. A breakdown of numbers of people expected in each category is actually a frequency distribution, as you learned in Chapter 1. Thus, a chi-square test is more formally described as comparing an **observed frequency** distribution to an **expected frequency** distribution. Overall, what the hypothesis testing involves is first figuring a number for the amount of mismatch between the observed frequencies and the expected frequencies, then seeing whether that number indicates a greater mismatch than you would expect by chance. This gives an idea as to how the chi-square test for goodness of fit came to have that name: the test shows *how well* an observed frequency distribution *fits* an expected (or predicted) frequency distribution.

Let's start with how you would come up with that mismatch number for the observed versus expected frequencies. The mismatch between observed and expected for any one category is just the observed frequency minus the expected frequency. For example, consider again the Harter and colleagues study. For self-focused men with an other-focused partner, the observed frequency of 50 is 16.33 more than the expected frequency of 33.67 (recall the expected frequency in this example is one-third of the 101 total). For the second category, the difference is −7.67. For the third, −8.67. These differences are shown in the "Difference" column of Table 13–1.

You do not use these differences directly. One reason is that some differences are positive and some are negative. Thus, they would cancel each other out. To get around this, you square each difference. (This is the same strategy we saw in Chapter 2 to deal with difference scores in figuring the variance.) In the relationship-style example, the squared difference for self-focused men with other-focused partners is 16.33 squared, or 266.67. For those men with self-focused partners, it is 58.83; for those with mutuality style partners, 75.17. These squared differences are shown in the Difference Squared column of Table 13–1.

A particular amount of difference between observed and expected has a different importance according to the size of the expected frequency. For example, a difference of 8 people between observed and expected is a much bigger mismatch if the expected frequency is 10 than if the expected frequency is 1,000. If the expected frequency is 10, a difference of 8 would mean that the observed frequency was 18 or 2, frequencies that are dramatically different from 10. But if the expected frequency is 1,000, a difference of 8 is only a slight mismatch. This would mean that the observed frequency was 1,008 or 992, frequencies that are only slightly different from 1,000.

How can you adjust the mismatch (the squared difference) between observed and expected for a particular category? What you need to do is adjust or weight the mismatch to take into account the expected frequency for that category. You can do this by dividing your squared difference for a category by the expected frequency for that category. Thus, if the expected frequency for a particular category is 10, you divide the squared difference by 10. If the expected frequency for the category is 1,000, you divide the squared difference by 1,000. In this way, you weight each squared difference by the expected frequency. This weighting puts the squared difference onto a more appropriate scale of comparison. In our example, for men with an other-focused partner, you would weight the mismatch by dividing the squared difference of 266.67 by 33.67, giving 7.92. For those with a self-focused partner, 58.83 divided by 33.67

chi-square test for goodness of fit hypothesis-testing procedure that examines how well an observed frequency distribution of a nominal variable fits some expected pattern of frequencies.

chi-square test for independence hypothesis-testing procedure that examines whether the distribution of frequencies over the categories of one nominal variable is unrelated to the distribution of frequencies over the categories of a second nominal variable.

observed frequency in a chi-square test, number of individuals actually found in the study to be in a category or cell.

expected frequency in a chi-square test, number of people in a category or cell expected if the null hypothesis were true.

gives 1.75. For those with a mutuality-style partner, 75.17 divided by 33.67 gives 2.23. These adjusted mismatches (squared differences divided by expected frequencies) are shown in the rightmost column of Table 13–1.

What remains is to get an overall number for the mismatch between observed and expected frequencies. This final step is done by adding up the mismatch for all the categories. In the Harter and colleagues example, this would be 7.92 plus 1.75 plus 2.23, for a total of 11.90. This final number (the sum of the weighted squared differences) is an overall indication of the amount of mismatch between the expected and observed frequencies. It is called the **chi-square statistic.** In terms of a formula,

> Chi-square is the sum, over all the categories, of the squared difference between observed and expected frequencies divided by the expected frequency.

$$\chi^2 = \sum \frac{(O - E)^2}{E} \tag{13–1}$$

In this formula, χ^2 is the chi-square statistic. Σ is the summation sign, telling you to sum over all the different categories. O is the observed frequency for a category (the number of people actually found in that category in the study). E is the expected frequency for a category (in the Harter and colleagues example, it is based on what you would expect if there were equal numbers in each category).

Applying the formula to the example,

$$\chi^2 = \sum \frac{(O - E)^2}{E} = \frac{(50 - 33.67)^2}{33.67} + \frac{(26 - 33.67)^2}{33.67} + \frac{(25 - 33.67)^2}{33.67} = 11.90.$$

TIP FOR SUCCESS

Notice in the chi-square formula that, for each category, you *first* divide the squared difference between observed and expected frequencies by the expected frequency, and *then* you sum the resulting values for all the categories. This is a slightly different procedure than you are used to from previous chapters (in which you often *first* summed a series of squared values in the numerator and *then* divided by a denominator value); so be sure to follow the formula carefully.

Steps for Figuring the Chi-Square Statistic

Here is a summary of what we've said so far in terms of steps:

- ❶ Determine the actual, observed frequencies in each category.
- ❷ Determine the expected frequencies in each category.
- ❸ In each category, take observed minus expected frequencies.
- ❹ Square each of these differences.
- ❺ Divide each squared difference by the expected frequency for its category.
- ❻ Add up the results of Step ❺ for all the categories.

The Chi-Square Distribution

Now we turn to the question of whether the chi-square statistic you have figured is a bigger mismatch than you would expect by chance. To answer that, you need to know how likely it is to get chi-square statistics of various sizes by chance. As long as you have a reasonable number of people in the study, the distribution of the chi-square statistic that would arise by chance follows quite closely a known mathematical distribution—the **chi-square distribution.**

chi-square statistic (χ^2) statistic that reflects the overall lack of fit between the expected and observed frequencies; sum, over all the categories or cells, of the squared difference between observed and expected frequencies divided by the expected frequency.

chi-square distribution mathematically defined curve used as the comparison distribution in chi-square tests; distribution of the chi-square statistic.

The exact shape of the chi-square distribution depends on the degrees of freedom. For a chi-square test, the degrees of freedom are the number of categories that are free to vary, given the totals. In the partners' relationship style example, there are three categories. If you know the total number of people and you know the number in any two categories, you could figure out the number in the third category; so only two are free to vary. That is, in a study like this one (which uses a chi-square test for goodness of fit), if there are three categories, there are two degrees of freedom. In terms of a formula,

> The degrees of freedom for the chi-square test for goodness of fit are the number of categories minus 1.

$$df = N_{\text{Categories}} - 1 \tag{13–2}$$

Chi-square distributions for several different degrees of freedom are shown in Figure 13–1. Notice that the distributions are all skewed to the right. This is because

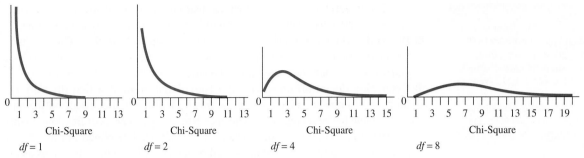

Figure 13–1 Examples of chi-square distributions for different degrees of freedom.

the chi-square statistic cannot be less than 0 but can have very high values. (Chi-square must be positive because it is figured by adding a group of fractions in each of which the numerator and denominator both have to be positive. The numerator has to be positive because it is squared. The denominator has to be positive because the number of people expected in a given category can't be a negative number; you can't expect less than no one!)

The Chi-Square Table

What matters most about the chi-square distribution for hypothesis testing is the cutoff for a chi-square to be extreme enough to reject the null hypothesis. A **chi-square table** gives the cutoff chi-squares for different significance levels and various degrees of freedom. Table 13–2 shows a portion of a chi-square table like the one in the Appendix (Table A–4). For our example, where there were two degrees of freedom, the table shows that the cutoff chi-square for the .05 level is 5.992. (Of course, as with other hypothesis testing procedures, when you carry out a chi-square using a statistics program like SPSS, you will be given an exact probability level, which you then check to see if it is less than the cutoff you set for the study, such as .05 or .01.)

In the Harter and colleagues (1997) example, we figured a chi-square of 11.90. This is clearly larger than the chi-square cutoff (using the .05 significance level) of 5.992 (see Figure 13–2). Thus, the researchers rejected the null hypothesis. That is, they rejected as too unlikely that the mismatch they observed could have come about if in the population of self-focused men there were an equal number of partners of each relationship style. It seemed more reasonable to conclude that there truly were different proportions of relationship styles of the partners of such men.

Steps of Hypothesis Testing

Let us review the chi-square test for goodness of fit using the same example, but this time systematically following the standard steps of hypothesis testing. In the process we also consider some fine points.

❶ **Restate the question as a research hypothesis and a null hypothesis about the populations.** There are two populations:

Population 1: Self-focused men like those in the study.
Population 2: Self-focused men whose partners are equally of the three relationship styles.

Table 13-2 Portion of a Chi-Square Table (with Cutoff Value Highlighted for the Harter et al. Example)

	Significance Level		
df	.10	.05	.01
1	2.706	3.841	6.635
2	4.605	5.992	9.211
3	6.252	7.815	11.345
4	7.780	9.488	13.277
5	9.237	11.071	15.087

Note: Full table is Table A–4 in the Appendix.

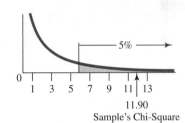

Figure 13-2 For the Harter et al. (1997) example, the chi-square distribution (*df* = 2) showing the cutoff for rejecting the null hypothesis at the .05 level and the sample's chi-square.

chi-square table table of cutoff scores on the chi-square distribution for various degrees of freedom and significance levels.

The research hypothesis is that the distribution of people over categories in the two populations is different; the null hypothesis is that they are the same.

❷ **Determine the characteristics of the comparison distribution.** The comparison distribution is a chi-square distribution with 2 degrees of freedom. (Once you know the total, there are only two category numbers still free to vary.)

❸ **Determine the cutoff on the comparison distribution at which the null hypothesis should be rejected.** You do this by looking up the cutoff on the chi-square table for your significance level and the study's degrees of freedom. In this example, we used the .05 significance level, and we determined in Step ❷ that there were 2 degrees of freedom. Based on the chi-square table, this gives a cutoff chi-square of 5.992 (see Figure 13–2).

❹ **Determine your sample's score on the comparison distribution.** Your sample's score is the chi-square figured from the sample. In other words, this is where you do all the figuring.

   ❹ **Determine the actual, observed frequencies in each category.** These are shown in the first column of Table 13–1.

   ❸ **Determine the expected frequencies in each category.** We figured these each to be 33.67 based on expecting an equal distribution of the 101 partners.

   ❹ **In each category, take observed minus expected frequencies.** These are shown in the third column of Table 13–1.

   ❶ **Square each of these differences.** These are shown in the fourth column of Table 13–1.

   ❶ **Divide each squared difference by the expected frequency for its category.** These are shown in the fifth column of Table 13–1.

   ❶ **Add up the results of Step ❶ for all the categories.** The result we figured earlier (11.90) is the chi-square statistic for the sample. It is shown in Figure 13–2.

❺ **Decide whether to reject the null hypothesis.** The chi-square cutoff to reject the null hypothesis (from Step ❸) is 5.992 and the chi-square of the sample (from Step ❹) is 11.90. Thus, you can reject the null hypothesis. The research hypothesis that the two populations are different is supported. That is, Harter and colleagues could conclude that the partners of self-focused men are not equally likely to be of the three relationship styles.

Another Example

A fictional research team of clinical psychologists want to test a theory that mental health is affected by the level of a certain mineral in the diet, called "mineral Q." The research team has located a region of the United States where mineral Q is found in very high concentrations in the soil. As a result, it is in the water people drink and in locally grown food. The researchers carry out a survey of older people who have lived in this area their whole life, focusing on mental health disorders. Of the 1,000 people surveyed, 138 had at some point in their life experienced an anxiety disorder, 99 had suffered from alcohol or drug abuse, 123 from a mood disorder (such as major chronic depression), and 111 from an impulse-control disorder (such as attention deficit hyperactivity disorder); 529 had never experienced any of these problems. (In this example, we ignore the problem of what happens when a person had more than one of these problems.)

The psychologists then compared their results to what would be expected based on large surveys of the U.S. public in general. In these surveys, 14.6% of adults at some point in their lives suffer from an anxiety disorder, 8.0% from alcohol or drug abuse, 11.0% from a mood disorder, and 12.8% from an impulse-control disorder; 53.6% do not experience any of these conditions (based on Kessler et al., 2005). If their sample

Table 13-3 Observed and Expected Frequencies and the Chi-Square Goodness of Fit Test for Types of Mental Health Disorders in a U.S. Region High in Mineral Q Compared to the General U.S. Population (Fictional Data)

Condition	Observed Ⓐ	Expected Ⓑ
Anxiety disorder	138	146 (14.6% × 1,000)
Alcohol or drug abuse	99	80 (8.0% × 1,000)
Mood disorder	123	110 (11.0% × 1,000)
Impulse-control disorder	111	128 (12.8% × 1,000)
None of these conditions	529	536 (53.6% × 1,000)

Degrees of freedom $= N_{Categories} - 1 = 5 - 1 = 4$ Ⓐ
Chi-square needed, $df = 4$, .05 level: 9.488 Ⓐ

$$\chi^2 = \sum \frac{(O - E)^2}{E} = \frac{(138 - 146)^2}{146} + \frac{(99 - 80)^2}{80} + \frac{(123 - 110)^2}{110} + \frac{(111 - 128)^2}{128} + \frac{(529 - 536)^2}{536} \text{Ⓒ}$$

$$= \frac{-8^2}{146} + \frac{19^2}{80} + \frac{13^2}{110} + \frac{-17^2}{128} + \frac{-7^2}{536} \text{Ⓓ}$$

$$= 0.44 + 4.51 + 1.54 + 2.26 + 0.09 \text{Ⓔ}$$

$$= 8.84 \text{Ⓕ}$$

Decision: Do not reject the null hypothesis.Ⓖ

---

of 1,000 is not different from the general U.S. population, 14.6% of them (146) should have had anxiety disorders, 8.0% of them (80) should have suffered from alcohol or drug abuse, and so forth. The question the clinical psychologists posed is, "On the basis of the sample we have studied, can we conclude that the rates of various mental health problems among people in this region are different from those of the general U.S. population?"

Table 13–3 shows the observed and expected frequencies and the figuring for the chi-square test.

❶ **Restate the question as a research hypothesis and a null hypothesis about the populations.** There are two populations:

Population 1: People in the U.S. region with a high level of mineral Q.
Population 2: People in the U.S. population in general.

The research hypothesis is that the distribution of numbers of people over the five mental health categories is different in the two populations; the null hypothesis is that it is the same.

❷ **Determine the characteristics of the comparison distribution.** The comparison distribution is a chi-square distribution with 4 degrees of freedom (that is, $df = N_{Categories} - 1 = 5 - 1 = 4$). See Figure 13–3.

❸ **Determine the cutoff sample score on the comparison distribution at which the null hypothesis should be rejected.** We will use the standard 5% significance level and we have just seen that there are 4 degrees of freedom. Thus, Table 13–2 (or Table A–4 in the Appendix) shows that the clinical psychologists need a chi-square of at least 9.488 to reject the null hypothesis. This is shown in Figure 13–3.

❹ **Determine your sample's score on the comparison distribution.** The chi-square figuring is shown in Table 13–3.

❺ **Determine the actual, observed frequencies in each category.** These are shown in the first column of Table 13–3.

TIP FOR SUCCESS

Note in this example that the expected frequencies are figured based on what would be expected in the U.S. population. This is quite different from the situations we have considered before where the expected frequencies were based on an even division. Thus, Population 2 in this example is people in the U.S. population in general, since that is the population that is being used to determine the expected frequencies.

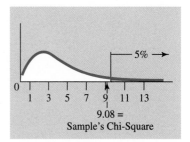

Figure 13–3 For the mineral Q example, the chi-square distribution ($df = 4$) showing the cutoff for rejecting the null hypothesis at the .05 level and the sample's chi-square.

❸ **Determine the expected frequencies in each category.** These are figured by multiplying the expected percentage by the total number. For example, with 14.6% expected to have anxiety disorders, the actual expected number to have anxiety disorders is 146 (that is, 14.6% of 1000). All of the expected frequencies are shown in Table 13–3.

❹ **In each category, take observed minus expected frequencies.** The result of these subtractions are shown in the numerators of the second formula line on Table 13–3.

❺ **Square each of these differences.** The results of these squarings are shown in the numerators of the third formula line on Table 13–3.

❻ **Divide each squared difference by the expected frequency for its category.** The result of these divisions are shown in the fourth formula line on Table 13–3.

❼ **Add up the results of Step ❻ for all the categories.** The sum comes out to 8.84. The addition is shown on Table 13–3; the location on the chi-square distribution is shown in Figure 13–3.

❺ **Decide whether to reject the null hypothesis.** The sample's chi-square (from Step ❹) of 8.84 is less extreme than the cutoff (from Step ❸) of 9.488. The researchers cannot reject the null hypothesis; the study is inconclusive. (Having failed to reject the null hypothesis with such a large sample, it is reasonable to suppose that, if there is any difference between the populations, it is quite small.)

How are you doing?

1. In what situation do you use a chi-square test for goodness of fit?
2. List the steps for figuring the chi-square statistic, and explain the logic behind each step.
3. Write the formula for the chi-square statistic and define each of the symbols.
4. (a) What is a chi-square distribution? (b) What is its shape? (c) Why does it have that shape?
5. Carry out a chi-square test for goodness of fit (using the .05 significance level) for a sample in which one category has 15 people, the other has 35 people, and the two categories are expected to have equal frequencies. (a) Use the steps of hypothesis testing and (b) sketch the distribution involved.

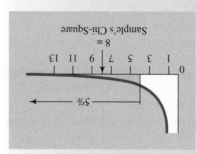

Figure 13–4 For "How Are You Doing?" question 5, the chi-square distribution ($df = 1$) showing the cutoff for rejecting the null hypothesis at the .05 level and the sample's chi-square.

❸ **Divide each squared difference by the expected frequency for its category.** These both come out to 4 (that is, 100/25 = 4).

❹ **Add up the results of Step ❸ for all the categories.** 4 + 4 = 8.

❺ **Decide whether to reject the null hypothesis.** The sample's chi-square of 8 is more extreme than the cutoff of 3.841. Reject the null hypothesis; people like those in the sample are different from the expected even breakdown.

(b) See Figure 13–4.

Ⓒ **In each category, take observed minus expected frequencies.** This is the direct comparison of the distribution for the sample versus the distribution representing the expected population.

Ⓓ **Square each of these differences.** This gets rid of the direction of the difference (since the interest is only in how much difference there is).

Ⓔ **Divide each squared difference by the expected frequency for its category.** This adjusts the degree of difference for the absolute size of the expected frequencies.

Ⓕ **Add up the results of Step Ⓔ for all the categories.** This gives you a statistic for the overall degree of discrepancy.

3. Formula for the chi-square statistic: $\chi^2 = \sum \dfrac{(O-E)^2}{E}$.

χ^2 is the chi-square statistic; $\sum$ tells you to sum over all the different categories; O is the observed frequency for a category; E is the expected frequency for a category.

4. (a) A chi-square distribution: for any particular number of categories, the distribution you would expect if you figured a very large number of chi-square statistics for samples from a population in which the distribution of people over categories is the expected distribution. (b) It is skewed to the right. (c) It has this shape because a chi-square statistic can't be less than 0 (since the numerator, a squared score, has to be positive, and its denominator, an expected number of individuals, also has to be positive), but there is no limit to how large it can be.

5. (a) ❶ **Restate the question as a research hypothesis and a null hypothesis about the populations.** There are two populations:

Population 1: People like those in the sample.

Population 2: People in general who have an equal distribution of the two categories.

The research hypothesis is that the distribution of numbers of people over categories is different in the two populations; the null hypothesis is that it is the same.

❷ **Determine the characteristics of the comparison distribution.** The comparison distribution is a chi-square distribution with 1 degree of freedom (that is, $df = N_{\text{categories}} - 1 = 2 - 1 = 1$).

❸ **Determine the cutoff sample score on the comparison distribution at which the null hypothesis should be rejected.** At the .05 level with $df = 1$, cutoff is 3.841.

❹ **Determine your sample's score on the comparison distribution.**

Ⓐ **Determine the actual, observed frequencies in each category.** As given in the problem, these are 15 and 35.

Ⓑ **Determine the expected frequencies in each category.** With 50 people and expecting an even breakdown, the expected totals are 25 and 25.

Ⓒ **In each category, take observed minus expected frequencies.** These come out to −10 (that is, $15 - 25 = -10$) and 10 (that is, $35 - 25 = 10$).

Ⓓ **Square each of these differences.** Both come out to 100 (that is, $-10^2 = 100$ and $10^2 = 100$).

The Chi-Square Test for Independence

So far, we have looked at the distribution of *one nominal variable* with several categories, such as the relationship style of men's partners. In fact, this kind of situation is fairly rare in research. We began with an example of this kind mainly as a stepping-stone to a more common actual research situation, to which we now turn.

The most common use of chi-square is when there are *two nominal variables,* each with several categories. For example, Harter and colleagues (1997) might have studied whether the breakdown of partners of self-focused men was the same as the breakdown of partners of other-focused men. If that were their purpose, we would have had two nominal variables. Relationship styles of partners would be the first nominal variable. Men's own relationship styles would be the second nominal variable. Hypothesis testing in this kind of situation is called a *chi-square test for independence.* You learn shortly why it has this name.

Suppose researchers at a large university survey 200 staff members who commute to work about the kind of transportation they use to get to work as well as whether they are "morning people" (prefer to go to bed early and awaken early) or "night people" (go to bed late and awaken late). Table 13–4 shows the results. Notice the two nominal variables: *types of transportation* (with three levels) and *sleep tendency* (with two levels).

Contingency Tables

contingency table two-dimensional chart showing frequencies in each combination of categories of two nominal variables.

Table 13–4 is a **contingency table,** a table in which the distributions of two nominal variables are set up so that you have the frequencies of their combinations as well as the totals. Thus, in Table 13–4, the 60 in the bus–morning combination is how many morning people ride the bus. (A contingency table is similar to the tables in factorial analysis of variance that you learned about in Chapter 10 where each cell had a mean

Table 13–4 Contingency Table of Observed Frequencies of Morning and Night People Using Different Types of Transportation (Fictional Data)

		Transportation			
		Bus	**Carpool**	**Own Car**	**Total**
Sleep Tendency	Morning	60	30	30	120 (60%)
	Night	20	20	40	80 (40%)
	Total	80	50	70	200 (100%)

of the scores of several people; but in a contingency table, the number in each cell is not a mean, but rather the *number of people that have a combination of variables.*)

Table 13–4 is a 3 × 2 contingency table because it has three levels of one variable crossed with two levels of the other. (Which dimension is named first does not matter.) It is also possible to have larger contingency tables, such as a 4 × 7 or a 6 × 18 table. Smaller tables, 2 × 2 contingency tables, are especially common.

Independence

The question in this example is whether there is any relation between the type of transportation people use and whether they are morning or night people. If there is no relation, the *proportion* of morning and night people is the same among bus riders, carpoolers, and those who drive their own cars. Or, to put it the other way, if there is no relation, the *proportion* of bus riders, carpoolers, and own car drivers is the same for morning and night people. However you describe it, the situation of no relation between the variables in a contingency table is called **independence.**[1]

Sample and Population

In the observed survey results in the example, the proportions of night and morning people in the sample vary with different types of transportation. For example, the bus riders are split 60–20; so three-fourths of the bus riders are morning people. Among people who drive their own cars, the split is 30–40. Thus, a slight majority are night people. Still, the sample is only of 200. It is possible that in the larger population, the type of transportation a person uses is independent of the person's being a morning or a night person. The big question is whether the lack of independence in the sample is large enough to reject the null hypothesis of independence in the population. That is, you need to do a chi-square test.

Determining Expected Frequencies

One thing that is new in a chi-square test for independence is that you now have to figure differences between observed and expected for each *combination* of categories—that is, for each **cell** of the contingency table. (When there was only one nominal variable, you figured these differences just for each category of that single nominal variable.) Table 13–5 is the contingency table for the example survey. This time, we have shown the expected frequency (in parentheses) next to each observed frequency.

The key idea to keep in mind when figuring expected frequencies in a contingency table is that "expected" is based on the two variables being independent. If they are independent, then the proportions up and down the cells of each column should be the same. In the example, overall, there are 60% morning people and 40% night people; thus, if the transportation method is independent of being a morning or night person,

independence situation of no relationship between two variables; term usually used regarding two nominal variables in a chi-square test for independence.

cell in chi-square, the particular combination of categories for two variables in a contingency table.

Table 13–5 Contingency Table of Observed (and Expected) Frequencies of Morning and Night People Using Different Types of Transportation (Fictional Data)

		Transportation			
		Bus	Carpool	Own Car	Total
Sleep Tendency	Morning	60 (48)[a]	30 (30)	30 (42)	120 (60%)
	Night	20 (32)	20 (20)	40 (28)	80 (40%)
	Total	80	50	70	200 (100%)

[a]Expected frequencies are in parentheses.

this 60%–40% split should hold for each column (each transportation type). First, the 60%–40% overall split should hold for the bus group. This would make an expected frequency in the bus cell for morning people of 60% of 80, which comes out to 48 people. The expected frequency for the bus riders who are night people is 32 (that is, 40% of 80 is 32). The same principle holds for the other columns: the 50 carpool people should have a 60%–40% split, giving an expected frequency of 30 morning people who carpool (that is, 60% of 50 is 30) and 20 night people who carpool (that is, 40% of 50 is 20), and the 70 own-car people should have a 60%–40% split, giving expected frequencies of 42 and 28.

Summarizing what we have said in terms of steps,

TIP FOR SUCCESS

Be sure to check that you are selecting the correct row percentage and column total for each cell. Selecting from the wrong row or column is a common mistake in figuring chi-square.

❶ **Find each row's percentage of the total.**
❷ **For each cell, multiply its row's percentage by its column's total.**

Applying these steps to the top left cell (morning persons who ride the bus),

❶ **Find each row's percentage of the total.** The 120 in the morning person row is 60% of the overall total of 200 (that is, $120/200 = 60\%$).
❷ **For each cell, multiply its row's percentage by its column's total.** The column total for the bus riders is 80; 60% of 80 comes out to 48 (that is, $.60 \times 80 = 48$).

These steps can also be stated as a formula,

A cell's expected frequency is the number in its row divided by the total, multiplied by the number in its column.

$$E = \left(\frac{R}{N}\right)(C) \qquad (13\text{–}3)$$

In this formula, E is the expected frequency for a particular cell. R is the number of people observed in this cell's row, and N is the number of people total (thus, R divided by N is the proportion of the total number of people that are in that row). C is the number of people observed in this cell's column. (Thus, for any given column, taking the result of R divided by N—the proportion in that row—and multiplying by C, the number in that column, gives you the number you would expect for that row to be in that column.)

Applying the formula to the same top left cell,

$$E = \left(\frac{R}{N}\right)(C) = \left(\frac{120}{200}\right)(80) = (.60)(80) = 48.$$

TIP FOR SUCCESS

As a check on your arithmetic, it is a good idea to make sure that the expected and observed frequencies add up to the same totals in each column (and overall).

Looking at the entire Table 13–5, notice that in each column (as well as overall) the expected frequencies add up to the same totals as the observed frequencies. (This is as it should be because the expected frequencies are just a different way of dividing up the column total.) For example, in the first column (bus), the expected frequencies of 48 and 32 add up to 80, just as the observed frequencies in that column of 60 and 20 do.

Figuring Chi-Square

You figure chi-square the same way as in the chi-square test for goodness of fit, except that you now figure the weighted squared difference for each *cell* and add these up. Here is how it works for our survey example:

$$\chi^2 = \sum \frac{(O - E)^2}{E} = \frac{(60 - 48)^2}{48} + \frac{(30 - 30)^2}{30} + \frac{(30 - 42)^2}{42}$$
$$+ \frac{(20 - 32)^2}{32} + \frac{(20 - 20)^2}{20} + \frac{(40 - 28)^2}{28}$$
$$= 3 + 0 + 3.43 + 4.5 + 0 + 5.14 = 16.07.$$

Table 13-6	Contingency Table Showing Marginal and Two Cells' Observed Frequencies to Illustrate Figuring of Degrees of Freedom				

		Transportation			
		Bus	**Carpool**	**Own Car**	**Total**
Sleep Tendency	Morning	60	30	—	120 (60%)
	Night	—	—	—	80 (40%)
	Total	80	50	70	200 (100%)

Degrees of Freedom

A contingency table with many cells may have relatively few degrees of freedom. In our example, there are six cells but only 2 degrees of freedom. Recall that the degrees of freedom are the number of categories free to vary once the totals are known. With a chi-square test for independence, the number of categories is the number of cells; the totals include the row and column totals—and if you know the row and column totals, you have a lot of information.

Consider the sleep tendency and transportation example. Suppose you know the first two cell frequencies across the top, for example, and all the row and column totals. You could then figure all the other cell frequencies just by subtraction. Table 13–6 shows the contingency table for this example with just the row and column totals and these two cell frequencies. Let's start with the "Morning/Own Car" cell. There is a total of 120 morning people and the other two morning-person cells have 90 in them (60 + 30). Thus, only 30 remain for the "Morning/Own Car" cell. Now consider the three night person cells. You know the frequencies for all the morning people cells and the column totals for each type of transportation. Thus, each cell frequency for the night people is its column's total minus the morning people in that column. For example, there are 80 bus riders and 60 are morning people. Thus, the remaining 20 must be night people.

What you can see in all this is that with knowledge of only two of the cells, you could figure out the frequencies in each of the other cells. Thus, although there are six cells, there are only 2 degrees of freedom—only two cells whose frequencies are really free to vary once we have all the row and column totals. However, rather than having to think all this out each time, there is a shortcut. In a chi-square test for independence, the degrees of freedom are the number of columns minus 1 multiplied by the number of rows minus 1. Put as a formula,

$$df = (N_{Columns} - 1)(N_{Rows} - 1) \qquad (13\text{–}4)$$

> The degrees of freedom for the chi-square test for independence are the number of columns minus 1 multiplied by the number of rows minus 1.

$N_{Columns}$ is the number of columns and N_{Rows} is the number of rows.

Using this formula for our survey example,

$$df = (N_{Columns} - 1)(N_{Rows} - 1) = (3 - 1)(2 - 1) = (2)(1) = 2.$$

Hypothesis Testing

With 2 degrees of freedom, Table 13–2 (or Table A–4) shows that the chi-square you need for significance at the .01 level is 9.211. The chi-square of 16.07 for our example is larger than this cutoff. Thus, you can reject the null hypothesis that the two variables are independent in the population.

Steps of Hypothesis Testing

Now let's go through the survey example again, this time following the steps of hypothesis testing.

❶ **Restate the question as a research hypothesis and a null hypothesis about the populations.** There are two populations:

Population 1: People like those surveyed.
Population 2: People for whom being a night or a morning person is independent of the kind of transportation they use to commute to work.

The null hypothesis is that the two populations are the same—that, in general the proportions using different types of transportation are the same for morning and night people. The research hypothesis is that the two populations are different, that among people in general the proportions using different types of transportation are different for morning and night people.

Put another way, the null hypothesis is that the two variables are independent (they are unrelated to each other). The research hypothesis is that they are not independent (that they are related to each other).

❷ **Determine the characteristics of the comparison distribution.** The comparison distribution is a chi-square distribution with 2 degrees of freedom (the number of columns minus 1 multiplied by the number of rows minus 1).

❸ **Determine the cutoff sample score on the comparison distribution at which the null hypothesis should be rejected.** You use the same table as for any chi-square test. In the example, setting a .01 significance level with 2 degrees of freedom, your need a chi-square of 9.211.

❹ **Determine your sample's score on the comparison distribution.**

  Ⓐ **Determine the actual, observed frequencies in each cell.** These are the results of the survey, as given in Table 13–4.

  Ⓑ **Determine the expected frequencies in each cell.** These are shown in Table 13–5. For example, for the bottom right cell ("Night Person/Own Car" cell),

  ❶ **Find each row's percentage of the total.** The 80 people in the night person's row are 40% of the overall total of 200 (that is, $80/200 = 40\%$).

  ⓐ **For each cell, multiply its row's percentage by its column's total.** The column total for those with their own car is 70; 40% of 70 comes out to 28 (that is, $.40 \times 70 = 28$).

  Ⓒ **In each cell, take observed minus expected frequencies.** For example, for the "Night Person/Own Car" cell, this comes out to 12 (that is, $40 - 28 = 12$).

  Ⓓ **Square each of these differences.** For example, for the "Night Person/Own Car" cell, this comes out to 144 (that is, $12^2 = 144$).

  Ⓔ **Divide each squared difference by the expected frequency for its cell.** For example, for the "Night Person/Own Car" cell, this comes out to 5.14 (that is, $144/28 = 5.14$).

  Ⓕ **Add up the results of Step Ⓔ for all the cells.** As we saw, this came out to 16.07.

❺ **Decide whether to reject the null hypothesis.** The chi-square needed to reject the null hypothesis is 9.211 and the chi-square for our sample is 16.07 (see Figure 13–5). Thus, you can reject the null hypothesis. The research hypothesis that the two variables are not independent in the population is supported. That is, the proportions of type of transportation used to commute to work are different for morning and night people.

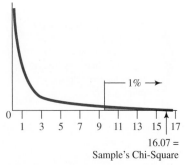

Figure 13–5 For the sleep tendency and transportation example, chi-square distribution $(df = 2)$ showing the cutoff for rejecting the null hypothesis at the .01 level and the sample's chi-square.

Table 13-7 Results and Figuring of the Chi-Square Test for Independence Comparing Whether First-Generation College Students Differ from Others in First Semester Dropouts

	Generation to Go to College		
	First Ⓐ Ⓑ	Other	Total
Dropped Out	73 (57.7)	89 (103.9)	162 (7.9%)
Did Not Drop Out	657 (672.3)	1,226 (1,211.1)	1,883 (92.1%)
Total	730	1,315	2,045

$df = (N_{Columns} - 1)(N_{Rows} - 1) = (2 - 1)(2 - 1) = (1)(1) = 1.$ ❷

Chi-square needed, $df = 1$, .01 level: 6.635. ❸

$$\chi^2 = \Sigma \frac{(O - E)^2}{E} = \frac{(73 - 57.7)^2}{57.7} + \frac{(89 - 103.9)^2}{103.9} + \frac{(657 - 672.3)^2}{672.3} + \frac{(1,226 - 1,211.1)^2}{1,211.1}$$

Ⓒ $= \dfrac{15.3^2}{57.7} + \dfrac{-14.9^2}{103.9} + \dfrac{-15.3^2}{672.3} + \dfrac{14.9^2}{1,211.1}$

Ⓓ $= \dfrac{234.1}{57.7} + \dfrac{222}{103.9} + \dfrac{234.1}{672.3} + \dfrac{222}{1,211.1}$

Ⓔ $= 4.06 + 2.14 + .35 + .18$

$= 6.73.$ Ⓕ

Decision: Reject the null hypothesis. ❺

Notes. 1. With a 2 × 2 analysis, the differences and squared differences (numerators) are the same for all four cells. In this example, the cells are a little different due to rounding error. 2. Data from Riehl (1994). The exact chi-square (6.73) is slightly different from that reported in the article (7.2), due to rounding error.

A Second Example

Riehl (1994) studied the college experience of students who were the first generation in their family to attend college. These students were compared to other students who were not the first generation in their family to go to college. (All students in the study were from Indiana University.) One of the variables Riehl measured was whether or not students dropped out during their first semester.

Table 13–7 shows the results along with the expected frequencies (shown in parentheses). Below the contingency table is the figuring for the chi-square test for independence.

❶ **Restate the question as a null hypothesis and a research hypothesis about the populations.** There are two populations:

Population 1: Students like those surveyed.

Population 2: Students whose dropping out or staying in college their first semester is independent of whether or not they are the first generation in their family to go to college.

The null hypothesis is that the two populations are the same—that, in general, whether or not students drop out of college is independent of whether or not they are the first generation in their family to go to college. The research hypothesis is that the populations are not the same. In other words, the research hypothesis is that students like those surveyed are different from the hypothetical population in which dropping out is unrelated to whether or not you are first generation.

❷ **Determine the characteristics of the comparison distribution.** This is a chi-square distribution with 1 degree of freedom.

❸ **Determine the cutoff sample score on the comparison distribution at which the null hypothesis should be rejected.** Using the .01 level and 1 degree of freedom. Table A–4 shows that you need a chi-square for significance is 6.635. This is shown in Figure 13–6.

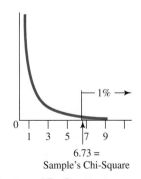

Figure 13–6 For the example from Reihl (1994), chi-square distribution ($df = 1$) showing the cutoff for rejecting the null hypothesis at the .01 level and the sample's chi-square.

❹ **Determine your sample's score on the comparison distribution.**

  ❹ **Determine the actual, observed frequencies in each cell.** These are the results of the survey, as given in Table 13–7.

  ❺ **Determine the expected frequencies in each cell.** These are shown in parentheses in Table 13–7.

  For example, for the top left cell ("First Generation/Dropped Out" cell),

    ❶ **Find each row's percentage of the total.** The "Dropped Out" row's 162 is 7.9% of the overall total of 2,045 (that is, $162/2,045 = 7.9\%$).

    ❷ **For each cell, multiply its row's percentage by its column's total.** The column total for the "First Generation" students is 730; 7.9% of 730 comes out to 57.7 (that is, $.079 \times 730 = 57.7$).

  ❻ **In each cell, take observed minus expected frequencies.** These are shown in Table 13–7. For example, for the "First Generation/Dropped Out" cell, this comes out to 15.3 (that is, $73 - 57.7 = 15.3$).

  ❼ **Square each of these differences.** These are also shown in Table 13–7. For example, for the "First Generation/Dropped Out" cell, this comes out to 234.1 (that is, $15.3^2 = 234.1$).

  ❽ **Divide each squared difference by the expected frequency for its cell.** Once again, these are shown in Table 13–7. For example, for the "First Generation/ Dropped Out" cell, this comes out to 4.06 (that is, $234.1/57.7 = 4.06$).

  ❾ **Add up the results of Step ❽ for all the cells.** As shown in Table 13–7, this comes out to 6.73. Its location on the chi-square distribution is shown in Figure 13–6.

❺ **Decide whether to reject the null hypothesis.** Your chi-square of 6.73 is larger than the cutoff of 6.635. Thus, you can reject the null hypothesis. That is, judging from a sample of 2,045 Indiana University students, first generation students are somewhat more likely to drop out during their first semester than are other students. (Remember, of course, that there could be many reasons for this result.)

The results of Riehl's (1994) study have been replicated in many other universities. For example, a recent study of this issue among college students across the United States also found that first generation students were more likely to drop out of college than other students (Chen, 2005).

How are you doing?

1. (a) In what situation do you use a chi-square test for independence? (b) How is this different from the situation in which you would use a chi-square test for goodness of fit?
2. (a) List the steps for figuring the expected frequencies in a contingency table. (b) Write the formula for expected frequencies in a contingency table and define each of its symbols.
3. (a) Write the formula for figuring degrees of freedom in a chi-square test for independence and define each of its symbols. (b) Explain the logic behind this formula.
4. Carry out a chi-square test for independence for the following observed scores (using the .10 significance level). (a) Use the steps of hypothesis testing, and (b) sketch the distribution involved.

		Nominal Variable A	
		Category 1	Category 2
Nominal Variable B	**Category 1**	10	10
	Category 2	50	10

4. (a) Chi-square test for independence:

❶ **Restate the question as a null hypothesis and a research hypothesis about the populations.** There are two populations:

Population 1: People like those studied.

Population 2: People whose being in a particular category of Nominal Variable A is independent of their being in a particular category of Nominal Variable B.

The null hypothesis is that the two populations are the same; the research hypothesis is that the populations are not the same.

❷ **Determine the characteristics of the comparison distribution.** This is a chi-square distribution with 1 degree of freedom. That is, $df = (N_{Columns} - 1)$ $(N_{Rows} - 1) = (2 - 1)(2 - 1) = 1$.

❸ **Determine the cutoff sample score on the comparison distribution at which the null hypothesis should be rejected.** From Table A–4 (in the Appendix), for the .10 level and 1 degree of freedom, the needed chi-square is 2.706.

❹ **Determine your sample's score on the comparison distribution.**

❶ **Determine the actual, observed frequencies in each cell.** These are shown in the contingency table for the problem.

❷ **Determine the expected frequencies in each cell.**

❶ **Find each row's percentage of the total.** For the top row 20/80 = 25%; for the second row, 60/80 = 75%.

❷ **For each cell, multiply its row's percentage by its column's total.** For the top left cell, 25% × 60 = 15; for the top right cell, 25% × 20 = 5; for the bottom left cell, 75% × 60 = 45; for the bottom right cell, 75% × 20 = 15.

❸ **In each cell, take observed minus expected frequencies.** For the four cells, 10 − 15 = −5; 10 − 5 = 5; 50 − 45 = 5; 10 − 15 = −5.

❹ **Square each of these differences.** This is 25 for each cell (that is, $5^2 = 25$ and $-5^2 = 25$).

❺ **Divide each squared difference by the expected frequency for its cell.** These come out to 25/15 = 1.67, 25/5 = 5, 25/45 = .56, and 25/15 = 1.67.

❻ **Add up the results of Step ❺ for all the cells.** 1.67 + 5 + .56 + 1.67 = 8.90.

❺ **Decide whether to reject the null hypothesis.** The sample's chi square of 8.90 is larger than the cutoff of 2.706. Thus, you can reject the null hypothesis: which category people are in on Nominal Variable A is not independent of which category they are in on Nominal Variable B.

(b) See Figure 13–7.

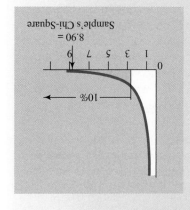

Figure 13-7 For "How Are You Doing?" question 4, chi-square distribution ($df = 1$) showing the cutoff for rejecting the null hypothesis at the .10 level and the sample's chi-square.

Assumptions for Chi-Square Tests

The chi-square tests of goodness of fit and for independence do not require the usual assumptions of normal population variances and such. There is, however, one key assumption: each score must not have any special relation to any other scores. This means that you can't use these chi-square tests if the scores are based on the same people being tested more than once. Consider a study in which 20 people are tested to see if the distribution of their preferred brand of breakfast cereal changed from before to after a recent nutritional campaign. The results of this study could not be tested with the usual chi-square, because the distributions of cereal choice before and after are from the same people. You may also hear about a rule that, for the results of a chi-square test to be valid, none of the expected frequencies should be less than 5. However, these days most statisticians no longer hold to this idea. We have more to say about this issue in the Controversy section later in this chapter.

Effect Size and Power for Chi-Square Tests for Independence

Effect Size

In chi-square tests for independence, you can use your sample's chi-square to figure a number that shows the degree of association of the two nominal variables.

With a 2×2 contingency table, the measure of association is called the **phi coefficient (ϕ).** Here is the formula:

$$\phi = \sqrt{\frac{\chi^2}{N}} \qquad (13\text{--}5)$$

The phi coefficient has a minimum of 0 and a maximum of 1, and it can be considered like a correlation coefficient (see Chapter 11).[2] Cohen's (1988) conventions for the phi coefficient are that .10 is a small effect size, .30 is a medium effect size, and .50 is a large effect size (the same as for an ordinary correlation coefficient).

For example, in the Riehl (1994) study of first generation college students, the sample's chi-square was 6.73 and there were 2,045 people in the study. Thus,

$$\phi = \sqrt{\frac{\chi^2}{N}} = \sqrt{\frac{6.73}{2,045}} = \sqrt{.00329} = .06.$$

This is a very small effect size. The fact that the chi-square of 6.73 was significant in this study tells you that the greater likelihood of first generation students dropping out that you saw in the sample is probably not due to the particular people that were randomly recruited to be in this sample. You can thus have some confidence that there is a pattern of this kind in the population. But the small phi coefficient tells you that this population tendency may not be a very important factor in practice.

You only use phi when you have a 2×2 situation. **Cramer's phi** is an extension of the ordinary phi coefficient that you can use for contingency tables larger than 2×2 (Cramer's phi is also known as *Cramer's V* and is sometimes written ϕ_C or V_C). You figure Cramer's phi the same way as the ordinary phi coefficient, except that instead of dividing by N, you divide by N times the degrees of freedom of the smaller side of the table. Stated as a formula,

$$\text{Cramer's } \phi = \sqrt{\frac{\chi^2}{(N)(df_{\text{Smaller}})}} \qquad (13\text{--}6)$$

In this formula, df_{Smaller} is the degrees of freedom for the smaller side of the contingency table.

In the sleep tendency and transportation preference example, the sample's chi-square was 16.07 and the total number of people surveyed was 200. There was one degree of freedom for the smaller side of the table (the rows in this example). Cramer's phi is the square root of what you get when you divide 16.07 by 200 multiplied by 1. This comes out to .28. In terms of the formula,

$$\text{Cramer's } \phi = \sqrt{\frac{\chi^2}{(N)(df_{\text{Smaller}})}} = \sqrt{\frac{16.07}{(200)(1)}} = \sqrt{.08} = .28.$$

Cohen's conventions for effect size for Cramer's phi depend on the degrees of freedom for the smaller side of the table. Table 13–8 shows Cohen's (1988) effect size conventions for Cramer's phi for tables in which the smallest side of the table is 2, 3, and 4. Notice that when the smallest side of the table is 2, there is one degree of freedom. Thus, the effect sizes given in the table for this situation are the same as for the ordinary phi coefficient.

Based on the table, in the transportation example there is an approximately medium effect size (.28), a medium amount of relationship between type of transportation one uses, and whether one is a morning or a night person.

phi coefficient (ϕ) effect-size measure for a chi-square test for independence with a 2×2 contingency table; square root of division of chi-square statistic by N.

Cramer's phi (Cramer's ϕ) measure of effect size for a chi-square test for independence with a contingency table that is larger than 2×2. Also known as *Cramer's V* and sometimes written as ϕ_C or V_C.

Table 13-8 Cohen's Conventions for Cramer's Phi

Smallest Side of Contingency Table	Effect Size		
	Small	Medium	Large
2 ($df_{Smaller} = 1$)	.10	.30	.50
3 ($df_{Smaller} = 2$)	.07	.21	.35
4 ($df_{Smaller} = 3$)	.06	.17	.29

Power

Table 13–9 shows the approximate power at the .05 significance level for small, medium, and large effect sizes and total sample sizes of 25, 50, 100, and 200. Power is given for tables with 1, 2, 3, and 4 degrees of freedom.[3]

Consider the power of a planned 2×4 study ($df = 3$) of 50 people with an expected medium effect size (Cramer's $\phi = .30$). The researchers will use the .05 level. From Table 13–9 you can find this study would have a power of .40. That is, if the research hypothesis is true, and there is a true medium effect size, there is about a 40% chance that the study will come out significant. Notice from this table two things about power for a chi-square test for independence. First, like all other hypothesis-testing situations, the more participants there are in the study, the more power there will be. Second, the more degrees of freedom there are (the more different categories that are crossed with each other), the less power there is. Thus, for maximum power, you want as many participants as possible with as simple a contingency table (that is, as few categories in each direction) as possible.

Table 13-9 Approximate Power for the Chi-Square Test for Independence for Testing Hypotheses at the .05 Significance Level

Total *df*	Total *N*	Effect Size		
		Small	Medium	Large
1	25	.08	.32	.70
	50	.11	.56	.94
	100	.17	.85	*
	200	.29	.99	*
2	25	.07	.25	.60
	50	.09	.46	.90
	100	.13	.77	*
	200	.23	.97	*
3	25	.07	.21	.54
	50	.08	.40	.86
	100	.12	.71	.99
	200	.19	.96	*
4	25	.06	.19	.50
	50	.08	.36	.82
	100	.11	.66	.99
	200	.17	.94	*

*Nearly 1.

Table 13-10	Approximate Total Number of Participants Needed for 80% Power for the Chi-Square Test for Independence for Testing Hypotheses at the .05 Significance Level		
	Effect Size		
Total _df_	**Small**	**Medium**	**Large**
1	785	87	26
2	964	107	39
3	1,090	121	44
4	1,194	133	48

Needed Sample Size

Table 13–10 gives the approximate total number of participants needed for 80% power with small, medium, and large effect sizes at the .05 significance level for chi-square tests for independence of 2, 3, 4, and 5 degrees of freedom.[4] Suppose you are planning a study with a 3×3 $(df = 4)$ contingency table. You expect a large effect size and will use the .05 significance level. According to the table, you would only need 48 participants. Again, the same principle holds that we emphasized earlier regarding the degrees of freedom when figuring power. In this case, it means that the more degrees of freedom there are (that is, the more categories in each variable being crossed), the more participants you need for the same amount of power.

How are you doing?

1. What are the assumptions for chi-square tests?
2. (a) What is the measure of effect size for a 2×2 chi-square test for independence? (b) Write the formula for this measure of effect size and define each of the symbols. (c) What are Cohen's conventions for small, medium, and large effect sizes? (d) Figure the effect size for a 2×2 chi-square test for independence in which there are a total of 100 participants and the chi-square is 12.
3. (a) What is the measure of effect size for a chi-square test for independence for a contingency table that is larger than 2×2? (b) Write the formula for this measure of effect size and define each of the symbols. (c) What is Cohen's convention for a small effect size for a 4×6 contingency table? (d) Figure the effect size for a 4×6 chi-square test for independence in which there are a total of 200 participants and the chi-square is 20.
4. What is the power of a planned 3×3 chi-square with 50 participants total and a predicted medium effect size?
5. What two factors affect the power of a study using a chi-square test for independence?
6. About how many participants do you need for 80% power in a planned 2×2 study in which you predict a medium effect size and will be using the .05 significance level?

6. Number of participants needed: 87.
5. Two factors that affect the power of a study using a chi-square test for independence: number of participants and degrees of freedom.

Answers

1. The only major assumption for chi-square tests is that the numbers in each cell or category are from separate persons.

2. (a) The measure of effect size for a 2 $\times$ 2 chi-square test for independence is the phi coefficient.

   (b) The formula for the measure of effect size is $\phi = \sqrt{\dfrac{\chi^2}{N}}$.

   ϕ is the phi coefficient (effect size for a chi-square test for independence with a 2 $\times$ 2 contingency table); χ^2 is the sample's chi-square; and N is the number of participants in the study.

   (c) Cohen's conventions: .10 is a small effect size, .30 is a medium effect size, and .50 is a large effect size.

   (d) Effect size: $\phi = \sqrt{\dfrac{12}{100}} = .35$.

3. (a) Effect size: Cramer's phi.

   (b) Formula: Cramer's $\phi = \sqrt{\dfrac{\chi^2}{(N)(df_{Smaller})}}$.

   Cramer's ϕ is Cramer's phi coefficient (effect size for a chi-square test for independence); χ^2 is the sample's chi-square; N is the number of participants in the study total; and $df_{Smaller}$ is the degrees of freedom for the smaller side of the contingency table.

   (c) Cohen's convention: .06.

   (d) Effect size: $\sqrt{20/[(200)(3)]} = .18$.

4. Power: .36.

Controversy: The Minimum Expected Frequency

Over a half century ago, Lewis and Burke (1949) published a landmark paper on the misuse of chi-square. They listed nine common errors that had appeared in published papers, giving many examples of each. With one exception, their work has held up very well through the years. The errors are still being made, and they are still seen as errors. (If you follow the procedures of this chapter, *you* won't be making them!)

The one exception to this critical picture is the error that Lewis and Burke considered the most common weakness in the use of chi-square: expected frequencies that are too low. Now, it seems that low expected numbers in cells may not be such a big problem after all. Lewis and Burke, like most statistics textbook authors of their time, held that every cell of a contingency table (and every category of a goodness of fit test) should have a reasonable-sized expected frequency. They recommended a minimum of 10, with 5 as the bottom limit. Others recommended figures ranging from 1 to 20. Even Sir Ronald Fisher (1938) previously had his own suggestion, recommending 10 as his minimum. Still others recommended that the minimum should be some proportion of the total or that it depended on whether the expected frequencies were equal or not. (Incidentally, notice that what was being debated were minimum *expected* frequencies, not observed frequencies.)

Since 1949, when Lewis and Burke published their article, there has been some systematic research on just what the effects of low expected frequencies are. (These studies use Monte Carlo methods; see Chapter 8, Box 8–1.) And what is the conclusion? As in most areas, the matter is still not completely settled. However, by the early 1980s, a major review of the research on the topic (Delucchi, 1983) and still the definitive word drew two main conclusions:

1. "As a general rule, the chi-square statistic may be properly used in cases where the expected values are much lower than previously considered permissible" (p. 168). Even expected frequencies as low as 1 per cell may be acceptable in terms of Type I error, provided that there are a reasonable number of individuals overall. The most important principle seems to be that there should be at least five times as many individuals as there are cells. For example, a cell with a very low expected frequency would be acceptable in a 2×2 contingency table if there were at least 20 participants in the study overall.[5]

2. However, Delucchi cited one researcher as concluding that, even though using chi-square with small expected frequencies may be acceptable (in the sense of not giving too many Type I errors in the long run), it may still not be a wise approach. This is because the chance of getting a significant result, even if your research hypothesis is true, may be quite slim. That is, with small expected frequencies, power is very low. Thus, you run the risk of Type II errors instead.

Chi-Square Tests in Research Articles

In research articles, chi-square tests usually include the frequencies in each category or cell as well as the degrees of freedom, number of participants, the sample's chi-square, and significance level. For example, Harter and colleagues (1997) reported their finding for the relationship style of the self-focused men as "$\chi^2 (2, n = 101) = 11.89, p < .005$" (p. 156).

Here is another example of a chi-square test for goodness of fit. Sandra Moriarty and Shu-Ling Everett (1994) had graduate students go to 55 different homes and observe people watching television for 45-minute sessions. In one part of their results, they compared the number of people they observed who fell into one of four distinct categories:

> Flipping [very rapid channel changing], the category dominated by the most active type of behavior, occurred most frequently in 33% of the sessions ($n = 18$). The grazing category [periods of browsing through channels] dominated 24% of the sessions ($n = 13$), and 22% were found to be in each of the continuous and stretch viewing categories ($n = 12$). These differences were not statistically significant ($\chi^2 = 1.79$, $df = 3, p > .05$). (p. 349)

Published reports of chi-square tests for independence provide the same basic chi-square information. For example, Durkin and Barber (2002) studied the relationship between playing computer games and positive development (such as being close to one's family, involved in activities, having positive mental health, and low disobedience to parents) among 16-year-old high school students in Michigan. As part of the study, the researchers tested whether male and female students differed in how often they played computer games. Students indicated how often they played computer games with a 7-point scale, from *never* (1) to *daily* (7). Here is how the researchers reported their results:

> The participants were categorized into three groups based on their frequency of play: "None" included participants who did not use computers at all, as well as those who used computers, but never for computer games; "Low" included participants who checked 2, 3, 4, or 5 for frequency of computer use to play computer games; and "High" included participants who checked 6 or 7 for frequency of computer game play.

A chi-square test [for independence] indicated that males and females were not evenly distributed across these three categories [χ^2 (2, $N = 1043$) = 62.39, $p < .001$]. Girls were overrepresented among the nonusers, with a majority never playing computer games (50.6%), compared to 29.4% of boys who never played. Boys were more than twice as likely (23.8%) as girls (9.9%) to be in the high use group. A substantial number of both girls (39.4%) and boys (46.8%) were in the low use group. (p. 381)

You may be interested to read the researchers' conclusions from the overall study: "No evidence was obtained of negative outcomes among game players. On several measures—including...[all of the positive development outcomes mentioned earlier]—game players scored more favorably than did peers who never played computer games. It is concluded that computer games can be a positive feature of a healthy adolescence" (Durkin & Barber, 2002, p. 373).

Durkin and Barber (2002) do not give the effect size for their significant result. However, you can figure it out from the chi-square, number of participants, and design of the study (2 × 3 in this example). Using the formula,

$$\phi = \sqrt{\chi^2/[(N)(df_{\text{Smaller}})]} = \sqrt{62.39[(1043)(1)]} = \sqrt{.060} = .24.$$

This suggests that there is something close to a moderate effect size.

Summary

1. Chi-square tests are used for hypothesis tests with *nominal variables.* A sample's chi-square statistic (χ^2) shows the amount of mismatch between expected and observed frequencies over several categories. It is figured by finding, for each category or combination of categories, the difference between observed frequency and expected frequency, squaring this difference (eliminating positive and negative signs), and dividing by the expected frequency (making the squared differences more proportionate to the numbers involved). The results are then added up for all the categories or combinations of categories. The distribution of the chi-square statistic is known and the cutoffs can be looked up in standard chi-square tables.

2. The chi-square test for goodness of fit is used to test hypotheses about whether a distribution of frequencies over two or more categories of a *single nominal variable* matches an expected distribution. (These expected frequencies are based, for example, on theory or on a distribution in another study or circumstance). In this test, the expected frequencies are given in advance or are based on some expected percentages (such as equal percentages in all groups). The degrees of freedom are the number of categories minus 1.

3. The chi-square test for independence is used to test hypotheses about the relation between *two nominal variables*—that is, about whether the breakdown over the categories of one variable has the same proportional pattern in each of the categories of the other variable. The frequencies are set up in a contingency table in which the two variables are crossed and the numbers in each combination are placed in each of the resulting cells. The frequency expected for a cell if the two variables are independent is the percentage of all the people in that cell's row multiplied by the total number of people in that cell's column. The degrees of freedom for the chi-square test for independence are the number of columns minus 1 multiplied by the number of rows minus 1.

4. Chi-square tests make no assumptions about normal distributions of their variables, but they do require that no individual be counted in more than one category or cell.
5. The estimated effect size for a chi-square test for independence (that is, the degree of association) for a 2 × 2 contingency table is the phi coefficient; for larger tables, Cramer's phi. Phi is the square root of the result of dividing your sample's chi-square by the number of persons. Cramer's phi is the square root of the result of dividing your sample's chi-square by the product of the number of persons multiplied by the degrees of freedom in the smaller side of the contingency table. These coefficients range from 0 to 1.
6. The minimum acceptable frequency for a category or cell has been a subject of controversy. Currently, the best advice is that even very small expected frequencies do not seriously increase the chance of a Type I error, provided that there are at least five times as many individuals as categories (or cells). However, low expected frequencies seriously reduce power and should be avoided if possible.

Key Terms

chi-square tests (p. 536)
chi-square test for goodness
  of fit (p. 539)
chi-square test for independence
  (p. 539)

observed frequency (p. 539)
expected frequency (p. 539)
chi-square statistic (χ^2) (p. 540)
chi-square distribution (p. 540)
chi-square table (p. 541)

contingency table (p. 546)
independence (p. 547)
cell (p. 547)
phi coefficient (ϕ) (p. 555)
Cramer's phi (Cramer's ϕ) (p. 555)

Example Worked-Out Problems

Chi-Square Test for Goodness of Fit

The expected distribution (from previous years) on an exam roughly follows a normal curve in which the highest scoring 2.5% of the students get As; the next highest scoring 14%, Bs; the next 67%, Cs; the next 14%, Ds; and the lowest 2.5%, Fs. A class takes a test using a new grading system and 10 get As, 34 get Bs, 140 get Cs, 10 get Ds, and 6 get Fs. Can you conclude that the new system produces a different distribution of grades (using the .01 level)? (a) Use the steps of hypothesis testing, and (b) make a sketch of the distribution involved.

Answers

(a) Table 13–11 shows the observed and expected frequencies and the figuring for the chi-square test.

❶ **Restate the question as a research hypothesis and a null hypothesis about the populations.** There are two populations:

Population 1: Students graded with the new system.
Population 2: Students graded with the old system.

The research hypothesis is that the populations are different; the null hypothesis is that the populations are the same.
❷ **Determine the characteristics of the comparison distribution.** The comparison distribution is a chi-square distribution with 4 degrees of freedom ($df = N_{Categories} - 1 = 5 - 1 = 4$).

Table 13-11   Figuring for Chi-Square Test for Goodness of Fit Example Worked-Out Problem

Grade	Observed ⒶA	Expected ⒷB
A	10	5 (2.5% × 200)
B	34	28 (14.0% × 200)
C	140	134 (67.0% × 200)
D	10	28 (14.0% × 200)
F	6	5 (2.5% × 200)

Degrees of freedom $= N_{\text{Categories}} - 1 = 5 - 1 = 4$ ❷

Chi-square needed, $df = 4$, .01 level: 13.277 ❸

$$\chi^2 = \Sigma \frac{(O - E)^2}{E} = \frac{(10 - 5)^2}{5} + \frac{(34 - 28)^2}{28} + \frac{(140 - 134)^2}{134} + \frac{(10 - 28)^2}{28} + \frac{(6 - 5)^2}{5}$$

$$= \frac{5^2}{5} + \frac{6^2}{28} + \frac{6^2}{134} + \frac{-18^2\,ⒸC}{28} + \frac{1^2}{5}$$

$$= \frac{25}{5} + \frac{36}{28} + \frac{36\,ⒹD}{134} + \frac{324}{28} + \frac{1}{5}$$

$$= 5 + 1.29 + .27 + 11.57 + .20 = 18.33. \quad ⒺE$$

Decision: Reject the null hypothesis. ❺

❸ **Determine the cutoff sample score on the comparison distribution at which the null hypothesis should be rejected.** Using the .01 level and $df = 4$, Table A–4 (in the Appendix) shows a needed chi-square of 13.277.

❹ **Determine your sample's score on the comparison distribution.** As shown in Table 13–11, this comes out to 18.33.

❺ **Decide whether to reject the null hypothesis.** The sample's chi-square of 18.33 is more extreme than the needed chi-square of 13.277. Thus, you can reject the null hypothesis and conclude that the populations are different; the new grading system produces a different distribution of grades than the previous one.

(b) Figure 13–8 shows the distribution.

Chi-Square Test for Independence

Janice Steil and Jennifer Hay (1997) conducted a survey of professionals (lawyers, doctors, bankers, and the like) regarding the people they compare themselves to when they think about their job situation (salary, benefits, responsibility, status, and so on). One

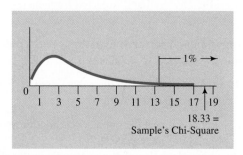

Figure 13–8   For the chi-square test for goodness of fit Example Worked-Out Problem, chi-square distribution ($df = 4$) showing the cutoff for rejecting the null hypothesis at the .01 level and the sample's chi-square.

question of special interest was how much professionals compare themselves to people of their own sex, the opposite sex, or both. Here are the results:

	Participant Gender	
	Men	Women
Comparison		
Same sex	29	17
Opposite sex	4	14
Both sexes	26	28

Can the researchers conclude that the gender of who people compare themselves to is different depending on their own gender (using the .05 level)? (a) Use the steps of hypothesis testing, and (b) make a sketch of the distribution involved.

Answers

(a) Table 13–12 shows the figuring for the chi-square test.

❶ **Restate the question as a null hypothesis and a research hypothesis about the populations.** There are two populations:

Population 1: Professionals like those surveyed.
Population 2: Professionals for whom own sex is independent of the sex of those to whom they compare their job situations.

The null hypothesis is that the two populations are the same—that, in general, professional men and women do not differ in the sex of those to whom they compare their job situations. The research hypothesis is that the populations are not the same, that professionals like those surveyed are unlike the hypothetical population in which men and women do not differ in the sex of those to whom they compare their job situations.

Table 13-12   Figuring for Chi-Square Test for Independence Example Worked-Out Problem

	Participant Gender		
	Men Ⓐ	Women Ⓑ	Total
Same sex	29 (23)	17 (23)	46 (39.0%)
Opposite sex	4 (9)	14 (9)	18 (15.3%)
Both sexes	26 (27)	28 (27)	54 (45.8%)
Total	59	59	118

Comparison (row label, left side)

$df = (N_{Columns} - 1)(N_{Rows} - 1) = (2 - 1)(3 - 1) = (1)(2) = 2.$ ❷

Chi-square needed, $df = 2$, .05 level: 5.992. ❸

$$\chi^2 = \Sigma\frac{(O - E)^2}{E} = \frac{(29 - 23)^2}{23} + \frac{(17 - 23)^2}{23} + \frac{(4 - 9)^2}{9} + \frac{(14 - 9)^2}{9} + \frac{(26 - 27)^2}{27} + \frac{(28 - 27)^2}{27}$$
Ⓒ

$$= \frac{6^2}{23} + \frac{-6^2}{23} + \frac{-5^2}{9} + \frac{5^2}{9} + \frac{-1^2}{27} + \frac{1^2}{27}$$
Ⓓ

$$= \frac{36}{23} + \frac{36}{23} + \frac{25}{9} + \frac{25}{9} + \frac{1}{27} + \frac{1}{27}$$
Ⓔ

$$= 1.57 + 1.57 + 2.78 + 2.78 + .04 + .04 = 8.78.$$ Ⓕ

Decision: Reject the null hypothesis. ❺

Note: Data from Steil and Hay (1997). The chi-square computed here (8.78) is slightly different from that reported in their article (8.76) due to rounding error.

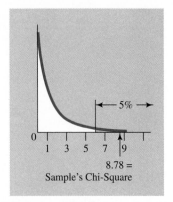

Figure 13–9 For the chi-square test for independence Example Worked-Out Problem, chi-square distribution ($df = 2$) showing the cutoff for rejecting the null hypothesis at the .05 level and the sample's chi-square.

Source: Data from Steil & Hay, 1997.

❷ **Determine the characteristics of the comparison distribution.** This is a chi-square distribution with 2 degrees of freedom.

❸ **Determine the cutoff sample score on the comparison distribution at which the null hypothesis should be rejected.** Using the .05 level and 2 degrees of freedom, the needed chi-square for significance is 5.992.

❹ **Determine your sample's score on the comparison distribution.** As shown in Table 13–12, this comes out to 8.78.

❺ **Decide whether to reject the null hypothesis.** The chi square of 8.78 is larger than the cutoff of 5.992; thus you can reject the null hypothesis: The gender of the people with whom professionals compare their job situations is likely to be different for men and women.

(b) Figure 13–9 shows the distribution.

Effect Size for a 2 × 2 Chi-Square Test for Independence

Figure the effect size for a study with 85 participants and a chi-square of 14.41.

Answer

$$\phi = \sqrt{\chi^2/N} = \sqrt{14.41/85} = \sqrt{.170} = .41.$$

Effect Size for a Chi-Square Test for Independence with a Contingency Table Greater Than 2 × 2

Figure the effect size for a 3 × 7 study with 135 participants and a chi-square of 18.32.

Answer

$$\text{Cramer's } \phi = \sqrt{\chi^2/[(N)(df_{\text{Smaller}})]} = \sqrt{18.32/[(135)(2)]}$$
$$= \sqrt{18.32/270} = \sqrt{.068} = .26.$$

Outline for Writing Essays for a Chi-Square Test for Goodness of Fit

1. Explain that chi-square tests are used for hypothesis testing with nominal variables. The chi-square test for goodness of fit is used to test hypotheses about whether a distribution of frequencies over two or more categories of a single nominal variable matches an expected distribution. Be sure to explain the meaning of the research hypothesis and the null hypothesis in this situation.

2. Describe the core logic of hypothesis testing in this situation. Be sure to mention that the hypothesis testing involves comparing observed frequencies (that is, frequencies found in the actual study) with expected frequencies (that is, frequencies that you would expect based on a particular theory or the results of previous research studies). The size of the discrepancy between the observed and expected frequencies determines whether the null hypothesis can be rejected.

3. Explain that the comparison distribution in this situation is a chi-square distribution. Be sure to mention that the shape of the chi-square distribution depends on the number of degrees of freedom. Describe how to determine the degrees of freedom and the cutoff chi-square value.

4. Describe how to figure the chi-square value for the sample. The key idea is to get a single number that indicates the overall discrepancy between what was found in the study and what would be expected based on some null hypothesis idea (such as the groups all being equal). To get this number you figure, for each group, the difference between the observed frequency and the expected

frequency, square it (because otherwise the sign of the differences would cancel each other out when you added them up), and divide the squared difference by the expected frequency (to adjust for the size of the numbers involved). You then add up all of the adjusted squared differences to get an overall number. (This should all be explained using the numbers in the study as an example.)

5. Explain how and why the scores from Steps ❸ and ❹ of the hypothesis-testing process are compared. Explain the meaning of the result of this comparison with regard to the specific research and null hypotheses being tested.

Outline for Writing Essays for a Chi-Square Test for Independence

Follow the preceding general outline for the chi-square test for goodness of fit, noting that the chi-square test for independence is used to test hypotheses about the relation between two nominal variables. Using the actual numbers in your study as examples, be sure also to explain the concept of independence and how and why you figure the expected frequency for each cell (in terms of the cells in each column having the same proportions of the column total as the cell's row total is a proportion of the overall total).

Practice Problems

These problems involve figuring. Most real-life statistics problems are done on a computer with special statistical software. Even if you have such software, do these problems by hand to ingrain the method in your mind. To learn how to use a computer to solve statistics problems like those in this chapter, refer to the Using SPSS section at the end of this chapter and the *Study Guide and Computer Workbook* that accompanies this text.

All data are fictional unless an actual citation is given.

Set I (for Answers to Set I Problems, see pp. 695–697)

1. Carry out a chi-square test for goodness of fit for each of the following studies (use the .05 level for each):

(a)

Category	Expected	Observed
A	20%	19
B	20%	11
C	40%	10
D	10%	5
E	10%	5

(b)

Category	Expected	Observed
I	30%	100
II	50%	100
III	20%	100

(c)

Category	Number in the Past	Observed
1	100	38
2	300	124
3	50	22
4	50	16

2. Carry out a chi-square test for goodness of fit for each of the following studies (use the .01 level for each). In each situation, the observed numbers are shown; the expected numbers are equal across categories.
   (a) Category A, 10; Category B, 10; Category C, 10; Category D, 10; Category E, 60.
   (b) Category A, 5; Category B, 5; Category C, 5; Category D, 5; Category E, 30.
   (c) Category A, 10; Category B, 10; Category C, 10; Category D, 10; Category E, 160.

3. A director of a small psychotherapy clinic is wondering whether there is any difference in the use of the clinic during different seasons of the year. Last year, there were 28 new clients in the winter, 33 in the spring, 16 in the summer, and 51 in the fall. On the basis of last year's data, should the director conclude that season makes a difference? (Use the .05 level.) (a) Carry out the five steps of hypothesis testing. (b) Make a sketch of the distribution involved. (c) Explain your answer to a person who has never taken a course in statistics. (This problem is a chi-square for a single nominal variable like the Harter and colleagues (1997) study of relationship styles at the beginning of the chapter. This is not a chi-square test for independence and does not involve any contingency tables.)

4. Folwell and others (1997) interviewed a group of adults, aged 54 and older, about their relationships with their siblings. One question they asked was whether there had been a change in emotional closeness over the years. They found that 43 of the respondents "perceived changes of emotional closeness in their sibling relationships . . . [and] 14 did not report a change in closeness in their sibling relationships" (p. 846). They also tested whether this difference was greater than you would expect by chance (which would be a 50-50 split). "A chi-square analysis revealed that respondents perceive changes in closeness in their sibling relationships ($\chi^2 = 14.75, df = 1, \alpha = .05$)" (p. 846).
   (a) Figure the chi-square yourself (your results should be the same, within rounding error). (b) Explain this result to a person who has never had a course in statistics.

5. Carry out a chi-square test for independence for each of the following contingency tables (use the .01 level). Also, figure the effect size for each contingency table.

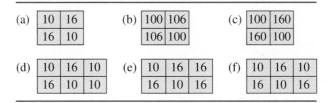

6. A developmental psychologist is interested in whether children of three different ages (5, 8, and 11) differ in their liking for a certain kind of music. The psychologist studies 200 children at a local elementary school. The results are shown in the table below. Is there a significant relationship between these two variables? (Use the .05 level.) (a) Carry out the steps of hypothesis testing, (b) make a sketch of the distribution, (c) figure the effect size, and (d) explain your answer to (a) to a person who has never taken a course in statistics.

		Age of Child		
		5	8	11
Liking for this kind of music	Yes	42	62	26
	No	18	38	14

7. A political psychologist is interested in whether the community a person lives in is related to that person's opinion on an upcoming water conservation ballot initiative. The psychologist surveys 90 people by phone with the following results. Is opinion related to community at the .05 level? (a) Carry out the steps of hypothesis testing, (b) make a sketch of the distribution, (c) figure the effect size, and (d) explain your answer to part (a) to a person who has never taken a course in statistics.

	Community A	Community B	Community C
For	12	6	3
Against	18	3	15
No opinion	12	9	12

8. Figure the effect size for the following studies:

	N	Chi-Square	Design
(a)	100	16	2×2
(b)	100	16	2×5
(c)	100	16	3×3
(d)	100	8	2×2
(e)	200	16	2×2

9. What is the power of the following planned studies using a chi-square test for independence with $p < .05$?

	Predicted Effect Size	Design	N
(a)	Small	2×2	25
(b)	Medium	2×2	25
(c)	Small	2×2	50
(d)	Small	2×3	25
(e)	Small	3×3	25
(f)	Small	2×5	25

10. About how many participants do you need for 80% power in each of the following planned studies using a chi-square test for independence with $p < 0.5$?

	Predicted Effect Size	Design
(a)	Medium	2×2
(b)	Large	2×2
(c)	Medium	2×5
(d)	Medium	3×3
(e)	Large	2×3

11. Lydon and his associates (1997) conducted a study that compared long-distance to local dating relationships. The researchers first administered questionnaires to a group of students one month prior to their leaving home to begin their first semester at McGill University (Time 1). Some of these students had dating partners who lived in the McGill area; others had dating partners who lived a long way from McGill. The researchers contacted the participants again late in the fall semester, asking them about the current status of their original dating relationships (Time 2). Here is how they reported their results:

> Of the 69 participants . . . 55 were involved in long-distance relationships, and 14 were in local relationships (dating partner living within 200 km of them). Consistent with our predictions, 12 of the 14 local relationships were still intact at Time 2 (86%), whereas only 28 of the 55 long-distance relationships were still intact (51%), $\chi^2(1, N = 69) = 5.55, p < .02$. (p. 108)

(a) Figure the chi-square yourself (your results should be the same, within rounding error). (b) Figure the effect size. (c) Explain this result to a person who has never had a course in statistics.

12. Wilfley and colleagues (2001), in a study of binge eating disorder, compared 37 women getting treatment in a clinic to a control group of 108 otherwise similar women from the general community. However, before beginning their analysis, they needed to check that the two groups were in fact not different in important ways. For example, they reported the following: "Equivalent proportions of women in the clinic ($N = 32$, 87%) and the community ($N = 89$, 82%) samples were obese . . . $\chi^2(1, N = 145) = 0.33, p = .56$" (p. 385).

(a) Figure the chi-square yourself (your results should be the same, within rounding error). (b) Figure the effect size. (c) Explain this result to a person who has never had a course in statistics.

Set II

13. Carry out a chi-square test for goodness of fit for each of the following studies (use the .01 level for each):

(a)	Category	Expected	Observed
	1	2%	5
	2	14%	15
	3	34%	90
	4	34%	120
	5	14%	50
	6	2%	20

(b)	Category	Proportion Expected	Observed
	A	1/3	10
	B	1/6	10
	C	1/2	10

14. Carry out a chi-square test for goodness of fit for each of the following studies (use the .05 level for each). In each situation, the observed numbers are shown; the expected numbers are equal across categories.
(a) Category I, 20; Category II, 20; Category III, 60.
(b) Category I, 20; Category II, 20; Category III, 20; Category IV, 60.

(c) Category I, 20; Category II, 20; Category III, 20; Category IV, 20; Category V, 60.

15. A researcher wants to be sure that the sample in her study is not unrepresentative of the distribution of ethnic groups in her community. Her sample includes 300 whites, 80 African Americans, 100 Latinos, 40 Asians, and 80 others. In her community, according to census records, there are 48% whites, 12% African Americans, 18% Latinos, 9% Asians, and 13% others. Is her sample unrepresentative of the population in her community? (Use the .05 level.) (a) Carry out the steps of hypothesis testing. (b) Make a sketch of the distribution involved. (c) Explain your answer to a person who has never taken a course in statistics. (This problem is a chi-square for a single nominal variable like the Harter and colleagues study of relationship styles at the beginning of the chapter. This is not a chi-square test for independence and does not involve any contingency tables.)

16. Stasser and colleagues (1989) conducted a study involving discussions of three different "candidates," which were described to participants in a way the researchers intended to make the candidates equally attractive. Thus, before analyzing their main results, they wanted to first test whether the three candidates were in fact seen as equally attractive. Of the 531 participants in their study, 197 initially preferred Candidate A; 120, Candidate B, and 214, Candidate C. The researchers described the following analysis:

> The relative frequencies of prediscussion preferences . . . suggested that we were not entirely successful in constructing equally attractive candidates. . . . [T]he hypothesis of equal popularity can be confidently rejected, $\chi^2(2, N = 531) = 28.35$, $p < .001$. (p. 71)

(a) Figure the chi-square yourself (your results should be the same, within rounding error). (b) Explain this result to a person who has never had a course in statistics.

17. Carry out a chi-square test for independence for each of the following contingency tables (use the .05 level). Also, figure the effect size for each contingency table.

(a)

0	18
18	0

(b)

0	0	18
9	9	0

(c)

0	0	9	9
9	9	0	0

(d)

20	40
0	40

18. Carry out a chi-square test for independence for each of the following contingency tables (use the .05 level). Also, figure the effect size for each contingency table.

(a)

8	8
8	16

(b)

8	8
8	32

(c)

8	8
8	48

(d)

8	8	8
8	8	8
8	8	16

(e)

8	8	8
8	8	8
8	8	32

(f)

8	8	8
8	8	8
8	8	48

19. The following results are of a survey of a sample of people buying ballet tickets, laid out according to the type of seat they purchased and how regularly they attend. Is there a significant relation? (Use the .05 level.) (a) Carry out the steps of hypothesis testing, (b) make a sketch of the distribution, (c) figure the effect size, and (d) explain your answer to part (a) to a person who has never taken a course in statistics.

		Attendance	
		Regular	Occasional
Seating Category	Orchestra	20	80
	Dress circle	20	20
	Balcony	40	80

20. A comparative psychologist tests rats, monkeys, and humans on a particular learning task. The following table shows the numbers of each species that were and were not able to learn the task. Is there a relation between species and ability to learn this task (use the .01 level)? (a) Carry out the steps of hypothesis testing. (b) Make a sketch of the distribution. (c) Explain your answer to a person who has never taken a course in statistics.

		Species		
		Rat	Monkey	Human
Learned Task	Yes	2	4	14
	No	28	16	6

21. Figure the effect size for the following studies:

	N	Chi-Square	Design
(a)	40	10	2 × 2
(b)	400	10	2 × 2
(c)	40	10	4 × 4
(d)	400	10	4 × 4
(e)	40	20	2 × 2

22. What is the power of the following planned studies, using a chi-square test for independence with $p < .05$?

	Predicted Effect Size	Design	N
(a)	Medium	2 × 2	100
(b)	Medium	2 × 3	100
(c)	Large	2 × 2	100
(d)	Medium	2 × 2	200
(e)	Medium	2 × 3	50
(f)	Small	3 × 3	25

23. About how many participants do you need for 80% power in each of the following planned studies, using a chi-square test for independence with $p < .05$?

	Predicted Effect Size	Design
(a)	Small	2 × 2
(b)	Medium	2 × 2
(c)	Large	2 × 2
(d)	Small	3 × 3
(e)	Medium	3 × 3
(f)	Large	3 × 3

24. Everett and colleagues (1997) mailed a survey to a random sample of physicians. Half were offered $1 if they would return the questionnaire (this was the experimental group); the other half served as a control group. The point of the study was to see if even a small incentive would increase the return rate for physician surveys. The researchers report their results as follows:

> Of the 300 surveys mailed to the experimental group, 39 were undeliverable, 2 were returned uncompleted, and 164 were returned completed. Thus, the response rate for the experimental group was 63% ($164/[300 - 39] = .63$). Of the 300 surveys mailed to the control group, 40 were undeliverable, and 118 were returned completed. Thus, the response rate for the control group was 45% ($118/[300 - 40]) = .45$). A chi-square test comparing the response rates for the experimental and control groups found the $1 incentive had a statistically significantly improved response rate over the control group [$\chi^2(1, N = 521) = 16.0, p < .001$].

(a) Figure the chi-square yourself (your results should be the same, within rounding error). (b) Figure the effect size. (c) Explain the results to (a) and (b) to a person who has never had a course in statistics.

25. Irving and Berel (2001) compared the effects of four kinds of programs (three actual programs and a control group) designed to make women more skeptical of media portrayals of female body image. After completing each program, the 110 participants were given stamped, addressed postcards that they could mail to a media activism organization ("About Face") if they so chose. Here are some of their results:

> . . . [P]ostcards were sent by approximately twice as many of the participants in the video-only condition (i.e., 36%) than in the internally oriented condition (19% of participants returned postcards) and the externally oriented condition (15% returned postcards). Only 5% of those in the no-intervention control group sent postcards to "About Face." Group differences in the rate of return were significant, $\chi^2(3, N = 110) = 8.79, p < .05$, suggesting that the intervention had a differential impact on intentions to engage in media activism. (p. 109)

(a) Figure the chi-square yourself (your results should be the same, within rounding error). (b) Figure the effect size. (c) Explain the results to a person who has never had a course in statistics.

Using SPSS

The ✑ in the following steps indicates a mouse click. (We used SPSS version 15.0 for Windows to carry out these analyses. The steps and output may be slightly different for other versions of SPSS.)

It is easier to learn the SPSS steps for chi-square tests using actual numbers. As an example, imagine you are a student in a class of 20 students and want to determine whether the students in the class are split equally among first- and second-year students (the class is not open to students in other year groups). We will use a chi-square test for goodness of fit to answer this question. Each student's year in college is shown in the first column of Figure 13–10.

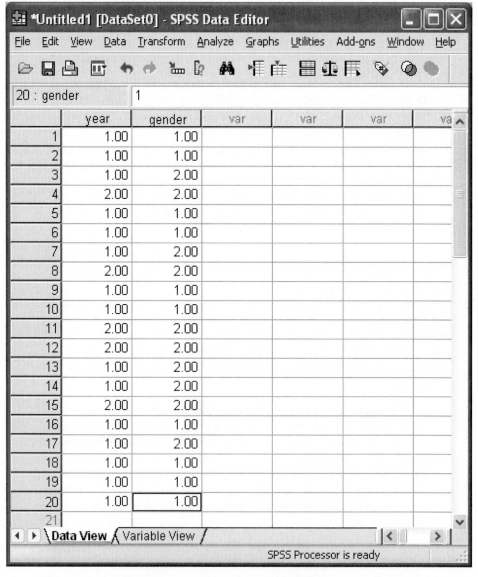

Figure 13–10 SPSS data editor window for a fictional study examining the distribution of first- and second-year college students and gender for a particular class.

Chi-Square Test for Goodness of Fit

❶ Enter the scores into SPSS. As shown in Figure 13–10, the score for each person is listed in a separate row. We labeled the variable "year." (For now, you can ignore the "gender" variable.)

❷ ✑ *Analyze.*

❸ ✑ *Nonparametric Tests,* ✑ *Chi-Square.*

❹ ✑ on the variable called "year" and then ✑ the arrow next to the box labeled "Test Variable List." This tells SPSS that the chi-square test for goodness of fit should be carried out on the scores for the nominal variable called "year." Notice in the "Expected Values" box that the option "All categories equal" is selected by default. This means that SPSS will carry out the chi-square to compare the observed frequency distribution in your sample with an expected frequency distribution based on an equal spread of scores across the categories. If you wish to use a different expected frequency distribution, select the "Values" option and enter the appropriate expected values.

❺ ✑ *OK.* Your SPSS output window should look like Figure 13–11.

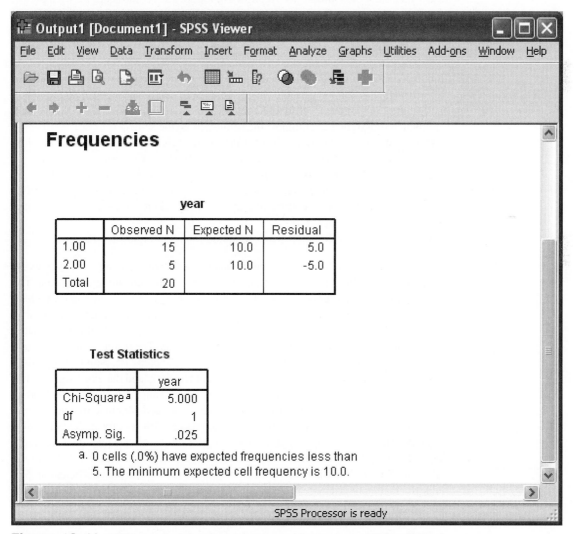

Figure 13–11   SPSS output window for a chi-square test for goodness of fit for a fictional study examining the distribution of first- and second-year college students for a particular class.

The first table in the SPSS output gives the observed frequencies, the expected frequencies, and the difference between the observed and expected frequencies (in the "Residual" column). The second table gives the value of chi-square, the degrees of freedom, and the exact significance level. The significance level of .025 (for the chi-square value of 5.00) is less than our .05 cutoff, which means that you can reject the null hypothesis. Thus, you can conclude that the students in the class are not split equally among first- and second-year students.

Chi-Square Test for Independence

Using the same example as for the chi-square test for goodness of fit, let's suppose you are interested in whether the distribution of first- and second-year students in the class is different for male and female students. To answer this question (which involves *two nominal variables*), we will use a chi-square test for independence.

❶ Enter the scores into SPSS. As shown in Figure 13–10, the score for each person is listed in a separate row. We labeled the variables "year" and "gender." (We assigned women a value of 1 for the gender variable and men a value of 2.)

❷ ✍ *Analyze.*

❸ ✍ *Descriptive Statistics,* ✍ *Crosstabs.*

❹ ✍ on the variable called "gender" and then ✍ the arrow next to the box labeled "Row(s)." ✍ on the variable called "year" and then ✍ the arrow next to the box labeled "Column(s)." (It doesn't matter which variable is assigned to rows and which is assigned to columns; the result will be the same.)

❺ ✍ *Statistics.* ✍ the box labeled *Chi-square* (this checks the box). ✍ the box labeled *Phi and Cramer's V* (this checks the box). ✍ *Continue.*

❻ ✍ *Cells.* ✍ the box labeled *Expected* (this checks the box). ✍ *Continue.* This step requests the expected frequencies to be included in the output. (Although this step is optional, we recommend that you always do it, as it reinforces the logic of the chi-square test.)

❼ ✍ *OK.* Your SPSS output window should look like Figure 13–12.

The first table in the SPSS output (which is not shown in Figure 13–12) gives the number of individuals for each variable and whether there are any missing data. The second table (labeled "gender * year Crosstabulation") gives the contingency table of observed and expected values for the two nominal variables ("gender" and "year"). The third table (labeled "Chi-Square Tests") shows the actual result of the chi-square test for independence, as well as the results of other tests. The results of the chi-square test for independence are provided in the first row (labeled "Pearson Chi-Square"), which shows the chi-square value, the degrees of freedom, and the exact significance level. The significance level of .010 (for the chi-square value of 6.667) is smaller than our .05 cutoff. Thus, you can reject the null hypothesis and conclude that the distribution of first- and second-year students in the class is different for male and female students. The final table (labeled "Symmetric Measures") shows the effect size measures. By default, SPSS always shows both the phi coefficient (labeled "Phi" in the table) and Cramer's φ (labeled "Cramer's V" in the table). The phi coefficient of .577 tells you that there is a large relationship between the year of students in the class and the students' gender.

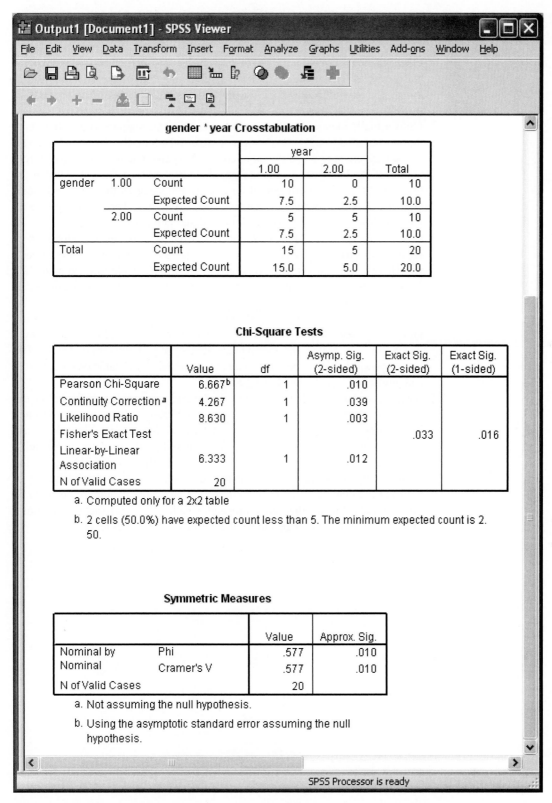

Figure 13–12   SPSS output window for a chi-square test for independence for a fictional study examining the distribution of first- and second-year college students and gender for a particular class.

Chapter Notes

1. Independence is typically used to talk about a lack of relation between two nominal variables. However, if you have studied Chapter 11, it may be helpful to think of independence as roughly the same as the situation of no correlation ($r = 0$).

2. Phi is actually identical to the correlation coefficient. Suppose you were to take the two variables in a 2×2 contingency table and arbitrarily make one of the values of each equal to 1 and the other equal to 2 (you could use any two different numbers). And suppose you then figured a correlation coefficient between the two variables. The result would be exactly the same as the phi coefficient. (Whether it was a positive or negative correlation, however, would depend on which categories in each variable got the higher number.)

3. Cohen (1988, pp. 228–248) gives more detailed tables. However, Cohen's tables are based on an effect size called w, which is equivalent to phi but not to Cramer's phi. He provides a helpful conversion table of Cramer's phi to w on page 222. There are also power calculators available on the Internet and power can be calculated using SPSS.

4. More detailed tables are provided in Cohen (1988, pp. 253–267). When using these tables, see Chapter Note 3. Also, Dunlap and Myers (1997) have shown that with a 2×2 table, the approximate number of participants needed for 80% to 90% power is $8/\phi^2$. There are also power calculators available on the Internet, and power can be calculated using SPSS.

5. Suppose you have a table larger than 2×2 with a category or cell that has an extremely small expected frequency (or even a moderately small expected frequency if the number of participants is also small). One solution is to combine related categories to increase the expected frequency and reduce the total number of cells. But this is a solution of last resort if you are making the adjustment based on the results of the experiment. The problem is that you are then taking advantage of knowing the outcome. The best solution is to add more people to the study. If this is not feasible, an alternative procedure, called Fisher's exact test, is sometimes possible. It is described in some intermediate statistics texts.

CHAPTER 14

Strategies When Population Distributions Are Not Normal

Data Transformations and Rank-Order Tests

Chapter Outline

- Assumptions in the Standard Hypothesis-Testing Procedures 578
- Data Transformations 580
- Rank-Order Tests 585
- Comparison of Methods 589
- Controversy: Computer-Intensive Methods 591
- Data Transformations and Rank-Order Tests in Research Articles 595

- Summary 596
- Key Terms 597
- Example Worked-Out Problems 597
- Practice Problems 597
- Using SPSS 602
- Chapter Notes 609

This chapter examines some strategies researchers use for hypothesis testing when the assumptions of normal population distributions and equal variances are clearly violated. (These assumptions are part of most ordinary hypothesis-testing procedures, such as the *t* test, analysis of variance, and the significance tests for correlation and prediction.) First, we briefly review the role of assumptions in the standard hypothesis-testing procedures. Then we examine two approaches psychology researchers use when assumptions have not been met: data transformations and rank-order tests.

Assumptions in the Standard Hypothesis-Testing Procedures

As you saw in previous chapters, you have to meet certain conditions (the assumptions) to get accurate results with a *t* test, analysis of variance, or the significance tests for correlation and prediction (regression). In these hypothesis-testing procedures, you treat the scores from a study as if they came from some larger, though unknown, populations. One assumption you have to make is that the populations involved follow a normal curve. The other main assumption you have to make is that the populations have equal variances.

You also learned in previous chapters that you get fairly accurate results when a study suggests that the populations even very roughly meet the assumptions of following a normal curve and having equal variances. Our concern here, however, is about the situation where it is clear that the populations are nowhere near normal or nowhere near having equal variances. In such situations, if you use the ordinary *t* test, analysis of variance, or the significance test for correlation or prediction, you can get quite incorrect results. For example, you could do all the figuring correctly and decide to reject the null hypothesis based on your results. Yet, if your populations do not meet the standard assumptions, this result could be wrong—wrong in the sense that instead of there actually being only a 5% chance of getting your results if the null hypothesis is true, in fact there might be a 15% or 20% chance! (It could also be 1% or 2%. The problem is that the usual cutoff can be a long way from accurate and you don't know in which direction.)

Remember: assumptions are about *populations,* not about *samples.* It is quite possible for a sample not to follow a normal curve even though it comes from a population that does follow a normal curve. Figure 14–1 shows histograms for several samples, each taken randomly from a population that follows a normal curve. (Notice that the smaller the sample is, the harder it is to see that it came from a normal population.) Of course, it is quite possible for nonnormal populations to produce any of these samples as well. Unfortunately, the sample is usually all you have to go on when doing a study. One thing researchers do is make a histogram for the sample; if it is not drastically different from normal, the researchers assume that the population it came from is roughly normal. (Also see the Using SPSS section at the end of this chapter.) When considering normality, most psychology researchers consider a distribution innocent until proven guilty. (The same principle applies to equal variances. For example, in a *t* test, the two samples could have quite different variances and yet come from populations with quite equal variances. Thus, here too we focus on the situation in which the samples are so very different in their variance that it seems unlikely they could come from populations with the same variance.)

One common situation where you doubt the assumption that the population follows a normal distribution is when there is a *ceiling* or *floor effect* (see Chapter 1). Another common situation that raises such doubts is when the sample has outliers, extreme scores at one or both ends of the sample distribution. Figure 14–2 shows some examples of samples with outliers. (Outliers also very greatly affect variances; so an outlier in a sample can also lead to quite misleading conclusions about whether the populations have equal variances.) Outliers are a big problem in the statistical methods we ordinarily use because these methods ultimately rely on squared deviations from the mean. Because it is so far from the mean, an outlier has a huge influence when you square its deviation from the mean. What this means is that a single outlier, if it is extreme enough, can drastically distort the results of a study

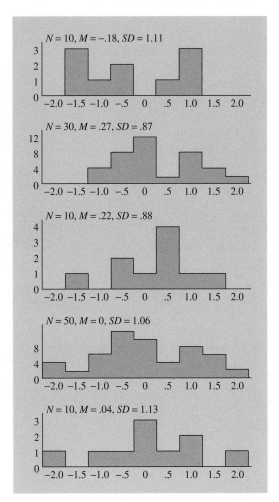

Figure 14–1 Histograms for several random samples, each drawn from a normal population with $\mu = 0$ and $\sigma = 1$.

(as you saw in the correlation example in Chapter 11). An outlier can cause a statistical test to give a significant result even when all the other scores would not. In other cases, an outlier can make a result not significant that would be significant without the outlier.

How are you doing?

1. What are the two main assumptions for *t* tests, the analysis of variance, and the significance tests for correlations and predictions (regression)?
2. (a) How do you check to see if you have met the assumptions? (b) Why is this problematic?
3. (a) What is an outlier? (b) Why are outliers likely to have an especially big distorting effect in most statistical procedures?

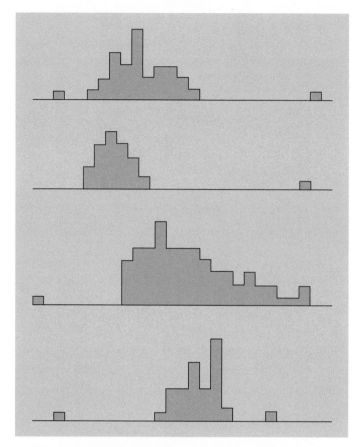

Figure 14–2 Distributions with outliers at one or both ends.

Data Transformations

One widely used procedure when the scores in the sample do not appear to come from a normal population is to change the scores! This is not done by fudging, although at first it may sound that way until we explain. The method is that the researcher applies some mathematical procedure to each score, such as taking its square root. The idea is to make a nonnormal distribution closer to normal. (Sometimes this can also make the variances of the different groups more similar.) This is called a **data transformation.**

data transformation mathematical procedure (such as taking the square root) used on each score in a sample, usually done to make the sample distribution closer to normal.

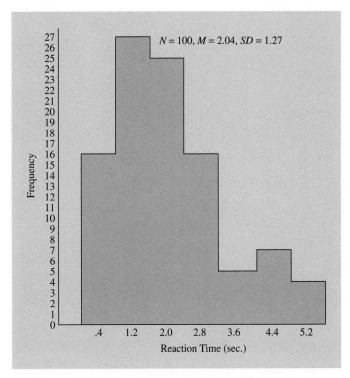

Figure 14–3   Skewed distribution of reaction times (fictional data).

Once you have made a data transformation that makes the scores in the sample appear to meet the normality assumption (and if the other assumptions are met), you can then go ahead with a usual *t* test, analysis of variance or significance test of a correlation or regression. Data transformation has an important advantage over other procedures of coping with nonnormal populations: once you have made a data transformation, you can use familiar and sophisticated hypothesis-testing procedures.

Consider an example. Measures of reaction time, such as how long it takes a research participant to press a particular key when a light flashes, are usually skewed to the right (positively skewed). There are many short (quick) responses, but usually a few quite long (slow) ones. It is unlikely that the reaction times shown in Figure 14–3 come from a population that follows a normal curve. The population of reaction-time scores itself is probably skewed.

However, suppose you take the square root of each reaction time. Most reaction times are affected only a little. A reaction time of 1 second stays 1; a reaction time of 1.5 seconds reduces to 1.22. However, very long reaction times, the ones that create the long tail to the right, are much reduced. For example, a reaction time of 9 seconds is reduced to 3, and a reaction time of 16 seconds (the person was really distracted and forgot about the task) reduces to 4. (Of course, if the reaction time is as long as 16 seconds when most are around 3 or 4, we might also consider that an outlier!) Figure 14–4 shows the result of taking the square root of each score in the skewed distribution shown in Figure 14–3. After a **square-root transformation,** this distribution of scores seems much more likely to have come from a population with a normal distribution (of transformed scores).

square-root transformation   data transformation using the square root of each score.

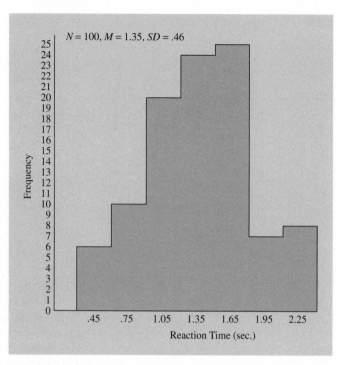

Figure 14–4 Distributions of scores from Figure 14–3 after square-root transformation.

Legitimacy of Data Transformations

Do you feel that this is somehow cheating? It would be if you did this knowingly in some way to make the result more favorable to your predictions. However, in actual research practice, the first step after the data are collected and recorded (and checked for accuracy) is to see if the data suggest that the populations meet assumptions. If the scores in your sample suggest that the populations do not meet assumptions, you do data transformations. Hypothesis testing is done only after this checking and any transformations have been performed.

Remember that you must do any transformation for *all* the scores on that variable, not just those in a particular group. Most important, no matter what transformation procedure you use, the order of the scores always stays the same. A person with an actual original score that is between the original scores of two other participating people, will still have a transformed score between those same two people's transformed scores.

The procedure may seem somehow to distort reality to fit the statistics. In some cases, this is a legitimate concern. Suppose you are looking at the difference in income between two groups of Americans. You probably do not care about how much the two groups differ in the square root of their income. What you care about is the difference in actual dollars.

On the other hand, consider a self-esteem questionnaire. Scores on the questionnaire do not have any absolute meaning. Higher scores mean greater self-esteem; lower scores, less self-esteem. However, each scale-point increase on the test is not necessarily related to an equal amount of increase in an individual's self-esteem. It is just as likely that the square root of each scale point's increase is directly related to the person's self-esteem.

Similarly, consider the example we used earlier of reaction time, measured in seconds. This would seem to have an absolute meaning: a second is a second. But even in this situation, the underlying variable, efficiency of processing of the nervous system, may not be directly related to the number of seconds. It is probably a complex operation that follows some unknown mathematical rule (though we would still expect that shorter times go with more efficient processing and longer times with less efficient processing).

In these examples, the underlying "yardstick" of the variable is not known. Thus, there is no reason to think that the transformed version is any less accurate a reflection of reality than the original version. And the transformed version may meet the normality assumption. Indeed, since most things in nature follow a normal curve, one could argue that the scores after being transformed to be closer to a normal curve are *more* likely to represent the true thing being measured.

Kinds of Data Transformations

There are several types of data transformations. We already have illustrated a square-root transformation: instead of using each score, you use the square root of each score. We gave an example in Figures 14–3 and 14–4. The general effect is shown in Figure 14–5. As you can see, a distribution that is skewed to the right (positively skewed) becomes less skewed to the right after a square-root transformation. To put it numerically, moderate numbers become only slightly lower and high numbers become much lower. The result is that the right side is pulled in toward the middle.

There are many other kinds of transformations you will see in psychology research articles. The square root transformation is actually quite common. Another common transformation is called a *log transformation,* in which, instead of the square root, the researcher takes the logarithm of each score. A log transformation has the same type of effect as the square root transformation, but the effect is stronger. Thus, a log transformation is better for distributions that are very strongly skewed to the right. An *inverse transformation* corrects distributions with an even stronger skew to the right than a log transformation. (In an inverse distribution, the researcher divides each score into 1. For example, a value of 10 becomes $1/10 = .1$.)

Note that all three of these common transformations—square root, log, or inverse—are designed for the situation in which the sample suggests the population is skewed to the *right.* This is the most common situation. However, sometimes a distribution is skewed to the *left.* If the distribution is skewed to the left, you can *reflect* all the scores; that is, subtract them all from some high number so that they are now all reversed. Then, using the square root, log, and inverse transformations will have the correct effect. However, you have to remember when looking at the final results that you have reversed the direction of scoring.

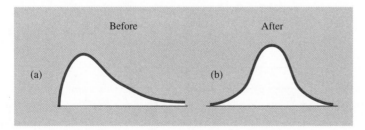

Figure 14–5 Distributions skewed to the right before (a) and after (b) taking the square root of each score.

Table 14–1 Results of a Study Comparing Highly Sensitive and Not Highly Sensitive Children on the Number of Books Read in the Past Year (Fictional Data)

| | Highly Sensitive | |
	No	Yes
	0	17
	3	36
	10	45
	22	75
Σ:	35	173
$M =$	8.75	43.25
$S^2 =$	95.58	584.25

We will not go into examples of all the kinds of transformations here. Just learning the square-root transformation will help you get the idea. The main thing to remember about other kinds of transformations is that they all use this same principle of taking each score and applying some arithmetic to it to make the set of scores come out more like a normal curve. Once again, whatever transformation you use, a score that is between two other scores always stays between those two other scores.

An Example of a Data Transformation

Consider a fictional study in which the researchers compare the number of books read in the past year by four children who score high on a test of being highly sensitive compared to four children who score low on the test of being highly sensitive. [The general idea of being a highly sensitive person is described in Aron (1996, 2002) and Aron & Aron (1997). Our examples in Chapter 10 were based on this concept as well.] Based on theory, the researcher predicts that highly sensitive children will read more books. Table 14–1 shows the results.

Ordinarily, in a study comparing two independent groups, you would use a *t* test for independent means. Yet the *t* test for independent means is like all of the procedures you have learned for hypothesis testing (except chi-square): It requires that the parent populations of scores for each group be normally distributed. In this study, however, the distribution of the sample is strongly skewed to the right; the scores tend to bunch up at the left, leaving a long tail to the right. It thus seems likely that the population of scores of number of books read (for both sensitive and nonsensitive children) is also skewed to the right. This shape for the population distribution also seems reasonable in light of what is being measured. A child cannot read fewer than zero books, but, once a child starts reading, it is easy to read a lot of books in a year.

Also note that the estimated population variances based on the two samples are dramatically different, 95.58 versus 584.25. This is another reason you would not want to go ahead with an ordinary *t* test.

However, suppose you do a square-root transformation on the scores (Table 14–2). Now both samples are much more like a normal curve; they have their middle scores bunched up in the middle (for example, for the Yes group, 6.00 and 6.71) and the more extreme (high and low) scores spread out a little from the mean (4.12 and 8.66). Also, the transformation seems reasonable in terms of the meaning of the numbers. The number of books read is meant as a measure of interest in things literary. Thus, the difference between 0 and 1 book is a much greater difference than the difference between 20 and 21 books.

Table 14–3 shows the *t* test analysis using the transformed scores.

Table 14–2 Square-Root Transformation of the Scores in Table 14–1

| Highly Sensitive | | | |
| No | | Yes | |
X	$\sqrt{X}$	X	$\sqrt{X}$
0	0.00	17	4.12
3	1.73	36	6.00
10	3.16	45	6.71
22	4.69	75	8.66

Table 14–3	Figuring for a *t* Test for Independent Means Using Square-Root Transformed Scores for the Study of Books Read by Highly Sensitive Versus Not Highly Sensitive Children (Fictional Data)

t needed for .05 significance level, $df = (4 - 1) + (4 - 1) = 6$, one-tailed $= -1.943$.

	Highly Sensitive	
	No	**Yes**
	0.00	4.12
	1.73	6.00
	3.16	6.71
	4.69	8.66
Σ:	9.58	25.49
$M =$	$9.58/4 = 2.40$	$25.49/4 = 6.37$
$S^2 =$	$12.03/3 = 4.01$	$10.56/3 = 3.52$

$$S^2_{Pooled} = 3.77$$

| $S^2_M =$ | $3.77/4 = .94$ | $3.77/4 = .94$ |

$$S^2_{Difference} = .94 + .94 = 1.88$$
$$S_{Difference} = \sqrt{1.88} = 1.37$$
$$t = (2.40 - 6.37)/1.37 = -2.90$$

Decision: Reject the null hypothesis.

How are you doing?

1. What is a data transformation?
2. Why is it done?
3. When is this legitimate?
4. Consider the following distribution of scores: 4, 16, 25, 25, 25, 36, 64. (a) Are these scores roughly normally distributed? (b) Why? (c) Carry out a square-root transformation for these scores (that is, list the square-root transformed scores). (d) Are the square-root transformed scores roughly normally distributed? (e) Why?

Answers

1. A data transformation is when each score is changed following some rule (such as take the square root, log, or inverse).
2. It is done to make the distribution more like a normal curve (or to make variances closer to equal across groups).
3. It is legitimate when it is done to all the scores, it is not done to make the results come out to fit the researcher's predictions, and the underlying meaning of the distance between scores is arbitrary.
4. (a) The scores are not roughly normally distributed. (b) They are skewed to the right. (c) Square-root transformation: 2, 4, 5, 5, 5, 6, 8. (d) The square-root transformed scores are roughly normally distributed. (e) The middle scores are bunched in the middle and the extremes spread out evenly on both sides.

Rank-Order Tests

Another way of coping with nonnormal distributions is to transform the scores to ranks. Suppose you have a sample with scores of 4, 8, 12, and 64. This would be a rather surprising sample if the population was really normal. A **rank-order transformation** would change the scores to 1, 2, 3, and 4; the 1 referring to the lowest

rank-order transformation changing a set of scores to ranks (for example, so that the lowest score is rank 1, the next highest rank 2, and so forth).

number in the group, the 2 to the second lowest and so forth. A complication with a rank-order transformation occurs when you have two or more scores that are tied. The usual solution to ties is to give them each the average rank. For example, the scores 12, 81, 81, 107, and 154 would be ranked 1, 2.5, 2.5, 4, and 5.

Changing ordinary scores to ranks is a kind of data transformation. But unlike square-root transformations, with a rank-order transformation you aren't trying to get a normal distribution. The distribution you get from a rank-order transformation is rectangular, with equal numbers of scores (one) at each value. Ranks have the effect of spreading the scores out evenly.

There are special hypothesis-testing procedures, called **rank-order tests,** that make use of rank-ordered scores. They also have two other common names. You can transform scores from a population with any shaped distribution into ranks. Thus, these tests are sometimes called **distribution-free tests.** Also, the shape of distributions of rank-order scores are known exactly rather than estimated. Thus, rank-order tests do not require estimating any parameters (population values). For example, there is no need to estimate a population variance, because you can determine exactly what it will be if you know that ranks are involved. Hence, hypothesis-testing procedures based on ranks are also called **nonparametric tests.**

The t test, analysis of variance, and the usual significance tests for correlation and prediction (regression) are examples of **parametric tests.**[1]

Rank-order tests also have the advantage that you can use them when the actual scores in the study are themselves ranks—for example, a study comparing the class standing of two types of graduates. Also, sometimes the exact numeric values of the measure used in a study are questionable. For example, a researcher intends the measure to be numeric in the usual sense, with a 7 being as much above a 5 as a 12 is above a 10 (the researcher intends this to be equal-interval measurement; see Chapter 1). However, in reality the researcher is sure only that the numbers are correctly ordered, with 7 higher than 5, 10 higher than 7, and so forth. In this case, the researcher might want to use rank-order measurement so as not to assume too much about the quality of the measurement.

The issue is actually somewhat controversial. Consider, for example, a scale marked "1 = Disagree, 2 = Mildly disagree, 3 = Mildly agree, and 4 = Agree." Are the underlying meanings of the numbers spread evenly across a numeric scale? It is clear that the results are meaningful as rank-order information; certainly, 2 shows more agreement than 1, 3 more than 2, and 4 more than 3. Hence, some psychologists argue that in most cases you should not assume that you have equal-interval measurements. Instead, they argue that you should convert your scores to ranks and use a rank-order significance test. Other researchers argue that even with true rank-order measurement, parametric statistical tests do a reasonably accurate job and that changing all the scores to ranks can lose valuable information. The issue remains unresolved.

Overview of Rank-Order Tests

Table 14–4 shows the name of the rank-order test that you would substitute for some of the parametric hypothesis-testing procedures you have learned. (Full procedures for using such tests are given in intermediate statistics texts; we describe the SPSS procedures for most of these at the end of the chapter.) For example, in a situation with three groups, you would normally do a one-way analysis of variance. But if you want to use a rank-order method, you would use the Kruskal-Wallis H test.[2]

Next, we will describe how such tests are done in a general way, including an example. However, we do not actually provide all the needed information (such as

rank-order test   hypothesis-testing procedure that uses rank-ordered scores.

distribution-free test   hypothesis testing procedure making no assumptions about the shape of populations. Also called a *nonparametric test.*

nonparametric test   hypothesis testing procedure making no assumptions about population parameters. Also called a *distribution-free test.*

parametric test   ordinary hypothesis-testing procedure, such as a t test or an analysis of variance, that requires assumptions about the shape or other parameters (such as the variance) of the populations.

Table 14–4   Major Rank-Order Tests Corresponding to Major Parametric Tests

Ordinary Parametric Test	Corresponding Rank-Order Test
t test for dependent means	Wilcoxon signed-rank test
t test for independent means	Wilcoxon rank-sum test or Mann-Whitney *U* test
Analysis of variance	Kruskal-Wallis *H* test
Pearson correlation (*r*)	Spearman's rho

the tables) for you to carry them out in practice. We introduce you to these techniques because you may see them used in articles you read and because their logic is the foundation of an alternative procedure that we do teach you to use (shortly). This alternative procedure does roughly the same thing as these rank-order tests and is closer to what you have already learned.

Basic Logic of Rank-Order Tests

Consider a study with an experimental group and a control group. (The situation in which you would use a *t* test for independent means if all the assumptions were met.) If you wanted to use a rank-order test, you would first transform all the scores into ranks, ranking all the scores from lowest to highest, regardless of whether a score was in the experimental or the control group. If the two groups were scores randomly taken from a single population, there should be about equal amounts of high ranks and low ranks in each group. (That is, if the null hypothesis is true, the ranks in the two groups should not differ much.) Because the distribution of ranks can be worked out exactly, statisticians can figure the exact probability of getting any particular division of ranks into two groups if in fact the two groups were randomly taken from identical distributions.

The way this actually works is that the researcher changes all the scores to ranks, adds up the total of the ranks in the group with the lower scores, and then compares this total to a cutoff from a special table of significance cutoffs for totals of ranks in this kind of situation. (Also, as with ordinary parametric tests, the major nonparametric tests can be done with SPSS or other statistical software programs.)

An Example of a Rank-Order Test

Table 14–5 shows the transformation to ranks and the figuring for the Wilcoxon rank-sum test for the kind of situation we have just described, using the books read by highly sensitive versus not highly sensitive children example. The logic is a little different from what you are used to; so be patient until we explain it.

Notice that we first set the significance cutoff, as you would in any hypothesis-testing procedure. (This cutoff is based on a table you don't have but is available in most intermediate statistics texts.) The next step is to rank all the scores from lowest to highest, then add up the ranks in the group you expect to have the smaller total. You then compare the smaller total to the cutoff. If this smaller total is less than or equal to the cutoff, you reject the null hypothesis. In the example, the sum of the ranks for the smaller total was actually equal to the cutoff; so the null hypothesis was rejected.

We used the Wilcoxon rank-sum test, though we could have used the Mann-Whitney *U* test. It gives an exactly mathematically equivalent final result and is based on the same logic. It differs only in the computational details when doing it by hand.

Table 14-5 Figuring for a Wilcoxon Rank-Sum Test for the Study of Books Read by Highly Sensitive Versus Not Highly Sensitive Children (Fictional Data)

Cutoff for significance: Maximum sum of ranks in the not highly sensitive group for significance at the .05 level, one-tailed (from a standard table) = 11.

Highly Sensitive			
No		**Yes**	
X	**Rank**	**X**	**Rank**
0	1	17	4
3	2	36	6
10	3	45	7
22	5	75	8
	Σ: 11		

Comparison to cutoff: Sum of ranks of group predicted to have lower scores, 11, equals but does not exceed cutoff for significance.

Decision: Reject the null hypothesis.

The Null Hypothesis in a Rank-Order Test

The null hypothesis in a rank-order test is not quite the same as in an ordinary parametric test. A parametric test such as the *t* test compares the *means* of the two groups; its null hypothesis is that the two populations have the same mean. The equivalent to the mean in a rank-order test is the middle rank (the *median* of the nonranked scores). Thus, we think of a rank-order test as comparing the medians of the two groups, that its null hypothesis is that the two populations have the same median.

Using Parametric Tests with Rank-Transformed Data

Two statisticians (Conover & Iman, 1981) have shown, instead of using the special procedures for rank-order tests, you get approximately the same results if you first transform the data into ranks and then just use the usual *t* test or analysis of variance procedures. (This also works for the significance tests for correlation and regression.)

The result of this shortcut (using a parametric test with scores transformed into ranks) will not be quite as accurate as either the ordinary parametric test or the rank-order test. It will not be quite as accurate because you are violating the assumption of normal population distributions. As we noted earlier, when you are using ranks, the population distribution is in fact rectangular (there are equal numbers—one—of each rank). Using this shortcut will also not be quite as accurate as the rank-order test. This is because the parametric test uses the *t* or *F* distribution instead of the special tables that rank-order tests use, which are based on exact probabilities of getting certain divisions of ranks. However, it turns out that, in practice, using an ordinary parametric test with ranks gives a result that is quite close to the true, accurate result you would get using the technically proper procedure.[3] Table 14–6 shows the figuring for an ordinary *t* test for independent means for the fictional sensitive children data, using each child's rank instead of the child's actual number of books read. Again we get a significant result. (In practice, carrying out an ordinary procedure like a *t* test with scores that have been transformed to ranks is least accurate with a very small sample like this. However, we used the small sample to keep the example simple.)

Table 14-6 Figuring for a *t* Test for Independent Means Using Ranks Instead of Raw Scores for the Study of Books Read by Highly Sensitive Versus Not Highly Sensitive Children (Fictional Data)

t needed for .05 significance level, $df = (4 - 1) + (4 - 1) = 6$, one-tailed $= -1.943$

	Highly Sensitive	
	No	**Yes**
	1	4
	2	6
	3	7
	$\underline{5}$	$\underline{8}$
Σ	11	25
$M =$	$11/4 = 2.75$	$25/4 = 6.25$
$S^2 =$	$8.75/3 = 2.92$	$8.75/3 = 2.92$
	$S^2_{Pooled} = 2.92$	
$S^2_M =$	$2.92/4 = .73$	$2.92/4 = .73$
	$S^2_{Difference} = .73 + .73 = 1.46$	
	$S_{Difference} = \sqrt{1.46} = 1.21$	
	$t = (2.75 - 6.25)/1.21 = -2.89$	

Decision: Reject the null hypothesis.

As shown in Table 14–4, Spearman's rho is a nonparametric equivalent of the Pearson correlation. Spearman's rho can be used when the assumptions for a Pearson correlation are not met, with certain kinds of curvilinear associations, or when the original scores are on a rank-ordered scale. Recall from Chapter 11 that Spearman's rho is a type of correlation coefficient that is figured by changing the scores into ranks (separately for each variable) and then carrying out the usual figuring for the Pearson correlation coefficient (r). So, in this case, the nonparametric test is actually figured by changing the scores to ranks and then using the equivalent parametric test.

Comparison of Methods

We have considered two methods of carrying out hypothesis tests when samples appear to come from nonnormal populations: data transformation and rank-order tests. How do you decide which to use?

Advantages and Disadvantages

Data transformations have the advantage of allowing you to use the familiar parametric techniques on the transformed scores. But transformations will not always work. For example, in an analysis of variance, there may not be any reasonable transformation that makes the scores normal or have equal variances in all groups. Also, as we discussed earlier, in some important situations, transformations may distort the scores in ways that lose the original meaning.

You can use rank-order methods regardless of the shape of the distributions of the original scores. Rank-order tests are, of course, especially appropriate when the original scores are ranks. They are also especially useful when the scores do not clearly follow a simple numeric pattern (such as equal-interval), which some psychologists think is a common situation. Further, the logic of rank-order methods is simple and direct, requiring no elaborate construction of hypothetical distributions or estimated parameters.

However, rank-order methods are not as familiar to readers of research, and rank-order methods have not been developed for many complex situations. Another problem is that the simple logic of rank-order tests breaks down if there are many ties in ranks. Finally, like data transformation methods, rank-order methods distort the original data, losing information. For example, in the same sample, a difference between 6.1 and 6.2 could be one rank, but the difference between 3.4 and 5.8 might also be one rank.[4]

Relative Risk of Type I and Type II Errors

How accurate are the various methods in terms of the 5% significance level really meaning that there is a 5% chance of incorrectly rejecting the null hypothesis (a Type I error)? And how do the different methods affect power?

When the assumptions for parametric tests are met, the parametric tests are as good as or better than any of the alternatives. This is true for protection against both Type I and Type II errors. This would be expected, because these are the conditions for which the parametric tests were designed.

However, when the assumptions for a parametric test are not met, the relative advantages of the possible alternative procedures we have considered (data transformations and rank-order tests) are not at all clear. In fact, the relative merits of the various procedures are topics of lively controversy, with many articles appearing in statistics-oriented journals every year.

How are you doing?

1. (a) What is a rank-order transformation? (b) Why is it done? (c) What is a rank-order test?
2. Transform the following scores to ranks: 5, 18, 3, 9, 2.
3. (a) If you wanted to use a standard rank-order test instead of a *t* test for independent means, what procedure would you use? (b) What are the steps of doing such a test? (c) What is the underlying logic?
4. (a) What happens if you change your scores to ranks and then figure an ordinary parametric test using the ranks? (b) Why will this not be quite accurate, even assuming that the transformation to ranks is appropriate? (c) Why will this result not be quite as accurate as using the standard rank-order test? (d) What are the advantages of using this procedure over a standard rank-order test?
5. If conditions are not met for a parametric test (a) what are the advantages and (b) disadvantages of data-transformation over rank-order tests, and what are the (c) advantages and (d) disadvantages of rank-order tests over data transformation?

tests.
methods; also, ties in ranks (which are common) distort the accuracy of these
(d) They are often unfamiliar and have not been developed for many complex
accurate.
reflect the true meaning of the measurement, and rank-order tests are very
(c) They can be used regardless of the distribution, rank-order may better
measurement.
(b) They will not always work and may distort the underlying meaning of the

Controversy: Computer-Intensive Methods

In recent years, thanks to the availability of computers, a whole new set of hypothesis-testing methods has become practical that some researchers argue should completely replace all the standard methods of hypothesis testing! The general name for these new procedures is **computer-intensive methods.** The main specific techniques are **randomization tests** and *bootstrap tests*. These procedures differ in important details, but their general logic is similar enough that we can give you the basic idea by focusing on one of them: randomization tests.

Suppose that you have two groups of scores, one for an experimental group and one for a control group. Suppose also that the means of the two groups differ by some amount. Now consider what happens if all these scores were mixed up, ignoring which group they came from. If you figure the difference between the means of these two randomly set up groups, what is the chance that this whole process would result in a mean difference as big as the one found in the original, proper grouping of the scores?

If the mean difference between the original groupings is quite small, it is likely that you could get that big a mean difference through chance groupings. But if the mean difference for the original groupings is quite large, creating chance groupings would not often produce a difference as large. If chance groupings would produce a result as big as the original groupings less than 5% of the time, we would feel confident

computer-intensive methods statistical methods, including hypothesis-testing procedures, involving large numbers of repeated computations.

randomization tests hypothesis-testing procedures (usually a computer-intensive method) that consider every possible reorganization of the data in the sample to determine if the organization of the actual sample data was unlikely to occur by chance.

that the original groupings were different from what you would expect by chance. Thus, the approach of comparing an actual grouping to chance groupings of scores is a way of doing a significance test.

When you do a randomization test for this kind of situation, the computer actually sets up every single possible division of the scores into two groups of these sizes. Then it counts how many of these possible organizations have a difference as extreme as (or more extreme than) the actual observed differences between your two groups. If fewer than 5% of the possible organizations have differences this extreme, your result is significant. You can reject the null hypothesis that the two groups could have been this different by a chance division. (This logic is like that used for working out the probabilities for rank-order tests, but in this case scores are not first converted to ranks.)

Table 14–7 shows what a computer would do for a randomization test for the example fictional two-group study of number of books read. Basically, what the table shows is

---

Table 14-7 Randomization Test Computations for the Study Comparing Highly Sensitive and Not Highly Sensitive Children on the Number of Books Read in the Past Year (Fictional Data)

Actual Results:

Highly Sensitive

	No	Yes
	0	17
	3	36
	10	45
	22	75
Σ	35	173
$M =$	8.75	43.25

Actual difference $= M_{Yes} - M_{No} = 34.5$

Needed to reject the null hypothesis: This mean difference must be in top 5% of mean differences. With 70 mean differences, it must be among the three highest differences.

All Possible Divisions (70) of the Eight Scores into Two Groups of Four Each:

Actual													
No	Yes	No	Yes	No	Yes	No	Yes	No	Yes	No	Yes	No	Yes
0	17	0	22	0	22	0	22	0	22	0	10	0	10
3	36	3	36	3	17	3	17	3	17	3	36	3	17
10	45	10	45	10	45	10	36	10	36	22	45	22	45
22	75	17	75	36	75	45	75	75	45	17	75	36	75

$M_{Yes} - M_{No}$: 34.5 — 37 — 27.5 — 23 — 8 — 31 — 21.5

No	Yes	No	Yes	No	Yes	No	Yes	No	Yes	No	Yes	No	Yes
0	10	0	10	0	10	0	10	0	10	0	10	0	10
3	17	3	17	3	22	3	22	3	22	3	22	3	22
22	36	22	36	17	45	17	36	17	36	36	17	36	17
45	75	75	45	36	75	45	75	75	45	45	75	75	45

$M_{Yes} - M_{No}$: 17 — 2 — 24 — 19.5 — 4.5 — 10 — −5

No	Yes	No	Yes	No	Yes	No	Yes	No	Yes	No	Yes	No	Yes
0	10	0	3	0	3	0	3	0	3	0	3	0	3
3	22	10	36	10	17	10	17	10	17	10	22	10	22
45	17	22	45	22	45	22	36	22	36	17	45	17	36
75	36	17	75	36	75	45	75	75	45	36	75	45	75

$M_{Yes} - M_{No}$: −9.5 — 27.5 — 18 — 13.5 — −1.5 — 20.5 — 16

(continued)

Table 14-7   *(continued)*

No	Yes	No	Yes	No	Yes	No	Yes	No	Yes	No	Yes	No	Yes
0	3	0	3	0	3	0	3	0	3	0	3	0	3
10	22	10	22	10	22	10	22	22	10	22	10	22	10
17	36	36	17	36	17	45	17	17	45	17	36	17	36
75	45	45	75	75	45	75	36	36	75	45	75	75	45

$M_{Yes} - M_{No}$: 1   6.5   −8.5   −13   14.5   10   −5

No	Yes	No	Yes	No	Yes	No	Yes	No	Yes	No	Yes	No	Yes
0	3	0	3	0	3	0	3	0	3	0	3	0	3
22	10	22	10	22	10	17	10	17	10	17	10	36	10
36	17	36	17	45	17	36	22	36	22	45	22	45	22
45	75	75	45	75	36	45	75	75	45	75	36	75	17

$M_{Yes} - M_{No}$: .5   −14.5   −19   3   −12   −16.5   −26

No	Yes	No	Yes	No	Yes	No	Yes	No	Yes	No	Yes	No	Yes
17	0	22	0	22	0	22	0	22	0	10	0	10	0
3	3	36	3	17	3	17	3	17	3	36	3	17	3
10	10	45	10	45	10	36	10	36	10	45	22	45	22
22	22	75	17	75	36	75	45	45	75	75	17	75	36

$M_{Yes} - M_{No}$: −34.5   −37   −27.5   −23   −8   −31   −21.5

No	Yes	No	Yes	No	Yes	No	Yes	No	Yes	No	Yes	No	Yes
10	0	10	0	10	0	10	0	10	0	10	0	10	0
17	3	17	3	22	3	22	3	22	3	22	3	22	3
36	22	36	22	45	17	36	17	36	17	17	36	17	36
75	45	45	75	75	36	75	45	45	75	75	45	45	75

$M_{Yes} - M_{No}$: −17   −2   −24   −19.5   −4.5   −10   5

No	Yes	No	Yes	No	Yes	No	Yes	No	Yes	No	Yes	No	Yes
10	0	3	0	3	0	3	0	3	0	3	0	3	0
22	3	36	10	17	10	17	10	17	10	22	10	22	10
17	45	45	22	45	22	36	22	36	22	45	17	36	17
36	75	75	17	75	36	75	45	45	75	75	36	75	45

$M_{Yes} - M_{No}$: 9.5   −27.5   −18   −13.5   1.5   −20.5   −16

No	Yes	No	Yes	No	Yes	No	Yes	No	Yes	No	Yes	No	Yes
3	0	3	0	3	0	3	0	3	0	3	0	3	0
22	10	22	10	22	10	22	10	10	22	10	22	10	22
36	17	17	36	17	36	17	45	45	17	36	17	36	17
45	75	75	45	45	75	36	75	75	36	75	45	45	75

$M_{Yes} - M_{No}$: −1   −6.5   8.5   13   −14.5   −10   5

No	Yes	No	Yes	No	Yes	No	Yes	No	Yes	No	Yes	No	Yes
3	0	3	0	3	0	3	0	3	0	3	0	3	0
10	22	10	22	10	22	10	17	10	17	10	17	10	36
17	36	17	36	17	45	22	36	22	36	22	45	22	45
75	45	45	75	36	75	75	45	45	75	36	75	17	75

$M_{Yes} - M_{No}$: −.5   14.5   19   −3   12   16.5   26

Seventy Differences Ordered From Lowest (Most Negative) to Highest:

−37, −34.5, −32, −27.5, −27.5, −26, −24, −23, −21.5, −20.5, −19.5, −19, −18, −17, −16.5, −16, −14.5, −14.5, −13.5, −13, −12, −10, −10, −9.5, −8.5, −8, −6.5, −5, −5, −4.5, −3, −2, −1.5, −1, −.5, .5, 1, 1.5, 2, 3, 4.5, 5, 5, 6.5, 8, 8.5, 9.5, 10, 10, 12, 13, 13.5, 14.5, 14.5, 16, 16.5, 17, 18, 19, 19.5, 20.5, 21.5, 23, 24, 26, 27.5, 27.5, 31, 34.5, 37

Decision: Actual mean difference is among the three highest. Reject the null hypothesis.

the worked-out difference between means for every one of the 70 possible combinations of eight scores into two groups of four scores each. Thus, for the actual two groups, the difference is 34.5; but for other ways of dividing up the eight scores, the difference in means can be as low as −37 and as high as +37. What is shown on the bottom, however, is that our particular result is one of the two highest of the 70, putting it in the top 5%. Thus, using this method, the researcher can conclude there is a significant difference—and do so without having made any assumptions whatsoever about population distributions!

Our example used a very small sample. Even so, there were 70 possible ways of dividing the scores into two equal groups. With larger (and more realistic) sample sizes, the number of different ways of dividing up the scores into groups quickly becomes unmanageable, even for most computers. For example, a comparison between two groups of seven participants each has 3,432 possible divisions; a comparison of 10 participants per group has 184,756. With 20 per group, there are 155,120,000! In practice, even most computers cannot handle true randomization tests, especially for complex analysis situations, with the size of samples common in psychology research.

To deal with this problem, statisticians have developed what are called *approximate randomization tests*. The computer randomly selects a large number of possible divisions of the sample—perhaps 1,000. The results using these randomly selected divisions are then considered representative of what you would find if you actually used every possible division. (This is similar to a Monte Carlo study, which we described in Chapter 8, Box 8–1. And how does something as orderly as a computer come up with so many random numbers? See Box 14–1.)

BOX 14–1 **Where Do Random Numbers Come From?**

To be random, numbers must be selected with equal odds. That is, the odds of each number's appearance have to be totally independent of the odds of the numbers appearing before and after it. One of the many important uses of random numbers is in computer-intensive statistical methods, as discussed in this chapter. They are also essential to Monte Carlo studies (see Chapter 8, Box 8–1), which are used to test the effect of violating normality and other assumptions of parametric statistical tests—one way for psychologists to know whether they need to use the methods described in this chapter. But random numbers in themselves are an interesting topic.

The first random number table was created in 1927. Before that, mechanical methods such as shuffling devices were used. Remember William S. ("Student") Gosset (Chapter 7, Box 7–1)? To obtain his random numbers, he shuffled and drew from a deck of 3,000 cards. Then, in 1927, Karl Pearson encouraged L. H. C. Tippett to publish a table. Tippett found drawing numbered cards from a bag "unsatisfactory"; so he selected digits from the 1925 census report. Later, in 1938, R. A. Fisher and Frank Yates published a list based on logarithms. At about the same time, a number of methods of checking for randomness were also introduced.

Later, more sophisticated physical solutions became common. Flashing a beam of light at irregular intervals onto a sectioned rotating disk was one. Another used the radiation of radioactive substances. It recorded the number of particles detected during a certain time span; if the number was odd, it set a counter to 1, and if even, to 0, and then generated lists of numbers from groupings of these binary digits. A third system employed an electronic valve that made noise that could be amplified; the fluctuating output values were random.

All of these physical methods were a nuisance: they required storing the numbers if they were to be reproduced or reused, and all this apparatus was hard to maintain. So computers are now often used to create "pseudorandom numbers," using some special equation, such as squaring large numbers and taking a central group of the resulting digits. But these numbers are in some subtle sense not random, but predictable because of the very fact that there was an intention in the equation's design: to create randomness (quite a paradox). There is also the problem of whether equations will "degenerate" and begin to repeat sequences. Finally, no matter how the list is generated, there is controversy about the consequences of the repeated use of the same table.

The whole topic of how difficult it is to create something free of order or intelligence seems to say something. What that is, we will leave for you to decide.

Computer-intensive methods, such as approximate randomization tests, do not require either of the two main assumptions of ordinary parametric tests. Further, like rank-order tests, they have a direct logic of their own that is very appealing, bypassing the whole process of estimated population distributions, distributions of means, and so forth. Computer-intensive methods are also extremely flexible. You can use them in almost any situation imaginable in which hypothesis testing could be applied. Thus, you can use them to analyze the results of a study when no test currently exists, parametric or otherwise.

The main disadvantage of the computer-intensive methods is that they are relatively new; so the details and relative advantages of various approaches have not been well worked out. Further, because they are new, in most cases the standard computer statistical packages include them in only a few specialized situations. But the number and importance of such situations is growing rapidly. For example, computer-intensive methods are increasingly the method of choice for handling the "too many *t* tests" problem in brain imaging studies, as discussed in Chapter 8. Computer-intensive methods are only beginning to appear in published articles, but their use is likely to increase rapidly. Indeed, they are starting to play a particularly important role in the analysis of results of cognitive and affective neuroscience brain imaging studies.

Data Transformations and Rank-Order Tests in Research Articles

The use of the procedures we have described in this chapter seems to wax and wane in popularity in different areas of psychology. In some fields, during certain years, you may see many studies using data transformations and never see a rank-order test. In other areas, during the same years, you may see just the reverse.

Data transformations are usually mentioned in the Results section of a research article, just prior to the description of the analysis that uses the scores that were transformed. For example, Sugerman and Carey (2007) studied the relationship between students' alcohol intake and their use of strategies to control drinking. (Examples of strategies they studied were spacing drinks over time and alternating alcoholic and nonalcoholic beverages when drinking.) Prior to presenting the main results, the researchers noted:

> Summary statistics were generated to evaluate the distributions of variables and to identify problems with skew that might require transformations. To correct for nonnormality due to positive skew, we square-root transformed the following variables: average drinks per week, average BAC [blood alcohol content], and heaviest BAC. (p. 341)

Here is an example of rank-order tests reported by Schwitzgebel and colleagues (2007). These researchers studied factors associated with how often people report dreaming in color. The participants in the study were 300 high school and university students in a central part of Eastern China. The students answered the question "Do you see colors in your dreams?" using response options of *never, rarely, occasionally, frequently,* and *very frequently.* The researchers noted at the start of the Results section of the article that "The data were treated as ranked and nonparametric" (p. 38).

They went on to state:

> Respondents with a principally urban childhood...reported significantly more colored dreaming (median *occasionally*) than respondents raised in rural areas (median *rarely*) (Mann-Whitney, one-tailed, $p < .0001$), and age of first regular exposure to colored TV and movies...was negatively correlated with report of colors in dreams (Spearman's rank correlation = .26, $p < .001$). (p. 40)

How often do *you* see colors in your dreams? Here is how a sample of 124 college students in Southern California answered that question: never, 4.7%; rarely, 14.3%; occasionally, 24.4%; frequently, 27.8%; very frequently, 28.7% (Schwitzgebel, 2003).

Summary

1. The *t* test, analysis of variance, and the significance tests for correlation and prediction (regression) are all parametric tests that assume that populations follow a normal curve and have equal variances. When samples suggest that the populations are very far from normal (as when they are highly skewed or have outliers) or have different variances, using the ordinary procedures gives incorrect results.

2. One approach when the populations appear to be violating these assumptions is to transform the scores, such as taking the square root of each score so that the distribution of the transformed scores appears to represent a normally distributed population. Other common transformations for skewed distributions are taking the log or inverse of each score. You can then use the ordinary hypothesis-testing procedures.

3. Another approach is to rank all of the scores in a study. Special rank-order tests (sometimes called nonparametric or distribution-free tests) use basic principles of probability to determine the chance of the ranks being unevenly distributed across groups. However, in many situations, using the rank-transformed scores in an ordinary parametric test gives a good approximation.

4. Data transformations allow you to use the familiar parametric techniques but cannot always be used and may distort the meaning of the scores. You can use rank-order methods in almost any situation, they are especially appropriate with rank or similar data, and they have a straightforward conceptual foundation. But rank-order methods are not widely familiar and they have not been developed for many complex data analysis situations. As with other data transformations, information may be lost or meaning distorted.

5. A randomization test is an example of a computer-intensive method that considers every possible rearrangement of the scores from a study to figure the probability that the actual arrangement (for example, the difference in means between the actual two groupings of scores) arose by chance. Computer-intensive methods have been proposed as an alternative to both parametric and nonparametric methods. They are widely applicable, sometimes to situations for which no other method exists. Also, they have an appealing direct logic. But they are unfamiliar to researchers; being new, their possible limitations are not well worked out, and they can be difficult to set up, because they are not provided on standard computer statistical software programs.

6. Research articles usually describe data transformations just prior to analyses using them. Rank-order methods are described much like any other kind of hypothesis test.

data transformation (p. 580)
square-root transformation (p. 581)
rank-order transformation (p. 585)

rank-order test (p. 586)
distribution-free test (p. 586)
nonparametric test (p. 586)

parametric test (p. 586)
computer-intensive methods (p. 591)
randomization test (p. 591)

Example Worked-Out Problems

The following problems are based on the following scores from a study with three groups:

Group A	Group B	Group C
15	21	18
4	16	19
12	49	11
14	17	22

Square-Root Transformation

Carry out a square-root transformation.

Answer

Group A	Group B	Group C
3.87	4.58	4.24
2.00	4.00	4.36
3.46	7.00	3.32
3.74	4.12	4.69

Rank-Order Transformation

Carry out a rank-order transformation.

Answer

Group A	Group B	Group C
5	10	8
1	6	9
3	12	2
4	7	11

Practice Problems

These problems involve figuring. Most real-life statistics problems are done on a computer with special statistical software. Even if you have such software, do these problems by hand to ingrain the method in your mind. To learn how to use a computer to solve statistics problems like those in this chapter, refer to the Using SPSS section at the end of this chapter and the *Study Guide and Computer Workbook* that accompanies this text.

All data are fictional unless an actual citation is given.

Set I (for Answers to Set I Problems, see pp. 697–698)

1. For each of the following sample distributions, say whether it suggests that the population distribution is probably not normal, and why.
   (a) 41, 52, 74, 107, 617
   (b) 221, 228, 241, 503, 511, 521
   (c) .2, .3, .5, .6, .7, .9, .11
   (d) −6, −5, −3, 10
   (e) 11, 20, 32, 41, 49, 62

2. For each of the following distributions, make a square-root transformation:
   (a) 16, 4, 9, 25, 36
   (b) 35, 14.3, 13, 12.9, 18

3. For the distribution of the following 30 scores, (a) make a grouped frequencies histogram of the scores as they are (intervals 0–4.9, 5–9.9 10–14.9, etc.); (b) carry out a square-root transformation; and (c) make a grouped histogram of the transformed scores (0–.9, 1–1.9, etc.):

   9, 28, 4, 16, 0, 7, 25, 1, 4, 10, 4, 2, 1, 9, 16, 11, 12, 1, 18, 2, 5, 10, 3, 17, 6, 4, 2, 23, 21, 20

4. A researcher compares the typical family size in 10 cultures, 5 from Language Group A and 5 from Language Group B. The figures for the Group A cultures are 1.2, 2.5, 4.3, 3.8, and 7.2. The figures for the Group B cultures are 2.1, 9.2, 5.7, 6.7, and 4.8. Based on these 10 cultures, does typical family size differ in cultures with different language groups? Use the .05 level. (a) Carry out a *t* test for independent means using the actual scores. (b) Carry out a square-root transformation (to keep things simple, round off the transformed scores to one decimal place). (c) Carry out a *t* test for independent means using the transformed scores. (d) Explain what you have done and why to someone who is familiar with the *t* test for independent means but not with data transformation.

5. A researcher is studying the effect of sleep deprivation on recall. Six participants are each tested twice on a recall task, once on a day when well rested (they had plenty of sleep the night before) and once when sleep deprived (they have had no sleep for 48 hours). Here are the recall scores:

Participant	Well Rested	Sleep Deprived
A	16	5
B	18	2
C	10	10
D	7	3
E	20	16
F	10	9

   Does sleep deprivation affect recall? (Use the .05 significance level.) (a) Carry out a *t* test for dependent means using the actual scores. (b) Carry out a square-root transformation of the difference scores (to keep things simple, round off the transformed scores to one decimal place). (c) Carry out a *t* test for dependent means using the transformed difference scores. (d) Explain what you have done and why to someone who is familiar with the *t* test for dependent means but not with data transformation.

6. A researcher randomly assigns participants to watch one of three kinds of films: one that tends to make people sad, one that tends to make people angry, and one that tends to make people exuberant. The participants are then asked to rate a series of photos of individuals on how honest they appear. The ratings for the sad-film group were 201, 523, and 614; the ratings for the angry-film group were 136, 340, and 301; and the ratings for the exuberant-film group were 838, 911, and 1,007. (a) Carry out an analysis of variance using the actual scores (use $p < .01$). (b) Carry out a square-root transformation of the scores (to keep things simple, round off the transformed scores to one decimal place). (c) Carry out an analysis of variance using the transformed scores. (d) Explain what you have done and why to someone who is familiar with analysis of variance but not with data transformation.

7. Miller (1997) conducted a study of commitment to a romantic relationship and how much attention a person pays to attractive alternatives. In this study, participants were shown a set of slides of attractive individuals. At the start of the results section, Miller notes, "The self-reports on the Attentiveness to Alternative Index and the time spent actually inspecting the attractive opposite-sex slides ... were positively skewed, so logarithmic transformations of the data were performed" (p. 760). Explain what is being described here (and why it is being done) to a person who understands ordinary parametric statistics but has never heard of data transformations.

8. Prior to reporting the results for the latency ms scores (reaction time scores in milliseconds) on each trial, Teachman and colleagues (2001) reported the following: "... trial latency data were reciprocally transformed (1,000/latency in ms)" (p. 230). Explain what is being described here (and why it is being done) to a person who understands ordinary parametric statistics but has never heard of data transformations.

9. Make a rank-order transformation for the scores in problems (a) 2a and (b) 2b.

10. For the distribution of 30 scores given in problem 3, (a) carry out a rank-order transformation and (b) make a grouped frequency histogram of the ranked scores (0–4.9, 5–9.9, etc.).

11. For the data in problems (a) 4, (b) 5, and (c) 6, carry out the appropriate test using the original scores (if you have not done so already), carry out a rank-transformation of the scores, carry out the appropriate statistical test (*t* test or analysis of variance) using the rank-transformed scores, and explain what you have done and why to someone who is familiar with the ordinary parametric procedures but not with rank-order transformations or rank-order tests.

12. Ford and colleagues (1997) were interested in the relation of certain personality factors to treatment for post-traumatic stress disorder (a psychological condition resulting from a traumatic event such as might be experienced during war or as a result of a violent attack). The personality factor of interest to the researchers was based on a modern version of Freudian psychoanalytic theory called "object relations." This refers to the psychological impact of our earliest relationships, mainly with our parents (the "objects" of these early relationships). The researchers based their measure of object relations on a clinical interview focusing on such things as the ability to invest in a close relationship and the ability to see others in a complex way (e.g., not seeing a person as all good or all bad). In reporting their results, they abbreviated the object relations clinical interview measure as "OR-C." The distribution of scores on the OR-C was not normal (it was bimodal).

One of their analyses focused on the relation of object relations to whether a person stays in treatment to completion or terminates prematurely. They reported their results as follows:

Six of the 74 participants prematurely terminated....The six premature terminators did not differ from the rest of the sample on any demographic or pretest variable.... They did differ statistically significantly from completers on OR-C ratings, scoring lower as tested by the nonparametric Mann-Whitney U Test ($Z = -3.43$, $p < .001$). (p. 554)

Explain, to a person who is familiar with the t test but not with rank-order tests, the general idea of what these researchers are doing (and why they didn't use an ordinary t test).

Set II

13. For each of the following sample distributions, say (a) whether it suggests that the population distribution is probably not normal, and (b) why.
    (a) 281, 283, 287, 289, 291, 300, 302
    (b) 1, 4, 6, 6, 7, 7, 9, 13
    (c) 7, 104, 104, 104, 1,245, 1,247, 1,248, 1,251
    (d) 68, 74, 76, 1,938
    (e) 407.2, 407.5, 407.6, 407.9
14. For each of the following distributions, make a square-root transformation:
    (a) 100, 1, 64, 81, 121
    (b) 45, 30, 17.4, 16.8, 47
15. For the distribution of the following 20 scores, (a) make a histogram of the scores as they are, (b) carry out a square-root transformation, and (c) make a histogram of the transformed scores:

    2, 207, 894, 107, 11, 79, 112, 938, 791, 3, 13, 89, 1,004, 92, 1,016, 107, 87, 91, 870, 921.

16. A study compared students' number of close friends during their first and second years in college. Here are the numbers of friends for five students tested.

Participant	First Year	Second Year
1	2	2
2	4	6
3	14	15
4	3	15
5	5	6

    Does the number of close friends increase from first to second year of college? (Use the .05 significance level.) (a) Carry out a t test for dependent means using the actual scores. (b) Carry out a square-root transformation of the difference scores (to keep things simple, round off the transformed scores to one decimal place). (c) Carry out a t test for dependent means using the transformed difference scores. (d) Explain what you have done and why to someone who is familiar with the t test for dependent means but not with data transformations.

17. A study compares performance on a novel task for people who do the task either alone, in the presence of a stranger, or in the presence of a friend. The scores for the participants in the alone condition are 1, 1, and 0; the scores of the participants in the stranger condition are 2, 6, and 1; and the scores for those in the friend condition are 3, 9, and 10. (a) Carry out an analysis of variance using the actual scores ($p < .05$). (b) Carry out a square-root transformation of the scores (to keep things simple, round off the transformed scores to one decimal place). (c) Carry out an analysis of variance using the transformed difference scores.

(d) Explain what you have done and why to someone who is familiar with analysis of variance but not with data transformation.

18. A researcher conducted an experiment organized around a televised major address by the U.S. president. Immediately after the address, three participants were randomly assigned to listen to the commentaries provided by the television network's political commentators. The other three were assigned to spend the same time with the television off, reflecting quietly about the speech. Participants in both groups then completed a questionnaire that assessed how much of the content of the speech they remembered accurately. The group that heard the commentators had scores of 4, 0, and 1. The group that reflected quietly had scores of 9, 3, and 8. Did hearing the commentary affect memory? Use the .05 level, one-tailed, predicting higher scores for the reflected-quietly group. (a) Carry out a t test for independent means using the actual scores. (b) Carry out a square-root transformation (to keep things simple, round off the transformed scores to one decimal place). (c) Carry out a t test for independent means using the transformed scores. (d) Explain what you have done and why to someone who is familiar with the t test for independent means but not with data transformation.

19. Carey and colleagues (1997) developed a program designed to enhance motivation for avoiding HIV infection risks. They then studied its effectiveness with a group of economically disadvantaged urban women who were randomly assigned to receive either the program or a control condition. All the women were measured before, 3 weeks after, and 12 weeks after the experimental group participated in the program. One of the measures in the study was sexual communication, such as the extent to which the women reported they had talked with their partners about safer sex and getting tested for HIV. Prior to describing their analyses on this variable, Carey and colleagues noted the following: "The communication scores were positively skewed at all three occasions; $\log_{10}(x + 1)$ transformations provided the best correction toward normality and were used in subsequent analyses" (p. 536). Explain what is being described here (and why it is being done) to a person who understands ordinary parametric statistics but has never heard of data transformations.

20. Connors and colleagues (1997) conducted a study focusing on the client-therapist alliance in alcoholism treatment. Prior to reporting the results of their study, they commented as follows:

> Variables such as percentage of days abstinent and drinks per day often depart from normality because of skewness and floor-ceiling effects. In response, the percentage of days abstinent variable was subjected to an arcsine transformation, and the drinks per drinking day variable was subjected to a square-root transformation, in each case to improve the distribution. (p. 592)

Explain what is being described here (and why it is being done) to a person who understands ordinary parametric statistics but has never heard of data transformations.

21. Martinez (2000) studied the link between homicide rates and immigrant status among Latinos in the United States. However, prior to presenting the results, Martinez noted, "…the dependent variables indicated skewed distributions. Thus, all Latino homicide types…were logarithmically transformed into natural logs." Explain what is being described here (and why it is being done) to a person who understands ordinary parametric statistics but has never heard of data transformations.

22. Make a rank-order transformation for the scores in problems (a) 14a and (b) 14b.

23. For the distribution of 20 scores given in problem 15, (a) carry out a rank-order transformation and (b) make a histogram of the ranked scores.

24. For the data in problems (a) 17 and (b) 18, carry out the appropriate test using original scores (if you have not done so already), carry out a rank-transformation of the scores, carry out the appropriate statistical test (*t* test or analysis of variance) using the rank-transformed scores, and explain what you have done and why to someone who is familiar with the normal parametric procedures but not with rank-order transformations or rank-order tests.

25. June and colleagues (1990) surveyed black students at a Midwestern university about problems in their use of college services. Surveys were conducted of about 250 students each time, at the end of the spring quarter over five different years. The researchers ranked the nine main problem areas for each of the years. One of their analyses then proceeded as follows: "A major question of interest was whether the ranking of most serious problems and use of services varied by years. Thus, a Kruskal-Wallis one-way analysis of variance (ANOVA) was performed on the rankings but was not significant. . . ." (p. 180). Explain why the researchers used the Kruskal-Wallis test instead of an ordinary analysis of variance and what conclusions can be drawn from this result.

26. As part of a larger study, Betsch and colleagues (2001) manipulated the attention to information presented in TV ads and then gave participants questions about the content of the ads as a check on the success of their manipulation. They reported:

> Participants who were instructed to attend to the ads answered 51.5%. . . of the questions correctly. In the other condition, only 41.1% of questions were answered correctly. This difference is significant according to the Mann-Whitney U test, $U(84) = 2317.0$, $p < .01$. This shows that the attention manipulation was effective. (p. 248)

Explain the general idea of what these researchers are doing (and why they didn't use an ordinary *t* test) to a person who is familiar with the *t* test but not with rank-order tests.

Using SPSS

The ⊲ in the following steps indicates a mouse click. (We used SPSS version 15.0 for Windows to carry out these analyses. The steps and output may be slightly different for other versions of SPSS.)

Checking for Normal Distributions

It is a good idea to check to see if each variable and each group in a study comes from a population with a normal distribution. In this case, the key thing to consider is the *skewness* of the distribution. As you learned in Chapter 1, skewness means a distribution is not normal because it is lopsided with a long tail on one side. First, have SPSS figure each variable's numerical skewness value. We will use the example of the square-root transformation of the scores from the study comparing highly sensitive and not highly sensitive children on the number of books read in the past year (see Tables 14–1 and 14–2 on p. 584). Since we have scores for two groups of students (highly sensitive and not highly sensitive) on the books variable, we will test for skewness in the book scores separately for each group.

❶ Enter the scores into SPSS. As shown in Figure 14–6, the score for each child is shown in the "books" column. The scores in the "sensitive" column show whether the child was not highly sensitive (a score of 0) or highly sensitive (a score of 1). Although the sensitive scores aren't needed at this point, they are

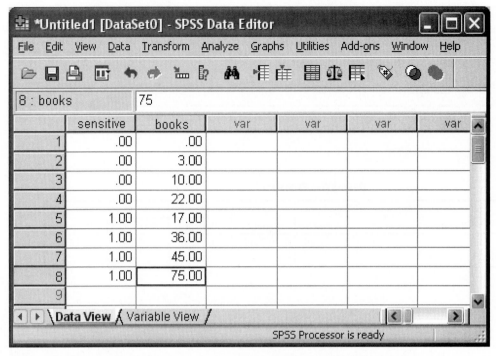

Figure 14–6   SPSS data editor window for the fictional study comparing highly sensitive and not highly sensitive children on the number of books read in the past year.

important for figuring a *t* test for independent means on the transformed scores (see Table 14–3).

❷ ✐ *Data.* ✐ *Split File.* ✐ the circle next to "Organize output by group". ✐ the "sensitive" variable and ✐ the arrow next to the box labeled "Groups Based on." ✐ *OK.* This step has the effect of telling SPSS to produce separate skewness statistics (which you will request in Steps ❸ through ❻) for the two "sensitive" groups.

❸ ✐ *Analyze.* ✐ *Descriptive Statistics,* ✐ *Descriptives.* This will bring up a "Descriptives" window.

❹ ✐ on the variable called "books" and then ✐ the arrow next to the box labeled "Variable(s)".

❺ ✐ *Options.* ✐ the box next to "Skewness" (this checks the box). ✐ *Continue.*

❻ ✐ *OK.* Your SPSS output window will look like Figure 14–7. SPSS gives one table of results for children with a value of 0 for the sensitive variable and a separate table for those with a value of 1 for the sensitive variable. In each table, the skewness statistic is shown in the second to last column of the table. A widely used informal rule is that a skewness statistic of greater than +1 or less than −1 indicates that a group or variable is highly skewed. In such cases, it is also a good idea to get a visual sense of the degree of skew. The best way to do this is to compare a histogram of the variable to the normal curve. Here are the SPSS steps to request such a diagram:

❶ ✐ *Graphs.* ✐ *Legacy Dialogs.* ✐ *Histogram.*

❷ ✐ on the variable called "books" and then ✐ the arrow next to the box labeled "Variable."

❸ ✐ the box next to "Display normal curve" (this checks the box).

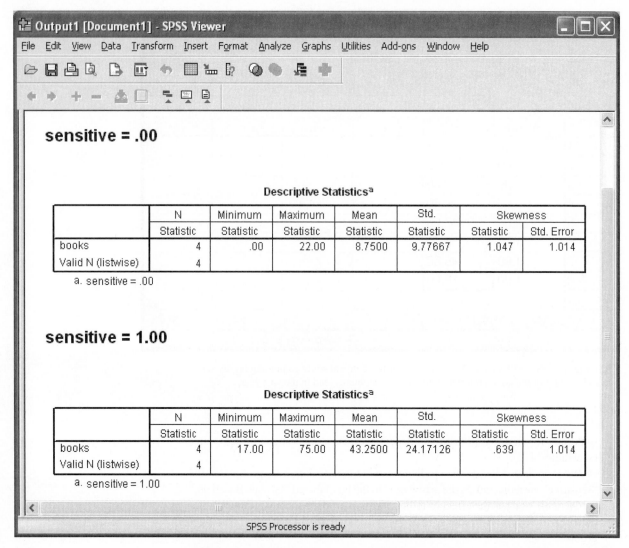

Figure 14–7 SPSS output window for the skewness of the "books" variable in a fictional study comparing highly sensitive and not highly sensitive children on the number of books read in the past year.

❹ ✑ *OK.* There will be two histograms (each with a normal curve on top of the histogram) in your SPSS output window. Figure 14–8 shows the first of these two histograms. There are scores for only four students shown in this first histogram (we used a small sample size in this example earlier in the chapter for learning purposes). However, the distribution shows some evidence of being skewed to the right, which suggests that the scores for the "books" variable do not come from a normal population. (In reality, you would conduct such a study with a larger sample, which would make it easier for you to examine the potential nonnormal distribution of the "books" scores.)

If you are now going to continue with the following SPSS examples below, you will need to turn off the "Split File" instruction that you gave to SPSS during Step ❷ of requesting the skewness statistic. Here is how to do that: ✑ *Data.* ✑ *Split File.* ✑ the circle next to "Analyze all cases, do not create groups". ✑ *OK.*

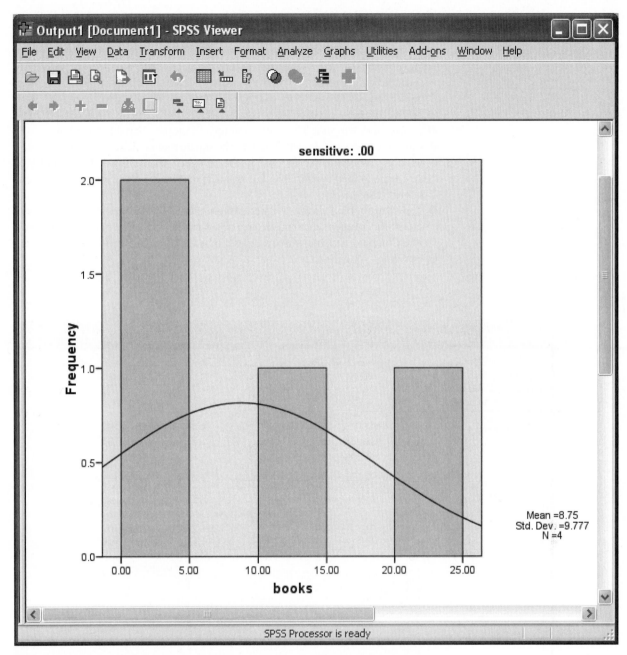

Figure 14–8 SPSS output window for a histogram and normal curve of the books variable in a fictional study comparing highly sensitive and not highly sensitive children on the number of books read in the past year.

Data Transformations

We will again use the example of the square-root transformation of the scores from the study comparing highly sensitive and not highly sensitive children on the number of books read in the past year (see Tables 14–1 and 14–2).

❶ Enter the scores into SPSS, as shown in Figure 14–6. Although the sensitive scores aren't needed for the data transformation, they are important for figuring a *t* test for independent means on the transformed scores (see Table 14–3). (A score of 0 in the "sensitive" column indicates that a child was not highly sensitive; and a score of 1 in the "sensitive" column indicates that a child was highly sensitive.)

❷ ✑ *Transform.*

❸ ✑ *Compute Variable.* This will bring up a "Compute Variable" window.

❹ Name the new variable (which will be the square root of the scores for the "books" variable) by typing "sqrtbooks" in the "Target Variable" box. (You could give any name to the new variable, but it is best to give it a name that describes how it was figured.)

❺ Type "sqrt(books)" in the "Numeric Expression" box. This tells SPSS to take the square root of each score and create a new variable with those transformed scores. The Compute Variable window should now look like Figure 14–9.

❻ ✑ *OK.*

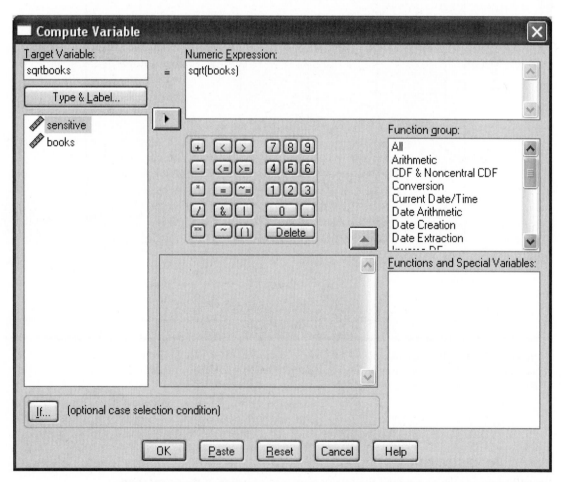

Figure 14–9 SPSS compute variable window for figuring the square root of the books scores for the fictional study comparing highly sensitive and not highly sensitive children on the number of books read in the past year.

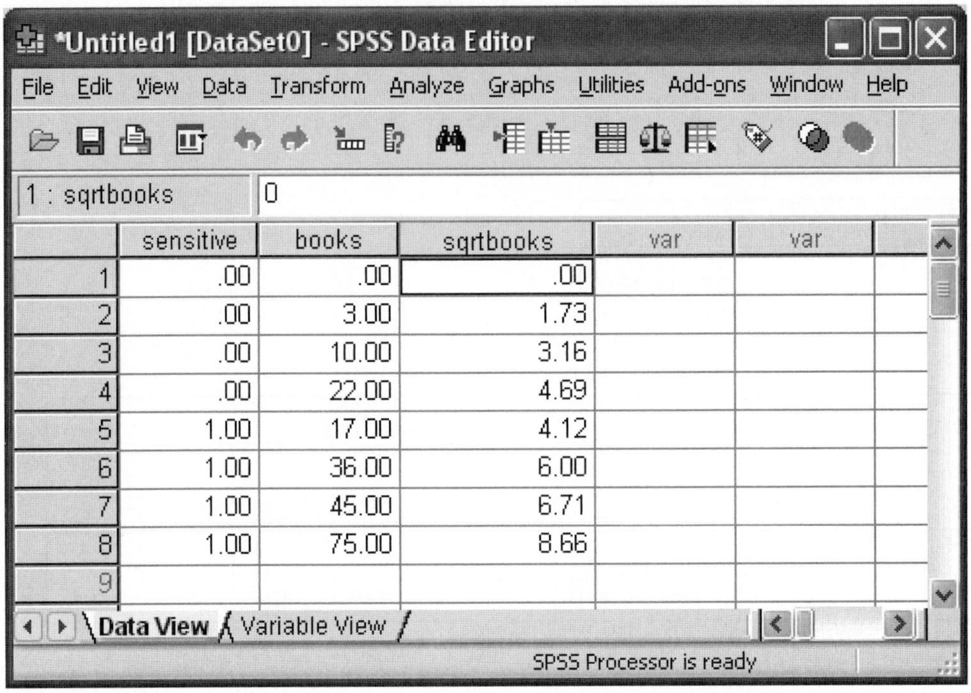

Figure 14–10   SPSS data editor window for the fictional study comparing highly sensitive and not highly sensitive children on the number of books read in the past year, including the scores for the books variable after a square root transformation.

Your SPSS data editor window should now look like Figure 14–10. You can now use the "sqrtbooks" scores in a *t* test for independent means to compare the scores of not highly sensitive and highly sensitive children. In Figure 14–11 we show the SPSS output of such a *t* test for independent means. The results of this *t* test are the same (within rounding error) as the results shown in Table 14–3 on p. 585.

TIP FOR SUCCESS

For extra practice with SPSS, follow the steps for using SPSS to figure a *t* test for independent means (see Chapter 8's Using SPSS section) for the transformed books scores. Check that your output for the *t* test is the same as that shown in Figure 14–11.

Rank-Order Tests

We will use the example of the Wilcoxon rank-sum test for the scores from the study comparing the highly sensitive and not highly sensitive children on the number of books read in the past year (see Table 14–5 on p. 588).

❶ Enter the scores into SPSS as shown in Figure 14–6. (A score of 0 in the "sensitive" column indicates that a child was not highly sensitive; and a score of 1 in the "sensitive" column indicates that a child was highly sensitive.)

❷ ✐ *Analyze.*

❸ ✐ *Nonparametric tests.*

❹ ✐ *2 Independent Samples.*

❺ ✐ on the variable called "books" and then ✐ the arrow next to the box labeled "Test Variable List." This tells SPSS that the rank-order test should be carried out on the scores for the "books" variable.

❻ ✐ the variable called "sensitive" and then ✐ the arrow next to the box labeled "Grouping Variable." This tells SPSS that the variable called "sensitive" shows which person is in which group. ✐ *Define Groups.* You now tell SPSS the

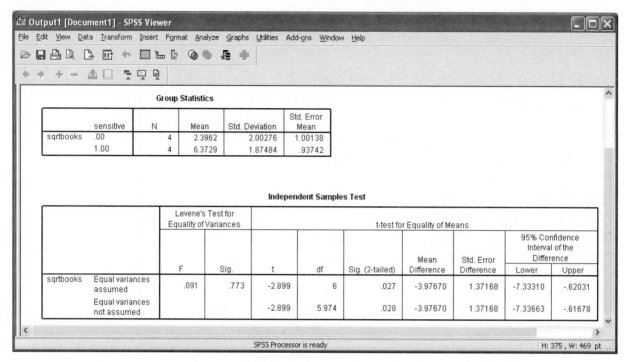

Figure 14–11 SPSS output window for a *t* test for independent means for the square-root transformed book scores from the fictional study comparing highly sensitive and not highly sensitive children on the number of books read in the past year.

values you used to label each group. Put "0" in the Group 1 box and put "1" in the Group 2 box. ✍ *Continue.*

❼ ✍ *OK.* Your SPSS output window should look like Figure 14–12.

You will notice that the heading under "NPar Tests" (which stands for nonparametric tests) is "Mann-Whitney Test." As we mentioned earlier in the chapter, the Mann-Whitney *U* test and the Wilcoxon rank-sum test differ in their computations but give mathematically equivalent final results. (As you will see in the second table in the SPSS output, the significance level is the same for Mann-Whitney and Wilcoxon rank-sum tests.) The first table in the SPSS output (labeled "Ranks") provides information about the two variables. The first column gives the levels of the "sensitive" grouping variable (0 and 1, which indicate the not highly sensitive and highly sensitive groups, respectively.) The second, third, and fourth columns give, respectively, the number of individuals (*N*), mean rank, and sum of ranks for each group.

The second table in the SPSS output (labeled "Test Statistics") shows the actual results of the nonparametric rank-ordered tests. We will focus here on the results for the Wilcoxon rank-sum test (but the overall significance level and conclusion is the same, regardless of which test result you consider). Notice that the value of 11.000 is the same as the sum of the ranks for the not highly sensitive group, as shown in Table 14–5. The exact significance level of .043 for this result [shown in the "Asymp. Sig. (2-tailed)" row] is for a two-tailed test. In this example, we were using a one-tailed test; so this two-tailed significance of .043 represents a one-tailed significance of .043/2, which is .0215. This significance level of .0215 is less than our .05 cutoff for this example, which means that you can reject the null hypothesis and the research hypothesis is supported.

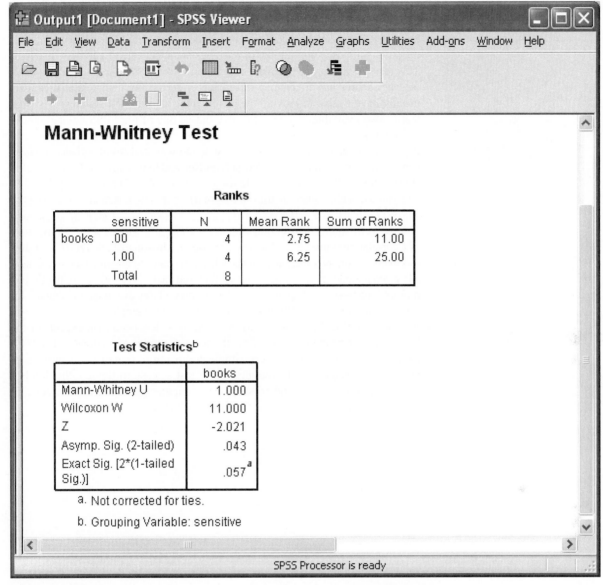

Figure 14-12 SPSS output window for a Wilcoxon rank-sum test for the fictional study comparing highly sensitive and not highly sensitive children on the number of books read in the past year.

Chapter Notes

1. Chi-square, like the rank-order tests, is considered a nonparametric test, but it is distribution-free only in the sense that no assumptions are made about the shape of the population distributions. However, the terms *distribution-free* and *nonparametric* are typically used interchangeably; the subtleties of differences between them are a matter of ongoing debate among statisticians.

2. There is one widely used nonparametric test, besides chi-square tests, that is not based on rank-order scores at all. This is called the *sign test,* which is used in

place of a *t* test for dependent means. You create your set of difference scores, then you just add up the number of difference scores that are positive. If there is no average difference, about half the difference scores should be positive and half negative. Suppose your number of positives are a lot more or a lot less than half. This result would argue against a null hypothesis that the true population of differences scores has an average difference of zero. Intermediate statistics texts usually have a table to look up the significance cutoffs for a sign test. The sign test is also available and easy to carry out as one of the SPSS nonparametric procedures.

3. If you want to be very accurate, for a *t* test or one-way analysis of variance, you can convert your result to what is called an *L* statistic and look it up on a chi-square table (Puri & Sen, 1985). The *L* statistic for a *t* test is $([N - 1] t^2)/(t^2 + [N - 2])$, and you use a chi-square distribution with $df = 1$. The *L* statistic for a one way analysis of variance is $([N - 1][df_{Between}]F)/([df_{Between}] F + df_{Within})$, and you use a chi-square distribution with $df = df_{Between}$. The *L* for the significance of a correlation is just $(N - 1)r^2$ and you use the chi-square table for $df = 1$. It is especially important to use the *L* statistic when using rank-transformed scores for more advanced parametric procedures, such as factorial analysis of variance (Chapter 10), multiple regression (Chapter 12), and those procedures discussed in Chapter 15. Thomas and colleagues (1999) give fully worked-out examples.

4. Another traditional advantage of rank-order tests has been that, except for the labor of changing the scores to ranks, the actual figuring (when done by hand) for most of these procedures is very simple compared to that of parametric tests. However, nowadays, with computers, it is just as easy to figure either kind of procedure. With some standard statistical computer packages, there is actually less trouble involved in figuring the parametric test.

CHAPTER 15

The General Linear Model and Making Sense of Advanced Statistical Procedures in Research Articles

Chapter Outline

- The General Linear Model   612
- Partial Correlation   617
- Reliability   618
- Multilevel Modeling   620
- Factor Analysis   622
- Causal Modeling   625
- Procedures that Compare Groups   634
- Analysis of Covariance (ANCOVA)   634
- Multivariate Analysis of Variance (MANOVA) and Multivariate Analysis of Covariance (MANCOVA)   635
- Overview of Statistical Techniques   636
- Controversy: Should Statistics Be Controversial?   637
- How to Read Results Using Unfamiliar Statistical Techniques   639
- Summary   641
- Key Terms   642
- Practice Problems   642
- Using SPSS   654
- Chapter Notes   662

Welcome to this final chapter. We will begin with a way to understand the big picture of what you have learned so far in this book, introducing what is called the *general linear model,* a fundamental idea in statistics that is the hidden common foundation of just about all the statistical methods psychologists use. (We provide a fuller introduction to the general linear model in a Web Chapter, available on

TIP FOR SUCCESS

To understand the advanced procedures in this chapter, you should have already covered the chapters on *t* tests, analysis of variance, correlation, and prediction.

the Web site for this book, *http://www.pearsonhighered.com/.* The Web Chapter also uses the general linear model as a platform for a broad review of the entire book.)

On the basis of this big picture and general integration, the main part of the chapter turns to a view of what lies ahead for you as you study more of the research at the basis of all psychology. Here we show you how to make sense in a general way of the advanced statistical procedures that are fairly widely used in psychology. Most research you will read as a psychology student uses one or more of the statistical procedures you have learned in this book. However, very often you will run into procedures that you will not learn to do yourself until you take more advanced statistics courses. Fortunately, most of these advanced procedures are direct extensions of what you have learned in this book. At the least, after reading this chapter, you should be able to make sense of the general idea of just about any statistical analysis in a research article.

The advanced techniques you will learn about first are partial correlation, reliability, multilevel modeling, factor analysis, and causal modeling. These are essentially elaborations of what you learned in Chapters 11 and 12 on correlation and regression. Later in this chapter you will learn about advanced statistical techniques that focus on differences among groups. These are essentially elaborations of what you learned in Chapters 9 and 10 on the analysis of variance. These procedures include the analysis of covariance, multivariate analysis of variance, and multivariate analysis of covariance. Finally, we consider what to do when you read a research article that uses a statistical technique you have never heard about.

The General Linear Model

More than 90% of the studies published in a typical year in the major social psychology journals use *t* tests, analysis of variance, correlation, or multiple regression (Reis & Stiller, 1992). This figure probably applies about equally well to all areas of psychology. By now you may have noticed many similarities among these four methods and the other statistical techniques that you have learned in this book. In fact, the techniques are even more closely related than you might have realized: many of them are simply mathematically equivalent variations of each other, and most of them can be derived from the same general formula. This is because there is a central logic behind all these methods based on a general formula that mathematical statisticians call the **general linear model.**

So let's focus on the Big Four (*t* tests, analysis of variance, correlation, and multiple regression), which are all special cases of the general linear model and therefore systematically related. Perhaps in the process, many of your half-sensed intuitions about what you've learned will emerge into the light.

To put it all briefly, the most general technique is multiple regression (Chapter 12), of which bivariate correlation and prediction (Chapters 11 and 12) are special cases. At the same time, the analysis of variance (Chapters 9 and 10) is also a special case of multiple regression. Finally, the *t* test (Chapters 7 and 8) can be derived directly from either bivariate correlation/prediction or the analysis of variance. Figure 15–1 shows these relationships.

When we say that one procedure is a *special case of another,* we mean that it can be derived from the formula for the other. Thus, when using the more specialized procedures, you get the same result as if you had used the more general procedure. To put this in more concrete terms, if you were going to a desert island to do psychology research and could take only one computer program with you to do statistical tests, you would want to choose multiple regression. With that one program, you could accomplish all of what is done by more specialized programs for bivariate

general linear model general formula that is the basis of most of the statistical methods covered in this text; describes a score as the sum of a constant, the weighted influence of several variables, and error.

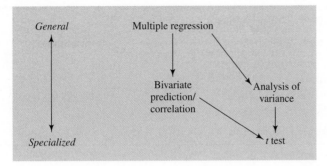

Figure 15-1 The relationships among the four major statistical techniques.

correlation, t tests, and analyses of variance. (To give a concrete example, if you were to do a one-way analysis of variance for just two groups, you would get the same result—in terms of statistical significance—as doing a t test for independent means for the two groups.)

One way of expressing the general linear model is as a mathematical relation between a criterion variable and one or more predictor variables. The general linear model is very closely related to multiple regression. As a reminder, here is the multiple regression linear prediction rule (shown for three predictor variables) you learned in Chapter 12: $\hat{Y} = a + (b_1)(X_1) + (b_2)(X_2) + (b_3)(X_3)$. In this formula, $\hat{Y}$ is the predicted score on the criterion variable; a is the regression constant; b_1, b_2, and b_3 are the regression coefficients for the first, second, and third predictor variables, respectively; and X_1, X_2, and X_3 are the person's scores on the first, second, and third predictor variables, respectively.

The principle of the general linear model is that any person's score on a particular criterion variable is the sum of several influences:

1. Some fixed influence that is the same for all individuals, such as the nature of the testing procedure.
2. Influences of variables you have measured on which people vary, such as amount of sleep the night before, how well one slept, and number of dreams.
3. Other influences that vary among individuals but are not or cannot be measured—this is what makes error.

Influence 1 corresponds to the regression constant (a) in the multiple regression linear prediction rule. Influence 2 corresponds to all of the b and X pairs—$(b_1)(X_1)$, $(b_2)(X_2)$, and so forth—in a multiple regression linear prediction rule. Influence 3 is about the errors in prediction. (If there were a 1.0 multiple correlation, there would be no error and thus no Influence 3.) Thus, the general linear model can be stated in symbols as follows:

$$Y = a + (b_1)(X_1) + (b_2)(X_2) + (b_3)(X_3) + \cdots + e \qquad \textbf{(15-1)}$$

In this formula, Y is a person's actual score on some criterion variable; a is the fixed influence that applies to all individuals (Influence 1); b_1 is the degree of influence of the first predictor variable (Influence 2); it is the regression coefficient, which you then multiply by the person's score on the first predictor variable, X_1. That is, b_2, b_3, and so forth are the influences of predictor variables 2, 3, and so forth. Again, e is the error, the sum of all other influences (Influence 3) on the person's score on Y. That is, e is what is left over after everything else has been taken into account in making the prediction. The formula for the general linear model is also summarized in Table 15-1.

A person's actual score on the criterion variable is the regression constant, plus the regression coefficient for the first predictor variable multiplied by the person's score on the first predictor variable, plus the regression coefficient for the second predictor multiplied by the person's score on the second predictor variable, plus the regression coefficient for the third predictor variable multiplied by the person's score on the third predictor variable, plus any additional regression coefficients multiplied by any additional scores on predictor variables, plus error.

Table 15–1 Summary of the General Linear Model

Verbal Description	Formula Symbol
Person's actual score on the criterion variable	Y
Some fixed influence	a
Influences of the measured variables	$(b_1)(X_1), (b_2)(X_2), (b_3)(X_3) \ldots$
Other influences that have not been measured (error)	e

Formula for the general linear model: $Y = a + (b_1)(X_1) + (b_2)(X_2) + (b_3)(X_3) + \cdots + e$

Notice that this formula is nearly identical to that for multiple regression, with two exceptions. First, instead of having the predicted Y value ($\hat{Y}$) on the left, you have the actual value of Y. Second, it includes an error term (e). This is because the formula is for the actual value of Y and because a and b values ordinarily don't predict perfectly. The error term (e) is added to account for the discrepancy from a perfect prediction of Y.

Thus, the general linear model is a statement of the influences that make up an individual's score on a particular variable. It is called a *linear model* because if you graphed the relationship between the criterion and predictor variables, the pattern would be a straight line (just as the regression line is a straight line in regression). That is, the relationship would be constant in the sense of not being curvilinear. In mathematical terms, the equation is said to be linear because there are no squared (or higher power) terms.[1]

You learned in Chapter 12 that multiple regression (and bivariate prediction) uses a *least-squares criterion*. This means that the a (regression constant) and b (regression coefficient) values of the multiple regression linear prediction rule for a particular criterion variable are figured in such a way as to create the smallest amount of squared error. Since multiple regression is virtually the same as the general linear model, you may not be surprised to learn that the general linear model is also based on a least-squares criterion.

How the Big Four Are Special Cases of the General Linear Model

We noted earlier that the main methods you have learned in this book are each a "special case" of the general linear model, in the sense that the formula for each can be derived from the general linear method formula (see Figure 15–1). We also just saw that multiple regression is basically the same thing as the general linear model. Thus, in practice, what we mean by "special case" for bivariate prediction and correlation, t test, and analysis of variance is that these procedures can all be done using multiple regression.

How is bivariate prediction a special case of multiple regression? Bivariate prediction is just the situation of multiple regression in which there is only one predictor variable. We saw in Chapter 12 that regression and correlation are basically the same thing (how much X predicts Y is exactly the same as how much X and Y are correlated). Thus, because bivariate prediction is a special case of multiple regression, so is bivariate correlation.

In a quite similar way, as we noted briefly earlier, the *t* test is a special case of the analysis of variance. An analysis of variance with two groups gives you exactly the same significance level as a *t* test comparing those two groups. This is because the underlying mathematics are the same. That is, if you start with the formulas for an analysis of variance with just two groups, with some algebra you can turn this into the formulas for the *t* test.

What often seems particularly obscure is how the analysis of variance or the *t* test can be a special case of regression. After all, the analysis of variance and the *t* test are about differences between groups; regression is about predicting a criterion variable from a predictor variable. To get the basic idea, let us consider how the *t* test is similar to bivariate prediction (regression). The *t* test compares two groups of scores on a measured variable. The measured variable is like a criterion variable in bivariate prediction (you want to know the effect on it). The distinction between the two groups in a *t* test is like the predictor variable in bivariate prediction. So you can think of a *t* test as being about whether there is any association between the variable that divides the group (for example, being in an experimental versus a control group) and the measured variable. The trick in understanding how this logic works is this: for the *t* test, you have to think of which group a person is in as a variable itself. We might call this variable *group,* and we could give one score on this variable to everyone in one of the groups (say, give a score of 1 on this *group* variable to everyone in the experimental group) and a different score to everyone in the other group (say, give a score of 2 on this *group* variable to everyone in the control group). We can now run a bivariate regression predicting the measured variable from the *group* variable. The significance of this regression will be exactly the same as the significance of the *t* test. The logic is that saying two groups are different on some measured variable is the same as saying that which group a person is in predicts the person's score on the measured variable. The exact equivalence of the two methods works because the underlying mathematics are the same. That is, if you start with the formulas for bivariate prediction, with some algebra you can turn them into the formulas for the *t* test. We have summarized the relation between bivariate prediction (regression) and the *t* test in Table 15–2.

In a Web Chapter (available on the Web site for this book, *http://www.pearson highered.com*), we go into the logic of the various "special case" ideas in some detail, including illustrating these ideas with concrete examples that highlight the practical links among the figuring of the different procedures. Studying this Web Chapter will much deepen your understanding of what you have learned in this book. It will also provide a quite thorough review of the main ideas.

Table 15-2   Relation Between Bivariate Prediction (Regression) and *t* Test

	Bivariate Prediction	***t* Test**
Variable 1	Predictor variable	Variable that divides the groups
Variable 2	Criterion variable	Measured variable
Relation tested	High scores on predictor go with high scores on criterion	Those in one group on the variable that divides the group have higher scores on the measured variable.

How are you doing?

1. (a) What does it mean for a procedure to be a "special case" of another procedure? (b) Describe which procedures are special cases of which.
2. Write the formula for the general linear model and define each of the symbols.
3. How is the general linear model different from multiple regression? (b) Why?
4. How is the *t* test a special case of analysis of variance?
5. How is the *t* test a special case of bivariate prediction?

Answers

1. (a) The special case can be mathematically derived from the other procedure; it is mathematically identical except that it applies in a more limited set of situations. (b) *t* test is a special case of analysis of variance and of bivariate correlation; analyses of variance and bivariate correlation (and bivariate prediction) are special cases of multiple regression.
2. Formula for the general linear model: $Y = a + (b_1)(X_1) + (b_2)(X_2) + (b_3)(X_3) + \cdots + e$; Y is a person's actual score on some criterion variable; a is the fixed influence that applies to all individuals; b_1, b_2, and b_3 are the degrees of influence of the first, second, and third predictor variables; X_1, X_2, and X_3 are the person's scores on the first, second, and third predictor variables, respectively; "... " is for any additional influences and scores on predictor variables (b_4, X_4, and so on); and e is the error, the sum of all other influences on the person's score on Y.
3. (a) The general linear model is for the actual (not the predicted) score on the criterion variable, and it includes a term for error. (b) To predict the actual score, you have to take into account that there will be error.
4. Analysis of variance focuses on the difference among two or more groups on a measured variable. The *t* test focuses on the difference between two groups on a measured variable. For a situation with two groups, the significance level from a *t* test is exactly the same as for the analysis of variance. Also, you can derive the *t* test formulas from the analysis of variance formulas.
5. You can turn a variable into a group that a person is in (giving people in one group one score, and those in the other group a different score). Then you can use prediction (regression) to predict the measured variable from this group variable. Being able to predict a person's score on a variable from which group they are in is the same thing as the two groups having different means on the variable. The significance you get for prediction is exactly the same as for the *t* test. This is because you can derive the *t* test formulas from the prediction formulas.

BOX 15–1   Two Women Make a Point About Gender and Statistics

One of the most useful advanced statistics books written so far is *Using Multivariate Statistics* by Barbara Tabachnick and Linda Fidell (2007), two experimental psychologists at California State University at Northridge. These two met at a faculty luncheon soon after Tabachnick was hired. Fidell recalls that she had just finished a course on French and one on matrix algebra, for the pleasure of learning them ("I was very serious at the time"). She was wondering what to tackle next when Tabachnick suggested that Fidell join her in taking a belly dancing course. Fidell thought, "Something frivolous for a change." Little did she know.

Thus, their collaboration began. After the lessons, they had long discussions about statistics. In particular, the two found that they shared a fascination—and consternation—with the latest statistics made possible through all the new statistical packages for computers. The problem was making sense of the results.

Fidell described it this way:

I had this enormous data set to analyze, and out came lots of pretty numbers in nice neat little columns, but I was not sure what all of it meant, or even whether my data had violated any critical assumptions. I knew there were some, but I didn't know anything about them. That was in 1975. I had been trained at the University of Michigan; I knew statistics up through the analysis of variance. But none of us were taught the multivariate analysis of variance at that time. Then along came these statistical packages to do it. But how to comprehend them?

Both Fidell and Tabachnick had gone out and learned on their own, taking the necessary courses, reading, and asking others who knew the programs better, trying out what would happen if they did this with the data, what would happen if they did that. Now the two women asked each other, "Why must this be so hard? Were others reinventing this same wheel at the very same time?" They decided to put their wheel into a book.

"And so began years of conflict-free collaboration," reports Fidell. (That is something to compare to the feuds recounted in other boxes in this book.) The authors had no trouble finding a publisher, and the book, now in its fifth edition (Tabachnick & Fidell, 2007), has sold "nicely." (This despite the fact that their preferred titles—*Fatima and Scheherazade's Multivariate Statistics Book: A Thousand and One Variables; The Fuzzy Pink Statistics Book; Weight Loss Through Multivariate Statistics*—were overruled by the publisher. However, if you looked closely at the first edition's cover, you saw a belly dancer buried in the design.)

Fidell emphasizes that both she and Tabachnick consider themselves data analysts and teachers, not statistics developers or theorists; they have not invented methods, merely popularized them by making them more accessible. But they can name dozens of women who have risen to the fore as theoretical statisticians. In Fidell's opinion, statistics is a field in which women seem particularly to excel and feel comfortable. In teaching new students, the math-shy ones in particular, she finds that once she can "get them to relax," they often find that they thoroughly enjoy statistics. She tells them, "I intend to win you over. And if you will give me half a chance, I will do it."

Whatever the reason, statistics is a branch of mathematics that, according to Fidell, women often come to find "perfectly logical, perfectly reasonable—and then, with time, something they can truly enjoy." That should be good news to many of you.

Source: Personal interview with Linda Fidell.

Partial Correlation

Partial correlation is widely used in personality, social, developmental, clinical, and various applied areas of psychology. Partial correlation is the amount of association between two variables, over and above the influence of one or more other variables. Suppose a researcher wants to know how the stress people experience in married life is related to how long they have been married. However, the researcher realizes that part of what might make marital stress and marriage length go together is whether couples have children. Having children or not could make stress and length go together, because those married longer are more likely to have children and having children may create marital stress. Thus, simply figuring the correlation between marital stress and marriage length would be misleading. The researcher wants to know what the relation between stress and marriage length would be if everyone had the same number of children. Or, to put it another way, the researcher wants somehow to subtract out the influence of number of children from the relation between marital stress and length.

In this example, the researcher would figure a partial correlation between marital stress and length of marriage, **partialing out** the number of children. Partialing out a variable is also called *holding constant, controlling for,* or *adjusting for* the variable held constant (such as number of children). These terms (partialing out, holding

partial correlation   the amount of association between two variables, over and above the influence of one or more other variables.

partialing out   removing the influence of a variable from the association between other variables.

constant, etc.) all mean the same thing and are used interchangeably. The actual statistic for partial correlation is called the **partial correlation coefficient.** Like an ordinary correlation coefficient, it goes from −1 to +1. Just remember that, unlike an ordinary correlation, one or more variables is being controlled for.

Here is another way to understand partial correlations. In the marriage example, you could figure the ordinary correlation between stress and marriage length using only people who have no children, then figure an ordinary correlation between stress and marriage length for only those with one child, and so on. Each of these correlations, by itself, is not affected by differences in the number of children (because the people included in any one of these correlations all have the same number of children). You could then figure a kind of average of these various correlations, each of which is not affected by number of children. This average of these correlations is the partial correlation. It is literally a correlation that *holds constant* the number of children. (The figuring for a partial correlation is fairly straightforward, and you do not actually have to figure all these individual correlations and average them. However, the result amounts to doing this.)

Here is an example from an actual study. Joiner and colleagues (2005) introduced their study as follows:

> Past suicidal behavior is related to future suicidal behavior. But is the relation meaningful (i.e., nonspurious), perhaps even causal, or is it fully accounted for by a set of third variables, such as enduring predispositions or various clinical conditions (e.g., mood disorders)? A full understanding of suicidal behavior hinges on this question. (p. 291)

The participants were 297 young adults who took part in a study testing the effectiveness of a treatment for suicidal individuals. Here is part of the results section of the research article:

> Controlling for age, gender, marital status, and ethnicity, family history of suicide, depression, bipolar disorder, and alcohol abuse, personal history of legal troubles as an adult and as a juvenile, current and past diagnoses of depression and bipolar disorder, and scores on indices of depression hopelessness, and problem-solving difficulties, borderline personality symptoms, drug dependence symptoms, alcohol dependence symptoms, and negative life events, the correlation between lifetime history of suicide attempts and…suicide scores [current suicidal symptoms] went from .24 to .20 ($ps <$ .05). (p. 294)

This study is an example of how researchers often use partial correlation to help sort out alternative explanations for the relations among variables. In this example, the correlation between past suicide attempts and current suicidal symptoms held up, even after controlling for many other variables that might explain the correlation. This result is reflected in the title of the research study: "Four Studies on How Past and Current Suicidality Relate Even When 'Everything But the Kitchen Sink' Is Covaried." As another example, if a correlation between marital stress and marital length holds up, even after controlling for the number of children, an alternative explanation about children is made unlikely.

partial correlation coefficient measure of the degree of correlation between two variables, over and above the influence of one or more other variables.

reliability degree of consistency or stability of a measure.

Reliability

The kinds of measures used in psychology research, such as questionnaires, systematic observation of behavior, physiological changes, and the like, are rarely perfectly consistent or stable over time. (We discussed this briefly in Chapter 11.) The degree of consistency or stability of a measure is called its **reliability.** Roughly speaking, the reliability of a measure is how much you would get the same result if you were to give the same measure again to the same person under the same circumstances. You will very often see reliability statistics in psychology research articles.

One way to assess a measure's reliability is to use the measure with the same group of people twice. The correlation between the two testings is called **test-retest reliability.** However, this approach often is not practical or appropriate. For example, you can't use this approach if taking a test once would influence the second taking (such as with an intelligence test).

For many measures, such as most questionnaires, you can also assess their reliability by correlating the average of the answers to half the questions with the average of the answers to the other half. For example, you could correlate the average score on all the odd-numbered questions with the average score on all the even-numbered questions. If the person is answering consistently, this should be a high correlation. This is called **split-half reliability.**

A problem with the split-half method is deciding which way to split the halves. Using odd-versus-even items makes sense in most situations, but by chance it could give too low or too high a correlation. Fortunately, there is a more general solution. You can divide the measure into halves in all possible ways and figure the correlation using each division, then average all these split-half correlations. A statistic called **Cronbach's alpha (α),** the most widely used measure of reliability, gives you what amounts to this average. Cronbach's alpha also can be thought of as telling you the overall internal consistency of the measure, how much high responses go with highs and lows with lows over all the items in the measure. Thus, Cronbach's alpha is a measure of what is called the **internal consistency reliability** of a measure: the extent to which the items of a measure assess a common characteristic. In general, in psychology, a good measure should have a Cronbach's alpha of at least .60 and preferably closer to .90.

Finally, in some research, the main measures are observations of behavior or coding of material written or spoken by participants. In these situations, there are often two or more raters of each participant's behavior or material, so that reliability is the similarity of the ratings between raters. This is called **interrater reliability.** (It is also called *interjudge reliability, interrater agreement, or interjudge agreement.*)

Reliabilities are nearly always discussed when a research article is mainly about the creation of a new measure. For example, Valk and colleagues (2001) developed a measure of disability in elderly nursing home residents. The test, which is filled out by staff about residents, initially included 26 items that assessed seven domains of functioning, such as Mobility (sample item, "Is the resident able to walk?") and Alertness (sample item, "Does the resident react if somebody speaks to him/her?"). They tested out their measure with 115 poorly functioning residents of Dutch nursing homes, with an average age of 81.5. For 111 of the residents, ratings were made by two different raters. All residents were assessed a second time a week later. Here is the reliability discussion from their results section:

> The associations of times with a domain, as measured by means of Cronbach's alpha, were obtained on each of the scales (lowest: Perception 0.54; highest: Mobility, 0.93). Table [15–3] presents the mean scores, *SD*, median, and Cronbach's alpha of the domains. The test-retest reliability was good to excellent; see Table [15–4]. Correlation coefficients ranged from 0.63 to 0.94. Interrater reliability for the scales Cognition, Incontinence, Mobility, and ADL was high (0.79 to 0.93), and moderate for Resistance to Nursing Assistance (0.51). Perception showed very low interrater reliability 0.33 (see Table [15–5]). (p. 188)

test-retest reliability one index of a measure's reliability, obtained by giving the test to a group of people twice; correlation between scores from the two testings.

split-half reliability one index of a measure's reliability, based on a correlation of the scores of items from the two halves of the test.

Cronbach's alpha (α) widely used measure of a test's *internal consistency reliability* that reflects the average of the split-half correlations from all possible splits into halves of the items on the test.

internal consistency reliability extent to which the items of a measure assess a common characteristic; usually measured using *Cronbach's alpha.*

interrater reliability similarity of ratings by two or more raters of each participant's behavior or material.

Table 15-3 Domains: Means, Standard Deviations, Cronbach's Alpha, and Range

Scale	n	Items	Mean	Median	SD	Cronbach's Alpha	Range
Incontinence	112	4	70.1	81.2	32.5	.88	0–8
Mobility	112	3	48.6	40	35.8	.93	0–10
Resistance	111	1	53.1	66.6	41.0	—	0–3
Alertness	111	6	30.8	27.7	22.0	.84	0–18
Cognition	112	7	69.3	72.7	28.9	.78	0–11
ADL	96	3	75.9	87.5	31.4	.90	0–8
Perception	88	2	.30	0	0.65	.54	0–4

Source: Valk, M., Post, M. W. M., Cools, H. J. M., & Shrijvers, G. A. J. P. (2001). Measuring disability in nursing home residents; Validity and reliability of a newly developed instrument. *Journal of Gerontology: Psychological Sciences, 56B,* 187–191. Copyright © The Gerontological Society of America. Reproduced by permission of the publisher.

Table 15-4 Reproducibility of the Questionnaire: After One Week

Scale	Correlation
Cognition	0.89
Mobility	0.94
ADL	0.90
Alertness	0.85
Incontinence	0.89
Resistance	0.63
Perception	0.76

Note: Spearman correlation coefficients, $p < .001$. *Source:* Valk, M., Post, M. W. M., Cools, H. J. M., & Shrijvers, G. A. J. P. (2001). Measuring disability in nursing home residents: Validity and reliability of a newly developed instrument. *Journal of Gerontology: Psychological Sciences, 56B,* 187–191. Copyright © The Gerontological Society of America. Reproduced by permission of the publisher.

Table 15-5 Interrater Reliability of the Questionnaire

Scale	Correlation
Cognition	0.79
Mobility	0.93
ADL	0.80
Alertness	0.71
Incontinence	0.88
Resistance	0.51
Perception	0.33

Note: Spearman correlation coefficients, $p < .001$. *Source:* Valk, M., Post, M. W. M., Cools, H. J. M., & Shrijvers, G. A. J. P. (2001). Measuring disability in nursing home residents: Validity and reliability of a newly developed instrument. *Journal of Gerontology: Psychological Sciences, 56B,* 187–191. Copyright © The Gerontological Society of America. Reproduced by permission of the publisher.

Looking at the tables, you can see, for example, that Alertness, with six items, has a Cronbach's alpha of .84, a test-retest reliability (labeled "Reproducibility of the Questionnaire: After One Week") of .85, and an interrater reliability of .71. This is thus a quite adequately reliable scale. On the other hand, consider Perception, which had two items. Here the reliabilities were .54, .76, and .33. Thus, the researchers dropped this domain (and its two items) from the scale, making the final scale 24 items assessing six domains. (Incidentally, you may have noticed from the notes at the bottom of the tables that the test-retest and interrater reliability were figured using the Spearman correlation. This is the rank-order correlation method we discussed in Chapter 11. Valk and colleagues used this kind of correlation because the items used rank-order measurement. Ordinarily, however, these kinds of reliabilities are figured using ordinary correlation coefficients.)

Multilevel Modeling

Regression (and correlation), whether bivariate or multiple, is about situations in which the individuals are not grouped in any particular way. However, the situation is more complicated when the participants in a study are grouped in some way. For example, suppose you are interested in how much the number of hours one spends studying for a statistics final exam predicts one's score on the exam. And suppose you have surveyed students in a dozen different statistics classes about their time studying for the final and found out the final exam score for each student. The problem is that things could be quite different in different courses. For example, in one course, the final exam might be the only test in the course; so, to get a good score, you would need to do many, many hours of studying. But in another course, there might have been many small tests and the final is not even cumulative but only on the last part of the course. In that class, many fewer hours of studying might lead to a good score. Also, different instructors might score the test more strictly or more leniently and might have very different difficulties of tests. Thus, if you were to run a regression using all the students and ignoring what class they were in, you might get a very misleading result. Too much mixing of apples and oranges.

An alternative solution would be to carry out the regression separately for each of the dozen courses (in each course, find the regression coefficient for hours studying predicting exam score), then average the regression coefficients across the different courses. This method would be much more accurate. (What you are doing here is like a partial correlation in which you are correlating the two lower-level variables, partialing out which group they are in.) In fact, with this method, you could even go further. You could see whether something like the experience of the teacher predicted test scores. Thus, you could run a regression analysis across the 12 classrooms to see if instructors' experience predicted average test scores in their classes. (That is, you would do a regression for the 12 classrooms with teacher experience as the predictor variable and each course's average test score as the criterion variable.)

The kind of analysis we just described is called **multilevel modeling.** The multiple levels in this case are a *lower level* (or *micro-level* or *level* 1), which is the individual students, and an *upper level* (or *macro level* or *level* 2), which is the course. Thus, the **lower-level variables** in the preceding example are study time and final test score. These lower-level variables are the variables for the people *within* each grouping. In this example there is also an **upper-level variable,** teacher experience. Upper-level variables are ones that are about the *grouping as a whole* (in this example, each course had many students, but just one instructor per course).

What used to be the standard procedure for a multilevel modeling situation (a research situation in which people are grouped in some way that could affect the pattern of scores) was what we described above: First, figure a regression in each grouping, then average the results across the groupings. Second, if there are upper-level variables (group level variables, like instructor's experience), do a further regression at the grouping level in which you predict from the upper-level variable, the average of each group's score on the criterion variable. This specific fairly straightforward analysis procedure (called *slopes as outcomes*), which used to be standard, has been replaced today by more sophisticated methods.

The more sophisticated methods take all the information at once, at all levels, and figure a slightly more accurate result. Even more important in practice than the added accuracy, these more recent sophisticated methods are also able to handle more complex research situations. Indeed, the existence of these new methods, along with the availability of user-friendly programs to carry them out, has led to a huge number of studies in recent years that could be analyzed only with multilevel modeling.

These new methods are widely used and have various names. The most common name is probably **hierarchical linear modeling (HLM),** after a widely used multilevel modeling computer program. Another common name is *random coefficients modeling* (a term having to do with technical aspects of how this procedure works).

These newer methods also use many special terms and symbols. However, you can understand the basic idea of the results of most studies using multilevel modeling by thinking about them using the logic of the old-fashioned, standard approach. That is, to make sense of a lower-level result using these more sophisticated methods, just think in terms of doing a regression analysis in each group and averaging those results. To make sense of a result involving an upper-level variable, think in terms of doing a regression using the upper-level variable to predict the average score in each grouping on the criterion variable.

Here is an example: Hutchison and Gibler (2007) used multilevel modeling to examine questions about political tolerance based on a worldwide survey of 17,977 respondents across 33 countries. Specifically, they were interested in whether various factors predicted political tolerance. In this survey, to measure political tolerance, the survey would "first ask respondents to select their least-liked group from a list of unpopular groups, and then ask . . . whether the respondent thinks the group should be allowed to publicly demonstrate [or] hold political office" (p. 133). There were two kinds of factors the researchers thought might predict tolerance. One kind of factor was the individual respondent's values and attitudes. Notice that both the criterion variable (political tolerance) and these predictor variables (individuals' values and attitudes) are

multilevel modeling   advanced type of regression analysis that handles a research situation in which people are grouped in some way that could affect the pattern of scores.

lower-level variable   in multilevel modeling, a variable that is about people *within* each grouping.

upper-level variable   in multilevel modeling, a variable that is about the grouping as a whole.

hierarchical linear modeling (HLM) sophisticated type of multilevel modeling that handles a research situation in which people are grouped in some way that could affect the pattern of scores.

lower-level variables, measured at the individual level. The researchers were also interested, however, in the influence of the situation in different countries, such as whether a country was currently involved in various kinds of international disputes. The country-level variables are upper-level variables. That is, in this study, individuals are grouped by country, and country would clearly seem to matter in relation to the things being studied.

With regard to the lower-level predictors, Hutchison and Gibler (2007) wrote that "the results of our multilevel political tolerance models . . . [show that] individual-level predictors [of] . . . democratic ideals, free speech priority, democratic activism, and education are all strongly and positively associated with political tolerance, while conformity and age both tend to decrease tolerant responses" (p.136). They then go on to report that they next "add the macrolevel [upper-level] component . . . to estimate the effects of external threat on political tolerance" (p. 136). They then report "a strong, negative relationship between disputes over territory and political tolerance . . . and no significant relationship with nonterritorial disputes" (p. 136). In other words, people living in countries facing threats about borders are much more intolerant than those in other countries. However, those living in countries facing other kinds of international disputes are not particularly more likely to be politically intolerant.[2]

Factor Analysis

Suppose you have measured a group of people on a large number of variables. (For example, you might have done a survey with questions about many different attitudes.) You use **factor analysis** to tell you which variables tend to clump together—which ones tend to be correlated with each other and not with other variables. Each such clump (group of variables) is called a **factor.** The correlation of an individual variable with a factor is called that variable's **factor loading** on that factor. Variables have loadings on each factor but usually have high loadings on only one. Factor loadings range from -1, a perfect negative correlation with the factor, through 0, no relation to the factor, to $+1$, a perfect positive correlation with the factor. Normally, psychology researchers consider a variable to contribute meaningfully to a factor only if it has a loading at least above .30 (or below $-.30$).

The factor analysis is done by computer based on a fairly complex set of formulas that begin with the correlations among all the variables and end up with a set of factor loadings. (It also provides other information, including how much each factor accounts for of the total amount of variation among the variables.) There are, in fact, several somewhat different approaches to factor analysis. Thus, the researcher has some leeway and can select from a variety of methods, each of which may give slightly different results.

However, the most subjective part of the process is the name the researcher gives to a factor. When reading about a factor analysis in a research article, think closely about the name the researcher gives to each factor. Do the names really do a good job of describing the variables that make up the factor?

Here is an example of a factor analysis from organizational psychology. Koslowsky and colleagues (2001) gave 232 nurses in Israeli hospitals the following instructions:

> Think about a time when you were being supervised in doing some task. Suppose your supervisor asked you to do your job somewhat differently and, though you were initially reluctant, you did exactly what you were asked.
>
> On the following pages there are a number of reasons why you might have done so. . . . Decide how likely it would be that you complied for this reason. (p. 461)

factor analysis statistical procedure applied in situations where many variables are measured and that identifies groups of variables that tend to be correlated with each other and not with other variables.

factor in factor analysis, group of variables that tend to correlate with each other and not with other variables.

factor loading in factor analysis, correlation of a variable with a factor.

Table 15-6 Factor Analysis Loadings for the Eleven Power Sources

Power Sources by Factor	Loadings	
	Factor 1	Factor 2
Harsh power bases		
Impersonal coercion	0.81	−0.17
Impersonal reward	0.80	0.05
Personal reward	0.78	0.31
Legitimate reciprocity	0.71	0.26
Personal coercion	0.66	0.32
Legitimate equity	0.61	0.17
Legitimate position	0.53	0.45
Soft power tactics		
Expertise	0.16	0.78
Information	−0.17	0.76
Reference	0.34	0.70
Legitimate dependence	0.36	0.56
Explained variance (%)	41.9	15.5
Internal consistency (alpha)	0.85	0.79

Source: Koslowsky, M., Schwarzwald, J., & Ashuri, S. (2001). On the relationship between subordinates' compliance to power sources and organizational attitudes. *Applied Psychology: An International Review, 50,* 455–476. Copyright © 2001 by Blackwell Publishing. Reprinted by permission of Blackwell Publishers Journals.

The nurses responded on a 7-point scale from 1, "definitely not a reason," to 7, "definitely a reason," to items relating to 11 power sources, such as coercion or providing information. As part of their study, the researchers carried out a factor analysis of the 11 power sources. They reported the following results: "The analysis yielded a two-factor solution [see Table 15–6]. The first factor, which explained 41.9 percent of the variance, included seven power sources [see Table 15–6].... The second factor, which explained 15.5 percent of the variance, included four power bases [see Table 15–6]" (pp. 465–466).

For example, Impersonal Coercion was included in the first factor because it had a high loading (.81) on this factor, but only a small loading (–.17) on the second factor. Expertise, on the other hand, was included in the second factor because it had a high loading on this factor (.78) but only a small loading (.16) on the first factor. Notice, however, that some items were not so clearly part of one factor or the other, such as Legitimate Position, which had a loading of .53 on the first factor and .45 on the second. This makes sense, since having a legitimate right to use power is somewhere between the harshness of such things as coercion and the softness of persuading by providing information. Also notice that the names the researchers chose to give to the factors seem reasonable in light of the variables included in them, though it is always possible that other researchers might see the variables in each factor as having a different overall meaning. Finally, notice that at the bottom of the table they also give the internal consistency (alpha), by which they mean Cronbach's alpha for the items in each factor (that is, the ones with high loadings on a factor) if you were to think of them as a scale. (In fact, based on this factor analysis, the researchers went on to use the items in the two factors as two scales, which they then related to other variables such as the nurse's job satisfaction.)

How are you doing?

1. (a) What is partial correlation? (b) What does it mean if a partial correlation is less than the original correlation? (c) What does it mean if a partial correlation is about the same as the original correlation? (d) How can partial correlation help sort out direction of causality in a correlational study?

2. (a) What is the reliability of a measure? (b), (c), and (d) List and define three kinds of reliability. (e) How does Cronbach's alpha relate to split-half reliability?

3. In the Valk and colleagues (2001) example of reliability (see Tables 15–3, 15–4, and 15–5), (a) indicate which is the most reliable scale, and (b), (c), and (d) give its reliabilities.

4. Under what conditions would you use multilevel modeling?

5. An organizational psychologist conducts a study of sales people in 38 department stores (with about 150 salespeople per store and with the stores varying from "big box" discount stores to exclusive high-end stores). The researcher plans to conduct a multilevel modeling analysis to find out whether length of time working at a store predicts job satisfaction, and also whether people working at stores with more prestige are more satisfied. (a) What are the lower-level variables? (b) What is the upper-level variable? (c) and (d) Describe the two steps you would use to carry out the analysis using the old-fashioned standard method.

6. (a) When do you use a factor analysis? (b) What information does it give you? (c) What is a factor? (d) What is a factor loading? (e) What is the most subjective part of factor analysis?

7. In the Koslowsky and colleagues (2001) example of factor analysis (see Table 15–6), what are personal reward's loadings on each factor?

7. The personal rewards loadings are .78 on the first factor and .31 on the second factor.

6. (a) You use a factor analysis when you have many measures of a group of people. (b) Factor analysis tells you the groupings of variables that are highly correlated with each other but not very correlated with variables in other groupings. (c) A factor is one of these groupings. (d) Factor loading is the correlation of a variable with a factor. (e) The most subjective part of factor analysis is deciding what to name a factor based on the variables with high loadings on it.

5. (a) The lower-level variables are length of time working in the store and job satisfaction. (b) The upper-level variable is the prestige of the store. (c) Figure a regression, among the employees at each store, in which you predict job satisfaction from length of time working in the store, then average the regression coefficients. (d) Figure a regression, across the 38 stores, predicting a store's average level of job satisfaction from the store's prestige.

4. You would use multilevel modeling when the scores of people tested are grouped in some way that would affect results.

3. (a) Mobility; (b) internal consistency reliability (Cronbach's alpha) = .93; (c) test-retest reliability (Spearman's correlation coefficient) = .94; (d) interrater reliability (Spearman's correlation coefficient) = .93.

(c) Internal consistency reliability, which is how much the different parts of the measure give similar results. (d) Interrater reliability, which is how much different raters give the same results. (e) Cronbach's alpha is like the average of the correlations between all possible pairs of halves of the measure.

Causal Modeling

As with factor analysis, you use causal modeling when you have measured people on a number of variables. Unlike factor analysis, the goal of causal modeling is to test whether the pattern of correlations among the variables in a sample fits with some specific theory about which variables are causing which.

Causal modeling methods are widely used in psychology. We first introduce the older (but still common) method of *path analysis,* often called ordinary path analy- sis. We then describe a specific type of path analysis called *mediational analysis.* Fi- nally, we describe an elaborate method of causal modeling, called *structural equation modeling* (which is also a kind of path analysis).

Path Analysis

In **path analysis,** you make a diagram with arrows connecting the variables. Each arrow, or **path,** shows what the researcher predicts to be the cause-and-effect con- nections between variables. Then, based on the correlations of these variables in a sample and the path diagram predicted by the researcher, you can figure path coeffi- cients for each path. The **path coefficient** is like a standardized regression coefficient (β) in multiple regression. In fact, if the path diagram is a correct description of the causal relationship among the variables, the path coefficient tells you how much of a standard deviation change on the variable at the end of the arrow is produced by a one standard deviation change in the predictor variable at the start of the arrow. (Also note that a path coefficient is like a partial correlation in that it is figured so that it partials out the influence of any other variables that have arrows to the variable at the end of the same arrow.)

Here is an example. Williamson and her colleagues (2001) studied 98 wives and 44 husbands who were caring for an elderly spouse living at home who was impaired in some way, such as with Alzheimer's disease. The research was testing a theory about what causes and what averts potentially harmful behavior by the caregiver to- ward the partner. Figure 15–2 shows their predicted pattern of cause-and-effect rela- tionships (along with the path coefficients figured from their results) among these different variables. For example, the arrows in the path diagram tell you that Caregiver Age is predicted to affect ADL (activities of daily living), which in turn is not predicted to affect any other variables in the model (that is, there are no arrows from ADL to other variables). However, Caregiver Age is also predicted to affect the degree of Care Recipient Dementia, which is one of the predicted causes of Current Relationship

path analysis   method of analyzing the correlations among a group of variables in terms of a predicted pattern of causal relations; usually the predicted pattern is diagrammed as a pattern of arrows from causes to effects.

path   an arrow in a path analysis or structural equation model that shows what the researcher predicts to be the cause-and-effect connections between variables.

path coefficient   degree of relation as- sociated with an arrow in a path analysis (including in structural equation model- ing); same as a standardized regression coefficient from a multiple regression prediction rule in which the variable at the end of the arrow is the criterion vari- able and the variable at the start of the arrow is the predictor, along with all the other variables that have arrows leading to that criterion variable.

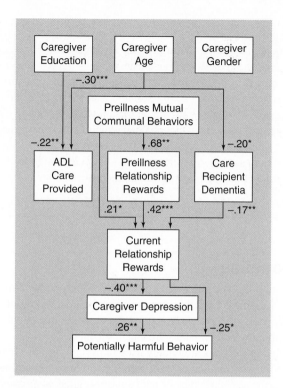

Figure 15–2 Significant pathways emerging in path analyses predicting potentially harmful caregiver behavior. ADL = activities of daily living.

*$p < .05$, **$p < .01$, ***$p < .001$.

Source: Williamson, G. M., Shaffer, D. R., & The Family Relationships in Late Life Project (2001). Relationships quality and potentially harmful behaviors by spousal caregivers: How we were then, how we are now. *Psychology and Aging, 16,* 217–226. Published by the American Psychological Association. Reprinted with permission.

Rewards, which in turn is predicted to affect Potentially Harmful Behavior in two ways: (1) indirectly through Caregiver Depression—high levels of rewards leading to less depression, which then reduces the likelihood of Potentially Harmful Behavior— and (2) directly, with high levels of rewards directly reducing the likelihood of Potentially Harmful Behavior. This path diagram lays out predictions based on a rich and complex theory.

Based on the correlations among these variables in their sample of caregivers, the path coefficients show the direction and degree of the predicted effects. The asterisks show the level of significance for a path. As is often done in ordinary path analyses, the researchers actually tested other possible paths, but included in the diagram only paths that were significant. (Thus, all paths in the model have at least one asterisk.)

Mediational Analysis

mediational analysis particular type of path analysis that tests whether a presumed causal relationship between two variables is due to some particular intervening variable (called a mediator variable).

As you will see shortly, path analysis as we have just described it ("ordinary path analysis") has largely given way to a more elaborate version, called structural equation modeling. However, there is one contemporary application of ordinary path analysis that is very widely used in psychology, **mediational analysis.** Mediational analysis is a procedure that you use to examine whether a presumed causal relationship between two variables, say, X and Y, is due to some particular intervening variable, which we will call M.

(*M* stands for *mediator variable,* which is another name for an intervening variable, a variable that explains the presumed causal relationship between two other variables.)

For example, imagine that a researcher shows that, when a woman is reminded of being a woman when taking a math test, she does worse and that this is because being reminded of being a woman when taking a math test makes her aware of the stereotype that women do worse in math (and thus she gets tense and does poorly). In this example, we are considering being reminded one is a woman as *X* (the cause), performance on the math test as *Y* (the effect), and salience of the stereotype that women do poorly in math as *M* (the mediator, variable). Figure 15–3 shows this predicted pattern as a path analysis. That is, the logic is that *M* is part of a causal path from *X* to *Y*, it "mediates" the effect of *X* on *Y*. In scientific research it is extremely important to identify underlying causes; so mediational analysis has become very widely used.

BOX 15–2 The Golden Age of Statistics: Four Guys Around London

The four most common statistical techniques were created by four Englishmen born within 68 years of each other, three of whom worked in the vicinity of London. (The fourth, Gosset, stuck at his brewery in Dublin, nevertheless visited London to study and kept in good touch with all that was happening in that city.) Clearly, their closeness and communication were important for creating the "critical mass" of minds sometimes associated with a golden age of discovery.

As is often the case with important discoveries, each man faced difficult practical problems or "anomalies" that pushed him to the solution at which he arrived—none simply set out to invent a statistical method in itself. Galton (Chapter 11, Box 11–1) was interested in the characteristics of parents and children, and Pearson (Chapter 13, Box 13–1) in measuring the fit between a set of observations and a theoretical curve. Gosset's (Chapter 7, Box 7–1) problem was small samples caused by the economics of the brewery industry, and Fisher (Chapter 9, Box 9–1) was studying the effects of manure on potatoes. (Age was not a factor—the age when these four made their major contributions ranged from 31 to 66.)

There were also three important social factors specific to this "golden age of statistics." First, there was biometrics, which was attempting to test the theory of evolution mathematically. Biometrics had its influence through Galton's reading of Darwin and Galton's subsequent influence on Pearson. Second, this period saw the beginning of mass hiring by industry and agriculture of university graduates with advanced mathematical training. Third, since the time of Newton, Cambridge University had been a special, centralized source of brilliant mathematicians for England. They could spread out through British industry and still, through their common alma mater, remain in contact with students and with each other and be conversant with the most recent breakthroughs.

Source: Tankard (1984).

Sir Francis Galton
(Corbis/Bettmann)

Sir Ronald Fisher
(Courtesy of the Library of Congress)

Karl Pearson
(Topham/The Image Works)

William S. Gosset
(The Granger Collection)

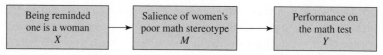

Figure 15-3 Path analysis diagram showing a hypothesized mediational relationship (variable *M* mediating the effect of variable *X* on variable *Y*).

Mediational analysis was introduced to most psychologists over 20 years ago in a famous paper by Robert Baron and David Kenny (1986). In that paper they spelled out four steps for establishing mediation:

Step 1: Show that *X* significantly predicts *Y*. If *X* does not predict *Y*, then it is unlikely *X* is a cause of *Y*. Thus, there would be no causal relationship to mediate.

Step 2: Show that *X* significantly predicts *M*. If *X* does not predict *M*, then it is unlikely *X* is a cause of *M*. Thus, *M* could not be part of a causal path from *X* to *Y*.

Step 3: Show that *M* predicts *Y* in the context of a multiple regression in which *X* is also included as a predictor. It is important that *M* predicts *Y*, or *M* cannot be part of a causal path from *X* to *Y*. It is important to include *X* as a predictor so we can be sure that the association of *M* and *Y* is not due to their being both caused by *X* (but not causing each other).

Step 4: Show that, when *M* is included as a predictor of *Y* (along with *X*), *X* no longer predicts *Y*. That is, there is no unique prediction of *X* to *Y* when *M* is taken into account; the original significant prediction drops to nonsignificance when *M* is included. Such a result is said to be consistent with *M* "fully mediating" the effect of *X* on *Y*. Whether or not there is significant mediation is usually tested with a procedure called *Sobel's test*. If the original significant prediction by *X* remains significant, but is weaker (as shown by a drop in its standardized regression coefficient) when *M* is included as a predictor of *Y*, this result is usually described as *M* "partially mediating" the effect of *X* on *Y*. This means that *M* explains some, but not all, of the effect of *X* on *Y*. [Some researchers are also beginning to use computer-intensive methods (see Chapter 14) to test the statistical significance of mediation (Shrout & Bolger, 2002).]

Here is an example. Fraley and Aron (2004) conducted an experiment in which pairs of strangers met under conditions in which they were doing something either humorous or not very humorous and found that those in the humor condition felt much closer to their partners afterward. Fraley and Aron, however, also wanted to show that this result was mediated in part by the humor distracting people from the discomfort of the initial meeting of a stranger. Thus they included a measure of distraction from discomfort in their study and conducted a mediational analysis. It is typical in mediation analysis for a research article to describe the analysis logic in some detail. Here is what Fraley and Aron wrote:

> The tests of . . . the mediation hypotheses . . . followed the logic outlined by Baron and Kenny (1986). That is, first we tested for whether the preconditions for mediation were satisfied: (a) that the overall effect of the distal cause (humor of the interaction) on the dependent [criterion] variable (closeness) was significant and (b) that the overall effect of the distal cause (humor) on the hypothesized mediator was significant. Next we tested the mediation by examining a regression equation predicting the dependent [criterion] variable (closeness) from both the distal cause (humor) and the mediator. In this analysis, partial mediation was considered as supported if (c) the mediator maintained a significant unique link with the dependent variable (closeness) but (d) the unique effect of the distal cause (humor) on the dependent

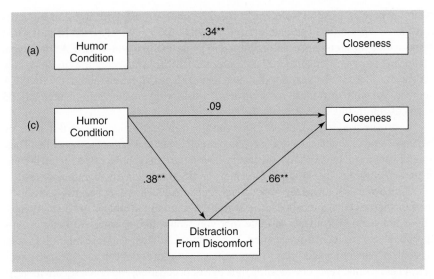

Figure 15–4   Results supporting hypothesized mediations of effect of a shared humorous experience on closeness. Shown are path diagrams with standardized path coefficients for (a) the model for the overall (unmediated) effect of humor condition on closeness, followed by models including hypothesized mediators of . . . (c) distraction from discomfort. . . . Mediation is supported . . . by the significant paths to and from the mediator and also by the reduction to nonsignificance of the humor-closeness association . . . as compared to the unmediated model a. (Sobel tests supporting this interpretation are given in the text.)

Note: **p < .01.

Source: Fraley, B., & Aron, A. (2004). The effect of a shared humorous experience on closeness in initial encounters. *Personal Relationships, 11,* 61–78. Copyright © 2004 by Blackwell Publishing. Reprinted by permission of Blackwell Publishers Journals.

variable (closeness) was reduced. Finally (e), the mediation should be significant using Sobel's test. (2004, p. 70)

Here is how they described their results:

> *The basic effect is . . . mediated by distraction from the discomfort of the initial encounter.* This hypothesis was supported. As shown in Figure [15–4] (compare model a to model c), including this variable in the regression equation reduced the beta for the experimental manipulation's effect on closeness from .34 to .09; $Z = 2.52$, $p < .01$. (2004, pp. 70–71)

Note that figures of mediational analysis, such as Figure 15–4, show the variables in a triangle arrangement in order to show the change in the relationship between the X and Y variables after taking into account the M (mediator) variable. On a conceptual level, however, these figures show the same type of relationship as the mediational path analysis shown in Figure 15–3.

Structural Equation Modeling

Structural equation modeling is a special elaboration of ordinary path analysis. It also involves a path diagram with arrows between variables and path coefficients for each arrow. However, structural equation modeling has several important advantages over the older path analysis method. One major advantage is that structural equation modeling gives you an overall measure of the fit, called a **fit index,** between the theory (as described by the path diagram) and the correlations among the scores in your

structural equation modeling sophisticated version of path analysis that includes paths with latent, unmeasured, theoretical variables and that also permits a kind of significance test and provides measures of the overall fit of the data to the hypothesized causal pattern.

fit index   in structural equation modeling, measure of how well the pattern of correlations in a sample corresponds to the correlations that would be expected based on the hypothesized pattern of causes and effects among those variables; usually ranges from 0 to 1, with 1 being a perfect fit.

sample. There are several different fit indexes, but for most, a fit of .90 or higher is considered a good fit. (The maximum is usually 1.00.) A widely used fit index that works a little differently is usually referred to by its abbreviation, **RMSEA** (root mean square error of approximation). The *smaller* the RMSEA, the better the fit. Fits below .05 are considered to be very good; below about .10, good. (Even though the RMSEA numbers are similar to those for significance tests, with smaller being better and .05 a typical cutoff, this is really only a coincidence.)

In structural equation modeling, you can also do a kind of significance test of the fit. We say a "kind of significance test" because the null hypothesis is that the theory fits. Thus, a significant result tells you that the theory does *not* fit. In other words, a researcher trying to demonstrate a theory hopes for a nonsignificant result in this significance test!

A second major advantage of structural equation modeling over ordinary path analysis is that it uses what are called latent variables. A **latent variable** is not actually measured, but stands for a true variable that you would like to measure but can only approximate with real-life measures. For example, a latent variable might be social class, which the researcher tries to approximate with several measured variables, such as level of income, years of education, prestige of occupation, and home square footage. No one of these measured variables by itself is a very good stand-in for social class.

In structural equation modeling, the mathematics is set up so that a latent variable is a combination of the measured variables, combined in such a way as to use only what they have in common with each other. What they have in common is the true score, the underlying variable they are all getting at parts of. (A latent variable is actually like a factor in factor analysis, in that the factor is not directly measured itself, but it represents a combination of several variables that make it up.)

In a structural equation modeling path diagram, the variables that are measured are usually shown in boxes and the latent variables, in circles or ovals. This is shown in Figure 15–5. Notice in the figure that the arrows from the latent variables (the ones in circles) go to the measured variables (the ones in boxes). The idea is that the latent variable is the underlying cause of the measured variables, the measured variables being the best we can do to get at the true latent variable.

RMSEA widely used fit index in structural equation modeling; low values indicate a good fit.

latent variable in structural equation modeling, unmeasured variable assumed to be the underlying cause of several variables actually measured in the study.

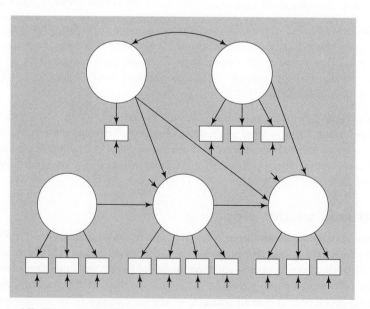

Figure 15–5 A structural equation model path diagram.

Also notice that all of the other arrows between variables are between latent variables. Structural equation modeling works in this way: the measured variables are used to make up latent variables, and the main focus of the analysis is on the causal relations (the paths) between the latent variables. (Notice, finally, the short arrows that seem to come from nowhere. These show that there is also error—other unmeasured causes—affecting the variable. These *error* or *disturbance* arrows are sometimes left out in published articles to keep the figure simple.)

An Example of Structural Equation Modeling

This example is from a study by Senecal and her colleagues (2001). They explain that

> The purpose of the present study was to propose and test a model of work-family conflict. . . . The model posits that positive interpersonal factors both at work (i.e., one's employer) and at home (e.g., one's spouse) influence work and family motivation. Moreover, the model proposes that low levels of self-determined family and work motivation both contributed to family alienation, which in turn influences the experience of work–family conflict. Finally, work–family conflict leads to feelings of emotional exhaustion. (p. 176)

The researchers measured the various variables in this model in a sample of 786 French Canadians who were all working at least part-time, were living with a relationship partner, and had at least one child.

Figure 15–6 shows the diagram of their model and the path coefficients. Notice that each latent variable (shown in ovals) has two to four measured variables associated with it. For example, Feeling Valued by One's Partner has three indicators (labeled V1, V2,

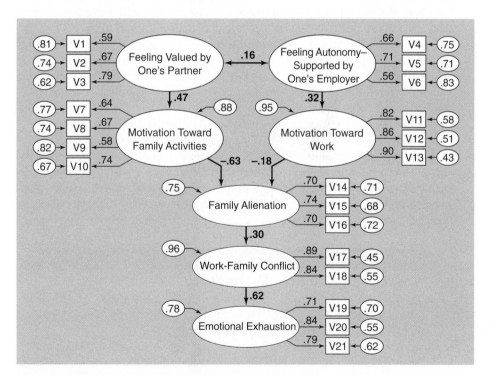

Figure 15–6 Results of the hypothesized model.

Source: Senecal, C., Vallerand, R. J., & Guay, F. (2001). Antecedents and outcomes of work-family conflict: Toward a motivational model. *Personality and Social Psychology Bulletin, 27*, 176–186. Copyright © 2001 by Sage Publications, Ltd. Reprinted by permission of Sage Publications, Thousands Oaks, London, and New Delhi.

and V3). The most important path coefficients are those between the latent variables. For example, Feeling Valued by One's Partner has a substantial path coefficient of .47 leading to Motivation Toward Family Activities. This means that, if the path model correctly shows the patterns of causality, a 1 standard deviation increase in Feeling Valued causes .47 of a standard deviation increase in Motivation Toward Family Activities.

Having laid out the model and figured the path coefficients, the authors then tested the fit of the correlations in their sample to the overall model: "The adequacy of the model was assessed by structural equation modeling . . ." (p. 181). In addition to looking at specific path coefficients, Senecal and colleagues (2001) considered the overall fit of their model, noting that all hypothesized paths had significant coefficients in the predicted direction and "the CFI = .94 and the NNFI = .93 [two fit indexes] were acceptable" (p. 182).

Some Limitations of Causal Modeling

It is important to realize how little magic there is behind these wonderful methods. They still rely entirely on a researcher's deep thinking. All the predicted paths in a path analysis diagram can be significant and a structural equation model can have an excellent fit, and yet it is still quite possible that other patterns of causality could work equally well or better.

Alternatives could have arrows that go in the opposite direction or make different connections, or the pattern could include additional variables not in the original diagram. Any kind of causal modeling shows at best that the correlations in the sample are consistent with the theory. The same correlations could also be consistent with quite different theories. Ideally, a researcher tries out reasonable alternative theories and finds that the correlations in the sample do not fit them well. Nevertheless, there can always be alternative theories the researcher did not think of to try.

In addition, causal modeling and all of the other techniques we have considered so far rely basically on correlations. Thus, they are all subject to the cautions we emphasized in Chapters 11 and 12. The most important caution is the one we just considered: correlation does not demonstrate direction of causality. Further, these techniques take only linear relationships directly into account. Finally, results are distorted (usually toward smaller path coefficients) if there is a restriction in range.

So don't be bowled over by the mathematical sophistication of a technique such as structural equation modeling. It is useful—sometimes wonderfully useful—but if you haven't used random assignment to groups, the direction of cause and effect cannot be determined beyond a reasonable doubt. If the underlying relationships are curvilinear, or if other limitations apply, such as restriction in range, the more sophisticated procedures are generally even more likely to give misleading results than simple bivariate correlations.

How are you doing?

1. What is the purpose of causal modeling?
2. (a) What is a path diagram? (b) What is a path? (c) What is a path coefficient? (d) In an ordinary path analysis, how do you evaluate whether there is a good fit of the model to the correlations in the sample?
3. (a) What is mediational analysis? (b) List the four steps for establishing mediation. (c) Explain the difference between a relationship that is fully mediated and one that is partially mediated.
4. (a) What is a fit index? (b) What is considered a good fit on most fit indexes? (c) What is considered a very good fit on the RMSEA?

5. (a) What is a latent variable? (b) What is its relation to measured variables? (c) What is the usual direction of causality between a latent variable and its associated measured variables? (d) Why?

6. (a) What is the meaning of a significance test of the overall fit in a structural equation model? (b) How is this different from an ordinary significance test?

7. What are two major limitations of structural equation modeling?

Answers

1. The purpose of causal modeling is to test whether the correlations in a sample are consistent with a predicted pattern of cause and effect among those variables (and also to figure the size of the relations among the variables given the predicted pattern and the correlations).

2. (a) A path diagram is a drawing of the predicted causal relationships among variables, showing causality as arrows from cause to effect. (b) A path is a predicted causal relation between two variables, shown as an arrow from the predicted cause to the predicted effect. (c) The path coefficient is the size of the causal influence based on the correlations among the variables in the sample and assuming the predicted relations in the path diagram are correct. Assuming the pattern of the path diagram is correct, it tells you the fraction of a standard deviation change in the effect variable produced by a 1 standard deviation change in the causal variable. (d) You check whether the path coefficients are all in the predicted direction and significant.

3. (a) Mediational analysis is a procedure that tests whether a presumed causal relationship between two variables is due to some intervening (or mediating) variable. (b) Step 1: Show that variable X significantly predicts variable Y. Step 2: Show that X significantly predicts variable M. Step 3: Show that M predicts Y in the context of a multiple regression in which X is also included as a predictor. Step 4: Show that, when M is included, along with X, as a predictor of Y, X no longer predicts Y. (c) The relationship between variable X and Y is fully mediated if a mediator variable M explains all of the effect of X on Y. The relationship is partially mediated if M explains some, but not all, of the effect of X on Y.

4. (a) A fit index is a number that tells you how well the predicted pattern of cause and effect in the path diagram is consistent with the correlations in the sample. (b) A good fit on most fit indexes is .90 or higher. (c) A very good fit on the RMSEA is below .05.

5. (a) A latent variable is a variable that is not directly measured, but that stands for the true value of the concept the variable is about. (b) A latent variable represents what a group of measured variables have in common. (c) The usual direction of causality between a latent variable and its associated measured variables is from latent variable to measured variables. (d) The underlying latent variable is the cause of the observed, measured variables.

6. (a) The significance test for the overall fit in a structural equation model is a test of the null hypothesis that the correlations in the sample are consistent with the predicted model shown in the path diagram. (b) A significant result means there is a bad fit.

7. First, no matter how good the fit, you can never know if there might be some other model that would fit equally well. Second, it is based on correlations and thus has all their limitations (such as not giving conclusive support for a particular direction of causality, being based entirely on linear relationships and being distorted by restriction in range).

Procedures That Compare Groups

So far in this chapter, we have looked at statistical procedures about associations among variables, essentially fancy elaborations of correlation and regression. Now we turn to procedures that focus on differences among group means, essentially fancy elaborations of the analysis of variance (Chapters 9 and 10).

In such procedures, there are two main kinds of variables. One is the kind that divides the groups from each other, such as experimental versus control group in a *t* test or the different groups in an analysis of variance (such as the Chapters 9 and 10 criminal record study example, which compared participants in the Criminal Record group, the Clean Record group, and the No Information group). A variable like this, especially when which group a person is in is based on the researcher's having randomly assigned participants to conditions, is called an **independent variable.** In a two-way factorial analysis of variance, there are actually two independent variables—for example, sensitivity (not high versus high) and test difficulty (easy versus hard) in the Aron and colleagues (2005) study we considered in Chapter 10.

The other kind of variable in a study that compares groups is the variable that is measured. In the criminal record example (from Chapter 9), it was ratings of innocence; in the Aron and colleagues (2005) study, it was individuals' reported level of negative mood. A variable like this, which is measured and represents the effect of the experimental procedure, is called a **dependent variable.** It is dependent in the sense that any participant's score on this variable depends on what happens in the experiment.

Note that an independent variable in a *t* test or analysis of variance is like a predictor variable in regression, and a dependent variable in a *t* test or analysis of variance is like the criterion variable in regression. Often, in fact, when discussing regression results, even in formal research articles, researchers use the independent–dependent variable terminology instead of the predictor–criterion variable terminology. But it is rare for researchers doing a *t* test or analysis of variance to use the predictor–criterion variable terminology.

We did not need to introduce these terms (*independent* and *dependent variables*) before because the situations we considered were relatively straightforward. However, it would be difficult to understand the remaining procedures covered in this chapter without knowing about the difference between them.

Analysis of Covariance (ANCOVA)

One of the most widely used elaborations of the analysis of variance is the **analysis of covariance (ANCOVA).** In this procedure, you do an ordinary analysis of variance, but one which adjusts the dependent variable for the effect of unwanted additional variables. The analysis of covariance does for the analysis of variance what partial correlation does for ordinary correlation. Each of the variables controlled for (or *"partialed out"* or *"held constant"*) is called a **covariate.** The rest of the results are interpreted like any other analysis of variance, with one main exception: when reporting results, instead of giving the means of each group, the researcher may give the **adjusted means,** the means of each group after adjusting (partialing out) the effect of the covariates.

Here is an example. Aron and colleagues (2000) had married couples come to their laboratory and participate in what they thought was an evaluation session in which they completed some questionnaires about the quality of their relationship, participated in a task together where they thought they were being observed for how they worked together during the task, and then completed some more questionnaires about their relationship. Actually, the first set of questionnaires was a pretest, the second set a posttest, and the task was experimentally manipulated so that some couples were randomly assigned to do a task together that was novel and physiologically arousing: they were tied

independent variable variable considered to be a cause, such as what group a person is in for a *t* test or analysis of variance.

dependent variable variable considered to be an effect; usually a measured variable.

analysis of covariance (ANCOVA) analysis of variance that controls for the effect of one or more additional variables.

covariate variable controlled for in an analysis of covariance.

adjusted mean mean of a group after adjusting for (partialing out) the effect of a covariate in analysis of covariance.

together at the wrist and ankles and then had to push a foam cylinder back and forth across a 30-foot gym mat, including going over a 3-foot barrier in the middle, without using their hands or teeth, trying to beat a time limit. Other couples were randomly assigned to do a more mundane task; they simply went back and forth across the mat.

Based on a theoretical model, the researchers predicted that "shared participation in the novel-arousing activities, compared with shared participation in mundane activities, increases experienced relationship quality" (p. 279). They then went on to describe their statistical analysis and results:

> To test this hypothesis, we conducted an analysis of covariance (ANCOVA) comparing the two experimental groups on couple average posttest experienced relationship quality with couple average pretest relationship quality (and relationship length) as a covariate.... [The hypothesis] was clearly supported, $F(1, 24) = 6.07$, $p < .05$, partial r [a measure of effect size] $= .45$. The adjusted means on the posttest experienced relationship quality index... were .30 for the novel-arousing-activity group and $-.35$ for the mundane-activity group. (pp. 279–280)

Notice that there were two covariates. First, the researchers wanted to look at change; so they compared posttest scores but adjusted them for pretest scores by making pretest scores a covariate. In addition, they wanted to be sure their results were not affected by differences in length of relationship; so they made length of relationship a second covariate. These are, in fact, the two main situations in which researchers use analysis of covariance. One is when they want to study change and they make the pretest measure a covariate. The other is when there are nuisance variables whose influence they want to hold constant.

Multivariate Analysis of Variance (MANOVA) and Multivariate Analysis of Covariance (MANCOVA)

In all of the procedures discussed so far in this book, there has been only one dependent variable. There may have been two or more independent variables, as in the factorial analysis of variance, but there has been only one dependent variable.

In this section we introduce **multivariate statistics,** which are procedures that can have more than one dependent variable. We will focus on the two most widely used multivariate procedures, multivariate versions of the analysis of variance and covariance.[3]

Multivariate analysis of variance (MANOVA) is an analysis of variance in which there is more than one dependent variable. Usually, the dependent variables are different measures of approximately the same thing, such as three different political involvement scales or two different reading ability tests. Suppose you study three groups and measure each participant on four dependent variables. The MANOVA would give an overall F and significance level for the difference among the three groups, in terms of how much they differ on the combination of the four dependent variables. The overall F is figured differently from an ordinary analysis of variance. In fact, there are several slightly different ways of figuring it, but the most common method is based on what is called *Wilk's lambda,* though you may also see other methods mentioned in computer outputs and research articles. However, it is still an F and it is interpreted in the same basic way; significance means you can reject the null hypothesis of no difference among groups in the population.

When you do find an overall significant difference among groups with MANOVA, this says that the groups differ on the combination of dependent variables. You then would want to know whether the groups differ on any or all of the dependent variables considered individually. Thus, you usually follow up a MANOVA with an ordinary analysis of variance for each of the dependent variables. These individual analyses of variance are called *univariate analyses of variance* (as opposed to the overall multivariate analysis), because each has only one dependent variable.

multivariate statistics statistical procedures involving more than one dependent variable.

multivariate analysis of variance (MANOVA) analysis of variance with more than one dependent variable.

An Example

Frydenberg and colleagues (2003) studied differences in how Australian, Colombian, German, and Palestinian adolescents cope with their problems. The researchers looked at three types of coping: "productive coping," which involves focusing on the problem; "nonproductive coping," which involves avoiding the problem; and "reference to others," in which a person asks other people for help. They described their results as follows:

> To consider the influence of Nationality on coping style, a MANOVA was completed using the 3 coping styles as dependent variables and Nationality as the independent variable.... The results show a significant multivariate effect for Nationality $(F(9, 1692) = 47.99; p < .001)$. (p. 63)

Having identified an overall difference in coping style among the adolescents from the different countries, the researchers then wanted to sort out effects on specific dependent variables. The results of the follow-up univariate ANOVAs indicated that: "All univariate tests were significant" (p. 63). For example, in one analysis, the researchers reported that ". . . Palestinians used this [productive coping] style more than did other students. Australian and Colombian subjects, while not differing in their mean use of this style, used it more than German subjects" (p. 63).

Multivariate Analysis of Covariance

An analysis of covariance in which there is more than one dependent variable is called a **multivariate analysis of covariance (MANCOVA).** The difference between it and an ordinary analysis of covariance is just like the difference between a MANOVA and an ordinary analysis of variance. Also, you can think of a MANCOVA as a MANOVA with covariates (variables adjusted for).

Overview of Statistical Techniques

Table 15–7 lays out the various procedures considered in this chapter, along with the other parametric procedures covered throughout the book. Just to prove to yourself how much you have learned, you might cover the right-hand column and play "Name That Statistic."

multivariate analysis of covariance (MANCOVA) analysis of covariance with more than one dependent variable.

Table 15-7 Major Statistical Techniques				
Association or Difference	**Number of Independent or Predictor Variables**	**Number of Dependent or Criterion Variables**	**Any Variables Controlled?**	**Name of Technique**
Association	1	1	No	Bivariate correlation/ regression
Association	Any number, grouped in some way	1	May be	Multilevel modeling
Association	1	1	Yes	Partial correlation
Association	Many, not differentiated		No	Reliability coefficients, Factor analysis
Association	Many, with specified causal patterns			Path analysis, Structural equation modeling
Difference	1	1	No	One-way ANOVA, *t* test
Difference	Any number	1	No	Factorial ANOVA
Difference	Any number	1	Yes	ANCOVA
Difference	Any number	Any number	No	MANOVA
Difference	Any number	Any number	Yes	MANCOVA

How are you doing?

1. In a *t* test or analysis of variance, (a) what is the independent variable, and (b) what is the dependent variable? (c) How do independent and dependent variables match up with criterion and predictor variables?
2. (a) What is an analysis of covariance? (b) How is it like partial correlation? (c) What is a covariate? (d) What are the two most common types of covariates?
3. How are multivariate statistics unlike all of the procedures covered previously in this book?
4. (a) What is multivariate analysis of variance, and how does it differ from an ordinary analysis of variance? (b) After finding a significant effect in a MANOVA, what is the usual next step? (c) What is multivariate analysis of covariance, and how does it differ from an ordinary analysis of covariance?
5. What method would you use if you had more than one independent variable, only one dependent variable, and one or more covariates?

Answers

1. (a) The independent variable is the variable that divides the groups. (b) The dependent variable is the variable that is measured. (c) The independent variable is like the predictor variable; the dependent variable is like the criterion variable.
2. (a) An analysis of covariance is an analysis of variance that controls for (or adjusts for or partials out) one or more variables. (b) An analysis of covariance is like partial correlation in that it finds results after controlling for another variable. (c) A covariate is the variable that is controlled for (or adjusted for or partialed out). (d) The two most common types of covariates are variables measured at pretest and nuisance variables that add unwanted variation to the analysis.
3. They can have more than one dependent variable.
4. (a) A multivariate analysis of variance is an analysis of variance with more than one dependent variable. (b) Carry out a series of univariate analyses of variance, that is, individual analyses of variance for each dependent variable. (c) A multivariate analysis of covariance is an analysis of covariance with more than one dependent variable.
5. If you had more than one independent variable, only one dependent variable, and one or more covariates, you would use analysis of covariance.

Controversy: Should Statistics Be Controversial?

Most statistics books, this one included, teach you statistical methods in a fairly cut-and-dried way, almost as if imparting absolute truth. But we have also tried to mess up this tidy picture with our discussions of controversies. Usually, this is thought to confuse students. (Although, when you learned other fields of psychology, your understanding was built, we hope, from the presentation of controversy: this person's research demonstrated one thing, but this other person's study showed a flaw, while that one's student showed that this was an exception, and so forth.) So, in this last section on controversy, we are going to try to mess things up even more!

In Box 15–3, we describe the historical development of today's statistics out of a hybrid of two views, known as the Fisher and the Neyman-Pearson approaches. This wedding was supposed to end the feud as to which was the better method, but in fact, although most psychologists are content with this hybrid, others, such as

BOX 15-3 The Forced Partnership of Fisher and Pearson

Let's take a final look at the history of statistical methods in psychology, adding some tidbits of interest. We told you in Box 9–1 that Sir Ronald Fisher more or less invented the experimental method as it is now employed; that he was a difficult man to get along with; and that Fisher and another great British statistician, Karl Pearson, were particular enemies.

Well, Pearson had a son, Egon, who worked at his father's Galton Laboratory at University College, London. In 1925, the young Egon formed a lasting friendship with Jerzy Neyman, a youthful lecturer at the University of Warsaw who had just arrived at the Galton Laboratory. In the next years, the two worked very closely.

In 1933, Karl Pearson retired. Ironically, Fisher was given Pearson's old position as head of the department of eugenics, originally founded by Galton. And because of the feud between Fisher and the senior Pearson, a new department of statistics was created to smooth the retiring bird's feathers, to be headed by Pearson's son, Egon.

As hard as Pearson and his friend Neyman claim to have tried to avoid the continuation of the old feud between Sir Ronald and the senior Pearson, it was soon as bitter as ever. The work of Neyman and the younger Pearson was actually more supportive of Fisher's ideas than of Pearson Senior's, but their extensions of Fisher's approaches, intended to be friendly, infuriated the cranky Sir Ronald.

There is more of interest about Neyman. He immigrated to the United States when Hitler invaded Poland, starting the statistics program at the University of California, Berkeley, where he remained until his death in 1981. He is especially remembered for his bringing David Blackwell, an African-American statistician, out of obscurity, because he had been unable to get a job due to his race. Neyman was also remembered for his afternoon department teas, ending with a toast to the "ladies," referring to the many women present, whose careers he also encouraged, leading to many prominent women statisticians.

Until Fisher died in 1962, however, Neyman was under constant attack from Fisher. Fisher had rejected what is called Bayesian theory, a whole approach to statistics, which holds the position that scientific research is conducted to adjust preexisting beliefs in the light of new evidence as it is collected. Fisher held that research is carried out mainly by objectively disproving the null hypothesis, not by testing prior probabilities arrived at subjectively. Fisher was exceptionally dogmatic about his ideas, referring to his approach as "absolutely rigorous" and the only case of "unequivocal inference." Fisher had a great mind, wrote a huge amount, and became very influential throughout the world.

Pearson and Neyman also rejected Bayesian theory, but they proposed the method of testing two opposing hypotheses rather than just the null hypothesis. As a result of this innovation, there would be two types of errors. Type I errors would be when the null hypothesis is rejected even though it is true (and they called its probability alpha, or the level of significance—does all this sound familiar?). Type II errors would be when the null hypothesis was not rejected even though it is false (and the probability of that error was beta—again familiar?). Which type of error you preferred to minimize depended on the impact of each on your purposes, because Neyman and Pearson were frequently thinking in terms of applied research. Fisher never talked about any hypothesis but the null and therefore never considered Type II errors.

Now you can see what happened: statistics today is a hybrid of Fisher's ideas, with Pearson's and Neyman's added when they could no longer be ignored. It was a wedding none of them would have probably approved of, for both camps eventually came to see their approaches as fundamentally in opposition. Fisher compared Neyman and Pearson to the stereotype of the Soviets of his day in their determination to reduce science to technology "in the comprehensive organized effort of a five-year plan for the nation" and remarked sarcastically after Neyman gave a talk before the Royal Statistical Society in London that Neyman should have chosen a topic "on which he could speak with authority." Neyman, for his part, stated that Fisher's methods of testing were in a "mathematically specifiable sense worse than useless." Ah, how rational.

As we have noted throughout these boxes, statistics is, for better and for worse, a product of human intellect and human passions operating together (ideally, for the sake of science, though the latter to a lesser extent). The results have not always been perfect, but they can be far more interesting than they might seem on the surface.

Sources: Peters (1987); Salsburg (2001); Stigler (1986); Tankard (1984).

Gigerenzer and his associates (Gigerenzer & Murray, 1987; Gigerenzer et al., 1989; Sedlmeier & Gigerenzer, 1989), are not at all content. Neither are Jacob Cohen (1990) and Robert Rosenthal (e.g., Rosnow & Rosenthal, 1989), two psychologists who are very well-known for their contributions to statistical techniques and whose work on topics such as power, effect size, the null hypothesis, meta-analysis, and other topics we have mentioned throughout the book.

Gigerenzer and Murray (1987) argue that the viewpoints of Fisher and of Pearson and Neyman—which to these early statisticians themselves were always fundamentally contradictory—have been misunderstood and misused as a result of being blended. The marriage was entirely one of convenience, with little thought given to long-term effects. Gigerenzer and Murray regard the hybrid as the result of so many of the first statistics textbooks having been written under the influence of the dogmatic and persuasive Sir Ronald Fisher (recall Box 9–1). But then, after World War II, the Pearson-Neyman view became known and had to be integrated without admitting that the original texts could have been wrong. (The desire was to present psychology as a science, having as its basis a unified, mechanical, flawless method of decision making.)

The result of all of this, Gigerenzer and Murray claim, is a neglect of controversy and of alternative approaches, and statistics textbooks "filled with conceptual confusion, ambiguity, and errors" (p. 23). Further, they argue that these dominant statistical methods, which were originally only tools, are now shaping the way psychologists view human cognition and perception itself (recall Box 10–1).

More generally, the current hot debates about significance tests we considered in Chapters 4, 5, and 6 are part of this larger trend of reopening the long-buried controversies.

As a last word on all this, we must say that the majority of psychologists and statisticians are fairly comfortable with the methods found in today's textbooks. Time and careful thinking will tell whether this majority ought to be so complacent. But no one is going to figure it out for us. We will have to do it together. Therefore, we truly hope that, once you master the methods in this book, you will have the confidence to look further and not be content to continue applying these methods in a mindless, rote way 20 years from now. If you become a psychologist who either reads research or does it, then whatever else your interests, you must also be a good citizen within the larger discipline. Keep up at least a little with developments in methods of data analysis, accepting and even demanding change when it is warranted. After all, if our tools become dated, what hope is there for our findings?

How to Read Results Using Unfamiliar Statistical Techniques

Based on this chapter and what you have learned throughout this book, you should be well prepared to read and understand, at least in a general way, the results in most psychology research articles. However, you will still now and then come up against new techniques (and sometimes unfamiliar names for old techniques). This happens even to seasoned researchers. So what do you do when you run into something you have never heard of before?

First, don't panic. Usually, you can figure out the basic idea. Ask yourself if the technique may be related to one that you already know. Imagine you read the results section of a research article and the researchers state that they conducted a logistic regression (a technique that you have not learned about in this book). It is a good starting point if you assume that this technique, because it has the word "regression" in it, is probably somewhat similar to the kind of regression that you are familiar with. By reading the rest of the results section and the others sections of the article, it may be possible for you to get a good sense of what kind of analysis the researchers used.

Almost always there will be a *p* level, and it should be clear just what pattern of results is being considered significant or not. In addition, there will usually be some indication of the degree of association or the size of the difference. If the statistic is about the association among some variables, it is probably stronger as the result gets closer to 1 and weaker as the result gets closer to 0. You should not expect to understand every word in a situation like this, but do try to grasp as much as you can about the meaning of the result.

Suppose you really can't figure out anything about a statistical technique used in a research article. In that situation, you can try to look up the procedure in a statistics book. Intermediate and advanced textbooks are sometimes a good bet, but we have to warn you that trying to make sense of an intermediate or advanced statistics text on your own can be difficult. Many such texts are heavily mathematically oriented. Even a quite accessible textbook will use its own set of symbols. Thus, it can be hard to make sense of a description of a particular method without having read the whole book. Perhaps a better solution in this situation is to ask for help from a professor or graduate student. If you know the basics as you have learned them in this book, you should be able to understand the essentials of their explanations. Table 15–8 summarizes the various approaches you can use when you come across results that use unfamiliar statistical techniques.

If you are often coming upon statistics you don't understand, the best solution is to take more statistics courses. Usually, the next course after this one would be an intermediate course that focuses mainly on analysis of variance and may go into multiple regression to some extent. You will find such a course particularly useful if you are planning to go to graduate school in psychology, where statistics will be a crucial tool in all the research you do. It will help prepare you for graduate school. Also, a strong performance in such a course is extremely impressive to those evaluating applications to the top graduate programs. (It is also our experience that you are especially likely to enjoy the other students you meet in such a course. Those who take the intermediate statistics course in psychology are not all whizzes at statistics, but they are almost always highly motivated, bright students who will share your goals.) In fact, some people find statistics so fascinating that they choose to make a career of it. You might too!

More generally, new statistical methods are being invented constantly. Psychologists all encounter unfamiliar numbers and symbols in the research articles they read. They puzzle them out, and so will you. We say that with confidence because you have arrived, safe and knowledgeable, at the back pages of this book. You have mastered a thorough introduction to a complex topic. That should give you complete confidence that, with a little time and attention, you can understand anything further in statistics. Congratulations on your accomplishment.

TIP FOR SUCCESS

When faced with an unfamiliar statistical technique, focus on what you can understand about the technique. This may allow you to get the general idea of the result.

TIP FOR SUCCESS

You might also try doing a search on the Internet for information about an unfamiliar statistical technique. However, as with textbooks, you may encounter difficulties with symbols and complex descriptions. Also, you will have to decide whether the content of a particular Web site is likely to be accurate.

Table 15–8 Approaches for Reading Results Using Unfamiliar Statistical Techniques

- Don't panic
- Focus on what you *can* understand about the technique
- Look to see if the technique may be related to one that you already know
- Look for a *p* level to see if the results are statistically significant
- Look for a statistic that may show the degree of association or size of difference
- Look up the technique on the Internet or in an intermediate or advanced textbook
- Ask for help from a professor or graduate student

Summary

1. The general linear model is a statement of the influences that make up an individual's score on a particular variable. The general linear model states that the value of a variable for any individual is the sum of a constant, plus the weighted influence of each of several other variables, plus error. Bivariate and multiple correlation and regression (and associated significance tests), the t test, and the analysis of variance are all special cases of the general linear model.
2. Partial correlation is the correlation between two variables while holding one or more other variables constant.
3. Reliability coefficients tell you how much scores on a test are internally consistent (usually with Cronbach's alpha), consistent over time (test–retest reliability), or give comparable scores from different raters (interrater reliability).
4. Multilevel modeling is used when scores are grouped in some way that matters for the scores, so that scores within each grouping are lower-level variables, scores for the grouping as a whole are upper-level variables. A traditional method for studying the relation between lower-level variables is to do a regression in each grouping and average the results; a next step might be to see if an upper-level variable predicts average group scores on a lower-level variable. More sophisticated statistical methods are actually used today in practice, such as hierarchical linear modeling (HLM).
5. Factor analysis identifies groupings of variables, called factors, that correlate maximally with each other and minimally with other variables. A factor loading is the correlation of a variable with a factor.
6. Causal modeling analysis examines whether the correlations among several variables in a sample are consistent with a systematic, hypothesized pattern of causal relationships among them. Path analysis describes these relationships with arrows, each pointing from cause to effect. Each arrow has a path coefficient indicating the influence of the theorized causal variable on the theorized effect variable. Mediational analysis is a type of path analysis that tests whether a presumed casual relationship between two variables is due to some intervening (or mediating) variable. Structural equation modeling is an advanced version of path analysis that includes latent, unmeasured variables (each of which represents the common elements of several measured variables). It also provides measures of the overall fit of the hypothesized causal pattern to the correlations in the sample.
7. In a t test, analysis of variance, and other procedures that compare groups, variables that divide the groups and are considered the cause are called independent variables; variables that are measured and considered the effect are called dependent variables.
8. The analysis of covariance (ANCOVA) is an analysis of variance that controls for one or more variables (called covariates). The multivariate analysis of variance (MANOVA) is an analysis of variance that has more than one dependent variable. The multivariate analysis of covariance (MANCOVA) is an analysis of covariance that has more than one dependent variable.
9. In recent years psychologists have begun to reexamine the basics of the statistics they use, opening up the possibility of controversy about what had been in the past often taken as incontrovertible.
10. It is often possible to get the main idea of an unfamiliar statistical procedure by keeping several things in mind. First, the procedure probably tells you about association among variables or differences among groups. Second, p values tell you about the significance of that association or difference. Finally, you will probably be given some numbers from which you can get a sense of the degree of association or amount of difference.

Key Terms

general linear model (p. 612)
partial correlation (p. 617)
partialing out (p. 617)
partial correlation coefficient (p. 618)
reliability (p. 618)
test-retest reliability (p. 619)
split-half reliability (p. 619)
Cronbach's alpha (α) (p. 619)
internal consistency reliability (p. 619)
interrater reliability (p. 619)
multilevel modeling (p. 621)
lower-level variable (p. 621)
upper-level variable (p. 621)

hierarchical linear modeling
  (HLM) (p. 621)
factor analysis (p. 622)
factor (p. 622)
factor loading (p. 622)
path analysis (p. 625)
path (p. 625)
path coefficient (p. 625)
mediational analysis (p. 626)
structural equation modeling (p. 629)
fit index (p. 629)
RMSEA (p. 630)
latent variable (p. 630)

independent variable (p. 634)
dependent variable (p. 634)
analysis of covariance
  (ANCOVA) (p. 634)
covariate (p. 634)
adjusted mean (p. 634)
multivariate statistics (p. 635)
multivariate analysis of variance
  (MANOVA) (p. 635)
multivariate analysis of covariance
  (MANCOVA) (p. 636)

Practice Problems

For the problems below that ask you to explain results, you need to explain only the general meaning of the results, using only the same level of detail as used when the procedures were described in the chapter. You do not need to describe the logic of the statistical procedures covered here in the way that you have been doing in previous chapters.

All studies for which we do not give an actual citation are fictional.

Set I (for Answers to Set I Problems, see pp. 698–700)

1. Zimmer-Gembeck and colleagues (2001) studied dating practices in a sample of 16-year-olds in Minneapolis. As part of their study they examined the relation of dating involvement, experience, and quality with various aspects of self-concept and self-worth (that is, how positively the 16-year-olds rated themselves on such things as scholastic competence, social acceptance, and so on). However, the researchers were concerned that the correlations among these variables would be inappropriately influenced by differences in the appearance of physical maturity (how old the person looks). Thus, their results, shown in Table 15–9, provide correlations "controlling for appearance of physical maturity" (p. 327).

   Explain this method and the pattern of a few example results to a person who is familiar with correlation and multiple regression but is unfamiliar with partial correlation.

2. Boyd and Gullone (1997) studied anxiety and depression in a sample of 783 adolescents attending schools in and around Melbourne, Australia. To measure anxiety, they used the Revised Children's Manifest Anxiety Scale (RCMAS). The RCMAS measures a number of different domains of anxiety (such as physiological anxiety and anxiety related to social concerns). In discussing the measure in their methods section, they note the following: "Alpha coefficient reliability estimates of internal consistency for the RCMAS range from .42 to .87" (p. 192). Explain these results to someone who is familiar with correlation but is unfamiliar with reliability or the statistics associated with it.

3. Ryan and colleagues (1998) conducted a study to examine whether sixth-grade students' tendency to avoid seeking help in the classroom was related to student and classroom characteristics. The participants were 516 students from 63 different

Table 15-9 Partial Correlations (Controlling for Appearance of Physical Maturity) of Dating and Self-Concept at Age 16

Self-Concept/Self-Worth	Overinvolvement with Dating	Level of Dating Experience	Quality of Romantic Relationship
Scholastic competence	−0.10	0.08	−0.03
Social acceptance	0.04	0.24 **	0.29**
Physical appearance	0.06	0.24**	0.11
Job competence	−0.12	0.12	0.07
Romantic appeal	0.10	0.35***	0.36***
Behavioral conduct	−0.33***	−0.17*	−0.04
Close friendship	0.00	0.09	0.09
Global self-worth	−0.11	0.05	0.18*

N ranged from 125 (when examining quality of romantic relationships) to 166.
*$p < 0.05$, **$p < 0.01$, ***$p < 0.001$
Source: Zimmer-Gembeck, M. J., Siebenbruner, J., & Collins, A. W. (2001). Diverse aspects of dating: Associations with psychosocial functioning from early to middle adolescence. *Journal of Adolescence, 24,* 313–336. Copyright © 2001 with permission of Elsevier.

math classrooms. In describing their results, the researchers noted: "We used hierarchical linear modeling (HLM) to examine our research questions. . . . Our questions were hierarchical, in that we were interested in both student-level characteristics and classroom-level characteristics that were related to avoidance of help seeking" (p. 530). One of the student-level characteristics that the researchers examined was academic self-efficacy, which refers to students' beliefs about their ability to complete their schoolwork successfully. One of the classroom-level characteristics examined was teachers' ratings of their role in students' social and emotional well-being. The researchers summarized the results of their study as follows: "This study extended previous examinations of help seeking by including individual- and classroom-level predictors. By using multilevel analysis techniques, we found that avoidance of help seeking is related to both individual characteristics of students and characteristics of the classroom" (p. 532).

Explain these results to someone who is familiar with regression (prediction), but has not heard of multilevel modeling.

4. Fawzi and colleagues (1997) studied whether the usual way of thinking about posttraumatic stress disorder (PTSD), as described in the fourth edition of the standard *Diagnostic and Statistical Manual of Mental Disorders* (DSM-IV), applies to Vietnamese refugees in the United States. As part of their study, 74 refugees were interviewed (in their native language) regarding various PTSD symptoms and the traumatic events they had experienced, such as torture. As expected, the number of PTSD symptoms correlated with the number of traumatic events. In a further analysis of the pattern of symptoms (which symptoms go together with which), they conducted a factor analysis that resulted in four factors.

> In correspondence with the DSM-IV, the first three factors represented dimensions of arousal, avoidance, and reexperiencing, respectively (see Table [15–10]). However, in contrast to the DSM-IV defined subcategories where avoidance represents one dimension of symptomatology, avoidance appeared to be separated into two factors in this sample. The second factor reflected avoidance associated with general withdrawal or numbing of responsiveness, with high factor loadings for "unable to feel emotions" and "less interest in daily activities." The fourth factor reflected avoidance of stimuli related to the traumatic event(s). (p. 104)

Table 15-10 Factor Loading for Principal Components Analysis (Factor Analysis) of PTSD-IV Symptoms for 74 Vietnamese Refugees

Symptom Dimension	Factor Loading
Arousal	
Recurrent nightmares	.79
Difficulty concentrating	.78
Feeling irritable/outburst of anger	.77
Inability to remember parts of the most traumatic events	.74
Trouble sleeping	.73
Avoiding activities that remind you of traumatic events	.70
Feeling jumpy, easily startled	.67
% Variance explained	44%
Avoidance/withdrawal	
Unable to feel emotions	.79
Less interest in daily activities	.70
Feeling detached or withdrawn	.65
Feeling jumpy, easily startled	.51
Feeling as if you don't have a future	.51
% Variance explained	24%
Reexperiencing	
Recurrent thoughts/memories of most terrifying events	.83
Feeling as though the event is happening again	.83
Sudden emotional or physical reaction when reminded of most traumatic events	.57
% Variance explained	22%
Avoidance of stimuli related to trauma event(s)	
Avoiding thoughts or feeling associated with traumatic events	.71
% Variance explained	11%

Source: Fawzi, M. C. S., Pham, T., Lin, L., Nguyen, T. V., Ngo, D., Murphy, E., & Mollica, R. F. (1997). The validity of posttraumatic stress disorder among Vietnameses refugees. *Journal of Traumatic Stress, 10*, 101–108. Copyright © 1997 by the International society for Traumatic Stress Studies. Reprinted with permission.

Explain these results to a person who is familiar with correlation but is unfamiliar with factor analysis.

5. MacKinnon-Lewis and her colleagues (1997) were interested in predictors of social acceptance by peers of 8- to 10-year-old boys. The main predictors they used were the child's rating of parental acceptance and rejection, peers' ratings of acceptance and aggression, and conflict with siblings as observed in a laboratory interaction. They tried several different possible causal models, and concluded that the best was what they called Model 1.

The standardized path coefficients of Model 1 are presented in Figure [15–7], which shows that siblings whose mothers were perceived and observed to be more rejecting were observed and reported to be more aggressive with one another than were siblings whose mothers were less rejecting. Moreover, boys who experienced more aggressive sibling interactions were more likely to be nominated by their peers as being aggressive and were less accepted by their peers. Although fathering failed to evince a direct influence on sibling aggression, an indirect effect was evidence as a result of the fact that less accepting fathering was related to more rejecting mothering. (p. 1027)

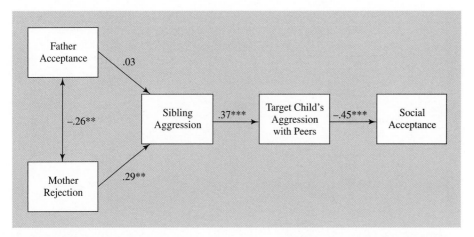

Figure 15–7 Path model of associations among parenting variables, sibling aggression, peer aggression, and social acceptance. Standardized path coefficients are given.
$**p < .01, ***p < .001.$

Source: MacKinnon-Lewis, C., Starnes, R., Volling, B., & Johnson, S. (2001). Perceptions of parenting as predictors of boys' sibling and peer relations. *Developmental Psychology, 22,* 1024–1031. Published by the American Psychological Association. Reprinted with permission.

Explain the method they used, illustrating it with some sample results, to a person who is familiar with multiple regression and partial correlation in a general way but not with path analysis.

6. Recall from Chapter 11 the study by Aron and colleagues (2000, Study 1) in which 113 married people completed a newspaper survey about their relationships. The study participants completed a series of measures, including a single question regarding how exciting the things are that they do with their partner, a measure about their relationship quality, and a measure of boredom with the relationship. Aron and colleagues tested a mediational relationship that is outlined in the two study hypotheses. "*Hypothesis 1:* Shared participation in novel-arousing activities is associated with higher levels of experienced relationship quality. *Hypothesis 2:* This association is mediated by the extent to which the relationship is perceived as boring (versus exciting)" (p. 275). Here is how they reported the results of the study:

Regarding Hypothesis 1, as predicted, there was a strong positive association between responses to the exciting activities question and experienced relationship quality ($r = .51, p < .001$). . . . Hypothesis 2 was that this association would be mediated by boredom with the relationship. The results clearly support this hypothesis. As shown in Figure 15–8, the beta of .51 between exciting activities and experienced relationship quality became nonsignificant and dropped to a beta of .10 (*ns*) when boredom with the relationship was included in the model. At the same time, boredom with the relationship, which correlated −.56 with exciting activities and −.79 with quality, retained a significant beta of −.74 ($p < .001$) with quality when the exciting activities variable was included in the model. (p. 276)

Explain the method they used, and the actual results of the analysis, to a person who understands correlation and prediction but has never heard of mediational analysis.

7. Aron and colleagues (1998) studied experiences of unreciprocated love, loving someone who does not love you. One of their predictions focused on the intensity

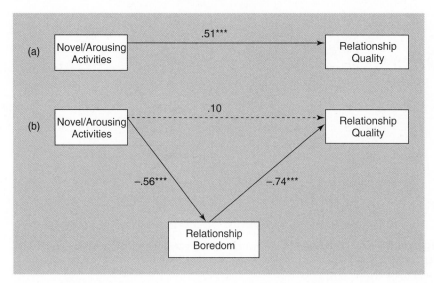

Figure 15–8 Results for the test of Hypothesis 2 based on newspaper survey data (Study 1: $N = 112$). The path diagrams show mediation by reported relationship boredom of the association between novel-arousing activities (reported participation in "exciting" activities) and experienced relationship quality (scores on the Dyadic Satisfaction subscale of Spanier's, 1976, Dyadic Adjustment Scale). Path coefficients shown are standardized regression coefficients.

***$p < .001$.

Source: Aron, A., Norman, C. C., Aron, E. N., Mckenna, C., & Heyman, R. E. (2000). Couples' shared participation in novel and arousing activities and experienced relationship quality. *Journal of Personality and Social Psychology, 78,* 273–284.

of the experience (how much you think about it, how much it disrupts your life). The researchers hypothesized that intensity would be predicted by desirability (how much the lover thought a relationship with the beloved would be wonderful), probability (how much the beloved had led the lover to believe a relationship might develop), and desirability of the state (how much the lover thought it was desirable to be in love, even though it was not reciprocated). Aron and colleagues carried out a structural equation model analysis testing this model. The results are shown in Figure 15–9 (reproduced from their Figure 1).

(a) Explain the pattern of results. (b) Using this diagram as an example, explain the general principles of interpreting a path diagram (including the limitations) to a person who understands multiple regression in a general way but who is unfamiliar with path diagrams or structural equation modeling.

8. In each of the following studies, which variable is the independent variable and which is the dependent variable?

   (a) A study comparing a group given two different kinds of medication on their level of anxiety.

   (b) A study looking at heart rate change while watching one of three kinds of movies (horror movie, love story, or comedy).

   (c) A study of number of touches between two infants playing in the same room, comparing when their mothers are present versus when their mothers are not present.

9. Roeser and colleagues (2001) conducted a cross-cultural study of self-esteem comparing adolescents from the United States and the Netherlands. In their article they had a section labeled "Covariates" in which they note, "A measure of

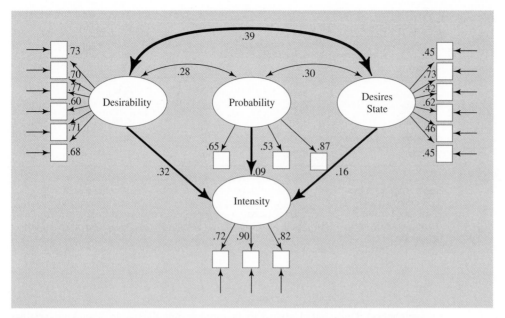

Figure 15–9   Latent variable model based on a three-factor framework of motivation in unreciprocated love that was fitted to data for 743 participants who reported experiencing un-reciprocated love.

Note: Bentler-Bonnett normed fixed index (NFI) = .90; nonnormed fit index (NNFI) = .92; average standardized residuals = .04; $\chi^2(129)$ = 430.88; $p < .01$. All parameter estimates shown were significantly different from 0, at least at the .05 level. The key result is that each of the major causal paths to intensity, from desirability, probability, and desirability of the state, were positive and significant, confirming the hypothesis that each of these variables independently predicts intensity.
Source: Aron, A., Aron, E. N., & Allen, J. (1998). Motivations for unreciprocated love. *Personality and Social Psychology Bulletin, 24,* 787–796. Copyright © 1998 by Sage Publications, Ltd. Reprinted by permission of Sage Publications, Thousands Oaks, London, and New Delhi.

social desirability was included in each analysis because prior research has shown that self-report measures of mental health often elicit socially desirable response patterns" (p. 120). (That is, social desirability was a kind of nuisance variable they were concerned would disturb their pattern of results.) They then reported a series of analyses of covariance. Here is one of their results: "ANCOVA results for the CBCL [a measure of emotional/behavioral problems] . . . revealed only one significant effect: After covarying out the effect of social desirability . . . , American adolescents reported significantly more externalizing problems than their Dutch peers, $F(1, 136) = 9.80$, $p < .01$, Eta squared = .07" (p. 123). Explain what is being done, using this result as an example, to someone who is familiar with ordinary analysis of variance and with partial correlation but who is not familiar with the analysis of covariance.

10. Gire (1997) studied the preferred methods of resolving conflicts, comparing people in individualistic versus collectivistic cultures. Participants were 90 Nigerians (Nigeria was considered an example of a relatively collectivist society) and 95 Canadians (Canada was considered an example of a relatively individualistic society). All participants answered questions about how much they preferred each of five methods of resolving conflicts. Half the participants in each country answered the questions regarding an interpersonal conflict (a conflict between two neighbors) and half regarding an intergroup conflict (between two groups of

Table 15-11 Method Preferences as a Function of Culture and Type of Conflict

Method	Nigerians		Canadians	
	IP	IG	IP	IG
Threats*	2.09	1.50	1.35	1.61
Accept the situation*	2.72	3.16	3.43	2.71
Negotiation	6.07	6.11	5.56	5.64
Mediation	4.70	4.77	4.87	5.13
Arbitration*	3.05	4.90	5.20	5.42

Note: One asterisk (*) indicates that the means of the culture by type of conflict interaction on a given method was significant at $p < .05$ level. The larger the number, the higher the preference for the method. IP = Interpersonal Conflict; IG = Intergroup Conflict.
Source: Gire, J. T. (1997). The varying effect of individualism-collectivism on reference for methods of conflict resolution. *Canadian Journal of Behavioral Science, 29,* 38–43. Copyright © 1997 by the Canadian Psychological Association. Reprinted with permission.

neighbors). This created a two-way factorial design: the two independent variables were culture (Nigeria versus Canada) and the type of conflict interaction (interpersonal versus intergroup). The five dependent variables were five measures of conflict resolution preferences.

> These data were analyzed by using the multivariate analysis of variance (MANOVA) procedure. The 2-way MANOVA yielded a significant main effect of culture $F(5, 173) = 6.37$, $p < .001$. An examination of the univariate analyses and the means suggests that Nigerians preferred negotiation to a greater extent than Canadians, while the reverse was the case on arbitration, as predicted. There was also a significant culture by type of conflict interaction, $F(5, 173) = 3.84$, $p < .002$. The univariate analyses and the means, presented in Table [15–11], reveal that significant differences occurred on three procedures— threats, acceptance of the situation, and arbitration. (p. 41)

Explain these results to someone who understands factorial analysis of variance but is not familiar with multivariate analysis of variance.

11. For each of the following studies, what would be the most appropriate statistical technique?
    (a) A study in which the researcher has a complex theory of the pattern of cause and effect among several variables.
    (b) A study of the association between two variables.
    (c) A study of whether a questionnaire scale is consistent internally (that is, that the items correlate with each other) and consistent over time in giving the same result.
    (d) A two-way factorial design with three dependent measures.
    (e) A study in which the association between elementary school class size and student satisfaction is examined across 10 different schools.
    (f) A study in which a researcher measures 16 variables and wants to explore whether there are any simpler groupings of variables underlying these 16.
    (g) A study in which an experimental group and a control group are being compared on a single dependent variable.
    (h) A study comparing five groups of individuals on a single dependent variable.

Set II

12. Frank and her colleagues (1997) studied adolescents' depressive concerns and their relation with their parents. These researchers focused on two aspects of depressive concerns, a self-critical preoccupation and an interpersonal preoccupation. They also focused on two aspects of what they called "separation-individuation conflict" with parents, how much the adolescents perceived their parents as constraining them (exerting strong control over their behaviors) and how insecure the adolescents felt about their parents. The researchers reported their analysis and results as follows:

> We then correlated the mother and father versions of the Perceived Constraint and Insecurity scales with scores for self-critical and interpersonal concerns. Bivariate and partial correlational analyses are summarized in Table [15–12]. Partial analyses controlled for one aspect of separation-individuation conflict . . . and each type of depressive concern. (p. 211)

Explain this method and illustrate your answer by focusing on some example results to a person who is familiar with correlation and, in a general way, with ordinary multiple regression but is unfamiliar with partial correlation.

13. Schmader and colleagues (2001), as part of a study of students' beliefs about ethnic injustice in a university setting, describe one of their key measures as follows: "Beliefs about systemic ethnic injustice were assessed with four items ($\alpha = .69$)" (p. 101). [Here is an example item: "Differences in status between ethnic groups are the result of injustice" (p. 101).] Explain the meaning of "$\alpha = .69$" to someone familiar with correlation but not with reliability or Cronbach"s alpha.

14. McClelland and colleagues (2007) studied the association between behavioral regulation and academic achievement in a sample of 310 preschool children from 54 different classrooms. Behavioral regulation refers to basic skills in regulating behavior, such as paying attention and following instructions. The researchers noted that: "To account for the nesting of children in classrooms, we used Hierarchical Linear Modeling to . . . investigate the associations between

Table 15–12 Bivariate and Partial Correlations Showing Relations Between the Constraint and Insecurity Scales and Self-Critical and Interpersonal Preoccupations

Scale	Bivariate r		Partial r	
	Interpersonal	Self-Critical	Interpersonal	Self-Critical
Constraint				
Fathers	.12	.23***	.00	.18**
Mothers	.08	.23***	−.12*	.14**
Insecurity				
Fathers	.24***	.13	.20*	.02
Mothers	.33***	.12*	.29***	−.07

Note: Partial correlation analyses assessing relations between constraint (or insecurity) and depressive concerns control for insecurity (or constraint) as well as adolescent depression.

*$p < .05$. **$p < .01$. ***$p < .001$.

Source: Frank, S. J., Poorman, M. O., Van Egeren, L. A., & Fields, D. T. (1997). Perceived relationships with parents among adolescent impatients with depressive preoccupations and depressed mood. *Journal of Clinical Child Psychology, 26,* 205–215. Copyright © 1997 by Lawrence Erlbaum Associates, Inc. Reprinted with permission.

behavioral regulation and achievement" (p. 953). Explain, to a person who is familiar with regression but not with multilevel modeling, why the researchers used multilevel modeling instead of regular regression to analyze the study results.

15. Crick and colleagues (1997) developed a teachers' rating measure of "relational aggression" in preschoolers. Ordinary, overt aggression harms others directly, but "relational aggression harms others through damage to their peer relationships (e.g., using social exclusion or rumor spreading as a form of retaliation)" (p. 579). As part of this study, they first administered a 23-item teacher rating scale of preschoolers' social behavior. They described the key analysis of this measure as follows:

> A . . . factor analysis . . . was first conducted to assess whether . . . relational aggression would emerge as a separate factor independent of overt aggression. The analysis yielded the four predicted factors, relational aggression, overt aggression, prosocial behavior, and depressed affect. (p. 582)

Table 15–13 shows the factor loadings. Explain their results to a person who is familiar with correlation but is unfamiliar with factor analysis.

Table 15-13   Factor Loadings for the Teacher Measure of Social Behavior (PSBS-T)

Item	Relational Aggression	Overt Aggression	Prosocial Behavior	Depressed Affect
Tells a peer that he or she won't play with that peer or be that peer's friend unless he or she does what this child asks	.84			
Tells others not to play with or be a peer's friend	.83			
When mad at a peer, this child keeps that peer from being in the play group	.81			
Tells a peer that they won't be invited to their birthday party unless he or she does what the child wants	.88			
Tries to get others to dislike a peer	.89			
Verbally threatens to keep a peer out of the play group if the peer doesn't do what the child asks	.85			
Kicks or hits others		.81		
Verbally threatens to hit or beat up other children		.75		
Ruins other peer's things when he or she is upset		.82		
Pushes or shoves other children		.72		
Hurts other children by pinching them		.83		
Verbally threatens to physically harm a peer in order to get what they want		.81		
Is good at sharing and taking turns			.76	
Is helpful to peers			.83	
Is kind to peers			.62	
Says or does nice things for other kids			.75	
Doesn't have much fun				.90
Looks sad				.87
Doesn't smile much				.82

Note: All cross-loadings were less than .40. PSBS-T = Preschool Social Behavior Scale—Teacher Form.
Source: Crick, N. R., Casas, J. F., & Mosher, M. (1997). Relational and overt aggression in preschool. *Developmental Psychology, 33,* 579–588. Published by the American Psychological Association. Reprinted with permission.

16. Penedo and colleagues (2003) conducted a study looking at the relationship among optimism, perceived stress management skills, and positive mood in a sample of 46 men who underwent surgery for prostate cancer. They conducted a mediational analysis "to determine whether the relationship between optimism and positive mood was explained through perceived stress management skills" (p. 221). The researchers carried out their mediational analysis using the four-step Baron and Kenny (1986) approach you learned in this chapter. The results of the mediational analysis supported the hypothesized mediational relationship and showed full mediation. Explain to a person who understands correlation and prediction what variables Penedo and colleagues used in each of the four steps of their mediation analysis and, given that full mediation was found, describe the results they found for each step.

17. Kwan and her colleagues (1997) predicted that the relation of self-esteem and social harmony to life satisfaction would be different in different cultures. In more communal cultures, such as many Asian cultures, social harmony would matter more. However, in more individualistic cultures, such as most North American and European cultures, self-esteem would matter more. As part of the focus on cultural differences, the researchers also measured independent self-construal (how much a person emphasizes personal development and achievement) and interdependent self-construal (how much a person emphasizes getting along and fitting in with others). The participants in the study were 389 college students from the United States and Hong Kong. Figure 15–10 shows their basic results. Note that Kwan and colleagues give two path coefficients for each path: the ones not in parentheses are for the Hong Kong sample; those in parentheses are for the U.S. sample.

    (a) Explain the pattern of results. (b) Using this diagram as an example, explain the general principles of interpreting a path diagram (including any limitations) to a person who understands multiple regression in a general way but is unfamiliar with path diagrams or structural equation modeling.

18. DeGarmo and Forgatch (1997) studied the social support divorced mothers received from their closest confidant. The researchers measured a number of variables and then examined the predicted relationships among the variables using structural equation modeling. Figure 15–11 shows the results.

    (a) Explain the pattern of results. (b) Using this diagram as an example, explain the general principles of interpreting a path diagram (including any limitations) to a person who understands multiple regression in a general way but is unfamiliar with path diagrams or structural equation modeling.

19. In each of the following studies, indicate which variable is the independent variable and which is the dependent variable:
    (a) A study of speed of performance on a complex task, in which one group does the task at night and the other in the morning.
    (b) A study comparing college women and men on their attitudes toward psychotherapy.
    (c) A study of voting preferences of people from three different regions of Canada.

20. Thompson and colleagues (2001) conducted a study of the "Mozart effect"—that listening to music written by Mozart improves performance on tasks involving spatial abilities. In their initial analysis, the researchers found that participants did better on a paper-folding task after listening to a Mozart sonata than after an equivalent period of silence or after listening to a piece by another classical composer (an Albioni adagio). However, they then repeated their analyses, but this time

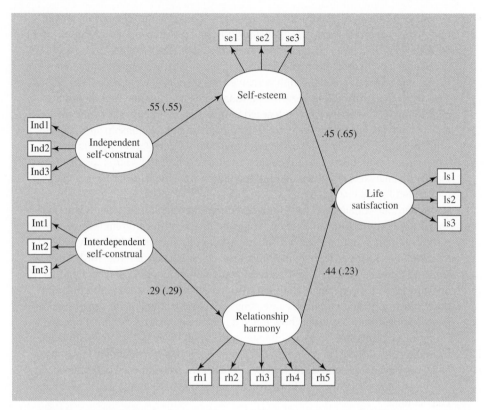

Figure 15–10 The final Self-Construal Scale model, $N = 194$ for the Hong Kong sample; $N = 194$ for the U.S. sample. Ellipses (ovals) represent latent constructs, boxes represent indicators, arrows pointing from latent constructs to indicators depict factor loadings, and arrows relating latent constructs represent path coefficients. Standardized path coefficients are shown; factor loadings and measurement errors are omitted for clarity. Numbers inside parentheses are coefficients for the U.S. sample; numbers outside parentheses are coefficients for the Hong Kong sample. All these coefficients were significant at $p < .05$ or less.

Source: Kwan, V. S., Bond, M. A., & Singelis, T. M. (1997). Pancultural explanations for life satisfaction: Adding relationship harmony to self-esteem. *Journal of Personality and Social Psychology, 73,* 1038–1051. Published by the American Psychological Association. Reprinted with permission.

> . . . a series of analyses of covariance . . . tested whether the Mozart effect would remain in evidence when individual differences in enjoyment, arousal, and mood were statistically controlled. For each analysis . . . the covariate represented the scores on one of [these] measures. Although the Mozart effect remained significant when . . . mood scores were partialed out, $F(1, 10) = 12.93$, $p < .05$, it was no longer reliable when enjoyment ratings, . . . arousal scores, or subjective mood-arousal ratings were held constant. (p. 250)

Explain what is being done, using this result as an example, to someone who is familiar with ordinary analysis of variance, but who is not familiar with the analysis of covariance.

21. This question refers to another part of the study by DeGarmo and Forgatch (1997), described in problem 18. These researchers studied a group of divorced mothers, focusing on the support they received from their closest confidant. That confidant was sometimes a close friend, sometimes a family member, and sometimes a cohabiting partner. In the study, both the mothers and the confidants were

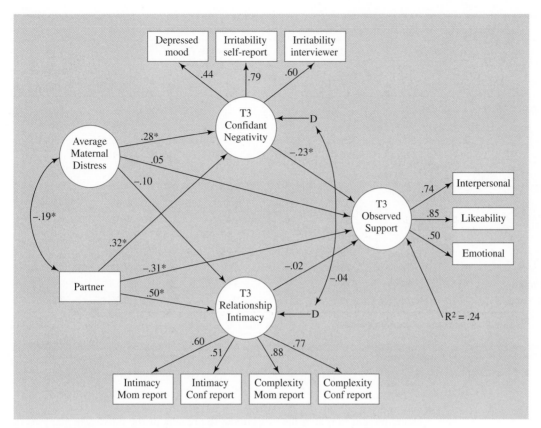

Figure 15–11 Support process model with mother, confidant, and relationship characteristics, controlling for repartnering with a man and for change in maternal distress. T3 = Time 3; Conf = Confidant. $\chi^2(67, N = 138) = 84.82$, $p = .07$; comparative fit index = .962: *$p < .05$.
Source: DeGarmo, D. S., & Forgatch, M. S. (1997). Determinants of observed confidant support for divorced mothers. *Journal of Personality and Social Psychology, 72,* 336–345. Published by the American Psychological Association. Reprinted with permission.

interviewed on various measures; they were also videotaped interacting in a special laboratory task, and the interaction was systematically coded by the researchers. These various approaches created quite a few measures of the relationship between the mother and her closest confidant, including three measures of confidant support, four measures of confidant negativity, and four measures of the intimacy of their relationship.

One aspect of the study focused on how the relationship with the confidant differed for confidants who were friends, family members, or cohabiting partners. DeGarmo and Forgatch described the analysis as follows:

> Multivariate and univariate analyses of variance were conducted on the indicators of support, negativity, and intimacy for close friends, family members, and cohabiting partners. The mean values, tests of differences, and significant contrasts are displayed in Table [15–14].
>
> Significant differences were found among relationship types in the multivariate analysis of variance (MANOVA) on the indicators, $F(20, 254) = 4.10$, $p < .001$. (p. 340)

Table 15-14 Means and Standard Deviations for Construct Indicators by Confidant Relationship Types

Construct Indicator	Friend (1)		Family (2)		Partner (3)		F(2, 135)	Significant Contrasts
	M	SD	M	SD	M	SD		
Observed confidant support								
Interpersonal	3.34	.67	3.35	.63	2.92	.65	5.93**	1, 2 > 3
Likeability	3.39	.86	3.24	.94	2.68	1.21	6.58**	1, 2 > 3
Emotional	1.04	.36	.96	.37	.69	.35	12.17***	1, 2 > 3
Confidant negativity								
Self-report, irritability	1.91	.84	1.70	.70	2.25	.65	5.27**	3 > 2
Intimacy-report irritability	1.36	.50	1.33	.35	1.48	.40	1.65	
Depressed mood	1.06	.32	.93	.36	.95	.34	2.02	
Relationship intimacy								
Mother-report intimacy	3.18	.73	3.19	.75	3.65	.58	5.94**	3 > 1, 2
Confidant-report intimacy	3.05	.78	3.29	.69	3.48	.64	4.62**	3 > 1
Mother-report complexity	1.91	.84	2.29	.74	2.87	.33	22.52***	3 > 1, 2
Confidant-report complexity	2.01	.74	2.19	.75	2.73	.55	13.36***	3 > 1, 2

Note: ns = 65, 33, and 40 for the friend, family, and partner relationship types, respectively.

**p < .01. ***p < .001.

Source: DeGarmo, D. S., & Forgatch, M. S. (1997). Determinants of observed confidant support for divorced mothers. *Journal of Personality and Social Psychology, 72,* 336–345. Published by the American Psychological Association. Reprinted with permission.

Degarmo and Forgatch then discussed the results of the univariate analyses of variance. For example, they noted that the "analysis of variance showed a pattern in which partners were observed to provide less support" (p. 340).

Explain these results to a person familiar with analysis of variance but not with MANOVA.

22. In a recent issue of a journal in an area of psychology that especially interests you, find an article that uses one of the statistical procedures described in this chapter. Write a brief summary of the study, and explain the result of the statistical procedure. With your answer, include a photocopy or printout of the article, marking clearly the part that reports the statistics you describe.

23. In a recent issue of a journal in an area of psychology that especially interests you, find an article that uses a statistical procedure not covered anywhere in this book. Write a brief summary of the study you found, and do your best to explain the result of the statistical procedure. With your answer, include a photocopy or printout of the article, marking clearly the part that reports the statistics you describe.

Using SPSS

The ⬤ in the following steps indicates a mouse click. (We used SPSS version 15.0 for Windows to carry out these analyses. The steps and output may be slightly different for other versions of SPSS.) You will learn how to use SPSS to carry out three of the procedures you learned about in this chapter: partial correlation, internal consistency reliability, and ANCOVA. Among the procedures covered in this chapter, these are the ones that are most straightforward to carry out in SPSS without significant additional understanding. Nevertheless, given that you have learned only the most basic aspects of even these three procedures, you should be very cautious in drawing conclusions from your analyses. There may well be fine points you are not aware of that need to be taken into account.

Finding the Partial Correlation Coefficient

As usual, it is easiest to follow the steps using an example. So we will use the sleep and mood example from Chapter 11. In that study, a researcher asked six students how many hours of sleep they had last night and how happy they felt right now (from 0, *not at all happy,* to 8, *extremely happy*). The correlation between sleep and mood was statistically significant, with $r = .853$, $p = .031$ (see Figure 11–22, p. 485). This tells you that there is an association between the amount of sleep people have and the level of happiness they report the next day (such that more sleep is linked with greater happiness and less sleep with less happiness). While it is entirely plausible that having less sleep makes people unhappy the next day, it is also possible that some other variable—such as general anxiety level—may affect both the amount of sleep a person gets and the level of happiness. So imagine that the researcher also asked students to rate how anxious they had been feeling in the last week (from 0, *not at all anxious,* to 5, *extremely anxious*). You can use a partial correlation coefficient to test whether the correlation between sleep and mood remains after partialing out (or controlling for) people's level of anxiety. The (fictional) scores for the three variables—sleep, mood, and anxiety—are shown in the SPSS data editor window in Figure 15–12.

❶ Enter the scores into SPSS. Enter the scores as shown in Figure 15–12.
❷ ✍ *Analyze.*
❸ ✍ *Correlate.*

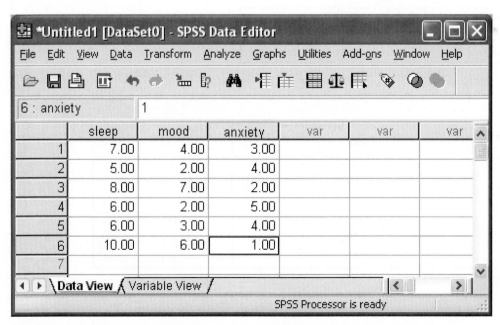

Figure 15–12   SPSS data editor window for the fictional study of the relationship between hours slept last night and mood, including anxiety variable.

❹ ✍ *Partial.*

❺ ✍ on the variable called "mood" and then ✍ the arrow next to the box labeled "Variables." ✍ on the variable called "sleep" and then ✍ the arrow next to the box labeled "Variables." This tells SPSS to figure the correlation between the "mood" and "sleep" variables. (If you wanted to find the correlation between each of several variables, you would put all of them into the "Variables" box.)

❻ ✍ on the variable called "anxiety" and then ✍ the arrow next to the box labeled "Controlling for." This tells SPSS to control for (or partial out) the "anxiety" variable when figuring the association between the "mood" and "sleep" variables.

❼ ✍ *Options.* ✍ the box labeled "Means and standard deviations". ✍ *Continue.* (Although this step is optional, we strongly recommend that you always request these additional statistics for a partial correlation.)

❽ ✍ *OK.* Your SPSS output window should look like Figure 15–13. The first table gives the mean and standard deviation for each variable. The second table gives the actual result of the partial correlation analysis. As you can see, the partial correlation between mood and sleep (after controlling for anxiety) is $r = .151$, with $p = .808$. The p value is greater than our usual .05 cutoff. Thus, the partial

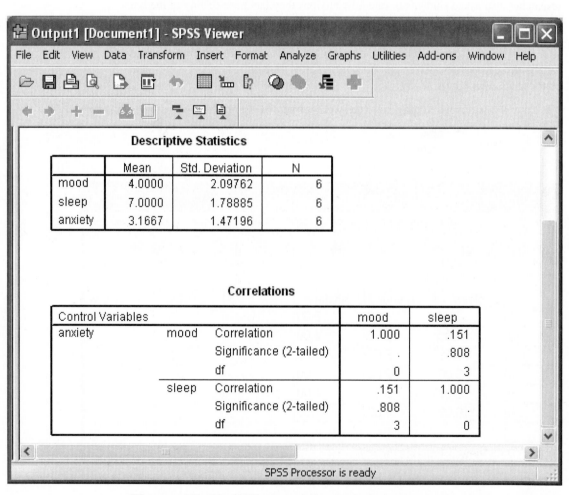

Figure 15–13 SPSS output window for the fictional study of the relationship between hours slept last night and mood, controlling for anxiety.

correlation coefficient is not statistically significant. This tells you that mood is not associated with the amount of sleep the previous night, after controlling for level of anxiety. The partial correlation coefficient is not statistically significant. Recall that without controlling for anxiety, the correlation between mood and sleep was $r = .853$, $p = .031$. So, in this example, the previously significant and strong correlation between mood and sleep becomes nonsignificant and considerably smaller after controlling for anxiety.

Figuring Internal Consistency Reliability

Internal consistency reliability is a measure of the extent to which the items of a measure assess a common characteristic. Imagine that you ask 10 people to complete a 6-item measure of their optimistic beliefs. Each item uses a 5-point response scale, from 1 = *disagree a lot,* to 5 = *agree a lot*. Example items include: "In uncertain times, I usually expect the best" and "I'm always optimistic about my future." (These are actual items from a widely used measure of optimism; Scheier et al., 1994.)

❶ Enter the scores into SPSS. Enter the scores as shown in Figure 15–14. We labeled the six items "optimism1," "optimism2," and so on. As usual, each row of the SPSS data editor window shows the responses of a single person.

❷ ✎ *Analyze.*

❸ ✎ *Scale.* ✎ *Reliability Analysis.* This will open up a Reliability Analysis window.

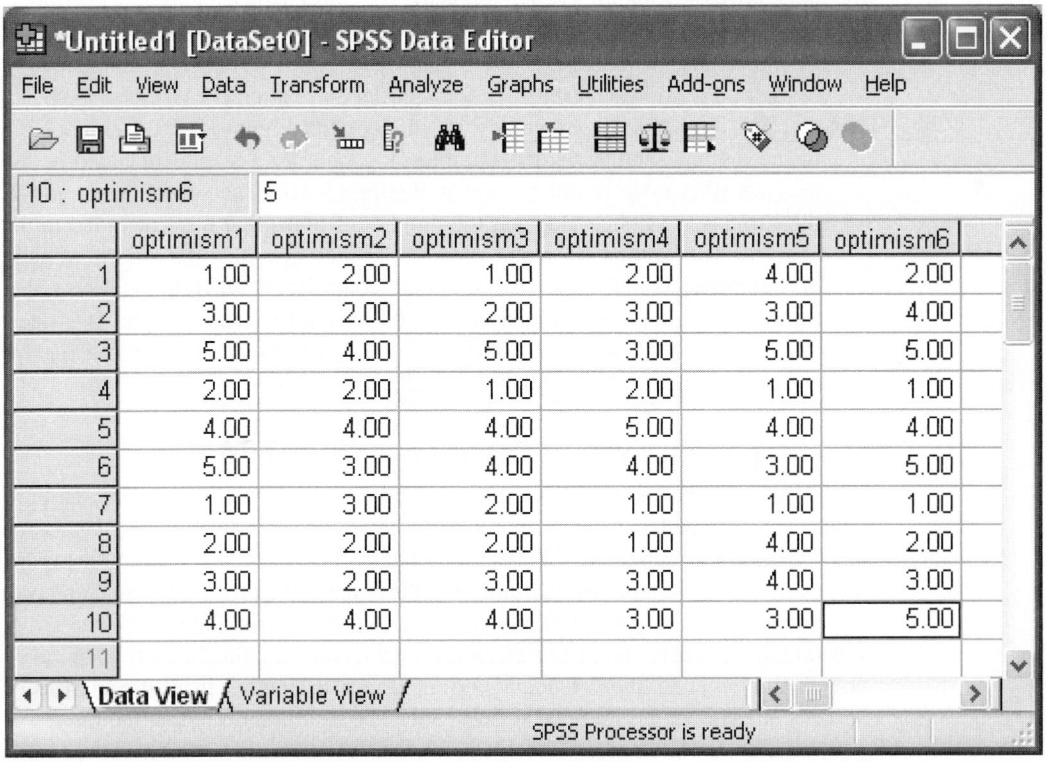

	optimism1	optimism2	optimism3	optimism4	optimism5	optimism6
1	1.00	2.00	1.00	2.00	4.00	2.00
2	3.00	2.00	2.00	3.00	3.00	4.00
3	5.00	4.00	5.00	3.00	5.00	5.00
4	2.00	2.00	1.00	2.00	1.00	1.00
5	4.00	4.00	4.00	5.00	4.00	4.00
6	5.00	3.00	4.00	4.00	3.00	5.00
7	1.00	3.00	2.00	1.00	1.00	1.00
8	2.00	2.00	2.00	1.00	4.00	2.00
9	3.00	2.00	3.00	3.00	4.00	3.00
10	4.00	4.00	4.00	3.00	3.00	5.00
11						

Figure 15–14 SPSS data editor window for a fictional study of 10 people's responses to a 6-item measure of optimistic beliefs.

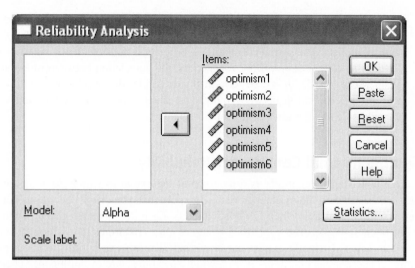

Figure 15–15 Reliability analysis window for a fictional study of 10 people's responses to a 6-item measure of optimistic beliefs.

❹ ✐ on the variable called "optimism1" and ✐ the arrow next to the box labeled "Items." Repeat this process for the remaining five items. Your Reliability Analysis window should now look like Figure 15–15. (Notice that by default the term *Alpha* is shown in the "Model" box in the bottom left corner of the Reliability Analysis window. This tells SPSS to figure Cronbach's alpha measure of internal consistency reliability that you learned in this chapter.)

❺ ✐ *Statistics*. Under the "Descriptives for" heading, ✐ the box labeled "Item". ✐ *Continue*. (Although this step is optional, we strongly recommend that you always request these additional statistics for a partial correlation.)

❻ ✐ *OK*. Your SPSS output window should look like Figure 15–16. The first table in the output summarizes the number of people (or "cases") included in the analysis (this table is not shown in Figure 15–16). The second table shows the Cronbach's alpha value and the number of items that were included in the analysis. The Cronbach's alpha value of .915 tells you that the 6-item measure of optimistic beliefs has good internal consistency reliability. (Recall that the general rule is a good measure should have a Cronbach's alpha of at least .60, and ideally closer to .90.) The third table gives the descriptive statistics for each item included in the reliability analysis.

Figuring an Analysis of Covariance (ANCOVA)

Let us consider the analysis of variance example from Chapter 9, in which 15 individuals rated the guilt of a defendant (on a scale from 1 = *completely sure of innocence* to 10 = *completely sure of guilt*) after being randomly assigned to one of three groups that were given different information about the defendant's previous criminal record. Specifically, one group was told that the defendant had a criminal record, one group was told that the defendant had a clean criminal record, and the third group received no information about the defendant's criminal record. The results of the analysis of variance are shown in Figure 9–11 on p. 366. The results showed that the ratings of guilt were not the same across the three groups ($F = 4.063$, $p = .045$). These results suggest that the information a person receives about a defendant's criminal record has an effect on that person's rating of the guilt of the defendant. However, it is also

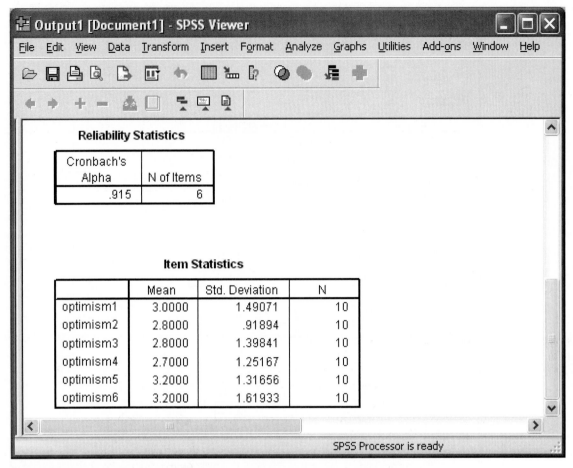

Figure 15–16   SPSS output window for the internal consistency reliability of a 6-item measure of optimistic beliefs that was completed by a sample of 10 people (fictional study).

possible that the results were affected by some unmeasured factor. For example, people vary in the degree to which they generally see other people as being suspicious. Differences in this belief across study participants in the different groups might account for the study results. So, imagine that the 15 study participants also completed a measure of their tendency to see people as being suspicious (ideally measured prior to the experimental manipulation), using a scale from 1 = *no suspicious beliefs* to 7 = *strong suspicious beliefs*. We can carry out an ANCOVA to test whether the group differences in ratings of guilt remain after controlling for participant's general tendency to hold suspicious beliefs.

❶ Enter the scores into SPSS. The scores are shown in Figure 15–17. In the first column (labeled "group"), we used the number *1* to indicate that a person is in the Criminal Record group, the number *2* to indicate a person in the Clean Record group, and the number *3* to indicate a person in the No Information group. The second column (labeled "guilt") shows each participant's rating as to the guilt of the defendant. The third column (labeled "suspicious") shows each participant's tendency to hold suspicious beliefs.

❷ ✐ *Analyze.*

❸ ✐ *General Linear Model.* ✐ *Univariate.* This will open up a Univariate window.

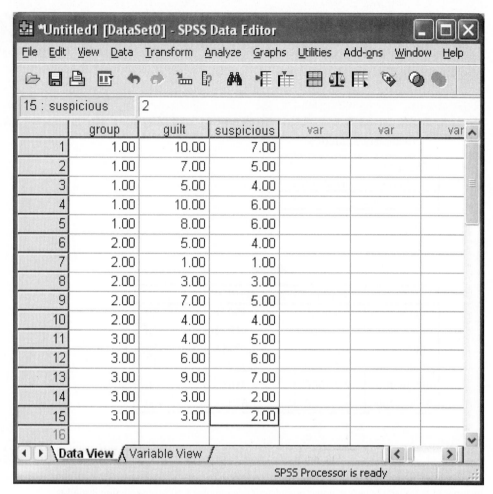

Figure 15–17 SPSS data editor window for an analysis of covariance (ANCOVA) for the criminal record example, in which 15 individuals indicated their general level of suspicious beliefs and also rated the guilt of a defendant after being randomly assigned to one of three groups that were given different information about the defendant's criminal record.

❹ ✍ the variable called "guilt" and then ✍ the arrow next to the box labeled "Dependent Variable". This tells SPSS that the ANCOVA should be carried out on the scores for the "guilt" variable.

❺ ✍ on the variable called "group" and then ✍ the arrow next to the box labeled "Fixed Factor(s)." This tells SPSS that the variable called "group" shows which person is in which group.

❻ ✍ on the variable called "suspicious" and then ✍ the arrow next to the box labeled "Covariate(s)." This tells SPSS that the variable called "suspicious" should be controlled for (or partialed out) in the analysis of variance (ANOVA). This is what makes this particular analysis an ANCOVA (analysis of covariance), since you have a covariate in the analysis.

❼ ✍ *Options*. This will open a Univariate: Options window. ✍ the box labeled "Descriptive statistics" (this checks the box). This tells SPSS to provide descriptive statistics (such as the mean) for each group. ✍ on the variable called "group" and ✍ the arrow next to the box labeled "Display means for group." This tells

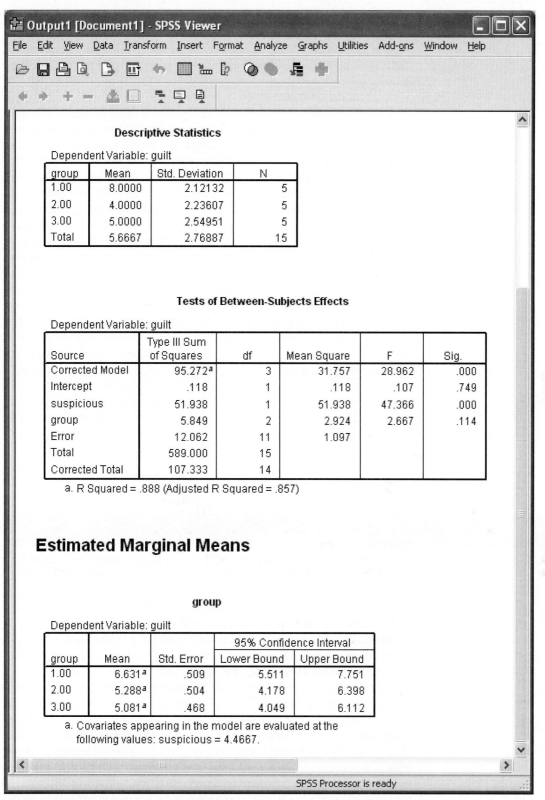

Figure 15–18 SPSS output window for an analysis of covariance (ANCOVA) for the criminal record example, in which 15 individuals indicated their general level of suspicious beliefs and also rated the guilt of a defendant after being randomly assigned to one of three groups that were given different information about the defendant's criminal record.

SPSS to provide the adjusted mean of each group. ✐ *Continue.* (Although this step is optional, we strongly recommend that you always request these additional statistics for an ANCOVA.)

❽ ✐ *OK.* Your output should look like Figure 15–18. The first table in the output (which is not shown in Figure 15–18) tells you the number of people who were in each group (5 in our example). The second table shows you the mean and standard deviation for the "guilt" dependent variable for each of the three groups in the study. The third table shows you the actual result of the ANCOVA. The first column in the table lists the types of population variance estimates. The most important estimate for our purposes is the one for the "group" variable. Looking across the row for the "group" variable, you can see that it had an F ratio of 2.667 with a significance level of $p = .114$. Since the significance level is higher than our usual .05 cutoff, the result is not statistically significant. This tells you that participants' ratings of the defendant's guilt did not differ according to which criminal record group they were in, after controlling for participants' general suspiciousness beliefs. The final table shows the adjusted means for the guilt dependent variable for each of the three groups in the study. These are the means for each group for the guilt variable, after controlling for (or partialing out) the "suspicious" variable. SPSS refers to these adjusted means as *marginal means.* The adjusted means are shown in the "Means" column of the table. The adjusted means are 6.631, 5.288, and 5.081. Notice that these adjusted means are closer together than the unadjusted means, which were 8.000, 4.000, and 5.000 (as shown in the second table in the output). This shows you that controlling for the suspicious variable in the ANCOVA made the group means on the guilt variable closer together than they were when the suspicious variable was not controlled for.

Chapter Notes

1. There are clever ways of sneaking squared and higher power terms into linear model procedures. For example, you could create a new, transformed variable in which each score was squared. This transformed variable could then be used in a linear model equation as an ordinary variable. Thus, no squared term would actually appear in the equation. It turns out that this little trick can be extraordinarily valuable. For example, you can use this kind of procedure to handle curvilinear relationships with statistical methods designed for linear relationships (Cohen et al., 2003; Darlington, 1990).

2. Another approach to multilevel modeling applies the same principle to what amounts to a repeated measures or within-subject situation. These are situations in which each individual is tested many times on the same variables. For example, people might record their stress level and their marital conflicts every night for 2 weeks. Then you would want to know if, on those days when stress level is high, is the person on that day more prone to have marital conflicts? To analyze this, you would, in effect want to do a regression, for each individual, with the predictor variable being a day's stress level and the criterion variable being the amount of marital conflict that day. To get the overall result you would average, across all the individuals, the regression coefficients you had figured for each individual. As an additional analysis, you might want to see if those individuals with

more education might have fewer conflicts overall (that is, whether they have lower average conflict levels averaged across the 2 weeks). In this example, the grouping variable is the individual! The lower level is days and the lower-level variables are daily level of stress and daily marital conflicts. The upper-level variable would be each individual's level of education.

3. There are also multivariate versions of correlation and regression in which there is more than one criterion variable, such as *canonical correlation*. But these are not widely used. Also, in addition to multivariate analysis of variance and covariance, multilevel modeling, factor analysis, and structural equation modeling, which are widely used, are technically considered multivariate procedures.

Appendix: Tables

Table A-1 Normal Curve Areas: Percentage of the Normal Curve Between the Mean and the Z Scores Shown and Percentage of Scores in the Tail for the Z Scores Shown

Z	% Mean to Z	% in Tail	Z	% Mean to Z	% in Tail
.00	0.00	50.00	.30	11.79	38.21
.01	0.40	49.60	.31	12.17	37.83
.02	0.80	49.20	.32	12.55	37.45
.03	1.20	48.80	.33	12.93	37.07
.04	1.60	48.40	.34	13.31	36.69
.05	1.99	48.01	.35	13.68	36.32
.06	2.39	47.61	.36	14.06	35.94
.07	2.79	47.21	.37	14.43	35.57
.08	3.19	46.81	.38	14.80	35.20
.09	3.59	46.41	.39	15.17	34.83
.10	3.98	46.02	.40	15.54	34.46
.11	4.38	45.62	.41	15.91	34.09
.12	4.78	45.22	.42	16.28	33.72
.13	5.17	44.83	.43	16.64	33.36
.14	5.57	44.43	.44	17.00	33.00
.15	5.96	44.04	.45	17.36	32.64
.16	6.36	43.64	.46	17.72	32.28
.17	6.75	43.25	.47	18.08	31.92
.18	7.14	42.86	.48	18.44	31.56
.19	7.53	42.47	.49	18.79	31.21
.20	7.93	42.07	.50	19.15	30.85
.21	8.32	41.68	.51	19.50	30.50
.22	8.71	41.29	.52	19.85	30.15
.23	9.10	40.90	.53	20.19	29.81
.24	9.48	40.52	.54	20.54	29.46
.25	9.87	40.13	.55	20.88	29.12
.26	10.26	39.74	.56	21.23	28.77
.27	10.64	39.36	.57	21.57	28.43
.28	11.03	38.97	.58	21.90	28.10
.29	11.41	38.59	.59	22.24	27.76

Table A-1 (continued)

Z	% Mean to Z	% in Tail	Z	% Mean to Z	% in Tail
.60	22.57	27.43	1.03	34.85	15.15
.61	22.91	27.09	1.04	35.08	14.92
.62	23.24	26.76	1.05	35.31	14.69
.63	23.57	26.43	1.06	35.54	14.46
.64	23.89	26.11	1.07	35.77	14.23
.65	24.22	25.78	1.08	35.99	14.01
.66	24.54	25.46	1.09	36.21	13.79
.67	24.86	25.14	1.10	36.43	13.57
.68	25.17	24.83	1.11	36.65	13.35
.69	25.49	24.51	1.12	36.86	13.14
.70	25.80	24.20	1.13	37.08	12.92
.71	26.11	23.89	1.14	37.29	12.71
.72	26.42	23.58	1.15	37.49	12.51
.73	26.73	23.27	1.16	37.70	12.30
.74	27.04	22.96	1.17	37.90	12.10
.75	27.34	22.66	1.18	38.10	11.90
.76	27.64	22.36	1.19	38.30	11.70
.77	27.94	22.06	1.20	38.49	11.51
.78	28.23	21.77	1.21	38.69	11.31
.79	28.52	21.48	1.22	38.88	11.12
.80	28.81	21.19	1.23	39.07	10.93
.81	29.10	20.90	1.24	39.25	10.75
.82	29.39	20.61	1.25	39.44	10.56
.83	29.67	20.33	1.26	39.62	10.38
.84	29.95	20.05	1.27	39.80	10.20
.85	30.23	19.77	1.28	39.97	10.03
.86	30.51	19.49	1.29	40.15	9.85
.87	30.78	19.22	1.30	40.32	9.68
.88	31.06	18.94	1.31	40.49	9.51
.89	31.33	18.67	1.32	40.66	9.34
.90	31.59	18.41	1.33	40.82	9.18
.91	31.86	18.14	1.34	40.99	9.01
.92	32.12	17.88	1.35	41.15	8.85
.93	32.38	17.62	1.36	41.31	8.69
.94	32.64	17.36	1.37	41.47	8.53
.95	32.89	17.11	1.38	41.62	8.38
.96	33.15	16.85	1.39	41.77	8.23
.97	33.40	16.60	1.40	41.92	8.08
.98	33.65	16.35	1.41	42.07	7.93
.99	33.89	16.11	1.42	42.22	7.78
1.00	34.13	15.87	1.43	42.36	7.64
1.01	34.38	15.62	1.44	42.51	7.49
1.02	34.61	15.39	1.45	42.65	7.35

(continued)

Table A-1 *(continued)*

Z	% Mean to Z	% in Tail	Z	% Mean to Z	% in Tail
1.46	42.79	7.21	1.88	46.99	3.01
1.47	42.92	7.08	1.89	47.06	2.94
1.48	43.06	6.94	1.90	47.13	2.87
1.49	43.19	6.81	1.91	47.19	2.81
1.50	43.32	6.68	1.92	47.26	2.74
1.51	43.45	6.55	1.93	47.32	2.68
1.52	43.57	6.43	1.94	47.38	2.62
1.53	43.70	6.30	1.95	47.44	2.56
1.54	43.82	6.18	1.96	47.50	2.50
1.55	43.94	6.06	1.97	47.56	2.44
1.56	44.06	5.94	1.98	47.61	2.39
1.57	44.18	5.82	1.99	47.67	2.33
1.58	44.29	5.71	2.00	47.72	2.28
1.59	44.41	5.59	2.01	47.78	2.22
1.60	44.52	5.48	2.02	47.83	2.17
1.61	44.63	5.37	2.03	47.88	2.12
1.62	44.74	5.26	2.04	47.93	2.07
1.63	44.84	5.16	2.05	47.98	2.02
1.64	44.95	5.05	2.06	48.03	1.97
1.65	45.05	4.95	2.07	48.08	1.92
1.66	45.15	4.85	2.08	48.12	1.88
1.67	45.25	4.75	2.09	48.17	1.83
1.68	45.35	4.65	2.10	48.21	1.79
1.69	45.45	4.55	2.11	48.26	1.74
1.70	45.54	4.46	2.12	48.30	1.70
1.71	45.64	4.36	2.13	48.34	1.66
1.72	45.73	4.27	2.14	48.38	1.62
1.73	45.82	4.18	2.15	48.42	1.58
1.74	45.91	4.09	2.16	48.46	1.54
1.75	45.99	4.01	2.17	48.50	1.50
1.76	46.08	3.92	2.18	48.54	1.46
1.77	46.16	3.84	2.19	48.57	1.43
1.78	46.25	3.75	2.20	48.61	1.39
1.79	46.33	3.67	2.21	48.64	1.36
1.80	46.41	3.59	2.22	48.68	1.32
1.81	46.49	3.51	2.23	48.71	1.29
1.82	46.56	3.44	2.24	48.75	1.25
1.83	46.64	3.36	2.25	48.78	1.22
1.84	46.71	3.29	2.26	48.81	1.19
1.85	46.78	3.22	2.27	48.84	1.16
1.86	46.86	3.14	2.28	48.87	1.13
1.87	46.93	3.07	2.29	48.90	1.10

Table A-1 (*continued*)

Z	% Mean to Z	% in Tail	Z	% Mean to Z	% in Tail
2.30	48.93	1.07	2.67	49.62	.38
2.31	48.96	1.04	2.68	49.63	.37
2.32	48.98	1.02	2.69	49.64	.36
2.33	49.01	.99	2.70	49.65	.35
2.34	49.04	.96	2.71	49.66	.34
2.35	49.06	.94	2.72	49.67	.33
2.36	49.09	.91	2.73	49.68	.32
2.37	49.11	.89	2.74	49.69	.31
2.38	49.13	.87	2.75	49.70	.30
2.39	49.16	.84	2.76	49.71	.29
2.40	49.18	.82	2.77	49.72	.28
2.41	49.20	.80	2.78	49.73	.27
2.42	49.22	.78	2.79	49.74	.26
2.43	49.25	.75	2.80	49.74	.26
2.44	49.27	.73	2.81	49.75	.25
2.45	49.29	.71	2.82	49.76	.24
2.46	49.31	.69	2.83	49.77	.23
2.47	49.32	.68	2.84	49.77	.23
2.48	49.34	.66	2.85	49.78	.22
2.49	49.36	.64	2.86	49.79	.21
2.50	49.38	.62	2.87	49.79	.21
2.51	49.40	.60	2.88	49.80	.20
2.52	49.41	.59	2.89	49.81	.19
2.53	49.43	.57	2.90	49.81	.19
2.54	49.45	.55	2.91	49.82	.18
2.55	49.46	.54	2.92	49.82	.18
2.56	49.48	.52	2.93	49.83	.17
2.57	49.49	.51	2.94	49.84	.16
2.58	49.51	.49	2.95	49.84	.16
2.59	49.52	.48	2.96	49.85	.15
2.60	49.53	.47	2.97	49.85	.15
2.61	49.55	.45	2.98	49.86	.14
2.62	49.56	.44	2.99	49.86	.14
2.63	49.57	.43	3.00	49.87	.13
2.64	49.59	.41	3.50	49.98	.02
2.65	49.60	.40	4.00	50.00	.00
2.66	49.61	.39	4.50	50.00	.00

Table A-2   Cutoff Scores for the *t* Distribution

	One-Tailed Tests			Two-Tailed Tests		
df	.10	.05	.01	.10	.05	.01
1	3.078	6.314	31.821	6.314	12.706	63.657
2	1.886	2.920	6.965	2.920	4.303	9.925
3	1.638	2.353	4.541	2.353	3.182	5.841
4	1.533	2.132	3.747	2.132	2.776	4.604
5	1.476	2.015	3.365	2.015	2.571	4.032
6	1.440	1.943	3.143	1.943	2.447	3.708
7	1.415	1.895	2.998	1.895	2.365	3.500
8	1.397	1.860	2.897	1.860	2.306	3.356
9	1.383	1.833	2.822	1.833	2.262	3.250
10	1.372	1.813	2.764	1.813	2.228	3.170
11	1.364	1.796	2.718	1.796	2.201	3.106
12	1.356	1.783	2.681	1.783	2.179	3.055
13	1.350	1.771	2.651	1.771	2.161	3.013
14	1.345	1.762	2.625	1.762	2.145	2.977
15	1.341	1.753	2.603	1.753	2.132	2.947
16	1.337	1.746	2.584	1.746	2.120	2.921
17	1.334	1.740	2.567	1.740	2.110	2.898
18	1.331	1.734	2.553	1.734	2.101	2.879
19	1.328	1.729	2.540	1.729	2.093	2.861
20	1.326	1.725	2.528	1.725	2.086	2.846
21	1.323	1.721	2.518	1.721	2.080	2.832
22	1.321	1.717	2.509	1.717	2.074	2.819
23	1.320	1.714	2.500	1.714	2.069	2.808
24	1.318	1.711	2.492	1.711	2.064	2.797
25	1.317	1.708	2.485	1.708	2.060	2.788
26	1.315	1.706	2.479	1.706	2.056	2.779
27	1.314	1.704	2.473	1.704	2.052	2.771
28	1.313	1.701	2.467	1.701	2.049	2.764
29	1.312	1.699	2.462	1.699	2.045	2.757
30	1.311	1.698	2.458	1.698	2.043	2.750
35	1.306	1.690	2.438	1.690	2.030	2.724
40	1.303	1.684	2.424	1.684	2.021	2.705
45	1.301	1.680	2.412	1.680	2.014	2.690
50	1.299	1.676	2.404	1.676	2.009	2.678
55	1.297	1.673	2.396	1.673	2.004	2.668
60	1.296	1.671	2.390	1.671	2.001	2.661
65	1.295	1.669	2.385	1.669	1.997	2.654
70	1.294	1.667	2.381	1.667	1.995	2.648
75	1.293	1.666	2.377	1.666	1.992	2.643
80	1.292	1.664	2.374	1.664	1.990	2.639
85	1.292	1.663	2.371	1.663	1.989	2.635
90	1.291	1.662	2.369	1.662	1.987	2.632
95	1.291	1.661	2.366	1.661	1.986	2.629
100	1.290	1.660	2.364	1.660	1.984	2.626
∞	1.282	1.645	2.327	1.645	1.960	2.576

Table A-3 Cutoff Scores for the F Distribution

Denom-inator df	Signi-ficance Level	Numerator Degrees of Freedom					
		1	2	3	4	5	6
1	.01	4,052	5,000	5,404	5,625	5,764	5,859
	.05	162	200	216	225	230	234
	.10	39.9	49.5	53.6	55.8	57.2	58.2
2	.01	98.50	99.00	99.17	99.25	99.30	99.33
	.05	18.51	19.00	19.17	19.25	19.30	19.33
	.10	8.53	9.00	9.16	9.24	9.29	9.33
3	.01	34.12	30.82	29.46	28.71	28.24	27.91
	.05	10.13	9.55	9.28	9.12	9.01	8.94
	.10	5.54	5.46	5.39	5.34	5.31	5.28
4	.01	21.20	18.00	16.70	15.98	15.52	15.21
	.05	7.71	6.95	6.59	6.39	6.26	6.16
	.10	4.55	4.33	4.19	4.11	4.05	4.01
5	.01	16.26	13.27	12.06	11.39	10.97	10.67
	.05	6.61	5.79	5.41	5.19	5.05	4.95
	.10	4.06	3.78	3.62	3.52	3.45	3.41
6	.01	13.75	10.93	9.78	9.15	8.75	8.47
	.05	5.99	5.14	4.76	4.53	4.39	4.28
	.10	3.78	3.46	3.29	3.18	3.11	3.06
7	.01	12.25	9.55	8.45	7.85	7.46	7.19
	.05	5.59	4.74	4.35	4.12	3.97	3.87
	.10	3.59	3.26	3.08	2.96	2.88	2.83
8	.01	11.26	8.65	7.59	7.01	6.63	6.37
	.05	5.32	4.46	4.07	3.84	3.69	3.58
	.10	3.46	3.11	2.92	2.81	2.73	2.67
9	.01	10.56	8.02	6.99	6.42	6.06	5.80
	.05	5.12	4.26	3.86	3.63	3.48	3.37
	.10	3.36	3.01	2.81	2.69	2.61	2.55
10	.01	10.05	7.56	6.55	6.00	5.64	5.39
	.05	4.97	4.10	3.71	3.48	3.33	3.22
	.10	3.29	2.93	2.73	2.61	2.52	2.46
11	.01	9.65	7.21	6.22	5.67	5.32	5.07
	.05	4.85	3.98	3.59	3.36	3.20	3.10
	.10	3.23	2.86	2.66	2.54	2.45	2.39
12	.01	9.33	6.93	5.95	5.41	5.07	4.82
	.05	4.75	3.89	3.49	3.26	3.11	3.00
	.10	3.18	2.81	2.61	2.48	2.40	2.33
13	.01	9.07	6.70	5.74	5.21	4.86	4.62
	.05	4.67	3.81	3.41	3.18	3.03	2.92
	.10	3.14	2.76	2.56	2.43	2.35	2.28
14	.01	8.86	6.52	5.56	5.04	4.70	4.46
	.05	4.60	3.74	3.34	3.11	2.96	2.85
	.10	3.10	2.73	2.52	2.40	2.31	2.24

(*continued*)

Table A-3 *(continued)*

Denom- inator *df*	Signi- ficance Level	Numerator Degrees of Freedom					
		1	2	3	4	5	6
15	.01	8.68	6.36	5.42	4.89	4.56	4.32
	.05	4.54	3.68	3.29	3.06	2.90	2.79
	.10	3.07	2.70	2.49	2.36	2.27	2.21
16	.01	8.53	6.23	5.29	4.77	4.44	4.20
	.05	4.49	3.63	3.24	3.01	2.85	2.74
	.10	3.05	2.67	2.46	2.33	2.24	2.18
17	.01	8.40	6.11	5.19	4.67	4.34	4.10
	.05	4.45	3.59	3.20	2.97	2.81	2.70
	.10	3.03	2.65	2.44	2.31	2.22	2.15
18	.01	8.29	6.01	5.09	4.58	4.25	4.02
	.05	4.41	3.56	3.16	2.93	2.77	2.66
	.10	3.01	2.62	2.42	2.29	2.20	2.13
19	.01	8.19	5.93	5.01	4.50	4.17	3.94
	.05	4.38	3.52	3.13	2.90	2.74	2.63
	.10	2.99	2.61	2.40	2.27	2.18	2.11
20	.01	8.10	5.85	4.94	4.43	4.10	3.87
	.05	4.35	3.49	3.10	2.87	2.71	2.60
	.10	2.98	2.59	2.38	2.25	2.16	2.09
21	.01	8.02	5.78	4.88	4.37	4.04	3.81
	.05	4.33	3.47	3.07	2.84	2.69	2.57
	.10	2.96	2.58	2.37	2.23	2.14	2.08
22	.01	7.95	5.72	4.82	4.31	3.99	3.76
	.05	4.30	3.44	3.05	2.82	2.66	2.55
	.10	2.95	2.56	2.35	2.22	2.13	2.06
23	.01	7.88	5.66	4.77	4.26	3.94	3.71
	.05	4.28	3.42	3.03	2.80	2.64	2.53
	.10	2.94	2.55	2.34	2.21	2.12	2.05
24	.01	7.82	5.61	4.72	4.22	3.90	3.67
	.05	4.26	3.40	3.01	2.78	2.62	2.51
	.10	2.93	2.54	2.33	2.20	2.10	2.04
25	.01	7.77	5.57	4.68	4.18	3.86	3.63
	.05	4.24	3.39	2.99	2.76	2.60	2.49
	.10	2.92	2.53	2.32	2.19	2.09	2.03
26	.01	7.72	5.53	4.64	4.14	3.82	3.59
	.05	4.23	3.37	2.98	2.74	2.59	2.48
	.10	2.91	2.52	2.31	2.18	2.08	2.01
27	.01	7.68	5.49	4.60	4.11	3.79	3.56
	.05	4.21	3.36	2.96	2.73	2.57	2.46
	.10	2.90	2.51	2.30	2.17	2.07	2.01
28	.01	7.64	5.45	4.57	4.08	3.75	3.53
	.05	4.20	3.34	2.95	2.72	2.56	2.45
	.10	2.89	2.50	2.29	2.16	2.07	2.00

Table A-3 (*continued*)

Denom- inator *df*	Signi- ficance Level	Numerator Degrees of Freedom					
		1	2	3	4	5	6
29	.01	7.60	5.42	4.54	4.05	3.73	3.50
	.05	4.18	3.33	2.94	2.70	2.55	2.43
	.10	2.89	2.50	2.28	2.15	2.06	1.99
30	.01	7.56	5.39	4.51	4.02	3.70	3.47
	.05	4.17	3.32	2.92	2.69	2.53	2.42
	.10	2.88	2.49	2.28	2.14	2.05	1.98
35	.01	7.42	5.27	4.40	3.91	3.59	3.37
	.05	4.12	3.27	2.88	2.64	2.49	2.37
	.10	2.86	2.46	2.25	2.11	2.02	1.95
40	.01	7.32	5.18	4.31	3.83	3.51	3.29
	.05	4.09	3.23	2.84	2.61	2.45	2.34
	.10	2.84	2.44	2.23	2.09	2.00	1.93
45	.01	7.23	5.11	4.25	3.77	3.46	3.23
	.05	4.06	3.21	2.81	2.58	2.42	2.31
	.10	2.82	2.43	2.21	2.08	1.98	1.91
50	.01	7.17	5.06	4.20	3.72	3.41	3.19
	.05	4.04	3.18	2.79	2.56	2.40	2.29
	.10	2.81	2.41	2.20	2.06	1.97	1.90
55	.01	7.12	5.01	4.16	3.68	3.37	3.15
	.05	4.02	3.17	2.77	2.54	2.38	2.27
	.10	2.80	2.40	2.19	2.05	1.96	1.89
60	.01	7.08	4.98	4.13	3.65	3.34	3.12
	.05	4.00	3.15	2.76	2.53	2.37	2.26
	.10	2.79	2.39	2.18	2.04	1.95	1.88
65	.01	7.04	4.95	4.10	3.62	3.31	3.09
	.05	3.99	3.14	2.75	2.51	2.36	2.24
	.10	2.79	2.39	2.17	2.03	1.94	1.87
70	.01	7.01	4.92	4.08	3.60	3.29	3.07
	.05	3.98	3.13	2.74	2.50	2.35	2.23
	.10	2.78	2.38	2.16	2.03	1.93	1.86
75	.01	6.99	4.90	4.06	3.58	3.27	3.05
	.05	3.97	3.12	2.73	2.49	2.34	2.22
	.10	2.77	2.38	2.16	2.02	1.93	1.86
80	.01	6.96	4.88	4.04	3.56	3.26	3.04
	.05	3.96	3.11	2.72	2.49	2.33	2.22
	.10	2.77	2.37	2.15	2.02	1.92	1.85
85	.01	6.94	4.86	4.02	3.55	3.24	3.02
	.05	3.95	3.10	2.71	2.48	2.32	2.21
	.10	2.77	2.37	2.15	2.01	1.92	1.85
90	.01	6.93	4.85	4.01	3.54	3.23	3.01
	.05	3.95	3.10	2.71	2.47	2.32	2.20
	.10	2.76	2.36	2.15	2.01	1.91	1.84

(*continued*)

Table A-3 *(continued)*

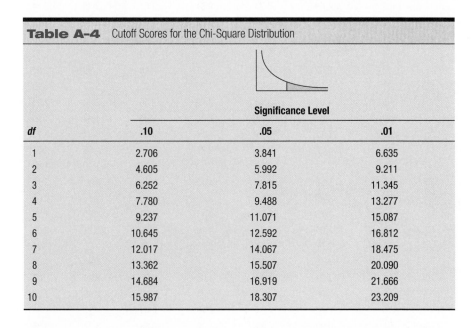

Denominator df	Significance Level	\multicolumn{6}{c}{Numerator Degrees of Freedom}						
		1	**2**	**3**	**4**	**5**	**6**
95	.01	6.91	4.84	4.00	3.52	3.22	3.00
	.05	3.94	3.09	2.70	2.47	2.31	2.20
	.10	2.76	2.36	2.14	2.01	1.91	1.84
100	.01	6.90	4.82	3.98	3.51	3.21	2.99
	.05	3.94	3.09	2.70	2.46	2.31	2.19
	.10	2.76	2.36	2.14	2.00	1.91	1.83
∞	.01	6.64	4.61	3.78	3.32	3.02	2.80
	.05	3.84	3.00	2.61	2.37	2.22	2.10
	.10	2.71	2.30	2.08	1.95	1.85	1.78

Table A-4 Cutoff Scores for the Chi-Square Distribution

df	\multicolumn{3}{c}{Significance Level}		
	.10	**.05**	**.01**
1	2.706	3.841	6.635
2	4.605	5.992	9.211
3	6.252	7.815	11.345
4	7.780	9.488	13.277
5	9.237	11.071	15.087
6	10.645	12.592	16.812
7	12.017	14.067	18.475
8	13.362	15.507	20.090
9	14.684	16.919	21.666
10	15.987	18.307	23.209

Table A-5 Index to Power Tables and Tables Giving Number of Participants Needed for 80% Power

Hypothesis-Testing Procedure	Chapter	Power Table	Number of Participants Table
t test for dependent means	7	p. 248	p. 249
t test for independent means	8	p. 289	p. 290
One-way analysis of variance	9	p. 341	p. 341
Two-way analysis of variance	10	p. 409	p. 410
Correlation coefficient (*r*)	11	p. 465	p. 465
Chi-square test for independence	13	p. 556	p. 557

Answers to Set I Practice Problems

Chapter 1

1. (a) Satisfaction with the vocational counselor; (b) 1, 2, 3, or 4; (c) 3.
2. (a) Nominal (or categorical); (b) numeric (or quantitative)—more precisely, equal interval; (c) numeric (or quantitative)—more precisely, rank order (or ordinal).
3. (a) Frequency table:

Number of Children	Frequency	Percent
6	1	5
5	0	0
4	1	5
3	2	10
2	7	35
1	5	25
0	4	20

(b) Histogram:

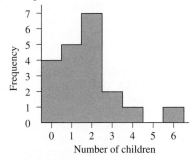

Number of children

(c) Unimodal, skewed to the right.

4. (a) Frequency table:

Hours	Frequency	Percent	Hours	Frequency	Percent
18	1	2	8	5	10
17	0	0	7	11	22
16	0	0	6	4	8
15	1	2	5	2	4
14	0	0	4	3	6
13	2	4	3	4	8
12	1	2	2	2	4
11	3	6	1	1	2
10	5	10	0	1	2
9	4	8			

(b) Histogram is based on the preceding frequency table. See answer to question 3 for an example.

(c) Approximately unimodal, slightly skewed to the right.

5. (a) Frequency table:

Score	Frequency	Percent	Score	Frequency	Percent
96	1	4	72	0	0
95	0	0	71	1	4
94	0	0	70	1	4
93	0	0	69	1	4
92	1	4	68	2	8
91	1	4	67	1	4
90	0	0	66	0	0
89	0	0	65	0	0
88	0	0	64	2	8
87	1	4	63	0	0
86	0	0	62	0	0
85	1	4	61	0	0
84	0	0	60	0	0
83	2	8	59	1	4
82	0	0	58	0	0
81	1	4	57	0	0
80	1	4	56	0	0
79	0	0	55	0	0
78	0	0	54	0	0
77	0	0	53	0	0
76	2	8	52	0	0
75	2	8	51	0	0
74	1	4	50	1	4
73	1	4			

(b) Based on the preceding frequency table. See answer to question 3b for an example.

(c) Grouped frequency table:

Interval	Frequency	Percent
90–99	3	12
80–89	6	24
70–79	8	32
60–69	6	24
50–59	2	8

(d) Based on frequency table in (c) above. See answer to question 3b for an example.

(e) Unimodal, approximately symmetrical (slightly skewed to the left).

6. (a) Similar to question 5a.

(b) Grouped frequency table:

Interval	Frequency	Percent
80–89	10	29.4
70–79	0	0
60–69	5	14.7
50–59	0	0
40–49	5	14.7
30–39	7	20.6
20–29	7	20.6

(c) Histogram:

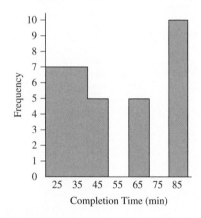

(d) Roughly rectangular.

7. (a) Bimodal; (b) approximately normal (or unimodal or symmetrical); (c) multimodal.

8. (a) Any distribution that is symmetrical (that is, the pattern of frequencies on the left and right side of the distribution are mirror images of each other); (b) any distribution in which all values have approximately the same frequency; (c) any distribution in which the scores are piled up on the left side of the distribution and are spread out on the right side of the distribution.

9. (a) A distribution is the way a group of numbers is spread out over the possible values the numbers can have. You can describe such a distribution with a graph, called a histogram—a kind of bar graph with one bar for each possible value with one unit of height for each time its particular value occurs. In a histogram, a symmetrical distribution has a symmetrical shape (the right and left halves are mirror images). A unimodal distribution is one in which this graph has a single high point, with the other values gradually decreasing around it.

(b) A negatively skewed unimodal distribution has a single high point, is not symmetrical, and its tail—the long, low side—extends to the left (where the negative scores go on the graph).

10. (a) This is called a frequency table because it lays out how frequently (how many times) each category occurs for nine different categories. A frequency table makes the pattern of numbers easy to see. For example, of the 90 college students in the study, 19 gave bad news about Relationship with family (the first category). The table also gives the percentages. For example, 19 students is 19/90 of the total, or 21.1 percent.

(b) The most bad news is given in four of the nine categories: Relationship with family, Relationship with actual/potential girlfriend/boyfriend, Relationship with friends, and Health of family member/friend. All of these categories had to do with family members or friends and most with relationships, and there were few cases in the other categories (which had little directly to do with family or friends).

Chapter 2

1. (a) $M = (\Sigma X)/N = 261/9 = 29$; (b) 28; (c) $\Sigma(X - M)^2 = (32 - 29)^2 + (28 - 29)^2 + (24 - 29)^2 + (28 - 29)^2 + (28 - 29)^2 + (31 - 29)^2 + (35 - 29)^2 + (29 - 29)^2 + (26 - 29)^2 = 86$; (d) $SD^2 = \Sigma(X - M)^2/N = 86/9 = 9.56$; (e) $SD = \sqrt{SD^2} = \sqrt{9.56} = 3.09$.

2. (a) 4; (b) 4; (c) 26; (d) 3.25; (e) 1.80.

3. (a) 4.3125; (b) 4.5550; (c) 10.7637; (d) 2.6909; (e) 1.6404.

4. The average temperature, in the sense of adding up the 10 readings and dividing by 10, was −7 degrees Celsius. This is the *mean.* However, if you line up the temperatures from highest to lowest, the middle two numbers are both −5 degrees. The middle number is the *median.* The specific temperature that came up most often is the *mode;* there are two modes, −1 and −5.

As for the variation (the amount of variability), one approach is the *variance*—the average of each temperature's squared deviation from the mean temperature, which is 46.8. You get a more direct sense of how much a group of numbers vary among themselves if you take the square root of the variance, which gives the standard deviation; the square root of 46.8 is 6.84. This means, roughly, that on an average day the temperature differs by 6.84 degrees from the average of −7 degrees.

5. (a) .4000; (b) .1446; (c) similar to question 4.

6. The mean, mode, and median for a normal curve are all located at the same midpoint of the curve (that is also the highest point in the distribution). The mode is the highest point in the distribution, which for a normal curve falls exactly at the midpoint of the distribution. This midpoint is the median value, since half of the scores in the distribution are below that point and half are above that point. The mean also falls at the same point because the normal curve is symmetrical about the midpoint, and every score in the left hand side of the curve has a matching score on the right hand side.

7. The mean is the ordinary arithmetic average: add up the total number of anxiety attacks and divide by the number of people. The mean number of anxiety attacks over a two-week period was 6.84. The *SD* (standard deviation), roughly speaking, is the average amount that the number of anxiety attacks are spread out from their average—in this case, by 3.18 attacks. This is quite a lot of spread. To be more

precise, you figure the standard deviation by taking each person's number of anxiety attacks and subtracting 6.84 from it and squaring this difference; the standard deviation is the square root of the average of these differences.

8. Like the answer to question 7, focusing on means of 5.02, 5.11, 32.27, and 31.36 and on standard deviations of 2.16, 2.08, 20.36, and 21.08.

Chapter 3

1. (a) $Z = (X - M)/SD = (91 - 79)/12 = 1$; (b) $-.92$; (c) 2.
2. (a) If IQ = 107, $Z = (X - M)/SD = (107 - 100)/16 = .44$; $X = (Z)(SD) + M = (.44)(41) + 231 = 249$. (We rounded off to a whole number because the actual score on the test is the number of items correct, which cannot be a fraction.) (b) $Z = -1.06$; $X = 188$; (c) $Z = 0$; $X = 231$.
3. Wife: $Z = (X - M)/SD = (63 - 60)/6 = .5$. Husband: $Z = (59 - 55)/4 = 1$. The husband has adjusted better in relation to other divorced men than the wife has adjusted in relation to other divorced women.

   For wives, a score of 63 is 3 points better than the average of 60 for divorced women in general. (The mean in the problem is the ordinary average—the sum of the scores divided by the number of scores.) There is, of course, some variation in scores among divorced women. The approximate average amount that women's scores differ from the average is 6 points; this is the *SD* (standard deviation) referred to in the problem. (*SD* is only approximately the average amount scores differ from the mean. To be precise, *SD* is the square root of the average of the square of the difference of each score from the mean.) Thus, the wife's score is only half as far as above the mean of wives' scores. This gives her what is called a *Z* score of $+.5$, which gives her location on a scale that compares her score to that of divorced women in general. Using the same logic, the husband's divorce adjustment is as much above the mean as the average amount that men differ from the mean; that is, he has a *Z* score of $+1$. What this all means is that both have adjusted better than average for their gender, but the husband has adjusted better in relation to other divorced men than the wife has adjusted in relation to other divorced women.
4. (a) 50%; (b) 16%; (c) 98%; (d) 84%; (e) 50%; (f) 84%; (g) 2%; (h) 16%.
5. (a) 50; (b) 45; (c) 40; (d) 35; (e) 30.
6. (a) From the normal curve table, 43.32% (.4332) have *Z* scores between the mean and 1.5. By definition, 50% have *Z* scores below the mean. Thus, the total percentage below 1.5 is 50% + 43.32% = 93.32%; (b) 6.68%; (c) 6.68%; (d) 93.32%; (e) 1.79%; (f) 98.21%; (g) 32.64%; (h) 3.75%; (i) 4.65%.
7. (a) $Z = (16 - 15)/5 = .2$; from the normal curve table, percentage in the tail for a *Z* score of $.2 = 42.07\%$; (b) 34.46%; (c) 27.43%; (d) 72.57%; (e) 42.07%.
8. (a) Top 40% means 40% in the tail; the nearest *Z* score from the normal curve table for 40% in the tail is .25; a *Z* score of .25 equals a raw score of $(.25)(5) + 15 = 16.25$; (b) 17.6; (c) 19.2.
9. (a) 21.90%; (b) 22.24%; (c) 42.79%; (d) 44.06%; (e) 21.90%.
10. (a) Needed $Z = 1.64$; this corresponds to a raw score of $(1.64)(10) + 50 = 66.4$. (b) The scores for many things you

measure, in nature and in psychology, tend approximately to follow the particular pattern shown in the figure shown here, called a "normal curve." In a normal curve, most of the scores are near the middle, with fewer numbers of scores at each extreme. Because the normal curve is mathematically defined, the precise proportion of scores in any particular section of it can be calculated, and these have been listed in special tables. (Then explain mean and standard deviation as in answers to Chapter 2 problems, and *Z* scores as in question 3.) The normal curve table tells the percentage of score in the normal curve between the mean and any particular *Z* score, and the percentage of scores in the tail for any *Z* score.

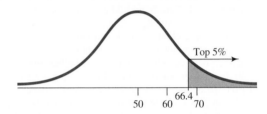

The coordination test scores are known to follow a normal curve. Thus, you can look up in the table the *Z* score for the point on the normal curve at which 5% of the scores are in the tail. This is a *Z* score of 1.64 (actually, there is not an exact point on the table for 5% in the tail; so I could have used either 1.64 or 1.65). With a standard deviation of 10, a *Z* score of 1.64 is 16.4 points above the mean, Adding that to the mean of 50 makes the score needed to be in the top 5% turn out to 66.4.

11. A *sample* is a group of people studied that represents the entire group to which the results are intended to apply, called the *population*. (In this example, the population is the U.S. adult public.) You study a sample because it would be impractical or impossible to test the entire population. One way of ensuring that the sample is not systematically unrepresentative is to select the sample randomly. This does not mean haphazardly. For example, just taking adults who are easily available to test would be haphazard sampling. But this would not be a good method because whatever factors make them easily available—such as living in a nearby town—might make them unrepresentative of the population as a whole. By using randomly selected telephone numbers to select the sample, the researchers are trying to produce a sample that is representative of the whole population.
12. (a) 10/50: $p = 10/50 = .2$; (b) .4; (c) $(10 + 20)/50 = .6$; (d) .6; (e) 1. (f) The probability of a particular thing happening is usually defined as the number of possible ways the thing could happen (the number of *possible successful outcomes*) divided by the number of possible ways things like this could happen (the number of *all possible outcomes*). For part (a) there are 10 different drug/alcohol people you might pick out of a total of 50 people you are picking from. Thus, the probability is $10/50 = .2$. The same principle applies for parts (b) through (e).

Chapter 4

1. (a) Hypothesis-testing procedure: the logical, statistical procedure for determining the likelihood of your study having

gotten a particular pattern of results if the null hypothesis is true. (b) .05 Significance level: the situation in hypothesis testing in which you decide to reject the null hypothesis because the probability of getting your particular results if the null hypothesis were true is less than 5%. (c) Two-tailed test: a procedure used in hypothesis testing when the research hypothesis does not specify a particular direction of difference; it tests for extreme results that are either higher or lower than would be expected by chance.

2. It is possible that the research hypothesis is correct but the result in the particular sample was not extreme enough to be able to reject the null hypothesis.

3.   i. (a) Population 1: Canadian children of librarians; Population 2: All Canadian children. (b) Population 1 children have a higher average reading ability than Population 2 children. (c) Population 1's average reading ability is not higher than Population 2's. (d) One-tailed, because the question is whether they "score higher"; only one direction of difference is of interest.
    ii. (a) Population 1: People who live in a particular city; Population 2: All people who live in the region. (b) Populations 1 and 2 have different mean incomes. (c) Populations 1 and 2 have the same mean income. (d) Two-tailed, because the question is whether the income of the people in the city is "different" from those in the region as a whole; a difference in either direction would be of interest.
   iii. (a) Population 1: People who have experienced an earthquake; Population 2: People in general. (b) Populations 1 and 2 have different mean levels of self-confidence. (c) Populations 1 and 2 have the same mean level of self-confidence. (d) Two-tailed, because the question specifies "more or less"; a difference in either direction would be of interest.

4.

Study	Cutoff	Z Score on Comparison Distribution	Decision
A	+1.64	2	Reject null hypothesis
B	±1.96	2	Reject null hypothesis
C	+2.33	2	Inconclusive
D	±2.57	2	Inconclusive
E	+1.64	1	Inconclusive

5.

Study	Cutoff	Z Score on Comparison Distribution	Decision
A	+1.64	1	Inconclusive
B	±2.57	4	Reject null hypothesis
C	±2.57	3	Reject null hypothesis
D	±2.57	2.5	Inconclusive
E	−1.64	−2	Reject null hypothesis

6. (a) ❶ **Restate the question as a research hypothesis and a null hypothesis about the populations.** There are two populations of interest:
Population 1: Students who are prevented from using their sense of smell.
Population 2: Students in general.

The research hypothesis is that students prevented from using their sense of smell (Population 1) will do worse on the taste task than students in general (Population 2). The null hypothesis is that students prevented from using their sense of smell (Population 1) will not do worse on the taste task than students in general (Population 2).
❷ **Determine the characteristics of the comparison distribution.** The comparison distribution will be the same as Population 2. As stated in the problem, $\mu = 14$ and $\sigma = 4$. We assume it follows a normal curve.
❸ **Determine the cutoff sample score on the comparison distribution at which the null hypothesis should be rejected.** For a one-tailed test at the .05 level, the cutoff is −1.64. (The cutoff is a *negative value,* because the research hypothesis is that Population 1 will *do worse* on the task than Population 2—that is, Population 1 will have a *lower score* on the task than Population 2.)
❹ **Determine your sample's score on the comparison distribution.** The sample's score was 5. $Z = (5 - 14)/4 = -2.25$.
❺ **Decide whether to reject the null hypothesis.** A Z score of −2.25 is more extreme than the cutoff of −1.64. Thus, you can reject the null hypothesis. The research hypothesis is supported—not having a sense of smell makes for fewer correct identifications.
(b) In brief, you solve this problem by considering the likelihood that being without a sense of smell makes no difference. If the sense of smell made no difference, the probability of the student studied getting any particular number correct is simply the probability of students in general getting any particular number correct. We know the distribution of the number correct that students get in general. Thus, you can figure that probability. It turns out that it would be fairly unlikely to get only five correct; so the researcher concludes that not having the sense of smell does make a difference.

To go into the details a bit, the key issue is determining these probabilities. We assumed that the number correct for the students in general follows a normal curve—a specific bell-shaped mathematical pattern in which most of the scores are in the middle and there are fewer scores as the number correct gets higher or lower. There are tables showing exactly what proportions are between the middle and any particular Z score on the normal curve.

When considering what to conclude from a study, researchers often use a convention that, if a result could have happened by chance less than 5% of the time under a particular scenario, the scenario will be considered unlikely. The normal curve tables show that the top 5% of the normal curve begins with a Z score of 1.64. The normal curve is completely symmetrical; thus, the bottom 5% includes all Z scores below −1.64. Therefore, the researcher would probably set the following rule: the scenario in which being without the sense of smell makes no difference will be rejected as unlikely if the number correct (converted to a

Z score using the mean and standard deviation for students in general) is less than −1.64.

The actual number correct for the student who could not use the sense of smell was 5. The normal curve for students in general had a mean of 14 and a standard deviation of 4. Getting 5 correct is 9 below the mean of 14; in terms of standard deviations of 4 each, it is 9/4 below the mean. A Z score of −2.25 is more extreme than −1.64. Thus, the researcher concludes that the scenario in which being without smell has no effect is unlikely. This is shown in what I have drawn here:

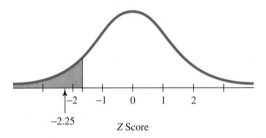

7. Cutoff (.01 level, one-tailed) = −2.33; Z score on comparison distribution for patient studied = 1.20; the experiment is inconclusive. Hypothesis testing steps, explanation, and sketch are similar to those of question 6.
8. Cutoff (.05 level, two-tailed) = ±1.96; Z score on comparison distribution for the police chief studied = .81; the experiment is inconclusive. Hypothesis testing steps, explanation, and sketch similar to question 6.
9. The two Ms (5.7 and 4.8) and the p < .05 are crucial. M stands for *mean,* the average of the scores in a particular group. The average number of times per day the high narcissism participants looked in the mirrors was 5.7, while the average for the low narcissism participants was only 4.8. The p < .05 tells us that this difference is statistically significant at the .05 level. This means that, if a person's level of narcissism made no difference in how often the person looked in the mirror, the chances of getting two groups of participants who were this different on looking in the mirror just by chance would be 5%. Hence, you can reject that possibility as unlikely and conclude that the level of narcissism does make a difference in how often people look in the mirror.
10. Similar to question 9.

Chapter 5

1. The standard deviation of the distribution of means is generally smaller than the standard deviation of the distribution of the population of individuals because there is less variation among means of samples of more than one score than there are among individual scores. This is because the likelihood of two extreme scores in the same direction randomly ending up in the same sample is less than the probability of each of those extreme scores being chosen individually.
2. (a) $\sigma^2 = 10^2 = 100$; $\sigma_M^2 = \sigma^2/N = 100/2 = 50$; $\sigma_M = \sqrt{\sigma_M^2} = \sqrt{50} = 7.07$; (b) 5.77; (c) 5; (d) 3.33.
3. (a) $\sigma^2 = 20^2 = 400$; $\sigma_M^2 = \sigma^2/N = 400/2 = 200$; $\sigma_M = \sqrt{\sigma_M^2} = \sqrt{200} = 14.14$; (b) 11.55; (c) 10; (d) 6.67.

4. (a) The best estimate of the population mean is the sample mean of 100. From question 2a, the standard deviation of the distribution of means (σ_M) is 7.07. For the 95% confidence limits, the Z scores you want are −1.96 and +1.96. Lower limit = (−1.96)(7.07) + 100 = 86.14; upper limit = (1.96)(7.07) + 100 = 113.86; (b) 88.69, 111.31; (c) 90.2, 109.8; (d) 93.47, 106.53.
5. (a) The best estimate of the population mean is the sample mean of 10. From question 3a, the standard deviation of the distribution of means (σ_M) is 14.14. For the 99% confidence limits, the Z scores you want are −2.57 and +2.57. Lower limit = (−2.57)(14.14) + 10 = −26.34; upper limit = (2.57)(14.14) + 10 = 46.34; (b) −19.68, 39.68; (c) −15.70, 35.70; (d) −7.14, 27.14.
6. (a) ❶ **Restate the question as a research hypothesis and a null hypothesis about the populations.** There are two populations of interest:
Population 1: People given the experimental treatment.
Population 2: People in general (who do not get the experimental treatment).

The research hypothesis is that the population given the experimental treatment (Population 1) has a different mean score than people in general (Population 2). The null hypothesis is that Population 1's mean is the same as Population 2's.
❷ **Determine the characteristics of the comparison distribution.** Comparison distribution is a distribution of means of samples of 10 taken from the distribution of Population 2. $\mu_M = \mu = 40$; $\sigma_M^2 = \sigma^2/N = 6^2/10 = 3.6$; $\sigma_M = \sqrt{\sigma_M^2} = \sqrt{3.6} = 1.90$. Because the population is normal, the distribution of means is normal.
❸ **Determine the cutoff sample score on the comparison distribution at which the null hypothesis should be rejected.** For a two-tailed test at the .05 level, the cutoffs are −1.96 and 1.96.
❹ **Determine your sample's score on the comparison distribution.** $Z = (44 − 40)/1.90 = 2.11$.
❺ **Decide whether to reject the null hypothesis.** 2.11 is more extreme than 1.96. Thus, you can reject the null hypothesis. The research hypothesis is supported; those who receive the experimental treatment score differently from the general population. The distributions involved are shown on the next page.
(b) Hypothesis-testing steps similar to part (a). $\sigma_M = 6$; $Z = (48 − 40)/6 = 1.33$; do not reject null hypothesis; study is inconclusive as to whether those who receive the experimental treatment are different from those in the general population. (c) For part (a), 95% confidence interval: Lower limit = (−1.96)(1.9) + 44 = 40.28; upper limit = (1.96)(1.9) + 44 = 47.72. For part (b), 95% confidence interval: 36.24 to 59.76.
7. Hypothesis-testing steps and drawing similar to question 6. (a) $\sigma_M = .8$; $Z = (82 − 81)/.8 = 1.25$; do not reject null hypothesis. (b) $\sigma_M = 2.53$; $Z = (84 − 81)/2.53 = 1.19$; do not reject null hypothesis. (c) For part (a), 99% confidence interval: 79.94 to 84.06. For part (b), 99% confidence interval: 77.50 to 90.50.
8. (a) and (b) Hypothesis-testing steps and drawing similar to question 6. $\sigma_M = .1$; $Z = (1.5 − 1.8)/.1 = −3$; reject the null hypothesis.

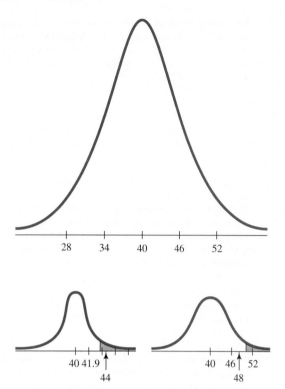

6 (a)   6 (b)

was 3 standard deviations below the mean of the distribution of means, making it clearly more extreme than the cutoff. Thus, you can reject the null hypothesis and conclude that the results support the hypothesis that elderly women who take part in the special program have lower reaction times.

(d) 99% confidence interval: 1.24 to 1.76. The confidence interval is an estimate (based on your sample's mean and the standard deviation of the distribution of means) of the range of values that is likely to include the true population mean for the group studied (Population 1: in this example, women who receive the special reaction-time program). A 99% confidence interval is the range of values you are 99% confident include the true population mean. The lower limit of this interval is the mean of the lowest distribution of means that would have a 99% chance of including this sample mean; its upper limit is the mean of the highest distribution of means that would have a 99% chance of including this sample mean.

To figure the confidence interval, you first consider that the best single estimate of the mean of Population 1 is the sample's mean (in this case, 1.5). You then assume that the standard deviation of the distribution of means for this population is the same as for the known population (which we figured earlier to be .1). Based on this information, if the true population mean was 1.5, 99% of the time, sample means would fall between a Z score of -2.57 (the point on the normal curve that includes 49.5% of the scores below the mean) and $+2.57$. In our example, these Z scores correspond to raw scores of 1.24 and 1.76.

It turns out that the values figured in this way are the limits of the confidence interval. Why? Suppose the true population mean was 1.24. In this case, there would be a .5% chance of getting a mean as large as or larger than 1.5. (That is, with a mean of 1.24 and a standard deviation of .1, 1.5 is exactly 2.57 standard deviations above the mean, which is the point that corresponds to the cutoff for the top .5% of this curve.) Similarly, if the true population mean was 1.76, there would only be a .5% chance of getting a mean lower than 1.5.

9. (a) and (b) Hypothesis-testing steps and drawing similar to question 6. $\sigma_M = .2$; $Z = (5.9 - 5.5)/.2 = 2$; reject the null hypothesis. (c) Similar to question 8c, plus an explanation of material from previous chapter on hypothesis testing, normal curve, means, and standard deviations. (d) 95% confidence interval: 5.51 to 6.29.

10. The error bars are the lines that go above and below the top of each bar. The error bars show, for each particular group, the standard deviation of the distribution of means for people like those in this group. (Then explain a distribution of means as in question 8c.)

11. Similar to question 8d.

(c) This is a standard hypothesis-testing problem, with one exception. You can't compare directly the reaction times for the group of 25 women tested to a distribution of reaction times for individual women. The probability of a group of scores having an extreme mean just by chance is much less than the probability of any single individual having an extreme score just by chance. (When taking a group of scores at random, any extreme individual scores are likely to be balanced out by less extreme or oppositely extreme scores.) Thus, you need to compare the mean of the group of 25 reaction times to a distribution of what would happen if you were to take many random groups of 25 reaction time scores and find the mean of each group of 25 scores.

Such a distribution of many means of samples has the same mean as the original distribution of individual scores (there is no reason for it to be otherwise). However, it is a narrower curve. This is because the chances of extremes are less. In fact, its variance will be exactly the variance of the original distribution of individuals divided by the number of scores in each sample. In this example, this makes a distribution of means with a mean of 1.8 and a standard deviation of .1 (that is, the square root of the result of $.5^2$ divided by 25). This will be a normal distribution because a distribution of many means from a normally distributed population is also normal.

The cutoff for significance, using the .01 level and a one-tailed test, is -2.33. The mean reaction time of the group of 25 women who received the special program, 1.5,

Chapter 6

1. *Alpha* is the probability of rejecting the null hypothesis when the null hypothesis is actually true (that is, the probability of making a Type I error). *Beta* is the probability of failing to reject the null hypothesis when in fact the null hypothesis is false (that is, the probability of making a Type II error).

2. (a)

	Real Situation	
	Null Hypothesis True	**Research Hypothesis True**
Research Hypothesis Supported (Reject null)	*Type I Error* Decide more recess time improves behavior, but it really doesn't	*Correct Decision* Decide more recess time improves behavior, and it really does
Study Inconclusive (Do not reject null)	*Correct Decision* Decide effect of recess time on behavior is not shown in this study; actually more recess time doesn't improve behavior	*Type II Error* Decide effect of recess time on behavior is not shown in this study; actually more recess time improves behavior

(Conclusion from Hypothesis Testing)

(b) and (c) Answers are similar to those of question 2a.

3. (a) $d = (\mu_1 - \mu_2)/\sigma = (19 - 25)/12 = -.50$, medium; (b) $-.25$, small; (c) 0, no effect; (d) .42, medium; (e) .83, large.

4. (a) $d = (\mu_1 - \mu_2)/\sigma = (50 - 50)/5 = 0$, no effect; (b) .40, medium; (c) .80, large; (d) 1.20, large; (e) $-.60$, medium.

5. A small positive effect size is .20; Predicted $\mu_1 = \mu_2 + (d)(\sigma) = 15 + (.20)(2) = 15.4$; (b) 14; (c) 16.6; (d) 15.7; (e) 12.

6.

	Z Needed for Significance	**σ_M**	**Score for Significance**
(a)	1.64	.4	90.66
(b)	1.64	.4	90.66
(c)	1.64	.2	90.33
(d)	1.64	1.0	91.64
(e)	2.33	.4	90.93
(f)	1.96	.4	90.78

	Z for Significance on the Predicted Population	**Beta**	**Power**	**Effect Size**
(a)	$(90.66 - 91)/.4 = -.85$	.20	.80	.25
(b)	$(90.66 - 92)/.4 = -3.35$	<.01	>.99	.50
(c)	$(90.33 - 91)/.2 = -3.35$	<.01	>.99	.50
(d)	$(91.64 - 91)/1 = .64$	.74	.26	.25
(e)	$(90.93 - 91)/.4 = -.18$	.43	.57	.25
(f)	$(90.78 - 91)/.4 = -.55$	.29	.71	.25

Drawing of overlapping distributions for part (a) follows.

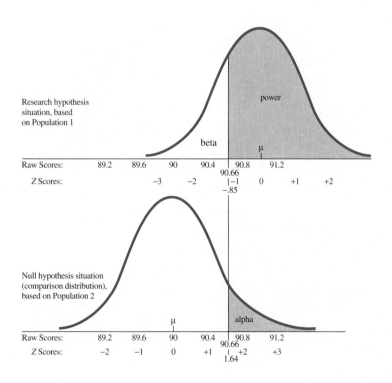

7. (a) Not affected; (b) possibly of small importance; (c) regarding situation (a), the significance tells you the probability of getting your results if the null hypothesis is true; sample size is already taken into account in figuring the significance. Regarding situation (b), it is possible to get a significant result with a large sample even when the actual practical effect is slight, such as when the mean of your sample (which is your best estimate of the mean of the population that gets the experimental treatment) is only slightly higher than the mean of the known population. This is possible because significance is based on the difference between the mean of your sample and the known population mean divided by the standard deviation of the distribution of means. If the sample size is very large, then the standard deviation of the distribution of means is very small (because it is figured by taking the square root of the result of dividing the population variance by the sample size). Thus, even a small difference between the means when divided by a very small denominator can give a large overall result, making the study significant.

8. Power is the chance of rejecting the null hypothesis if the research hypothesis is true. In other words, the power of a study represents the likelihood that you will get a statistically significant result in your study, if in fact the research hypothesis is true. Ideally, a study should have power of 80% or more. If a study has low power and does not get a statistically significant result, the result of the study is entirely inconclusive. This is because it is not clear whether the nonsignificant result is due to the low power of the study or because the research hypothesis is in fact false.

   Effect size can be thought of as the degree to which populations do not overlap. The larger the effect size is, the greater the power will be. As noted by Aron and colleagues,

their study had a high level of power (about 90%) for detecting both large and medium-sized effects. Given this high level of power, the researchers were able to conclude that the most likely reason for the nonsignificant study results is that the research hypothesis is in fact false. As the researchers noted, with such a high level of power, it is very unlikely that the results of the study would be nonsignificant if there were in fact a medium-sized or large effect in the population. Since smaller effect sizes are associated with lower power, the researchers were careful not to rule out the possibility that there is in fact a small effect in the population (which may not have been detected in the study due to the lower power for identifying a small effect size).

9. (a) Increases power; (b) decreases power; (c) increases power; (d) decreases power; (e) decreases power.

10. (i) When planning an experiment, to permit changes of various kinds (or even abandon the project) if power is too low (or possibly to make the study less costly, for example by reducing the number of participants, if power is higher than reasonably needed). (ii) After a study is done that had nonsignificant results, to evaluate whether the result should be attributed to the null hypothesis being false (in the high-power situation) or to inadequate power so that it is still reasonable to think that future research might have a chance of being significant. (Also, in the case of a significant result with a large sample, if power is very high, this suggests that a low effect size is possible, so that, although the result is significant, it may not be very important.)

11. (a) ❶ $\sigma_M = 2$; ❷ significance cutoff: $Z = 1.64$; raw = $50 + (1.64)(2) = 53.28$; ❸ corresponding Z on predicted distribution = $(53.28 - 55)/2 = -.86$; ❹ from Z table, power = .81, beta = .19.
   (b)

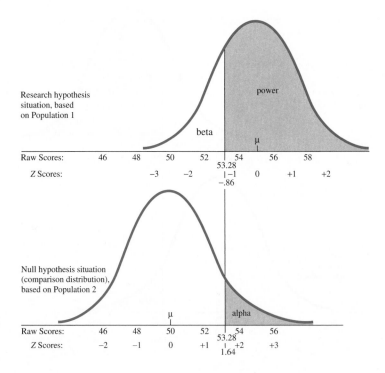

(c) Power is the chance of rejecting the null hypothesis if the research hypothesis is true. To find power, you first need the standard deviation of the comparison distribution (2 here) and the cutoff to reject the null hypothesis in raw score terms (this is a one-tailed test at the .05 level; so it is a Z of 1.64, which for this distribution's mean and standard deviation is 53.28). You also have to be able to assume that the distributions of both the known population (Population 2) and the distribution for the population based on the research hypothesis (Population 1) follow a normal curve and have the same variance. Then comes the power figuring. The researcher hypothesizes that the mean of the population of artists (Population 1) is 55. The distribution of means from this population would be normal with mean = 55 and $\sigma_M = 2$. We already figured that any mean above 53.28 will be significant in terms of the comparison distribution. But a score of 53.28 has a Z score of only $-.86$ on the distribution of means based on the researcher's hypothesis. Using the normal curve table, 81% is above $-.86$. Assuming that the research's predictions are correct, there is an 81% chance that a sample of 36 artists will produce a result high enough to reject the null hypothesis. That is, power is 81%.

12. (a) ❶ $\sigma_M = .89$; predicted mean on Population 1 = 11 + (.80)(.89) = 11.71. ❷ significance cutoff: $Z = 2.57$; raw = 11 + (2.57)(.89) = 13.29; ❸ corresponding Z on predicted distribution = $(11.71 - 13.29)/.89 = -1.78$; ❹ from Z table, power = .96, beta = .04. (b) and (c) are similar to questions 11b and c, with an additional explanation of effect size.

Chapter 7

1. (a) t needed $(df = 63, p < .05,$ one-tailed$) = -1.671$; $S_M^2 = S^2/N = 9/64 = .141$. $S_M = \sqrt{S_M^2} = \sqrt{.141} = .38$; $t = (M - \mu)/S_M = (11 - 12.40)/.38 = -3.68$; reject null hypothesis. (b) t needed $= -2.690, 2.690$; $S_M = 2.55$; $t = 1.32$; do not reject null hypothesis. (c) t needed $= 2.364$; $S_M = .13$; $t = 3.15$; reject null hypothesis.

2. (a) ❶ **Restate the question as a research hypothesis and a null hypothesis about the populations.** There are two populations of interest:
Population 1: Response times under the new sheriff.
Population 2: Response times under the old sheriff.

The research hypothesis is that the two populations are different. The null hypothesis is that the two populations are the same.
❷ **Determine the characteristics of the comparison distribution.** Population 2: shape = assumed normal; $\mu = 30$; The estimated population variance is $S^2 = [\Sigma(X - M)^2]/df = (124)/(10 - 1) = 13.78$. Distribution of means: shape = $t (df = 9)$; mean of the distribution of means = 30; variance of the distribution of means is $S_M^2 = S^2/N = 13.78/10 = 1.378$; standard deviation of the distribution of means is $S_M = \sqrt{S_M^2} = \sqrt{1.378} = 1.17$.
❸ **Determine the cutoff sample score on the comparison distribution at which the null hypothesis should be rejected.** t needed $(df = 9, p < .05,$ one-tailed$) = -1.833$.
❹ **Determine your sample's score on the comparison distribution.** $M = (\Sigma X)/N = 280/10 = 28$; $t = (M - \mu)/S_M = (28 - 30)/1.17 = -1.71$.
❺ **Decide whether to reject the null hypothesis.** -1.71 is not more extreme than -1.833; do not reject the null hypothesis.

(b)

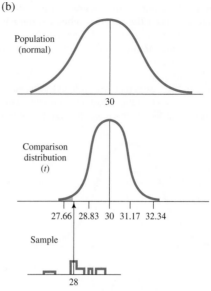

(c) Similar to question 5c, except, instead of difference scores, actual scores are used here, and the expected population mean is the 30 minutes that the sheriff had promised to do better than the current sheriff.

3. (a) and (b) Hypothesis testing steps and sketch similar to questions 2a and b; t needed $= -2.776, 2.776$; $t = (M - \mu)/S_M = (46 - 40)/2.3 = 2.61$; do not reject the null hypothesis. (c) Similar to question 5c, except, instead of difference scores, actual scores are used here, and the expected population mean is the 40 questions that people usually get correct.

4. (a) t needed $(df = 19, p < .05,$ one-tailed$) = 1.729$; $S_M^2 = S^2/N = 8.29/20 = .415$; $S_M = \sqrt{S_M^2} = \sqrt{.415} = .64$; $t = (M - \mu)/S_M = (1.7 - 0)/.64 = 2.66$; reject null hypothesis. (b) t needed $= -1.984, 1.984$; $S_M^2 = S^2/N = 414.53/164 = 2.53$; $S_M = \sqrt{S_M^2} = \sqrt{2.53} = 1.59$; $t = (2.3 - 0)/1.59 = 1.45$; do not reject null hypothesis. (c) t needed $= -2.625$; $S_M^2 = S^2/N = 4/15 = .27$; $S_M = \sqrt{S_M^2} = \sqrt{.27} = .52$; $t = -4.23$; reject null hypothesis.

5. (a) ❶ **Restate the question as a research hypothesis and a null hypothesis about the populations.** There are two populations of interest:
Population 1: Cities like those who participated in the antilittering program.
Population 2: Cities that do not change in the amount of litter over a one-year period.

The research hypothesis is that Population 1 has a greater mean decrease in litter than Population 2. The null hypothesis is that Population 1 doesn't have a greater mean decrease in litter than Population 2.
❷ **Determine the characteristics of the comparison distribution.** Population 2: shape = assumed normal; $\mu = 0$; the estimated population variance is $S^2 = [\Sigma(X - M)^2]/df = (50)/(4 - 1) = 16.67$. Distribution of means: shape = $t (df = 3)$; mean of the distribution of means of difference scores = 0; variance of the distribution of means of difference scores is $S_M^2 = S^2/N = 16.67/4 = 4.17$; standard deviation of the distribution of means of difference scores is $S_M = \sqrt{S_M^2} = \sqrt{4.17} = 2.04$.

❸ **Determine the cutoff sample score on the comparison distribution at which the null hypothesis should be rejected.** *t* needed ($df = 3, p < .01$, one-tailed) $= -4.541$.

❹ **Determine your sample's score on the comparison distribution.** Change scores $= -7, -6, 1, -8; M = -20/4 = -5; t = (M - \mu)/S_M = (-5 - 0)/2.04 = -2.45$.

❺ **Decide whether to reject the null hypothesis.** -2.45 (from Step ❹) is not more extreme than the cutoff of -4.541 (from Step ❸); do not reject the null hypothesis.

(b)

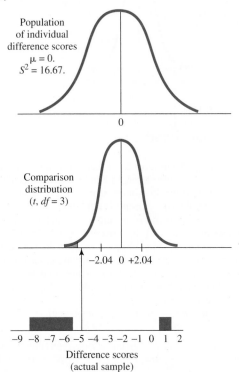

Population of individual difference scores $\mu = 0$. $S^2 = 16.67$.

Comparison distribution ($t, df = 3$)

$-2.04 \quad 0 \quad +2.04$

$-9 \ -8 \ -7 \ -6 \ -5 \ -4 \ -3 \ -2 \ -1 \ 0 \ 1 \ 2$

Difference scores (actual sample)

(c) The first thing I did was to simplify things by converting the numbers to difference scores—postprogram (2008) litter minus preprogram (2007) litter for each city. Then I found the mean of these difference scores, which was -5. That is, there is an average decrease of five pounds of litter per block per day.

The next step was to see whether this result, found in these four cities, indicates some real difference more generally due to being in this program. The alternative is the possibility that this much change could have happened in four randomly selected cities just by chance even if in general the program has no real effect. That is, we imagine that the average change for cities in general is actually 0, and maybe this study just happened to pick four cities that would have decreased this much anyway.

I then considered just how much a group of four cities would have to change before I could conclude that they have changed too much to chalk it up to chance. This required figuring out the characteristics of this imagined population of cities in which, on the average, there is no change. An average of no change is the same as saying it has a mean of 0 change. Since I didn't know the variance of this hypothetical distribution of cities that don't change, I

estimated it from the information in the sample of four cities. If the sample cities were just a chance drawn from the hypothetical distribution of no change, the variance of these cities should reflect the variance of this distribution (which would be the distribution they come from). However, the variance figured from a particular group (sample) from a larger population will in general be slightly smaller than the true population's variance. Thus, I had to modify the variance formula to take this into account: instead of dividing the sum of the squared deviations by the number of scores, I divided it by the degrees of freedom, which is the number of scores minus 1—in this case, 3. (This adjustment exactly accounts for the tendency of the variance in the sample to underestimate the true population variance.) As shown in the calculations in the steps of hypothesis testing, this gave an estimated population variance (S^2) of 16.67.

I was interested not in individual cities but in a group of four. Thus, what I really needed to know was the characteristics of a distribution of means of samples of four taken from this hypothetical population of individual city change scores. Such a distribution of means will have the same mean of 0 (since there is no reason to expect the means of such groups of four drawn randomly to be systematically higher or lower than 0). However, such a distribution will have a much smaller variance (because the average of a group of four scores is a lot less likely to be extreme than any individual score). Fortunately, it is known (and can be proved mathematically) that the variance of a distribution of means is the variance of the distribution of individuals divided by the number of individuals in each sample. In our example, this works out to 16.67 divided by 4, which is 4.17. The standard deviation of this distribution is thus the square root of 4.17, or 2.04.

It also turns out that if we assume that the hypothetical population of individual cities' change scores is normally distributed (and we have no reason to think otherwise), the distribution of means of samples from that distribution can be thought of as having a precise known shape, called a *t* distribution (which has slightly thicker tails than a normal curve). Thus, I looked in a table for a *t* distribution for the situation in which there are 3 degrees of freedom used to estimate the population variance. The table shows that there is less than a 1% chance of getting a score that is -4.541 standard deviations from the mean of this distribution.

The mean change score for the sample of four cities was -5, which is 2.45 (that is, $5/-2.04$) standard deviations below the mean of 0 change on this distribution of means of change scores. This is not as extreme as -4.541. Thus, there is more than a 1% chance that these results could have come from a hypothetical distribution with no change. Therefore, the researcher would not rule out that possibility, and the experiment would be considered inconclusive.

6. (a), (b), and (c). Hypothesis-testing steps, sketch, and explanation similar to question 5. *t* needed $= -2.776, 2.776$; $t = (M - \mu)/S_M = (-.014 - 0)/.005 = -2.8$; reject the null hypothesis. (*Note:* This result is very close to the cutoff level; if you round off slightly, your result might not be significant. This is one of those rare situations in which different ways of rounding can produce different results.)

7. (a) $d = (\mu_1 - \mu_2)/\sigma = (20 - 0)/32 = .63$, medium effect size; (b) .50, medium; (c) .25, small; (d) .20, small.

8. From Table 7–11: (a) .22; (b) .71; (c) .86; (d) .77; (e) .99.

9. From Table 7–12: (a) 33; (b) 12; (c) 156.

10. Similar to question 5c, except focusing on this study and the simpler situation involving just a single sample; you also do not need to explain the basic logic of hypothesis testing (only what is added when you have an unknown population variance).

11. Similar to questions 5b and 5c, except the explanation should focus on this study; also, material on mean, standard deviation, and variance should be added, as in the answers to Chapter 2 problems.

12. (a) Anxiety: $S_M^2 = S^2/N = 1.85^2/100 = .0342$; $S_M = \sqrt{S_M^2} = \sqrt{.0342} = .185$; $t = 1.50/1.85 = 8.11$. Depression: $S_M = .423$; $t = 7.28$; Introversion: $S_M = .222$; $t = -1.04$; Neuroticism: $S_M = .421$; $t = 2.11$.

(b) Similar to question 5c, except focusing on this study; also, material on mean, standard deviation, and variance should be added, as in the answers to Chapter 2 problems.

Chapter 8

1. (a) Independent; (b) dependent; (c) dependent.
2. (a) $S_{Pooled}^2 = (df_1/df_{Total})(S_1^2) + (df_2/df_{Total})(S_2^2) = (19/38)(1) + (19/38)(2) = 1.5$; $S_{M_1}^2 = S_{Pooled}^2/N_1 = 1.5/20 = .075$; $S_{M_2}^2 = .075$; $S_{Difference}^2 = S_{M_1}^2 + S_{M_2}^2 = .075 + .075 = .15$; $S_{Difference} = .39$. (b) .35; (c) .32; (d) .27; (e) .35.
3. (a) t needed $(df = 58, p < .05, \text{two-tailed}) = -2.004, 2.004$; $S_{Pooled}^2 = (df_1/df_{Total})(S_1^2) + (df_2/df_{Total})(S_2^2) = (29/58)(2.4) + (29/58)(2.8) = 2.6$; $S_{M_1}^2 = S_{Pooled}^2/N_1 = 2.6/30 = .087$; $S_{M_2}^2 = .087$; $S_{Difference}^2 = S_{M_1}^2 + S_{M_2}^2 = .087 + $

.087 = .174. $S_{Difference} = .417$; $t = (M_1 - M_2)/S_{Difference} = (12 - 11.1)/.417 = 2.16$. Conclusion: Reject the null hypothesis. The difference is significant.

(b) $S_{Pooled}^2 = 2.67$; $S_{Difference} = .45$; $t = 2.00$; do not reject the null hypothesis. (c) $S_{Pooled}^2 = 2.60$; $S_{Difference} = .417$; $t = 2.16$; reject the null hypothesis.

4. (a) ❶ **Restate the question as a research hypothesis and a null hypothesis about the populations.** There are two populations of interest:

Population 1: People who get their news from TV.
Population 2: People who get their news from the Internet.

The research hypothesis is that the two populations have different means. The null hypothesis is that the two populations have the same mean.

❷ **Determine the characteristics of the comparison distribution.** $S_{Pooled}^2 = (60/80)(4) + (20/80)(6) = 4.5$; mean of the comparison distribution (distribution of difference between means) = 0; $S_{Difference} = .54$; Shape = $t (df = 80)$.

❸ **Determine the cutoff sample score on the comparison distribution at which the null hypothesis should be rejected.** t needed $(df = 80, p < .01, \text{two-tailed}) = -2.639, 2.639$.

❹ **Determine your sample's score on the comparison distribution.** $t = (24 - 26)/.54 = -3.70$.

❺ **Decide whether to reject the null hypothesis.** -3.70 is more extreme than -2.639; reject the null hypothesis; the prediction is supported by the experiment.

(b)

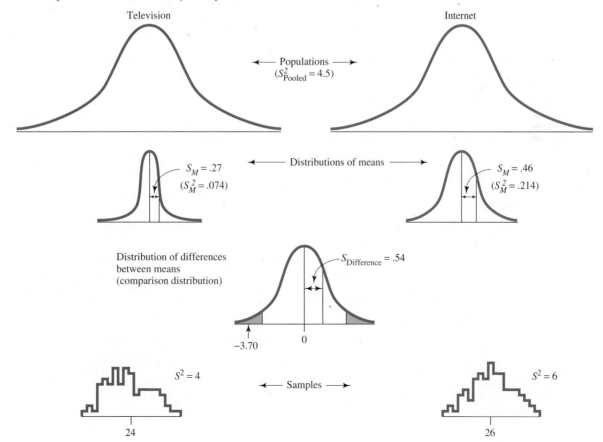

Television

Internet

Populations
($S_{Pooled}^2 = 4.5$)

Distributions of means

$S_M = .27$
($S_M^2 = .074$)

$S_M = .46$
($S_M^2 = .214$)

Distribution of differences between means (comparison distribution)

$S_{Difference} = .54$

-3.70 0

$S^2 = 4$

Samples

$S^2 = 6$

24

26

(c) In this situation, I am testing whether the two samples come from identical populations. I have two estimates of those identical populations, one from each sample. Thus, to get the most accurate overall estimate of the population variance, I can average the two estimates of the population variance. To give more weight to the estimate based on the larger degrees of freedom, I figure a weighted average, multiplying each estimate by its proportion of the total degrees of freedom and adding up the results. This pooled estimate of the population variance comes out to 4.5.

Because I was interested not in individual scores but in the difference between the mean of a group of 61 and the mean of another group of 21, I needed to figure out what would be the characteristics of a distribution of differences between means of groups of 61 and 21 that are randomly taken from the two identical populations whose variance I just estimated. This required two steps. First, I figured the characteristics of the distribution of means in the usual way for the population associated with each sample, but using my pooled estimate for the variance of each population of individuals. This came out to .074 for the TV group and .214 for the Internet group. The second step is directly about the distribution of differences between means. It is like a distribution you would get if you took a mean from the distribution of means for the TV group, took one from the distribution of means for the Internet group, and figured their difference. After doing this many times, the distribution of these differences would make up a new distribution, called a distribution of differences between means. Because we are assuming (if Internet versus TV made no difference) that the two original populations have the same means, on average, the difference between a mean taken from the TV group and a mean taken from the Internet group should come out to 0 (because sometimes one will be bigger and sometimes the other, but in the long run these random fluctuations should balance out). The variance of this distribution of differences between means is affected by the variation in both distributions of means; in fact, it is just the sum of the two. Thus, its variance is .074 plus .214, or .288. Its square root, the standard deviation of the distribution of differences between means, is .54.

Because this whole process is based on estimated variances, the distribution of means is a *t* distribution with degrees of freedom equal to the total number of degrees of freedom that went into the two estimates; thus $df = 80$. Looking this up on the *t* table for .01 two-tailed gives a cutoff needed of -2.639 and 2.639. The *t* for my sample is the difference between the two groups divided by the standard deviation of the distribution of differences between means: $(24 - 26)/.54 = -3.70$. This is more extreme than the cutoff; so I can reject the null hypothesis.

5. (a), (b), and (c). Hypothesis-testing steps, sketch, and explanation similar to question 4 [except part (c) also needs to include basic material as in answers to previous chapters' problems]. *t* needed $= -2.262, 2.262$; $S^2_{\text{Pooled}} = (5/9)(5.6) + (4/9)(19.3) = 11.69$; $S^2_{\text{Difference}} = 1.95 + 2.34 = 4.29$; $S_{\text{Difference}} = 2.07$; $t = (6 - 9.6)/2.07 = -1.74$. Do not reject the null hypothesis; the experiment is inconclusive as to whether including the child's name makes a difference. (*Note:* The scores in this problem seem to violate the

assumption of equal population variances. However, because the result was not significant even using the ordinary procedure, it would probably not be significant using a modified procedure.)

6. (a), (b), and (c). Hypothesis-testing steps, sketch, and explanation similar to question 4. *t* needed $= 1.943$; $S^2_{\text{Pooled}} = (4/6)(6.7) + (2/6)(12.33) = 8.58$; $S^2_{\text{Difference}} = 2.86 + 1.72 = 4.58$; $S_{\text{Difference}} = 2.14$; $t = (5.33 - 5.2)/2.14 = .06$. Do not reject the null hypothesis; the experiment is inconclusive as to whether older children do better.

7. (a) Estimated $d = (M_1 - M_2)/S_{\text{Pooled}} = (24 - 26)/\sqrt{4.5} = -.94$; (b) -1.05; (c) .04. (d) Effect size represents the degree to which two populations do not overlap. The less that two populations overlap, the larger the effect size will be. In psychology, we often want to know not just whether a result is significant, but how big the effect is; effect size provides a measure of how big the effect is. Effect size for the *t* test for independent means is the difference between the population means divided by the standard deviation of the population of individuals. However, you do not know the population means; so you estimate them using the sample means. You also do not know the standard deviation of the population of individuals; so you estimate it by using the pooled estimate of the population standard deviation. So, in part (a), the effect size was the difference between the sample means (24 minus 26, which gives -2), divided by the pooled estimate of the population standard deviation (which was the square root of 4.5, or 2.12). This gave an estimated effect size of $-.94$, which is a large effect size according to Cohen's effect size conventions for the *t* test for independent means.

8. From Table 8–4: (a) .19; (b) nearly 1; (c) .72; (d) .97.

9. (a) Harmonic mean $= 2(N_1)(N_2)/(N_1 + N_2) = (2)(3)(57)/(3 + 57) = 5.7$; from Table 8–4 approximate power $= .11$; (b) harmonic mean $= 16.7$, power $= .15$; (c) harmonic mean $= 26.7$, power $= .19$; (d) harmonic mean $= 30$, power $= .19$.

10. (a) Estimated $d = (M_1 - M_2)/S_{\text{Pooled}} = (107 - 149)/84 = -.50$, medium effect size; needed N (from Table 8–5) $= 50$ per group, 100 total. (b) Estimated $d = .20$; needed $N = 393$ per group, 786 total. (c) Estimated $d = .80$; needed $N = 20$ per group, 40 total. (d) Estimated $d = -.80$; needed $N = 26$ per group, 52 total.

11. Along with the following, include a full explanation of all terms and concepts as in question 4c and answers to previous chapters' explanation problems. (a) and (b) This study shows that using a conventional .05 significance level, German children who receive low levels of support—whether from their mother, father, or classmates—showed lower levels of self-worth. Further, the effect sizes were fairly large (.78 and .69) with regard to support from mother or father; however, the effect size was only small to moderate (.35) with regard to support from classmates. This would seem to imply that support from parents is more important than support from classmates in terms of a child's feeling of self-worth. The power of the study for a large effect size is .98. (This assumes there were about equal numbers of children in the high and low support groups, that the test is two-tailed, and uses the figure for 50 in each group.) The power for a medium effect size is .70. Because we already know

that the results are significant and we know the effect sizes, the power calculations are not very important.
12. Similar to question 4c, focusing on the results of this study.

Chapter 9

1. (a) F needed ($df = 2, 27; p < .05) = 3.36$; $S_M^2 = [\Sigma(M - GM)^2]/df_{Between}) = [(7.4 - 7)^2 + (6.8 - 7)^2 + (6.8 - 7)^2]/2 = .12$; $S_{Between}^2 = (S_M^2)(n) = (.12)(10) = 1.2$; $S_{Within}^2 = (S_1^2 + S_2^2 + \cdots + S_{Last}^2)/N_{Groups} = (.82 + .90 + .80)/3 = .84$; $F = 1.2/.84 = 1.43$; do not reject the null hypothesis.
(b) F needed ($df = 3, 96; p < .05) = 2.70$ (actually using $df = 3, 95$); $S_M^2 = 164.67$; $S_{Between}^2 = (164.67)(25) = 4116.75$; $S_{Within}^2 = 736.5$; $F = 5.59$; reject the null hypothesis.
2. (a) F needed ($df = 2, 9; p < .01) = 8.02$; Group 1: $M = 8$, $S^2 = .67$; Group 2: $M = 6, S^2 = .67$; Group 3: $M = 4, S^2 = .67$; $S_{Between}^2 = (4)(4) = 16$; $S_{Within}^2 = .67$; $F = 16/.67 = 23.88$; reject the null hypothesis.
(b) F needed ($df = 2, 9; p < .01) = 8.02$; Group 1: $M = 8$, $S^2 = 21.33$; Group 2: $M = 6, S^2 = 21.33$; Group 3: $M = 4$, $S^2 = 21.33$; $S_{Between}^2 = (4)(4) = 16$; $S_{Within}^2 = 21.33$; $F = 16/21.33 = .75$; do not reject the null hypothesis.
(c) For part (a), $R^2 = (S_{Between}^2)(df_{Between})/[(S_{Between}^2)(df_{Between}) + (S_{Within}^2)(df_{Within})] = (16)(2)/[(16)(2) + (.67)(9)] = .84$. For part (b), $R^2 = (S_{Between}^2)(df_{Between})/[(S_{Between}^2)(df_{Between}) + (S_{Within}^2)(df_{Within})] = (16)(2)/[(16)(2) + (21.33)(9)] = .14$.
(d)

| Group 1 | | | | | | |
X	X − GM Dev	Dev²	X − M Dev	Dev²	M − GM Dev	Dev²
8	2	4	0	0	2	4
8	2	4	0	0	2	4
7	1	1	−1	1	2	4
9	3	9	1	1	2	4
Σ 32		18		2		16

$M = 32/4 = 8$.

| Group 2 | | | | | | |
X	X − GM Dev	Dev²	X − M Dev	Dev²	M − GM Dev	Dev²
6	0	0	0	0	0	0
6	0	0	0	0	0	0
5	−1	1	−1	1	0	0
7	1	1	1	1	0	0
Σ 24		2		2		0

$M = 24/4 = 6$.

| Group 3 | | | | | | |
X	X − GM Dev	Dev²	X − M Dev	Dev²	M − GM Dev	Dev²
4	−2	4	0	0	−2	4
4	−2	4	0	0	−2	4
3	−3	9	−1	1	−2	4
5	−1	1	1	1	−2	4
Σ 16		18		2		16

$M = 16/4 = 4$.
$GM = (32 + 24 + 16)/12 = 72/12 = 6$.
$SS_{Total} = 18 + 2 + 18 = 38$.
$SS_{Within} = 2 + 2 + 2 = 6$.
$SS_{Between} = 16 + 0 + 16 = 32$.

Analysis of variance table:

Source	SS	df	MS	F
Between	32	2	16	23.88
Within	6	9	.67	
Total	38	11		

Conclusion: Reject the null hypothesis

3. (a) ❶ **Restate the question as a research hypothesis and a null hypothesis about the populations.** There are three populations of interest:

Population 1: Patients with affective disorders.
Population 2: Patients with cognitive disorders.
Population 3: Patients with drug-related conditions.

The research hypothesis is that the three population means differ. The null hypothesis is that the three populations have the same mean.
❷ **Determine the characteristics of the comparison distribution.** F distribution with 2 and 9 degrees of freedom.
❸ **Determine the cutoff sample score on the comparison distribution at which the null hypothesis should be rejected.** 5% level, $F (df = 2, 9)$ needed $= 4.26$.
❹ **Determine your sample's score on the comparison distribution.** $S_{Between}^2 = (5.33)(4) = 21.32$; $S_{Within}^2 = (.67 + 3.33 + 2.67)/3 = 2.22$; $F = 21.32/2.22 = 9.60$.
❺ **Decide whether to reject the null hypothesis.** F from Step ❹ (9.60) is more extreme than cutoff F from Step ❸ (4.26); reject the null hypothesis.

(b)

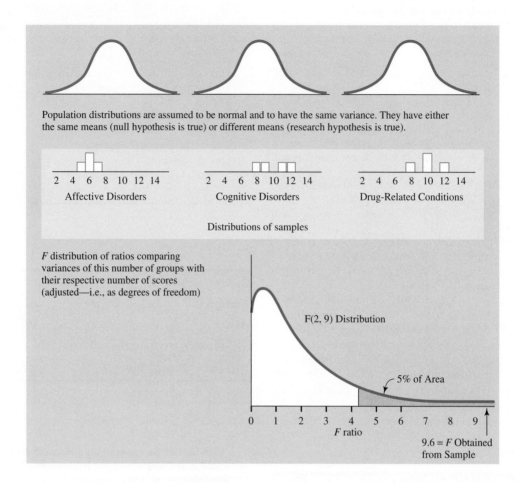

Population distributions are assumed to be normal and to have the same variance. They have either the same means (null hypothesis is true) or different means (research hypothesis is true).

| 2 4 6 8 10 12 14 | 2 4 6 8 10 12 14 | 2 4 6 8 10 12 14 |
| Affective Disorders | Cognitive Disorders | Drug-Related Conditions |

Distributions of samples

F distribution of ratios comparing variances of this number of groups with their respective number of scores (adjusted—i.e., as degrees of freedom)

F(2, 9) Distribution

5% of Area

0 1 2 3 4 5 6 7 8 9

F ratio

9.6 = *F* Obtained from Sample

(c) $R^2 = (S^2_{\text{Between}})(df_{\text{Between}})/[(S^2_{\text{Between}})(df_{\text{Between}}) + (S^2_{\text{Within}}(df_{\text{Within}})] = (21.32)(2)/[(21.32)(2) + (2.22)(9)] = .68$.

(d) The null hypothesis is that the three groups are from populations of length-of-stay scores with equal means (and, as with a *t* test, we must be able to assume that they have equal variances). If this null hypothesis is true, then you can estimate the variance of these equal populations in two ways:

(i) You can estimate from the variation within each of the three groups and then average them. (This is just what you would do in a *t* test for independent means, except now you are averaging three variances instead of just two. Also in a *t* test you would weight these variances according to the degrees of freedom they contribute to the overall estimate. However, because all three groups have equal numbers, you can simply average them—in effect weighting them equally.) In this example, the three variance estimates were .67, 3.33, and 2.67, which gave a pooled estimate of 2.22. This is called the within-groups estimate of the population variance.

(ii) You can estimate the variance using the three means. If we assume the null hypothesis is true, the means of the three groups are based on samples taken from identical populations. Each of these identical populations will have an identical

distribution of means of samples taken from that population. The means of our three samples are all from identical populations, which is the same as if they were all from the same population. Thus, the amount of variation among our three means should reflect the variation in the distribution of means that they can be thought of as coming from. As a result, I can use these three means (6, 10, and 10) to estimate the variance in this distribution of means. Using the usual formula for estimating a population variance, I get 5.33.

However, what we want is the variance of a distribution of individuals. So the question is, what would be the distribution of individuals that would produce a distribution of means (of four scores each) with a variance of 5.33? To find the distribution of means from a distribution of individuals, you divide the variance of the distribution of individuals by the size of the samples. In this case, you want to do the reverse. Thus, you multiply the variance of the distribution of means by the size of the samples to get the variance of the distribution of individuals. This comes out to 5.33 times 4, or 21.32. This is called the between-groups estimate of the population variance.

If the null hypothesis is true, the within-groups and between-groups estimates of the population variance should be about the same because they are estimates of essentially the same population. Thus, the ratio of the between-groups estimate divided by the within-groups estimate should be about 1.

However, suppose the null hypothesis is false and the three populations from which these groups come have different means. In that situation, the estimate based on the variation among the group means will be bigger than the one based on the variation within the groups. The reason it will be bigger is as follows. If the null hypothesis is true, the only reason that the means of our groups vary is because of the variance inside of each of the three identical distributions of means. But if the null hypothesis is false, each of those distributions of means also has a different mean. Thus, the variation in our means is due to *both* the variation inside of each of these now *not* identical distributions of means, and also to the differences in the means of these distributions of means. Thus, there is an additional source of variation in the means of our groups. If you estimate the variance of the population using these three means, it will be larger than if the null hypothesis were true. On the other hand, the within-groups variance is not affected by whether the three groups have different means, because it considers variation only within each of the groups. The within-groups variance thus does not get any bigger if the null hypothesis is false. Therefore, when the null hypothesis is false, the ratio of the between-groups variance to the within-groups variance will be more than 1.

The ratio of the between-groups estimate to the within-groups estimate is called an F ratio. In this example, our F ratio is 21.32 to 2.22; 21.32/2.22 = 9.60.

Statisticians have made tables of what happens when you figure F ratios based on the situation in which you randomly take a group of four scores from each of three identical populations. This is the situation in which the null hypothesis is true. Looking at these tables, it turns out that there is less than a 5% chance of getting an F ratio larger than 4.26. Because our actual F ratio is bigger than this, we can reject the null hypothesis.

(e) F needed ($df = 1, 9; p < .05$) = 5.12; S^2_{Between} (for two means) = (8)(4) = 32; S^2_{Within} (from overall analysis) = 2.22; $F = 32/2.22 = 14.41$; reject the null hypothesis.

(f) $S^2_{\text{Between}} = (0)(4) = 0$; $F = 0/2.22 = 0$; do not reject the null hypothesis.

(g) In a study with more than two groups, researchers often make predictions for differences between specific pairs of groups; these are called planned contrasts. To test a planned contrast, you do a special analysis of variance in which the between-groups estimate is based on just the two groups being compared, but the within-groups estimate uses the information from all groups in the overall analysis of variance. (The variation in all populations is assumed to be the same, so this method lets you take advantage of the information in all the groups when figuring the within-groups population variance estimate.) Thus, for the first planned contrast (Affective versus Drug-Related Conditions), I figured the between-groups estimate using the estimated variance of the distribution of means based on means of these two groups (6 and 10, which came out to $S^2_M = 8$) and then multiplied this by the number in each group (4). The result was 32. Dividing this by the overall within-groups estimate I'd figured earlier in the problem, which was 2.22, gave an F ratio of 14.41. This was bigger than the needed F for df of 1 (the number of df in figuring

the between-groups estimate). Thus, I could reject the null hypothesis. Following the same procedure for the second planned contrast gave an F of 0, which of course was not significant.

4. (a), (b), (c), and (d). Hypothesis-testing steps, sketch of distributions, effect size, and explanation similar to question 3 [except (d) needs to include material similar to explanations from earlier chapters' practice problems]. F needed ($df = 2, 147; p < .05$) = 3.09 (actually using $df = 2, 100$); S^2_{Between} = (.09)(50) = 4.5; $S^2_{\text{Within}} = (5.2 + 5.8 + 4.8)/3 = 5.27$; $F = .85$; do not reject the null hypothesis. $R^2 = (4.5)(2)/[(4.5)(2) + (5.27)(147)] = .01$.

5. (a), (b), (c), and (d). Hypothesis-testing steps, sketch of distributions, effect size, and explanation similar to question 3 [except (d) needs to include material similar to explanations from earlier chapters' practice problems]. F needed ($df = 3, 28; p < .01$) = 4.57; S^2_{Between} = (155)(8) = 1240; $S^2_{\text{Within}} = (3.5^2 + 4.6^2 + 3.8^2 + 4.9^2)/4 = 17.97$; $F = 69.0$; reject the null hypothesis. $R^2 = (1240)(3)/[(1240)(3) + (17.97)(28)] = .88$.

(e) Bonferroni corrected significance level = .05/5 = .01; F needed ($df = 1, 28; p < .01$) = 7.64; S^2_{Between} (for two means) = (4.5)(8) = 36, S^2_{Within} (from overall analysis) = 17.97, $F = 36/17.97 = 2.00$, do not reject the null hypothesis.

(f) $S^2_{\text{Between}} = (364.5)(8) = 2916$, $F = 2916/17.97 = 162.27$, reject the null hypothesis.

(g) $S^2_{\text{Between}} = (8)(8) = 64$, $F = 64/17.97 = 3.56$, do not reject the null hypothesis.

(h) $S^2_{\text{Between}} = (288)(8) = 2304$, $F = 2304/17.97 = 128.21$, reject the null hypothesis.

(i) $S^2_{\text{Between}} = (264.5)(8) = 2116$, $F = 2116/17.97 = 117.75$, reject the null hypothesis.

(j) (Explanation of planned contrasts similar to question 3d.) Bonferroni correction is done to take into account that, when testing many contrasts, the chance of any one of them coming out significant is greater than the supposed significance level. This is corrected by using for each contrast a significance level based on dividing the overall significance level by the number of contrasts. In this problem with five contrasts and an overall significance level of .05, each of the five contrasts is tested at the .05/5 = .01 level of significance.

6. (a) .05/2 = .025; (b) .0125; (c) .0033; (d) .002.

7. (a) Overall study's $df_{\text{Between}} = 5 - 1 = 4$; $df_{\text{Within}} = 9 + 9 + 9 + 9 + 9 = 45$. Scheffé corrected $F = 17.21/4 = 4.30$. Overall study's .05 cutoff $F(df = 4, 45)$ is 2.58. Thus, even with the Scheffé correction, this comparison is significant. (b) Scheffé corrected $F = 17.21/5 = 3.44$. Overall study's .05 cutoff $F (df = 5, 54$, actually using $df = 5, 50$ from the table) is 2.40, significant comparison. (c) Scheffé corrected $F = 17.21/4 = 4.30$. Overall study's .05 cutoff $F (df = 4, 95)$ is 2.47, significant comparison. (d) Scheffé corrected $F = 17.21/4 = 4.30$. Overall study's .01 cutoff $F (df = 4, 45)$ is 3.77, significant comparison.

8. From Table 9–9: (a) .09; (b) .12; (c) .10; (d) .38.

9. From Table 9–10: (a) 322; (b) 21; (c) 274; (d) 52.

10. Similar to question 3d (and also including material from Chapter 8), but focusing on this study's results.

11. Similar to questions 3d and 3g (and including material from previous chapters) but focusing on this study's results.

12. (a) Acceptance, emotional extremes, jealousy; (b) emotional extremes, jealousy, obsessive preoccupation, sexual attraction, desire for union, desire for reciprocation, love at first sight; (c) happiness, friendship, trust, fear of closeness, emotional extremes, jealousy; (d) emotional extremes, jealousy. (e) After conducting an overall analysis of variance among more than two groups, researchers often go on to conduct an exploratory analysis comparing each pair of groups; these are called post hoc (after the fact) comparisons. The problem is that, with many comparisons, it is possible that some will be significant just by chance more often than the supposed significance level of, say, 5%. When doing post hoc tests, special procedures have been developed to protect against this problem so that the researcher can be confident that any difference found will be truly no more likely to have occurred by, say, 5% (if that is the significance level chosen) if the null hypothesis is true. The Scheffé test is an example of this kind of procedure.

Chapter 10

1. i. (a) and (b)

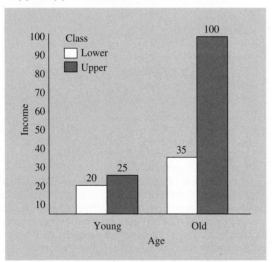

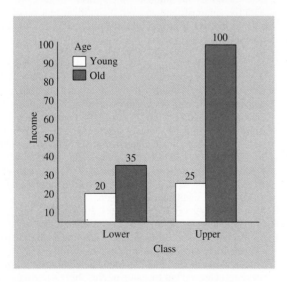

(c) Main effects model for class and age, interaction effect; (d) income is greater in general for upper-class and for older individuals, but the combination of older and upper class has a higher income than would be expected just from the effects of either variable alone.

ii. (a) and (b) Graphs of the same kind as in part (i) (a) and (b); (c) no main effects, interaction effect; (d) neither type of college nor type of major, by itself, predicts grades, but there is a clear pattern if one considers the combinations: grades are highest for community college arts majors and for liberal arts college science majors.

iii. (a) and (b) Graphs of the same kind as in part (i) (a) and (b); (c) both main effects significant; no interaction; (d) females miss fewer days per month than males; those who exercise miss fewer days per month than controls. Each combination misses the number of days you would expect knowing their level of each variable separately.

2. i. (a) and (b) Graphs of the same kind as in question 1 (i) (a) and (b); (c) main effect for relationship and an interaction; (d) conversations are longer with friends, but the difference is much greater for personal than for nonpersonal topics.

ii. (a) and (b) Graphs of the same kind as in question 1 (i) (a) and (b); (c) main effect for city and cost, plus an interaction; (d) restaurant quality is different in different cities, with New York highest and Chicago lowest. Restaurant quality is different in different price ranges, with expensive the best and inexpensive the least. The two factors do not simply combine, however, because price makes more difference in New York than in other cities.

iii. (a) and (b) Graphs of the same kind as in question 1 (i) (a) and (b); (c) main effects for brand and type and an interaction; (d) flavor is rated on the average more positively for regular than decaf, and brands Z and X are rated more favorably than Y. However, there is an interaction in which there is no difference between regular and decaf for brand Z, but for brands Z and Y, regular is rated 2 points higher.

3. Example answers.

		Sport			
	(a)	*Baseball*	*Football*	*Basketball*	
Condition	*With motivational program*	10	5	6	7
	Without motivational program	10	5	6	7
		10	5	6	

		Sport			
	(b)	*Baseball*	*Football*	*Basketball*	
Condition	*With motivational program*	6	6	6	6
	Without motivational program	10	10	10	10
		8	8	8	

		Sport			
	(c)	*Baseball*	*Football*	*Basketball*	
Condition	*With motivational program*	6	7	8	7
	Without motivational program	8	9	10	9
		7	8	9	

(d)

Condition		Baseball	Football	Basketball	
	With motivational program	6	7	8	7
	Without motivational program	10	9	8	9
		8	8	8	

(e)

Condition		Baseball	Football	Basketball	
	With motivational program	6	7	8	7
	Without motivational program	6	8	10	8
		6	7.5	9	

4. As expected, participants with extreme stereotypes about PR agents being extroverted, compared to participants with only moderate stereotypes of this kind, described PR agents as more extroverted. This result was statistically significant, meaning that you can be reasonably confident that the pattern of the result applies not just to the particular people studied, but to people like those studied in general. (More precisely, the researchers were able to conclude that, if there was no average difference in the general population between extreme and moderate stereotype people, there is less than a .0001 chance that this experiment could have produced a result that strong.) In addition, and most important, this tendency was surprisingly much stronger for participants who were given a description of a particular PR agent who was highly introverted. This result was also statistically significant. (In this case, the chance was less than 5% of getting a result this strong if in the general population there was no average tendency of this kind.)

On average, those exposed to the extreme introvert tended to give higher ratings of extroversion. This result was of "marginal" statistical significance, meaning that it was on the borderline of being too unlikely to have come up if there were no true average difference in the population. More important, this result is not very interesting because, as you can see from the graph, it is entirely due to the extreme stereotype participants; if anything, the moderate stereotype participants showed an opposite pattern of effect.
5. Similar to question 4.
6. F needed for each effect in (a), (b), and (c) $(df = 1, 8, p < .05) = 5.32$. Graphs as the same kind as in question 1 (i) (a) or (b).

(a)

		Experimental Condition		
		A	B	Overall
Group	1	.67	2.67	1.67
	2	2.67	.67	1.67
Overall		1.67	1.67	

Source	SS	df	MS	F	
Group	0	1	0	0	Do not reject null.
Condition	0	1	0	0	Do not reject null.
Interaction	12	1	12	35.29	Reject null.
Within cells	2.68	8	.34		

(b)

		Experimental Condition		
		A	B	Overall
Group	1	.67	.67	.67
	2	2.67	2.67	2.67
Overall		1.67	1.67	

Source	SS	df	MS	F	
Group	12	1	12	35.29	Reject null.
Condition	0	1	0	0	Do not reject null.
Interaction	0	1	0	0	Do not reject null.
Within cells	2.68	8	.34		

(c)

		Experimental Condition		
		A	B	Overall
Group	1	.67	2.67	1.67
	2	.67	2.67	1.67
Overall		.67	2.67	

Source	SS	df	MS	F	
Group	0	1	0	0	Do not reject null.
Condition	12	1	12	35.29	Reject null.
Interaction	0	1	0	0	Do not reject null.
Within cells	2.68	8	.34		

7. (a) F needed for main effect for Diagnosis $(df = 1, 6) = 5.99$; for main effect for Therapy and interaction $(df = 2, 6) = 5.14$.

Source	SS	df	MS	F	
Therapy	8	2	4	1.33	Do not reject null.
Diagnosis	108	1	108	36	Reject null.
Interaction	0	2	0	0	Do not reject null.
Within cells	18	6	3		

(b) Means:

	A	B	C	
I	4	2	3	3
II	10	8	9	9
	7	5	6	

(c) Similar to question 1 (i) (a).
(d) There is a significant difference in effectiveness between the two diagnostic categories: therapy is more effective for those with Diagnosis II. However, there is no

significant difference among types of therapy, and the types of therapy are not significantly differentially effective for the different diagnostic types.

8. (a) *F* needed for each effect ($df = 1, 8$) $= 5.32$.

Source	SS	df	MS	F	
Likability	0	1	0	0	Do not reject null.
Nervousness	0	1	0	0	Do not reject null.
Interaction	48	1	48	32	Reject null.
Within cells	12	8	1.5		

(b) Means

	Likable	Not Likable	
Nervous	7	3	5
Not Nervous	3	7	5
	5	5	

(c) Similar to question 1 (i) (a).

(d) These results indicate that there is a significant interaction between nervousness and likability: The defendant who is likable is more likely to be rated innocent if he is nervous; but the defendant who is not likable is more likely to be rated innocent if he is not nervous. There was no overall significant effect for likable or not or for nervous or not, though with the very small sample sizes involved, failures to reject the null hypothesis should not be taken as evidence that such an effect does not exist.

The figuring of the significance is like a one-way analysis of variance using the structural model approach. The within-groups sum of squares and degrees of freedom are figured in the usual way, considering each cell as its own group. However, the between-groups deviations from the mean are divided into three parts: one is the variation between likability versus not (based on each participant's liking versus not-liking group's mean minus the grand mean); another is the variation between nervous versus not. The degrees of freedom for each is the number of levels (2 in each case) minus 1.

However, following this procedure, some of the between-groups effect is left over—the variation between likability groups that is different according to which nervousness group they are in. This is an example of what is called an interaction effect. You figure its mean squares based on the deviation of the score from the overall grand mean minus the other three deviations (the score minus its group's mean from the grand mean). Its degrees of freedom are what are left over in the total between-groups degrees of freedom (with four subgroups, between-groups $df = 3$ minus 1 for likability and minus another 1 for nervousness).

9. (a) $R^2_{\text{Columns}} = (S^2_{\text{Columns}})(df_{\text{Columns}})/$
$[(S^2_{\text{Columns}})(df_{\text{Columns}}) + (S^2_{\text{Within}})(df_{\text{Within}})];$
$R^2_{\text{Condition}} = (0)(1)/[(0)(1) + (.34)(8)] = 0,$
$R^2_{\text{Group}} = 0, R^2_{\text{Interaction}} = .82;$ (b) $R^2_{\text{Condition}} = 0,$
$R^2_{\text{Group}} = .82, R^2_{\text{Interaction}} = 0;$ (c) $R^2_{\text{Condition}} = .82,$

$R^2_{\text{Group}} = 0, R^2_{\text{Interaction}} = 0;$ (d) $R^2_{\text{Therapy}} = .31,$
$R^2_{\text{Diagnosis}} = .86, R^2_{\text{Interaction}} = 0;$ (e) $R^2_{\text{Likability}} = 0,$
$R^2_{\text{Nervousness}} = 0, R^2_{\text{Interaction}} = .80.$

10. From Table 10–15: (a) .19; (b) .29; (c) .26; (d) .21; (e) .78.

11. From Table 10–16: (a) 197; (b) 197; (c) 33; (d) 132; (e) 162; (f) 162.

Chapter 11

1. (a) Curvilinear; (b) linear, positive, large; (c) linear, negative, large; (d) linear, positive, large; (e) linear, positive, small to moderate; (f) no correlation.

2. (a)

(b) Positive linear correlation—as therapist empathy goes up, so does patient satisfaction.

(c) Therapist empathy $M = 62$; patient satisfaction $M = 3$.

Therapist Empathy (*X*)		Patient Satisfaction (*Y*)		Products of Deviation Scores
Deviation	Deviation Squared	Deviation	Deviation Squared	$(X - M_X)$ $(Y - M_Y)$
$X - M_X$	$(X - M_X)^2$	$Y - M_Y$	$(Y - M_Y)^2$	
8	64	1	1	8
32	1024	2	4	64
−26	676	−1	1	26
−14	196	−2	4	28
	$SS_X = 1960$		$SS_Y = 10$	$\Sigma = 126$

$r = 126/\sqrt{(1960)(10)} = .90$

(d) Comparison distribution is a *t* distribution with $df = N - 2 = 4 - 2 = 2$. The *t* tables (Table A–2 in the Appendix) shows that for a two-tailed test at the .05 level, with 2 degrees of freedom, the cutoff *t* scores are 4.303 and −4.303. Using the formula $t = r/\sqrt{(1 - r^2)/(N - 2)} = .90/\sqrt{(.19)/(2)} = 2.92$. This *t* value is not more extreme than the cutoffs; do not reject the null hypothesis.

(e) The first thing I did was make a graph, called a scatter diagram, putting one variable on each axis; I then put a dot where each person's pair of scores goes on that graph. This gives a picture of the pattern of relationship between the two variables. In this example, high scores generally go with high scores and lows with lows. The scores are going together in a systematic pattern makes this a *correlation;* that highs go with highs and lows with lows makes this correlation *positive;* that dots fall roughly near a straight line makes this positive correlation *linear.*

Next, I figured the *correlation coefficient,* a number describing the degree of linear correlation (in a positive correlation, how consistently highs go with highs and lows with lows). To do this, I figured deviation scores for each variable, then figured the products of the pairs of deviation scores and summed those products. I then squared the deviation scores for each variable. Summing these squared scores for each variable gives the sum of squares for the therapist empathy variable and the sum of squares for the patient satisfaction variable. I figured the correlation coefficient by dividing the sum of products of deviation scores by a correction number, which is the square root of the result of multiplying the sum of squares for the *X* variable by the sum of squares for the *Y* variable. This correction number takes into account the number of people in the study and the variability of each variable's scores. The correlation coefficient will be a positive number if there is a positive correlation. This is because, with a positive correlation, the sum of products of deviation scores will be a positive number, because positive deviations will mostly have been multiplied by positive deviations and negative with negative, giving positive products. Correlation coefficients can vary from -1 (a perfect negative correlation) to $+1$ (a perfect positive correlation). In this example, the correlation coefficient (r) of .90 indicates a large positive linear correlation between therapist empathy and patient satisfaction.

To test the statistical significance of a correlation coefficient, you determine a *t* score for the correlation coefficient and compare that *t* score to a cutoff *t* value from a *t* table. The formula for finding the *t* score from the correlation coefficient involves dividing the correlation coefficient by the square root of what you get when you divide 1 minus the correlation coefficient squared by 2 less than the number of people in the study. The degrees of freedom for the *t* test are 2 less than the number of people in the study. In this example, there were 2 degrees of freedom, which gave *t* cutoffs (from the *t* table) of 4.303 and –4.303. The *t* value for the correlation coefficient was 2.92, which was not more extreme than the cutoff values; so the null hypothesis (of no correlation between therapist empathy and patient satisfaction in the population) was not rejected.
(f) (i) If a therapist has more empathy, this causes the patient to feel more satisfied (empathy causes satisfaction); (ii) if a patient feels more satisfied, this causes the therapist to feel more empathic toward the patient (satisfaction causes empathy); or (iii) some third factor, such as a good match of the patient's problem with the therapist's ability, causes patients to be more satisfied and therapists to be more empathic (third factor causes both satisfaction and empathy).
3. (a) See question 2a for example scatter diagram. (b) Positive linear correlation: as hours studied go up, so do test grades. (c) $r = .84$. (d) $df = N - 2 = 5 - 2 = 3$; cutoff *t* scores are 3.182 and -3.182; $t = 2.69$; do not reject the null hypothesis. (e) Like question 2e. (f) (i) Studying more

causes improved test grades; (ii) getting a better test grade causes more hours studied; note that, although this is theoretically possible, in reality it is not possible to have a future event (the score on the test) cause a previous event (hours studied); or (iii) a third factor, such as interest in the subject matter, could be causing the student to study more and also to do better on the test.
4. (a) See question 2a for example scatter diagram. (b) Positive linear correlation: as self-disclosure goes up, so does liking for partner. (c) $r = .47$. (d) $df = N - 2 = 5 - 2 = 3$; cutoff *t* scores are 3.182 and -3.182; $t = .92$; do not reject the null hypothesis.
5. Set A:

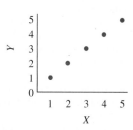

	X		**Y**		**Products of**
Deviation	**Deviation Squared**		**Deviation**	**Deviation Squared**	**Deviation Scores**
$X - M_X$	$(X - M_X)^2$		$Y - M_Y$	$(Y - M_Y)^2$	$(X - M_X)$ $(Y - M_Y)$
-2	4		-2	4	4
-1	1		-1	1	1
0	0		0	0	0
1	1		1	1	1
2	4		2	4	4
	$SS_X = 10$			$SS_Y = 10$	$\Sigma = 10$

$$r = 10/\sqrt{(10)(10)} = 1.00$$

$df = N - 2 = 5 - 2 = 3$; cutoff *t* scores are 3.182 and -3.182; using the formula gives $t = 1/0$, which is undefined (since you can't divide a number by 0). However, any perfect correlation is statistically significant; so we can reject the null hypothesis and the research hypothesis is supported.
Set B: $r = .90$; $t = 3.58$; reject the null hypothesis; the research hypothesis is supported.
Set C: $r = -.60$; $t = -1.30$; do not reject the null hypothesis.
Set D: $r = .60$; $t = 1.30$; do not reject the null hypothesis.
6. (a) The measures may have low reliability, thus reducing (attenuating) the possible correlation between them. (b) There is restriction in range: among millionaires, there may not be a very great range of comfort of living situation (they probably all have quite comfortable situations); so the correlation with any variable (including happiness) is limited.
7. From Table 11–7: (a) .11; (b) .92; (c) .83; (d) .60; (e) .17.

8. From Table 11–8: (a) 28; (b) 68; (c) 783.

9. (a) This table shows the degree of association among scores on several measures given to pregnant women and their partners. (Here continue with an explanation of the correlation coefficient like that in question 2e, except in this problem you also need to explain the mean and deviation scores, which you do in the same way as in answering the problems in Chapter 2.) For example, the correlation of .17 between women's reports of stress and men's reports of stress indicates that the association between these two measures is quite weak. That is, how much stress a woman is under is not highly related to how much stress her partner believes she is under. On the other hand, the correlation of .50 (near the middle of the first column of correlations) tells you that there is a much stronger association between a woman's report of stress and her depressed mood in the second interview. That is, women who report being under stress are also likely to report being depressed; those reporting being under not much stress are likely to report not being very depressed.

(b) In general, the correlations shown in this table are strongest among the stress, support, and mood items; correlations of these variables with demographics (age, ethnicity, etc.) were fairly weak. Partner support seemed to be strongly correlated with stress and mood, and depressed mood at the second testing was particularly related to the other variables.

(c) Just because two variables are correlated, even strongly correlated, does not mean that you can know the particular direction of causality that creates that association. For example, there is a strong negative correlation between partner support at time 1 and depressed mood at time 2. There are three logically possible directions of causality here: (1) support can be causing lower depression, (2) lower depression can be causing support, or (3) some third factor can be causing both. You can rule out the second possibility, since something in the future (low depression) cannot cause the past (initial support). However, the other two possibilities remain. It is certainly plausible that having her partner's support helps reduce depression, but it is also possible that a third factor is causing both. For example, consider level of income. Perhaps when a couple has more income, the partner has more time and energy to provide support and the greater comfort of living keeps depression down.

Chapter 12

1. (a) Score on knowledge of physiology; (b) number of injuries; (c) linear prediction rule formula is $\hat{Y} = a + (b)(X)$, so predicted number of injuries = $10.30 - (.70)$ (knowledge of physiology); (d) $10.30 - (.70)(0) = 10.30$; (e) 9.60; (f) 8.90; (g) 6.80; (h) 6.10.

2. (a) Midterm exam score; (b) final exam score; (c) predicted final exam score = $40 + (.5)$(midterm exam score); (d) $40 + (.5)(30) = 55$; (e) 60; (f) 65; (g) 70; (h) 75; (i) 80; (j) 85; (k) 90.

3. (a) $\hat{Y} = 1.5 + (.8)(X)$; (b) $\hat{Y} = 10.0 - (.40)(X)$; (c) $\hat{Y} = 2.0 + (.2)(X)$; (d) $\hat{Y} = 9.5 - (.8)(X)$.

(e)

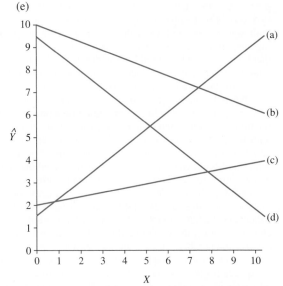

4. (a) Use the formula $b = \Sigma[(X - M_X)(Y - M_Y)]/SS_X$. Figure $\Sigma[(X - M_X)(Y - M_Y)]$ and SS_X using the procedure shown in Chapter 11 question 2c (or use your results from question 3 in Chapter 11). In this study, $\Sigma[(X - M_X)(Y - M_Y)] = 210$ and $SS_X = 56$. Thus, $b = 210/56 = 3.75$. $a = M_Y - (b)(M_X) = 73 - (3.75)(6) = 50.50$. Therefore, predicted test grade = $50.50 + (3.75)$(hours studied).

(b)

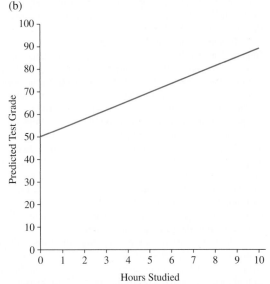

(c) $50.50 + (3.75)(3) = 61.75$; (d) 69.25; (e) 76.75; (f) $\beta = (b)(\sqrt{SS_X}/\sqrt{SS_Y})$. Figure SS_Y using the procedure shown in Chapter 11 question 2c (or use your results from question 3 in Chapter 11). $SS_Y = 1110$. Therefore, $\beta = (3.75)(\sqrt{56}/\sqrt{1110}) = .84$.

(g) Prediction is a statistical procedure used to predict scores on one variable (called a criterion variable) from scores on another variable (called a predictor variable). You use a linear prediction rule to make predictions. The linear prediction rule says that, to predict a person's score on a criterion variable (*Y*), start with a particular number (called a regression constant) and add to it the result of multiplying a particular number (called a regression coefficient) by the person's score on the predictor variable (*X*). The regression constant (which is labeled *a*) is a fixed value that you always add in to the prediction. The regression coefficient (which is labeled *b*) is called a coefficient because it is a number you multiply by something.

There are formulas for determining the values of *a* (the regression constant) and *b* (the regression coefficient) that give the best linear prediction rule. The best linear prediction rule is the one that that gives the lowest sum of squared errors between the actual scores on the criterion variable and the predicted scores on the criterion variable. The linear prediction rule can be written as a formula: $\hat{Y} = a + (b)(X)$. $\hat{Y}$ means the predicted value of *Y*, that is, the predicted value of the criterion variable (the variable you are trying to predict). In this example, the linear prediction rule was predicted test grade = 50.50 + (3.75)(hours studied). The linear prediction rule can be shown as a line on a graph. This line is called a regression line. The regression line shows the relationship between values for the *X* variable and predicted values for the *Y* variable. You draw the regression line by using the linear prediction rule to predict the value of the *Y* for a low value of *X* and marking that point on a graph, then predicting the value of *Y* for a high value of *X* and marking that point on a graph, and then finally you join the two dots. The slope of the regression line is *b* (the regression coefficient). The regression coefficient is the predicted amount of increase in units for the criterion variable when the predictor variable increases by one unit. So the regression coefficient of 3.75 in this example means that every one-hour increase in the number of hours studied gives a predicted increase of 3.75 points on the test grade. The point where the regression line crosses the vertical axis—which is called the intercept—is *a* (the regression constant). In this example, the regression line crosses the vertical axis at 50.50 (which is the value of *a*). I used the linear prediction rule to figure the predicted test grade of the students who studied for different amounts of time.

The scale used for the predictor and criterion variables will affect the value of *b* (the regression coefficient) in the linear prediction rule. This can make it hard to compare linear prediction rules across studies. You can avoid this problem by figuring a standardized regression coefficient, which is referred to using the Greek symbol β (beta). The standardized

regression coefficient shows the predicted amount of change in standard deviation units of the criterion variable if the value of the predicted variable increases by one standard deviation. The standardized regression coefficient can be figured by multiplying the regression coefficient by the result of dividing the square root of the sum of squared deviations for the predictor variable by the square root of the sum of squared deviations for the criterion variable. The standardized regression coefficient of .84 in this example means that, for every standard deviation increase in hours studied, the predicted test grade increases by .84 of a standard deviation.

(h)

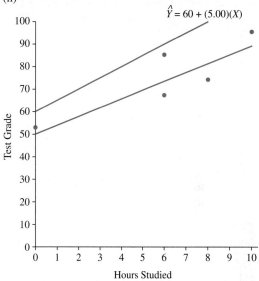

$$\hat{Y} = 60 + (5.00)(X)$$

(i) The regression line figured in part (b) does a better job of coming close to the dots. The regression line from part (b) is a visual equivalent of the linear prediction rule figured in part (a). Since that linear prediction rule is the best linear prediction rule (in terms of giving the lowest sum of squared errors between actual scores on the criterion variable and the predicted scores on the criterion variable), the regression line equivalent of that rule is the line that does the best job of coming close (in squared units) to the actual scores (shown by the dots).

(j) $\hat{Y} = 50.50 + (3.75)(X)$; the sum of squared errors using the prediction rule from (a) is 322.5. The sum of squared errors using the prediction rule $\hat{Y} = 60 + (5.00)(X)$ is 1855.0.

Hours Studied	Test Grade	Rule: $\hat{Y} = 50.50 + (3.75)(X)$			Rule: $\hat{Y} = 60 + (5.00)(X)$		
		Predicted Test Grade	Error	Squared Error	Predicted Test Grade	Error	Squared Error
X	*Y*	$\hat{Y}$	$(Y - \hat{Y})$	$(Y - \hat{Y})^2$	$\hat{Y}$	$(Y - \hat{Y})$	$(Y - \hat{Y})^2$
0	52	50.5	1.5	2.25	60.0	−8.0	64.0
10	95	88.0	7.0	49.00	110.0	−15.0	225.0
6	83	73.0	10.0	100.00	90.0	−7.0	49.0
8	71	80.5	−9.5	90.25	100.0	−29.0	841.0
6	64	73.0	−9.0	81.00	90.0	−26.0	676.0
				Σ = 322.5			Σ = 1855.0

(k) Proportionate reduction in error = $(SS_{Total} - SS_{Error})/SS_{Total}$. From (j) above, $SS_{Error} = 322.5$. SS_{Total} is the same as SS_Y, which from (c) above was 1110. So, proportionate reduction in error = $(1110 - 322.5)/1110 = .71$.

5. (a) Predicted hours studied = $-7.87 + (.19)$(test grade); (b) similar to question 4b; (c) 5.43; (d) 6.38; (e) 7.33; (f) $\beta = (b)(\sqrt{SS_X}/\sqrt{SS_Y}) = (.19)(\sqrt{1110}/\sqrt{56}) = .85$.

6. (a) Use the formula $b = \Sigma[(X - M_X)(Y - M_Y)]/SS_X$. Figure $\Sigma[(X - M_X)(Y - M_Y)]$ and SS_X using the procedure shown in Chapter 11 question 2c. In this study, $\Sigma[(X - M_X)(Y - M_Y)] = 126$ and $SS_X = 1960$. Thus, $b = 126/1960 = .06$. $a = M_Y - (b)(M_X) = 3 - (.06)(62) = -.72$. Therefore, predicted satisfaction = $-.72 + (.06)$ (empathy).

(b)

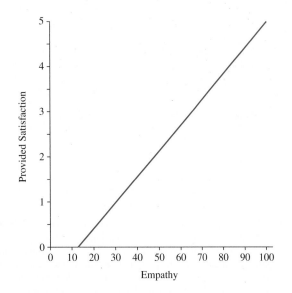

(c) $-.72 + (.06)(50) = 2.28$; (d) 3.12; (e) 4.08; (f) $\beta = (b)(\sqrt{SS_X}/\sqrt{SS_Y})$. Figure SS_Y using the procedure shown in Chapter 11 question 2c. $SS_Y = 10$. Therefore, $\beta = (.06)(\sqrt{1960}/\sqrt{10}) = .84$. (g) Similar to 4g above.

(h) Proportionate reduction in error = $(SS_{Total} - SS_{Error})/SS_{Total}$. Using the same procedure as in 4j above, $SS_{Error} = 1.94$. SS_{Total} is the same as SS_Y, which from part (f) above was 10. So, proportionate reduction in error = $(10 - 1.94)/10 = .81$.

7. (a) Predicted empathy = $24.2 + (12.6)$(satisfaction);   (b) similar to question 6b; (c) 62.0; (d) 49.4; (e) 36.8; (f) $\beta = (b)(\sqrt{SS_X}/\sqrt{SS_Y}) = (12.6)(\sqrt{10}/\sqrt{1960}) = .9$.

8. (a) Use the formula $b = \Sigma[(X - M_X)(Y - M_Y)]/SS_X = 73.20/2831.20 = .03$. $a = M_Y - (b)(M_X) = 2.6 - (.03)(68.6) = .54$. Therefore, predicted satisfaction = $.54 + (.03)$ (empathy).

(b) Figure like question 6b; (c) 2.04; (d) 2.46; (e) 2.94; (f) $\beta = (.03)(\sqrt{2831.20}/\sqrt{13.20}) = .44$. (g) In this question, we added an extra person to the study. The therapist empathy value for that person was a very high score (95) and the patient satisfaction was a very low score (1). The best way to compare the relationship between therapist empathy and patient satisfaction in the original case (question 6) and with the addition of the new person is to look at the standardized regression coefficients (βs). In question 6, the β was .84. This tells you that every increase of one standard deviation on therapist empathy is associated with a .84 standard deviation change in patient satisfaction. After adding the new person into the study, the β was .44. This tells you that every one standard deviation increase in therapist empathy is associated with a .44 standard deviation in patient satisfaction. Thus, by adding this new person to the study, the overall association between therapist empathy and patient satisfaction has become weaker. This makes sense because the patient we added to the study was quite different from the other patients. In question 6, there was a very strong tendency for high scores on therapist empathy to be associated with high sores on patient satisfaction (and low scores with low scores). The new patient we added in this question has a very high score on therapist empathy but a very low score on patient satisfaction. So the new patient can be thought of as an outlier, which in this case has the effect of making the association between therapist empathy and patient satisfaction less strong than it was without the outlier.

9. (a) $\hat{Y} = a + (b_1)(X_1) + (b_2)(X_2) + (b_3)(X_3) = 1.5 + (.8)(X_1) - (.3)(X_2) + (9.99)(X_3)$.
(b) $\hat{Y} = 10.0 - (.4)(X_1) + (11.0)(X_2) - (8.62)(X_3)$.
(c) $\hat{Y} = 2.0 + (.2)(X_1) + (6.13)(X_2) + (2.12)(X_3)$.
(d) $\hat{Y} = 9.5 - (.8)(X_1) + (21.23)(X_2) + (1.02)(X_3)$.
(e) $\hat{Y} = 1.5 + (.8)(2) - (.3)(5) + (9.99)(9) = 91.51$.

10. First, explain prediction as in question 4g and correlation as in Chapter 11. The two graphs show regression lines separately for each experimental group. The left graph shows that Expectation of Success provides little information to predict Number of Plans for either the Positive Fantasy or Negative Reality group, but for the Contrast group, there is a fairly strong positive relation between Expectation of Success and Number of Plans. The right graph, which shows the regression lines for predicting Taking Responsibility from Expectation of Success, indicates that there is a moderate negative relation for the Positive Fantasy group, a small negative relation for the Negative Reality group, and a strong positive relation for the Contrast group.

11. In bivariate prediction, you are predicting scores on a single criterion variable from scores on a single predictor variable. In multiple regression, you are predicting scores on a single criterion variable from scores on two or more predictor variables. The Peer Acceptance part of the table actually shows the results of two multiple regression analyses. In the first multiple regression analysis (Equation 1), the researchers predicted peer acceptance (the criterion variable) from scores on nonsocial teaching (one predictor variable) and scores on social coaching (a second predictor variable). In the second multiple regression analysis (Equation 2), the researchers predicted peer acceptance (the criterion variable) from scores on responsive style (one predictor variable) and scores on social coaching (a second predictor variable). In

the first multiple regression analysis, the standardized regression coefficients were .10 and .32. These standardized regression coefficients can be interpreted in the same manner as in bivariate prediction. However, it is important to note that the regression coefficients in multiple regression reflect what each predictor variable contributes to the prediction, over and above what the other predictor variables contribute. Thus, the ordinary correlations between each predictor variable and the criterion variable can show a quite different pattern. The R^2 of .14 for the first regression is the proportionate reduction in error or proportion of variance accounted for. This means that the two predictor variables together accounted for 14% (that is, $.14 \times 100 = 14\%$) of the variation in peer acceptance scores. (The square root of the proportionate reduction in error, .37, is the multiple correlation coefficient.)

Chapter 13

1. (a) χ^2 needed ($df = 5 - 1 = 4$, .05 level) = 9.488.

Category	O	Expected	O − E	(O − E)²	(O − E)²/E
A	19	(.2)(50) = 10	9	81	8.10
B	11	(.2)(50) = 10	1	1	.10
C	10	(.4)(50) = 20	−10	100	5.00
D	5	(.1)(50) = 5	0	0	0.00
E	5	(.1)(50) = 5	0	0	0.00
Total	50		50	0	$\chi^2 = 13.20$

Conclusion: Reject the null hypothesis

(b) χ^2 needed = 5.992; $\chi^2 = 44.45$, reject the null hypothesis; (c) χ^2 needed = 7.815; $\chi^2 = 1.23$, do not reject the null hypothesis.

2. χ^2 needed for (a), (b), and (c): ($df = 5 - 1 = 4$, 1%) = 13.277;

(a)

Category	O	Expected	O − E	(O − E)²	(O − E)²/E
A	10	20	−10	100	5
B	10	20	−10	100	5
C	10	20	−10	100	5
D	10	20	−10	100	5
E	60	20	40	1600	80
Total	100	100	0		$\chi^2 = 100$

Conclusion: Reject the null hypothesis

(b) $\chi^2 = 50$, reject the null hypothesis; (c) $\chi^2 = 450$, reject the null hypothesis.

3. (a) ❶ **Restate the question as a research hypothesis and a null hypothesis about the populations.** There are two populations of interest:

Population 1: Clients like those of this psychotherapy clinic. **Population 2:** Clients for whom season makes no difference in when they use the psychotherapy clinic.

The research hypothesis is that the distribution over seasons of when clients use the psychotherapy clinic is different between the two populations. The null hypothesis is that the distributions over seasons of when clients use the psychotherapy clinic is not different between the populations. ❷ **Determine the characteristics of the comparison distribution.** Chi-square distribution with 3 degrees of freedom ($df = 4$ categories $- 1 = 3$). ❸ **Determine the cutoff sample score on the comparison distribution at which the null hypothesis should be rejected.** .05 level, $df = 3$: χ^2 needed = 7.815. ❹ **Determine your sample's score on the comparison distribution.**

Season	O	Expected	O − E	(O − E)²	(O − E)²/E
Winter	28	(1/4)(128) = 32	−4	16	.50
Spring	33	(1/4)(128) = 32	1	1	.03
Summer	16	(1/4)(128) = 32	−16	256	8.00
Fall	51	(1/4)(128) = 32	19	361	11.28
Total	128	128	0		$\chi^2 = 19.81$

❺ **Decide whether to reject the null hypothesis.** 19.81 is larger than 7.815; reject the null hypothesis; the research hypothesis is supported.

(b)

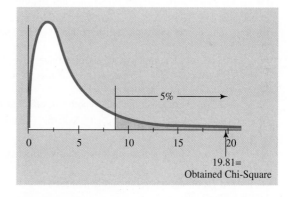

(c) If the season makes no difference, you would expect about 25% of clients to use the psychotherapy clinic each season (for last year, 25% of 128 is 32). Are last year's actual numbers in each season so discrepant from these expectations that you should conclude that in general the numbers of new clients are not equally distributed over the seasons? The chi-square statistic reflects the discrepancy between observed and expected results. For each category (such as the four seasons), you figure that discrepancy, square it, and divide by the expected number; then you add up the results. In the winter, 28 less than 32 is −4, squared is 16, divided by 32 is .50. Doing the same for the other three seasons and adding up the four gives a total chi-square of 19.81. (Chi-square uses squared discrepancies so that the result is not affected by the directions of the differences. You divide by the expected number to reduce the impact of the raw number of cases on the result.)

Statisticians have determined mathematically what would happen if you took an infinite number of samples from a population with a fixed proportion of cases in each category and figured chi-square for each sample. This distribution depends only on how many categories are free to take on different expected values. (The total number expected is the total number of cases; thus, if you know the expected for any three categories, you can just subtract to get the number expected for the fourth). A table of the chi-square distribution when three categories are free to vary shows that there is only a 5% chance of getting a chi-square of 7.815 or greater. Because our chi-square is larger than this, the observed result differs from the expected more than you would reasonably expect by chance; the number of new clients, in the long run, is probably not equal over the four seasons.

4. (a) You should get the same result within rounding error. (b) Similar to question 3c.

5. For (a), (b), and (c): $df = (N_{\text{Columns}} - 1)(N_{\text{Rows}} - 1) = (2 - 1)(2 - 1) = 1$; χ^2 needed $= 6.635$.

(a)

10 (13)	16 (13)	26	(50%)
16 (13)	10 (13)	26	(50%)
26	26	52	

$\chi^2 = (10 - 13)^2/13 + (16 - 13)^2/13 + (16 - 13)^2/13 + (10 - 13)^2/13 = 2.76$. Do not reject the null hypothesis: effect size, $\phi = \sqrt{\chi^2/N} = \sqrt{2.76/52} = \sqrt{0.53} = .23$.

(b) $\chi^2 = .36$, do not reject the null hypothesis; effect size, $\phi = .03$.

(c) $\chi^2 = 27.68$, reject the null hypothesis; effect size, $\phi = .23$. For (d), (e), and (f): $df = (N_{\text{Columns}} - 1)(N_{\text{Rows}} - 1) = (3 - 1)(2 - 1) = 2$; χ^2 needed $= 9.211$.

(d) $\chi^2 = 2.76$, do not reject the null hypothesis; effect size, Cramer's $\phi = \sqrt{\chi^2/[(N)(df_{\text{Smaller}})]} = \sqrt{2.76/[(72)(1)]} = \sqrt{.0383} = .20$.

(e) $\chi^2 = 2.76$, do not reject the null hypothesis; effect size, Cramer's $\phi = .18$.

(f) $\chi^2 = 3.71$, do not reject the null hypothesis; effect size, Cramer's $\phi = .22$.

6. (a) ❶ **Restate the question as a research hypothesis and a null hypothesis about the populations.** There are two populations of interest:

Population 1: Children like those surveyed.
Population 2: Children for whom age is independent of whether or not they like this kind of music.

The research hypothesis is that the two populations are different. The null hypothesis is that the two populations are the same.

❷ **Determine the characteristics of the comparison distribution.** Chi-square distribution with two degrees of freedom. $df = (N_{\text{Columns}} - 1)(N_{\text{Rows}} - 1) = (3 - 1)(2 - 1) = 2$.

❸ **Determine the cutoff sample score on the comparison distribution at which the null hypothesis should be rejected.** .05 level, $df = 2$: χ^2 needed $= 5.992$.

❹ **Determine your sample's score on the comparison distribution.**

		Age of Child			
		5	8	11	
Likes Type of Music	Yes	42 (39)	62 (65)	26 (26)	130 (65%)
	No	18 (21)	38 (35)	14 (14)	70 (35%)
		60	100	40	200

$\chi^2 = (42 - 39)^2/39 + (62 - 65)^2/65 + (26 - 26)^2/26 + (18 - 21)^2/21 + (38 - 35)^2/35 + (14 - 14)^2/14 = 1.06$.

❺ **Decide whether to reject the null hypothesis.** 1.06 is less extreme than 5.992; do not reject the null hypothesis; the study is inconclusive.

(b)

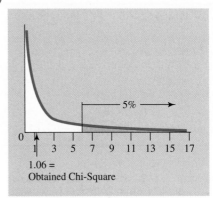

1.06 =
Obtained Chi-Square

(c) Cramer's $\phi = \sqrt{\chi^2/[(N)(df_{\text{Smaller}})]} = \sqrt{1.06/[(200)(1)]} = \sqrt{.0053} = .07$.

(d) In this example, 65% of all children liked the particular kind of music. Thus, if age and liking of this kind of music are not related, 65% of the children in each age group should like this kind of music. For example, you'd expect 39 of the 60 8-year-olds to like this music. Are the survey results so discrepant from these expectations that you should conclude that age is related to what kind of music children like?

The chi-square statistic reflects the discrepancy between observed and expected results. For each combination of the 2 × 3 arrangement, you figure that discrepancy between observed and expected, square it, and divide by the expected number; then you add up the results. In the yes-8-year-old combination, 42 minus 39 is 3, squared is 9, divided by 39 is .23. Doing the same for the other five combinations and adding them all up gives 1.06. (Chi-square uses squared discrepancies so that the result is not affected by the directions of the differences. It is divided by the expected number to adjust for the impact of relatively different numbers expected in the combinations.)

The rest is similar to question 3c, except for the following about degrees of freedom. For each age group, if you know the totals and the figure for children who like this kind of music, you can figure the number who do not by subtraction. And of the three age groups, if you know the total and any two of them, you can figure the third by subtraction. So only two combinations are "free to vary."

7. (a) ❶ **Restate the question as a research hypothesis and a null hypothesis about the populations.** There are two populations of interest:

Population 1: People like those surveyed.
Population 2: People for whom the community they live in is independent of their opinion on the upcoming ballot initiative.

The research hypothesis is that the two populations are different (the community people live in is not independent of their opinion on the upcoming ballot initiative). The null hypothesis is that the two populations are the same (the community people live in is independent of their opinion on the upcoming ballot imitative).
❷ **Determine the characteristics of the comparison distribution.** Chi-square distribution with four degrees of freedom. $df = (N_{Columns} - 1)(N_{Rows} - 1) = (3 - 1)(3 - 1) = 4$.
❸ **Determine the cutoff sample score on the comparison distribution at which the null hypothesis should be rejected.** .05 level, $df = 4$: χ^2 needed $= 9.488$.
❹ **Determine your sample's score on the comparison distribution.** $\chi^2 = (12 - 9.8)^2/9.8 + (6 - 4.2)^2/4.2$
$+ (3 - 7)^2/7 + (18 - 16.8)^2/16.8 + (3 - 7.2)^2/7.2$
$+ (15 - 12)^2/12 + (12 - 15.4)^2/15.4 + (9 - 6.6)^2/6.6$
$+ (12 - 11)^2/11 = .49 + .77 + 2.29 + .09 + 2.45$
$+ .75 + .75 + .87 + .09 = 8.55$.
❺ **Decide whether to reject the null hypothesis.** χ^2 in Step ❹ (8.55) is less extreme than Step ❸ cutoff (9.488). Therefore, do not reject the null hypothesis; the study is inconclusive.
(b) Similar to question 6b.
(c) Cramer's $\phi = \sqrt{[8.55/(90)(2)]} = \sqrt{[8.55/180]} = \sqrt{.05} = .22$.
(d) Similar to question 6d but focusing on this study's results.

8. (a) $\phi = \sqrt{\chi^2/N} = \sqrt{16/100} = .40$;
(b) Cramer's
$\phi = \sqrt{\chi^2/[(N)(df_{Smaller})]} = \sqrt{16/[(100)(1)]} = .40$;
(c) Cramer's $\phi = .28$;
(d) $\phi = .28$;
(e) $\phi = .28$.

9. From Table 13–9: (a) .08; (b) .32; (c) .11; (d) .07; (e) .06; (f) .06.

10. From Table 13–10: (a) 87; (b) 26; (c) 133; (d) 133; (e) 39.

11. (a) You should get the same results within rounding error.
(b) $\phi = \sqrt{\chi^2/N} = \sqrt{5.55/69} = .28$;
(c) Similar to question 6d but focusing on this study's results.

12. (a) You should get the same results within rounding error.
(b) $\phi = \sqrt{\chi^2/N} = \sqrt{.33/145} = .05$;
(c) Similar to question 6d but focusing on this study's results.

Chapter 14

1. The following are probably not normal: (a) skewed to the right; (b) bimodal; (d) skewed to the right; (e) approximately rectangular.
2. (a) 4, 2, 3, 5, 6; (b) 5.92, 3.78, 3.61, 3.59, 4.24.
3. (a)

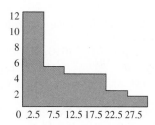

(b) 3, 5.3, 2, 4, 0, 2.6, 5, 1, 2, 3.2, 2, 1.4, 1, 3, 4, 3.3, 3.5, 1, 4.2, 1.4, 2.2, 3.2, 1.7, 4.1, 2.4, 2, 1.4, 4.8, 4.6, 4.5.
(c)

4. (a) t needed ($df = 8$, $p < .05$, two-tailed) $= -2.306, 2.306$; Group A: $M = 3.8$, $S^2 = 5.06$; Group B: $M = 5.7$, $S^2 = 6.76$; $S^2_{Pooled} = 5.91$; $S_{Difference} = 1.54$; $t = -1.23$; do not reject the null hypothesis.
(b) Group A: 1.1, 1.6, 2.1, 1.9, 2.7; Group B: 1.4, 3.0, 2.4, 2.6, 2.2.
(c) t needed $= -2.306, 2.306$; Group A: $M = 1.88$, $S^2 = .35$; Group B: $M = 2.32$, $S^2 = .35$; $S^2_{Pooled} = .35$; $S_{Difference} = .37$; $t = -1.19$; do not reject the null hypothesis.
(d) It would not have been correct to carry out a t test on the numbers as they were (without transforming them). This is because the distributions of the samples were very skewed for both language groups. Thus, it seemed likely that the population distributions were also seriously skewed. That would clearly violate the assumption for a t test that the underlying population distributions are normal. Thus, I took the square root of each score. This had the advantage of making the sample distributions much closer to normal. This suggests that the population distributions of square roots of family sizes are probably nearly normally distributed. I realize that taking the square root of each family size distorts its straightforward meaning, but the impact for the individuals in the family of each additional child is probably not equal. That is, going from no children to 1 child has a huge impact. Going from 1 to 2 has less, and going from 7 to 8 probably makes much less difference for the family.

In any case, having taken the square root of each score, I then carried out an ordinary t test for independent means using these transformed scores. As with the original *t* test, the result was inconclusive (the null hypothesis could not be rejected), but at least I could be confident that I had done the analysis correctly.

5. (a) *t* needed ($df = 5, p < .05$, two-tailed) $= -2.571, 2.571$; $t = (M - \mu)/S_M = (6 - 0)/2.54 = 2.36$; do not reject the null hypothesis.

(b) 3.32, 4, 0, 2, 2, 1.

(c) $t = (2.05 - 0)/.6 = 3.42$; reject the null hypothesis.

(d) Similar to question 4d.

6. (a) *F* needed ($df = 2, 6; p < .01$) $= 10.93$; Sad: $M = 446$, $S^2 = 47,089$; Angry: $M = 259, S^2 = 11,727$; Exuberant: $M = 918.67, S^2 = 7,184$; $S^2_{Between} = 346,775.22$; $S^2_{Within} = 22,000$; $F = 15.76$; reject the null hypothesis.

(b) 14.2, 22.9, 24.8; 11.7, 18.4, 17.3; 28.9, 30.2, 31.7.

(c) $M = 20.63, S^2 = 31.94$; $M = 15.8, S^2 = 12.91$; $M = 30.27, S^2 = 1.96$; $S^2_{Between} = 162.82$; $S^2_{Within} = 15.60$; $F = 10.44$; do not reject the null hypothesis.

(d) Similar to question 4d, except note that the square root transformation does *not* solve the problem of skew and that it also creates distributions very likely to violate the assumption of equal population variances.

7. Miller wanted to examine the relationships among the variables he was studying, probably including various parametric hypothesis-testing techniques such as the *t* test, analysis of variance, or testing the significance of bivariate or multiple correlation or regression results. Such procedures are based on the assumption that the distributions of the variables in the population follow a normal curve. However, Miller first checked the distributions of the variables he was studying and found that the scores on two key measures were skewed, suggesting that the population distributions for these variables probably violated the normal distribution assumption. (Rest of your answer similar to question 4d.)

8. Similar to question 7.

9. (a) 3, 1, 2, 4, 5; (b) 5, 3, 2, 1, 4.

10. (a) 16.5, 30, 10.5, 22.5, 1, 15, 29, 3, 10.5, 18.5, 10.5, 6, 3, 16.5, 22.5, 20, 21, 3, 25, 6, 13, 18.5, 8, 24, 14, 10.5, 6, 28, 27, 26.

(b)

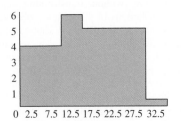

11. (a) Test using original scores in 4a above. Ranks: Group A, 1, 3, 5, 4, 9; Group B, 2, 10, 7, 8, 6; Group A: $M = 4.4$, $S^2 = 8.8$; Group B: $M = 6.6$, $S^2 = 8.8$; $S^2_{Pooled} = 8.8$; $S_{Difference} = 1.88$; $t = -1.17$; do not reject the null hypothesis. *Explanation:* Similar to question 4d, except instead of explaining square root transformation, explain rank-order transformation. I changed each of the scores to its rank

among all the scores. This makes the distribution roughly rectangular. Some statisticians recommend that if the assumptions are questionable for an ordinary parametric test, you change the scores to ranks first and then proceed, and that gives more accurate results. There are special procedures you can use for a *t* test for independent means with ranks. But the figuring is mathematically equivalent to what you do with an ordinary *t* test with ranks. The difference is that the rank-order procedure goes with special tables that are more accurate in this situation than the *t* table. However, statisticians have found that the results using an ordinary *t* table in this situation are usually a good approximation.

(b) Ranks: 5, 6, 1, 3.5, 3.5, 2; $t = (M - \mu)/S_M = (3.5 - 0)/.75 = 4.67$; reject the null hypothesis.

(c) Ranks: 2, 5, 6; 1, 4, 3; 7, 8, 9; $S^2_{Between} = 22.32$; $S^2_{Within} = 2.56$; $F = 8.72$; reject the null hypothesis.

12. Similar to questions 4d and 11a, but note that the researchers used one of the special rank-order tests.

Chapter 15

1. "Controlling for" refers to partial correlation, a procedure based on multiple regression in which you figure the correlation between two variables, subtracting out the influence of one or more other variables (the variables that are controlled for). It amounts to figuring the correlation between your variables at each level of the controlled-for variable and then averaging these correlations.

For example, in this study, the moderately strong correlation between romantic appeal and level of dating experience can't be explained as both being due somehow to appearance of physical maturity, because appearance of physical maturity is controlled for.

2. Boyd and Gullone are describing the reliability of the study's measures. Reliability is how much a test measures something consistently. One method of assessing reliability is by looking at how one-half of the test correlates with the other half of the test, the idea being that the same person is taking two tests (the two halves of the test) at the same time under the same circumstances. A more general way to assess the reliability of a measure is to divide the measure into halves in all possible ways and figure the correlation between halves using each division; averaging all of these correlations gives a statistic called Cronbach's alpha (which Boyd and Gullone refer to as an alpha coefficient). Cronbach's alpha is a measure of the internal consistency reliability of a measure, which is the extent to which the items of a measure assess a common characteristic. An alpha of .60 or .70 is usually considered a minimum adequate level of reliability; that some of Boyd and Gullon's measures had lower alphas means that some of the variables studied may not be giving very precise information and may not be doing a good job of assessing a common characteristic.

3. In this study, the participants are students who are grouped into different classrooms. This grouping into classrooms means that you can not use a regular regression approach to test whether the tendency to avoid seeking help is related to various student and classroom characteristics. So the researchers used a technique called multilevel modeling instead of regular regression. This type of analysis takes into account the fact that there are groupings of students in the

study. In this example, characteristics of the individual students (such as their level of self-efficacy) are called lower-level variables. These lower-level variables are the variables for the students in each classroom. The classroom characteristics (such as teachers' ratings of their role in students' social and emotional well-being) are called upper-level variables. These upper-level variables are ones that are about each classroom as a whole (because everyone in that classroom has the same teacher). One way to think about this kind of analysis is to imagine that the researchers conducted a separate regression for each of the 63 different math classrooms. The predictor variables in each regression would be the student characteristics, and the criterion variable would be the students' tendency to avoid seeking help. The researchers could then average the regression coefficients across the 63 regressions to get a sense of the overall association between student characteristics and their tendency to avoid seeking help. Then the researchers could conduct another set of regression for each of the 63 different classrooms. In each of these regressions, the predictor variables would be the classroom-level variables, and the criterion variable would be the average of each group's scores on the tendency to avoid seeking help measure. The researchers could then average the regression coefficients to give the overall association between the classroom level variables and students' tendency to avoid seeking help. Fortunately, these days researchers can use sophisticated methods that take all the information on all the levels at once and figure a slightly more accurate result. In this study, the researchers used such a method, called hierarchical linear modeling (HLM).

4. You use a factor analysis to uncover the underlying pattern among a large number of variables—to find out which variables group together in the sense of correlating with each other but not with other variables in other groupings. Fawzi and colleagues' results suggest that the best underlying pattern among the 16 PTSD symptom ratings has four groupings or factors (called "dimensions" in their table). The table shows the correlation, called "Factor Loadings," of each individual variable with the grouping. (In this table, the researchers listed only each symptom's factor loading on the factor on which it had the highest loading. Each variable has a loading on each factor, but ordinarily has a high loading on only one factor, and it is thought of as being part of that factor.) The researchers note that the first three factors correspond to the three key aspects of PTSD as it is usually understood. Their fourth factor (which has only one item), however, suggested that there is an additional and somewhat separate aspect of avoidance that has not been considered in previous work as being a separate aspect.

5. The procedure described here is path analysis, an elaboration of ordinary multiple regression in which you make specific predictions about the pattern of causality among your variables (your casual model), usually including making a diagram showing the causality as arrows between boxes, as in the figure by MacKinnon-Lewis and colleagues. You then figure the regression coefficients (called "path coeffients"). These researchers tried several possible models, and the figure shows the one that they decided was best (in terms of the strongest coefficients overall). In this model,

for example, father acceptance (after partialing out mother rejection) has little direct influence on sibling aggression, but mother rejection (after partialing out father acceptance) has a moderate effect on it. According to the rest of this model, sibling aggression has a moderate effect on aggression with peers, which in turn has a fairly large effect on aggression with peers, which in turn has a fairly large negative effect on social acceptance.

6. (Explanation of path analysis as in question 6.) Aron and colleagues conducted a mediational analysis, which is a particular type of path analysis. Mediational analysis allows you to test whether a presumed causal relationship between two variables is due to some particular intervening variable (called a mediator variable). In this study, the researchers examined whether boredom with a relationship explained the association between participating in exciting activities and relationship quality. To test the mediation, the researchers first examined whether exciting activities (the predictor variable) predicted relationship quality (the criterion variable). This prediction was significant (standardized regression coefficient = .51, $p < .001$). They also examined whether exciting activities (the predictor variable) predicted relationship boredom (the mediator variable). This prediction was significant (standardized regression coefficient = $-.56$, $p < .001$). Finally, Aron and colleagues examined whether exciting activities and relationship boredom predicted relationship quality in a multiple linear regression analysis. Consistent with mediation, relationship boredom predicted relationship quality (standarized regression coefficient = .74, $p < .001$), and exciting activities no longer predicted relationship quality (standardized regression coefficient = .10, *ns*). So the results of the mediational analysis were consistent with the researchers' mediation hypothesis that relationship boredom explains the effect of engaging in exciting activities on relationship quality.

7. (a) In the context of the proposed model, the key result is that all three hypothesized paths to intensity were significant. However, you can also see that the path from desirability to intensity was strongest and the path from probability to intensity, though significant, was not very strong. This means that how intensely one feels unrequited love is very strongly predicted by how desirable one finds the beloved, moderately by how much one finds the state of being in love desirable, but only slightly by one's belief that the other will eventually reciprocate.

(b) Structural equation modeling is a statistical technique in which you specify a pattern of causal links among variables, diagrammed with arrows connecting each cause to its effects. You can also specify that some variables measured in the study may actually be indicators of an underlying unmeasured latent variable. In this example, the researcher has specified paths from the three motivational factors to intensity. Further, each of the motivational factors and intensity (shown in ovals) are actually latent variables that are seen as the underlying causes of several measured variables (shown here as boxes; if there were not a shortage of space, each of these boxes would have a name for the specific questionnaire items it stands for).

A key statistical aspect of structural equation modeling involves using the correlations among variables to compute a "path coefficient" for each arrow. This tells the degree to which changes on the variable at the tail of the arrow are associated with changes in the variable at the head of the arrow (under conditions in which all other causes for that effect variable are held constant). That is, the path coefficient is a standardized regression coefficient (a beta) for the causal variable in a prediction model in which the effect variable is the criterion variable and all of the causal variables are predictor variables. For example, the path of .32 from desirability to intensity means that holding constant probability and desires state, for each standard deviation of change in desirability, there would be .32 of a standard deviation of change in intensity.

8. (a) Independent: the type of medication; dependent: level of anxiety.
(b) Independent: kind of movie; dependent: heart rate change.
(c) Independent: whether or not mother is present; dependent: number of touches between the two infants.

9. ANCOVA, or analysis of covariance, is analysis of variance in which one or more variables have been controlled for; ANCOVA is to ordinary ANOVA as a partial correlation is to ordinary correlation. In this example, Roeser and colleagues are making the point that the country main effect in their factorial ANOVA holds up even after social desirability is controlled for.

10. MANOVA, or multivariate analysis of variance, is ordinary analysis of variance, except that it looks at the overall effect on more than one dependent variable. In this example, there were five measures of conflict resolution preference. The significant "main effect of culture" means that the two cultures differed significantly when considering the entire set of dependent variables at once. Similarly, the significant "culture by type of conflict interaction" means that the effect of culture on the set of dependent variables varies according to the type of conflict. To understand which of the several conflict resolution variables were accounting for these overall effects, the researchers carried out univariate analyses, ordinary analyses of variance on one dependent variable at a time. The pattern of results was quite different according to the specific dependent variable considered.

11. (a) Causal modeling (path analysis or structural equation modeling);
(b) bivariate correlation and regression;
(c) reliability statistics, such as Cronbach's alpha and test-retest reliability;
(d) multivariate analysis of variance, probably followed up by univariate analyses of variance;
(e) multilevel modeling;
(f) factor analysis;
(g) *t* test for independent means;
(h) one-way analysis of variance.

Glossary

Numbers in parentheses refer to chapters in which the term is introduced or substantially discussed.

adjusted mean mean of a group after adjusting for (partialing out) the effect of a covariate in analysis of covariance. (15)

adjusting for same as *partialing out.* (15)

alpha (α) probability of making a Type I error; the probability of getting statistical significance if the null hypothesis is actually true; same as *significance level.* (6) Also short for *Cronbach's alpha.* (15)

analysis of covariance (ANCOVA) analysis of variance that controls for the effect of one or more additional variables. (15)

analysis of variance (ANOVA) hypothesis-testing procedure for studies with three or more groups. (9, 15)

analysis of variance table chart showing the major elements in figuring an analysis of variance using the structural model approach. (9)

assumption condition, such as a population's having a normal distribution, required for carrying out a particular hypothesis-testing procedure; a part of the mathematical foundation for the accuracy of the tables used in determining cutoff values. (7)

beta (β) probability of making a Type I error. (6) Also, a standardized regression coefficient. (12)

between-groups estimate of the population variance ($S^2_{Between}$, $MS_{Between}$) estimate of the variance of the population of individuals based on the variation among the means of the groups studied. Also called *mean squares between.* (9)

between-groups (or numerator) degrees of freedom ($df_{Between}$) degrees of freedom used in the between-groups estimate of the population variance in an analysis of variance (the numerator of the F ratio); number of scores free to vary (number of means minus 1) in figuring the between-groups estimate of the population variance. (9)

biased estimate estimate of a population parameter that is likely systematically to overestimate or underestimate the true value of the population parameter. For example, SD^2 would be a biased estimate of the population variance (it would systematically underestimate it). (7)

bimodal distribution frequency distribution with two approximately equal frequencies, each clearly larger than any of the others. (1)

bivariate prediction prediction of scores on one variable based on scores of one other variable. Also called *bivariate regression.* (12)

Bonferroni procedure multiple-comparison procedure in which the total alpha percentage is divided among the set of comparisons so that each is tested at a more stringent significance level. (9)

categorical variable same as *nominal variable.* (1)

ceiling effect situation in which many scores pile up at the high end of a distribution (creating skewness) because it is not possible to have a higher score. (1)

cell in a factorial research design, the particular combination of levels of the variables that divide the groups. (10) In a chi-square test for independence, the particular combination of categories for two variables in a contingency table. (13)

cell mean mean of a particular combination of levels of the variables that divide the groups in a factorial design in analysis of variance. (10)

central tendency typical or most representative value of a group of scores, such as the mean, median, or mode. (2)

chi-square distribution mathematically defined curve used as the comparison distribution in chi-square tests; distribution of the chi-square statistic. (13)

chi-square statistic (χ^2) statistic that reflects the overall lack of fit between the expected and observed frequencies; sum, over all the categories or cells, of the squared difference between observed and expected frequencies divided by the expected frequency. (13)

chi-square table table of cutoff scores on the chi-square distribution for various degrees of freedom and significance levels. (13)

chi-square test for goodness of fit hypothesis-testing procedure that examines how well an observed frequency distribution of a single nominal variable fits some expected pattern of frequencies. (13)

chi-square test for independence hypothesis-testing procedure that examines whether the distribution of frequencies over the categories of one nominal variable are unrelated to (independent of) the distribution of frequencies over the categories of a second nominal variable. (13)

chi-square tests hypothesis-testing procedures used when the variables of interest are nominal variables. (13)

comparison distribution distribution used in hypothesis testing. It represents the population situation if the null hypothesis is true. It is the distribution to which you compare the score based on your sample's results. It is made up of the same kinds of numbers as those of the sample's results (such as sample means, differences between sample means, *F* ratios, or chi squares). (4)

computational formula equation mathematically equivalent to the definitional formula. It is easier to use when figuring by hand but does not directly show the meaning of the procedure. (2)

computer-intensive methods statistical methods, including hypothesis-testing procedures, involving large numbers of repeated computations. (14)

confidence interval (CI) roughly speaking, the range of scores (that is, the scores between an upper and lower value) that is likely to include the true population mean; more precisely, the range of possible population means from which it is not highly unlikely that you could have obtained your sample mean. (5)

confidence limit upper or lower value of a confidence interval. (5)

contingency table two-dimensional chart showing frequencies in each combination of categories of two nominal variables, as in a chi-square test for independence. (13)

continuous variable variable for which, in theory, there are an infinite number of values between any two values. (1)

controlling for same as *partialing out*. (15)

conventional levels of significance ($p < .05, p < .01$) levels of significance (alpha levels) widely used in psychology. (4)

correlation association between scores on two or more variables. (11)

correlational research design any research design other than a true experiment. (11)

correlation coefficient (*r*) measure of degree of linear correlation between two variables ranging from -1 (a perfect negative linear correlation) through 0 (no correlation) to $+1$ (a perfect positive correlation). (11)

correlation matrix common way of reporting the correlation coefficients among several variables in a research article; table in which the variables are named on the top and along the side and the correlations among them are all shown. (11)

covariate variable controlled for in an analysis of covariance. (15)

Cramer's phi (Cramer's ϕ) measure of effect size for a chi-square test for independence used with a contingency table that is larger than 2×2. Also known as *Cramer's V* and sometimes written as ϕ_C or V_C. (13)

criterion variable (usually *Y*) in prediction, a variable that is predicted. (12)

Cronbach's alpha (α) widely used measure of a test's *internal consistency reliability* that reflects the average of the split-half correlations from all possible splits into halves of the items on the test. (15)

curvilinear correlation relation between two variables that shows up on a scatter diagram as dots following a systematic pattern that is not a straight line. (11)

cutoff sample score in hypothesis testing, the point on the comparison distribution at which, if reached or exceeded by the sample score, you reject the null hypothesis. Also called *critical value*. (4)

data transformation mathematical procedure (such as taking the square root) used on each score in a sample, usually done to make the sample distribution closer to normal. (14)

decision error incorrect conclusion in hypothesis testing in relation to the real (but unknown) situation, such as deciding the null hypothesis is false when it is really true. (6)

definitional formula equation for a statistical procedure directly showing the meaning of the procedure. (2)

degrees of freedom (*df*) number of scores free to vary when estimating a population parameter; usually part of a formula for making that estimate—for example, in the formula for estimating the population variance from a single sample, the degrees of freedom is the number of scores minus 1. (7)

dependent variable variable considered to be an effect; usually a measured variable. (15)

descriptive statistics procedures for summarizing a group of scores or otherwise making them more comprehensible. (1)

deviation score score minus the mean. (2)

dichotomizing dividing the scores for a variable into two groups. Also called *median split*. (10)

difference score difference between a person's score on one testing and the same person's score on another testing; often an after-score minus a before-score, in which case it is also called a *change score*. (7)

direction of causality path of causal effect; if *X* is thought to cause *Y* then the direction of causality is from *X* to *Y*. (11)

directional hypothesis research hypothesis predicting a particular direction of difference between populations—for example, a prediction that one population has a higher mean than another population. (4)

discrete variable variable that has specific values (such as whole numbers) and that cannot have values between these specific values (such as fractional values). (1)

distribution of differences between means distribution of differences between means of pairs of samples such that, for each pair of means, one mean is from one population and the other mean is from a second population; the comparison distribution in a *t* test for independent means. (8)

distribution of means distribution of means of samples of a given size from a population (also called a *sampling distribution of the mean*); comparison distribution when testing hypotheses involving a single sample of more than one individual. (5)

distribution-free test hypothesis-testing procedure making no assumptions about the shape of populations. Also called a *nonparametric test*. (14)

effect size conventions standard rules about what to consider a small, medium, and large effect size, based on what is typical in psychology research; also known as Cohen's conventions. (6)

effect size in studies involving means of one or two groups, measure of difference (lack of overlap) between populations;

the usual standardized effect size measure increases with greater differences between means and decreases with greater standard deviations in the populations, but it is not affected by sample size. There are also conventional effect size measures for other kinds of studies (correlations, analysis of variance and chi-square test situations); these describe the standardized degree of association in the population. (6)

equal-interval variable variable in which the numbers stand for approximately equal amounts of what is being measured. (1)

error in prediction, the difference between a person's predicted score on the criterion variable and the person's actual score on the criterion variable. (12)

eta squared (η^2) common name for the R^2 measure of effect size for the analysis of variance. Also called *correlation ratio*. (9)

expected frequency (E) in a chi-square test, number of people in a category or cell expected if the null hypothesis were true. (13)

expected relative frequency in figuring probabilities, number of successful outcomes divided by the number of total outcomes you would expect to get if you repeated an experiment a large number of times. (3)

factor in factor analysis, group of variables that tend to correlate with each other and not with other variables. (15)

factor analysis statistical procedure applied in situations where many variables are measured and that identifies groups of variables that tend to be correlated with each other and not with other variables. (15)

factorial analysis of variance analysis of variance for a factorial research design. (10)

factorial research design way of organizing a study in which the influence of two or more variables is studied at once by setting up the situation so that a different group of people are tested for each combination of the levels of the variables; for example, in a 2×2 factorial research design there would be four groups: those high on variable 1 and high on variable 2, those high on variable 1 but low on variable 2, those low on variable 1 but high on variable 2, and those low on variable 1 and low on variable 2. (10)

factor loading in factor analysis, correlation of a variable with a factor. (15)

F distribution mathematically defined curve that is the comparison distribution used in an analysis of variance. (9)

fit index in structural equation modeling, measure of how well the pattern of correlations in a sample corresponds to the correlations that would be expected based on the hypothesized pattern of causes and effects among those variables; usually ranges from 0 to 1, with 1 being a perfect fit. (15)

floor effect situation in which many scores pile up at the low end of a distribution (creating skewness) because it is not possible to have any lower score. (1)

F ratio in analysis of variance, ratio of the between-groups population variance estimate to the within-groups population variance estimate. Also called simply *F*. (9)

frequency distribution pattern of frequencies over the various values; what a frequency table, histogram, or frequency polygon describes. (1)

frequency table listing of number of individuals having each of the different values for a particular variable. (1)

F table table of cutoff scores on the F distribution. (9)

general linear model general formula that is the basis of most of the statistical methods covered in this text; describes a score as the sum of a constant, the weighted influence of several variables, and error. (15)

grand mean (GM) overall mean of all the scores, regardless of what group they are in; when group sizes are equal, mean of the group means. (9)

grouped frequency table frequency table in which the number of individuals (frequency) is given for each interval of values. (1)

grouping variable a variable that separates groups in analysis of variance (and t tests); also see *independent variable*. (10)

harmonic mean special average influenced disproportionately by smaller numbers; in a t test for independent means when the number of scores in the two groups differ, the harmonic mean is used as the equivalent of each group's sample size when determining power. (8)

hierarchical linear modeling (HLM) sophisticated type of multilevel modeling that handles a research situation in which people are grouped in some way that could affect the pattern of scores. (15)

histogram barlike graph of a frequency distribution in which the values are plotted along the horizontal axis and the height of each bar is the frequency of that value; the bars are usually placed next to each other without spaces, giving the appearance of a city skyline. (1)

holding constant same as *partialing out*. (15)

hypothesis prediction, often based on informal observation, previous research, or theory, that is tested in a research study. (4)

hypothesis testing procedure for deciding whether the outcome of a study (results for a sample) support a particular theory or practical innovation (which is thought to apply to a population). (4)

independence situation of no relationship between two variables; term usually used regarding two nominal variables in a chi-square test for independence. (13)

independent variable variable considered to be a cause, such as what group a person is in for a t test or analysis of variance. (15)

inferential statistics procedures for drawing conclusions based on the scores collected in a research study but going beyond them. (1)

interaction effect situation in a factorial analysis of variance in which a combination of variables has an effect that could not be predicted from the effects of the two variables individually; situation in which the effect of one grouping variable on the measured variable is different across the levels of the other grouping variable. (10)

intercept the point where the regression line crosses the vertical axis; the regression constant (a). (12)

internal consistency reliability extent to which the items of a measure assess a common characteristic; usually measured using *Cronbach's alpha*. (15)

interrater reliability similarity of ratings by two or more raters of each participant's behavior or material. (15)

interval range of values in a grouped frequency table that are grouped together. (For example, if the interval size is 10, one of the intervals might be from 10 to 19.) (1)

kurtosis extent to which a frequency distribution deviates from a normal curve in terms of whether its curve in the middle is more peaked or flat than the normal curve. (1)

latent variable in structural equation modeling, unmeasured variable assumed to be the underlying cause of several variables actually measured in the study. (15)

levels of measurement types of underlying numerical information provided by a measure, such as equal-interval, rank-order, and nominal (categorical). (1)

linear correlation relation between two variables that shows up on a scatter diagram as the dots roughly following a straight line. (11)

linear prediction rule formula for making predictions; that is, formula for predicting a person's score on a criterion variable based on the person's score on one or more predictor variables; also called *linear prediction model*. (12)

long-run relative-frequency interpretation of probability understanding of probability as the proportion of a particular outcome that you would get if the experiment were repeated many times. (3)

lower-level variable in multilevel modeling, a variable that is about people *within* each grouping. (15)

main effect difference between groups on one grouping variable in a factorial design in analysis of variance; result for a grouping variable, averaging across the levels of the other grouping variable(s). (10)

marginal mean in a factorial design in analysis of variance, mean score for all the participants at a particular level of one of the grouping variables. (10)

mean (M, μ) arithmetic average of a group of scores; sum of the scores divided by the number of scores. (2)

mean of a distribution of means (μ_M) the mean of a distribution of means of samples of a given size from a population; the same as the mean of the population of individuals (μ). (5)

mean squares between ($MS_{Between}$) same as *between-groups estimate of the population variance* ($S^2_{Between}$). (9)

mean squares within (MS_{Within}) same as *within-groups estimate of the population variance* (S^2_{Within}). (9)

median middle score when all the scores in a distribution are arranged from lowest to highest. (2)

mediational analysis particular type of path analysis that tests whether a presumed causal relationship between two variables is due to some particular intervening variable (called a mediator variable). (15)

meta-analysis statistical method for combining effect sizes from different studies. (6)

mode value with the greatest frequency in a distribution. (2)

multilevel modeling advanced type of regression analysis that handles a research situation in which people are grouped in some way that could affect the pattern of scores. (15)

multimodal distribution frequency distribution with two or more high frequencies separated by a lower frequency; a bimodal distribution is the special case of two high frequencies. (1)

multiple correlation correlation of a criterion variable with two or more predictor variables. (12)

multiple correlation coefficient (R) in multiple regression, the correlation between the criterion variable and all the predictor variables taken together. It is a measure of degree of multiple correlation; positive square root of the proportionate reduction in error (R^2) in a multiple regression analysis. (12)

multiple regression procedure for predicting scores on a criterion variable from scores on two or more predictor variables. (12)

multivariate analysis of covariance (MANCOVA) analysis of covariance with more than one dependent variable. (15)

multivariate analysis of variance (MANOVA) analysis of variance with more than one dependent variable. (15)

multivariate statistics statistical procedures involving more than one dependent variable. (15)

negative correlation relation between two variables in which high scores on one go with low scores on the other, mediums with mediums, and lows with highs; on a scatter diagram, the dots roughly follow a straight line sloping down and to the right; a correlation coefficient (r) less than 0. (11)

95% confidence interval confidence interval in which, roughly speaking, there is a 95% chance that the population mean falls within this interval. (5)

99% confidence interval confidence interval in which, roughly speaking, there is a 99% chance that the population mean falls within this interval. (5)

no correlation no systematic relationship between two variables; also used for correlation coefficient (r) equal to 0. (11)

nominal variable variable with values that are categories (that is, they are names rather than numbers). Also called *categorical variable*. (1)

nondirectional hypothesis research hypothesis that does not predict a particular direction of difference between populations. (4)

nonparametric test hypothesis-testing procedure making no assumptions about population parameters. Also called a *distribution-free test*. (14)

normal curve specific, mathematically defined, bell-shaped frequency distribution that is symmetrical and unimodal; distributions observed in nature and in research commonly approximate it. (1, 3)

normal curve table table showing percentages of scores associated with the normal curve; the table usually includes percentages of scores between the mean and various numbers of standard deviations above the mean and percentages of scores more positive than various numbers of standard deviations above the mean. (3)

normal distribution frequency distribution that follows a normal curve. (3)

null hypothesis statement about a relation between populations that is the opposite of the research hypothesis; statement that in the population there is no difference (or a difference opposite to that predicted) between populations; contrived statement set up to examine whether it can be rejected as part of hypothesis testing. (4)

numeric variable variable whose values are numbers (as opposed to a nominal variable); also called *quantitative variable.* (1)

observed frequency (*O*) in a chi-square test, number of individuals actually found in the study to be in a category or cell. (13)

one-tailed test hypothesis-testing procedure for a directional hypothesis; situation in which the region of the comparison distribution in which the null hypothesis would be rejected is all on one side (or tail) of the distribution. (4)

one-way analysis of variance analysis of variance in which there is only one grouping variable. (10)

outcome term used in discussing probability for the result of an experiment (or almost any event, such as a coin coming up heads or it raining tomorrow). (3)

outlier score with an extreme value (very high or very low) in relation to the other scores in the distribution. (2, 11)

parametric test ordinary hypothesis-testing procedure, such as a *t* test or an analysis of variance, that requires assumptions about the shape or other parameters (such as the variance) of the populations. (14)

partial correlation the amount of association between two variables, over and above the influence of one or more other variables. (15)

partial correlation coefficient measure of the degree of correlation between two variables, over and above the influence of one or more other variables. (15)

partialing out removing the influence of a variable from the association between other variables; same as *holding constant, controlling for,* and *adjusting for.* (15)

path an arrow in a path analysis or structural equation model that shows what the researcher predicts to be the cause-and-effect connections between variables. (15)

path analysis method of analyzing the correlations among a group of variables in terms of a predicted pattern of causal relations; usually the predicted pattern is diagrammed as a pattern of arrows from causes to effects. (15)

path coefficient degree of relation associated with an arrow in a path analysis (including in structural equation modeling); same as a regression coefficient from a multiple regression prediction rule in which the variable at the end of the arrow is the criterion variable and the variable at the start of the arrow is the predictor, along with all the other variables that have arrows leading to that criterion variable. (15)

phi coefficient (ϕ) effect-size measure for a chi-square test for independence with a 2 × 2 contingency table; square root of division of chi-square statistic by *N*. (13)

planned contrast comparison in which the particular means to be compared were decided in advance. Also called *planned comparison.* (9)

pooled estimate of the population variance (S^2_{Pooled}) in a *t* test for independent means, weighted average of the estimates of the population variance from two samples (each estimate weighted by the proportion consisting of its sample's degrees of freedom divided by the total degrees of freedom for both samples). (8)

population entire group of people to which a researcher intends the results of a study to apply; larger group to which inferences are made on the basis of the particular set of people (sample) studied. (3)

population parameter actual value of the mean, standard deviation, and so on, for the population; usually population parameters are not known, though often they are estimated based on information in samples; population parameters are usually symbolized by Greek letters. (3)

positive correlation relation between two variables in which high scores on one go with high scores on the other, mediums with mediums, and lows with lows; on a scatter diagram, the dots roughly follow a straight line sloping up and to the right; a correlation coefficient (*r*) greater than 0. (11)

post hoc comparisons multiple comparisons, not specified in advance; procedure conducted as part of an exploratory analysis after an analysis of variance. (9)

power table table for a hypothesis-testing procedure showing the statistical power of studies with various effect sizes and sample sizes. (6)

predictor variable (usually *X*) in prediction, variable that is used to predict scores of individuals on another variable. (12)

probability (*p*) expected relative frequency of an outcome; the proportion of successful outcomes to all outcomes. (3)

product of deviation scores the result of multiplying the deviation score on one variable by the deviation score on another variable. (11)

proportionate reduction in error (r^2) measure of association between variables that is used when comparing associations. Also called *proportion of variance accounted for.* (11)

proportion of variance accounted for (R^2) proportion of the total variation of scores from the grand mean that is accounted for by the variation between the means of the groups. (9)

quantitative variable same as *numeric variable.* (1)

randomization test hypothesis-testing procedure (usually a computer-intensive method) that considers every possible reorganization of the data in the sample to determine if the organization of the actual sample data were unlikely to occur by chance. (14)

random selection method for selecting a sample that uses truly random procedures (usually meaning that each person in the population has an equal chance of being selected); one procedure is for the researcher to begin with a complete list of all the people in the population and select a group of them to study using a table of random numbers. (3)

rank-order test hypothesis-testing procedure that uses rank-ordered scores. (14)

rank-order transformation changing a set of scores to ranks (for example, so that the lowest score is rank 1, the next highest rank 2, and so forth). (14)

rank-order variable numeric variable in which the values are ranks, such as class standing or place finished in a race. Also called *ordinal variable.* (1)

ratio scale equal-interval variable measured on a ratio scale if it has an *absolute zero point* (such as age or number of children), meaning that the value of zero on the variable indicates a complete absence of the variable. (1)

raw score ordinary score (or any number in a distribution before it has been made into a Z score, deviation score, or otherwise transformed). (3)

rectangular distribution frequency distribution in which all values have approximately the same frequency. (1)

regression coefficient (*b*) number multiplied by a person's score on a predictor variable as part of a linear prediction rule. (12)

regression constant (*a*) in a linear prediction rule, particular fixed number added into the prediction; same as *intercept.* (12)

regression line line on a graph such as a scatter diagram showing the predicted value of the criterion variable for each value of the predictor variable; visual equivalent of the linear prediction rule. (12)

reliability degree of consistency or stability of a measure. (15)

repeated-measures analysis of variance analysis of variance for a repeated-measures design in which each person is tested more than once so that the levels of the grouping variable(s) are different times or types of testing for the same people. (10)

repeated-measures design research strategy in which each person is tested more than once; same as *within-subjects design.* (7)

research hypothesis statement in hypothesis testing about the predicted relation between populations. (4)

restriction in range situation in which you figure a correlation but only a limited range of the possible values on one of the variables is included in the sample studied. (11)

RMSEA (root mean square error of approximation) widely used fit index in structural equation modeling; low values indicate a good fit. (15)

robustness extent to which a particular hypothesis-testing procedure is reasonably accurate even when its assumptions are violated. (7)

sample scores of the particular group of people studied; usually considered to be representative of the scores in some larger population. (3)

sample statistic descriptive statistic, such as the mean or standard deviation, figured from the scores in a group of people studied. (3)

scatter diagram graph showing the relationship between two numeric variables: the values of one variable (often the predictor variable) are along the horizontal axis and the values of the other variable (often the criterion variable) are along the vertical axis; each score is shown as a dot in this two-dimensional space. (11)

Scheffé test method of figuring the significance of post hoc comparisons that takes into account all possible comparisons that could be made. (9)

score particular person's value on a variable. (1)

significance level same as *alpha* (α). (6)

skewed distribution distribution in which the scores pile up on one side of the middle and are spread out on the other side; distribution that is not symmetrical. (1)

slope steepness of the angle of a regression line in a graph of the relation of scores on a predictor variable and predicted scores on a criterion variable; number of units the line goes up for every unit it goes across. (12)

Spearman's rho the equivalent of a correlation coefficient for rank-ordered scores. (11)

split-half reliability one index of a measure's reliability, based on a correlation of the scores of items from the two halves of the test. (15)

squared deviation score square of the difference between a score and the mean. (2)

square-root transformation data transformation using the square root of each score. (14)

standard deviation (*SD, S,* σ) square root of the average of the squared deviations from the mean; the most common descriptive statistic for variation; approximately the average amount that scores in a distribution vary from the mean. (2)

standard deviation of a distribution of means (σ_M, S_M) square root of the variance of a distribution of means; also called *standard error of the mean (SEM)* and *standard error (SE).* (5)

standard deviation of the distribution of differences between means ($S_{\text{Difference}}$) In a *t* test for independent means, square root of the variance of the distribution of differences between means. (8)

standard error (*SE*) same as *standard deviation of a distribution of means*; also called *standard error of the mean (SEM).* (5)

standard error of the mean (*SEM*) same as *standard deviation of a distribution of means.* Also called *standard error (SE).* (5)

standardized regression coefficient (β) regression coefficient in standard deviation units. It shows the predicted amount of change in standard deviation units of the criterion variable if the value of the predictor variable increases by one standard deviation. (12)

statistical power probability that a study will give a significant result if the research hypothesis is true. (6)

statistically significant conclusion that the results of a study would be unlikely if in fact the sample studied represents a population that is no different from the population in general; an outcome of hypothesis testing in which the null hypothesis is rejected. (4)

statistics branch of mathematics (and set of research tools used by psychologists) that focuses on the organization, analysis, and interpretation of a group of numbers. (1)

structural equation modeling sophisticated version of path analysis that includes paths with latent, unmeasured, theoretical variables and that also permits a kind of significance test and provides measures of the overall fit of the data to the hypothesized causal pattern. (15)

structural model way of understanding the analysis of variance as a division of the deviation of each score from the overall mean into two parts: the variation in groups (its deviation from its group's mean) and the variation between groups (its group's mean's deviation from the overall mean); an alternative (but mathematically equivalent) way of understanding the analysis of variance. (9)

subjective interpretation of probability way of understanding probability as the degree of one's certainty that a particular outcome will occur. (3)

sum of squared deviations (SS) total of all the scores of each score's squared difference from the mean; also called *sum of squares.* (2)

sum of squares (SS) same as *sum of squared deviations.* (2)

sum of the squared errors (SS_{Error}) sum of the squared differences between each predicted score and actual score on the criterion variable. (12)

symmetrical distribution distribution in which the pattern of frequencies on the left and right side are mirror images of each other. (1)

t distribution mathematically defined curve that is the comparison distribution used in a t test. (7)

test-retest reliability one index of a measure's reliability, obtained by giving the test to a group of people twice; correlation between scores from the two testings. (15)

theory set of principles that attempt to explain one or more facts, relationships, or events; psychologists often derive specific predictions from theories that are then tested in research studies. (4)

total squared error when predicting from the mean (SS_{Total}) sum of squared differences of each score on the criterion variable from the predicted score when predicting from the mean. (12)

t score on a t distribution, number of standard deviations from the mean (like a Z score, but on a t distribution). (7)

t table table of cutoff scores on the t distribution for various degrees of freedom, significance levels, and one- and two-tailed tests. (7)

t test hypothesis-testing procedure in which the population variance is unknown; it compares t scores from a sample to a comparison distribution called a t distribution. (7)

t test for a single sample hypothesis-testing procedure in which a sample mean is being compared to a known population mean and the population variance is unknown. (7)

t test for dependent means hypothesis-testing procedure in which there are two scores for each person and the population variance is not known; it determines the significance of a hypothesis that is being tested using difference or change scores from a single group of people. (7)

t test for independent means hypothesis-testing procedure in which there are two separate groups of people tested and in which the population variance is not known. (8)

two-tailed test hypothesis-testing procedure for a nondirectional hypothesis; the situation in which the region of the comparison distribution in which the null hypothesis would be rejected is divided between the two sides (tails) of the distribution. (4)

two-way analysis of variance analysis of variance for a two-way factorial research design. (10)

two-way factorial research design factorial research design in analysis of variance with two grouping variables. (10)

Type I error rejecting the null hypothesis when in fact it is true; getting a statistically significant result when in fact the research hypothesis is not true. (6)

Type II error failing to reject the null hypothesis when in fact it is false; failing to get a statistically significant result when in fact the research hypothesis is true. (6)

unbiased estimate of the population variance (S^2) estimate of the population variance, based on sample scores, which has been corrected so that it is equally likely to overestimate or underestimate the true population variance; the correction used is dividing the sum of squared deviations by the sample size minus 1, instead of the usual procedure of dividing by the sample size directly. (7)

unimodal distribution frequency distribution with one value clearly having a larger frequency than any other. (1)

upper-level variable in multilevel modeling, a variable that is about the grouping as a whole. (15)

value possible number or category that a score can have. (1)

variable characteristic that can have different values. (1)

variance (SD^2, S^2, σ^2, MS) measure of how spread out a set of scores are; average of the squared deviations from the mean. (2)

variance of a distribution of differences between means ($S^2_{Difference}$) one of the numbers figured as part of a t test for independent means; it equals the sum of the variances of the distributions of means associated with each of the two samples. (8)

variance of a distribution of means (S^2_M, σ^2_M) variance of the population divided by the number of scores in each sample. (5)

weighted average average in which the scores being averaged do not have equal influence on the total, as in figuring the pooled variance estimate in a t test for independent means. (8)

within-groups (or denominator) degrees of freedom (df_{Within}) degrees of freedom used in the within-groups estimate of the population variance in an analysis of variance, denominator of the F ratio; number of scores free to vary (number of scores in each group minus 1, summed over all the groups) in figuring the within-groups population variance estimate. (9)

within-groups estimate of the population variance ($S^2_{Within}, MS_{Within}$) estimate of the variance of the population of individuals based on the variation among the scores in each of the actual groups studied. (9)

Z score number of standard deviations that a score is above (or below, if it is negative) the mean of its distribution; it is thus an ordinary score transformed so that it better describes the score's location in a distribution. (3)

Z test hypothesis-testing procedure in which there is a single sample and the population variance is known. (5)

Glossary of Symbols

Numbers in parentheses refer to chapters in which the term is introduced or substantially discussed.

α Significance level, such as .05 or .01; probability of a Type I error in hypothesis testing. (6) Also Cronbach's alpha, a measure of internal consistency reliability. (15)

β Probability of a Type II error in hypothesis testing. (6) Also a standardized regression coefficient. (12)

μ Population mean. (3)

μ_M Mean of a distribution of means. (5)

σ Population standard deviation. (3)

σ_M Standard deviation of a distribution of means. (5)

σ^2 Population variance. (3)

σ_M^2 Variance of a distribution of means. (5)

Σ Sum of; add up all the scores following. (2)

ϕ Phi coefficient; effect size in chi-square analysis of a 2×2 contingency table. (14)

χ^2 Chi-square statistic. (13)

a Regression constant. (12)

b Regression coefficient. (12)

d Effect size for studies involving one or two means. (6–8)

df Degrees of freedom. (7–13)

$df_1, df_2,$ **and so on**   Degrees of freedom for the first group, second group, and so on. (8–10)

$df_{Between}$ Between-groups (numerator) degrees of freedom in the analysis of variance. (9)

$df_{Columns}, df_{Rows}, df_{Interaction}$ Degrees of freedom for columns, rows, and interaction (in the factorial analysis of variance). (10)

df_{Total} Total degrees of freedom over all groups. (8–10)

df_{Within} Within-groups (denominator) degrees of freedom in the analysis of variance. (9)

F ratio   In an analysis of variance, ratio of between-groups population variance estimate to within-groups population variance estimate. (9, 10)

GM Grand mean; mean of all scores in the analysis of variance. (9, 10)

M Mean. (2)

$M_1, M_2,$ **and so on**   Mean of the first group, second group, and so on. (8–10)

M_{Column}, M_{Row} Mean of the scores in a particular column or a particular row (in the factorial analysis of variance). (10)

$MS_{Between}$ Mean squares (mean of the squared deviations from the mean) between. (9)

$MS_{Columns}, MS_{Rows}, MS_{Interaction}$ Mean squares (mean of the squared deviations from the mean) between for columns, rows, interaction (in the factorial analysis of variance). (10)

MS_{Error} Mean squares (mean of the squared deviations from the mean) error. (9)

MS_{Within} Mean squares (mean of the squared deviations from the mean) within. (9)

n Number of scores in each group in the analysis of variance. (9)

N Number of scores overall. (2)

$N_1, N_2,$ **and so on**   Number of scores in the first group, second group, and so on. (8–10)

$N_{Categories}$ Number of categories in a chi-square test for goodness of fit. (13)

$N_{Columns}, N_{Rows}$ Number of columns, number of rows (in a factorial analysis of variance and in a contingency table in a chi-square test for independence). (10, 13)

N_{Cells} Number of cells in a factorial design. (10)

N_{Groups} Number of groups in the analysis of variance. (9, 10)

p Probability. (3)

r Correlation coefficient. (11)

r^2 Proportionate reduction in error (proportion of variance accounted for) in bivariate regression. (11)

R Multiple correlation coefficient. (12)

R^2 Proportionate reduction in error (proportion of variance accounted for) in multiple regression and analysis of variance. (9, 10, 12, 15)

$R_{Columns}^2, R_{Rows}^2, R_{Interaction}^2$ Proportion of variance accounted for by columns, rows, interaction (measure of effect size in the factorial analysis of variance). (10)

S Unbiased estimate of the population standard deviation. (7)

S^2 Unbiased estimate of the population variance. (7)

S_1^2, S_2^2, **and so on**   Unbiased estimate of the population variance based on scores in the first sample, second sample, and so on. (8–10)

S_{Between}^2 Between-groups estimate of the population variance. (9)

S_{Columns}^2, S_{Rows}^2, $S_{\text{Interaction}}^2$ Estimated population variance between groups for columns, rows, interaction (in factorial analysis of variance). (10)

$S_{\text{Difference}}$ Standard deviation of the distribution of differences between means. (8)

$S_{\text{Difference}}^2$ Variance of the distribution of differences between means. (8)

SE Standard error (standard deviation of the distribution of means. (5)

S_M Standard deviation of the distribution of means based on an estimated population variance; same as *standard error (SE)*. (7)

S_M^2 Variance of a distribution of means based on an estimated population variance in a *t* test or as estimated from the variation among means of groups in the analysis of variance. (7, 9)

$S_{M_1}^2$, $S_{M_2}^2$, **and so on**   Variance of the distribution of means based on a pooled population variance estimate, corresponding to the first sample, second sample, and so on. (8, 9)

S_{Pooled} Pooled estimate of the population standard deviation. (8)

S_{Pooled}^2 Pooled estimate of the population variance. (8)

S_{Within}^2 Within-groups estimate of the population variance. (9)

SD Standard deviation. (2)

SD^2 Variance. (2)

SS Sum of squared deviations from the mean. (9)

SS_{Between} Sum of squared deviations (from the mean) between groups. (9)

SS_{Columns}, SS_{Rows}, $SS_{\text{Interaction}}$ Sum of squared deviations (from the mean) between columns or rows or due to interaction (in the factorial analysis of variance). (10)

SS_{Error} In prediction, sum of squared error when predicting from the linear prediction rule. (12)

SS_{Total} Total sum of squared deviations from the mean (or from the grand mean, in the analysis of variance). (2, 9, 10)

SS_{Within} Sum of squared deviations (from the mean) within groups (or within cells). (9, 10)

t **score**   Number of standard deviations from the mean on a *t* distribution. (7, 8, 11)

X Score on a particular variable; in prediction (regression), X is usually for the predictor variable. (1, 2, 11, 12)

X_1, X_2, **and so on**   First predictor variable, second predictor variable, and so on. (12)

Y Score on a particular variable; in prediction (regression), Y is usually for the criterion variable. (11, 12)

$\hat{Y}$ Predicted value of criterion variable Y. (12)

Z A score's number of standard deviations from the mean. (3)

References

Abelson, R. P. (1997). On the surprising longevity of flogged horses: Why there is a case for the significance test. *Psychological Science, 8,* 12–15.

Altman, D. G., Levine, D. W., Howard, G., & Hamilton, H. (1997). Tobacco farming and public health: Attitudes of the general public and farmers. *Journal of Social Issues, 53,* 113–128.

American Psychological Association (2001). *Publication manual of the American Psychological Association* (5th ed.). Washington, DC: American Psychological Association.

Anderson, J. E., Carey, J. W., & Taveras, S. (2000). HIV testing among the general US population and persons at increased risk: information from national surveys, 1987–1996. *American Journal of Public Health, 90,* 1089–1095.

Aron, A., & Aron, E. N. (1989). *The heart of social psychology.* Lexington, MA: Heath.

Aron, A., Aron, E. N., & Allen, J. (1998). Motivations for unreciprocated love. *Personality and Social Psychology Bulletin, 24,* 787–796.

Aron, A., Aron, E. N., & Smollan, D. (1992). Inclusion of Other in the Self Scale and the structure of interpersonal closeness. *Journal of Personality and Social Psychology, 63,* 596–612.

Aron, A., Fisher, H. E., Mashek, D. J., Strong, S., Li, H.-F., & Brown, L. L. (2005). Reward, motivation and emotion systems associated with early-stage intense romantic love. *Journal of Neurophysiology, 94,* 327–337.

Aron, A., Melinat, E., Aron, E. N., Vallone, R., & Bator, R. (1997). The experimental generation of interpersonal closeness: A procedure and some preliminary findings. *Personality and Social Psychology Bulletin, 23,* 363–377.

Aron, A., Norman, C. C., Aron, E. N., McKenna, C., & Heyman, R. E. (2000). Couples' shared participation in novel and arousing activities and experienced relationship quality. *Journal of Personality and Social Psychology, 78,* 273–284.

Aron, A., Paris, M., & Aron, E. N. (1995). Falling in love: Prospective studies of self-concept change. *Journal of Personality and Social Psychology, 69,* 1102–1112.

Aron, E. N. (1996). *The highly sensitive person.* New York: Birch/Lane.

Aron, E. N. (2002). *The highly sensitive child.* New York: Broadway Books.

Aron, E. N., & Aron, A. (1997). Sensory processing sensitivity and its relation to introversion and emotionality. *Journal of Personality and Social Psychology, 73,* 345–368.

Aron, E., Aron, A., & Davies, K. M. (2005). Adult shyness: The interaction of temporal sensitivity and an adverse childhood environment. *Personality and Social Psychology Bulletin, 31,* 1–17.

Bakeman, R. (2006). The practical importance of findings. *Monographs of the Society for Research in Child Development, 71,* 127–145.

Baldwin, K. M., Baldwin, J. R., & Ewald, T. (2006). The relationship among shame, guilt, and self-efficacy. *American Journal of Psychotherapy, 60,* 1–21.

Balluerka, N., Gómez, J., & Hidalgo, D. (2005). The controversy over null hypothesis significance testing revisited. *Methodology, 1,* 55–70.

Baron, R. M., & Kenny, D. A. (1986). The moderator-mediator variable distinction in social psychological research: Conceptual, strategic, and statistical considerations. *Journal of Personality and Social Psychology, 51,* 1173–1182.

Bates, D. W., Leape, L. L., Cullen, D. J., Laird, N., Petersen, L. A., Teich, J. M., et al. (1998). Effect of computerized physician order entry and a team intervention on prevention of serious medication errors. *Journal of the American Medical Association, 280,* 1311–1316.

Beilock, S. L., Rydell, R. J., & McConnell, A. R. (2007). Stereotype threat and working memory: Mechanisms, alleviation, and spillover. *Journal of Experimental Psychology: General, 136,* 256–276.

Berndsen, M., McGarty, C., van der Pligt, J., & Spears, R. (2001). Meaning-seeking in the illusory correlation paradigm: The active role of participants in the categorization process. *British Journal of Social Psychology, 40,* 209–233.

Betsch, T., Plessner, H., Schwieren, C., & Gutig, R. (2001). I like it but I don't know why: A value-account approach to implicit attitude formation. *Personality and Social Psychology Bulletin, 27,* 242–253.

Bezeau, S., & Graves, R. (2001). Statistical power and effect sizes of clinical neuropsychology research. *Journal of Clinical and Experimental Neuropsychology, 23,* 399–406.

Bleeker, M. M., & Jacobs, J. E. (2004). Achievement in math and science: Do mothers' beliefs matter twelve years later? *Journal of Educational Psychology, 96,* 97–109.

Block, N. (1995). How heritability misleads about race. *Cognition, 56,* 99–128.

Bohnert, A. M., Aikins, J. W., & Edidin, J. (2007). The role of organized activities in facilitating social adaptation across the transition to college. *Journal of Adolescent Research, 22,* 189–208.

Bourgeois, M. M. (1997). A powerful, effective statistics text [Review of A. Aron & E. Aron, *Statistics for Psychology,* 1st edition]. *Contemporary Psychology, 42,* 993–994.

Boyd, C. P., & Gullone, E. (1997). An investigation of negative affectivity in Australian adolescents. *Journal of Clinical Child Psychology, 26,* 190–197.

Brickman, P., Coates, D., & Janoff-Bulman, R. (1978). Lottery winners and accident victims: Is happiness relative? *Journal of Personality and Social Psychology, 36,* 917–927.

Brockner, J., Ackerman, G., Greenberg, J., Gelfand, M. J., Francesco, A. M., Chen, Z. X., Leung, K., Bierbrauer, G., Gomez, C., Kirkman, B. L., & Shapiro, D. (2001). Culture and procedural justice: The influence of power distance on reactions to voice. *Journal of Experimental Social Psychology, 37,* 300–315.

Buss, D. M., & Schmitt, D. P. (1993). Sexual strategies theory: An evolutionary perspective on human mating. *Psychological Review, 100,* 204–232.

Carey, M. P., Maisto, S. A., Kalichman, S. C., Forsyth, A. D., Wright, E. M., & Johnson, B. T. (1997). Enhancing motivation to reduce the risk of HIV infection for economically disadvantaged urban women. *Journal of Consulting and Clinical Psychology, 65,* 531–541.

Carver, C. S. (2004). Negative affects deriving from the behavioral approach system. *Emotion, 4,* 3–22.

Caspi, A., Begg, D., Dickson, N., Harrington, H., Langley, J., Moffitt, T. E., & Silva, P. A. (1997). Personality differences predict health-risk behaviors in young adulthood: Evidence from a longitudinal study. *Journal of Personality and Social Psychology, 73,* 1052–1063.

Catanzaro, D., & Taylor, J. C. (1996). The scaling of dispersion and correlation: A comparison of least-squares and absolute deviation statistics. *British Journal of Mathematical and Statistical Psychology, 49,* 171–188.

Cavallera, G. M., & Giudici, S. (2008). Morningness and eveningness personality: A survey in literature from 1995 up till 2006. *Personality and Individual Differences, 44,* 3–21.

Chambless, D. L., & Hollon, S. D. (1998). Defining empirically supported therapies. *Journal of Consulting and Clinical Psychology, 66,* 7–19.

Chapman, H. A., Hobfoll, S. E., & Ritter, C. (1997). Partners' stress underestimations lead to women's distress: A study of pregnant inner-city women. *Journal of Personality and Social Psychology, 73,* 418–425.

Chen, X. (2005). First generation students in postsecondary education: A look at their college transcripts (NCES 2005-171). U.S. Department of Education, National Center for Education Statistics. Washington, DC: U.S. Government Printing Office.

Chow, S. L. (1988). Significance test or effect size. *Psychological Bulletin, 103,* 105–110.

Chow, S. L. (1996). *Statistical significance: Rationale, validity, and utility.* London: Sage.

Christakis, N. A., & Fowler, J. H. (2007). The spread of obesity in a large social network over 32 years. *New England Journal of Medicine, 353,* 370–379.

Clark-Carter, D. (1997). The account taken of statistical power in research published in the *British Journal of Psychology. British Journal of Psychology, 88,* 71–83.

Cohen, J. (1962). The statistical power of abnormal-social psychological research: A review. *Journal of Abnormal and Social Psychology, 65,* 145–153.

Cohen, J. (1969). *Statistical power analysis for the behavioral sciences* (1st ed.). New York: Academic Press. (2nd ed., 1988, Hillsdale, NJ: Erlbaum.)

Cohen, J. (1983). The cost of dichotomization. *Applied Psychological Measurement, 7,* 249–253.

Cohen, J. (1990). Things I have learned (so far). *American Psychologist, 45,* 1304–1312.

Cohen, J. (1992). A power primer. *Psychological Bulletin, 112,* 155–159.

Cohen, J. (1994). The Earth is round ($p < .05$). *American Psychologist, 49,* 997–1003.

Cohen, J., & Cohen, P. (1983). *Applied multiple regression/ correlation analysis for the behavioral sciences* (2nd ed.). Hillsdale, NJ: Erlbaum.

Cohen, J., Cohen, P., Aiken, S. G., & West, L. S. (2003). *Applied multiple regression/correlation analysis for the behavioral sciences* (3rd ed.). Mahwah, NJ: Erlbaum.

Connors, G. J., Carroll, K. M., DiClemente, C. C., Longabaugh, R., & Donovan, D. M. (1997). The therapeutic alliance and its relationship to alcoholism treatment participation and outcome. *Journal of Consulting and Clinical Psychology, 65,* 588–598.

Conover, W., & Iman, R. L. (1981). Rank transformations as a bridge between parametric and nonparametric statistics. *American Statistician, 35,* 124–129.

Cook, T. D., & Campbell, D. T. (1979). *Quasi-experimentation: Design and analysis issues for field settings.* Skokie, IL: Rand McNally.

Cooper, S. E., & Robinson, D. A. G. (1989). The influence of gender and anxiety on mathematics performance. *Journal of College Student Development, 30,* 459–461.

Cortina, J. M., & Dunlop, W. P. (1997). On the logic and purpose of significance testing. *Psychological Methods, 2,* 161–172.

Crick, N. R., Casas, J. F., & Mosher, M. (1997). Relational and overt aggression in preschool. *Developmental Psychology, 33,* 579–588.

Croizet, J-C., & Claire, T. (1998). Extending the concept of stereotype threat to social class: The intellectual underperformance of students from low socioeconomic backgrounds. *Personality and Social Psychology Bulletin, 24,* 588–594.

Dahlstrom, W. G., Larbar, D., & Dahlstrom, L. E. (1986). *MMPI patterns of American minorities.* Minneapolis: University of Minnesota Press.

Dane, F. C., & Wrightsman, L. S. (1982). Effects of defendants' and victims' characteristics on jurors' verdicts. In N. L. Kerr & R. M. Bray (Eds.), *The psychology of the courtroom* (pp. 83–115). Orlando, FL: Academic Press.

Dawes, R. M., Faust, D., & Meehl, P. E. (1993). Statistical prediction versus clinical prediction: Improving what works. In G. Keren & C. Lewis (Eds.), *A handbook for data analysis in the behavioral sciences: Methodological issues* (pp. 351–367). Hillsdale, NJ: Erlbaum.

Day, J. C., & Newburger, E. C. (2002). The big payoff: Educational attainment and synthetic estimates of work-life earnings. Current Population Reports, Special Studies, P23–210. Washington, DC: U.S. Department of Commerce, Economics and Statistics Administration, U.S. Census Bureau. Available at *http://www.census.gov/prod/2002pubs/p23-210.pdf*.

DeCarlo, L. T. (1997). On the meaning and use of kurtosis. *Psychological Methods, 2,* 292–307.

DeGarmo, D. S., & Forgatch, M. S. (1997). Determinants of observed confidant support for divorced mothers. *Journal of Personality and Social Psychology, 72,* 336–345.

Delucchi, K. L. (1983). The use and misuse of chi-square: Lewis and Burke revisited. *Psychological Bulletin, 94,* 166–176.

Denenberg, V. H. (1999). A critique of Mody, Studdert-Kennedy, and Brady's "Speech perception deficits in poor readers: Auditory processing or phonological coding?" *Journal of Learning Disabilities, 32,* 379–383.

Diener, E., Lucas, R. E., & Scollon, C. N. (2006). Beyond the hedonic treadmill: Revising the adaptation theory of well-being. *American Psychologist, 61,* 305–314.

Dodge, T., & Kaufman, A. (2007). What makes consumers think dietary supplements are safe and effective? The role of disclaimers and FDA approval. *Health Psychology, 26,* 513–517.

Dunlap, W. P., & Myers, L. (1997). Approximating power for significance tests with one degree of freedom. *Psychological Methods, 2,* 186–191.

Durkin, K., & Barber, B. (2003). Not so doomed: Computer game play and positive adolescent development. *Applied Developmental Psychology, 23,* 373–392.

Dwinell, P. E., & Higbee, J. L. (1991). Affective variables related to mathematics achievement among high-risk college freshmen. *Psychological Reports, 69,* 399–403.

Endler, N. S., & Magnusson, D. (1976). Toward an interactional psychology of personality. *Psychological Bulletin, 83,* 956–974.

Eppley, K. R., Abrams, A. I., & Shear, J. (1989). Differential effects of relaxation techniques on trait anxiety: A meta-analysis. *Journal of Clinical Psychology, 45,* 957–974.

Escudero, V., Rogers, L. E., & Gutierrez, E. (1997). Patterns of relational control and nonverbal affect in clinic and nonclinic couples. *Journal of Social and Personal Relationships, 14,* 5–29.

Evans, R. (1976). *The making of psychology.* New York: Knopf.

Everett, S. A., Price, J. H., Bedell, A. W., & Telljohann, S. K. (1997). The effect of a monetary incentive in increasing the return rate of a survey to family physicians. *Evaluation and the Health Professions, 20,* 207–214.

Eysenck, H. J. (1981). *A model for personality.* Berlin: Springer-Verlag.

Fawzi, M. C. S., Pham, T., Lin, L., Nguyen, T. V., Ngo, D., Murphy, E., & Mollica, R. F. (1997). The validity of posttraumatic stress disorder among Vietnamese refugees. *Journal of Traumatic Stress, 10,* 101–108.

Fraley, B., & Aron, A. (2004). The effect of a shared humorous experience on closeness in initial encounters. *Personal Relationships, 11,* 61–78.

Fidler, F., Cumming, G., Thomason, N., Pannuzzo, D., Smith, J., Fyffe, P., Edmonds, H., Harrington, C., & Schmitt, R. (2005). Toward improved statistical reporting in the Journal of Consulting and Clinical Psychology. *Journal of Consulting and Clinical Psychology, 73,* 136–143.

Fisher, R. A., & Yates, F. (1938). *Statistical tables for biological, agricultural and medical research.* London: Oliver and Boyd.

Fiske, S. T. (1998). Stereotyping, prejudice, and discrimination. In D. T. Gilbert, S. T. Fiske, & G. Lindzey (Eds.) *The handbook of social psychology* (4th ed., pp. 357–411). New York: McGraw-Hill.

Folwell, A. L., Chung, L. C., Nussbaum, J. F., Bethea, L. S., & Grant, J. A. (1997). Differential accounts of closeness in older adult sibling relationships. *Journal of Social and Personal Relationships, 14,* 843–849.

Ford, J. D., Fisher, P., & Larson, L. (1997). Object relations as a predictor of treatment outcome with chronic posttraumatic stress disorder. *Journal of Consulting and Clinical Psychology, 65,* 547–559.

Frank, S. J., Poorman, M. O., Van Egeren, L. A., & Field, D. T. (1997). Perceived relationships with parents among adolescent inpatients with depressive preoccupations and depressed mood. *Journal of Clinical Child Psychology, 26,* 205–215.

Franz, M. L. von. (1979). *The problem of puer aeternus.* New York: Springer-Verlag.

Frattaroli, J. (2006). Experimental disclosure and its moderators: A meta-analysis. *Psychological Bulletin, 132,* 823–865.

Frick, R. W. (1995). Accepting the null hypothesis. *Memory and Cognition, 23,* 132–138.

Frick, R. W. (1996). The appropriate use of null hypothesis testing. *Psychological Methods, 1,* 379–390.

Frick, R. W. (1998). Interpreting statistical testing: Process and propensity, not population and random sampling. *Behavior Research Methods, Instruments, and Computers, 30,* 527–535.

Friend, R. (2001). Effects of strategy instruction on summary writing of college students. *Contemporary Educational Psychology, 26,* 3–24.

Frydenberg, E., Lewis, R., Kennedy, G., Ardila, R., Frindte, W., & Hannoun, R. (2003). Coping with concerns: An exploratory comparison of Australian, Colombian, German, and Palestinian adolescents. *Journal of Youth and Adolescence, 32,* 59–66.

Furr, M. R., & Rosenthal, R. (2003). Evaluating theories efficiently: The nuts and bolts of contrast analysis. *Understanding Statistics, 2,* 45–67.

Gable, S., & Lutz, S. (2000). Household, parent, and child contributions to childhood obesity. *Family Relations, 49,* 293–300.

Gallagher-Thompson, D., Dal Canto, P. G., Jacob, T., & Thompson, L. W. (2001). A comparison of marital interaction patterns between couples in which the husband does or does not have Alzheimer's disease. *The Journals of Gerontology Series B: Psychological Sciences and Social Sciences, 56,* S140–S150.

Gallup, D. G. H. (1972). *The Gallup poll: Public opinion, 1935–1971.* New York: Random House.

Galton, F. (1889). *Natural inheritance.* London: Macmillan.

Gerbert, B., Bronstone, A., Maurer, T., Hofmann, R., & Berger, T. (1999). Decision support software to help primary care physicians triage skin cancer: A pilot study. *Archives of Dermatology, 135,* 187–192.

Gibbons, J. L., Wilson, S. L., & Rufener, C. A. (2006). Gender attitudes mediate gender differences in attitudes towards adoption in Guatemala. *Sex Roles, 54,* 139–145.

Gigerenzer, G., & Murray, D. J. (1987). *Cognition as intuitive statistics.* Hillsdale, NJ: Erlbaum.

Gigerenzer, G., Swijtink, Z., Porter, Y., Daston, L., Beatty, J., & Kruger, L. (1989). *The empire of chance.* Cambridge, England: Cambridge University Press.

Gire, J. T. (1997). The varying effect of individualism-collectivism on preference for methods of conflict resolution. *Canadian Journal of Behavioural Science, 29,* 38–43.

Gilbert, D. (2006). *Stumbling on happiness.* New York: Knopf.

Gonzaga, G. C., Keltner, D., Londahl, E. A., & Smith, M. D. (2001). Love and the commitment problem in romantic relations and friendship. *Journal of Personality and Social Psychology, 81,* 247–262.

Gonzales, P. M., Blanton, H., & Williams, K. J. (2002). The effect of stereotype threat and double minority status on the test performance of Latino women. *Personality and Social Psychology Bulletin, 28,* 659–670.

Graham, S., Weiner, B., & Zucker, G. S. (1997). An attributional analysis of punishment goals and public reactions to O. J. Simpson. *Personality and Social Psychology Bulletin, 23,* 331–346.

Greene, E., & Dodge, M. (1995). The influence of prior record evidence on juror decision making. *Law and Human Behavior, 19,* 67–78.

Grilo, C. M., Walker, M. L., Becker, D. F., Edell, W. S., & McGlashan, T. H. (1997). Personality disorders in adolescents with major depression, substance use disorders, and coexisting major depression and substance use disorders. *Journal of Consulting and Clinical Psychology, 65,* 328–332.

Gump, B. B., & Kulik, J. A. (1997). Stress, affiliation, and emotional contagion. *Journal of Personality and Social Psychology, 72,* 305–319.

Gump, B. B., Reihman, J., Stewart, P., Lonky, E., Darvill, T., & Matthews, K. A. (2007). Blood lead (Pb) levels: A potential environmental mechanism explaining the relation between socioeconomic status and cardiovascular reactivity in children. *Health Psychology, 26,* 296–304.

Hahlweg, K., Fiegenbaum, W., Frank, M., Schroeder, B., & von Witzleben, I. (2001). Short- and long-term effectiveness of an empirically supported treatment for agoraphobia. *Journal of Consulting and Clinical Psychology, 69,* 375–382.

Halpern, D. F., & Wai, J. (2007). The world of competitive Scrabble: Novice and expert differences in visuospatial and verbal abilities. *Journal of Experimental Psychology: Applied, 13,* 79–94.

Hamilton, D. (1981). *Cognitive processes in stereotyping and intergroup behavior.* Hillsdale, NJ: Erlbaum.

Hamilton, D., & Gifford, R. (1976). Illusory correlation in interpersonal perception: A cognitive basis of stereotypic judgments. *Journal of Experimental Social Psychology, 12,* 392–407.

Harris, R. J. (1997). Significance tests have their place. *Psychological Science, 8,* 8–11.

Harter, S., Waters, P. L., Pettitt, L. M., Whitesell, N., Kofkin, J., & Jordan, J. (1997). Autonomy and connectedness as dimensions of relationship styles in men and women. *Journal of Social and Personal Relationships, 14,* 147–164.

Hazan, C., & Shaver, P. (1987). Romantic love conceptualized as an attachment process. *Journal of Personality and Social Psychology, 52,* 511–524.

Heller, K. A., & Ziegler, A. (1996). Gender differences in mathematics and the natural sciences: Can attributional retraining improve the performance of gifted females? *Gifted Child Quarterly, 40,* 200–210.

Hermann, C., Blanchard, E. B., & Flor, H. (1997). Biofeedback treatment for pediatric migraine: Prediction of treatment outcome. *Journal of Consulting and Clinical Psychology, 65,* 611–616.

Heyman, R. E., Feldbau-Kohn, S. R., Ehrensaft, M. K., Langhinrichsen-Rohling, J., & O'Leary, K. D. (2001). Can questionnaire reports correctly classify relationship distress and partner physical abuse? *Journal of Family Psychology, 15,* 334–346.

Hindley, C., Filliozat, A., Klackenberg, G., Nicolet-Meister, D., & Sand, E. (1966). Differences in age of walking in five European longitudinal samples. *Human Biology, 38,* 364–379.

Holden, G. W., Thompson, E. E., Zambarano, R. J., & Marshall, L. A. (1997). Child effects as a source of change in maternal attitudes. *Journal of Social and Personal Relationships, 14,* 481–490.

Holzworth, R. J. (1996). Policy capturing with ridge regression. *Organizational Behavior and Human Decision Processes, 68,* 171–179.

Hopkins, K. D., & Glass, G. V. (1978). *Basic statistics for the behavioral sciences.* Englewood Cliffs, NJ: Prentice Hall.

Hunter, J. E. (1997). Needed: A ban on the significance test. *Psychological Science, 8,* 3–7.

Husserl, E. (1970). *The crisis of European sciences and transcendental phenomenology: An introduction to phenomenological philosophy* (D. C. Carr, Trans.). Evanston, IL: Northwestern University Press.

Hutchison, M. L., & Gibler, D. M. (2007). Political tolerance and territorial threat: A cross-national study. *Journal of Politics, 69,* 128–142.

Iacobucci, D. (2005). From the editor: On *p*-values. *Journal of Consumer Research, 32.*

Insko, C. A. (2003). Editorial. *Journal of Personality and Social Psychology, 83,* 1330–1332.

Irving, L. M., & Berel, S. R. (2001). Comparison of media-literacy programs to strengthen college women's resistance to media images. *Psychology of Women Quarterly, 25,* 103–111.

Jackson, L. A., Ervin, K. S., Gardner, P. D., & Schmitt, N. (2001). Gender and the Internet: Women communicating and men searching. *Sex Roles, 44,* 363–379.

Johnson, C., & Mullen, B. (1994). Evidence for the accessibility of paired distinctiveness in distinctiveness-based illusory correlation in stereotyping. *Personality and Social Psychology Bulletin, 20,* 65–70.

Joiner, T. E., Jr., Yeates, C., Fitzpatrick, K. K., Witte, T. K., Schmidt, N. B., Berlim, M. T., Fleck, M. P. A., & Rudd, M. D. (2005). Four studies on how past and current suicidality relate even when "everything but the kitchen sink" is covaried. *Journal of Abnormal Psychology, 114,* 291–303.

Jones, L. V., & Tukey, J. W. (2000). A sensible formulation of the significance test. *Psychological Methods, 5,* 411–414.

June, L. N., Curry, B. P., & Gear, C. L. (1990). An 11-year analysis of black students' experience of problems and use of services: Implications for counseling professionals. *Journal of Counseling Psychology, 37,* 178–184.

Kagan, J. (1994). *Galen's prophecy: Temperament in human nature.* New York: Basic Books.

Kammrath, L. K., Mendoza-Denton, R., & Mischel, W. (2005). Incorporating if . . . then . . . personality signatures in person perception: Beyond the person-situation dichotomy. *Journal of Personality and Social Psychology, 88,* 605–618.

Kenny, D. A. (1995). Relationship science in the 21st century. *Journal of Social and Personal Relationships, 12,* 597–600.

Kessler, R. C., Berglund, P., Demler, O., Jin, R., Merikangas, K. R., & Walters, E. E. (2005). Lifetime prevalence and age-of-onset distributions of DSM-IV disorders in the National Comorbidity Survey Replication. *Archives of General Psychiatry, 62,* 593–602.

Kleinmuntz, B. (1990). Why we still use our heads instead of formulas: Toward an integrative approach. *Psychological Bulletin, 107,* 296–310.

Koslowsky, M., Schwarzwald, J., & Ashuri, S. (2001). On the relationship between subordinates' compliance to power sources and organisational attitudes. *Applied Psychology: An International Review, 50,* 455–476.

Kraemer, H. C., & Thiemann, S. (1987). *How many subjects? Statistical power analysis in research.* Newbury Park, CA: Sage.

Kunda, Z., & Oleson, K. C. (1997). When exceptions prove the rule: How extremity of deviance determines the impact of deviant examples on stereotypes. *Journal of Personality and Social Psychology, 72,* 965–979.

Kwan, V. S. Y., Bond, M. H., & Singelis, T. M. (1997). Pancultural explanations for life satisfaction: Adding relationship harmony to self-esteem. *Journal of Personality and Social Psychology, 73,* 1038–1051.

Larson, R., Dworkin, J., & Verma, S. (2001). Men's work and family lives in India: The daily organization of time and emotions. *Journal of Family Psychology, 15,* 206–224.

Lee, K., Byatt, G., & Rhodes, G. (2000). Caricature effects, distinctiveness, and identification: Testing the face-space framework. *Psychological Science, 11,* 379–385.

Leventhal, L., & Huyn, C-L. (1996). Directional decisions for two-tailed tests: Power, error rates, and sample size. *Psychological Methods, 1,* 278–292.

Lewandowski, G. W., Aron, A., & Gee, J. (2007). Personality goes a long way: The malleability of opposite-sex physical attractiveness perceptions. *Personal Relationships, 14,* 571–585.

Lewis, D., & Burke, C. J. (1949). The use and misuse of the chi-square test. *Psychological Bulletin, 46,* 433–489.

Li, K. Z. H., Linderberger, U., Freund, A. M., & Baltes, P. B. (2001). Walking while memorizing: Age-related differences in compensatory behavior. *Psychological Science, 12,* 230–237.

Li, N. P., Bailey, J. M., Kenrick, D. T., & Linsenmeier, J. A. (2002). The necessities and luxuries of mate preferences: Testing the tradeoffs. *Journal of Personality and Social Psychology, 82,* 947–955.

Lydon, J., Pierce, T., & O'Regan, S. (1997). Coping with moral commitment to long-distance dating relationships. *Journal of Personality and Social Psychology, 73,* 104–113.

MacCallum, R. C., Zhang, S., Preacher, K. J., & Rucker, D. D. (2002). On the practice of dichotomization of quantitative variables. *Psychological Methods, 7,* 19–40.

MacKinnon-Lewis, C., Starnes, R., Volling, B., & Johnson, S. (1997). Perceptions of parenting as predictors of boys' sibling and peer relations. *Developmental Psychology, 33,* 1024–1031.

Maddock, J. E., & Rossi, J. S. (2001). Statistical power of articles published in three health-psychology related journals. *Health Psychology, 20,* 76–78.

Maggi, S., Hertzman, C., & Vaillancourt, T. (2007). Changes in smoking behaviors from late childhood to adolescence: Insights from the Canadian National Longitudinal Survey of Children and Youth. *Health Psychology, 26,* 232–240.

Martinez, R. (2000). Immigration and urban violence: The link between immigrant Latinos and types of homicide. *Social Science Quarterly, 81,* 363–374.

Maxwell, S. E., & Delaney, H. D. (1993). Bivariate median splits and spurious statistical significance. *Psychological Bulletin, 113,* 181–190.

Maxwell. (2004). The persistence of underpowered studies in psychological research: Causes, consequences, and remedies. *Psychological Methods, 9,* 147–163.

McClelland, M. M., Cameron, C. E., Connor, C. M., Farris, C. L., Jewkes, A. M., & Morrison, F. J. (2007). Links between behavioral regulation and preschoolers' literacy, vocabulary, and math skills. *Developmental Psychology, 43,* 947–959.

McConnell, A. R. (2001). Implicit theories: Consequences for social judgment of individuals. *Journal of Experimental Social Psychology, 37,* 215–227.

McConnell, A. R., Sherman, S. J., & Hamilton, D. L. (1994). Illusory correlation in the perception of groups: An extension of the distinctiveness-based account. *Journal of Personality and Social Psychology, 67,* 414–429.

McCracken, G. (1988). *The long interview.* London: Sage.

McKee, T. L. E., & Ptacek, J. T. (2001). I'm afraid I have something bad to tell you: Breaking bad news from the perspective of the giver. *Journal of Applied Social Psychology, 31,* 246–273.

McLaughlin-Volpe, T., Aron, A., & Reis, H. T. (2001, February). *Closeness during interethnic social interactions and prejudice: A diary study.* Paper presented at the Annual Meeting of the Society for Personality and Social Psychology, San Antonio, TX.

Meehl, P. E. (1954). *Clinical versus statistical prediction: A theoretical analysis and a review of the evidence.* Minneapolis: University of Minnesota Press.

Micceri, T. (1989). The unicorn, the normal curve, and other improbable creatures. *Psychological Bulletin, 105,* 156–166.

Mikulincer, M. (1998). Attachment working models and the sense of trust: An exploration of interaction goals and affect regulation. *Journal of Personality and Social Psychology, 74,* 1209–1224.

Mikulincer, M., & Shaver, P. R. (2007). *Attachment in adulthood: Structure, dynamics, and change.* New York: Guilford.

Miller, L. C., & Fishkin, S. A. (1997). On the dynamics of human bonding and reproductive success: Seeking windows on the adapted-for human-environmental interface. In J. Simpson & D. T. Kenrick (Eds.), *Evolutionary social psychology* (pp. 197–235). Hillsdale, NJ: Erlbaum.

Miller, R. S. (1997). Inattentive and contented: Relationship commitment and attention to alternatives. *Journal of Personality and Social Psychology, 73,* 758–766.

Mirvis, P., & Lawler, E. (1977). Measuring the financial impact of employee attitudes. *Journal of Applied Psychology, 62,* 1–8.

Mischel, W. (1968). *Personality and assessment.* New York: Wiley.

Mischel, W. (2004). Toward an integrative science of the person. *Annual Review of Psychology, 55,* 1–22.

Mischel, W. (2007). Walter Mischel. In L. Gardner & W. M. Runyan (Eds.), *A history of psychology in autobiography, Vol. IX* (pp. 229–267). Washington, DC: American Psychological Association.

Mize, J., & Pettit, G. S. (1997). Mothers' social coaching, mother-child relationship style, and children's peer competence: Is the medium the message? *Child Development, 68,* 312–332.

Mody, M., Studdert-Kennedy, M., & Brady, S. (1997). Speech perception deficits in poor readers: Auditory processing or phonological coding? *Journal of Experimental Child Psychology, 64,* 1–33.

Morehouse, E., & Tobler, N. S. (2000). Preventing and reducing substance use among institutionalized adolescents. *Adolescence, 35,* 1–28.

Moriarty, S. E., & Everett, S-L. (1994). Commercial breaks: A viewing behavior study. *Journalism Quarterly, 71,* 346–355.

Mouradian, V. E. (2001). Applying schema theory to intimate aggression: Individual and gender differences in representation of contexts and goals. *Journal of Applied Social Psychology, 31,* 376–408.

Murphy, K. R. (1998). Obituary. The passing of giants: Raymond B. Cattell and Jacob Cohen. *The Industrial-Organizational Psychologist, 35* (4). Available online: *http://www.siop.org/tip/backissues/TIPApril98/obituary.aspx.*

Nancy, R., & Cordes, D. (2007). A semi-parametric approach to estimate the family-wise error rate in fMRI using resting-state data. *Neuroimage, 34,* 1562–1576.

National Center for Education Statistics, U.S. Department of Education. (2001). *Digest for educational statistics, 2001.* Washington, DC: Government Printing Office.

Nezlek, J. B., Kowalski, R. M., Leary, M. R., Blevins, T., & Holgate, S. (1997). Personality moderators of reactions to interpersonal rejection: Depression and trait self-esteem. *Personality and Social Psychology Bulletin, 23,* 1235–1244.

Nichols, T., & Hayasaka, S. (2003). Controlling the familywise error rate in functional neuroimaging: A comparative review. *Statistical Methods in Medical Research, 12,* 419–446.

Nickerson, R. S. (2000). Null hypothesis significance testing: A review of an old and continuing controversy. *Psychological Methods, 5,* 241–301.

Norcross, J. C., Kohout, J. L., & Wicherski, M. (2005). Graduate study in psychology: 1971 to 2004. *American Psychologist, 60,* 959–975.

Nownes, A. J. (2000). Policy conflict and the structure of interest communities: A comparative state analysis. *American Politics Quarterly, 28,* 309–327.

Oakes, M. (1982). Intuiting strength of association from a correlation coefficient. *British Journal of Psychology, 73,* 51–56.

Oettingen, G., Schnetter, K., & Pak, H. (2001). Self-regulation of goal setting: Turning free fantasies about the future into binding goals. *Journal of Personality and Social Psychology, 80,* 736–753.

Olthoff, R. K. (1989). *The effectiveness of premarital communication training.* Unpublished doctoral dissertation, California Graduate School of Family Psychology, San Francisco.

Orbach, I., Mikulincer, M., King, R., Cohen, D., & Stein, D. (1997). Thresholds and tolerance of physical pain in suicidal and nonsuicidal adolescents. *Journal of Consulting and Clinical Psychology, 65,* 646–652.

Owen, S. V., & Froman, R. D. (2005). Why carve up your continuous data? *Research in Nursing and Health, 28,* 496–503.

Payne, B. K. (2001). Prejudice and perception: The role of automatic and controlled processes in misperceiving a weapon. *Journal of Personality and Social Psychology, 81,* 181–192.

Pearson, K. (1978). *The history of statistics in the 17th and 18th centuries.* London: Griffin.

Pecukonis, E. V. (1990). A cognitive/affective empathy training program as a function of ego development in aggressive adolescent females. *Adolescence, 25,* 59–76.

Pedersen, W. C., Miller, L. C., Putcha-Bhagavatula, A. D., & Yang, Y. (2002). Evolved sex differences in the number of partners desired? The long and the short of it. *Psychological Science, 13,* 157–161.

Peeters, M. A. G., & Rutte, C. G. (2005). Time management behavior as a moderator for the job demand–control interaction. *Journal of Occupational Health Psychology, 10,* 64–75.

Penedo, F. J., Dahn, J. R., Gonzalez, J. S., Molton, I., Carver, C. S., Antoni, M. H., Roos, B. A., & Schneiderman, N. (2003). Perceived stress management skill mediates the relationship between optimism and positive mood following radical prostatectomy. *Health Psychology, 22,* 220–222.

Pennebaker, J. W., & Beall, S. K. (1986). Confronting a traumatic event: Towards an understanding of inhibition and disease. *Journal of Abnormal Psychology, 95,* 274–281.

Perna, F. M., Antoni, M. H., Baum, A., Gordon, P., & Schneiderman, N. (2003). Cognitive behavioral stress management effects on injury and illness among competitive athletes: A randomized clinical trial. *Annals of Behavioral Medicine, 25,* 66–73.

Peters, W. S. (1987). *Counting for something: Statistical principles and personalities.* New York: Springer-Verlag.

Pettigrew, T. F., & Tropp, L. R. (2006). A meta-analytic test of intergroup contact theory. *Journal of Personality and Social Psychology, 90,* 751–783.

Prenda, K. M., & Lachman, M. E. (2001). Planning for the future: A life management strategy for increasing control and life satisfaction in adulthood. *Psychology and Aging, 16,* 206–216.

Prentice, D. A., & Miller, D. T. (1992). When small effects are impressive. *Psychological Bulletin, 112,* 160–164.

Punnett, B. J., Greenidge, D., & Ramsey, J. (2007). Job attitudes and absenteeism: A study in the English speaking Caribbean. *Journal of World Business, 42,* 214–227.

Puri, M. L., & Sen, P. K. (1985). *Nonparametric methods in general linear models.* New York: Wiley.

Rashotte, L. S., & Webster, M., Jr. (2005). Gender status beliefs. *Social Science Research, 34,* 618–633.

Raskauskas, J., & Stoltz, A. D. (2007). Involvement in traditional and electronic bullying among adolescents. *Developmental Psychology, 43,* 564–575.

Raymore, L. A., Barber, B. L., & Eccles, J. S. (2001). Leaving home, attending college, partnership and parenthood: The role of life transition events in leisure pattern stability from adolescence to young adulthood. *Journal of Youth and Adolescence, 30,* 197–223.

Reber, P. J., & Kotovsky, K. (1997). Implicit learning in problem solving: The role of working memory capacity. *Journal of Experimental Psychology: General, 126,* 178–203.

Riehl, R. J. (1994). Academic preparation, aspirations, and first-year performance of first-generation students. *College and University, 70,* 14–19.

Risen, J. L., Gilovich, T., & Dunning, D. (2007). One-shot illusory correlations and stereotype formation. *Personality and Social Psychology Bulletin, 33,* 1492–1502.

Roberts, B. W., Walton, K. E., & Viechtbauer, W. (2006). Patterns of mean-level change in personality traits across the life course: A meta-analysis of longitudinal studies. *Psychological Bulletin, 132,* 1–25.

Robins, R. W., & John, O. P. (1997). Effects of visual perspective and narcissism on self-perception: Is seeing believing? *Psychological Science, 8,* 37–42.

Roeser, R. W., van der Wolf, K., & Strobel, K. R. (2001). On the relation between social-emotional and school functioning during early adolescence: Preliminary findings from Dutch and American samples. *Journal of School Psychology, 39,* 111–139.

Rosnow, R. L., & Rosenthal, R. (1989) Statistical procedures and the justification of knowledge in psychological science. *American Psychologist, 44,* 1276–1284.

Ruscio, J. (2000). The role of complex thought in clinical prediction: Social accountability and the need for cognition. *Journal of Consulting and Clinical Psychology, 68,* 145–154.

Rushton, J. P., & Jensen, A. R. (2005). Thirty years of research on race differences in cognitive ability. *Psychology, Public Policy, and Law, 11,* 235–294.

Russell, D., Peplau, L. A., & Cutrona, C. E. (1980). The revised UCLA Loneliness Scale: Concurrent and discriminant validity evidence. *Journal of Personality and Social Psychology, 39,* 472–480.

Ryan, A. M., Gheen, M. H., & Midgley, C. (1998). Why do some students avoid asking for help? An examination of the interplay among students' academic efficacy, teachers' social-emotional role, and the classroom goal structure. *Journal of Educational Psychology, 90,* 528–535.

Salsburg, D. (2001). *The lady tasting tea: How statistics revolutionized science in the twentieth century.* New York: Freeman.

Sawilowsky, S. S., & Blair, R. C. (1992). A more realistic look at the robustness and Type II error properties of the *t* test to departures from population normality. *Psychological Bulletin, 111,* 352–360.

Scheier, M. F., Carver, C. S., & Bridges, M. W. (1994). Distinguishing optimism from neuroticism (and trait anxiety, self-mastery, and self-esteem): A re-evaluation of the Life Orientation Test. *Journal of Personality and Social Psychology, 67,* 1063–1078.

Schmader, T., Major, B., & Gramzow, R. H. (2001). Coping with ethnic stereotypes in the academic domain: Perceived injustice and psychological disengagement. *Journal of Social Issues, 57,* 93–111.

Schmidt, F. L. (1996). Statistical significance testing and cumulative knowledge in psychology: Implications for training of researchers. *Psychological Methods, 1,* 115–129.

Schmidt, F. L., & Hunter, J. E. (1997). Eight common but false objections to the discontinuation of significance testing in the analysis of research data. In L. L. Harlow, S. A. Mulaik, & J. H. Steiger (Eds.), *What if there were no significance tests?* (pp. 37–64). Mahwah, NJ: Erlbaum.

Schmitt, N., Oswald, F. L., Kim, B. H., Imus, A., Merritt, S., Friede, A., & Shivpuri, S. (2007). The use of background and ability profiles to predict college student outcomes. *Journal of Applied Psychology, 92,* 165–179.

Schram, C. M. (1996). A meta-analysis of gender differences in applied statistics achievement. *Journal of Educational and Behavioral Statistics, 21,* 55–70.

Schreider, Yu. A. (1966). Preface to the English edition. In N. P. Bushlenko, D. I. Golenko, Yu. A. Schreider, L. M. Sobol, & V. G. Sragovich (Yu. A. Schreider, Ed.), *The Monte Carlo method: The method of statistical trials* (G. J. Tee, Trans.) (p. vii). Elmsford, NY: Pergamon Press.

Schuster, M. A., Stein, B. D., Jaycox, L. H., Collins, R. L., Marshall, G. N., Elliott, M. N., Zhou, A. J., Kanouse, D. E., Morrison, J. L., & Berry, S. H. (2001). A national survey of stress reactions after the September 11, 2001, terrorist attacks. *New England Journal of Medicine, 345,* 1507–1512.

Schwitzgebel, E. (2003). Why did we think we dreamed in black and white? *Studies in History and Philosophy of Science, 33,* 649–660.

Schwitzgebel, E., Huang, C., & Zhou, Y. (2006). Do we dream in color? Cultural variations and scepticism. *Dreaming, 16,* 36–42.

Sedlmeier, P., & Gigerenzer, G. (1989). Do studies of statistical power have an effect on the power of studies? *Psychological Bulletin, 105,* 309–316.

Selwyn, N. (2007). Hi-tech = guy-tech? An exploration of undergraduate students' gendered perceptions of information and communication technologies. *Sex Roles, 56,* 525–536.

Senecal, C., Vallerand, R. J., & Guay, F. (2001). Antecedents and outcomes of work-family conflict: Toward a motivational model. *Personality and Social Psychology Bulletin, 27,* 176–186.

Shevlin, M. (2005). Review of A. Aron & E. Aron, *Statistics for Psychology,* 3rd edition. *Psychology Learning and Teaching, 4,* issue 2.

Siegel, M., & Biener, L. (1997). Evaluating the impact of statewide anti-tobacco campaigns: The Massachusetts and California Tobacco Control Programs. *Journal of Social Issues, 53,* 147–168.

Sigall, H., & Ostrove, N. (1975). Beautiful but dangerous: Effects of offender attractiveness and nature of the crime on juridic judgments. *Journal of Personality and Social Psychology, 31,* 410–414.

Sinclair, L., & Kunda, Z. (2000). Motivated stereotyping of women: She's fine if she praised me but incompetent if she criticized me. *Personality and Social Psychology Bulletin, 26,* 1329–1342.

Skinner, B. F. (1956). A case history in scientific method. *American Psychologist, 11,* 221–233.

Smith, M. L., & Glass, G. V. (1977). Meta-analysis of psychotherapy outcome studies. *American Psychologist, 32,* 752–760.

Soproni, K., Miklosi, A., Csanyi, V., & Topal, J. (2001). Comprehension of human communicative signs in pet dogs (*Canis familiaris*). *Journal of Comparative Psychology, 115,* 122–126.

Speed, A., & Gangstead, S. W. (1997). Romantic popularity and mate preferences: A peer-nomination study. *Personality and Social Psychology Bulletin, 23,* 928–935.

Spencer, S. J., Steele, C. M., & Quinn, D. M. (1999). Stereotype threat and women's math performance. *Journal of Experimental Social Psychology, 35,* 4–28.

Stankiewicz, B. J., Legge, G. E., Mansfield, J. S., & Schlicht, E. J. (2006). Lost in Virtual Space: Studies in Human and Ideal Spatial Navigation. *Journal of Experimental Psychology: Human Perception and Performance, 32,* 688–704.

Stanley, S. M., Amato, P. R., Johnson, C. A., & Markman, H. J. (2006). Premarital education, marital quality, and marital stability: Findings from a large, random household survey. *Journal of Family Psychology, 20,* 117–126.

Stasser, G., Taylor, L. A., & Hanna, C. (1989). Information sampling in structured and unstructured discussions of three- and six-person groups. *Journal of Personality and Social Psychology, 57,* 67–78.

Steele, C. M. (1997). A threat in the air: How stereotypes shape intellectual identity and performance. *American Psychologist, 52,* 613–629.

Steen, L. A. (1987). Forward. In S. Tobias, *Succeed with math: Every student's guide to conquering math anxiety* (pp. xvii–xviii). New York: College Entrance Examination Board.

Steering Committee of the Physicians Health Study Research Group. (1988). Preliminary report: Findings from the aspirin component of the ongoing Physicians Health Study. *New England Journal of Medicine, 318,* 262–264.

Steil, J. M., & Hay, J. L. (1997). Social comparison in the work place: A study of 60 dual-career couples. *Personality and Social Psychology Bulletin, 23,* 427–438.

Stigler, S. M. (1986). *The history of statistics.* Cambridge, MA: Belknap Press.

Sugerman, D. E., & Carey, K. B. (2007). The relationship between drinking control strategies and college student alcohol use. *Psychology of Addictive Behaviors, 21,* 338–345.

Suh, E., Diener, E., & Fijita, F. (1996). Events and subjective well-being: Only recent events matter. *Journal of Personality and Social Psychology, 70,* 1091–1102.

Suzuki, L., Aronson, J. (2005). The cultural malleability of intelligence and its impact on the racial/ethnic hierarchy. *Psychology, Public Policy, and Law, 1,* 320–327.

Tankard, J., Jr. (1984). *The statistical pioneers.* Cambridge, MA: Schenkman.

Taylor, A. B., West, S. G., & Aiken, L. S. (2006). Loss of power in logistic, ordinal logistic, and probit regression when an outcome variable is coarsely categorized. *Educational and Psychological Measurement, 66,* 228–239.

Teachman, B. A., Gregg, A. P., & Woody, S. R. (2001). Implicit associations for fear-relevant stimuli among individuals with snake and spider fears. *Journal of Abnormal Psychology, 110,* 226–235.

Thomas, J. R., Nelson, J. K., & Thomas, K. T. (1999). A generalized rank-order method for nonparametric analysis of data from exercise science: A tutorial. *Research Quarterly for Exercise and Sport, 70,* 11–27.

Thompson, B. (2007). Effect sizes, confidence intervals, and confidence intervals for effect sizes. *Psychology in the Schools, 44,* 423–432.

Thompson, W. F., Schellenberg, E. G., & Husain, G. (2001). Arousal, mood, and the Mozart effect. *Psychological Science, 12,* 248–251.

Tobias, S. (1982, January). Sexist equations. *Psychology Today,* pp. 14–17.

Tobias, S. (1987). *Succeed with math: Every student's guide to conquering math anxiety.* New York: College Entrance Examination Board.

Tobias, S. (1995). *Overcoming math anxiety.* New York: W. W. Norton.

Tufte, E. R. (1983). *The visual display of quantitative information.* Cheshire, CT: Graphic Press.

Valenzuela, M. (1997). Maternal sensitivity in a developing society: The context of urban poverty and infant chronic undernutrition. *Developmental Psychology, 33,* 845–855.

Valk, M., Post, M. W. M., Cools, H. J. M., & Shrijvers, G. A. J. P. (2001). Measuring disability in nursing home residents: Validity and reliability of a newly developed instrument. *Journal of Gerontology: Psychological Sciences, 56,* 187–191.

Van Aken, M. A. G., & Asendorpf, J. B. (1997). Support by parents, classmates, friends, and siblings in preadolescence: Covariation and compensation across relationships. *Journal of Social and Personal Relationships, 14,* 79–93.

Van Prooijen, J.-W., Van den Bos, K., & Wilke, H. A. M. (2004). Group belongingness and procedural justice: Social inclusion and exclusion by peers affects the psychology of voice. *Journal of Personality and Social Psychology, 87,* 66–79.

VanLaningham, J., Johnson, D. R., & Amato, P. (2001). Marital happiness, marital duration, and the U-shaped curve: Evidence from a five-wave panel study. *Social Forces, 79,* 1313–1341.

Viswanath, K., Breen, N., Meissner, H., Moser, R. P., Hesse, B., Randolph Steele, W., & Rakowski, W. (2006). Cancer knowledge and disparities in the information age. *Journal of Health Communication, 11,* 1–17.

Walberg, H. J., & Lai, J.-S. (1999). Meta-analytic effects for policy. In G. J. Cizek (Ed.), *Handbook of educational policy* (pp. 419–453). San Diego, CA: Academic Press.

Walberg, H. J., Strykowski, B. F., Rovai, E., & Hung, S. S. (1984). Exceptional performance. *Review of Educational Research, 54,* 87–112.

Warner, L. J., Lumley, M. A., Casey, R. J., Pierantoni, W., Salazar, R., Zoratti, E. M., Enberg. R., & Simon, M. R. (2006). Health effects of written emotional disclosure in adolescents with asthma: A randomized, controlled trial. *Journal of Pediatric Psychology, 31,* 557–568.

Weller, A., & Weller, L. (1997). Menstrual synchrony under optimal conditions: Bedouin families. *Journal of Comparative Psychology, 111,* 143–151.

Whitecotton, S. M. (1996). The effects of experience and a decision aid on the slope, scatter, and bias of earnings forecasts. *Organizational Behavior and Human Decision Processes, 66,* 111–121.

Wilfley, D. E., Pike, K. M., Dohm, F., Striegel-Moore, R. H., & Fairburn, C. G. (2001). Bias in binge eating disorder: How representative are recruited clinic samples? *Journal of Consulting and Clinical Psychology, 69,* 383–388.

Wilkinson, L., & Task Force on Statistical Inference. (1999). Statistical methods in psychology journals: Guidelines and explanations. *American Psychologist, 54,* 594–604.

Williamson, G. M., Shaffer, D. R., & The Family Relationships in Late Life Project. (2001). Relationship quality and potentially harmful behaviors by spousal caregivers: How we were then, how we are now. *Psychology and Aging, 16,* 217–226.

Wiseman, H. (1997). Interpersonal relatedness and self-definition in the experience of loneliness during the transition to university. *Personal Relationships, 4,* 285–299.

Woods, S. P., Rippeth, J. D., Conover, E., Carey C. L., Parsons, T. D., & Tröster A. I. (2006). Statistical power of studies examining the cognitive effects of subthalamic nucleus deep brain stimulation in Parkinson's disease. *Clinical Neuropsychology, 20,* 27–38.

Xu, X., Aron, A., Fisher, H., Brown, L. L., Cao, G., Feng, T., & Weng, X. (May 2007). *Reward/motivation systems associated with early stage romantic love in Chinese students: An fMRI study.* Presented at the Neural Systems of Social Behavior Conference, Austin, TX.

Yamagishi, N., & Melara, R. D. (2001). Informational primacy of visual dimensions: Specialized roles for luminance and chromaticity in figure-ground perception. *Perception and Psychophysics, 63,* 824–846.

Yorges, S. L., Bloom, A. J., & Difonzo, K. M. (2007). Great expectations? Student reactions when courses don't measure up. *Psychology and Education: An Interdisciplinary Journal, 44,* 18–29.

Zeidner, M. (1991). Statistics and mathematics anxiety in social science students: Some interesting parallels. *British Journal of Education, 61,* 319–329.

Zimmer-Gembeck, M. J., Siebenbruner, J., & Collins, A. W. (2001). Diverse aspects of dating: Associations with psychosocial functioning from early to middle adolescence. *Journal of Adolescence, 24,* 313–336.

Index

A

Abelson, R. P., 162
Absolute zero point, 4
Adams, John, 6
Addition rule, 96–97
Adjusted means, 634
Alpha (α), 177
  Cronbach's alpha, 619–20
  statistical power and, 200–201
American Psychological Association
  (APA), 125–26
  Publication Manual of the, 162, 181,
  205–6
Analysis of covariance (ANCOVA),
  634–35, 636
  in SPSS, 658–62
Analysis of variance (ANOVA), 310–69.
  See also Factorial analysis of
  variance
  assumptions in, 331–32
  between-groups estimates of the
  population variance,
  313–17, 321–23
  carrying out, 319–27
  definition of, 311
  effect size and, 339–40
  examples of, 371–77
  extensions and special cases
  in, 389–90
  F distribution and, 317–18, 323–24
  F ratio and, 317, 323
  F table and, 317–18, 324–25
  general linear model and, 612–13,
  614–15
  hypothesis testing with, 327–31
  logic of, 311–19
  multivariate, 635–36
  one-way, 365–68, 373, 636
  planned contrasts and, 334–37
  post hoc comparisons and, 337–39
  power and, 340–41
  repeated-measures, 390
  in research articles, 344–45
  sample size and, 341–42
  in SPSS, 364–68

structural model in, 345–51,
  395–96
summary of steps for, 331, 350–51
tables, 349
three-way and higher, 389–90
two-way, 373, 386–89, 395–406
within-groups estimates of the
  population variance, 312, 316–17,
  320–21
And rule, 97
ANOVA. *See* Analysis of variance
  (ANOVA)
Anxiety, reducing, 12–13
APA. *See* American Psychological
  Association
A posteriori comparisons. *See* Post hoc
  comparisons
A priori comparisons. *See* Planned
  contrasts
Arbuthnot, John, 6
Aron, A., 51, 371, 584, 628–29
Aron, E. N., 51, 371, 374, 377, 386, 392,
  399, 401, 584, 634
Assumptions
  in analysis of variance, 331–32
  for chi-square tests, 554
  definition of, 247
  in factorial analysis of variance, 389
  for significance testing of correlation
  coefficients, 454–55
  in standard hypothesis testing,
  578–80
  for t tests, 247
  for t tests for independent means,
  286–87
Attenuation, 462

B

Bar graphs, 14, 19–20, 380–84
  in SPSS, 429–31
Baron, Robert, 628
Bayesian theory, 638
Behaviorism, 52
Beta (β), 177, 503–5
  correlation coefficient and, 505,
  509–10

Between-groups degrees of
  freedom, 324
Between-groups estimates of
  the population variance,
  313–16
  comparing with within-groups
  estimates, 316–17
  figuring, 321–23
Biased estimates, 225–26
Bimodal frequency distributions, 15–16
Biometrika (Pearson), 537
Bivariate prediction, 506, 636
  general linear model and, 612–13,
  614–15
  multiple regression vs., 507–8
  in SPSS, 532–35
Blackwell, David, 638
Bonferroni procedure, 336
Bootstrap tests, 591
Brickman, P., 117
Burke, C. J., 558
Bush, George H. W., 86

C

Categorical variables, 4, 5
Causality, 456–58
Causal modeling, 625–33
  limitations of, 632
  mediational analysis, 626–29
  path analysis, 625–26
  structural equation modeling,
  629–32
Ceiling effect, 18, 578
Cell mean, 373, 377
Cells, 373, 547–48
Central limit theorem, 74, 143
Central tendency, 33–36. *See also*
  Mean (M); Median; Mode
  definition of, 34
  in research articles, 55–57
  summary of measures, 42
Change scores, 237
Chi-square distribution, 540–41
  cutoff scores for, 672
Chi-square statistic (χ^2), 540
Chi-square table, 541

Chi-square tests, 536–76
  assumptions for, 554
  chi-square distribution and, 540–41
  chi-square statistic and, 540
  chi-square table and, 541
  contingency tables and, 546–47
  definition of, 536
  degrees of freedom and, 549
  effect size and, 554–55
  expected frequencies in, 538–39,
    547–48
  figuring, 540, 548
  for goodness of fit, 538–46, 573–74
  hypothesis testing and, 541–44,
    549–52
  for independence, 539, 546–54,
    574–75
  minimum expected frequency,
    controversy on, 558–59
  misuse of, 558–59
  phi coefficient and, 555–56
  power and, 556
  in research articles, 559–60
  sample and population in, 547
  sample size and, 557
  in SPSS, 572–75
Chow, S. L., 209
Clark, Margaret, 52
Clinical vs. Statistical Prediction
    (Meehl), 510
Cohen, Jacob, 126, 183, 184, 199, 288,
    392, 466, 555–56, 639
Comparison distributions, 111
  distribution of means and, 138,
    146–47
  sample mean's score on, 230
  t distribution, 227–28
  in *t* test for independent means and,
    271–78
  in *Z* tests, 146–53
Computational formulas, 49
Computer-intensive methods, 591–95
Conditional probabilities, 97
Confidence intervals (CI), 156–61
  controversy over, 162
  definition of, 157
  hypothesis testing and, 160–61
  logic of, 159–60
  95%, 157–61
  99%, 157–58
  in research articles, 163
  significance tests vs., 162
Confidence limits, 157, 158–59
Constant. *See* Regression constant
Contingency tables, 546–47
  phi coefficient and, 555–56
Continuous variables, 4
Conventional levels of significance, 113.
    See also Significance levels;
    Statistical significance
Correction number, 445

Correlation, 432–86
  causality and, 456–58
  coefficient, 443–52, 458–64
  controversy over "large", 466–67
  curvilinear, 437–40, 463
  definition of, 433
  graphing, 434–37, 482–83
  illusory, 460–61
  interpreting, 458–64
  linear, 437–40, 443–46
  multiple, 506
  negative, 439–40
  no correlation, 439
  partial, 617–18
  patterns of, 437–43
  positive, 439–40
  in research articles, 467–69
  in SPSS, 482–85
  statistical procedures vs. research
    methods, 457–58
  strength of, 440
Correlational research design, 458
Correlation coefficients (*r*), 443–52,
    458–64
  assumptions for significance testing
    of, 454–55
  definition of, 446
  effect size and power and, 464–65
  examples of figuring, 448–51, 454
  figuring linear correlation and, 443–46
  formula for, 448
  interpreting, 446–48, 458–64
  measurement unreliability and, 461–62
  multiple (*R*), 507
  outliers and, 462
  partial, 618, 655–57
  proportionate reduction in error (*r*²),
    458–59, 516–17
  regression coefficients vs., 509–10
  restriction in range and, 459–60
  sample size and, 464–65
  significance of, 452–56
  size of (what is "large"?), 466–67
  Spearman's rho and, 463
  in SPSS, 483–85, 655–57
  standardized regression coefficient
    and, 505
  steps for figuring, 448
Correlation matrix, 468–69
Covariance, analysis of, 634–35, 636,
    658–62
Covariates, 634–35
Cramer's phi, 555–56
Criterion variables (*Y*), 488,
    613–14, 636
Critical values. *See* Cutoff sample
    scores
Cronbach's alpha (α), 619–20
Cumulative frequencies, 7
Curvilinear correlations, 437–39
  Spearman's rho and, 463

Cutoff sample scores, 111–13
  for the chi-square distribution, 672
  determining with two-tailed tests,
    120–21
  for the *F* distribution, 669–72
  for the *t* distribution, 229–30, 668
  t tables and, 229–30

D

d (effect size), 182
Darwin, Charles, 446
Data transformations, 580–85
  advantages and disadvantages of, 589
  definition of, 580
  example of, 584–85
  kinds of, 583–84
  legitimacy of, 582–83
  rank-order tests, 585–89
  in research articles, 595–96
  in SPSS, 605–9
Davies, K. M., 371
Da Vinci, Leonardo, 89
Decision aids, 511
Decision errors, 175–78
  in research articles, 210–12
Definitional formulas, 49
Degrees of freedom (*df*), 226–27
  between-groups, 324
  chi-square test for independence
    and, 549
  in two-way analysis of variance,
    398–99
  within-groups, 324–25
Delaney, H. D., 392
Delucchi, K. L., 559
De Moivre, Abraham, 74
Denenberg, V. H., 211–12
Denominator degrees of freedom. *See*
    Within-groups degrees of freedom
Dependent variable, 634
Descriptive statistics, definition, 2
Deviation scores, 44, 443–46
Dewey, Thomas, 86
Dichotomizing, 391–92
Diener, E., 117
Difference scores, 236–37
Directional hypotheses, 119, 121
Direction of causality, 456–58
Discrete variables, 4
Distribution-free tests, 586
Distribution of differences between
    means, 271–78
  definition of, 271
  logic of, 272
  mean of, 273
  population variance estimation
    and, 273–74
  shape of, 276
  standard deviation of, 275–76
  t score for, 276
  variance of, 274–75

Distribution of means, 138–46
  building, 138–40
  compared with other distributions, 145
  comparison distributions and, 138, 146–47
  definition of, 138
  determining characteristics of, 140–44
  example of determining, 144–45
  figuring the Z score of a sample's mean on the, 147–48
  hypothesis testing with, 146–53
  mean of the (μ_M), 140–41, 145
  rules and formulas for, 140–44, 145
  standard deviation of the (σ_M), 142, 145, 227
  standard error/standard error of the mean (*SE/SEM*), 142
  in t tests, 227–28
  variance of the (σ_M^2), 141–42, 145
Duncan procedure, 338

E

Effect size, 179–87
  analysis of variance and, 339–40
  chi-square tests and, 554–55
  conventions, 183–84
  correlation coefficients and, 464
  definition of, 180
  in factorial analysis of variance, 406–8
  figuring, 182–83
  meta-analysis and, 184–86
  in research articles, 210–12
  statistical power and, 191–95, 202, 203–4
  statistical significance vs., 208–10
  t test for dependent means and, 247–48
  t test for independent means and, 288
Ellsworth, Phoebe, 154
Eppley, K. R., 184
Equal-interval variables, 4, 5
Error, 613–14
  decision, 175–78
  definition of, 498
  least squared error, 498–503
  in prediction, 514–18, 613–14
  proportionate reduction in, 514–18
  sampling, 147
  standard error (*SE*), 142, 157–61
  Type I and Type II, 176–78, 590
Error bars, 155–56
Estimation, 156–61, 182
Eta squared (η^2), 340
Ethnicity, math performance and, 53–54
Expected frequencies
  chi-square test for independence and, 538–39
  definition of, 539

  determining, 547–48
  minimum, controversy on, 558–59
Expected relative frequency, 89

F

F distributions, 317–18, 323–24
  cutoff scores for, 669–72
F ratios, 317
  figuring, 323
  interaction effects and, 388–89
  in two-way analysis of variance, 386–89
F tables, 317–18, 324–25
Factor, definition of, 622
Factor analysis, 622–23, 636
Factorial analysis of variance, 370–431, 636
  assumptions in, 389
  dichotomizing variables in, 391–92
  examples of, 371–77
  factorial research design and, 370, 372–75
  interaction effects and, 372–73, 376–86, 388–89
  logic of, 371–76
  power and effect size in, 406–10
  in research articles, 393–95
  sample size in, 409–10
  in SPSS, 426–31
  terminology in, 373–75
Factorial research design, 370, 372–75
Factor loading, 622
Fermat, Pierre de, 90
Fidell, Linda, 616–17
Fisher, Ronald, 126, 317, 537, 558, 594, 627, 638
Fit index, 629–30
Floor effect, 17, 578
Formulas, computational/definitional, 49
Fraley, B., 628–29
Frequency distributions, 15–19
  bimodal, 15–16
  comparison of types of, 15–16
  definition of, 15
  kurtotic, 18
  multimodal, 15
  normal, 18
  rectangular, 15
  skewed, 16–18
  symmetrical, 16–17
  t distributions, 227–28
  unimodal, 15, 38
Frequency graphs
  frequency polygons, 15, 17
  histograms, 10–15
  misleading, 19–21
Frequency polygons, 15, 17
  misleading, 19–21
Frequency tables, 7–10
  constructing, 7–8, 24–25
  definition of, 7

  examples of, 7–9
  grouped, 9–10
  for nominal variables, 8
  in research articles, 21–22
  in SPSS, 29–30
Frick, R. W., 208
Froman, R. D., 392

G

Gallup poll, 86
Galton, Francis, 94, 446, 627
Gaussian distribution. *See* Normal curves
Gauss, Karl Friedrich, 73, 74
Gender
  math performance and, 53–54
  statistics and, 53–54, 616–17
General linear model, 611–16
Gibler, D. M., 621–22
Gigerenzer, G., 639
Gilbert, Daniel, 117
Goodness of fit, chi-square test for, 538–46, 573–74
Gosset, William S., 223, 224, 251, 537, 594, 627
Grand mean (*GM*), 321
Graphs
  bar, 19–20
  frequency, 10–15
  misleading, 19–21
  scatter diagrams, 434–36, 482–83
Graziano, Bill, 52
Grouped frequency tables, 9–10, 19
Group/grouping variable, 373, 615
Groups, comparing, 634
Gump, B. B., 393–95, 467

H

Harmonic mean, 294
Harter, S., 537–38, 541, 546
Hazan, Cindy, 310–11
Heart of Social Psychology, The (Aron, Aron), 51
Hierarchical linear modeling (HLM), 621
Highly sensitive persons, 13
Histograms, 10–15
  constructing, 13–14
  definition of, 10
  examples of, 11–12
  frequency polygons from, 15
  misleading, 19–21
  in research articles, 22–23
  in SPSS, 30–32
Hunter, J. E., 125
Husserl, E., 52
Hutchison, M. L., 621–22
Hypothesis, defined, 107
Hypothesis testing, 92, 107–74
  analysis of variance in, 327–31
  assumptions in, 578–80
  chi-square tests in, 541–44, 549–52
  comparison distribution in, 111

Hypothesis testing (*continued*)
  computer-intensive methods for, 591–95
  confidence intervals and, 160–61
  cutoff sample scores in, 111–13, 120–21
  decision errors and, 175–78
  definition of, 107
  with distribution of means, 146–53
  estimation, as alternative to, 156–61
  examples of, 108–9, 110–18
  logic of, 109–10, 115
  with means of samples, 137–74
  with nonnormal distributions, 577–610
  null and research hypotheses in, 110–11, 113–15, 125
  one-tailed and two-tailed tests in, 119–23
  possible outcomes of, 178, 179
  prediction and, 505
  process and steps for, 110–15
  in research articles, 127–28, 154–56
  significance levels and, 113
  significance testing and, 124–26
  statistical power and, 201–2
  steps in, 110–15
  t tests for dependent means, 236–44
  t tests for independent means in, 278–85
  t tests, single sample, 223–36
  two-way analysis of variance in, 386–89
  Z test for, 146–53

I

Illusory correlation, 460–61
Independence
  chi-square test for, 539, 546–54
  definition of, 547
Independent variable, 634
Inferential statistics, 2, 67–106
  normal curve and, 73–83
  probability and, 88–93
  samples and populations in, 83–88
  Z scores and, 68–72
Insko, Chet, 154
Interaction effects, 372–73, 376–86
  examples of, 377–80, 387
  F ratios and, 388–89
  identifying, 377–84
  main effects and, 383–84
  personality and, 387
  recognizing and interpreting, 376–86
Intercepts, 493
Internal consistency reliability, 619
Interrater reliability, 619
Intervals, 9, 19. *See also* Confidence intervals
Inverse transformations, 583

J

Jefferson, Thomas, 6
Jung, Carl, 53

K

Kenny, David, 628
Koslowsky, M., 622–23
Kruskal-Wallis *H* test, 586, 587
Kulik, J. A., 393–95
Kurtosis, 18–19

L

Lai, J.-S., 184
Lanarkshire milk experiment, 251
Laplace, Pierre, 74
Latane, Bibb, 51–52
Latent variable, 630
Least squared error principle, 498–503
Least squares criterion, 499, 614
Levels of measurement, 3–5
Lewis, D., 558
Linear contrasts. *See* Planned contrasts
Linear correlations, 437–40
  figuring, 443–46
Linear prediction rule, 488–91
  examples of, 490–91
  finding the best, 496–98
  in SPSS, 532–35
Log transformations, 583
Long-run relative-frequency interpretation of probability, 89
LoSchiavo, Frank, 153
Lower-level variables, 621–22

M

MacCallum, R. C., 392
Maddock, J. E., 199
Main effects, 373
  interaction effects and, 383–84
  in two-way analysis of variance, 386–88
Mann-Whitney *U* test, 587
Marginal means, 373
Marginal significance, 153–54
Math anxiety/performance, 12–13
Maxwell, S. E., 199, 392
McLaughlin-Volpe, T., 8
Mean (*M*), 34–37, 42
  adjusted, 634
  cell, 373, 377
  definition of, 34, 42
  distribution of differences between, 271–78
  distribution of means, 138–46
  estimating, 156–61
  examples of figuring, 34–37
  formula for, 35–36
  grand mean (*GM*), 321
  harmonic, 294
  hypothesis tests with, 137–74
  marginal, 373

median and mode vs., 39–42
  normal curves and, 41–42, 74–76
  in research articles, 55–57
  spread around (variability), 43–44
  in SPSS, 62
  steps in figuring, 37
  tyranny of the, 52–53
  when used, 42
  of *Z* scores, 72
Mean of a population (μ), 87, 156–57
Mean of the distribution of means (μ_M), 140–41
  figuring *Z* score of, 147–48
Measurement, 3–5
  unreliability of, 461–62
Median, 39, 42
  mean and mode vs., 39–42
  in research articles, 55–57
  in SPSS, 62
  steps for finding, 39
  when used, 42
Mediational analysis, 626–29
Mediator variable (*M*), 627
Meditation, effect sizes and, 184–85
Meehl, Paul, 510–11
Méré, Chevalier de, 89
Meta-analysis, 184–86
Miccerri, T., 93–94
Michell, John, 6
Mikulincer, M., 328–31
Miller, R. S., 466
Mischel, Walter, 387
Misleading graphs, 19–21
Mode, 37–39, 42
  definition of, 37, 42
  mean and median vs., 39–42
  in SPSS, 62
  when used, 39, 42
Mody, M., 211–12
Monte Carlo methods, 286–87, 558, 594
Morehouse, E., 210
$MS_{Between}$, 322
MS_{Within}, 320–21
μ (mean of a population), 87, 145
μ_M (mean of a distribution of means), 141, 145
Multilevel modeling, 620–22, 636
Multimodal distributions, 15–16
Multiple correlation, 506
Multiple correlation coefficient (*R*), 507
Multiple regression, 506–8
  bivariate prediction vs., 507–8
  relationship of techniques to, 612–15
Multiplication rule, 97
Multivariate analysis of covariance (MANCOVA), 636
Multivariate analysis of variance (MANOVA), 635–36
Murray, D. J., 639

N

N (number), 36
Negative correlation, 439–40
Nelson, Todd, 153
Neuman-Keuls procedure, 338
Newton, Isaac, 74
New York Times, misleading graphs in, 19, 20
Neyman, Jerzy, 638
No correlation, 439
Nominal variables, 4–5
  chi-square tests and, 536, 538, 546
  frequency tables for, 8
  mode and, 39
Nondirectional hypotheses, 119, 121
Nonnormal population distributions, 577–610
  comparison of methods, 589–90
  computer-intensive methods, 591–95
  data transformations, 580–85
  rank-order tests, 585–89
Nonparametric statistics, 94
Nonparametric tests, 586
Nonrandom samples, 94–95
Normal curves, 18, 73–83
  areas, 77, 664–67
  commonness in nature, 73–74
  controversies over, 93–94
  definition of, 18, 73
  discovery/invention of, 74
  figuring percentages of scores using, 78–80, 99–100
  figuring *Z* scores and raw scores using, 80–83
  percentage of scores between mean and standard deviations in, 74–76
  probability and, 91–92
  in research articles, 95–96
  tables of, 76–77, 664–67
Normal distribution, 73. *See also* Normal curves
  in SPSS, 602–5
Null hypothesis, 110–15, 125, 638
  cutoff sample scores and, 111–13, 116–17, 229–30
  deciding whether to reject, 113–14, 117, 230
  definition of, 110
  implications of rejecting or failing to reject, 114–15, 125
  population variance and, 312–18
  in rank-order tests, 588
  research hypothesis and, 110–11
  t tables and, 229–30
Numerator degrees of freedom. *See* Between-groups degrees of freedom
Numeric variables, 4, 391–92

O

Oakes, Michael, 466
Observed frequency, 539
Oettingen, G., 512
Olthoff, R. K., 237, 240, 252
Omnibus tests, 343–44
One-sample *t* tests. *See t* tests, single sample
One-tailed tests, 119
  statistical power and, 201, 202, 204
  when to use, 120
One-way analysis of variance, 365–68, 373, 636
Orbach, I., 343
Ordinal variables, 4
Or rule, 96–97
Outcomes, 89, 178, 179
  independent, 97
  mutually exclusive, 96–97
Outliers, 39, 462, 578–79
Owen, S. V., 392

P

Pacioli, Luca, 89
Parametric tests, 586, 587, 636
  with rank-transformed data, 588–89
  Type I and II errors with, 590
Partial correlation, 617–18, 636
Partial correlation coefficient, 618
  in SPSS, 655–57
Partialing out, 617
Pascal, Blaise, 89–90
Path analysis, 625–26, 636
Path coefficient, 625
Pearson, Egon, 638
Pearson, Karl, 74, 446, 536–37, 594, 627, 638
Pearson chi-square. *See* Chi-square tests
Percentiles, 7
Phi coefficient (φ), 555–56
Planned comparisons. *See* Planned contrasts
Planned contrasts, 334–37
  Bonferroni procedure and, 336
  example of, 334–35
  figuring, 334
  omnibus tests vs., 343–44
Polls, 86–87, 147
Pooled estimate of the population variance (S^2_{Pooled}), 273–74
Population parameters, 87–88
Populations, 83–88
  assumptions about, 578–80
  biased estimates of, 225–26
  chi-square test and, 547
  definition of, 83
  distribution of differences between means and, 145
  distributions of, 145
  estimating, 156–57, 312–18
  examples of, 84–85
  mean of (μ), 87, 156–57
  nonnormal distributions of, 577–610
  probability and, 92

in research articles, 95–96
  samples vs. in psychology studies, 83
  standard deviation of (σ), 87, 145
  statistical terminology for, 87–88
  variance of (σ^2), 87, 225–26
  variance of, between-groups estimates of, 313–17, 321–23
  variance of, pooled estimate of (S^2_{Pooled}), 273–74
  variance of, within-groups estimates of, 312, 316–17, 320–21
Positive correlation, 439–40
Post hoc comparisons, 337–39, 367–68
Power. *See* Statistical power
Power tables, 190, 672
Prediction, 487–535
  bivariate, 506, 507–8
  clinical vs. statistical, 510–11
  comparing predictors, 509–10
  general linear model and, 612–13, 614–15
  hypothesis as, 107
  hypothesis testing and, 505
  issues in, 503–6
  least squared error principle and, 498–503
  limitations of, 508
  linear prediction rule, 488–91, 496–98
  multiple regression and, 506–8
  proportionate reduction in error and, 514–18
  regression coefficients and, 489–505, 509–10
  regression lines in, 492–96
  in research articles, 511–14
  in SPSS, 532–35
Predictor variables (*X*), 488, 615, 636
Prentice, D. A., 466
Probability (*p*), 88–93
  addition rule and, 96–97
  conditional, 97
  definition of, 89
  figuring, 89–90, 101–2
  interpretations of, 89
  multiplication rule and, 97
  normal distribution and, 91–92
  Pascal and, 89–90
  range of, 90
  in research articles, 95–96
  rules, 91, 96–97
  samples and populations and, 92
  statistical significance and, 113
  steps for finding, 90
  symbols for, 90–91
  Z scores and, 91–92
Procedural satisfaction, 393
Products of deviation scores, 443–44
Proportionate reduction in error, 514–18
  figuring, 515–16
  as r^2, 458–59, 516–17

Proportion of variance accounted for, 339, 458–59
Proportions, exaggeration of, 19–21
Pseudorandom numbers, 594

Q

Quantitative variables, 4

R

Random (Brownian) motion, 286
Random coefficients modeling, 621
Randomization tests, 591–95
Random numbers, 594
Random selection, 85–86
Rank-order tests, 585–89
  advantages and disadvantages of, 589–90
  definition of, 586
  examples of, 587–88
  logic of, 587
  null hypothesis in, 588
  overview of, 586–87
  in research articles, 595–96
  in SPSS, 607–9
Rank-order transformation, 585
Rank-order variables, 4, 5
Ratio scales, 4
Raw scores
  changing to Z scores, 70–72, 99
  changing Z scores to, 70–72, 99
  definition of, 69
  effect size, 182
  figuring from normal curve tables, 80–83
Rectangular distributions, 15
Regression. *See also* Prediction
  multiple, 506–8
  special cases of, 614–15
Regression coefficient (b), 489, 613, 614
  finding for least squares linear prediction rule, 499–501
  standardized (β), 503–5
  standardized vs. unstandardized, 509–10
Regression constant (a), 489, 613, 614
  finding for least squares linear prediction rule, 499–501
Regression lines, 492–96
  drawing, 493–95
  intercepts of, 493
  slope of, 492–93
Reis, Harry, 51
Reliability, 618–20, 636
  internal consistency, in SPSS, 657–58
  of measurement, 461–62
Repeated-measures analysis of variance, 390
Repeated-measures designs, 236. *See also* t tests, for dependent means
  advantages and disadvantages of, 250–52

Representative values, 33
Research articles
  analysis of variance in, 344–45
  central tendency and variability in, 55–57
  chi-square tests in, 559–60
  confidence intervals in, 163
  correlation in, 467–69
  data transformations in, 595–96
  decision errors in, 210–12
  effect size in, 210–12
  factorial analysis of variance in, 393–95
  frequency tables in, 21–22
  histograms in, 22–23
  hypothesis tests in, 127–28, 154–56
  normal curves in, 95–96
  populations in, 95–96
  prediction in, 511–14
  probabilities in, 95–96
  rank-order tests in, 595–96
  samples in, 95–96
  significance levels in, 127–29
  standard errors in, 154–56
  statistical power in, 210–12
  t tests for independent means in, 292–93
  t tests, single sample and dependent means in, 252–53
  unfamiliar techniques in, 639–40
  Z scores in, 95–96
  Z tests in, 154–56
Research design
  correlational, 458
  factorial, 370, 372–75
  repeated-measures, 236, 250–52
  three-way factorial, 374
Research hypothesis, 110–11
  statistical power and, 187
Restriction in range, 459–60
Richardson, Deborah, 51
Riehl, R. J., 551
RMSEA (root mean square error of approximation), 630
Robustness, 247
Rosenthal, R., 154, 343–44, 466, 639
Rosnow, R. L., 154, 343–44, 466
Rossi, J. S., 199

S

S^2_{Between}, 322
S^2_{Within}, 320–21
Samples, 83–88
  chi-square test and, 547
  definition of, 83
  distributions of, 145
  examples of, 84–85
  mean of, 145, 156
  methods of sampling, 85–86
  nonrandom, 94–95
  populations vs., in psychology studies, 83

probability and, 92
  random selection, 85–86
  in research articles, 95–96
  statistical terminology for, 87–88
  surveys, polls, and "free samples", 86–87
Sample size. *See also* specific testing procedures
  figuring needed size, 197–200, 249
  statistical power and, 195–200
  unequal, 87–88
Sample statistics, 87–88
Sampling distributions. *See* Comparison distributions
Sampling error, 147
Sampling methods, 85–86
Scatter diagrams (scatterplots), 434–36
  in SPSS, 482–83
Scheffé test, 338
Schuster, M. A., 96
Scores, 3
  change, 237
  deviation, 44
  difference, 236–37
  outliers, 39
  raw, 70–72, 80–83
  standard, 72
  t, 230, 276
  Z, 68–72
SD. *See* Standard deviation
SD^2. *See* Variance
Sedlmeier, P., 199
Senecal, C., 631
Shaver, Philip, 310–11
Shreider, Y. A., 287
Sigma
  Σ (sum of), 35
  σ (standard deviation of a population), 87, 145
  σ_M (standard deviation of a distribution of means), 142, 145
  σ^2 (variance of a population), 87, 145
  σ^2_M (variance of the distribution of means), 142, 145
Significance levels, 113
  alpha (α), 177, 200–201
  beta (β), 177, 503–5
  conventional, 113
  correlation coefficients and, 452–56
  marginal, 153–54
  in research articles, 127–28, 129
  statistically significant, 113
  statistical power and, 200–201, 202, 204
Significance tests
  confidence intervals vs., 162
  controversy over, 124–26, 129, 162
  correlation coefficient and, 454–55
Simpson, Thomas, 74
Skewed distributions, 16–18
  mean, mode, and median in, 51

Skinner, B. F., 52
Slope, 492–93
　slopes as outcomes, 621
Snedecor, George, 317
Soproni, K., 252
Spearman, Charles, 463
Spearman's rho, 463, 587, 589
Split-half reliability, 619
SPSS, 2
　analysis of covariance in, 658–62
　analysis of variance in, 364–68
　bivariate linear prediction rule in, 532–35
　chi-square tests in, 572–75
　correlation coefficients in, 483–85
　data transformations in, 605–9
　factorial analysis of variance in, 426–31
　frequency tables in, 29–30
　histograms in, 30–32
　mean, mode, and median in, 62
　normal distributions in, 602–5
　partial correlation coefficients in, 655–57
　rank-order tests in, 607–9
　reliability, internal consistency in, 657–58
　scatter diagrams in, 482–83
　t tests for dependent means in, 266–68
　t tests for independent means in, 305–9
　t tests, single sample, in, 265–66
　variance and standard deviation in, 62–65
Squared deviation score, 44, 45
Square-root transformations, 581–82, 584
SS. See Sum of squared deviations
Standard deviation (*SD*), 45–49
　of a population (σ), 87, 145
　computational and definitional formulas for, 49
　definition of, 45
　of the distribution of differences between means ($S_{\text{Difference}}$), 275–76
　of the distribution of means (σ_M), 142, 145, 227
　examples of figuring, 47–49
　formula for, 45–47
　normal curves and, 74–76
　in research articles, 55–57, 155
　in SPSS, 62–65
　as SS/N, 46–47
　steps in figuring, 45
　of *Z* scores, 72
Standard error (*SE*), 142, 157–61
　in research articles, 154–56
Standard error of the mean (*SEM*), 142
　in research articles, 155
Standardized effect size, 182
Standardized regression coefficients (β), 503–5, 509–10
Standard scores, 72. *See also Z* scores

Stangor, Charles, 154
Statistical mood, 53
Statistical power, 187–207
　analysis of variance and, 340–41
　chi-square tests and, 556
　correlation coefficients and, 464
　definition of, 187
　determining, 190
　determining from predicted effect sizes, 195
　effect size and, 191–95, 202, 203–4, 208–10
　in factorial analysis of variance, 408–9
　figuring, 212–13
　hypothesis testing procedures and, 201–2, 204
　influences on, 191–202
　interpreting study results and, 205–7
　one- vs. two-tailed tests and, 201, 202, 204
　planning studies and, 203–4
　power tables, 190, 672
　in research articles, 210–12
　role when results not statistically significant, 206, 207
　sample size and, 195–200, 202, 204, 207
　significance level and, 200–202, 204, 208–10
　statistical vs. practical significance and, 205–6, 208–10
　t test for dependent means and, 248–49
　t test for independent means and, 288–89, 293–94
　of typical psychology experiments, 199
Statistical significance, 113, 127–28, 175–221. *See also* Statistical power
　effect size vs., 208–10
　practical significance vs., 205–6
　statistical power and, 200–202, 204
Statistics
　branches of, 2
　concepts and terminology, 3–6
　controversy in, 637–39
　definition of, 2
　golden age of, 627
　historical development of, 637–39
　joy of, 51–52
　techniques in, overview, 636
　trivia on, 6
　unfamiliar techniques, reading results using, 639–40
Statistics anxiety, 12–13
Steele, C. M., 53
Stereotype threat, 53–54
St. Jean, Richard, 154
Structural equation modeling, 629–32, 636
Structural model, 345–51
　analysis of variance tables in, 349
　example of, 347–49

principles of, 345–47
　summary of procedures for, 350–51
　in two-way analysis of variance, 395–96
Student's *t* test. *See t* tests
Stumbling on Happiness (Gilbert), 117
Subjective interpretation of probability, 89
Sum of (Σ), 35
Sum of squared deviations (*SS*), 44, 46, 50, 345–46
Sum of squares (*SS*), 46
Sum of the squared errors (SS_{Error}), 498–99, 514–16
Surveys, 86–87
Symbols, statistical, 35–36
Symmetrical distributions, 16–17

T

t distributions, 227–28
　cutoff scores for, 229–30, 668
t scores, 230, 276
t tables, 229–30
t tests, 222–69, 636
　advantages and disadvantages of, 250–52
　basic principle of, 225–26
　bivariate prediction, relationship with, 615
　comparison of types of, 290–91
　definition of, 223
　general linear model and, 612–13, 614–15
　problem of too many, 291–92, 595
　with rank-transformed data, 588–89
t tests, for dependent means, 236–44
　advantages and disadvantages of, 250–52
　assumptions of, 247
　comparison with other tests, 244, 291
　definition of, 236
　difference scores and, 236–37
　effect size and, 247–49
　examples of, 237–43
　for pairs of research participants, 243–44
　power for, 248–49
　in research articles, 252–53
　sample size and, 249
　in SPSS, 266–68
　summary of steps for, 241
t tests, for independent means, 270–309
　assumptions of, 286–87
　comparison with other tests, 291
　definition of, 270
　distribution of differences between means and, 271–78
　effect size and, 288
　examples of, 278–84
　hypothesis testing with, 278–85
　power and, 288–89, 293–94

t tests, for independent means (*continued*)
in research articles, 292–93
sample size and, 289–90
in SPSS, 305–9
summary of steps for, 281
t tests, single sample, 223–36
assumptions of, 247
comparison with other tests, 230–31, 244, 291
definition of, 223
degrees of freedom and, 226–27
example of, 231–33
null hypothesis rejection and, 230
population variance estimation from sample scores, 225–26
in research articles, 252–53
in SPSS, 265–66
standard deviation of distribution of means and, 227
summary of steps for, 233–34
t distribution and, 227–28
t score and, 230
t table and, 229–30
Z test compared with, 230–31
Tabachnick, Barbara, 616–17
Test anxiety, 12–13
Test-retest reliability, 619
Theory, defined, 107
Thorngate, Warren, 154
Three-way factorial design, 374
Tippett, L. H. C., 594
Tobias, S., 12, 54
Tobler, N. S., 210
Total squared error when predicting from the mean (SS_{Total}), 515
Transcendental Meditation (TM), 184–85
Truman, Harry, 86
Tufte, E. R., 19
Tukey test, 338
2×3 factorial design, 375
Two-tailed tests, 119–23
definition of, 119
determining cutoff scores with, 120–21
example of hypothesis testing with, 121–23
statistical power and, 201, 202
when to use, 120
Two-way analysis of variance, 373, 386–89
degrees of freedom in, 398–99
figuring, 395–406
F ratios in, 386–89
in SPSS, 426–29
steps for, 396–98
summary of procedures for, 403
variance tables for, 399, 400, 404
Two-way factorial research design, 373
Type I error, 176–78
parametric tests and, 590

Type II error, 177–78
parametric tests and, 590
statistical power and, 190

U

Unbiased estimates of the population variance (S^2), 226
Unimodal frequency distributions, 15, 38
Upper-level variable, 621

V

Valenzuela, M., 282, 288
Valk, M., 619–20
Values, 3
representative, 33
Van Prooijen, J. W., 393
Variability, 43–44
computational formulas for, 49
definitional formulas for, 49
examples of figuring, 47–49
formulas for, 45–47
importance in psychology research, 49–50
in research articles, 55–57
SS/N, 46–47
$SS/(N - 1)$, 50
standard deviation, 45
variance, 45–46
Variables, 3–5, 634
continuous, 4
criterion, 488, 613–14, 636
definition of, 3
dependent, 634
dichotomizing, 391–92
discrete, 4
equal-interval, 4, 5
independent, 634
kinds of, 3–5
latent, 630
lower-level, 621–22
mediator, 627
nominal, 4–5
predictor, 488, 615, 636
rank-order, 4, 5
upper-level, 621
X and *Y*, 35
Variance (SD^2), 44–45. *See also* Analysis of variance (ANOVA); Factorial analysis of variance
definition of, 44
examples of figuring, 45
formulas for, 45–47, 49, 145
pooled estimate of the population variance (S^2_{Pooled}), 273–74
proportion of accounted for (R^2), 339
in SPSS, 62–65
as SS/N, 46–47
steps in figuring, 44
Variance of a population (σ^2), 87, 225–26

Variance of the distribution of differences between means ($S^2_{Difference}$), 275
Variance of the distribution of means (σ^2_M), 141–42, 145, 274–75
Verbal fillers, 152
Viswanath, K., 95
Von Franz, Marie Louise, 53

W

Walberg, H. J., 184
Washburn, David, 154
Weighted averages, 273–74
Wilcoxon rank-sum test, 587–88
Wilcoxon signed-rank test, 587
Williamson, G. M., 625–26
Wiseman, H., 154–55
Within-groups degrees of freedom, 324–25
Within-groups estimates of the population variance, 312
comparing with between-groups estimates, 316–17
figuring, 320–21
Within-subjects analysis of variance. *See* Repeated-measures analysis of variance

X

X, 35, 488

Y

Y, 488
Yates, Frank, 594
Yurak, Tricia, 154

Z

Z scores, 68–72
as a scale, 69
changing raw scores to, 70–72, 99
changing to raw scores, 70–72, 99
definition of, 68
figuring for sample's mean on the distribution of means, 147–48
figuring from normal curve tables, 80–83
figuring from percentages, 100–101
figuring percentage above or below, 78–80, 99–100
mean of, 72
normal curve table and, 76–77
probability and, 91–92
in research articles, 95–96, 98
standard deviation of, 72
Z test, 146–53
compared with *t* tests, 230–31, 244
definition of, 138
examples of, 148–52
in research articles, 154–56

Steps of Hypothesis Testing for Major Procedures

	Z Test (Ch. 5)	t Test for a Single Sample (Ch. 7)	t Test for Dependent Means (Ch. 7)	t Test for Independent Means (Ch. 8)	One-Way Analysis of Variance (Ch. 9)
❶	Restate the question as a research hypothesis and a null hypothesis about the populations.	Restate the question as a research hypothesis and a null hypothesis about the populations.	Restate the question as a research hypothesis and a null hypothesis about the populations.	Restate the question as a research hypothesis and a null hypothesis about the populations.	Restate the question as a research hypothesis and a null hypothesis about the populations.
❷	Determine the characteristics of the comparison distribution. $\mu_M = \mu$; $\sigma_M^2 = \sigma^2/N$; $\sigma_M = \sqrt{\sigma_M^2}$; approximately normal if population normal or $N > 30$.	Determine the characteristics of the comparison distribution. (a) The mean of the distribution of means is the same as the population mean. (b) Figure its standard deviation: ❹ $S^2 = SS/df$ ❸ $S_M^2 = S^2/N$ ❻ $S_M = \sqrt{S_M^2}$ (c) t distribution, $df = N - 1$.	Determine the characteristics of the comparison distribution. (a) All based on difference scores. (b) Figure mean of the difference scores. (c) Its mean will be 0. (d) Figure its standard deviation: ❹ $S^2 = SS/df$ ❸ $S_M^2 = S^2/N$ ❻ $S_M = \sqrt{S_M^2}$ (e) t distribution, $df = N - 1$.	Determine the characteristics of the comparison distribution. (a) Its mean will be 0. (b) Figure its standard deviation: ❹ For each population. $S^2 = SS/(N-1)$ ❸ $S_{Pooled}^2 = (df_1/df_{Total})(S_1^2) + (df_2/df_{Total})(S_2^2)$; $df_1 = N_1 - 1$ and $df_2 = N_2 - 1$; $df_{Total} = df_1 + df_2$. ❻ $S_{M_1}^2 = S_{Pooled}^2/N_1$; $S_{M_2}^2 = S_{Pooled}^2/N_2$ ❶ $S_{Difference}^2 = S_{M_1}^2 + S_{M_2}^2$ ❸ $S_{Difference} = \sqrt{S_{Difference}^2}$ (c) t distribution, degrees of freedom $= df_{Total}$	Determine the characteristics of the comparison distribution. (a) F distribution. (b) $df_{Between} = N_{Groups} - 1$. (c) $df_{Within} = df_1 + df_2 + \cdots + df_{Last}$.
❸	Determine the cutoff sample score on the comparison distribution at which the null hypothesis should be rejected. Use normal curve table.	Determine the cutoff sample score on the comparison distribution at which the null hypothesis should be rejected. Use t table.	Determine the cutoff sample score on the comparison distribution at which the null hypothesis should be rejected. Use t table.	Determine the cutoff sample score on the comparison distribution at which the null hypothesis should be rejected. Use t table.	Determine the cutoff sample score on the comparison distribution at which the null hypothesis should be rejected. Use F table.
❹	Determine your sample's score on the comparison distribution. $Z = (M - \mu_M)/\sigma_M$	Determine your sample's score on the comparison distribution. $t = (M - \mu)/S_M$	Determine your sample's score on the comparison distribution. $t = (M - \mu)/S_M$	Determine your sample's score on the comparison distribution. $t = (M_1 - M_2)/S_{Difference}$	Determine your sample's score on the comparison distribution. (a) Figure $S_{Between}^2$: (i) Figure the mean of each group. ❹ $S_M^2 = \sum(M - GM)^2/df_{Between}$ ❸ $S_{Between}^2 = (S_M^2)(n)$ (b) Figure S_{Within}^2 ❶ For each group, $S^2 = \sum(X - M)^2/(n - 1) = SS/df$ ❷ $S_{Within}^2 = (S_1^2 + S_2^2 + \cdots + S_{Last}^2)/N_{Groups}$ (c) $F = S_{Between}^2/S_{Within}^2$
❺	Decide whether to reject the null hypothesis. Compare scores from Steps ❸ and ❹.	Decide whether to reject the null hypothesis. Compare scores from Steps ❸ and ❹.	Decide whether to reject the null hypothesis. Compare scores from Steps ❸ and ❹.	Decide whether to reject the null hypothesis. Compare scores from Steps ❸ and ❹.	Decide whether to reject the null hypothesis. Compare scores from Steps ❸ and ❹.